# World Civilizations

# World Civilizations

## *The Global Experience*

**VOLUME II**

FIFTH EDITION

**Peter N. Stearns**
*George Mason University*

**Michael Adas**
*Rutgers University*

**Stuart B. Schwartz**
*Yale University*

**Marc J. Gilbert**
*Hawaii Pacific University*

New York San Francisco Boston
London Toronto Sydney Tokyo Singapore Madrid
Mexico City Munich Paris Cape Town Hong Kong Montreal

Senior Acquisitions Editor: Janet Lanphier
Development Editor: Stephanie Ricotta
Supplements Editor: Kristi Olson
Media Producer: Melissa Edwards
Executive Marketing Manager: Sue Westmoreland
Production Manager: Eric Jorgensen
Project Coordination, Text Design, and Electronic Page Makeup: Electronic Publishing Services Inc., New York City
Cover Designer/Manager: Wendy Ann Fredericks
Cover Art: Emmanuel Taiwo Jedege, Ona Ayo—Path of Joy 1993. Private collection, The October Gallery, London
Photo Researcher: Linda Sykes
Senior Manufacturing Buyer: Alfred C. Dorsey
Printer and Binder: Quebecor World Dubuque
Cover Printer: Coral Graphic Services

For permission to use copyrighted material, grateful acknowledgment is made to the copyright holders on p. C-1, which is hereby made part of this copyright page.

**Library of Congress Cataloging-in-Publication Data**
World civilizations : the global experience / Peter N. Stearns ... [et al.]. — 5th ed.
p. cm.
Includes bibliographical references and index.
ISBN 0-321-39192-6 — ISBN 0-321-40984-1 (v. 1) — ISBN 0-321-40981-7 (v. 2) 1. Civilization—History. 2. Civilization—History—Sources. I. Stearns, Peter N. II. Title.
CB69.W666 2006
909—dc22
2006009656



Please visit us at www.ablongman.com

ISBN 0-321-39192-6 (Single Volume Edition)
ISBN 0-321-40984-1 (Volume 1)
ISBN 0-321-40981-7 (Volume 2)
ISBN 0-132-20699-4 (AP Edition)

1 2 3 4 5 6 7 8 9 10——QWD——09 08 07 06

# Brief Contents

# DETAILED CONTENTS

## PART VI
## THE NEWEST STAGE OF WORLD HISTORY: 1914–PRESENT 746

# MAPS

# PREFACE

When we began to work on the first edition of *World Civilizations: The Global Experience* in the early 1990s, we did so out of the conviction that it was time for a world history textbook truly global in its approach and coverage and yet manageable and accessible for today's college students. Our commitment to that goal continues with this fifth edition. We seek to present a truly global history—one that discusses the evolution and development of the world's leading civilizations—and balances that coverage with examination of the major stages in the nature and degree of interactions among different peoples and societies around the globe. We view world history not as a parade of facts to be memorized or a collection of the individual histories of various societies, but rather as a study of historical events in a global context. The study of world history combines meaningful synthesis of independent development within societies with comparative analysis of the results of contacts between societies.

Several decades of scholarship in world history and in area studies by historians and other social scientists have yielded a wealth of information and interpretive generalizations. The challenge is to create a coherent and comprehensible framework for organizing all this information. Our commitment to world history stems from our conviction that students will understand and appreciate the present world by studying the myriad forces that have shaped that world and created our place within it. Furthermore, study of the past in order to make sense of the present will help them prepare to meet the challenges of the future.

Many world historians argue that there is, or should be, a world history common to all of humanity. This history would capture key developments that all societies have experienced, albeit sometimes in different ways—developments like the emergence of agriculture or industry, or the results of new kinds of religious or biological contacts. The "big picture" of human history must be supplemented, of course, with an understanding of separate developments in particular places. It provides the core, however, of what world history is all about, and why it provides important perspective in an increasingly global age. World history explains the emergence of the world today, and it is hard to imagine a more important topic.

## Approach

The two principal distinguishing characteristics of this book are its global orientation and its analytical emphasis. This is a true *world* history textbook. It deals seriously with the Western tradition but does not award it pride of place or a preeminence that diminishes other areas of the world. *World Civilizations: The Global Experience* examines the histories of all areas of the world and all peoples according to their growing or waning importance. It also considers what happened across regions by examining cross-civilizational developments such as migration, trade, the spread of religion, exposure to new diseases, plant exchange, and cultural interchange.

Many world history textbooks function as factual compendia, leaving analytical challenge to the classroom. Our goal throughout this book has been to relate fact to interpretation while still allowing ample opportunity for classroom exploration. Our analytical emphasis focuses on how key aspects of the past and present have been shaped by global forces such as the exchange of technology and ideas. By encouraging students to learn how to assess continuity and change, we seek to help them relate the past to the present. Through analysis and interpretation students become active, engaged learners, rather than passive readers of the facts of historical events.

## Periodization

This text pays a great deal of attention to periodization, an essential requirement for coherent presentation. *World Civilizations: The Global Experience* identifies six periods in world history, each period determined by three basic criteria: a geographical rebalancing among major civilizational areas, an increase in the intensity and extent of contact across civilizations (or, in the case of the earliest period, cross-regional contact), and the emergence of new and roughly parallel developments in most, if not all, of these major civilizations. The book is divided into six parts corresponding to these six major periods of world history. In each part, basic characteristics of each period are referred to in chapters that discuss the major civilizations in the Middle East, Africa, Asia, Europe, and the Americas, and in several cross-cutting chapters that address larger world trends. Part introductions identify the fundamental new characteristics of parallel or comparable developments and regional or international exchange that define each period.

Part 1, From Hunting and Gathering to Civilizations, 2.5 Million–1000 B.C.E.: Origins, sketches the hunting-and-gathering phase of human existence, then focuses on the rise of agriculture and the emergence of civilization in parts of Asia, Africa, Central America, and southeastern Europe—the sequence of developments that set world history in motion from the origin of the human species until about 3000 years ago.

Part 2, The Classical Period, 1000 B.C.E.–500 C.E.: Uniting Large Regions, deals with the growing complexity of major civilizations in several areas of the world. During the classical period, civilizations developed a new capacity to integrate large regions and diverse groups of people through overarching cultural and political systems. Yet many regions and societies remained unconnected to the increasingly complex centers of civilization. Coverage of the classical period of world history, then, must consider both types of societies.

The period covered in Part 3, The Postclassical Period, 500–1450: New Faith and New Commerce, saw the emergence of new commercial and cultural linkages that brought most civilizations into contact with one another and with nomadic groups. The decline of the great classical empires, the rise of new civilizational centers, and the emergence of a network of world contacts, including the spread of major religions, are characteristics of the postclassical era.

Developments in world history over the three centuries from 1450 to 1750 mark a fourth period in world history, which is covered in Part 4, The Early Modern Period: The World Shrinks. The rise of the West, the intensification of global contacts, the growth of trade, and the formation of new empires define this period and separate it from the preceding postclassical period.

Part 5, The Dawn of the Industrial Age, 1750–1914, covers the period of world history dominated by the advent of industrialization in western Europe and growing European imperialism. The increase and intensification of commercial interchange, technological innovations, and cultural contacts all reflected the growth of Western power and the spread of Western influence.

The Newest Stage of World History: 1914–Present, the focus of Part 6, defines the characteristics of this period as the retreat of Western imperialism, the rise of new political systems such as communism, the surge of the United States and the Soviet Union, and a variety of economic innovations, including the achievements of Japan, China, Korea, and the Pacific Rim. Part 6 deals with this most recent period of world history and some of its portents for the future.

## Themes

We make world history accessible to today's students by using several themes as filters for the vast body of information that constitutes the subject. These themes provide a perspective and a framework for understanding where we have come from, where we are now, and where we might be headed.

### Commonalities Among Societies

*World Civilizations: The Global Experience* traces several key features of all societies. We look at the technologies people have developed—for humans were toolmaking animals from an early date—and at the impact of technological change on the physical environment. We examine social structure, including the inequalities between the two genders and among different social classes. We also detail the intellectual and cultural developments occurring within various societies. These three areas—technology and the environment, inequalities and reactions to inequalities, and intellectual and cultural development—are filters through which to examine any human society.

### Contacts Among Civilizations

Large regional units that defined aspects of economic exchange, political institutions, and cultural values began to spring up more than 5000 years ago. These civilizations—that is, societies that generate and use an economic surplus beyond basic survival needs—created a general framework for the lives of most people ever since. But different regions had a variety of contacts, involving migration, trade, religious missionaries, exchanges of diseases and plants, and wars. Formal relations between societies—what we now call international relations—also were organized. Many aspects of world history can be viewed in terms of whether societies had regular connections, haphazard interchange, or some mix of the two.

## Features

The features in *World Civilizations: The Global Experience* have been carefully constructed and honed over the course of five editions. Our aim has been to provide students with tools to help them learn how to analyze change and continuity.

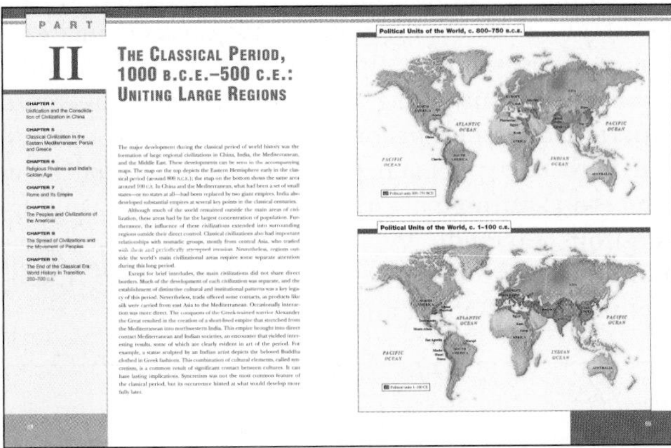


### *New!* Part Introductions

Part introductions, wholly rewritten for this edition, discuss the conditions that set the stage for the developments that define each new period in world history, identify the characteristics of the period of world history covered in the part, and recap the continuities that exist from one period to the next. The title of each part signals the key themes to be explored in the chapters that follow. A counterpoint to the account of broad changes in each period is a discussion of some aspect of ordinary human experience (old age, childhood, work, leisure) and how it changed during the period. Two world maps at the beginning of each part introduction provide a graphic reference for the major changes of the period. Part timelines list the major events of the chronological period covered.

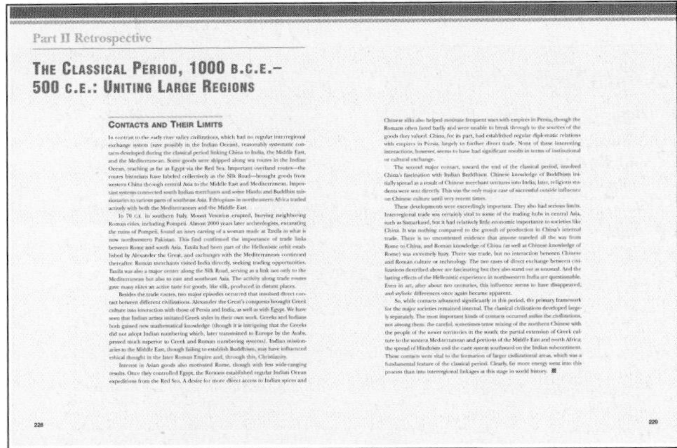


### *New!* Part Retrospectives

Following the final chapter in each part is a retrospective essay that recaps the dominant cross-civilizational (or cross-regional) contacts and divisions that occurred during the era under examination. These sections encourage analysis of the dominant contact patterns in the period as well as the relationship to them of major individual societies.

### *New!* Chapter Introductions

The chapter introductions are all new in this edition. Each tells a compelling story about a particular pattern, individual, or incident to spark students' interest and introduce chapter material in an engaging and dramatic way. The opening story concludes with an explanation of how the story relates to the chapter content and the key themes and analytical issues that will be examined in the chapter.

### *New!* Complete Redesign

The fifth edition of *World Civilizations: The Global Experience* has been thoroughly redesigned. The student-friendly text, maps, and global orientation help students easily recognize and distinguish geographical features and areas. Maps in the part introductions highlight major developments during each period and familiarize students with all areas of the world. Full-color photos help bring history to life.

### *New!* Document Analysis Questions

Found at the end of the book, these questions about original documents not only test students' analytical skills in interpreting documentary evidence but also test how they use it to develop and defend their response to an historical question based on the sources provided. Using the documents to answer the question allows students to simulate the work of an historian in examining and analyzing historical sources. Each of the major periods in world history is covered by three questions, and different types of documents, including both written and visual sources, are employed.

## Timelines

In addition to the timeline in each part introduction, each chapter includes a timeline that orients the student to the period, countries, and key events of the chapter.

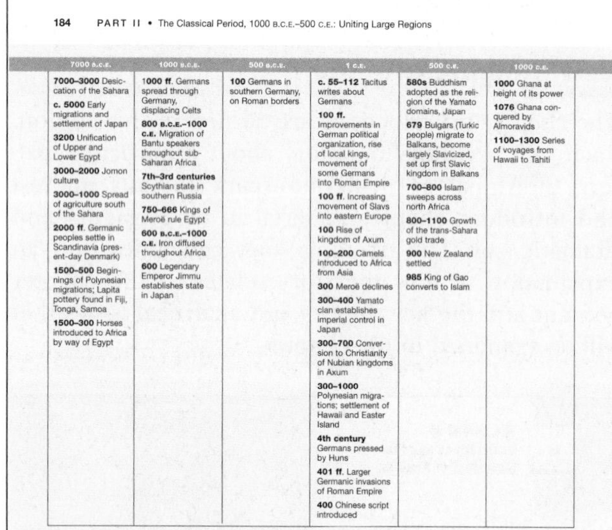

184 PART II • The Classical Period, 1000 B.C.E.–500 C.E.: Uniting Large Regions

| 7000 B.C.E. | 1000 B.C.E. | 500 B.C.E. | 1 C.E. | 500 C.E. | 1000 C.E. |
|---|---|---|---|---|---|
| **7000–3000** Desiccation of the Sahara<br>**c. 5000** Early migrations and settlement of Japan<br>**3200** Unification of Upper and Lower Egypt<br>**3000–2000** Jomon culture<br>**3000–1000** Spread of agriculture south of the Sahara<br>**2000 ff.** Germanic peoples settle in Scandinavia (present-day Denmark)<br>**1500–500** Beginnings of Polynesian migrations; Lapita pottery found in Fiji, Tonga, Samoa<br>**1500–300** Horses introduced to Africa by way of Egypt | **1000 ff.** Germans spread through Germany, displacing Celts<br>**800 B.C.E.–1000 C.E.** Migration of Bantu speakers throughout sub-Saharan Africa<br>**7th–3rd centuries** Scythian state in southern Russia<br>**750–666** Kings of Meroë rule Egypt<br>**600 B.C.E.–1000 C.E.** Iron diffused throughout Africa<br>**600** Legendary Emperor Jimmu establishes state in Japan | **100** Germans in southern Germany, on Roman borders | **c. 55–112** Tacitus writes about Germans<br>**100 ff.** Improvements in German political organization, rise of local kings, movement of some Germans into Roman Empire<br>**100 ff.** Increasing movement of Slavs into eastern Europe<br>**100** Rise of kingdom of Axum<br>**100–200** Camels introduced to Africa from Asia<br>**300** Meroë declines<br>**300–400** Yamato clan establishes imperial control in Japan<br>**300–700** Conversion to Christianity of Nubian kingdoms in Axum<br>**300–1000** Polynesian migrations; settlement of Hawaii and Easter Island<br>**4th century** Germans pressed by Huns<br>**401 ff.** Larger Germanic invasions of Roman Empire<br>**400** Chinese script introduced | **580s** Buddhism adopted as the religion of the Yamato domains, Japan<br>**679** Bulgars (Turkic people) migrate to Balkans, become largely Slavicized, set up first Slavic kingdom in Balkans<br>**700–800** Islam sweeps across north Africa<br>**800–1100** Growth of the trans-Sahara gold trade<br>**900** New Zealand settled<br>**985** King of Gao converts to Islam | **1000** Ghana at height of its power<br>**1076** Ghana conquered by Almoravids<br>**1100–1300** Series of voyages from Hawaii to Tahiti |

## Section-Opening Focal Points

Focal points listed below each main chapter heading identify for students the principal points to be explored in the section.

### The Spread of Civilization in Africa

- Africa, the continent where the earliest humans developed and the home of Egypt's remarkable civilization, experienced climatic changes, such as the drying of the Sahara between 7000 and 3000 B.C.E., and foreign influences, such as the introduction of the horse around 1000 B.C.E. and of iron around 500 B.C.E. These developments set in motion a series of cultural changes. The migration of Bantu-speaking peoples from West Africa across the continent often was accompanied by the introduction of iron and agriculture. Kingdoms such as Axum in Ethiopia and Ghana in the western Sudan represented the growth of African civilizations.

Africa is a vast continent, almost 12 million square miles, which is about three times the size of the United States. Most of it lies in the tropics, and although we

## Visualizing the Past

The Visualizing the Past feature of each chapter supports visual literacy by showing students how to read and analyze visual material such as maps, charts, graphs, tables, or photos to interpret historical patterns. Text accompanying the illustrations provides a level of analysis, and a series of questions draws the students into providing their own analyses.

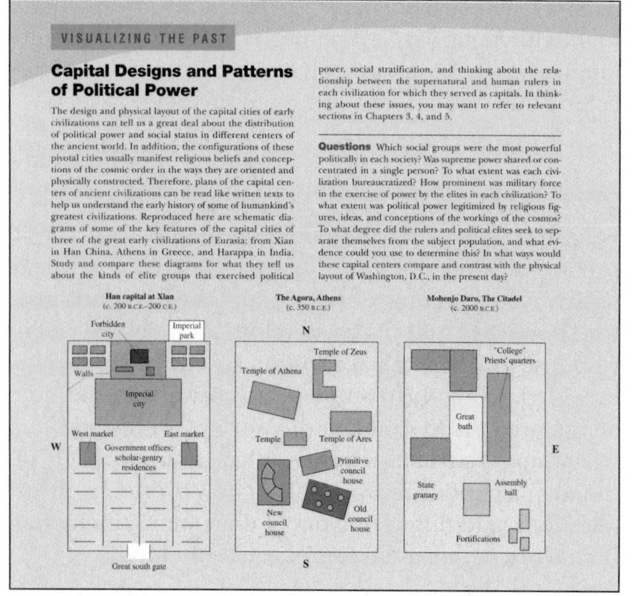

VISUALIZING THE PAST

### Capital Designs and Patterns of Political Power

The design and physical layout of the capital cities of early civilizations can tell us a great deal about the distribution of political power and social status in different centers of the ancient world. In addition, the configurations of these pivotal cities usually manifest religious beliefs and conceptions of the cosmic order in the ways they are oriented and physically constructed. Therefore, plans of the capital centers of ancient civilizations can be read like written texts to help us understand the early history of some of humankind's greatest civilizations. Reproduced here are schematic diagrams of some of the key features of the capital cities of three of the great early civilizations of Eurasia: from Xian in Han China, Athens in Greece, and Harappa in India. Study and compare these diagrams for what they tell us about the kinds of elite groups that exercised political power, social stratification, and thinking about the relationship between the supernatural and human rulers in each civilization for which they served as capitals. In thinking about these issues, you may want to refer to relevant sections in Chapters 3, 4, and 5.

**Questions** Which social groups were the most powerful politically in each society? Was supreme power shared or concentrated in a single person? To what extent was each civilization bureaucratized? How prominent was military force in the exercise of power by the elites in each civilization? To what extent was political power legitimized by religious figures, ideas, and conceptions of the workings of the cosmos? To what degree did the rulers and political elites seek to separate themselves from the subject population, and what evidence could you use to determine this? In what ways would these capital centers compare and contrast with the physical layout of Washington, D.C., in the present day?



## Documents

Substantial excerpts from selected original documents put students in contact with diverse voices of the past. We share a firm commitment to include social history involving women, the nonelite, and experiences and events outside the spheres of politics and high culture. Each document is preceded by a brief scene-setting narration and followed by probing questions to guide the reader through an understanding of the document and to encourage interpretive reflection and analysis.

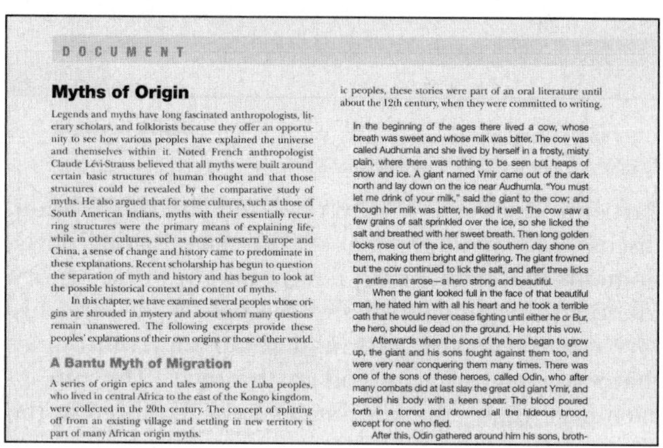

DOCUMENT

### Myths of Origin

Legends and myths have long fascinated anthropologists, literary scholars, and folklorists because they offer an opportunity to see how various peoples have explained the universe and themselves within it. Noted French anthropologist Claude Lévi-Strauss believed that all myths were built around certain basic structures of human thought and that those structures could be revealed by the comparative study of myths. He also argued that for some cultures, such as those of South American Indians, myths with their essentially recurring structures were the primary means of explaining life, while in other cultures, such as those of western Europe and China, a sense of change and history came to predominate in these explanations. Recent scholarship has begun to question the separation of myth and history and has begun to look at the possible historical context and content of myths.

In this chapter, we have examined several peoples whose origins are shrouded in mystery and about whom many questions remain unanswered. The following excerpts provide these peoples' explanations of their own origins or those of their world.

#### A Bantu Myth of Migration

A series of origin epics and tales among the Luba peoples, who lived in central Africa to the east of the Kongo kingdom, were collected in the 20th century. The concept of splitting off from an existing village and settling in new territory is part of many African origin myths.

ic peoples, these stories were part of an oral literature until about the 12th century, when they were committed to writing.

In the beginning of the ages there lived a cow, whose breath was sweet and whose milk was bitter. The cow was called Audhumla and she lived by herself in a frosty, misty plain, where there was nothing to be seen but heaps of snow and ice. A giant named Ymir came out of the dark north and lay down on the ice near Audhumla. "You must let me drink of your milk," said the giant to the cow; and though her milk was bitter, he liked it well. The cow saw a few grains of salt sprinkled over the ice, so she licked the salt and breathed with her sweet breath. Then long golden locks rose out of the ice, and the southern day shone on them, making them bright and glittering. The giant frowned but the cow continued to lick the salt, and after three licks an entire man arose—a hero strong and beautiful.

When the giant looked full in the face of that beautiful man, he hated him with all his heart and he took a terrible oath that he would never cease fighting until either he or Bur, the hero, should lie dead on the ground. He kept this vow.

Afterwards when the sons of the hero began to grow up, the giant and his sons fought against them too, and were very near conquering them many times. There was one of the sons of these heroes, called Odin, who after many combats did at last slay the great old giant Ymir, and pierced his body with a keen spear. The blood poured forth in a torrent and drowned all the hideous brood, except for one who fled.

After this, Odin gathered around him his sons, broth-

## In Depth

Each chapter contains an analytical essay on a topic of broad application related to the chapter's focus but extending across chronological and geographical boundaries. Critical thinking questions at the end of each In Depth essay prompt the reader to think

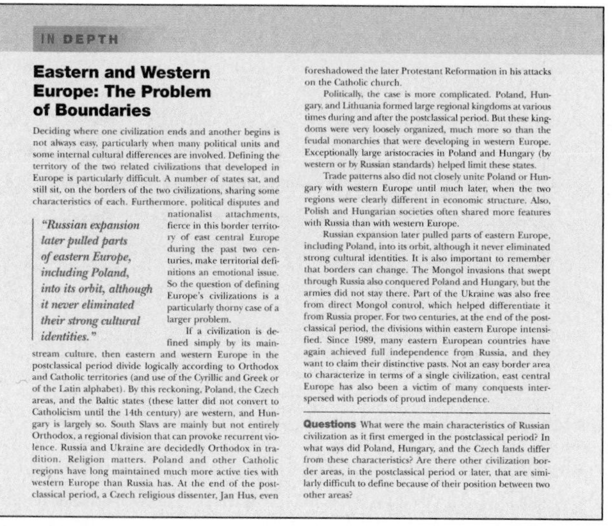

IN DEPTH

### Eastern and Western Europe: The Problem of Boundaries

Deciding where one civilization ends and another begins is not always easy, particularly when many political units and some internal cultural differences are involved. Defining the territory of the two related civilizations that developed in Europe is particularly difficult. A number of states sat, and still sit, on the borders of the two civilizations, sharing some characteristics of each. Furthermore, political disputes and nationalist attachments, fierce in this border territory of east central Europe during the past two centuries, make territorial definitions an emotional issue. So the question of defining Europe's civilizations is a particularly thorny case of a larger problem.

> *"Russian expansion later pulled parts of eastern Europe, including Poland, into its orbit, although it never eliminated their strong cultural identities."*

If a civilization is defined simply by its mainstream culture, then eastern and western Europe in the postclassical period divide logically according to Orthodox and Catholic territories (and use of the Cyrillic and Greek or of the Latin alphabet). By this reckoning, Poland, the Czech areas, and the Baltic states (these latter did not convert to Catholicism until the 14th century) are western, and Hungary is largely so. South Slavs are mainly but not entirely Orthodox, a regional division that can provoke recurrent violence. Russia and Ukraine are decidedly Orthodox in tradition. Religion matters. Poland and other Catholic regions have long maintained much more active ties with western Europe than Russia has. At the end of the postclassical period, a Czech religious dissenter, Jan Hus, even foreshadowed the later Protestant Reformation in his attacks on the Catholic church.

Politically, the case is more complicated. Poland, Hungary, and Lithuania formed large regional kingdoms at various times during and after the postclassical period. But these kingdoms were very loosely organized, much more so than the feudal monarchies that were developing in western Europe. Exceptionally large aristocracies in Poland and Hungary (by western or by Russian standards) helped limit these states.

Trade patterns also did not closely unite Poland or Hungary with western Europe until much later, when the two regions were clearly different in economic structure. Also, Polish and Hungarian societies often shared more features with Russia than with western Europe.

Russian expansion later pulled parts of eastern Europe, including Poland, into its orbit, although it never eliminated strong cultural identities. It is also important to remember that borders can change. The Mongol invasions that swept through Russia also conquered Poland and Hungary, but the armies did not stay there. Part of the Ukraine was also free from direct Mongol control, which helped differentiate it from Russia proper. For two centuries, at the end of the postclassical period, the divisions within eastern Europe intensified. Since 1989, many eastern European countries have again achieved full independence from Russia, and they want to claim their distinctive pasts. Not an easy border area to characterize in terms of a single civilization, east central Europe has also been a victim of many conquests interspersed with periods of proud independence.

**Questions** What were the main characteristics of Russian civilization as it first emerged in the postclassical period? In what ways did Poland, Hungary, and the Czech lands differ from these characteristics? Are there other civilization border areas, in the postclassical period or later, that are similarly difficult to define because of their position between two other areas?

beyond the "who, what, where, and when" of historical events and consider instead the far-reaching implications of historical developments.

### Global Connections

Each chapter ends with a Global Connections section that reinforces the key themes and issues raised in the chapter and makes clear their importance not only to the areas of civilization discussed in the chapter but also to the world as a whole.

o positions of leadership and to
ivities such as making war and

d not support full-time specialists,
gious and craft experts were rec-
f several kinds, varying according
nctions. The most esteemed were
also trained as priests. The chief-
ommunal ceremonies and knew
protect the tribe or hapu. The
with spirits, gods, and goddesses
tantly in human affairs. At the
scale were shamans, who special-
erved as the mediums by which
their desires known to humans.

**ociety** In addition to priests,
wide variety of experts, ranging
canoes, to woodcarvers and tat-
ost important experts, however,
relating to making war. Maori
with war. During the appropriate
pus fought regularly with their
t confederations. Young men
warriors, and leaders could not
positions without demonstrating
Much of the time and energy of
d to planning campaigns against
r building the intricate hilltop
roughout the north island.
fe in Maori wars was low by Euro-
combats were fierce. Hand-to-
ears and exquisitely carved war
ed mode of combat. Successful
se attacks were highly admired.

the Maori from achieving the full occupational specialization that, as we have seen, was critical to the advance to true civilization elsewhere. Isolation limited Maori technological advances and their resistance to disease. These limits rendered them vulnerable to peoples such as the Europeans, who had more sophisticated tools and weapons and transmitted diseases that decimated the tribes of New Zealand. Although their skills in war and their adaptability allowed the Maori to survive in the long run, they could do little to prevent the disintegration of their culture and the destruction of much of the world they had known before the coming of the Europeans.

GLOBAL CONNECTIONS

**The Emerging Cultures**

Two important features were shared by the societies that formed on the fringes of the major core of world civilizations during the classical period and slightly beyond. First, as they adopted or imported agriculture, they were able to form more structured political units and develop a more complex social hierarchy. Second, each of the emerging societies exhibited important characteristics from its own past. These characteristics carried forward into the history of these regions, even as other influences were encountered.

Most of the fringe societies obviously participated in a new range of contacts, either through migration into greater interaction with an established civilization or, as with Japan, through deliberate imitation. Nomadic peoples more generally also enhanced contacts, bringing new influences through trade, migration, or invasion.

### Further Readings

Each chapter includes several annotated paragraphs of suggested readings. Students receive reliable guidance on a variety of books: source materials, standards in the field, encyclopedic coverage, more readable general-interest titles, and the like.

### On the Web

Each chapter ends with a list of Web sites with annotations to give students the key words necessary to search for similar sites.

### Chapter Updates

20th century materials have been substantially revised, with particular attention to greater clarity and emphasis on the end of the cold war and ensuing developments. The emergence of globalization and resistance to globalization have also been reexamined. All of the other chapters have been reviewed and updated as necessary.

### Glossary

The comprehensive glossary is another feature that sets this book apart. It includes conceptual terms, frequently used foreign terms, and names of important geographic regions and key characters on the world stage. Much of world history will be new to most students, and this glossary will help them develop a global vocabulary.

## Acknowledgments

Grateful acknowledgment is made to the following colleagues and reviewers, who made many useful suggestions during the development of the text.

J. Michael Allen, Brigham Young University, Hawaii campus

Anthony Cheeseboro, Southern Illinois University, Edwardsville

Scott Cotton, University of Texas, Dallas

Patricia O'Neill, Central Oregon Community College

Jim Ross-Nazzal, Montgomery College

Sharlene Sayegh, California State University, Long Beach

David R. Smith, California State Polytechnic, Pomona

Christopher J. Ward, Clayton State University

PETER N. STEARNS

MICHAEL ADAS

STUART B. SCHWARTZ

MARC JASON GILBERT

# SUPPLEMENTS

With the best of Longman's multimedia solutions for history in one easy-to-use place, MyHistoryLab offers instructors a state-of-the-art interactive instructional solution for World History courses organized according to the textbook. Available from non-course-management or course-management platforms (CourseCompass™, Blackboard™, and WebCT™), MyHistoryLab is designed to be used as a supplement to a traditional lecture course or to administer a completely online course. MyHistoryLab provides helpful tips, review materials, and activities to make the study of history an enjoyable learning experience. Icons in the book lead students to specific assets. **MyHistoryLab includes the following features:**

### Primary Source Documents and Comparative Case Studies

Each chapter contains primary source documents and comparative case studies with accompanying discussion questions for students to review and assess. The most prominent documents in each chapter can be assigned, and the results of the quiz will report to the grade book.

### History Bookshelf

Read, download, or print more than 50 of the most commonly assigned works.

### History Toolkit

A number of useful tools and tutorials, including "How to Analyze Primary Sources" and "Everything You Need to Know About Your History Course," help students with their historical research and classroom studies. "Best of History Web Sites," "The History News Network," and "The History Link Library" are kept up to date and provide the most relevant and accurate links for research assignments.

### Resource Index

This master index lists all of the images, maps, documents, videos, and case studies that appear on MyHistoryLab throughout all of the chapters in the book, with a link to each asset.

### Map Room

This part of the site contains a full index of all of the maps that are available in each chapter throughout the site. The Map Room also contains map activities that allow students to assess a map from the time period covered and take a brief map quiz for that chapter.

### Pre-Test and Post-Test Quizzes and Individualized Study Plan

Each chapter contains a pre-test and a post-test quiz to allow students to review their knowledge of the material. Feedback provides links that take students directly to the relevant section of the textbook online, and a personalized Study Plan allows students to assess their proficiency.

### Chapter Review Materials

The Study Guide, PowerPoint™ presentations, flashcards, and other features help students master the contents of the textbook and prepare for exams.

### Chapter Exam

Each chapter has a chapter exam. Student results are reported to an online gradebook.

### The Textbook Online

Students can read the book online or print out sections of the book to read anywhere. Icons in the book pages link to relevant MyHistoryLab assets.

### Writing Resources

This part of the site contains a number of resources to help students improve their history writing. Assets include information about typical classroom assignments and research, writing support, style guidelines, and a tutorial for how to avoid plagiarism.

### Research Navigator™

The EBSCO ContentSelect, Academic Journal and Abstract Database, the *New York Times* Search by Subject Archive, "Best of the Web" Link Library, and *Financial Times* Article Archive and Company Financials offer thousands of credible and reliable articles and Web sites to get the research process started.

### Test Bank

Course management users can create their own exams using the Test Bank from the text and place them in MyHistoryLab for students to take as practice quizzes or as graded exams.

### The Tutor Center

On-call qualified help is available to answer student questions about MyHistoryLab. The Tutor Center is open Sunday through Thursday from 5 P.M. to midnight, EST.

## For Qualified College Adopters

### Instructor's Manual

0-321-41756-9
Prepared by Pamela Marquez of Metropolitan State College of Denver, the manual includes chapter summaries, discussion suggestions, critical thinking exercises, map exercises, primary source analysis suggestions, and term paper and essay topics. A special "Instructor's Tool Kit" by George Jewsbury of Oklahoma State University includes audiovisual suggestions.

### Test Bank

0-321-44257-1
Written by John Lyons of Joliet Junior College, this supplement contains more than 2000 multiple-choice and essay questions. All questions are referenced by topic, type, and text page number.

### TestGen-EQ Computerized Testing System

0-321-44256-3
This flexible, easy-to-master, computerized test bank on a dual-platform CD-ROM includes all of the items in the printed test bank and allows instructors to select specific questions, edit existing questions, and add their own items to create exams. Tests can be printed in several fonts and formats and can include figures, such as graphs and tables.

### Instructor Resource Center (IRC)

www.ablongman.com/irc
Through the Instructor Resource Center, instructors can log into premium online products, browse and download book-specific instructor resources, and receive immediate access and instructions for installing course management content. Instructors who already have access to CourseCompass™ or Supplements Central can log in to the IRC immediately using their existing login and password. First-time users can register at the IRC welcome page at www.ablongman.com/irc.

### History Digital Media Archive CD-ROM

0-321-14976-9
The Digital Media Archive CD-ROM contains electronic images, interactive and static maps, and media elements such as video. These media assets are fully customizable and ready for classroom presentation or easy downloading into PowerPoint™ or any other presentation software.

### Discovering World History Through Maps and Views

0-321-21647-4
This updated second edition is by Gerald A. Danzer, University of Illinois, Chicago, winner of the AHA's James Harvey Robinson Award for his work in developing map transparencies. This set of over 100 four-color downloadable transparencies is an unparalleled supplement that contains four-color historical reference maps, source maps, views and photos, urban plans, building diagrams, and works of art. These transparencies are available to adopters as downloadable PDFs on the Instructor Resource Center.

### Text-Specific Transparency Set

0-321-44382-9
Instructors can download files with which to make full-color transparency map acetates taken from the text at www.ablongman.com/irc.

### World History Companion Web Site

www.ablongman.com/worldhistory
Instructors can take advantage of the online course companion that supports the world history course. The instructor section includes a list of instructor links as well as a link to the Instructor Resource Center.

## Supplements for Students

### Research Navigator and *Research Navigator Guide*

0-205-40838-9
Research Navigator is a comprehensive Web site comprising three exclusive databases of credible and reliable source material for research and for student assignments: EBSCO's ContentSelect Academic Journal Database, the

*New York Times* Search-by-Subject Archive, and "Best of the Web" Link Library. The site also includes an extensive help section. The *Research Navigator Guide* provides students with access to the Research Navigator Web site and includes reference material and hints about conducting online research.

### Mapping World History

0-06-500560-0
This workbook was created for use in conjunction with *Discovering World History Through Maps and Views.* It is designed to teach students how to interpret and analyze cartographic materials as historical documents.

### Study Guide

Volume I: 0-321-41755-0
Volume II: 0-321-44381-0
Prepared by Theron Corse of Tennessee State University, each volume includes chapter outlines, timelines, map exercises, multiple-choice practice tests, and critical thinking and essay questions.

### *World History Map Workbook,* Second Edition

Volume I: 0-321-06632-4
Volume II: 0-321-06633-2
Created by Glee Wilson of Kent State University, this two-volume workbook contains more than 40 maps accompanied by more than 120 pages of exercises. Each volume is designed to teach the location of various countries and their relationship to one another. Also includes exercises that enhance students' critical thinking abilities.

### Documents in World History

Volume 1, *The Great Tradition: From Ancient Times to 1500*
0-321-33054-4
Volume 2, *The Modern Centuries: From 1500 to the Present*
0-321-33258-X
Edited by Peter N. Stearns, Stephan S. Gosch, and Erwin P. Grieshaber. This collection of primary source documents illustrates the human characteristics of key civilizations during major stages of world history.

### Study Card for World History

0-321-29234-0
Colorful, and packed with useful information, Longman's Study Cards make studying easier, more efficient, and more enjoyable. Course information is distilled down to the basics to allow for quickly mastering the fundamentals, reviewing a subject for understanding, or preparing for an exam.

### *Longman Atlas of World History*

0-321-20998-2
The 52 four-color maps of this atlas from Longman and Maps.com provide comprehensive global coverage for the major historical periods, ranging from the earliest of civilizations to the present. Each map has been designed to be colorful, easy to read, and informative, making history and geography more comprehensible.

### Penguin-Longman Partnership

Students and professors alike will love the value and quality of the Penguin books offered at a deep discount when bundled with *World Civilizations: The Global Experience* for qualified college adopters. For a complete listing of titles, go to www.ablongman.com/penguin.

### Longman Library of World Biography Series

Each interpretive biography in the new Library of World Biography Series focuses on a figure whose actions and ideas significantly influenced the course of world history. Pocket-sized and brief, each book relates the life of its subject to the broader themes and developments of the times. Series titles include:

- *Ahmad al-Mansur: Islamic Visionary,* Richard L. Smith
- *Alexander the Great: Legacy of a Conqueror,* Winthrop Lindsay Adams
- *Benito Mussolini: The First Fascist,* Anthony L. Cardoza
- *Fukuzawa Yûkichi: From Samurai to Capitalist,* Helen M. Hopper
- *Ignatius of Loyola: Founder of the Jesuits,* Patrick Donnelly
- *Jacques Coeur: Entrepreneur and King's Bursar,* Kathryn L. Reyerson
- *Katô Shidzue: A Japanese Feminist,* Helen M. Hopper
- *Simón Bolívar: Liberation and Disappointment,* David Bushnell
- *Vasco da Gama: Renaissance Crusader,* Glenn J. Ames
- *Zheng He: China and the Oceans in the Early Ming Dynasty, 1405–1433,* Edward L. Dreyer

### Longman World History Series

These books focus on the historical significance of a particular movement, experience, or interaction. Concise and inexpensive, they bring the global connections and consequences of these events to the fore, showing students how events that happened long ago or far away can still affect them. Titles include:

- *Colonial Encounters in the Age of High Imperialism,* Scott B. Cook
- *Environmentalism: A Global History,* Ramachandra Guha
- *Expansion and Global Interaction: 1200–1700,* David Ringrose

# About the Authors

## Peter N. Stearns

Peter N. Stearns is provost and professor of history at George Mason University. He received his Ph.D. from Harvard University. Before moving to George Mason University, he taught at Rutgers University, the University of Chicago, and Carnegie Mellon, where he won the Robert Doherty Educational Leadership Award and the Elliott Dunlap Smith Teaching Award. He has taught world history for more than 15 years. He currently serves as chair of the Advanced Placement World History Committee and also founded and is the editor of the *Journal of Social History*. In addition to textbooks and readers, he has written studies of gender and consumerism in a world history context. Other books address modern social and cultural history and include studies on gender, old age, work, dieting, and emotion. His most recent book in this area is *American Fear: Causes and Consequences of High Anxiety.*

## Michael Adas

Michael Adas is the Abraham Voorhees Professor of History and a board of governor's chair at Rutgers University in New Brunswick, New Jersey. Over the past couple of decades his teaching has focused on patterns and processes of global and comparative history. His courses on race and empire in the early modern and industrial eras and on world history in the 20th century have earned him a number of teaching prizes. In addition to texts on world history, Adas has written mainly on the comparative history of colonialism and its impact on the peoples and societies of Asia and Africa. His books include *Machines as the Measure of Men: Science, Technology, and Ideologies of Western Dominance*, which won the Dexter Prize, and the recently published *Dominance by Design: Technological Imperatives and America's Civilizing Mission.* He is currently writing a global history of the First World War.

## Stuart B. Schwartz

Stuart B. Schwartz was born and educated in Springfield, Massachusetts, and then attended Middlebury College and the Universidad Autonoma de Mexico. He has an M.A. and Ph.D. from Columbia University in Latin American history. He taught for many years at the University of Minnesota and joined the faculty at Yale University in 1996. He has also taught in Brazil, Puerto Rico, Spain, France, and Portugal. He is a specialist on the history of colonial Latin America, especially Brazil, and is the author of numerous books, notably *Sugar Plantations in the Formation of Brazilian Society* (1985), which won the Bolton Prize for the best book in Latin American History. He is also the author of *Slaves, Peasants, and Rebels* (1992), *Early Latin America* (1983), and *Victors and Vanquished* (1999). He has held fellowships from the Guggenheim Foundation and the Institute for Advanced Study (Princeton). For his work on Brazil he was recently decorated by the Brazilian government. He continues to read widely in the history and anthropology of Latin America, Africa, and early modern Europe.

## Marc Jason Gilbert

Marc Jason Gilbert is the holder of an NEH-supported Chair in World History at Hawaii Pacific University in Honolulu, Hawaii. He is a former University System of Georgia Distinguished Professor of Teaching and Learning. He received his Ph.D in history in 1978 at UCLA, where he built his own program in world history out of a mixture of more traditional fields. He is a founding member of the World History Association and one of its initial elected officers. More than a decade ago, he founded and served as executive director of the Southeastern World History Association. He has co-directed two Summer Institutes for Teaching Advanced Placement World History. He has attempted to bring a global dimension to the study of south and southeast Asian history in numerous articles and books, such as *Why the North Won the Vietnam War.*

# PROLOGUE

The study of history is the study of the past. Knowledge of the past gives us perspective on our societies today. It shows different ways in which people have identified problems and tried to resolve them, as well as important common impulses in the human experience. History can inform through its variety, remind us of some human constants, and provide a common vocabulary and examples that aid in mutual communication.

The study of history is also the study of change. Historians analyze major changes in the human experience over time and examine the ways in which those changes connect the past to the present. They try to distinguish between superficial and fundamental change, as well as between sudden and gradual change. They explain why change occurs and what impact it has. Finally, they pinpoint continuities from the past along with innovations. History, in other words, is a study of human society in motion.

World history has become a subject in its own right. It involves the study of historical events in a global context. It does not attempt to sum up everything that has happened in the past. World history focuses on two principal subjects: the evolution of leading societies and the interaction among different peoples around the globe.

## The Emergence of World History

Serious attempts to deal with world history are relatively recent. Many historians have attempted to locate the evolution of their own societies in the context of developments in a larger "known world": Herodotus, though particularly interested in the origins of Greek culture, wrote also of developments around the Mediterranean; Ibn Khaldun wrote of what he knew about developments in Africa and Europe as well as in the Muslim world. But not until the 20th century, with an increase in international contacts and a vastly expanded knowledge of the historical patterns of major societies, did a full world history become possible. In the West, world history depended on a growing realization that the world could not be understood simply as a mirror reflecting the West's greater glory or as a stage for Western-dominated power politics. This hard-won realization continues to meet some resistance. Nevertheless, historians in several societies have attempted to develop an international approach to the subject that includes, but goes beyond, merely establishing a context for the emergence of their own civilizations.

Our understanding of world history has been increasingly shaped by two processes that define historical inquiry: detective work and debate. Historians are steadily uncovering new data not just about particular societies but about lesser-known contacts. Looking at a variety of records and artifacts, for example, they learn how an 8th-century battle between Arab and Chinese forces in central Asia brought Chinese prisoners who knew how to make paper to the Middle East, where their talents were quickly put to work. And they argue about world history frameworks: how central European actions should be in the world history of the past 500 years, and whether a standard process of modernization is useful or distorting in measuring developments in modern Turkey or China. Through debate come advances in how world history is understood and conceptualized, just as the detective work advances the factual base.

## What Civilization Means

Humans have always shown a tendency to operate in groups that provide a framework for economic activities, governance, and cultural forms such as beliefs and artistic styles. These groups, or societies, may be quite small; hunting-and-gathering bands often numbered no more than 60 people. World history usually focuses on somewhat larger societies, with more extensive economic relationships (at least for trade) and cultures.

One vital kind of grouping is called civilization. The idea of civilization as a type of human society is central to most world history, though it also generates debate and though historians are now agreed that it is not the only kind of grouping that warrants attention. Civilizations, unlike some other societies, generate surpluses beyond basic survival needs. This in turn promotes a variety of specialized occupations and heightened social differentiation, as well as regional and long-distance trading networks. Surplus production also spurs the growth of cities and the development of formal states, with some bureaucracy, in contrast to more informal methods of governing. Most civilizations have also developed systems of writing.

Civilizations are not necessarily better than other kinds of societies. Nomadic groups have often demonstrated great creativity in technology and social relationships, and some were more vigorous than settled civilizations in promoting global contacts. Moreover, there is disagreement about exactly what defines a civilization—for example, what about cases like the Incas where there was no writing?

Used carefully, however, the idea of civilization as a form of human social organization, and an unusually extensive one, has merit. Along with agriculture (which developed earlier), civilizations have given human groups the capacity to fundamentally reshape their environments and to dominate most other living creatures. The history of civilizations embraces most of the people who have ever lived; their literature, formal scientific discoveries, art, music, architecture, and inventions; their most elaborate social, political, and economic systems; their brutality and destruction caused by conflicts; their exploitation of other species; and their degradation of the environment—a result of changes in technology and the organization of work.

The study of civilizations always involves more, however, than case-by-case detail. World history makes sense only if civilizations are compared, rather than treated separately. Equally important, civilizations (and other societies) developed important mutual contacts, which could have wide impact in reshaping several societies at the same time. And civilizations responded to still wider forces, like migration, disease, or missionary activity, that could reshape the frameworks within which they operated. Civilizations in these wider contexts—as they changed through internal dynamics, mutual interactions, and responses to broader forces—form the basic patterns of world history for the past 5000 years.

160°W
140°W
120°W
100°W
80°W
60°W
40°W
20°W
80°N
ARCTIC OCEAN
GREENLAND
Arctic Circle
Yukon R.
ICELAND
60°N
BERING SEA
GULF OF ALASKA
HUDSON BAY
ALEUTIAN ISLANDS
ROCKY MOUNTAINS
NORTH AMERICA
St. Lawrence R.
APPALACHIAN MTS.
40°N
Mississippi R.
PACIFIC OCEAN
Rio Grande
ATLANTIC OCEAN
GULF OF MEXICO
Tropic of Cancer
WEST INDIES
20°N
HAWAIIAN ISLANDS
CARIBBEAN SEA
GUIANA HIGHLANDS
0° Equator
Amazon R.
SOUTH AMERICA
ANDES MOUNTAINS
BRAZILIAN HIGHLANDS
20°S
ATACAMA DESERT
Tropic of Capricorn
Paraná R.
PACIFIC OCEAN
40°S
60°S
Antarctic Circle
80°S

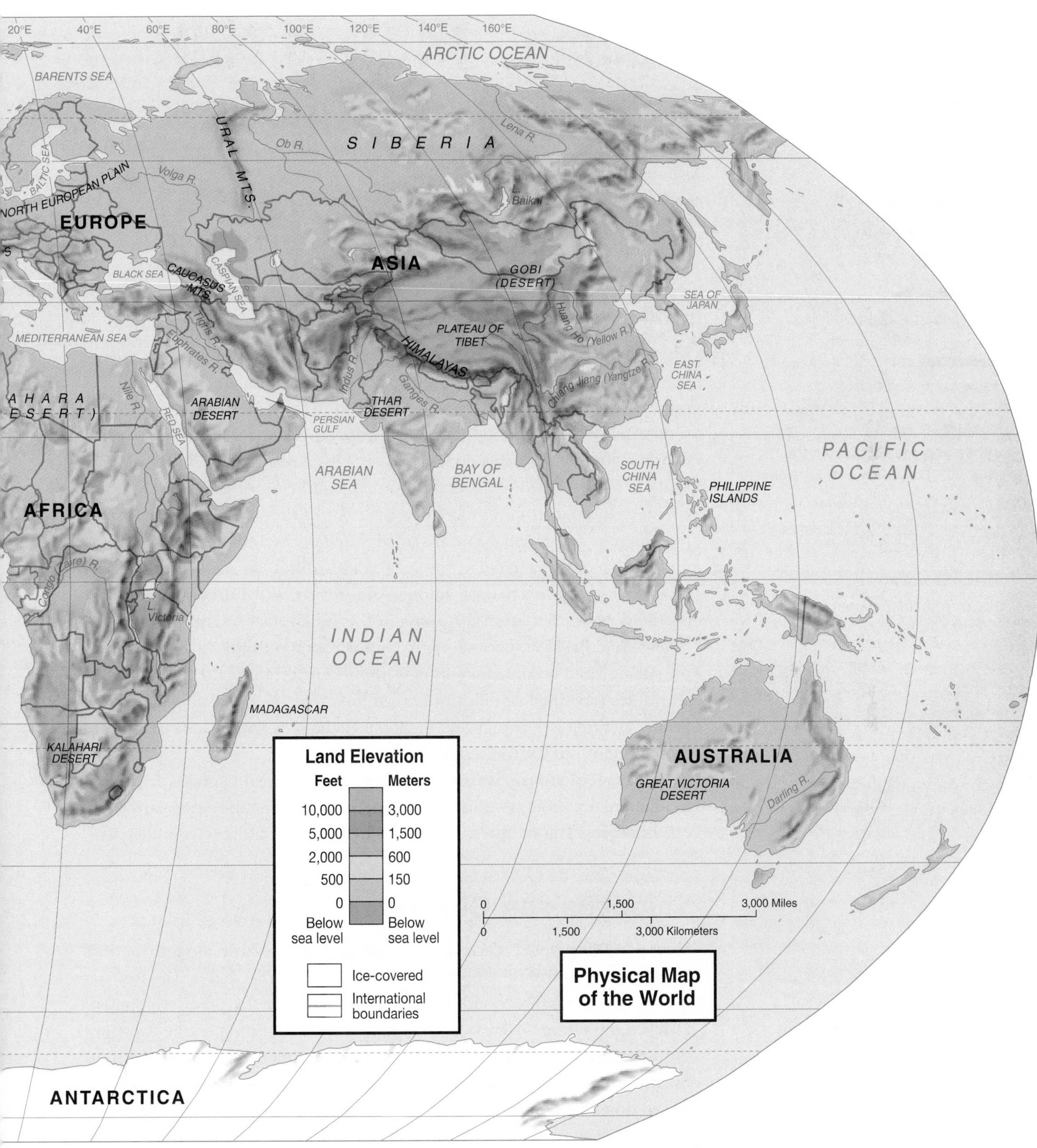
20°E
40°E
60°E
80°E
100°E
120°E
140°E
160°E
ARCTIC OCEAN
BARENTS SEA
SIBERIA
Lena R.
Ob R.
URAL MTS.
BALTIC SEA
NORTH EUROPEAN PLAIN
Volga R.
Baikal
EUROPE
ASIA
BLACK SEA
CAUCASUS MTS.
CASPIAN SEA
GOBI (DESERT)
SEA OF JAPAN
PLATEAU OF TIBET
Huang Ho (Yellow R.)
MEDITERRANEAN SEA
Tigris R.
Euphrates R.
HIMALAYAS
EAST CHINA SEA
Indus R.
Ganges R.
Chiang Jiang (Yangtze R.)
SAHARA DESERT)
Nile R.
ARABIAN DESERT
THAR DESERT
RED SEA
PERSIAN GULF
PACIFIC OCEAN
ARABIAN SEA
BAY OF BENGAL
SOUTH CHINA SEA
PHILIPPINE ISLANDS
AFRICA
Congo (Zaire) R.
L. Victoria
INDIAN OCEAN
MADAGASCAR
KALAHARI DESERT
AUSTRALIA
GREAT VICTORIA DESERT
Darling R.
Land Elevation
Feet
Meters
10,000
5,000
2,000
500
0
Below sea level
3,000
1,500
600
150
0
Below sea level
Ice-covered
International boundaries
0
1,500
3,000 Miles
0
1,500
3,000 Kilometers
Physical Map of the World
ANTARCTICA

PART

# IV

# The Early Modern Period, 1450–1750: The World Shrinks



## The World Map Changes

These maps depict two of the big changes in world history that occurred between 1450 and 1750. Over these centuries, a number of new empires came into being, replacing smaller political units characteristic of the preceding postclassical period. Several European countries acquired overseas empires the first time this option had ever been so dramatically developed, while new land-based empires arose in Asia and eastern Europe. The Russian and Ottoman empires extended over both European and Asian territory, while the new Mughal Empire ruled much of the Indian subcontinent.

The second big change involved trade routes. In 1450 international trade focused on exchanges among Asia, Africa, and Europe across some overland routes but also via seaways in the Indian Ocean and the Mediterranean Sea. By 1750, oceangoing routes across the Pacific and particularly the Atlantic had become increasingly important, although the Indian Ocean sea routes remained significant. For the first time, the Americas and, soon, Pacific Oceania were caught up in global exchanges, with results not only in these regions but for the rest of the world as well.

Change, of course, is never complete. Even as world geography shifted fundamentally, some political features persisted during the three early modern centuries. Trade routes also maintained some holdovers from the past.

## Triggers for Change

Several developments marked the beginning of the early modern period, distinguishing it from the postclassical period that preceded it. The first was the revival of empire building. A striking example of this development involved the Ottoman Turks, who conquered Constantinople, the capital of the Byzantine Empire. Soon the Ottomans extended their rule over most Byzantine territories and beyond, putting a Muslim power in charge of one of the great Christian cities and territories of the past. Worried Christian leaders elsewhere in the world turned to new activities to compensate for the loss of influence and territory. The second development visible by 1450—the steady progression of explorations by Europeans along the Atlantic coast of

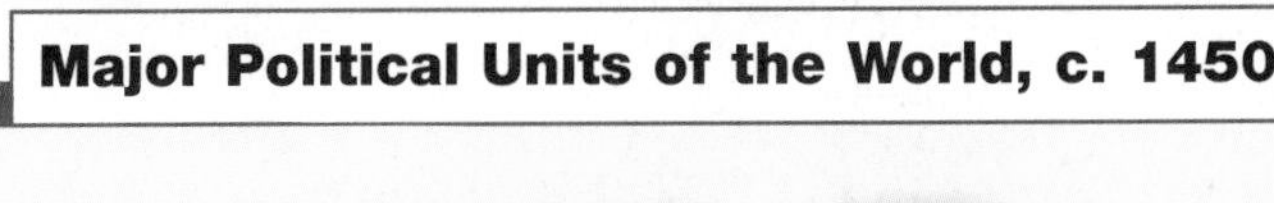

## Major Political Units of the World, c. 1450

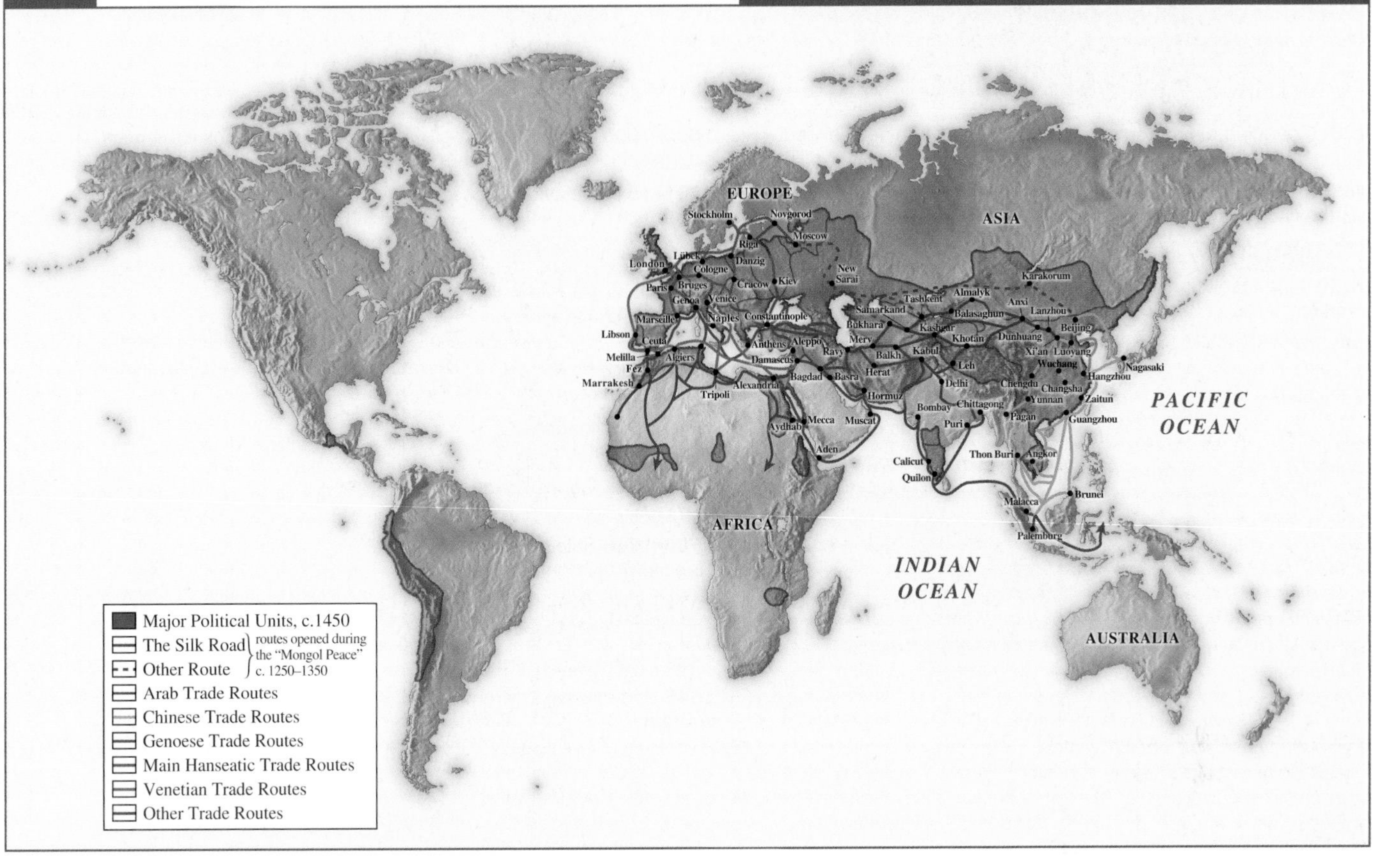

- Major Political Units, c.1450
- The Silk Road } routes opened during the "Mongol Peace" c. 1250–1350
- Other Route } routes opened during the "Mongol Peace" c. 1250–1350
- Arab Trade Routes
- Chinese Trade Routes
- Genoese Trade Routes
- Main Hanseatic Trade Routes
- Venetian Trade Routes
- Other Trade Routes

## Major Political Units of the World, c. 1750

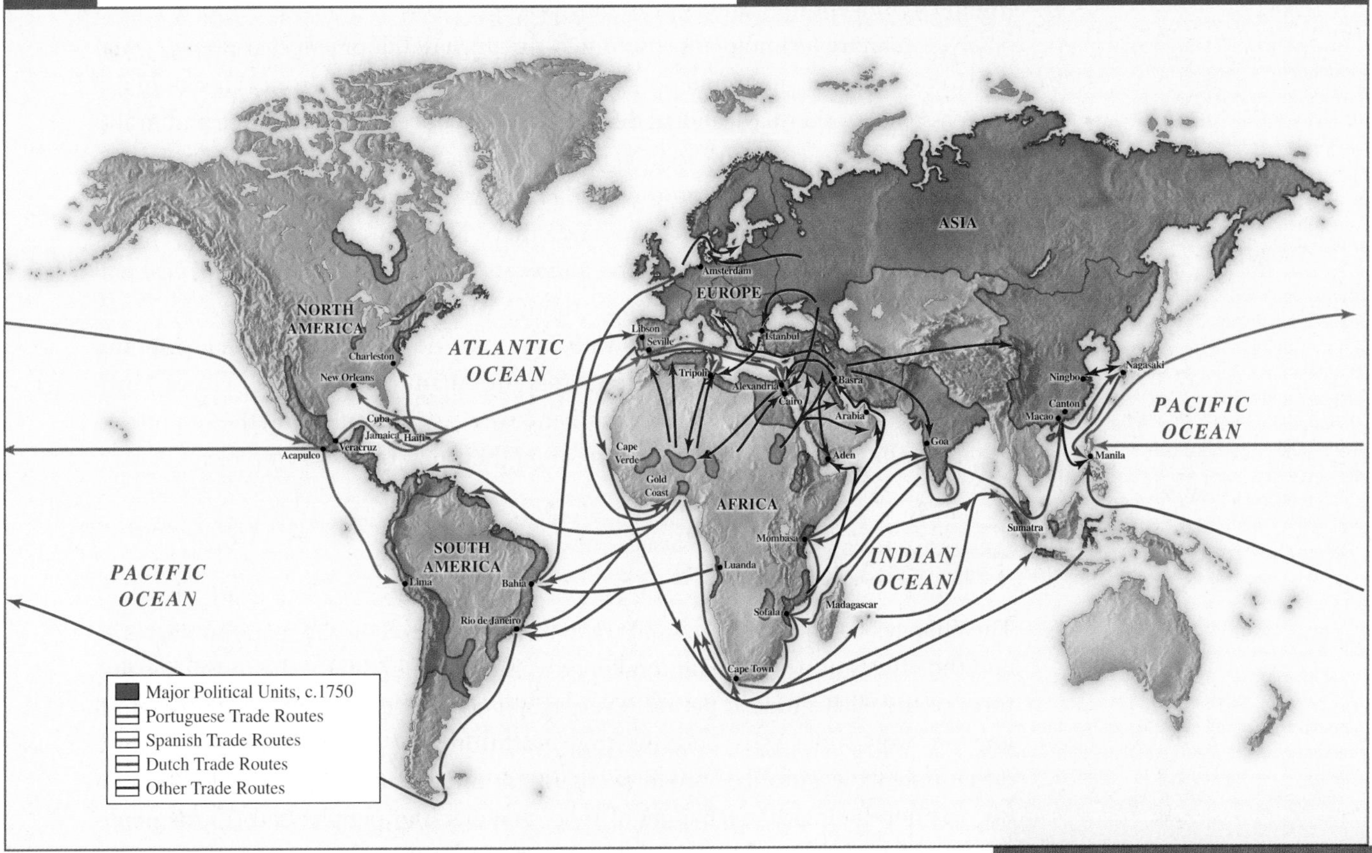

- Major Political Units, c.1750
- Portuguese Trade Routes
- Spanish Trade Routes
- Dutch Trade Routes
- Other Trade Routes

| 1300 C.E. | 1400 C.E. | 1500 C.E. | 1550 C.E. |
|---|---|---|---|
| **1281** Founding of Ottoman dynasty<br>**1350s** Ottoman invasion of southeastern Europe<br>**1368** Ming dynasty in China<br>**1390** ming restrictions in overseas trade | **1405–1433** Chinese expedition period<br>**1434–1498** Portuguese expeditions down west African coast<br>**1441** Beginning of European slave trade in Africa<br>**1453** Ottoman conquest of Constantinople<br>**1480** Moscow region free of Mongol control<br>**1492** Columbus expeditions<br>**1498–1499** Vasco da Gama expedition opens seas to Asia | **1500–1600** Europe's commercial revolution<br>**1501–1510** Safavid conquest of Iran<br>**1509** Spanish colonies on American mainland<br>**1510–1511** Portugal conquers Goa (India), Malacca (Malaysia)<br>**1517–1541** Protestant Reformation (Europe)<br>**1519–1521** Magellan circumnavigates globe<br>**1519–1524** Cortés conquers Mexico<br>**1520–1566** Suleiman the Magnificent (Ottoman)<br>**1526** Babur conquest in northern India (Mughal)<br>**1533** Pizarro wins Peru<br>**1548** Portuguese government in Brazil | **1552** Russia begins expansion in central Asia and western Siberia<br>**1570** Portuguese colony of Angola (Africa)<br>**1571** Ottoman naval defeat of Lepanto<br>**1590** Hideyoshi unifies Japan<br>**1591** Fall of Songhay (Africa) |

Africa—was motivated in part by the desire to find ways to trade with east Asia that would circumvent the centers of Islamic power.

New military technologies constituted the third development that played a vital role in defining the new framework for this period. European mariners began to use compasses and other navigational devices, first introduced by the Chinese and Arabs. Europeans also learned how to design better sailing ships. The most important new military technology was the growing use of guns and gunpowder, another Chinese invention now adapted by Europeans and others. New guns played a vital role in the creation of new empires both on land and overseas. Guns also affected political patterns within Africa, Japan, and Europe, though with less sweeping results.

Larger, sturdier ships, armed with cannon and featuring greater shipping capacity, sailed the new trade routes across the Atlantic and Pacific oceans. Europeans exercised disproportionate dominance over these routes, and they employed the new military technologies in establishing their new overseas empires.

## THE BIG CHANGES

The changes in world empires and trade routes depicted on the maps on page 453 and the effects of new naval and military technologies highlight the distinctive features of the early modern period. Every major society reacted differently, depending on world position and existing tradition. In general, however, these developments led to three broad changes: (a) the forging of a new global economy; (b) new biological exchanges of food, animals, and people; and (c) the emergence of new, large empires based on guns and gunnery.

| 1600 C.E. | 1650 C.E. | 1700 C.E. | 1750 C.E. |
|---|---|---|---|
| **1600** Dutch and British merchants begin activity in India<br>**1600–1690** Scientific Revolution (Europe)<br>**1603** Tokugawa shogunate<br>**1607** First British colonies in North America<br>**1608** First French North American colonies<br>**1637** Russian pioneers to Pacific<br>**1640s** Japan moves into isolation<br>**1641** Dutch colonies in Indonesia<br>**1642–1727** Isaac Newton<br>**1644** Qing dynasty, China | **1652** Dutch colony South Africa<br>**1658–1707** Aurangzeb reign, beginning of Mughal decline<br>**1682–1699** Turks driven from Hungary<br>**1689–1725** Peter the Great (Russia) | **1713** New Bourbon dynasty, Spain<br>**1722** Fall of Safavid dynasty (Iran)<br>**1759–1788** Reforms of Latin American colonial administration | **1756–1763** Seven Years War<br>**1763** Britain acquires "New France"<br>**1764** British East India Company controls Bengal (India)<br>**1770s** European–Bantu conflicts in southern Africa<br>**1772–1795** Partition of Poland<br>**1775–1783** American Revolution<br>**1781** Indian revolts in New Grenada and Peru (Latin America)<br>**1792** Slave uprising in Haiti |

## A New Global Economy

International trade increased, for the first time including the Americas in the exchange. This was a major step in bringing the various regions of the world closer together and exposing them more widely to international influences.

## Biological Exchange

The inclusion of the Americas in the global trade set in motion a number of biological exchanges of enormous consequence. Foods from the Americas, like corn and the potato, began to be grown in Asia and, later, Europe. Combined with local improvements in agriculture, these new foods resulted in population increases. Europeans introduced new diseases into the Americas and Pacific island territories, decimating the native populations. Population loss encouraged new migrations, particularly from Europe and Africa, into the Americas. The massive African slave trade was in part a response to a labor shortage in the Americas. New animals, like the horse, greatly altered life in the Americas. These biological exchanges, called the "Columbian exchange," altered many relationships among populations. New foods helped generate population increase worldwide, trumping the devastation wrought by new diseases. But new diseases and unprecedented levels of death were agonizing realities for many regions.

## New Empires

The gunpowder empires formed large political units. Building and maintaining these new political structures required huge energies and huge expenses. New empires in India, the Middle East, southeastern Europe, and Russia challenged political traditions in their imperial territories, while Spain, Portugal, France, England, and the Netherlands exerted pressure on their new overseas holdings.

These three main developments—the new global economy, the biological exchange, and the emergence of new empires—involved considerable shifts in world power. The world position of western Europe increased most obviously. Russia gained a new role as well. New masters ruled over many parts of the Americas, while portions of Africa found themselves immersed in novel orbits. New economic and military agents and competitors challenged many established societies in Asia and Africa. Systematic patterns of inequality began to characterize some of the societies that supplied foods and raw materials to western Europe. Europe became wealthier and ever more powerful as it supplied processed goods and commercial services to these same regions.

## Continuity

Change is never complete. Even as world geography shifted, some political features persisted during the three centuries of the early modern period. Some existing trade routes continued to be important avenues of global exchange.

Many societies reacted to the big changes of the early modern period by preserving key features of their past. No sweeping, global cultural change occurred during this era. Notable developments took place within individual societies, such as the new influence of science in western Europe or the rise of Japanese Confucianism. The spread of world religions continued, with Islam reaching southeast Asia and parts of southeastern Europe and, even more dramatically, with conversions to Christianity in the Americas. But cultural stability described much of the world, and global contacts did not overturn regional culture patterns.

No systematic changes occurred in gender relations in the early modern period. The new African slave trade affected gender balances on both sides of the Atlantic. More men than women were seized in Africa; as a result, the lack of adequate numbers of husbands encouraged African polygamy. New ideas sparked some debate over women's conditions in western Europe, though little real change. Relations between men and women in most other societies adhered to established patterns.

Aside from the new developments in the military sphere, there were no technological breakthroughs until after 1750. Many societies participated only gradually in the use of guns and gunnery. Manufacturing techniques changed modestly, and little change, took place in agriculture beyond the foodstuffs.

While political change, signaled by the rise of empires, was more general, several societies emphasized continuity in this realm as well. China prided itself on reviving and then maintaining its system of government. Many African societies preserved earlier traditions of divine kinship.

## Impact on Daily Life: Work

Changes of the early modern period profoundly affected ordinary people in many parts of the world. Indians in the Americas died by the thousands as European and African immigrants brought diseases like smallpox and measles. Europeans used silver to pay for desirable Chinese goods. Flush with new wealth, the Chinese government began to require that taxes be paid in silver, thus compelling ordinary Chinese to find new ways to obtain money. Often such efforts were unsuccessful, and as a result many Chinese fell ever deeper into poverty. Millions of Africans were seized from their homes and subjected to a terrifying and often deadly passage to the Americas. Those who managed to survive the voyage discovered that they were now compelled to live out their lives as slaves.

The most general social change during the early modern period was a growing pressure to work harder. The early modern world was increasingly commercial and crowded. Population increases in some regions demanded more from workers to help sustain larger families and villages. Many manufacturers and landowners tried to force their workers to increase their pace. The new forms of race-based slavery in the Americas placed greater emphasis on production. In western Europe, for example, Protestantism preached a work ethic that convinced many people that labor was a way to demonstrate God's grace.

People of all ages responded to the pressure to work harder. Child labor increased in many regions. Many European children were pressed into service as indentured laborers; for example, whole groups of orphans might be transported to work sites. By the 18th century, London orphans might be sent to work in new English factories or to North America as indentured servants. Even in old age, adults had to work if they wanted to survive. Master artisans, from makers of porcelain in China to gunsmiths in Europe, tried to compel their workers and apprentices to turn out more product. The pressure to work harder and longer was a personal side to the systemic changes that were reshaping the world.

The name commonly given to this period—early modern—captures complexity. The period is more recognizably modern than its predecessor. The renewed emphasis on political structures may strike a modern chord as well. But if modern, this was still early: many features, including the continued dominance of traditional agriculture even in the most advanced economies, make it clear that there were still many changes to come in world history after 1750.

## Trends and Societies in the Early Modern Period

The chapters that follow examine the differing reactions to the major developments and changes of the early modern period. Chapter 21 offers an overview of the new global trading patterns that followed from the changes in naval technology and warfare. New trading opportunities and colonial expansion were closely related to significant changes within western Europe, the subject of Chapter 22. European changes would ultimately affect other parts of the world as well. Russia, selecting aspects of Western society as a model for change, developed one of the most novel gunpowder empires, with major impact on the power balance in eastern Europe, east Asia, and part of the Muslim world. The story of Russia's rise is told in Chapter 23. Chapters 24 and 25 return to the Atlantic world. The early modern era was a formative period for a new society in Latin America, born of interactions among native populations, Europeans, and Africans. Chapter 26, on the new Muslim states in the Middle East and southern Asia, concentrates on the emergence of other gunpowder empires. East Asia responded in its own, largely successful way to the new world economy. In these areas internal dynamics had more to do with developments that occurred between 1450 and 1750.

Each of the chapters in this part deals with reactions to world trade, biological exchange, and new pressures on labor. Each also highlights the diversity of patterns emerging in different parts of the world, depending on cultural orientation and shifts in positions of world power.

CHAPTER 21

# The World Economy



How did silver mined by conscripted South American Indians change China's tax system? Silver quickly became the global currency of the early modern period. Production and use of silver show the power of the new **world economy** emerging after 1500. Silver had long been valued, of course, but new sources of production made it a commonly traded commodity. Japanese mines raised their output, trading with Europe and China. But it was European discoveries of silver in the Americas that really turned the tide. Mexican silver mines were important, but the big find, in the mid-16th century, was at Potosi, in Bolivia, where there was an enormous vein of ore. Desperate for labor, the Spanish revived *mita*—the Inca system of drafting workers for short stints. By 1600 there were 150,000 miners at Potosi, more than a third of them conscripted through the mita system.

Silver was a godsend to Europeans. The Spanish crown kept a fifth of the silver its colonies produced, and this was its chief gain from the American colonies. Silver allowed Spain to build massive armies and grand new public buildings. But most of the silver sent to Europe passed through Spain to merchants elsewhere. They, in turn, used silver primarily to buy Asian goods that had long been sought, such as Indian spices and Chinese porcelain and silk. The Spanish also sent considerable silver to the Philippines, where it was traded for Chinese products sent to elites in the Americas and Europe. Silver greased the wheels of international commerce, allowing Europeans to buy Asian imports that could not otherwise have been afforded.

China and India were the largest recipients of New World silver—a clear sign of Asia's dynamism in the new world economy. Silver encouraged economic growth in Asia. It began to replace paper money. Merchants required silver even for purchases of common items like food. The Ming dynasty required periodic tax payments in silver. This reduced the number of tax collections—a reform known as "one whip of the lash." Silver imports helped sustain a standard of living in China that, into the early 19th century, was superior to that of western Europe.

**FIGURE 21.1** This engraving of the Potosi silver mine in 1590 shows a cut-away view of a mountain. Inside, Native American miners work by torchlight.

But there were also worries. Many Chinese observers thought that silver was creating a wider gap between rich and poor, and they pointed out that the poor had to struggle to find the silver needed to pay their taxes. A few Europeans mused about expending so much effort to obtain silver that would only be swallowed up in Asia, but most agreed that the new consumer goods were well worth the trouble. A very few Europeans, but undoubtedly lots of ordinary Latin Americans, worried about the harsh working conditions in the mines.

This chapter deals with the consequences of some key developments long celebrated in American school texts: the voyages of Columbus and other explorers and the empires built by European conquerors and missionaries. The result was a power shift in world affairs, but another set of crucial developments in world history also resulted: the redefinition of interchanges among major societies in the world.

The story is not, however, simply the familiar one. European countries did play a disproportionate role in change, particularly the huge shifts affecting the Americas and Africa. But African and Asian contributions were active as well.

| 1400 C.E. | 1500 C.E. | 1600 C.E. | 1700 C.E. |
|---|---|---|---|
| **1394–1460** Life of Prince Henry the Navigator<br>**1433** China ends its great expeditions<br>**1434** Portugal extends expeditions along west African coast<br>**1488** Portuguese round Cape of Good Hope<br>**1492** Columbus's first expedition<br>**1497–1498** Vasco da Gama sails to India | **1509** First Spanish colonies on Latin American mainland<br>**1514** Portuguese expedition to Indonesia<br>**1519–1521** Magellan circumnavigates the globe<br>**1534** First French explorations in Canada<br>**1542** Portuguese reach Japan<br>**1562** Britain begins its slave trade<br>**1571** Ottoman fleet defeated in Battle of Lepanto<br>**1588** British defeat Spanish Armada<br>**1597** Japan begins isolation policy | **1607** First permanent British colony in Virginia<br>**1608** First French colonies in Canada; England gains first trading concession in India<br>**1641** Dutch begin conquests of Java (Indonesia)<br>**1652** Dutch launch colony in southern Africa | **1744** French–British wars in India<br>**1756–1763** Seven Years War in Europe, India, and North America<br>**1763** British acquire New France<br>**1775–1783** American Revolution<br>**1756** "Black hole" of Calcutta<br>**1764** East India Company controls Bengal |

## The West's First Outreach: Maritime Power

**European merchant fleets seized control of key international trading routes. Initial Spanish and Portuguese leadership was followed by growing efforts from Britain, France, and Holland.**

Various European leaders, particularly merchants but also some princes and clergy, had become increasingly aware of the larger world around them since 1100. The Crusades brought knowledge of the Islamic world's superior economy and the goods that could be imported from Asia. The Mongol Empire, which sped up exchanges between the civilizations of Asia, also spurred European interest. The fall of the khans in China disrupted this interchange, as China became once again a land of mystery to Europeans. Europe's upper classes had by this time become accustomed to imported products from southeast Asia and India, particularly spices. These goods were transported to the Middle East in Arab ships, then brought overland, where they were loaded again onto vessels (mainly from Genoa and Venice, in Italy) for the Mediterranean trade.

Europeans entered into this era of growing contacts with several disadvantages. They remained ignorant of the wider world. Viking adventurers from Scandinavia had crossed the Atlantic in the 10th century, reaching Greenland and then North America, which they named Vinland. However, they quickly lost interest beyond establishing settlements on Greenland and Iceland, in part because they encountered indigenous warriors whose weaponry was good enough to cause them serious problems. And although scientists elsewhere knew otherwise, many Europeans continued to believe that the earth was flat; this belief made them fearful of distant voyages lest they fall off the world's edge.

As Europeans launched a more consistent effort at expansion from 1291 onward, they were pressed by new problems: fear of the strength of the emerging Ottoman Empire and the lack of gold to pay for Asian imports. Initial settlements in island groups in the south Atlantic fed their hopes for further gains. However, the first expeditions were limited by the small, oar-propelled ships used in the Mediterranean trade, which could not travel far into the oceans.

### New Technology: A Key to Power

During the 15th century, a series of technological improvements began to change the equation. Europeans developed deep-draft, round-hulled sailing ships for the Atlantic, capable of carrying heavy armaments. They were using and improving the compass. Mapmaking and other navigational devices improved as well. Finally, European knowledge of explosives, another Chinese invention, was adapted into gunnery. European metalwork, steadily advancing in sophistication, allowed Western metalsmiths to devise the first guns and cannons. Though not very accurate, these weapons were awesome by the standards of the time (and terrifying to many Europeans, who had reason to fear the new destructive power of their own armies and navies). The West began to forge a military advantage over all other civilizations of the world, at first primarily on the seas—an advantage it would retain into the 20th century. With an unprecedented ability to kill and intimidate from a distance, western Europe was ready for its big push.

## Portugal and Spain Lead the Pack

The specific initiative came from the small kingdom of Portugal, whose Atlantic location made it well-suited for new initiatives. Portugal's rulers were drawn by the excitement of discovery, the harm they might cause to the Muslim world, and a thirst for wealth—a potent mix. A Portuguese prince, Henry the Navigator (Figure 21.2), organized a series of expeditions along the African coast and also outward to islands such as the Azores. Beginning in 1434 the Portuguese began to press down the African coast, each expedition going a little farther than its predecessor. They brought back slaves, spices such as pepper, and many stories of gold hoards they had not yet been able to find.

Portuguese Travelers in Africa

Later in the 15th century, Portuguese sailors ventured around the **Cape of Good Hope** in an attempt to find India, where direct contact would give Europeans easier access to luxury cloths and spices. They rounded the cape in 1488, but weary sailors forced the expedition back before it could reach India. Then, after news of Columbus's discovery of America for Spain in 1492, Portugal redoubled its efforts, hoping to stave off the new Spanish competition. Vasco da Gama's fleet of four ships reached India in 1498, with the aid of a Hindu pilot picked up in east Africa. The Portuguese mistakenly believed that the Indians were Christians, for they thought the Hindu temples were churches. They faced the hostility of Muslim merchants, who had long dominated trade in this part of the world, and they brought only crude goods for sale, like iron pots. But fortunately they had some gold as well. They managed to return with a small load of spices. A later trip involved more violence, as Europeans substituted force for their lack of attractive items for world trade. Da Gama used ships' guns to intimidate, and his forces killed or tortured many Indian merchants to set an example.

Da Gama's success set in motion an annual series of Portuguese voyages to the Indian Ocean, outlined in Map 21.1. One expedition, blown off course, reached Brazil, where it proclaimed Portuguese sovereignty (Figure 21.3). Portugal began to set up forts on the African coast and also in India—the forerunners of such Portuguese colonies as Mozambique, in east Africa, and Goa, in India. By 1514 the Portuguese had reached the islands of Indonesia, the center of spice production, and China. In 1542 one Portuguese expedition arrived in Japan, where a missionary effort was launched that met with some success for several decades.

**FIGURE 21.2** Prince Henry the Navigator financed annual expeditions down the western coast of Africa in an effort to find a sea route to the Indies, establish trade with Africa, and find the fabled Christian kingdom of Prester John.

Meanwhile, only a short time after the Portuguese quest began, the Spanish reached out with even greater force. Here also was a country only recently freed from Muslim rule, full of missionary zeal and a desire for riches. The Spanish had traveled into the Atlantic during the 14th century. Then in 1492, the same year that the final Muslim fortress was captured in Spain, the Italian navigator **Christopher Columbus,** operating in the name of the newly united Spanish monarchy, set sail for a westward route to India, convinced that the round earth would make his quest possible. As is well known, he failed, reaching the Americas instead and mistakenly naming their inhabitants "Indians." Although Columbus believed

Christopher Columbus in the "New World"

Christopher Columbus and the Round World

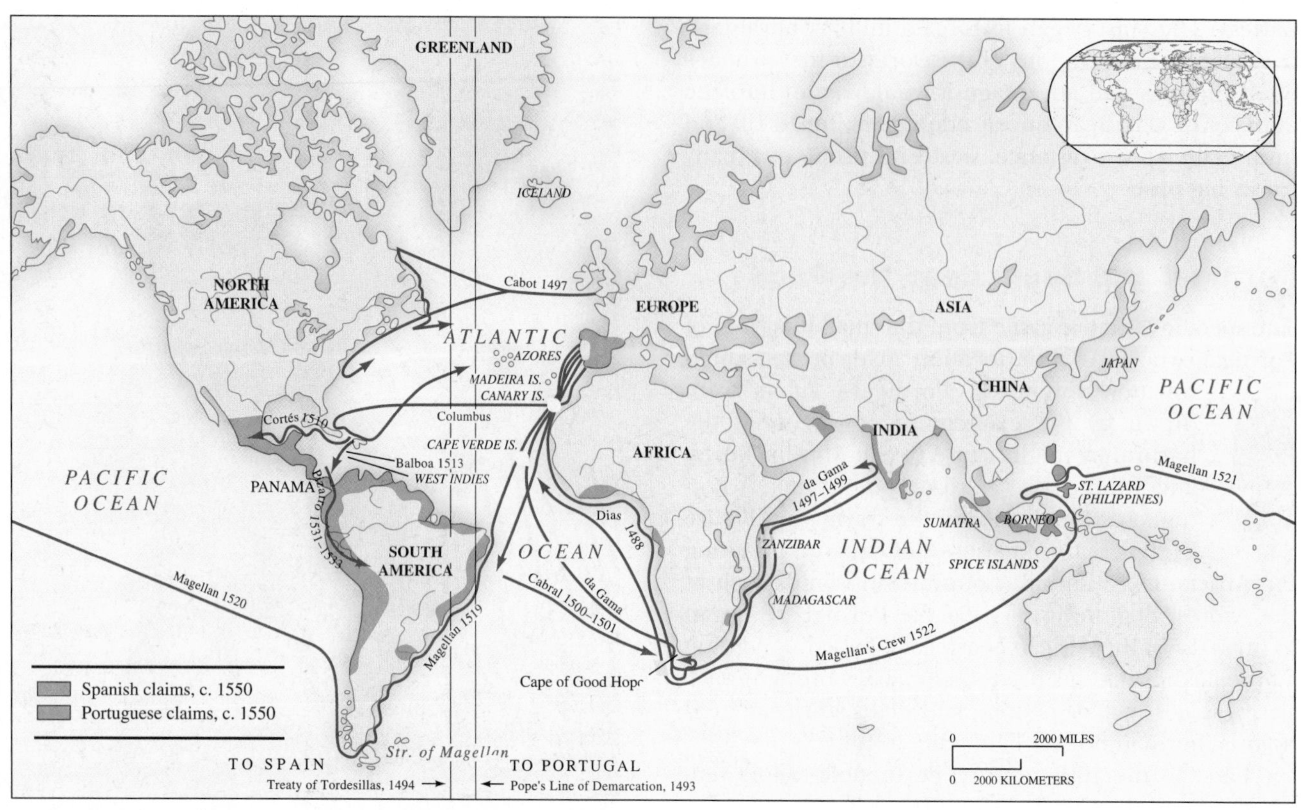


**MAP 21.1 Spain and Portugal: Explorations and Colonies.** In the early years of exploration, Spanish and Portuguese voyagers surveyed much of the coast of South America and some choice ports in Africa and Asia.

to his death that he had sailed to India, later Spanish explorers realized that they had voyaged to a region where Europeans, Africans, and Asians had not traveled previously. One expedition, headed by Amerigo Vespucci, gave the New World its name. Spain, eager to claim this new land, won papal approval for Spanish dominion over most of what is now Latin America, although a later treaty awarded Brazil to Portugal.

Finally, a Spanish expedition under **Ferdinand Magellan** set sail westward in 1519, passing the southern tip of South America and sailing across the Pacific, reaching the Indonesian islands in 1521 after incredi-

**FIGURE 21.3** This 1505 woodcut is the earliest known European portrayal of Native Americans. It was done by an unknown German artist who had never been to America but based his drawing on the testimony of those who had. The accompanying text reported: "The people are thus naked, handsome, brown. . . . They also eat each other . . . and hang the flesh of them in the smoke. They become a hundred and fifty years of age, and have no government."

ble hardships. It was on the basis of this voyage, the first trip around the world, that Spain claimed the Philippines, which it held until 1898.

Portugal emerged from this first round of exploration with coastal holdings in parts of Africa and in the Indian port of Goa, a lease on the Chinese port of Macao, short-lived interests in trade with Japan, and finally, the claim on Brazil. Spain asserted its hold on the Philippines, various Pacific islands, and the bulk of the Americas. During the 16th century, the Spanish backed up these claims by military expeditions to Mexico and South America. The Spanish also held Florida and sent expeditions northward from Mexico into California and other parts of what later became the southwestern United States.

Europeans in the World, Fifteenth and Sixteenth Centuries

## Northern European Expeditions

Later in the 16th century, the lead in exploration passed to northern Europe, as newly strong monarchies, such as France and England, got into the act and zealous Protestants in Britain and Holland strove to rival Catholic gains (Map 21.2). In part this shift in dynamism occurred because Spain and Portugal were busy digesting the gains they had already made; in part it was because northern Europeans, particularly the Dutch and the British, improved the design of oceanic vessels, producing lighter, faster ships than those of their Catholic adversaries. Britain won a historic sea battle with Spain in 1588, routing the massive Spanish Armada. From this point onward, the British, the Dutch, and to some extent the French vied for dominance on the seas, although in the Americas they aimed mainly northward because they could not challenge the Spanish and Portuguese colonies. Only in the sugar-rich West Indies did northern Europe seize islands initially claimed by Spain.

The new adventurers, like their Spanish and Portuguese predecessors, appreciated the economic potential of such voyages. Two 16th-century English explorers, trying to find an Arctic route to China, were told to keep an eye out for any native populations en route, for such people would provide a perfect market for warm English woolens. And if the territory was unpopulated, it might be put to use as a source of fish for Britain. A quest for profit had become a dominant policy motive.

French explorers crossed the Atlantic first in 1534, reaching Canada, which they claimed. In the 17th

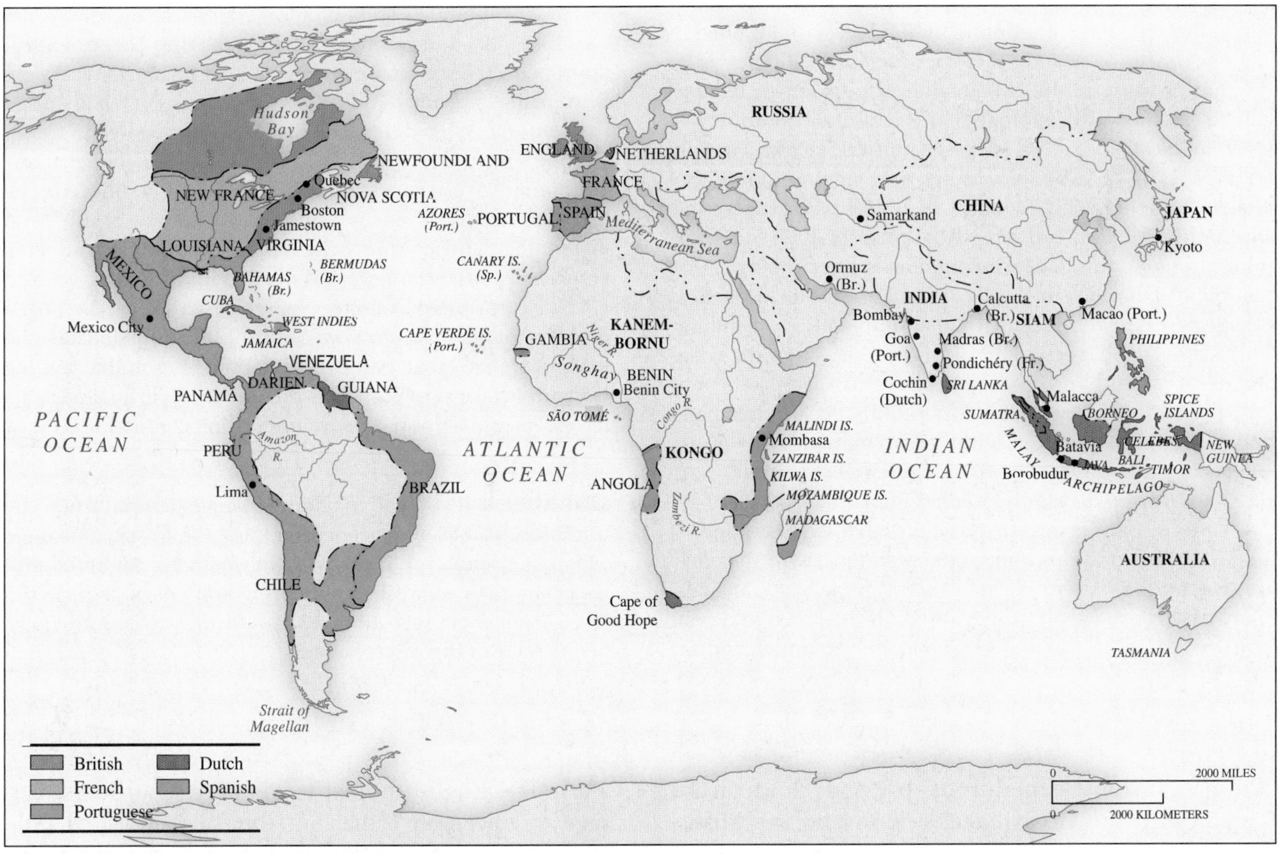

**MAP 21.2 French, British, and Dutch Holdings, c. 1700.** During the 17th century, northwestern Europe took the initiative in explorations, venturing into North America and seeking convenient trading stations elsewhere.

IN DEPTH

## Causation and the West's Expansion

Because of their interest in social change, historians inevitably deal with causation. What prompted the fall of Rome? Why did Islam spread so widely? What factors explain why most agricultural civilizations developed patriarchal family structures?

Historical causation differs from the kinds of causation many scientists test. When experiments or observations can be repeated, scientists can gain a fairly precise understanding of the factors that produce a phenomenon: remove an ingredient, for example, and the product changes. Historical causation is more complex. Major developments may resemble each other, but they never happen the same way twice. Definitive proof that factor *X* explains 40 percent of the spread of Buddhism in east Asia is impossible. This is why historians often disagree about causation. But if precision is impossible, high probability is not. We can get a fairly good sense of why things happen, and sloppy causation claims can be disproved. Furthermore, probing causation helps us explore a phenomenon itself. We know more about the nature of Western expansion in the 15th and 16th centuries if we discuss what caused it.

> *"[S]ome historians used to claim 'great men' as the prime movers in history."*

Some historians and other social scientists look to a single kind of cause as the explanation of a variety of circumstances. Some anthropologists are cultural determinists. They judge that a basic set of cultural factors, usually assumed to be very durable, causes the ongoing differences between societies: Chinese and Greeks, on average, respond differently to emotional stimuli because of their different cultural conditioning. More common is a technological or economic determinism. Some historians see technological change as setting other changes in motion. Others, including Marxists, argue that economic arrangements—how the economy is structured and what groups control it—produce at least the basic framework for innovations. At another pole, some historians used to claim "great men" as the prime movers in history. The causes of change thus became Chinggis Khan or Ashoka, with no need to look much further.

Various approaches to causation have been applied to the West's explorations and colonial conquests in the early modern period. There is room for a "great man" analysis. Many descriptive accounts that dwell on explorers and conquerors (Vasco da Gama and Cortés, for example) and on leaders who sponsored them (such as Henry the Navigator) suggest that the key cause of the West's new role stemmed from the daring and vision of exceptional individuals.

Cultural causation can also be invoked. Somehow, Europe's expansion must relate to the wonders of innovation introduced by the Renaissance. The link with Christian culture is even easier to prove, for a missionary spirit quickly supplemented the efforts of early explorers, leading to more voyages and settlements in Asia and the Americas.

Political causation enters in, if not in causing the initial surge, at least in confirming it. Starting in the 16th century, rivalries between the nation-states motivated a continuing quest for new trade routes and colonies.

There is also room for a simpler, technologically determinist approach. In this view, Europe's gains came from a handful of new inventions. Benefiting from knowledge of advances in China and the Middle East, Europeans introduced naval cannons. Along with steady improvements in navigation and ship design, new techniques explain why Europe gained as it did. Except in the Americas, where they had larger technical and organizational advantages, Europeans advanced in areas they could reach by sea and dominate by ships' guns—port cities, islands, and trade routes—and not elsewhere. Put simply, Europe gained because of these few technological edges.

Like all determinisms, however, this technological approach raises as many questions as it answers. Why were Europeans so ready to adopt new inventions? (What caused the cause?) Why did other societies that were aware of Europe's innovations, such as China, deliberately scorn any adoption of Western naval techniques? Here a different culture determined a reaction different from that of the West. Technology and culture went hand in hand. Clearly, some combined causal framework is needed in this case.

We cannot expect uniform agreement on a precise ordering of causation. However, we can expect fruitful debate—the kind of debate that has already moved our understanding beyond surface causes, such as the powerful personalities of a few people, to a grasp of more underlying contexts.

---

**Questions** If you had to choose a single determinism (cultural, technological, or economic) as basic to social change, which one would you pick? Why? In what ways might the professed motives of Western explorers and colonists have differed from their real motives? Would they necessarily have been aware of the discrepancy?

---

century, various expeditions pressed down from Canada into the Great Lakes region and the Mississippi valley.

The British also turned their attention to North America, starting with a brief expedition as early as 1497. The English hoped to discover a northwest passage to spice-rich India, but they accomplished little beyond exploration of the Hudson Bay area of Canada during the 16th century. England's serious work began in the 17th century, with the colonization of the east coast of North America. Holland also had holdings in North America and, for a time, in Brazil.

The Dutch entered the picture after winning independence from Spain, and Holland quickly became a major competitor with Portugal in southeast Asia. The Dutch sent many sailors and ships to the region, ousting the Portuguese from the Indonesian islands by the early 17th century. Voyagers from the Netherlands explored the coast of Australia, though without much immediate result. Finally, toward the mid-17th century, Holland established a settlement on the southern tip of Africa, mainly to provide a relay station for its ships bound for the East Indies.

The Netherlands, Britain, and France all chartered great trading companies, such as the **Dutch East India Company.** These companies were given government monopolies of trade in the regions designated, but they were not rigorously supervised by their own states. They had rights to raise armies and coin money on their own. Thus, semiprivate companies, amassing great commercial fortunes, long acted almost like independent governments in the regions they claimed. For some time, a Dutch trading company effectively ruled the island of Taiwan off the coast of China. The **British East India Company** played a similar role in parts of India during much of the 18th century. The companies in North America traded actively in furs.

No matter where in Europe they came from, explorers and their crews faced many hardships at sea. The work was tiring and uncertain, with voyages lasting many months or years, and diseases such as scurvy were rampant. One expedition accepted only bachelors for its crew because married men would miss their families too much. A sailor on another trip complained that "he was tired of being always tired, that he would rather die once than many times, and that they might as well shut their eyes and let the ship go to the bottom."

## Toward a World Economy

■ **Europe's maritime dominance generated three wider changes, developing from the 1490s onward. One was the Columbian exchange of foods, diseases, and people. A second was new export-import patterns that created durable economic inferiorities. A third was the emergence of new overseas empires.**

### The Columbian Exchange of Disease and Food

The impact of wider exchange became visible quickly. The extension of international contacts spread disease (see Chapter 20). The victims were millions of Native Americans who had not previously been exposed to Afro-Eurasian diseases such as smallpox and measles and who therefore had no natural immunities (Figure 21.4). During the 16th and 17th centuries, they died in huge numbers. Overall, in North and South America, more than half the native population would die; some estimates run as high as 80 percent. Whole island populations in the West Indies were wiped out. This was a major blow to earlier civilizations in the Americas as well as an opportunity for Europeans to forge a partially new population of their own citizens and slaves imported from Africa. The devastation occurred over a 150-year period, although in some areas it was more rapid. When Europeans made contact with Polynesians and Pacific Coast peoples in the 18th century, the same dreadful pattern played out, again devastating vibrant cultures.

FIGURE 21.4 This 16th-century print portrays Aztecs suffering from smallpox during the Cortés invasion (1518–1519).

Other exchanges were less dire. New World crops were spread rapidly via Western merchants. American corn and sweet potatoes were taken up widely in China (where merchants learned of them from Spaniards in the Philippines), the Mediterranean, and parts of Africa. In some cases these productive new crops, along with local agricultural improvements, triggered large population increases. For example, China began to experience long-term population pressure in the 17th century, and new crops played a key role. When Europeans introduced the potato around 1700, major population upheaval occurred there as well.

Indeed, food played a key role in the world system created during the early modern period. About 30 percent of the foods consumed in the world today come from plants of American origin. Corn became a staple in the African diet. Europeans, ironically, were more conservative. Rumors spread that American foods spread the plague. Some worried about consuming foods that were not mentioned in the Bible. It took more than a century for the potato to gain ground, but fried potatoes (French fries) were being sold on the streets of Paris by the 1680s.

Animal husbandry became more similar across the world as European and Asian animals, such as horses and cattle, were introduced to the New World. The spread of basic products and diseases formed an important backdrop to world history from the 16th century on, with varying effects on population structures in diverse regions.

## The West's Commercial Outreach

Europeans did not displace all Asian shipping from the coastal waters of China and Japan, nor did they completely monopolize the Indian Ocean (see Chapter 27). Along the east African coast, while a few European bases were established, Muslim traders remained active, and commerce continued to move toward the Middle East. Generally, however, western Europe dominated a great deal of oceanic shipping, even muscling in on trade between other societies, as between India and southeast Asia. This greatly increased Europe's overall profits, and disproportionate control by the great merchant companies increased the European ability to determine the framework for international trade. In the eastern Mediterranean, for example, a Spanish-directed fleet defeated the navy of the Ottoman Empire in the battle of **Lepanto** in 1571. With this setback, any hope of successful Muslim rivalry against European naval power ended. The Turks rebuilt their fleet and continued their activity in the eastern Mediterranean, but they could not challenge the Europeans on the larger international routes.

Although western Europe did not conquer much inland territory in Africa or Asia, it did seek a limited network of secure harbors. Led by Spain and Portugal, then followed by the various northern powers, European ports spread along the west coast of Africa, several parts of the Indian subcontinent, and the islands of southeast Asia by the 17th century. Even in China, where unusually strong governments limited the Europeans' ability to seize harbors outright, the Portuguese won effective control over the island port of Macao. European-controlled ports served as areas for contact with overland traders (usually local merchants) and provided access to inland goods not directly within the reach of the West.

Discovery and Exploration: Africa

Where direct control was not feasible, European influence led to the formation of special Western enclaves in existing cities, where Western traders won special legal rights. This was the pattern in the Ottoman Empire, where Western merchants set up colonies within Constantinople, and in Russia, where Western factors (shipping agents) set up first in Moscow and then in St. Petersburg. Elements of this system even emerged in Japan after a firm isolationist policy was launched about 1600, as Dutch traders had some special access to the port of Nagasaki. The point was obvious: international trade gained growing importance in supplementing regional economies. Because western Europe now ran this trade, it won special rights of access.

## Imbalances in World Trade

The most active competition in world trade emerged between European nations themselves. Spain briefly dominated, thanks to its imports of silver from the Americas. But it lacked a good banking system and could not support a full commercial surge. England, France, and Holland, where merchants had firmer status, soon pulled in the lion's share of profits from world trade. Western Europe quickly expanded its manufacturing operations, so that it could export expensive finished goods, such as guns and cloth, in return for unprocessed goods, such as silver and sugar, traded by other societies. Here was another margin for profit.

The dominant **core nations** in the new world system supplemented their growing economic prowess by self-serving political policies. The doctrines of **mercantilism,** which urged that a nation-state not import goods from outside its own empire but sell exports as widely as possible in its own ships, both reflected and encouraged the new world system. Tariff policies discouraged manufacturing in colonial areas and stimulated home-based manufacturing.

Beyond western Europe lay areas that were increasingly enmeshed in the world economy but as dependants to the core nations. These areas produced low-cost goods: precious metals and cash crops such as

VISUALIZING THE PAST

## West Indian Slaveholding

The following table describes the rise of the plantation system, and attendant slaveholding, on the British West Indian island of Antigua, where sugar growing for export gained increasing hold. Trends of the sort indicated in this table raise further analytical issues about cause and effect. What might have caused the main changes in Antigua's estate system? How might the changes have related to the larger framework of the world economy? What do the trends suggest about the European demand for sugar and about production methods used to meet this demand?

What impact would the trends have had on slaves themselves? Laws in the British Caribbean soon began to enforce the estate system, exempting masters from murder charges when slaves died from beatings administered as punishment and fining groups such as the Quakers for daring to bring slaves to religious meetings. How do the statistical trends help explain the imposition of new laws of this sort?

| | 1688 | 1706 | 1767 |
|---|---|---|---|
| Taxables | 53 | 36 | 65 |
| Slaveholders | 16 | 30 | 65 |
| Planters with 20+ slaves | 6 | 16 | 46 |
| Planters with 100+ slaves | 0 | 4 | 22 |
| Slaves | 332 | 1,150 | 5,610 |
| Acreage | 5,811 | 5,660 | 12,350 |

**Questions** What trends in the social and economic structure of this part of Antigua during the 18th century do these figures suggest? What were the main changes in the relationship of slaveholding to property ownership? In the size of estates? In the comparative growth rates of owner and slave populations? Did the estate economy become more or less labor intensive, given the acreage involved? What do the trends suggest about the nature of the European-born or European-derived elite of Antigua?

sugar, spice, tobacco, and later cotton. Human labor was a vital item of exchange. Parts of sub-Saharan Africa entered the new world economy mainly as suppliers of slaves. The earlier west African patterns of trade across the Sahara yielded to a dominant focus on the Atlantic and therefore to activities organized by Western shippers. In return for slaves and unprocessed goods, Europeans traded their manufactured items, including guns, while profiting from their control of commercial and shipping services.

### A System of International Inequality

The new world economic relationships proved highly durable. Most of the areas established as dependants by the 17th century still carry some special burdens in world trade today. The core–dependant system should not be exaggerated, in part because most of the world, including most of Asia and much of Africa, was not yet fully embraced by it. In dependent areas such as Latin America and the slave-supplying parts of Africa, not all people were mired in poverty. African slave traders and princes who taxed the trade might grow rich. In Latin America the silver mines and commercial estates required regional merchants and farmers to supply food. Furthermore, many peasants in Latin America and even more in Africa were not yet involved in a market economy at all—whether regional or international—but rather produced for local subsistence with traditional motives and methods. However, significant minorities were involved in production for the world market. Also, most African and Latin American merchants and landlords did not fully control their own terms of trade. They might prosper, but their wealth did not stimulate much local manufacturing or general economic advance. Rather, they tended to import European-made goods, including (in the case of American planters) art objects and luxury items.

Coercive labor systems spread. Because dependent economies relied on cheap production of unprocessed goods, there was a tendency to build a system of forced labor that would cost little even when the overall labor supply was precarious. In the Americas, given the population loss from disease, this led to the massive importation of African slaves. Also, for many Native Americans and **mestizos** (people of mixed European and Native American blood), systems of estate management developed that demanded large amounts of labor. More limited examples of estate agriculture, in which peasants were forced into labor without the legal freedom to leave, arose for spice production in the Dutch East Indies and, by the 18th century, in British-dominated agricultural operations in India.

### How Much World in the World Economy?

Huge areas of the world were not yet caught up in contact with the world economy. The societies that remained outside the world system did not gain ground as rapidly as the core areas of Europe because they did not have the profit opportunities in international trade. Their technologies changed less rapidly. But until the 18th century or beyond, they did not face great international problems.

China clearly benefited from the world economy, while participating less actively than Europe did. The Chinese government, having renounced large-scale international trade of its own early in the 15th century, deliberately avoided involvement with international trade on someone else's terms. It did copy some firearms manufacturing from the Europeans, but at a fairly low level. Beyond this it depended on extensive government regulation, backed up by a coastal navy, to keep European activities in check. Most of the limited trade that existed was channeled through Macao. European visitors wrote scornfully of China's disdain for military advances. A Jesuit wrote that "the military . . . is considered mean among them." The Chinese were also disparaged for adhering to tradition. One Western missionary in the 17th century described how, in his opinion, the Chinese could not be persuaded "to make use of new instruments and leave their old ones without an especial order from the Emperor to that effect. They are more fond of the most defective piece of antiquity than of the most perfect of the modern, differing much in that from us who are in love with nothing but what is new."

So China managed to avoid trying to keep up with European developments while also avoiding subservience to European merchants. The world economy played only a subordinate role in Chinese history through the 18th century. Chinese manufacturing gains led to a strong export position, which is why Europeans sent a great deal of American silver to China to pay for the goods they wanted. But official isolation persisted. Indeed, at the end of the 18th century, a famous British mission, appealing to the government to open the country to greater trade, was rebuffed. The imperial court, after insisting on extreme deference from the British envoy, haughtily informed him that the Chinese had no need for outside goods. European eagerness for Chinese goods—attested to by the habit adopted in the 17th century of calling fine porcelain "china"—was simply not matched by Chinese enthusiasm, but a trickle of trade continued. Westerners compensated in part by developing their own porcelain industry by the 18th century, which contributed to the early Industrial Revolution, particularly in Britain. Still, there were hopes for commercial entry to China that remained unfulfilled.

Japan, though initially attracted by Western expeditions in the 16th century, also more fully pulled back. So did Korea. The Japanese showed some openness to Christian missions, and they were fascinated by Western advances in gunnery and shipping. Artists captured the interest in exotic foreigners. Guns had particular relevance to Japan's ongoing feudal wars, for there was no disdain here for military life. Yet Japanese leaders soon worried about undue Western influence and the impact this could have on internal divisions among warring lords, as well as the threat guns posed to samurai military dominance. They encouraged a local gunmaking industry that matched existing European muskets and small cannon fairly readily, but having achieved this they cut off most contact with any world trade. Most Japanese were forbidden to travel or trade abroad, the small Christian minority was suppressed, and from the 17th until the 19th centuries Japan entered a period of almost complete isolation except for some Chinese contact and trading concessions to the small Dutch enclave near Nagasaki.

Several other societies were not deeply affected by new world trade, participating at levels too low to have significant impact. The rulers of India's new Mughal Empire in the 16th century were interested in Western traders and even encouraged the establishment of small port colonies. India also sold goods in return for New World silver. Most attention, however, was riveted on internal development and land-based expansion and commerce; world trade was a sideline. The same held true for the Ottoman and Safavid empires in the Middle East through the 17th century, despite the presence of small European enclaves in key cities. Russia also lay outside the world economic orbit until the 18th century. A largely agricultural society, Russia conducted much of its trade with nomadic peoples in central Asia, which further insulated it from west European demands. Finally, much of Africa, outside the slave-trading orbit in western regions, was untouched by world trade patterns.

## The Expansionist Trend

The world economy was not stationary; it tended to gain ground over time. South America, the West Indies, a part of North America, and some regions in west Africa were first staked out as dependencies beginning in the 16th century, and the list later expanded. Portions of southeast Asia that produced for world markets, under the dominance of the great Western trading companies, were brought into the orbit by the 17th century.

By the late 17th century, Western traders were advancing in India as the Mughal Empire began to fall apart. The British and French East India Companies staked out increasing roles in internal trade and administration. Early in the 18th century, Britain passed tariffs against the import of cotton cloth made in India as a means of protecting Britain's own cotton industry. The intent was to use India as a market for British-processed goods and a source of outright payments of gold, which the British were requiring by the late 18th century. Indian observers were aware of the shifting balance. An 18th-century account noted,

> But such is the little regard which they [the British] show to the people of this kingdom, and such their apathy and indifference for their welfare, that the people under their dominion groan everywhere, and are reduced to poverty and distress.

India maintained a complex regional economy still, with much internal manufacturing and trade; it was not forced into such complete dependency as Latin America, for example. However, what had initially been a position outside the world economy was changing, to India's disadvantage. Manufacturing began to decline.

Eastern Europe also was brought into a growing relationship with the world economy and the west European core. The growth of cities in the West created a growing market for imported grains by the 18th century. Much of this demand was met by east European growers, particularly in Prussia and Poland but also in Russia. Export grains, in turn, were produced mainly on large estates by serfs, who were subjected to prolonged periods of labor service. This relationship was similar to that which prevailed in Latin America, with one exception: outside of Poland, east European governments were much stronger than their Latin American counterparts.

## Colonial Expansion

- **Europe developed a network of overseas colonies, particularly in the Americas but also in a few parts of Africa and Asia. By the 18th century, growing European inroads in India marked a decisive change in south Asia.**

### The Americas: Loosely Controlled Colonies

Opportunities to establish colonies were particularly inviting in the Americas, where European guns, horses, and iron weapons offered special advantages and where political disarray and the population losses provided openings in many cases (see Chapter 24). Spain moved first. The Spanish colonized several West Indian islands soon after Columbus's first voyage, starting with Hispaniola and then moving into Cuba, Jamaica, and Puerto Rico. Only in 1509 did they begin settlement on the mainland, in search of gold. The first colony was established in what is now Panama, under an able but unscrupulous adventurer, **Vasco de Balboa.** Several expeditions fanned out in Central America, and then a separate expedition from Cuba launched the Spanish conquest of the Aztecs in Mexico. Another expedition headed toward the Inca realm in the Andes in 1531, where hard fighting was needed before ultimate victory. From this base several colonial expeditions spread to Colombia, other parts of the Andes, and portions of Argentina.

Discovery and Exploration: "The New World"

Expansion resulted from the efforts of a motley crew of adventurers, many of them violent and treacherous, like **Francisco Pizarro** (1478–1541), admittedly one of the more successful examples (Figure 21.5). Pizarro first came to the Americas in 1502 and settled on the island of Hispaniola. Later, he joined Balboa's colony in Panama, where he received a cattle ranch. Learning of wealth in Peru, he joined with an illiterate soldier and a priest, mounting two expeditions that failed. In 1528 he returned to Spain to gain the king's support and also his agreement that he would be governor of the new province. With these pledges and a force of about 180 men, he attacked the divided Inca Empire. Capturing Emperor Atahuallpa, he accepted a large ransom and then strangled him. Several revolts

FIGURE 21.5 Francisco Pizarro.

DOCUMENT

## Western Conquerors: Tactics and Motives

In the first passage quoted here, Columbus writes to the Spanish monarchy on his way home from his 1492 expedition. In the second passage, the brother of Francisco Pizarro, the Spanish conqueror of Peru, describes in 1533 how the Inca ruler, Atahuallpa, was defeated.

### Columbus's 1492 Expedition

Sir, believing that you will take pleasure in hearing of the great success which our Lord has granted me in my voyage, I write you this letter, whereby you will learn how in thirty-three days' time I reached the Indies with the fleet which the most illustrious King and Queen, our Sovereigns, gave to me, where I found very many islands thickly peopled, of all which I took possession without resistance for their Highnesses by proclamation made and with the royal standard unfurled. To the first island that I found I gave the name of *San Salvador,* in remembrance of His High Majesty, who hath marvelously brought all these things to pass; the Indians call it *Guanaham*. . . .

*Espanola* is a wonder. Its mountains and plains, and meadows, and fields, are so beautiful and rich for planting and sowing, and rearing cattle of all kinds, and for building towns and villages. The harbours on the coast, and the number and size and wholesomeness of the rivers, most of them bearing gold, surpass anything that would be believed by one who had not seen them. There is a great difference between the trees, fruits, and plants of this island and those of *Juana*. In this island there are many spices and extensive mines of gold and other metals. The inhabitants of this and of all the other islands I have found or gained intelligence of, both men and women, go as naked as they were born, with the exception that some of the women cover one part only with a single leaf of grass or with a piece of cotton, made for that purpose. They have neither iron, nor steel, nor arms, nor are they competent to use them, not that they are not well-formed and of handsome stature, but because they are timid to a surprising degree. . . .

Although I have taken possession of all these islands in the name of their Highnesses, and they are all more abundant in wealth than I am able to express . . . yet there was one large town in *Espanola* of which especially I took possession, situated in a locality well adapted for the working of the gold mines, and for all kinds of commerce, either with the main land on this side, or with that beyond which is the land of the great Khan, with which there is great profit. . . .

I have also established the greatest friendship with the king of that country, so much so that he took pride in calling me his brother, and treating me as such. Even should these people change their intentions towards us and become hostile, they do not know what arms are, but, as I have said, go naked, and are the most timid people in the world; so that the men I have left could, alone, destroy the whole country, and this island has no danger for them, if they only know how to conduct themselves. . . . Finally, and speaking only of what has taken place in this voyage, which has been so hasty, their Highnesses may see that I shall give them all the gold they require, if they will give me but a very little assistance; spices also, and cotton, as much as their Highnesses shall command to be shipped; and mastic, hitherto found only in Greece . . . slaves, as many of these idolators as their Highnesses shall command to be shipped. . . .

But our Redeemer hath granted this victory our illustrious King and Queen and their kingdoms, which have acquired great fame by an event of such high importance, in which all Christendom ought to rejoice, and which it ought to celebrate with great festivals and the offering of solemn thanks to the Holy Trinity with many solemn prayers, both for the great exaltation which may accrue to them in turning so many nations to our holy faith, and also

followed during Pizarro's rule from Lima, a coastal city he founded. But the Spanish king ennobled Pizarro for his success. At a dinner in 1541, Pizarro was assassinated by a group of Inca rebels.

Early colonies in the Americas typically were developed by small bands of gold-hungry Europeans, often loosely controlled by colonial administrations back home. Colonial rulers often established only loose controls over native populations at first, content to exact tribute without imposing detailed administration and sometimes leaving existing leaders in place. Gradually, more formal administration spread as agricultural settlements were established and official colonial systems took shape under control of bureaucrats sent from Spain and Portugal. Active missionary efforts, designed to Christianize the native peoples, added another layer of detailed administration throughout the Spanish holdings in North and South America.

France, Britain, and Holland, though latecomers to the Americas, also staked out colonial settlements. French explorations along the St. Lawrence River in Canada led to small colonies around Quebec, from 1608 onward, and explorations in the Mississippi River basin. Dutch and English settlers moved into portions of the Atlantic coastal regions early in the 17th century. Also in the 17th century, all three countries seized for the temporal benefits which will bring great refreshment and gain, not only to Spain, but to all Christians.

## Why and How Atahuallpa Was Defeated

The messengers came back to ask the Governor to send a Christian to Atahuallpa, that he intended to come at once, and that he would come unarmed. The Governor sent a Christian, and presently Atahuallpa moved, leaving the armed men behind him. He took with him about five or six thousand Indians without arms, except that under their shirts they had small darts and slings with stones.

He came in a litter, and before went three or four hundred Indians in liveries, cleaning straws from the road and singing. Then came Atahuallpa in the midst of his chiefs and principal men, the greatest among them being also borne on men's shoulders. . . . A Dominican Friar, who was with the Governor, came forward to tell him, on the part of the Governor, that he waited for him in his lodgings, and that he was sent to speak with him. The Friar then told Atahuallpa that he was a Priest, and that he was sent there to teach the things of the Faith, if they should desire to be Christians. He showed Atahuallpa a book . . . and told him that book contained the things of God. Atahuallpa asked for the book, and threw it on the ground, saying: "I will not leave this place until you have restored all that you have taken in my land. I know well who you are, and what you have come for." . . . The Friar went to the Governor and reported what was being done, and that no time was to be lost. The Governor sent to me; and I had arranged with the Captain of the artillery that, when a sign was given, he should discharge his pieces, and that, on hearing the reports, all the troops should come forth at once. This was done, and as the Indians were unarmed, they were defeated without danger to any Christian. Those who carried the litter, and the chiefs who surrounded Atahuallpa, were all killed, falling around him. The Governor came out and seized Atahuallpa, and in protecting him, he received a knife cut from a Christian in the hand. The troops continued the pursuit as far as the place where the armed Indians were stationed, who made no resistance whatever, because it was night. All were brought into town, where the Governor was quartered.

Next morning the Governor ordered us to go to the camp of Atahuallpa, where we found forty thousand pesos worth of gold and two or three pounds of silver. . . . The Governor said that he had not come to make war on the Indians, but that our Lord the Emperor, who was Lord of the whole world, had ordered him to come that he might see the land, and let Atahuallpa know the things of our Faith. . . . The Governor also told him that that land, and all other lands, belonged to the Emperor, and that he must acknowledge him as his Lord. He replied that he was content, and, observing that the Christians had collected some gold, Atahuallpa said to the Governor that they need not take such care of it, as if there was so little; for that he could give them ten thousand plates, and that he could fill the room in which he was up to a white line, which was the height of a man and a half from the floor.

**Questions** What were the main bases for initial European judgments about the characteristics of Native American? How might the native peoples have judged the Europeans? What motives does Columbus appeal to in trying to interest Spanish rulers in the new land?

These documents raise obvious problems of interpretation. They interpret interactions with another, very foreign culture from the European standpoint only. They also attribute motives to the adventurers that may or may not have been predominant. Figuring out how to gain useful, valid information from documents of this sort, which are undeniably revealing of key passages in world history, is a major challenge. What parts of the accounts seem most reliable, and what criteria can be used to sort out degrees of accuracy?

and colonized several West Indian islands, which they soon involved in the growing slave trade.

## British and French North America: Backwater Colonies

Colonies of European settlers developed in North America, where patterns differed in many respects from those in Latin America and the Caribbean. English colonies along the Atlantic received religious refugees, such as the Calvinists who fled religious tensions in Britain to settle in New England. Government grants of land to major proprietors such as William Penn led to explicit efforts to recruit settlers. New York began as a Dutch settlement but was taken over easily by an English expedition in 1664.

In Canada, the first substantial European settlements were launched by the French government under Louis XIV. The initial plan involved setting up manorial estates under great lords whose rights were carefully restricted by the state. French peasants were urged to emigrate, although it proved difficult to develop an adequate labor force. However, birth rates were high, and by 1755 **New France** had about 55,000 settlers in a peasant society that proved extremely durable as it fanned out around the fortress of Quebec.

**FIGURE 21.6** British naval power allowed the light infantry to scale the French fort from the St. Lawrence River and capture Quebec in 1759. The battle was a turning point in Canadian history: the beginning of the end of French rule.

Strong organization by the Catholic church completed this partial replica of French provincial society. Britain attacked the French strongholds (Figure 21.6) as part of a worldwide colonial struggle between the two powers, the **Seven Years War.** France lost its colony under the terms of the **Treaty of Paris,** which in 1763 settled the war. France eagerly regained its West Indian sugar islands, along with trading posts in Africa, and Britain took control of Canada and the Mississippi basin. Relations between British officials and the French Canadian community remained strained as British settlements developed in eastern Canada and in Ontario. The flight of many American loyalists after the 1776 revolution added to the English-speaking contingent in Canada.

Colonial holdings along the Atlantic and in Canada were generally of modest interest to Western colonial powers in the 17th and even the 18th centuries. The Dutch were more attached to their Asian colonies. British and French leaders valued their West Indian holdings much more than their North American colonies. The value of North American products, such as timber and furs, was not nearly as great as profits from the Caribbean or Latin America, so much less attention was given to economic regulation. As a result, some merchant and manufacturing activities emerged among the new Americans.

However, the American colonies that would become the United States had a population of a mere 3 million, far smaller than the powerful colonies in Latin America. Southern colonies that produced tobacco and sugar, and then cotton, became important. Patterns there were similar to those of Latin America, with large estates based on imported slave labor, a wealthy planter class bent on importing luxury products from western Europe, and weak formal governments. Still, in world historical terms, the Atlantic colonies in North America were a backwater amid the larger colonial holdings staked out in the early modern centuries.

Yet European settlers did arrive. Driven by religious dissent, ambition, and other motives, Europeans, many from the British Isles, colonized the Atlantic coastal region, where native populations were quickly reduced by disease and war. The society that developed in the British colonies was far closer to west European forms than was that of Latin America. The colonies operated their own assemblies, which provided the people with political experience. Calvinist and Quaker church assemblies gave governing power to groups of elders or wider congregations. Many colonists thus had reason to share with some west Europeans a sense of the importance of representative institutions and self-government.

Colonists were also avid consumers of political theories written in Europe, such as the parliamentary ideas of John Locke. There was also wide reading and discussion of Enlightenment materials. Institutions such as the 18th-century American Philosophical Society deliberately imitated European scientific institutes, and hundreds of North Americans contributed scientific findings to the British Royal Society. The colonies remained modest in certain cultural attainments. Art was rather primitive, although many stylistic cues came from Europe. There was no question that in formal culture, North American leaders saw themselves as part of a larger Western world.

By the late 18th century, some American merchants were trading with China, their ships picking up medicinal herbs along the Pacific coast and exchanging them for Chinese artifacts and tea. Great Britain tried to impose firmer limits on this modestly thriving local economy after the Seven Years War. It hoped to win greater tax revenues and to guarantee markets for British goods and traders, but the effort came too late and helped encourage rebellion in key colonies. Unusual among the colonies, North America developed a merchant class and some stake in manufacturing in a pattern similar to that taking shape in western Europe itself.

The spread of Western values in the Atlantic colonies and in British and French settlements in Canada was facilitated by the modest impact of Native Americans in these settled areas (Figure 21.7). The native population of this part of North America had always been less dense than in Central America or the Andes region. Because few Native American groups in these regions practiced settled agriculture, instead combining hunting with slash and burn corn growing, European colonists found it easy to displace them from large stretches of territory. The ravages of European-imported disease reduced the indigenous population greatly. Many forest peoples were pushed westward. Some abandoned agriculture, turning to a new horse-based hunting economy on the plains (the horse was brought to Mexico by the Spaniards). Many territorial wars further distracted the Native American groups. The net result of these factors was that although European colonists interacted with Native Americans, learned from them, and feared and mistreated them, the colonists did not combine with them to forge new cultural groups like those emerging in much of Latin America.

**FIGURE 21.7** Watercolor by John White (c. 1590) of the Native American settlement of Secoton, Virginia. White was the governor of the pioneer colony of Roanoke, in what is now North Carolina. When he returned from a desperate voyage back to England to obtain supplies, he found the settlement abandoned. Historians have never been able to determine what happened to the men, women, and children of the "Lost Colony."

By 1700, the importation of African slaves proved to be a more important addition to the North American experience, particularly in the southern colonies. The practice of slaveholding and interactions with African culture distinguished North American life from its European counterpart. By the 18th century, 23 percent of the population of the English colonies was of African origin.

## North America and Western Civilization

On balance, most white settlers intended to transplant key Western habits into their new setting. For example, family patterns were similar. American colonists were able to marry slightly earlier than ordinary western Europeans because of the greater abundance of land, and they had larger families. Still, they reproduced most features of the European-style family, including the primary emphasis on the nuclear unit. The new Americans did have unusual concern for children, if only because they depended so heavily on their work in a labor-scarce environment. European visitors commented on the child-centeredness of American families and the freedom of children to speak up. These variations, though significant, played on trends also becoming visible in Europe, such as the new emphasis on family affection.

Even when key colonies rebelled against European control, as they did in 1776, they moved in the name of Western political ideas and economic goals against the dependency the British tried to impose. They established a government that responded to the new Western political theories, implementing some key ideas for the first time.

## Africa and Asia: Coastal Trading Stations

In Africa, Europeans for the most part contented themselves with small coastal fortresses, negotiating with African kings and merchants but not trying to claim large territories on their own. Generally, Europeans were deterred by climate, disease, and nonnavigable rivers from trying to reach into the interior. There were two important exceptions. From initial coastal settlements, Portugal sent expeditions into Angola in search of slaves. These expeditions had a more direct and more disruptive impact in this part of southwestern Africa than elsewhere along the Atlantic coast. More important still was the **Cape Colony** planted by the Dutch on the Cape of Good Hope in 1652. The intent was to form another coastal station to supply Dutch ships bound for Asia. But some Dutch farmers were sent, and these **Boers** (the Dutch word for farmers) began to fan out on large farms in a region still lightly populated by Africans. They clashed with local hunting groups, enslaving some of them. Only after 1770 did the expanding Boer settlements directly conflict with Bantu farmers, opening a long battle for control of southern Africa that raged until the late 20th century in the nation of South Africa.

European colonies in Asia were also exceptional. Spain set up an administration for the Philippines and sent active Catholic missionaries. The Dutch East India company administered portions of the main islands of present-day Indonesia and also (for a time) Taiwan, off the China coast.

Colonization in Asia entered a new phase as the British and French began to struggle for control of India, beginning in the late 17th century when the Mughal Empire weakened. Even before the Mughals faltered after the death in 1707 of their last great emperor, Aurangzeb, French and British forts dotted the east and west coasts, along with Portuguese Goa. As Mughal inefficiency increased, with a resultant surge of regional states ruled by Indians, portions of the subcontinent became an arena for the growing international rivalry between Britain and France.

The British East India Company had two advantages in this competition. Through negotiation with local princes, it had gained a station at **Calcutta,** which gave it some access to the great wealth of the Ganges valley. Furthermore, the company had enormous influence over the British government and, through Britain's superior navy, excellent communication on the ocean routes. Its French rivals, in contrast, had less political clout at home, where the government often was distracted by European land wars. The French also were more interested in missionary work than the British, for Protestants became deeply committed to colonial missions only in the 19th century. Before then, the British were content to leave Hindu customs alone and devote themselves to commercial profits.

French–British rivalry raged bitterly through the mid-18th century. Both sides recruited Indian princes and troops as allies. Outright warfare erupted in 1744 and then again during the Seven Years War. In 1756, an Indian ruler in Bengal attacked and captured the British base at Calcutta. In the aftermath of the battle, English prisoners were placed in their own jail, where humidity and overcrowding led to perhaps as many as 120 deaths before Indian officials became aware of their plight and released them. The English used this incident, which they dubbed the "black hole of Calcutta," to rally their forces. The East India Company's army recaptured Calcutta and then seized additional Indian and French territory, aided by abundant bribes to many regional princes. French power in India was destroyed, and the East India Company took over administration of the Bengal region, which stretched inland from Cal-

FIGURE 21.8 This Indian portrait of two women in European dress illustrates the English influence in 18th-century India.

cutta. Soon after this, the British also gained the island of Ceylon (Sri Lanka) from the Dutch.

The full history of British India did not begin until late in the 18th century, when the British government took a more active hand in Indian administration, supplementing the unofficial government of the East India Company (Figure 21.8). Indeed, British control of the subcontinent was incomplete. The Mughal Empire remained, although it was increasingly weak and it controlled scant territory, as did other regional kingdoms, including the Sikh state. Britain gained some new territories by force but was also content to form alliances with local princes without disturbing their internal administration.

In most colonies, European administration long remained fairly loose. Few settlers arrived, except in south Africa and the Americas. Outside the Americas, cultural impositions were slight. Missionary activity won many converts in the Philippines but not elsewhere in Asia or in Africa at this point. The main impact of colonies supplemented the more general development of the world economy: colonial administrations pressed for economic advantage for the home country by opening markets and prompting commercial production of cheap foods and raw materials. Here, of course, the consequences to colonial peoples were very real.

## Impact on Western Europe

Western Europe was hugely affected by its own colonial success, not only economically but also diplomatically. Colonial rivalries and wars added to the existing hostilities between key nation-states. England and Holland early turned against Spanish success, with great effect. The Dutch and the English competed, engaging in many skirmishes in the 17th century. Then attention turned to the growing competition between the British and the French.

This contest had extensive geographic scope: the Seven Years War (1756–1763), fought in Europe, India, and North America, has been called the first world war.

There were also less obvious but equally dramatic effects on European society, including daily life. For example, from the mid-17th century onward, the use of colonially produced sugar spread widely. Previously, sugar had been a costly, upper-class item. Now for the first time, except for salt, a basic product available to ordinary people was being traded over long distances. The spread of sugar had cultural as well as social and economic significance in giving ordinary Europeans the ability to obtain pleasurable sensations in quick doses—an interesting foreshadowing of later features of Western consumer behavior. It also promoted a growing role for dentists by the 18th century.

More broadly, the profits Europeans brought in from world trade, including the African slave trade, added wealth and capital. Many Europeans turned to manufacturing operations, as owners and workers, partly because of opportunities for export in world trade. These developments enhanced Europe's commercial character, while reducing dependence on agriculture alone. They provided additional tax revenues for growing governments and their military ambitions.

## The Impact of a New World Order

The development of the world economy and European colonialism had immense impact. The imposition of unfree labor systems, to supply goods for world trade, was increasingly widespread. Slavery and serfdom deeply affected Latin America and eastern Europe, while the slave trade disrupted west Africa, and millions of individual lives as well.

Yet the world economy brought benefits as well as hardships, quite apart from the profits to Europe. New foods and wider trade patterns helped some societies deal with scarcity. Individual merchants and landowners gained new wealth virtually everywhere. China prospered from the imports of silver, though rapid population growth limit gains overall. The mixture of profits and compulsion brought more and more people and regions into the world economy network.

**GLOBAL CONNECTIONS**

## The World Economy—And the World

Buoyed by its growing role in the world, western Europe unquestionably saw its economy and military power increase more rapidly than those of any other society during the early modern period. As the next chapter shows, Europe changed internally as well, often in dramatic ways. Because of these facts, it is tempting to see the early modern centuries as a European drama in which other regions either played supporting roles or watched in awe.

Yet the relationships to the world economy were in fact quite complex. They ranged from conscious isolation to controlled participation to undeniable dependency. Many societies retained vibrant political systems and internal economies. Some, although attracted to certain Western features, wanted to stand apart from the values and institutions that world economic success seemed to involve.

Even societies that had changes thrust upon them, like Latin America, were hardly passive. Pressed by missionaries, Latin Americans did not simply adopt European-style Christianity, but rather blended in traditional beliefs and practices and many distinctive artistic forms. The world was growing closer, but it was not necessarily becoming simpler.

## Further Readings

Excellent discussions of Western exploration and expansion are Carlo Cipolla, *Guns, Sails, and Empires: Technological Innovation and the Early Phases of European Expansion 1400–1700* (1997); J. H. Parry, *The Age of Reconnaissance* (1982); Richard S. Dunn, *Sugar and Slaves: The Rise of the Planter Class in the English West Indies, 1624–1713* (1972); and D. Boorstin, *The Discoverers* (1991). Recent works include Alan K. Smith, *Creating a World Economy: Merchant Capital, Colonialism, and World Trade 1460–1825* (1991); and James Tracy, ed., *The Rise of Merchant Empires* (1986) and *The Political Economy of Merchant Empires* (1991). Somewhat more specific facets are treated in D. K. Fieldhouse, *The Colonial Empires* (1971); J. H. Parry, *The Discovery of South America* (1979); and S. Subrahmanyam, *The Portuguese Empire in Asia, 1500–1700* (1993). A vital treatment of the international results of new trading patterns of foods and disease is Alfred Crosby, *The Columbian Exchange: Biological and Cultural Consequences of 1492* (1972); see also Elinor G. Melville, *A Plague of Sheep: Environmental Consequences of the Conquest of Mexico* (1994). For a stimulating reemphasis on Asia, see Andre Geuder Frank, *ReOrient: Global Economy in the Asian Age* (1998).

On slavery and its trade, see Eric Williams, *Capitalism and Slavery* (1964); Orlando Patterson, *Slavery and Social Death: A Comparative Study* (1982); and D. B. Davis, *Slavery and Human Progress* (1984); the last two are important comparative and analytical statements in a major field of recent historical study. See also Philip D. Curtin, *Atlantic Slave Trade* (1972), and his edited volume, *Africa Remembered: Narratives by West Africans from the Era of the Slave Trade* (1967). A good recent survey of developments in Africa and in the period is Paul Bohannan and Philip Curtin, *Africa and Africans* (1988).

New world trading patterns, including Asia's role in them, are discussed in K. N. N. Shanduri, *Trade and Civilization in the Indian Ocean* (1985); Stephan Frederic Dale, *Indian Merchants and Eurasia Trade: 1600–1750* (1994); Scott Levi, *The Indian*

*Diaspora in Central Asia and Its Trade 1550–1900.* (2002); and Philip Curtin, *Cross-Cultural Trade in World History* (1984). A controversial theoretical statement about new trade relationships and their impact on politics and social structure is found in Immanuel Wallerstein, *The Modern World System: Capitalist Agriculture and the Origins of the European World Economy in the Sixteenth Century* (1974), and *The Modern World System: Mercantilism and the Consolidation of the European World Economy 1600–1750* (1980); see also his *Politics of the World Economy: The States, the Movements, and the Civilizations (1984).*

For discussions on where colonial North America fits in this period of world history, see Jack Greene and J. R. Pole, eds., *Colonial British America: Essays on the New History of the Early Modern Era* (1984); William J. Eccles, *France in America,* rev. ed. (1990); and Gary Nash, *Red, White, and Black: The Peoples of Early America,* rev. ed. (1982).

## On the Web

Biographies of leaders of the European age of discovery, from Henry the Navigator to Vasco da Gama, are offered at http://www.win.tue.nl/cs/fm/engels/discovery/. This site also traces the lives of the world's great explorers of every region and era. Though seemingly a lesson plan, http://www.yale.edu/ynhti/curriculum/units/1992/2/92.02.01.x.html#a offers excellent overviews of Euro-American contacts and a superb bibliography.

A virtual version of an exhibit mounted by the Library of Congress and other materials that look at the multicultural dimensions of the events of 1492, the life of Christopher Columbus, and the Colombian exchange his voyages initiated can be found at http://www.loc.gov/exhibits/1492/. Other such exhibits and analyses of his career can be found at http://www.ibiblio.org/expo/1492.exhibit/c-Columbus/columbus.html and http://xroads.virginia.edu/~CAP/COLUMBUS/col3.html.

Most discussions on the nature of that exchange rightly focus on the material outcomes of the Atlantic slave trade, such as the development of plantation economies and the exchange of crops, animals, and diseases. However, http://daphne.palomar.edu/scrout/colexc.htm also examines what it admits to be the controversial notion that the indigenous peoples of the Americas may have contributed toward the evolution of important modern ideas, including Western conceptions of liberty, ecology, and even corporate structure. At the very least, such speculation reminds us that the relationship between the indigenous people of the Americas and their European conquerors was complex.

The relationship between conquistador Hernán Cortés and Donna Maria, La Malinche, his female Nahuatl-speaking translator, certainly was as complicated as Cortés's relations with his Aztec-hating Mesoamerica allies. Both relationships are discussed at http://thedagger.com/conquest.html. Another site, http://www.fordham.edu/halsall/mod/aztecs1.html, offers a text of the discussions between Cortés and Moctezuma that Malinche facilitated as a translator and that foreshadowed the end of the Aztec Empire. Malinche's role in the Columbian exchange is examined at http://www.mexconnect.com/mex_/history/malinche.html and http://thedagger.com/archive/conquest/malinche.html.

Francisco Pizarro's encounter with Inca leaders and the imposition of Spanish rule over their empire is presented at http://www.ucalgary.ca/applied_history/tutor/eurvoya/inca.html.

The controversy over the demographic catastrophe that accompanied the conquest of Mexico is analyzed from the perspective of contemporary Spanish and Nahuatl records at http://www.hist.umn.edu/~rmccaa/vircatas/vir6.htm (or scroll down to this subject in 1998 files at http://www.hist.umn.edu/~rmccaa/).

The importance of the trade in commodities such as silver and sugar in the emerging global economy is discussed at http://www.learner.org/channel/courses/worldhistory/unit_main_15.html, http://www.silverinstitute.org/facts/history.php, and http://www.zum.de/whkmla/economy/plants/sugarcane.html.

Dutch and British traders soon outstripped their Iberian competitors in the new global economy, a process glimpsed at http://www.colonialvoyage.com/, http//www.bbc.co.uk/history/state/empire/east_india_01.shtml, and http://www.fordham.edu/halsall/mod/modsbook03.html. The latter site also contains the chief primary documentation for the early modern world system and includes a summary of Immanuel Wallerstein's World System Theory (http://www.fordham.edu/halsall/mod/wallerstein.html). The pattern of the then emerging new world order can be glimpsed through a virtual visit to the Dutch factory at Batavia (http://batavia.ugent.be/).

CHAPTER

22

# The Transformation of the West, 1450–1750



In 1960, a French historian named Philippe Ariès dropped something of a bombshell on his fellow historians. He published a book called *Centuries in Childhood* and made startling claims about what he said was a great difference between the way Western parents treated their children in premodern versus modern times. The subject itself was new: very few serious historians had ever studied childhood. Even newer were the claims: Ariès contended that premodern Western society had not distinguished the period we call childhood, instead treating children either as infants or young adults. Changes, he argued, began in the 16th century, with more explicit identification of children as creatures different from adults and deserving of special affection and attention. Ariès believed that the premodern approach was superior to the modern one, but most readers interpreted his work as saying that modern Westerners had learned to recognize a natural period of childhood and therefore to treat children decently.

Ariès based much of his work on art. He argued that premodern Western art either neglected children in favor of strictly adult subjects or treated them in ways that suggested little explicit interest in their status as children. Thus children figured only in religious art, as small instances of piety more than as small people. Their faces were stylized, with little indication of individual character, and more often than not, when they were shown at all, they were strictly in the background. All this began to change in paintings between the 16th and 18th centuries. Dutch family paintings, for example, began to show children in the foreground with clear personalities. They took delight in portraying children as active parts of the family, sitting with the family at mealtimes or listening to music after dinner. And of course their subjects were secular—of this world. Ariès and other historians after him believed that these changes mirrored changes in real life and culture. People began to place new value on children, to give them more individualized names, to play with them, and to invest more deeply with them emotionally. By the 18th century the old custom of swaddling young children—wrapping them tightly in cloth so that they could not move easily—was dropped in western Europe. This showed a new interest in the young and willingness to spend more time actively supervising them.

**FIGURE 22.1** This portrait of the Dutch Hoopesads family by Pieter de Hooch in the 17th century gives attention to the individual children while also suggesting that they are somewhat apart—at least the daughters. How does this compare with a more fully "modern" family portrait in Western culture?

Changes of this sort are hard to explain. Perhaps greater prosperity allowed more attention to children. The Dutch paintings, for example, mainly showed successful business families. Cultural change was certainly important. Gradually, the older Christian emphasis on children as sinners whose wills must be brought into submission gave way to new beliefs that children should be thought of as innocents, open to education and improvement.

The results of changes are also important. How would this new treatment of children affect their capacities as adults? How might these changes affect the way Europeans viewed children in other cultures? What role, in other words, did changes in ideas and practices about childhood play in larger history of the early modern West and its interactions with other societies?

| 1300 C.E. | 1450 C.E. | 1500 C.E. | 1550 C.E. | 1650 C.E. | 1750 C.E. |
|---|---|---|---|---|---|
| **1300–1450** Italian Renaissance | **1450–1519** Life of Leonardo da Vinci<br>**1450–1600** Northern Renaissance<br>**1455** First European printing press, Mainz, Germany<br>**1469–1527** Life of Machiavelli<br>**1475–1514** Life of Michelangelo<br>**1490s** France and Spain invade Italian city-states; beginning of Italian decline | **1500–1600** Commercial revolution<br>**1515–1547** Reign of Francis I, France<br>**1517** Luther's 95 theses; beginning of Protestant Reformation<br>**1534** Beginning of Church of England<br>**1541–1564** Calvin in Geneva<br>**1543** Copernican revolution; Copernicus's work on astronomy | **1550–1649** Religious wars in France, Germany, and Britain<br>**1555–1603** Reign of Elizabeth I, England<br>**1564–1642** Life of Galileo<br>**1588** English defeat the Spanish Armada<br>**17th century** Scientific Revolution<br>**1609** Independence of Netherlands<br>**1618–1648** Thirty Years War<br>**1642–1649** English Civil War<br>**1642–1727** Life of Isaac Newton<br>**1643–1715** Reign of Louis XIV, France; absolute monarchy<br>**1647–1648** Culmination of popular rebellions in western Europe | **1670–1692** Decline of witchcraft trials<br>**1682–1699** Habsburgs drive Turks from Hungary<br>**1688–1690** Glorious Revolution in Britain; parliamentary monarchy; some religious toleration; political writing of John Locke<br>**18th century** Enlightenment<br>**1712–1786** Life of Frederick the Great of Prussia, enlightened despot<br>**1730–1850** European population boom<br>**1733** James Kay invents flying shuttle loom<br>**1736** Beginnings of Methodism | **1756–1763** Seven Years War: France, Britain, Prussia, and Austria<br>**1776** Adam Smith's *Wealth of Nations*<br>**1780–1790** Reign of Joseph II, first Habsburg emperor<br>**1792** Mary Wollstonecraft's *Vindication of the Rights of Women* |

Sweeping historical interpretations like Ariès's are always debated. Many historians objected to Ariès's use of art—arguing that art was too strictly upper class to serve as the basis for claims about society as a whole. Many contended that Ariès was wrong about the neglect of childhood in the premodern West, and most historians now agree that Ariès overdid the modern–premodern contrast. But there remains fairly wide agreement that important changes in the treatment of children did take place amidst the larger transformations of early modern western Europe. And if these transformations affected something as fundamental as childhood, what else did they change?

## The First Big Changes: Culture and Commerce, 1450–1650

- **The Renaissance emphasized new styles and beliefs. The Protestant Reformation and the Catholic response to it caused even wider changes in the West. The western European economy became steadily more commercial.**

### A New Spirit

The Italian writer Francesco Petrarch (1304–1374) once climbed Ventoux, a mountain in southern France. He wrote of his ascent, proud of his own skill and using the climb as a symbol of what he could achieve. There was a new spirit in this work, intended to be published, compared to the more religious Middle Ages. But Petrarch did not abandon religion, and in later life he talked about how he had given up poetry in favor of reading Christian texts, finding "hidden sweetness which I had once esteemed but lightly."

### The Italian Renaissance

The move away from earlier patterns began with the Renaissance, which first developed in Italy during the 14th and 15th centuries. Largely an artistic movement, the Renaissance challenged medieval intellectual values and styles. It also sketched a new, brasher spirit that may have encouraged a new Western interest in exploring strange waters or urging that old truths be reexamined.

Italy was already well launched in the development of Renaissance culture by the 15th century, based on its

Vasari on Leonardo da Vinci (1550)

Machiavelli's *The Prince*

unusually extensive urban, commercial economy and its competitive city-state politics. Writers such as Petrarch and Boccaccio had promoted classical literary canons against medieval logic and theology, writing in Italian as well as the traditional Latin and emphasizing secular subjects such as love and pride. Painting turned to new realism and classical and human-centered themes. Religion declined as a central focus. The Italian Renaissance blossomed further in the 15th and early 16th centuries. This was a great age of Western art, as Leonardo da Vinci advanced the realistic portrayal of the human body and Michelangelo applied classical styles in painting and sculpture. In political theory, **Niccolo Machiavelli** emphasized realistic discussions of how to seize and maintain power. Like the artists, Machiavelli bolstered his realism with Greek and Roman examples.

Overall, Italian Renaissance culture stressed themes of **humanism:** a focus on humankind as the center of intellectual and artistic endeavor. Religion was not attacked, but its principles were no longer predominant. Historians have debated the reasons for this change. Italy's more urban, commercial environment was one factor, but so was the new imitation of classical Greek and Roman literature and art.

These Renaissance themes had some bearing on politics and commerce. Renaissance merchants improved their banking techniques and became more openly profit-seeking than their medieval counterparts had been. City-state leaders experimented with new political forms and functions. They justified their rule not on the basis of heredity or divine guidance but more on the basis of what they could do to advance general well-being and their city's glory. Thus, they sponsored cultural activities and tried to improve the administration of the economy. They also developed more professional armies, for wars among the city-states were common, and gave new attention to military tactics and training. They also rethought the practice of diplomacy, introducing the regular exchange of ambassadors for the first time in the West. Clearly, the Renaissance encouraged innovation, although it also produced some dependence on classical models.

## The Renaissance Moves Northward

Italy began to decline as a Renaissance center by about 1500. French and Spanish monarchs invaded the peninsula, reducing political independence. At the same time, new Atlantic trade routes reduced the importance of Mediterranean ports, a huge blow to the Italian economy.

As Renaissance creativity faded in its Italian birthplace, it passed northward. The **Northern Renaissance**—focused in France, the Low Countries, Germany, and England—began after 1450. Renaissance styles also affected Hungary and Poland in east central Europe. Classical styles in art and architecture became the rage. Knowledge of Greek and Latin literature gained ground, although many northern humanists wrote in their own languages (English, French, and so on). Northern humanists were more religious than their Italian counterparts, trying to blend secular interests with continued Christian devotion. Renaissance writers such as Shakespeare in England and Rabelais in France mixed classical themes with an earthiness—a joy in bodily functions and human passions—that maintained elements of medieval popular culture. Renaissance literature established a new set of classics for literary traditions in the major Western languages, such as the writings of Shakespeare in England and Cervantes in Spain.

Sir Thomas More, *Utopia* (1516)

The Northern Renaissance produced some political change, providing another move toward greater state powers. As their revenues and operations expanded, Renaissance kings increased their pomp and ceremony. Kings such as **Francis I** in France became patrons of the arts, importing Italian sculptors and architects to create their classical-style palaces. By the late 16th century, many monarchs were sponsoring trading companies and colonial enterprises. Interest in military conquest was greater than in the Middle Ages. Francis I was even willing to ally with the Ottoman sultan, the key Muslim leader. His goal was to distract his main enemy, the Habsburg ruler of Austria and Spain. In fact, it was an alliance in name only, but it illustrated how power politics was beginning to abandon the feudal or religious justifications that had previously clothed it in the West.

Yet the impact of the Renaissance should not be overstated, particularly outside Italy. Renaissance kings were still confined by the political powers of feudal landlords. Ordinary people were little touched by Renaissance values; the life of most peasants and artisans went on much as before. Economic life also changed little, particularly outside the Italian commercial centers. Even in the upper classes, women sometimes encountered new limits as Renaissance leaders touted men's public bravado over women's domestic roles.

## Changes in Technology and Family

More fundamental changes were brewing in Western society by 1500, beneath the glittering surface of the Renaissance. Spurred by trading contacts with Asia, workers in the West improved the quality of pulleys and pumps in mines and learned how to forge stronger iron products. Printing was introduced in the 15th century when the German **Johannes Gutenberg** introduced movable type, building on Chinese printing technology. Soon books were distributed in greater quantities in the West, which helped expand the audience for Renaissance writers and disseminated religious ideas.

Literacy began to gain ground and became a fertile source of new kinds of thinking.

Family structure was also changing. A **European-style family** pattern came into being by the 15th century. This pattern involved a late marriage age and a primary emphasis on nuclear families of parents and children rather than the extended families characteristic of most agricultural civilizations. The goal was to limit family birth rates. By the 16th century, ordinary people usually did not marry until their late 20s—a marked contrast to most agricultural societies. These changes emphasized the importance of husband–wife relations. They also closely linked the family to individual property holdings, for most people could not marry until they had access to property.

European Population Density, c. 1600

## The Protestant and Catholic Reformations

In the 16th century, religious upheaval and a new commercial surge began to define the directions of change more fully. In 1517, a German monk named **Martin Luther** nailed a document containing 95 *theses,* or propositions, to the door of the castle church in Wittenberg. He was protesting claims made by a papal representative in selling *indulgences,* or grants of salvation, for money, but in fact his protest went deeper. Luther's reading of the Bible convinced him that only faith could gain salvation. Church sacraments were not the path, for God could not be manipulated. Luther's protest, which was rebuffed by the papacy, soon led him to challenge many Catholic beliefs, including the authority of the pope. Luther would soon argue that monasticism was wrong, that priests should marry (as he did), and that the Bible should be translated from Latin so ordinary people could have direct access to its teachings. Luther did not want to break Christian unity, but the church he wanted should be on his terms (or, as he would have argued, the terms of the true faith).

Martin Luther, Sermon at the Castle Pleissenburg

Luther picked up wide support for his views during the mid-16th century and beyond. Many Germans, in a somewhat nationalist reaction, resented the authority and taxes of the Roman pope. German princes saw an opportunity to gain more power. Their nominal leader, the Holy Roman emperor, remained Catholic. Thus, princes who turned Protestant could increase their independence and seize church lands. The Lutheran version of **Protestantism** (as the general wave of religious dissent was called) urged state control of the church as an alternative to papal authority, and this had obvious political appeal.

There were reasons for ordinary people to shift their allegiance as well. Some German peasants saw Luther's attack on authority as a sanction for their own social rebellion against landlords, although Luther specifically renounced this reading. Some townspeople were drawn to Luther's approval of work in the world. Because faith alone gained salvation, Lutheranism could sanction moneymaking and other earthly pursuits more wholeheartedly than did traditional Catholicism. Unlike Catholicism, Lutherans did not see special vocations as particularly holy; monasteries were abolished, along with some of the Christian bias against moneymaking.

Once Christian unity was breached, other Protestant groups sprang forward. In England, Henry VIII began to set up an **Anglican church,** initially to challenge papal attempts to enforce his first marriage, which had failed to produce a male heir. (Henry ultimately had six wives in sequence, executing two of them, a particularly graphic example of the treatment of women in power politics.) Henry was also attracted to some of the new doctrines, and his most durable successor, his daughter Elizabeth I, was Protestant outright.

Still more important were the churches inspired by **Jean Calvin,** a French theologian who established his base in the Swiss city of Geneva. Calvinism insisted on God's *predestination,* or prior determination, of those who would be saved. Calvinist ministers became moral guardians and preachers of God's word. Calvinists sought the participation of all believers in local church administration, which promoted the idea of a wider access to government. They also promoted broader popular education so that more people could read the Bible. Calvinism was accepted not only in part of Switzerland but also in portions of Germany, in France (where it produced strong minority groups), in the Netherlands, in Hungary, and in England and Scotland. By the early 17th century, Puritan exiles brought it to North America.

Calvin on Predestination

The Catholic church did not sit still under Protestant attack. It did not restore religious unity, but it defended southern Europe, Austria, Poland, much of Hungary, and key parts of Germany for the Catholic faith. Under a **Catholic Reformation,** a major church council revived Catholic doctrine and refuted key Protestant tenets such as the idea that priests had no special sacramental power and could marry. They also attacked popular superstitions and remnants of magical belief, which meant that Catholics and Protestants alike were trying to find new ways to shape the outlook of ordinary folk. A new religious order, the **Jesuits,** became active in politics, education, and missionary work, regaining some parts of Europe for the church. Jesuit fervor also sponsored Catholic missionary activity in Asia and the Americas.

Ignatius Loyola, Rules for Thinking with the Church

Council of Trent

## The End of Christian Unity in the West

The Protestant and Catholic Reformations had several results in Europe during the late 16th and early 17th cen-

Account of the Massacre of Saint Bartholomew

Europe After the Treaty of Westphalia, 1648

turies. Most obvious was an important series of religious wars. France was a scene of bitter battles between Calvinist and Catholic forces. These disputes ended only with the granting of tolerance to Protestants through the **edict of Nantes** in 1598, although in the next century French kings progressively cut back on Protestant rights. In Germany, the **Thirty Years War** broke out in 1618, pitting German Protestants and allies such as Lutheran Sweden against the Holy Roman emperor, backed by Spain. The war was so devastating that it reduced German power and prosperity for a full century, cutting population by as much as 60 percent in some regions (Figure 22.2). It was ended only by the 1648 **Treaty of Westphalia,** which agreed to the territorial tolerance concept: Some princely states and cities chose one religion, some another. This treaty also finally settled a rebellion of the Protestant Netherlands against Spain, giving the former its full independence.

Religious fighting punctuated British history, first before the reign of Elizabeth in the 16th century, then in the **English Civil War** in the 1640s. Here too, religious issues combined with other problems, particularly in a battle between the claims of parliament to rights of control over royal actions and some rather tactless assertions of authority by a new line of English kings. The civil war ended in 1660 (well after King Charles I had been beheaded; Figure 22.3), but full resolution

James I on the Divine Right of Kings

FIGURE 22.2 Hans Holbein's *The Dance of Death*, published in 1538, illustrated social upheaval resulting from the continuing plague as well as from religious conflict.

FIGURE 22.3 Civil war over religious issues and the relative power of king and parliament resulted in the beheading of Charles I in London in 1649. As this painting suggests, the regicide was one of the most controversial events in English history.

came only in 1688–1689, when limited religious toleration was granted to most Protestants, though not to Catholics.

Religious issues thus dominated European politics for almost a century. The religious wars led to a grudging and limited acceptance of the idea of religious pluralism. Christian unity could not be restored, although in most individual countries the idea of full religious liberty was still in the future. The religious wars persuaded some people that religion itself was suspect; if there was no dominant single truth, why all the cruelty and carnage? Finally, the wars affected the political balance of Europe, as Map 22.1 shows. After a period of weakness during its internal strife, France was on the upswing. The Netherlands and Britain were galvanized toward a growing international role. Spain, briefly ascendant, fell back. Internally, some kings and princes benefited from the decline of papal authority by taking a stronger role in religious affairs. This was true in many Catholic and Protestant domains. In some cases, however, Protestant dissent encouraged popular political movements and enhanced parliamentary power.

Religious Diversity in Western Europe

The Decline of Spanish Power in Europe, 1640–1714

The impact of religious change went well beyond politics. Popular beliefs changed most in Protestant areas, but Catholic reform produced new impulses as well. Western people gradually became less likely to see an intimate connection between God and nature. Protestants resisted the idea of miracles or other interventions in nature's course. Religious change also promoted greater concentration on family life. Religious writers encouraged love between husband and wife. As one English Protestant put it, "When love is absent between husband and wife, it is like a bone out of joint: there is no ease, no order." This promotion of the family had ambiguous implications for women. Protestantism, abolishing religious convents, made marriage more necessary for women than before; there were fewer alternatives for women who could not marry. Fathers were also responsible for the religious training of the children. On the other hand, women's emotional role in the family improved with the new emphasis on affection.

The Ideal Wife

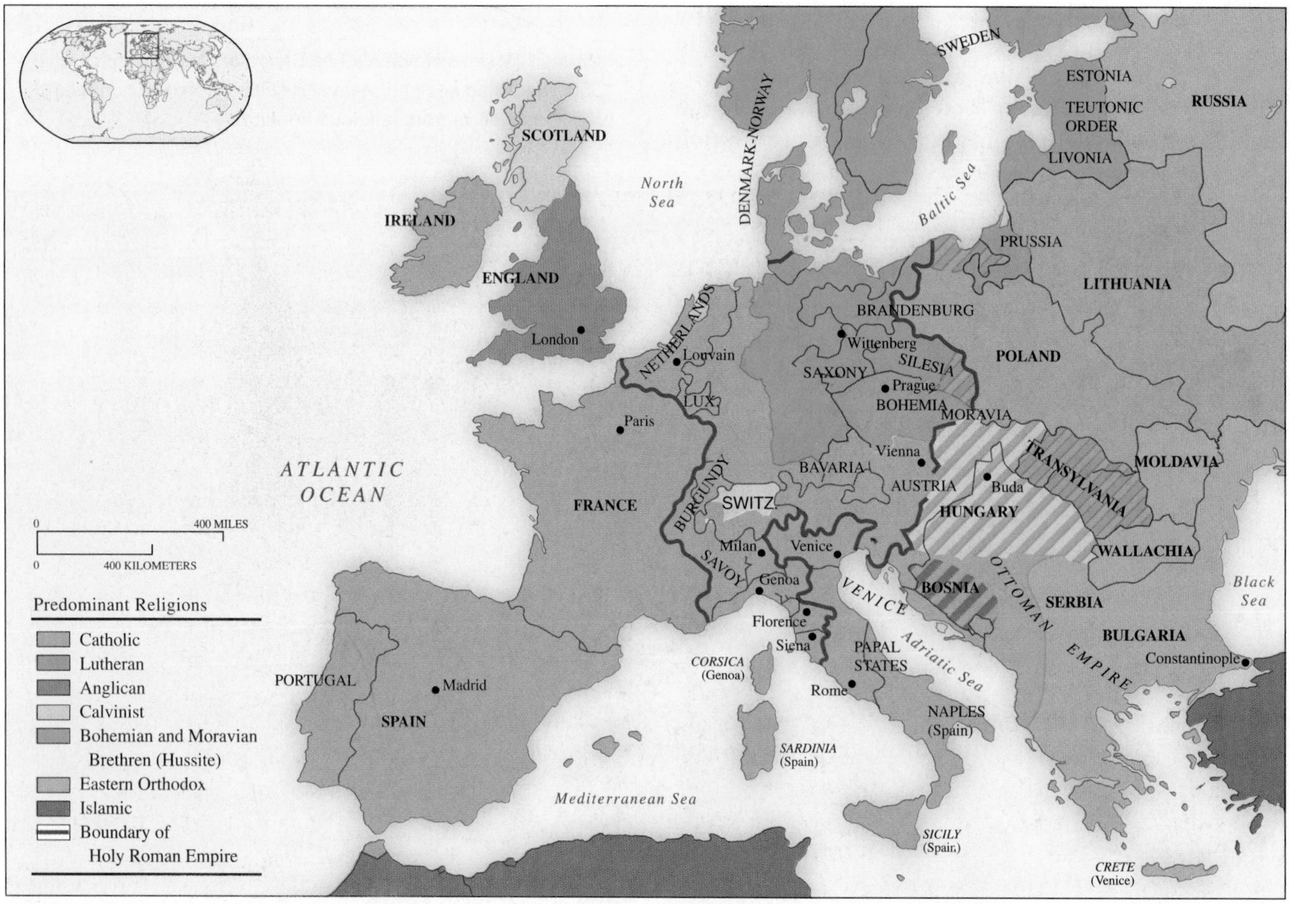

**MAP 22.1 Western Europe During the Renaissance and Reformation.** Different Protestant denominations made inroads in much of northwestern Europe with the Reformation, but Catholicism maintained its hold on significant portions of the continent.

Religious change accompanied and promoted growing literacy along with the spread of the printing press. In the town of Durham, England, around 1570, only 20 percent of all people were literate, but by 1630 the figure had climbed to 47 percent. Growing literacy opened people to additional new ideas and ways of thinking.

## The Commercial Revolution

Along with religious upheaval during the 16th century, the economic structure of the West was fundamentally redefined. The level of European trade rose sharply, and many Europeans had new goods available to them. Involvement with markets and merchants increased. Here was the clearest impact of the new world economy in western Europe.

A basic spur to greater commercialization was the price inflation that occurred throughout western Europe during the 16th century. The massive import of gold and silver from Spain's new colonies in Latin America forced prices up. The availability of more money, based on silver supply, generated this price rise. New wealth heightened demand for products to sell, both in the colonies and in Europe, but Western production could not keep pace, hence the price inflation. Inflation encouraged merchants to take new risks, for borrowing was cheap when money was losing value. A sum borrowed one year would be worth less, in real terms, five years later, so it made sense to take loans for new investments.

Inflation and the new colonial opportunities led to the formation of the great trading companies, often with government backing, in Spain, England, the Netherlands, and France. Governments granted regional monopolies to these giant concerns; thus, the Dutch East Indies Company long dominated trade with the islands of Indonesia. European merchants brought new profits back to Europe and developed new managerial skills and banking arrangements.

Colonial markets stimulated manufacturing. Most peasants continued to produce mainly for their own needs, but agricultural specialty areas developed in the production of wines, cheeses, wool, and the like. Some of these industries favored commercial farming and the use of paid laborers on the land. Shoemaking, pottery, metalworking, and other manufacturing specializations arose in both rural villages and the cities. Technical improvements followed in many branches of manufacture, particularly in metals and mining.

Prosperity increased for many ordinary people as well as for the great merchants. One historian has estimated that by about 1600 the average Western peasant or artisan owned five times as many "things" as his or her counterpart in southeastern Europe. A 16th-century Englishman noted that whereas in the past a peasant and his family slept on the floor and had only a pan or two as kitchenware, by the final decades of the century a farmer might have "a fair garnish of pewter in his cupboard, three or four feather beds, so many coverlets and carpets of tapestry, a silver salt, a bowl for wine . . . and a dozen spoons." It was about this time that French peasants began to enjoy wine fairly regularly rather than simply at special occasions—the result of higher productivity and better trade and transport facilities.

## Social Protest

There were victims of change as well. Growing commercialization created the beginnings of a new **proletariat** in the West—people without access to wealth-producing property. Population growth and rising food prices hit hard at the poor, and many people had to sell their small plots of land. Some proletarians became manufacturing workers, depending on orders from merchant capitalists to keep their tools busy in their cottages. Others became paid laborers on agricultural estates, where landlords were eager for a more manipulable workforce to take advantage of business opportunities in the cities. Others pressed into the cities, and a growing problem of beggars and wandering poor began to affect Western society. By blaming the poor for moral failings, a new, tough attitude toward poverty took shape that has lasted to some extent to the present day.

Not surprisingly, the shifts in popular economic and cultural traditions provoked important outcries. A huge wave of popular protest in western Europe developed at the end of the 16th century and extended until about 1650. Peasants and townspeople alike rose for greater protection from poverty and loss of property. The uprisings did not deflect the basic currents of change, but they revealed the massive insecurity of many workers.

The popular rebellions of the 17th century revealed social tension and new ideas of equality. Peasant songs voiced such sentiments as this: "The whole country must be overturned, for we peasants are now to be the lords, it is we who will sit in the shade." Uprisings in 1648 produced demands for a popular political voice; an English group called the Levelers gained 100,000 signatures on a petition for political rights. Elsewhere, common people praised the kings while attacking their "bad advisors" and high taxes. One English agitator said that "we should cut off all the gentlemen's heads. . . . We shall have a merrier world shortly." In France, Protestant and Catholic peasants rose together against landlords and taxes: "They seek only the ruin of the poor people for our ruin is their wealth."

An unprecedented outburst against suspected witches arose in the same decades in various parts of western Europe and also in New England. Although attacks on witches had developed before, the new scale reflected intense social and cultural upheaval. Between 60,000 and 100,000 suspected witches were accused and killed. The **witchcraft persecution** reflected new resentments against the poor, who were often accused of witchcraft by communities unwilling to accept responsibility for their poverty. The hysteria also revealed new tensions about family life and the role of women, who were the most common targets of persecution. A few of the accused witches actually believed they had magical powers, but far more were accused by fearful or self-serving neighbors. The whole witchcraft experience revealed a society faced with forces of unusual complexity.

## Science and Politics: The Next Phase of Change

- **A revolution in the nature and status of science occurred during the 17th century. The European state took on new forms and functions.**

The revolution in science, culminating in the 17th century, set the seal on the cultural reorientation of the West. Although the **Scientific Revolution** most obviously affected formal intellectual life, it also promoted changes in popular outlook. At the same time, after the political upheavals of the Reformation, a more decisive set of new government forms arose in the West, centering on the emergence of the nation-state. The functions of the state expanded. The Western nation-state was not a single form, because key variants such as absolute monarchies and parliamentary regimes emerged, but there were some common patterns beneath the surface.

### Did Copernicus Copy?

This is a chapter about big changes in western Europe during the early modern period. Big changes are always complex. One key development was the rise of science in intellectual life. A key first step here was the discovery by the Polish monk **Copernicus,** in the 16th century, that the planets moved around the sun rather than the earth, as the Greeks had thought. This discovery set other scientific advances in motion, and more generally showed that new thinking could improve on tradition. Copernicus is usually taken as a quiet hero of Western science and rationalism.

Nicolaus Copernicus: On the Revolution of the Heavenly Spheres

Copernicus based his findings on mathematics, understanding that the Greek view of earth as central raised key problems in calculating planetary motion. Historians have recently uncovered similar geometrical findings by two Arabs, al-Urdi and al-Tusi, from the 13th and 14th centuries. Did Copernicus copy, as Westerners had previously done from the Arabs, while keeping quiet because learning from Muslims was now unpopular? Or did he discover independently? It's also worth noting that scientists in other traditions, such as Chinese, Indian, and Mayan, had already realized the central position of the sun. Change, again, is complicated.

Copernicus's Drawing of the Heliocentric Theory

What is certain is that based on discoveries like that of Copernicus, science began to take on more importance in Western intellectual life than had ever been the case in the intellectual history of other societies, including classical Greece. Change may be complicated but it does occur.

God and Nature

### Science: The New Authority

During the 16th century, scientific research quietly built on the traditions of the later Middle Ages. After Copernicus, Johannes Kepler (1571–1630; Figure 22.4) was another important early figure in the study of planetary

**FIGURE 22.4** Johannes Kepler, one of the leading figures in the Scientific Revolution.

motion. Unusual for a major researcher, Kepler was from a poor family; his father abandoned the family outright, and his mother, once tried for witchcraft, was unpleasant. But Kepler made his way to university on scholarship, aiming for the Lutheran ministry but drawn to astronomy and mathematics. Using the work of Copernicus and his own observations, he resolved basic issues of planetary motion. He also worked on optics and, with the mixed interests so common in real intellectual life, also practiced astrology, casting horoscopes for wealthy patrons. Also around 1600, anatomical work by the Belgian Vesalius gained greater precision. These key discoveries not only advanced knowledge but also implied a new power for scientific research in its ability to test and often overrule accepted ideas.

A series of empirical advances and wider theoretical generalizations extended the possibilities of science from the 1600s onward. New instruments such as the microscope and improved telescopes allowed gains in biology and astronomy. The Italian **Galileo** publicized Copernicus's discoveries while adding his own basic findings about the laws of gravity and planetary motion. Condemned by the Catholic church for his innovations, Galileo proved the inadequacy of traditional ideas about the universe. He also showed the new pride in scientific achievement, writing modestly how he, "by marvelous discoveries and clear demonstrations, had enlarged a thousand times" the knowledge produced by "the wise men of bygone ages." Chemical research advanced understanding of the behavior of gasses. English physician **William Harvey** demonstrated the circular movement of the blood in animals, with the heart as the "central pumping station."

Galileo Galilei, Letter to the Grand Duchess Christina

These advances in knowledge were accompanied by important statements about science and its impact. Francis Bacon urged the value of careful empirical research and predicted that scientific knowledge could advance steadily, producing improvements in technology as well. **René Descartes** established the importance of a skeptical review of all received wisdom, arguing that human reason could develop laws that would explain the fundamental workings of nature.

The capstone to the 17th-century Scientific Revolution came in 1687, when **Isaac Newton** published his *Principia Mathematica.* This work drew the various astronomical and physical observations and wider theories together in a neat framework of natural laws. Newton set forth the basic principles of all motion (for example, that a body in motion maintains uniform momentum unless affected by outside forces such as friction). Newton defined the forces of gravity in great mathematical detail and showed that the whole universe responded to these forces, which among other things explained the planetary orbits described by Kepler. Finally, Newton stated the basic scientific method in terms of a mixture of rational hypothesis and generalization and careful empirical observation and experiment. Here was a vision of a natural universe that could be captured in simple laws (although increasingly complex mathematics accompanied the findings). Here was a vision of a method of knowing that might do away with blind reliance on tradition or religious faith.

The Scientific Revolution was quickly popularized among educated Westerners. Here was a key step in the cultural transformation of western Europe in the early modern period. New scientific institutes were set up, often with government aid, to advance research and disseminate the findings. Lectures and easy-to-read manuals publicized the latest advances and communicated the excitement that researchers shared in almost all parts of Europe. Attacks on beliefs in witchcraft became more common, and magistrates grew increasingly reluctant to entertain witchcraft accusations in court. Public hysteria began to die down after about 1670. There were growing signs of a new belief that people could control and calculate their environment. Insurance companies sprang up to help guard against risk. Doctors increased their attacks on popular healers, promoting a more scientific diagnosis of illness. Newsletters, an innovation by the late 17th century, began to advertise "lost and found" items, for there was no point leaving this kind of problem to customary magicians, called "cunning men," who had poked around with presumably enchanted sticks.

By the 1680s writers affected by the new science, though not themselves scientists, began to attack traditional religious ideas such as miracles, for in the universe of the Scientific Revolution there was no room for disruption of nature's laws. Some intellectuals held out a new conception of God, called **Deism,** arguing that although there might be a divinity, its role was simply to set natural laws in motion. In England, **John Locke** argued that people could learn everything they needed to know through their senses and reason; faith was irrelevant. Christian beliefs in human sinfulness crumbled in the view of these intellectuals, for they saw human nature as basically good. Finally, scientific advances created wider assumptions about the possibility of human progress. If knowledge could advance through concerted human effort, why not progress in other domains? Even literary authorities joined this parade, and the idea that past styles set timeless standards of perfection came under growing criticism.

Science had never before been central to intellectual life. Science had played important roles in other civilizations, as in China, classical Greece, Central America, and Islam. Generally, however, wider religious or philosophical interests predominated. In China most notably, despite some real interest in generalizations

VISUALIZING THE PAST

## Versailles

This picture shows Louis XIV's grand 17th-century palace at Versailles. It displays the sheer opulence of this absolute monarchy, in what was Europe's richest and most populous and influential nation. It also shows the renewed hold of a classical style, seen to be most prestigious for public buildings. What else does it suggest?

Architecture is sometimes thought to be the most socially and historically revealing of all the arts because it depends most heavily on public support; it is harder for architects, particularly dealing with public buildings, to be as idiosyncratic as painters or poets.

**Questions** What kinds of intentions on the part of Louis and his advisors does this building represent? How can Versailles be interpreted as a statement of absolute monarchy in addition to its obvious showiness? What are the relationships to nature and to spatial arrangement? What would the palace represent to an ordinary French person? To an aristocrat?

The palace at Versailles.

about the physical universe derived from Daoism, science continued to be construed mainly in terms of practical, empirical advances. The Western passion for combining empiricism with more sweeping rational formulations—the idea of general laws of nature—clearly built on traditions that had come from Greek thought as mediated by Christian theology and Islamic philosophy during the postclassical period. In sum, the West was not alone in developing crucial scientific data, but it now became the leading center for scientific advance, and its key thinkers stood alone for some time in seeing science as the key to gaining and defining knowledge.

## Absolute and Parliamentary Monarchies

The feudal monarchy—the balance between king and nobles—that had defined Western politics since the late postclassical period finally came undone in the 17th century. In most countries, after the passions of religious wars finally cooled, monarchs gained new powers, curtailing the tradition of noble pressure or revolt. At the same time, more ambitious military organization, in states that defined war as a central purpose, required more careful administration and improved tax collection.

The model for this new pattern was France, now the West's most important nation. French kings steadily built up their power in the 17th century. They stopped convening the medieval parliament and passed laws as they saw fit, although some provincial councils remained strong. They blew up the castles of dissident nobles, another sign that gunpowder was undercutting the military basis of feudalism. They appointed a growing bureaucracy drawn from the merchants and lawyers. They sent direct representatives to the outlying provinces. They professionalized the army, giving more formal training to officers, providing uniforms and support, and creating military hospitals and pensions.

So great was the power of the monarch, in fact, that the French system became known as **absolute monarchy.** Its most glorious royal proponent, King **Louis XIV,** summed up its principles succinctly: "I am the state." Louis became a major patron of the arts, giving government a cultural role beyond any previous levels in the West. His academies not only encouraged science but also worked to standardize the French language. A sumptuous palace at Versailles was used to keep nobles busy with social functions so that they could not interfere with affairs of state.

Louis XIV Writes to His Son

Using the new bureaucratic structure, Louis and his ministers developed additional functions for the state. They reduced internal tariffs, which acted as barriers to trade, and created new, state-run manufacturing. The reigning economic theory, mercantilism, held that governments should promote the internal economy to improve tax revenues and to limit imports from other nations, lest money be lost to enemy states. Therefore, absolute monarchs such as Louis XIV set tariffs on imported goods, tried to encourage their merchant fleets, and sought colonies to provide raw materials and a guaranteed market for manufactured goods produced at home.

The basic structure of absolute monarchy developed in other states besides France (Map 22.2). Spain tried to imitate French principles in the 18th century, which resulted in efforts to tighten control over its Latin American colonies. However, the most important spread of absolute monarchy occurred in the central European states that were gaining in importance. A series of kings in Prussia, in eastern Germany, built a strong army and bureaucracy. They promoted economic activity and began to develop a state-sponsored school system. Habsburg kings in Austria–Hungary, though still officially rulers of the Holy Roman Empire, concentrated increasingly on developing a stronger monarchy in the lands under their direct control. The power of these Habsburg rulers increased after they pushed back the last Turkish invasion threat late in the 17th century and then added the kingdom of Hungary to their domains.

Most absolute monarchs saw a strong military as a key political goal, and many hoped for territorial expansion. Louis XIV used his strong state as the basis for a series of wars from the 1680s onward. The wars yielded some new territory for France but finally attracted an opposing alliance system that blocked further advance. Prussian kings, though long cautious in exposing their proud military to the risk of major war, turned in the 18th century to a series of conflicts that won new territory.

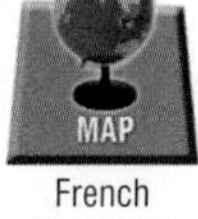

French Territorial Acquisitions, 1679–1714

Britain and the Netherlands, both growing commercial and colonial powers, stood apart from the trend toward absolute monarchy in the 17th century. They emphasized the role of the central state, but they also built parliamentary regimes in which the kings shared power with representatives selected by the nobility and upper urban classes. The English civil wars produced a final political settlement in 1688 and 1689 (the so-called **Glorious Revolution**) in which parliament won basic sovereignty over the king. The English parliament no longer depended on the king to convene, for regular sessions were scheduled. Its rights to approve taxation allowed it to monitor or initiate most major policies.

The English Bill of Rights

Furthermore, a growing body of political theory arose in the 17th century that built on these parliamentary ideas. John Locke and others argued that power came from the people, not from a divine right to royal rule. Monarchs should therefore be restrained by institutions that protected the public interest, including certain general rights to freedom and property. A right of revolution could legitimately oppose unjust rule.

Overall, western Europe developed important diversity in political forms, between absolute monarchy

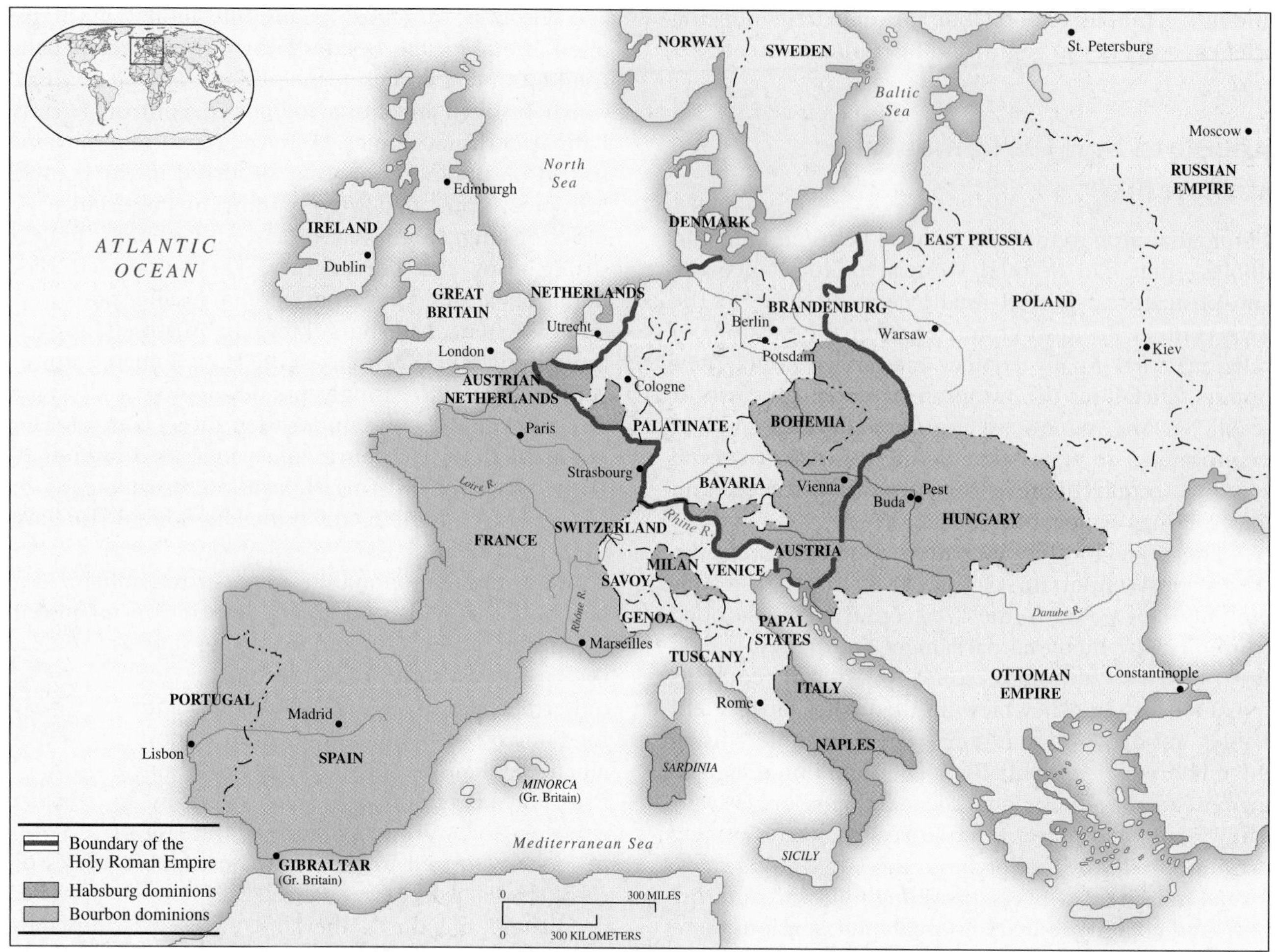


**MAP 22.2 Europe Under Absolute Monarchy, 1715.** The rise of absolute monarchies led to consolidation of national borders as states asserted full control of areas within their boundaries. For example, a recent study shows that villages that straddled the French–Spanish border were undifferentiated before 1600, but by 1700 they showed marked national differences because of different state policies and the greater impact of belonging to one state or another.

and a new kind of **parliamentary monarchy.** It maintained a characteristic tension between government growth and the idea that there should be some limits to state authority. This tension was expressed in new forms, but it recalled some principles that had originated in the Middle Ages.

## The Nation-State

The absolute monarchies and the parliamentary monarchies shared important characteristics as nation-states. Unlike the great empires of many other civilizations, they ruled peoples who shared a common culture and language, some important minorities apart. They could appeal to a certain loyalty that linked cultural and political bonds. This was as true of England, where the idea of special rights of Englishmen helped feed the parliamentary movement, as it was of France. Not surprisingly, ordinary people in many nation-states, even though not directly represented in government, increasingly believed that government should act for their interests. Thus, Louis XIV faced recurrent popular riots based on the assumption that when bad harvests drove up food prices, the government was obligated to help people out.

In sum, nation-states developed a growing list of functions, particularly under the banner of mercantilism, whose principles were shared by monarchists and parliamentary leaders alike. They also promoted new political values and loyalties that were very different from the political traditions of other civilizations. They kept the West politically divided and often at war.

IN DEPTH

## Elites and Masses

What caused the end of witchcraft hysteria in the West by the later 17th century? Did wise rulers calm a frenzied populace or did ordinary people themselves change their minds? One explanation focuses on new efforts by elites, such as local magistrates, to discipline mass impulses. Authorities stopped believing in demonic disruptions of natural processes, and so forced an end to persecutions. But many ordinary people were also thinking in new ways. Without converting fully to a scientific outlook, they became open to new ideas about how to handle health problems, reducing their belief in magical remedies; they needed witches less. Potential "witches" may have become more cautious. Older women, threatened by growing community suspicion, learned to maintain a lower profile and to emphasize benign, grandmotherly qualities rather than seeking a more independent role. Without question, there was a decline both in witchcraft beliefs, once a key element in the Western mentality, and in the hysteria specifically characteristic of the 16th and 17th centuries. This decline reflected new ways of thinking about strangeness and disruption. It involved complex interactions between various segments of Western society: magistrates and villagers, scientists and priests, husbands and widows.

*"Some historians have suggested that the rise of science opened a new gap between the ways educated upper classes and masses thought."*

The transformation of Western society after 1450 raises fascinating questions about the role of elites—particularly powerful groups and creative individuals—versus the ordinary people in causing change. The growing importance of social history has called attention to ordinary people, as we have seen, but it has not answered all the questions about their actual role. This role varies by place and time, of course. Some social historians tend to see ordinary people as victims of change, pushed around by the power groups. Others tend to stress the positive historical role of ordinary people in partly shaping the context of their own lives and affecting the larger course of history.

It is easy to read the early modern transformation of western Europe as an operation created by elites, with the masses as passively watching or futilely protesting. Not only the Renaissance and Reformation but also the commercial revolution required decisive action by key leadership groups. Leading merchants spurred economic change, and they ultimately began to farm out manufacturing jobs. The resultant rise of dependent wage labor, which tore a growing minority of western Europeans away from property and so from economic control of their lives, illustrates the power disparities in Western society. Ordinary people knuckled under or protested, but they were reacting, not initiating.

The rise of science rivets our attention on the activities of extraordinarily creative individuals, such as Newton, and elite institutions, such as the scientific academies. Some historians have suggested that the rise of science opened a new gap between the ways educated upper classes and masses thought.

Yet the ordinary people of western Europe were not passive, nor did they simply protest change in the name of tradition. Widespread shifts came from repeated decisions by peasants and artisans, not just from those at the top. The steady technological improvements in manufacturing thus flowed upward from practicing artisans, not downward from formal scientists. The European-style family that had taken shape by the 16th century was an innovation by ordinary people long ignored by the elite. It encouraged new parent–child relations and new tensions between young adults and the old that might spur other innovations, including a willingness to settle distant colonies in search of property. The fact that young people often had to wait to marry until their property-owning fathers died could induce many to seek new lands or new economic methods. In other words, ordinary people changed their habits too, and these changes had wide impact.

**Questions** Did elites gain new power over the masses in early modern Western society? Are ordinary people more conservative by nature, more suspicious of change, than groups at the top? Can you describe at least two other historical cases in which it is important to determine whether change was imposed on ordinary people from above or whether ordinary people themselves produced important innovations?

## The West by 1750

- **Warfare continued due to rivalries among Europe's monarchs. The Enlightenment expanded the range of intellectual innovation. Changes in daily life accelerated as a result of cultural forces and new pressures from commercial and population growth.**

### Political Patterns

Many of the key changes in modern Europe drew together by the mid-18th century. Political changes were least significant. During much of the century, English politics settled into a bloated parliamentary routine in which key political groups competed for influence without major policy differences. Absolute monarchy in France changed little institutionally, but it became less effective. It could not force changes in the tax structure that would give it more solid financial footing because aristocrats refused to surrender their traditional exemptions.

Political developments were far livelier in central Europe. In Prussia, **Frederick the Great,** building on the military and bureaucratic organization of his predecessors, introduced greater freedom of religion while expanding the economic functions of the state. His government actively encouraged better agricultural methods; for example, it promoted use of the American potato as a staple crop. It also enacted laws promoting greater commercial coordination and greater equity; harsh traditional punishments were cut back. Rulers of this sort claimed to be enlightened despots, wielding great authority but for the good of society at large.

The Growth of Brandenburg-Prussia

Enlightened or not, the policies of the major Western nation-states produced recurrent warfare. France and Britain squared off in the 1740s and again in the Seven Years War (1756–1763); their conflicts focused on battles for colonial empire. Austria and Prussia also fought, with Prussia gaining new land. Wars in the 18th century were carefully modulated, without devastating effects, but they demonstrated the continued linkage between statecraft and war that was characteristic of the West.

## Enlightenment Thought and Popular Culture

In culture, the aftermath of the Scientific Revolution spilled over into a new movement known as the **Enlightenment,** centered particularly in France but with adherents throughout the Western world. Enlightenment thinkers continued to support scientific advance. Although there were no Newton-like breakthroughs, chemists gained new understanding of major elements, and biologists developed a vital new classification system for the natural species.

The Enlightenment also pioneered in applying scientific methods to the study of human society, sketching the modern social sciences. The basic idea was that rational laws could describe social as well as physical behavior and that knowledge could be used to improve policy. Thus, criminologists wrote that brutal punishments failed to deter crime, whereas a decent society would be able to rehabilitate criminals through education. Political theorists wrote about the importance of carefully planned constitutions and controls over privilege, although they disagreed about what political form was best. A new school of economists developed. In his classic book *Wealth of Nations,* Scottish philosopher **Adam Smith** set forth a number of principles of economic behavior. He argued that people act according to their self-interest but, through competition, promote general economic advance. Government should avoid regulation in favor of the operation of individual initiative and market forces. This was an important statement of economic policy and an illustration of the growing belief that general models of human behavior could be derived from rational thought.

Adam Smith, Intro to the *Wealth of Nations* (1776)

Single individuals could sum up part of the Enlightenment's impressive range. Denis Diderot (1713–1784; Figure 22.5) was a multifaceted leader of

**FIGURE 22.5** Denis Diderot, one of the key figures in the definition and dissemination of the Enlightenment.

DOCUMENT

## Controversies About Women

Changes in family structure and some shifts in the economic roles of women, as well as ambivalent Protestant ideas about women that emphasized the family context but urged affection and respect between wives and husbands, touched off new gender tensions in Western society by the 17th century. Some of these tensions showed in witchcraft trials, so disproportionately directed against women. Other tensions showed in open debate about women's relationships to men; women not content with a docile wifeliness vied with new claims of virtue and prowess by some women. Although the debate was centered in the upper class of Protestant nations such as England, it may have had wider ramifications. Some of these ramifications, though quieter during the 18th century, burst forth again in arguments about inequality and family confinement in the 19th century, when a more durable feminist movement took shape in the West. In the selections here, the antiwoman position is set forth in a 1615 pamphlet by Joseph Swetham; the favorable view implicitly urging new rights is in a 1640 pamphlet pseudonymously authored by "Mary Tattle-Well and Ioane Hit-Him-Home, spinsters."

### Swetham's "Arraignment of Women"

Men, I say, may live without women, but women cannot live without men: for Venus, whose beauty was excellent fair, yet when she needed man's help, She took Vulcan, a clubfooted Smith. . . .

For women have a thousand ways to entice thee and ten thousand ways to deceive thee and all such fools as are suitors unto them: some they keep in hand with promises, and some they feed with flattery, and some they delay with dalliances, and some they please with kisses. They lay out the folds of their hair to entangle men into their love; betwixt their breasts in the vale of destruction; and in their beds there is hell, sorrow and repentance. Eagles eat not men till they are dead, but women devour them alive. . . .

It is said of men that they have that one fault, but of women it is said that they have two faults: that is to say, they can neither say well nor do well. There is a saying that goeth thus: that things far fetched and dear bought are of us most dearly beloved. The like may be said of women; although many of them are not far fetched, yet they are dear bought, yea and so dear that many a man curseth his hard pennyworths and bans his own heart. For the pleasure of the fairest woman in the world lasteth but a honeymoon; that is, while a man hath glutted his affections and reaped the first fruit, his pleasure being past, sorrow and repentance remaineth still with him.

### Tattle-Well and Hit-Him-Home's "Women's Sharp Revenge"

But it hath been the policy of all parents, even from the beginning, to curb us of that benefit by striving to keep us under and to make us men's mere Vassals even unto all posterity. How else comes it to pass that when a Father hath a numerous issue of Sons and Daughters, the sons forsooth they must be first put to the Grammar school, and after perchance sent to the University, and trained up in the Liberal Arts and Sciences, and there (if they prove not Blockheads) they may in time be book-learned? . . .

When we, whom they style by the name of weaker Vessels, though of a more delicate, fine, soft, and more pliant flesh therefore of a temper most capable of the best Impression, have not that generous and liberal Education, lest we should be made able to vindicate our own injuries, we are set only to the Needle, to prick our fingers, or else to the Wheel to spin a fair thread for our own undoing, or perchance to some more dirty and debased drudgery. If we be taught to read, they then confine us within the compass of our Mother Tongue, and that limit we are not suffered to pass; or if (which sometimes happeneth) we be brought up to Music, to singing, and to dancing, it is not for any benefit that thereby we can engross unto ourselves, but for their own particular ends, the better to please and content their licentious appetites when we come to our maturity and ripeness. And thus if we be weak by Nature, they strive to make us more weak by our Nurture; and if in degree of place low, they strive by their policy to keep us more under.

Now to show we are no such despised matter as you would seem to make us, come to our first Creation, when man was made of the mere dust of the earth. The woman had her being from the best part of his body, the Rib next to his heart, which difference even in our complexions may be easily decided. Man is of a dull, earthy, and melancholy aspect, having shallows in his face and a very forest upon his Chin, when our soft and smooth Cheeks are a true representation of a delectable garden of intermixed Roses and Lilies. . . . Man might consider that women were not created to be their slaves or vassals; for as they had not their Original out of his head (thereby to command him), so it was not out of his foot to be trod upon, but in a medium out of his side to be his fellow feeler, his equal, and companion. . . .

Thus have I truly and impartially proved that for Chastity, Charity, Constancy, Magnanimity, Valor, Wisdom, Piety, or any Grace or Virtue whatsoever, women have always been more than equal with men, and that for Luxury, Surquidant obscenity, profanity, Ebriety, Impiety, and all that may be called bad we do come far short of them.

**Questions** What are the main disagreements in these 17th-century texts? What kind of approach was more novel, judging by the Western gender tradition to that point? What conditions prompted a more vigorous public debate about gender in the 17th century? How does it connect to religious, commercial, and political change? How does the favorable argument compare with more modern views about women? What kinds of change does it advocate? Did the new arguments about women's conditions suggest that these conditions were improving?

the French Enlightenment, best known for his editorial work on the *Encyclopédie* that compiled scientific and social scientific knowledge. Trained initially by the Jesuits, Diderot also wrote widely on philosophy, mathematics, and the psychology of deaf-mutes and also tried his hand at literature. An active friend of other philosophers, Diderot also traveled to foreign courts as advisor and visiting intellectual. He visited Catherine the Great of Russia in 1773–1774, for example, to thank her for generous patronage.

More generally still, the Enlightenment produced a set of basic principles about human affairs: Human beings are good, at least improvable, and they can be educated to be better; reason is the key to truth, and religions that rely on blind faith or refuse to tolerate diversity are wrong. Enlightenment thinkers attacked the Catholic church with particular vigor. Progress was possible, even inevitable, if people could be set free. Society's goals should center on improving material and social life.

Although it was not typical of the Enlightenment's main thrust, a few thinkers applied these general principles to other areas. A handful of socialists argued that economic equality and the abolition of private property must become important goals. A few feminist thinkers, such as **Mary Wollstonecraft** in England, argued—against the general male-centered views of most Enlightenment thinkers—that new political rights and freedoms should extend to women. Several journals written by women for women made their first appearance during this extraordinary cultural period. Madame de Beaumere took over the direction of the French *Journal des Dames* from a man, and in Germany, Marianne Ehrmann used her journal to suggest that men might be partly to blame for women's lowly position.

The popularization of new ideas encouraged further changes in the habits and beliefs of many ordinary people. Reading clubs and coffeehouses allowed many urban artisans and businessmen to discuss the latest reform ideas. Leading writers and compilations of scientific and philosophical findings, such as the *Encyclopaedia Britannica,* won a wide audience and, for a few people, a substantial fortune from the sale of books.

Other changes in popular outlook paralleled the new intellectual currents, although they had deeper sources than philosophy alone. Attitudes toward children began to shift in many social groups. Older methods of physical discipline were criticized in favor of more restrained behavior that would respect the goodness and innocence of children. Swaddling—wrapping infants in cloth so they could not move or harm themselves—began to decline as parents became interested in freer movement and greater interaction for young children. Among wealthy families, educational toys and books for children reflected the idea that childhood should be a stage for learning and growth.

Family life generally was changed by a growing sense that old hierarchies should be rethought and revised toward greater equality in the treatment of women and children in the home. Love between family members gained new respect, and an emotional bond in marriage became more widely sought. This was the point at which new imagery about children clearly took hold. Change affected older children as well: parents grew more reluctant to force a match on a son or daughter if the emotional vibrations were not right. Here was a link not only with Enlightenment ideas of proper family relations but with novels such as Richardson's *Pamela* that poured out a sentimental view of life.

## Ongoing Change in Commerce and Manufacturing

Ongoing economic change paralleled changes in popular culture and intellectual life. Commerce continued to spread. Ordinary Westerners began to buy processed products, such as refined sugar and coffee or tea obtained from Indonesia and the West Indies, for daily use. This was a sign of the growing importance of Europe's new colonies for ordinary life and of the beginnings of mass consumerism in Western society. Another sign of change was the growing use of paid professional entertainment as part of popular leisure, even in rural festivals. Circuses, first introduced in France in the 1670s, began to redefine leisure to include spectatorship and a taste for the bizarre.

Agriculture began to change. Until the late 17th century, western Europe had continued to rely largely on the methods and techniques characteristic of the Middle Ages—a severe economic constraint in an agricultural society. The three-field system still meant that a full third of all farmland was left unplanted each year to restore fertility. First in the Netherlands and then elsewhere, new procedures for draining swamps added available land. Reformers touted nitrogen-fixing crops to reduce the need to leave land idle. Stockbreeding improved, and new techniques such as seed-drills and the use of scythes instead of sickles for harvesting increased productivity. Some changes spread particularly fast on large estates, but other changes affected ordinary peasants as well. Particularly vital in this category was the spread of the potato from the late 17th century onward.

A New World crop, the potato had long been shunned because it was not mentioned in the Bible and was held to be the cause of plagues. Enlightened government leaders, and the peasants' desire to win greater economic security and better nutrition, led to widespread use of this crop. In sum, the West improved its food supply and agricultural efficiency, leaving more labor available for other pursuits.

**FIGURE 22.6** A family of woolmakers at home—an example of domestic manufacturing.

These changes, along with the steady growth of colonial trade and internal commerce, spurred increased manufacturing. Capitalism—the investment of funds in hopes of larger profits—also spread from big trading ventures to the production of goods. The 18th century witnessed a rapid spread of household production of textiles and metal products, mostly by rural workers who alternated manufacturing with some agriculture. Here was a key use of labor that was no longer needed for food. Hundreds of thousands of people were drawn into this domestic system, in which capitalist merchants distributed supplies and orders and workers ran the production process for pay (Figure 22.6). Although manufacturing tools were still operated by hand, the spread of domestic manufacturing spurred important technological innovations designed to improve efficiency. In 1733, John Kay in England introduced the flying shuttle, which permitted automatic crossing of threads on looms; with this, an individual weaver could do the work of two. Improvements in spinning soon followed as the Western economy began to move toward a full-fledged Industrial Revolution (see Chapter 28).

Human changes accompanied and sometimes preceded technology. Around 1700, most manufacturers who made wool cloth in northern England were artisans, doing part of the work themselves. By 1720, a group of loom owners were becoming outright manufacturers with new ideas and behaviors. How were manufacturers different? They spent their time organizing production and sales rather than doing their own work. They moved work out of their homes. They stopped drinking beer with their workers. And they saw their workers as market commodities, to be treated as the conditions of trade demanded. In 1736, one such manufacturer coolly wrote that because of slumping sales, "I have turned off [dismissed] a great many of my makers, and keep turning more off weekly."

Finally, agricultural changes, commercialism, and manufacturing combined, particularly after about 1730, to produce a rapidly growing population in the West. With better food supplies, more people survived, particularly with the aid of the potato. Furthermore, new manufacturing jobs helped landless people support themselves, promoting earlier marriage and sexual relationships. Population growth, in turn, promoted further economic change, heightening competition and producing a more manipulable labor force. The West's great population revolution, which continued into the 19th century, both caused and reflected the civilization's dynamism, although it also produced great strain and confusion.

## Innovation and Instability

By the 18th century, the various strands of change were increasingly intertwined in Western civilization. Stronger governments promoted agricultural improvements, which helped prod population growth. Changes in popular beliefs were fed by new economic structures; both encouraged a reevaluation of the family and the roles of children. New beliefs also raised new political challenges. Enlightenment ideas about liberty and fundamental human equality could be directed against existing regimes. New family practices might have political implications as well. Children, raised with less adult restraint and encouraged to value their individual worth through parental love and careful education, might see traditional political limitations in new ways.

There was no perfect fit, no inevitable match, in the three strands of change that had been transforming the West for two centuries or more: the commercial, the cultural, and the political. However, by 1750 all were in place. The combination had already produced an unusual version of an agricultural civilization, and it promised more upheaval in the future.

GLOBAL CONNECTIONS

## Europe and the World

In 1450, Europeans were convinced that their Christianity made them superior to other people. But they also understood that many societies were impressive in terms of cities and wealth and the strength of their governments. As Europe changed and prospered, its outlook toward the world changed as well. We saw in the previous chapter how Europeans began to use technology as a measure of society, arguing that other societies that were less interested in technological change were inferior. By the 18th century, criticisms of the superstitions of other people began to surface among Europeans proud of their science and rationalism.

The wider world could still provide a sense of wonder, but increasingly this was focused on natural phenomena and the strange animals being imported to European zoos. The Enlightenment generated the idea of a "noble savage"—a person uncorrupted by advanced civilization and urban ways. But this was largely a fiction designed to comment on Europe itself, not a source of real admiration for other peoples. Increasingly, European power and the rapid changes within Western civilization led to a sense that most other societies were backward, perhaps not even civilized. The idea had powerful impact, not only on European attitudes but also on the ways other societies perceived themselves and reacted.

## Further Readings

For an overview of developments in Western society during this period, with extensive bibliographies, see Sheldon Watts, *A Social History of Western Europe, 1450–1720* (1984); Michael Anderson, *Approaches to the West European Family* (1980); and Peter N. Stearns, *Life and Society in the West: The Modern Centuries* (1988). Charles Tilly, *Big Structures, Large Processes, Huge Comparisons* (1985), offers an analytical framework based on major change; see also Tilly's edited volume, *The Formation of National States in Western Europe* (1975).

On more specific developments and periods, J. R. Hale, *The Civilization of Europe in the Renaissance* (1994); J. H. Plumb, *The Italian Renaissance* (1986); F. H. New, *The Renaissance and Reformation: A Short History* (1977); O. Chadwick, *The Reformation* (1983); and Steven Ozment, *The Age of Reform, 1520–1550* (1980), and his *Protestants: The Birth of a Revolution* (1992), are fine introductions to early changes. See also Hubert Jedin and John Dolan, eds., *Reformation and Counter Reformation* (1980). H. Baron, *The Crisis of the Early Italian Renaissance* (1996), examines the place of civic life in Italian humanism. E. Amt, ed., *Women's Lives in the Medieval Europe: A Source-Book* (1992); and A. Vickery, *The Gentleman's Daughter: Women's Lives in Georgian England* (1998), survey the growth or retreat of opportunities for women over time.

Later changes are sketched in Thomas Munck, *Seventeenth Century Europe: 1598–1700* (1990); and Jeremy Black, *Eighteenth Century Europe: 1700–1789* (1990). On England in the civil war period, see Christopher Hill, *A Nation of Change and Novelty* (1990).

Key aspects of social change in this period can be approached through Peter Burke, *Popular Culture in Early Modern Europe* (1978); Robin Biggs, *Communities of Belief: Cultural and Social Tensions in Early Modern France* (1989); Keith Thomas, *Religion and the Decline of Magic* (1971); Lawrence Stone, *The Family, Sex and Marriage in England 1500–1800* (1977); and James Sharpe, *Instruments of Darkness: Witchcraft in Early Modern England* (1997). On popular protest, see Charles Tilly, *The Contentious French* (1986); and H. A. F. Kamen, *The Iron Century: Social Change in Europe 1550–1660* (1971).

On science, A. R. Hall, *From Galileo to Newton, 1630–1720* (1982), is a fine introduction. Relations between science and technology are covered in C. Cipolla, *Before the Industrial Revolution* (1976).

## On the Web

Daily life in Renaissance Italy can be explored through links identified at http://tudorhistory.org/links/life.html and http://www.twingroves.district96.k12.il.us/Renaissance/GeneralFiles/RenLinksDaily.html. The lives and art of Leonardo da Vinci (http://www.mos.org/leonardo/), Michelangelo (http://www.michelangelo.com/buonarroti.html), and Raphael (http://www.theartgallery.com.au/ArtEducation/greatartists/Raphael/about/) were closely intertwined with the city of Florence, whose history is addressed at http://www.mega.it/eng/egui/epo/secrepu.htm.

Martin Luther's life and the course of the Protestant Reformation and Catholic Reformation are discussed at http://www.iep.utm.edu/l/luther.htm, http://mars.acnet.wnec.edu/~grempel/courses/wc2/lectures/catholicreform.html, and http://www.fordham.edu/halsall/sbook1y.html. The art and literature of the Northern Renaissance is examined at http://www.urtonart.com/history/Renaissance/northrenaiss.htm and http://www.msu.edu/~cloudsar/nrweb.htm, while http://communication.ucsd.edu/bjones/Books/luther.html illustrates the role of the printing press in the Reformation.

The Web provides insight into the role of two of the leading absolute monarchs of Europe, Frederick the Great (http://members.tripod.com/~Nevermore/king7.html) and Louis XIV (http://www.royalty.nu/Europe/France/LouisXIV.html and http://www.chateauversailles.fr/). Virtual visits of their palaces can be made at http://www.chateauversailles.fr/en/, http://www.bc.edu/bc_org/avp/cas/fnart/arch/versailles.html, http://www.courses.psu.edu/nuc_e/nuc_e405_g9c/potsdam/park/schloss.html, and http://en.wikipedia.org/wiki/Sanssouci. Isaac Newton's life and letters can be examined at http://www.cannylink.com/historyissacnewton.htm, while links to other leading figures of the Scientific Revolution can be explored at http://www.fordham.edu/halsall/mod/modsbook09.html, http://libraries.brookline.mec.edu/bookmarks/Science/ScientificRevolution.html, and http://www.historyteacher.net/GlobalHistory-1/WebLinks/WebLinks-ScientificRevolution.htm.

The development of modern political and economic theory can be traced through the life and work of Niccolo Machiavelli (http://www.philosophypages.com/ph/macv.htm and http://www.constitution.org/mac/prince00.htm), the Medici family (http://www.pbs.org/empires/medici/medici/index.html), Adam Smith (http://www.econlib.org/library/Enc/bios/Smith.html), and through the study of the Glorious Revolution of 1688 (http://www.victorianweb.org/history/Glorious_Revolution.html). Sites addressing Renaissance women and their texts can be found at http://www.yesnet.yk.ca/schools/projects/renaissance/renaissancewomen.html, http://www.allsands.com/History/People/womanoftheren_vzp_gn.htm, http://womenshistory.miningco.com/cs/medieval/, and http://www.wwp.brown.edu/texts/rwoentry.html.

CHAPTER 23

# The Rise of Russia



New rulers often face a special challenge of legitimacy: why should people accept their rule and their policies? The Russian tsars of the 15th and 16th century faced just such a challenge. They claimed the right to dominate Russia and orchestrate steady expansion of territory. How could they persuade the people that their power was legitimate? Early tsars, particularly Ivan III and Ivan IV, proved particularly inventive. First, they pointed to their family tree, noting their descent from the line of Rurik, the legendary founder of Russia. Ivan IV had huge genealogy books prepared, ignoring the claims of other descendants. The early tsars also invoked the example of the Roman Empire, speaking of Russia as the "third Rome"—after Byzantium and Rome itself. This had appeal: Rome was a much admired state from the classical past, and Byzantium added an element of Christian mission. Russia could be presented as protector of the faith. Ivan IV's genealogies were thus filled with lives of the saints and church resolutions, designed to show how God's purpose, from creation onward, had been to found a truly Christian empire and how Russia was now called to fulfill this purpose. Russia's ruler was often portrayed in religious terms, as leader of the holy church and as part of a divine mission.

But even this was not enough. As Ivan IV campaigned in central Asia, he also invoked the heritage of the Mongols. Russia should rule in central Asia, according to this argument, because it was the long-standing property of the Rurik dynasty (which was nonsense historically but sounded good); because it was "his duty as a Christian monarch to extirpate the rule of the infidel"; and because, having defeated the Mongols, he had become a khan himself. And sure enough, at the time and thereafter, Muslim leaders often took oaths of loyalty to the tsar on the Qur'an, and the tsar styled himself, in that region, the "khan of the north."

Three lessons may be taken from all this that are important for Russian and world history alike. First, tsars claimed a lot. Second, their claims embodied significant contradictions. Were they khans, claiming arbitrary authority over the masses, or were they benevolent, gentle Christians? And third, precisely because Russian expansion touched so many different regions and traditions, the new empire would inevitably be complex and multifaceted.

**FIGURE 23.1** Early Russian tsar Ivan V, 1682–1696. Ivan was actually sickly and ineffective, and soon gave way to Peter the Great. But the portrait suggests the symbolism with which the tsars were invested.

| 1450 C.E. | 1600 C.E. | 1750 C.E. |
|---|---|---|
| **1462** Much of Russia freed from Tatars by Ivan III (Ivan the Great)<br>**1480** Moscow region free; Russian expansion presses south<br>**1533–1584** Life of Ivan IV (Ivan the Terrible), first to emphasize the title of tsar, boyar power reduced<br>**1552–1556** Russian expansion in central Asia, western Siberia | **1604–1613** Time of Troubles<br>**1613–1917** Romanov dynasty<br>**1637** Russian pioneers to Pacific<br>**1649** Law enacted making serfdom hereditary<br>**1689–1725** Reign of Peter the Great<br>**1700–1721** Wars with Sweden<br>**1703** Founding of St. Petersburg | **1762–1796** Reign of Catherine the Great<br>**1773–1775** Pugachev revolt<br>**1772, 1793, 1795** Partition of Poland<br>**1785** Law enacted tightening landlord power over serfs |

## Russia's Expansionist Politics Under the Tsars

■ **Russia's early modern development first emphasized territorial expansion and the strengthening of tsarist rule.**

Russia's emergence as a new power in eastern Europe and central Asia initially depended on its gaining freedom from Mongol (Tatar) control. The Duchy of Moscow was the center for the liberation effort beginning in the 14th century. Local princes began to carve out greater autonomy, and the effectiveness of Mongol control began to diminish. Ironically, the Moscow princes initially gained political experience as tax collectors for the Mongols, but gradually they moved toward regional independence. Under **Ivan III**—Ivan the Great, who claimed succession from the Rurik dynasty and the old Kievan days—a large part of Russia was freed after 1462. Ivan organized a strong army, giving the new government a military emphasis it would long retain. By 1480, Moscow had been freed from any payment to the Mongols and had gained a vast territory running from the borders of the Polish Lithuanian kingdom to the Ural Mountains.

Russia's rise had some similarities to earlier Macedonian and Roman expansion: a new state, on the fringes of the "civilized world," suddenly and steadily gaining great power.

### The Need for Revival

Mongol control never reshaped basic Russian values, for the rulers were interested in tribute, not full government. Many Russian landlords adopted Mongol styles of dress and social habits. However, most Russians remained Christians, and most local administrative issues remained in the hands of regional princes, landlords, or peasant villages. In these senses, Russia was set to resume many of its earlier patterns when full independence was achieved. On the other hand, the Mongol period reduced the vigor of Russian cultural life, lowering the levels of literacy among the priesthood, for example. Economic life deteriorated as well: with trade down and manufacturing limited, Russia had become a purely agricultural economy dependent on peasant labor. In these senses, independence brought a challenge for revival and reform.

Ivan the Great claimed an earlier tradition of centralized rule, which went back to the Rurik dynasty and Byzantine precedents, and added to it the new sense of imperial mission. He married the niece of the last Byzantine emperor, which gave him the chance to assert control over all Orthodox churches whether in Russia or not. The idea of Russia as a third Rome explained why Ivan called himself tsar, or caesar, the "autocrat of all the Russias."

The next important tsar, **Ivan IV,** justly called Ivan the Terrible, continued the policy of Russian expansion. He also placed greater emphasis on controlling the tsarist autocracy, earning his nickname by killing many of the Russian nobles, or *boyars,* whom he suspected of conspiracy. Russian aristocrats lacked the tradition of political assertion of their counterparts in western Europe, and Ivan's policies of terror confirmed this fact.

IMAGE Ivan the Terrible

### Patterns of Expansion

The territorial expansion policy focused particularly on central Asia. It was motivated by a desire to push the former Mongol overlords farther back. Russia was a country of vast plains, with few natural barriers to invasion. The early tsars turned this drawback to an advantage by pushing southward toward the Caspian Sea; they also moved east into the Ural mountains and beyond. Both Ivan III and Ivan IV recruited peasants to migrate to the newly seized lands, particularly in the south. These peasant-adventurers, or **cossacks,** were Russian pioneers, combining agriculture with daring military feats on horseback. The expansion territories long had a rough-and-ready frontier quality, only gradually settling down to more regular administration. The cossack spirit provided volunteers for further expansion, for many of the pioneers—like their American counterparts in the 19th century—chafed under detailed tsarist control and were eager to move on to new settlements. During the 16th century, the cossacks not only conquered the Caspian Sea area but also moved into western Siberia, across the Urals, beginning the gradual takeover and settlement of these vast plains, which previously had been sparsely inhabited by nomadic Asian peoples (Map 23.1).

Expansion also offered tsars a way to reward loyal nobles and bureaucrats by giving them estates in new territories. This practice provided new agricultural areas and sources of labor; Russia used slaves for certain kinds of production work into the 18th century. Although Russia never became as dependent on expansion for social control and economic advance as the later Roman Empire or the Ottoman Empire, it certainly had many reasons to continue the policy. Russia also created trading connections with its new Asian territories and their neighbors.

Russia's early expansion, along with that of the Ottoman Empire to the south, eliminated independent central Asia—that age-old source of nomadic cultures and periodic invasions in both the east and the west. The same expansion, though driven by the movement of Russian peasants and landlords to new areas, also added to Russia diverse new peoples, making this a multicultural empire, like that of the Mughals and Ottomans. Particularly important was the addition of a large Muslim minority, overseen by the tsarist government but not pressed to integrate with Russian culture.

Russia, 1462–1914

## Western Contact and Romanov Policy

Along with expansion and enforcement of tsarist primacy, the early tsars added one element to their overall approach: carefully managed contacts with western Europe. The tsars realized that Russia's cultural and economic subordination to the Mongols had put them at a commercial and cultural disadvantage. Ivan III was eager to launch diplomatic missions to the leading Western states. During the reign of Ivan IV, British merchants established trading contacts with Russia, selling manufactured products in exchange for furs and other raw materials. Soon, Western merchants established outposts in Moscow and other Russian centers. The tsars also imported Italian artists and architects to design church buildings and the magnificent royal palace in the Kremlin in Moscow. The foreign architects modified Renaissance styles to take Russian building traditions into account, producing the ornate, onion-shaped domes that became characteristic of Russian (and other east European) churches and creating a distinctive form of classicism. A tradition of

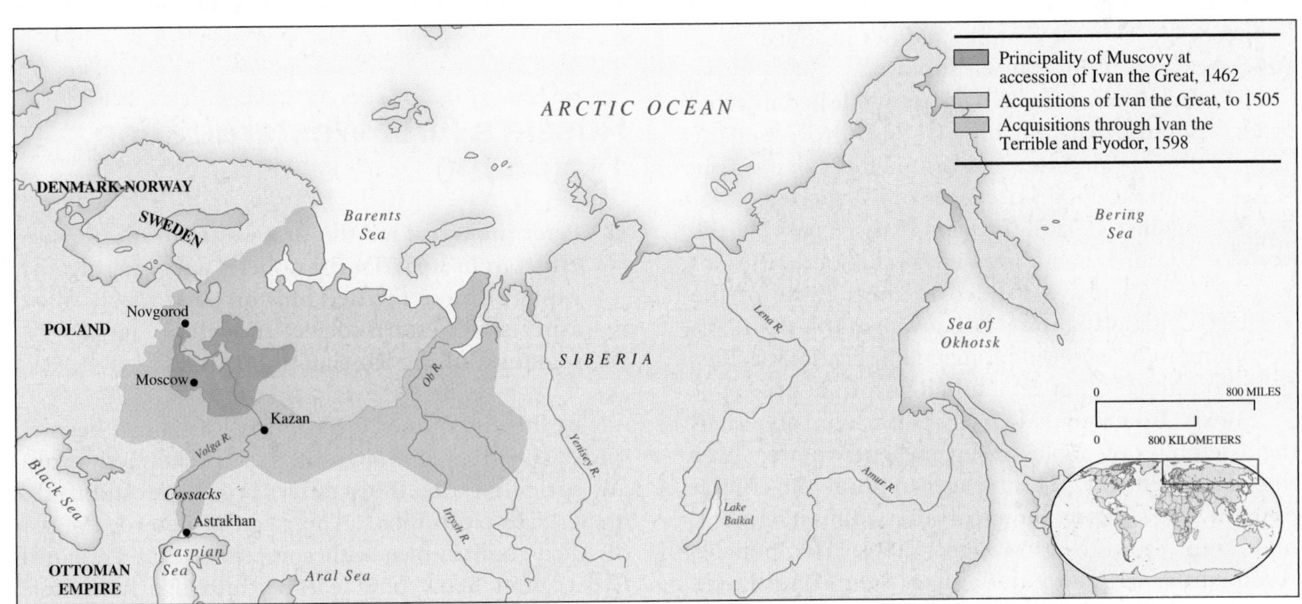


**MAP 23.1 Russian Expansion Under the Early Tsars, 1462–1598.** From its base in the Moscow region, Russia expanded in three directions; the move into Siberia involved pioneering new settlements, as the government encouraged Russians to push eastward. Political controls extended gradually as well.

**FIGURE 23.2** This icon, from the early 15th century, depicts Mary and the Christ Child. The Russian icon tradition used styles derived from Byzantine art. By the 17th century, under Western influence, they had become more naturalistic.

looking to the West, particularly for emblems of upper-class art and status, was beginning to emerge by the 16th century, along with some reliance on Western commercial initiative (Figure 23.2).

Ivan IV died without an heir. This led to some new power claims by the boyars—the **Time of Troubles**—plus Swedish and Polish attacks on Russian territory. In 1613, however, an assembly of boyars chose a member of the Romanov family as tsar. This family, the **Romanov dynasty,** was to rule Russia until the great revolution of 1917. Although many individual Romanov rulers were weak, and tensions with the claims of nobles recurred, the Time of Troubles did not produce any lasting constraints on tsarist power.

The first Romanov, Michael, reestablished internal order without great difficulty. He also drove out the foreign invaders and resumed the expansionist policy of his predecessors. A successful war against Poland brought Russia part of the Ukraine, including Kiev. In the south, Russia's boundaries expanded to meet those of the Ottoman Empire. Expansion at this point was beginning to have new diplomatic implications as Russia encountered other established governments.

Michael Romanov

**Alexis Romanov,** Michael's successor, abolished the assemblies of nobles and gained new powers over the Russian church. He was eager to purge the church of many superstitions and errors that, in his judgment, had crept in during Mongol times. His policies resumed the Orthodox tradition of state control over the church. Dissident religious conservatives, called **Old Believers,** were exiled to Siberia or to southern Russia, where they maintained their religion and extended Russia's colonizing activities.

## Russia's First Westernization, 1690–1790

■ **Peter the Great led the first westernization effort in history. Tsarist policies encouraging westernization focused only on particular aspects of Western society and left out large segments of the Russian population.**

By the end of the 17th century Russia had become one of the great land empires, but it remained unusually agricultural by the standards of the West and the great Asian civilizations. The reign of **Peter I,** the son of Alexis and known with some justice as Peter the Great, built many new features into this framework between 1689 and 1725. In essence, Peter extended his predecessors' policies of building up tsarist control and expanding Russian territory (Map 23.2). He added a more definite interest in changing selected

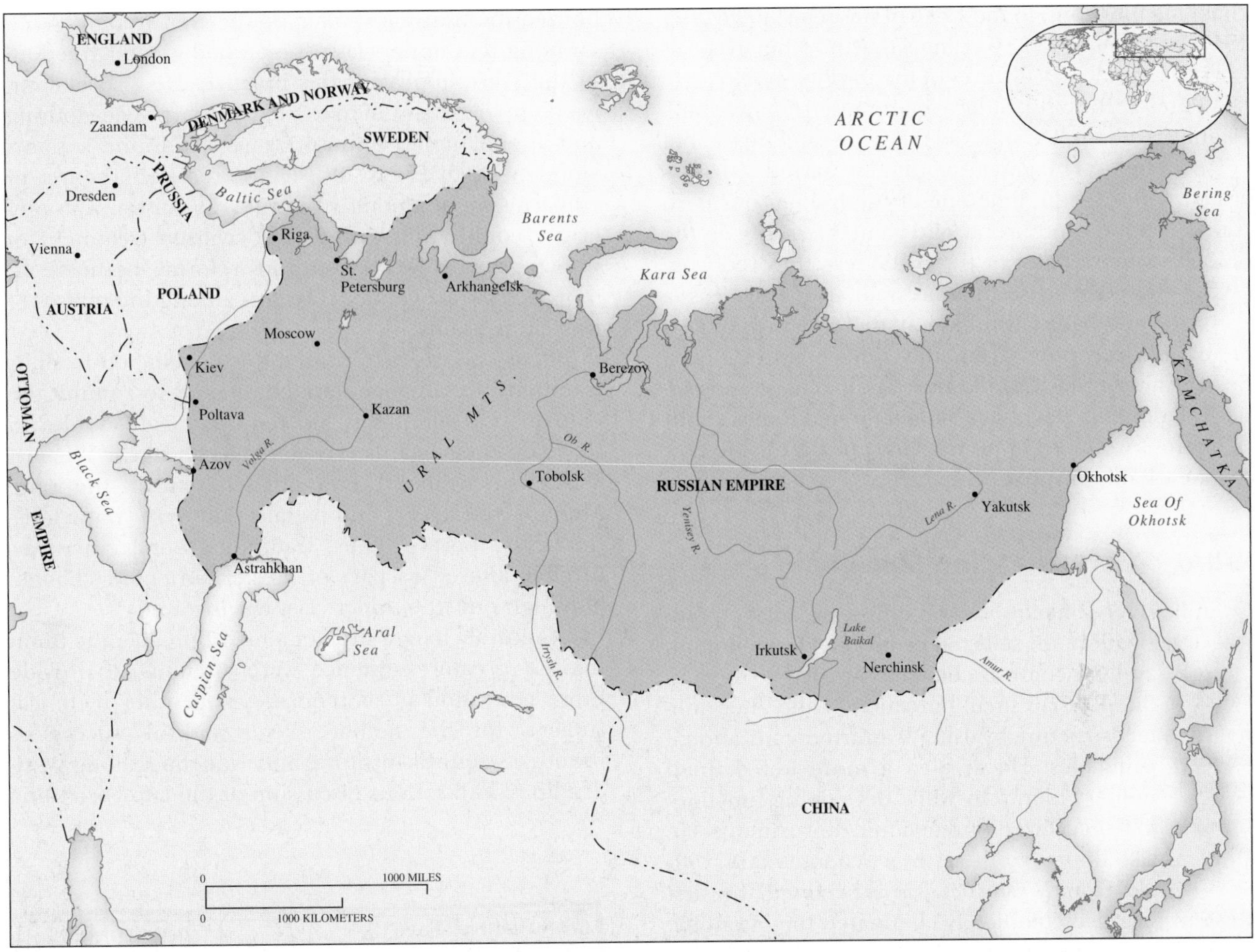

**MAP 23.2 Russia Under Peter the Great.** From 1696 to 1725, Peter the Great allowed his country only one year of peace. For the rest of this reign he radically changed the form of his government to pursue war. By the end, he had established his much-desired "Window on the West" on the southern shores of the Baltic Sea, where he founded the new city of St. Petersburg.

aspects of Russian economy and culture by imitating Western forms.

Peter the Great was a vigorous leader of exceptional intelligence and ruthless energy. A giant, standing 6 feet 8 inches, he was eager to move his country more fully into the Western diplomatic and cultural orbit without making it fully Western. He traveled widely in the West, incognito, seeking Western allies for a crusade against Turkish power in Europe—for which he found little enthusiasm. He also visited many Western manufacturing centers, even working as a ship's carpenter in Holland; through these activities he gained an interest in Western science and technology. He brought scores of Western artisans back with him to Russia.

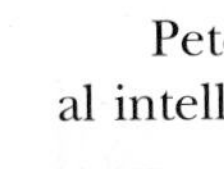

Peter the Great

## Tsarist Autocracy of Peter the Great

In politics, Peter was clearly an autocrat. He put down revolts against his rule with great cruelty, in one case executing some of the ringleaders personally. He had no interest in the parliamentary features of Western centers such as Holland, seizing instead on the absolutist currents in the West at this time. Peter enhanced the power of the Russian state by using it as a reform force, trying to show that even aristocratic habits could be modified by state decree. Peter also extended an earlier policy of recruiting bureaucrats from outside aristocratic ranks and giving them noble titles to reward bureaucratic service. Here was a key means of freeing the state from exclusive dependence on aristocratic officials.

Peter imitated Western military organization, creating a specially trained fighting force that put down local militias. Furthermore, he set up a secret police to prevent dissent and to supervise the bureaucracy. Here he paralleled an earlier Chinese innovation but went well beyond the bureaucratic control impulses of Western absolutists at that time. Peter's Chancery of Secret Police survived, under different names and with changing functions, to the 1990s; it was reinstituted after 1917 by a revolutionary regime that in other respects worked to undo key features of the tsarist system.

Peter's foreign policy maintained many well-established lines. He attacked the Ottoman Empire, but he won no great victories. He warred with Sweden, at the time one of the leading northern powers in Europe, and gained territory on the eastern coast of the Baltic Sea, thus reducing Sweden to second-rate military status. Russia now had a window on the sea, including a largely ice-free port. From this time onward, Russia became a major factor in European diplomatic and military alignments. The tsar commemorated Russia's shift of interests westward by moving his capital from Moscow to a new Baltic city that he named St. Petersburg.

Battle of Poltava, 1709

## What Westernization Meant

Overall, Peter concentrated on improvements in political organization, on selected economic development, and on cultural change. He tried to streamline Russia's small bureaucracy and alter military structure by using Western organizational principles. He created a more well-defined military hierarchy while developing functionally specialized bureaucratic departments. He also improved the army's weaponry and, with aid from Western advisors, created the first Russian navy. He completely eliminated the old noble councils, creating a set of advisors under his control. Provincial governors were appointed from St. Petersburg, and although town councils were elected, a tsar-appointed town magistrate served as final authority. Peter's ministers systematized law codes to extend through the whole empire and revised the tax system, with taxes on ordinary Russian peasants increasing steadily. New training institutes were established for aspiring bureaucrats and officers—one way to bring talented nonnobles into the system.

Lomonosov: Panegyric to the Sovereign Emperor Peter the Great

Peter's economic efforts focused on building up metallurgical and mining industries, using Russia's extensive iron holdings to feed state-run munitions and shipbuilding facilities. Without urbanizing extensively or developing a large commercial class, Peter's reforms changed the Russian economy. Landlords were rewarded for using serf labor to staff new manufacturing operations. This was a limited goal but a very important one, giving Russia the internal economic means to maintain a substantial military presence for almost two centuries.

Finally, Peter was eager to make Russia culturally respectable in Western eyes. Before Peter the Great, it was a custom in upper-class marriages for the father of the bride to pass a small whip to the groom. This symbolized the transfer of male power over women. Peter, knowing that upper-class women had greater freedom in the West, abolished this practice. He also encouraged upper-class women to wear Western-style clothing and attend public cultural events. He found support among women as a result. He also reduced a source of embarrassment among Westerners in Russia, who otherwise could easily point to uncivilized treatment of women. But, as with most of his reforms, he made no move to change gender relations among the masses of Russian peasants.

Peter was eager to cut the Russian elite off from its traditions, to enhance state power, and to commit the elite to new identities. He required male nobles to shave off their beards (Figure 23.3) and wear Western clothes; in symbolic ceremonies he cut off the long, Mongol-type sleeves and pigtails that were characteristic of the boyars. Thus, traditional appearance was forcibly altered as part of Western-oriented change, although only the upper class was involved.

Cultural change supplemented bureaucratic training. Of greater substance were attempts to provide more education in mathematics and other technical subjects for the nobility. Peter and his successors founded scientific institutes and academies along Western lines, and serious discussion of the latest scientific

**FIGURE 23.3** This contemporary Russian cartoon lampoons Peter the Great's order to his nobility to cut off their beards.

and technical findings became common. At the elite level, Peter built Russia into a Western cultural zone, and Western fads and fashions extended easily into the glittering new capital city. Ballet, initially encouraged in the French royal court, was imported and became a Russian specialty. The use of Christmas trees came from Germany.

This westernization effort had several features that can be compared with imitation processes in other societies later on. In the first place, the changes were selective. Peter did not try to touch the ordinary people of Russia or to involve them in the technological and intellectual aspects of westernization. New manufacturing involved serf labor that was partially coerced, not the wage-labor spreading in the West. There was no interest in building the kind of worldwide export economy characteristic of the West. Peter wanted economic development to support military strength rather than to achieve wider commercial goals. Finally, westernization was meant to encourage the autocratic state, not to challenge it with some of the new political ideas circulating in the West. This was real change, but it did not fold Russia into Western civilization outright. Selectivity was crucial, and there was no interest in abandoning particularly Russian goals.

Furthermore, the westernization that did occur brought hostile responses. Many peasants resented the westernized airs and expenses of their landlords, some of whom no longer even knew Russian but spoke only French. Elements of the elite opposed Peter's thirst for change, arguing that Russian traditions were superior to those of the West. As one priest wrote to Tsar Alexis, "You feed the foreigners too well, instead of bidding your folk to cling to the old customs." This tension continued in Russian history from this point forward, leading to important cycles of enthusiasm and revulsion toward Western values.

Reflections on the Accomplishments of Peter the Great

FIGURE 23.4 Catherine the Great in the costume of Minerva, the Roman goddess of wisdom, war, and the arts.

## Consolidation Under Catherine the Great

The death of Peter the Great in 1724 was followed by several decades of weak rule, dominated in part by power plays among army officers who guided the selection of several ineffective emperors and empresses. The weakness of tsardom in these years encouraged new grumblings about undue westernization and some new initiatives by church officials eager to gain more freedom to maneuver, but no major new policy directions were set. Russian territorial expansion continued, with several clashes with the Ottoman Empire and further exploration and settlement in Siberia. In 1761, Peter III, nephew of Peter the Great's youngest daughter, reached the throne. He was retarded, but his wife, a German-born princess who changed her name to Catherine—and was later known as **Catherine the Great**—soon took matters in hand. After Peter III's death, she ruled as Catherine II (see Figure 23.4). Catherine resumed Peter the Great's interests in several respects. She defended the powers of the central monarch. She put down a vigorous peasant uprising, led by Emelian Pugachev, butchering Pugachev himself. She used the **Pugachev rebellion** as an excuse to extend the powers of the central government in regional affairs.

Catherine II (the Great) (1729–1796) is one of the fascinating women leaders of history. Born a Prussian princess, she converted to the Orthodox faith after her marriage to the heir to the Russian throne was arranged. Her married life was miserable, with frequent threats of divorce from her husband. She also disliked her son, the future Tsar Paul I. Carefully cultivating the Russian court, Catherine benefited from a plot to dethrone her husband, Peter III, after an unpopular foreign policy move. Officers of the palace guard installed her as empress in 1762. The tsar was later murdered, possibly with Catherine's consent. Catherine's reign combined genuine Enlightenment interests with her need to consolidate power as a truly Russian ruler—a combination that explains the complexities of her policies. Like many male rulers, Catherine maintained an active personal life and had a succession of lovers, some of them politically influential.

IMAGE
Catherine the Great

Like Peter the Great, Catherine was a selective westernizer, as her "instruction of 1767" (see the Document section) clearly demonstrated. She flirted with the ideas of the French Enlightenment, importing several French philosophers for visits and patronizing the arts and sciences. She summoned various reform commissions to discuss new law codes and other Western-style measures, including reduction of traditionally severe punishments.

DOCUMENT
Catherine the Great's Constitution (1767)

Catherine's image was not always consistent with her policies, however. She was a centralizer and certainly an advocate of a strong tsarist hand. But Catherine also gave new powers to the nobility over their serfs, maintaining a trade-off that had been developing over the previous two centuries in Russia. In this trade-off, nobles served a strong central government and staffed it as bureaucrats and officers. They were in this sense a service aristocracy, not an independent force. They also accepted into their ranks newly ennobled officials chosen by the tsars. In return, however, most of the actual administration over local peasants, except for those on government-run estates, was wielded by the noble landlords. These landlords could requisition peasant labor, levy taxes in money and goods, and even impose punishments for crimes because landlord-dominated courts administered local justice. Catherine increased the harshness of punishments nobles could decree for their serfs.

Catherine patronized Western-style art and architecture, continuing to build St. Petersburg in the classical styles popular at the same time in the West and encouraging leading nobles to tour the West and even send their children to be educated there. But she also tried to avoid cultural influence from the West. When the great French Revolution broke out in 1789, Catherine was quick to close Russia's doors to the "seditious" writings of liberals and democrats. She also censored a small but emerging band of Russian intellectuals who urged reforms along Western lines. One of the first Western-inspired radicals, a noble named Radishev, who sought abolition of serfdom and more liberal political rule, was vigorously harassed by Catherine's police, and his writings were banned.

Catherine pursued the tradition of Russian expansion with energy and success. She resumed campaigns against the Ottoman Empire, winning new territories in central Asia, including the Crimea, bordering the Black Sea. The Russian–Ottoman contest became a central diplomatic issue for both powers, and Russia became increasingly ascendant. Catherine accelerated the colonization of Russia's holdings in Siberia and encouraged further exploration, claiming the territory of Alaska in Russia's name. Russian explorers also moved down the Pacific coast of North America into what is now northern California, and tens of thousands of pioneers spread over Siberia.

Finally, Catherine pressed Russia's interests in Europe, playing power politics with Prussia and Austria, though without risking major wars. She increased Russian interference in Polish affairs. The Polish government was extremely weak, almost paralyzed by a parliamentary system that let members of the nobility veto any significant measure, and this invited interest by more powerful neighbors. Russia was able to win agreements with Austria and Prussia for the **partition of Poland.** Three partitions, in 1772, 1793, and 1795, eliminated Poland as an independent state, and Russia held the lion's share of the spoils. The basis for further Russian involvement in European affairs had obviously been created, and this would show in Russia's ultimate role in putting down the French armies of Napoleon after 1812—the first time Russian troops moved into the heartland of western Europe.

IMAGE
*The Cake of Kings—First Partition of Poland,* 1773 Engraving

By the time of Catherine's death in 1796, Russia had passed through three centuries of extraordinary development. It had won independence and constructed a strong central state, though one that had to maintain a balance with the local political and economic interests of a powerful nobility. It had brought new elements into Russia's culture and economy, in

DOCUMENT

## The Nature of Westernization

Peter the Great and Catherine the Great were the two chief reformist rulers in Russia before 1800. In the first of the following edicts, Peter focuses on educational change; his approach reflected a real desire for innovation, Russia's autocratic tradition in government, and its hierarchical social structure. Catherine's "Instruction" borrowed heavily from Western philosophers and was hailed by one French intellectual as "the finest monument of the century." This document also showed distinctively Russian traditions and problems. However, the reforms in law and punishment were not put into practice, and the document itself was banned as subversive by Catherine's successor, as Russia's rulers began to fear the subversive qualities of Western influence after the French Revolution.

### Decrees on Compulsory Education of the Russian Nobility, January 12 and February 28, 1714

Send to every *gubernia* [region] some persons from mathematical schools to teach the children of the nobility—except those of freeholders and government clerks—mathematics and geometry; as a penalty [for evasion] establish a rule that no one will be allowed to marry unless he learns these [subjects]. Inform all prelates to issue no marriage certificates to those who are ordered to go to schools. . . .

The Great Sovereign has decreed: in all *gubernias* children between the ages of ten and fifteen of the nobility, of government clerks, and of lesser officials, except those of freeholders, must be taught mathematics and some geometry. Toward that end, students should be sent from mathematical schools [as teachers], several into each *gubernia,* to prelates and to renowned monasteries to establish schools. During their instruction these teachers should be given food and financial remuneration of three altyns and two dengas per day from *gubernia* revenues set aside for that purpose by personal orders of His Imperial Majesty. No fees should be collected from students. When they have mastered the material, they should then be given certificates written in their own handwriting. When the students are released they ought to pay one ruble each for their training.

Without these certificates they should not be allowed to marry or receive marriage certificates.

### From the "Instruction" of 1767

6. Russia is a European State.

7. This is clearly demonstrated by the following Observations: The Alterations which Peter the Great undertook in Russia succeeded with the greater Ease, because the Manners, which prevailed at that Time, and had been introduced amongst us by a Mixture of different Nations, and the Conquest of foreign Territories, were quite unsuitable to the Climate. Peter the First, by introducing the Manners and Customs of Europe among the European People in his Dominions, found at that Time such Means as even he himself was not sanguine enough to expect.

8. The Possessions of the Russian Empire extend upon the terrestrial Globe to 32 Degrees of Latitude, and to 165 of Longitude.

9. The Sovereign is absolute; for there is no other Authority but that which centers in his single Person, that can act with a Vigour proportionate to the Extent of such a vast Dominion.

10. The Extent of the Dominion requires an absolute Power to be vested in that Person who rules over it. It is expedient so to be, that the quick Dispatch of Affairs, sent from distant Parts, might make ample Amends for the delay occasioned by the great Distance of the Places.

11. Every other Form of Government whatsoever would not only have been prejudicial to Russia, but would even have proved its entire Ruin.

12. Another Reason is: That it is better to be subject to the Laws under one Master, than to be subservient to many.

13. What is the true End of Monarchy? Not to deprive People of their natural Liberty; but correct their Actions, in order to attain the supreme Good. . . .

272. The more happily a People live under a government, the more easily the Number of the Inhabitants increases. . . .

519. It is certain, that a high opinion of the *Glory* and *Power* of the Sovereign, would *increase* the *Strength* of his Administration; but a *good Opinion of his Love of Justice, will increase it at least as much.*

520. All this will never please those flatterers, who are daily instilling this pernicious Maxim into all the Sovereign on Earth, That their People are created for them only. But We think, and esteem it Our Glory to declare, "That We are created for Our People; and, of this Reason, We are obliged to Speak of Things just as they ought to be." For God forbid! That, after this Legislation is finished, any Nation on Earth should be more just; and, consequently, should flourish, more than Russia; otherwise the Intention of Our Laws would be totally frustrated; an Unhappiness which I do not wish to survive.

---

**Questions** In what sense did reformist measures strengthen Russian autocracy? Why might 18th-century Western thinkers admire reformist tsars? What relationships to the West did the reform measures suggest? What do the documents suggest about the motivations of leaders such as Peter and Catherine? Were they similar? Which westernizer maintained a closer match between their claims and appearances and Russia's real conditions?

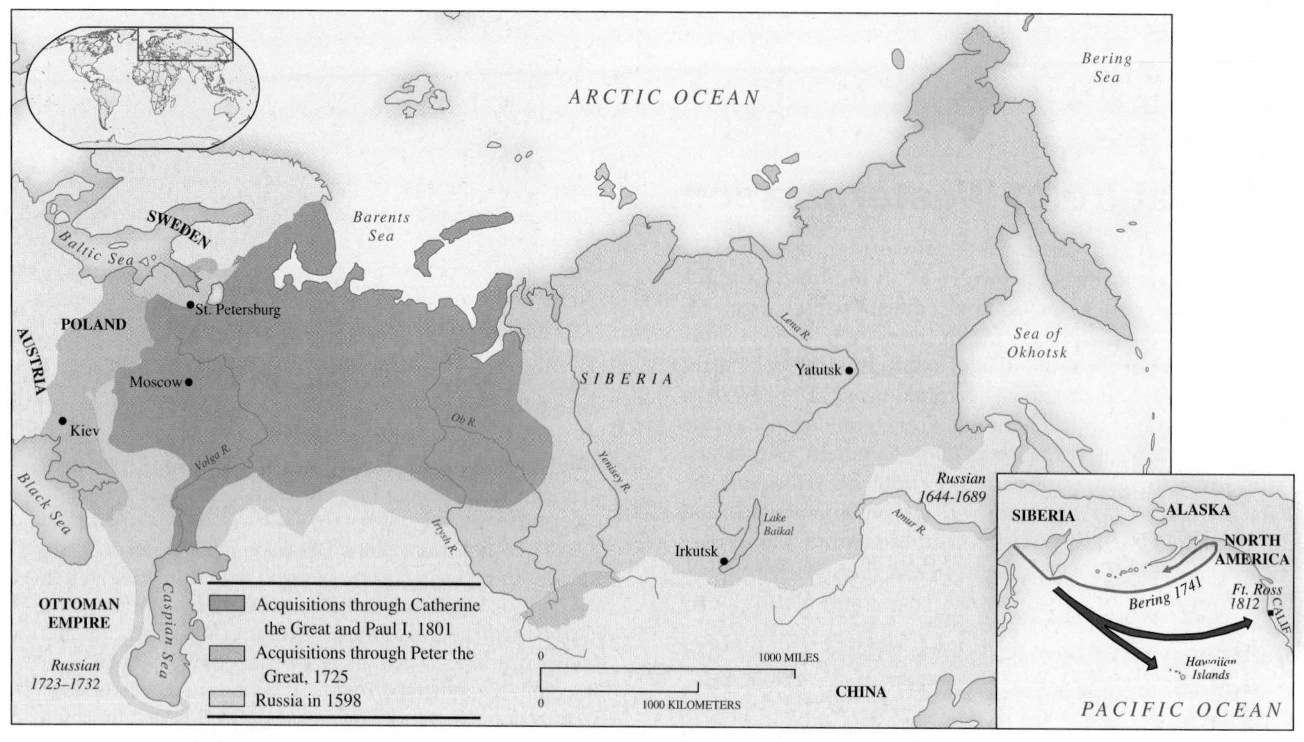


**MAP 23.3 Russia's Holdings by 1800.** Expansion fluctuated from one decade to the next but persisted, bringing Russia into encounters with Europe, the Ottoman Empire, and East Asia.

part by borrowing from the West. And it had extended its control over the largest land empire in the world (Map 23.3). In the east it bordered China, where an 18th-century Amur River agreement set new frontiers. A tradition of careful but successful military aggrandizement had been established, along with a real pioneering spirit of settlement. It is no wonder that not long after 1800, a perceptive French observer, Alexis de Tocqueville, likened the expanded and increasingly important Russia to the new country emerging in the Western Hemisphere, the United States of America—the two giants of future world history.

# Themes in Early Modern Russian History

- **Russian serfdom constituted a distinctive social and economic system.**

Because of its great estates, its local political power, and its service to the state, the Russian nobility maintained a vital position in Russian society. In Russia and in eastern Europe generally, landed nobles tended to be divided between a minority of great magnates, who lived in major cities and provided key cultural patronage, and smaller landowners, whose culture was less westernized and whose lifestyle was much less opulent.

## Serfdom: The Life of East Europe's Masses

During the 17th and 18th centuries, the power of the nobility over the serfs increased steadily. Before the Mongol conquest, Russian peasants had been largely free farmers with a legal position superior to that of their medieval Western counterparts. After the expulsion of the Tatars, however, increasing numbers of Russian peasants fell into debt and had to accept servile status to the noble landowners when they could not repay. They retained access to much of the land, but not primary ownership. The Russian government actively encouraged this process from the 16th century onward. Serfdom gave the government a way to satisfy the nobility and regulate peasants when the government itself lacked the bureaucratic means to extend direct controls over the common people. As new territories were added to the empire, the system of serfdom was extended accordingly, sometimes after a period of free farming.

Russian Serfs

VISUALIZING THE PAST

## Oppressed Peasants

This painting is from the early 20th century (1907), when revolutionary currents were swirling in Russia and the status of the peasantry was widely discussed. This raises obvious issues of interpretation. The subject of the painting, tax collection and the poor material conditions of 17th-century peasants, is valid for the 17th century, but the artist was also trying to score contemporary points.

**Questions** Does this painting suggest early 20th-century rather than 17th-century sympathies in Russian culture? If so, in what ways? Given the lack of popular art from the 17th century, except religious art, does the painting provide useful material for understanding peasant conditions? What elements were probably guesswork on the artist's part? What aspects of the tax collector's appearance suggest that the artist was striving for an accurate rendition of the ways officials looked *before* the reforms of Peter the Great?

By 1800, half of Russia's peasantry was enserfed to the landlords, and much of the other half owed comparable obligations to the state. Laws passed during the 17th and 18th centuries tied the serfs to the land and increased the legal rights of the landlords. An act in 1649 fixed the hereditary status of the serfs, so that people born to that station could not legally escape it.

Russia was setting up a system of serfdom very close to outright slavery in that serfs could be bought and sold, gambled away, and punished by their masters. The system was a very unusual case in which a people essentially enslaved many of its own members, in contrast to most slave systems, which focused on "outsiders."

Rural conditions in many other parts of eastern Europe were similar. Nobles maintained estate agriculture in Poland, Hungary, and elsewhere. They used the system to support their political control and distinctive lifestyle, as in Russia.

The intensification of estate agriculture and serf labor also reflected eastern Europe's growing economic subordination to the West; in this sense the systems should be compared with developments in Latin

America, despite very different specific origins (see Chapter 24). Coerced labor was used to produce grain surpluses sold to Western merchants for the growing cities of western Europe. In return, Western merchants brought in manufactured goods, including the luxury furnishings and clothing essential to the aristocratic lifestyle.

Serfs on the estates of eastern Europe were taxed and policed by their landlords. In Russia, whole villages were sold as manufacturing labor—a process Peter the Great actively encouraged. Peasants were not literally slaves. They continued to use village governments to regulate many aspects of their lives, relying more heavily on community ties than their counterparts in the Western countryside. Yet most peasants were illiterate and quite poor. They paid high taxes or obligations in kind, and they owed extensive labor service to the landlords or the government—a source not only of agricultural production but also of mining and manufacturing. The labor obligation tended to increase steadily. Both the economic and the legal situation of the peasantry continued to deteriorate. Although Catherine the Great sponsored a few model villages to display her enlightenment to Western-minded friends, she turned the government of the serfs over to the landlords more completely than ever before. A law of 1785 allowed landlords to punish harshly any serfs convicted of major crimes or rebellion.

## Trade and Economic Dependence

In between serfs and landlords, there were few layers of Russian society. Cities were small, and 95 percent of the population remained rural. (Most manufacturing took place in the countryside, so there was no well-defined artisan class.) Government growth encouraged some nonnoble bureaucrats and professionals. Small merchant groups existed as well, although most of Russia's European trade was handled by Westerners posted to the main Russian cities and relying on Western shipping. The nobility, concerned about this potential social competition, prevented the emergence of a substantial merchant class.

Russia's social and economic system worked well in many respects. It produced enough revenue to support an expanding state and empire. Russia was able to trade in furs and other commodities with areas in central Asia outside its boundaries, which meant that its export economy was not totally oriented toward the more dynamic West. It underwrote the aristocratic magnates and their glittering, westernized culture. The system, along with Russia's expansion, yielded significant population growth: Russia's population doubled during the 18th century to 36 million. For an empire burdened by a harsh climate in most regions, this was no small achievement. Despite periodic famines and epidemics, there was no question that the overall economy had advanced.

Yet the system suffered from important limitations. Most agricultural methods were highly traditional, and there was little motivation among the peasantry for improvement because increased production usually was taken by the state or the landlord. Landlords debated agricultural improvements in their academies, but when it came time to increase production, they concentrated on squeezing the serfs. Manufacturing lagged behind Western standards, despite the important extension developed under Peter the Great.

## Social Unrest

Russia's economic and social system led to protest. By the end of the 18th century, a small but growing number of Western-oriented aristocrats such as Radishev were criticizing the regime's backwardness, urging measures as far-reaching as the abolition of serfdom. Here were the seeds of a radical intelligentsia that, despite government repression, would grow with time. More significant still were the recurring peasant rebellions. Russian peasants for the most part were politically loyal to the tsar, but they harbored bitter resentments against their landlords, whom they accused of taking lands that were rightfully theirs. Periodic rebellions saw peasants destroy manorial records, seize land, and sometimes kill landlords and their officials.

Peasant rebellions had occurred from the 17th century onward, but the Pugachev rebellion of the 1770s was particularly strong. Pugachev (Figure 23.5), a cossack chieftain who claimed to be the legitimate tsar, promised an end to serfdom, taxation, and military conscription along with the abolition of the landed aristocracy. His forces roamed over southern Russia until they were finally defeated. Pugachev was brought to Moscow in a case and cut into quarters in a public square. The triumph of Catherine and the nobility highlighted the mutual dependence of government and the upper class but did not end protest. Radishev, finding peasants barely able to work their own plots of land and sometimes tortured to work harder, thought he saw the handwriting on the wall: "Tremble, cruel hearted landlord! On the brow of each of your peasants I see your condemnation written."

Emelyan Pugachev Awaits Punishment for Leading Peasant Revolt

## Russia and Eastern Europe

Russian history did not include the whole of eastern Europe after the 15th century. Regions west of Russia

FIGURE 23.5 The Cossack leader Emelian Pugachev attracted supporters by appealing to the popular belief that Peter III, Catherine's husband, was still alive. Claiming to be Peter III, he led a revolt in 1773–1774 that threatened Catherine's throne. When the revolt was defeated, Pugachev was brutally executed as an example to other potential revolutionaries.

Eastern Europe, c. 1550

continued to form a fluctuating borderland between western European and eastern European influences. Even in the Balkans, under Ottoman control, growing trade with the West sparked some new cultural exchange by the 18th century, as Greek merchants, for example, picked up many Enlightenment ideas.

Areas such as present-day Poland or the Czech and Slovak regions operated more fully within the Western cultural orbit. The Polish scientist Copernicus was an early participant in fundamental discoveries in what became the Scientific Revolution. Western currents such as the Reformation also echoed in parts of east central Europe such as Hungary.

At the same time, many smaller eastern European nationalities lost political autonomy during the early modern era. Hungary, freed from the Ottomans, became part of the German-dominated Habsburg Empire. This empire also took over the Czech lands, then called Bohemia. Prussian territory pushed eastward into Polish areas.

The decline of Poland was particularly striking. In 1500, Poland, formed in 1386 by a union of the regional kingdoms of Poland and Lithuania, was the largest state in eastern Europe aside from Russia. Polish cultural life, linked with the West through shared Roman Catholicism, flourished in the 16th century. By 1600, however, economic and political setbacks mounted. Polish aristocrats, charged with electing the king, began deliberately choosing weak figures. As in Russia, urban centers, and thus a merchant class, were lacking. The aristocratic parliament vetoed any reform efforts until late in the 18th century, after Poland began to be partitioned by its more powerful neighbors. The eclipse of Poland highlighted Russian emergence on the European as well as the Eurasian stage.

Poland-Lithuania and Russia

IN DEPTH

## Multinational Empires

Of all the new multinational empires created in the early modern period, Russia's was the most successful, lasting until 1991 and to an extent beyond. In contrast, India's Mughal Empire disappeared completely by the mid-19th century, and the Ottoman and Habsburg empires flickered until after World War I. All the multinational empires were reasonably tolerant of internal diversity (like the Roman and Arab empires of the past, two other multinational entities). The Russian tsar, for example, called himself "Khan of the North" to impress central Asian people and took oaths of loyalty from this region on the Qur'an. However, Russia differed from Asian empires and the Habsburgs in having a larger core of ethnic groups ready to fan out to the frontiers and establish pioneer settlements that sometimes developed into larger Russian enclaves. Russia also benefited from its willingness and ability to copy the West selectively, in contrast most obviously to the Ottoman Empire in the same period. This copying provided access to new military technologies and some new organizational forms.

> *"The Russian tsar, for example, called himself 'Khan of the North' to impress central Asian people and took oaths of loyalty from this region on the Qur'an."*

Ironically, the same period that saw the creation of so many new empires also confirmed the importance of the culturally more cohesive nation-state, the dominant form in western Europe. England and France, prototypical nation-states, were not culturally homogeneous; they had important pockets of minorities who differed linguistically or religiously from the majority culture. But both maintained a clear basis for joining the political unit to the cultural one to foster loyalty. Efforts by the 17th-century French kings to purify and standardize the French language, or by English parliamentarians to claim empowerment from the "rights of freeborn Englishmen," were early signs that politics and national culture were coming together.

The clash between national loyalties and multinational empires did not become serious until the 19th century, and it has continued into the 21st. In the long run, most multinational states have not been able to sustain themselves in the face of increasing demands from individual national groups. The collapse of several multinational units in the 20th century—the Ottomans in the Middle East, the Habsburgs in east central Europe, and the Russians—created new diplomatic trouble spots quite obvious in the world today, for stable nation-states have had a hard time developing in these regions.

**Questions** Why have nation-states been more successful, as political units, in modern world history than multinational empires have been? In what ways did the Russian Empire develop some nation-state characteristics? What were its principal multinational features? Amid new needs for international economic coordination in the 21st century, is it possible to build multinational organizations on some new basis?

GLOBAL CONNECTIONS

## Russia and the World

From a world history standpoint, Russia's emergence as a key player both in Europe and in Asia was a crucial development in the early modern period. Today, Russia spans 10 time zones, and much of this territory had been acquired by the late 18th century. By this point, Russia was affecting diplomatic and military developments in Europe, in the Middle East (through its frequent battles with the Ottoman Empire), and in east Asia. It had gained a direct hold in central Asia. The spread of Russian claims to Alaska, and expeditions even to Hawaii, hinted at an even larger role. This was a different kind of empire from those that Western nations were building, but it had huge impact.

### Further Readings

For excellent survey coverage on this period, as well as additional bibliography, see Nicholas Riasanovsky, *History of Russia* (1992). Two excellent source collections for this vital period of Russian history are T. Riha, ed., *Readings in Russian Civilization, Vol. 2, Imperial Russia 1700–1917* (1969), and Basil Dmytryshyn, *Imperial Russia: A Sourcebook 1700–1917* (1967).

On important regimes, see P. Dukes, *The Making of Russian Absolutism: 1613–1801* (1982); J. L. I. Fennell, *Ivan the Great of Moscow* (1961); L. Hughes, *Russia in the Age of Peter the Great* (1998); R. Massie, *Peter the Great* (1981); and N. V. Riasanovsky, *The Image of Peter the Great in Russian History and Thought* (1985). This last book is a very interesting interpretive effort. On Catherine, see I. de Madariaga, *Russia in the Age of Catherine the Great* (1981).

Three good studies deal with cultural history: H. Rogger, *National Consciousness in Eighteenth Century Russia* (1963);

Marc Raeff, *Origins of the Russian Intelligentsia: The Eighteenth Century Nobility* (1966); and Marc Raeff, ed., *Russian Intellectual History* (1986).

For economic and social history, A. Kahan, *The Knout and the Plowshare: Economic History of Russia in the 18th Century* (1985), is an important treatment. For the vital peasant question, see Jerome Blum, *Lord and Peasant in Russia from the Ninth to the Nineteenth Century* (1961); see also Richard Hellie, *Slavery in Russia, 1450–1725* (1982). For an analytical overview, see Marc Raeff, *Understanding Imperial Russia: State and Society in the Old Regime* (1984). A very revealing comparison is Peter Kolchin, *Unfree Labor: American Slavery and Russian Serfdom* (1987). A fine recent survey on military and diplomatic strategy is William Fuller, *Strategy and Power in Russia, 1600–1914* (1992).

## On the Web

A vivid introduction to Russian history is offered at http://www.geographia.com/russia/rushis01.htm with sections devoted to ancient Russia (http://www.geographia.com/russia/rushis04.htm), the Mongol impact (http://www.geographia.com/russia/rushis03.htm), and the Romanovs (http://www.geographia.com/russia/rushis04.htm), and also http://www.alexanderpalace.org/. Peter the Great's maritime interests are examined at http://www.maritimeheritage.org/ports/europe/russia.html. The lives of Peter the Great and Catherine the Great are seen against the backdrop of early modern Russia at http://emuseum.mnsu.edu/history/russia/peter.html and http://emuseum.mnsu.edu/history/russia/catherine.html. A virtual tour of their palaces at St. Petersburg is available at http://www.cityvision2000.com/city_tour/index.htm and http://www.hermitagemuseum.org/html_En/index.html.

Cossack life is presented at http://www.sfu.ca/archaeology/museum/russia/cossack.htm and http://en.wikipedia.org/wiki/History_of_the_Cossacks. Catherine the Great's response to the rebellion led by the cossack Emelian Pugachev, and how it illuminated the differences in the political landscape of revolutionary France and absolutist Russia, is described at http://mars.acnet.wnec.edu/~grempel/courses/russia/lectures/16catherine.html. An overview of Pugachev's rebellion can be supplemented by reading his *ukaz,* or order, recorded at http://artsci.shu.edu/reesp/documents/pugachev.htm.

CHAPTER 24

# Early Latin America



In September 1589 Captain Mancio Serra de Leguizamon lay dying in his bed in Cuzco, the ancient capital of the Incas in the highlands of Peru. His mind was still clear, but his body was failing, and he knew his time was approaching. He needed to set his affairs in order with his heirs, his king, and with God. He called a priest and a notary to his bedside to draw up his last will and testament.

Born in Castile to a Basque family, like many young Spanish men he had been attracted to the New World by its fabled wealth and opportunities for advancement. When he was 16, he sailed for the New World in search of adventure. Sometime in 1532 he joined the 168 men under the Spanish conqueror Francisco Pizarro, who were embarked on the conquest of the Inca Empire. Mancio Serra claimed in his will that he was the first Spaniard to enter Cuzco when the Spaniards laid siege to the city in 1533. Legend has it that, in the looting that followed, he seized a great golden disk representing the sun that had hung on the walls of the principal temple of the sun in Cuzco. But that very night he fell to drinking and gambling and lost the treasure. In Spanish today, there is an expression, "to gamble the sun before it rises," that has come to mean "to fritter away your time." Its origins are in the story of Mancio Serra, who never got over his love of gambling.

But all was not lost with the disk of gold: for his efforts, Mancio received grants of Indian laborers and a site in the city where, using an Inca stonework foundation, he built a fine home. There were more expeditions, civil wars, an Indian mistress, a marriage to an Inca noblewoman and, later, to a Spanish woman. There were numerous children, some legitimate and some not. Mancio Serra became a respected leader in Peru, for a while mayor of Cuzco, a man of substance with many servants, slaves, and retainers. The details of his life recapitulate many of the general trends of the larger story of the European conquest of the Americas, carried out, as the Spaniards had always claimed, to spread Christianity and expand the domains of their king as well as to make their fortunes. But on his deathbed, Mancio Serra had second

**FIGURE 24.1** By the end of the 17th century, a society that fused Hispanic culture and indigenous elements had emerged in Spanish America. In this painting of a Corpus Christi procession celebrated in Cuzco, Peru, in the 1670s, native Andean artists working in the genre of Spanish religious painting show members of the Inca nobility paying homage to the colonial civil and religious authorities in the presence of the saint's images. This representation of the diverse social elements of colonial society in joint celebration of Catholicism was designed to demonstrate the unity of the faith and the order of colonial society.

| 1450 C.E. | 1500 C.E. | 1600 C.E. | 1750 C.E. |
|---|---|---|---|
| **1492** Fall of Granada, last Muslim kingdom in Spain; expulsion of the Jews; Columbus makes landfall in the Caribbean<br>**1493** Columbus's second expedition; beginnings of settlement in the Indies<br>**1493–1520** Exploration and settlement in the Caribbean<br>**1494** Treaty of Tordesillas | **1500** Cabral lands in Brazil<br>**1519–1524** Cortés leads conquest of Mexico<br>**1533** Cuzco, Peru, falls to Francisco Pizarro<br>**1540–1542** Coronado explores area that is now the southwestern United States<br>**1541** Santiago, Chile, founded<br>**1549** Royal government established in Brazil<br>**1580–1640** Spain and Portugal united under same rulers | **1630–1654** Dutch capture northeastern Brazil<br>**1654** English take Jamaica<br>**1695** Gold discovered in Brazil<br>**1702–1713** War of the Spanish succession; Bourbon dynasty rules Spain | **1755–1776** Marquis of Pombal, prime minister of Portugal<br>**1759** Jesuits expelled from Brazil<br>**1756–1763** Seven Years War<br>**1759–1788** Carlos III rules Spain; Bourbon reforms<br>**1763** Brazilian capital moved to Rio de Janeiro<br>**1767** Jesuits expelled from Spanish America<br>**1781** Comunero revolt in New Granada; Tupac Amaru rebellion in Peru<br>**1788** Conspiracy for independence in Minas Gerais, Brazil |

thoughts about the justice of what he had done. Before assigning his property to his heirs, calling himself the last of the conquerors still alive and so the last who could give eye-witness testimony, in his will he addressed the king of Spain:

> We found these realms in such order that there was not a thief, nor a vicious man, nor an adulteress, nor were there prostitutes, nor were there immoral people, each being content and honest in their labor. And that their lands, forests, mines, pastures and dwellings and produce were regulated in such a manner that each person possessed his own property without any other seizing or occupying it. . . . All things, from the greatest to the smallest, had their place and order. . . . I wish Your Catholic Majesty to understand the motive that moves me to make this statement is the peace of my conscience and because of the guilt I share. For we have destroyed by our evil behavior such a government as was enjoyed by these natives.

Mancio Serra went on to say that the actions and abuses of the Spaniards had ruined the inhabitants, introduced bad habits, and reduced the ancient nobility to poverty. He had seen and lived it all, it burdened his soul and his conscience, and he believed it was a matter for the royal conscience as well. "I inform Your Majesty that there is no more I can do to alleviate these injustices other than by my words, in which I beg God to pardon me." In an earlier will he had declared that everything produced from his grant of indigenous workers, including his landed estate, should belong to them, "since it was once their own."

The conquests of Spain and Portugal during the 15th and 16th centuries tell the story of glory, personal gain, the creation of empires, and the resulting questions about what was just in the relationship between an expanding Europe and the peoples of the world. Spain and Portugal created empires in the Americas by conquest and settlement. These lands, which became Latin America, were immediately drawn into a new world economy, providing silver, gold, new crops, and other goods. The emerging hierarchy of world economic relationships shaped conditions in this new civilization for several centuries.

The societies of Latin America also created important new political and cultural forms. The Spaniards and Portuguese, often collectively called Iberians because all came from the Iberian peninsula in Europe, mixed with Native Americans and adopted aspects of their culture while introducing the religion, technologies, and many aspects of their culture to the indigenous peoples. Both groups were also influenced by the cultures of the slaves imported from Africa. The formative period for Latin American civilization extended from initial contacts in the 1490s through the 18th century, when colonial structures began to decline. This period included a number of stages, from raw conquest to growing social, economic, and political complexity by the 18th century.

New societies, created by the intrusion of Spaniards and Portuguese and by the incorporation or destruction of Native American cultures, arose throughout the American continents. Both Europeans and Native Americans drew heavily on their previous experiences as they grappled with the problems created by their encounter. Much of what the Iberians did in the Americas followed the patterns and examples of their European traditions. The Native Americans who survived, although they were battered and profoundly transformed, showed a vitality and resiliency that shaped later societies in many ways. What resulted drew on European and Native American precedents, but it was something new: the world's latest addition to the list of distinctive civilizations.

Various European peoples sought the same ends in the New World: economic gain and social mobility. The Portuguese, English, Spanish, Dutch, and French all created large landed estates, or plantations, worked by coerced laborers—ultimately African slaves—wherever tropical conditions and European demand made such enterprises feasible. The Europeans exploited precious metals when they were discovered, and those who were not so fortunate followed rumors of gold or emeralds.

## Spaniards and Portuguese: From Reconquest to Conquest

■ **The Spaniards and Portuguese came from societies long in contact with peoples of other faiths and cultures in which warfare and conquest were well-established activities. American realities and the resistance of indigenous peoples modified these traditions, but by the 1570s, much of the Americas had been brought under Iberian control.**

The Spanish and Portuguese peoples who inhabited the Iberian peninsula had long lived at the frontier of Mediterranean Europe. During the Middle Ages their lands were a cultural frontier between Christianity and Islam. Conflicts created a strong tradition of military conquest and rule over peoples of other beliefs and customs. Christian kingdoms emerged, such as Portugal on the Atlantic coast, Aragon in eastern Spain, and in the center of the peninsula, Castile, the largest of all. By the mid-15th century, the rulers **Ferdinand of Aragon** and his wife **Isabella of Castile** carried out a program of unification that sought to eliminate the religious and ethnic diversity in their kingdoms. With the fall in 1492 of Granada, the last Muslim kingdom, the cross triumphed throughout the peninsula. Moved by political savvy and religious fervor, Isabella ordered the Jews of her realm to convert or leave the country. As many as 200,000 people may have left, severely disrupting some aspects of the Castilian economy. It was also in 1492, with the Granada war at an end and religious unification established, that Isabella and Ferdinand were willing to support the project of a Genoese mariner named Christopher Columbus, who hoped to reach the East Indies by sailing westward around the globe.

Christian Reconquest of Muslim Spain

### Iberian Society and Tradition

Like many Mediterranean peoples, the Spanish and Portuguese were heavily urban, with many peasants living in small towns and villages. That pattern was also established in America, where Europeans lived in cities and towns surrounded by a rural native population. Many commoners who came to America as conquerors sought to recreate themselves as a new nobility, with native peoples as their serfs. The patriarchal family was readily adapted to Latin America, where large estates and **encomiendas**—grants of American Indian laborers—provided the framework for relations based on economic dominance. The Iberian peninsula had maintained a tradition of holding slaves—part of its experience as an ethnic frontier—in contrast to most of medieval Europe, and African slaves had been imported from the trans-Sahara trade. The extension of slavery to America built on this tradition.

The political centralization of both Portugal and Castile depended on a professional bureaucracy, usually made up of men trained as lawyers and judges. This system is worthy of comparison with the systems in China and other great empires. Religion and the church served as the other pillar of Iberian politics; close links between church and state resulted from the reconquest of the Iberian peninsula from the Muslims, and these links, including royal nomination of church officials, were also extended to the New World.

Spanish and particularly Portuguese merchants also shaped traditions that became relevant in the American colonies. Portugal had been moving down the African coast since 1415, establishing trading posts rather than outright colonies. In the Atlantic islands, however, more extensive estates were established, leading to a slave trade with Africa and a highly commercial agricultural system based on sugar. Brazil would extend this pattern, starting out as a trade factory but then shifting, as in the Atlantic islands, to plantation agriculture.

### The Chronology of Conquest

The Spanish and Portuguese conquest and colonization of the Americas falls roughly into three periods during the early modern centuries. First came an era of conquest from 1492 to about 1570 (Map 24.1), during which the main lines of administration and economy were set out. The second phase was one of consolidation and maturity from 1570 to about 1700 in which the colonial institutions and societies took their definite form. Finally, during the 18th century, a period of reform and reorganization in both Spanish America and Portuguese Brazil intensified the colonial relationship and planted the seeds of dissatisfaction and revolt.

The period from 1492 to about 1570 witnessed a remarkable spurt of human destruction and creation. During roughly a century, vast areas of two continents and millions of people were brought under European control. Immigration, commerce, and exploitation of native populations linked these areas to an emerging Atlantic economy. These processes were accompanied and made possible by the conquest and destruction of many American Indian societies and the transformation of others, as well as by the introduction in some places of African slaves. Mexico and Peru, with their large sedentary populations and mineral resources, attracted the Spaniards and became the focus of immigration and institution building. Other conquests radiated outward from the Peruvian and Mexican centers.

## The Caribbean Crucible

The **Caribbean** experience served Spain as a model for its actions elsewhere in the Americas. After Columbus's original voyage in 1492, a return expedition in the next year established a colony on the island of Santo Domingo, or **Hispaniola** (Figure 24.2). From there and from Spain, expeditions carried out new explorations and conquests. Puerto Rico (1508) and Cuba (1511) fell under Spanish control, and by 1513 settlements existed in Panama and on the northern coast of South America.

Spanish and Portuguese Explorations, 1400–1600

In the Caribbean, the agricultural Taino people of the islands provided enough surplus labor to make their distribution to individual Spaniards feasible, and thus began what would become the encomienda, or grant of indigenous people to individual Spaniards in a kind of serfdom. The holder of an encomienda, an **encomendero,** was able to use the people as workers or to tax them. Gold hunting, slaving, and European diseases rapidly depopulated the islands, and within two decades little was left there to hold Spanish attention. A few strongly fortified ports, such as Havana, San Juan, and Santo Domingo, guarded Spain's commer-

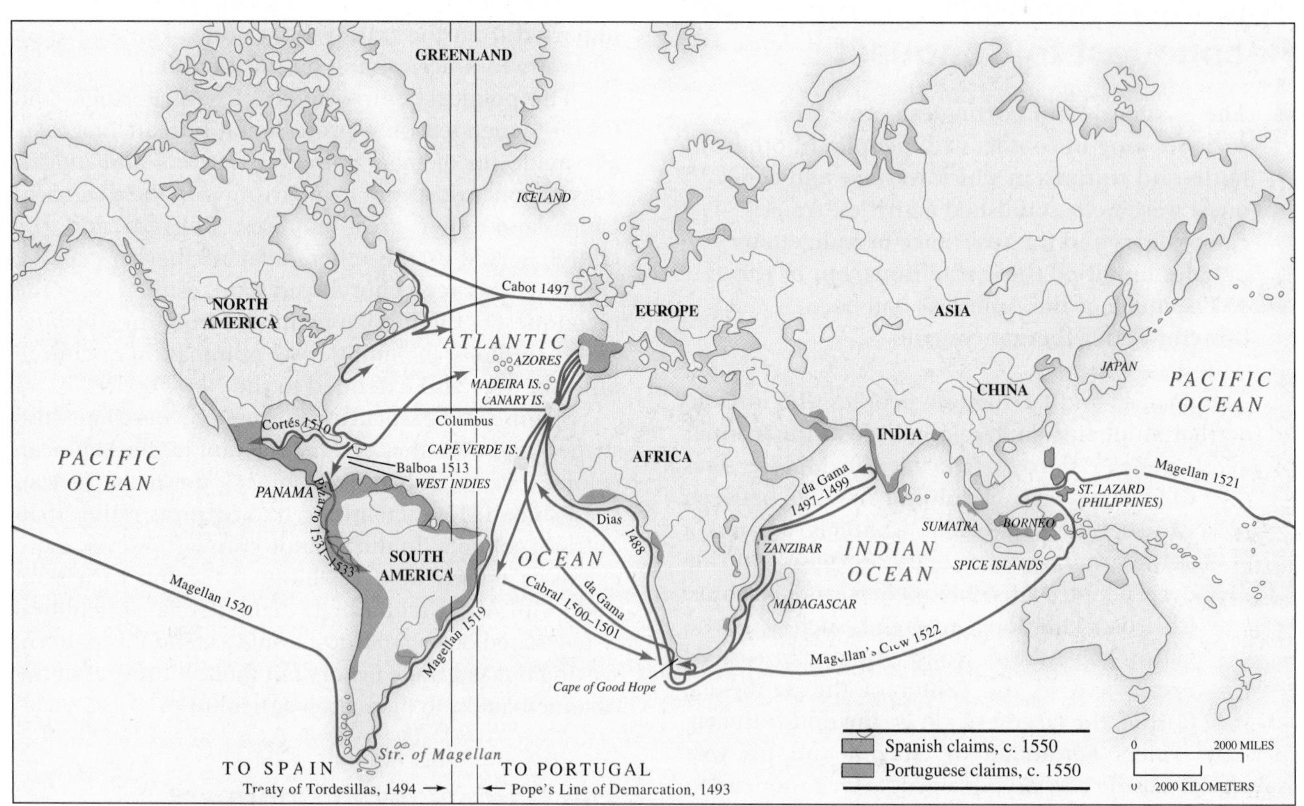


**MAP 24.1** Spanish and Portuguese Explorations, 1400–1600

**FIGURE 24.2** The port city of Santo Domingo was the principal Spanish settlement in the Caribbean in the 16th century.

cial lifeline, but on the whole the Caribbean became a colonial backwater for the next two centuries, until sugar and slaves became the basis of its resurgence.

In the 40 years between the first voyage of Columbus and the conquest of Mexico, the Caribbean served as a testing ground. The Spaniards established Iberian-style cities but had to adapt them to American realities. Hurricanes and the native peoples' resistance caused many towns to be moved or abandoned, but the New World also provided opportunities to implant new ideas and forms. Unlike cities in Europe, Spanish American cities usually were laid out according to a grid plan or checkerboard form, with the town hall, major church, and governor's palace in the central plaza (Figure 24.3). Spaniards applied Roman models and rational town planning ideas to the new situation. Conquest came to imply settlement.

To rule, Spain created administrative institutions: the governorship, the treasury office, and the royal court of appeals staffed by professional magistrates. Spanish legalism was part of the institutional transfer. Notaries accompanied new expeditions, and a body of laws was developed, based on those of Spain and augmented by American experience. The church, represented at first by individual priests and then by missionaries such as the Dominicans, participated in the enterprise. By 1530, a cathedral was being built on Hispaniola, and a university soon followed.

Rumors and hopes stimulated immigration from Spain, and by the 1510s the immigrants included larger numbers of Spanish women. Also, Spanish and Italian merchants began to import African slaves to work on the few sugar plantations that operated on the islands. The arrival of both Spanish women and African slaves represented a shift from an area of conquest to one of settlement. The gold-hunting phase had given out in the islands by the 1520s and was replaced by the establishment of ranches and sugar

**FIGURE 24.3** St. Augustine, Florida. As the oldest city in the United States (founded in 1565), it was established to guard the Spanish sea route from the Caribbean that the silver fleets traveled back to Spain.

plantations. The adventurous, the disappointed, and the greedy repeated the pattern as expeditions spun off in new directions.

Disease and conquest virtually annihilated the native peoples of the Caribbean. Depopulation of the laboring population led to slaving on other islands, and in 30 years or so, most of the indigenous population had died or been killed. The people of the lesser Antilles, or "Caribs," whom the Spanish accused of cannibalism and who were thus always subject to enslavement, held out longer because their islands were less attractive to European settlement. To meet the labor needs of the islands, African slaves were imported. As early as 1510, the mistreatment and destruction of the American Indians led to attempts by clerics and royal administrators to end the worst abuses. The activities of men such as Dominican friar **Bartolomé de Las Casas** (1484–1566; Figure 24.4), a conquistador turned priest, initiated the struggle for justice.

**FIGURE 24.4** Father Bartolomé de Las Casas.

Expeditions leaped from island to island. Where the native peoples and cultures were more resilient, their impact on the societies that emerged was greater than in the Caribbean, but the process of contact was similar. By the time of the conquest of Mexico in the 1520s and Peru in the 1530s, all the elements of the colonial system of Latin America were in place. Even in Brazil, which the Portuguese began to exploit after 1500, a period of bartering with the Native Americans was slowly replaced by increasing royal control and development of a sugar plantation economy. There, as in the Caribbean, resistance and subsequent depopulation of the native peoples led to the importation of African laborers.

DOCUMENT

## A Vision from the Vanquished

History usually is written by the victors, so it is rare to find a detailed statement from the vanquished. In the 17th century, Guaman Poma de Ayala, an acculturated Peruvian Indian who claimed to trace his lineage to the provincial nobility of Inca times, composed a memorial outlining the history of Peru under the Incas and reporting on the current conditions under Spanish rule. Guaman Poma was a Christian and a loyal subject. He hoped that his report would reach King Philip III of Spain, who might then order an end to the worst abuses, among which were the Spanish failure to recognize the rank and status of Indian nobles. His book was not published in his lifetime and was not recovered until the 20th century.

Guaman Poma was an educated, bilingual Indian who spoke Quechua as well as Spanish and who had a profound understanding of Andean culture. His book is remarkable for its revelations of Indian life, for its detailed criticism of the abuses suffered by the Indians, and especially because Guaman Poma illustrated his memorial with a series of drawings that give his words a visual effect. The illustrations also reveal the worldview of this interesting man. The drawings and text offer a critical inside view not of the laws, but of the workings of Spain's empire in America from an Indian point of view.

### Miners

At the mercury mines of Huancavelica the Indian workers are punished and ill-treated to such an extent that they die like flies and our whole race is threatened with extermination. Even the chiefs are tortured by being suspended by their feet. Conditions in the silver-mines of Potosí and Chocllococha, or at the gold-mines of Carabaya are little better. The managers and supervisors, who are Spaniards or mestizos, have virtually absolute power. There is no reason for them to fear justice, since they are never brought before the courts.

Beatings are incessant. The victims are mounted for this purpose on a llama's back, tied naked to a round pillar or put in stocks. Their hair is cut off and they are deprived of food and water during detention.

Any shortage in the labor gangs is made an excuse for punishing the chiefs as if they were common thieves or traitors instead of the nobility of the country. The work itself is so hard as to cause permanent injury to many of those who survive it. There is no remuneration for the journey to the mines and a day's labor is paid at the rate for half a day.

### Proprietors

Your Majesty has granted large estates, including the right to employ Indian labor, to a number of individuals of whom some are good Christians and the remainder are very bad ones. These encomenderos, as they are termed, may boast about their high position, but in reality they are harmful both to the labor force and to the surviving Indian nobility. I therefore propose to set down the details of their life and conduct.

They exude an air of success as they go from their card games to their dinners in fine silk clothes. Their money is squandered on these luxuries, as well it may, since it costs them no work or sweat whatever. Although the Indians ultimately pay the bill, no concern is ever felt for them or even for Your Majesty or God himself.

Official posts like those of royal administrator and judge ought not to be given to big employers or mine-owners or to their obnoxious sons, because these peoples have enough to live on already. The appointments ought to go to Christian gentlemen of small means, who have rendered some service to the Crown and are educated and humane, not just greedy.

Anybody with rights over Indian labor sees to it that his own household is well supplied with servant girls and indoor and outdoor staff. When collecting dues and taxes, it is usual to impose penalties and detain Indians against their will. There is no redress since, if any complaint is made, the law always favors the employer.

The collection of tribute is delegated to stewards, who make a practice of adding something in for themselves. They too consider themselves entitled to free service and obligatory presents, and they end up as bad as their masters. All of them, and their wives as well, regard themselves as entitled to eat at the Indians' expense.

The Indians are seldom paid the few reales a day which are owed to them, but they are hired out for the porterage of wine and making rope or clothing. Little rest is possible either by day or night and they are usually unable to sleep at home.

It is impossible for servant girls, or even married women, to remain chaste. They are bound to be corrupted and prostituted because employers do not feel any scruple about threatening them with flogging, execution, or burial alive if they refuse to satisfy their master's desires.

The Spanish grandees and their wives have borrowed from the Inca the custom of having themselves conveyed in litters like the images of saints in processions. These Spaniards are absolute lords without fear of either God or retribution. In their own eyes they are judges over our people, whom they can reserve for their personal service or their pleasure, to the detriment of the community.

Great positions are achieved by favour from above, by wealth or by having relations at Court in Castile. With some notable exceptions, the beneficiaries act without consideration for those under their control. The encomenderos call themselves conquerors, but their Conquest was achieved by uttering the words: Ama mancha noca Inca, or "Have no fear. I am Inca." This false pretense was the sum total of their performance.

---

**Questions** What are the main abuses Guaman Poma complains about? What remedies does he recommend? What relationship do his views have to traditional Inca values? How might a white landlord or colonial official have answered his attacks?

## The Paths of Conquest

> No other race can be found that can penetrate through such rugged lands, such dense forests, such great mountains and deserts and cross such broad rivers as the Spaniards have done . . . solely by the valor of their persons and the forcefulness of their breed.

These words, written by Pedro Cieza de Leon, one of the conquistadors of Peru, underlined the Spaniards' pride in their accomplishments. In less than a century, a large portion of two continents and islands in an inland sea, inhabited by millions of people, was brought under Spanish control. Spanish expeditions, usually comprising 50 to 500 men, provided the spearhead of conquest, and in their wake followed the women, missionaries, administrators, and artisans who began to form civil society.

The conquest was not a unified movement but rather a series of individual initiatives that usually operated with government approval. The conquest of the Americas was two pronged: one prong was directed toward Mexico; the other was aimed at South America.

We can use the well-documented campaign in Mexico as an example of a conquest. In 1519 **Hernán Cortés,** an educated man with considerable ability as a leader, led an expedition of 600 men to the coast of Mexico. After hearing rumors of a great kingdom in the interior, he began to strike inland. Pitched battles were fought with towns subject to the Aztec Empire, but after gaining these victories, Cortés was able to enlist the defeated peoples' support against their overlords. With the help of the Indian allies, Cortés eventually reached the great Aztec island capital of Tenochtitlan. By a combination of deception, boldness, ruthlessness, and luck, the Aztec emperor **Moctezuma II** was captured and killed. Cortés and his followers were forced to flee the Aztec capital and retreat toward the coast, but with the help of the Aztecs' traditional enemies, they cut off and besieged Tenochtitlan. Although the Aztec confederacy put up a stiff resistance, disease, starvation, and battle brought the city down in 1521. Tenochtitlan was replaced by **Mexico City.** The Aztec poets later remembered,

Second Letter of Hernan Cortéz to King Charles V of Spain

> We are crushed to the ground,
> we lie in ruins.
> There is nothing but grief and suffering
> in Mexico and Tlatelolco,
> where once we saw beauty and valor.

By 1535, most of central Mexico, with its network of towns and its dense, agricultural populations, had been brought under Spanish control as the kingdom of **New Spain.** From there, the Spanish pushed their conquest southward into Central America and northward into the area of the nomadic peoples of north central Mexico.

Excerpts from the "Account of Alva Ixtlilxochitl"

The second trajectory of conquests led from the Caribbean outposts to the coast of northern South America and Panama. From Panama, the Spaniards followed rumors of a rich kingdom to the south. In 1532, after a false start, Francisco Pizarro led his men to the conquest of the Inca Empire, which was already weakened by a long civil war. Once again, using guile and audacity, fewer than 200 Spaniards and their Indian allies brought down a great empire. The Inca capital of Cuzco, high in the Andes, fell in 1533, but the Spanish decided to build their major city, Lima, closer to the coast. By 1540, most of Peru was under Spanish control, although an active resistance continued in remote areas for another 30 years.

From the conquests of densely populated areas, such as Mexico and Peru, where there were surpluses of food and potential laborers, Spanish expeditions spread out in search of further riches and strange peoples. They penetrated the zones of semisedentary and nomadic peoples, who often offered stiff resistance. From 1540 to 1542, in one of the most famous expeditions, **Francisco Vázquez de Coronado,** searching for mythical cities of gold, penetrated what is now the southwestern United States as far as Kansas. At the other end of the Americas, **Pedro de Valdivia** conquered the tenacious Araucanians of central Chile and set up the city of Santiago in 1541, although the Araucanians continued to fight long after. Buenos Aires, in the southern part of the continent, founded by an expedition from Spain in 1536, was abandoned because of resistance and was not refounded until 1580. Other expeditions penetrated the Amazon basin, and explored the tropical forests of Central and South America during these years, but there was little there to attract permanent settlement to those areas. By 1570, there were 192 Spanish cities and towns throughout the Americas, one-third of which were in Mexico and Central America.

European Empires in Latin America, 1660

## The Conquerors

The Spanish captains led by force of will and personal power. "God in the sky, the king in Spain, and me here" was the motto of one captain, and sometimes, absolute power could lead to tyranny. The crown received one-fifth of all treasure. Men signed up on a shares basis; those who brought horses or who had special skills might get double shares. Rewards were made according to the contract, and premiums were paid for special service and valor. There was a tendency for leaders to reward their friends, relatives, and men from their home province more liberally than others, so that after each conquest there was always a group of unhappy and dissatisfied conquerors ready to organize a new expedition. As one observer put it, "if each man was given the governorship, it would not be enough."

Few of the conquerors were professional soldiers; they represented all walks of Spanish life, including a scattering of gentlemen. Some of the later expeditions included a few Spanish women such as Ines Suárez, the heroine of the conquest of Chile, but such cases were rare. In general, the conquerors were men on the make, hoping to better themselves and serve God by converting the heathen at the same time. Always on the lookout for treasure, most conquerors were satisfied by encomiendas. These adventurous men, many of humble origins, came to see themselves as a new nobility entitled to dominion over a new peasantry: the American Indians.

The reasons for Spanish success were varied. Horses, firearms, and more generally steel weapons gave them a great advantage over the stone technology of the native peoples. This technological edge, combined with effective and ruthless leadership, produced remarkable results. Epidemic disease also proved to be a silent ally of the Europeans. Finally, internal divisions and rivalries within American Indian empires, and their high levels of centralization, made the great civilizations particularly vulnerable. It is no accident that the peoples who offered the stiffest and most continuous resistance were usually the mobile, tough, nomadic tribes rather than the centralized states of sedentary peasants.

By about 1570, the age of the conquest was coming to a close. Bureaucrats, merchants, and colonists replaced the generation of the conquerors as institutions of government and economy were created. The transition was not easy. In Peru a civil war erupted in the 1540s, and in Mexico there were grumblings from the old followers of Cortés. But the establishment of viceroys in the two main colonies and the creation of law courts in the main centers signaled that Spanish America had become a colony rather than a conquest.

### Conquest and Morality

Conquest involved violence, domination, and theft. The Spanish conquest of the Americas created a series of important philosophical and moral questions for Europeans. Mancio Serra was not alone in questioning the conquest. Who were the Indians? Were they fully human? Was it proper to convert them to Christianity? Was the conquest of their lands justified? Driven by greed, many of the conquistadors argued that conquest was necessary to spread the gospel and that control of Indian labor was essential for Spain's rule. In 1548 Juan Gines de Sépulveda, a noted Spanish scholar, basing his arguments on Aristotle, published a book claiming that the conquest was fully justified. The Spaniards had come to free the Indians from their unjust lords and to bring the light of salvation. Most importantly, he argued, the Indians were not fully human, and some peoples "were born to serve."

In 1550 the Spanish king suspended all further conquests and convoked a special commission in Valladolid to hear arguments for and against this position. Father Bartolomé de Las Casas—former conqueror and encomendero, Dominican priest, bishop of Chiapas, untiring defender of the Indians, and critic of Spanish brutality—presented the contrary opinion against Sépulveda. Las Casas had long experience in the West Indies, and he believed that the inhabitants were rational people who, unlike the Muslims, had never done harm to Christians. Thus, the conquest of their lands was unjustified. The Indians had many admirable customs and accomplishments, he said. He argued that "the Indians are our brothers and Christ has given his life for them." Spanish rule in order to spread the Christian faith was justified, but conversion should take place only by peaceful means.

Excerpt from Bartolomé de Las Casas in Defense of the Indians

The results of the debate were mixed. The crown had reasons to back Las Casas against the dangerous ambitions of the Spanish conquerors. Sépulveda's book was censored, but the conquests nevertheless continued. Although some of the worst abuses were moderated, in reality the great period of conquest was all over by the 1570s. It was too little, too late. Still, the Spanish government's concern with the legality and morality of its actions and the willingness of Spaniards such as Las Casas to speak out against abuses are also part of the story. The interests of many other conquerors and officials, however, ran in the opposite direction.

## The Destruction and Transformation of American Indian Societies

- **To varying degrees, all indigenous societies suffered the effects of European conquest. Population loss was extreme in many areas. The Spanish created institutions such as the encomienda and later the mita to tax the native population or to make them work. These policies disrupted indigenous societies.**

The various American peoples responded in many different ways to the invasion of their lands and the transformation of their societies. All of them suffered a severe decline of population—a demographic catastrophe (Figure 24.5). On the main islands of the Caribbean, the indigenous population had nearly disappeared by 1540 as the result of slaving, mistreatment, and disease. In central Mexico, war, destruction, and above all disease brought the population from an estimated 25 million in 1519 to less than 2 million in 1580. In Peru a similar process brought a loss from 10 million to 1.5 million between 1530 and 1590. Elsewhere in the Americas a similar but less well documented process took place. Smallpox, influenza, and measles wreaked havoc on the American Indian population, which had developed no immunities against these diseases.

Although epidemic was the major cause of depopulation, the conquest and the weakening of indigenous societies contributed to the losses. Population declines of this size disrupted Indian societies in many ways. For example, in central Mexico the contraction of the Indian population led the Spanish to concentrate the remaining population in fewer towns, and this led in turn to the seizure of former communal farming lands by Spanish landowners. Demographic collapse made maintaining traditional social and economic structures very difficult.

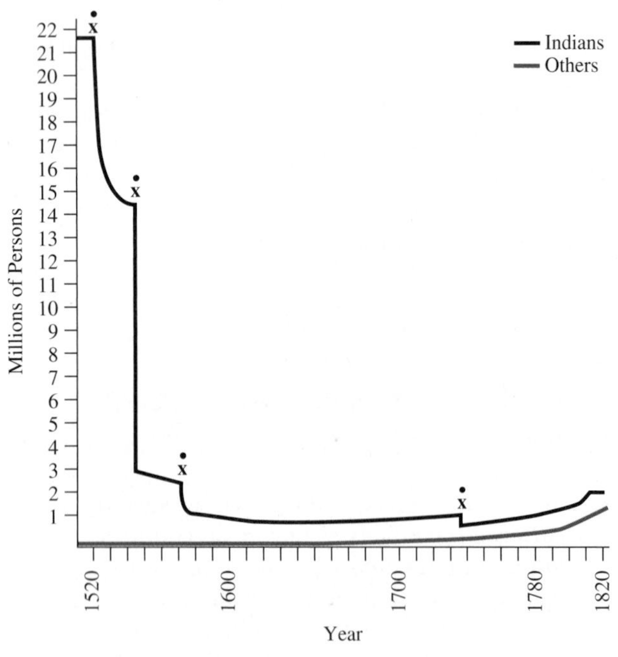


FIGURE 24.5 Population decline in New Spain.

The case of Mexico is particularly stark. The tremendous decline of the Indian population was matched by the rapid increase in European livestock. Cattle, sheep, and horses flourished on the newly created Spanish farms or on unclaimed lands. In a way, European livestock replaced the Indian population of Mexico (Figure 24.6).

## Exploitation of the Indians

The Spaniards did not interfere with aspects of American Indian life that served colonial goals or at least did not openly conflict with Spanish authority or religion. Thus, in Mexico and Peru, while the old Indian religion and its priestly class were eliminated, the traditional Indian nobility remained in place, supported by Spanish authority, as middlemen between the tax and labor demands of the new rulers and the majority of the population.

The enslavement of Indians, except those taken in war, was prohibited by the mid-16th century in most of Spanish America. Instead, different forms of labor or taxation were imposed. At first, encomiendas were given to the individual conquerors of a region. The holders of these grants were able to use their Indians as workers and servants or to tax them. Whereas commoners had owed tribute or labor to the state in the Inca and Aztec empires, the new demands were arbitrary, often excessive, and usually without the reciprocal obligation and protection characteristic of the Indian societies. In general, the encomiendas were destructive to Indian societies. The Spanish crown, unwilling to see a new nobility arise in the New World among the conquerors with their grants of Indian serfs, moved to end the institution in the 1540s. The crown limited the inheritability of encomiendas and prohibited the right to demand certain kinds of labor from the Indians. Although encomiendas continued to exist in marginal regions at the fringes of the empire, they were all but gone by the 1620s in the central areas of Mexico and Peru. Colonists increasingly sought grants of land rather than Indians as the basis of wealth.

The New Laws of the Indies for the Good Treatment and Preservation of the Indians (1542)

Meanwhile, the colonial government increasingly extracted labor and taxes from native peoples. In many places, communities were required to send groups of laborers to work on state projects, such as church construction or road building, or in labor gangs for mining or agriculture. This forced labor, called the *mita* in Peru, mobilized thousands of Indians to work in the mines and on other projects. Although the Indians were paid a wage for this work, there were many abuses of the system by the local offi-

**FIGURE 24.6** The contact between Europeans, Africans, and Native Americans eventually produced large numbers of castas, people considered to be of mixed racial origin. By the 18th century, especially in New Spain, a genre of painting flourished that depicted a husband and wife of different racial categories and their child who would fit one of the casta designations. The purpose and public for these paintings is unclear, but they illustrate domestic relations and material culture as well as racial ideology.

cials, and community labor requirements often were disruptive and destructive to Indian life. By the 17th century, many Indians left their villages to avoid the labor and tax obligations, preferring instead to work for Spanish landowners or to seek employment in the cities. This process eventually led to the growth of a wage labor system in which Indians, no longer resident in their villages, worked for wages on Spanish-owned mines and farms or in the cities.

In the wake of this disruption, Native American culture also demonstrated great resiliency in the face of Spanish institutions and forms, adapting and modifying them to indigenous ways. In Peru and Mexico, native peoples learned to use the Spanish legal system and the law courts so that litigation became a way of life. At the local level, many aspects of Native American life remained, and Native Americans proved to be selective in their adaptation of European foods, technology, and culture.

IN DEPTH

## The Great Exchange

The arrival of the Spaniards and the Portuguese in the Americas began one of the most extensive and profound changes in the history of humankind. The New World, which had existed in isolation since the end of the last ice age, was now brought into continual contact with the Old World. The peoples and cultures of Europe and Africa came to the Americas through voluntary or forced immigration. Between 1500 and 1850, perhaps 10 to 15 million Africans and 5 million Europeans crossed the Atlantic and settled in the Americas as part of the great migratory movement. Contact also initiated a broader biological and ecological exchange that changed the face of both the Old World and the New World—the way people lived, what they ate, and how they died, indeed how many people there were in different regions—as the animals, plants, and diseases of the two hemispheres were transferred. We have seen that these biological contacts were a vital aspect of the establishment of the new world economy.

> *"The replacement of Native Americans by cattle became a metaphor of the conquest of Mexico."*

It was historian Alfred Crosby who first called this process the **Columbian exchange,** and he has pointed out its profound effects as the first stage of the "ecological imperialism" that accompanied the expansion of the West. In this chapter we have discussed the devastating impact of Old World disease on Native American peoples. Long separated from the populations of the Old World and lacking immunities to diseases such as measles and smallpox, populations throughout the Americas suffered disastrous losses after initial contact. Not only among the dense populations in Peru and Mexico, but in the forests of Brazil and the woodlands of North America, contact with Europeans and Africans resulted in epidemics that devastated the indigenous populations. Only after many generations did immunities build up in the remaining populations that allowed them to withstand the diseases.

Disease may have also moved in the other direction. Some authorities believe that syphilis had an American origin and was brought to Europe only after 1492. In general, however, forms of life in the Old World—diseases, plants, and animals—were more complex than those in the Americas and thus displaced the New World varieties in open competition. The diseases of Eurasia and Africa had a greater impact on America than American diseases had on the Old World.

With animals also, the major exchange was from the Old World to the New World. From the beginning of contact, Europeans noted with curiosity the strange fauna of America, so different from that of Europe. The birds were a hit. Parrots were among the first creatures brought to Europe from America. Many early observers commented on the smaller size of the mammals in the New World and the absence of certain types, not realizing that mastodons, horses, camels, and other animals that had once roamed the Americas had long since disappeared. Native Americans had domesticated dogs, guinea pigs, some fowl, and llamas, but in general domesticated animals were far less important in the Americas than in the Old World. Protein resources were thus also more restricted. The absence of cattle and horses had also left the peoples of the Americas without beasts of burden except for the llamas of the Andes.

In the first years of settlement in the Caribbean, the Spanish introduced horses, cattle, sheep, chickens, and domestic goats and pigs, all of which were considered essential for civilized life as the Iberians understood it. Some of these animals thrived in the New World. In the scrub brush and prairies of North America, in the tropical grasslands of Venezuela, and on the South American pampas, vast herds of cattle began to roam freely. A hundred head of cattle abandoned by the Spanish in the Rio de la Plata area in 1587 had become 100,000 head 20 years later. For meat, tallow, and hides in the Americas, and eventually for the export of hides and meat to Europe and the rest of the world, the arrival of cattle in the Americas was a revolutionary occurrence. In Mexico, livestock and Spanish haciendas grew as rapidly as the Native American populations declined and their communities contracted. The replacement of Native Americans by cattle became a metaphor of the conquest of Mexico.

The success of other European livestock was no less impressive. In the Andes and in Mexico, sheep thrived and

## Colonial Economies and Governments

- **Agriculture and mining were the basis of the Spanish colonial economy. Eventually, Spanish farms and ranches competed with Native American villages, but they also depended on Native Americans as laborers. Over this economy Spain built a bureaucratic empire in which the church was an essential element and a major cultural factor.**

Spanish America was an agrarian society in which perhaps 80 percent of the population lived and worked on the land. Yet in terms of America's importance to supported an active textile industry, which eventually supplied most of the local needs. Horses were adopted quickly by the nomadic peoples of North and South America. This adaptation transformed their societies and gave them added mobility, allowing them to meet the Europeans on an almost equal basis. With horses, the Apaches of Arizona and the Indians of the Argentine pampas were able to hold off the Europeans for 300 years.

European livestock, even pigs and chickens, transformed indigenous life in America. Native Americans acquired some animals, such as oxen, slowly, but other animals, such as horses and sheep, had obvious benefits and were acquired more rapidly. The chieftain in Panama who answered that the greatest benefit Spain had brought to his people was the chicken egg may have disappointed his questioner, but his statement reflected a keen appreciation of the importance of the interchange. The newly introduced animals changed the ecological balance in the New World. Not only animals that were purposefully introduced, but species such as the sparrow and the brown rat, whose arrival was unplanned, changed the nature of life in the Americas.

The Europeans also brought their crops and their weeds. It was hard for Iberians to live without the Mediterranean necessities: wheat bread, olive oil, and wine. Columbus on his second voyage in 1499 introduced wheat, peas, melons, onions, grapes, and probably olives as well as sugar cane. Some crops, such as sugar cane, thrived and provided the basis for the rise of plantation economies; other crops such as wheat, olives, and grapes needed cooler or drier environments and had to wait until the Spanish reached the more temperate zones before they flourished. Later, Europeans introduced all of their own crops and even some crops such as bananas, coconut trees, coffee, and breadfruit that they had found in Africa, Asia, and the Pacific. They also inadvertently introduced other plants, such as tumbleweed, which spread quickly.

In the exchange of foods and stimulants, the contribution of America probably outweighed that of Europe, however. It is difficult today to imagine the diet of the Old World before the discovery of America. New World plants, such as tomatoes, squash, sweet potatoes, types of beans, and peppers, became essential foods in Europe. Tobacco and cacao, or chocolate, both American in origin, became widely distributed throughout the world.

Even more important were basic crops, such as the potato, maize, and manioc, all of which yielded more calories per acre than all the Old World grains except rice. The high yield of calories per acre of maize and potatoes had supported the high population densities of the American civilizations. After the Columbian voyages, these foods began to produce similar effects in the rest of the world. Manioc, or casava (we know it as tapioca), was a basic Indian food in the Caribbean and tropical South America. Particularly well suited to the tropics, manioc was never popular in Europe, but it spread widely in Asia and Africa, where it became a basic food by the 18th century. The potato, a staple of the Andean civilizations, was easy to grow and yielded large numbers of calories. By the 18th century it was well known from Ireland to Russia. Maize was a great success. It yielded as many calories per acre as rice, but it was easier to grow and could flourish in a wide variety of situations. By the 17th century it had spread to Spain and France, and by the 18th century it was found in Italy, Turkey, Greece, and Russia. The Europeans also introduced it to west Africa and China. Maize became a staple across the globe. At present, at least one-third of the crops raised to feed the world's population are of New World origin.

After 1750, the world population experienced a dramatic rise. The reasons for this expansion were many, but the contribution of the American foodstuffs with their high yields was a central one. Manioc, potatoes, sweet potatoes, and maize—to say nothing of peanuts, beans, and tomatoes—greatly expanded the food resources available throughout the world and continue to do so today. The balance sheet of the Columbian exchange was mixed, but the world was undeniably different after it began.

---

**Questions** Why and in what ways was the Columbian exchange a particularly significant case of global contact? Was western Europe the chief beneficiary of the exchange? What balance was there between the economic dependency of the Americas and the ideas, technology, and goods they received from Europe?

Spain, mining was the essential activity and the basis of Spain's rule in the West Indies. It was precious metals that first began to fit Latin America into the developing world economy.

Although the booty of conquest provided some wealth, most of the precious metal sent across the Atlantic came from the postconquest mining industry. Gold was found in the Caribbean, Colombia, and Chile, but it was silver far more than gold that formed the basis of Spain's wealth in America.

## The Silver Heart of Empire

The major silver discoveries were made in Mexico and Peru between 1545 and 1565. Great silver mining towns developed. **Potosí** in upper Peru (in what is now

Bolivia) was the largest mine of all, producing about 80 percent of all the Peruvian silver. In the early 17th century, more than 160,000 people lived and worked in the town and its mine. Peru's Potosí and Mexico's Zacatecas became wealthy mining centers with opulent churches and a luxurious way of life for some. As one viceroy of Peru commented, it was not silver that was sent to Spain "but the blood and sweat of Indians."

Mining labor was provided by a variety of workers. The early use of American Indian slaves and encomienda workers in the 16th century gradually was replaced by a system of labor drafts. By 1572 the mining mita in Peru was providing about 13,000 workers a year to Potosí alone. Similar labor drafts were used in Mexico, but by the 17th century the mines in both places also had large numbers of wage workers willing to brave the dangers of mining in return for the good wages.

Although indigenous methods were used at first, most mining techniques were European in origin. After 1580, silver mining depended on a process of amalgamation with mercury to extract the silver from the ore-bearing rock. The Spanish discovery of a mountain of mercury at **Huancavelica** in Peru aided American silver production. Potosí and Huancavelica became the "great marriage of Peru" and the basis of silver production in South America.

According to Spanish law, all subsoil rights belonged to the crown, but the mines and the processing plants were owned by individuals, who were permitted to extract the silver in return for paying one-fifth of production to the government, which also profited from its monopoly on the mercury needed to produce the silver (Figure 24.7).

Mining stimulated many other aspects of the economy, even in areas far removed from the mines. Workers had to be fed and the mines supplied. In Mexico, where most of the mines were located beyond the area of settled preconquest Indian population, large Spanish-style farms developed to raise cattle, sheep, and wheat. The Peruvian mines high in the Andes were supplied from distant regions with mercury, mules, food, clothing, and even coca leaves, used to deaden hunger and make the work at high altitudes less painful. From Spain's perspective, mining was the heart of the colonial economy.

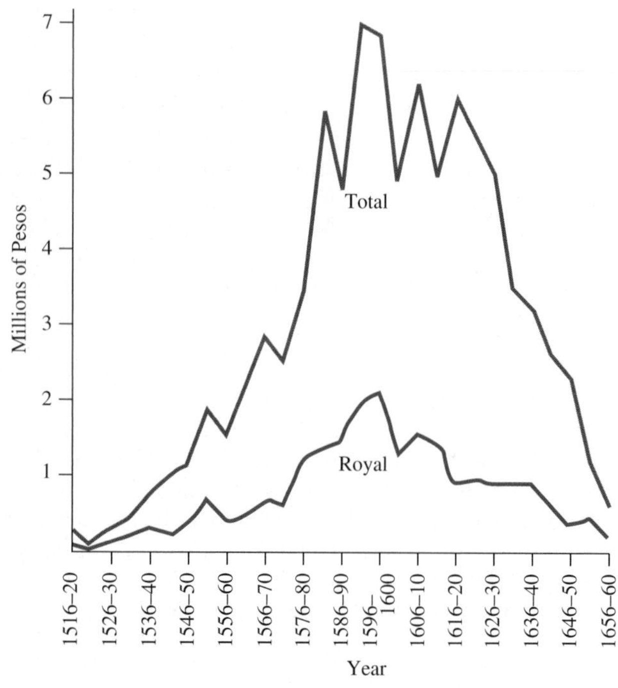


**FIGURE 24.7** Silver production in Spanish America, 1516–1660.

## Haciendas and Villages

Spanish America remained predominantly an agrarian economy, and wherever large sedentary populations lived, Indian communal agriculture of traditional crops continued. As populations dwindled, Spanish ranches and farms began to emerge. The colonists, faced with declining Indian populations, also found land ownership more attractive. Family-owned rural estates, which produced grains, grapes, and livestock, developed throughout the central areas of Spanish America. Most of the labor force on these estates came from Native Americans who had left the communities and from people of mixed Native American and European heritage. These rural estates, or **haciendas,** producing primarily for consumers in America, became the basis of wealth and power for the local aristocracy in many regions. Although some plantation crops, such as sugar and later cacao, were exported to Europe from Spanish America, they made up only a small fraction of the value of the exports in comparison with silver. In some regions where Native American communities continued to hold traditional farming lands, an endemic competition between haciendas and village communities emerged.

## Industry and Commerce

In areas such as Ecuador, New Spain, and Peru, sheep raising led to the development of small textile sweatshops, where common cloth was produced, usually by women. America became self-sufficient for its basic foods and material goods and looked to Europe only for luxury items not locally available.

Still, from Spain's perspective and that of the larger world economy taking shape in the early modern centuries, the American "kingdoms" had a silver heart, and the whole Spanish commercial system was organized around that fact. Spain allowed only Spaniards to trade with America and imposed tight restrictions. All American trade from Spain after the mid-16th century passed through the city of Seville and, later, through the nearby port of Cadiz. A Board of Trade in Seville controlled all commerce with America, registered ships and passengers, kept charts, and collected taxes. It often worked in conjunction with a merchant guild, or **consulado,** in Seville that controlled goods shipped to America and handled much of the silver received in return. Linked to branches in Mexico City and Lima, the consulados kept tight control over the trade and were able to keep prices high in the colonies.

Other Europeans looked on the West Indies trade with envy. To discourage foreign rivals and pirates, the Spanish eventually worked out a convoy system in which two fleets sailed annually from Spain, traded their goods for precious metals, and then met at Havana, Cuba, before returning to Spain.

The fleet system was made possible by the large, heavily armed ships, called **galleons,** that were used to carry the silver belonging to the crown. Two great galleons a year also sailed from Manila in the Philippines to Mexico loaded with Chinese silks, porcelain, and lacquer. These goods were then shipped on the convoy to Spain along with the American silver. In the Caribbean, heavily fortified ports, such as Havana and Cartagena (Colombia), provided shelter for the treasure ships, while coast guard fleets cleared the waters of potential raiders. Although cumbersome, the convoys (which continued until the 1730s) were successful. Pirates and enemies sometimes captured individual ships, and some ships were lost to storms and other disasters, but only one fleet was lost—to the Dutch in 1627.

In general, the supply of American silver to Spain was continuous and made the colonies seem worth the effort, but the reality of American treasure was more complicated. Much of the wealth flowed out of Spain to pay for Spain's European wars, its long-term debts, and the purchase of manufactured goods to be sent back to the West Indies. Probably less than half of the silver remained in Spain itself. The arrival of American treasure also contributed to a sharp rise in prices and a general inflation, first in Spain and then throughout western Europe during the 16th century. At no time did the American treasure make up more than one-fourth of Spain's state revenues; the wealth of Spain depended more on the taxes levied on its own population than it did on the exploitation of its Native American subjects. However, the seemingly endless supply of silver stimulated bankers to continue to lend money to Spain because the prospect of the great silver fleet was always enough to offset the falling credit of the Spanish rulers and the sometimes bankrupt government. As early as 1619, Sancho de Moncada wrote that "the poverty of Spain resulted from the discovery of the Indies." But there were few who could see the long-term costs of empire.

## Ruling an Empire: State and Church

Spain controlled its American empire through a carefully regulated bureaucratic system. Sovereignty rested with the crown, based not on the right of conquest but on a papal grant that awarded the West Indies to Castile in return for its services in bringing those lands and peoples into the Christian community. Some Native Americans found this a curious idea, and European theologians agreed, but Spain was careful to bolster its rule in other ways. The **Treaty of Tordesillas** (1494) between Castile and Portugal clarified the spheres of influence and right of possession of the two kingdoms by drawing a hypothetical north–south line around the globe and reserving to Portugal the newly discovered lands (and their route to India) to the east of the line and to Castile all lands to the west. Thus, Brazil fell within the Portuguese sphere. Other European nations later raised their own objections to the Spanish and Portuguese claims.

The Spanish Empire became a great bureaucratic system built on a juridical core and staffed to a large extent by **letrados,** university-trained lawyers from Spain. The modern division of powers was not clearly defined in the Spanish system, so that judicial officers also exercised legislative and administrative authority. Laws were many and contradictory at times, but the **Recopilación** (1681) codified the laws into the basis for government in the colonies.

The king ruled through the **Council of the Indies** in Spain, which issued the laws and advised him. Within the West Indies, Spain created two **viceroyalties** in the 16th century, one based in Mexico City and the other in Lima. Viceroys, high-ranking nobles who were direct representatives of the king, wielded broad military, legislative, and, when they had legal training, judicial powers. The viceroyalties of New Spain and Peru were then subdivided into 10 judicial divisions controlled by superior courts, or **audiencias,** staffed by professional royal magistrates who helped to make law as well as apply it. At the local level, royally appointed magistrates applied the laws, collected taxes, and assigned the work required of American Indian communities. It is little wonder that they often were highly criticized for bending the law and taking advantage of the Indians under their control. Below them were many minor officials who made bureaucracy both a living and a way of life.

To some extent, the clergy formed another branch of the state apparatus, although it had other functions and goals as well. Catholic religious orders such as the

Franciscans, Dominicans, and Jesuits carried out the widespread conversion of the Indians, establishing churches in the towns and villages of sedentary Indians and setting up missions in frontier areas where nomadic peoples were forced to settle.

Taking seriously the pope's admonition to Christianize the peoples of the new lands as the primary justification for Spain's rule, some of the early missionaries became ardent defenders of Indian rights and even admirers of aspects of Indian culture. For example, Franciscan priest Fray Bernardino de Sahagún (1499–1590) became an expert in the Nahuatl language and composed a bilingual encyclopedia of Aztec culture, which was based on methods very similar to those used by modern anthropologists. Other clerics wrote histories, grammars, and studies of Indian language and culture. Some were like Diego de Landa, Bishop of Yucatán (1547), who admired much about the culture of the Maya but who so detested their religion that he burned all their ancient books and tortured many Maya suspected of backsliding from Christianity. The recording and analysis of Indian cultures were designed primarily to provide tools for conversion.

In the core areas of Peru and New Spain, the missionary church eventually was replaced by an institutional structure of parishes and bishoprics. Archbishops sat in the major capitals, and a complicated church hierarchy developed. Because the Spanish crown nominated the holders of all such positions, the clergy tended to be major supporters of state policy as well as a primary influence on it.

The Catholic church profoundly influenced the cultural and intellectual life of the colonies in many ways. The construction of churches, especially the great baroque cathedrals of the capitals, stimulated the work of architects and artists, usually reflecting European models but sometimes taking up local themes and subjects. The printing presses, introduced to America in the early 16th century, always published a high percentage of religious books as well as works of history, poetry, philosophy, law, and language. Much intellectual life was organized around religion. Schools—such as those of Mexico City and Lima, founded in the 1550s—were run by the clergy, and universities were created to provide training primarily in law and theology, the foundations of state and society. Eventually, more than 70 universities flourished in Spanish America. A stunning example of colonial intellectual life was the nun **Sor Juana Inés de la Cruz** (1651–1695; Figure 24.8), author, poet, musician, and social thinker. Sor Juana was welcomed at the court of

Sor Juana Inez de la Cruz, from *La Respuesta*

**FIGURE 24.8** Sor Juana Inés de la Cruz was a remarkable Mexican poet and writer whose talents won her recognition rarely given to women for intellectual or artistic achievements in colonial Latin America.

the viceroy in Mexico City, where her beauty and intelligence were celebrated. She eventually gave up secular concerns and her library, at the urging of her superiors, to concentrate on purely spiritual matters.

To control the morality and orthodoxy of the population, the tribunal of the Inquisition set up offices in the major capitals. Although American Indians usually were exempt from its jurisdiction, Jews, Protestants, and other religious dissenters were prosecuted and sometimes executed in an attempt to impose orthodoxy. Overall, church and state combined to create an ideological and political framework for the society of Spanish America.

## Brazil: The First Plantation Colony

■ **In Brazil the Portuguese created the first great plantation colony of the Americas, growing sugar with the use of Native American and then African slaves. In the 18th century, the discovery of gold opened up the interior of Brazil to settlement and the expansion of slavery.**

The first official Portuguese landfall on the South American coast took place in 1500 when **Pedro Alvares Cabral,** leader of an expedition to India, stopped briefly on the tropical Brazilian shore. There was little at first to attract European interest except for the dyewood trees that grew in the forests, and thus the Portuguese crown paid little attention to Brazil for 30 years, preferring instead to grant licenses to merchants who agreed to exploit the dyewood. Pressure from French competitors finally moved the Portuguese crown to military action. The coast was cleared of rivals and a new system of settlement was established in 1532. Minor Portuguese nobles were given strips of land along the coast to colonize and develop. The nobles who held these **capitaincies** combined broad, seemingly feudal powers with a strong desire for commercial development. Most of them lacked the capital needed to carry out the colonization, and some had problems with the indigenous population. In a few places, towns were established, colonists were brought over, relations with the Native Americans were peaceful, and, most importantly, sugar plantations were established using first Native American, then African slaves.

In 1549 the Portuguese king sent a governor general and other officials to create a royal capital at Salvador. The first Jesuit missionaries also arrived. By 1600, indigenous resistance had been broken in many places by military action, missionary activity, or epidemic disease. A string of settlements extended along the coast, centered on port cities such as Salvador and Rio de Janeiro. These served roughly 150 sugar plantations, a number that doubled by 1630. The plantations were increasingly worked by African slaves. By 1600, the Brazilian colony had about 100,000 inhabitants: 30,000 Europeans, 15,000 black slaves, and the rest Native Americans and people of mixed origin.

### Sugar and Slavery

During most of the next century, Brazil held its position as the world's leading sugar producer. Sugar cane had to be processed in the field. It was cut and pressed in large mills, and the juice was then heated to crystallize into sugar. This combination of agriculture and industry in the field demanded large amounts of capital for machinery and large quantities of labor for the backbreaking work (Figure 24.9). Although there were always some free workers who had skilled occupations, slaves did most of the work. During the 17th century, about 7000 slaves a year were imported from Africa. By the end of the century, Brazil had about 150,000 slaves—about half its total population.

On the basis of a single crop produced by slave labor, Brazil became the first great plantation colony and a model that later was followed by other European nations in their own Caribbean colonies. Even after the Brazilian economy became more diverse, Brazil's social hierarchy still reflected its plantation and slave origins. The white planter families became an aristocracy linked by marriage to resident merchants and to the few Portuguese bureaucrats and officials, and they dominated local institutions. At the bottom of society were the slaves, distinguished by their color and their status as property. However, a growing segment of the population was composed of people of mixed origins, the result of miscegenation between whites, Indians, and Africans who—alongside poorer whites, freed blacks, and free Indians—served as artisans, small farmers, herders, and free laborers. In many ways, society as a whole reflected the hierarchy of the plantation.

Like Spain, Portugal created a bureaucratic structure that integrated this colony within an imperial system. A governor general ruled from Salvador, but the governors in each capitaincy often acted independently and reported directly to the overseas council in Lisbon. The missionary orders were particularly important in Brazil, especially the Jesuits. Their extensive cattle ranches and sugar mills supported the construction of churches and schools as well as a network of missions with thousands of Native American residents.

As in Spanish America, royal officials trained in the law formed the core of the bureaucracy. Unlike the Spanish Empire, which except for the Philippines was almost exclusively American, the Portuguese Empire included colonies and outposts in Asia, Africa, and Brazil. Only gradually, in the 17th century, did Brazil

FIGURE 24.9 Sugar was introduced to the Caribbean in 1493, and Brazil became the greatest producer by the next century. Sugar plantations using slave labor characterized Brazil and the Caribbean. This early European engraving is wrong in some details, but it does convey an image of the factory-like conditions in the sugar mills.

become the predominant Portuguese colony. Even then, Brazil's ties to Portugal were in some ways stronger and more dependent than those between Spanish America and Spain. Unlike Spanish America, Brazil had neither universities nor printing presses. Thus, intellectual life was always an extension of Portugal, and Brazilians seeking higher education and government offices or hoping to publish their works always had to turn to the mother country. The general economic dependency of Latin America was matched by an intellectual subordination more intense in Brazil than in Spanish America.

## Brazil's Age of Gold

As overseas extensions of Europe, the American colonies were particularly susceptible to changes in European politics. For 60 years (1580–1640), the Habsburg kings of Spain also ruled Portugal, a situation that promoted their cooperation and gave these rulers a truly worldwide empire. From 1630 to 1654, as part of a global struggle against Spain, the Dutch seized a portion of northeastern Brazil and controlled its sugar production. Although the Dutch were expelled from Brazil in 1654, by the 1680s the Dutch, English, and French had established their own plantation colonies in the Caribbean and were producing sugar with slave laborers. This competition, which led to a rising price for slaves and a falling world price for sugar, undercut the Brazilian sugar industry, and the colony entered into hard times. Eventually, each European nation tried to establish an integrated set of colonies that included plantations (the Caribbean, Brazil), slaving ports (Africa), and food-producing areas (New England, southern Brazil).

Although Brazil's domination of the world sugar market was lost, throughout the 17th century **Paulistas,** hardy backwoodsmen from São Paulo (an area with few sugar plantations), had been exploring the interior, capturing Indians, and searching for precious metals. These expeditions not only established Portuguese claims to much of the interior of the continent but eventually were successful in their quest for wealth. In 1695, gold strikes were made in the mountainous interior in a region that came to be called **Minas Gerais** (General Mines), and the Brazilian colony experienced a new boom.

A great gold rush began. People deserted coastal towns and plantations to head for the gold washings, and they were soon joined by waves of about 5000 immigrants a year who came directly from Portugal. Slaves provided labor in the mines, as in the plantations. By 1775, there were over 150,000 slaves (out of a total population of 300,000 for the region) in Minas Gerais. Wild mining camps and a wide-open society eventually coalesced into a network of towns such as the administrative center of Ouro Prêto, and the government, anxious to control the newfound wealth, imposed a heavy hand to collect taxes and rein in the unruly population. Gold production reached its height between 1735 and 1760 and averaged about 3 tons a year in that period, making Brazil the greatest source of gold in the Western world.

The discovery of gold—and later of diamonds—was a mixed blessing in the long run. It opened the interior to settlement, once again with disastrous effects on the indigenous population and with the expansion of slavery. The early disruption of coastal agriculture caused by the gold strikes was overcome by government control of the slave trade, and exports of sugar and tobacco continued to be important to the colony. Mining did stimulate the opening of new areas to ranching and farming, to supply the new markets in the mining zone. **Rio de Janeiro,** the port closest to the mines, grew in size and importance. It became capital of the colony in 1763. In Minas Gerais, a distinctive society developed. The local wealth was used to sponsor the building of churches, which in turn stimulated the work of artists, architects, and composers. Like the rest of Brazil, however, the hierarchy of color and the legal distinctions of slavery marked life in the mining zones, which were populated by large numbers of slaves and free persons of color.

Finally, gold allowed Portugal to continue economic policies that were detrimental in the long run. With access to gold, Portugal could buy the manufactured goods it needed for itself and its colonies, as few industries were developed in the mother country. Much of the Brazilian gold flowed from Portugal to England to pay for manufactured goods and to compensate for a trade imbalance. After 1760, as the supply of gold began to dwindle, Portugal was again in a difficult position—it had become in some ways an economic dependency of England.

## Multiracial Societies

**The mixture of whites, Africans, and Indians created the basis of multiracial societies in which hierarchies of color, status, and occupation all operated. By the 18th century, the castas, people of mixed origin, began to increase rapidly and had become a major segment of the population.**

The conquest and settlement of Latin America created the conditions for the formation of multiethnic societies on a large scale. The three major groups—Indians, Europeans, and Africans—had been brought together under very different conditions: the Europeans as conquerors and voluntary immigrants, the Indians as conquered peoples, and the Africans as slaves. This situation created hierarchies of masters and servants, Christians and pagans, that reflected the relationships of power and the colonial condition. In central Mexico, where an Indian nobility had existed, aspects of preconquest social organization were maintained because they served the ends of Spanish government. In theory, there was a separation between the "republic of the Spaniards," which included all non-Indians, and the "republic of the Indians," which was supposed to have its own social rankings and its own rules and laws. This separation was never a reality, however, and the "republic of the Indians" always formed the base on which all society rested. Indians paid tribute, something not required of others in society.

### The Society of Castas

Spaniards had an idea of society drawn from their own medieval experience, but American realities soon altered that concept. The key was miscegenation. The conquest had involved the sexual exploitation of Indian women and occasional alliances formed by the giving of concubines and female servants. Marriages with indigenous women, especially of the Indian nobility, were not unknown. With few European women available, especially in frontier regions, mixed marriages and informal unions were common. The result was the growth of a large population of mixed background, the so-called mestizos. Although they were always suspected of illegitimacy, their status, especially in the early years, was higher than that of Indians. More acculturated than the Indians and able to operate in two worlds, mestizos became members of an intermediate category, not fully accepted as equals to Spaniards and yet expected to live according to the standards of Spanish society and often acting as auxiliaries to it. A similar process took place in areas such as Brazil and the Caribbean coasts, where large numbers of African slaves were imported. Slave owners exploited their female slaves or took slave women as mistresses, and then sometimes freed their mulatto children. The result was the growth of a large population of mixed background.

Throughout the Spanish Indies, European categories of noble, priest, and commoner continued, as did hierarchies based on wealth and occupation. But American realities created new distinctions in which race and place of birth also played a crucial role. This was the **sociedad de castas,** based on racial origins, in which Europeans or whites were at the top, black slaves or Native Americans were at the bottom, and the many kinds of mixes filled the intermediate categories. This accompanied the great cultural fusion in the formation of Latin America.

From the three original ethnic categories, many combinations and crosses were possible: mestizo, mulatto, and so on. By the 18th century, this segment of the population had grown rapidly, and there was much confusion and local variation in terminology. A whole genre of painting developed simply to identify

VISUALIZING THE PAST

## Race or Culture? A Changing Society

The process of marriage or sexual contact between Spaniards, Indians, and Africans began to complicate the demographic and social structures of the American colonies. The rise of a significant number of people of mixed origin could be noted in both Peru and Mexico. These graphs point out the differences in the two areas and may imply something about the situation of the indigenous communities as well as that of the castas. We should also remember that these categories were not necessarily biological and that Indians might be classified as castas if they spoke Spanish or wore Spanish-style clothes. What seems to be precise demographic measurement may, in fact, be imprecise social definition.

**Question** Do modern censuses that use cultural or "racial" labels face the same problems of definition that the early censuses in the colonial Americas confronted?

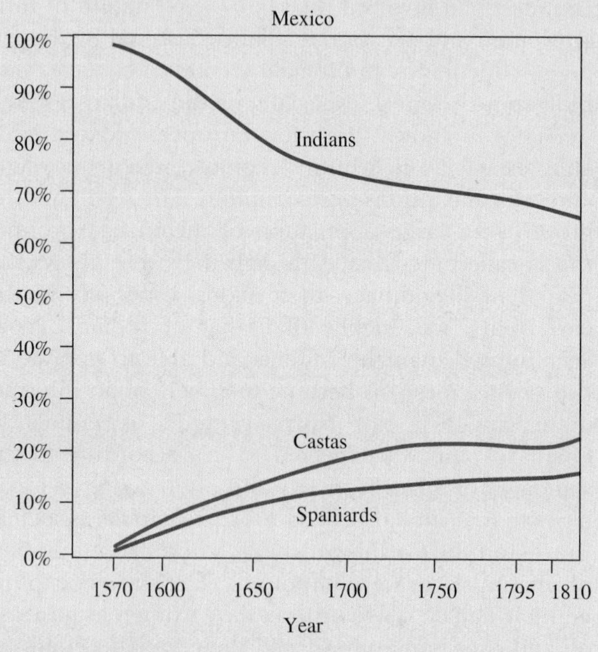


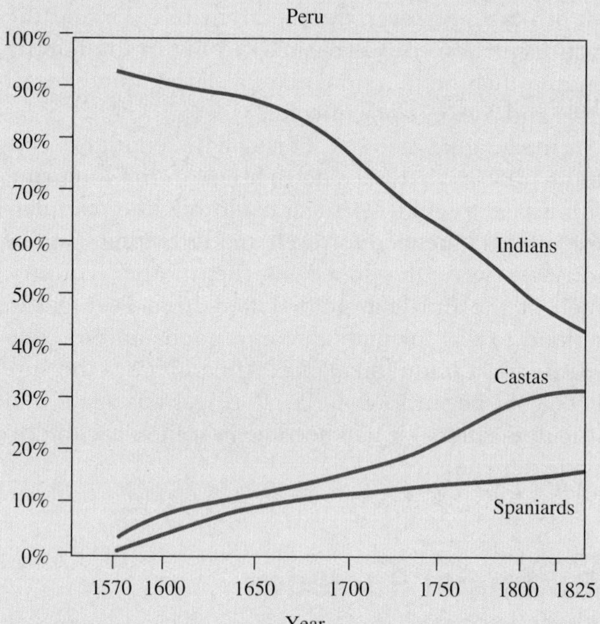


Changing ratios of ethnic categories in Mexico and Peru.

and classify the various combinations. Together, the people of mixed origins were called the castas, and they tended to be shopkeepers and small farmers. In 1650 the castas made up perhaps 5 to 10 percent of the population of Spanish America, but by 1750 they made up 35 to 40 percent (see Visualizing the Past). In Brazil, still dominated by slavery, free people of color made up about 28 percent of the population—a proportion equal to that of whites. Together, however, free and slave blacks and mulattos made up two-thirds of the inhabitants of Brazil in the late 18th century.

As the mixed population grew in Spanish America, increasing restrictions were placed on them, but their social mobility could not be halted. A successful Indian might call himself a mestizo; a mestizo who married a Spanish woman might be called white. The ranks of the castas were also swelled by former slaves who had been given or had bought their freedom and by Indians who left their communities, spoke Spanish, and lived within the orbit of the Hispanic world. Thus, physical characteristics were only one criterion of rank and status, but color and ethnicity mattered, and they created a pseudoracial hierarchy. European or white status was a great social advantage. Not every person of European background was wealthy, but most of the wealthy merchants, landowners, bureaucrats, and min-

FIGURE 24.10 Women in colonial Latin America engaged in agriculture and manufacturing, especially in textile workshops, but social ideology still reserved the household and the kitchen as the proper sphere for women, as seen in this scene of a kitchen in a large Mexican home.

ers were white. As one visitor wrote, "In America, every white is a gentleman."

Originally, all whites had shared the privileged status of Spaniards regardless of the continent of their birth, but over time distinctions developed between **peninsulares,** or those actually born in Spain, and **Creoles,** or those born in the New World. Creoles thought of themselves as loyal American Spaniards, but with so many mestizos around, the shadow of a possible Indian ancestor and illegitimacy always made their status suspect as far as the Europeans were concerned. Still, Creoles dominated the local economies, held sway over large numbers of dependents at their haciendas and mines, and stood at the top of society, second only to the peninsulares. Increasingly, they developed a sense of identity and pride in their accomplishments, and they were sensitive to any suggestion of inferiority or to any discrimination because of their American birth. That growing sense of self-identity eventually contributed to the movements for independence in Latin America.

The hierarchy of race intersected with traditional Iberian distinctions based on gender, age, and class. The father of a family had legal authority over his children until they were 25. Women were in a subordinate position; they could not serve in government and were expected to assume the duties of motherhood and household (Figure 24.10). After marriage, women came under the authority of their husbands, but many a widow assumed the direction of her family's activities. Lower-class women often controlled small-scale commerce in towns and villages, worked in the fields, and labored at the looms of small factories. Marriages often were arranged and accompanied by the payment of a dowry, which remained the property of the woman throughout the marriage. Women also had full rights to inheritance. Upper-class women who did not marry at a young age were placed in convents to prevent contacts or marriages with partners of unsuitable backgrounds.

## The 18th-Century Reforms

- **Increasing attacks on the Iberian empires by foreign rivals led to the Bourbon reforms in Spanish America and the reforms of Pombal in Brazil. These changes strengthened the two empires but also generated colonial unrest that eventually led to movements for independence.**

No less than in the rest of Europe, the 18th century was a period of intellectual ferment in Spain and Portugal as well as in their empires. In Spain and its colonies, small clubs and associations, calling themselves **amigos del país,** or friends of the country, met in many cities to discuss and plan all kinds of reforms. Their programs were for material benefits and improvements, not political changes. In Portugal, foreign influences and ideas created a group of progressive thinkers and bureaucrats open to new ideas in economy, education, and philosophy. Much of the change that came in both empires resulted as much from the changing European economic and demographic realities as from new ideas. The expansion of population and economy in Europe, and the increased demands for American products, along with the long series of wars in the 18th century, gave the American colonies a new importance. Both the Spanish and Portuguese empires revived, but with some long-term results that eventually led to the fall of both.

### The Shifting Balance of Politics and Trade

By the 18th century, it was clear that the Spanish colonial system had become outmoded and that Spain's exclusive hold on the Indies was no longer secure. To some extent the problem lay in Spain itself. Beset by foreign wars, increasing debt, declining population, and internal revolts, a weakened Spain was threatened by a powerful France and by the rising mercantile strength of England and Holland, whose Protestantism also made them natural rivals of Catholic Spain. Since the 16th century, French, Dutch, and English ship captains had combined contraband trade with raiding in the Spanish Empire, and although Spain's European rivals could not seize Mexico or Peru, the sparsely populated islands and coasts of the Caribbean became likely targets. Buccaneers, owing allegiance to no nation, raided the Caribbean ports in the late 17th century. Meanwhile, the English took Jamaica in 1654, the French took control of western Hispaniola (Haiti) by 1697, and other islands fell to the English, French, and Dutch. Many of the islands turned to sugar production and the creation of slave and plantation colonies much like those in Brazil. These settlements were part of a general process of colonization, of which the English settlement of eastern North America and the French occupation of Canada and the Mississippi valley were also part.

Less apparent than the loss of territories, but equally important, was the failure of the Spanish mercantile and political system. The annual fleets became irregular. Silver payments from America declined, and most goods shipped to the West Indies and even the ships that carried them were non-Spanish in origin. The colonies became increasingly self-sufficient in basic commodities, and as central government became weaker, local aristocrats in the colonies exercised increasing control over the economy and government of their regions, often at the expense of the Native American and the lower-class populations. Graft and corruption were rampant in many branches of government. The empire seemed to be crumbling. What is most impressive is that Spain was able to retain its American possessions for another century.

Even with Spain in decline, the West Indies still seemed an attractive prize coveted by other powers, and the opportunity to gain them was not long in coming. A final crisis was set in motion in 1701 when the Spanish king, Charles II, died without an heir. Other European nations backed various claimants to the Spanish throne, hoping to win the prize of the Spanish monarchy and its American colonies. Philip of Anjou, a Bourbon and thus a relative of the king of France, was named successor to the Spanish throne. The **War of the Spanish Succession** (1702–1713) ensued, and the result at the Treaty of Utrecht (1713) was recognition of a branch of the Bourbon family as rulers of Spain; the price was some commercial concessions that allowed French merchants to operate in Seville and permitted England to trade slaves in Spanish America (and even to send one ship per year to trade for silver in the Americas). Spain's commercial monopoly was now being broken not just by contraband trade but by legal means as well.

## The Bourbon Reforms

The new and vigorous Bourbon dynasty in Spain launched a series of reforms aimed at strengthening the state and its economy. In this age of "enlightened despotism," the Spanish Bourbon monarchs, especially **Charles III** (r. 1759–1788), were moved by economic nationalism and a desire for strong centralized government to institute economic, administrative, and military reforms in Spain and its empire. The goal of these rulers and their progressive ministers was to revive Spain within the framework of its traditional society. Their aim was to make government more effective, more powerful, and better able to direct the economy. Certain groups or institutions that opposed these measures or stood in the way might be punished or suppressed. The Jesuit order, with its special allegiance to Rome, its rumored wealth, and its missions in the New World (which controlled almost 100,000 Indians in Paraguay alone), was a prime target. The Jesuits were expelled from Spain and its empire in 1767, as they had been from the Portuguese empire in 1759. In general, however, the entrenched interests of the church and the nobility were not frontally attacked as long as they did not conflict with the authority of the crown. The reforms were aimed at material improvements and a more powerful state, not social or political upheaval. French bureaucratic models were introduced. The system of taxation was tightened. The navy was reformed, and new ships were built. The convoy fleet system was abandoned, and in 1778 new ports were opened in Spain and America for the West Indies trade, although trade still was restricted to Spaniards or to ships sailing under Spanish license.

In the West Indies, the Bourbons initiated a broad program of reform. New viceroyalties were created in New Granada (1739) and the Rio de la Plata (1778) to provide better administration and defense to the growing populations of these regions. Royal investigators were sent to the Indies. The most important of them, **José de Gálvez,** spent six years in Mexico before returning to Spain to become minister of the Indies and a chief architect of reform. His investigations, as well as reports by others, revealed the worst abuses of graft and corruption, which implicated the local magistrates and the Creole landowners and aristocracy. Gálvez moved to eliminate the Creoles from the upper bureaucracy of the colonies. New offices were created. After 1780, the *corregidores,* or local magistrates, were removed from the Indian villages, and that office was replaced by a new system of intendants, or provincial governors, based on French models. This intendancy system was introduced throughout the Indies. Such measures improved tax collection and made government more effective, but the reforms also disrupted the patterns of influence and power, especially among the Creole bureaucrats, miners, and landowners as their political power declined.

Many of the reforms in America were linked directly to defense and military matters. During the century, Spain often was allied with France, and the global struggle between England and France for world hegemony made Spain's American possessions a logical target for English attack. During the Seven Years War (1756–1763), the loss of Florida and the English seizure of Havana shocked Spain into action, particularly because when England held Havana in 1762, Cuban trade boomed. Regular Spanish troops were sent to New Spain, and militia units, led by local Creoles who were given military rank, were created throughout the empire. Frontiers were expanded, and previously unoccupied or loosely controlled regions, such as California, were settled by a combination of missions and small frontier outposts. In the Rio de la Plata, foreign competitors were resisted by military means. Spain sought every means to strengthen itself and its colonies.

During the Bourbon reforms, the government took an active role in the economy. State monopolies were established for items the government considered essential, such as tobacco and gunpowder. Whole new areas of Spanish America were opened to development. Monopoly companies were granted exclusive rights to develop certain colonial areas in return for developing the economies of those regions.

The commerce of the Caribbean greatly expanded under the more liberal trading regulations. Cuba became another full-scale plantation and slave colony, exporting sugar, coffee, and tobacco and importing large numbers of Africans. Buenos Aires, on the Rio de la Plata, proved to be a great success story. Its population had grown rapidly in the 18th century, and by 1790 it had a booming economy based on ranching and the export of hides and salted beef. A newly prosperous merchant community in Buenos Aires dominated the region's trade.

The commercial changes were a double-edged sword. As Spanish and English goods became cheaper and more accessible, they undercut locally produced goods so that some regions that had specialized in producing cloth or other goods were unable to compete with the European imports. Links to international trade tightened as the diversity of Latin America's economy decreased. Later conflicts between those who favored free trade and those who wanted to limit imports and protect local industry often were as much about regional interests as about economic philosophy.

Finally, and most importantly, the major centers of the Spanish Empire also experienced rapid growth in the second half of the 18th century. Mining inspectors and experts had been sent to Peru and New Spain to suggest reforms and introduce new techniques. These improvements, as well as the discovery of new veins, allowed production to expand, especially in New Spain, where silver output reached new heights. In fact, silver production in Mexico far outstripped that of Peru, which itself saw increased production.

All in all, the Bourbon reforms must be seen from two vantage points: Spain and America. Undoubtedly, in the short run, the restructuring of government and economy revived the Spanish Empire. In the long run, the removal of Creoles from government, the creation of a militia with a Creole officer corps, the opening of commerce, and other such changes contributed to a growing sense of dissatisfaction among the elite, which only their relative well-being and the existing social tensions of the sociedad de castas kept in check.

## Pombal and Brazil

The Bourbon reforms in Spain and Spanish America were paralleled in the Portuguese world during the administration of the **Marquis of Pombal** (1755–1776), Portugal's authoritarian prime minister. Pombal had lived as ambassador in England and had observed the benefits of mercantilism at firsthand. He hoped to use these same techniques, along with state intervention in the economy, to break England's hold on the Portuguese economy, especially on the flow of Brazilian gold from Portugal to England. This became crucial as the production of Brazilian gold began to decline after 1760. In another example of "enlightened despotism," Pombal brutally suppressed any group or institution that stood in the way of royal power and his programs. He developed a particular dislike for the Jesuits because of their allegiance to Rome and their semi-independent control of large areas in Brazil. Pombal expelled the Jesuits from the Portuguese Empire in 1759.

Pombal made Brazil the centerpiece of his reforms. Vigorous administrators were sent to the colony to enforce the changes. Fiscal reforms were aimed at eliminating contraband, gold smuggling, and tax evasion. Monopoly companies were formed to stimulate agriculture in older plantation zones and were given the right to import large numbers of slaves. New crops were introduced. Just as in Spanish America, new regions in Brazil began to flourish. Rio de Janeiro became the capital, and its hinterland was the scene of agricultural growth. The undeveloped Amazonian region, long dominated by Jesuit missionaries, received new attention. A monopoly company was created to develop the region's economy, and it stimulated the development of cotton plantations and the export of wild cacao from the Amazonian forests. These new exports joined the traditional sugar, tobacco, and hides as Brazil's main products.

Pombal was willing to do some social tinkering as part of his project of reform. He abolished slavery in Portugal to stop the import of slaves there and to ensure a steady supply to Brazil, the economic cornerstone of the empire. Because Brazil was vast and needed to be both occupied and defended, he removed Indians from missionary control in the Amazon and encouraged whites to marry them. Immigrant couples from Portugal and the Azores were sent to colonize the Amazon basin and the plains of southern Brazil, which began to produce large quantities of wheat and cattle. Like the Bourbons in Spain, Pombal hoped to revitalize the colonies as a way of strengthening the mother country. Although new policies were instituted, little changed within the society. Brazil was just as profoundly based on slavery in the late 18th century as it had ever been: The levels of slave imports reached 20,000 a year.

Even in the long run, Pombal's policies were not fully effective. Although he reduced Portugal's trade imbalance with England during this period, Brazilian trade suffered because the demand for its products on the world market remained low. This was a classic problem for the American colonies. Their economies were so tied to the sale of their products on the European market and so controlled by policies in the metropolis that the colonies' range of action was always limited. Although Pombal's policies were not immediately successful, they provided the structure for an economic boom in the last 20 years of the 18th century that set the stage for Brazilian independence.

## Reforms, Reactions, and Revolts

By the mid-18th century, the American colonies of Spain and Portugal, like the rest of the world, were experiencing rapid growth in population and productive capacity. By the end of the century, Spanish America had a population of almost 13 million. Between 1740 and 1800, the population of Mexico, the most populous area, increased from 3.5 million to almost 6 million, about half of whom were Indians. In Brazil the population reached about 2 million by the end of the century. This overall increase resulted from declining mortality rates, increasing fertility levels, increasing immigration from Europe, and the thriving slave trade. The opening of new areas to development and Europe's increasing demand for American products accompanied the population growth. The American colonies were experiencing a boom in the last years of the 18th century.

Reformist policies, tighter tax collection, and the presence of a more activist government in both Spanish America and Brazil disrupted old patterns of power and influence, raised expectations, and sometimes provoked violent colonial reactions. Urban riots, tax revolts, and Indian uprisings were not unknown before 1700, but serious and more protracted rebellions broke out after that date. In New Granada (present-day Colombia), popular complaints against the government's control of tobacco and liquor consumption, and rising prices as well as new taxes, led to the widespread **Comunero Revolt** in 1781. A royal army was defeated, the viceroy fled from Bogota, and a rebel army almost took the capital. Only tensions between the various racial and social groups, and concessions by the government, brought an end to the rebellion.

At the same time, in Peru, an even more threatening revolt erupted. A great Indian uprising took place under the leadership of Jose Gabriel Condorcanqui, known as **Tupac Amaru.** A mestizo with a direct link to the family of the Incas, Tupac Amaru led a rebellion against "bad government." For almost three years the whole viceroyalty was thrown into turmoil while more than 70,000 Indians, mestizos, and even a few Creoles joined in rebellion against the worst abuses of the colonial regime. Tupac Amaru was captured and brutally executed, but the rebellion smoldered until 1783. It failed mostly because the Creoles, although they had their own grievances against the government, feared that a real social upheaval might take place if they upset the political balance.

This kind of social upheaval was not present in Brazil, where a government attempt to collect back taxes in the mining region led in 1788 to a plot against Portuguese control. A few bureaucrats, intellectuals, and miners planned an uprising for independence, but their conspiracy was discovered. The plotters were arrested, and one conspirator, a militia officer nicknamed Tiradentes, was hanged.

Despite their various social bases, these movements indicated that activism by governments increased dissatisfaction in the American colonies. The new prosperity of the late 18th century contributed to a sense of self-confidence and economic interest among certain colonial classes, which made them sensitive to restrictions and control by Spain and Portugal. Different groups had different complaints, but the sharp social and ethnic divisions within the colonies acted as a barrier to cooperation for common goals and tended to undercut revolutionary movements. Only when the Spanish political system was disrupted by a crisis of legitimacy at the beginning of the 19th century did real separation and independence from the mother countries become a possibility.

GLOBAL CONNECTIONS

## Latin American Civilization and the World Context

In three centuries, Spain and Portugal created large colonial empires in the Americas. These American colonies provided a basis of power to their Iberian mother countries and took a vital place in the expanding world economy as suppliers of precious minerals and certain crops to the growing economy of Europe. By the 18th century, the weakened positions of Spain and Portugal within Europe allowed England and France to benefit directly from the Iberian trade with American colonies. To their American colonies, the Iberian nations transferred and imposed their language, laws, forms of government, religion, and institutions. Large numbers of immigrants, first as conquerors and later as settlers, came to the colonies. Eventually, the whole spectrum of Iberian society was recreated in the New World as men and women came to seek a better life, bringing with them their customs, ideas, religion, laws, and ways of life. By government and individual action, a certain homogeneity was created, both in Spanish America and in Brazil. That seeming unity was most apparent among the Europeanized population.

In fact, despite the apparent continuity with Spain and Portugal and homogeneity among the various colonies, there were great variations. Latin America, with its distinct environments, its various economic possibilities, and its diverse indigenous peoples, imposed new realities. In places such as Mexico and Peru, Native American cultures emerged from the shock of conquest, battered but still vibrant. Native American communities adapted to the new colonial situation. A distinctive multiethnic and multiracial society developed, drawing on Iberian precedents but also dependent on the native population, the imported Africans, and the various mixed racial categories. Argentina with few Native Americans, Cuba with its slaves and plantations, and Mexico with its large rural indigenous populations all shared the same Hispanic traditions and laws, and all had a predominantly white elite, but their social and economic realities made them very different places. Latin America developed as a composite civilization—distinct from the West but related to it—combining European and Native American culture and society or creating the racial hierarchies of slave societies in places such as Brazil.

The empires of Spain and Portugal in Latin America bear comparison with the Russian Empire that had been formed at about the same time. While Iberian expansion had been maritime and Russian expansion over land, the process of colonization and the conquest of indigenous peoples created many parallels, including the development of coerced labor. The creation of all of these empires also demonstrated the impact of gunpowder. But the cultural impact of the West was different in the Iberian and Russian empires. Whereas the Russian rulers had decided, quite selectively, what aspects of Western culture to adopt, in Latin America Western forms were often simply imposed on the populations, but not without resistance.

From the perspective of the world economy, despite the ultimate decline in production of precious metals, Latin American products remained in great demand in Europe's markets. As Latin Americans began to seek political independence in the early 19th century, they were confronted by this basic economic fact and by their continued dependence on trade with the developing global economy. Latin America's world economic position, with its dependent and coerced labor force and outside commercial control, revealed its colonial status, but in its often bitter history of cultural clash and accommodation a new civilization had been born.

## Further Readings

James Lockhart and Stuart B. Schwartz, *Early Latin America* (1983), provides an interpretation and overview. Lyle N. Macalister, *Spain and Portugal in the New World* (1984), is particularly good on the Iberian background and the formation of societies in Latin America. The relevant chapters of Leslie Bethell, ed., *The Cambridge History of Latin America,* vols. 1 and 2 (1985), are a good starting point for a discussion of commerce and government. Matthew Restall, *Seven Myths of the Spanish Conquest* (2003), provides a fresh look at that process. On the conquest period there are excellent regional studies. Geographer Carl O. Sauer, *The Early Caribbean* (1966), describes the discovery, settlement, and conquest of that region, with much attention to Indian culture. James Lockhart, *Spanish Peru* (1968), is a model reconstruction of conquest society. The story of Mancio Serra is told in Stuart Stirling, *The Last Conquistador* (1999). The conquest of Mexico can be seen from two different angles in Bernal Díaz del Castillo, *The Discovery and Conquest of Mexico,* trans. A. P. Maudsley (1956), and in James Lockhart's edition of the Aztec testimony gathered after the conquest by Bernardino de Sahagún, published as *We Peoples Here* (1962). Many sources are collected in S. Schwartz, ed., *Victors and Vanquished* (2000).

The transformation of Indian societies has been studied in books such as Steve J. Stern, *Peru's Indian Peoples and the Challenge of Spanish Conquest* (1982), on the early colonial era; Ward Stavig, *The World of Tupac Amaru* (1999), on 18th-century Peru; and Matthew Restall, *The Maya World* (1997), on Yucatan. Other approaches to the impact of conquest are presented in Noble David Cook, *Born to Die: Disease and New World Conquest, 1492–1650* (1998), and Carolyn Dean, *Inka Bodies and the Bodies of Christ* (1999). Particularly sensitive to Indian views are Nancy Farriss, *Maya Society Under Colonial Rule* (1984), and Kenneth Mills, *Idolatry and Its Enemies* (1997).

Social and economic history have received considerable attention. The establishment of colonial economies has been studied in detail in books such as Eric Van Young, *Hacienda and Market in Eighteenth-Century Mexico* (1981); Stuart Schwartz, *Sugar Plantations and the Formation of Brazilian Society* (1985); and Kris Lane, *Quito, 1599* (2003). Very good social history is now being written. For example, Susan Socolow, *Women in Colonial Latin America* (2000), examines the changing role of women. In Louisa Schell Hoberman and Susan Migden Socolow, eds., *Cities and Society in Colonial Latin America* (1986), urban social types are examined. Arnold Bauer, *Goods, Power, and History* (2001), discusses material culture. A different kind of social history that examines popular thought can be seen in Serge Gruzinski, *The Conquest of Mexico* (1993).

The best starting place on the Bourbon reforms is David Brading, *Miners and Merchants in Bourbon Mexico* (1971). John L. Phelan, *The Comunero Revolt: The People and the King* (1978), examines the Bourbon reforms' unintended effects. The revolt of Tupac Amaru is analyzed in Sinclair Thomson, *We Alone Will Rule* (2002). Dauril Alden's *Royal Government in Colonial Brazil* (1968) and Kenneth Maxwell's *Conflicts and Conspiracies* (1973) show Pombal's effects on Brazil.

## On the Web

The methods by which Europeans extracted wealth from Latin America by the manipulation of old or imposition of new patterns of mining, labor, and land ownership (the *mita* and *encomendero* systems) and the impact these new patterns of economic life had on both the indigenous population and the imported African slave population are collectively examined at http://www.emory.edu/

COLLEGE/CULPEPER/BAKEWELL/index.html and http://www.hist.umn.edu/~rmccaa/colonial/potosi/. These sites also illuminate the efforts of Portugal's Marquis of Pombal and the Spanish throne to control the economies of Latin America.

Indigenous resistance to Latin America's dependent economic position is given a human face through a discussion of the rebellions of Tupac Amaru and Juan Santos Atahualpa at http://www.dickshovel.com/500.html.

Some of the syncretic or composite elements of modern Latin American civilization are revealed in the "Day of the Dead" celebration, which is explored at http://www.public.iastate.edu/~rjsalvad/scmfaq/muertos.html and http://teacherlink.ed.usu.edu/tlresources/units/Byrnes-celebrations/Day.html. A traditional Day of the Dead altar can be constructed using illustrations provided at http://www.mexweb.com/muertos.htm.

CHAPTER 25

# Africa and the Africans in the Age of the Atlantic Slave Trade



Sometimes a single, extraordinary life can represent the forces and patterns of a whole historical era. Born in the early 19th century, Mahommah Gardo Baquaqua was a young man from the trading town of Djougou in what is now the Benin Republic in west Africa. A Muslim, he could speak Arabic, Hausa, and a number of other languages, as was common among the trading peoples from which he came. At a young age, Baquaqua was captured and enslaved during a war with a neighboring African state; after gaining his freedom, he was enslaved again, and around 1845 he was sold into the Atlantic slave trade.

Baquaqua was taken first to northeastern Brazil and from there was purchased by a ship captain from Rio de Janeiro. After a number of voyages along the Brazilian coast, his ship eventually sailed for New York. After a failed attempt to use the American courts to gain his freedom (a strategy that many slaves attempted), Baquaqua fled to Boston with the help of local abolitionists. In that city he was befriended by antislavery Baptist missionaries. With them, he sailed for Haiti. Eventually he learned French and English and studied at a college in upstate New York in order to prepare for missionary work in his native Africa. His life was not easy. Eventually, because of racial incidents, he moved to Canada.

Although Baquaquahad had left the Baptist college, he did not abandon his desire to return to Africa, and he continued to seek ways to make that voyage. In 1854, in an attempt to get the money he needed to realize his dream, he published his autobiography, *An Interesting Narrative: Biography of Mahommah G. Baquaqua.* In it he was able to provide his personal observations on his experiences. On the slave ship, he reported:

> O the loathsomeness and filth of that horrible place will never be effaced from my memory; nay as long as my memory holds her seat in this distracted brain, will I remember that. My heart, even at this day, sickens at the thought of it. Let those *humane individuals,* who are in favor of slavery, only allow themselves to take the slave's position in the noisome hold of a slave ship, just for one trip

**FIGURE 25.1** Image of African slave trade. The French artist Auguste François Biard painted this scene of the west African slave trade in 1840 in an attempt to show its cruelties. Represented here are not only the European merchants and sailors receiving the slaves but west African merchants and soldiers involved in supplying them. The painting was eventually acquired by an ardent English abolitionist.

> from Africa to America, and without going into the horrors of slavery further than this, if they do not come out thorough-going abolitionists, then I have no more to say in favor of abolition.

The only place worse than the hold of a slave ship, said Baquaqua, was the place to which slave owners would be condemned in the next life. We do not know whether Baquaqua finally returned to the land of his birth, but the life of this African, while singular in many aspects, represents the stories of millions of Africans in the age of the slave trade, and these make up an important part of world history.

| 1400 C.E. | 1500 C.E. | 1600 C.E. | 1700 C.E. | 1800 C.E. |
|---|---|---|---|---|
| **1415** Portuguese capture Ceuta (Morocco); beginning of European expansion<br>**1441** First shipment of African slaves brought directly from Africa to Portugal<br>**1481** Portuguese fort established at El Mina (Ghana) | **1562** Beginnings of English slave trade<br>**1570** Portuguese establish colony in Angola<br>**1591** Fall of Songhay Empire | **1652** Dutch establish colony at Cape of Good Hope | **1700–1717** Osei Tutu unifies the Asante kingdom<br>**1713** English get right to import slaves to Spanish Empire<br>**1720s** Rise of the kingdom of Dahomey<br>**1790s** Abolitionist movement gains strength in England<br>**1792** Slave uprising in Haiti | **1804** Usuman Dan Fodio leads Hausa expansion<br>**1815** Cape colony comes under formal British control<br>**1818–1828** Shaka forges Zulu power and expansion; mfecane under way<br>**1833** Great Britain abolishes slavery in the West Indies<br>**1834** Boers make "Great Trek" into Natal |

Sub-Saharan Africa, previously linked to the Muslim world in many ways, moved at its own pace even as it was pulled in new directions during the early modern centuries. Islam remained important, and in eastern Africa so did trade with western Asia, but the rise of the West and of the Western-dominated world economy proved to be a powerful force in recasting the framework of African history. The strength of earlier African cultural and political traditions persisted in many places, but the impact of the West was the newest influence in Africa and in some respects an immensely powerful one. African history had its own pace, and this chapter therefore exceeds the chronological boundaries of the early modern period. The influences of Islam and the West initiated or intensified processes of religious conversion, political reorganization, and social change that persisted in some cases into the 19th century. The distinctive nature and chronology of African history should not blind us to its role in world history.

During the age of European maritime and commercial expansion, large areas of Africa were brought into the orbit of the expanding world economy and were influenced by the transformation that was taking place. Not all parts of Africa were influenced in the same way or at the same time. After 1450, the growing and often bitter contacts between Europeans and Africans, primarily through the slave trade, linked the destiny of Africa to the broader external trends of the emerging world economy. These contacts also resulted in a diaspora of millions of Africans to the Middle East, Europe, and especially the Americas. Not all European contact with Africa was centered on the slave trade, nor was the desire for slaves the only impulse behind European explorations, but the slave trade after 1600 overshadowed other activities until the mid-19th century. Along with Latin America and Europe itself, sub-Saharan Africa was most deeply affected by the world economy during the early modern period, but its patterns, including its involvements with the West, remained distinctive.

Changing global interactions had a direct impact on certain areas of Africa, and they also made Africans an important element in the shifting balance of world civilizations. The forced movement of Africans as captive laborers and the creation of slave-based societies in the Americas were major aspects of the formation of the modern world and the growth of the economies of western Europe. This forced migration was part of the international exchange of foods, diseases, animals, and ideas that marked the era and had a profound influence on the indigenous peoples in various regions, as we saw in the case of the Americas. Moreover, in the large areas of the Americas colonized by Europeans where slavery came to be the predominant form of labor, African culture became part of a complex mixture of cultures, contributing to the creation of new cultural forms. In this chapter we examine the history of parts of Africa in the age of the slave trade and the creation of slave societies in the Atlantic world as part of the general process of European expansion and the creation of a world economy.

Although much of the analysis in this chapter emphasizes the increasing linkage between Africa and the wider world, it should be made clear at the outset that many fundamental processes of African development continued throughout this period. Almost all of Africa remained independent of outside political control, and most cultural development was autonomous as well. Africa differed profoundly from Latin America in these respects during the early modern centuries.

A variety of trends affected various parts of the sub-Saharan region. Islam consolidated its position in east Africa and the Sudan. In Ethiopia the Christian kingdom of the highlands continued to hold off its Muslim rivals. In many places in Africa, as in Europe, independent states continued to form and expand, perhaps as a result of a population expansion that followed the spread of iron tools and improved agriculture. Kingdoms spread to new areas. Scholars disagree on the extent to which these long-term developments were affected by Europeans and the rise of the Atlantic slave trade. Some argue that the enlarged political scale—the growth of large kingdoms through much of the subcontinent—was the dominant theme of the period and that slavery was one of its byproducts. Others see European demand as a major impulse in political expansion. In this chapter we emphasize the impact of slavery and the slave trade because our focus is not simply the geographic region of Africa but the Africans who, like Baquaqua, and so many others, were swept into the expanding international economy.

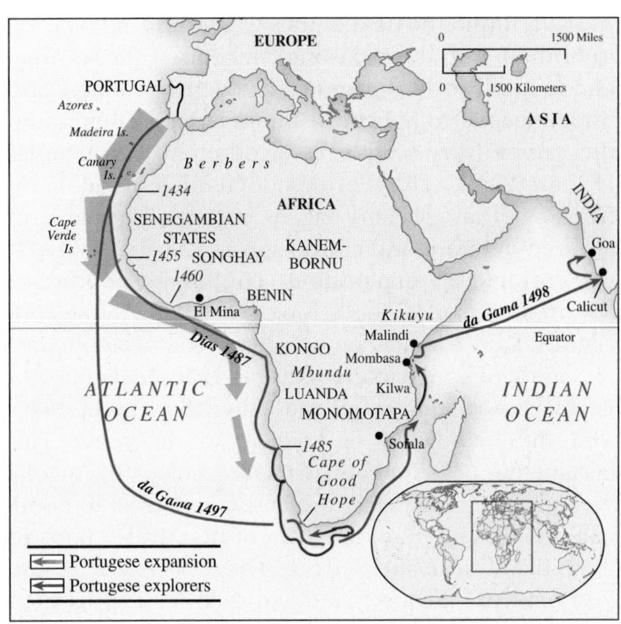


**MAP 25.1** Portuguese Expansion and Major African Kingdoms

## The Atlantic Slave Trade

■ **Early Portuguese contacts set the patterns for contact with the African coast. The slave trade expanded to meet the demand for labor in the new American colonies, and millions were exported in an organized commerce that involved both Europeans and Africans.**

Portuguese ships pushed down the west African coast and finally reached the Cape of Good Hope in 1487 (Map 25.1). Along the coast, the Portuguese established **factories:** forts and trading posts with resident merchants. The most important of these was **El Mina** (1482) in the heart of the gold-producing region of the forest zone. These forts allowed the Portuguese to exercise some control with few personnel. Although the early voyagers carried out some raids, once their cannon range was exceeded the Portuguese simply were not powerful enough to enforce their will on the larger west African states. Therefore, most forts were established with the consent of local rulers, who benefited from access to European commodities and sometimes from the military support the Portuguese provided in local wars.

Africans acquired goods from the Portuguese, who sometimes provided African rulers with slaves brought from other stretches of the coast. In return, the Portuguese received ivory, pepper, animal skins, and gold. From El Mina, Accra, and other trade forts, routes led directly into the gold-producing regions of the interior, so that the Portuguese eventually traded with Mande and Soninke merchants from Mali and Songhay. Much of the Portuguese success resulted from their ability to penetrate the existing African trade routes, to which they could also add specialized items. Portuguese and African Portuguese mulatto traders struck out into the interior to establish trade contacts and collection points.

Trade was the basis of Portuguese relations with Africans, but in the wake of commerce followed political, religious, and social relations. The small states of the Senegambian coast did not impress the Portuguese, who were particularly suspicious of Muslims, their traditional enemies. When they reached the Gold Coast (modern Ghana) and found the kingdom of Benin, they were impressed both by the power of the ruler and by the magnificence of his court. Other large African states also provoked similar responses.

Missionary efforts were made to convert the rulers of Benin, Kongo, and other African kingdoms. The Portuguese contacted the Kongo kingdom south of the Zaire River about 1484. The missionaries achieved a major success in Kongo, where members of the royal family were converted. The ruler, **Nzinga Mvemba** (r. 1507–1543), with the help of Portuguese advisors and missionaries, brought the whole kingdom to Christianity. Attempts were made to "Europeanize" the kingdom. Portugal and Kongo exchanged ambassadors and dealt with each other with a certain equality in this early period, but eventually enslavement of his subjects led Nzinga Mvemba to try to end the slave trade and limit Portuguese activities. He was only partially successful because of Portugal's control of Kongo's ability to communicate with the outside world and its dominance over Kongo's trade.

These first contacts were marked by cultural preconceptions as well as by appreciation and curiosity.

Africans found the newcomers strange and at first tried to fit them into their existing concepts of the spiritual and natural world. Images of Portuguese soldiers and traders began to appear in the bronzes of Benin and the carved ivory sculptures of other African peoples (Figure 25.2). The Portuguese tended to look on Africans as savages and pagans but also as capable of civilized behavior and conversion to Christianity.

Portuguese exploration continued southward toward the Cape of Good Hope and beyond in the 16th century. Early contacts were made with the Mbundu peoples south of Kongo in the 1520s, and a more permanent Portuguese settlement was established there in the 1570s with the foundation of **Luanda** on the coast. This became the basis for the Portuguese colony of Angola. As we have already seen, the Portuguese tried to dominate the existing trading system of the African ports in the Indian Ocean and Red Sea. They established an outpost on Mozambique Island and then secured bases at Kilwa, Mombasa, Sofala, and other ports that gave them access to the gold trade from Monomotapa (Mwenemutapa) in the interior. In east Africa, as on the west African coast, the number of permanent Portuguese settlers was minimal. The Portuguese effort was primarily commercial and military, although it was always accompanied by a strong missionary effort.

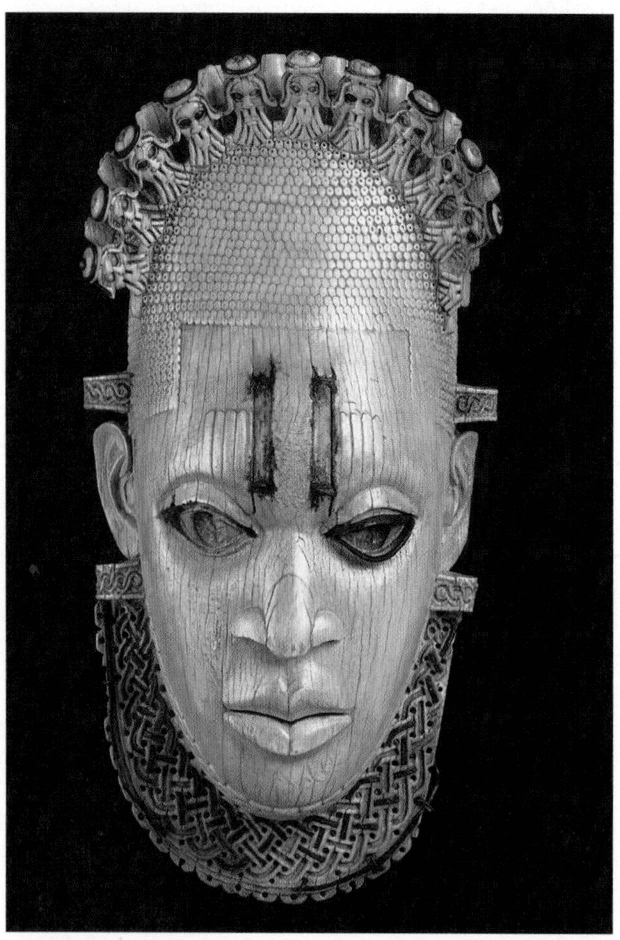

FIGURE 25.2 African artists were impressed by the strangeness of Europeans and sometimes incorporated them in their own work, as can be seen in the headpiece of this beautifully carved ivory head of a Benin monarch. Europeans in turn employed African artisans to produce decorative luxury goods.

The patterns of contact established by the Portuguese were followed by others. In the 17th century, the Dutch, English, French, and others competed with the Portuguese and displaced them to some extent, but the system of fortified trading stations, the combination of force and diplomacy, alliances with local rulers, and the predominance of commercial relations continued as the principal pattern of European contact with Africa.

Although for a long time Portugal's major interest was in gold, pepper, and other products, a central element in this pattern was the slave trade. Slavery as an institution had been extensive in the Roman Empire but had greatly declined in most of Europe during the Middle Ages, when it was replaced by serfdom. In the Mediterranean and in Iberia, however, where there was an active military frontier between Christians and Muslims, it had remained important. Moreover, the trans-Saharan slave trade had brought small numbers of black Africans into the Mediterranean throughout the period. The Portuguese voyages now opened a direct channel to sub-Saharan Africa. The first slaves brought directly to Portugal from Africa arrived in 1441, and after that date slaves became a common trade item. The Portuguese and later other Europeans raided for slaves along the coast, but the numbers acquired in this way were small. After initial raids, Europeans found that trade was a much more secure and profitable way to get these human cargoes. For example, the Portuguese sent about 50 slaves per year to Portugal before 1450, when raiding was prevalent, but by 1460 some 500 slaves per year arrived in Portugal as a trade with African rulers developed. Whether the victims were acquired by raiding or by trade, the effects on them were similar. An eyewitness to the unloading of slaves in Portugal in 1444 wrote,

"Voyage from Lisbon to the Island of São Thomé," by an Anonymous Portuguese Pilot, c. 1540

> But what heart could be so hard as not to be pierced with piteous feelings to see that company? For some kept their heads low and their faces bathed in tears, looking one upon another; others stood groaning very dolorously, looking up to the height of heaven, fixing their eyes upon it, crying out loudly, as if asking help of the Father of Nature.

The slave trade was given added impetus when the Portuguese and the Spanish began to develop sugar plantations on the Atlantic islands of Madeira (Portugal) and the Canaries (Spain) and off the African coast on the Portuguese-held island of São Tomé. Sugar produc-

**TABLE 25.1 Slave Exports from Africa, 1500–1900 (in thousands)**

| | 1500–1600 (%) | 1600–1700 (%) | 1700–1800 (%) | 1800–1900 (%) | Total |
|---|---|---|---|---|---|
| Red Sea | 200 (17) | 200 (7) | 200 (3) | 450 (8) | 1050 (6) |
| Trans-Sahara | 550 (47) | 700 (24) | 700 (9) | 1200 (22) | 3150 (19) |
| East Africa and Indian Ocean | 100 (9) | 100 (4) | 400 (5) | 442 (8) | 1042 (6) |
| Trans-Atlantic | 325 (28) | 1868 (65) | 6133 (83) | 3330 (61) | 11,656 (69) |
| | | | | | 16,898 |

*Source*: Adapted from Paul Lovejoy, *Transformations in Slavery: A History of Slavery in Africa* (1983).

tion demanded many workers and constant labor under difficult conditions, usually in a tropical or subtropical environment. The plantation system of organization associated with sugar, in which managers were able to direct and control laborers over long periods with little restraint, was later extended to America and then to other crops. Although the system did not depend only on Africans, they became the primary plantation laborers in the Atlantic world. The slave trade grew significantly in volume and complexity after 1550 as the American plantation colonies, especially Brazil, began to develop. By 1600, the slave trade predominated over all other kinds of commerce on the African coast.

## Trend Toward Expansion

Although debate and controversy surround many aspects of the history of slavery, it is perhaps best to start with the numbers. Estimates of the volume of the trade vary widely, and scholars still debate the figures and their implications, but the range of calculations has been narrowed by recent research. Between 1450 and 1850, it is estimated that about 12 million Africans were shipped across the Atlantic (Table 25.1). With a mortality rate of 10 to 20 percent on the ships, about 10 or 11 million Africans actually arrived in the Americas. How many people died in Africa as a result of the slaving wars or in the forced marches to the coast is unknown, but estimates have been as high as one-third of the total captured. The volume changed over time. In the 16th century, the numbers were small, but they increased to perhaps 16,000 per year in the 17th century. The 18th century was the great age of the Atlantic slave trade; probably more than 7 million slaves, or more than 80 percent of all those embarked, were exported between 1700 and 1800. By the latter date, about 3 million slaves lived in the Americas. Even in the 19th century, when slavery was under attack, the slave trade to some places continued. Cuba received some 700,000 slaves, and Brazil took more than 1 million in that century alone.

The high volume of the slave trade was necessary to the slave owners because, in most of the slave regimes in the Caribbean and Latin America, slave mortality was high and fertility was low (partly because more men than women were imported). Thus, over time there was usually a loss of population. The only way to maintain or expand the number of slaves was by importing more from Africa. The one exception to this pattern was the southern United States, where the slave population grew, perhaps because of the temperate climate and the fact that few worked in the most dangerous and unhealthy occupations, such as sugar growing and mining. By 1860, almost 6 million slaves worked in the Americas, about 4 million of them in the southern United States, an area that depended more on natural population growth than on the Atlantic slave trade. In terms of total population, however, slaves in British North America were never more than one-fourth of the whole population, whereas in the British and French Caribbean they made up 80 to 90 percent of the population.

The dimensions of the trade varied over time, reflecting the economic and political situation in the Americas. From 1530 to 1650, Spanish America and Brazil received the majority of African slaves, but after the English and French began to grow sugar in the Caribbean, the islands of Jamaica, Barbados, and St. Domingue (Haiti) became important terminals for the slavers. By the 18th century, Virginia and the Carolinas in North America had also become major destinations, although they never rivaled the Caribbean or Brazil (Table 25.2).

**TABLE 25.2 Estimated Slave Imports into the Americas by Importing Region, 1519–1866**

| Region and Country | Slaves |
|---|---|
| Brazil | 3,902,000 |
| British Caribbean | 2,238,200 |
| Spanish America | 1,267,800 |
| French Caribbean | 1,092,600 |
| Guianas* | 403,700 |
| British North America | 361,100 |
| Dutch Caribbean | 129,700 |
| Danish Caribbean | 73,100 |
| | 9,468,200 |

*Includes Dutch, French, and British colonies, namely, Berbice, Cayenne, Demerara, Essequebo, and Surinam.

IN DEPTH

## Slavery and Human Society

Slavery is a very old and widespread institution. It has been found at different times all over the globe, among simple societies and in the great centers of civilization. In some of these societies, it has been a marginal or secondary form of labor, whereas in others it became the predominant labor form or "mode of production" (in the jargon of Marxist analysis). The need for labor beyond the capacity of the individual or the family unit is very old, and as soon as authority, law, or custom could be established to set the conditions for coercion, the tribe, the state, the priests, or some other group or institution extracted labor by force. Coerced labor could take different forms. There are important distinctions between indentured servants, convict laborers, debt-peons, and chattel slaves.

> *"To paraphrase English historian Charles Boxer, no people can enslave another for 400 years without developing an attitude of superiority."*

Although most societies placed some limits on the slaveholder's authority or power, the denial of the slave's control over his or her own labor and life choices was characteristic of this form of coercion throughout history. In most societies that had a form of chattel slavery, the slave was denied a sense of belonging in the society—the idea of kinship. The honor associated with family or lineage was the antithesis of slavery. The Old Testament figure Joseph might rise to a high position, and so might a vizier of a Turkish sultan, but as slaves they were instruments of their masters' will. In fact, because they were slaves and thus unconstrained by kinship or other ties and obligations, they could be trusted in positions of command.

Because slaves became nonpersons—or, as one modern author has put it, because they suffered a "social death"—it was always easier to enslave "others" or "outsiders": those who were different in some way. Hebrews enslaved Canaanites, Greeks enslaved "barbarians," and Muslims made slaves of nonbelievers. If the difference between slave and master was readily seen, it made enforcement of slave status that much easier. Racism as such did not cause modern slavery, but differences in culture, language, color, and other physical characteristics always facilitated enslavement. The familiarity of Europeans and Muslims with black Africans in an enslaved status contributed to the development of modern racism. To paraphrase English historian Charles Boxer, no people can enslave another for 400 years without developing an attitude of superiority.

Slavery was not only a general phenomenon that existed in many societies. Rarely questioned on any grounds, it was seen as a necessary and natural phenomenon. Slavery is accepted in the texts of ancient India, the Old Testament, and the writings of classical Greece. Aristotle specifically argued that some people were born to rule and others to serve. In Christian theology, although all people might be free in spirit in the kingdom of God, servitude was considered a necessary reality. Voices might be raised arguing for fair treatment or against the enslavement of a particular group, but the condition of servitude usually was taken as part of the natural order of the world.

In this context, the attack on slavery in Western culture that grew from the Enlightenment and the social and economic changes in western Europe and its Atlantic colonies at the end of the 18th century was a remarkable turning point in world history. Whether one believes that slavery was an outdated labor form that was incompatible with industrial capitalism and was therefore abolished, or that it was

Between 1550 and 1850, Brazil alone received 3.5 to 5 million Africans, or about 42 percent of all those who reached the New World. The Caribbean islands, dedicated to sugar production, were the other major destination of Africans. The island colonies of St. Domingue and Jamaica each received more than 1 million slaves in the 18th century alone.

It should be emphasized that these figures represent only the volume in the Atlantic slave trade. The older trans-Sahara, Red Sea, and east African slave trades in the hands of Muslim traders continued throughout the period and added another 3 million people to the total of Africans exported as slaves in this period (Table 25.1).

The Atlantic slave trade drew slaves from across the continent, and its concentration shifted over time. In the 16th century, the majority of slaves were exported from the Senegambia region, but by the 17th century, west central Africa (modern Zaire and Angola) was the major supplier. Also important were the areas of the Gold Coast and the Slave Coast—Dahomey and Benin—at the end of the century, when Benin alone was exporting more than 10,000 slaves per year. In the century that followed, wars for control of the interior created the large states of Asante among the Akan peoples of the Gold Coast and Dahomey among the Fon peoples. These wars were both the cause and the result of increasing slave exports from these regions.

### Demographic Patterns

The majority of the trans-Saharan slave trade consisted of women to be used as concubines and domestic servants in north Africa and the Middle East, but the destroyed because its immorality became all too obvious, its demise was quick. In about a century and a half, the moral and religious underpinning of chattel slavery was cut away and its economic justifications were questioned seriously. Although slavery lingered in at least a few places well into the 20th century, few people were willing to defend the institution publicly.

Although slavery historically existed in many places, it has become intimately associated with Africa because of the scope of the Atlantic slave trade and the importance of slavery in forming the modern world system. There was nothing inevitable about Africa's becoming the primary source of slaves in the modern world. Europeans did use Native American and European indentured workers when they could, but historical precedents, maritime technology, and availability combined to make Africa the source of labor for the expanding plantation colonies of Europe.

African slavery obviously played an important role in shaping the modern world. The African slave trade was one of the first truly international trades, and it created an easy access to labor that enabled Europeans to exploit the Americas. Some have argued that it was an important, even a necessary feature in the rise of capitalism and the international division of labor. Others disagree. In this question, as in nearly every other question about modern slavery, controversies still abound.

In the context of African history, the interpretation of slavery is still changing rapidly. A recent and careful estimate of the volume involved in the Atlantic trade (10–12 million) has been questioned seriously, especially by African scholars, who see this new figure as an attempt to downplay the exploitation of Africa. Another debate centers on the impact of the trade on the population and societies within Africa. The slave trade was important to the economy of the Atlantic, but how important was this external trade in Africa itself? Reacting to the preabolitionist European self-justifications that the slave trade was no great crime because Africans had long become familiar with slavery and were selling already enslaved people, early researchers argued that African slavery often was an extension of kinship or other forms of dependency and was quite unlike the chattel slavery of western Europe. But further research has demonstrated that in many African societies, slavery was an integral part of the economy, and although specific conditions sometimes differed greatly from those in the Americas, the servile condition in Africa had much in common with chattel slavery. For example, the Sokoto caliphate in the 19th century had a proportion of slaves similar to that in Brazil and the southern United States. Slave societies did exist in Africa.

Controversy rages over the extent to which the development of African slavery resulted from the long-term impact of the slave trade and the European demand for captive labor. African societies did not live in isolation from the pressures and examples of the world economy into which they were drawn. The extent to which that contact transformed slavery in Africa is now in question. These controversies among historians reflect current concerns and a realization that the present social and political situation in Africa and in many places in the Americas continues to bear the burden of a historical past in which slavery played an essential role. In evaluating slavery, as in all other historical questions, what we think about the present shapes our inquiry and our interpretation of the past.

**Questions** Why did Africa become the leading source of slaves in the early modern world economy? What are some of the leading issues in interpreting African slavery? What were the roles of Africans and Europeans in the early modern slave trade?

Atlantic slave trade concentrated on men. To some extent this was because planters and mine owners in the Americas were seeking workers for heavy labor and were not eager to risk buying children because of the high levels of mortality. Also, African societies that sold captives into slavery often preferred to sell the men and keep the women and children as domestic slaves or to extend existing kin groups.

The Atlantic trade seems to have had a demographic impact on at least certain parts of west and central Africa. One estimate is that the population of about 25 million in 1850 in those regions was about one-half what it would have been had there been no slave trade. It is true that the trans-Atlantic trade carried more men than women and more women than children, but captive women and children who remained in Africa swelled the numbers of enslaved people and skewed the proportion of women to men in the African enslaving societies. Finally, as the Atlantic trade developed, new crops, such as maize and manioc, were introduced to Africa that provided new food resources for the population and helped it recover from the losses to the slave trade.

## Organization of the Trade

The patterns of contact and trade established by the Portuguese at first were followed by rival Europeans on the African coast. Control of the slave trade or a portion of it generally reflected the political situation in Europe. For one and a half centuries, until about 1630, the Portuguese controlled most of the coastal trade and were the major suppliers of their own colony of Brazil and the Spanish settlements in America. The growth of slave-based plantation colonies in the Caribbean and elsewhere led other Europeans to compete with the Portuguese. The Dutch became major competitors when they seized El Mina in 1637. By the 1660s, the English were eager to have their own source of slaves for their growing colonies in Barbados, Jamaica, and Virginia. The **Royal African Company** was chartered for that purpose. The French made similar arrangements in the 1660s, but not until the 18th century did France become a major carrier. Like other small European nations, even Denmark had its agents and forts on the African coast.

Each nation established merchant towns or trade forts from which a steady source of captives could be obtained. For the Europeans stationed on the coast, Africa was also a graveyard because of the tropical diseases they encountered. Fewer than 10 percent of the employees of the Royal Africa Company who went to Africa ever returned to England, and the majority died in the first year out. European mortality among the crews of slave ships was also very high because of tropical diseases such as malaria. The slave trade proved deadly to all involved, but at least some of the Europeans had a choice, whereas for the enslaved Africans there was none.

West African Slave Fort

European agents for the companies often had to deal directly with local rulers, paying a tax or offering gifts. Various forms of currency were used, such as iron bars, brass rings, and cowrie shells. The Spanish developed a complicated system in which a healthy man was called an **Indies piece,** and children and women were priced at fractions of that value. Slaves were brought to the coast by a variety of means. Sometimes, as in Angola, European military campaigns produced captives for slaves, or African and mulatto agents purchased captives at interior trade centers. In Dahomey a royal monopoly was established to control the flow of slaves. Some groups used their position to tax or control the movement of slaves from the interior to the coast. Although African and European states tried to establish monopolies over the trade, private merchants often circumvented restrictions.

Clearly, both Europeans and Africans were actively involved in the slave trade. It was not always clear which side was in control. One group of English merchants on the Gold Coast complained of African insolence in 1784 because in negotiations the Africans had emphasized that "the country belongs to them." In any case, the result of this collaboration was to send millions of Africans into bondage in foreign lands.

Historians have long debated the profitability of the slave trade. Some argue that the profits were so great and constant that they were a major element in the rise of commercial capitalism and, later, the origins of the Industrial Revolution. Undoubtedly, many people profited from the trade in African slaves. A single slaving voyage might make a profit of as much as 300 percent, and merchants in the ports that specialized in fitting out ships for the slave trade, such as Liverpool, England, or Nantes, France—as well as African suppliers—derived a profit from the slave trade. But the slave trade also involved risks and costs, so that in the long run, profitability levels did not remain so high. In the late 18th century, profitability in the English slave trade probably ran from 5 to 10 percent on average, and in the French and Dutch trades it was slightly lower. The slave trade was little more profitable in the long run than most business activities of the age, and by itself was not a major source of the capital needed in the Industrial Revolution.

However, it is difficult to calculate the full economic importance of slavery to the economies of Europe because it was so directly linked to the plantation and mining economies of the Americas. During some periods, a **triangular trade** existed in which slaves were carried to the Americas; sugar, tobacco, and other goods were then carried to Europe; and European products were sent to the coast of Africa to begin the triangle again. Were profits from the slave trade accumulated in Liverpool invested in the textile industry of England? And if so, how important were these investments for the growth of that industry? We would need to calculate the value of goods produced in Europe for exchange in the slave trade as well as the profits derived from the colonies to measure the importance of slavery to the growth of the European economies. Still, the very persistence of the slave trade indicates its viability. The slave trade surely contributed to the formation of emerging capitalism in the Atlantic world. In Africa itself, the slave trade often drew economies into dependence on trade with Europeans and suppressed the growth of other economic activities.

It is clear that by the late 18th century, the slave trade and slavery were essential aspects of the economy of the Atlantic basin, and their importance was increasing. More than 40 percent of all the slaves that crossed the Atlantic embarked during the century after 1760, and the plantation economies of Brazil, the Caribbean, and the southern United States were booming in the early 19th century. The slave trade was profitable enough to keep merchants in it, and it contributed in some way to the expanding economy of western Europe. It was also the major way in which Africa was linked to the increasingly integrated economy of the world.

## African Societies, Slavery, and the Slave Trade

- **The slave trade influenced African forms of servitude and the social and political development of African states. Newly powerful states emerged in west Africa; in the Sudan and east Africa, slavery also produced long-term effects.**

Europeans in the age of the slave trade sometimes justified the enslavement of Africans by pointing out that slavery already existed on that continent. However, although forms of bondage were ancient in Africa, and the Muslim trans-Sahara and Red Sea trades already were established, the Atlantic trade interacted with and transformed these earlier aspects of slavery.

"A Defense of the Slave Trade," July 1740

African societies had developed many forms of servitude, which varied from a peasant status to something much more like chattel slavery in which people were considered things: "property with a soul," as Aristotle put it. African states usually were nonegalitarian, and because in many African societies all land was owned by the state or the ruler, the control of slaves was one of the few ways, if not the only way, in which individuals or lineages could increase their wealth and status. Slaves were used as servants, concubines, soldiers, administrators, and field workers. In some cases, as in the ancient empire of Ghana and in Kongo, there were whole villages of enslaved dependants who were required to pay tribute to the ruler. The Muslim traders of west Africa who linked the forest region to the savanna had slave porters as well as villages of slaves to supply their caravans. In many situations, these forms of servitude were fairly benign and were an extension of lineage and kinship systems. In others, however, they were exploitive economic and social relations that reinforced the hierarchies of various African societies and allowed the nobles, senior lineages, and rulers to exercise their power. Among the forest states of west Africa, such as Benin, and in the Kongo kingdom in central Africa, slavery was already an important institution before the European arrival, but the Atlantic trade opened up new opportunities for expansion and intensification of slavery in those societies.

Despite great variation in African societies and the fact that slaves sometimes attained positions of command and trust, in most cases slaves were denied choice about their lives and actions. They were placed in dependent or inferior positions, and they were often considered aliens. It is important to remember that the enslavement of women was a central feature of African slavery. Although slaves were used in many ways in African societies, domestic slavery and the extension of lineages through the addition of female members remained a central feature in many places. Some historians believe that the excess of women led to polygyny (having more than one wife at a time) and the creation of large harems by rulers and merchants, whose power was increased by this process, and the position of women was lowered in some societies.

In the Sudanic states of the savanna, Islamic concepts of slavery had been introduced. Slavery was viewed as a legitimate fate for nonbelievers but was illegal for Muslims. Despite the complaints of legal scholars such as Ahmad Baba of Timbuktu (1556–1627) against the enslavement of Muslims, many of the Sudanic states enslaved their captives, both pagan and Muslim. In the Niger valley, slave communities produced agricultural surpluses for the rulers and nobles of Songhay, Gao, and other states. Slaves were used for gold mining and salt production and as caravan workers in the Sahara. Slavery was a widely diffused form of labor control and wealth in Africa.

The existence of slavery in Africa and the preexisting trade in people allowed Europeans to mobilize the commerce in slaves quickly by tapping existing routes and supplies. In this venture they were aided by the rulers of certain African states, who were anxious to acquire more slaves for themselves and to supply slaves to the Europeans in exchange for aid and commodities. In the 16th-century Kongo kingdom, the ruler had an army of 20,000 slaves as part of his household, and this gave him greater power than any Kongo ruler had ever held. In general, African rulers did not enslave their own people, except for crimes or in other unusual circumstances; rather, they enslaved their neighbors. Thus, expanding, centralizing states often were the major suppliers of slaves to the Europeans as well as to societies in which slavery was an important institution.

## Slaving and African Politics

As one French agent put it, "The trade in slaves is the business of kings, rich men, and prime merchants." European merchants and royal officials were able to tap existing routes, markets, and institutions, but the new and constant demand also intensified enslavement in Africa and perhaps changed the nature of slavery itself in some African societies.

In the period between 1500 and 1750, as the gunpowder empires and expanding international commerce of Europe penetrated sub-Saharan Africa, existing states and societies often were transformed. As we saw in Chapter 13, the empire of Songhay controlled a vast region of the western savanna until its defeat by a Moroccan invasion in 1591, but for the most part the many states of central and western Africa were small and fragmented. This led to a situation of instability caused by competition and warfare as states tried to expand at the expense of their neighbors or to consolidate power by incorporating subject provinces. The warrior or soldier emerged in this situation as an important social type in states such as the Kongo kingdom and Dahomey as well as along the Zambezi River. The endless wars promoted the importance of the military and made the sale of captives into the slave trade an extension of the politics of regions of Africa. Sometimes, as among the Muslim states of the savanna or the Lake Chad region, wars took on a religious overtone of

Africa, 1500–1800

believers against nonbelievers, but in much of west and central Africa that was not the case. Some authors see this situation as a feature of African politics; others believe it was the result of European demand for new slaves. In either case, the result was the capture and sale of millions of human beings. Although increasing centralization and hierarchy could be seen in the enslaving African societies, a contrary trend of self-sufficiency and anti-authoritarian ideas developed among the peoples who bore the brunt of the slaving attacks.

One result of the presence of Europeans on the coast was a shift in the locus of power within Africa. Just as states such as Ghana and Songhay in the savanna took advantage of their position as intermediaries between the gold of the west African forests and the trans-Saharan trade routes, the states closer to the coast or in contact with the Europeans could play a similar role. Those right on the coast tried to monopolize the trade with Europeans, but European meddling in their internal affairs and European fears of any coastal power that became too strong blocked the creation of centralized states under the shadow of European forts. Just beyond the coast it was different. With access to European goods, especially firearms, iron, horses, cloth, tobacco, and other goods, western and central African kingdoms began to redirect trade toward the coast and to expand their influence. Some historians have written of a gun and slave cycle in which increased firepower allowed these states to expand over their neighbors, producing more slaves, which they traded for more guns. The result was unending warfare and the disruption of societies as the search for slaves pushed ever farther into the interior.

## Asante and Dahomey

Perhaps the effects of the slave trade on African societies are best seen in some specific cases. Several large states developed in west Africa during the slave trade era. Each represented a response to the realities of the European presence and the process of state formation long under way in Africa. Rulers in these states grew in power and often surrounded themselves with ritual authority and a luxurious court life as a way of reinforcing the position that their armies had won (Figures 25.3 and 25.4).

In the area called the Gold Coast by the Europeans, the empire of **Asante** (Ashanti) rose to prominence in the period of the slave trade. The Asante were members of the Akan people (the major group of modern Ghana) who had settled in and around Kumasi, a region of gold and kola nut production that lay between the coast and the Hausa and Mande trading centers to the north. There were at least 20 small states, based on the matrilineal clans that were common to all the Akan peoples, but those of the Oyoko clan predominated. Their cooperation and their access to firearms after 1650 initiated a period of centralization and expansion. Under the vigorous **Osei Tutu** (d. 1717), the title **asantehene** was created to designate the supreme civil and religious leader. His golden stool became the symbol of an Asante union that was created by linking the many Akan clans under the authority of the asantehene but recognizing the autonomy of subordinate areas. An all-Asante council advised the ruler, and an ideology of unity was used to overcome the traditional clan divisions. With this new structure and a series of military reforms, conquest of the area began. By 1700, the Dutch on the coast realized that a new power had emerged, and they began to deal directly with it.

With control of the gold-producing zones and a constant supply of prisoners to be sold as slaves for more firearms, Asante maintained its power until the 1820s as the dominant state of the Gold Coast. Although gold continued to be a major item of export, by the end of the 17th century, slaves made up almost two-thirds of Asante's trade.

FIGURE 25.3 The annual yam harvest festival was an occasion when the power and authority of the Asante ruler could be displayed. The English observers who painted this scene were impressed by the might of this west African kingdom.

**FIGURE 25.4** The size of African cities and the power of African rulers often impressed European observers. Here the city of Loango, capital of a kingdom on the Kongo coast, is depicted as a bustling urban center. At this time it was a major port in the slave trade.

Farther to the east, in the area of the Bight of Benin (between the Volta and Benin rivers on what the Europeans called the Slave Coast), several large states developed. The kingdom of Benin was at the height of its power when the Europeans arrived. It traced its origins to the city of Ife and to the Yoruba peoples that were its neighbors, but it had become a separate and independent kingdom with its own well-developed political and artistic traditions, especially in the casting of bronze. As early as 1516, the ruler, or *oba,* limited the slave trade from Benin, and for a long time most trade with Europeans was controlled directly by the king and was in pepper, textiles, and ivory rather than slaves. Eventually, European pressure and the goals of the Benin nobility combined to generate a significant slave trade in the 18th century, but Benin never made the slave trade its primary source of revenue or state policy.

The kingdom of **Dahomey,** which developed among the Fon (or Aja) peoples, had a different response to the European presence. It began to emerge as a power in the 17th century from its center at Abomey, about 70 miles from the coast. Its kings ruled with the advice of powerful councils, but by the 1720s access to firearms allowed the rulers to create an autocratic and sometimes brutal political regime based on the slave trade. In the 1720s, under King Agaja (1708–1740), the kingdom of Dahomey moved toward the coast, seizing in 1727 the port town of Whydah, which had attracted many European traders. Although Dahomey became to some extent a subject of the powerful neighboring Yoruba state of Oyo, whose cavalry and archers made it strong, Dahomey maintained its autonomy and turned increasingly to the cycle of firearms and slaves. The trade was controlled by the royal court, whose armies (including a regiment of women) were used to raid for more captives.

As Dahomey expanded it eliminated the royal families and customs of the areas it conquered and imposed its own traditions. This resulted in the formation of a unified state, which lasted longer than some of its neighbors. Well into the 19th century, Dahomey was a slaving state, and dependence on the trade in human beings had negative effects on the society as a whole. More than 1.8 million slaves were exported from the Bight of Benin between 1640 and 1890.

This emphasis on the slave trade should not obscure the creative process within many of the African states. The growing divine authority of the rulers paralleled the rise of absolutism in Europe. It led to the development of new political forms, some of which had the power to limit the role of the king. In the Yoruba state of Oyo, for example, a governing council shared power with the ruler. In some states, a balance of offices kept central power in check. In Asante the traditional village chiefs and officials whose authority was based on their lineage were increasingly challenged by new officials appointed by the asantehene as a state bureaucracy began to form.

The creativity of these societies was also seen in traditional arts. In many places, crafts such as bronze casting, woodcarving, and weaving flourished. Guilds of artisans developed in many societies, and their specialization produced crafts executed with great skill. In Benin and the Yoruba states, for example, remarkable and lifelike sculptures in wood and ivory continued to be produced. Often, however, the best artisans labored for the royal court, producing objects designed to honor the ruling family and reinforce the civil and religious authority of the king. This was true in architecture, weaving, and the decorative arts as well. Much of this artistic production also had a religious function or contained religious symbolism; African artists made the spiritual world visually apparent.

Europeans came to appreciate African arts and skills. In the 16th century, the Portuguese began to employ African artists from Benin, Sierra Leone, and Kongo to work local ivory into ladles, saltcellars (containers), and other decorative objects that combined African and European motifs in beautifully carved designs (Figure 25.5). Although works were commissioned by Europeans and sometimes including European religious and political symbols, African artists found ways to incorporate traditional symbols and themes from motherhood to royal power. Many of these objects ended up in the collections of nobles and kings throughout Renaissance Europe. They demonstrated the growing contact between Africa and the wider world.

**FIGURE 25.5** Ivory hunting horn.

## East Africa and the Sudan

West Africa obviously was the region most directly influenced by the trans-Atlantic slave trade, but there and elsewhere in Africa, long-term patterns of society and economy continued and intersected with the new external influences. On the east coast of Africa, the Swahili trading cities continued their commerce in the Indian Ocean, adjusting to the military presence of the Portuguese and the Ottoman Turks. Trade to the interior continued to bring ivory, gold, and a steady supply of slaves. Many of these slaves were destined for the harems and households of Arabia and the Middle East, but a small number were carried away by the Europeans for their plantation colonies. The Portuguese and Indo-Portuguese settlers along the Zambezi River in Mozambique used slave soldiers to increase their territories, and certain groups in interior east Africa specialized in supplying ivory and slaves to the east African coast. Europeans did establish some plantation-style colonies on islands such as Mauritius in the Indian Ocean, and these depended on the east African slave trade.

On Zanzibar and other offshore islands, and later on the coast itself, Swahili, Indian, and Arabian merchants followed the European model and set up clove-producing plantations using African slave laborers. Some of the plantations were large, and by the 1860s Zanzibar

VISUALIZING THE PAST

## Symbols of African Kingship

In many African societies, the symbols of authority and kingship had a ritual power. African kings were sacred, or sacredness resided in the symbols of their authority. Art and design, by creating impressive ritual and civil objects, were often used to emphasize the power and prestige of the ruler and the links between the community and the king. In Dahomey, for example, royal treasures were paraded by the people as a way of creating a sense of pride and awe among the viewers. Among the Fante people, young males of the chief's family carry staffs and decorative swords, each of which carries a message or symbolic meaning. Such ceremonies solidify the image of the king and link the generations. Arts can serve kingship, and by mobilizing artists and by defining the images and messages to be conveyed, rulers help to create culture. This was a technique of rule in no way limited to Africa.

**Questions** What kinds of symbols are used by Western societies to bolster authority? Has secularization of some societies changed the way in which symbols are viewed? Can symbols have different meanings to different groups within a society?

Symbols of authority.

had a slave population of about 100,000. The sultan of Zanzibar alone owned more than 4000 slaves in 1870. Slavery became a prominent feature of the east African coast, and the slave trade from the interior to these plantations and to the traditional slave markets of the Red Sea continued until the end of the 19th century.

Much less is known about the interior of eastern Africa. Large and small kingdoms were supported by the well-watered and heavily populated region of the great lakes of the interior. Bantu speakers predominated, but many peoples inhabited the region. Linguistic and archeological evidence suggests that pastoralist peoples from the upper Nile valley with a distinctive late Iron Age technology moved southward into what is today western Kenya and Uganda, where they came into contact with Bantu speakers and with the farmers and herders who spoke another group of languages called Cushitic. The Bantu states absorbed the immigrants, even when the newcomers established ruling dynasties. Later Nilotic migrations, of people who spoke languages of the Nilotic group, especially of the **Luo** peoples, resulted in the construction of related dynasties among the states in the area of the large lakes of east central Africa. At Bunyoro, the Luo eventually established a ruling dynasty among the existing Bantu population. This kingdom exercised considerable power in the 16th and 17th centuries. Other related states formed in the region. In Buganda, near Lake Victoria, a strong monarchy ruled a heterogeneous population and dominated the region in the 16th century. These developments in the interior, as important as they were for the history of the region, were less influenced by the growing contact with the outside world than were other regions of Africa.

Across the continent in the northern savanna at the end of the 18th century, the process of Islamization, which had been important in the days of the Mali and Songhay empires, entered a new and violent stage that not only linked Islamization to the external slave trade and the growth of slavery in Africa but also produced other long-term effects in the region. After the breakup of Songhay in the 16th century, several successor states had developed. Some, such as the Bambara kingdom of Segu, were pagan. Others, such as the Hausa kingdoms in northern Nigeria, were ruled by Muslim royal families and urban aristocracies but continued to contain large numbers of animist subjects, most of whom were rural peasants. In these states the degree of Islamization was slight, and an accommodation between Muslims and animists was achieved.

Beginning in the 1770s, Muslim reform movements began to sweep the western Sudan. Religious brotherhoods advocating a purifying Sufi variant of Islam extended their influence throughout the Muslim trade networks in the Senegambia region and the western Sudan. This movement had an intense impact on the **Fulani** (Fulbe), a pastoral people who were spread across a broad area of the western Sudan.

In 1804 Usuman Dan Fodio, a studious and charismatic Muslim Fulani scholar, began to preach the reformist ideology in the Hausa kingdoms. His movement became a revolution when in 1804, seeing himself as God's instrument, he preached a jihad against the Hausa kings, who, he felt, were not following the teachings of Muhammad. A great upheaval followed in which the Fulani took control of most of the Hausa states of northern Nigeria in the western Sudan. A new kingdom, based in the city of Sokoto, developed under Dan Fodio's son and brother. The Fulani expansion was driven not only by religious zeal but by political ambitions, as the attack on the well-established Muslim kingdom of Bornu demonstrated. The result of this upheaval was the creation of a powerful Sokoto state under a caliph, whose authority was established over cities such as Kano and Zaria and whose rulers became emirs of provinces within the Sokoto caliphate.

By the 1840s, the effects of Islamization and the Fulani expansion were felt across much of the interior of west Africa. New political units were created, a reformist Islam that tried to eliminate pagan practices spread, and social and cultural changes took place in the wake of these changes. Literacy became more widely dispersed, and new centers of trade, such as Kano, emerged in this period. Later jihads established other new states along similar lines. All of these changes had long-term effects on the region of the western Sudan.

These upheavals, moved by religious, political, and economic motives, were affected by the external pressures on Africa. They fed into the ongoing processes of the external slave trade and the development of slavery within African societies. Large numbers of captives resulting from the wars were exported down to the coast for sale to the Europeans, while another stream of slaves crossed the Sahara to north Africa. In the western and central Sudan, the level of slave labor rose, especially in the larger towns and along the trade routes. Slave villages, supplying royal courts and merchant activities as well as a plantation system, developed to produce peanuts and other crops. Slave women spun cotton and wove cloth for sale, slave artisans worked in the towns, and slaves served the caravan traders, but most slaves did agricultural labor. By the late 19th century, regions of the savanna contained large slave populations—in some places as much as 30 to 50 percent of the whole population. From the Senegambia region of Futa Jallon, across the Niger and Senegal basins, and to the east of Lake Chad, slavery became a central feature of the Sudanic states and remained so through the 19th century.

## White Settlers and Africans in Southern Africa

**In southern Africa, a Dutch colony eventually brought Europeans into conflict with Africans, especially the southern Bantu-speaking peoples. One of these groups, the Zulu, created under Shaka a powerful chiefdom during the early 19th century in a process of expansion that affected the whole region.**

One area of Africa little affected by the slave trade in the early modern period was the southern end of the continent. As we saw in Chapter 13, this region was still occupied by non-Bantu hunting peoples, the San (Bushmen); by the Khoikhoi (Hottentots), who lived by hunting and sheep herding; and, after contact with the Bantu, by cattle-herding peoples. Peoples practicing farming and using iron tools were living south of the Limpopo River by the 3rd century C.E. Probably Bantu speakers, they spread southward and established their villages and cattle herds in the fertile lands along the eastern coast, where rainfall was favorable to their agricultural and pastoral way of life. The drier western regions toward the Kalahari Desert were left to the Khoikhoi and San. Mixed farming and pastoralism spread throughout the region in a complex process that involved migration, peaceful contacts, and warfare.

By the 16th century, Bantu-speaking peoples occupied much of the eastern regions of southern Africa. They practiced agriculture and herding; worked iron and copper into tools, weapons, and adornments; and traded with their neighbors. They spoke related languages such as Tswana and Sotho as well as the Nguni languages such as Zulu and Xhosa. Among the Sotho, villages might have contained as many as 200 people; the Nguni lived in hamlets made up of a few extended families. Men worked as artisans and herders; women did the farming and housework and sometimes organized their labor communally.

Politically, chiefdoms of various sizes—many of them small, but a few with as many as 50,000 inhabitants—characterized the southern Bantu peoples. Chiefs held power with the support of relatives and with the acceptance of the people, but there was great variation in chiefly authority. The Bantu-speaking peoples' pattern of political organization and the splitting off of junior lineages to form new villages created a process of expansion that led to competition for land and the absorption of newly conquered groups. This situation became intense at the end of the 18th century, either because of the pressures and competition for foreign trade through the Portuguese outposts on the east African coast or because of the growth of population among the southern Bantu. In any case, the result was farther expansion southward into the path of another people who had arrived in southern Africa.

In 1652 the Dutch East India Company established a colony at the Cape of Good Hope to serve as a provisioning post for ships sailing to Asia. Large farms developed on the fertile lands around this colony. The Cape Colony depended on slave labor brought from Indonesia and Asia for a while, but it soon enslaved local Africans as well. Expansion of the colony and its labor needs led to a series of wars with the San and Khoikhoi populations, who were pushed farther to the north and west. By the 1760s, the Dutch, or Boer, farmers had crossed the Orange River in search of new lands. They saw the fertile plains and hills as theirs, and they saw the Africans as intruders and a possible source of labor. Competition and warfare resulted. By about 1800 the Cape Colony had about 17,000 settlers (or Afrikaners, as they came to be called), 26,000 slaves, and 14,000 Khoikhoi.

As the Boers were pushing northward, the southern Bantu were extending their movement to the south. Matters were also complicated by European events when Great Britain seized the Cape Colony in 1795 and then took it under formal British control in 1815. While the British government helped the settlers to clear out Africans from potential farming lands, government attempts to limit the Boer settlements and their use of African labor were unsuccessful. Meanwhile, competition for farming and grazing land led to a series of wars between the settlers and the Bantu during the early 19th century.

Various government measures, the accelerating arrival of English-speaking immigrants, and the lure of better lands caused groups of Boers to move to the north. These *voortrekkers* moved into lands occupied by the southern Nguni, eventually creating a number of autonomous Boer states. After 1834, when Britain abolished slavery and imposed restrictions on landholding, groups of Boers staged their **Great Trek** far to the north to be free of government interference. This movement eventually brought them across the Orange River and into Natal on the more fertile east coast, which the Boers believed to be only sparsely inhabited by Africans. They did not realize or care that the lack of population resulted from a great military upheaval taking place among the Bantu peoples of the region.

## The Mfecane and the Zulu Rise to Power

Among the Nguni peoples, major changes had taken place. A unification process had begun in some of the northern chiefdoms, and a new military organization had emerged. In 1818 leadership fell to Shaka, a brilliant military tactician, who reformed the loose forces into regiments organized by lineage and age. Iron discipline and new tactics were introduced, including the use of a short stabbing spear to be used at close range. The army was made a permanent institution, and the regiments were housed together in separate villages. The fighting men were allowed to marry only after they had completed their service.

Shaka's own Zulu chiefdom became the center of this new military and political organization, which began to absorb or destroy its neighbors (Figure 25.6). Shaka demonstrated talent as a politician, destroying the ruling families of the groups he incorporated into the growing Zulu state. He ruled with an iron hand, destroying his enemies, acquiring their cattle, and crushing any opposition. His policies brought power to the Zulu, but his erratic and cruel behavior also earned him enemies among his own people. Although he was assassinated in 1828, Shaka's reforms remained in place, and his successors built on the structure he had created. Zulu power was still growing in the 1840s, and the Zulu remained the most impressive military force in black Africa until the end of the century.

The rise of the Zulu and other Nguni chiefdoms was the beginning of the **mfecane,** or wars of crushing and wandering. As Zulu control expanded, a series of campaigns and forced migrations led to constant fighting as other peoples sought to survive by fleeing, emulating, or joining the Zulu. Groups spun off to the north and south, raiding the Portuguese on the coast, clashing with the Europeans to the south, and fighting with neighboring chiefdoms. New African states, such as the **Swazi,** that adapted aspects of the Zulu model emerged among the survivors. One state, **Lesotho,** successfully resisted the Zulu example. It combined Sotho and Nguni speakers and defended itself against Nguni armies. It eventually developed as a kingdom far less committed to military organization, one in which the people had a strong influence on their leaders.

The whole of the southern continent, from the Cape Colony to Lake Malawi, had been thrown into turmoil by raiding parties, remnants, and refugees.

FIGURE 25.6 This Zulu royal kraal, drawn in the 1830s, gives some idea of the power of the Zulu at the time that Shaka was forging Zulu dominance during the mfecane.

Superior firepower allowed the Boers to continue to hold their lands, but it was not until the Zulu Wars of the 1870s that Zulu power was crushed by Great Britain, and even then only at great cost. During that process, the basic patterns of conflict between Africans and Europeans in the largest settler colony on the continent were created. These patterns included competition between settlers and Africans for land, the expanding influence of European government control, and the desire of Europeans to use Africans as laborers.

## The African Diaspora

- **Despite African resistance to enslavement, the slave trade and the horrifying Middle Passage carried millions of Africans from their original homelands. In the Americas, especially in plantation colonies, they became a large segment of the population, and African cultures were adapted to new environments and conditions.**

The slave trade was the means by which the history of the Americas and Africa became linked and a principal way in which African societies were drawn into the world economy. The import into Africa of European firearms, Indian textiles, Indonesian cowrie shells, and American tobacco in return for African ivory, gold, and especially slaves demonstrated Africa's integration into the mercantile structure of the world. Africans involved in the trade learned to deal effectively with this situation. Prices of slaves rose steadily in the 18th century, and the terms of trade increasingly favored the African dealers. In many African ports, such as Whydah, Porto Novo, and Luanda, African or Afro-European communities developed that specialized in the slave trade and used this position to advantage.

### Slave Lives

For the slaves themselves, slavery meant the destruction of their villages or their capture in war, separation from friends and family, and then the forced march to an interior trading town or to the slave pens at the coast. Conditions were deadly; perhaps as many as one-third of the captives died along the way or in the slave pens. Eventually the slaves were loaded onto the ships. Cargo sizes varied and could go as high as 700 slaves crowded into the dank, unsanitary conditions of the slave ships, but most cargoes were smaller. Overcrowding was less of a factor in mortality than the length of the voyage or the point of origin in Africa; the Bights of Benin and Biafra were particularly dangerous. The average mortality rate for slaves varied over time, but it ran at about 18 percent or so until the 18th century, when it declined somewhat. Still, losses could be catastrophic on individual ships, as on a Dutch ship in 1737, where 700 of the 716 slaves died on the voyage.

The **Middle Passage,** or slave voyage to the Americas, was traumatic. Taken from their homes, branded, confined, and shackled, the Africans faced not only the dangers of poor hygiene, dysentery, disease, and bad treatment but also the fear of being beaten or worse by the Europeans. Their situation sometimes led to suicide or resistance and mutiny on the ships. However traumatic, the Middle Passage certainly did not strip Africans of their culture, and they arrived in the Americas retaining their languages, beliefs, artistic traditions, and memories of their past.

Diagram of Slave Ship Filled for Middle Passage

## Africans in the Americas

The slaves carried across the Atlantic were brought mainly to the plantations and mines of the Americas. Landed estates using large amounts of labor, often coerced, became characteristic of American agriculture, at first in sugar production and later for rice, cotton, and tobacco. The plantation system already used for producing sugar on the Atlantic islands of Spain and Portugal was transferred to the New World. After attempts to use Native American laborers in places such as Brazil and Hispaniola, Africans were brought in. West Africans, coming from societies in which herding, metallurgy, and intensive agriculture were widely practiced, were sought by Europeans for the specialized tasks of making sugar. In the English colonies of Barbados and Virginia, indentured servants from England eventually were replaced by enslaved Africans when new crops, such as sugar, were introduced or when indentured servants became less available.

In any case, the plantation system of farming with a dependent or enslaved workforce characterized the production of many tropical and semitropical crops in demand in Europe, and thus the plantation became the locus of African and American life. But slaves did many other things as well, from mining to urban occupations as artisans, street vendors, and household servants. In short, there was almost no occupation that slaves did not perform, although most were agricultural laborers (Figure 25.7).

**FIGURE 25.7** Africans performed all kinds of labor in the Americas, from domestic service to mining and shipbuilding. Most worked on plantations like this sugar mill in the Caribbean.

DOCUMENT

## An African's Description of the Middle Passage

During the era of the slave trade, enslaved Africans by one means or another succeeded in telling their stories. These accounts, with their specific details of the injustice and inhumanities of slavery, became particularly useful in the abolitionist crusade. The autobiography of Frederick Douglass is perhaps the most famous of these accounts. The biography of Olaudah Equiano, an Ibo from what is today eastern Nigeria on the Niger River, presents a personal description of enslavement in Africa and the terrors of the Middle Passage. Equiano and his sister were kidnapped in 1756 by African slave hunters and sold to British slave traders. Separated from his sister, Equiano was carried to the West Indies and later to Virginia, where he became servant to a naval officer. He traveled widely on his master's military campaigns and was later sold to a Philadelphia Quaker merchant, who eventually allowed him to buy his freedom. Later, he moved to England and became an active member in the movement to end slavery and the slave trade. His biography was published in 1789. The political uses of this kind of biography and Equiano's association with the abolitionists should caution us against accepting the account at face value, but it does convey the personal shock and anguish of those caught in the slave trade.

> The first object which saluted my eyes when I arrived on the coast was the sea, and a slaveship, which was riding at anchor, and waiting for its cargo. These filled me with astonishment, which was soon converted into terror, which I am yet at a loss to describe, nor the then feelings of my mind. When I was carried on board I was immediately handled, and tossed up, to see if I were sound, by some of the crew; and I was now persuaded that I had got into a world of bad spirits, and that they were going to kill me. Their complexions too differing so much from ours, their long hair, and the language they spoke, which was very different from any I had ever heard, united to confirm me in this belief. Indeed, such were the horrors of my views and fears at that moment, that if ten thousand worlds had been my own, I would have freely parted with them all to have exchanged my condition with that of the meanest slave in my own country. When I looked round the ship too, and saw a large furnace or copper boiler, and a multitude of black people of every description chained together, every one of their countenances expressing dejection and sorrow, quite overpowered with horror and anguish, I fell motionless on the deck and fainted. When I recovered a little, I found some black people about me, who I believed were some of those who brought me on board, and had been receiving their pay; they talked to me in order to cheer me, but all in vain. I asked them if we were not to be eaten by those white men with horrible looks, red faces, and long hair. They told me I was not. . . . I now saw myself deprived of all chance of returning to my native country, or even the least glimpse of hope of gaining the shore, which I now considered as friendly; and I even wished for my former slavery, in preference to my present situation, which was filled with horrors of every kind, still heightened by my ignorance of what I was to undergo. I

### American Slave Societies

Each American slave-based society reflected the variations of its European origin and its component African cultures, but there were certain similarities and common features. Each recognized distinctions between African-born **saltwater slaves,** who were almost invariably black (by European standards) and their American-born descendants, the **Creole slaves,** some of whom were mulattos as a result of the sexual exploitation of slave women or other forms of miscegenation. In all American slave societies, a hierarchy of status evolved in which free whites were at the top, slaves were at the bottom, and free people of color had an intermediate position. In this sense, color and "race" played a role in American slavery it had not played in Africa. Among the slaves, slaveholders also created a hierarchy based on origin and color. Creole and especially mulatto slaves were given more opportunities to acquire skilled jobs or to work as house servants rather than in the fields or mines. They were also more likely to win their freedom by manumission, the voluntary freeing of slaves.

This hierarchy was a creation of the slaveholders and did not necessarily reflect perceptions among the slaves. There is evidence that important African nobles or religious leaders, who for one reason or another were sold into slavery, continued to exercise authority within the slave community. Still, the distinctions between Creole and African slaves tended to divide that community, as did the distinctions between different African groups whose members maintained their ties and affiliations in America. Many of the slave rebellions in the Caribbean and Brazil were organized along African ethnic and political lines. In Jamaica there were several Akan-led rebellions in the 18th century, and the was not long suffered to indulge my grief; I was soon put down under decks, and there I received such a salutation in my nostrils as I had never experienced in my life; so that with the loathsomeness of the stench, and the crying together, I became so sick and low that I was not able to eat, nor had I the least desire to taste anything. I now wished for the last friend, death, to relieve me; but soon, to my grief two white men offered me eatables; and on my refusing to eat, one of them held me fast by the hands, and laid me across, I think, the windlass, and tied my feet while the other flogged me severely. I had never experienced anything of this kind before; and, although not being used to the water, I naturally feared that element the first time I saw it; yet, nevertheless, could I have got over the nettings, I would have jumped over the side; but I could not; and, besides the crew used to watch us very closely who were not chained down to the decks, lest we should leap into the water; and I have seen some of these poor African prisoners most severely cut for attempting to do so, and hourly whipped for not eating. This indeed was often the case with myself. In a little time after amongst the poor chained men, I found some of my own nation, which in a small degree gave ease to my mind. I inquired of them what was to be done with us? They gave me to understand we were to be carried to these white people's country to work for them. I then was a little revived, and thought, if it were no worse than working, my situation was not so desperate; but still I feared I should be put to death, the white people looked and acted, as I thought, in so savage a manner; for I had never seen among any people such instances of brutal cruelty; and this was not only shown to us blacks, but also to some of the whites themselves. . . .

At last when the ship we were in had got in all her cargo, they made ready with many fearful noises, and we were all put under deck, so that we could not see how they managed the vessel. But this disappointment was the least of my sorrow. The stench of the hold while we were on the coast was so intolerably loathsome, that it was dangerous to remain there for any time, and some of us had been permitted to stay on deck for the fresh air; but now the whole ship's cargo was confined together, it became absolutely pestilential. The closeness of the place, and the heat of the climate, added to the number in the ship, which was so crowded that each had scarcely room to turn himself, almost suffocated us. This produced copious perspirations, so that the air soon became unfit for respiration, from a variety of loathsome smells, and brought on a sickness amongst the slaves, of which many died, thus falling victims to the improvident avarice, as I may call it, of their purchasers. This wretched situation was again aggravated by the galling of the chains, now become insupportable; and the filth of the necessary tubs, into which the children fell, and were almost suffocated. The shrieks of the women, and the groans of the dying, rendered the whole a scene of horror almost inconceivable.

**Questions** In what ways does Equiano's description contradict a previous understanding of the slave trade? What opportunities existed for the captives to resist? What effect might the experience of Africans on the slave ships have had on their perceptions of each other and of the Europeans?

largest escaped slave community in 17th-century Brazil apparently was organized and led by Angolans.

Although economic factors imposed similarities, the slave-based societies also varied in their composition. In early 17th-century Lima, Peru, the capital of Spain's colony in South America, blacks outnumbered Europeans. In the 18th century, on the Caribbean islands where the indigenous population had died out or had been exterminated and where few Europeans settled, Africans and their descendants formed the vast majority. In Jamaica and St. Domingue, slaves made up more than 80 percent of the population; a large proportion of them were African born. Brazil also had large numbers of imported Africans, but its more diverse population and economy, as well as a tradition of manumitting slaves and high levels of miscegenation, meant that slaves made up only about 35 percent of the population. However, free people of color, the descendants of former slaves, made up about another one-third, so that together slaves and free colored people made up two-thirds of the total population.

North American cities such as Charleston and New Orleans also developed a large slave and free African population. But the southern colonies of British North America differed significantly from the Caribbean and Brazil, by depending less on imported Africans because of natural population growth among the slaves. In North America, Creole slaves predominated, but manumission was less common, and free people of color made up less than 10 percent of the total Afro-American population. The result was that slavery in North America was less influenced by Africa. By the mid-18th century, the slave population in most places in North America was reproducing itself. By 1850, fewer than 1 percent of the slaves there were African born. The combination of natural growth and the small direct trade from Africa reduced the degree of African cultural reinforcement.

## The People and Gods in Exile

Africans brought as slaves to the Americas faced a peculiar series of problems. Working conditions were exhausting, and life for most slaves often was difficult and short. Family formation was made difficult because of the general shortage of female slaves; the ratio of men to women was as much as three to one in some places. To this was added the insecurity of slave status: family members might be separated by sale or by a master's whim. Still, most slaves lived in family units, even though their marriages were not always sanctioned by the religion of their masters. Throughout the Americas, wherever Africans were brought, aspects of their language, religion, artistic sensibilities, and other cultural elements survived. To some extent, the amount of continuity depended on the intensity and volume of the slave trade from a particular area. Some slaveholders tried to mix up the slaves on their plantations so that strong African identities would be lost, but colonial dependence on slavers who consistently dealt with the same region tended to undercut such policies. In the Americas, African slaves had to adapt and to incorporate other African peoples' ideas and customs into their own lives. Moreover, the ways and customs of the masters were also imposed. Thus, what emerged as Afro-American culture reflected specific African roots adapted to a new reality. Afro-American culture was dynamic and creative in this sense.

Religion was an obvious example of continuity and adaptation. Slaves were converted to Catholicism by the Spaniards and the Portuguese, and they showed fervent devotion as members of Black Catholic brotherhoods, some of which were organized by African origins. In North America and the British Caribbean they joined Protestant denominations. Still, African religious ideas and practices did not die out. In the English islands, **obeah** was the name given to the African religious practices, and the men and women knowledgeable in them were held in high regard within the community. In the practices of Brazilian **candomble** (Yoruba) and Haitian **vodun** (Aja), fully developed versions of African religions flourished and continue today, despite attempts to suppress them.

The reality of the Middle Passage meant that religious ideas were easier to transfer than the institutional aspects of religion. Without religious specialists or a priestly class, aspects of African religions were changed by contact with other African peoples as well as with colonial society. In many cases, slaves held their new faith in Christianity and their African beliefs at the same time, and tried to fuse the two. For Muslim Africans this was more difficult. In 1835 in Bahia, the largest slave rebellion in Brazil was organized by Muslim Yoruba and Hausa slaves and directed against the whites and against nonbelievers.

Resistance and rebellion were other aspects of African American history. Recalcitrance, running away, and direct confrontation were present wherever slaves were held. As early as 1508, African runaways disrupted communications on Hispaniola, and in 1527, a plot to rebel was uncovered in Mexico City. Throughout the Americas, communities of runaway slaves formed. In Jamaica, Colombia, Venezuela, Haiti, and Brazil, runaway communities were persistent. In Brazil during the 17th century, **Palmares,** an enormous runaway slave kingdom with many villages and a population of perhaps 8000 to 10,000 people, resisted Portuguese and Dutch attempts to destroy it for a century. In Jamaica the runaway Maroons were able to gain some independence and a recognition of their freedom. So-called ethnic slave rebellions organized by a particular African group were common in the Caribbean and Brazil in the 18th century. In North America, where reinforcement from the slave trade was less important, resistance was also important, but it was based less on African origins or ethnicities.

Slave Revolt in Saint Domingue, 1791

Perhaps the most remarkable story of African American resistance is found in the forests of **Suriname,** a former Dutch plantation colony. There, large numbers of slaves ran off in the 18th century and mounted an almost perpetual war in the rain forest against the various expeditions sent to hunt them down. Those captured were brutally executed, but eventually a truce developed. Today about 50,000 Maroon descendants still live in Suriname and French Guiana. The Suriname Maroons maintained many aspects of their west African background in terms of language, kinship relations, and religious beliefs, but these were fused with new forms drawn from European and American Indian contacts resulting from their New World experience. From this fusion based on their own creativity, a truly Afro-American culture was created (Figure 25.8).

## The End of the Slave Trade and the Abolition of Slavery

The end of the Atlantic slave trade and the abolition of slavery in the Atlantic world resulted from economic, political, and religious changes in Europe and its overseas American colonies and former colonies. These changes, which were manifestations of the Enlightenment, the age of revolution, Christian revivalism, and perhaps the Industrial Revolution, were external to

FIGURE 25.8 African, American, or both? In Suriname, descendants of escaped slaves maintain many aspects of African culture but have adapted, modified, and transformed them in various ways. This wooden door shows the imaginative skills of African American carvers.

Africa, but once again they determined the pace and nature of change within Africa.

Like much else about the history of slavery, there is disagreement about the end of the slave trade. It is true that some African societies began to export other commodities, such as peanuts, cotton, and palm oil, which made their dependence on the slave trade less important, but the supply of slaves to European merchants was not greatly affected by this development. In general, the British plantation economies were booming in the period from 1790 to 1830, and plantations in Cuba, Brazil, and the southern United States flourished in the decades that followed. Thus, it is difficult to find a direct and simple link between economic self-interest and the movement to suppress the slave trade.

Opponents of slavery and the brutality of the trade had appeared in the mid-18th century, in relation to new intellectual movements in the West. Philosopher Jean-Jacques Rousseau in France and political economist Adam Smith in England both wrote against it. Whereas in ancient Rome during the spread of Christianity and Islam, and in 16th-century Europe, the enslavement of "barbarians" or nonbelievers was seen as positive—a way to civilize others—slavery during the European Enlightenment and bourgeois revolution came to be seen as backward and immoral. The slave trade was particularly criticized. It was the symbol of slavery's inhumanity and cruelty.

An African Pamphleteer Attacks Slavery (1787)

England, as the major maritime power of the period, was the key to the end of the slave trade. Under the leadership of religious humanitarians, such as John Wesley and **William Wilberforce,** an abolitionist movement gained strength against the merchants and the West Indies interests. After much parliamentary debate, the British slave trade was abolished in 1807. Having set out on this course, Britain tried to impose abolition of the slave trade on other countries throughout the Atlantic. Spain and Portugal were pressured to gradually suppress the trade, and the British navy was used to enforce these agreements by capturing illegal slave ships. By the 19th century, the moral and intellectual justifications that had supported the age of the slave trade had worn thin and the movement to abolish slavery was growing in the Atlantic world. The full end of slavery in the Americas did not occur until 1888, when it was abolished in Brazil.

## GLOBAL CONNECTIONS

## Africa and the African Diaspora in World Context

Africa was drawn into the world economy in the era of the slave trade, at first slowly, but with increasing intensity after 1750. Its incorporation produced differing effects on African societies, reinforcing authority in some places, creating new states in others, and sometimes provoking social, religious, and political reactions. Although many aspects of African life followed traditional patterns, contact with the world economy forced many African societies to adjust in ways that often placed them at a disadvantage and facilitated Europe's colonization of Africa in the 19th century. Well into the 20th century, as forced labor continued in Africa under European direction, the legacy of the slave trade era proved slow to die.

Part of that legacy was the movement of millions of Africans far from their continent. Taken against their will, they and their descendants drew on the cultures and practices of Africa as they coped with slavery. Eventually, they created vibrant new cultural forms, which along with their labor and skills contributed to the growth of new societies.

## Further Readings

Aside from the general books on Africa already mentioned in the Further Readings for previous chapters, some specific readings are particularly useful. Martin Hall, *The Changing Past: Farmers, Kings, and Traders in Southern Africa* (1987), discusses the use of archeological evidence in African history. D. Birmingham and Phyllis Martin, eds., *History of Central Africa*, 2 vols. (1983), presents extended essays on a number of regions. On west Africa in the age of the slave trade, a good introduction is J. F. A. Ajayi and Michael Crowder, eds., *History of West Africa*, 2 vols. (1975), especially volume 2. On southern Africa, Leonard Thompson's *A History of South Africa* (1990) presents a broad survey, and J. D. Omer-Cooper's *The Zulu Aftermath* (1969) is a classic account.

There are many histories of the slave trade, but Herbert S. Klein, *The Atlantic Slave Trade* (1999), provides an up-to-date and intelligent overview. A large general history is Hugh Thomas, *The Slave Trade* (1997). On the quantitative aspects of the slave trade, Philip Curtin, *The Atlantic Slave Trade: A Census* (1969), is the proper starting point, while David Eltis, *The Rise of African Slavery in the Americas* (2000), is an important newer study. All new quantitative studies will depend on the CD-ROM edited by David Eltis et al. entitled *The Atlantic Slave Trade* (1998). Roger Anstey, *The Atlantic Slave Trade and British Abolition* (1975), deals with the economic and religious aspects of the end of the slave trade.

On Africa, Paul Lovejoy's *Transformations in Slavery: A History of Slavery in Africa* (1983) and Patrick Manning's *Slavery and African Life* (1990) provide comprehensive overviews. J. E. Inikori, *Forced Migration: The Impact of the Export Slave Trade on African Societies* (1982), brings together essays by leading scholars. Robert Harms, *The Diligent: Voyage Through the Worlds of the Slave Trade* (2002), uses one voyage to examine the whole system of the Atlantic slave trade. Joseph Miller, *Way of Death* (1989), is a detailed study of the effects of the slave trade on Angola and a fine example of an in-depth study of one region.

John K. Thornton, *Africa and Africans in the Making of the Atlantic World* (1994), is an excellent argument for the centrality of slavery in Africa. Walter Rodney's essay "Africa in Europe and the Americas," in *Cambridge History of Africa*, vol. 4, 578–622, is a succinct overview of the African diaspora. In a similar vein with a cultural emphasis is Michael Gomez, *Reversing Sail: A History of the African Diaspora* (2005). Herbert Klein, *African Slavery in Latin America and the Caribbean* (1987), is a useful survey. S. Schwartz, *Tropical Babylons* (2004), examines the early association of plantations and slavery. Excellent overviews based on the best secondary literature are Robin Blackburn's *The Making of New World Slavery* (1997) and his *The Overthrow of Colonial Slavery* (1988).

On the general theoretical issues of slavery, Orlando Patterson, *Slavery and Social Death* (1982), is a broad comparative sociological study. David B. Davis, *Slavery and Human Progress* (1984), takes a historical approach to many of the same questions and then places the abolitionist movement in context. Some of the best recent scholarship is collected in G. Heuman and J. Walvin, eds., *The Slavery Reader* (2003)

## On the Web

The starting point for Web-based examination of the African slave trade is http://www.antislavery.org/, while best Web resources for the study of the Atlantic slave trade are http://www.bbc.co.uk/worldservice/africa/features/storyofafrica/9chapter4.shtml and http://hitchcock.itc.virginia.edu/Slavery/, which contains vivid images of the trade from capture to plantation settlements. For the Arab slave trade in Africa and African slavery in the Middle East, see http://www.bbc.co.uk/worldservice/africa/features/storyofafrica/9chapter6.shtml and http://www.fordham.edu/halsall/med/lewis1.html. The east African slave trade is closely examined at http://www.geocities.com/CollegePark/Classroom/9912/easterntrade.html and http://worldhistoryconnected.press.uiuc.edu/1.1/gilbert.html.

Though their present histories elide it, the states of Ashante (http://www.uiowa.edu/~africart/toc/people/Asante.html), Dahomey (http://www.zum.de/whkmla/region/westafrica/dahomeykgd.html), Oyo (http://www.ijebu.org/oyo/), Sokoto (http://www.dawodu.com/paden1.htm and http://countrystudies.us/nigeria/9.htm), and Kongo (http://www.uiowa.edu/~africart/toc/people/Kongo.html) were closely linked to the Atlantic slave trade, while Mozambique and Kilwa (http://www.kilwa.net/Kilwa_English/Kilwa_Area/kilwa_area.html and http://www.utalii.com/Off_the_normal_path/kilwa.htm) were centers of the east African slave trade. Africans who encountered European settlers in southern Africa (http://www.geocities.com/Athens/Styx/6497/SouthAfrica.html and http://www.historyworld.net/wrldhis/PlainTextHistories.asp?historyid=ad33) fared little better, though the Zulu Empire (http://www.urscene.com/Black_History_Pages/Shaka_Zulu.html), with innovative leadership provided by Shaka (http://www.carpenoctem.tv/military/shaka.html), had an imperial thrust of its own (called by its victims the mfecane, or troubles), and more than held its own for a time.

A biography of Ibo slave Olaudah Equiano and links to the text of his narrative of the slave life can be found at http://www.brycchancarey.com/equiano/ and http://docsouth.unc.edu/neh/equiano1/menu.html. Quobna Ottoba Cugoano, a former African slave living in Great

Britain, published a critique of slavery in 1787, extracts from which can be found at http://www.brycchancarey.com/cugoano/extract1.htm. Narratives of the lives of African slaves in the United States are collected at http://xroads.virginia.edu/~hyper/wpa/wpahome.html. Links to similar sources are offered at http://www.wested.org/basrc/bandl/library/slavery/slavery.html. Principal slave revolts in the United States are identified at http://www.historyguy.com/slave_rebellions_usa.htm.

The lives of early British abolitionists are explored at http://www.brycchancarey.com/abolition/index.htm. The controversies over the impact of the replacement of the slave trade by Europeans in Africa with so-called legitimate trade (in other words, whatever its intent, it served to mask or justify great European penetration) are explored in Robin Law, "The Transition from the Slave Trade to 'Legitimate' Commerce" in *Studies in the World History of Slavery, Abolition and Emancipation,* Volume I, number 1 (1996), available at http://www.h-net.msu.edu/~slavery/essays//esy9601law.html.

For the persistence of slavery in Africa today, see http://www.africaonline.com/site/Articles/1,3,48750.jsp, http://www.pbs.org/wonders/Episodes/Epi5/5_retel3.htm, http://www.zum.de/whkmla/region/eastafrica/tangpre1815.html, http://www.international.ucla.edu/article.asp?parentid=4416, http://news.bbc.co.uk/hi/english/world/africa/newsid_313000/313365.htm, http://www.cc.jyu.fi/~aphamala/pe/issue2/sudan.htm, http://www.worldtrek.org/odyssey/teachers/malilessons.html, http://www.humanities.ualberta.ca/History111/from_henry_gates.htm, and http://www.thewhitefathers.org.uk/304ati.html.

CHAPTER 26

# The Muslim Empires



Babur (known to his troops as "The Tiger") was the first Mughal emperor of India. Claiming descent on his mother's side from Chinggis Khan and on his father's side from the ruthless Turkish conqueror Timur, he was himself a skilled warrior and a cultured man who was known for his high spirits and love of beauty. But in April 1526, as the 44-year-old Babur led his armies into India, his future looked bleak. Though battle-hardened, his soldiers were far from their base of support and they were headed into combat with a force that outnumbered them 10 to 1. For nearly a century the Lodis had ruled an empire that stretched across north India. Babur, in contrast, had repeatedly been defeated in his attempts to win back Ferghana, the kingdom he had inherited and lost, and been driven from his ancestral home in the fabled city of Samarkand (see Map 26.4). Although in the years before his foray into India he had been able to build a small kingdom centered around Kabul in present-day Afghanistan, Babur had had little success in his attempts to recoup his earlier losses, and his plans for the conquest of Persia to the west had been foiled by the rise of the powerful Safavid dynasty in the early 1500s.

Babur decided to meet the enemy just north of the Lodi capital at Delhi, from which a succession of Muslim dynasties had dominated north India since the early 13th century. He ordered his troops to use leather strips to lash together the matchlock cannon that were positioned at the center of his army. Arrayed against them, under the command of the Lodi sultan, Ibrahim, were more than a thousand war elephants that would lead the charge to crush Babur's unimposing band of warriors. When the battle was joined at mid-morning on April 21, the roar and fire of the cannon panicked the surging elephants and they fled, trampling the Lodi soldiers marching into battle behind them. Making good use of his superior firepower—the enemy apparently had few cannons or muskets—Babur routed the massive army and went on to capture Delhi.

Babur's warriors were buoyed by their victory and the treasure seized in the capital. In the battles that followed against a Hindu alliance and an army raised by Ibrahim's brother, they effectively deployed the batteries of cannon they had arduously transported from Kabul. By the end of 1530, the Tiger was master of northern India and the founder of a new dynasty, the Mughal, that would rule varying portions of the subcontinent for nearly 300 years.

**FIGURE 26.1** Babur superintending the planting of gardens in India. The rulers of each of the three great Muslim empires of the early modern era were lavish patrons of the arts and splendid architecture.

| 1250 C.E. | 1400 C.E. | 1500 C.E. | 1525 C.E. | 1550 C.E. | 1650 C.E. | 1700 C.E. |
|---|---|---|---|---|---|---|
| **1243** Mongol invasion of Asia Minor<br>**1281** Founding of Ottoman dynasty<br>**1334** Death of first Safavid Sufi master at Ardabil<br>**1350s** Ottoman invasion of Europe; conquest of much of the Balkans and Hungary | **1402** Timur's invasion; Ottoman setbacks under Bayazid<br>**c. 1450s** Shi'a influences enter Safavid teachings<br>**c. 1450s** Beginning of large-scale recruitment of Janissary troops<br>**1453** Ottoman capture of Constantinople | **1501–1510** Safavid conquest of Persia (present-day Iran)<br>**1507** Portuguese victory over Ottoman-Arab fleet at Diu in Indian Ocean<br>**1514** Ottoman victory over Safavids at Chaldiran<br>**1517** Ottoman capture of Syria and Egypt<br>**1520–1566** Rule of Suleyman the Magnificent; construction of Suleymaniye mosque in Constantinople | **1526** Battle of Panipat; Babur's conquest of India<br>**1529** First Ottoman siege of Vienna<br>**1540** Babur's successor, Humayan, driven from India<br>**1540–1545** Humayan in exile at the Safavid court | **1556** Mughal Empire reestablished in north India<br>**1556–1605** Reign of Akbar<br>**1571** Battle of Lepanto<br>**1582** Akbar's proclamation of a new religion, designed to unite Hindus and Muslims<br>**1588–1629** Reign of Abbas I (the Great) in Persia | **1657–1658** Great war of succession between sons of Shah Jahan<br>**1658–1707** Reign of Aurangzeb<br>**1683** Last Ottoman siege of Vienna<br>**1680s** Rajput and peasant revolts in north India<br>**1699** Treaty of Carlowitz; Ottomans cede territories in Europe | **1722** First Turkish-language printing press<br>**1722** Fall of the Safavid dynasty<br>**1730** Ottoman armies are defeated by Persian forces under Nadir Khan (later Nadir Shah, emperor of Persia)<br>**1730s** First Western-modeled military schools established in Constantinople<br>**1736–1747** Reign of Nadir Shah<br>**1739** Nadir Shah invades India from Persia, sacks Mughal capital at Delhi |

Babur's rapid conquest of north India represents several key themes found in the rise of each of the three major Muslim dynasties whose empires stretched from the Mediterranean to the Bay of Bengal throughout the early modern phase of global history (see Map 26.1). Like the warrior leaders who founded the **Ottoman** and **Safavid** empires to the west, Babur and his followers were from Turkic-speaking nomadic groups in central Asia. In each case, the warrior leaders who founded these dynasties took advantage of the power vacuum left by the breakup of the Mongol empire and the devastation wrought by Timur's assaults on the Islamic heartlands of the Middle East and Muslim-ruled northern India. Babur's **Mughal Empire** was the last of the three to be established, and he drew on many of the precedents set by both the Ottomans and Safavids. Like them—and the military of all of the great Eurasian empires in the early modern era—his armies relied heavily on large cannons and, increasingly, on muskets. In many instances their adversaries lacked or were less skilled at deploying these weapons, which were transforming warfare across the globe. In fact, at the Battle of Khanua, Babur copied Turkish techniques in massing his muskets and cannon to defeat yet another much larger army, led by a great Hindu warrior.

The Middle East

In contrast to the founders of the Ottoman and Safavid dynasties, Babur and the four Mughal rulers who succeeded him did not launch their conquests out of religious fervor. Like the Mughal monarchs, once in power, most of the Ottoman and Safavid rulers showed great tolerance for the faiths of the non-Muslim peoples who became their subjects. But the same tolerance was often not shown to rival Muslim sects. The Sunni–Shi'a split, which, as we have seen, arose early in the history of Islamic civilization, fueled often violent rivalries between the Ottomans and the Safavids. And sectarian identities frequently intensified ethnic divisions found in each of the great Muslim empires and across much of the Islamic world. Wars between the empires and the constant need for rulers to be attentive to shifting alliances and military innovations introduced by rival dynasties within the far-flung Muslim community also go far toward explaining the inward-looking quality of much of Islamic society in this era. Whether they were emperor's advisors, scholars, merchants, or artisans, most Muslims had come to view the vast and diverse Islamic world as a self-sufficient entity that had much more to offer the rest of the world than it could ever hope to receive from societies outside the Islamic fold. As we shall see, in each of these civilizations there were visionaries who insisted that Muslims needed to pay a good deal more attention to

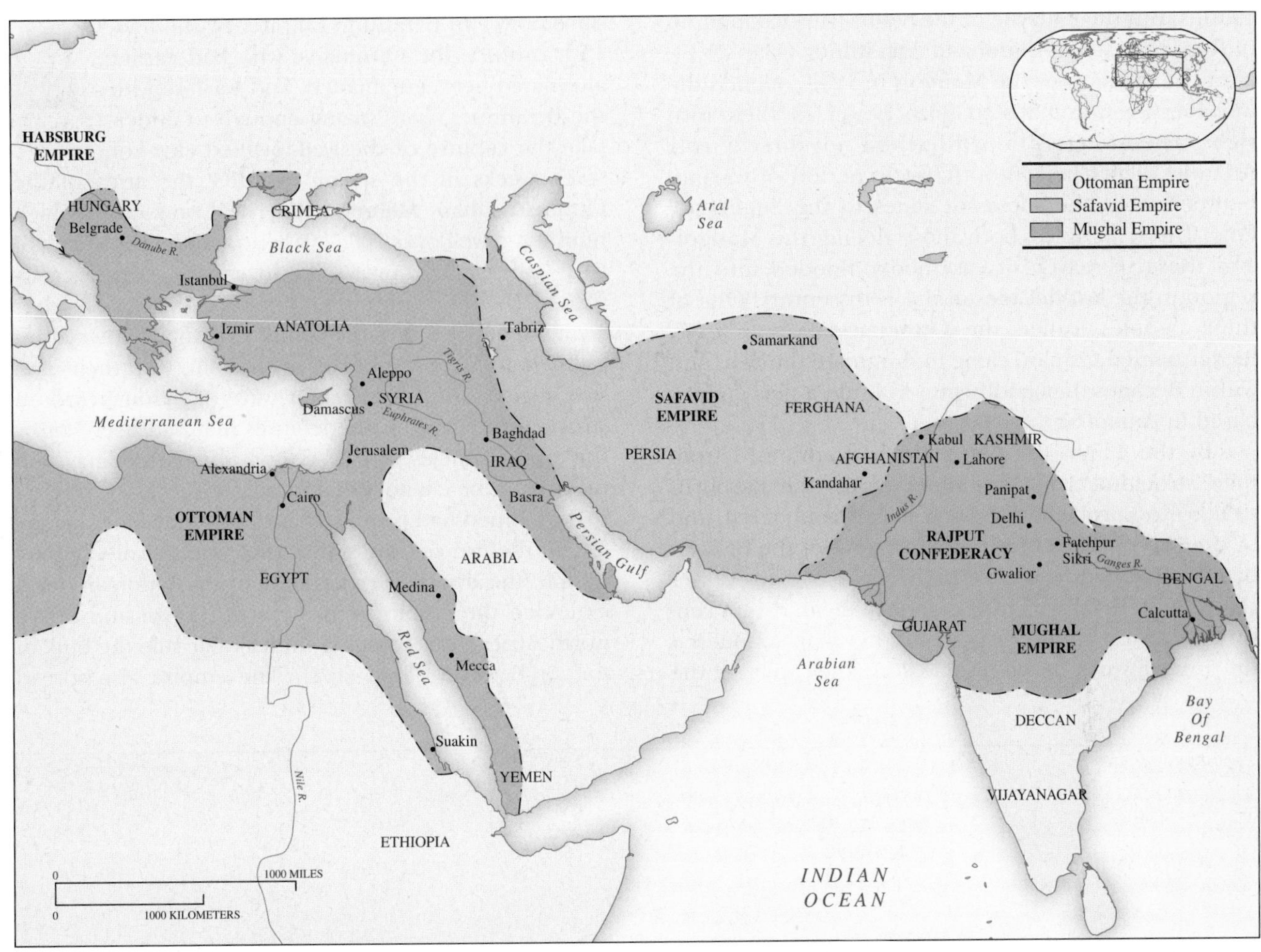


**MAP 26.1** The Ottoman, Safavid, and Mughal Empires

changes taking place in the West, and leaders who worked vigorously to counter the aggressive expansion of the Portuguese and other European nations in the Mediterranean and across the Indian Ocean.

Compared with the Abbasid era, new discoveries in the sciences dropped off during this period, but the transmission of Indian and Greco-Arab learning may have accelerated in the Muslim world. Far more impressive were the influences that the artists and architects from each of these Muslim empires exerted on each other. Contravening the Muslim prohibition of the depiction of human figures, miniature painting—typically of shahs and sultans, epic sagas, social scenes, and battles—reached a level of perfection seldom equaled. And especially between Persia and India, artists, techniques, and fashions in painting were shared extensively, although regional styles could be quite distinct. Though few of the monumental buildings commissioned by Babur in India remain, all were heavily influenced by Ottoman tastes and methods of construction. In each of these fields and in every instance of emulation, borrowing, and reworking, this cross-fertilization between disparate cultures and peoples built on a tradition of exchange that had been a hallmark of Islamic civilization from its beginnings.

## The Ottomans: From Frontier Warriors to Empire Builders

■ **In the 13th and 14th centuries, the Ottomans built an empire in the eastern Mediterranean that rivaled the Abbasid imperium at its height. Though the Ottomans patterned much of their empire on the ideas and institutions of earlier Muslim civilizations, in warfare, architecture, and engineering they carried Islamic civilization to new levels of attainment.**

For centuries before the rise of the Ottoman dynasty, Turkic-speaking peoples from central Asia played key roles in Islamic civilization as soldiers and administrators, often in the service of the Abbasid caliphs. But the collapse of the Seljuk Turkic kingdom of Rum in eastern Anatolia in Asia Minor (Map 26.2), after the invasion by the Mongols in 1243, opened the way for the Ottomans to seize power in their own right. The Mongols raided but did not directly rule Anatolia, which fell into a chaotic period of warfare between would-be successor states to the Seljuk sultans. Turkic peoples, both those fleeing the Mongols and those in search of easy booty, flooded into the region in the last decades of the 13th century. One of these peoples, called the **Ottomans** after an early leader named Osman, came to dominate the rest, and within decades they had begun to build a new empire based in Anatolia.

By the 1350s, the Ottomans had advanced from their strongholds in Asia Minor across the Bosporus straits into Europe. Thrace was quickly conquered, and by the end of the century large portions of the Balkans had been added to their rapidly expanding territories (Map 26.2). In moving into Europe in the mid-14th century, the Ottomans had bypassed rather than conquered the great city of Constantinople, long the capital of the once powerful Byzantine Empire. By the mid-15th century, the Ottomans, who had earlier alternated between alliances and warfare with the Byzantines, were strong enough to undertake the capture of the well-fortified city. For seven weeks in the spring of 1453, the army of the Ottoman sultan, **Mehmed II,** "The Conqueror," which numbered well over 100,000, assaulted the triple ring of land walls that had protected the city for centuries (Figure 26.2). The outnumbered forces of the defenders repulsed attack after attack until the sultan ordered his gunners to batter a portion of the walls with their massive siege cannon. Wave after wave of Ottoman troops struck at the gaps in the defenses that had been cut by the guns, quickly overwhelmed the defenders, and raced into the city to loot and pillage for the three days that Mehmed had promised as their reward for victory.

Mehmed II

In the two centuries after the conquest of Constantinople, the armies of a succession of able Ottoman rulers extended the empire into Syria and Egypt and across north Africa, thus bringing under their rule the bulk of the Arab world (Map 26.2). The empire also spread

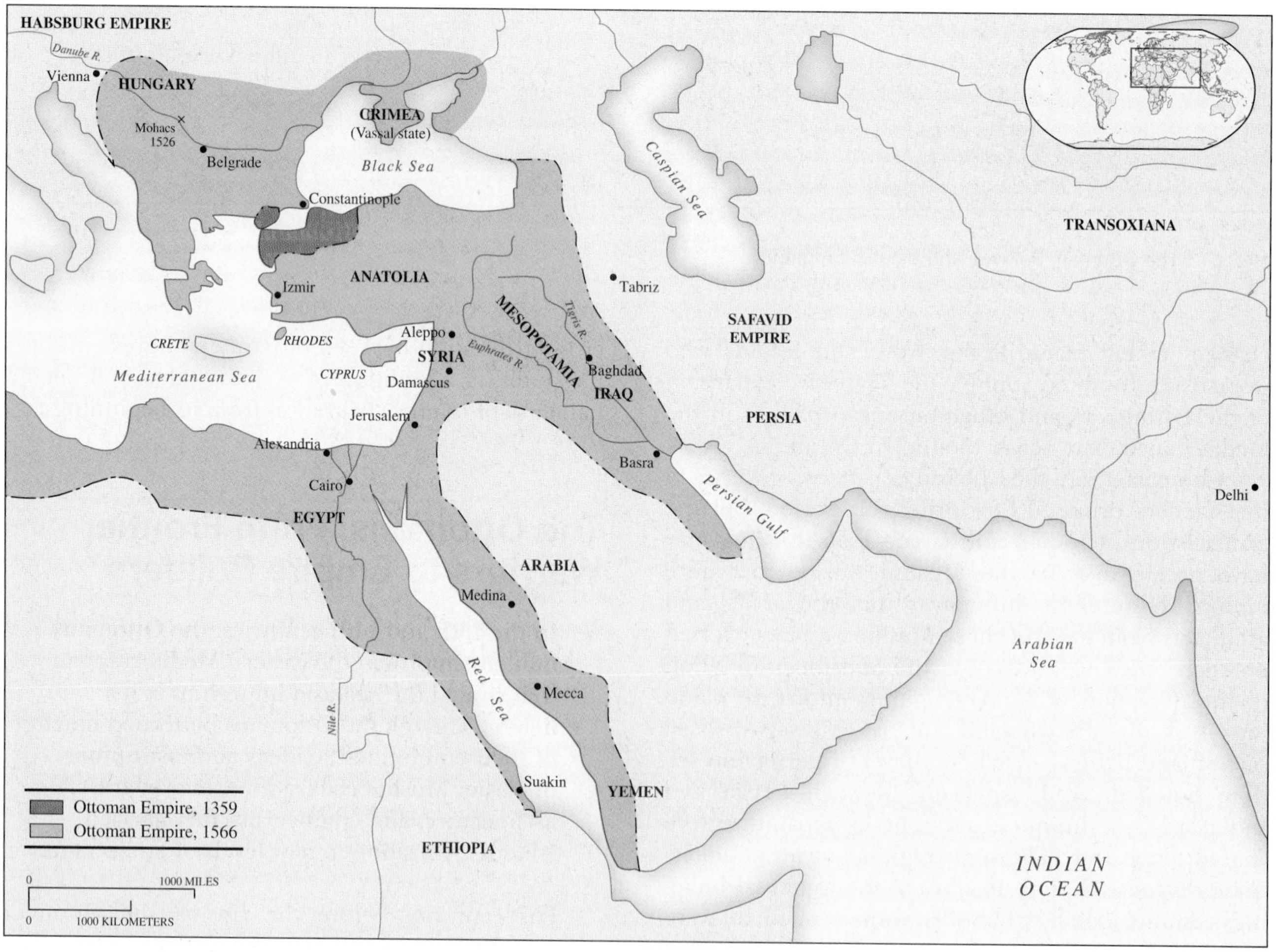

**MAP 26.2** The Expansion of the Ottoman Empire

FIGURE 26.2 An illuminated French manuscript from the 15th century shows the Ottoman siege of Constantinople in 1453. The Muslim capture of the great eastern bastion of Christian Europe aroused fears throughout the continent, resulting in demands for new Crusades to recapture the city. The advance of the Ottomans in the east also provided impetus to the overseas expansion of nations such as Spain and Portugal on the western coasts of Europe. Both of these Catholic maritime powers saw their efforts to build overseas empires as part of a larger campaign to outflank the Muslim powers and bring areas that they controlled into the Christian camp.

The Ottoman Empire

through the Balkans into Hungary in Europe and around the Black and Red seas. The Ottomans became a formidable naval power in the Mediterranean Sea. Powerful Ottoman galley fleets made possible the capture of major island bases on Rhodes, Crete, and Cyprus. The Ottoman armies also drove the Venetians and Genoese from much of the eastern Mediterranean and threatened southern Italy with invasion on several occasions. From their humble origins as frontier vassals, the Ottomans had risen to become the protectors of the Islamic heartlands and the scourge of Christian Europe. As late as 1683, Ottoman armies were able to lay siege to the capital of the Austrian Habsburg dynasty at Vienna. Even though the Ottoman Empire was in decline by this time, and the threat the assault posed to Vienna was far less serious than a previous attack in the early 16th century, the Ottomans remained a major force in European politics until the late 19th century.

## A State Geared to Warfare

Military leaders played a dominant role in the Ottoman state, and the economy of the empire was geared to warfare and expansion. The Turkic cavalry, chiefly responsible for the Ottomans' early conquests from the 13th to the 16th centuries, gradually developed into a warrior aristocracy. They were granted control over land and peasant producers in annexed areas for the support of their households and military retainers. From the 15th century onward, members of the warrior class also vied with religious leaders and administrators drawn from other social groups for control of the expanding Ottoman bureaucracy. As the power of the warrior aristocracy shrank at the center, they built up regional and local bases of support. These inevitably competed with the sultans and the central bureaucracy for revenue and labor control.

From the mid-15th century, the imperial armies were increasingly dominated by infantry divisions made up of troops called **Janissaries.** Most of the Janissaries had been forcibly conscripted as adolescent boys in conquered areas, such as the Balkans, where the majority of the population retained its Christian faith. Sometimes the boys' parents willingly turned their sons over to the Ottoman recruiters because of the opportunities for advancement that came with service to the Ottoman sultans. Though legally slaves, the youths were given fairly extensive schooling for the time and converted to Islam. Some of them went on to serve in the palace or bureaucracy, but most became Janissaries.

Because the Janissaries controlled the artillery and firearms that became increasingly vital to Ottoman success in warfare with Christian and Muslim adversaries, they rapidly became the most powerful component in the Ottoman military machine. Their growing importance was another factor contributing to the steady decline of the role of the aristocratic cavalry. Just like the mercenary forces that had earlier served the caliphs of Baghdad, the Janissaries eventually tried to translate military service into political influence. By the late 15th century they were deeply involved in court politics; by the mid-16th century they had the power to depose sultans and decide which one of a dying ruler's sons would mount the throne.

## The Sultans and Their Court

Nominally, the Ottoman rulers were absolute monarchs. But even the most powerful sultan maintained his position by playing factions in the warrior elite off each other and pitting the warriors as a whole against the Janissaries and other groups. Chief among the latter were the Islamic religious scholars and legal experts, who retained many of the administrative functions they had held under the Arab caliphs of earlier centuries. In addition to Muslim traders, commerce within the empire was in the hands of Christian and Jewish merchants, who as dhimmis, or "people of the book," were under the protection of the Ottoman rulers. Although they have often been depicted in Western writings as brutal and corrupt despots, some Ottoman sultans, especially in the early centuries of their sway, were very capable rulers. Ottoman conquest often meant effective administration and tax relief for the peoples of areas annexed to the empire.

Like the Abbasid caliphs, the Ottoman sultans grew more and more distant from their subjects as their empire increased in size and wealth. In their splendid marble palaces and pleasure gardens, surrounded by large numbers of slaves and the many wives and concubines of their harems, Ottoman rulers followed elaborate court rituals based on those of earlier Byzantine, Persian, and Arab dynasties. Day-to-day administration was carried out by a large bureaucracy headed by a grand **vizier** (*wazir* in Arabic). The vizier was the overall head of the imperial administration, and he often held more real power than the sultan. Early sultans took an active role in political decisions and often personally led their armies into battle.

Like earlier Muslim dynasties, however, the Ottomans suffered greatly because they inherited Islamic principles of political succession that remained vague and contested. The existence of many talented and experienced claimants to the throne meant constant danger of civil strife. The death of a sultan could, and increasingly did, lead to protracted warfare among his sons. Defeated claimants sometimes fled to the domains of Christian or Muslim rulers hostile to the Ottomans, thereby becoming rallying points for military campaigns against the son who had gained the throne.

## Constantinople Restored and the Flowering of Ottoman Culture

An empire that encompassed so many and such diverse cultures from Europe, Africa, and Asia naturally varied greatly from one province to the next in its social arrangements, artistic production, and physical appearance. But the Ottomans' ancient and cosmopolitan capital at Constantinople richly combined the disparate elements of their extensive territories. Like the Byzantine Empire as a whole, Constantinople had fallen on hard times in the centuries before the Ottoman conquest in 1453. Soon after Mehmed II's armies had captured and sacked the city, however, the Ottoman ruler set about restoring its ancient glory. He had the cathedral of Saint Sophia converted into one of the grandest mosques in the Islamic world, and new mosques and palaces were built throughout the city. This construction benefited greatly from architectural advances the Ottomans derived from the Byzantine heritage. Aqueducts were built from the surrounding hills to supply the growing population with water, markets were reopened, and the city's defenses were repaired.

Hagia Sophia

Each sultan who ruled in the centuries after Mehmed strove to be remembered for his efforts to beautify the capital. The most prominent additions were further mosques that represent some of the most sublime contributions of the Ottomans to Islamic and human civilization. The most spectacular of these was the Suleymaniye, pictured in Figure 26.3. As its name suggests, the mosque was built at the behest of the most successful of the sultans, Suleyman the Magnificent (r. 1520–1566). Although it smacks of hometown pride, the following description by a 17th-century Ottoman chronicler of the reaction of some Christian visitors to the mosque conveys a sense of the awe that the structure still evokes:

The Suleymaniye Mosque

> The humble writer of these lines once himself saw ten Frankish infidels skillful in geometry and architecture, who, when the door-keeper had changed their shoes for slippers, and had introduced them into the mosque for the purpose of showing it to them, laid their finger on their mouths, and each bit his finger from astonishment when they saw the minarets; but when they beheld the dome they tossed up their hats and cried Maria! Maria! and on observing the four arches which supported the dome . . . they could not find terms to express their admiration, and the ten . . . remained a full hour looking with astonishment on those arches. [One of them said] that nowhere was so much beauty, external and internal, to be found united, and that in the whole of Frangistan [Christian Europe] there was not a single edifice which could be compared to this.

In addition to the mosques, sultans and powerful administrators built mansions, rest houses, religious schools, and hospitals throughout the city. Both public and private gardens further beautified the capital, which Ottoman writers compared to paradise itself. The

FIGURE 26.3 Built in the reign of Suleyman I in the 1550s and designed by the famous architect Sinan, the Suleymaniye mosque is among the largest domed structures in the world, and it is one of the great engineering achievements of Islamic civilization. The pencil-thin minarets flanking the great central dome are characteristic of Ottoman architecture, which was quite distinct from its Safavid and Mughal counterparts.

city and its suburbs stretched along both sides of the Bosporus, the narrow strait between the Mediterranean and Black seas that separates Europe from Asia (Map 26.2). Its harbors and the Golden Horn, a triangular bay that formed the northern boundary of the city, were crowded with merchant ships from ports throughout the region. Constantinople's great bazaars were filled with merchants and travelers from throughout the empire and places as distant as England and Malaya. They offered all manner of produce, from the spices of the East Indies and the ivory of Africa to slaves and forest products from Russia and fine carpets from Persia. Coffeehouses—places where men gathered to smoke tobacco (introduced from America in the 17th century by English merchants), gossip, do business, and play chess—were found in all sections of the city. They were pivotal to the social life of the capital. The coffeehouses also played a major role in the cultural life of Constantinople as places where poets and scholars could congregate, read their latest works aloud, and debate about politics and the merits of each other's ideas.

Beneath the ruling classes, a sizeable portion of the population of Constantinople and other Ottoman cities belonged to the merchant and artisan classes. The Ottoman regime closely regulated commercial exchanges and handicraft production. Government inspectors were employed to ensure that standard weights and measures were used and to license the opening of new shops. They also regulated the entry of apprentice artisans into the trades and monitored the quality of the goods they produced. Like their counterparts in medieval European towns, the artisans were organized into guilds. Guild officers set craft standards, arbitrated disputes between their members, and provided financial assistance for needy members. They even arranged popular entertainments, often linked to religious festivals.

The early Ottomans had written in Persian, and Arabic remained an important language for works on law and religion throughout the empire's history. But by the 17th century, the Turkish language of the Ottoman court had become the preferred mode of expression for poets and historians as well as the language of the Ottoman bureaucracy. In writing as in the fine arts, the Ottomans' achievements have been somewhat overshadowed by those of their contemporary Persian and Indian rivals. Nonetheless, the authors, artists, and artisans of the Ottoman Empire left a considerable legacy, particularly in poetry, ceramics, carpet manufacturing, and above all in architecture.

## The Problem of Ottoman Decline

Much of the literature on the Ottoman Empire concentrates on its slow decline from the champion of the Muslim world and the great adversary of Christendom to the "sick man" of Europe in the 18th and 19th centuries. This approach provides a very skewed view of Ottoman history as a whole. Traced from its origins in the late 13th century, the Ottoman state is one of the great success stories in human political history. Vigorous and expansive until the late 17th century, the Ottomans were able to ward off the powerful enemies who surrounded their domains on all sides for nearly four centuries. The dynasty endured for more than 600 years, a feat matched by no other in all human history.

Venetian Observations on the Ottoman Empire

DOCUMENT

## An Islamic Traveler Laments the Muslims' Indifference to Europe

Although most of the travelers and explorers in this era were Europeans who went to Africa, Asia, and the Americas, a few people from these lands visited Europe. One of these, Abu Taleb, was a scholar of Turkish and Persian descent whose family had settled in India. At the end of the 18th century, Abu Taleb traveled in Europe for three years and later wrote an account in Persian of his experiences there. Although his was one of the few firsthand sources of information about Europe available to Muslim scholars and leaders, Abu Taleb was deeply disturbed by the lack of interest shown by other Muslims in his observations and discoveries.

When I reflect on the want of energy and the indolent dispositions of my countrymen, and the many erroneous customs which exist in all Mohammedan countries and among all ranks of Mussulmans, I am fearful that my exertions [in writing down his experiences in Europe] will be thrown away. The great and the rich intoxicated with pride and luxury, and puffed up with the vanity of their possessions, consider universal science as comprehended in the circle of their own scanty acquirements and limited knowledge; while the poor and common people, from the want of leisure, and overpowered by the difficulty of procuring a livelihood, have not time to attend to his personal concerns, much less to form desires for the acquirement of information of new discoveries and inventions, although such a person has been implanted by nature in every human breast, as an honour and an ornament to the species. I therefore despair of their reaping any fruit from my labours, being convinced that they will consider this book of no greater value than the volumes of tales and romances which they peruse merely to pass away their time, or are attracted thereto by the easiness of the style. It may consequently be concluded, that as they will find no pleasure in reading a work which contains a number of foreign names, treats on uncommon subjects, and alludes to other matters which cannot be understood at first glance, but require a little time for consideration, they will, under pretense of zeal for their religion, entirely abstain and refrain from perusing it.

**Questions** What reasons does Abu Taleb give for his fellow Muslims' indifference to his travel reports on Europe? What other factors can be added as a result of our study of long-standing Islamic attitudes toward Europe and conditions in the Ottoman Empire in this period? In what ways might the Muslims' neglect of events in Europe have hindered their efforts to cope with this expansive civilization in the centuries that followed? Were there Western counterparts to Abu Taleb in these centuries, and how were their accounts of distant lands received in Europe?

From one perspective, the long Ottoman decline, which officials and court historians actively discussed from the mid-17th century onward, reflects the great strength of the institutions on which the empire was built. Despite internal revolts and periodic conflicts with such powerful foreign rivals as the Russian, Austrian, Spanish, and Safavid empires, the Ottomans ruled into the 20th century. Yet the empire had reached the limits of its expansive power centuries earlier, and by the late 17th century the long retreat from Russia, Europe, and the Arab lands had begun. In a sense, some contraction was inevitable. Even when it was at the height of its power, the empire was too large to be maintained, given the resource base that the sultans had at their disposal and the primitive state of transport and communications in the preindustrial era.

The Decline of the Ottomans

The Ottoman state had been built on war and steady territorial expansion. As possibilities for new conquests ran out and lands began to be lost to the Ottomans' Christian and Muslim enemies, the means of maintaining the oversized bureaucracy and army shrank. The decline in the effectiveness of the administrative system that held the empire together was signaled by the rampant growth of corruption among Ottoman officials. The venality and incompetence of state bureaucrats prompted regional and local officials to retain more revenue for their own purposes. Poorly regulated by the central government, many local officials, who also controlled large landed estates, squeezed the peasants and the laborers who worked their lands for additional taxes and services. At times the oppressive demands of local officials and estate owners sparked rebellions. Peasant uprisings and flight resulted in the abandonment of cultivated lands and in social dislocations that further drained the resources of the empire.

From the 17th century onward, the forces that undermined the empire from below were compounded by growing problems at the center of imperial administration. The early practice of assigning the royal princes administrative or military positions, to prepare them to rule, died out. Instead, possible successors to the throne were kept like hostages in special sections of the palace, where they remained until one

FIGURE 26.4 The clash of the galley fleets at Lepanto was one of the greatest sea battles in history. But despite devastating losses, the Ottomans managed to replace most of their fleet and go back on the offensive against their Christian adversaries within a year. Here the epic encounter is pictured in one of the many paintings devoted to it in the decades that followed. The tightly packed battle formations that both sides adopted show the importance of ramming rather than cannon fire in naval combat in the Mediterranean in this era. This pattern was reversed in the Atlantic and the other oceanic zones into which the Europeans had been expanding since the 14th century.

of them ascended the throne. The other princes and potential rivals were also, in effect, imprisoned for life in the palace. Although it might have made the reigning sultan more secure, this solution to the problem of contested succession produced monarchs far less prepared to rule than those in the formative centuries of the dynasty. The great warrior-emperors of early Ottoman history gave way, with some important exceptions, to weak and indolent rulers, addicted to drink, drugs, and the pleasures of the harem. In many instances, the later sultans were little more than pawns in the power struggles of the viziers and other powerful officials with the leaders of the increasingly influential Janissary corps. Because the imperial apparatus had been geared to strong and absolute rulers, the decline in the caliber of Ottoman emperors had devastating effects on the empire as a whole. Civil strife increased, and the discipline and leadership of the armies on which the empire depended for survival deteriorated.

## Military Reverses and the Ottoman Retreat

Debilitating changes within the empire were occurring at a time when challenges from without were growing rapidly. The Ottomans had made very effective use of artillery and firearms in building their empire. But their reliance on huge siege guns, and the Janissaries' determination to block all military changes that might jeopardize the power they had gained within the state, caused the Ottomans to fall farther and farther behind their European rivals in the critical art of waging war. With the widespread introduction of light field artillery into the armies of the European powers in the 17th century, Ottoman losses on the battlefield multiplied rapidly, and the threat they posed for the West began to recede.

On the sea, the Ottomans were eclipsed as early as the 16th century. The end of their dominance was presaged by their defeat by a combined Spanish and Venetian fleet at Lepanto in 1571. The great battle is depicted in the painting in Figure 26.4. Although the Ottomans had completely rebuilt their war fleet within a year after Lepanto and soon launched an assault on north Africa that preserved that area for Islam, their control of the eastern Mediterranean had been lost. Even more ominously, in the decades before Lepanto, the Ottomans and the Muslim world had been outflanked by the Portuguese seafarers who sailed down and around the coast of Africa. The failure in the early 1500s of the Ottomans and their Muslim allies in the Indian Ocean to drive the Portuguese from Asian waters proved far more harmful in the long run than Ottoman defeats in the Mediterranean.

Portuguese naval victories in the Indian Ocean revealed the decline of the Ottoman galley fleets and Mediterranean-style warships more generally. The trading goods, particularly spices, that the Portuguese carried around Africa and back to Europe enriched the Ottomans' Christian rivals. In addition, the fact that a large portion of the flow of these products was no longer transmitted to European ports through Muslim trading centers in the eastern Mediterranean meant that merchants and tax collectors in the Ottoman Empire lost critical revenues. As if this were not enough, from the late 16th century on, large amounts of silver flowed into the Ottomans' lands from mines worked by Native American laborers in the Spanish empire in Peru and Mexico. This sudden influx of bullion into the rigid and slow-growing economy of the Ottoman Empire set off a long-term inflationary trend that further undermined the finances of the empire.

Several able sultans took measures to shore up the empire in the 17th century. The collapse of the Safavid dynasty in Persia and conflicts between the European powers at this time also gave the Ottomans hope that their earlier dominance might be restored. But their reprieve was temporary. With the scientific, technological, and commercial transformations occurring in Europe (discussed in Chapter 22), the Ottomans were falling behind their Christian rivals in most areas. But the growing gap was most critical in trade and warfare. The Ottomans inherited from their Arab, Persian, and Turkic predecessors the conviction that little of what happened in Europe was important. This belief, which is seen as a major cause of Ottoman decline by the traveler Abu Taleb quoted in the Document feature, prevented them from taking seriously the revolutionary changes that were transforming western Europe. The intense conservatism of powerful groups such as the Janissaries, and to a lesser extent the religious scholars, reinforced this fatal attitude. Through much of the 17th and 18th centuries, these groups blocked most of the Western-inspired innovations that reform-minded sultans and their advisors tried to introduce. As a result of these narrow and potentially dangerous attitudes, the isolated Ottoman imperial system proved incapable of checking the forces that were steadily destroying it.

Abu Taleb on the West and Western Influence

## The Shi'a Challenge of the Safavids

- **In the first years of the 16th century, the Safavids founded a dynasty that conquered what is now Iran. Restoring Persia (as it was then called) as a major center of political power and cultural creativity, they also established it as one of the strongest and most enduring centers of Shi'ism within the Islamic world.**

Like the Ottomans, the Safavid dynasty arose from the struggles of rival Turkic nomadic groups in the wake of the Mongol and Timurid invasions of the 13th and 14th centuries. Also like the Ottomans, the Safavids rose to prominence as the frontier warrior champions of a highly militant strain of Islam. But unlike the Ottomans, who became the champions of the Sunni majority of the Muslim faithful, the Safavids espoused the Shi'a variant of Islam. As we saw in Chapter 11, in the early decades of Muslim expansion a split developed in the community of the faithful between the Sunnis, who recognized the legitimacy of the first three successors to Muhammad (Abu Bakr, Umar, and Uthman), and the Shi'a, who believed that only the fourth successor (Ali, Mohammed's cousin and son-in-law) had the right to succeed the prophet. Over time, differences in doctrine, ritual, and law were added to the disagreements over succession that originally divided the Islamic community. Divisions have also arisen within both the Shi'a and Sunni groupings, but bitter hostility and violent conflict most often have developed along Sunni–Shi'a lines. The long rivalry between the Sunni Ottomans and the Shi'a Safavids proved to be one of the most pivotal episodes in the long history of these sectarian struggles.

The Safavid dynasty had its origins in a family of Sufi mystics and religious preachers, whose shrine center was at Ardabil near the Caspian Sea (Map 26.3). In the early 14th century, one of these Sufis, **Sail al-Din,** who gave the dynasty its name, began a militant campaign to purify and reform Islam and spread Muslim teachings among the Turkic tribes of the region. In the chaos that followed the collapse of Mongol authority in the mid-14th century, Sail al-Din and other Safavid Sufi leaders gained increasing support. But as the numbers of the **Red Heads** (as the Safavids' followers were called because of their distinctive headgear) grew, and as they began in the mid-15th century to preach Shi'a doctrines, their enemies multiplied. After decades of fierce local struggles in which three successive Safavid leaders perished, a surviving Sufi commander, **Ismâ'il,** led his Turkic followers to a string of victories on the battlefield. In 1501, Ismâ'il's armies took the city of Tabriz, where he was proclaimed *shah,* or emperor.

In the next decade, Ismâ'il's followers conquered most of Persia, drove the Safavid's ancient enemies, the Ozbegs—a neighboring nomadic people of Turkic stock—back into the central Asian steppes, and advanced into what is now Iraq. The Safavid successes and the support their followers received in the Ottoman

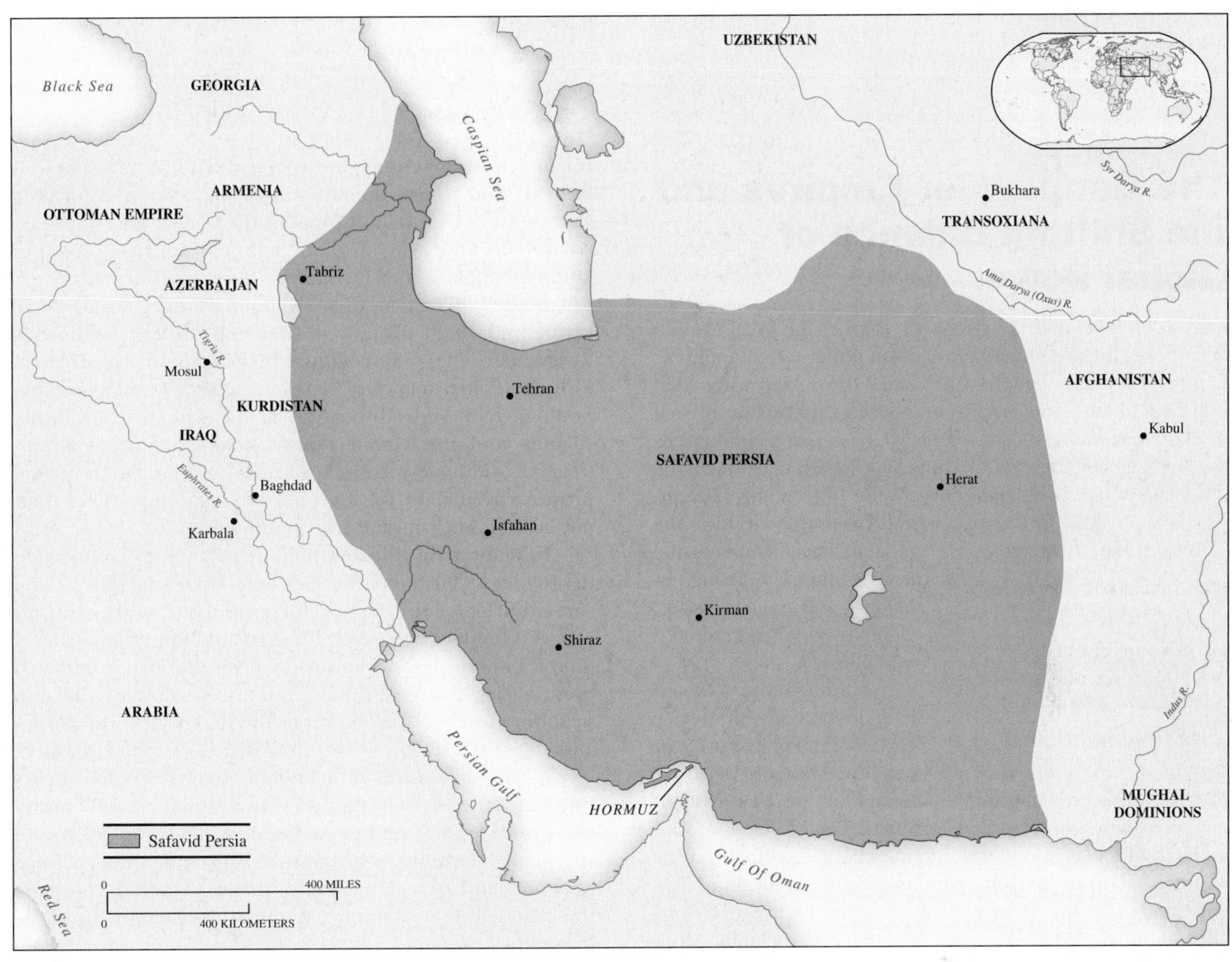


**MAP 26.3** The Safavid Empire

borderlands from Turkic-speaking peoples brought them into conflict with Ottoman rulers. In August 1514, at **Chaldiran** in northwest Persia, the armies of the two empires met in one of the most fateful battles in Islamic history. Chaldiran was more than a battle between the two most powerful dynasties in the Islamic world at the time. It was a clash between the champions of the Shi'a and Sunni variants of Islam. The religious fervor with which both sides fought the battle was intensified by the long-standing Safavid persecutions of the Sunnis and the slaughter of Shi'a living in Ottoman territories by the forces of the Ottoman sultan, Selim.

The battle also demonstrated the importance of muskets and field cannon in the gunpowder age. Because his artillery was still engaged against enemies far to the east, Ismâ'il hoped to delay a decisive confrontation with the Ottoman forces under the Sultan Selim. When battle could not be avoided, Ismâ'il threw his cavalry against the cannon and massed muskets of the Ottoman forces. Despite desperate attempts to make up through clever maneuvers what he lacked in firepower, Ismâ'il's cavalry proved no match for the well-armed Ottomans.

The Safavids were dealt a devastating defeat. Thus, their victory at Chaldiran buttressed the Ottomans' efforts to build the most powerful empire in the Islamic world. But the Ottomans could not follow up the battle with conquests that would have put an end to their Safavid rivals. The latter's capital at Tabriz was too far from Ottoman supply areas to be held through the approaching winter. The withdrawal of the Ottoman armies gave the Safavids the breathing space they needed to regroup their forces and reoccupy much of the territory they had originally conquered. Nonetheless, defeat at Chaldiran put an end to Ismâ'il's dreams of further westward expansion, and most critically it checked the rapid spread of conversions to Shi'a Islam in the western borderlands that had resulted from the Safavid's recent successes in battle. The outcome at Chaldiran determined that Shi'ism would be concentrated mainly in Persia, or present-day Iran, and neighboring areas in what is today southern Iraq.

IN DEPTH

## The Gunpowder Empires and the Shifting Balance of Global Power

Like so many of their predecessors, each of the great Muslim dynasties of the premodern era came to power with the support of nomadic warrior peoples. Each based the military forces that won and sustained its empire on massed cavalry. But in each case, there was a significant divergence from past conditions. As the outcome of the critical battle of Chaldiran between the Ottomans and Safavids made clear, by the 16th century firearms had become a decisive element in armed conflict—the key to empire building. In military and political terms, global history had entered a new phase.

*"In feudal Europe and somewhat later in Japan . . . siege cannons reduced feudal castles to rubble."*

Although the Chinese had invented gunpowder and were the first to use it in war, the Mongols were the first to realize the awesome potential of the new type of weaponry based on explosive formulas. The Mongols continued to build their armies around swift cavalry and their skill as mounted archers. But siege cannons became critical to Mongol conquests once they ventured into the highly urbanized civilizations that bordered on their steppe homelands. Mongol successes against intricately walled and heavily fortified cities in China, Russia, and the Islamic heartlands impressed their sedentary and nomadic adversaries with the power of the new weaponry and contributed much to its spread throughout the Eurasian world in the late 13th and 14th centuries.

Innovation in the use of gunpowder spread quickly to many areas, especially Europe and the Muslim Middle East. By the late 15th century, muskets and field cannons, however heavy and clumsy the latter might be, were transforming warfare from Europe to China. In the Middle East, Janissary musketeers and heavy artillery became the driving force of Ottoman expansion. The Safavids' lack of artillery was critical to their defeat at Chaldiran. In Europe, armies were increasingly built around musket and artillery regiments. Rival states vied to attract gunsmiths who could provide them with the latest weaponry or, even better, invent guns that would give them decisive advantages over their rivals. In the Atlantic and the Mediterranean, handguns and cannons were introduced into sea warfare—an innovation that proved essential to the Europeans' ability to project their power overseas from the 16th century onward.

In many areas, the new military technology contributed to broader social and political changes. In feudal Europe and somewhat later in Japan, for example, siege cannons reduced feudal castles to rubble. In so doing, they struck a mortal blow at the warrior aristocracies that had dominated these societies for centuries. But the success of the new weaponry forced a revolution in the design of fortifications and defense strategies. The defense systems that resulted, which were expensive and elaborate, spawned corps of professional officers and engineers, vast military supply industries, and urban centers enclosed by low-lying walls and star-shaped bastions. The cost of the field artillery, siege weapons, and new defense industries promoted state centralization, as the experience of the Muslim empires and the history of Europe and Japan in the gunpowder age demonstrate. Rulers with national or imperial ambitions had the firepower to level the fortresses of regional lords and thus more effectively control the populations and resources of their domains.

Although the new weaponry was vital to the rise and sustenance of nation-states and empires, some political systems were more compatible than others with efforts to exploit and

### Politics and War Under the Safavid Shahs

After his defeat at Chaldiran, Ismâ'il, once a courageous warrior and a popular leader, retreated to his palace and tried to escape his troubles through drink. His seclusion, along with struggles between the factions backing each of his sons for the right to succeed him, left openings for subordinate Turkic chiefs to attempt to seize power. After years of turmoil, a new shah, Tahmasp I (r. 1534–1576), won the throne and set about restoring the power of the dynasty. The Turkic chiefs were foiled in their bid for supreme power, and the Ozbegs were again and again driven from the Safavid domains. Under Shah Abbas I (r. 1587–1629), the empire reached the height of its strength and prosperity, although the territories it controlled remained roughly equivalent to those ruled by Ismâ'il and Tahmasp I.

Under Tahmasp I and his successors, repeated efforts were made to bring the Turkic chiefs under control. They were gradually transformed into a warrior nobility comparable to that in the Ottoman domains. Like their Ottoman counterparts, the Safavid warrior nobles were assigned villages, whose peasants were required to supply them and their troops with food and labor. The most powerful of the warrior leaders occupied key posts in the imperial administration, and from the defeat at Chaldiran onward they posed a constant threat to the Safavid improve on it. At one extreme, the Chinese scholar-gentry limited innovations in gunpowder weaponry and its use in warfare because they feared that these changes would lead to the dominance of the military in Ming and later Qing society. After the early 1600s, the shoguns, or military leaders, of neighboring Japan virtually banned the firearms that had done so much to bring them to power. In this case, a military caste feared that the spread of firearms to the general populace would destroy what was left of the feudal order they had built centuries earlier.

The obstacles faced by nomadic peoples such as the Mongols were very different. Their sparse populations and arid lands simply did not generate the resources or sustained invention that would allow them to keep up with their sedentary neighbors in the expensive arms races that the new technology spawned. As the advantages of sedentary societies grew more pronounced in the 17th and 18th centuries, nomadic peoples found not only that they could no longer raid or conquer the agrarian cores but also that sedentary adversaries could advance into and occupy their homelands on the steppe and desert fringes.

Nomadic dynasties, such as the Ottomans, Safavids, and Mughals, who had won their empires in the early stages of the gunpowder revolution, did control the agrarian bases and skilled artisans needed to supply their armies with muskets and siege cannons. But they were confronted by internal conflicts and, perhaps more critically in the long run, formidable external rivals. To begin with, their military technology was far in advance of the transport and communication systems of their far-flung empires. This fact, and their failure to build effective imperial bureaucracies, left them at the mercy of the warrior elites who brought them to power. In each of the three empires, the regional bases of the warrior classes became increasingly independent of the ruling dynasty. This meant that the rulers were denied revenue and other resources that were vital to maintaining competitive military establishments. Their fragile and overstretched administrative systems proved difficult to reform and more and more ineffective at administering the peasant populations in their charge. Internal revolts further sapped the resources of the hard-pressed Muslim dynasties.

In each Muslim empire, decline was hastened by the rise of European rivals, who proved more adept at taking advantage of the gunpowder revolution. The smaller but highly competitive nation-states of western Europe were better able to mobilize more limited human and natural resources than their Muslim counterparts. Constant struggles for survival in the multistate European system also made the elites of Spain, England, and France more receptive to technological innovation, which became a central ingredient of political success in the gunpowder era. Emulating the more advanced states of western Europe, for example, Peter the Great forced social reforms and military innovations that transformed a weak and backward Russia into a powerful adversary of the Ottomans and the nomadic peoples of the steppes. Thus, although it began in China and was initially spread by the Mongol nomads, the gunpowder revolution eventually tipped the global balance of power in favor of the peoples of Christian Europe. This shift was an essential condition for Europe's rise to global power in the centuries that followed.

**Questions** What advantages would gunpowder weaponry give to those who used it over those who did not in the early modern era? Were these advantages as decisive as they were later in the industrial age? Why would the use of muskets and early field cannons take a higher level of military organization and troop discipline and training than had been needed in earlier time periods? What made the new military technology so expensive? Why did the Europeans adopt it more readily than most other peoples, and why were they so intent on improving it?

monarchs. To counterbalance this threat, Safavid rulers recruited Persians for positions at the court and in the rapidly expanding imperial bureaucracy. The struggle for power and influence between Turkic and Persian notables was further complicated by the practice, initiated by Ismâ'il's successor, Tahmasp I, of recruiting into the bureaucracy and army slave boys who were captured in campaigns in southern Russia. Like the Janissaries in the Ottoman Empire, many of these slaves rose to positions of power. Also like the Janissaries, the slave regiments soon became a major force in Safavid political struggles.

Of all of the Safavid shahs, Abbas I, known also as **Abbas the Great,** made the greatest use of the youths who were captured in Russia and then educated and converted to Islam. They not only came to form the backbone of his military forces but were granted provincial governorships and high offices at court. Like the Janissaries, "slave" regiments, which were wholly dependent on Abbas's support, monopolized the firearms that had become increasingly prominent in Safavid armies. The Persians had artillery and handguns long before the arrival of the Portuguese by sea in the early 16th century. But Abbas and his successors showed little reluctance to call on the knowledgeable but infidel Europeans for assistance in their wars with the Ottomans. Of special importance were the Sherley brothers from England. They provided instruction in the casting of cannons and trained Abbas's slave infantry and a special regiment of musketeers recruited from the Iranian peasantry. By the end of his reign, Abbas had built up a standing army of nearly 40,000 troops and an elite bodyguard. These measures to strengthen his armies and his victories on the battlefield appeared to promise security for the Safavid domains for decades to come—a promise that was not fulfilled.

## State and Religion

The Safavid family was originally of Turkic stock, and early shahs such as Ismâ'il wrote in Turkish, unlike their Ottoman rivals, who preferred to write in Persian. After Chaldiran, however, Persian gradually supplanted Turkish as the language of the court and bureaucracy. Persian influences were also felt in the organization of court rituals and in the more and more exalted position of the Safavid shahs. Abandoning all pretense of the egalitarian camaraderie that had marked their earlier dealings with the warrior chiefs, the Safavids took grand titles, such as *padishah,* or king of kings, often derived from those used by the ancient Persian emperors. Like the Ottoman rulers, the Safavids presided from their high thrones over opulent palace complexes crowded with servants and courtiers. The pattern of palace life was set by elaborate court rituals and social interaction governed by a refined sense of etiquette and decorum. Although the later Safavid shahs played down claims to divinity that had been set forth under Ismâ'il and his predecessors, they continued to claim descent from one of the Shi'a **imams,** or successors of Ali.

Changes in the status accorded to the Safavid rulers were paralleled by shifts in the religious impulses that had been so critical to their rise to power. The militant, expansive cast of Shi'a ideology was modified as the faith became a major pillar of dynasty and empire. The early Safavids imported Arabic-speaking Shi'a religious experts. But later shahs came to rely on Persian religious scholars who entered into the service of the state and were paid by the government. **Mullahs,** who were both local mosque officials and prayer leaders, were also supervised by the state and given some support from it. All religious leaders were required to curse the first three caliphs and mention the Safavid ruler in the Friday sermon. Teaching in the mosque schools was also planned and directed by state religious officials.

Through these agents, the bulk of the Iranian population was converted to Shi'ism during the centuries of Safavid rule. Sunni Muslims, Christians, Jews, Zoroastrians, and the followers of Sufi preachers were pressured to convert to Shi'ism. Shi'a religious festivals, such as that commemorating the martyrdom of Husayn (a son of Ali) and involving public flagellation and passion plays, and pilgrimages to Shi'a shrines, such as that at Karbala in central Iraq, became the focal points of popular religion in Iran. Thus, Shi'ism not only provided ideological and institutional support for the Safavid dynasty but also came to be an integral part of Iranian identity, setting the people of the region off from most of their Arab and Turkic neighbors.

**FIGURE 26.5** Occupying one side of the great square of the Safavid capital at Isfahan, the blue-tiled Shah Mosque was one of the architectural gems of the early modern era worldwide.

## Elite Affluence and Artistic Splendor

Although earlier rulers had built or restored mosques and religious schools and financed public works projects, Abbas I surpassed them all. After securing his political position with a string of military victories, Abbas I set about establishing his empire as a major center of international trade and Islamic culture. He had a network of roads and rest houses built, and he strove to make merchants and travelers safe within his domains. He set up workshops to manufacture the silk textiles and splendid Persian carpets that were in great demand. Abbas I encouraged Iranian merchants to trade not only with their Muslim neighbors and India and China to the east but also with the Portuguese—and later the Dutch and English—whose war and merchant ships were becoming a familiar sight in the Persian Gulf and Arabian Sea.

Although Abbas I undertook building projects throughout his empire, he devoted special attention to his capital at **Isfahan.** The splendid seat of Safavid power was laid out around a great square, which was lined with two-story shops interspersed with great mosques, government offices, and soaring arches that opened onto formal gardens. Abbas I founded several colleges and oversaw the construction of numerous public baths and rest houses. He patronized workshops where intricately detailed and brilliantly colored miniatures were produced by master painters and their apprentices.

Above all, the great mosques that Abbas I had built at Isfahan were the glory of his reign. The vividly colored ceramic tiles, which Iranian builders had begun to use centuries earlier, turned the massive domes and graceful minarets of Safavid mosques and royal tombs into creations of stunning beauty. Geometric designs, floral patterns, and verses from the Qur'an written in stylized Arabic added movement and texture to the deep blue tiles that distinguished the monumental construction of the Safavid era. Gardens and reflecting pools were built near the mosques and rest houses. By combining graceful arches, greenery, and colorful designs, Persian architects and artisans created lush, cool refuges (perhaps duplicating heaven itself, as it is described in the Qur'an) in a land that is dry, dusty, and gray-brown for much of the year.

## Society and Gender Roles: Ottoman and Safavid Comparisons

Although the Ottomans and Safavids were bitter political rivals and religious adversaries, the social systems that developed under the two dynasties had much in common. Both were dominated, particularly in their earliest phases, by warrior aristocracies, which shared power with the absolutist monarchs of each empire and enjoyed prestige and luxury in the capital and on rural estates. In both cases, the warrior aristocrats gradually retreated to the estates, making life increasingly difficult for the peasants on whom they depended for the support of their grand households and many retainers. As the real power of the rulers of each empire diminished and as population increases reduced the uncultivated lands to which peasants might flee, the demands of the landlord class grew harsher. Foreign invasions, civil strife, and the breakdown in vital services once provided by the state added to the growing misery of the peasantry. The resulting spread of banditry, peasant uprisings, and flight from the land further drained the resources of both empires and undermined their legitimacy.

The early rulers of both the Ottoman and the Safavid empires encouraged the growth of handicraft production and trade in their realms. Both dynasties established imperial workshops where products ranging from miniature paintings and rugs to weapons and metal utensils were manufactured. The rulers of each empire lavishly patronized public works projects that provided reasonably well-paid work for engineers, stonemasons, carpenters, and other sorts of artisans. Some of the more able emperors of these dynasties also pursued policies that they believed would increase both internal and international trade. In these endeavors, the Ottomans gained in the short run from the fact that large-scale traders in their empire often were from minority groups, such as Christians and Jews, who had extensive contacts with overseas traders that the bazaar merchants of the Safavid realm normally lacked. Although Safavid cooperation with Portuguese traders remedied this shortcoming to some extent, the Safavid economy remained much more constricted, less market oriented, and more technically backward than that of their Ottoman rivals.

Women in Islamic societies under Ottoman or Safavid rule faced legal and social disadvantages comparable to those we have encountered in most civilized areas so far. Within the family, women were subordinated to their fathers and husbands. They seldom had political or religious power, and they had surprisingly meager outlets for artistic or scholarly expression. Even women of nomadic Turkic and Mongol backgrounds gradually lost their independence when they settled in the towns of conquered areas. There, the dictates of increasingly patriarchal codes and restrictive practices such as seclusion and veiling were imposed on women of all classes, but most strictly on those of the elite.

However, recent evidence suggests that many women in the Islamic heartlands in this era, perhaps clinging to the memory of the lives led by their nomadic predecessors, struggled against these restrictions. Travelers to Persia in the time of Abbas I remarked on the brightly colored robes worn by

FIGURE 26.6 A portrait of a Safavid notable, probably Shah Suleyman I (1667–1693), by a Persian court artist. He is surrounded by courtiers, including a European visitor bearing presents for the Persian leader. From the time of Abbas, Europeans nations vied fiercely for influence at the Safavid court.

women in the capital and elsewhere, and noted that many women made no effort to cover their faces in public. At both the Ottoman and Safavid courts, the wives and concubines of the rulers and royal princes continued to exert influence behind the throne and remained deeply involved in palace conspiracies. More important for ordinary women in each of these societies was the fact that many were active in trade and some in money-lending. Court records also suggest that women often could invoke provisions in Islamic law that protected their rights to inheritance, decent treatment by their spouses, and even divorce in marital situations that had become intolerable.

How typical these instances of assertion and expression were is not clear. Although some women were a good deal better off than we had once thought, perhaps as well off as or even better off than their counterparts in China and India, most women probably lived unenviable lives. Limited largely to contacts with their own families and left with little more than household chores and domestic handicrafts such as embroidery to occupy their time, the overwhelming majority of women in effect disappeared from the history of two of the great centers of Islamic civilization.

## The Rapid Demise of the Safavid Empire

Given the power and splendor the Safavid Empire had achieved by the end of the reign of Abbas I, its collapse was stunningly rapid. Abbas's fears of usurpation by one of his sons, which were fed by plots on the part of several of his closest advisors, had led during his reign to the death or blinding of all who could legitimately succeed him. A grandson, who was weak and thus thought by high state officials to be easily manipulated, was placed on the throne after Abbas's death. From this point, the dynasty's fortunes declined. As was true of the Ottomans, the practice of confining the princes to the atmosphere of luxury and intrigue that permeated the court led to a sharp fall in the quality of Safavid rulers. Able shahs, such as Abbas II (r. 1642–1666), were too few to halt the decline of the imperial administration or to deal effectively with the many foreign threats to the empire. Factional disputes and rebellions shook the empire from within, and nomadic raiders and Ottoman and Mughal armies steadily reduced the territory the Safavids could tap for labor and revenue.

By March 1722, Isfahan was besieged by Afghani tribes. In October, after over 80,000 of the capital's inhabitants had died of starvation and disease, the city fell and Safavid power was ended. One of those who fought for the throne in the decade of war and destruction that followed claimed descent from the Safavid line. But a soldier-adventurer named **Nadir Khan Afshar** eventually emerged victorious from these bloody struggles. Although he began as a champion of Safavid restoration, Nadir Khan proclaimed himself shah in 1736. Despite the title, his dynasty and those that followed were short-lived. The area that had once made up the Safavid Empire was reduced for generations to a battleground for its powerful neighbors and a tempting target for nomadic raiders.

## The Mughals and the Apex of Muslim Civilization in India

■ **Under the rule of the Mughal dynasty, Islam reached the peak of its influence as a political and cultural force in south Asian history. Under the Mughal emperors, a blend of Hindu and Islamic civilizations produced some of the world's most sublime architecture and art.**

Despite the fact that the founder of the Mughal dynasty, **Babur,** traced his descent on one side from the Mongol khans, the Mughal in the dynasty's name was not derived from the earlier nomadic conquerors. Babur was also descended from the Turkic conqueror Timur, and most of his followers were from Turkic or mixed nomadic origins. Unlike the Ottomans and Safavids, Babur's motives for conquest and empire building had little to do with religious fervor. Originally, he directed raids into the fertile and heavily populated plains of north India only to gain booty to support his campaigns to win back his lost kingdom, Ferghana. Although India had much greater potential as a base on which to build an empire, Babur cared little for the green and well-watered subcontinent. Even after he conquered India, he continued to long for the arid steppes and blue-domed mosques of his central Asian birthplace. But after decades of wars on the steppes that repeatedly ended in defeat, he was forced to give up his dream of reclaiming his homeland and to turn his full energies to the conquest of northern India. Within two years, his armies had conquered large portions of the Indus and Ganges plains and he had laid the foundations for a dynasty that would last more than 300 years.

The founder of the Mughal dynasty was a remarkable man. He was a fine military strategist and fierce fighter who went into battle alongside his troops. But Babur also cultivated a taste for the arts and music over the course of the decades when he was continually fighting for survival. He wrote one of the great histories of India, was a fine musician, and designed wonderful gardens for his new capital at Delhi. But he was a better conqueror than administrator. Babur did little to reform the very ineffective Lodi bureaucracy he had taken over—a project that would have solidified the Mughals' hold on the empire he had conquered. In 1530, at the age of 48, he suddenly fell ill and died, leaving his son, **Humayan,** to inherit the newly founded kingdom.

Like his father, Humayan was a good soldier; in fact, he had won his first battle at age 18. But Babur's death was the signal for his enemies to strike from all sides. One of Humayan's brothers disputed his succession, and armies from Afghanistan and the Rajput states of western India marched on his capital (Map 26.4). By 1540, with his armies shattered, Humayan was forced to flee to Persia. There he remained in exile, an embarrassed guest at the Safavid court, for nearly a decade. Having gained a foothold at Kabul in 1545, Humayan launched a series of campaigns into India that restored Mughal rule to the northern plains by 1556. But Humayan did not live to savor his victory. Shortly after entering Delhi in triumph, he was hurrying down his library steps, his arms full of books, to answer the call to prayer. He stumbled and fell, hitting his head. He died within days.

### Akbar and the Basis for a Lasting Empire

Humayan's sudden death once again imperiled the Mughal dynasty. His son and successor, **Akbar,** was only 13 years old, and the Mughals' enemies moved quickly to take advantage of what they saw as a very favorable turn of events. Their expectations were soon dashed because Akbar proved to be one of the greatest leaders

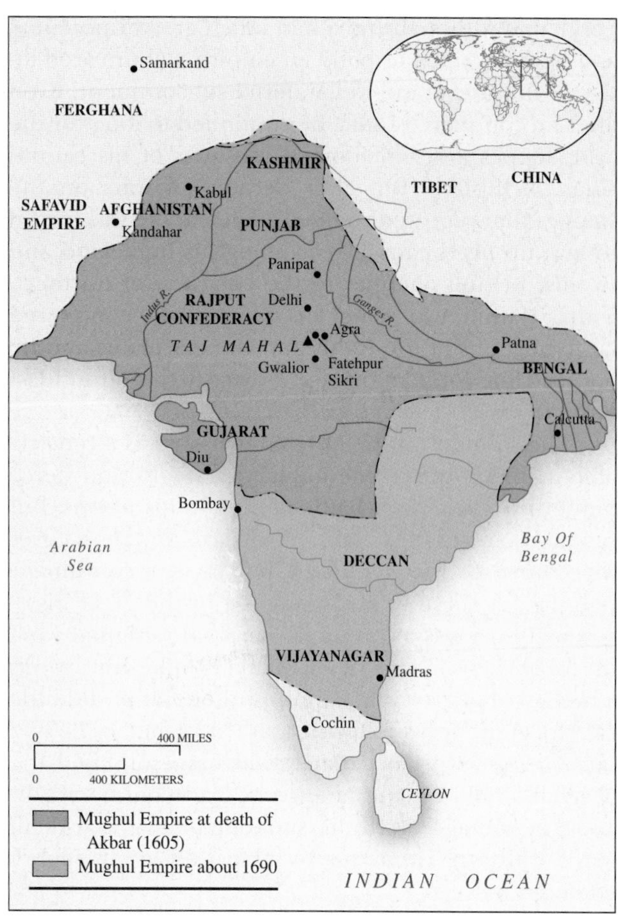


MAP 26.4 The Growth of the Mughal Empire, from Akbar to Aurangzeb

Akbar, Emperor of India

of all history. Interestingly, Akbar's reign was contemporaneous with those of several other remarkable monarchs, including Elizabeth I of England, Philip of Spain, and the Muslim rulers Suleyman the Magnificent and Abbas I. Akbar was a match for any one of these very formidable rivals.

Like his father and grandfather, Akbar was a fine military commander with great personal courage. But unlike his predecessors, Akbar also had a vision of empire and sense of mission that hinged on uniting India under his rule. A workaholic who seldom slept more than three hours a night, Akbar personally oversaw the building of the military and administrative systems that would form the backbone of the Mughal Empire for centuries. He also patronized the arts and entered into complex religious and philosophical discussions with learned scholars from throughout the Muslim, Christian, and Hindu worlds. In addition, Akbar found time to carry out social reforms and invent his own universalistic religion. Though illiterate—there had been little time for book learning when his father fought for survival in the wilderness—Akbar had an insatiable curiosity and an incredible memory. By having others read aloud to him, he became educated in many fields.

At first with the help of senior advisors, but soon on his own, Akbar routed the enemies who had hoped to capitalize on the Mughals' misfortunes. In the decades after 1560, when he took charge of the government, Akbar's armies greatly extended the empire with conquests throughout north and central India. But it was Akbar's social policies and administrative genius that made it possible to establish the foundations of a lasting dominion in the subcontinent. He pursued a policy of reconciliation and cooperation with the Hindu princes and the Hindu majority of the population of his realm. He encouraged intermarriage between the Mughal aristocracy and the families of the Hindu Rajput rulers. Akbar also abolished the much-hated *jizya,* or head tax, that earlier Muslim rulers had levied on Hindu unbelievers. He promoted Hindus to the highest ranks in the government, ended a long-standing ban on the building of new Hindu temples, and ordered Muslims to respect cows, which the Hindu majority viewed as sacred.

Despite the success of these policies in reconciling the Hindu majority to Muslim rule, Akbar viewed tolerance as merely the first stage in a longer strategy to put an end to sectarian divisions in the subcontinent. Blending elements of the many religions with which he was familiar, he invented a new faith, the **Din-i-Ilahi,** that he believed could be used to unite his Hindu and Muslim subjects. If the adherents of India's diverse religions could be convinced to embrace this common creed, Akbar reasoned, sectarian quarrels and even violent conflict could be brought to an end.

Akbar and the Jesuits

Like their counterparts in the Ottoman and Safavid empires, the Muslim and Hindu warrior aristocrats who formed the core of the supporters of the Mughal dynasty were granted peasant villages for their support. In turn, they were required to maintain a specified number of cavalry and to be on call if the emperor needed their services. The court and the central bureaucracy were supported by revenues drawn from the tribute paid by the military retainers and from taxes on lands set aside for the support of the imperial household. Because of a shortage of administrators, in most areas local notables, many of whom were Hindu, were left in place as long as they swore allegiance to the Mughal rulers and paid their taxes on time. These arrangements left the control and welfare of the village population largely in the hands of the military retainers of the dynasty and local power brokers.

## Social Reform and Social Change

In addition to his administrative reforms, Akbar pushed for social changes that he believed would

VISUALIZING THE PAST

## The Basis of Imperial Power in the Rival Muslim Empires

The table provides the vital statistics of each of the three great Muslim empires of the early modern era. Use the data to determine the relative strengths and weaknesses of each of the empires. Also make use of the maps provided throughout this chapter to include geographical factors and incorporate points from the text with relevance to the questions posed below.

**Questions** Which of the rival empires has the largest resource base? On the basis of your impressions from the text discussion, which was the most formidable in terms of artisan production and external trade? Which empire did geography favor the most in terms of defending itself and projecting its power? Which was the most secure? Which was the most threatened by (a) rival powers and (b) internal enemies? Which of these threats proved the most powerful and why? How would you rank the three empires in terms of overall military strength? What long-term problems can you identify regarding the survival of these imperial systems in the changing global system of the early modern era?

**Vital Statistics of the Gunpowder Empires**

| | Land Area | Approximate Population | Religious Composition | Estimated Size of Military Forces | Source of Cannon/Firearms |
|---|---|---|---|---|---|
| Ottoman Empire c. 1566 | c.1,200,000 sq. mi. | 30–35 million | Large majority Sunni Muslim; Significant Jewish and Christian minorities | Largest army recorded: 200,000 cavalry, infantry, artillery; +90 warships | Produced locally |
| Safavid Empire, 1600 | c. 750.000 sq. mi. | No reliable consensus; perhaps 10–15 million | Majority Shi'a Muslim; small Sunni, Jewish, and Christian minorities | 40,000–50,000 cavalry, infantry, artillery; no navy | Imported cannon not widely used, except by European mercenaries |
| Mughal Empire, c. 1600 | c. 1,000,000 sq. mi. | 105–110 million | 10–15% Muslim (divided Sunni/ Shi'a); great majority Hindu and Sikh, Jewish, Christian minorities | Armies in hundreds of thousands reported; cavalry, infantry, artillery; no navy | Imported and produced locally |

Note: c. = approximations or rough estimates.

greatly benefit his subjects. Beyond the public works typically favored by able Muslim rulers, Akbar sought to improve the calendar, to establish living quarters for the large population of beggars and vagabonds in the large cities, and to regulate the consumption of alcohol. Whatever success the latter campaign may have had in Indian society as a whole, it apparently failed in Akbar's own household, for one of his sons was reputed to drink 20 cups of double-distilled wine per day.

More than any of Akbar's many reform efforts, those involving the position of women demonstrated how far the Mughal ruler was in advance of his time. He encouraged widow remarriage, at that point taboo for both Hindus and Muslims, and discouraged child marriages. The latter were so widespread among the upper classes that he did not try to outlaw them, and it is doubtful that his disapproval did much to curb the practice. Akbar did legally prohibit sati, or the burning of high-caste Hindu women on their husbands' funeral pyres (Figure 26.7). Because this custom was deeply entrenched among the Rajput princes and warrior classes that were some of his most faithful allies, this was a risky move on Akbar's part. But he was so determined to eradicate sati, particularly in cases where the widow was pressured to agree to be burned alive, that he once personally rescued a young woman despite the protestations of her angry relatives. He also tried to provide relief for women

FIGURE 26.7 This engraving from a late 16th-century German traveler's account of India shows a European artist's impression of an Indian widow committing sati. Not surprisingly, this practice of burning high-caste widows in some parts of India and among certain social groups on their deceased husbands' funeral pyres often was described at great length by European visitors in this era. There was some disagreement in their accounts as to whether the women went willingly into the fire, as some early authors claimed. Later inquiries in the British period revealed that some of the widows had been drugged and others tied to the funeral pyre. It is likely that many simply caved in to pressure applied by their dead spouse's relatives and at times even their own children.

trapped in purdah, or seclusion in their homes, by encouraging the merchants of Delhi and other cities to set aside special market days for women only.

## Mughal Splendor and Early European Contacts

Despite his many successes and the civil peace and prosperity his reign brought to much of northern India, Akbar died a lonely and discouraged man. By 1605 he had outlived most of his friends and faced revolts by sons eager to claim his throne. Above all, he died knowing that Din-i-Ilahi, the religion he had created to reconcile his Hindu and Muslim subjects, had been rejected by both.

Although neither of his successors, Jahangir (r. 1605–1627) or Shah Jahan (r. 1627–1658), added much territory to the empire Akbar had left them, in their reigns Mughal India reached the peak of its splendor. European visitors marveled at the size and opulence of the chief Mughal cities: Delhi, Agra, and Lahore. The huge Mughal armies, replete with elephant and artillery corps, dwarfed those of even the most powerful European rulers at the time. Some of the more perceptive European observers, such as François Bernier, also noted the poverty in which the lower classes in both town and countryside lived and the lack of discipline and training of most of the soldiers in the Mughal armies. Perhaps most ominously, Bernier added that in invention and the sciences, India had fallen far behind western Europe in most areas.

Nonetheless, by the late 17th century, Mughal India had become one of the major overseas destinations for European traders. They brought products from throughout Asia, though little from Europe itself, to exchange for a variety of Indian manufactures, particularly the subcontinent's famed cotton textiles. The trade gap that the demand for Indian cotton cloth and clothing had created in the West in Roman times persisted millennia later. The importance of the Indian textile trade to the West is suggested by the names we still use for different kinds of cotton cloth, from calico (after the Indian port city of Calicut) to chintz and muslin, as well as by our names for cotton clothes such as pajamas.

The English in South Asia and the Indian Ocean

Because they were easily washed and inexpensive, Indian textiles first won a large market among the working and middle classes in Britain and elsewhere in Europe. In the reigns of Queen Mary and Queen Anne, fine Indian cloth came into fashion at the court as well. An incident from the reign of the Mughal emperor **Aurangzeb,** who succeeded Shah Jahan, suggests just how fine the cloth in question was. Aurangzeb, a religious zealot, scolded his favorite daughter for appearing in his presence in garments that revealed so much of her body. The daughter protested that she had on three layers of fine cotton clothing. It is thus no wonder that even after industrialization had revolutionized cotton textile manufacture in England, European visitors to India continued to observe and write in great detail about the techniques Indian artisans used to weave and dye cotton cloth. The popularity of madras cloth today demonstrates that this interest has not died out.

Two Very Different Mughal Emperors

## Artistic Achievement in the Mughal Era

Both Jahangir and Shah Jahan continued Akbar's policy of tolerance toward the Hindu majority and retained most of the alliances he had forged with Hindu princes and local leaders. They made little attempt to change the administrative apparatus they had inherited from Akbar, and they fought their wars in much the same way as the founders of the dynasty had. Both mounted campaigns to crush potential enemies and in some cases to enlarge the empire. But neither was as interested in conquest and politics as in enjoying the good life. Both were fond of drink, female dancers, and the pleasure gardens they had laid out from Kashmir to Allahabad. Both were delighted by polo matches (a game invented by the princes of India), ox and tiger or elephant fights, and games of pachisi, which they played on life-sized boards with palace dancers as chips. Both took great pleasure in the elaborate court ceremonies that blended Indian and Persian precedents, lavish state processions, their palaces and jewel-studded wardrobes, and the scented and sweetened ices that were rushed from the cool mountains in the north to their capitals on the sweltering plains.

Jahangir and Shah Jahan are best remembered as two of the greatest patrons of the fine arts in human history. They expanded the painting workshops that had been started by the early Mughals so that thousands of exquisite miniature paintings could be produced during their reigns. Both Jahangir and Shah Jahan also devoted massive resources to building some of the most stunning architectural works of all time. The best known of these is the **Taj Mahal** (Figure 26.8), which has become a symbol for India itself. But structures such as the audience hall in the Red Fort at Delhi, Akbar's tomb at Sikandra, and the tomb of Itimad al-Dowleh at Agra rival the Taj Mahal in design and perhaps surpass it in the beauty of their detail and decoration.

Taj Mahal, India

At its best, Mughal architecture blends what is finest in the Persian and Hindu traditions. It fuses the Islamic genius for domes, arches, and minarets and the balance between them with the Hindu love of ornament. In place of the ceramic tiles that the Persians used to finish their mosques and tombs, Indian artisans substituted gleaming white marble, inset with semiprecious stones arranged in floral and geometric patterns. Extensive use was also made of marble reflecting pools, the most famous of which mirrors the beauty of the Taj Mahal. When these pools were inlaid with floral patterns and provided with fountains, the rippling water appeared to give life to the stone plant forms. Like the architects and artisans of the Ottoman Empire and Safavid Persia, those who served the Mughal rulers strove to create paradise on earth, an aspiration that was carved in marble on the audience hall of the Red Fort at Delhi. Around the ceiling of the great hall, it is written "If there is paradise on earth—It is here . . . it is here."

## Court Politics and the Position of Elite and Ordinary Women

Not surprisingly, two rulers who were so absorbed in the arts and the pursuit of pleasure left most of the mundane tasks of day-to-day administration largely in the hands of subordinates. In both cases, strong-willed

FIGURE 26.8 Perhaps no single building has come to symbolize Indian civilization more than the Taj Mahal. The grace and elegance of the tomb that Shah Jahan built in his wife's honor provide an enduring source of aesthetic delight. The white marble of the tomb is inlaid with flowers and geometric designs cut from semiprecious stones. The windows of the central chamber, which houses the tombs of Shah Jahan and Mumtaz Mahal, are decorated with carved marble screens, which add a sense of lightness and delicacy to the structure.

wives took advantage of their husbands' neglect of politics to win positions of power and influence at the Mughal court. Jahangir's wife, **Nur Jahan,** continually amassed power as he became more and more addicted to wine and opium. She packed the court with able male relatives, and her faction dominated the empire for most of the later years of Jahangir's reign. Nur Jahan was a big spender, but not only on pomp and luxury. She became a major patron of much-needed charities in the major cities. Despite her success at pursuits that were normally reserved for males, she was defeated in the end by the roles of wife and mother to which many felt she should confine herself. She died giving birth to her 19th child.

Shah Jahan's consort, **Mumtaz Mahal,** also became actively involved in court politics. But Shah Jahan was a much more engaged and able ruler than Jahangir, and thus her opportunities to amass power behind the throne were more limited. She is remembered not for her political acumen but for the love and devotion Shah Jahan bestowed upon her, a love literally enshrined in the Taj Mahal, the tomb where she is buried. Shah Jahan's plans to build a companion tomb for himself in black marble across the Jumna River were foiled by the revolt of his sons and by his imprisonment. He was buried next to his wife in the Taj Mahal, but her tomb is central and far larger than that of her husband.

Although the position of women at the Mughal court improved in the middle years of the dynasty's power, that of women in the rest of Indian society declined. Child marriage grew more popular, and the age limit was lowered. It was not unheard of for girls to be married at age nine. Widow remarriage among Hindus nearly died out. Seclusion was more and more strictly enforced for upper-caste women, both Hindu and Muslim. Muslim women rarely ventured forth from their homes unveiled, and those who did risked verbal and even physical abuse. The governor of one of the provinces of the Mughal Empire divorced his wife because she was seen scrambling for her life, unveiled, from a runaway elephant. Among upper-caste Hindus, the practice of sati spread despite Shah Jahan's renewed efforts to outlaw it. The dwindling scope of productive roles left to women, combined with the burden of the dowry that had to be paid to marry them off, meant that the birth of a girl was increasingly seen as an inauspicious event. At court as well as in the homes of ordinary villagers, only the birth of a son was greeted with feasting and celebrations.

## The Beginnings of Imperial Decline

Aurangzeb, Shah Jahan's son and successor, seized control of an empire that was threatened by internal decay and growing dangers from external enemies. For decades, the need for essential administrative, military, and social reforms had been ignored. The Mughal bureaucracy had grown bloated and corrupt. The army was equally bloated and backward in weaponry and tactics. Peasants and urban workers had seen their productivity and living standards fall steadily. The Taj Mahal and other wonders of the Mughal artistic imagination had been paid for by the mass of the people at a very high price.

Though not the cruel bigot he is often portrayed as, Aurangzeb was not the man to restore the dynasty's declining fortunes. Courageous, honest, intelligent, and hard-working, he seemed an ideal successor to two rulers who had so badly neglected the affairs of state. But Aurangzeb was driven by two ambitions that proved disastrous to his schemes to strengthen the empire. He was determined to extend Mughal control over the whole of the Indian subcontinent, and he believed that it was his duty to purify Indian Islam and rid it of the Hindu influences he was convinced were steadily corrupting it.

Aurangzeb, Mughal River

The first ambition increased the number of the empire's adversaries, strained the allegiance of its vassals and allies, and greatly overextended its huge but obsolete military forces. By the time of his death in 1707, after a reign of nearly 50 years, Aurangzeb had conquered most of the subcontinent and extended Mughal control as far north as Kabul in what is now Afghanistan. But the almost endless warfare of his years in power drained the treasury and further enlarged an inefficient bureaucracy and army without gaining corresponding increases in revenues to support them.

Equally critically, the long wars occupied much of Aurangzeb's time and energies, diverting him from the administrative tasks and reforms essential to the dynasty's continued strength. While he was leading his massive armies in the south, there were peasant uprisings and revolts by Muslim and Hindu princes in the north. Perhaps even more harmful to the imperial system was the growing autonomy of local leaders, who diverted more and more revenue from the central administration into their own coffers. On the northern borders, incursions by Persian and Afghan warrior bands were increasing.

While Aurangzeb's military campaigns strained the resources of the empire, his religious policies gravely weakened the internal alliances and disrupted the social peace Akbar had so skillfully established. Aurangzeb continued to employ Hindus in the imperial service; in fact, he did not have the Muslim replacements to do without them. But non-Muslims were given far fewer posts at the upper levels of the bureaucracy, and their personal contact with the emperor was severely restricted. Aurangzeb also took measures that he and his religious advisors felt would help rid their Muslim faith and culture of the Hindu influences that had permeated it over the centuries. He forbade the building of new temples and put an end to Hindu religious festivals at court. Aurangzeb also reinstated the hated head tax on unbelievers—a measure he hoped might prod them to convert to Islam. The tax fell heavily on the Hindu poor and in some cases drove them to support sectarian movements that rose up to resist Aurangzeb.

By the end of Aurangzeb's reign, the Mughal Empire was far larger than it had been under any of the earlier emperors, but it was also more unstable. Internal rebellions, particularly those mounted by the **Marattas** in western India, put an end to effective Mughal control over large areas. The rise of new sects, such as the **Sikhs** in the northwest, further strained the declining resources of an imperial system that was clearly overextended. The early leaders of the Sikhs originally tried to bridge the differences between Hindu and Muslim. But Mughal persecution of the new sect, which was seen as religiously heretical and a political threat to the dynasty, eventually transformed Sikhism into a staunchly anti-Muslim force within the subcontinent. In addition, Muslim kingdoms in central and east India continued to resist Mughal hegemony, and Islamic invaders waited at the poorly guarded passes through the Himalayas to strike and plunder once it was clear that the Mughals could no longer fend them off.

Islamic Commentators in India

GLOBAL CONNECTIONS

## Gunpowder Empires and the Restoration of the Islamic Bridge Between Civilizations

The formation of the Ottoman, Safavid, and Mughal dynasties warrants comparison with the steadily expanding land empires of the Russian tsars and the Ming emperors, each of which also included substantial Muslim populations. And although the emerging nation-states of western Europe expanded mainly by sea, they also shared a good deal with the vast land empires of Eurasia. All were highly centralized politically and organized around absolute and hereditary rulers. Each empire's power and capacity to expand was dependent on new military technologies and modes of military organization deployed on both land and sea. In contrast to the Muslim empires, which were established by pastoral peoples, those of Russia and China expended much of their expansive energies to contain and subdue nomadic peoples. Western Europeans confronted nomadic peoples—some of whom practiced agriculture, but most of whom were primarily hunters and gatherers—in their American and south African settler colonies.

Changes in the position of the three great Islamic empires relative to the Russian, Chinese, and western European empires of the early modern era were gradual and complex. The Ottoman, Safavid, and Mughal empires retained active programs of overseas trade which, as we have seen, was a defining feature of early modern history worldwide. Arabs, for example, continued to interact with the peoples of the east African coast and their trade in slaves, spices, and other goods. Europeans sought luxury products both in the Middle East and in India. In fact, Indian merchants made large profits from the spices and textiles they exported and that the Europeans paid for in silver from the Americas. But the Europeans were increasingly assertive, setting up their own merchant groupings in Istanbul, for example, where they followed their laws rather than those of the Ottoman Empire.

European disdain for the slower pace of scientific and technological change in the Muslim—as well as the Chinese and Russian—empires also grew as the political and military power of the dynasties that ruled these decreased. The internal causes of decline discussed in this chapter for the early modern Muslim empires were probably sufficient to destroy within a matter of decades the great gunpowder empires of Islam. But each was also undermined by further weaknesses that had profound significance for Islamic civilization as a whole. Captivated by their rivalries with each other and the problems of holding together their empires, none of the dynasties took the rising threat from Europe seriously. They called on Western travelers and missionaries for advice in casting cannons or military tactics, but none of the officials of the great Islamic empires systematically monitored technological advances in Europe. Eventually, the decline of the Mughals opened the door for growing political and military intervention by Europeans in the Indian subcontinent, particularly the British and French, who formed alliances with rival princes in an increasingly decentralized society. A British empire in India was actively forming by the end of the early modern centuries.

The failure to take strong measures to meet the challenges that European overseas expansion was creating for Islamic civilization was also responsible for the weakening of the economic basis of each of the empires. Key tax revenues and merchant profits were drained off by the rise of European trading empires in Asia (see Chapters 21, 22, and 27). The Europeans' gains in ways to generate wealth and economic growth meant increasing losses for Muslim societies and political systems. These setbacks eventually proved critical to the failure of Muslim efforts to compete politically and militarily with their Christian rivals.

### Further Readings

The Lapidus survey suggested in the earlier chapters on Islam provides a fine introduction to the empires that are the focus of this chapter. For a comparative look at the subject, see William H. McNeill, *The Age of Gunpowder Empires, 1450–1800* (1989).

The best detailed studies of the Ottoman Empire can be found in the works of Halil Inalcik, especially his chapters in *The Cambridge History of Islam* (1977). For a different perspective on the Ottomans, see Stanford Shaw's *History of the Ottoman Empire and Modern Turkey*, vol. 1 (1780–1808) (1976). Bernard Lewis's *Istanbul and the Civilization of the Ottoman Empire* (1963) provides internal perspectives of life at the center of the Ottoman Empire. For the most recent and approachable exploration of the origins of the Ottoman state, see C. Kafadar, *Between Two Worlds: The Construction of the Ottoman State* (1995). G. Necipoglu, *Architecture, Ceremonial, and Power: The Topkapi Palace in the Fifteenth and Sixteenth Centuries* (1991), illuminates the potent political symbolism embedded in the Ottoman Empire's greatest artistic achievement. S. S. Blair and J. Bloom, *The Art and Architecture of Islam, 1250–1800* (1994), can be used to extend this analysis across the Muslim world. Peter F. Sugar, *Southeastern Europe Under Ottoman Rule, 1354–1804* (1977), is a fine account of life in the Christian portions of the empire. Afaf Lutfi al-Sayyid Marsot, *Women and Men in Late Eighteenth Century Egypt* (1995), explores gender roles in the age of the Ottomans.

R. M. Savory's writings, including *Iran Under the Safavids* (1980), and his chapters in *The Cambridge History of Iran* (1986), are the most reliable of a very limited literature in

English on the Safavid period. Though quite specialized, Michel Mazzaoui, *The Origins of the Safavids* (1972), provides the fullest account of the beginnings and rise of the Safavid dynasty. The contributions to the volume that Savory edited on *Islamic Civilization* (1976) include good discussions of the arts and society in the Turkic and Persian sectors of the Islamic heartland. The introductory sections of Nikki Keddi's *Roots of Revolution* (1981) provide a good discussion of the relationship between religion and the state in the Safavid period.

The Ikram and Ahmad books cited in Chapter 12 on expansion of Islam in India are also good resources on the Mughals. Though specialized, the works of Irfan Habib, M. Athar Ali, Richard Eaton, John F. Richards, and Douglas Streusand on the Mughal Empire are also critical, as is Muzzafar Alam's *The Crisis of the Empire in Mughal North India* (1993), one of many recent works reexamining the decline of the Mughal Empire. Of the many works on Mughal art and architecture, Gavin Hambly's *Mughal Cities* (1968) has some of the best color plates and an intelligent commentary.

The role of women in the Islamic Gunpowder Empires is addressed in several recent studies, many of which take India's Nur Jahan as their touchstone. These include Stephen P. Blake, "Contributors to the Urban Landscape: Women Builders in Safavid Isfahan and Mughal Shahjahanabad," in Gavin Hambly, ed., *Women in the Medieval Islamic World* (1998); Ellison Banks Findly, *Nur Jahan: Empress of Mughal India* (1993); Stanley K. Freiberg, *Jahanara: Daughter of the Taj Mahal* (1999); and D. Fairchild Ruggles, ed., *Women, Patronage, and Self-Representation in Islamic Societies* (2000).

Trade between the Muslim gunpowder empires is one of the issues explored in Ashin Das Gupta and M. N. Pearson, eds., *India and the Indian Ocean, 1500–1800* (1987), and in Michael Adas, ed., *Islamic and European Expansion* (1993).

## On the Web

Virtual visits to the palaces of the Ottomans (http://www.ee.bilkent.edu.tr/~history/topkapi.html), the Safavids (http://isfahan.anglia.ac.uk./glossary/hist8.htm) (click on the photograph to the right), the Mughals (http://rohini.ncst.ernet.in/fatehpur/, http://ignca.nic.in/agra001.htm, http://www.mughalgardens.org/html/fortress_gardens.html, and http://www.taj-mahal.net), and their splendid gardens (see, for example, http://www.mughalgardens.org/intro.html) provide clear evidence of the splendor of their empires.

The career of the Ottoman sultan Suleyman, justifiably called the "magnificent," is traced at http://www.byegm.gov.tr/yayinlarimiz/NEWSPOT/1997/2/N9.htm and http://www.wsu.edu:8001/~dee/OTTOMAN/SULEYMAN.HTM.

Studies of the life and work of the Mughal emperor Akbar (http://sangha.net/messengers/akbar.htm, http://www.wsu.edu:8080/~dee/MUGHAL/AKBAR.HTM, and http://www.kamat.com/kalranga/mogul/akbar.htm) lend insight into his relations with his tutors, his skill as an empire-builder, his view of Islamic polity and religious orthodoxy, and his program of religious toleration as embodied in his Din-i-Ilahi, or divine discipleship, that was promoted by his coinage (http://prabhu.50g.com/mughal/mug_akbar.html).

The brilliant art and literary record left by some Mughal and Ottoman emperors provides glimpses into the working of their regimes, as is revealed by the Akbarnama (http://www.bampfa.berkeley.edu/exhibits/indian/u0300.html). Among the lavish illustrations that are included in this work are those illuminating the building of the Mughal city of Fatephur Sikri (http://rubens.anu.edu.au/htdocs/surveys/charlotte/bycountry/display00310.html). Insight into warfare of the period and the role of Janissaries, slave troops, and slavery in gunpowder empires can be obtained at http://i-cias.com/e.o/janissaries.htm, http://www.fordham.edu/halsall/islam/1493janissaries.html, and http://www.fordham.edu/halsall/mod/1555busbecq.html. The prominent role of women in the Mughal Empire is traced at http://www.skidmore.edu/academics/arthistory/ah369/Intropg2.htm, which offers links for further study (see http://www.skidmore.edu/academics/arthistory/ah369/LINKSPG2.HTM). The study of the role of women in the Ottoman Empire and the ultimate advancement of the education of women toward the end of that dynasty is supported by resources at http://www.turkishculture.org/lifestyles/womeneducation.html, http://chnm.gmu.edu/wwh/lessons/lesson3/lesson3.php?s=0, and http://www.womeninworldhistory.com/toc-10.html.

CHAPTER 27

# Asian Transitions in an Age of Global Change





After savoring the exhilaration that only those who have made a breakthrough discovery can know, Vasco da Gama and his Portuguese crews received a number of rude shocks on the last legs of their epic voyage to India in 1498. Da Gama's exploratory probes were conducted in sailing ships that were a good deal smaller than the Portuguese merchant vessel depicted arriving in Japan a century later in the wonderful silk screen painting (Figure 27.8) on page 611. After nearly five months at sea, his tiny flotilla of four ships made its way through the treacherous waters off the Cape of Good Hope on the southern tip of Africa and sailed into the Indian Ocean.

After rounding the cape, da Gama's expedition followed the African coastline northward in search of other Christians and a port to take on fresh supplies (Map 27.1). To their chagrin, most of the towns they encountered were controlled by Muslim Arabs. Some of the Arabs, including those at Mombasa—the largest commercial center on the coast—became hostile once they realized that the Portuguese were Christians. Conversations with the much friendlier sultan, traders, and townspeople farther north at Malindi, however, left no doubt that da Gama's expedition had indeed discovered a sea route from Europe to the fabled Indies.

Da Gama and his compatriots were, of course, delighted and perhaps a bit awed by what they had achieved even before they crossed to India. Their very entry into the Indian Ocean meant that they had won a momentous victory over Spain. They had bested their Iberian rivals in a contest to find a sea route to the East Indies that both nations had pursued at considerable expense for decades. And their triumph was all the more satisfying because they had proved correct the long-standing conviction of Portuguese navigators and mapmakers that the Indian Ocean could be reached by sailing around Africa. And that in turn confirmed the Portuguese claim that Christopher Columbus's much-touted voyage across the Atlantic had been a failure. Columbus had not reached the Indies after all. He had made landfall at islands hitherto unknown to the Europeans, and of undetermined value.

Learning that the goal of da Gama's expedition was India, the sultan at Malindi generously offered the Portuguese captain general a pilot to guide his ships across the Arabian Sea to the lands of spices and gems. Nearly a month later, da

**FIGURE 27.1** Vasco da Gama's arrival in Calicut on India's Malabar coast as depicted in a 16th-century European tapestry. As the pomp and splendor captured in the scene convey, da Gama's voyage was regarded by European contemporaries as a major turning point in world history.

Gama's ships arrived at Calicut on India's Malabar coast (Map 27.1). An ancient and thriving commercial emporium controlled by a Hindu ruler who the Portuguese at first thought might be a Christian, Calicut seemed an ideal place to conclude their long voyage from Lisbon. Da Gama and his crew scrambled ashore eager to trade for the spices, fine textiles, and other Asian products that were among the main objectives of the voyages of exploration. Delighted by the fine quality and abundance of the products from all over Asia that were available in the town's great marketplace, the Portuguese were startled to learn that the local merchants had little interest in the products they had brought to trade. In fact, their cast-iron pots, coarse cloth, and glass and coral beads elicited little more than sneers from the merchants they approached.

Da Gama and his crew faced the humbling prospect of returning home to Lisbon with little proof that they had reached Asia and begun to tap its legendary wealth. Reluctantly, they concluded that they had little choice but to use the small supply of silver bullion they had brought along for emergencies. They found that the Asian merchants were quite willing to take their precious metal. But they also realized that their meager supply of bullion would not go very far toward filling the holds of their ships with Asian treasures.

| 1350 C.E. | 1500 C.E. | 1550 C.E. | 1600 C.E. | 1650 C.E. | 1700 C.E. |
|---|---|---|---|---|---|
| **1368** Ming dynasty comes to power in China<br>**1368–1398** Reign of the Hongwu emperor<br>**1390** Ming restrictions on overseas commerce<br>**1403–1424** Reign of the Yunglo emperor in China<br>**1405–1423** Zhenghe expeditions from China to southeast Asia, India, and east Africa<br>**1498–1499** Vasco da Gama opens the sea route around Africa to Asia | **1507** Portuguese defeat combined Muslim war fleet near Diu off western India<br>**1510** Portuguese conquest of Goa in western India<br>**1511** Portuguese conquer Malacca on the tip of Malayan peninsula<br>**1540s** Francis Xavier makes mass converts in India | **1573** End of the Ashikaga shogunate<br>**1573–1620** Reign of the Wanli emperor<br>**1580s** Jesuits arrive in China<br>**1590** Hideyoshi unifies Japan<br>**1592** First Japanese invasion of Korea<br>**1597** Second Japanese invasion of Korea | **1600s** Dutch and British assault on Portuguese Empire in Asia; decline of Portuguese power<br>**1603** Tokugawa shogunate established<br>**1614** Christianity banned in Japan<br>**1619–1620** Dutch East India Company established at Batavia on Java<br>**1640s** Japan moves into self-imposed isolation<br>**1641** Dutch capture Malacca from Portuguese; Dutch confined to Deshima Island off Nagasaki<br>**1644** Nomadic Manchus put an end to Ming dynasty; Manchu Qing dynasty rules China | **1654–1722** Reign of the Kangxi emperor in China | **1755–1757** Dutch become paramount power on Java; Qing conquest of Mongolia |

Much of the enterprise that occupied the Europeans who went out to Asia in the 16th and 17th centuries was devoted to working out the implications of that first encounter in Calicut. The very fact of da Gama's arrival demonstrated not only the seaworthiness of their **caravel** ships but also that the Europeans' needs and curiosity could drive them halfway around the world. Their stops at Calicut and ports on the eastern coast of Africa also confirmed reports of earlier travelers that the Portuguese had arrived in east Africa and south and southeast Asia long after their Muslim rivals. This unpleasant discovery promised resistance to Portuguese trading and empire building in Asia. It also meant major obstacles to their plans for converting the peoples of the area to Roman Catholicism. The Portuguese and the other Europeans who came after them found that their Muslim adversaries greatly outnumbered them and had long-standing and well-entrenched political and economic connections from east Africa to the Philippines. They soon concluded that only the use of military force would allow them to break into the vast Indian Ocean trading system.

Although da Gama's voyage marked a major turning point for western Europe, its impact on Asia was much less decisive. As was the case with the Mughal and Safavid empires (see Chapter 26), the central themes in the history of Asian civilizations in the 16th and 17th centuries often had little or nothing to do with European expansion. The development of Asian states and empires emerged from long-term processes rooted in the inner workings of these ancient civilizations and in their interactions with neighboring states and nomadic peoples. Although the European presence was felt in each of the areas considered in this chapter, the impact of Europe's global expansion was of secondary importance except in the islands of southeast Asia, which were especially vulnerable to Western sea power. Most Asian rulers, merchants, and religious leaders refused to take seriously the potential threat posed by what was, after all, a handful of strangers from across the world.

## The Asian Trading World and the Coming of the Europeans

■ **In the centuries following da Gama's voyage, most European enterprise in the Indian Ocean centered on efforts to find the most profitable ways to carry Asian products back to Europe. Some Europeans went to Asia not for personal gain but to convert others to Christianity, and these missionaries, as well as some traders, settled in coastal enclaves.**

As later voyages by Portuguese fleets revealed, Calicut and the ports of east Africa, which Vasco da Gama

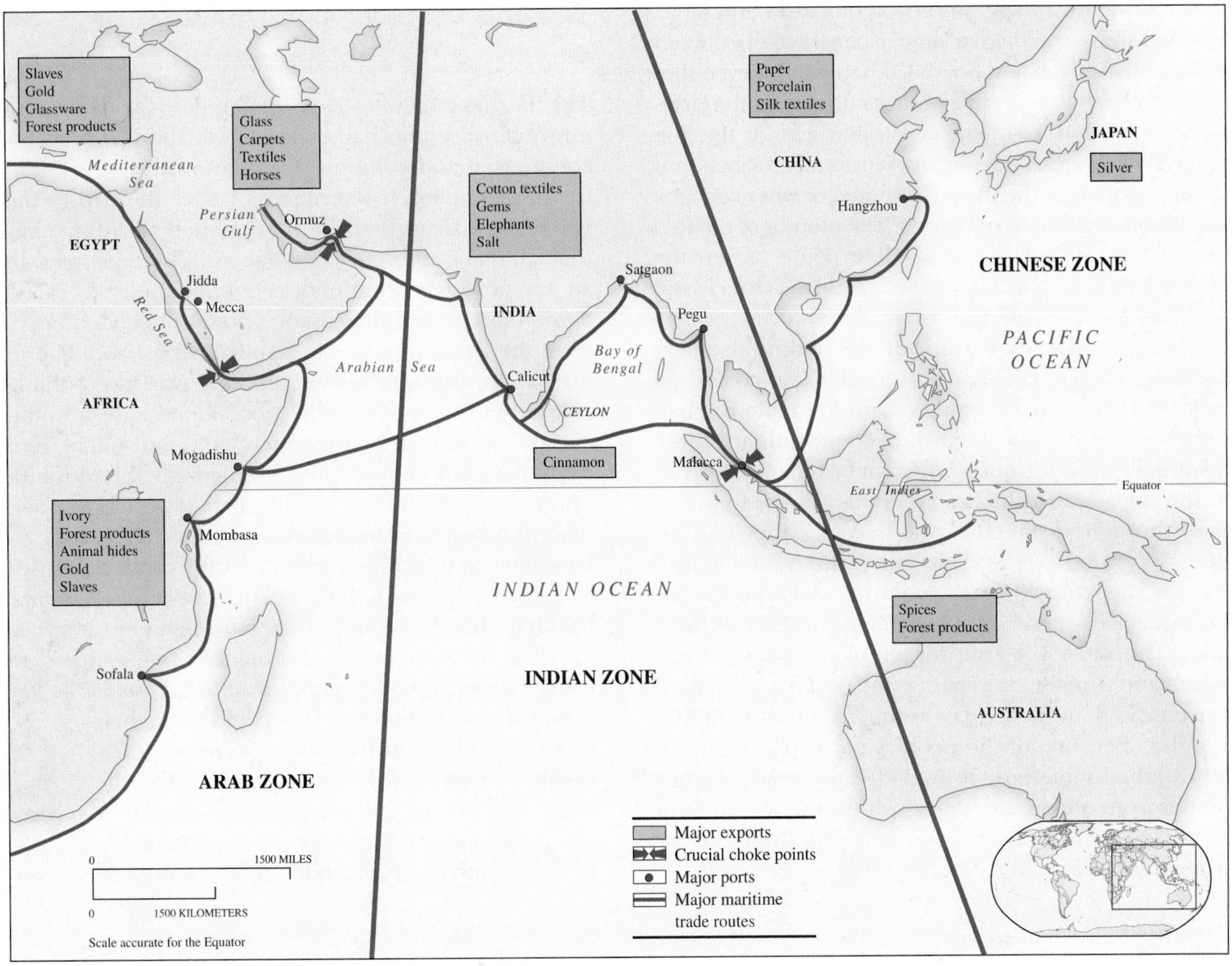

**MAP 27.1** Routes and Major Products Exchanged in the Asian Trading Network, c. 1500

had found on the initial foray into Asia, made up only a small segment of a larger network of commercial exchange and cultural interaction. This trading system stretched thousands of miles from the Middle East and Africa along all the coasts of the giant Asian continent. Both the products exchanged in this network and the main routes followed by those who sailed it had been established for centuries—in many cases, millennia.

In general, the **Asian sea trading network** can be broken down into three main zones, each of which was focused on major centers of handicraft manufacture (Map 27.1). In the west was an Arab zone anchored on the glass, carpets, and tapestries of the Islamic heartlands at the head of the Red Sea and the Persian Gulf. India, with its superb cotton textiles, dominated the central portions of the system. China, which excelled in producing paper, porcelain, and silk textiles, formed the eastern pole. In between or on the fringes of the three great manufacturing centers were areas such as Japan, the mainland kingdoms and island states of southeast Asia, and the port cities of east Africa that fed mainly raw materials—precious metals, foods, and forest products—into the trading network.

Trade Routes to Asia

Of the raw materials circulating in the system, the broadest demand and highest prices were paid for spices, which came mainly from Ceylon and the islands at the eastern end of what is today the Indonesian archipelago. Long-distance trade was largely in high-priced commodities such as spices, ivory from Africa, and precious stones. But silk and cotton textiles also were traded over long distances. Bulk items, such as rice, livestock, and timber, normally were exchanged between the ports within each of the main trading zones.

Since ancient times, monsoon winds and the nature of the ships and navigational instruments available to sailors had dictated the main trade routes in the Asian network. Much navigation was of the coasting variety, that is, sailing along the shoreline and charting distances and location with reference to towns and natural landmarks.

The Arabs and Chinese, who had compasses and large, well-built ships, could cross large expanses of open water such as the Arabian and South China seas. But even they preferred established coastal routes rather than the largely uncharted and less predictable open seas. As the Portuguese quickly learned, there were several crucial points where segments of the trade converged or where geography funneled it into narrow areas. The mouths of the Red Sea and Persian Gulf were two of these points, as were the Straits of Malacca, which separated mainland from island southeast Asia (Map 27.1).

Two general characteristics of the trading system at the time of the Portuguese arrival were critical to European attempts to regulate and dominate it. First, there was no central control. Second, military force was usually absent from commercial exchanges within it. Although Arab sailors and merchants were found in ports throughout much of the network, they had no sense of common cause. They sailed and traded to provide for their own livelihood and to make profits for the princes or merchants who financed their expeditions. The same was true for the Chinese, southeast Asian, and Indian merchants and sailors who were concentrated in particular segments of the trading complex. Because all the peoples participating in the network had something to trade for the products they wanted from others, exchanges within the system were largely peaceful. Trading vessels were lightly armed for protection against attack by pirates.

## Trading Empire: The Portuguese Response to the Encounter at Calicut

The Portuguese were not prepared to abide by the informal rules that had evolved over the centuries for commercial and cultural exchanges in the great Asian trading complex. It was apparent after the trip to the market in Calicut that the Portuguese had little, other than gold and silver, to exchange with Asian peoples. In an age in which prominent economic theorists, called *mercantilists,* taught that a state's power depended heavily on the amount of precious metals a monarch had in his coffers, a steady flow of bullion to Asia was unthinkable. It was particularly objectionable because it would enrich and thus strengthen merchants and rulers from rival kingdoms and religions, particularly the Muslims, whose position the Portuguese had set out to undermine through their overseas enterprises (Figure 27.2). Unwilling to forgo the possibilities for profit that a sea route to Asia presented, the Portuguese resolved to take by force what they could not get through fair trade.

The decision by the Portuguese to use force to extract spices and other goods from Asia resulted largely from their realization that they could offset their lack of numbers and trading goods with their superior ships and weaponry. Except for the huge war fleets of Chinese junks, no Asian people could muster fleets able to withstand the firepower and maneuverability of the Portuguese

Portuguese Church in Southern India

FIGURE 27.2 In the 15th and 16th centuries, the port of Lisbon in tiny Portugal was one of the great centers of international commerce and European overseas exploration. Although aspects of the early, streamlined caravel design can be detected in the ships pictured here, additional square sails, higher fore and aft castles, and numerous cannons projecting from holes cut in the ships' sides exemplify a later stage of naval development.

squadrons. Their sudden appearance in Asian waters and their interjection of sea warfare into a peaceful trading system gained the European intruders an element of surprise that kept their adversaries off balance in the critical early years of empire building. The Portuguese forces were small in numbers but united in their drive for wealth and religious converts. This allowed them to take advantage of the deep divisions that separated their Asian competitors and the Asians' inability to combine their forces effectively in battle. Thus, when da Gama returned on a second expedition to Asian waters in 1502, he was able to force ports on both the African and Indian coasts to submit to a Portuguese tribute regime. He also assaulted towns that refused to cooperate. When a combined Egyptian and Indian fleet was finally sent in reprisal in 1509, it was defeated off Diu on the western Indian coast. The Portuguese would not have to face so formidable an alliance of Asian sea powers again.

The Portuguese soon found that sea patrols and raids on coastal towns were not sufficient to control the trade in the items they wanted, especially spices. Thus, from 1507 onward they strove to capture towns and build fortresses at a number of strategic points on the Asian trading network (see map in Visualizing the Past). In that year they took **Ormuz** at the southern end of the Persian Gulf; in 1510 they captured **Goa** on the western Indian coast. Most critical of all, in the next year they successfully stormed Malacca on the tip of the Malayan peninsula. These ports served both as naval bases for Portuguese fleets patrolling Asian waters and as *factories,* or points where spices and other products could be stored until they were shipped to Europe. Ships and naval stations became the key components of a Portuguese trading empire that was financed and directed by the kings of Portugal.

The aim of the empire was to establish Portuguese monopoly control over key Asian products, particularly spices such as cinnamon (Figure 27.3). Ideally, all the spices produced were to be shipped in Portuguese galleons to Asian or European markets. There they would be sold at high prices, which the Portuguese could dictate because they controlled the supply of these goods. The Portuguese also sought, with little success, to impose a licensing system on all merchant ships that traded in the Indian Ocean from Ormuz to Malacca. The combination of monopoly and the licensing system, backed by force, was intended to give the Portuguese control of a sizeable portion of the Asian trading network.

FIGURE 27.3 Although today nutmeg is a minor condiment, in the early modern era it was a treasured and widely used spice. In this manuscript illustration from the 16th century, slices of an oversized nutmeg are being weighed in preparation for sale on the international market.

## Portuguese Vulnerability and the Rise of the Dutch and English Trading Empires

The plans for empire that the Portuguese drew up on paper never became reality. They managed for some decades to control much of the flow of spices, such as nutmeg and mace, which were grown in very limited areas. But control of the market in key condiments, such as pepper and cinnamon, eluded them. At times the Portuguese resorted to severe punishments such as cutting off the hands of the rival traders and ships' crews caught transporting spices in defiance of their monopoly. But they simply did not have the soldiers or the ships to sustain their monopolies, much less the licensing system. The resistance of Asian rivals, poor military discipline, rampant corruption among crown officials, and heavy Portuguese shipping losses caused by overloading and poor design had taken a heavy toll on the empire by the end of the 16th century.

The overextended and declining Portuguese trading empire proved no match for the Dutch and English rivals, whose war fleets challenged it in the early 17th century. Of the two, the Dutch emerged, at least in the short term, as the victors. They captured the critical Portuguese

VISUALIZING THE PAST

# Intruders: The Pattern of Early European Expansion into Asia

Compare the map shown here with Map 27.1. Note the new routes, major port centers, and fortified factory centers added by the different European powers as they moved into Asia. Compare these with the traditional regions of spice growing, textile manufacture, and other industries.

Also note the areas where the different European powers began to establish substantial territorial empires and the dates when these areas were brought under Western control. Compare the routes favored by the Portuguese, Dutch, English, French, and Spanish, and the areas where their fortified outposts and territorial conquests are centered.

**Questions** What do the shifting areas where European routes and fortified trading centers are located tell us about the main goals and relative power of each of the European countries? What advantages did those who entered later in the process have in this regard? On the basis of the discussion in Chapters 21 and 22, which of these states would you argue had the strongest power base in Europe itself? Why was the Spanish pattern of expansion so radically different from those of the other powers? Which areas of Asia were the most impervious to European expansionism in this period, and why?

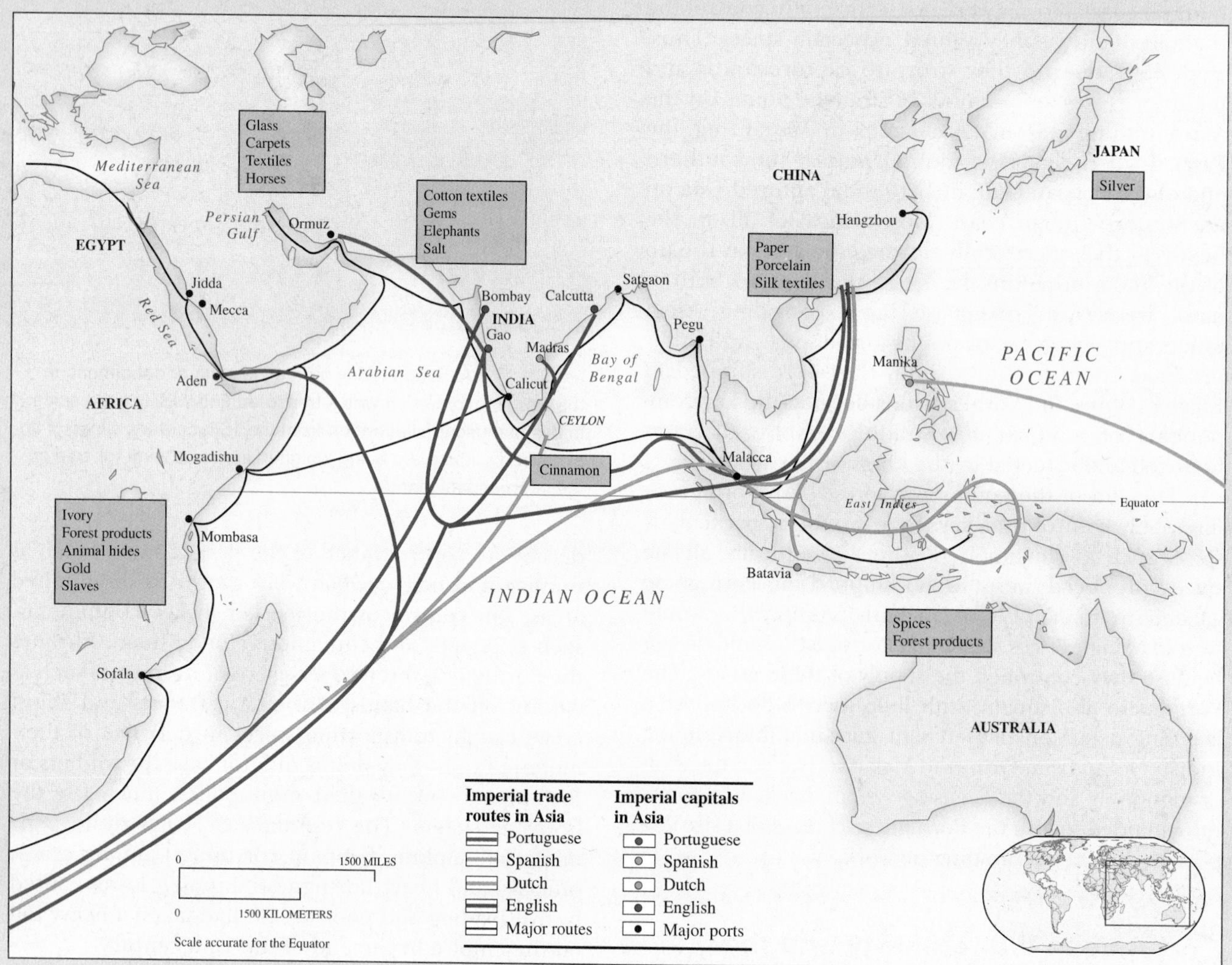

port and fortress at Malacca and built a new port of their own in 1620 at **Batavia** on the island of Java. The latter location, which was much closer to the island sources of key spices, reflected the improved European knowledge of Asian geography. It also reflected the Dutch decision to concentrate on the monopoly control of certain spices rather than on Asian trade more generally. The English, who fought hard but lost the struggle for control of the Spice Islands, were forced to fall back to India.

The **Dutch trading empire** (see Visualizing the Past) was made up of the same basic components as the Portuguese: fortified towns and factories, warships on patrol, and monopoly control of a limited number of products. But the Dutch had more numerous and better armed ships and went about the business of monopoly control in a much more systematic fashion. To regulate the supply of cloves, nutmeg, and mace, for example, they uprooted the plants that produced these spices on islands they did not control. They also forcibly removed or wiped out island peoples who cultivated these spices without Dutch supervision and dared to sell them to their trading rivals.

Although the profits from the sale of these spices in Europe in the mid-17th century helped sustain Holland's golden age, the Dutch found that the greatest profits in the long run could be gained from peacefully working themselves into the long-established Asian trading system. The demand for spices declined and their futile efforts to gain control over crops such as pepper that were grown in many places became more and more expensive. In response, the Dutch came to rely mainly (as they had long done in Europe) on the fees they charged for transporting products from one area in Asia to another. They also depended on profits gained from buying Asian products, such as cloth, in one area and trading them in other areas for goods that could be sold in Europe at inflated prices. The English also adopted these peaceful trading patterns, although their enterprises were concentrated along the coasts of India and on the cloth trade rather than on the spices of southeast Asia.

## Going Ashore: European Tribute Systems in Asia

Their ships and guns allowed the Europeans to force their way into the Asian trading network in the 16th and 17th centuries. But as they moved inland and away from the sea, their military advantages and their ability to dominate the Asian peoples rapidly disappeared. Because the vastly superior numbers of Asian armies offset the Europeans' advantage in weapons and organization for waging war on land, even small kingdoms such as those on Java and in mainland southeast Asia were able to resist European inroads into their domains. In the larger empires such as those in China, India, and Persia, and when confronted by martial cultures such as Japan's, the Europeans quickly learned their place. That they were often reduced to kowtowing or humbling themselves before the thrones of Asian potentates is demonstrated by the instructions given by a Dutch envoy about the proper behavior for a visit to the Japanese court:

> Our ministers have no other instruction to take there except to look to the wishes of that brave, superb, precise nation in order to please it in everything, and by no means to think on anything which might cause greater antipathy to us. . . . That consequently the Company's ministers frequenting the scrupulous state each year must above all go armed in modesty, humility, courtesy, and amity, always being the lesser.

In certain situations, however, the Europeans were drawn inland away from their forts, factories, and war fleets in the early centuries of their expansion into Asia. The Portuguese, and the Dutch after them, felt compelled to conquer the coastal areas of Ceylon to control the production and sale of cinnamon, which grew in the forests of the southern portions of that island. The Dutch moved slowly inland from their base at Batavia into the highlands of western Java. They discovered that this area was ideal for growing coffee, which was in great demand in Europe by the 17th century. By the mid-18th century, the Dutch not only controlled the coffee-growing areas but were the paramount power on Java.

The Spanish, taking advantage of the fact that the Philippine Islands lay in the half of the world the pope had given them to explore and settle in 1493, invaded the islands in the 1560s. The conquest of **Luzon** and the northern islands was facilitated by the fact that the animistic inhabitants lived in small states the Spanish could subjugate one by one. The repeated failure of Spanish expeditions to conquer the southern island of **Mindanao,** which was ruled by a single kingdom whose Muslim rulers were determined to resist Christian dominance, dramatically underscores the limits of the Europeans' ability to project their power on land in this era.

In each area where the Europeans went ashore in the early centuries of expansion, they set up tribute regimes that closely resembled those the Spanish imposed on the Native American peoples of the New World (see Chapter 24). The European overlords were content to let the indigenous peoples live in their traditional settlements, controlled largely by hereditary leaders drawn from their own communities. In most areas, little attempt was made to interfere in the daily lives of the conquered peoples as long as their leaders met the tribute quotas set by the European conquerors. The tribute was paid in the form of agricultural products grown by the peasantry under forced labor systems supervised by the peasants' own elites. In some cases, the indigenous peoples continued to harvest crops they had produced for centuries, such as the bark of the cinnamon plant. In other areas new crops, such as coffee and sugar cane, were introduced. But in all cases, the demands for tribute took into account the local peasants' need to raise the crops on which they subsisted.

## Spreading the Faith: The Missionary Enterprise in South and Southeast Asia

Although the Protestant Dutch and English were little interested in winning converts to Christianity during the early centuries of overseas expansion, the spread of Roman Catholicism was a fundamental part of the global mission of the Portuguese and Spanish. After the widespread conversion of Native American peoples, the meager returns from the Iberian missionary offensive in Asia were disappointing. The fact that Islam had arrived in much of maritime south and southeast Asia centuries before da Gama's arrival had much to do with the indifference or open hostility the Portuguese met when they tried to convert the peoples of these regions to Christianity. The dream of a Christian Asia joining the Iberian crusade against the Muslims was also dealt a setback by the discovery that the Hindus, whom da Gama and some of his entourage had originally believed to be Christians, had a sophisticated and deeply entrenched set of religious ideas and rituals.

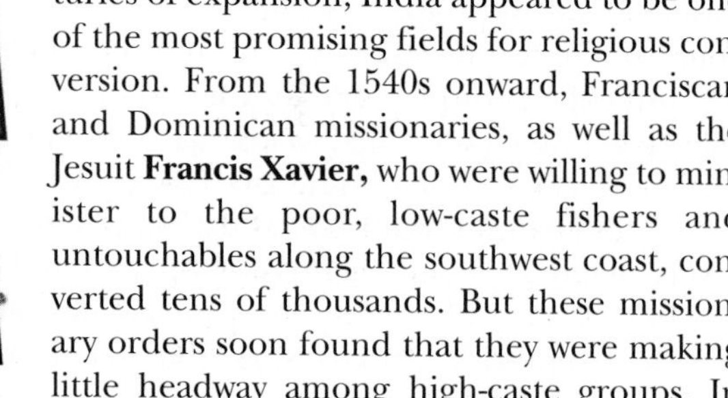

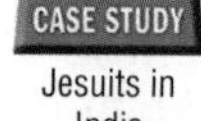

CASE STUDY
Jesuits in India

DOCUMENT
St. Francis Xavier, Jesuit in India

Despite these setbacks, of all the Asian areas where European enclaves were established in the early centuries of expansion, India appeared to be one of the most promising fields for religious conversion. From the 1540s onward, Franciscan and Dominican missionaries, as well as the Jesuit **Francis Xavier,** who were willing to minister to the poor, low-caste fishers and untouchables along the southwest coast, converted tens of thousands. But these missionary orders soon found that they were making little headway among high-caste groups. In fact, taboos against contact with untouchables and other low-caste groups made it nearly impossible for the missionaries to approach prospective upper-caste converts.

To overcome these obstacles, an Italian Jesuit named **Robert di Nobili** devised a different conversion strategy in the early 1600s. He learned several Indian languages, including Sanskrit, which allowed him to read the sacred texts of the Hindus. He donned the garments worn by Indian brahmans and adopted a vegetarian diet. All these measures were calculated to win over the upper-caste Hindus in south India, where he was based. Di Nobili reasoned that if he succeeded in Christianizing the high-caste Hindus, they would then bring the lower Hindu castes into the fold. But, he argued, because the ancient Hindu religion was sophisticated and deeply entrenched, Indian brahmans and other high-caste groups would listen only to those who adopted their ways. Meat eaters would be seen as defiling; those who were unfamiliar with the Hindus' sacred texts would be considered ignorant.

Despite some early successes, di Nobili's strategy was undone by the refusal of high-caste Hindu converts to worship with low-caste groups and to give up many of their traditional beliefs and religious rituals. Rival missionary orders, particularly the Dominicans and Franciscans, denounced his approach. In assimilating to Hindu culture, they claimed, di Nobili and his co-workers, not the Indians, were the ones who had been converted. His rivals also pointed out that the refusal of di Nobili's high-caste converts to worship with untouchable Christians defied one of the central tenets of Christianity: the equality of all believers before God. His rivals finally won the ear of the pope, and di Nobili was recalled to Rome. Deprived of his energy and knowledge of Indian ways, his mission in south India quickly collapsed.

Beyond socially stigmatized groups such as the untouchables, the conversion of the general populace in Asia occurred only in isolated areas. Perhaps the greatest successes of the Christian missions occurred in the northern islands of the Philippines, which had not previously been exposed to a world religion such as Islam or Buddhism. Because the Spanish had conquered the island of Luzon and the smaller islands to the south, and then governed them as part of their vast intercontinental empire, they were able to launch a major missionary effort. The *friars,* as the priests and brothers who went out to convert and govern the rural populace were called, became the main channel for transmitting European influences. The friars first converted local Filipino leaders. These leaders then directed their followers to build new settlements that were centered, like those in Iberia and the New World, on town squares where the local church, the residences of the missionary fathers, and government offices were located. Beyond tending to the spiritual needs of the villagers in their congregation, the friars served as government officials.

Like the Native Americans of Spain's New World empire, most Filipinos were formally converted to Catholicism. But also like the Native Americans, the Filipinos' brand of Christianity represented a creative blend of their traditional beliefs and customs and the religion preached by the friars. Because key tenets of the Christian faith were taught in Spanish for fear that they would be corrupted if put in the local languages, it is doubtful that most of the converts had a very good grasp of Christian beliefs. Many converted because Spanish dominance and their own leaders' conversion gave them little choice. Others adopted the new faith because they believed that the Christian God could protect them from illness or because they were taken with the notion that they would be equal to their Spanish overlords in heaven.

Almost all Filipinos clung to their traditional ways and in the process seriously compromised Christian beliefs and practices. The peoples of the islands continued public bathing, which the missionaries condemned as immodest, and refused to give up ritual drinking. They also continued to commune with deceased members of their families, often in sessions that were disguised as public recitations of the rosary. Thus, even in the Asian area where European control was the strongest and pressures for acculturation to European ways the greatest, much of the preconquest way of life and approach to the world was maintained.

## Ming China: A Global Mission Refused

- **With the restoration of ethnic Chinese rule and the reunification of the country under the Ming dynasty (1368–1644), Chinese civilization enjoyed a new age of splendor. Renewed agrarian and commercial growth supported a population that was the largest of any center of civilization at the time, probably exceeding that of all western Europe.**

Zhu Yuanzhang, a military commander of peasant origins who founded the Ming dynasty, had suffered a great deal under the Mongol yoke. Both his parents and two of his brothers had died in a plague in 1344, and he and a remaining brother were reduced to begging for the land in which to bury the rest of their family. Threatened with the prospect of starvation in one of the many famines that ravaged the countryside in the later, corruption-riddled reigns of the Mongols, Zhu alternated between begging and living in a Buddhist monastery to survive. When the neighboring countryside rose in rebellion in the late 1340s, Zhu left the monastery to join a rebel band. His courage in combat and his natural capacity as a leader soon made him one of the more prominent of several rebel warlords attempting to overthrow the Yuan dynasty. After protracted military struggles against rival rebel claimants to the throne and the Mongol rulers themselves, Zhu's armies conquered most of China. Zhu declared himself the **Hongwu** emperor in 1368. He reigned for 30 years.

Immediately after he seized the throne, Zhu launched an effort to rid China of all traces of the "barbarian" Mongols. Mongol dress was discarded, Mongol names were dropped by those who had adopted them and were removed from buildings and court records, and Mongol palaces and administrative buildings in some areas were raided and sacked. The nomads themselves fled or were driven beyond the Great Wall, where Ming military expeditions pursued them on several occasions.

### Another Scholar-Gentry Revival

Because the Hongwu emperor, like the founder of the earlier Han dynasty, was from a peasant family and thus poorly educated, he viewed the scholar-gentry with some suspicion. But he also realized that their cooperation was essential to the full revival of Chinese civilization. Scholars well versed in the Confucian classics were again appointed to the very highest positions in the imperial government. The generous state subsidies that had supported the imperial academies in the capital and the regional colleges were fully restored. Most critically, the civil service examination system, which the Mongols had discontinued, was reinstated and greatly expanded. In the Ming era and the Qing that followed, the examinations played a greater role in determining entry into the Chinese bureaucracy than had been the case under any earlier dynasty.

In the Ming era, the examination system was routinized and made more complex than before. Prefectural, or county, exams were held in two out of three years. The exams were given in large compounds, like the one depicted in Figure 27.4, surrounded by walls and watchtowers from which the examiners could keep an eye on the thousands of candidates. Each candidate was assigned a small cubicle where he struggled to answer the questions, slept, and ate over the several days that it took to complete the arduous exam. Those who passed and received the lowest degree were eligible to take the next level of exams, which were given in the provincial capitals every three years. Only the most gifted and ambitious went on because the process was fiercely competitive—in some years as many as 4000 candidates competed for 150 degrees. Success at the provincial level brought a rise in status and opened the way for appointments to positions in the middle levels of the imperial bureaucracy. It also permitted particularly talented scholars to take the

**FIGURE 27.4** A 19th-century engraving shows the cubicles in which Chinese students and bureaucrats took the imperial civil service examinations in the capital at Beijing. Candidates were confined to the cubicles for days and completed their exams under the constant surveillance of official proctors. They brought their own food, slept in the cubicles, and were disqualified if they were found talking to others taking the exams or going outside the compound where the exams were being given.

imperial examinations, which were given in the capital every three years. Those who passed the imperial exams were eligible for the highest posts in the realm and were the most revered of all Chinese, except members of the royal family.

## Reform: Hongwu's Efforts to Root Out Abuses in Court Politics

Hongwu was mindful of his dependence on a well-educated and loyal scholar-gentry for the day-to-day administration of the empire. But he sought to put clear limits on their influence and to institute reforms that would check the abuses of other factions at court. Early in his reign, Hongwu abolished the position of chief minister, which had formerly been the key link between the many ministries of the central government. The powers that had been amassed by those who occupied this office were transferred to the emperor. Hongwu also tried to impress all officials with the honesty, loyalty, and discipline he expected from them by introducing the practice of public beatings for bureaucrats found guilty of corruption or incompetence. Officials charged with misdeeds were paraded before the assembled courtiers and beaten a specified number of times on their bare buttocks. Many died of the wounds they received in the ordeal. Those who survived never recovered from the humiliation, which was to a certain extent shared by all the scholar-gentry by virtue of the very fact that such degrading punishments could be meted out to any of them.

Hongwu also introduced measures to cut down on the court factionalism and never-ending conspiracies that had eroded the power of earlier dynasties. He decreed that the emperor's wives should come only from humble family origins. This was intended to put an end to the power plays of the consorts from high-ranking families, who built palace cliques that were centered on their influential aristocratic relatives. He warned against allowing eunuchs to occupy positions of independent power and sought to limit their numbers within the Forbidden City. To prevent plots against the ruler and fights over succession, Hongwu established the practice of exiling all potential rivals to the throne to estates in the provinces, and he forbade them to become involved in political affairs. On the darker side, Hongwu condoned thought control, as when he had some sections from Mencius's writings that displeased him deleted forever from the writings included on the imperial exams. Although many of these measures went far to keep peace at court under Hongwu and his strong successor, the Yunglo emperor (r. 1403–1424), they were allowed to lapse under later, less capable, rulers, with devastating consequences for the Ming Empire.

## A Return to Scholar-Gentry Social Dominance

Perhaps because his lowly origins and personal suffering made him sensitive to the plight of the peasantry, Hongwu introduced measures that would improve the lot of the common people. Like most strong emperors, he promoted public works projects, including dike building and the extension of irrigation systems aimed at improving the farmers' yields. To bring new lands

DOCUMENT

## Exam Questions as a Mirror of Chinese Values

The subjects and specific learning tested on the Chinese civil service exams give us insight into the behavior and attitudes expected of the literate, ruling classes of what was perhaps the best-educated preindustrial civilization. Sample questions from these exams can tell us a good deal about what sorts of knowledge were considered important and what kinds of skills were necessary for those who aspired to successful careers in the most prestigious and potentially the most lucrative field open to Chinese youths: administrative service in the imperial bureaucracy. The very fact that such a tiny portion of the Chinese male population could take the exams and an even smaller number could successfully pass them says a lot about gender roles and elitism in Chinese society. In addition, the often decisive role of a student's calligraphy—the skill with which he was able to brush the Chinese characters—reflects the emphasis the Chinese elite placed on a refined sense of aesthetics.

Question 1: Provide the missing phrases and elaborate on the meaning of the following:

The Duke of She observed to Confucius: "Among us there was an upright man called Kung who was so upright that when his father appropriated a sheep, he bore witness against him." Confucius said . . .

[The missing phrases are, "The upright men among us are not like that. A father will screen his son and a son his father . . . yet uprightness is to be found in that."]

Question 2: Write an eight-legged essay [one consisting of eight sections] on the following:

Scrupulous in his own conduct and lenient only in his dealings with the people.

Question 3: First unscramble the following characters and then comment on the significance of this quotation from one of the classic texts:

Beginning, good, mutually, nature, basically, practice, far, near, men's

[The correct answer is, "Men's beginning nature is basically good. Nature mutually near. Practice mutually far."]

**Questions** Looking at the content of these questions, what can we learn about Chinese society and attitudes? For example, where do the Chinese look for models to orient their social behavior? What kinds of knowledge are important to the Chinese? Do they stress specialist skills or the sort of learning that we associate with a broad liberal arts education? If we take SAT exams as equivalent gauges of our social values, how would you compare Ming China and modern America? What are the advantages and drawbacks of each system?

under cultivation and encourage the growth of a peasant class that owned the lands it toiled so hard to bring into production, Hongwu decreed that unoccupied lands would become the tax-exempt property of those who cleared and cultivated them. He lowered forced labor demands on the peasantry by both the government and members of the gentry class. Hongwu also promoted silk and cotton cloth production and other handicrafts that provided supplemental income for peasant households.

Although these measures led to some short-term improvement in the peasants' condition, they were all but offset by the growing power of rural landlord families, buttressed by alliances with relatives in the imperial bureaucracy. Gentry households with members in government service were exempted from land taxes and enjoyed special privileges, such as permission to be carried about in sedan chairs and to use fans and umbrellas. Many gentry families engaged in moneylending on the side; some even ran lucrative gambling dens. Almost all added to their estates either by buying up lands held by peasant landholders or by foreclosing on loans made to farmers in times of need in exchange for mortgages on their family plots. Peasants displaced in these ways had little choice but to become tenants of large landowners or landless laborers moving about in search of employment.

More land meant ever larger and more comfortable households for the gentry class. They justified the growing gap between their wealth and the poverty of the peasantry by contrasting their foresight and industry with the lazy and wasteful ways of the ordinary farmers. The virtues of the gentry class were celebrated in stories and popular illustrations. The latter showed members of gentry households hard at work weaving and storing grain to see them through the cold weather, while commoners who neglected these tasks wandered during the winter, cold and hungry, past the walled compounds and closed gates of gentry households.

At most levels of Chinese society, the Ming period continued the subordination of youths to elders and women to men that had been steadily intensifying in earlier periods. If anything, neo-Confucian thinking was even more influential than under the late Song and Yuan dynasties. Some of its advocates proposed draconian measures to suppress challenges to the increasingly

**FIGURE 27.5** The varied diversions of the wives and concubines of Ming emperors are depicted in this scene of court life. In addition to court intrigues and maneuvers to win the emperor's favor, women of the imperial household occupied themselves with dance, music, games, and polite conversation. With eunuchs, officials, and palace guards watching them closely, the women of the palace and imperial city spent most of their lives in confined yet well-appointed spaces.

rigid social roles. For example, students were expected to venerate and follow the instructions of their teachers, no matter how muddle-headed or tipsy the latter might be. A terrifying lesson in proper decorum was drawn from an incident in which a student at the imperial academy dared to dispute the findings of one of his instructors. The student was beheaded, and his severed head was hung on a pole at the entrance to the academy. Not surprisingly, this rather unsubtle solution to the problem of keeping order in the classroom merely drove student protest underground. Anonymous letters critical of poorly prepared teachers continued to circulate among the student body.

Women were also driven to underground activities to ameliorate their subordination and, if they dared, expand their career opportunities. At the court, they continued, despite Hongwu's measures, to play strong roles behind the scenes. Even able rulers such as Hongwu were swayed by the advice of favorite wives or dowager mothers and aunts. On one occasion, Hongwu chided the empress Ma for daring to inquire into the condition of the common people. She replied that because he was the father of the people, she was the mother, and thus it was quite proper for her to be concerned for the welfare of her children.

Even within the palace, the plight of most women was grim. Hundreds, sometimes thousands of attractive young women were brought to the court in the hope that they would catch the emperor's fancy and become one of his concubines or perhaps even be elevated to the status of wife. Because few actually succeeded, many spent their lives in loneliness and inactivity, just waiting for the emperor to glance their way.

In society at large, women had to settle for whatever status and respect they could win within the family. As before, their success in this regard hinged largely on bearing male children and, when these children were married, moving from the status of daughter-in-law to mother-in-law. The daughters of upper-class families were often taught to read and write by their parents or brothers, and many composed poetry, painted, and played musical instruments (Figure 27.5).

For women from the nonelite classes, the main avenues for some degree of independence and self-expression remained becoming courtesans or entertainers. The former should be clearly distinguished from prostitutes because they served a very different clientele and were literate and often accomplished in painting, music, and poetry. Although courtesans often enjoyed lives of luxury, even the most successful made their living by gratifying the needs of upper-class men for uninhibited sex and convivial companionship.

## An Age of Growth: Agriculture, Population, Commerce, and the Arts

The first decades of the Ming period were an age of buoyant economic growth in China that both was fed by and resulted in unprecedented contacts with other civilizations overseas. The territories controlled by the Ming emperors were never as extensive as those ruled by the Tang dynasty. But in the Ming era, the great commercial boom and population increase that had begun in the late Song were renewed and accelerated. The peopling of the Yangtze region and the areas to the south was given a great boost by the importation, through Spanish and Portuguese merchant intermediaries, of new food crops from the Americas, particularly root crops from the Andes highlands. Three plants—maize (corn), sweet potatoes, and peanuts—were especially important. Because these crops could be grown on inferior soils without irrigation, their cultivation spread quickly through the hilly and marginal areas that bordered on the irrigated rice lands of southern China. They became vital supplements to the staple rice or millet diet of the Chinese people, particularly those of the rapidly growing southern regions.

Because these plants were less susceptible to drought, they also became an important hedge against famine. The introduction of these new crops was an important factor behind the great surge in population growth that was under way by the end of the Ming era. By 1600 the population of China had risen to about 120 million from 80 to 90 million in the 14th century. Two centuries later, in 1800, it had more than doubled and surpassed 300 million.

Agrarian expansion and population increase were paralleled in early Ming times by a renewal of commercial growth. The market sector of the domestic economy became ever more pervasive, and overseas trading links multiplied. Because China's advanced handicraft industries produced a wide variety of goods, from silk textiles and tea to fine ceramics and lacquerware, that were in high demand throughout Asia and in Europe, the terms of trade ran very much in China's favor. This is why China received more American silver (brought by European merchants) than any other single society in the world economy of the early modern period. In addition to the Arab and Asian traders, Europeans arrived in increasing numbers at the only two places—**Macao** and, somewhat later and more sporadically, **Canton**—where they were officially allowed to do business in Ming China.

Not surprisingly, the merchant classes, particularly those engaged in long-distance trade, reaped the biggest profits from the economic boom. But a good portion of their gains was transferred to the state in the form of taxes and to the scholar-gentry in the form of bribes for official favors. Much of the merchants' wealth was invested in land rather than plowed back into trade or manufacturing, because land owning, not commerce, remained the surest route to social status in China.

Ming prosperity was reflected in the fine arts, which found generous patrons both at court and among the scholar-gentry class more generally. Although the monochromatic simplicity of the work of earlier dynasties was sustained by the ink brush paintings of artists such as Xuwei, much of the Ming output was busier and more colorful. Portraits and scenes of court, city, or country life were more prominent. Nonetheless, the Chinese continued to delight in depicting individual scholars or travelers contemplating the beauty of mountains, lakes, and marshes that dwarf the human observers.

Whereas the painters of the Ming era concentrated mainly on developing established techniques and genres, major innovation was occurring in literature. Most notable in this regard was the full development of the Chinese novel, which had had its beginnings in the writings of the Yuan era. The novel form was given great impetus by the spread of literacy among the upper classes in the Ming era. This was facilitated by the growing availability of books that had resulted from the spread of woodblock printing from the 10th century onward. Ming novels such as *The Water Margin*, *Monkey*, and *The Golden Lotus* were recognized as classics in their own time and continue to set the standard for Chinese prose literature today.

## An Age of Expansion: The Zhenghe Expeditions

The seemingly boundless energy of the Chinese in early decades of Ming rule drove them far beyond the traditional areas of expansion in central Asia and the regions south of the Yangtze. In the reign of the third Ming emperor, Yunglo, they launched a series of expeditions that had no precedent in Chinese history. Between 1405 and 1423, the admiral Zhenghe, one of Yunglo's most trusted subordinates, led seven major expeditions overseas (Map 27.2). A mix of motives, including a desire to explore other lands and proclaim the glory of the Ming Empire to the wider world, prompted the voyages. The early expeditions were confined largely to southeast Asian seas and kingdoms. The last three expeditions reached as far as Persia, southern Arabia, and the east coast of Africa—distances comparable to those covered by the Portuguese in their early voyages around Africa.

Voyages of Zheng-he

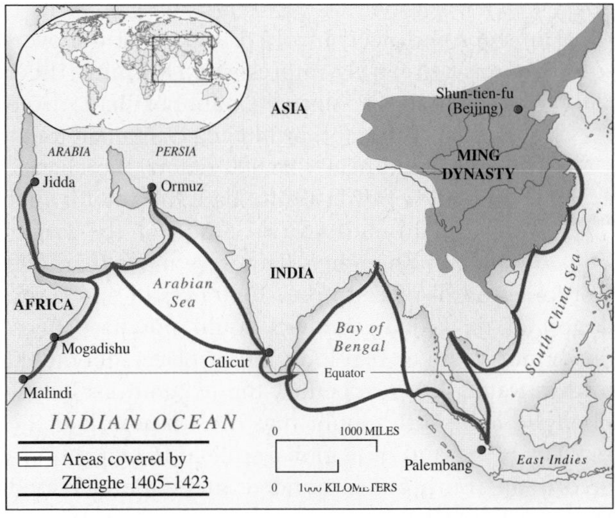


**MAP 27.2** Ming China and the Zhenghe Expeditions, 1405–1423

IN DEPTH

## Means and Motives for Overseas Expansion: Europe and China Compared

Given China's capacity for overseas expansion and the fateful consequences for global history that resulted from the fact that Europe, not China, eventually took the lead, the reasons for the Chinese failure to follow up on their early voyages of exploration merit serious examination. The explanations for the Chinese refusal to commit to overseas expansion can be best understood if they are contrasted with the forces that drove the Europeans with increasing determination into the outside world. In broad terms, such a comparison underscores the fact that although both the Europeans and the Chinese had the means to expand on a global scale, only the Europeans had strong motives for doing so.

> *"Why . . . were the impressive Zhenghe expeditions a dead end, whereas the more modest probes of Columbus and da Gama were the beginning of half a millennium of European overseas expansion and global dominance?"*

The social and economic transformations that occurred in European civilization during the late Middle Ages and the early Renaissance had brought it to a level of development that compared favorably with China in many areas (see Chapters 15 and 17). Although the Chinese empire was far larger and more populous than tiny nation-states such as Portugal, Spain, and Holland, the European kingdoms had grown more efficient at mobilizing their more limited resources. Rivalries between the states of a fragmented Europe had also fostered a greater aggressiveness and sense of competition on the part of the Europeans than the Chinese rulers could even imagine. China's armies were far larger than those of any of the European kingdoms, but European soldiers were on the whole better led, armed, and disciplined. Chinese wet rice agriculture was more productive than European farming, and the Chinese rulers had a far larger population to cultivate their fields, build their dikes and bridges, work their mines, and make tools, clothing, and weapons. But on the whole, the technological innovations of the medieval period had given the Europeans an advantage over the Chinese in the animal and machine power they could generate—a capacity that did much to make up for their deficiencies in human power.

Despite their differences, both civilizations had the means for sustained exploration and expansion overseas, although the Chinese were ready to undertake such enterprises a few centuries earlier than the Europeans. As the voyages of da Gama, Columbus, and Zhenghe demonstrated, both civilizations had the shipbuilding and navigational skills and technology needed to tackle such ambitious undertakings. Why, then, were the impressive Zhenghe expeditions a dead end, whereas the more modest probes of Columbus and da Gama were the beginning of half a millennium of European overseas expansion and global dominance?

The full answer to this question is as complex as the societies it asks us to compare. But we can learn a good deal by looking at the groups pushing for expansion within each civilization and the needs that drove them into the outside

The ships and fleets involved in each of the overseas missions were truly impressive. The initial fleet contained 62 ships (Columbus had three ships in 1492, and in 1498 da Gama had four) that carried nearly 28,000 sailors, merchants, and soldiers (da Gama had 150 for his first voyage around Africa). Some of the larger ships in Zhenghe's fleet were more than 400 feet long and displaced up to 1500 tons of water; the largest of da Gama's caravels could not have been much more than 60 feet long and displaced about 300 tons of water. Taken together, the expeditions led by Zhenghe leave little doubt that the Chinese had the capacity to expand on a global scale at least a century before the Europeans rounded the Cape of Good Hope and entered Asian waters.

A Ming Naval Expedition

### Chinese Retreat and the Arrival of the Europeans

Just over a half century after the last of the Zhenghe expeditions, China had purposely moved from the position of a great power reaching out overseas to an increasingly isolated empire. In 1390 the first imperial edict aimed at limiting Chinese overseas commerce was issued. In the centuries that followed, the Ming war fleet declined dramatically in the number and quality of its ships, and strict limits were placed on the size and number of masts with which a seagoing ship might be fitted. As the Chinese shut themselves in, the Europeans probed ever farther across the globe and were irresistibly drawn to the most legendary of all

A European View of Asia

world. There was widespread support for exploration and overseas expansion in seafaring European nations such as Portugal, Spain, Holland, and England. European rulers financed expeditions they hoped would bring home precious metals and trade goods that could be sold at great profits. Both treasure and profits could be translated into warships and armies that would strengthen these rulers in their incessant wars with European rivals and, in the case of the Iberian kingdoms, with their Muslim adversaries.

European traders looked for much the same benefits from overseas expansion. Rulers and merchants also hoped that explorers would find new lands whose climates and soils were suitable for growing crops such as sugar that were in high demand and thus would bring big profits. Leaders of rival branches of the Christian faith believed that overseas expansion would give their missionaries access to unlimited numbers of heathens to be converted or would put them in touch with the legendary lost king, Prester John, who would ally with them in their struggle with the infidel Muslims.

By contrast, the Chinese Zhenghe expeditions were very much the project of a single emperor and a favored eunuch, whose Muslim family origins may go a long way toward accounting for his wanderlust. Yunglo appears to have been driven by little more than curiosity and the vain desire to impress his greatness and that of his empire on peoples whom he considered inferior. Although some Chinese merchants went along for the ride, most felt little need for the voyages. They already traded on favorable terms for all the products Asia, and in some cases Europe and Africa, could offer. The merchants had the option of waiting for other peoples to come to them, or, if they were a bit more ambitious, of going out in their own ships to southeast Asia.

The scholar-gentry were actively hostile to the Zhenghe expeditions. The voyages strengthened the position of the much-hated eunuchs, who vied with the scholar-gentry for the emperor's favor and the high posts that went with it. In addition, the scholar-gentry saw the voyages as a foolish waste of resources that the empire could not afford. They believed it would be better to direct the wealth and talents of the empire to building armies and fortifications to keep out the hated Mongols and other nomads. After all, the memory of foreign rule was quite fresh.

As had happened so often before in their history, the Chinese were drawn inward, fixated on internal struggles and the continuing threat from central Asia. Scholar-gentry hostility and the lack of enthusiasm for overseas voyages displayed by Yunglo's successors after his death in 1424 led to their abandonment after 1430. As the Chinese retreated, the Europeans surged outward. It is difficult to exaggerate the magnitude of the consequences for both civilizations and all humankind.

**Questions** How might history have been changed if the Chinese had mounted a serious and sustained effort to project their power overseas in the decades before da Gama rounded the Cape of Good Hope? Why did the Chinese fail to foresee the threat that European expansion would pose for the rest of Asia and finally for China itself? Did other civilizations have the capacity for global expansion in this era? What prevented them from launching expeditions similar to those of the Chinese and Europeans? In terms of motivation for overseas expansion, were peoples such as the Muslims, Indians, and Native Americans more like the Europeans or the Chinese?

overseas civilizations, the Middle Kingdom of China. In addition to the trading contacts noted earlier, Christian missionaries infiltrated Chinese coastal areas and tried to gain access to the court, where they hoped to curry favor with the Ming emperors. While religious orders such as the Franciscans and Dominicans toiled to win converts among the common people and made modest progress that could be counted in the tens of thousands, the Jesuits adopted the top-down strategy that di Nobili had pursued in India (Figure 27.6). In China, however, a single person, the Ming emperor, instead of a whole caste, sat at the top of the social hierarchy, and for that reason the rulers and their chief advisors became the prime targets of the Jesuit mission.

Some Chinese scholars showed interest in Christian teachings and Western thinking more generally. But the Jesuit missionaries who made their way to Beijing clearly recognized that their scientific knowledge and technical skills were the keys to maintaining a presence at the Ming court and eventually interesting the Chinese elite in Christianity. Beginning in the 1580s, a succession of brilliant Jesuit scholars, such as **Matteo Ricci** and **Adam Schall,** spent most of their time in the imperial city, correcting faulty calendars, forging cannons, fixing clocks imported from Europe, and astounding the Chinese scholar-gentry with the accuracy of their instruments and their ability to predict eclipses. They won a few converts among the elite. However, most court officials were suspicious of these strange-looking "barbarians" with

Two Jesuits and Sixteenth- and Seventeenth-Century China

Matteo Ricci's Journals

large noses and hairy faces, and they tried to limit their contacts with the imperial family. Some at the court, especially the scholar-officials who were humiliated by the foreigners' corrections to their calendars, were openly hostile to the Jesuits. Despite serious harassment, however, the later Ming emperors remained sufficiently fascinated by these very learned and able visitors that they allowed a handful to remain.

## Ming Decline and the Chinese Predicament

By the late 1500s, the Ming retreat from overseas involvement had become just one facet of a familiar pattern of dynastic decline. The highly centralized, absolutist political structure, which had been established by Hongwu and had been run well by able successors such as Yunglo, became a major liability under the mediocre or incompetent men who occupied the throne through much of the last two centuries of Ming rule. Decades of rampant official corruption, exacerbated by the growing isolation of weak rulers by the thousands of eunuchs who gradually came to dominate life within the Forbidden City, eventually eroded the foundations on which the empire was built.

Public works projects, including the critical dike works on the Huanghe (Yellow River), fell into disrepair, and floods, drought, and famine soon ravaged the land. Peasants in afflicted districts were reduced to eating the bark from trees or the excrement of wild geese. Some peasants sold their children into slavery to keep them from starving, and peasants in some areas resorted to cannibalism. Rapacious local landlords built huge estates by taking advantage of the increasingly desperate peasant population. As in earlier phases of dynastic decline, farmers who had been turned off their land and tortured for taxes, or had lost most of the crops they had grown, turned to flight, banditry, and finally open rebellion to confiscate food and avenge their exploitation by greedy landlords and corrupt officials.

True to the pattern of dynastic rise and fall, internal disorder resulted in and was intensified by foreign threats and renewed assaults by nomadic peoples from beyond the Great Wall. One of the early signs of the seriousness of imperial deterioration was the inability of Chinese bureaucrats and military forces to put an end to the epidemic of Japanese (and ethnic Chinese) pirate attacks that ravaged the southern coast in the

**FIGURE 27.6** Jesuits in Chinese dress at the emperor's court. The Jesuits believed that the best way to convert a great civilization such as China was to adopt the dress, customs, language, and manners of its elite. They reasoned that once the scholar-gentry elite had been converted, they would bring the rest of China's vast population into the Christian fold.

mid-16th century. Despite an official preoccupation with the Mongols early in the Ming era and with the Manchus to the northeast of the Great Wall in later times, the dynasty was finally toppled in 1644, not by nomads but by rebels from within. By that time, the administrative apparatus had become so feeble that the last Ming emperor, **Chongzhen,** did not realize how serious the rebel advance was until enemy soldiers were scaling the walls of the Forbidden City. After watching his wife withdraw to her chambers to commit suicide, and after bungling an attempt to kill his young daughter, the ill-fated Chongzhen retreated to the imperial gardens and hanged himself rather than face capture.

## Fending Off the West: Japan's Reunification and the First Challenge

**In the mid-16th century, the Japanese found leaders who had the military and diplomatic skills and ruthlessness needed to restore unity under a new Shogunate, the Tokugawa. By the early 1600s, with the potential threat from the Europeans looming ever larger, the Tokugawa shoguns succeeded in enveloping the islands in a state of isolation that lasted nearly two and a half centuries.**

By the 16th century, the daimyo stalemate and the pattern of recurring civil war were so entrenched in Japanese society that a succession of three remarkable military leaders was needed to restore unity and internal peace. **Nobunaga,** the first of these leaders, was from a minor warrior household. But his skills as a military leader soon vaulted him into prominence in the ongoing struggles for power among the daimyo lords. As a leader, Nobunaga combined daring, a willingness to innovate, and ruthless determination—some would say cruelty. He was not afraid to launch a surprise attack against an enemy that outnumbered him ten to one, and he was one of the first of the daimyos to make extensive use of the firearms that the Japanese had begun to acquire from the Portuguese in the 1540s.

In 1573 Nobunaga deposed the last of the Ashikaga shoguns, who had long ruled in name only. By 1580 he had unified much of central Honshu under his command (Map 27.3). As his armies drove against the powerful western daimyo in 1582, Nobunaga was caught off guard by one of his vassal generals and was killed when the Kyoto temple where he had taken refuge was burned to the ground.

At first it appeared that Nobunaga's campaigns to restore central authority to the islands might be undone. But his ablest general, **Toyotomi Hideyoshi** (Figure 27.7), moved quickly to punish those who had betrayed Nobunaga and to renew the drive to break the power of the daimyos who had not yet submitted to him. Though the son of a peasant, Hideyoshi matched

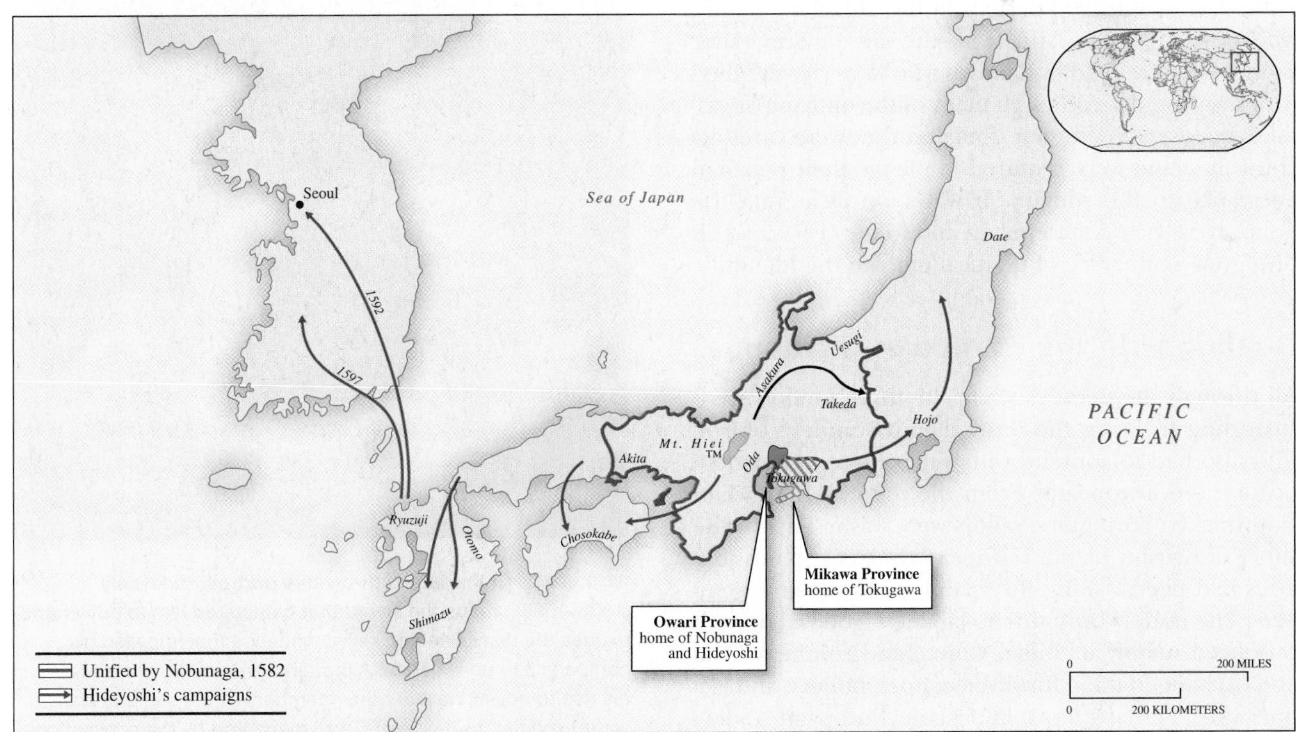


MAP 27.3 Japan During the Rise of the Tokugawa Shogunate

his master in military prowess but was far more skillful at diplomacy. A system of alliances and a string of victories over the last of the resisting daimyos made Hideyoshi the military master of Japan by 1590.

The ambitious overlord had much more grandiose schemes of conquest in mind. He dreamed of ruling China and even India, although he knew little about either place. Hideyoshi also threatened, among others, the Spanish in the Philippines. Apparently as the first step toward fulfilling this vision of empire building on a grand scale, Hideyoshi launched two attacks on Korea in 1592 and 1597, each of which involved nearly 150,000 soldiers. After initial successes, both campaigns stalled. The first ended in defeat; the second was still in progress when Hideyoshi died in 1598.

Although Hideyoshi had tried to ensure that he would be succeeded by his son, the vassals he had appointed to carry out his wishes tried to seize power for themselves after his death. One of these vassals, **Tokugawa Ieyasu,** had originally come from a minor daimyo house. But as an ally of Hideyoshi, he had been able to build up a powerful domain on the heavily populated Kanto plain. Ieyasu soon emerged triumphant from the renewed warfare that resulted from Hideyoshi's death. Rather than continue Hideyoshi's campaigns of overseas expansion, Ieyasu concentrated on consolidating power at home. In 1603 he was granted the title of shogun by the emperor, an act that formally inaugurated centuries of rule by the Tokugawa shogunate.

Under Ieyasu's direction, the remaining daimyos were reorganized. Most of the lands in central Honshu either were controlled directly by the Tokugawa family, who now ruled the land from the city of **Edo** (later Tokyo), or were held by daimyos who were closely allied with the shoguns. Although many of the outlying or vassal daimyos retained their domains, they were carefully controlled and were required to pledge their personal allegiance to the shogun. It was soon clear that the Tokugawas' victory had put an end to the civil wars and brought a semblance of political unity to the islands.

## Dealing with the European Challenge

All through the decades when the three unifiers were struggling to bring the feisty daimyos under control, they also had to contend with a new force in Japanese history: the Europeans. From the time in 1543 when shipwrecked Portuguese sailors were washed up on the shore of Kyushu island, European traders and missionaries had been visiting the islands in increasing numbers. The traders brought the Japanese goods that were produced mainly in India, China, and southeast Asia and exchanged them for silver, copper, pottery, and lacquerware. Perhaps more important, European traders and the missionaries who followed them to the islands brought firearms, printing presses, and other Western devices such as clocks. The firearms, which the Japanese could themselves manufacture within years and were improving in design within a generation, revolutionized Japanese warfare and contributed much to the victories of the unifiers. Commercial contacts with the Europeans also encouraged the Japanese to venture overseas to trade in nearby Formosa and Korea and in places as distant as the Philippines and Siam.

Soon after the merchants, Christian missionaries (Figure 27.8) arrived in the islands and set to work converting the Japanese to Roman Catholicism. Beginning in the outlying daimyos' domains, the missionaries worked their way toward the political center that was beginning to coalesce around Nobunaga and his followers by the 1570s. Seeing Christianity as a counterforce to the militant Buddhist orders

A Japanese View of European Missionaries

FIGURE 27.7 In this late 16th-century portrait, Hideyoshi (1536–1598) grasps the sword that catapulted him to power and exudes the discipline and self-confidence that impelled his campaigns to unify Japan. Although warrior skills were vital in his rise to power, he and other members of the samurai class were expected to be literate, well mannered by the conventions of the day, and attuned to the complex and refined aesthetics of rock gardens and tea ceremonies.

FIGURE 27.8 A number of the major forms of interaction between expansive European peoples and those of Asia are vividly illustrated in this panoramic Japanese silkscreen painting from the early 1600s. The strong impression made by the size and power of the Portuguese ship that has just arrived in harbor is evident in the artist's exaggeration of the height of its fore and aft castles. The trade goods being unloaded, mainly Chinese silks, which are also being sold in the marketplace at the right of the painting, but also exotic products such as peacocks and tiger skins, demonstrate the ways in which the Portuguese had become carriers between different areas in Asia, including Japan. The cluster of black-robed missionaries waiting to greet the arriving Portuguese sea captain (under the umbrella in the center) suggests that efforts to convert the Japanese to Christianity were in full swing, at least in this area of the kingdom.

that were resisting his rise to power, Nobunaga took the missionaries under his protection and encouraged them to preach their faith to his people. The Jesuits, adopting the same top-down strategy of conversion that they had followed in India and China, converted many of the daimyos and their samurai retainers. Some of the Jesuits were also convinced that they were on the verge of winning over Nobunaga, who delighted in wearing Western clothes, encouraged his artists to copy Western paintings of the Virgin Mary and scenes from the life of Christ, and permitted the missionaries to build churches in towns throughout the islands. The missionaries were persuaded that Nobunaga's conversion would bring the whole of the Japanese people into the Christian fold. Even without it, they reported converts in the hundreds of thousands by the early 1580s.

In the late 1580s, quite suddenly, the missionaries saw their carefully mounted conversion campaign collapse. Nobunaga was murdered, and his successor, Hideyoshi, though not yet openly hostile, was lukewarm toward the missionary enterprise. In part, the missionaries' fall from favor resulted from the fact that the resistance of the Buddhist sects had been crushed. More critically, Hideyoshi and his followers were alarmed by reports of converts refusing to obey their overlords' commands when they believed them to be in conflict with their newly adopted Christian beliefs. Thus, the threat that the new religion posed for the established social order was growing more apparent. That threat was compounded by signs that the Europeans might follow up their commercial and missionary overtures with military expeditions aimed at conquering the islands. The Japanese had been strongly impressed with the firearms and pugnacity of the Europeans, and they did not take threats of invasion lightly.

## Japan's Self-Imposed Isolation

Growing doubts about European intentions, and fears that both merchants and missionaries might subvert the existing social order, led to official measures to restrict foreign activities in Japan, beginning in the late 1580s. First, Hideyoshi ordered the Christian missionaries to leave the islands—an order that was not rigorously enforced, at least at the outset. By the mid-1590s, Hideyoshi was actively persecuting Christian missionaries and converts. His successor, Ieyasu, continued this persecution and then officially banned the faith in 1614. European missionaries were driven out of the islands; those who remained underground were hunted down and killed or expelled. Japanese converts were compelled to renounce their faith; those who refused were imprisoned, tortured, and executed. By the 1630s, the persecutions, even against Christians who tried to practice their faith in secret, had become so intense that thousands of converts in the western regions joined in hard-fought but hopeless rebellions against the local daimyos and the forces of the shogun. With the suppression of these uprisings, Christianity in Japan was reduced to an underground faith of isolated communities.

"Closed Country Edict of 1635" and "Exclusion of the Portuguese, 1639" by Tokugawa Ieyasu

Under Ieyasu and his successors, the persecution of the Christians grew into a broader campaign to isolate

Japan from outside influences. In 1616 foreign traders were confined to a handful of cities; in the 1630s all Japanese ships were forbidden to trade or even sail overseas. One after another, different European nations were either officially excluded from Japan (the Spanish) or decided that trading there was no longer worth the risk (the English). By the 1640s only a limited number of Dutch and Chinese ships were allowed to carry on commerce on the small island of **Deshima** in Nagasaki Bay. The export of silver and copper was greatly restricted, and Western books were banned to prevent Christian ideas from reentering the country. Foreigners were permitted to live and travel only in very limited areas.

By the mid-17th century, Japan's retreat into almost total isolation was complete. Much of the next century was spent in consolidating the internal control of the Tokugawa shogunate by extending bureaucratic administration into the vassal daimyo domains throughout the islands. In the 18th century, a revival of neo-Confucian philosophy, which had marked the period of the Tokugawa's rise to power, increasingly gave way to the influence of thinkers who championed the **school of National Learning.** As its name implies, the new ideology laid great emphasis on Japan's unique historical experience and the revival of indigenous culture at the expense of Chinese imports such as Confucianism. In the centuries that followed, through contacts with the small Dutch community at Deshima, members of the Japanese elite also followed developments in the West. Their avid interest in European achievements contrasted sharply with the indifference of the Chinese scholar-gentry in this period to the doings of the "hairy barbarians" from Europe.

## GLOBAL CONNECTIONS

## An Age of Eurasian Closure

In 1700, after two centuries of European involvement in south and southeast Asia, most of the peoples of the area had been little affected by efforts to build trading empires and win Christian converts. European sailors had added several new routes to the Asian trading network. The most important of these were the link around the Cape of Good Hope between Europe and the Indian Ocean and the connection between the Philippine Islands and Mexico in the Americas. The Europeans' need for safe harbors and storage areas led to the establishment and rapid growth of trading centers such as Goa, Calicut, and Batavia. It also resulted in the gradual decline of existing indigenous commercial centers, especially the Muslim cities on the east coast of Africa and somewhat later the fortress town of Malacca. The Europeans introduced the principle of sea warfare into what had been a peaceful commercial world. But the Asian trading system as a whole survived the initial shock of this innovation, and the Europeans eventually concluded that they were better off adapting to the existing commercial arrangements rather than dismantling them.

Because exchanges had been taking place between Europe and Asia for millennia, few new inventions or diseases were spread in the early centuries of expansion. This low level of major exchanges was particularly striking compared with the catastrophic interaction between Europe and the Americas. But, as in Africa, European discoveries in the long-isolated Western Hemisphere did result in the introduction of important new food plants into India, China, and other areas from the 1600s onward. The import of silver was also an addition to wealth and adornment in China. Otherwise, Europeans died mainly of diseases that they contracted in Asia, such as new strains of malaria and dysentery. They spread diseases only to the more isolated parts of Asia, such as the Philippines, where the coming of the Spanish was accompanied by a devastating smallpox epidemic. The impact of European ideas, inventions, and modes of social organization was also very limited during the first centuries of expansion. Key European devices, such as clocks, were seen as toys by Asian rulers to whom they were given as presents.

During the early modern period in global history, the West's surge in exploration and commercial expansion touched most of Asia only peripherally. This was particularly true of east Asia, where the political cohesion and military strength of the vast Chinese empire and the Japanese warrior-dominated states blocked all hope of European advance. Promising missionary inroads in the 16th century were stifled by hostile Tokugawa shoguns in the early 17th century. They were also carefully contained by the Ming emperors and the nomadic Qing dynasty in the mid-1600s. Strong Chinese and Japanese rulers limited trading contacts with the aggressive Europeans and confined European merchants to a few ports—Macao and Canton in China, Deshima in Japan—that were remote from their respective capitals. In its early decades, the Ming dynasty also pursued a policy of overseas expansion that had no precedent in Chinese history. But when China again turned inward in the last centuries of the dynasty, a potentially formidable obstacle to the rise of European dominance in maritime Asia was removed. China's strong position in global trade continued, in marked contrast to Japan's greater isolation. But even China failed to keep pace with changes in European technology and merchant activity, with results that would show more clearly in the next stage of global interconnections.

## Further Readings

The account of da Gama's epic voyage that opens the chapter is based heavily on J. H. Parry's superb *The Discovery of the Sea* (1981). C. G. F. Simkins, *The Traditional Trade of Asia* (1968), and Anthony Reid, *Southeast Asia in the Age of Commerce, 1450–1680* (1988), provide overviews of the Asian trading network from ancient times until about the 18th century. Much more detailed accounts of specific segments of the system, as well as the impact upon it of the Dutch and Portuguese, can be found in the works of J. C. van Leur, M. A. P. Meilink-Roelofsz, K. N. Chaudhuri, Ashin Das Gupta, Sanjay Subrahmanyam, and Michael Pearson. C. R. Boxer's *The Portuguese Seaborne Empire* (1969) and *The Dutch Seaborne Empire* (1965) are still essential reading, although the latter has little on the Europeans in Asia. Boxer's *Race Relations in the Portuguese Colonial Empire, 1415–1852* (1963) provides a stimulating, if contentious, introduction to the history of European social interaction with overseas peoples in the early centuries of expansion. Important correctives to Boxer's work can be found in the more recent contributions of George Winius.

Louise Levathes, *When China Ruled the Seas: The Treasure Fleet of the Dragon Throne, 1405–33* (1994), is an entertaining account of China's global reach. G. B. Sansom, *The Western World and Japan* (1968), includes a wealth of information on the interaction between Europeans and, despite its title, peoples throughout Asia, and it has good sections on the missionary initiatives in both China and Japan.

The period of the Ming dynasty has been the focus of broader and more detailed studies than the dynasties that preceded it. An important early work is Charles O. Hucker, *The Censorial System of Ming China* (1966). Two essential and more recent works are Albert Chan's *The Glory and Fall of the Ming Dynasty* (1982) and Edward Dreyer's more traditional political history, *Early Ming China, 1355–1435* (1982). See also F. Mote and D. Twitchett, eds., *The Cambridge History of China: The Ming Dynasty 1368–1644,* vols. 6 and 7 (1988, 1998).

There are also wonderful insights into daily life at various levels of Chinese society in Roy Huang's very readable *1587: A Year of No Significance: The Ming Dynasty in Decline* (1981), and into the interaction between the Chinese and the Jesuits in Jonathan Spence's *The Memory Palace of Matteo Ricci* (1984). Frederic Wakeman Jr., *The Great Enterprise,* 2 vols. (1985), is essential to an understanding of the transition from Ming to Manchu rule. The early chapters of Spence's *The Search for Modern China* (1990) also provide an illuminating overview of that process.

Perhaps the best introductions to the situation in Japan in the early phase of European expansion are provided by G. B. Sansom's survey, *A History of Japan, 1615–1867* (1963), and Conrad Totman's *Politics in the Tokugawa Bakufu, 1600–1843* (1967). Numerous studies on the Europeans in Japan include those by Donald Keene, Grant Goodman, Noel Perrin, and C. R. Boxer. Intellectual trends in Japan in this era are most fully treated in H. D. Harootunian's *Toward Restoration: The Growth of Political Consciousness in Tokugawa Japan* (1970).

## On the Web

The achievement of the Ming and later Qing dynasties are on view at virtual tours of their versions of the Great Wall and Forbidden City offered at http://www.chinavista.com/travel/greatwall/greatwall.html and http://www.chinavista.com/beijing/gugong/map.html.

Perhaps the finest of all virtual tour sites on the Web is that which provides a glimpse into the rich cultural life of the Tokugawa capital of Edo at http://www.us-japan.org/EdoMatsu/. This shogunate was established after a civil war that followed the reigns of Nobunaga Oda (http://ox.compsoc.net/~gemini/simons/historyweb/oda-nobunaga.html) and Toyotomi Hideyoshi, developer of the grand Osaka Castle (http://www.tourism.city.osaka.jp/en/castle/mainmenu.htm).

Hideyoshi's death may or may not have been hastened by the great losses Japan sustained as a result of his two failed invasions of Korea (for a Korean view of these events, known as the Imjin Wars, see http://en.wikipedia.org/wiki/Imjin_War and http://www.geocities.com/yisun-shi_sun_shin_adm/yisun-shisunshin.html). However, his passing hastened the ascension of Tokugawa Ieyasu (http://www.samurai-archives.com/ieyasu.html and http://www.japan-guide.com/e/e2128.html), whose shogunate paved the way for the construction of modern Japan.

The era that saw the rise and development of the Tokugawa witnessed much exchange between Asians and Christian missionaries elsewhere in Asia. An exceptional online study of these exchanges and the lives of Mateo Ricci, Adam Schall, and Robert di Nobili can be found at http://acc6.its.brooklyn.cuny.edu/~phalsall/texts/ric-jour.html and http://archive.ncsa.uiuc.edu/SDG/Experimental/vatican.exhibit/exhibit/i-rome_to_china/Rome_to_china.html.

These exchanges were made possible by earlier developments in seagoing transportation, trade, and exploration, such as the travels of Zhenghe (or Chengho) (http://chinapage.com/chengho.html), the development of the caravel (http://www.mariner.org/age/portuguese.html and http://www.pfri.hr/pov/pov07.html), and the development of Portuguese and Dutch trading empires (http://www.geocities.com/Athens/Styx/6497/).

Web pages devoted to the activities of the Dutch East India Company (http://batavia.rug.ac.be/index.html, http://www.tanap.net/_resources/images/deshima.jpg, http://en.wikipedia.org/wiki/Deshima, and http://batavia.UGent.be/) provide luminous virtual tours of both Batavia and Deshima that demonstrate the still peripheral role of Europeans in Asia at this time.

Part IV Retrospective

# A Look Back at the Early Modern Period

## Contacts and Their Limits

In the context of world history, all the basic changes during the early modern period involved new levels of contacts. Merchants from many parts of the world participated in the new world economy. Their military superiority at sea allowed Europeans to reach new areas, especially along coasts and islands. Chinese merchants continued to trade in southeast Asia, encountering Europeans in the Philippines as well as through the port of Macao. The Columbian exchange was based on contacts—Asians learning of new foodstuffs, like the sweet potato, from the Americas, or Americans experiencing diseases brought by contacts with Europeans and Africans. An obvious result of new contacts was the emergence of overseas empires, but even land-based empires brought new connections. Russians, for example, came into contact with new Muslim and Jewish minorities as their conquests expanded, while the Ottoman Empire included Muslims, Jews, and Christians, not only in the general population but in the state bureaucracy as well.

On the whole, the contacts of the early modern period moved things—types of foods, germs, and goods—more than ideas. New foods from the Americas reached China, for example, which also took in massive amounts of New World silver. But the Chinese did not incorporate many new ideas or technologies from their new contacts. Small numbers of European missionaries, seen as harmless, were tolerated, and many of them took on European dress and habits. Early in the 18th century, even this tolerance declined as China began to repress Christian missionary efforts. Europeans gladly welcomed new products and wealth from other parts of the world. Indeed, many Europeans became dependent on items like sugar, one of the first great international consumer goods that involved mass taste. Europeans also eagerly imported the habit of coffee drinking, and coffee houses, initially developed in the Middle East, sprang up throughout Europe. European rulers, however, criticized coffee drinking as a foreign and dissolute habit and urged their subjects to stick to beer and wine. A new sense of superiority limited Europeans' openness to institutions and ideas from other regions than had been the case in the postclassical period. The Ottoman Empire also kept a lid on many kinds of contacts, even as it experienced growing interaction with European as well as African and Asian merchants. Despite knowledge of the printing press, for example, Ottoman rulers forbade presses in the empire until the mid-18th century, on grounds they might be used to spread subversive ideas. Ottoman rulers did import Western doctors, who actually knew no more than their local counterparts; otherwise, outside scientific developments were largely ignored.

There were exceptions to this standard rule of exchange of goods outweighing interchange of ideas. Extensive Christian conversions in the Philippines, where the Spanish occupied directly, contrasted with the experience in most of Asia, where European Christian missionaries made only limited inroads on established affiliations to

Buddhism, Hinduism, or Islam. Japan reacted to the changes of the early modern era in yet another way. Initially Japan showed great interest in European firearms and some receptivity to Christianity. But at the end of the 16th century, new Japanese leaders sought to protect local traditions, including feudal military skills, and cut off both missionary activity and most gun production. For the next century and beyond, Japan remained relatively isolated from the rest of the world. India's Mughal rulers displayed considerable interest in cultural contacts with different parts of Asia as well as the West, but here too tolerance declined over time. Russia, in contrast, became an avid imitator of Western techniques and styles, though only at the elite level of society.

In Latin America outside goods—germs, animals, but also European-manufactured guns and art work—were imported extensively. Europeans also introduced new ideas, especially pressure to convert to Christianity. Native Americans combined these imports with local traditions, merging some of their own gods with the roster of Christian saints or using traditional native art in Christian celebrations. The outcome, a classic result of contact, contained the outlines of a new culture that was neither traditional nor fully Western. In some regions, imported African rituals and habits added to this mix of influences.

The point is obvious: the early modern period introduced many opportunities for new levels and types of contact. The results were, however, highly varied, with less widespread cultural exchange than might have been anticipated. Many peasant groups, in the interiors of Asia and Africa, experienced few new contacts of any sort. Even where trade and biological exchange penetrated, leaders and even ordinary people had some leeway about accepting other influences. Many people chose to stick to the tried and true; others, like the Japanese, launched a more internal pattern of cultural change. Americans, particularly those living along the coasts, were the great exception, but even here the native populations might modify unusual contacts and pressures to make them more recognizable and acceptable. The centuries of the early modern period are a somewhat transitional period. The increased number and level of contacts of the era set new patterns in motion, but people responded to those new patterns in widely diverse ways.

At the same time, a few examples of striking cosmopolitanism emerged during this period—not typical, but far beyond what had been achieved by travelers in the earlier, postclassical era. A number of European missionaries became quite comfortable with Hindu or Confucian customs. Ottoman diplomats and merchants in Europe were very familiar with their surroundings, even if they imported few new ideas back home. In the later 18th century, a Muslim from India, Abu Taleb Khan, living in London, reported on his own mixed reactions to the world around him. He disliked what he saw as England's lack of religious faith, its arrogance, and its greed for money, but he very much appreciated the fairness of the English courts and (he said) the English ability to keep women in line, by force if necessary, despite women's freedom to mix in public. ■

PART

# V

# THE DAWN OF THE INDUSTRIAL AGE, 1750–1914



Maps tell two related stories for the "long" 19th century—a period whose characteristics ran from the late 18th century to 1914. First, a radically new kind of technology and economy arose in a few parts of the world, in what began to be called the Industrial Revolution. The Industrial Revolution greatly increased industrial production as well as the speed and volume of transportation. Areas that industrialized early gained a huge economic lead over other parts of the world.

Industrial countries also gained power advantages over the rest of the world, thanks to new, mass-produced weaponry, steamships, and developments in communications. Western Europe led a new and unprecedented round of imperialism, taking over Africa, Oceania, and many parts of Asia. Even countries that began industrialization a bit later, like Russia and Japan, were adding to their empires by 1914.

Industrialization reached into every aspect of human endeavor. In movements like Futurism, some modern artists tried to render the new world of speed and mechanization. Other artists used new knowledge of color to create images of nature that would contrast with the ugliness of machines. Impressionists, arguing that literal realism in art had been made unnecessary by the development of photography, concentrated on the essentials of natural and other settings.

## TRIGGERS FOR CHANGE

By 1750 Europe's trading advantage over much of the rest of the world was increasing. Other gunpowder empires that had flourished during the Early Modern period were encountering difficulties; for example, the Ottoman Empire began to lose territory in wars with Russia. In this context, Great Britain began to introduce revolutionary new technologies, most notably the steam engine. This core innovation soon led to further inventions that increased western Europe's economic advantage over most other parts of the world.

An impressive series of inventions emerged from Britain, France, the United States, and a few other countries at this time in world history, because Europeans knew they could make money in the world economy by selling manufactured goods to other societies in return for cheap foods and raw

## World Centers of Industrialization, c. 1910

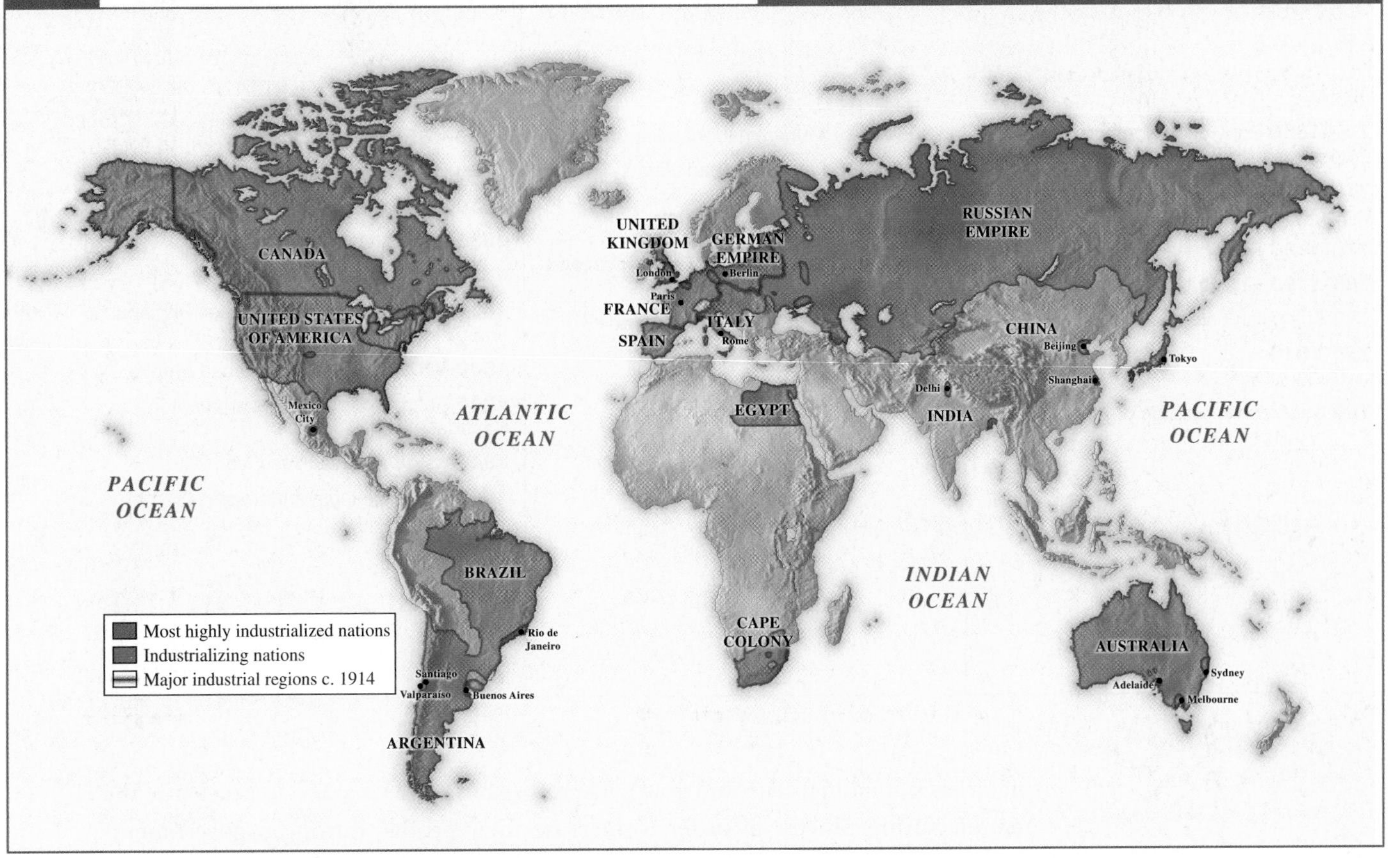
CANADA
UNITED STATES OF AMERICA
Mexico City
PACIFIC OCEAN
ATLANTIC OCEAN
BRAZIL
Rio de Janeiro
Santiago
Valparaiso
Buenos Aires
ARGENTINA
UNITED KINGDOM
London
Paris
FRANCE
SPAIN
GERMAN EMPIRE
Berlin
ITALY
Rome
EGYPT
CAPE COLONY
RUSSIAN EMPIRE
CHINA
Beijing
Shanghai
Tokyo
Delhi
INDIA
INDIAN OCEAN
PACIFIC OCEAN
AUSTRALIA
Adelaide
Sydney
Melbourne
Most highly industrialized nations
Industrializing nations
Major industrial regions c. 1914

## Major World Empires, c. 1910

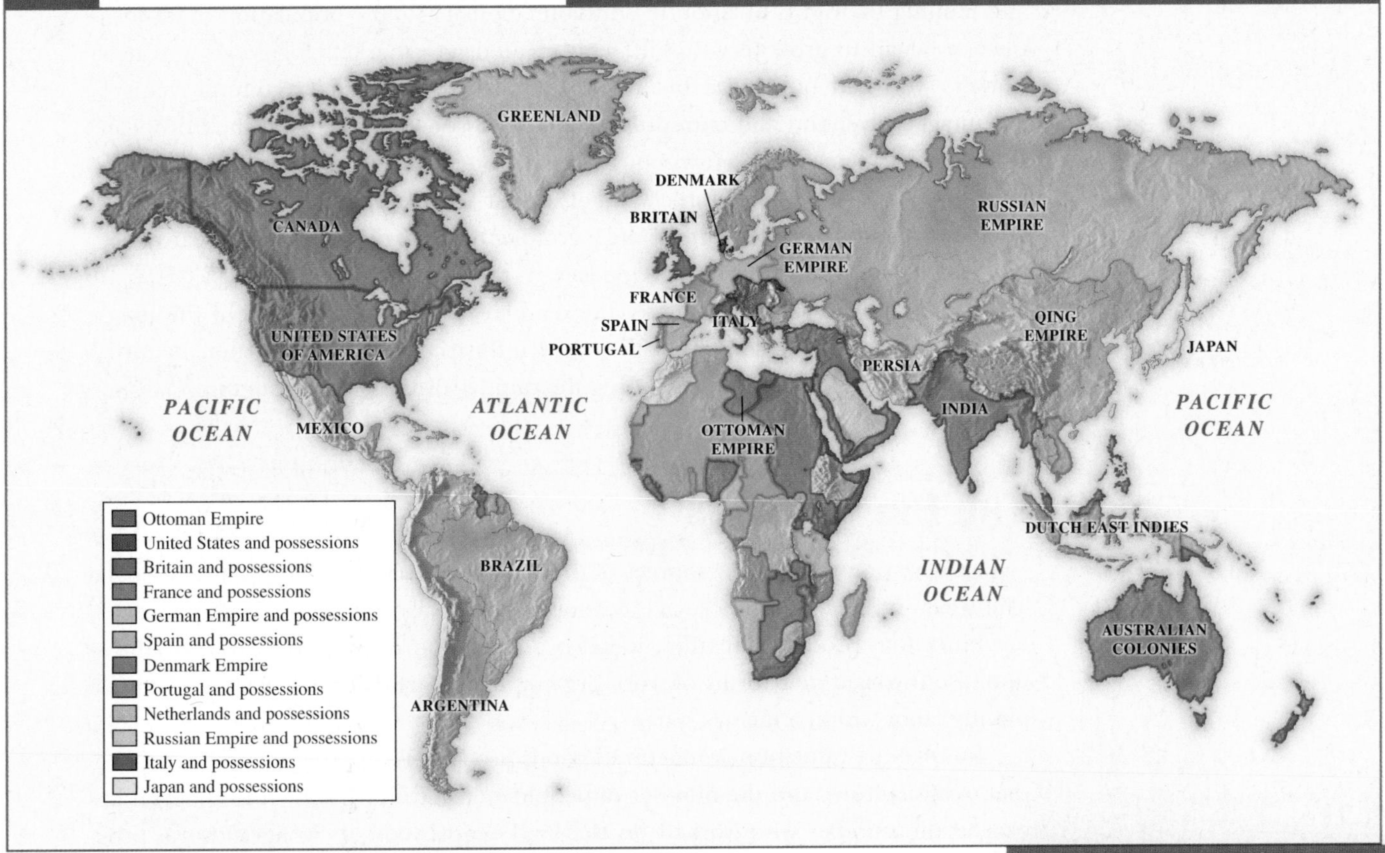
GREENLAND
CANADA
UNITED STATES OF AMERICA
MEXICO
PACIFIC OCEAN
ATLANTIC OCEAN
BRAZIL
ARGENTINA
DENMARK
BRITAIN
GERMAN EMPIRE
FRANCE
SPAIN
PORTUGAL
ITALY
OTTOMAN EMPIRE
PERSIA
RUSSIAN EMPIRE
QING EMPIRE
JAPAN
INDIA
PACIFIC OCEAN
DUTCH EAST INDIES
INDIAN OCEAN
AUSTRALIAN COLONIES
Ottoman Empire
United States and possessions
Britain and possessions
France and possessions
German Empire and possessions
Spain and possessions
Denmark Empire
Portugal and possessions
Netherlands and possessions
Russian Empire and possessions
Italy and possessions
Japan and possessions

| 1700 C.E. | 1800 C.E. | 1825 C.E. |
|---|---|---|
| **1730–1850** Population boom in western Europe<br>**1770** James Watt's steam engine; beginning of Industrial Revolution<br>**1776–1783** American Revolution<br>**1786–1790** First British reforms in India<br>**1788** Australian colonization begins<br>**1789–1815** French Revolution and Napoleon<br>**1789** Napoleon's invasion of Egypt | **1805–1849** Muhammad Ali rules Egypt<br>**1808–1825** Latin American wars of independence<br>**1815** Vienna settlement<br>**1815** British annexation of Cape Town and region of southern Africa<br>**1822** Brazil declares independence<br>**1823** Monroe Doctrine | **1825–1855** Repression in Russia<br>**1826** New Zealand colonization begins<br>**1830, 1848** Revolutions in Europe<br>**1835** English education in India<br>**1838** Ottoman trade treaty with Britain<br>**1839–1841** Opium War between England and China<br>**1839–1876** Reforms in Ottoman Empire<br>**1840** Semiautonomous government in Canada<br>**1846–1848** Mexican-American War<br>**1848 ff.** Beginnings of Marxism |

materials (including silver and gold). Therefore businesses worked to accelerate the manufacturing process in order to increase their profits. European governments also began to create conditions designed to encourage industrial growth by improving roads and canals, developing new central banks, holding technology expositions, and limiting the rights of labor. In addition, about 1730, the population of western Europe began to grow very rapidly. This created new markets for goods and new workers who had no choice but to accept factory jobs. Finally, cultural changes encouraged invention and entrepreneurship. The rise of science and the European Enlightenment created an environment in which new discoveries seemed both possible and desirable. A rising appreciation of secular achievement encouraged businesspeople to undertake new ventures, and a growing number of western Europeans were interested in and could afford new goods.

So a combination of factors set the context for the replacement of the longstanding agricultural economy with a new industrial order. This order, in turn, would spark further changes, including the rapid growth of European imperialism.

## The Big Changes

Industrialization meant new sources of power, founded initially on the use of coal. The steam engine was the crucial development. It was used to transmit power to machines that produced textiles, metal products, and other goods. Industrialization also involved new forms of work organization, particularly massing and disciplining labor within a factory system.

By 1840 the value of manufactured goods produced each year began to surpass that of agriculture, and the number of people engaged in manufacturing began to exceed the number who worked on the land. Improvements in agricultural production were vital supports to the process of industrialization.

| 1850 C.E. | 1875 C.E | 1900 C.E. |
|---|---|---|
| **1850–1864** Taiping Rebellion in China<br>**1853** Perry expedition to Edo Bay in Japan<br>**1854–1856** Crimean War<br>**1858** British assume control over India<br>**1860–1868** Civil strife in Japan<br>**1861** Emancipation of serfs in Russia<br>**1861–1865** American Civil War<br>**1863** Emancipation of slaves in U.S.<br>**1864–1871** German unification<br>**1868–1912** Meiji (reform) era in Japan<br>**1870–1910** Acceleration of "demographic transition" in western Europe and the U.S.<br>**1870–1910** Expansion of commercial export economy in Latin America<br>**1871–1912** High point of European imperialism | **1877–1878** Ottomans out of most of Balkans; Treaty of San Stefano<br>**1879–1890s** Partition of west Africa<br>**1882** British takeover of Egypt<br>**1885** Formation of National Congress Party in India<br>**1886–1888** Slavery abolished in Cuba and Brazil<br>**1890** Japanese constitution<br>**1890s** Partition of east Africa<br>**1894–1895** Sino Japanese War<br>**1895** Cuban revolt against Spain<br>**1898** Formation of Marxist Social Democratic Party in Russia<br>**1898** Spanish–American War; U.S. acquires the Philippines, Puerto Rico, and Hawaii; United States intervenes in Cuba<br>**1898–1901** Boxer Rebellion in China | **1901** Commonwealth of Australia<br>**1903** Construction of Panama Canal begins<br>**1904–1905** Russo-Japanese War<br>**1905–1906** Revolution in Russia; limited reforms<br>**1908** Young Turk rising<br>**1910** Japan annexes Korea<br>**1911–1912** Revolution in China; end of empire<br>**1914–1918** World War I |

The Industrial Revolution had two broad sets of consequences in the 19th century. First, in the industrial countries, the rise of the factory system changed many aspects of life. Work became more specialized and more closely supervised. The changes in work brought about by industrialization deeply affected families. Work moved out of the home, challenging traditional family life, in which all family members had participated in production. Though child labor was used early in the process of industrialization, increasingly childhood was redefined in industrial societies, away from work and toward schooling. Industrialization spurred the growth of cities. While new opportunities were involved, there was also great tension and, for a time, pockets of dreadful misery amid urban slums and machine-driven labor conditions.

Industrialization changed politics. New, middle-class groups, expanding on the basis of industrial growth, sought a political voice. As urban workers grew restive, governments had to strengthen police forces and also, gradually, to expand the right to vote among the lower classes. New nationalist loyalties involved ideological change away from primarily local and religious attachments, but they also provided identities for people whose traditional values were disrupted by industrial life and movement to the cities. A few societies outside the West even sought to industrialize early on. Egypt tried and largely failed, in the first half of the 19th century; a bit later, Japan and Russia launched industrial revolutions of their own.

For some societies, the main effect of industrialization was to increase pressures to turn out food supplies and cheap raw materials for the industrial world, even though these societies were largely non-industrial. Western dominance in the world economy increased, and involvement in this economy became more widespread. For Latin America this meant even more such production, with newly introduced products like coffee and increased output of resources like copper. Parts of Asia that had previously profited from the world economy were now pressed into more low-cost production. All over the world, cheap manufactured goods from Western factories put hundreds of thousands of traditional manufacturing workers, many of them women, out of a job.

While industrial transformations of the world economy exerted the greatest pressure for change, they also provided the context for European imperial expansion into many new areas. When they took over in places like Africa, Europeans moved quickly to intensify low-cost production of foods, minerals, and (sometimes) simple manufactured goods.

Two other key changes accompanied this process of global economic change. First, the institution of slavery increasingly came under attack. The Atlantic slave trade was legally abolished early in the 19th century. Then slave and serf systems were progressively eliminated in the Americas, Europe, Russia, and Africa. New ideas about human rights and new confidence in "free wage labor" facilitated the change. Significant population growth provided new sources of labor to replace slaves. Immigrants poured out of Europe to the Americas and Australia. Indenture systems brought massive numbers of Asians to Oceania, the Americas, and Africa. As slavery ended, harsh, low-paid "free" labor intensified in many places. Second, the massive economic changes brought about by the Industrial Revolution impacted the environment. In industrial societies, smoke and the steady increase of chemical and urban wastes worsened regional air and water quality. The expansion of export production in other parts of the world also affected the environment in negative ways. The introduction of crops like coffee and cotton, for example, to new parts of Africa and Latin America often caused significant soil erosion.

## Continuity

In the first place, although industrialization was indeed revolutionary, its consequences were spread out over many decades. Dramatic innovations such as department stores should not conceal the fact that such stores controlled only about 5 percent of all retail commerce in major Western cities—the rest centered on more traditional shops, peddling, and outdoor markets.

Continuity also shows in the different ways specific groups and regions reacted to change. The need to respond to Western economic and, often, military pressure was quite real around the world. But reactions varied in part because of the impact of different traditions. Japanese society had to be adapted considerably to facilitate industrialization. The feudal system was abolished outright, but its legacy helped to shape Japanese business organizations, and the absence of a comparable legacy may have reduced Chinese flexibility for some time. The spread of literacy in Russia in the later 19th century—part of Russia's efforts to reform—created new opportunities for popular literature, as had occurred earlier in the West. But in contrast to Western literature, which often celebrated outlaws, Russian adventure stories always included the triumph of the state over disorder. The cultural differences illustrated by these comparisons did not necessarily persist without alteration, but they continued to influence regional patterns.

Response to change also included the "invention" of traditions. Many societies sought to balance disruption by appealing to apparent sources of stability that drew on traditional themes. Many Western leaders emphasized the sanctity of the family and domestic roles for women, hoping that the home would provide a "haven" amid rapid economic change. The ideas of the family as a haven and of the special domestic virtues of women were partly myths, even as both took on the status of tradition. In the 1860s the U.S. government instituted Thanksgiving as a national holiday, and many Americans assumed that this was simply an official recognition of a long-standing celebration; in fact, Thanksgiving had been only rarely and fitfully observed before this new holiday, designed to promote family and national unity, was newly established.

## Impact on Daily Life: Leisure

The Industrial Revolution transformed leisure. Leaders in industrial centers wanted to discourage traditional festivals, because they took too much time away from work and sometimes led to rowdiness on the part of workers. Factory rules also limited napping, chatting, wandering around, and drinking on the job. In the early decades of industrialization, leisure declined at first—replaced by long and exhausting work days—just as it had when agriculture replaced hunting and gathering.

With time, however, industrial societies introduced new kinds of leisure. Professional sports began to take shape around the middle of the 19th century. A bit later, new forms of popular theater attracted many people in the cities. The idea of vacations also spread: workers took same-day train excursions to beaches and travel companies formed to assist the middle classes in more ambitious trips. Much of the new leisure depended on professional entertainers, with the bulk of the population turning into spectators.

While the most dramatic innovations in leisure occurred in industrial societies, here too there was quick connection to the wider world. Many mine and plantation owners sought to curb traditional forms of leisure activity in the interests of more efficient production. Although they had less success than factory owners did, they did have some impact. New forms of leisure pioneered in western Europe or the United States also caught on elsewhere. Soccer began to win interest in Latin America by the 1860s. Baseball began to spread from the United States to the rest of the Americas and Japan by the 1890s. By the 1920s, movies had won global attention as well. While most societies retained traditional, regional leisure forms, something of a global leisure culture was beginning to emerge.

## Societies and Trends

Chapters in this section begin with developments in the West, where industrialization and new political ideas first emerged. The West also spawned new settler societies in the United States, Canada, Australia, and New Zealand. These developments are described in Chapter 28. Chapter 29 focuses on the world economy and imperialism, tracing the effects of Western industrialization on the nonindustrial world. Chapter 30 describes the balance between new forces within Latin America. Chapter 31 describes developments in key parts of Asia as they responded to the challenges of Western power and economic change. Chapter 32 deals with two non-Western societies, Russia and Japan, that launched ambitious plans for industrialization in the late 19th century; the comparative study of the processes of industrialization in Russia, Japan, and the West sheds new light on the varied forms this process could take.

CHAPTER 28

# The Emergence of Industrial Society in the West, 1750–1914



Why did an anti-Chinese riot break out in Milwaukee in 1889 when there were only 16 Chinese immigrants living in the whole state of Wisconsin? The riot occurred in March. It followed press reports that Chinese laundrymen were seducing European American girls. One paper claimed there was a sinister ring transporting girls to Chicago where they would be forced to marry Chinese men. The headlines were inflammatory: "Chinese Horrors. Twenty-two Children Are Lured into the Dens." Following accusations, police did arrest two Chinese. But court procedures were too slow for the public. Large crowds gathered, calling for lynchings, abusing Chinese effigies, and burning and looting Chinese stores. After a tense few days, most of the Chinese immigrants left town.

From a world history standpoint, this incident is not significant, but it is suggestive. First, it occurred after several decades of Chinese immigration into the United States, where initially many worked on western railways. This in turn was part of a larger movement of people from Asia to the Americas and elsewhere, as population growth in Asian nations combined with a deteriorating position in the world economy. More than a million Chinese emigrated to various parts of the Americas in the decades before and after 1900, and there was massive movement from India, Japan, and the Philippines as well. This new migration from Asia to the Americas was a major departure in world history, and it would continue into the 21st century.

Second, of course, the Milwaukee incident illustrates the anxieties that contact with Asians caused among many Americans. The 1880s saw massive anti-Chinese rioting in the western United States, with more than 140 Chinese murdered and more than 10,000 forced to leave their homes and stores. In 1882 the first of several measures was passed to limit Chinese immigration, an exclusionary policy that would last until 1943. Anxiety focused both on Chinese competition with American labor and on accusations of predatory sexual behavior. It proved difficult, for several decades, for Chinese Americans to assimilate more fully into national life. And of course, as with many immigrants, some did not want to. For example, many Chinese spent considerable sums to send the bodies of their deceased relatives back to China, the only place, in their view, where ancestors could be properly accommodated.

FIGURE 28.1 A Chinese laundry shop, 1855. Chinese workers began to reach the United States in the mid-19th century, part of a larger stream of Asian labor migrations to many areas in the world. The mostly uneducated and unskilled Chinese workers first came to America in response to advertising by railroad companies, who wanted cheap labor to build the Western railroads. Although the new immigrants faced resentment from American workers, both because of job competition and because of real or imagined differences in values, the Chinese managed to establish themselves in some additional types of work, especially laundries. These enterprises were attractive to the Chinese because they required little specialized skill or capital, and American men did not object to Chinese laundries, as they considered laundry to be "women's work."

While Western history in the 19th century seemed dominated by internal developments—new political movements, expansion into settler societies like the United States, and the **Industrial Revolution**—it is important to remember the international contacts, some of them quite new, that provided a larger framework. Change is measured by befores and afters. In 1750 western Europe consisted almost entirely of monarchies. By 1914 many monarchies had been overthrown, and everywhere powerful legislatures, based on extensive voting systems, defined much of the political apparatus. In 1750 North America was a minor player in Western and world history. By 1914 the United States and other settler societies had made an increasing mark on the economy and politics of the West. But also by 1914, western Europe had generated an alliance system that was about to plunge much of the world into chaos.

## The Age of Revolution

- **New ideas helped stimulate a wave of revolutions in the West from the 1770s to 1848. Revolutionary patterns would gain international influence; they also interacted with the early effects of Western industrialization.**

### Optimism Against All Odds

In 1793 a French aristocrat, the Marquis de Condorcet, was hiding from the dominant party of the French Revolution. He had not voted to execute the French king, and his life was in danger as a result. While in hiding, he wrote a book titled *Progress of the Human Mind,* demonstrating that progress had become inevitable in the modern world because of growing education and

| 1700 C.E. | 1820 C.E. | 1840 C.E. | 1860 C.E. | 1880 C.E. | 1900 C.E. |
|---|---|---|---|---|---|
| **1730 ff.** Massive population rise<br>**c. 1770** James Watt's steam engine; beginning of Industrial Revolution<br>**1788** First convict settlement in Australia<br>**1789** George Washington first president of the United States<br>**1789–1799** French Revolution<br>**1790 ff.** Beginning of per capita birth rate decline (United States)<br>**1793** First free European settlers in Australia<br>**1793–1794** Radical phase of French Revolution<br>**1799–1815** Reign of Napoleon<br>**1800–1850** Romanticism in literature and art<br>**1803** Louisiana Purchase (United States)<br>**1810–1826** Rise of democratic suffrage in United States.<br>**1815** Congress of Vienna ushers in a more conservative period in Europe | **1820** Revolutions in Greece and Spain; rise of liberalism and nationalism<br>**1820s ff.** Industrialization in United States<br>**1823** First legislative council in Australia<br>**1826–1837** Active European colonization begins in New Zealand<br>**1829** Andrew Jackson seventh president of United States<br>**1830** Revolutions in several European countries<br>**1832** Reform Bill of 1832 (England)<br>**1837** Rebellion in Canada<br>**1837–1842** U.S.-Canada border clashes<br>**1839** New British colonial policy allows legislature and more autonomy | **1840** Union act reorganizes Canada, provides elected legislature<br>**1843–1848** First Maori War, New Zealand<br>**1846–1848** Mexican-American War<br>**1848 ff.** Writings of Karl Marx; rise of socialism<br>**1848–1849** Revolutions in several European countries<br>**1850** Australia's Colonies Government Act allows legislature and more autonomy<br>**1852** New constitution in New Zealand; elected councils<br>**1859** Darwin's *Origin of Species*<br>**1859–1870** Unification of Italy | **1860–1870** Second Maori War<br>**1861–1865** American Civil War<br>**1863** Emancipation Proclamation, United States<br>**1864–1871** German unification<br>**1867** British North America Act unites eastern and central Canada<br>**1870–1879** Institution of Third Republic, France<br>**1870s ff.** Rapid birth rate decline<br>**1870s ff.** Spread of compulsory education laws<br>**1871–1914** High point of European imperialism<br>**1879–1907** Alliance system: Germany-Austria (1879); Germany-Austria-Russia (1881); Germany-Italy-Austria (1882); France-Russia (1891); Britain-France (1904); Britain-Russia (1907) | **1880s ff.** High point of impressionism in art<br>**1881–1914** Canadian Pacific Railway<br>**1881–1889** German social insurance laws enacted<br>**1882** United States excludes Chinese immigrants<br>**1891–1898** Australia and New Zealand restrict Asian immigration<br>**1893** Women's suffrage in New Zealand<br>**1898** Spanish-American War; United States acquires Puerto Rico, Guam, Philippines<br>**1898** United States annexes Hawaii<br>**1899** United States acquires part of Samoa | **1901** Commonwealth of Australia creates national federation<br>**1907** New Zealand gains dominion status in British Empire<br>**1912–1913** Balkan Wars<br>**1914** Beginning of World War I |

wider literacy; mankind was on the verge of virtual perfection. After eight months of hiding, Condorcet was caught and put in jail, where he died. His last years testify to the harsh downside of political upheaval in modern Europe, but also to the firm hold of hope in better things to come.

Against the backdrop of intellectual challenge, commercial growth, and population pressure, the placid politics of the 18th century were shattered by the series of revolutions that took shape in the 1770s and 1780s. This was the eve of the **age of revolution,** a period of political upheaval beginning roughly with the American Revolution in 1775 and continuing through the French Revolution of 1789 and other movements for change up to 1848. The wave of revolutions caught up many social groups with diverse motives, some eager to use revolution to promote further change and some hoping to turn back the clock and recover older values.

## Forces of Change

Three forces were working to shatter Europe's calm by the mid-18th century. The first of the forces was cultural, for intellectual ferment was running high. Enlightenment thinkers challenged regimes that did not grant full religious freedom or that insisted on aristocratic privilege, and a few called for widespread popular voice in government. Jean-Jacques Rousseau argued for government based on a general will, and this could be interpreted as a plea for democratic voting. A gap had opened between leading intellectuals and established institutions, and this played a role in the revolutions that lay ahead. Enlightenment thinkers also encouraged economic and technological change and policies that would promote industry; manufacturers and political reformers alike could take inspiration from these ideas.

Along with cultural change, ongoing commercialization continued to stir the economy. Businesspeople, gaining new wealth, might well challenge the idea that aristocrats alone should hold the highest political offices. They certainly were growing interested in new techniques that might spur production. Commercial practices might also draw attack, from artisans or peasant villagers who preferred older economic values. This could feed revolution as well.

A final source of disruption was occurring more quietly at all social levels. Western Europe experienced its huge population jump after about 1730. Within half a century, the population of France rose by 50 percent; that of Britain and Prussia rose 100 percent. This **population revolution** was partly the result of better border policing by the efficient nation-state governments, which reduced the movement of disease-bearing animals. More important was improved nutrition resulting from the growing use of the potato. These factors reduced the death rate, particularly for children; instead of more than 40 percent of all children dying by age 2, the figure by the 1780s was closer to 33 percent. More children surviving also meant more people living to have children of their own, so the birth rate increased as well.

Population pressure at this level always has dramatic impact. Upper-class families, faced with more surviving children, tried to tighten their grip on existing offices. In the late 18th century, it became harder for anyone who was not an aristocrat to gain a high post in the church or state. This reaction helped feed demands for change by other groups. Above all, population pressure drove many people into the working class as they lost any real chance of inheriting property, creating new motives for protest.

The population growth of the 18th century prompted a rapid expansion of domestic manufacturing in western Europe and, by 1800, in the United States. Hundreds of thousands of people became full- or part-time producers of textile and metal products, working at home but in a capitalist system in which materials, work orders, and sales depended on urban merchants. This development has been called **proto-industrialization,** and it ultimately encouraged new technologies to expand production further because of the importance of new market relationships and manufacturing volume.

Population upheaval and the spread of a propertyless class that worked for money wages had a sweeping impact on a variety of behaviors in Western society, including North America. Many villagers began to change their dress to more urban styles; this suggests an early form of new consumer interest. Premarital sex increased, and out-of-wedlock births rose to 10 percent of all births. Among groups with little or no property, parental authority began to decline because the traditional threat of denying inheritance had no meaning. Youthful independence became more marked, and although this was particularly evident in economic behavior as many young people looked for jobs on their own, the new defiance of authority might have had political implications as well.

## The American Revolution

When Britain's Atlantic colonies rebelled in 1775, it was primarily a war for independence rather than a full-fledged revolution. A large minority of American colonists resisted Britain's attempt to impose new taxes and trade controls on the colonies after 1763. Many settlers also resented restrictions on movement into the frontier areas. The colonists also invoked British political theory to argue that they should not be taxed without representation. The Stamp Act of 1765, imposing taxes on documents and pamphlets, particularly roused protest against British tyranny. Other grievances were involved. Crowding along the eastern seaboard led some younger men to seek new opportunities, including political office, that turned them against the older colonial leadership. Growing commerce antagonized some farmers and artisans, who looked for ways to defend the older values of greater social equality and community spirit.

The Bostonians Paying the Excise Man

With the start of the **American Revolution,** colonial rebels set up a new government, which issued the Declaration of Independence in 1776 and authorized a formal army to pursue its war. The persistence of the revolutionaries was combined with British military blunders and significant aid from the French government, designed to embarrass its key enemy. After several years of fighting, the United States won its freedom and, in 1789, set up a new constitutional structure based on Enlightenment principles, with checks and balances between the legislature and the executive branches of government, and formal guarantees of individual liberties. Voting rights, though limited, were widespread, and the new regime was for a time the most advanced in the world. Socially, the revolution accomplished less; slavery was untouched.

The Declaration of Independence (1776)

## Crisis in France in 1789

The next step in the revolutionary spiral occurred in France. It was the **French Revolution** that most clearly set in motion the political restructuring of western Europe. Several factors combined in the 1780s in what became a classic pattern of revolutionary causation. Ideological insistence on change won increasing attention from the mid-18th century onward, as Enlightenment thinkers urged the need to limit the powers of the Catholic church, the aristocracy, and the monarchy. Social changes reinforced the ideological challenge. Some middle-class people, proud of their business or professional success, wanted a greater political role. Many peasants, pressed by population growth, wanted fuller freedom from landlords' demands.

The French government and upper classes proved incapable of reform. Aristocrats tightened their grip in response to their own population pressure, and the government proved increasingly ineffective—a key ingredient in any successful revolution. Finally, a sharp economic slump in 1787 and 1788, triggered by bad harvests, set the seal on revolution.

Madame de Staël on the Ancien Regime

The French king, **Louis XVI,** called a meeting of the traditional parliament to consider tax reform for his financially pinched regime. But middle-class representatives, inspired by Enlightenment ideals, insisted on turning this assembly (which had not met for a century and a half) into a modern parliament, with voting by head (that is, each representative with a vote, rather than a single vote for each estate) and with majority representation for nonnoble property owners. The fearful king caved in after some street riots in Paris in the summer of 1789, and the revolution was under way.

Oath of the Tennis Court

Events that summer were crucial. The new assembly, with its middle-class majority, quickly turned to devising a new political regime. A stirring ***Declaration of the Rights of Man and the Citizen*** proclaimed freedom of thought. Like the American Declaration of Independence, this law enacted natural rights to "liberty, property, security, and resistance to oppression" and specifically guaranteed free expression of ideas. A popular riot stormed a political prison, the Bastille, on July 14, in what became the revolution's symbol; ironically, almost no prisoners were there. Soon after this, peasants seized manorial records and many landed estates. This triggered a general proclamation abolishing manorialism, giving peasants clear title to much land and establishing equality under the law. Although aristocrats survived for some time, the principles of aristocratic rule were undercut. The privileges of the church were also attacked, and church property was seized. A new constitution proclaimed individual rights, including freedom of religion, press, and property. A strong parliament was set up to limit the king, and about one-half the adult male population—those with property—were eligible to vote.

*Declaration of the Rights of Man and the Citizen*

## The French Revolution: Radical and Authoritarian Phases

By 1792 the initial push for reform began to turn more radical. Early reforms provoked massive opposition in the name of church and aristocracy, and civil war broke out in several parts of France. Monarchs in Britain, Prussia, and Austria trumpeted their opposition to the revolution, and France soon moved toward European war as well. These pressures led to a takeover by radical leaders, who wanted to press the revolution forward and to set up firmer authority in the revolution's defense. The radicals abolished the monarchy. The king was decapitated on the **guillotine,** a new device introduced, Enlightenment-fashion, to provide more humane executions, but instead it became a symbol of revolutionary bloodthirst. The radicals also executed several thousand opponents in what was named the Reign of Terror, even though by later standards it was mild.

The leader of the radical phase was Maximilien Robespierre (1758–1794), a classic example of a revolutionary ideologue. Born into a family of lawyers, he gained his law degree in 1781 and soon was publishing Enlightenment-style political tracts. The new philosophies inspired passion in Robespierre, particularly the democratic ideas of Rousseau. Elected to all the initial revolutionary assemblies, Robespierre headed the prosecution of the king in 1792 and then took over the leadership of government. He put down many factions, sponsored the Terror, and worked to centralize the government. In 1794 he set up a civic religion, the "cult of the Supreme Being," to replace Catholicism. Personally incorruptible, Robespierre came to symbolize the single-minded revolutionary. But he shied away from significant social reforms that might have drawn urban support. He was convinced that he knew the people's will. Opposition mounted, and when he called for yet another purge of moderate leaders, he was arrested and guillotined on the same day, abandoned by the popular factions that had once spurred him on.

Saint-Just on Democracy, Education, and Terror

While in power, Robespierre and his colleagues pushed revolutionary reforms. A new constitution, never fully put into practice, proclaimed universal adult male suffrage. The radicals introduced a metric system of weights and measures, the product of the rationalizing genius of the Enlightenment. Slavery was abolished in the French colonies, though this measure was reversed after the radical regime collapsed. Robe-

VISUALIZING THE PAST

## The French Revolution in Cartoons

This cartoon, titled *The Former Great Dinner of the Modern Gargantua with His Family,* appeared in 1791 or 1792, as the French Revolution was becoming more radical. It pictures the king as a latter-day Gargantua, referring to a French literary figure who was a notoriously great eater.

**Questions** How does the cartoon characterize the relationship between French society and economy and the monarchy? What social structure is implied? What conclusions might readers of the cartoon draw about what should happen to the monarchy? With improvements in printing and literacy, cartoons were becoming more available, and they have continued to be important into the present day. Why were they effective as a means of communicating ideas? Did they spur people to action, or might they deflect action by provoking a good laugh?

spierre and his allies also proclaimed universal military conscription, arguing that men who were free citizens owed loyalty and service to the government. And revolutionary armies began to win major success. Not only were France's enemies driven out, but the regime began to acquire new territory in the Low Countries, Italy, and Germany, spreading revolutionary gains farther in western Europe.

A new spirit of popular **nationalism** surfaced during the revolution's radical phase. Many French people felt an active loyalty to the new regime—to a state they believed they had helped create. A new symbol was a revolutionary national anthem (the world's first), with its rousing first lines, "Come, children of the nation, the day of glory has arrived." Nationalism could replace older loyalties to church or locality.

The fall of the radicals led to four years of moderate policies. Then in 1799 the final phase of the revolution was ushered in with the victory of **Napoleon Bonaparte,** a leading general who soon converted the revolutionary republic to an authoritarian empire. Napoleon reduced the parliament to a rubber stamp, and a powerful police system limited freedom of expression. However, Napoleon confirmed other liberal gains, including religious freedom,

Madame de Ržmusat on the Rise of Napoleon

while enacting substantial equality—though for men, not women—in a series of new law codes. To train bureaucrats, Napoleon developed a centralized system of secondary schools and universities.

Driven by insatiable ambition, Napoleon devoted most of his attention to expansion abroad (Map 28.1). A series of wars brought France against all of Europe's major powers, including Russia. At its height, about 1812, the French Empire directly held or controlled as satellite kingdoms most of western Europe, and its success spurred some reform measures even in Prussia and Russia. The French Empire crumbled after this point. An attempt to invade Russia in 1812 failed miserably. French armies perished in the cold Russian winter even as they pushed deep into the empire. An alliance system organized by Britain crushed the emperor definitively in 1814 and 1815. Yet Napoleon's campaigns had done more than dominate European diplomacy for one and a half decades. They had also spread key revolutionary legislation—the idea of equality under the law and the attack on privileged institutions such as aristocracy, church, and craft guilds—throughout much of western Europe.

The Empire of Napoleon in 1812

Napoleon's Exile to St. Helena

The revolution and Napoleon encouraged popular nationalism outside of France as well as within. French military success continued to draw great excitement at home. Elsewhere, French armies tore down local governments, as in Italy and Germany, which whetted appetites there for greater national unity. And the sheer fact of French invasion made many people more conscious of loyalty to their own nations; popular resistance to Napoleon, in parts of Spain and Germany, played a role in the final French defeat.

## A Conservative Settlement and the Revolutionary Legacy

The allies who had brought the proud French emperor down met at Vienna in 1815 to reach a peace settlement that would make further revolution impossible. Diplomats at the **Congress of Vienna** did not try to punish France too sternly, on the grounds that the European balance of power should be restored. Still, a series of stronger powers was established around France, which meant gains for Prussia within Germany and for the hitherto obscure nation

Europe After the Congress of Vienna, 1815

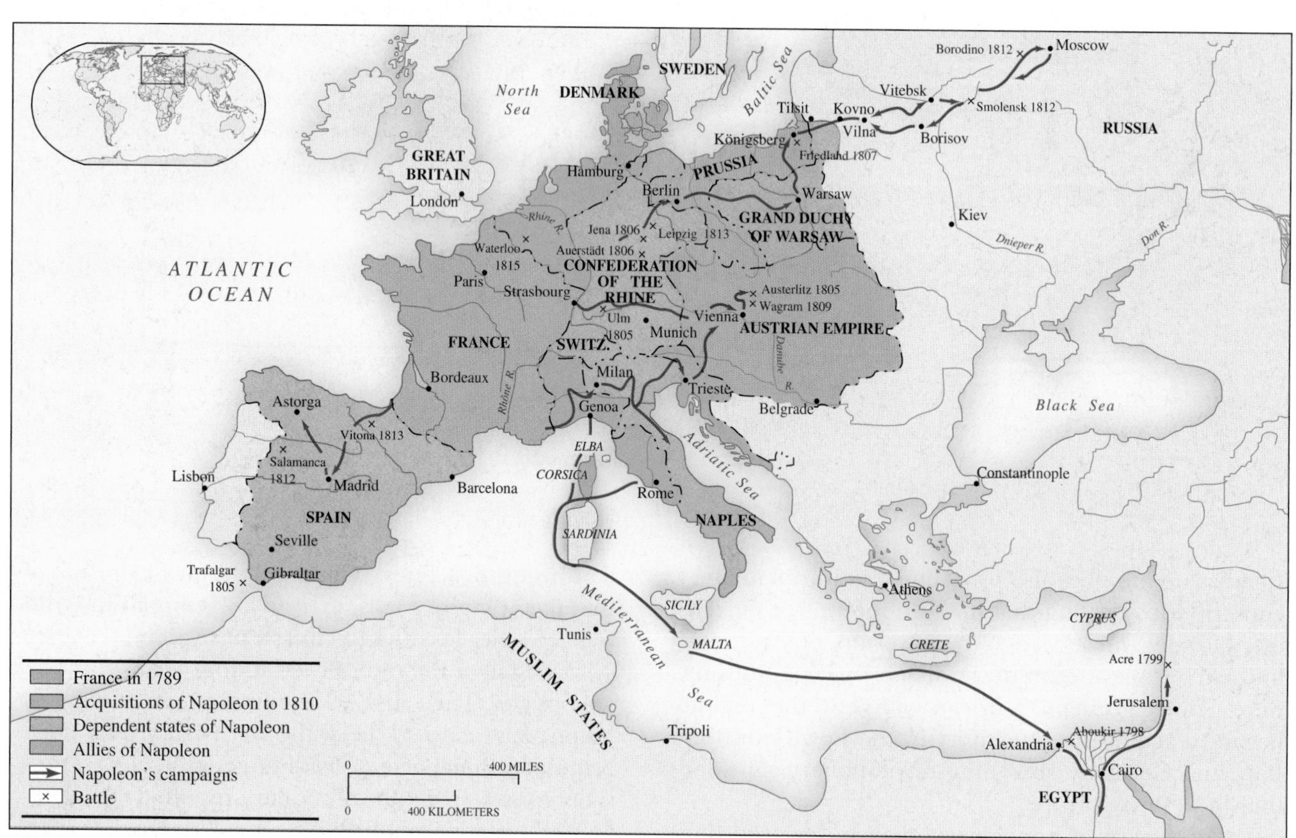


**MAP 28.1 Napoleon's Empire in 1812.** By 1812, France dominated Europe to the borders of Russia, but Napoleon's decision to invade Russia proved disastrous, as his army was soon mired in the bitter cold and deep snows of a harsh Russian winter. Defeated in 1814, Napoleon was exiled to the island of Elba (shown above) but he escaped and returned to power. After final defeat at the Battle of Waterloo (1815), he was exiled to the remote South Atlantic island of St. Helena.

of Piedmont in northern Italy. The old map was not restored, and the realignments ultimately facilitated national unifications. Britain gained new colonial territories, confirming its lead in the scramble for empire in the wider world. Russia, newly important in European affairs, maintained its hold over most of Poland.

These territorial adjustments kept Europe fairly stable for almost half a century—a major achievement, given the crisscrossed rivalries that had long characterized Western society. But the Vienna negotiators were much less successful in promoting internal peace. The idea was to restore monarchy in France and to link Europe's major powers in defense of churches and kings. This was a key statement of the growing movement of **conservatives** in Europe, who defined themselves in opposition to revolutionary goals.

But political movements arose to challenge conservatism. They involved concrete political agitation but also an explosion of ideals. Many of the ideals would resonate in many parts of the world during the 19th and 20th centuries. **Liberals** focused primarily on issues of political structure. They looked for ways to limit state interference in individual life and urged representation of propertied people in government. Liberals touted the importance of constitutional rule and protection for freedoms of religion, press, and assembly. Largely representing the growing middle class, many liberals also sought economic reforms, including better education, which would promote industrial growth.

John Stuart Mill on Women's Rights

**Radicals** accepted the importance of most liberal demands, but they also wanted wider voting rights. Some advocated outright democracy. They also urged some social reforms in the interest of the lower classes. A smaller current of socialism urged an attack on private property in the name of equality and an end to capitalist exploitation of workers. Nationalists, often allied with liberalism or radicalism, urged the importance of national unity and glory.

Political protest found support among students and among urban artisans, concerned about economic changes that might displace craft skills. Revolutions broke out in several places in 1820 and again in 1830. The 1820 revolts involved a nationalist **Greek Revolution** against Ottoman rule—a key step in gradually dismantling the Ottoman Empire in the Balkans—and a rebellion in Spain. Another French Revolution of 1830 installed a different king and a somewhat more liberal monarchy. Uprisings also occurred in key states in Italy and Germany, though without durable result; the Belgian Revolution of 1830 produced a liberal regime and a newly independent nation.

Britain and the United States also participated in the process of political change, though without revolution. Key states in the United States granted universal adult male suffrage (except for slaves) and other political changes in the 1820s, leading to the election of a popular president, Andrew Jackson, in 1828. In Britain, the **Reform Bill of 1832,** a response to popular agitation, gave the parliamentary vote to most middle-class men. By the 1830s, regimes in France, Britain, Belgium, and several other countries had solid parliaments (the equivalent of Congress in the United States), some guarantees for individual rights against arbitrary state action, religious freedom not only for various Christian sects but also for Jews, and voting systems that ranged from democratic (for men) to the upper-middle class, plus aristocracy alone.

Reform Bill of 1832

## Industrialization and the Revolutions of 1848

By the 1830s and 1840s, industrialization began to add pressures to Europe's revolutionary ferment. The 1832 Reform Bill in England, for example, responded in part to growing working-class agitation, though it did not extend the vote to workers and led to further political protest. By this time France, Belgium, and Germany, as well as the United States, were fully engaged in the early stages of the Industrial Revolution, based in part on copying British models. These developments spurred some direct unrest among factory workers. They raised even more concerns among artisans, worried for the future of traditional skilled labor, and these groups provided much of the muscle that went into the final phase of the age of revolution.

Key lower-class groups turned to political protest as a means of compensating for industrial change. Artisans and workers in Britain generated a new movement to gain the vote in the 1830s and 1840s. This **Chartist movement** hoped that a democratic government would regulate new technologies and promote popular education.

The extraordinary wave of revolutions of 1848 and 1849 brought protest to a head. Paris was again the center. In the popular uprising that began in February 1848, the French monarchy was once again expelled, this time for good, and a democratic republic was established briefly. Urban artisans pressed for serious social reform—perhaps some version of socialism, and certainly government-supported jobs for the unemployed. Groups of women schoolteachers agitated for the vote and other rights for women. The social demands were far wider than those of the great uprising of 1789.

European Centers of Rebellion and Revolution, 1820–1848

Revolution quickly spread to other centers. Major revolts occurred in Germany (Figure 28.2), Austria, and Hungary. Revolutionaries in these areas devised

FIGURE 28.2 The 1848 revolution in Berlin. After months of maneuvering, negotiation, and street clashes, the revolutionaries agreed on a liberal constitution that would have established a constitutional monarchy. When they offered the crown under these terms to King Friedrich Wilhelm IV, who had initially given in to the demands of the crowds, he politely declined, saying in private that he could not accept a crown "from the gutter." Friedrich Wilhelm believed he ruled by divine right—not by the consent of the governed. The great difference between the king's and the reformers' views of constitutional monarchy was indicative of the chasm that existed in mid-19th-century Europe between advocates of aristocratic and democratic government.

Metternich on the Revolutions of 1848

liberal constitutions to modify conservative monarchies, artisans pressed for social reforms that would restrain industrialization, and peasants sought a complete end to manorialism. Revolts in central Europe also pressed for nationalist demands: German nationalists worked for the unity of their country, and various nationalities in Austria–Hungary, including Slavic groups, sought greater autonomy. A similar liberal nationalist revolt occurred in various parts of Italy.

The revolutionary fires burned only briefly. The social demands of artisans and some factory workers were put down quickly; not only conservatives but middle-class liberals opposed these efforts. Nationalist agitation also failed for the moment, as the armies of Austria–Hungary and Prussia restored the status quo to central Europe and Italy. Democracy persisted in France, but a nephew of the great Napoleon soon replaced the liberal republic with an authoritarian empire that lasted until 1870. Peasant demands were met, and serfdom was fully abolished throughout western Europe. Many peasants, uninterested in other gains, supported conservative forces.

The substantial failure of the revolutions of 1848 drew the revolutionary era in western Europe to a close. Failure taught many liberals and working-class leaders that revolution was too risky; more gradual methods should be used instead. Improved transportation reduced the chance of food crises, the traditional trigger for revolution in Western history. Bad harvests in 1846 and 1847 had driven up food prices and helped promote insurgency in the cities, but famines of this sort did not recur in the West. Many governments also installed better riot control police.

By 1850 an industrial class structure had come to predominate. Earlier revolutionary gains had reduced the aristocrats' legal privileges, and the rise of business had eroded their economic dominance. With industrialization, social structure came to rest less on privilege and birth and more on money. Key divisions by 1850 pitted middle-class property owners against workers of various sorts. The old alliances that had produced the revolutions were now dissolved.

## The Consolidation of the Industrial Order, 1850–1914

**The unification of Italy and Germany created new rivalries in western Europe. European countries developed new functions for governments, responding to industrial pressures, including socialism.**

In most respects, the 65 years after 1850 seemed calmer than the frenzied period of political upheaval and initial industrialization. Railroads and canals linked cities across Europe and spurred industrialization and urbanization (Map 28.2). City growth continued in the West; indeed, several countries, starting with Britain, passed the 50 percent mark in urbanization—the first time in human history that more than a minority of a population lived in cities. City governments began to gain ground on the pressing problems growth had created. Sanitation improved, and death rates fell below birth rates for the first time in urban history. Parks, museums, effective regulation of food and housing facilities, and more efficient police forces all added to the safety and the physical and cultural amenities of urban life. Revealingly, crime rates began to stabilize or even drop in several industrial areas, a sign of more effective social control but also of a more disciplined population.

Industrialization in Europe

### Adjustments to Industrial Life

Family life adjusted to industrialization (Figure 28.3). Birth rates began to drop as Western society began a demographic transition to a new system that promoted fairly stable population levels through a new combination of low birth rates and low death rates. Children were now seen as a source of emotional satisfaction and parental responsibility, not as workers contributing to a family economy. As the Document feature shows, arguments about women's special family duties gained ground.

Material conditions generally improved after 1850. By 1900 probably two-thirds of the Western population enjoyed conditions above the subsistence level. People could afford a few amenities such as newspapers and family outings, their diet and housing improved, and their health got better. The decades from 1880 to 1920 saw a real revolution in children's health, thanks in part to better hygiene during childbirth and

Industrial Society and Factory Conditions

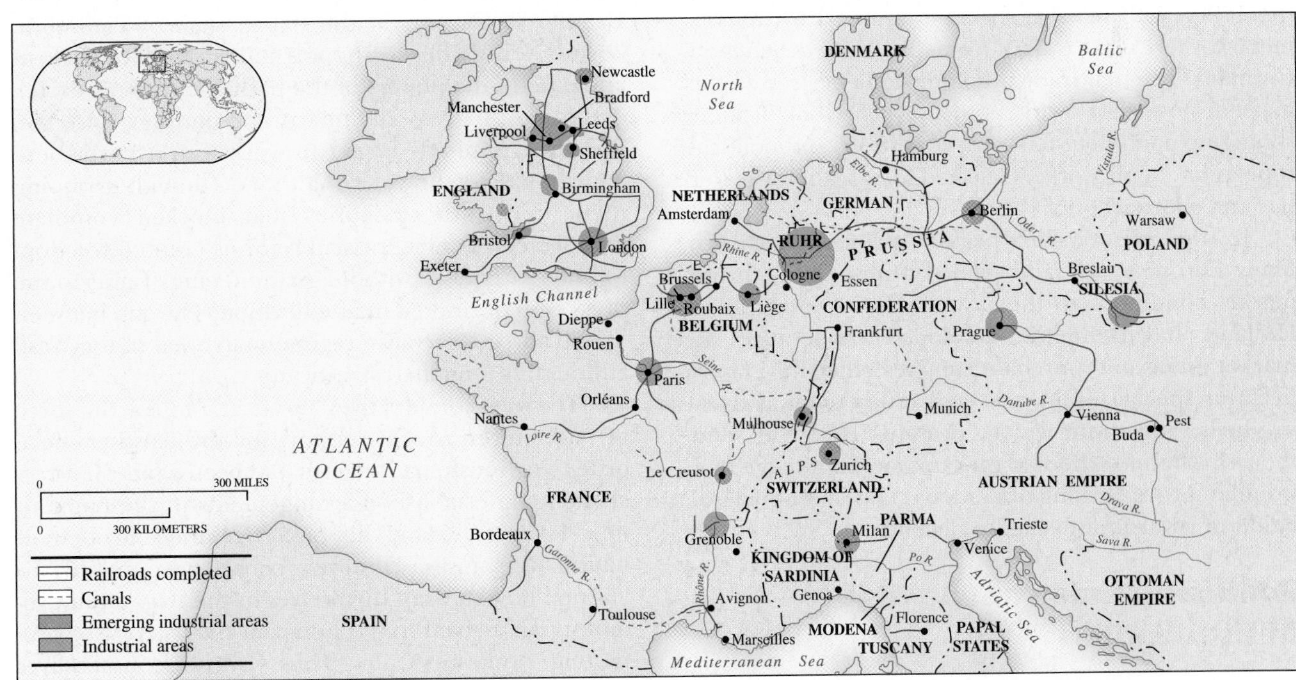


**MAP 28.2 Industrialization in Europe, c. 1850.** By the mid-19th century, industrialization had spread across Europe, aided by the development of railroad links and canals that brought resources to the new factories and transported their finished goods to world markets.

FIGURE 28.3 Respectable middle-class leisure in western Europe.

better parental care. Infancy and death separated for the first time in human history: Instead of one-third or more of all children dying by age 10, child death rates fell to less than 10 percent and continued to plummet. The discovery of germs by **Louis Pasteur** led by the 1880s to more conscientious sanitary regulations and procedures by doctors and other health care specialists; this reduced the deaths of women in childbirth. Women began to outlive men by a noticeable margin, but men's health also improved.

In little more than a decade, between 1860 and 1873, the number of corporations in western Europe doubled. The rise of corporations, drawing on stockholder investment funds, was a major change in business and organizational life. Important labor movements took shape among industrial workers by the 1890s, with massive strike movements by miners, metalworkers, and others from the United States to Germany. The new trade union movement stressed the massed power of workers. Hosts of labor leaders sprang up amid detested work conditions and political repression. Many workers learned to bargain for better pay and shorter hours.

In the countryside, peasant protests declined. Many European peasants gained a new ability to use market conditions to their own benefit. Some, as in Holland and Denmark, developed cooperatives to market goods and purchase supplies efficiently. Many peasants specialized in new cash crops, such as dairy products. Still more widely, peasants began to send their children to school to pick up new knowledge that would improve farming operations. The traditional isolation of rural areas began to decline.

## Political Trends and the Rise of New Nations

Western politics consolidated after the failed revolutions of 1848. Quite simply, issues that had dominated the Western political agenda for many decades were largely resolved within a generation. The great debates about fundamental constitutions and government structure, which had emerged in the 17th century with the rise of absolutism and new political theory and then raged during the decades of revolution, at last grew quiet.

Many Western leaders worked to reduce the need for political revolution after 1850. Liberals decided that revolution was too risky and became more willing to compromise. Key conservatives strove to develop reforms that would save elements of the old regime, including power for the landed aristocracy and the monarchy. A British conservative leader, **Benjamin Disraeli,** took the initiative of granting the vote to working-class men in 1867. **Count Camillo di Cavour,** in the Italian state of Piedmont, began even earlier to support industrial development and extend the powers of the parliament to please liberal forces. In Prussia a new prime minister, **Otto von Bismarck,** similarly began to work with a parliament and to extend the vote to all men (though grouping them in wealth categories that blocked complete democracy). Other Prussian reforms granted freedom to Jews, extended (without guaranteeing) rights to the press, and promoted mass education. The gap between liberal and conservative regimes narrowed in the West, although it remained significant.

A Letter from Otto von Bismarck (1866)

The new conservatives also began to use the force of nationalism to win support for the existing social order. Previously, nationalism had been a radical force, challenging established arrangements in the name of new loyalties. Many liberals continued to defend nationalist causes. However, conservative politicians learned how to wrap themselves in the flag, often promoting an active foreign policy in the interest of promoting domestic calm. Thus, British conservatives became champions of expanding the empire, while in the United States, by the 1890s, the Republican party became increasingly identified with imperialist causes.

The most important new uses of nationalism in the West occurred in Italy and Germany. After wooing liberal support, Cavour formed an alliance with France that enabled him to attack Austrian control of northern Italian provinces in 1858. The war set in motion a nationalist rebellion in other parts of the peninsula that allowed Cavour to unite most of Italy under the Piedmontese king (Map 28.3). This led to a reduction of the political power of the Catholic pope, already an opponent of liberal and nationalist ideas—an important part of the general reduction of church power in Western politics.

The Unification of Italy, 1859–1870

Following Cavour's example, Bismarck in Prussia staged a series of wars in the 1860s that expanded Prussian power in Germany. He was a classic diplomatic military strategist, a key example of an individual agent seizing on larger trends such as nationalism to produce results that were far from inevitable. For example, in 1863 Bismarck used the occasion of Danish incorporation of two heavily German provinces, Schleswig and Holstein, to justify the Prussian and Austrian defeat of Denmark. Then he maneuvered a pretext for a Prussian declaration of war against Austria. In 1866 Prussia emerged as the supreme German power. A final war, against France, led to outright German unity in 1871 (Map 28.4). The new German Empire boasted a national parliament with a lower house based on universal male suffrage and an upper house that favored conservative state governments. This kind of compromise, combined with the dizzying joy of nationalist success, won support for the new regime from most liberals and many conservatives.

The Unification of Germany, 1815–1871

Other key political issues were resolved at about the same time. The bloody **American Civil War**—the first war based extensively on industrial weaponry and transport systems, carefully watched by European military observers—was fought between 1861 and 1865. The war resolved by force the simmering dispute over sectional rights between the North and South and also brought an end to slavery in the nation. France, after its defeat by Germany in 1870, overthrew its short-lived echo of the Napoleonic Empire and established a conservative republic with votes for all men, a reduction of church power, and expansion of education, but no major social reform. Just as conservative Bismarck could be selectively radical, France proved that liberals could be very cautious.

Almost all Western nations now had parliamentary systems, usually democracies of some sort, in which religious and other freedoms were widely protected. In this system, liberal and conservative ministries could alternate without major changes of internal policy. Indeed, Italy developed a process called **trasformismo**, or transformism, in which parliamentary deputies, no

MAP 28.3 The Unification of Italy

MAP 28.4 The Unification of Germany, 1815–1871

DOCUMENT

## Women in the Industrial Revolution

The West's Industrial Revolution changed the situation of women in many ways. Some of the changes have recurred more recently in other civilizations; others were particularly characteristic of the 19th-century West. Industrialization cut into women's traditional work and protest roles (for example, in spearheading bread riots as attention shifted to work-based strikes), but it tended to expand the educational opportunities for women. Some new work roles and protest outlets, including feminism, developed by 1914. Important changes occurred in the home as well. New ideas and standards elevated women's position and set up more demanding tasks. Relationships between women were also affected by the growing use of domestic servants (the most common urban job for working-class women) and new attitudes of middle- and lower-class women. The first document that follows sketches the idealization of middle-class women; it comes from an American moral tract of 1837, written anonymously, probably by a man. The second document, written by a woman and published in an English women's magazine, shows new household standards of another sort, with a critical tone also common in middle-class literature. Finally, a British housewife discusses her servant problems, reflecting yet another facet of women's lives. How could women decide what their domestic roles were and whether they brought satisfaction?

### Women as Civilizers (1837)

As a sister, she soothes the troubled heart, chastens and tempers the wild daring of the hurt mind restless with disappointed pride or fired with ambition. As a mistress, she inspires the nobler sentiment of purer love, and the sober purpose of conquering himself for virtue's sake. As a wife, she consoles him in grief, animates him with hope in despair, restrains him in prosperity, cheers him in poverty and trouble, swells the pulsations of his throbbing breast that beats for honorable distinction, and rewards his toils with the undivided homage of a grateful heart. In the important and endearing character of mother, she watches and directs the various impulses of unfledged genius, instills into the tender and susceptible mind the quickening seeds of virtue, fits us to brave dangers in time of peril, and consecrates to truth and virtue the best affections of our nature.

### Motherhood as Power and Burden (1877)

Every woman who has charge of a household should have a practical knowledge of nursing, simple doctoring and physicianing. The professional doctor must be called in for real illness. But the Home Doctor may do so much to render professional visits very few and far between. And her knowledge will be of infinite value when it is necessary to carry out the doctor's orders. . . .

### The Mother Builder

It is a curious fact that architects who design and builders who carry out their plans must have training for this work. But the Mother Builder is supposed to have to know by instinct how to put in each tiny brick which builds up the "human." The result of leaving it to "instinct" is that the child starts out with bad foundations and a jerry-built constitution. . . .

When one considers that one child in every three born dies before the age of five years, it is evident how wide-spread must be the ignorance as to the feeding and care of these little ones. It is a matter of surprise to those who understand the constitution and needs of infants that, considering the conditions under which the large number of them are reared, the mortality is not greater. . . .

matter what platforms they professed, were transformed once in Rome to a single-minded pursuit of political office and support of the status quo.

## The Social Question and New Government Functions

The decline of basic constitutional disputes by the 1870s promoted the fuller development of an industrial-style state in the West. A new set of political movements emerged.

Government functions and personnel expanded rapidly throughout the Western world after 1870. All Western governments introduced civil service examinations to test applicants on the basis of talent rather than on connections or birth alone, thus unwittingly imitating Chinese innovations more than a thousand years before. With a growing bureaucracy and improved recruitment, governments began to extend their regulatory apparatus, inspecting factory safety, the health of prostitutes, hospital conditions, and even (through the introduction of passports and border controls) personal travel.

Schooling expanded, becoming generally compulsory up to age 12. Governments believed that education provided essential work skills and the basis for new levels of political loyalty. Many American states by 1900 began also to require high school education, and most Western nations expanded their public secondary

## The Risks Babies Run

To begin with, the popular superstition that a young baby must be "hungry" because it lives on milk, and is on this plea the recipient of scraps and bits of vegetables, potato and gravy, crusts, and other heterogeneous articles of diet, has much to answer for. Then, the artistic sense of the mother which leads her to display mottled necks, dimpled arms, and chubby legs, instead of warmly covering these charming portions of baby's anatomy, goes hugely to swell the death-rate. Mistakes in feeding and covering have much to answer for in the high mortality of infants.

## The Servant "Problem" (1860)

So we lost Mary, and Peggy reigned in her stead for some six weeks. . . .

But Peggy differed greatly from her predecessor Mary. She was not clean in her person, and my mother declared that her presence was not desirable within a few feet. Moreover she had no notion of putting things in their places, but always left all her working materials in the apartment where they were last used. It was not therefore pleasant, when one wanted a sweeping brush, to have to sit down and think which room Peggy had swept the last, and so on with all the paraphernalia for dusting and scrubbing. But this was not the worst. My mother, accustomed to receive almost reverential respect from her old servants could not endure poor Peggy's familiar ways. . . .

Now, though I am quite willing to acknowledge the mutual obligation which exists between the employer and employed, I do not agree with my charwoman that she is the only person who ought to be considered as conferring a favor. I desire to treat her with all kindness, showing every possible regard to her comfort, and I expect from her no more work than I would cheerfully and easily perform in the same time. But when I scrupulously perform my part of the bargain, both as regards food and wages, not to mention much thought and care in order to make things easy for her and which were not in the agreement at all, I think she ought not only to keep faith with me if possible, but to abstain from hinting at the obligation she confers in coming.

It is not pleasant, as my mother says, to beg and pray for the help for which we also pay liberally. But it is worse for my kitchen helper to be continually reminding me that she need not go out unless she likes, and that it was only to oblige me she ever came at all. I do not relish this utter ignoring of her wages, etc., or her being quite deaf because I choose to offer a suggestion as to the propriety of dusting out the corners, or when I mildly hint that I should prefer her doing something in my way. . . .

But if I were to detail all my experiences, I should never have done. I have had many good and willing workers; but few on whose punctuality and regularity I could rely.

---

**Questions** In what ways did industrialization increase differences between women and men in the 19th-century West? What were the main changes in women's roles and ideals? How did middle-class and working-class women differ? These magazine articles were prescriptive, suggesting what women should be like. Middle-class audiences consumed vast amounts of this kind of prescriptive literature from the 19th century onward, as sources of both praise and constructive criticism. Did the women's images projected in these materials bolster or undermine women's position? Would they generate contentment or dissatisfaction among their readers? Finally, do they reflect real life or merely idealized standards (for wives, mothers, and servants)? What are the problems in using prescriptive materials to describe 19th-century women's history?

school systems. Here was a huge addition to the ways in which governments and individuals interacted. The new school systems promoted literacy; by 1900, 90 to 95 percent of all adults in western Europe and the United States could read. Schools also encouraged certain social agendas. Girls were carefully taught about the importance of home and women's moral mission in domestic science programs. Schools also carefully propounded nationalism, teaching the superiority of the nation's language and history as well as attacking minority or immigrant cultures.

Governments also began to introduce wider welfare measures, replacing or supplementing traditional groups such as churches and families. Bismarck was a pioneer in this area in the 1880s as he tried to wean German workers from their attraction to socialism. His tactic failed, as socialism steadily advanced, but his measures had lasting importance. German social insurance began to provide assistance in cases of accident, illness, and old age. Some measures to aid the unemployed were soon added, initially in Britain. These early welfare programs were small and their utility limited, but they sketched a major extension of government power.

Accompanying the quiet revolution in government functions was a realignment of the political spectrum in the Western world during the late 19th century. Constitutional issues were replaced by social issues—what people of the time called the **social question**—as the key criteria for political partisanship. Socialist and feminist movements surged to the political fore, placing liberals and conservatives in a new defensive posture.

The rise of **socialism** depended above all on the power of grievances of the working class, with allies from other groups. It also reflected a redefinition of political theory by German theorist **Karl Marx.** Early socialist doctrine, from the Enlightenment through 1848, had focused on human perfectibility: set up a few exemplary communities where work and rewards would be shared, and the evils of capitalism would end. Marx's socialism, worked out between 1848 and 1860, was tough-minded, and he blasted earlier theorists as giddy utopians. Marx saw socialism as the final phase of an inexorable march of history, which could be studied dispassionately and scientifically.

Karl Marx on the Question of Free Trade

History for Marx was shaped by the available means of production and who controlled those means, an obvious reflection of the looming role of technology in the industrial world forming at that time. According to Marx, class struggle always pitted a group out of power with the group controlling the means of production; hence, in the era just passed, the middle class had battled the feudal aristocracy and its hold on the land. Now the middle class had won; it dominated production and, through this, the state and the culture as well. But it had created a new class enemy, the propertyless proletariat, that would grow until revolution became inevitable. Then, after a transitional period in which proletarian dictatorship would clean up the remnants of the bourgeois social order, full freedom would be achieved. People would benefit justly and equally from their work, and the state would wither away; the historic class struggle would at last end because classes would be eliminated.

Marx's vision was a powerful one. It clearly identified capitalist evil. It told workers that their low wages were exploitive and unjust. It urged the need for violent action but also ensured that revolution was part of the inexorable tides of history. The result would be heaven on earth—ultimately, an Enlightenment-like vision of progress.

Capitalism Challenged: *The Communist Manifesto*

By the 1860s, when working-class activity began to revive, Marxist doctrine provided encouragement and structure. Marx himself continued to concentrate on ideological development and purity, but leaders in many countries translated his doctrine into practical political parties. Germany led the way. As Bismarck extended the vote, socialist leaders in the 1860s and 1870s were the first to understand the implications of mass electioneering. Socialist movements provided fiery speakers who courted popular votes. By the 1880s, socialists in Germany were cutting into liberal support, and by 1900, the party was the largest single political force in the nation. Socialist parties in Austria, France, and elsewhere followed a roughly similar course, everywhere emerging as a strong minority force.

The rise of socialism terrified many people in Western society, who took the revolutionary message literally. In combination with major industrial strikes and unionization, it was possible to see social issues portending outright social war. But socialism itself was not unchanging. As socialist parties gained strength, they often allied with other groups to achieve more moderate reforms. A movement called **revisionism** arose, which argued that Marx's revolutionary vision was wrong and that success could be achieved by peaceful democratic means. Many socialist leaders denounced revisionism but put their energies into building electoral victories rather than plotting violent revolution.

Socialism: The Gotha Program

Socialism was not the only challenge to the existing order. By 1900 powerful **feminist movements** had arisen. These movements sought various legal and economic gains for women, such as equal access to professions and higher education as well as the right to vote. Feminism won support particularly from middle-class women, who argued that the very moral superiority granted to women in the home should be translated into political voice. Many middle-class women also chafed against the confines of their domestic roles, particularly as family size declined. In several countries, feminism combined with socialism, but in Britain, the United States, Australia, and Scandinavia, a separate feminist current arose that petitioned widely and even conducted acts of violence in order to win the vote. Several American states and Scandinavian countries extended the vote to women by 1914, in a pattern that would spread to Britain, Germany, and the whole United States after 1918.

Recommendations of the Salem Convention

The new feminism, like the labor movement, was no mere abstraction but the fruit of active, impassioned leadership, largely from the middle classes. Emmeline Pankhurst (1858–1928; Figure 28.4) was typical of the more radical feminist leadership both in background and tactics. Born to a reform-minded English middle-class family, she was active in women's rights issues, as was her husband. She collaborated with Richard Pankhurst, whom she had married in 1879, to work for improvements in women's property rights, and she participated in the Socialist Fabian Society. But then she turned more radical. She formed a suffrage organization in 1903 to seek the vote for women. With her daughter Christabel, she sponsored attention-getting public disturbances, including planting a bomb in St. Paul's Cathedral. Window-smashing, arson, and hunger strikes rounded out her spectacular tactical arsenal. Often arrested, she engaged in a huge strike in 1912. The suffragists' support of the war effort in 1914 gained them public sympathy. Pankhurst

FIGURE 28.4 Emmeline Goulden Pankhurst. In her 1914 autobiography, Pankhurst recalled the early stirrings of feminism in her childhood: "The education of the English boy, then as now, was considered a much more serious matter than the education of the English boy's sister. . . . Of course [I] went to a carefully selected girls' school, but beyond the facts that the head mistress was a gentlewoman and that all the pupils were girls of my own class, nobody seemed concerned. A girl's education at that time seemed to have for its prime object the art of 'making home attractive'—presumably to migratory male relatives. It used to puzzle me to understand why I was under such a particular obligation to make home attractive to my brothers. We were on excellent terms of friendship, but it was never suggested to them as a duty that they make home attractive to me. Why not? Nobody seemed to know."

moved to Canada for a time, leaving the English movement to her daughter, but returned as a respected figure to run for parliament after women had gained the vote in 1928.

## Cultural Transformations

- Dramatic changes in daily life reflected the pressures and opportunities of industrialization. Cultural changes involved steady advances in sciences and increasingly defiant innovation in the arts.

### Emphasis on Consumption and Leisure

Key developments in popular culture differentiated Western society after 1850 from the decades of initial industrialization. Better wages and the reduction of work hours gave ordinary people new opportunities. Alongside the working class grew a large white-collar labor force of secretaries, clerks, and salespeople, who served the growing bureaucracies of big business and the state. These workers, some of them women, adopted many middle-class values, but they also insisted on interesting consumption and leisure outlets.

The middle class itself became more open to the idea that pleasure could be legitimate.

Furthermore, the economy demanded change. Factories could now spew out goods in such quantity that popular consumption had to be encouraged simply to keep pace with production. Widespread advertising developed to promote a sense of need where none had existed before. Product crazes emerged. The bicycle fad of the 1880s, in which middle-class families flocked to purchase the new machine, was the first of many consumer fads in modern Western history. People just had to have them. Bicycles also changed previous social habits, as women needed less cumbersome garments and young couples could outpedal chaperones during courtship.

**Mass leisure culture** began to emerge. Popular newspapers, with bold headlines and compelling human interest stories, won millions of subscribers in the industrial West. They featured shock and entertainment more than appeals to reason or political principle. Crime, imperialist exploits, sports, and even comics became the items of the day. Popular theater soared. Comedy routines and musical revues drew thousands of patrons to music halls. After 1900 some of these entertainment themes dominated the new medium of motion pictures. Vacation trips became increasingly common, and seaside resorts grew to the level of big business.

The rise of team sports readily expressed the complexities of the late 19th-century leisure revolution. Here was another Western development that soon had international impact. Soccer, American football, and baseball surged into new prominence at both amateur and professional levels. These new sports reflected industrial life. Though based on traditional games, they were organized by means of rules and umpires. They taught the virtues of coordination and discipline and could be seen as useful preparation for work or military life. They were suitably commercial: sports equipment, based on the ability to mass-produce rubber balls, and professional teams and stadiums quickly became major businesses. But sports also expressed impulse and violence. They expressed irrational community loyalties and even, as the Olympic games were reintroduced in 1896, nationalist passions.

Overall, new leisure interests suggested a complex set of attitudes on the part of ordinary people in Western society. They demonstrated growing secularism. Religion still counted among some groups, but religious practice had declined as people increasingly looked for worldly entertainments. Many people would have agreed that progress was possible on this earth through rational planning and individual self-control. Yet mass leisure also suggested a more impulsive side to popular outlook, one bent on the display of passion or at least vicarious participation by spectators in emotional release.

## Advances in Scientific Knowledge

Science and the arts took separate paths, with influential developments in each area. The size of the intellectual and artistic community in the West expanded steadily with rising prosperity and advancing educational levels. A growing audience existed for various intellectual and artistic products. The bulk of the new activity was resolutely secular. Although new churches were built as cities grew, and missionary activity reached new heights outside the Western world, the churches no longer served as centers for the most creative intellectual life. Continuing advances in science kept alive the rationalist tradition. Universities and other research establishments increasingly applied science to practical affairs, linking science and technology in the popular mind under a general aura of progress. Improvements in medical pathology and the germ theory combined science and medicine, although no breakthrough therapies resulted yet. Science was applied to agriculture through studies of seed yields and chemical fertilizers, with Germany and then the United States in the lead.

The great advance in theoretical science came in biology with the evolutionary theory of **Charles Darwin,** whose major work was published in 1859. Darwin argued that all living species had evolved into their present form through the ability to adapt in a struggle for survival. Biological development could be scientifically understood as a process taking place over time, with some animal and plant species disappearing and others—the fittest in the survival struggle—evolving from earlier forms. Darwin's ideas clashed with traditional Christian beliefs that God had fashioned humankind as part of initial creation, and the resultant debate further weakened the hold of religion. Darwin also created a more complex picture of nature than Newton's simple physical laws had suggested. In this view, nature worked through random struggle, and people were seen as animals with large brains, not as supremely rational.

Reactions to Darwin

Developments in physics continued as well, with work on electromagnetic behavior and then, about 1900, increasing knowledge of the behavior of the atom and its major components. New theories arose, based on complex mathematics, to explain the behavior of planetary motion and the movement of electrical particles, where Newtonian laws seemed too simple. After 1900, **Albert Einstein** formalized this new work through his theory of relativity, adding time as a factor in physical measurement. Again, science seemed to be steadily advancing in its grasp of the physical universe, although it is also important to note that its complexity surpassed the understanding even of educated laypeople.

The social sciences also continued to use observation, experiment, and rationalist theorizing. Great efforts went into compiling statistical data about populations, economic patterns, and health conditions. Sheer empirical knowledge about human affairs had never been more extensive. At the level of theory, leading economists tried to explain business cycles and the causes of poverty, and social psychologists studied the behavior of crowds. Toward the end of the 19th century, Viennese physician **Sigmund Freud** began to develop his theories of the workings of the human subconscious. He argued that much behavior is determined by impulses but that emotional problems can be relieved if they are brought into the light of rational discussion.

## New Directions in Artistic Expression

A second approach in Western culture developed in the 19th century. This approach emphasized artistic values and often glorified the irrational. To be sure, many novelists, such as Charles Dickens in England, bent their efforts toward realistic portrayals of human problems, trying to convey information that would inspire reform. Many painters built on the discoveries of science, using knowledge of optics and color. For example, French painter Georges Seurat was inspired by findings about how the eye processes color, applying tiny dots of paint to his canvasses so that they would blend into a coherent whole in a style aptly called pointillism.

Nevertheless, the central artistic vision, beginning with **romanticism** in the first half of the century, held that emotion and impression, not reason and generalization, were the keys to the mysteries of human experience and nature. Artists portrayed intense passions, even madness, not calm reflection. Romantic novelists wanted to move readers to tears, not philosophical debate; painters sought empathy with the beauties of nature or the storm-tossed tragedy of shipwreck (Figure 28.5). Romantics and their successors after 1850 also deliberately tried to violate traditional Western artistic standards. Poetry did not have to rhyme; drama did not necessarily need plot; painting could be evocative, not literal (Figure 28.6). (For literal portrayals, painters could now argue, use a camera.) Each generation of artists proved more defiant than the last. By 1900 painters and sculptors were becoming increasingly abstract, and musical composers worked with atonal scales that defied long-established conventions. Some artists talked of art for art's sake, arguing essentially that art had its own purposes unrelated to the larger society around it.

At neither the formal nor the popular levels, then, did Western culture produce a clear synthesis in the 19th century. New scientific discipline and rationalism warred with impulse—even with evocations of violence. The earlier certainties of Christianity and even the Enlightenment gave way to greater debate. Some observers worried that this debate also expressed tensions between different facets of the same modern mind and that these tensions could become dangerous. Perhaps the Western world was not put together quite as neatly as the adjustments and consolidations after 1850 might suggest.

**FIGURE 28.5** Romantic painters delighted in evocative scenes and rural nostalgia, as depicted by John Constable in *The Cornfields*.

# Western Settler Societies

- **The expansion of settler societies strongly influenced by European institutions and values was a leading development of the 19th century.**

The Industrial Revolution prompted a major expansion of the West's power in the world. Western nations could pour out far more processed goods than before, which meant that they needed new markets. They also needed new raw materials and agricultural products,

**FIGURE 28.6** Paul Cézanne's *The Large Bathers* (1898–1905). This painting illustrates the artist's abandonment of literal pictorial realism to concentrate on what he considered fundamental. This, along with his use of nudity, alienated the "respectable" public but, by the time of his death in 1906, was beginning to win him critical acclaim. Cézanne painted slowly and was wholly absorbed in his work, spending little time with friends and family. "The landscape," he said, "becomes human, becomes a thinking, living being within me. I become one with my picture. . . . We merge in an iridescent chaos."

which spurred the development of more commercial agriculture in places such as Africa and Latin America. The vast ships and communication networks created by industrial technology spurred the intensification of the Western-led world economy (see Chapter 29).

Industrialization also extended the West's military advantage in the wider world. Steamships could navigate previously impassable river systems, bringing Western guns inland as never before. The invention of the repeating rifle and machine gun gave small Western forces superiority over masses of local troops. These new means combined with new motives: European nations competed for new colonies as part of their nationalistic rivalry, businesspeople sought new chances for profit, and missionaries sought opportunities for conversion. Haltingly before 1860, then rapidly, Europe's empires spread through Africa, southeast Asia, and parts of China and the Middle East.

Many of the same forces, and also massive European emigration, created or expanded Western settler societies overseas in areas where indigenous populations were decimated by disease. Some settler societies maintained sizeable local populations, sometimes even a considerable majority. South Africa was a case in point, discussed in Chapter 29. But some societies filled with an overwhelming majority of immigrants, mostly of European origin, and also brought in so many institutions and beliefs from Europe that they gained a close link with Western history. Some, perhaps, were part of the West outright. The most important overseas Western nation, and the only one to become a major world force before 1914, was the United States.

Most of the older settler societies, and also Australia and New Zealand, were influenced by the results of the age of political revolution. Revolution formed the United States directly. To avoid a repetition, Britain treated other settler societies, like Canada, with greater care, facilitating the spread of parliamentary governments and liberal constitutions.

## Emerging Power of the United States

The country that was to become the United States did not play a substantial role in world history in its colonial period. Its export products were far less significant than those of Latin America and the Caribbean. The American Revolution caused a stir in Europe, but the new nation emphasized internal development through the early 19th century. The Monroe Doctrine (1823) warned against European meddling in the Americas, but it was British policy and naval power that kept the hemisphere free from new colonialism. American energies were poured into elaboration of the new political system, internal commercial growth and early industrialization, and westward expansion. The Louisiana Purchase, the acquisition of Texas, and the rush to California rapidly extended the United States beyond the Mississippi River. The nation stood as a symbol of freedom to many Europeans, and it was often invoked in the revolutions of 1848, as in the earlier Latin American wars for independence. It began to receive a new stream of immigrants, particularly from Ireland and Germany, during the 1840s. Its industrialists also borrowed heavily from European investors to fund national expansion.

The crucial event for the United States in the 19th century was the Civil War, fought between 1861 and 1865. Profound differences separated the increasingly industrial North, with its growing farms, from the slave-holding South, with its export-oriented plantation economy and distinctive value system. Disputes over slaveholding led the southern states to try secession; the North opposed these actions in the interests of preserving national unity and, somewhat hesitantly, ending the slavery system. The Civil War produced an anguishing level of casualties and maimings. The North's victory brought important gains for the freed slave minority, although by the late 1870s, white politicians in the South had begun to severely constrain the political and economic rights of African Americans.

The Civil War also accelerated American industrialization. Heavy industry boomed in a push to produce for the war effort. The completion of a rail link to the Pacific opened the west to further settlement, leading to the last bitter round of wars with Native Americans. Economic expansion brought the United States into the industrial big leagues, its growth rivaling that of Germany. After the Civil War, American armaments manufacturers began to seek export markets. Other industrial producers soon followed as the United States became a major competitor worldwide. American firms, such as the Singer sewing machine company, set up branches in other countries. American agriculture, increasingly mechanized, began to pour out exports of grain and meats (the latter thanks to the development of refrigerated shipping), particularly to European markets where peasant producers could not fully compete.

American diplomacy was not particularly influential outside the Western Hemisphere, although a wave of imperialist expansion from the late 1890s onward brought American interests to the Pacific and Asia. American culture was also seen as largely parochial. Despite increasingly varied art and literature, American work had little impact abroad. Many artists and writers, such as Henry James and James McNeill Whistler, sought inspiration in European centers, sometimes becoming expatriates. Even in technology, American borrowing from Europe remained extensive, and American scientific work gained ground only in the late 19th century, partly through the imitation of German-style research universities. These developments confirmed the role of the new giant in extending many larger Western patterns.

## European Settlements in Canada, Australia, and New Zealand

During the 19th century, Canada, Australia, and New Zealand filled with immigrants from Europe and established parliamentary legislatures and vigorous commercial economies that aligned them with the dynamics of Western civilization (Map 28.5). Sparse and disorganized hunting-and-gathering populations (particularly in Canada and Australia) offered little resistance. Like the

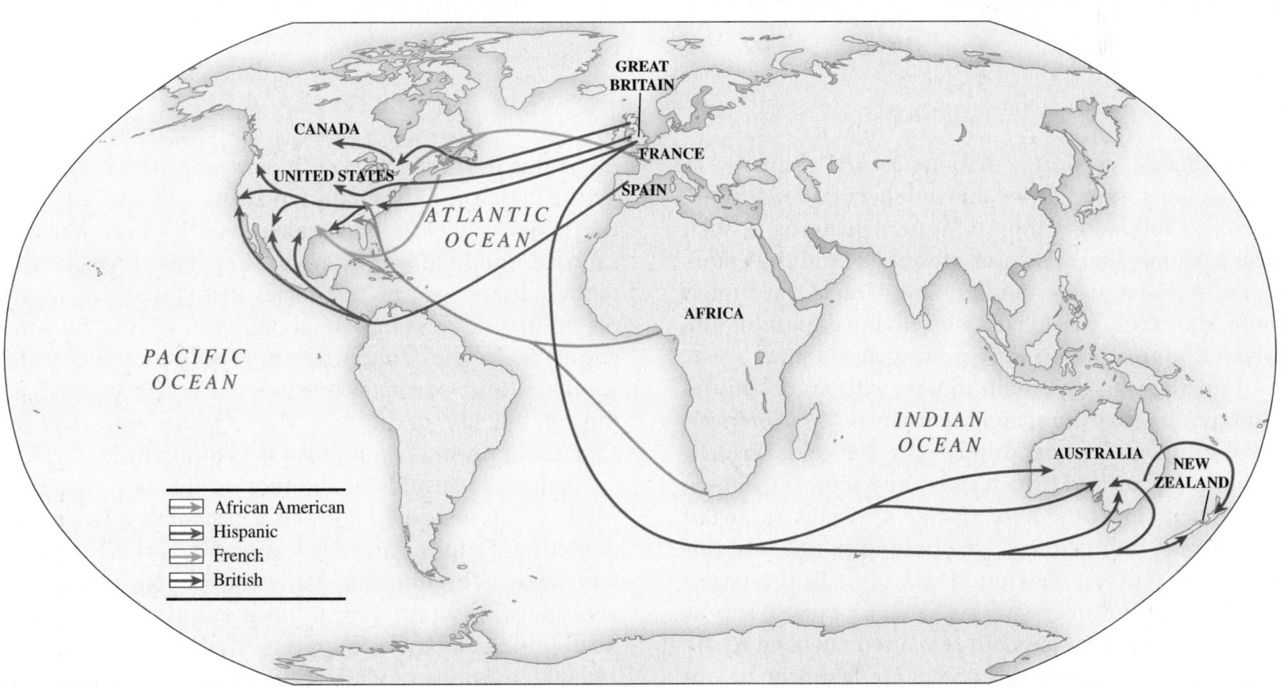


**MAP 28.5 Early 19th-Century Settlement in the United States, Canada, Australia, and New Zealand.** Immigration led European settlers (and, in North America, enslaved Africans) to key areas previously populated by peoples vulnerable to imported diseases.

IN DEPTH

## The United States in World History

Placing the history of the United States in the context of world history raises some important issues. Should the United States be treated as a separate civilization, perhaps along with Canada and other places that mixed dominant Western settlement with frontier conditions? Latin America, because of its ongoing position in the world economy and its blending of European, Native American, and African influences, usually is not treated as part of Western civilization. Does the same hold true for the United States?

Because the United States is so often treated separately in history courses, there is a ready assumption of American uniqueness. The United States had purer diplomatic motives than did western Europe—look at the idealism of Woodrow Wilson. It had its own cultural movements, such as the religious Great Awakening of the 18th century and transcendentalism in the 19th. The United States had the unique experience of wave after wave of immigrants reaching its shores, contributing great cultural diversity but also promoting cultural and social integration under the banners of Americanization. Many thoughtful historians argue for American exceptionalism—that is, the United States as its own civilization, not as part of larger Western patterns. *American exceptionalists* do not contend that the United States was immune from contact with western Europe, which would be ridiculous, but they argue that this contact was incidental to the larger development of the United States on its own terms.

> *"The American exceptionalist argument often appeals particularly to things Americans like to believe about themselves."*

American exceptionalists can point to several factors that caused the development of a separate U.S. civilization. Although colonial immigrants often intended to duplicate European styles of life, the vastness and wealth of the new land quickly forced changes. As a result, American families gave greater voice to women and children, and abundant land created a class of independent farmers rather than a traditional peasantry with tight-knit villages. The successful revolution continued to shape a political life different from that of western Europe. The frontier, which lasted until the 1890s and had cultural impact even beyond that date, would continue to make Americans unusually mobile and restless while draining off some of the social grievances that arose in western Europe.

Distinctive causes produced distinctive results. There is no question that the United States, into the 20th century, had a different agricultural setup from that of western Europe. American politics, with the exception of the Civil War, emphasized small disagreements between two major political parties; third-party movements typically were pulled into the mainstream rather quickly. There was less political fragmentation and extremism than in western Europe and more stability (some would say boredom). No strong socialist movement took shape. Religion was more important in American than in European life by the late 19th century. Religion served immigrants as a badge of identity and helped

United States, these new nations looked primarily to Europe for cultural styles and intellectual leadership. They also followed common Western patterns in such areas as family life, the status of women, and the extension of mass education and culture. Unlike the United States, however, these nations remained part of the British Empire, though with growing autonomy.

Canada, won by Britain in wars with France in the 18th century, had remained apart from the American Revolution. Religious differences between French Catholic settlers and British rulers and settlers troubled the area recurrently, and several uprisings occurred early in the 19th century. Determined not to lose this colony as it had lost the United States, the British began in 1839 to grant increasing self-rule. Canada set up its own parliament and laws but remained attached to the larger empire. Initially, this system applied primarily to the province of Ontario, but other provinces were included, creating a federal system that describes Canada to this day. French hostilities were eased somewhat by the creation of a separate province, Quebec, where the majority of French speakers was located. Massive railroad building, beginning in the 1850s, brought settlement to the western territories and a great expansion of mining and commercial agriculture in the vast plains. As in the United States, new immigrants from southern and particularly eastern Europe poured in during the last decades of the century, attracted by Canada's growing commercial development.

Britain's Australian colonies originated in 1788, when a ship deposited convicts to establish a penal settlement at Sydney. Australia's only previous inhabitants had been a hunting-and-gathering people called the aborigines, and they were in no position to resist European settlement and exploration. By 1840 Australia had 140,000 European inhabitants, engaged mainly in a prosperous sheep-raising agriculture that provided needed wool for British industries. The exportation of all Americans, building a new society, retain some sense of their moorings. The absence of established churches in the United States kept religion out of politics, in contrast to Europe, where churches got caught up in more general attacks on the political establishment.

The American exceptionalist argument often appeals particularly to things Americans like to believe about themselves—more religious than people in other societies, less socialistic, full of the competence that came from taming a frontier—but it must embrace some less savory distinctiveness as well. The existence of slavery, and then the racist attitudes and institutions that arose after its abolition, created ongoing issues in American life that had no direct counterpart in western Europe. Correspondingly, Europe had less direct contact with African culture; jazz was one of the key products of this aspect of American life.

Yet from a world history standpoint, the United States must be seen also, and perhaps primarily, as an offshoot of Western civilization. The colonial experience and the revolution showed the powerful impact of Western political ideas, culture, and even family styles. American history in the 19th century followed patterns common in western Europe. The development of parliamentary life and the spread of democracy, though occurring unusually early in the United States, fit a larger Western pattern. American industrialization was a direct offshoot of that in Europe and followed a common dynamic. Labor strikes and trade unionism spread in similar ways in western Europe and the United States in the late 19th century. American intellectuals kept in close contact with European developments, and there were few purely American styles. Conditions for women and wider patterns of family life, in areas such as birth control and disciplining children, were similar on both sides of the North Atlantic, which shows that the United States not only imitated western Europe but paralleled it.

In some important cases, because the United States was freer from peasant and aristocratic traditions, it pioneered developments that surfaced later in western Europe. This was true in the development of mass consumer culture and mass media (such as the popular press and popular films).

American exceptions remain, such as the Civil War, racial issues, and the absence of serious socialism. American distinctiveness remains in another respect: the United States was rising to world power just as key European nations, notably Britain, began to decline. The trajectory of American history is somewhat different from that of western Europe, and the 20th century revealed a growing American ability to play power politics in western Europe itself. Just as American exceptionalists must admit crucial western European influences, those who see the United States as part of the West must factor in special features and dynamics.

The main point is to analyze American history in careful comparative terms, removing the nation's history from the isolation in which it is so often taught and viewed.

---

**Questions** Which argument has the greater strength in describing 19th-century history: the United States as a separate civilization or the United States as part of the West? Have the United States and western Europe become more or less similar in the 21st century? Why?

convicts ceased in 1853, by which time most settlers were free immigrants. The discovery of gold in 1851 spurred further pioneering, and by 1861 the population had grown to more than a million. As in Canada, major provinces were granted self-government with a multiparty parliamentary system. A unified federal nation was proclaimed on the first day of the 20th century. By this time, industrialization, a growing socialist party, and significant welfare legislation had taken shape.

Finally, New Zealand, visited by the Dutch in the 17th century and explored by the English in 1770, began to receive British attention after 1814. Here the Polynesian hunting-and-gathering people, the Maoris, were well organized politically (see Chapter 9). Missionary efforts converted many of them to Christianity between 1814 and the 1840s. The British government, fearful of French interest in the area, moved to take official control in 1840, and European immigration followed. New Zealand settlers relied heavily on agriculture (including sheep raising), selling initially to Australia's booming gold-rush population and then to Britain. Wars with the Maoris plagued the settlers during the 1860s, but after the Maori defeat, generally good relations were established, and the Maoris won some representation in parliament. As in Canada and Australia, a parliamentary system was created that allowed the new nation to rule itself as a dominion of the British Empire without interference from the mother country.

Canada, New Zealand, and Australia each had distinct national flavors and national issues. These new countries were far more dependent on the European, particularly the British, economy than was the United States. Industrialization did not overshadow commercial agriculture and mining, even in Australia, so that exchanges with Europe remained important. Nevertheless, despite their distinctive features, these countries followed the basic patterns of Western civilization, from political forms to key leisure activities.

The currents of liberalism, socialism, modern art, and scientific education that described Western civilization to 1900 and beyond largely characterized these important new extensions.

It was these areas, along with the United States and part of Latin America, particularly Brazil and Argentina, that received new waves of European emigrants during the 19th century. Although Europe's population growth rate slowed after 1800, it still advanced rapidly on the basis of previous gains as more children reached adulthood and had children of their own. Europe's export of people helped explain how Western societies could take shape in such distant areas.

The spread of the Western settler societies also reflected the new power of Western industrialization. Huge areas could be settled quickly, thanks to steamships and rails, while remaining in close contact with western Europe.

## Diplomatic Tensions and World War I

■ **By the end of the 19th century, diplomatic and military tensions were escalating in Europe. Tensions reflected domestic developments, including social protest and competitive nationalisms.**

The unification of Germany and its rapid industrial growth profoundly altered the power balance within Europe. Bismarck was very conscious of this, and during the 1870s and 1880s, still a skilled manipulator, he built a complex alliance system designed to protect Germany and divert European attention elsewhere. France, Germany's deepest enemy, was largely isolated. But even the French concentrated on imperialist expansion in Africa and Asia.

By 1900, however, few parts of the world were available for Western seizure. Latin America was independent but under extensive U.S. influence, so a new intrusion of colonialism was impossible. Africa was almost entirely carved up. The few final colonies taken after 1900—Morocco by France and Tripoli (Libya) by Italy—caused great diplomatic furor on the part of other colonial powers worried about the balance of forces. China and the Middle East were technically independent but were in fact crisscrossed by rivalries between the Western powers and Russia (and in China's case, Japan). No agreement was possible on further takeovers.

Yet imperialist expansion had fed the sense of rivalry between key nation-states. Britain, in particular, grew worried about Germany's overseas drive and its construction of a large navy. Economic competition between a surging Germany and a lagging Britain added fuel to the fire. France, eager to escape the Bismarck-engineered isolation, was willing to play down its traditional rivalries with Britain. The French also took the opportunity to ally with Russia, when after 1890 Germany dropped this particular alliance because of Russian–Austrian enmity.

### The New Alliance System

By 1907 most major European nations were paired off in two alliance systems: Germany, Austria–Hungary, and Italy formed the **Triple Alliance.** Britain, Russia, and France formed the newer **Triple Entente.** Three against three seemed fair, but Germany grew increasingly concerned about facing potential enemies to the east (Russia) and west (France). These powers steadily built up their military arsenals in what turned out to be the first of several arms races in the 20th century. All powers save Britain had instituted peacetime military conscription to provide large armies and even larger trained reserves. Artillery levels and naval forces grew steadily—the addition of a new kind of battleship, the dreadnought, was a key escalation—and discussions about reducing armament levels went nowhere. Each alliance system depended on an unstable partner. Russia suffered a revolution in 1905, and its allies worried that any further diplomatic setbacks might paralyze the eastern giant. Austria–Hungary was plagued by nationality disputes, particularly by minority Slavic groups; German leaders fretted that a diplomatic setback might bring chaos. Both Austria and Russia were heavily involved in maneuverings in the Balkans, the final piece in what became a nightmare puzzle.

Small Balkan nations had won independence from the Ottoman Empire during the 19th century; as Turkish power declined, local nationalism rose, and Russian support for its Slavic neighbors paid off. But the nations were intensely hostile to one another. Furthermore, **Balkan nationalism** threatened Austria, which had a large southern Slav population. Russia and Austria nearly came to blows on several occasions over Balkan issues. Then, in 1912 and 1913, the Balkan nations engaged in two internal wars, which led to territorial gains for several states but satisfied no one (Map 28.6). Serbia, which bordered Austria to the south, had hoped for greater stakes. At the same time, Austria grew nervous over the gains Serbia had achieved. In 1914 a Serbian nationalist assassinated an Austrian archduke on behalf of Serbian claims. Austria vowed to punish Serbia. Russia rushed to the defense of Serbia and mobilized its troops against Austria. Germany, worried about Austria and also eager to

Nationalities Within the Hapsburg Empire

MAP 28.6 The Balkans Before the Regional Wars, 1912

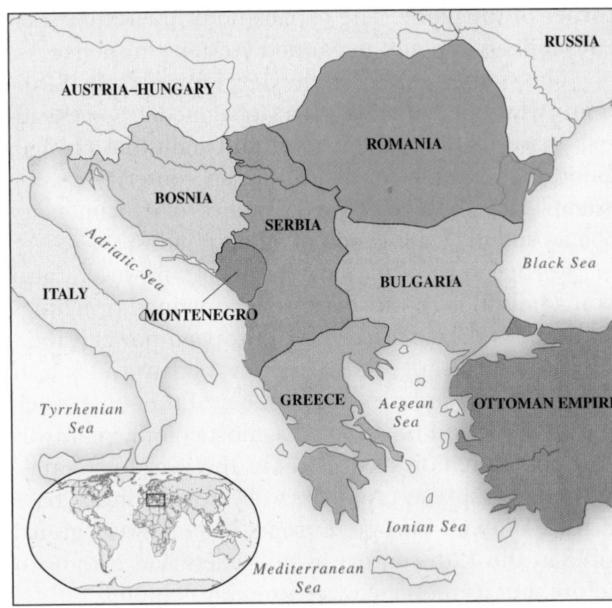


The Balkans After the Regional Wars, 1913

be able to strike against France before Russia's cumbersome mobilization was complete, called up its reserves and then declared war on August 1. Britain hesitated briefly, then joined its allies. World War I had begun, and with it came a host of new problems for Western society.

## Diplomacy and Society

The tensions that spiraled into major war are not easy to explain. Diplomatic maneuverings can seem quite remote from the central concerns of most people, if only because key decisions—for example, with whom to ally—are made by a specialist elite. Even as the West became more democratic, few ordinary people placed foreign affairs high on their election agendas.

The West had long been characterized by political divisions and rivalries. In comparison with some other civilizations, this was an inherent weakness of the Western political system. In a sense, what happened by the late 19th century was that the nation-state system got out of hand, encouraged by the absence of serious challenge from any other civilizations. The rise of Germany and new tensions in the Balkans simply complicated the growing nationalist competition.

This diplomatic escalation also had some links to the strains of Western society under the impact of industrialization. Established leaders in the West continued to worry about social protest. They tended to seek diplomatic successes to distract the people. This procedure worked nicely for a few decades when imperialist gains came easily. But then it backfired. Around 1914 German officials, fearful of the power of the socialists, wondered whether war would aid national unity. British leaders, beset by feminist dissent and labor unrest, failed to think through their own diplomatic options. Leaders also depended on military buildups for economic purposes. Modern industry, pressed to sell the soaring output of its factories, found naval purchases and army equipment a vital supplement. Mass newspapers, which fanned nationalist pride with stories of conquest and tales of the evils of rival nations, helped shape a belligerent popular culture.

Thus, just a few years after celebrating a century of material progress and peace, ordinary Europeans went to war almost gaily in 1914. Troops departed for the front convinced that war would be exciting, with quick victories. Their departure was hailed by enthusiastic civilians, who draped their trains with flowers. Four years later, almost everyone would agree that war had been unmitigated hell. However, the complexities of industrial society were such that war's advent seemed almost a welcome breath of the unexpected, a chance to get away from the disciplined stability of everyday life.

GLOBAL CONNECTIONS

## Industrial Europe and the World

Europe's growing power during the 19th century transformed the world. Imperialism and the redefinition of the world economy pushed European interests to every corner of the globe. The expansion of the settler societies reflects and also expanded Western influence.

This same power made developments in 19th-century Europe something of a global model. Some leaders, aware of Europe's political and industrial change, found the example repellent. Russian conservatives, for example, warned against the divisiveness of parliamentary politics and the exploitation of modern industry.

Europe's revolutionary heritage, however, also won admiration, partly because it contained principles that could be used to counter European power. Liberalism, radicalism, and socialism began to spread beyond the boundaries of Europe and the settler societies. They could be directed against colonial controls or the exploitation of workers in the world economy. Nationalism spread rapidly as well, from its initial base in revolutionary Europe. Europe, in sum, was a global force in the 19th century as no society had ever been before, but its message was extremely complex.

By 1914 Europe's world role promoted new anxieties within the West. Novel contacts, like Asian immigration into the United States, spurred new fears. On a wider scale, some leaders warned of competition from Asia. Ironically, growing internal tensions within the West ultimately predominated, though the results would have international effects as well.

## Further Readings

Two excellent studies survey Europe's Industrial Revolution: Sidney Pollard, *Peaceful Conquest: The Industrialization of Europe* (1981); and David Landes, *The Unbound Prometheus: Technological Change and Industrial Development in Western Europe from 1700 to the Present* (1969). See also Phyllis Deane, *The First Industrial Revolution* (1980), on Britain. For a more general survey, see Peter N. Stearns, *The Industrial Revolution in World History* (1993). On the demographic experience, see Thomas McKeown, *The Modern Rise of Population* (1977).

For the French Revolution and political upheaval, Isser Woloch's *The New Regime: Transformations of the French Civic Order, 1789–1829* (1994) is a useful introduction. Lynn Hunt's *Politics, Culture, and Class in the French Revolution* (1984) is an important study. Other revolutionary currents are treated in *The Crowd in History: Popular Disturbances in France and England* (1981) by George Rudé and *1848: The Revolutionary Tide in Europe* (1974) by Peter Stearns.

The impact of the Industrial Revolution on gender relations is analyzed in A. Clarke, *The Struggle for the Breeches: Gender and the Making of the British Working Class* (1995). Major developments concerning women and the family are covered in Louise Tilly and Joan Scott, *Women, Work, and Family* (1978); and Steven Mintz and Susan Kellogg, *Domestic Revolutions: A Social History of American Family Life* (1989). See also R. Evans, *The Feminists: Women's Emancipation in Europe, Americ,a and Australia* (1979). An important age group is treated in John Gillis, *Youth and History* (1981). An influential generation receives its due in T. Hoppen, *The Mid-Victorian Generation, 1846–1886* (1998).

For an overview of social change, see Peter Stearns and Herrick Chapman, *European Society in Upheaval* (1991). On labor history, see Michael Hanagan, *The Logic of Solidarity* (1981); and Albert Lindemann, *History of European Socialism* (1983). Eugen Weber, *Peasants into Frenchmen: The Modernization of Rural France* (1976), and Harvey Graff, ed., *Literacy and Social Development in the West* (1982), deal with important special topics.

On political and cultural history, see Gordon Wright, *France in Modern Times* (1981); Gordon Craig, *Germany, 1866–1945* (1978); and Louis Snyder, *Roots of German Nationalism* (1978). J. H. Randall's *The Making of the Modern Mind* (1976) is a useful survey; see also O. Chadwick's *The Secularization of the European Mind in the Nineteenth Century* (1976). On major diplomatic developments, see D. K. Fieldhouse, *Economics and Empire, 1830–1914* (1970); and David Kaiser, *Politics and War: European Conflict from Philip II to Hitler* (1990).

The impact of these winds of change as they swept across the American sociopolitical landscape is examined in W. Cronon, *Nature's Metropolis: Chicago and the Great West* (1991); R. M. Utley, *The Indian Frontier and the American West, 1846–1890* (1984); Robert Dahl, *How Democratic Is the American Constitution?* (2002); S. M. Lipsett, *American Exceptionalism: A Double-Edged Sword* (1996); and T. Dublin, *Women at Work: The Transformation of Work and Community in Lowell, Massachusetts, 1826–1860* (1979).

## On the Web

Links to the sights, sounds, and songs of the French Revolution of 1789 are offered at http://www.andrew.cmu.edu/user/sc24/frenchrev.html, http://history.hanover.edu/modern/FRENCHRV.html, http://userwww.port.ac.uk/andressd/frlinks.htm, http://chnm.gmu.edu/revolution/, http://marseillaise.org/english/, and http://www.admi.net/marseillaise.html. One of the French Revolution's most lasting achievements, abolition of the feudal system in France, is recorded at http://history.hanover.edu/texts/abolfeud.htm.

The American Revolution and the Revolutionary War are explored in documents, site visits, and publications at http://www.revwar.com/links/document.html. Major sites addressing the war include http://www.nps.gov/revwar/, http://revolution.h-net.msu.edu/, http://www.pbs.org/ktca/liberty/, and http://revolution.h-net.msu.edu/bib.html.

A glimpse into the role of women in the American Revolution, and a useful bibliography of that role is offered at http://userpages.aug.com/captbarb/femvets.html and http://www.carleton.ca/~pking/arbib/z.htm, respectively. Many Web pages offer insight into the personalities of the age of revolution, such as Marie Antoinette (http://www2.lucidcafe.com/lucidcafe/library/95nov/antoinette.html), Napoleon (http://www.napoleon.org/en/home.asp, http://www.napoleon-series.org/, http://www.napoleonbonaparte.nl/, and http://www.pbs.org/empires/napoleon/), and Thomas Paine (http://

odur.let.rug.nl/~usa/B/tpaine/paine.htm).

Also readily available are Web resources that can provide an overview of the Industrial Revolution (http://www.scholars.nus.edu.sg/victorian/technology/ir/irov.html and http://mars.acnet.wnec.edu/~grempel/courses/wc2/lectures/industrialrev.html) or surveys of the lives of key figures of that watershed in world history, such as James Watt (whose reconception of the steam engine can be found at http://www.geocities.com/Athens/Acropolis/6914/watte.htm, http://www.spartacus.schoolnet.co.uk/SCwatt.htm, and http://homepages.westminster.org.uk/hooke/issue10/watt.htm), Eli Whitney (http://www.eliwhitney.org/), and Ned Ludd (http://www.spartacus.schoolnet.co.uk/PRluddites.htm), whose name became synonymous with resistance to technological change.

The life of industrial workers in 19th-century England is examined at http://www.fordham.edu/halsall/mod/1844engels.html, http://www.galbithink.org/fw.htm, http://www.womeninworldhistory.com/lesson7.html, and http://dbhs.wvusd.k12.ca.us/Chem-History/Faraday-Letter.html.

Web sites illuminating the world of women and child workers include http://www.fordham.edu/halsall/mod/1842womenminers.html, http://www.womeninworldhistory.com/textile.html, http://www.fordham.edu/halsall/mod/robinson-lowell.html, and http://www.spartacus.schoolnet.co.uk/Twork.htm.

The impact of industrialization gave thrust to the writings of Karl Marx and others whose critiques and assessments of the future of capitalism were to usher in a new revolutionary period in human history. A brief essay at http://www.scholars.nus.edu.sg/victorian/philosophy/phil2.html illuminates key forms of Marxian analysis, including the role of ideology in human society. Two of the best sites for accessing and comparing the ideas of Marxist writers are http://www.marxists.org/index.htm and http://www.anu.edu.au/polsci/marx/marx.html (which includes a very clear RealAudio file of the "Internationale" sung by an Irish folksinger accompanied on the guitar).

CHAPTER 29

# Industrialization and Imperialism: The Making of the European Global Order



On January 22, 1879, at the height of its century-long reign as the paramount global power, Great Britain suffered one of the most devastating defeats ever inflicted by a non-Western people on an industrialized nation. The late-Victorian painting shown in Figure 29.1 depicts the Battle of Isandhlwana at which more than 20,000 Zulu soldiers outmaneuvered a much smaller but overconfident British army invading their kingdom. Taking advantage of the British commander's foolhardy decision to divide his forces, the Zulus attacked the main British encampment from all directions and, in a fiercely fought battle lasting only a couple of hours, wiped out 950 European troops and nearly 850 African irregulars. Divided and caught off guard, the British could not form proper firing lines to repel the much larger and well-led Zulu *impis*—the equivalent of a division in a Western army. The flight of the African irregulars, who made up a sizeable portion of the British army, left gaps in the British force that were quickly exploited by the Zulu fighters. Soon after the main battle was joined, most of the British and mercenary African soldiers in the camp at Isandhlwana were dead or in desperate flight to a river nearby, where most were hunted down by impis positioned to block their retreat.

The well-drilled Zulu impis who routed the British forces at Isandhlwana skillfully wielded the cattle-hide shields and short stabbing spears, or *assegais,* that had been the Zulus' trademark for more than half a century. In the early 1800s, warriors and weapons had provided the military power for an ambitious young leader named Shaka to forge a powerful kingdom in the southeastern portions of what would later become the Union of South Africa (Map 29.4). The Zulus' imposing preindustrial military organization had triumphed over all African rivals and later proved the most formidable force resisting the advance of both the Dutch-descended Boers (later called Afrikaners) and British imperial armies in southern Africa.

The British defeat was shocking in large part because it seemed implausible, given the great and ever-growing disparity between the military might of the European colonial powers and the African and Asian peoples they had come to dominate in unprecedented ways. Technological innovations and mass production made it possible for European states to supply advanced weaponry and other war materiel to sizeable naval and land forces across the globe. The

FIGURE 29.1 A romantic depiction of the 1879 Battle of Isandhlwana in the Natal province of South Africa. The battle demonstrated that, despite their superior firepower, the Europeans could be defeated by well-organized and determined African or Asian resistance forces.

enhanced firepower and mobility that resulted made it possible for Western warships and regiments to crush the preindustrial military resistance of adversaries as diverse as the armies of the vast Qing Empire in China, the revivalist religious state founded by the Mahdi in the Sudan, and the legendary Zulu impis in south Africa.

| 1600 C.E. | 1700 C.E. | 1750 C.E. | 1800 C.E. | 1850 C.E. | 1900 C.E. |
|---|---|---|---|---|---|
| **1619** Dutch establish trading post at Batavia in Java<br>**1620s** Sultan of Mataram's attacks on Batavia fail<br>**1652** First Dutch settlement in south Africa at Cape Town<br>**1661** British port-trading center founded at Bombay<br>**1690** Calcutta established at center of British activities in Bengal | **1707** Death of Mughal emperor, Aurangzeb; beginning of imperial breakdown<br>**1739** Nadir Shah's invasion of India from Persia<br>**1740–1748** War of Austrian Succession; global British–French struggle for colonial dominance | **1750s** Civil war and division of Mataram; Dutch become the paramount power on Java<br>**1756–1763** Seven Years War, British–French global warfare<br>**1757** Battle of Plassey; British become dominant power in Bengal<br>**1769–1770** Great Famine in Bengal<br>**1775–1783** War for independence by American colonists; another British–French struggle for global preeminence<br>**1786–1790** Cornwallis's political reforms in India<br>**1790–1815** Wars of the French Revolution and Napoleonic era<br>**1798** Napoleon's invasion of Egypt | **1815** British annex Cape Town and surrounding area<br>**1830** Boers begin Great Trek in south Africa<br>**1835** Decision to give support for English education in India; English adopted as the language of Indian law courts | **1850s** Boer republics established in the Orange Free State and Transvaal<br>**1853** First railway line constructed in India<br>**1857** Calcutta, Madras, and Bombay universities founded<br>**1857–1858** "Mutiny" or Great Rebellion in north India<br>**1858** British parliament assumes control over India from the East India Company<br>**1867** Diamonds discovered in Orange Free State<br>**1869** Opening of the Suez Canal<br>**c. 1879–1890s** Partition of west Africa<br>**1879** Zulu victory over British at Isandhlwana; defeat at Rorke's Drift<br>**1882** British invasion of Egypt<br>**1885** Indian National Congress Party founded in India<br>**1885** Gold discovered in the Transvaal<br>**1890s** Partition of east Africa<br>**1898** British–French crisis over Fashoda in the Sudan<br>**1899–1902** Anglo-Boer War in south Africa | **1902** Anglo-Japanese Treaty<br>**1904** Anglo-Russian crisis at Dogger Bank<br>**1904–1905** First Moroccan crisis<br>**1911** Second Moroccan crisis; Russo-Japanese War<br>**1914** Outbreak of World War I |

The aftermath of the Zulu triumph at Isandhlwana demonstrated that the British defeat was a fluke, a dramatic but short-lived exception to what had become a pervasive pattern of European (and increasingly American) political and military supremacy worldwide. Estimates of Zulu losses at Isandhlwana, for example, range from two to three times those for British units and "native" levees combined. Within hours of their utter destruction of most of the main British column, a force of some 3000 Zulu warriors was decimated in the siege of a small outpost at nearby Rorke's Drift. There a cluster of farm buildings was successfully defended by just over a hundred British soldiers, many of whom were wounded from earlier clashes. Not even the courageous and disciplined Zulu impis could overcome the withering firepower of well-led British battalions armed with breech-loading, repeating rifles.

As was the case in equally stunning massacres of the expeditionary forces of industrial powers in other colonial settings, most notably Custer's last stand in the American West, revenge for the defeat inflicted by the Zulus at Isandhlwana was massive and swift. Additional troops were drawn from throughout the far-flung British Empire and, within months, a far larger British force was advancing on the Zulu capital at Ulundi. Like the coalition of Indian tribes that had joined to destroy Custer's units of the Seventh Cavalry, the Zulu impis that had turned back the first British invasion dispersed soon after the clashes at Isandhlwana and Rorke's Drift. By late August, the Zulu ruler, Cetshwayo, had surrendered to the British and been shipped into exile at Cape Town. Assuming a rather calculated pose of naivete, Cetshwayo captured the sense of awe and helplessness felt by so many African and Asian leaders who sought to resist the advance of European colonizers in his much publicized admission that he was "only a child, and the British government [was] his father."

The British advances into the heart of Cetshwayo's kingdom in the last of the wars between the Europeans and the Zulus exemplified many of the fundamental shifts in the balance of world power in the turn-of-the-century decades of the great "scramble" for overseas territories that did so much to set the stage for World War I. Like their French, Dutch, Belgian, German, Russian, Japanese, and American competitors, the British plunged deep into Africa, the Middle East, and Asia. In contrast to the earlier centuries of overseas expansion, the European powers were driven in the late-19th century by rivalries with each other, and in some instances with the Japanese and Americans, rather than fears of Muslim kingdoms in the Middle East and north Africa or powerful empires in Asia.

In most of the areas they claimed as colonial possessions, the Europeans established direct rule, where they had once been mainly content to subjugate and control local rulers and their retainers. The 1879 Anglo-Zulu war had been precipitated by British demands, including the right to station a resident in the Zulu kingdom and the breakup of the Zulu military machine, that would have reduced Cetshwayo to the status of a vassal. Though the British and other colonizers would continue to govern through indigenous officials in many areas, their subordinates were increasingly recruited from new elites, both professional and commercial, who emerged from schools where the languages and customs of the imperial powers were taught to growing numbers of colonized peoples.

## The Shift to Land Empires in Asia

■ **From the mid-18th century onward, the European powers began to build true empires in Asia similar to those they had established in the Americas beginning in the 16th century. In the first phase of the colonization process, Europeans overseas were willing to adapt their lifestyles to the climates and cultures of the lands they had gone out to rule.**

Although we usually use the term *partition* to refer to the European division of Africa at the end of the 19th century, the Western powers had actually been carving up the globe into colonial enclaves for centuries (Map 29.1). At first this process was haphazard and often quite contrary to the interests and designs of those in charge of European enterprises overseas. For example, the directors who ran the Dutch and English East India companies (which were granted monopolies of the trade between their respective countries and the East in the 17th and 18th centuries) had little interest in territorial acquisitions. In fact, they were actively opposed to involvement in the political rivalries of the Asian princes. Wars were expensive, and direct administration of African or Asian possessions was even more so. Both cut deeply into the profits gained through participation in the Asian trading system, and profits—not empires—were the chief concern of the Dutch and English directors.

Colonization in Africa

Whatever policies company directors may have instructed their agents in Africa and Asia to follow, these "men-on-the-spot" were often drawn into local power struggles. And before the Industrial Revolution produced the telegraph and other methods of rapid communication, company directors and European prime ministers had very little control over those who actually ran their trading empires. In the 18th century, a letter took months to reach Calcutta from London; the reply took many months more. Thus, commanders in the field had a great deal of leeway. They could conquer whole provinces or kingdoms before home officials even learned that their armies were on the move.

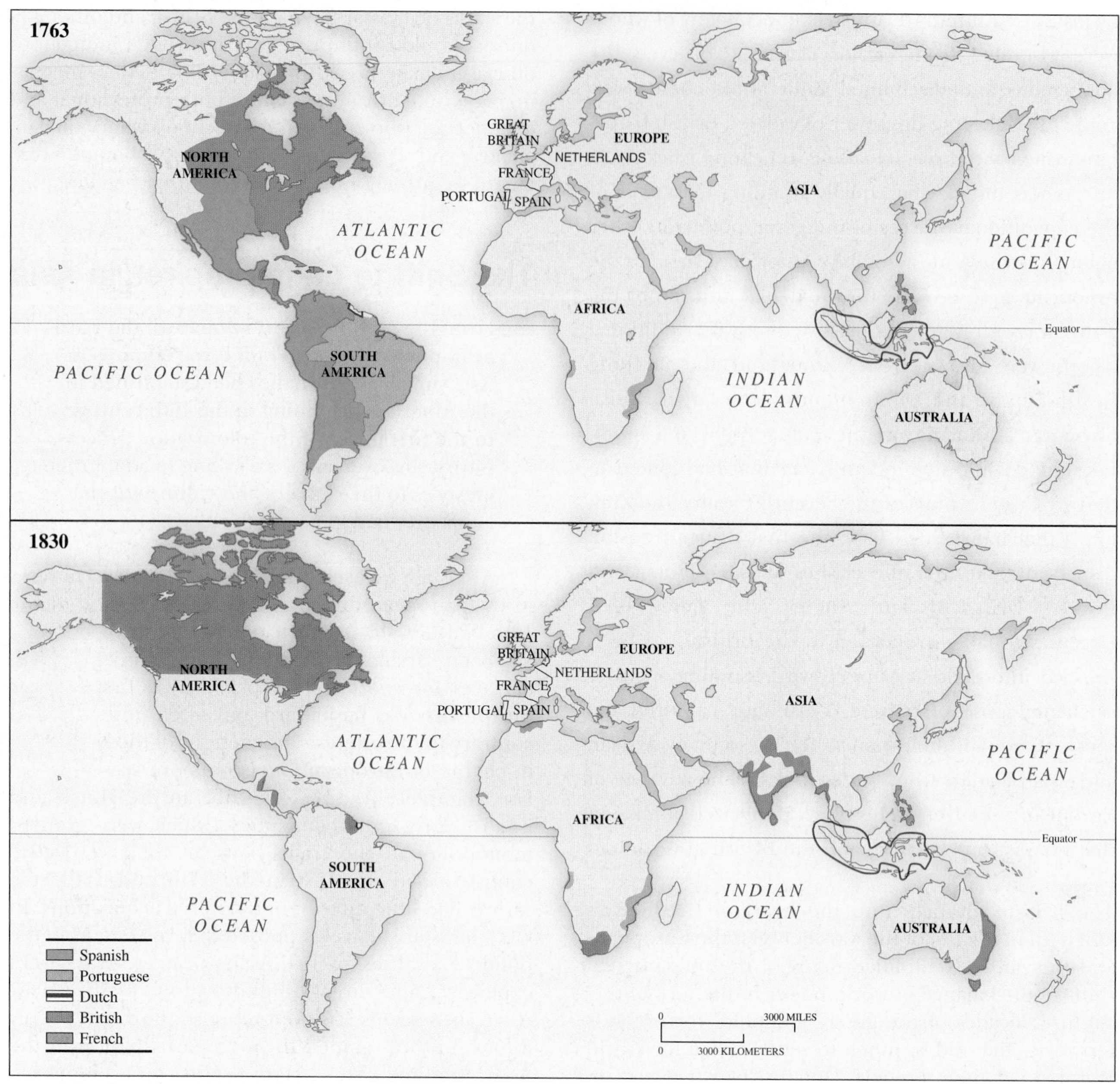


MAP 29.1 European Colonial Territories, Before and After 1800

## Prototype: The Dutch Advance on Java

One of the earliest empires to be built in this fashion was that pieced together in the late 17th and 18th centuries by the Dutch in Java (Map 29.2). Java was then and is now the most populous of the hundreds of islands that make up the country of Indonesia. In the early years after the Dutch established their Asian headquarters at Batavia on the northwest coast of the island in 1619, it was a struggle just to survive. The Dutch were content to become the vassals of and pay tribute to the sultans of **Mataram,** who ruled most of Java. In the decades that followed, the Dutch concentrated on gaining monopoly control over the spices produced on the smaller islands of the Indonesian archipelago to the east. But in the 1670s, the Dutch repeatedly intervened in the wars between rival claimants to the throne of Mataram, and they backed the side that eventually won. As the price for their assistance, the Dutch demanded that the territories around Batavia be turned over to them to administer.

This episode was the first of a long series of Dutch interventions in the wars of succession between the princes of Mataram. Dutch armies were made up mainly of troops recruited from the island peoples of the

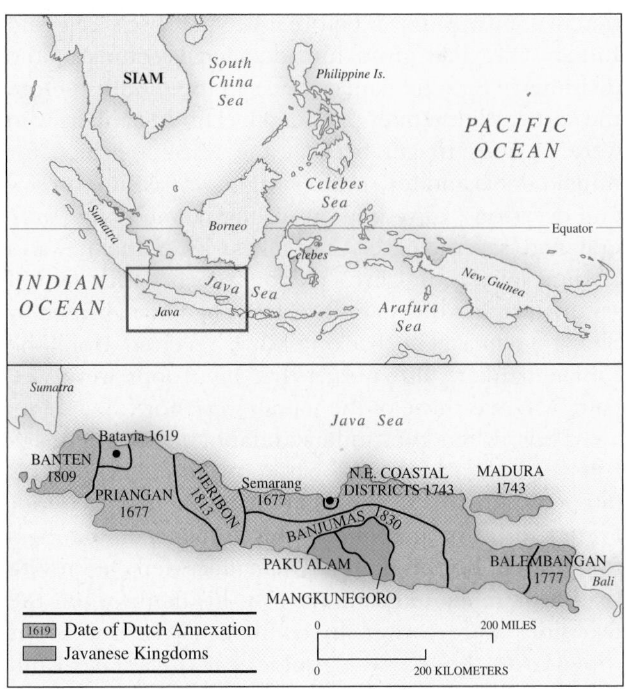


**MAP 29.2** The Stages of Dutch Expansion in Java

eastern Indonesian archipelago, led by Dutch commanders. Their superior organization and discipline, even more than their firearms, made the Dutch a potent ally of whichever prince won them to his side. But the price the Javanese rulers paid was very high. Each succession dispute and Dutch intervention led to more and more land being ceded to the increasingly land-hungry Europeans. By the mid-18th century, the sultans of Mataram controlled only the south central portions of Java (Map 29.2). A failed attempt by Sultan Mangkubumi to restore Mataram's control over the Dutch in the 1750s ended with a Dutch-dictated division of the kingdom that signified Dutch control of the entire island. Java had been transformed into the core of an Asian empire that would last for 200 years.

**FIGURE 29.2** Indian soldiers, or sepoys, made up a large portion of the rank-and-file troops in the armies of British India. Commanded by European officers and armed, uniformed, and drilled according to European standards, troops such as those pictured here were recruited from the colonized peoples and became one of the mainstays of all European colonial regimes. The European colonizers preferred to recruit these soldiers from subject peoples whom they saw as particularly martial. In India, these included the Sikhs (pictured here) and Marattas, as well as Gurkhas recruited from neighboring but independent Nepal.

## Pivot of World Empire: The Rise of the British Rule in India

In many ways, the rise of the British as a land power in India resembled the Dutch capture of Java. The directors of the British East India Company were as hostile as the Dutch financiers to territorial expansion. But British agents of the company in India repeatedly meddled in disputes and conflicts between local princes. In these interventions, the British, adopting a practice pioneered by the French, relied heavily on Indian troops, called **sepoys** (some of whom are pictured in Figure 29.2) recruited from peoples throughout the subcontinent. As had been the case in Java, Indian princes regarded the British as allies whom they could use and control to crush competitors from within India or put down usurpers who tried to seize their thrones. As had happened in Java, the European pawns gradually emerged as serious rivals to the established Indian rulers and eventually dominated the region.

Partly because the struggle for India came later, there were also important differences between the patterns of colonial conquest in India and Java as well as between the global repercussions of each. In contrast to the Dutch march inland, which resulted largely from responses to local threats and opportunities, the rise of the **British Raj** (the Sanskrit-derived name for the British political establishment in India) owed much to the fierce global rivalry between the British and the French. In the 18th century, the two powers found themselves on opposite sides in five major wars. These struggles were global in a very real sense. On land and sea, the two old adversaries not only fought in Europe but also squared off in the Caribbean, where each had valuable plantation colonies; in North America; and on the coasts and bays of the Indian Ocean. With the exception of the American War of Independence (1775–1783), these struggles ended in British victories. The British loss of the American colonies was more than offset by earlier victories in the Caribbean and especially in India. These triumphs gradually gave the British control of the entire south Asian subcontinent.

Although the first victories of the British over the French and the Indian princes came in the south in the late 1740s, their rise as a major land power in Asia hinged on victories won in Bengal to the northeast (Map 29.3). The key battle at **Plassey** in 1757, in which fewer than 3000 British troops and Indian sepoys defeated an Indian army of nearly 50,000, is traditionally pictured as the heroic triumph of a handful of brave and disciplined Europeans over a horde of ill-trained and poorly led Asians. The battle pitted Sirãj ud-daula, the teenage *nawab,* or ruler, of Bengal, against **Robert Clive,** the architect of the British victory in the south. The prize was control of the fertile and populous kingdom of Bengal. The real reasons for Clive's famous victory tell us a good deal about the process of empire building in Asia and Africa.

The Sequence of British Territorial Acquisitions in India, 1765–1856

The numbers on each side and the maneuvers on the field had little to do with the outcome of a battle that in a sense was over before it began. Clive's well-paid Indian spies had given him detailed accounts of the divisions in Sirãj ud-daula's ranks in the months before the battle. With money provided by Hindu bankers who were anxious to get back at the Muslim prince for unpaid debts and for confiscating their treasure on several occasions, Clive bought off the nawab's chief general and several of his key allies. Even the nawab's leading spy was on Clive's payroll, which somewhat offset the fact that the main British spy had been bribed by Sirãj ud-daula. The backing Clive received from the Indian bankers also meant that his troops were well paid, whereas those of the nawab were not.

Thus, when the understandably nervous teenage ruler of Bengal rode into battle on June 23, 1757, his fate was already sealed. The nawab's troops under French officers and one of his Indian commanders fought well. But his major Indian allies defected to the British or remained stationary on his flanks when the two sides were locked in combat. These defections wiped out the nawab's numerical advantage, and Clive's skillful leadership and the superiority of his artillery did the rest. The British victors had once again foiled their French rivals. As the nawab had anticipated, they soon took over the direct administration of the sizeable Bengal-Bihar region. The foundations of Britain's Indian and global empire had been laid.

## The Consolidation of British Rule

In the decades after Plassey, the British officials of the East India Company repeatedly went to war with Indian princes whose kingdoms bordered on the company's growing possessions (Map 29.3). These entanglements

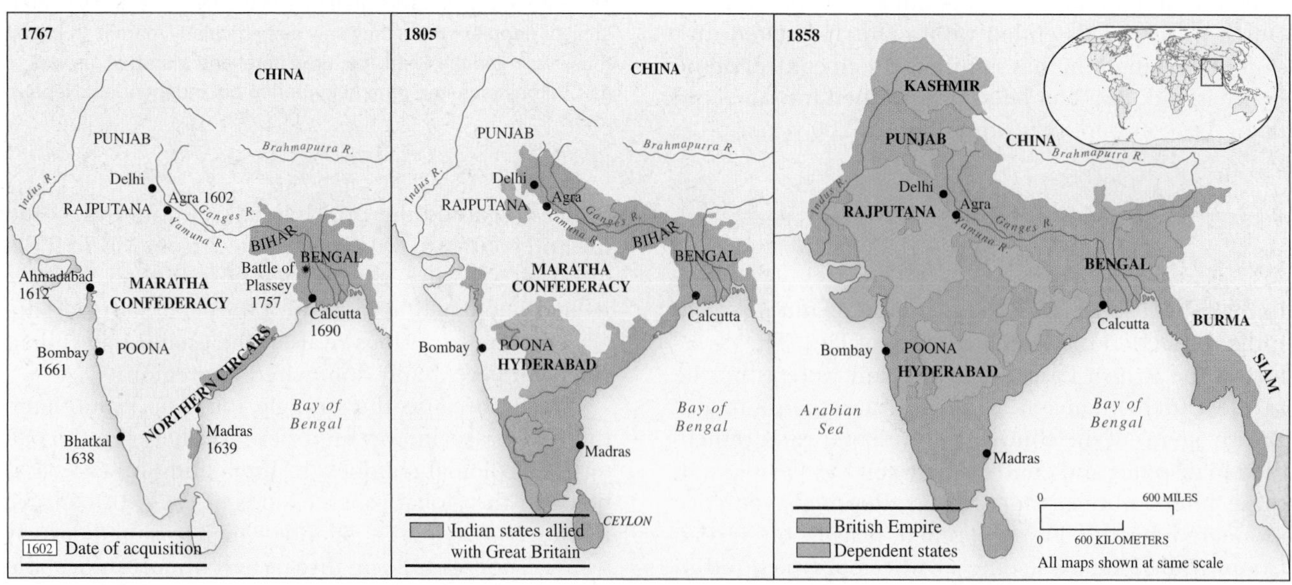

**MAP 29.3** The Growth of the British Empire in India, from the 1750s to 1858

grew stronger and stronger as the Mughal Empire broke down more fully in the last decades of the century. In its ruins, regional Indian princes fought to defend or expand their territories at the expense of their neighbors. Interventions in these conflicts or assaults on war-weakened Indian kingdoms allowed the British to advance steadily inland from their three trading towns on the Indian coast: Madras, Bombay, and Calcutta. These cities became the administrative centers of the three **presidencies** that eventually made up the bulk of the territory the British ruled directly in India. In many areas, the British were content to leave defeated or allied Indian princes on the thrones of their **princely states** and to control their kingdoms through agents stationed at the rulers' courts.

Because there was no sense of Indian national identity, it was impossible for Muslim or Hindu rulers to appeal to the defense of the homeland or the need for unity to drive out the foreigners. Indian princes continued to fear and fight with each other despite the ever growing power of the British Raj. Old grudges and hatreds ran deeper than the new threat of the British. Many ordinary Indians were eager to serve in the British regiments, which had better weapons, brighter uniforms, and higher and more regular pay than all but a handful of the armies of the Indian rulers. By the mid-19th century, Indian soldiers in the pay of the British outnumbered British officers and enlisted men in India by almost five to one.

From the first decades of the 19th century, India was clearly the pivot of the great empire being built by Britain on a global scale. Older colonies with large numbers of white settlers, such as Canada and Australia, contributed more space to the total square miles of empire the British were so fond of calculating. But India had by far the greater share of colonized peoples. Britain's largest and most powerful land forces were the armies recruited from the Indian peoples, and these were rapidly becoming the police of the entire British Indian empire. In the mid-19th century, Indian soldiers were sent to punish the Chinese and Afghans, conquer Burma and Malaya, and begin the conquest of south and east Africa. Indian ports were essential to British sea power east of the Cape of Good Hope. As the century progressed, India became the major outlet for British overseas investments and manufactured goods as well as a major source of key raw materials.

Growth of British Control in India

## Early Colonial Society in India and Java

Although they slowly emerged as the political masters of Java and India, the Dutch and the British were at first content to leave the social systems of the peoples they ruled pretty much as they had found them. The small numbers of European traders and company officials who lived in the colonies for any length of time simply formed a new class atop the social hierarchies that already existed in Java and different parts of India. Beneath them, the aristocratic classes and often the old ruling families were preserved. They were left in charge of the day-to-day administration at all but the very highest levels. At the highest levels, the local rulers were paired with an agent of the imperial power (Figure 29.3).

To survive in the hot tropical environments of south and southeast Asia, the Dutch and English were forced to adapt to the ancient and sophisticated host

**FIGURE 29.3** The close alliances that the European colonizers often struck with the "native" princes of conquered areas are graphically illustrated by this photo of the Susuhunan of Surakarta, a kingdom in central Java, standing arm-in-arm with a high Dutch official. At the upper levels of the administration, Dutch leaders were paired with Javanese rulers and aristocrats. The Dutch official always had the last say in joint decisions. But his Javanese "partner" was closely linked to subordinate administrators and often had a good deal more to say about how effectively the decision was carried out.

IN DEPTH

## Western Education and the Rise of an African and Asian Middle Class

To varying degrees and for many of the same reasons as the British in India, all European colonizers educated the children of African and Asian elite groups in Western-language schools. The early 19th-century debate over education in India was paralleled by an equally hard-fought controversy among French officials and missionaries regarding the proper schooling for the peoples of Senegal in west Africa. The Dutch did not develop European-language schools for the sons of the Javanese elite until the mid-19th century, and many young Javanese men continued to be educated in the homes of the Dutch living in the colonies until the end of the century. Whatever their particular views on education, all colonial policymakers realized that they needed administrative assistants and postal clerks and that they could not begin to recruit enough Europeans to fill these posts. Therefore, all agreed that Western education for some segments of the colonized population was essential for the maintenance of colonial order.

> *"Western education in the colonies . . . within a generation or two would produce major challenges to European colonial dominance."*

One of the chief advantages of having Western-educated African and Asian subordinates—for they were always below European officials or traders—was that their salaries were much lower than what Europeans would have been paid for doing the same work. The Europeans had no trouble rationalizing this inequity. Higher pay for the Europeans was justified as compensation for the sacrifices involved in colonial service. Colonial officials also assumed that European employees would be more hard-working and efficient.

Beyond the need for government functionaries and business assistants, each European colonizer stressed different objectives in designing Western-language schools for the children of upper-class families. The transmission of Western scientific learning and production techniques was a high priority for the British in India. The goal of educational policymakers, such as Macaulay, was to teach the Indians Western literature and manners and to instill in them a Western sense of morality. As Macaulay put it, the British hoped that English-language schools would turn out brown English gentlemen, who would in turn teach their countrymen the ways of the West.

The French, at least until the end of the 19th century, went even further. Because they conceived of French nationalism as a matter of culture rather than birth, it was of prime importance that Africans and other colonial students master the French language and the subtleties of French cuisine, dress, and etiquette. The French also saw the process of turning colonial subjects into black, brown, and yellow French citizens as a way to increase their stagnant population to keep up with rival nations, especially Germany and Great Britain. Both of these rivals and the United States had much higher birth rates in this period.

When the lessons had been fully absorbed and the students fully assimilated to French culture, they could become full citizens of France, no matter what their family origins or skin color. Only a tiny minority of the population of any French colony had the opportunity for the sort of schooling

cultures of their Asian colonies. After establishing themselves at Batavia, for example, the Dutch initially tried to create a little Holland in Java. They built high, close-packed houses overlooking canals, just like those they had left behind in Amsterdam and Rotterdam. But they soon discovered that the canals were splendid breeding grounds for insects and microbes that (though the Europeans did not make the connection until somewhat later) carried debilitating or lethal diseases such as malaria, dysentery, and typhoid. By the late 17th century, the prosperous merchants and officials of Batavia had begun to move away from the unhealthy center of the city to villas in the suburbs. Their large dwellings were set in gardens and separated by rice paddies and palm groves. The tall houses of the inner city gave way in the countryside to low, sprawling dwellings with many open spaces to catch the tropical breezes. Each was ringed with long porches with overhanging roofs to block the heat and glare of the sun. Similar dwellings, from which we get our term *bungalow*, came into fashion in India in the 18th century.

Europeans living in the tropical colonies also adopted, to varying degrees, the dress, the eating and work habits, and even the political symbols and styles of the Asian peoples they ruled. Some Englishmen refused to give up their tight-fitting woolen clothing, at least in public. But many (one suspects most of those who survived) took to wearing looser-fitting cotton clothing. Dutch gentlemen even donned the long skirt-like sarongs of the Javanese aristocrats. British and Dutch officials learned to appreciate the splendid cuisines of India and Java—a taste that the Dutch would never lose and the British would revive at home in the postindependence era. Englishmen smoked Indian *hookahs*, or water pipes, and delighted in performances of Indian "dancing girls." Adjusting to the that would qualify them for French citizenship. But by the early 20th century, there were thousands of Senegalese and hundreds of Vietnamese and Tunisians who could carry French passports, vote in French elections, and even run for seats in the French parliament. Other European colonial powers adopted either the British or the French approach to education and its aims. The Dutch and the Germans followed the British pattern, whereas the Portuguese pushed assimilation for even smaller numbers of the elite classes among the peoples they colonized.

Western education in the colonies succeeded in producing clerks and railway conductors, brown Indian gentlemen, and black French citizens. It also had effects that those who shaped colonial educational policy did not intend, effects that within a generation or two would produce major challenges to European colonial dominance. The population of most colonized areas was divided into many different ethnic, religious, and language groups with separate histories and identities. Western-language schools gave the sons (and, in limited instances, the daughters) of the leading families a common language in which to communicate. The schools also spread common attitudes and ideas and gave the members of diverse groups a common body of knowledge. In all European colonial societies, Western education led to similar occupational opportunities: in government service, with Western business firms, or as professionals (e.g., lawyers, doctors, journalists). Thus, within a generation after their introduction, Western-language schools had created a new middle class in the colonies that had no counterpart in precolonial African or Asian societies.

Occupying social strata and economic niches in the middle range between the European colonizers and the old aristocracy on one hand and the peasantry and urban laborers on the other, Western-educated Africans and Asians became increasingly aware of the interests and grievances they had in common. They often found themselves at odds with the traditional rulers or the landed gentry, who, ironically, were often their fathers or grandfathers. Members of the new middle class also felt alienated from the peasantry, whose beliefs and way of life were so different from those they had learned in Western-language schools.

For more than a generation they clung to their European tutors and employers. Eventually, however, they grew increasingly resentful of their lower salaries and of European competition for scarce jobs. They were also angered by their social segregation from the Europeans, which intensified in the heightened racist atmosphere of the late 19th century. European officials and business managers often made little effort to disguise their contempt for even the most accomplished Western-educated Africans and Asians. Thus, members of the new middle class in the colonies were caught between two worlds: the traditional ways and teachings of their fathers and the modern world of their European masters. Finding that they would be fully admitted to neither world, they rejected the first and set about supplanting the Europeans and building their own versions of the second, or modern, world.

---

**Questions** Why did the Europeans continue to provide Western-language education for Africans and Asians once it was clear they were creating a class that might challenge their position of dominance? What advantages did Western-educated Africans and Asians have as future leaders of resistance to the European colonial overlords? Do you think the European colonial rule would have lasted longer if Western-language education had been denied to colonized peoples?

heat of the colonies, both the Dutch and the English worked hard in the cool of the morning, took a long lunch break (often with a siesta), and then returned to the office for the late afternoon and early evening.

Because the Europeans who went to Asia until the mid-19th century were overwhelmingly male, Dutch and British traders and soldiers commonly had liaisons with Asian women. In some cases these involved little more than visits to the local brothel. But very often European men lived with Asian women, and sometimes they married them. Before the end of the 18th century, mixed marriages on the part of prominent traders or officers were widely accepted, particularly in Java. Examples of racial discrimination against the subject peoples on the basis of their physical appearance can certainly be found during the early decades of European overseas empire. But the frequency of liaisons that cut across racial boundaries suggests a social fluidity and a degree of interracial interaction that would be unthinkable by the last half of the 19th century, when the social distance between colonizers and colonized was consciously marked in a variety of ways.

## Social Reform in the Colonies

Until the early 19th century, neither the Dutch nor the British had much desire to push for changes in the social or cultural life of their Asian subjects. The British enforced the rigid divisions of the Hindu caste system, and both the British and the Dutch made it clear that they had little interest in spreading Christianity among the Indians or the Javanese. In fact, for fear of offending Hindu and Muslim religious sentiments, the British refused to allow Christian missionaries to preach in their territories until the second decade of the 19th century.

Beginning in the 1770s, however, rampant corruption on the part of company officials forced the British parliament to enact significant reforms in the administration of the East India Company and its colonies. By that time most of those who served in India saw their brief tenure as a chance to strike it rich quickly. They made great fortunes by cheating the company and exploiting the Indian peasants and artisans. The bad manners and conspicuous consumption of these upstarts, whom their contemporaries scornfully called **nabobs,** were satirized by leading English novelists of the age.

When the misconduct of the nabobs resulted in the catastrophic Bengal famine of 1770, in which as much as one-third of the population of that once prosperous province died, their abuses could no longer be ignored. The British parliament passed several acts that restructured the company hierarchy and made it much more accountable to the British government. A succession of political reforms culminated in sweeping measures taken in the 1790s by the same **Lord Charles Cornwallis** whose surrender at Yorktown had sealed Britain's loss of the American colonies. By cleaning up the courts and reducing the power of local British administrators, Cornwallis did much to check widespread corruption. Because of his mistrust of Indians, his measures also severely limited their participation in governing the empire.

In this same period, forces were building, in both India and England, that caused a major shift in British policy toward social reform among the subject peoples. The Evangelical religious revival, which had seen the spread of Methodism among the English working classes, soon spilled over into Britain's colonial domains. Evangelicals were in the vanguard of the struggle to put an end to the slave trade, and their calls for reforms in India were warmly supported by Utilitarian philosophers such as Jeremy Bentham and James Mill. These prominent British thinkers believed that there were common principles by which human societies ought to be run if decent living conditions were to be attained by people at all class levels. Mill and other Utilitarians were convinced that British society, though flawed, was far more advanced than Indian society. Thus, they pushed for the introduction of British institutions and ways of thinking in India, as well as the eradication of what they considered Indian superstitions and social abuses.

Both Utilitarians and Evangelicals agreed that Western education was the key to revitalizing an ancient but decadent Indian civilization. Both factions were contemptuous of Indian learning. Influential British historian Thomas Babington Macaulay put it most bluntly when he declared in the 1830s that one shelf of an English gentleman's library was worth all the writings of Asia. Consequently, the Evangelicals and the Utilitarians pushed for the introduction of English-language education for the children of the Indian elite. These officials also pushed for major reforms in Indian society and advocated a large-scale infusion of Western technology.

At the center of the reformers' campaign was the effort to put an end to sati, the ritual burning of Hindu widows on the funeral pyres of their deceased husbands. This practice, which was clearly a corruption of Hindu religious beliefs, had spread fairly widely among upper-caste Hindu groups by the era of the Muslim invasions in the 11th and 12th centuries. In fact, the wives of proud warrior peoples, such as the Rajputs, had been encouraged to commit mass suicide rather than risk dishonoring their husbands by being captured and molested by Muslim invaders. By the early 19th century, some brahman castes and even lower-caste groups in limited areas had adopted the practice of sati.

In the 1830s, bolstered by the strong support and active cooperation of Western-educated Indian leaders, such as **Ram Mohun Roy,** the British outlawed sati. One confrontation between the British and those affected by their efforts to prevent widow burnings illustrates the confidence of the reformers in the righteousness of their cause and the sense of moral and social superiority over the Indians that the British felt in this era. A group of brahmans complained to a British official, Charles Napier, that his refusal to allow them to burn the widow of a prominent leader of their community was a violation of their social customs. Napier replied,

> The burning of widows is your custom. Prepare the funeral pyre. But my nation also has a custom. When men burn women alive, we hang them and confiscate all their property. My carpenters shall therefore erect gibbets on which to hang all concerned when the widow is consumed. Let us all act according to our national customs.

The range and magnitude of the reforms the British enacted in India in the early 19th century marked a watershed in global history. During these years, the alien British, who had become the rulers of one of the oldest centers of civilization, consciously began to transmit the ideas, inventions, modes of organization, and technology associated with western Europe's scientific and industrial revolutions to the peoples of the non-Western world. English education, social reforms, railways, and telegraph lines were only part of a larger project by which the British tried to remake Indian society along Western lines. India's crop lands were measured and registered, its forests were set aside for "scientific" management, and its people were drawn more and more into the European-dominated global market economy. British officials promoted policies that they believed would teach the

Indian peasantry the merits of thrift and hard work. British educators lectured the children of India's rising middle classes on the importance of emulating their European masters in matters as diverse as being punctual, exercising their bodies, and mastering the literature and scientific learning of the West. Ironically, the very values and ideals that the British preached so earnestly to the Indians would soon be turned against colonizers by those leading India's struggle for independence from Western political domination.

## Industrial Rivalries and the Partition of the World, 1870–1914

**The spread of the Industrial Revolution from the British Isles to continental Europe and North America resulted in ever higher levels of European and American involvement in the outside world. Beginning in the 1870s, the Europeans indulged in an orgy of overseas conquests that reduced most of Africa, Asia, and the Pacific Ocean region to colonial possessions by the time of the outbreak of World War I in 1914.**

Although science and industry gave the Europeans power over the rest of the world, they also heightened economic competition and political rivalries between the European powers. In the first half of the 19th century, industrial Britain, with its seemingly insurmountable naval superiority, was left alone to dominate overseas trade and empire building. By the last decades of the century, Belgium, France, and especially Germany and the United States were challenging Britain's industrial supremacy and actively building (or in the case of France, adding to) colonial empires of their own. Many of the political leaders of these expansive nations saw colonies as essential to states that aspired to status as great powers. Colonies were also seen as insurance against raw material shortages and the loss of overseas market outlets to European or North American rivals.

Criticism of British Free Trade Policy

Thus, the concerns of Europe's political leaders were both political and economic. The late 19th century was a period of recurring economic depressions in Europe and the United States. The leaders of the newly industrialized nations had little experience in handling the overproduction and unemployment that came with each of these economic crises. They were deeply concerned about the social unrest and, in some cases, what appeared to be stirrings of revolution that each phase of depression created. Some political theorists argued that as destinations to which unemployed workers might migrate and as potential markets for surplus goods, colonies could serve as safety valves to release the pressure built up in times of industrial slumps.

Imperialism in African (1880s)

In the era of the scramble for colonial possessions, political leaders in Europe played a much more prominent role in decisions to annex overseas territories than they had earlier, even in the first half of the 19th century. In part, this was because of improved communications. Telegraphs and railways made it possible to transmit orders much more rapidly from the capitals of Europe to their representatives in the tropics. But more than politicians were involved in late 19th-century decisions to add to the colonial empires. The development of mass journalism and the extension of the vote to the lower middle and working classes in industrial Europe and the United States made public opinion a major factor in foreign policy. Although stalwart explorers might on their own initiative make treaties with local African or Asian potentates who assigned their lands to France or Germany, these annexations had to be ratified by the home government. In most cases, ratification meant fierce parliamentary debates, which often spilled over into press wars and popular demonstrations. Empires had become the property and pride of the nations of Europe and North America.

Stanley and Kingsley in Africa

### Unequal Combat: Colonial Wars and the Apex of European Imperialism

Industrial change not only justified the Europeans' grab for colonial possessions but made them much easier to acquire. By the late 19th century, scientific discoveries and technological innovations had catapulted the Europeans far ahead of all other peoples in the capacity to wage war. The Europeans could tap mineral resources that most peoples did not even know existed, and European chemists mixed ever more deadly explosives. Advances in metallurgy made possible the mass production of light, mobile artillery pieces that rendered suicidal the massed cavalry or infantry charges that were the mainstay of Asian and African armies. Advances in artillery were matched by great improvements in hand arms. Much more accurate and faster firing, breech-loading rifles replaced the clumsy muzzle-loading muskets of the first phase of empire building. By the 1880s, after decades of experimentation, the machine gun had become an effective battlefield weapon. Railroads gave the Europeans the mobility of the swiftest African or Asian cavalry and the ability to supply large armies in

Africa Before the Scramble, 1876; Africa After the Scramble, 1914

**FIGURE 29.4** This striking painting captures the sleek majesty of the warships that were central to British success in building a global empire. Here the *Prince of Wales* puts ashore British soldiers in Bengal in the northeast of Britain's Indian empire.

the field for extended periods of time. On the sea, Europe's already formidable advantages (amply illustrated in Figure 29.4) were increased by industrial transformations. After the opening of the Suez Canal in 1869, steam power supplanted the sail, iron hulls replaced wood, and massive guns, capable of hitting enemy vessels miles away, were introduced into the fleets of the great powers.

The dazzling array of new weaponry with which the Europeans set out on their expeditions to the Indian frontiers or the African bush made the wars of colonial conquest very lopsided. This was particularly true when the Europeans encountered resistance from peoples such as those in the interior of Africa or the Pacific islands (Maps 29.4 and 29.5). These areas had been cut off from most preindustrial advances in technology, and thus their peoples were forced to fight European machine guns with spears, arrows, and leather shields. One African leader, whose followers struggled with little hope to halt the German advance into east Africa, resorted to natural imagery to account for the power of the invaders' weapons:

> On Monday we heard a shuddering like Leviathan, the voice of many cannon; we heard the roar like waves of the rocks and rumble like thunder in the rains. We heard a crashing like elephants or monsters and our hearts melted at the number of shells. We knew that we were hearing the battle of Pangani; the guns were like a hurricane in our ears.

Not even peoples with advanced preindustrial technology and sophisticated military organization, such as the Chinese and the Vietnamese, could stand against, or really comprehend, the fearful killing devices of the Europeans. In advising the Vietnamese emperor to give in to European demands, one of his officials, who had led the fight against the French invaders, warned, "Nobody can resist them. They go where they choose. . . . Under heaven, everything is feasible to them, save only the matter of life and death."

Despite the odds against them, African and Asian peoples often fiercely resisted the imposition of colonial rule. West African leaders, such as Samory and Ahmadou Sekou, held back the European advance for decades. When rulers such as the Vietnamese emperors

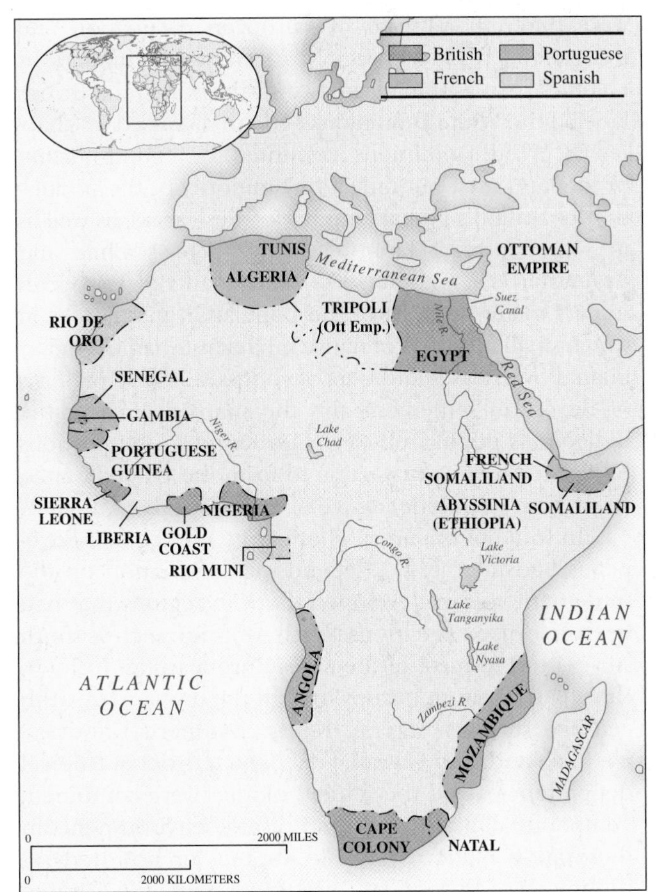


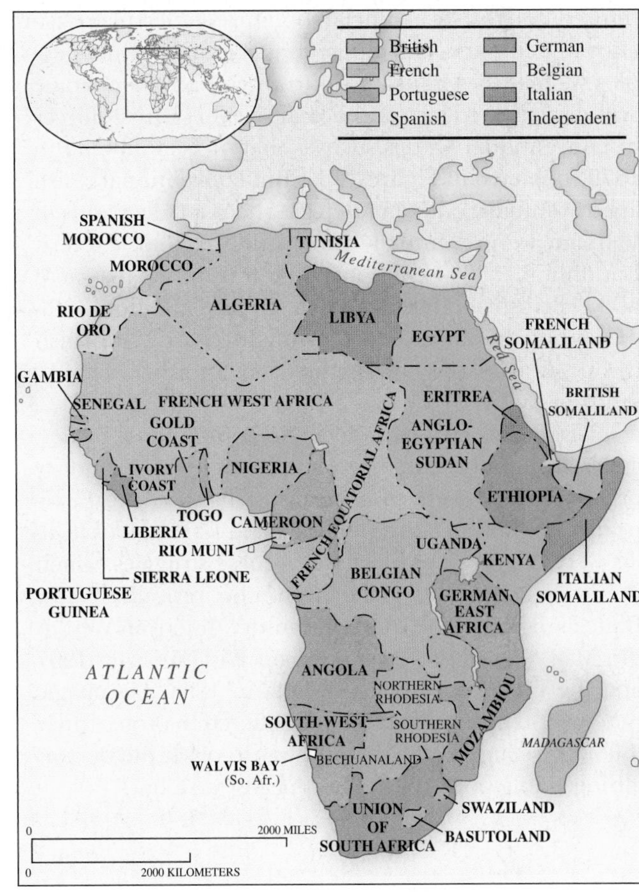


MAP 29.4 The Partition of Africa Between c. 1870 and 1914

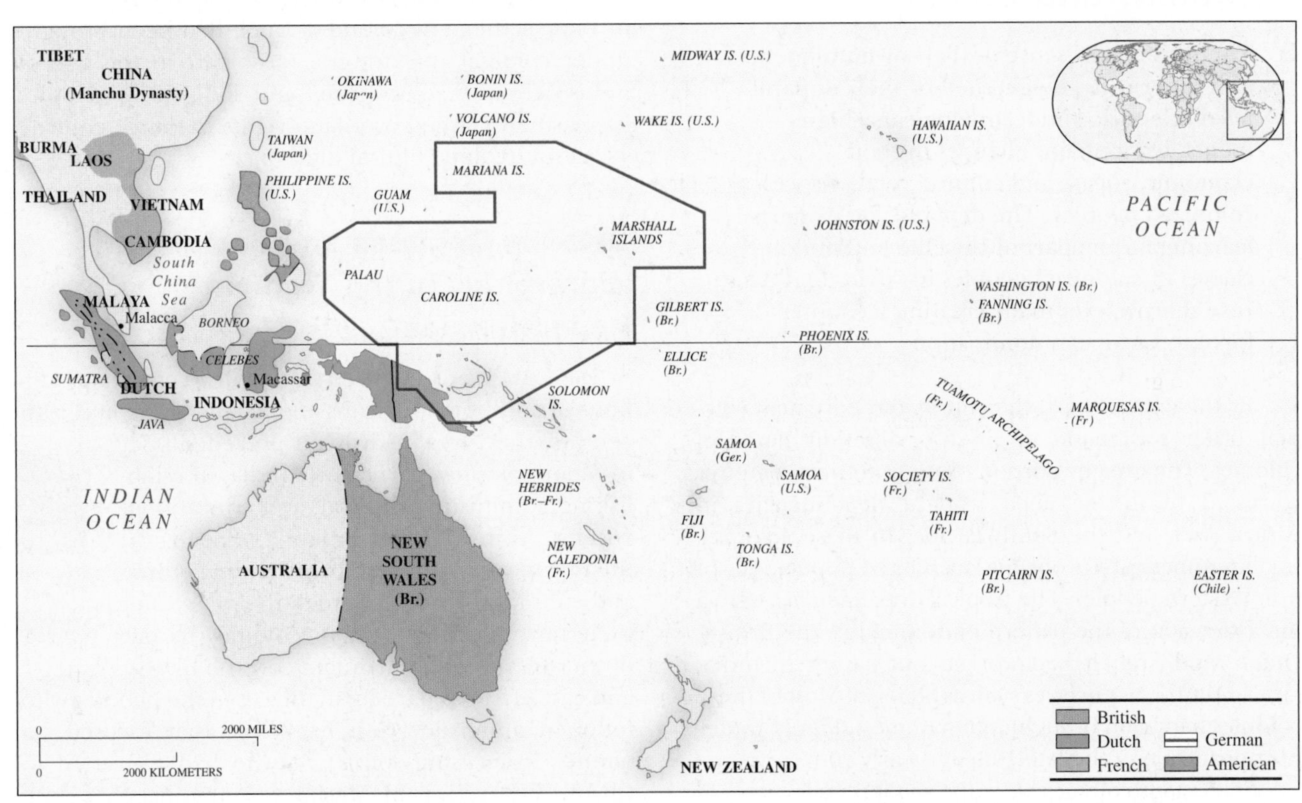


MAP 29.5 The Partition of Southeast Asia and the Pacific to 1914

refused to fight, local officials organized guerrilla resistance in defense of the indigenous regime. Martial peoples such as the Zulus in south Africa had the courage and discipline to face and defeat sizeable British forces in conventional battles such as that at **Isandhlwana** in 1879 (depicted in Figure 29.1). But conventional resistance eventually ended in defeat. The guerrilla bands in Vietnam were eventually run to the ground. Even at Isandhlwana, 3000 Zulus lost their lives in the massacre of 800 British and 500 African troops. In addition, within days of the Zulu victory, a tiny force of 120 British troops at a nearby outpost held off an army of thousands of Zulus.

Given European advantages in conventional battles, guerrilla resistance, sabotage, and in some cases banditry proved the most effective means of fighting the Europeans' attempts to assert political control. Religious leaders were often in the forefront of these struggles, which occurred across the globe, from the revivalist Ghost Dance religion in the late 19th-century American West to the Maji Maji uprisings in German East Africa in 1907 and the Boxer Rebellion in China in 1898. The magic potions and divine assistance they offered to protect their followers seemed to be the only way to offset the demoralizing killing power of the Europeans' weapons.

## Patterns of Dominance: Continuity and Change

■ **The Europeans' sense of their own uniqueness and superiority, heightened by their unparalleled scientific and technological achievements, led to major changes in their economic, social, and cultural relations with colonized peoples. The demand for Western learning on the part of the elite and middle classes of colonized peoples in Africa and Asia rose sharply, eventually creating a counterforce to European domination.**

By the end of the 19th century, the European colonial order was made up of two different kinds of colonies. The greater portion of the European empires consisted of the so-called tropical dependencies in Africa, Asia, and the South Pacific. In these colonies, small numbers of Europeans ruled large populations of non-Western peoples. The tropical dependencies were a vast extension of the pattern of dominance the British, Dutch, and French had worked out earlier in India, Java, and African enclaves such as Senegal. Most of these colonies had been brought, often quite suddenly, under European rule in the late 19th and early 20th century.

**Settlement colonies** were the second major type of European overseas possession, but within this type there were different patterns of European occupation and indigenous response. One pattern was exhibited by colonies such as Canada and Australia, which the British labeled the **White Dominions** and are discussed in Chapter 28. White Dominions accounted for a good portion of the land area but only a tiny minority of the population of Britain's global empire. In these areas, as well as in some parts of Latin America, such as Chile and Argentina (see Chapter 30), descendants of European settlers made up most of the population in colonies in which small numbers of native inhabitants had been decimated by diseases and wars of conquest. These patterns of European settlement and the sharp decline of the indigenous population were also found in the portions of North America that came to form the United States, which won its independence in the late 18th century.

In some of the areas where large numbers of Europeans had migrated, a second major variation on the settlement colony developed. Both in regions that had been colonized as early as North America, such as south Africa, and in most of the areas Europeans and Americans had begun to occupy only in the mid- or late 19th century, such as Algeria, Kenya, Southern Rhodesia, New Zealand, and Hawaii, key characteristics of tropical dependencies and the settler colonies were combined. Temperate climates and mild disease environments in these areas made it possible for tens or hundreds of thousands of Europeans to settle permanently. Despite the Europeans' arrival, large indigenous populations survived and then began to increase rapidly. As a result, in these settlement colonies, which had been brought under colonial rule for the most part in the age of industrialization, Europeans and indigenous peoples increasingly clashed over land rights, resource control, social status, and cultural differences.

### Colonial Regimes and Social Hierarchies in the Tropical Dependencies

As the Europeans imposed their rule over tens of millions of additional Africans and Asians in the late 19th century, they drew heavily on precedents set in older colonies, particularly India, in establishing administrative, legal, and educational systems. As in India (or in Java and Senegal), the Europeans exploited long-standing ethnic and cultural divisions between the peoples of their new African or Asian colonies to put down resistance and maintain control. In west and east Africa in particular, they used the peoples who followed animistic religions (those that focused on nature or ancestral spirits) or who had converted to Christianity against the Muslim communities that existed in most colonies. In official reports and censuses,

European Powers in Southeast Asia

VISUALIZING THE PAST

## Capitalism and Colonialism

In the century since the European powers divided up much of Africa, Asia, and the Pacific into their colonial fiefdoms, historians have often debated how much this process had to do with capitalism. They have also debated, perhaps even more intensely, over how much economic benefit the European colonial powers and the United States were able to garner from their colonies. The table shown here compares Great Britain, the premier industrialized colonial power, with Germany, Europe, the United States, and key areas of the British Empire. For each Western society and colonized area, various indices of the amount or intensity of economic interaction are indicated. A careful examination of each set of statistics and a comparison among them should enable you to answer the questions that follow on the connections between capitalism and colonialism.

**Questions** To which areas did the bulk of British foreign investment flow? Which areas invested most heavily in Great Britain? With which areas did the British have the highest volume of trade? On which was it the most dependent for outlets for its manufactured goods? On which was it the most dependent for raw materials? On which for raw materials that had strategic importance? Do these patterns suggest that colonized areas were more or less important than independent nations; great power rivals, such as Germany and the United States; or settler colonies, such as Canada and Australia? On the basis of this information, would you say that Britain's "true" colonies (e.g., India, Malaya, sub-Saharan Africa) were vital to its economic well-being and defense? Which were the most important?

**British Investment Abroad on the Eve of the First World War (1913)**

| Circa 1913 | % of Total British Investment | % of Total British Imports | Main Products Exported to GB | % of Total British Exports | Main Products Imported fr. GB |
|---|---|---|---|---|---|
| Germany | 0.17 | 8.98 | Manufactures | 9.82 | Manufactures, Foodstuffs |
| Rest of Europe | 5.64 | 27 | Foodstuffs, Manufactures | 30 | Textiles, Machinery Manufactures |
| "White" Dominions (ANZAC) | 24.75 | 10.93 | Wool, Foodstuffs Ores, Textiles | 12.28 | Machinery, Textiles Foodstuffs |
| United States of America | 20.05 | 16.95 | Manufactures, Foodstuffs | 9.37 | Manufactures |
| India (may include Ceylon) | 10.07 | 6.30 | Cotton, Jute, Narcotics, Tea, Other Comestibles | 11.29 | Machinery Coal, Comestibles |
| Egypt | 1.29 | 0.74 | Cotton | 1.25 | Manufactures, Textiles, Coal |
| West Africa | 0.99 | | Foodstuffs, Plant Oils, Ores, Timber | | Manufactures, Textiles, Machinery |
| South Africa | 9.84 | 1.60 | Diamonds, Gold Wool, Other Ores | 3.79 | Machinery, Textiles, Consumer Products |

colonial administrators strengthened existing ethnic differences by dividing the peoples in each colony into "tribes." The label itself, with its connotations of primitiveness and backwardness, says a great deal about general European attitudes toward the peoples of sub-Saharan Africa. In southeast Asia, the colonizers attempted to use hill-dwelling "tribal" minorities against the majority populations that lived in the lowlands. In each colonial area, favored minorities, often Christians, were recruited into the civil service and police.

As had been the case in India, Java, and Senegal, small numbers of Europeans lived mainly in the capital city and major provincial towns. From these urban centers they oversaw the administration of the African and Asian colonies, which was actually carried out at the local level mainly by hundreds or thousands of African and Asian subordinates. Some of these subordinates, normally those in positions of the greatest authority, were Western educated. But the majority were recruited from indigenous elite groups, including village leaders, local notables, and regional lords (Figure 29.5). In Burma, Malaya, and east Africa, thousands of Indian administrators and soldiers helped the British to rule new additions to their empire.

In contrast to Java and India, where schools were heavily state supported, Western-language education in Africa was left largely to Protestant and Catholic

FIGURE 29.5 The importance of co-opting African and Asian rulers and elite social groups for European building is vividly illustrated by this 1861 painting of Queen Victoria and her consort Albert presenting a Bible to an African "chief" decked out in what Victorians imagined was dress attire for such a personage.

missionaries. As a result of deep-seated racial prejudices held by nearly all the colonizers, higher education was not promoted in Africa. As a result, college graduates were few in Africa compared with India, the Dutch East Indies, or even smaller Asian colonies such as Burma and Vietnam. This policy stunted the growth of a middle class in black Africa, a consequence that European colonial officials increasingly intended. As nationalist agitation spread among the Western-educated classes in India and other Asian colonies, colonial policymakers warned against the dangers posed by college graduates. According to this argument, those with advanced educations among the colonized aspired to jobs that were beyond their capacity and were disgruntled when they could not find employment.

## Changing Social Relations Between Colonizer and Colonized

In both long-held and newly acquired colonies, the growing tensions between the colonizers and the rising African and Asian middle classes reflected a larger shift in European social interaction with the colonized peoples. This shift had actually begun long before the scramble for colonies in the late 19th century. Its causes are complex, but the growing size and changing makeup of European communities in the colonies were critical factors. As more and more Europeans went to the colonies, they tended to keep to themselves on social occasions rather than mixing with the "natives." New medicines and increasingly segregated living quarters made it possible to bring to the colonies the wives and families of government officials and European military officers (but not of the rank and file until well into the 20th century). Wives and families further closed the social circle of the colonized, and European women looked disapprovingly on liaisons between European men and Asian or African women. Brothels were off limits for upper-class officials and officers, and mixed marriages or living arrangements met with more and more vocal disapproval within the constricted world of the colonial communities and back home in Europe. The growing numbers of missionaries and pastors for European congregations in the colonies obviously strengthened these taboos.

Historians of colonialism once put much of the blame on European women for the growing social gap between colonizer and colonized. But recent research has shown that male officials bore much of the responsibility. They established laws restricting or prohibiting miscegenation and other sorts of interracial liaisons. They also pushed for housing arrangements and police practices designed specifically to keep social contacts between European women and the colonized at a minimum. These measures locked European women in the colonies into an almost exclusively European world. They had many "native" servants and "native" nannies for their children. But they rarely came into contact with men or women of their own social standing from the colonized peoples. When they did, the occasions were highly public and strictly formal.

The trend toward social exclusivism on the part of Europeans in the colonies and their open disdain for the culture of colonized peoples were reinforced by notions of **white racial supremacy,** which peaked in acceptance in the decades before World War I. It was widely believed that the mental and moral superiority of whites over the rest of humankind, usually divided into

DOCUMENT

## Contrary Images: The Colonizer Versus the Colonized on the "Civilizing Mission"

Each of the following passages from novels written in the colonial era expresses a different view of the reasons behind European colonization in Africa and Asia and its consequences. The first is taken from an adventure story written by John Buchan titled *Prester John,* a favorite in the pre–World War I decades among English schoolboys, many of whom would go out as young men to be administrators in the colonies. Davie, the protagonist in the story, is a "tall, square-set lad . . . renowned [for his] prowess at Rugby football." In the novel, Davie summarizes key elements of the "civilizing mission" credo by which so many European thinkers and political leaders tried to justify their colonization of most of the rest of the world.

> I knew then [after his struggle to thwart a "native" uprising in South Africa] the meaning of the white man's duty. He has to take all the risks, reck[on]ing nothing of his life or his fortunes and well content to find his reward in the fulfillment of his task. That is the difference between white and black, the gift of responsibility, the power of being in a little way a king; and so long as we know this and practise it, we will rule not in Africa alone but wherever there are dark men who live only for the day and their own bellies. Moreover the work made me pitiful and kindly. I learned much of the untold grievances of the natives and saw something of their strange, twisted reasoning.

The second passage is taken from René Maran's *Batouala,* which was first published in 1921 just after World War I. Though a French colonial official in west Africa, Maran was an African American, born in Martinique, who was highly sensitive to the plight of the colonized in Africa. Here his protagonist, a local African leader named Batouala, complains of the burdens rather than the benefits of colonial rule and mocks the self-important European agents of the vaunted civilizing mission.

> But what good does it do to talk about it? It's nothing new to us that men of white skin are more delicate than men of black skin. One example of a thousand possible. Everyone knows that the whites, saying that they are "collecting taxes," force all blacks of a marriageable age to carry voluminous packages from when the sun rises to when it sets.
>
> These trips last two, three, five days. Little matter to them the weight of these packages which are called "sandoukous." They don't sink under the burden. Rain, sun, cold? They don't suffer. So they pay no attention. And long live the worst weather, provided the whites are sheltered.
>
> Whites fret about mosquito bites. . . . They fear mason bees. They are also afraid of the "prankongo," the scorpion who lives, black and venomous, among decaying roofs, under rubble, or in the midst of debris.
>
> In a word, everything worries them. As if a man worthy of the name would worry about everything which lives, crawls, or moves around him.

**Questions** What sorts of roles does Davie assume that the Europeans must play in the colonies? What benefits accrue to colonized peoples from their rule? What impression does he convey of the thinking and behavior of the colonized peoples? In what ways do Batouala's views of the Europeans conflict with Davie's assumptions about himself and other colonizers? Does Batouala agree with Davie's conviction that colonial rule is beneficial for the Africans? What sorts of burdens does Batouala believe it imposes? According to Batouala, what advantages do Africans have over Europeans?

racial types according to the crude criterion of skin color, had been demonstrated by what were then thought to be scientific experiments. Because the non-Europeans' supposedly inferior intelligence and weak sense of morality were seen as inherent and permanent, there seemed to be little motivation for Europeans to socialize with the colonized. There were also new reasons to fight the earlier tendency to adopt elements of the culture and lifestyle of subject peoples. As photos from the late 19th century reveal, stiff collars and ties for men and corsets and long skirts for women became obligatory for respectable colonial functionaries and their wives. The colonizers' houses were filled with the overstuffed furniture and bric-a-brac that the late Victorians loved so dearly. European social life in the colonies revolved around the infamous clubs, where the only "natives" allowed were the servants. In the heat of the summer, most of the administrators and nearly all of the colonizers' families retreated to hill stations, where the cool air and quaint architecture made it seem almost as if they were home again, or at least in a Swiss mountain resort.

"The White Man's Burden" Across Two Centuries

### Shifts in Methods of Economic Extraction

The relationship between the colonizers and the mass of the colonized remained much as it had been before.

District officers, with the help of many "native" subordinates, continued to do their paternal duty to settle disputes between peasant villagers, punish criminals, and collect taxes. European planters and merchants still relied on African or Asian overseers and brokers to manage laborers and purchase crops and handicraft manufactures. But late 19th-century colonial bureaucrats and managers tried to instruct African and Asian peasants in scientific farming techniques and to compel the colonized peoples more generally to work harder and more efficiently. These efforts involved an important extension of dependant status in the Western-dominated world economy.

A wide range of incentives was devised to expand export production. Some of them benefited the colonized peoples, such as cheap consumer goods that could be purchased with cash earned by producing marketable crops or working on European plantations. In many instances, however, colonized peoples were simply forced to produce, for little or no pay, the crops or raw materials that the Europeans wanted. Head and hut taxes were imposed that could be paid only in ivory, palm nuts, or wages earned working on European estates. Under the worst of these forced-labor schemes, such as those inflicted on the peoples of the Belgian Congo in the late 19th century, villagers were flogged and killed if they failed to meet production quotas, and women and children were held hostage to ensure that the men would deliver the products demanded on time (Figure 29.6).

Belgian King Crushing the Congo Free State

As increasing numbers of the colonized peoples were involved in the production of crops or minerals intended for export markets, the economies of most of Africa, India, and southeast Asia were reorganized to serve the needs of the industrializing European economies. Roads and railways were built primarily to move farm produce and raw materials from the interior of colonized areas to port centers from which they could be shipped to Europe. Benefiting from Europe's technological advances, mining sectors grew dramatically in most of the colonies. Vast areas that had previously been uncultivated or (more commonly) had been planted in food crops were converted to the production of commodities such as cocoa, palm oil, rubber, and hemp that were in great demand in the markets of Europe and, increasingly, the United States.

The profits from the precious metals and minerals extracted from Africa's mines or the rubber grown in Malaya went mainly to European merchants and industrialists. The raw materials themselves were shipped to Europe to be processed and sold or used to make industrial products. The finished products were intended mainly for European consumers. The African and Asian laborers who produced these products were generally poorly paid, if they were paid at all. The laborers and colonial economies as a whole were steadily reduced to dependence on the European-dominated global market. Thus, economic dependence complemented the political subjugation and social subordination of colonized African and Asian peoples in a world order loaded in favor of the expansionist nations of western Europe.

## Settler Colonies in South Africa and the Pacific

The settlement colonies where large numbers of Europeans migrated intending to make permanent homes exhibited many of the patterns of political control and economic exploitation found in the tropical dependencies. But the presence of substantial numbers of European settlers *and* indigenous peoples considerably altered the dynamic of political and social domination in this type of colony in comparison with societies like India or the Belgian Congo, where settlers were few and overwhelmingly outnumbered by colonized peoples.

**FIGURE 29.6** As this political cartoon of a vicious snake with Leopold II's head squeezing the life out of a defenseless African villager illustrates, an international campaign developed in the 1890s in opposition to the brutal forced-labor regime in what had become the Belgian king's personal fiefdom in the Congo after 1885. The much publicized scandal compelled the Belgian government to take over the administration of the colony in 1906.

From Algeria to Argentina, settler colonies varied widely. But those settled in the 19th century, with the exception of Australia, tended to be quite different from those occupied in North and South America in the early centuries of European overseas expansion. In these early settler colonies, which included areas that eventually formed the nations of Canada, the United States, Argentina, and Chile, conquest and especially diseases transmitted unwittingly by incoming European migrants had devastating effects on the indigenous peoples, whose numbers in most of these regions were sparse to begin with. By the end of the 19th century in all of these areas, including Australia, which had been settled late but very thinly peopled when the Europeans arrived, the surviving indigenous peoples had been displaced to the margins both geographically and socially. As discussed in Chapter 28, several of these older settler societies—and particularly the United States, Canada, and Australia—imported so many people, institutions, and beliefs from Europe that they now became a part of Western history.

In most of the settler colonies established in the 19th century, the indigenous peoples were both numerous when the Europeans arrived and, in north and sub-Saharan Africa at least, largely resistant to the diseases the colonizers carried with them. Even Pacific islands, such as New Zealand and Hawaii, which had been largely isolated until their first sustained contacts with the Europeans in the late-18th century, were quite densely populated by peoples who were able over time to build up immunities to the diseases the Europeans transmitted. As a result, the history of the newer settler colonies that were formed as the result of large-scale migrations from industrializing societies has been dominated by enduring competition and varying degrees of conflict between European settlers and indigenous peoples. As these divisions were hardened by ethnic, racial, and national identities, settlers also clashed with local representatives of the European powers and in many instances sought to forcibly gain independence from meddling missionaries and transient colonial officials.

## South Africa

The initial Dutch colony at Cape Town was established to provide a way station where Dutch merchant ships could take on water and fresh food in the middle of their long journey from Europe to the East Indies. The small community of Dutch settlers stayed near the coast for decades after their arrival. But the Boers (or farmers), as the descendants of the Dutch immigrants in south Africa came to be called, eventually began to move into the vast interior regions of the continent. There they found a temperate climate in which they could grow the crops and raise the livestock they were accustomed to in Europe. Equally important, they encountered a disease environment they could withstand.

South Africa

Like their counterparts in North America and Australia, the Boers found the areas into which they moved in this early period of colonization sparsely populated. Boer farmers and cattle ranchers enslaved the indigenous peoples, the *Khoikhoi,* while integrating them into their large frontier homesteads. Extensive miscegenation between the Boers and Khoikhoi produced the sizeable "colored" population that exists in South Africa today. The coloreds have historically been seen as distinct from the black African majority.

The arrival of the British overlords in south Africa in the early 19th century made for major changes in the interaction between the Boers and the indigenous peoples and transformed the nature of the settlement colony in the region. The British captured Cape Town during the wars precipitated by the French Revolution in the 1790s, when Holland was overrun by France, thus making its colonies subject to British attack. The British held the colony during the Napoleonic conflicts that followed, and they annexed it permanently in 1815 as a vital sea link to their prize colony, India. Made up mainly of people of Dutch and French Protestant descent, the Boer community differed from the British newcomers in almost every way possible. The Boers spoke a different language, and they lived mostly in isolated rural homesteads that had missed the scientific, industrial, and urban revolutions that transformed British society and attitudes. Most critically, the evangelical missionaries who entered south Africa under the protection of the new British overlords were deeply committed to eradicating slavery. They made no exception for the domestic pattern of enslavement that had developed in Boer homesteads and communities. By the 1830s, missionary pressure and increasing British interference in their lives drove a handful of Boers to open but futile rebellion, and many of the remaining Boers fled the Cape Colony.

In the decades of the Great Trek that followed, tens of thousands of Boers migrated in covered wagons pulled by oxen, first east across the Great Fish River and then over the mountains into the veld—the rolling grassy plains that make up much of the south African interior. In these areas, the Boers collided head-on with populous, militarily powerful, and well-organized African states built by Bantu peoples such as the Zulus and the Xhosa. The ever multiplying contacts that resulted transformed the settler society in south Africa from one where the indigenous peoples were marginalized, typical of those founded in the early centuries of expansion, into a deeply contested colonial realm akin to those established in the age of industrialization. Throughout the mid-19th century, the migrating Boers clashed again and again with Bantu peoples, who were determined to resist the seizure of the lands where they pastured their great herds of cattle and grew subsistence foods.

The British followed the Boer pioneers along the southern and eastern coast, eventually establishing a second major outpost at Durban in **Natal.** Tensions between the Boers and Britain remained high, but the imperial overlords were often drawn into frontier wars against the Bantu peoples, even though they were not always formally allied to the Boers.

In the early 1850s, the hard-liners among the Boers established two **Boer Republics** in the interior, named the Orange Free State and the Transvaal, which they tried to keep free of British influence. For more than a decade, the Boers managed to keep the British out of their affairs. But when diamonds were discovered in the Orange Free State in 1867, British entrepreneurs, including most famously **Cecil Rhodes,** and prospectors began to move in, and tensions between the Boers and the British began to build anew. In 1880–1881, these tensions led to a brief war in which the Boers were victorious. But the tide of British immigration into the republics rose even higher after gold was discovered in the Transvaal in 1885.

Cecil Rhodes Astride Africa

Although the British had pretty much left the Boers to deal as they pleased with the African peoples who lived in the republics, British miners and financiers grew more and more resentful of Boer efforts to limit their numbers and curb their civil rights. British efforts to protect these interlopers and bring the feisty and independent Boers into line led to the republics' declaration of war against the British in late 1899. Boer assaults against British bases in Natal, the Cape Colony, and elsewhere initiated the **Boer War** (1899–1902) that the British ultimately won but only at a very high cost in both lives and resources. British guilt over their brutal treatment of the Boers—men, women, and children—during the war also opened the way for the dominance of this settler minority over the black African majority that would prove to be the source of so much misery and violence in south African history through most of the 20th century.

The Boer War and Queen Victoria—Dutch Caricature

Creating Apartheid in South Africa

## Pacific Tragedies

The territories the Europeans, Americans, and Japanese claimed throughout the South Pacific in the 19th century were in some cases outposts of true empire and in others contested settler colonies. In both situations, however, the coming of colonial rule resulted in demographic disasters and social disruptions of a magnitude that had not been seen since the first century of European expansion into the Americas. Like the Native American peoples of the New World, the peoples of the South Pacific had long lived in isolation. This meant that, like the Native Americans, they had no immunities to many of the diseases European explorers and later merchants, missionaries, and settlers carried to their island homes from the 1760s onward. In addition, their cultures were extremely vulnerable to the corrosive effects of outside influences, such as new religions, different sexual mores, more lethal weapons, and sudden influxes of cheap consumer goods. Thus, whatever the intentions of the incoming Europeans and Americans—and they were by no means always benevolent—their contacts with the peoples of the Pacific islands almost invariably ushered in periods of social disintegration and widespread human suffering.

Of the many cases of contact between the expansive peoples of the West and the long-isolated island cultures of the South Pacific, the confrontations in New Zealand and Hawaii are among the most informative. As we have seen in Chapter 9, sophisticated cultures and fairly complex societies had developed in each of these areas. In addition, at the time of the European explorers' arrivals, the two island groups contained some of the largest population concentrations in the whole Pacific region. Both areas were subjected to European influences carried by a variety of agents, from whalers and merchants to missionaries and colonial administrators. With the great expansion of European settlement after the first decades of contact, the peoples of New Zealand and Hawaii experienced a period of crisis so severe that their continued survival was in doubt. In both cases, however, the threatened peoples and cultures rebounded and found enduring solutions to the challenges from overseas. Their solutions combined accommodation to outside influences, usually represented by the large numbers of European settlers living in their midst, with revivals of traditional beliefs and practices.

**New Zealand** The Maori of New Zealand actually went through two periods of profound disruption and danger. The first began in the 1790s, when timber merchants and whalers established small settlements on the New Zealand coast. Maori living near these settlements were afflicted with alcoholism and the spread of prostitution. In addition, they traded wood and food for European firearms, which soon revolutionized Maori warfare—in part by rendering it much more deadly—and upset the existing balance between different tribal groups. Even more devastating was the impact of diseases, such as smallpox, tuberculosis, and even the common cold, that ravaged Maori communities throughout the north island. By the 1840s, only 80,000 to 90,000 Maori remained of a population that had been as high as 130,000 less than a century earlier. But the Maori survived these calamities and began to adjust to the imports of the foreigners. They took up farming with European implements, and they grazed cattle purchased from European traders. They cut timber, built windmills, and traded extensively with the merchants who visited their shores. Many were converted to Christianity by the missionaries, who established their first station in 1814.

The arrival of British farmers and herders in search of land in the early 1850s, and the British decision to claim the islands as part of their global empire, again plunged the Maori into misery and despair. Backed by the military clout of the colonial government, the settlers occupied some of the most fertile areas of the north island. The warlike Maori fought back, sometimes with temporary successes, but they were steadily driven back into the interior of the island. In desperation, in the 1860s and 1870s they flocked to religious prophets who promised them magical charms and supernatural assistance in their efforts to drive out the invaders. When the prophets also failed them, the Maori seemed for a time to face extinction. In fact, some British writers predicted that within generations the Maori would die out entirely.

The Maori displayed surprising resilience. As they built up immunities to new diseases, they also learned to use European laws and political institutions to defend themselves and preserve what was left of their ancestral lands. Because the British had in effect turned the internal administration of the islands over to the settlers' representatives, the Maori's main struggle was with the invaders who had come to stay. Western schooling and a growing ability to win British colonial officials over to their point of view eventually enabled the Maori to hold their own in their ongoing legal contests and daily exchanges with the settlers. Though New Zealand was included in the White Dominions of the British Empire, it was in fact a multiracial society in which a reasonable level of European and Maori accommodation and interaction has been achieved. Over time the Maori have also been able to preserve much of value in their precontact culture.

**Hawaii** The conversion of Hawaii to settler colony status followed familiar basic imperialist patterns but with specific twists. Hawaii did not become a colony until the United States proclaimed annexation in 1898, although an overzealous British official had briefly claimed the islands for his nation in 1843. Hawaii came under increasing Western influence from the late 18th century onward—politically at the hands of the British, and culturally and economically from the United States, whose westward surge quickly spilled into the Pacific Ocean.

Although very occasional contact with Spanish ships during the 16th and 17th centuries probably occurred, Hawaii was effectively opened to the West through the voyages of **Captain James Cook** from 1777 to 1779 (Figure 29.7). Cook was first welcomed as a god, partly because he had the good luck to land during a sacred period when war was forbidden. A later and less well-timed visit brought Cook's death as Hawaiian warriors tried to take over his ship for its metal nails. These humble objects were much prized by a people whose elaborate culture rested on a Neolithic technology and thus was without iron or steel. The Cook expedition and later British visits convinced a young Hawaiian prince, Kamehameha, that some imitation of Western ways could produce a unified kingdom under his leadership, replacing the small and warring regional units that had previously prevailed. A series of vigorous wars, backed by British weapons and advisors, won Kamehameha his kingdom between 1794 and 1810. The new king and his successors promoted economic change, encouraging Western merchants to establish export trade in Hawaiian goods in return for increasing revenues to the royal treasury.

Hawaiian royalty began to imitate Western habits, in some cases traveling to Britain and often building Western-style palaces. Two powerful queens advanced the process of change by insisting that traditional taboos subordinating women be abandoned. In this context, vigorous missionary efforts from Protestant New England, beginning in 1819, brought extensive conversions to Christianity. As with other conversion processes, religious change had wide implications. Missionaries railed against traditional Hawaiian costumes, insisting that

FIGURE 29.7 One of the most famous, but ultimately tragic, cross-cultural encounters of the late 18th century was between Captain James Cook and the crew of the ship he commanded and the peoples of Hawaii. In this painting depicting his arrival in the islands, Cook, a renowned English explorer, is welcomed enthusiastically by the Hawaiians, who may have believed he was the god, Lono, whose festival had just begun. When Cook was later killed due to less fortunate timing and misunderstandings with the Hawaiians, he was lamented throughout Europe as one of the great lost heroes of his age.

women cover their breasts, and a new garment, the muumuu, was made from homespun American nightgowns with the sleeves cut off. Backed by the Hawaiian monarchy, missionaries quickly established an extensive school system, which by 1831 served 50,000 students from a culture that had not previously developed writing.

The combination of Hawaiian interest and Western intrusion produced creative political and cultural changes, though at the expense of previous values. Demographic and economic trends had more insidious effects. Western-imported diseases, particularly sexually transmitted diseases and tuberculosis, had the usual tragic consequences for a previously isolated people. By 1850 only about 80,000 Hawaiians remained of a prior population of about half a million. Because of the Hawaiian population decline, it was necessary to import Asian workers to staff the estates. The first Chinese contract workers had been brought in before 1800; after 1868, a larger current of Japanese arrived. Westerners began to more systematically exploit the Hawaiian economy. Whalers helped create raucous seaport towns. Western settlers from various countries (called *haoles* by the Hawaiians) experimented with potential commercial crops, soon concentrating on sugar. Many missionary families, impatient with the subsistence habits of Hawaiian commoners, turned to leasing land or buying it outright. Most settlers did not entirely forget their religious motives for migrating to the islands, but many families who came to Hawaii to do good ended by doing well.

Literal imperialism came as an anticlimax. The abilities of Hawaiian monarchs declined after 1872, in one case because of disease and alcoholism. Under a weakened state, powerful planter interests pressed for special treaties with the United States that would promote their sugar exports, and the American government claimed naval rights at the Pearl Harbor base by 1887. As the last Hawaiian monarchs turned increasingly to promoting culture, writing a number of lasting Hawaiian songs but also spending money on luxurious living, American planters concluded that their economic interests required outright United States control. An annexation committee persuaded American naval officers to "protect American lives and property" by posting troops around Honolulu in 1893. The Hawaiian ruler was deposed, and an imperialist-minded U.S. Congress formally took over the islands in 1898.

Platform of the American Anti-Imperialist League

As in New Zealand, Western control was combined with respect for Polynesian culture. Because Hawaiians were not enslaved and soon ceased to threaten those present, Americans in Hawaii did not apply the same degree of racism found in earlier relations with African slaves or Native Americans. Hawaii's status as a settler colony was further complicated by the arrival of many Asian immigrants. Nevertheless, Western cultural and particularly economic influence extended steadily, and the ultimate political seizure merely ratified the colonization of the islands.

GLOBAL CONNECTIONS

## A European-Dominated World Order

The Industrial Revolution not only gave the Europeans and North Americans the motives but also provided the means for them to become the agents of the first civilization to dominate the entire world. By the end of the 19th century, the Western industrial powers had directly colonized most of Asia and Africa, and (as we shall see in Chapter 31) indirectly controlled the remaining areas through the threat of military interventions or the manipulation of local elites. Political power made it possible for the Europeans to use their already well-established position in world trade to build a global economic order oriented to their industrial societies.

In many ways the first phase of globalization in the most meaningful sense of the term occurred in the four or five decades before the outbreak of World War I in 1914. The communications and commercial networks that undergirded the European colonial order made possible an unprecedented flow of foods and minerals from Africa, Asia, and Latin America to Europe and North America. Western industrial societies provided investment capital and machines to run the mines, plantations, and processing plants in colonized areas. European dominance also made it possible to extract cheap labor and administrative services from subject populations across the globe. Western culture, especially educational norms—but also manners, fashions, literary forms, and modes of entertainment—also became the first to be extensively exported to virtually all the rest of the world. No culture was strong enough to remain untouched by the European drive for global dominance in this era. None could long resist the profound changes unleashed by European conquest and colonization.

The European colonizers assumed that it was their God-given destiny to remake the world in the image of industrial Europe. But in pushing for change within colonized societies that had ancient, deeply rooted cultures and patterns of civilized life, the Europeans often aroused resistance to specific policies and to colonial rule more generally. The colonizers were able to put down protest movements led by displaced princes and religious prophets. But much more enduring and successful challenges to their rule came, ironically, from the very leaders their social reforms and Western-language schools had done so much to nurture. These Asian and African *nationalists* reworked European ideas and resurrected those of their own cultures. They borrowed European organizational techniques and used the communication systems and common language the Europeans had introduced into the colonies to mobilize the resistance to colonial domination that became one of the dominant themes of global history in the 20th century.

## Further Readings

The literature on various aspects of European imperialism is vast. An analytical and thematic overview that attempts to set forth the basic patterns in different time periods is provided by David B. Abernethy, *The Dynamics of Global Dominance: European Overseas Empires 1415–1980* (2000). Useful general histories on the different empires include Bernard Porter, *The Lion's Share: A Short History of British Imperialism 1850–1970* (1975); Raymond Betts, *Tricouleur* (1978); James J. Cooke, *The New French Imperialism, 1880–1910* (1973); Woodruff D. Smith, *The German Colonial Empire* (1978); and Frances Gouda, *Dutch Culture Overseas* (1995).

There is no satisfactory general history of the growth of the British Empire in India, but Edward Thompson and G. T. Garratt provide a lively chronology in *The Rise and Fulfillment of British Rule in India* (1962), which can be supplemented by the essays in R. C. Majumdar, ed., *British Paramountcy and Indian Renaissance, Part 1* (1963). More recent accounts of specific aspects of the rise of British power in India are available in C. A. Bayly's *Indian Society and the Making of the British Empire* (1988), and P. J. Marshall's *Bengal: The British Beachhead, 1740–1828* (1987), both part of *The New Cambridge History of India.* For the spread of Dutch power in Java and the "outer islands," see Merle Ricklets, *A History of Modern Indonesia* (1981).

Of the many contributions to the debate over late 19th-century imperialism, some of the most essential are those by D. C. M. Platt, Hans-Ulrich Wehler, William Appleman Williams, Jean Stengers, D. K. Fieldhouse, and Henri Brunschwig, as well as the earlier works by Lenin and J. A. Hobson. Winfried Baumgart's *Imperialism* (1982) provides a good overview of the literature and conflicting arguments. Very different perspectives on the partition of Africa can be found in Jean Suret-Canale's *French Colonialism in Tropical Africa, 1900–1945* (1971) and Ronald Robinson and John Gallagher's *Africa and the Victorians* (1961).

Most of the better studies on the impact of imperialism and social life in the colonies are specialized monographs, but Percival Spear's *The Nabobs* (1963) is a superb place to start on the latter from the European viewpoint, and the works of Frantz Fanon, Albert Memmi, and O. Mannoni provide many insights into the plight of the colonized. The impact of industrialization and other changes in Europe on European attitudes toward the colonized are treated in several works, including Philip Curtin, *The Image of Africa* (1964); William B. Cohen, *The French Encounter with Africans* (1980); and Michael Adas, *Machines as the Measure of Men* (1989). Ester Boserup, *Women's Role in Economic Development* (1970), provides a good overview of the impact of colonization on African and Asian women and families, but it should be supplemented by more recent monographs on the position of women in colonial settings. One of the best of these is Jean Taylor, *The Social World of Batavia* (1983).

## On the Web

The causes of imperialism in the 19th century are explored at http://mars.acnet.wnec.edu/~grempel/courses/wc2/lectures/imperialism.html and http://www.fordham.edu/halsall/mod/modsbook34.html. The nature and scope of British imperialism is examined at http://www.scholars.nus.edu.sg/victorian/history/empire/empireov.html and http://www.britishempire.co.uk. The Web also provides gateways for the study of German imperialism in China at http://www2.h-net.msu.edu/~german/gtext/kaiserreich/china.html and in Africa at http://web.jjay.cuny.edu/~jobrien/reference/ob22.html, http://www.cusd.chico.k12.ca.us/~bsilva/projects/imperialism/schuller.htm, and http://www.fordham.edu/halsall/mod/1901kaiser.html. American imperialism in the Philippines and the rest of Asia is examined at http://www.smplanet.com/imperialism/toc.html. Japanese imperialism in Korea is examined at http://kimsoft.com/korea/jp_hist1.htm and http://en.wikipedia.org/wiki/Period_of_Japanese_Rule_%28Korea%29, and included the use of chôngshindae or "comfort women" at http://www.koreasociety.org/KS_curriculum/HS/Z/Z–text/Z_143.htm and http://online.sfsu.edu/~son/w-links.htm.

The onset of British imperialism in India, including studies of key personalities, such as Robert Clive, and key events, such as the Battle of Plassey, receives careful treatment at http://www.sscnet.ucla.edu/southasia/History/British/Plassey.html. The life of Tipu Sultan, the Indian Muslim ruler who tried to defeat the British on their own terms, is examined at http://www.kamat.com/kalranga/itihas/tippu.htm.

The British debacle at Isandhlwana and the Zulu wars are given thorough treatment at http://www.rorkesdriftvc.com/isandhlwana/isandhlwana.htm and http://schwartz.eng.auburn.edu/zulu/zulu.html. An African nationalist perspective of these anticolonial struggles is offered at http://www.anc.org.za/ancdocs/history/misc/isandhlwana.html.

The "white man's burden" carried by Rudyard Kipling's prose and poetry is examined at http://www.geocities.com/Athens/Aegean/1457/, http://www.victorianweb.org/authors/kipling/Kipling.html and http://www.selfknowledge.com/238au.htm. The American anti-imperialist attack on Kipling's famous poem on race and empire is presented at http://www.boondocksnet.com/ai/kipling/kipling.html.

CHAPTER 30

# The Consolidation of Latin America, 1830–1920



On a rainy morning in 1867, on the Hill of Bells just outside the Mexican city of Queretaro, the handsome, erect figure of the young Austrian Archduke Maximilian stood, flanked by his loyal generals, before a Mexican firing squad. The story of his fall is a strange one. Just three years before, he and his wife, Carlota, had been sent by Carlota's grandfather, Napoleon III, to become emperor and empress of Mexico. They had replaced Benito Juárez, a reformist Mexican leader whose government had been toppled by Napoleon as a result of its refusal to pay the debts of its predecessors. Assured by Napoleon and the Conservative party of Mexico that the Mexican people enthusiastically awaited their arrival, Maximilian and Carlota believed they would bring stability to the troubled land.

Maximilian and Carlota were both well educated and well intentioned. They had tried to bring reforms to their adopted country and had even invited Juárez and other political opponents to join in the new government—an offer that was resolutely refused. In fact, Maximilian and Carlota had been gravely misled as to the attitude of the Mexican people toward their new rulers. Their authority rested on foreign bayonets, and their very presence was seen as an insult by the majority of Mexicans, who were determined to maintain the political independence they had won after a long and bitter struggle.

Juárez and Maximilian could not have been more different in most ways. Benito Juárez, the diminutive Zapotec Indian who had risen from poverty and obscurity to become Mexico's leading liberal politician, and Maximilian von Habsburg, the foreign-backed emperor who had blood ties to every royal house in Europe, represented two different visions of what Latin America should become. Their clash not only determined the fate of Mexico but also served as an example and a warning to other foreign states with imperialist designs.

Before the execution, Carlota had traveled all over Europe, pleading her husband's case, and numerous calls for clemency had reached Juárez's desk. But for the good of his country, Juárez refused to spare Maximilian, though

**FIGURE 30.1** Emperor Maximilian was finally captured after his attempt, with French help, to reestablish a monarchy in Mexico. Well-meaning, he eventually lost the support of the conservatives. Juárez refused to spare his life, as a warning to other ambitious nations that Mexico would remain independent. Manet's painting of the execution of Maximilian, shown here flanked by his two loyal generals facing the firing squad.

he confided to friends that he could not bring himself to meet the man for fear that his determination on this point would waver. Maximilian died a tragic figure; his last words were "Long live Mexico, long live independence." Carlota spent the next 60 years in seclusion. Even more tragically, by the time of Maximilian's death, hundreds of thousands of Mexicans had perished in the civil wars that had brought him to, and finally toppled him from, the throne.

| 1800 C.E. | 1820 C.E. | 1840 C.E. | 1860 C.E. | 1880 C.E. | 1900 C.E. |
|---|---|---|---|---|---|
| **1792** Slave rebellion in St. Domingue (Haiti)<br>**1804** Haiti declares independence<br>**1808–1825** Spanish-American wars of independence<br>**1808** Portuguese court flees Napoleon, arrives in Brazil; French armies invade Spain<br>**1810** In Mexico, Father Hidalgo initiates rebellion against Spain | **1821** Mexico declares independence; empire under Iturbide lasts to 1823<br>**1822** Brazil declares independence; empire established under Dom Pedro I<br>**1823** Monroe Doctrine indicates U.S. opposition to European ambitions in the Americas<br>**1829–1852** Juan Manuel de Roses rules Rio de la Plata<br>**1830** Bolívar dies; Gran Colombia dissolves into separate countries of Venezuela, Colombia, and Ecuador | **1846–1848** Mexican-American War<br>**1847–1855** Caste War in Yucatan<br>**1850s** Beginnings of railroad construction in Cuba, Chile, and Brazil<br>**1854** Benito Juárez leads reform in Mexico | **1862–1867** French intervention in Mexico<br>**1865–1870** War of the Triple Alliance (Argentina, Brazil, and Uruguay against Paraguay)<br>**1868–1878** Ten-year war against Spain in Cuba<br>**1869** First school for girls in Mexico<br>**1876–1911** Porfirio Díaz rules Mexico | **1886–1888** Cuba and Brazil abolish slavery<br>**1889** Fall of Brazilian Empire; republic established<br>**1895–1898** Cuban Spanish-American War; United States acquires Puerto Rico and Philippines | **1903** Panamanian independence; beginning of Panama Canal (opens in 1914) |

In the late 18th century the former colonies of Spain and Portugal were swept by the same winds of change that transformed Europe's society and economy and led to the independence of the United States. Although at present Latin America is sometimes considered part of the developing world along with many Asian and African nations, in reality its political culture was formed in the 18th century by the ideas of the Western Enlightenment. To a large degree, both Juárez and Maximilian shared these liberal ideals.

In the early 19th century, the various regions of Latin America fought for their political independence and created new nations, often based on the old colonial administrative units. But what kind of nations were these to be? The form of government, the kind of society, the role of religion, and the nature of the economy all had to be defined in each of the new countries, and deep divisions over these questions and others created bitter political struggles. Then too, there was always the shadow of foreign interference—from the old colonial powers, from new imperialist regimes, and from neighbors seeking territory or economic advantage. Latin America in the 19th century was shaped both by its internal struggles over these questions and by the dominant international forces of the day.

Despite their many differences, most 19th-century Latin American leaders shared with Western political figures a firm belief in the virtues of progress, reform, representational and constitutional government, and private property rights. At the same time, Latin American leaders faced problems very different from those of Europe and the United States. The colonial heritage had left little tradition of participatory government. A highly centralized colonial state had intervened in many aspects of life and had created both dependence on central authority and resentment of it. Class and regional interests deeply divided the new nations, and wealth was very unequally distributed. Finally, the rise of European industrial capitalism created an economic situation that often placed the new nations in a weak or dependent position. These problems and tensions are the focus of our examination of Latin America in the 19th century.

## From Colonies to Nations

**A combination of internal developments and the Napoleonic wars set Latin American independence movements in motion.**

By the late 18th century, the elites of American-born whites or Creoles (*criollos*) expressed a growing self-consciousness as they began to question the policies of Spain and Portugal. At the same time, these elites were joined by the majority of the population in resenting the increasingly heavy hand of government, as demonstrated by the new taxes and administrative reforms of the 18th century. But the shared resentment was not enough to overcome class conflicts and divisions. Early movements for independence usually failed because of the reluctance of the colonial upper classes to enlist the support of the American Indian, mestizo, and mulatto masses, who, they thought, might later prove too difficult to control. The actual movements were set in motion only when events in Europe precipitated actions in America.

## Causes of Political Change

Latin American political independence was achieved as part of the general Atlantic revolution of the late 18th and early 19th centuries, and Latin American leaders were moved by the same ideas as those seeking political change elsewhere in the Atlantic world. Four external events had a particularly strong impact on political thought in Latin America. The American Revolution, from 1775 to 1783, provided a model of how colonies could break with the mother country. The French Revolution of 1789 provoked great interest in Latin America, and its slogan, "liberty, equality, and fraternity," appealed to some sectors of the population. As that revolution became increasingly radical, however, it was rejected by the Creole elites, who could not support regicide, rejection of the church's authority, and the social leveling implied by the Declaration of the Rights of Man and the Citizen.

The third external event was partially an extension of the French Revolution but had its own dynamic. Torn by internal political conflict during the turmoil in France, the whites and free people of color in St. Domingue, France's great sugar colony in the Caribbean, became divided. The slaves seized the moment in 1791 to stage a general rebellion under able leadership by **Toussaint L'Overture.** Various attempts to subdue the island were defeated, and in 1804 the independent republic of Haiti was proclaimed. For Latin American elites, Haiti was an example to be avoided. It was not accidental that neighboring Cuba and Puerto Rico, whose elites had plantations and slaves and were acutely aware of events in Haiti, were among the last of Spain's colonies to gain independence. For slaves and free people of color throughout the Americas, however, Haiti became a symbol of freedom and hope.

What eventually precipitated the movements for independence in Latin America was the confused Iberian political situation caused by the French Revolution and its aftermath. France invaded Portugal and Spain, and a general insurrection erupted in 1808, followed by a long guerrilla war. During the fighting, a central committee, or junta central, ruled in the Spanish king's name in opposition to Napoleon's brother, whom Napoleon had appointed king.

Who was the legitimate ruler? By 1810 the confusion in Spain had provoked a crisis in the colonies. In places such as Caracas, Bogotá, and Mexico, local elites, pretending to be loyal to the deposed king Ferdinand, set up juntas to rule in his name, but they ruled on their own behalf. Soon the more conservative elements of the population—royal officials and those still loyal to Spain—opposed the movements for autonomy and independence. A crisis of legitimacy reverberated throughout the American colonies.

## Spanish American Independence Struggles

The independence movements divided into three major theaters of operation. In Mexico, a conspiracy among leading Creoles moved one of the plotters, the priest **Father Miguel de Hidalgo,** to call for help from the American Indians and mestizos of his region in 1810. He won a number of early victories but eventually lost the support of the Creoles, who feared social rebellion more than they desired independence. Hidalgo was captured and executed, but the insurgency smoldered in various parts of the country. Eventually, after 1820 when events in Spain weakened the king and the central government, conservative Creoles in Mexico were willing to move toward independence by uniting with the remnants of the insurgent forces. **Augustín de Iturbide,** a Creole officer at the head of an army that had been sent to eliminate the insurgents, drew up an agreement with them instead, and the combined forces of independence occupied Mexico City in September 1821. Soon thereafter, with the support of the army, Iturbide was proclaimed emperor of Mexico.

This was a conservative solution. The new nation of Mexico was born as a monarchy, and little recognition was given to the social aspirations and programs of Hidalgo and his movement. Central America was briefly attached to the Mexican Empire, which collapsed in 1824. Mexico became a republic, and the Central American states, after attempting union until 1838, split apart into independent nations.

In South America and the Caribbean, the chronology of independence was a mirror image of the conquest of the 16th century. Formerly secondary areas such as Argentina and Venezuela were among the first to opt for independence and the best able to achieve it. The old colonial center in Peru was among the last to break with Spain. The Caribbean islands of Cuba and Puerto Rico, fearful of slave rebellion and occupied by large Spanish garrisons, remained loyal until the end of the 19th century.

In northern South America, a movement for independence centered in Caracas had begun in 1810. After early reverses, **Simon Bolívar,** a wealthy Creole officer, emerged as the leader of the revolt against Spain (Figure 30.2). With considerable military skill and a passion for independence, he eventually mobilized support, and between 1817 and 1822 he won a series of victories in Venezuela, Colombia, and Ecuador. Until 1830, these countries were united into a new nation called **Gran Colombia.** Political differences and regional interests led to the breakup of Gran Colombia. Bolívar became disillusioned and fearful of anarchy. "America is ungovernable," he said, and "those who have served the revolution have plowed the sea." To his credit, however, Bolívar rejected all attempts to crown him as king, and he remained until his death in 1830 firmly committed to the cause of independence and republican government.

Simon Bolívar on Constitutional Government

The Great Liberator—Independence Leader, Caudillo, and Future President Simon Bolívar

Meanwhile, in southern South America, another movement had coalesced under **José de San Martín** in the Rio de la Plata. Buenos Aires had become a booming commercial center in the late 18th century, and its residents, called *porteños,* particularly resented Spanish trade restrictions. Pushing for freedom of trade, they opted for autonomy in 1810 but tried to keep the outlying areas, such as Paraguay, under their control. The myth of autonomy rather than independence was preserved for a while. By 1816, however, the independence of the United Provinces of the Rio de la Plata had been proclaimed, although the provinces were far from united. Upper Peru (Bolivia) remained under Spanish control, Paraguay declared independence in 1813, and the Banda Oriental (Uruguay) resisted the central authority of Buenos Aires.

In Buenos Aires, San Martín had emerged as a military commander willing to speak and act for independence. From Argentina his armies crossed the Andes to Chile to help the revolutionary forces in that colony. After winning victories there, the patriot forces looked northward. Peru was still under Spanish control. Its upper class was deeply conservative and not attracted to the movements for independence. San Martín's forces entered Peru, and Creole adherence was slowly won after major victories like the battle of Ayacucho in 1824, where royalist forces were defeated (Figure 30.3). By 1825 all of Spanish South America had gained its political independence. Despite various plans to create some form of monarchy in many of the new states, all of them emerged as independent republics with representative governments. The nations of Spanish America were born of the Enlightenment and the ideas of 19th-century liberalism. The wars of independence became the foundational moments of their heroic birth.

## Brazilian Independence

Although the movement for independence in Brazil was roughly contemporaneous with those in Spanish America, and many of the causes were similar, independence there was achieved by a very different process. By the end of the 18th century, Brazil had grown in population and economic importance. The growth of European demand for colonial products, such as sugar, cotton, and cacao, contributed to that growth and to the increase in slave imports to the

**FIGURE 30.2** Simon Bolívar (1783–1830) led the struggle for political independence in northern South America. Son of a wealthy Creole family, he became an ardent proponent of independence and a firm believer in the republican form of government. On his deathbed, Bolívar asked his closest aide to burn all of his letters and other writings. Knowing how valuable these papers would be to future historians, the aide disobeyed the order.

FIGURE 30.3 For more than a decade, insurgent armies formed in various parts of Spanish America to try to throw off the control of Spain. Often led by Creole officers and manned by soldiers from all levels of society, these armies became effective fighting forces. In the Rio de la Plata, José de San Martín (pictured right) emerged as an effective commander. After his victory there in 1816, he led an army of 4000 men across the Andes to aid the Chilean insurgents against Spain. He is depicted here in that epic march.

colony. Although Brazilian planters, merchants, and miners sometimes longed for more open trade and fewer taxes, they feared that any upsetting of the political system might lead to a social revolution or a Haitian-style general slave uprising. Thus, incipient movements for independence in Minas Gerais in 1788 and Bahia in 1798 were unsuccessful. As one official said, "Men established in goods and property were unwilling to risk political change."

The Napoleonic invasions provoked an outcome in Portugal different from that in Spain. When in 1807 French troops invaded Portugal, the whole Portuguese royal family and court fled the country and, under the protection of British ships, sailed to Brazil. Rio de Janeiro became the capital of the Portuguese Empire. Brazil was raised to equal status with Portugal, and all the functions of royal government were set up in the colony. As a partial concession to England and to colonial interests, the ports of Brazil were opened to world commerce, thus satisfying one of the main desires of the Brazilian elites. Unlike Spanish America, where the Napoleonic invasions provoked a crisis of authority and led Spanish Americans to consider ruling in their own name, in Brazil the transfer of the court brought royal government closer and reinforced the colonial relationship.

Until 1820, the Portuguese king, Dom **João VI,** lived in Brazil and ruled his empire from there. Rio de Janeiro was transformed into an imperial city with a public library, botanical gardens, and other improvements. Printing presses began to operate in the colony for the first time, schools were created, and commerce, especially with England, boomed in the newly opened ports. The arrival of many Portuguese bureaucrats and nobles with the court created jealousy and resentment, however. Still, during this period Brazil was transformed into the seat of empire, a fact not lost on its most prominent citizens.

Matters changed drastically in 1820 when, after the defeat of Napoleon in Europe and a liberal revolution in Portugal, the king was recalled and a parliament convoked. João VI, realizing that his return was inevitable, left his young son Pedro as regent, warning him that if independence had to come, he should lead the movement. Although Brazilians were allowed representation at the Portuguese parliament, it became clear that Brazil's new status was doomed and that it would be recolonized. After demands that the prince regent also return to Europe, Pedro refused, and in September 1822 he declared Brazilian independence. He became Dom **Pedro I,** constitutional emperor of Brazil. Fighting against Portuguese troops lasted a year, but Brazil avoided the long wars of Spanish America. Brazil's independence did not upset the existing social organization based on slavery, nor did it radically change the political structure. With the brief exception of Mexico, all of the former Spanish American colonies became republics, but Brazil became a monarchy under a member of the Portuguese ruling house.

## New Nations Confront Old and New Problems

- **The new nations confronted difficult problems: social inequalities, political representation, the role of the church, and regionalism. These problems led to political fragmentation. Leaders with strong personal followings, representing various interests and their own ambitions, rose to prominence.**

By 1830 the former Spanish and Portuguese colonies had become independent nations. The roughly 20 million inhabitants of these nations looked hopefully to the future. Many of the leaders of independence had shared ideals: representative government, careers open to talent, freedom of commerce and trade, the right to private property, and a belief in the individual as the basis of society. There was a general belief that the new nations should be sovereign and independent states, large enough to be economically viable and integrated by a common set of laws.

On the issue of freedom of religion and the position of the church, however, there was less agreement. Roman Catholicism had been the state religion and the only one allowed by the Spanish crown. While most leaders attempted to maintain Catholicism as the official religion of the new states, some tried to end the exclusion of other faiths. The defense of the church became a rallying cry for the conservative forces.

The ideals of the early leaders of independence often were egalitarian. Bolívar had received aid from Haiti and had promised in return to abolish slavery in the areas he liberated. By 1854 slavery had been abolished everywhere except Spain's remaining colonies, Cuba and Puerto Rico, as well as in Brazil; all were places where the economy was profoundly based on it. Despite early promises, an end to American Indian tribute and taxes on people of mixed origin came much more slowly, because the new nations still needed the revenue such policies produced. Egalitarian sentiments often were tempered by fears that the mass of the population was unprepared for self-rule and democracy. Early constitutions attempted to balance order and popular representation by imposing property or literacy restrictions on voters. Invariably, voting rights were reserved for men. Women were still disenfranchised and usually were not allowed to hold public office. The Creole elite's lack of trust of the popular classes was based on the fact that in many places the masses had not demonstrated a clear preference for the new regimes and had sometimes fought in royalist armies mobilized by traditional loyalties and regional interests.

Although some mestizos had risen to leadership roles in the wars of independence, the old color distinctions did not disappear easily. In Mexico, Guatemala, and the Andean nations, the large Indian population remained mostly outside national political life. The mass of the Latin American population—American Indians and people of mixed origins—waited to see what was to come, and they were suspicious of the new political elite, who were often drawn from the old colonial aristocracy but were also joined by a new commercial and urban bourgeoisie.

### Political Fragmentation

The new Latin American nations can be grouped into regional blocks (Map 30.1). Some of the early leaders for independence had dreamed of creating a unified nation in some form, but regional rivalries, economic competition, and political divisions soon made that hope impossible. Mexico emerged as a short-lived monarchy until a republic was proclaimed in 1823, but its government remained unstable until the 1860s because of military coups, financial failures, foreign intervention, and political turmoil. Central America broke away from the Mexican monarchy and formed a union, but regional antagonisms and resentment of Guatemala, the largest nation in the region, eventually led to dissolution of the union in 1838. Spain's Caribbean colonies, Cuba and Puerto Rico, suppressed early movements for independence and remained outwardly loyal. The Dominican Republic was occupied by its neighbor Haiti, and after resisting its neighbor as well as France and Spain, it finally gained independence in 1844.

Latin Americans Obtain Independence

In South America, the old colonial viceroyalty of New Granada became the basis for Gran Colombia, the large new state created by Bolívar that included modern Ecuador, Colombia, Panama, and Venezuela. The union, made possible to some extent by Bolívar's per-

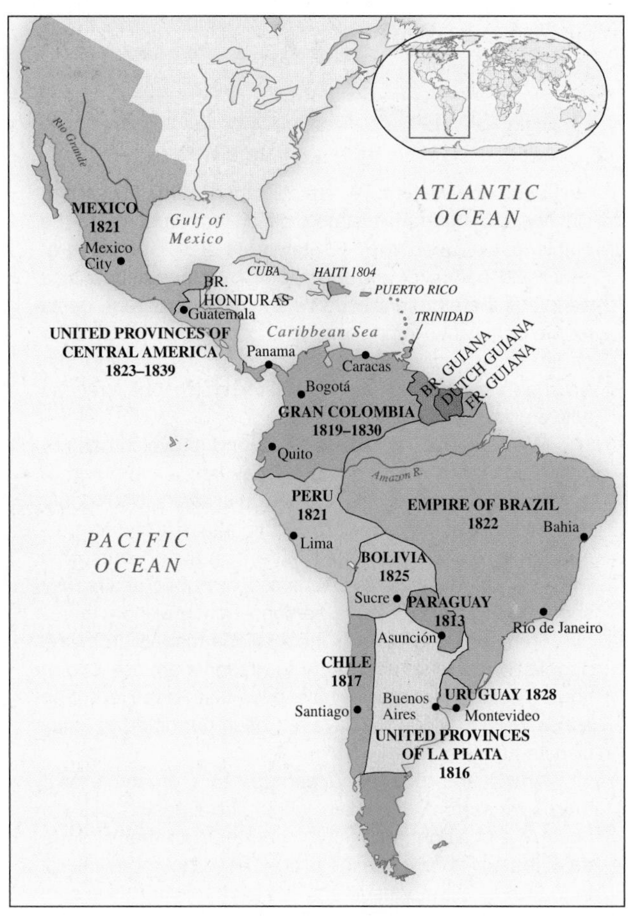


MAP 30.1 Independent States of Latin America in 1830

sonal reputation and leadership, disintegrated as his own standing declined, and it ended in 1830, the year of his death. In the south, the viceroyalty of the Rio de la Plata served as the basis for a state that the peoples of Argentina hoped to lead. Other parts of the region resisted. Paraguay declared and maintained its autonomy under a series of dictators. Modern Uruguay was formed by a revolution for independence against the dominant power of its large neighbors, Argentina and Brazil. It became an independent buffer between those two nations in 1828. The Andean nations of Peru and Bolivia, with their large Indian populations and conservative colonial aristocracies, flirted with union from 1829 to 1839 under the mestizo general **Andrés Santa Cruz,** but once again regional rivalries and the fears of their neighbors undermined the effort. Finally, Chile, somewhat isolated and blessed by the opening of trade in the Pacific, followed its own political course in a fairly stable fashion.

Most attempts at consolidation and union failed. Enormous geographic barriers and great distances separated nations and even regions within nations. Roads were poor and transportation rudimentary. Geography, regional interests, and political divisions were too strong to overcome. The mass of the population remained outside the political process. The problems of national integration were daunting. What is striking is not that Spanish America became 18 separate nations but that it did not separate into even more.

## Caudillos, Politics, and the Church

The problems confronting the new nations were many. More than a decade of warfare in places such as Venezuela, Colombia, and Mexico had disrupted the economies and devastated wide areas. The mobilization of large armies whose loyalty to regional commanders was often based on their personal qualities, rather than their rank or politics, led to the rise of **caudillos,** independent leaders who dominated local areas by force and sometimes seized the national government itself. In times of intense division between civilian politicians, a powerful regional army commander became the arbiter of power, and thus the army sometimes made and unmade governments. Keeping the army in the barracks became a preoccupation of governments, and the amount of money spent on the military far exceeded the needs. The military had become important in the 18th century as Spain tried to shore up the defense of its empire, but it became a preserver of order.

Military commanders and regional or national caudillos usually were interested in power for their own sake, but they could represent or mobilize different groups in society. Many often defended the interests of regional elites, usually landowners, but others were populists who mobilized and claimed to speak for American Indians, peasants, and the poor and sometimes received their unquestioning support. A few, such as the conservative Rafael Carrera, who ruled Guatemala from 1839 to 1865, sincerely took the interest of the American Indian majority to heart, but other personalist leaders disregarded the normal workings of an open political system and the rule of law.

Other common issues confronted many of the new nations. Most political leaders were agreed on the republic as the basic form of government, but they could not agree on what kind of republic. A struggle often developed between **centralists,** who wanted to create strong, centralized national governments with broad powers, and **federalists,** who wanted tax and commercial policies to be set by regional governments. Other tensions developed between liberals and conservatives. Liberals stressed the rights of the individual and attacked the corporate (based on membership in a group or organization) structure of colonial society. They dreamed of a secular society and looked to the United States and France as models. Often they wanted a decentralized, or federalist, form of government. Conservatives usually believed in a strong centralized state, and they often wanted to

DOCUMENT

## Confronting the Hispanic Heritage: From Independence to Consolidation

Simon Bolívar (1783–1830), "The Liberator," was a man of determination and perception. His campaigns for independence were defeated on several occasions, yet he did not despair. In 1815, while in exile on the island of Jamaica, he penned a letter to a newspaper that gave his evaluation of Latin America's situation and his vision for the future for its various parts. He advocated a republican form of government and rejected monarchy, but he warned against federalism and against popular democracies that might lead to dictatorships: "As long as our countrymen do not acquire the abilities and political virtues that distinguish our brothers to the north, wholly popular systems, far from working to our advantage, will, I greatly fear, bring about our downfall." Spain had left America unprepared, and in this letter Bolívar summarized many of the complaints of Latin Americans against Spanish rule and underlined the difficulty of the tasks of liberation—political, social, and economic. The famous "Letter of Jamaica" is one of the most candid writings by a leader of Latin American independence. The following excerpts suggest its tone and content.

### Bolívar's "Jamaica Letter" (1815)

> We are a young people. We inhabit a world apart, separated by broad seas. We are young in the ways of almost all the arts and sciences, although, in a certain manner, we are old in the ways of civilized society. I look upon the present state of America as similar to that of Rome after its fall. Each part of Rome adopted a political system conforming to its interest and situation or was led by the individual ambitions of certain chiefs, dynasties, or associations. But this important difference exists: those dispersed parts later reestablished their ancient nations, subject to the changes imposed by circumstances or extent. But we scarcely retain a vestige of what once was; we are, moreover, neither Indian nor European, but a species midway between the legitimate proprietors of this country and the Spanish usurpers. In short, although Americans by birth we derive our rights from Europe, and we have to assert these rights against the rights of the natives, and at the same time we must defend ourselves against the invaders. This places us in a most extraordinary and involved situation. . . .
>
> The role of the inhabitants of the American hemisphere has for centuries been purely passive. Politically they were nonexistent. We are still in a position lower than slavery, and therefore it is more difficult for us to rise to the enjoyment of freedom. . . . States are slaves because of either the nature or the misuse of their constitutions; a people is therefore enslaved when the government, by its nature or its vices infringes on and usurps the rights of the citizen or subject. Applying these principles, we find that America was denied not only its freedom but even an active and effective tyranny. . . .
>
> We have been harassed by a conduct which has not only deprived us of our rights but has kept us in a sort of permanent infancy with regard to public affairs. If we could have at least managed our domestic affairs and our internal administration, we could have acquainted ourselves with the processes and mechanics of public affairs. We should also have enjoyed a personal consideration, thereby commanding a certain unconscious respect from the people, which is so necessary to preserve amidst revolutions. That is why I say we have even been deprived of an active tyranny, since we have not been permitted to exercise its functions.
>
> Americans today, and perhaps to a greater extent than ever before, who live within the Spanish system occupy a position in society no better than that of serfs destined to labor, or at best they have no more status than that of mere consumers. Yet even this status is surrounded with galling restrictions, such as being forbidden to grow European crops, or to store products which are royal monopolies, or to establish factories of a type the Peninsula (Spain) itself does not possess. To this add the privileges, even in articles of prime necessity, and the barriers between the American provinces, designed to prevent all exchange of trade, traffic, and understanding. In short, do you wish to know what our future held?—simply the cultivation of the fields of indigo, grain, coffee, sugar cane, cacao, and cotton; cattle raising on the broad plains, hunting wild game in the jungles; digging in the earth to mine its gold—but even these limitations could never satisfy the greed of Spain. So negative was our existence that I can find nothing comparable in any other civilized society.

By mid-century, Latin American political leaders were advocating "progress" and attempting to bring Latin America closer to the norms of life set by Europe. For liberals such as Argentine soldier, statesman, and author Domingo F. Sarmiento (1811–1888), his nation's task was to overcome the "barbarism" of rural life and implant the "civilization" of the Europeanized cities. Sarmiento saw in the bands of mounted rural workers, or *gauchos,* and their caudillo leaders an anachronistic way of life that held the nation back. His comparison of the gauchos to the Berbers of north Africa demonstrates the ancient hostility of "civilized" urban-dwellers to the nomadic way of life. In a way, Sarmiento saw the dictatorship of Juan Manuel de Rosas as a result of the persistence of the gauchos and the manipulation of the lower classes—a sort of living example of what Bolívar had warned against. The following excerpt from Sarmiento's classic *Life in the Argentine Republic in the Days of the Tyrants, or Civilization and Barbarism* (1868) demonstrates his admiration for European culture, including that of Spain, and his desire to model his nation on it. That such a program might involve economic and cultural dependency did not concern Sarmiento and others like him.

## The Search for Progress

Before 1810 two distinct, rival, and incompatible forms of society, two differing kinds of civilization existed in the Argentine Republic: one being Spanish, European, and cultivated, the other barbarous, American, and almost wholly of native growth. The revolution which occurred in the cities acted only as the cause, the impulse, which set these two distinct forms of national existence face to face, and gave occasion for a contest between them, to be ended, after lasting many years, by the absorption of one into the other.

I have pointed out the normal form of association, or want of association, of the country people, a form worse a thousand times, than that of a nomad tribe. I have described the artificial associations formed in idleness, and the sources of fame among the gauchos—bravery, daring, violence and opposition to regular law, to the civil law, that is, of the city. These phenomena of social organization existed in 1810, and still exist, modified in many points, slowly changing in others, and yet untouched in several more. These foci about which were gathered the brave, ignorant, free, and unemployed peasantry, were found by thousands through the country. The revolution of 1810 carried everywhere commotion and the sound of arms. Public life, previously wanting in this Arabo-Roman society, made its appearance in all the taverns, and the revolutionary movement finally brought about provincial, warlike associations, called montoneras [mounted gaucho guerrilla bands], legitimate offspring of the tavern and the field, hostile to the city and to the army of revolutionary patriots. As events succeed each other, we shall see the provincial montoneras headed by their chiefs; the final triumph, in Facundo Quiroga [a caudillo leader], of the country over the cities throughout the land; and by their subjugation in spirit, government, and civilization, the final formation of the central consolidated despotic government of the landed proprietor, Don Juan Manuel de Rosas, who applied the knife of the gaucho to the culture of Buenos Aires, and destroyed the work of centuries—of civilization, law, and liberty. . . .

They [revolutions for independence] were the same throughout America, and sprang from the same source, namely, the progress of European ideas. South America pursued that course because all other nations were pursuing it. Books, events, and the impulses given by these, induced South America to take part in the movement imparted to France by North American demands for liberty, and to Spain by her own and French writers. But what my object requires me to notice is that the revolution—except in its external symbolic independence of the king—was interesting and intelligible only to the Argentine cities, but foreign and unmeaning to the rural districts. Books, ideas, municipal spirit, courts, laws, statues, education, all points of contact and union existing between us and the people of Europe, were to be found in the cities, where there was a basis of organization, incomplete and comparatively evil, perhaps, for the very reason it was incomplete, and had not attained the elevation which it felt itself capable of reaching, but it entered into the revolution with enthusiasm. Outside the cities, the revolution was a problematical affair, and [in] so far [as] shaking off the king's authority was shaking off judicial authority, it was acceptable. The pastoral districts could only regard the question from this point of view. Liberty, responsibility of power, and all the questions that the revolution was to solve, were foreign to their mode of life and to their needs. But they derived this advantage from the revolution, that it tended to confer an object and an occupation upon the excess of vital force, the presence of which among them has been pointed out, and was to add a broader base of union than that to which throughout the country districts the men daily resorted.

The Argentine Revolutionary War was twofold: first, a civilized warfare of the cities against Spain; second, a war against the cities on the part of the country chieftains with the view of shaking off all political subjugation and satisfying their hatred of civilization. The cities overcame the Spaniards, and were in their turn overcome by the country districts. This is the explanation of the Argentine Revolution, the first shot of which fired in 1810, and the last is still to be heard.

---

**Questions** To what extent did the leaders of independence see their problems as a result of their Hispanic heritage? What would have been the reaction of the mass of the population to Sarmiento's idea of progress? Were the leaders naive about Latin America's possibilities for political democracy?

maintain aspects of colonial society. They believed that a structure in which corporate groups (such as the American Indians), artisan guilds, or institutions (such as the church) provided the most equitable basis of social action should be recognized in law. To the conservatives, society was not based on open competition and individualism but was organic: each group was linked to the others like parts of a body whose health depended on the proper functioning of each part. Not all conservatives resisted change, and some—such as Mexican intellectual and politician Lucas Alamán—were among the most enlightened leaders in terms of economic and commercial reforms, but as a group the conservatives were skeptical of secularism and individualism and strove to keep the Catholic Iberian heritage alive.

The role of the church became a crucial issue in politics. It divided conservatives from the more secular liberals. In Mexico, for example, the church had played a major role in education, the economy, and politics. Few questioned its dogma, but liberals tried to limit its role in civil life. The church fought back with the aid of its pro-clerical supporters and with the power of the papacy, which until the 1840s refused to fill vacant positions in the hierarchy or to cooperate with the new governments.

Political parties, often calling themselves Liberal or Conservative, sprang up throughout Latin America. They struggled for power and tried to impose their vision of the future on society. However, their leaders usually were drawn from the same social class of landowners and urban bourgeoisie, with little to differentiate them except their position in the church or on the question of federalism versus centralization. The general population might be mobilized by the force and personality of a particular leader such as **Juan Manuel de Rosas** in Argentina or **Antonio López de Santa Anna** in Mexico, but political ideology rarely was an issue for most of the population.

The result was political turmoil and insecurity in much of Latin America in the first 50 years after independence. Presidents came and went quickly. Written constitutions, which both liberals and conservatives thought were a positive thing, were often short-lived and were overturned with a change in government because the margin for interpretation of the constitution was slight. Great efforts were made to make constitutions precise, specific, and definitive, but this resulted in an attempt to change them each time there was a change in government. Some nations avoided the worst aspects of instability. After enacting a constitution in 1833 that gave the president broad powers, Chile established a functioning political system that allowed compromise. Brazil, with its monarchical rule, despite a period of turmoil from 1832 to 1850, was able to maintain a political system of compromise, although it was dominated by the conservatives, who were favored by the emperor. Its 1824 constitution remained in force until 1889.

It is fair to say that in much of Latin America the basic questions of government and society remained unresolved after independence. Some observers attributed these problems to personalism, a lack of civic responsibility, and other defects in the "Latin" character. Nevertheless, the parallel experience of later emerging nations in the 20th century suggests that these problems were typical of former colonial dependencies searching for order and economic security in a world in which their options were constrained by their own potential and by external conditions.

## Latin American Economies and World Markets, 1820–1870

■ **Latin American economies stagnated in the aftermath of the wars of independence. Dependence on exports created neocolonial ties. Toward mid-century, a new prosperity began as some nations found new markets for their exports. The revenues allowed liberal governments to advocate a variety of social and political changes. Mexico, Argentina, and Brazil illustrate the general pattern from political instability or economic stagnation to the emergence of stable liberal regimes by the end of the century.**

The former colonies of Spain and Portugal now entered the world of diplomatic relations and international commerce. The new nations sought diplomatic recognition and security. In the 1820s, while Europe was undergoing the post-Napoleonic conservative reaction and monarchies were being restored, various plans to help Spain recolonize Latin America were put forward. Great Britain generally opposed those ideas, and because Great Britain was the dominant power at sea, its recognition of Latin American sovereignty was crucial. Moreover, the newly independent United States also felt an affinity and sympathy for the new nations to the south. The **Monroe Doctrine** of 1823 stated clearly that any attempt by a European power to colonize in the Americas would be considered an unfriendly act by the United States. The United States at the time probably could have done little to prevent such actions, but Britain could, and its support of Latin American independence provided needed protection.

There was a price for this support. During the turmoil of the 1820s, British foreign minister Lord Canning had once said, "Spanish America is free and if we do not mismanage our affairs sadly, she is English." He was referring to the broad economic and commercial advantages that the new nations offered. British commerce had legally penetrated the area in the 18th century, and Britain had profited from illegal trade as well. Now it could afford to offer its diplomatic recognition in exchange for the freedom to trade with the new nations. Although little capital had been invested directly in Latin America before 1850, Latin American governments now turned to foreign governments and banks for loans. Meanwhile, Britain became a major consumer of Latin American products. In return Britain sold about £5 million worth of manufactured goods to the new nations each year, about half of which went to Brazil, where British merchants were especially strong. Although some historians argue that this was a small portion of Britain's overseas trade, it was crucial for Latin America. In some ways, Britain replaced Spain as a dominant economic force over the area in a sort of neocolonial commercial system. Although other nations, notably France and the United States, also traded with Latin America, Britain remained predominant before 1860.

Open ports and the influx of foreign goods, often of better quality and cheaper than local products, benefited the port cities that controlled customhouses and the large landowners whose hides, sugar, and other products were exported. But these policies tended to damage local industries or regions that had specialized in producing for internal markets. Latin America became increasingly dependent on foreign markets and foreign imports and thereby reinforced the old colonial economic heritage in which land was the basis of wealth and prestige.

## Mid-Century Stagnation

From about 1820 to 1850, the economy of Latin America was stagnant. Wars had destroyed many industries, roads were poor, and much money was still tied up in land. Only Cuba, with its booming sugar economy, expanded, but Cuba was still a colony of Spain. After 1850, however, this situation began to change as the expansion of the European economy created new demands for Latin American products. Coffee in Brazil, hides and beef in Argentina, and minerals and grains in Chile provided the basis of growth and allowed some Latin American governments to address social issues. For example, Peru exploited enormous **guano** (bird droppings) deposits on islands off its coast. Between 1850 and 1880, exports of this fertilizer earned Peru more than £10 million, and this income allowed the government to end American Indian tribute and to abolish slavery by compensating the owners.

Latin American cities began to grow and provide good internal markets, and the introduction of steamships and railroads began to overcome the old problems of transportation. By the 1840s, steamship lines improved communication within countries and opened up new possibilities for international commerce, and by the 1860s, railroads like the one in Figure 30.4 were being built, usually to link export-producing regions to the ports. Landed wealth and exports continued to characterize the economies of the region, as they had in the colonial era. As the levels of exports and the governments' dependence on them increased, Latin America's vulnerability to the vagaries of the world economy increased as well.

Without detailing all the complex changes within the Latin American nations during the 19th century, we can discern a few general patterns. After the turmoil of independence, liberal reformers tried to institute a series of programs in the 1820s and 1830s intended to break the patterns of the colonial heritage and to follow the main social and economic trends of western Europe. These ideas often were imposed on societies and economies unprepared for drastic change, especially because the strength of opposing institutions, such as the church and the army, remained intact. By the 1840s, conservatives had returned to power in many places to slow or stop the reform measures. Some of them tried to speak for the lower classes or the American Indians, who wanted to see the paternal aspects of the old colonial state reimposed to protect them from the reforms of the liberals. In some ways, an alliance between the landowners and the peasantry emerged in opposition to the changes suggested by the middle-class, urban modernizers.

## Economic Resurgence and Liberal Politics

By the last quarter of the century, as the world economy entered a phase of rapid expansion, there was a shift in attitude and possibilities in Latin America. Liberals returned to power in many places in Latin America and initiated a series of changes that began to transform their nations. The ideological basis of the new liberal surge was also changing. Based on the ideas of **positivism** of the French philosopher **Auguste Comte,** who stressed observation and a scientific approach to the problems of society, Latin American politicians and intellectuals found a guiding set of principles and a justification of their quest for political stability and economic growth.

This shift was caused in large part by the general economic expansion of the second industrial revolution and the age of imperialism. The application of science to industry created new demands for Latin American products, such as copper and rubber, to accompany the increasing demand for its consumer products such as wheat, sugar, and coffee. The population of Latin

FIGURE 30.4 The drive for progress made Latin American nations eager to accept foreign investment. Railroads were needed to bring export goods to seaports so that they could be carried to foreign markets. They were built principally to serve the needs of foreign capital. Railroad workers, however, often proved to be the most radical segment of the Latin American workforce.

America doubled to more than 43 million inhabitants in the 60 years between 1820 and 1880. After 1850, economies grew rapidly; the timing varied greatly, but the expansion of exports in places such as Colombia, Argentina, and Brazil stimulated prosperity for some and a general belief in the advantages of the liberal programs. The desire to participate in the capitalist expansion of the Western economy dominated the thinking of Latin American leaders. Foreign entrepreneurs and bankers joined hands with philosophical liberals, landowners, and urban merchants in Latin America to back the liberal programs, which now became possible because of the increased revenues generated by exports.

The leaders of the post-1860 governments were a new generation of politicians who had matured during the chaotic years of postindependence politics. Their inspiration came from England, France, and the United States. They were firm believers in progress, education, and free competition within a secular society, but they were sometimes distrustful of the mass of their own people, who seemed to represent an ancient "barbarism" in contrast to the "civilization" of progress. That distrust and their sometimes insensitive application of foreign models to a very different reality in their own countries—what one Brazilian author has called "ideas out of place"—prevented many from achieving the progress they so ardently desired.

Economic growth and progress were costly. Responding to international demand, landowners increased their holdings, often aided by the governments they controlled or influenced. Peasant lands were expropriated in Chile, Peru, and Bolivia; small farmers were displaced in Brazil and Costa Rica; church lands were seized in Mexico. Labor was needed. Immigrants from Europe flooded into Argentina and Brazil, and in other countries new forms of tenancy, peonage, and disguised servitude developed.

## Mexico: Instability and Foreign Intervention

After the short monarchical experiment, a Mexican republic was established. Its constitution of 1824, based on the examples of France, the United States, and Spain, was a federalist document that guaranteed basic civil rights. Nevertheless, this constitution did not address the nation's continuing social problems and needs: the maldistribution of land, the status of the American Indians, the problems of education, and the situation of vast numbers of poor people among the approximately 7 million people in Mexico, the most populous of the new nations. Politics soon

The Plan of Iguala

From Monarchs to Masons: Mexico's Changing Political Arena

became a complicated struggle between the conservative centralists and the liberal federalists and was made even more complicated by jockeying for advantage by commercial agents of Great Britain and the United States. For a short period from 1832 to 1835, the liberals were in control and tried to institute a series of sweeping social and economic reforms, but their attack on the church led to violent reaction and the assumption of power by General Antonio López de Santa Anna.

The mercurial Santa Anna remained until his death the maker of Mexican politics. He was a typical caudillo, a personalist, autocratic leader. But Mexico's instability resulted not only from his personality. Santa Anna was merely the symptom of deeper problems.

Mexico's instability and financial difficulties made it a target for various foreign interventions. Even more threatening to the nation, Anglo-American settlers were occupying Texas, the vast area of Mexico's northern frontier. They brought their language, customs, and religion despite restrictions on the latter. Although the Texans at first sought more autonomy as federalists within the Mexican nation, as had been done in Yucatan and other Mexican provinces, ethnic and religious differences as well as Santa Anna's attempts to suppress the Texans in 1836 led to widespread fighting and the declaration of Texan independence. Santa Anna, captured for a while by the Texans, returned to dominate Mexican politics, but the question of Texas festered and became acute when in 1845 the United States, with its eye on California and **manifest destiny**—a belief that it was destined to rule the continent from coast to coast—voted to annex Texas.

The result was war. A border dispute and the breakdown of negotiations over California led to hostilities in 1846. Santa Anna, who had been in exile, returned to lead the Mexican forces, but U.S. troops seized California, penetrated northern Mexico, and eventually occupied the Mexican capital. Mexico was forced to sign the disadvantageous **Treaty of Guadalupe-Hidalgo** (1848), in which the United States acquired about one-half of Mexico's national territory but less than 5 percent of its population. The **Mexican-American War** and the treaty left a bitter legacy of distrust of the northern neighbor, not only in Mexico but throughout the region. For Mexico there was also a serious loss of economic potential, but the heroic battle against the better-equipped Americans produced a sense of nationalism and a desire to confront the nation's serious internal problems, which also bore some responsibility for the war and the defeat.

Politics could not revert to the prewar situation. Santa Anna did return to office for a while, more mercurial and despotic than ever, but now he was opposed by a new generation of liberals: intellectuals, lawyers, and some rural leaders, many of them from middle-class backgrounds, some of them mestizos and even a few American Indians. Perhaps the most prominent of them was **Benito Juárez** (1806–1872), a Zapotec Indian of humble origins who had received a legal education and eventually become the governor of his state (Figure 30.5). He shared the liberal vision of a secular society based on the rule of law in which the old privileges of the church and the army would be eliminated as a way of promoting economic change and growth.

The liberal revolt, called **La Reforma,** began in 1854 and triumphed within a year. In a series of laws integrated into a new constitution in 1857, the liberals set the basis for their vision of society. Military and clerical privileges were curtailed, and church property was placed on sale. Indian communal lands also were restricted, and the government forced the sale of these lands to individuals—to American Indians, it was hoped. The goal of these programs was to create a nation of small independent farmers. However, speculators or big landowners often bought up the lands, and the result was that the peasants and American Indians lost what land they had. By 1910 about half of Mexico's rural population was landless. Good intentions had brought disastrous results.

The liberal program produced the expected conservative reaction. The church threatened to excommunicate those who upheld the new constitution. Civil war erupted, and in reaction Juárez, now president, pushed forward even more radical measures. Losing ground in the war, the conservatives turned to Europe and convinced Napoleon III of France to intervene. Attracted by possible economic advantage, dreams of empire, and a desire to please Catholics in France, Napoleon III justified French intervention by claims of a shared "Latin" culture (this was the origin of the term *Latin America*). French forces landed in 1862 and soon took the capital. At the urging of the French, **Maximilian von Habsburg,** an Austrian archduke, was convinced to take the throne of Mexico. Well-intentioned but ineffective, Emperor Maximilian tried to get the support of Juárez and the liberals and even kept many of the laws of the Reforma in place, to the dismay of his conservative supporters. But Juárez absolutely rejected the idea of a foreign prince ruling Mexico. French troops and the United States' preoccupation with its own Civil War allowed Emperor Maximilian and his Empress Carlota to rule. When French troops were withdrawn, the regime crumbled. It was then, in 1867, that Maximilian and his loyal generals were captured and executed (as described in the chapter opening). Maximilian's death shocked Europeans. Juárez had sent a message to Europe: "hands off Mexico."

Juárez returned to office, but his administration was increasingly autocratic—a reality that he felt was unavoidable after so long a period of instability. By his

FIGURE 30.5 Benito Juárez, a Zapotec Indian from southern Mexico, rose to the presidency and began a series of sweeping reforms. His uncompromising resistance to foreign intervention and monarchy made him a symbol of Mexican sovereignty and independence. Juárez's stature as a nationalist and a man of law is portrayed in a mural by Mexican artist Diego Rivera.

death in 1872, the force of his personality, his concern for the poor, and his nationalist position against foreign intervention had identified liberalism with nationalism in Mexico and made Juárez a symbol of the nation. By 1880 Mexico was poised on the edge of a period of strong central government and relative political stability. One of Juárez's generals, Porfirio Díaz, became president and then virtual dictator. His government witnessed rapid economic growth, penetration of the economy by foreign capital, the expansion of the large landed estates, political repression, and eventually a revolution.

## Argentina: The Port and the Nation

Whereas Mexico and its silver had been the core of Spain's empire in America, the rolling plains, or pampas, of the Rio de la Plata in southern South America had been a colonial backwater until the 18th century, when direct trade began to stimulate its economy. The port of Buenos Aires and its merchants dominated the Rio de la Plata, but the other areas of the region had their own interests and resented the power and growth of the port city and its surrounding countryside. The United Provinces of the Rio de la Plata, which declared their independence in 1816, soon split apart, and local caudillos, able to call on the support of gauchos, dominated each region. In Buenos Aires, the liberals gained control in the 1820s and instituted a series of broad reforms in education, finance, agriculture, and immigration. These included a program of public land sales, which stimulated the growth of cattle ranches and the power of the rancher class.

As in Mexico, liberal reforms including freedom of religion produced a similar negative reaction from conservatives and the church. But the liberals' main sin was centralism, a desire to create a strong national government. Centralists (called *unitarians* in the Argentine context) provoked the reaction of the federalists, who by 1831 had taken power under Juan Manuel de Rosas, who commanded the loyalty of the gaucho employees of the ranchers.

Under Rosas, the federalist program of a weak central government and local autonomy was instituted, but Rosas's federalism favored the ranchers of the Buenos Aires province and the merchants of the great

DOCUMENT

Symbolism and Contested Identities in Argentina

port. He campaigned against the American Indians to the south to open new lands to the cattle ranchers. Exports of hides and salted meat increased, but the revenues collected at the port were not shared with the other provinces. Although popular with the gauchos and the urban poor and remembered today as a nationalist who resisted British and French economic pressure, Rosas proved to be a despotic leader, crushing his opponents and forcing people to display his slogan: "Death to the savage, filthy unitarians." His brand of populist, authoritarian, personalist politics drove liberal opponents into exile, where they plotted his overthrow. Eventually, the liberal exiles joined forces with the caudillos jealous of the advantages Rosas's brand of federalism had given Buenos Aires province. In 1852 this coalition defeated Rosas and drove him from power.

There followed a confused decade of rival governments because the questions of federalism and the role of Buenos Aires within the nation remained unresolved. A new constitution was issued in 1853 under the influence of Juan Bautista Alberdi, an able and progressive journalist who was also a strong believer in the need to encourage immigration. This constitution incorporated the programs of the federalists but guaranteed national unity through the power of the presidency over the provincial governors. By 1862, after considerable fighting, a compromise was worked out and the new, unified nation, now called the **Argentine Republic,** entered into a period of prosperity and growth under a series of liberal presidents whose programs paralleled the Reforma in Mexico. The age of the liberals was now in full swing.

Between 1862 and 1890, able and intelligent presidents like **Domingo F. Sarmiento** (1811–1888) initiated a wide series of political reforms and economic measures designed to bring progress to Argentina. Sarmiento was an archetype of the liberal reformers of the mid-century. A great admirer of England and the United States, a firm believer in the value of education, and an ardent supporter of progress, Sarmiento had been a constant opponent of Rosas and had been driven into exile. During that time, he wrote *Facundo,* a critique of the caudillo politics of the region, in which the "barbarism" of the gauchos and their leaders was contrasted to the "civilization" of the liberal reformers. (See the Document feature in this chapter.)

Now in power, Sarmiento and the other liberal leaders were able to put their programs into practice. They were aided by several factors. Political stability made investment more attractive to foreign banks and merchants. The expansion of the Argentine economy, especially exports of beef, hides, and wool, created the basis for prosperity. Foreign trade in 1890 was five times as great as it had been in 1860. The population tripled to more than 3 million as the agricultural expansion, high wages, and opportunities for mobility attracted large numbers of European immigrants. Buenos Aires became a great, sprawling metropolis. With increased revenues, the government could initiate reforms in education, transportation, and other areas, often turning to foreign models and foreign investors. There was also an increased feeling of national unity. A long and bloody war waged by Argentina, Brazil, and Uruguay against their neighbor Paraguay from 1865 to 1870 created a sense of unity and national pride.

That sense was also heightened by the final defeat of the Indians south of Buenos Aires by 1880 as more land was opened to ranching and agriculture. At about the same time as in the United States, the railroad, the telegraph, and the repeating rifle brought an end to the Indians' resistance and opened their lands to settlement. The American Indians, who were pushed far to the south, and the gauchos, whose way of life was displaced by the tide of immigrants, received little sympathy from the liberal government. By 1890, Argentina seemed to represent the achievement of a liberal program for Latin America.

## The Brazilian Empire

It was sometimes said that despite its monarchical form, Brazil was the only functioning republic in South America in the 19th century. At first glance it seemed that Brazil avoided much of the political instability and turmoil found elsewhere in the continent and that through the mediation of the emperor a political compromise was worked out. However, problems and patterns similar to those in Spanish America lay beneath that facade. The transition to nationhood was smooth, and thus the basic foundations of Brazilian society—slavery, large landholdings, and an export economy—remained securely in place, reinforced by a new Brazilian nobility created for the new empire.

Brazilian independence had been declared in 1822, and by 1824 a liberal constitution had been issued by Dom Pedro I, the young Brazilian monarch, although not without resistance from those who wanted a republic or at least a very weak constitutional monarchy. But Dom Pedro I was an autocrat. In 1831 he was forced to abdicate in favor of his young son, Pedro (later to become Dom Pedro II), but the boy was too young to rule, and a series of regents directed the country in his name. What followed was an experiment in republican government, although the facade of monarchy was maintained.

The next decade was as tumultuous as any in Spanish America. The conflict between liberalism and conservatism was complicated by the existence of monarchist and antimonarchist factions in Brazil. A series of regional revolts erupted, some of which took on aspects of social wars as people of all classes were mobilized in the fighting. The army suppressed these movements. By 1840, however, the politicians were willing to see the young Dom Pedro II begin to rule in his own name.

Meanwhile, Brazil had been undergoing an economic transformation brought about by a new export crop: coffee. Coffee provided a new basis for agricultural expansion in southern Brazil. In the provinces of Rio de Janeiro and then São Paulo, coffee estates, or **fazendas,** began to spread toward the interior as new lands were opened. By 1840 coffee made up more than 40 percent of Brazil's exports, and by 1880 that figure reached 60 percent.

Along with the expansion of coffee growing came an intensification of slavery, Brazil's primary form of labor. For a variety of humanitarian and economic reasons, Great Britain pressured Brazil to end the slave trade from Africa during the 19th century, but the slave trade continued on an enormous scale up to 1850. More than 1.4 million Africans were imported to Brazil in the last 50 years of the trade, and even after the trans-Atlantic slave trade ended, slavery continued. At mid-century, about one-fourth of Brazil's population were still enslaved. Although some reformers were in favor of ending slavery, a real abolitionist movement did not develop in Brazil until after 1870. Brazil did not finally abolish slavery until 1888.

As in the rest of Latin America, the years after 1850 saw considerable growth and prosperity in Brazil. Dom Pedro II proved to be an enlightened man of middle-class habits who was anxious to reign over a tranquil and progressive nation, even if that tranquility was based on slave labor. The trappings of a monarchy, a court, and noble titles kept the elite attached to the regime. Meanwhile, railroads, steamships, and the telegraph began to change communication and transportation. Foreign companies invested in these projects as well as in banking and other activities. In growing cities such as Rio de Janeiro and São Paulo, merchants, lawyers, a middle class, and an urban working class began to exert pressure on the government. Less wedded to landholding and slavery, these new groups were a catalyst for change, even though the right to vote was still very limited. Moreover, the nature of the labor force was changing.

After 1850 a tide of immigrants, mostly from Italy and Portugal, began to reach Brazil's shores, increasingly attracted by government immigration schemes. Between 1850 and 1875, more than 300,000 immigrants arrived in Brazil; more than two-thirds of them went to work in the coffee estates of southern Brazil. Their presence lessened the dependence on slavery, and by 1870 the abolitionist movement was gaining strength. A series of laws freeing children and the aged, the sympathy of Dom Pedro II, the agitation by abolitionists (both black and white), and the efforts of the slaves (who began to resist and run away in large numbers) brought in 1888 an end to slavery in Brazil, the last nation in the Western Hemisphere to abolish it.

Support for the monarchy began to wither. The long War of the Triple Alliance against Paraguay (1865–1870) had become unpopular, and the military began to take an active role in politics. Squabbles with the church undercut support from the clergy. The planters now turned increasingly to immigrants for their laborers, and some began to modernize their operations. The ideas of positivism, a modernizing philosophy that attempted to bring about material progress by applying scientific principles to government and society, attracted many intellectuals and key members of the army. Politically, a Republican party formed in 1871 began to gather support in urban areas from a wide spectrum of the population. The Brazilian monarchy, long a defender of the planter class and its interests, could not survive the abolition of slavery. In 1889 a nearly bloodless military coup deposed the emperor and established a republic under military men strongly influenced by positivist intellectuals and Republican politicians.

But such "progress" came at certain costs in many nations in Latin America. In the harsh backlands of northeastern Brazil, for example, the change to a republic, economic hardship, and the secularization of society provoked peasant unrest. Antonio Conselheiro, a religious mystic, began to gather followers in the 1890s, especially among the dispossessed peasantry. Eventually their community, Canudos, contained thousands. The government feared these "fanatics" and sent four military expeditions against Canudos, Conselheiro's "New Jerusalem." The fighting was bloody, and casualties were in the thousands. Conselheiro and his followers put up a determined guerrilla defense of their town and their view of the world. The tragedy of Canudos's destruction moved journalist Euclides da Cunha to write *Rebellion in the Backlands* (*Os sertões*, 1902), an account of the events. Like Sarmiento, he saw them as a struggle between civilization and barbarism. However, da Cunha maintained great sympathy for the followers of Antonio Conselheiro (Figure 30.6), and he argued that civilization could not be spread in the flash of a cannon. The book has become a classic of Latin American literature, but the problems of national integration and the disruption of traditional values in the wake of modernization and change remained unresolved.

Canudos: Millenarianism in Late-Nineteenth-Century Brazil

Inhabitants of Canudos

FIGURE 30.6 Refugees of Canudos.

## Societies in Search of Themselves

- There was a tension in cultural life between European influences and the desire to express an American reality, or between elite and folk culture. Social change came very slowly for American Indians, blacks, and women, but by the end of the century the desire for progress and economic resurgence was beginning to have social effects.

### Cultural Expression After Independence

The end of colonial rule opened up Latin America to direct influences from the rest of Europe. Scientific observers, travelers, and the just plain curious—often accompanied by artists—came to see and record, and while doing so introduced new ideas and fashions. Artistic and cultural missions sometimes were brought directly from Europe by Latin American governments.

The elites of the new nations adopted the tastes and fashions of Europe. The battles and triumphs of independence were celebrated in paintings, hymns, odes, and theatrical pieces in the neoclassical style in an attempt to use Greece and Rome as a model for the present. Latin Americans followed the lead of Europe, especially France. The same neoclassical tradition also was apparent in the architecture of the early 19th century.

In the 1830s, the generation that came of age after independence turned to romanticism and found the basis of a new nationality in historical images, the American Indian, and local customs. This generation often had a romantic view of liberty. They emphasized the exotic as well as the distinctive aspects of American society. In Brazil, for example, poet Antônio Gonçalves Dias (1823–1864) used the American Indian as a symbol of Brazil and America. In Cuba, novels sympathetic to

Brothers in Arms: Comparative Politics and Revolution

slaves began to appear by mid-century. In Argentina, writers celebrated the pampas and its open spaces. Sarmiento's critical account of the caudillos in *Facundo* described in depth the life of the gauchos, but it was José Hernández who in 1872 wrote *Martín Fierro*, a romantic epic poem about the end of the way of the gaucho. Historical themes and the writing of history became a political act because studying the past became a way of organizing the present. Many of Latin America's leading politicians were also excellent historians and the theme of their writing was the creation of the nation.

By the 1870s, a new realism emerged in the arts and literature that was more in line with the scientific approach of positivism and the modernization of the new nations. As the economies of Latin America surged forward, novelists appeared who were unafraid to deal with human frailties such as corruption, prejudice, and greed. Chilean Alberto Blest Gana and Brazilian mulatto J. Machado de Assis (1839–1908) wrote critically about the social mores of their countries during this era.

Throughout the century, the culture of the mass of the population had been little affected by the trends and tastes of the elite. Popular arts, folk music, and dance flourished in traditional settings, demonstrating a vitality and adaptability to new situations that was often lacking in the more imitative fine arts. Sometimes authors in the romantic tradition or poets such as Hernández turned to traditional themes for their subject and inspiration, and in that way they brought these traditions to the greater attention of their class and the world. For the most part, however, popular artistic expressions were not appreciated or valued by the traditional elites, the modernizing urban bourgeoisie, or the new immigrants.

## Old Patterns of Gender, Class, and Race

Although significant political changes make it appealing to deal with the 19th century as an era of great change and transformation in Latin America, it is necessary to recognize the persistence of old patterns and sometimes their reinforcement. Changes took place, to be sure, but their effects were not felt equally by all classes or groups in society, nor were all groups attracted by the promises of the new political regimes and their views of progress.

For example, women gained little ground during most of the century. They had participated actively in the independence movements. Some had taken up arms or aided the insurgent forces, and some—such as Colombian Policarpa (La Pola) Salvatierra, whose final words were "Do not forget my example"—had paid for their activities on the gallows. After independence, there was almost no change in the predominant attitudes toward women's proper role. Expected to be wives and mothers, women could not vote, hold public office, become lawyers, or in some places testify in a court of law. Although there were a few exceptions, unmarried women younger than 25 remained under the power and authority of their fathers. Once married, they could not work, enter into contracts, or control their own estates without permission of their husbands. As in the colonial era, marriage, politics, and the creation of kinship links were essential elements in elite control of land and political power, and thus women remained a crucial resource in family strategies.

Lower-class women had more economic freedom—often controlling local marketing—and also more personal freedom than elite women under the constraints of powerful families. In legal terms, however, their situation was no better—and in material terms, much worse—than that of their elite sisters. Still, by the 1870s women were an important part of the workforce.

The one area in which the situation of women began to change significantly was public education. There had already been a movement in this direction in the colonial era. At first, the idea behind education for girls and women was that because women were responsible for educating their children, they should be educated so that the proper values could be passed to the next generation. By 1842 Mexico City required girls and boys age 7 to 15 to attend school, and in 1869 the first girls' school was created in Mexico. Liberals in Mexico wanted secular public education to prepare women for an enlightened role within the home, and similar sentiments were expressed by liberal regimes elsewhere. Public schools appeared throughout Latin America, although their impact was limited. For example, Brazil had a population of 10 million in 1873, but only about 1 million men and half that number of women were literate.

The rise of secular public education created new opportunities for women. The demand for teachers at the primary level created the need for schools in which to train teachers. Because most teachers were women, these teacher training schools gave women access to advanced education. Although the curriculum often emphasized traditional female roles, an increasing number of educated women began to emerge who were dissatisfied with the legal and social constraints on their lives. By the end of the 19th century, these women were becoming increasingly active in advocating women's rights and other political issues.

In most cases, the new nations legally ended the old society of castes in which legal status and definition depended on color and ethnicity, but in reality much of that system continued. The stigma of skin color and former slave status created barriers to advancement. Indigenous peoples in Mexico, Bolivia, and Peru often continued to labor under poor conditions and to suffer the effects of government failures. There was conflict. In Yucatan, a great rebellion broke out, pitting the Maya against the central government and the whites, in 1839 and again in 1847. Despite the intentions of governments, American Indians resisted changes imposed from outside their communities and were willing to defend their traditional ways. The word *Indian* was still an insult in most places in Latin America. For some mestizos and others of mixed origin, the century presented opportunities for advancement in the army, professions, and commerce, but these cases were exceptions.

Race and Identity in Nineteenth-Century South America

In many places, expansion of the export economy perpetuated old patterns. Liberalism itself changed during the century, and once its program of secularization, rationalism, and property rights was made law, it became more restrictive. Positivists at the end of the century still hoped for economic growth, but some were willing to gain it at the expense of individual freedoms. The positivists generally were convinced of the benefits of international trade for Latin America, and large landholdings increased in many areas at the expense of small farms and Indian communal lands as a result. A small, white Creole, landed upper class controlled the economies and politics in most places, and they were sometimes joined in the political and economic functions by a stratum of urban middle-class merchants, bureaucrats, and other bourgeois types. The landed and mercantile elite tended to merge over time to create one group that, in most places, controlled the government. Meanwhile, new social forces were at work. The flood of immigration, beginning in earnest in the 1870s, to Argentina, Brazil, and a few other nations began to change the social composition of those places. Increasingly, rapid urbanization also changed these societies. Still, Latin America, though politically independent, began the 1880s as a group of predominantly agrarian nations with rigid social structures and a continuing dependency on the world market.

## The Great Boom, 1880–1920

Between 1880 and 1920, Latin America, like certain areas of Asia and Africa, experienced a tremendous spurt of economic growth, stimulated by the increasing demand in industrializing Europe and the United States for raw materials, foodstuffs, and specialized tropical crops. Mexico and Argentina are two excellent examples of the effects of these changes, but not all groups shared the benefits of economic growth. By the end of the 19th century, the United States was beginning to intervene directly in Latin American affairs.

Latin America was well prepared for export-led economic expansion. The liberal ideology of individual freedoms, an open market, and limited government intervention in the operation of the economy had triumphed in many places. Whereas this ideology had been the expression of the middle class in Europe, in Latin America it was adopted not only by the small urban middle class but also by the large landowners, miners, and export merchants linked to the rural economy and the traditional patterns of wealth and land owning. In a number of countries, a political alliance was forged between the traditional aristocracy of wealth and the new urban elements. Together they controlled the presidential offices and the congresses and imposed a business-as-usual approach to government at the expense of peasants and a newly emerging working class.

The expansion of Latin American economies was led by exports. Each nation had a specialty: bananas and coffee from the nations of Central America; tobacco and sugar from Cuba; rubber and coffee from Brazil; hennequen (a fiber for making rope), copper, and silver from Mexico; wool, wheat, and beef from Argentina; copper from Chile. In this era of strong demand and good prices, these nations made high profits. This allowed them to import large quantities of foreign goods, and it provided funds for the beautification of cities and other government projects. But export-led expansion was always risky because the world market prices of Latin American commodities ultimately were determined by conditions outside the region. In that sense, these economies were particularly vulnerable and in some ways dependent.

Also, export-led expansion could result in rivalry, hostility, and even war between neighboring countries. Control of the nitrates that lay in areas between Chile, Peru, and Bolivia generated a dispute that led to the War of the Pacific (1879–1883), pitting Chile against Bolivia and Peru. Although all were unprepared for a modern war at first, eventually thousands of troops were mobilized. The Chileans occupied Lima in 1881 and then imposed a treaty on Peru. Bolivia lost Antofagasta and its access to the Pacific Ocean and became a landlocked nation. Chile increased its size by a third and benefited from an economic boom during and after the war. In Peru and Bolivia, governments fell, and a sense of national crisis set in after the defeat in the "fertilizer war."

The expansion of Latin American trade was remarkable. It increased by about 50 percent between

IN DEPTH

## Explaining Underdevelopment

The terms *underdeveloped* and the more benign *developing* describe a large number of nations in the world with a series of economic and social problems. Because Latin America was first among what we now call the *developing nations* to establish its independence and begin to compete in the world economy, it had to confront the reasons for its relative position and problems early and without many models to follow. The Document section of this chapter offers two visions of Latin America's early problems that are similar because both emphasize the Hispanic cultural heritage, as well as its supposed deficiencies or strengths, as a key explanation for the region's history. Such cultural explanations were popular among 19th-century intellectuals and political leaders, and they continue today, although other general theories based on economics and politics have become more popular.

> ***"In 19th-century Latin America . . . early attempts to develop industry were faced with competition from the cheaper and better products of already industrialized nations such as England and France, so a similar path to development was impossible."***

At the time of Latin American independence, the adoption of European models of economy, government, and law seemed to offer great hope. But as "progress," republican forms of government, free trade, and liberalism failed to bring about general prosperity and social harmony, Latin Americans and others began to search for alternative explanations of their continuing problems as a first step in solving them. Some critics condemned the Hispanic cultural legacy; others saw the materialism of the modern world as the major problem and called for a return to religion and idealism. By the 20th century, Marxism provided a powerful analysis of Latin America's history and present reality, although Marxists themselves could not decide whether Latin American societies were essentially feudal and needed first to become capitalist or whether they were already capitalist and were ready for socialist revolution.

Throughout these debates, Latin Americans often implicitly compared their situation with that of the United States and tried to explain the different economic positions of the two regions. At the beginning of the 19th century, both regions were still primarily agricultural, and although a few places in North America were starting small industries, the mining sector in Latin America was far stronger than that of its northern neighbor. In 1850 the population of Latin America was 33 million, the population of the United States was 23 million, and the per capita income in both regions was roughly equal. By 1940, however, Latin America's population was much larger and its economic situation was far worse than in the United States. Observers were preoccupied by why and how this disparity arose. Was there some flaw in the Latin American character, or were the explanations to be found in the economic and political differences between the two areas, and how could these differences be explained? The answers to these questions were not easy to obtain, but increasingly they were sought not in the history of individual countries but in analyses of a world economic and political system.

There had long been a Marxist critique of colonialism and imperialism, but the modern Latin American analysis of underdevelopment grew from different origins. During the 1950s, a number of European and North American scholars developed the concept of *modernization,* or *westernization.* Basing their ideas on the historical experience of western Europe, they believed that development was a matter of increasing per capita production in any society, and that as development took place, various kinds of social changes would follow. The more industrialized, urban, and modern a society became, the more social change and improvement were possible as traditional patterns and attitudes were abandoned or transformed. Technology, communication, and the distribution of material goods were the means by which the transformation would take place. Some scholars also believed that as this process occurred, there would be a natural movement toward more democratic forms of government and popular participation.

*Modernization theory* held out the promise that any society could move toward a brighter future by following the path

1870 and 1890. Argentina's trade was increasing at about 5 percent a year during this period—one of the highest rates of growth ever recorded for a national economy. "As wealthy as an Argentine" became an expression in Paris, reflecting the fortunes that wool, beef, and grain were earning for some in Argentina. In Mexico, an oligarchic dictatorship, which maintained all the outward attributes of democracy but imposed "law and order" under the dictator Porfirio Díaz, created the conditions for unrestrained profits. Mexican exports doubled between 1877 and 1900. Similar figures could be cited for Chile, Costa Rica, and Bolivia.

This rapidly expanding commerce attracted the interest of foreign investors eager for high returns on taken earlier by western Europe. Its message was one of improvement through gradual rather than radical or revolutionary change, and thus it tended to be politically conservative. It also tended to disregard cultural differences, internal class conflicts, and struggles for power within nations. Moreover, sometimes it was adopted by military regimes that believed imposing order was the best way to promote the economic changes necessary for modernization.

The proponents of modernization theory had a difficult time convincing many people in the "underdeveloped" world, where the historical experience had been very different from that of western Europe. In 19th-century Latin America, for example, early attempts to develop industry were faced with competition from the cheaper and better products of already industrialized nations such as England and France, so a similar path to development was impossible. Critics argued that each nation did not operate individually but was part of a world system that kept some areas "developed" at the expense of others.

These ideas were first and most cogently expressed in Latin America. After World War II, the United Nations established an Economic Commission for Latin America (ECLA). Under the leadership of Argentine economist Raul Prebisch, the ECLA began to analyze the Latin American economies. Prebisch argued that "unequal exchange" between the developed nations at the center of the world economy and those like Latin America created structural blocks to economic growth. The ECLA suggested various policies to overcome the problems, especially the development of industries that would overcome the region's dependence on foreign imports.

From the structural analysis of the ECLA and from more traditional Marxist critiques, a new kind of explanation, usually called *dependency theory,* began to emerge in the 1960s. Rather than seeing underdevelopment or the lack of economic growth as the result of failed modernization, some scholars in Latin America began to argue that development and underdevelopment were not stages but part of the same process. They believed that the development and growth of some areas, such as western Europe and the United States, were achieved at the expense of, or because of, the underdevelopment of dependent regions such as Latin America. Agricultural economies at the periphery of the world economic system always were at a disadvantage in dealing with the industrial nations of the center, and thus they would become poorer as the industrial nations got richer. The industrial nations would continually draw products, profits, and cheap labor from the periphery. This basic economic relationship of dependency meant that external forces determined production, capital accumulation, and class relations in a dependent country. Some theorists went further and argued that Latin America and other nations of the Third World were culturally dependent in their consumption of ideas and concepts. Both modernization theory and Mickey Mouse were seen as the agents of a cultural domination that was simply an extension of economic reality. These theorists usually argued that socialism offered the only hope for breaking out of the dependency relationship.

These ideas, which dominated Latin American intellectual life, were appealing to other areas of Asia and Africa that had recently emerged from colonial control. Forms of dependency analysis became popular in many areas of the world in the 1960s and 1970s. By the 1980s, however, dependency theory was losing its appeal. As an explanation of what had happened historically in Latin America, it was useful, but as a theory that could predict what might happen elsewhere, it provided little help. Marxists argued that it overemphasized the circulation of goods (trade) rather than how things were produced and that it ignored the class conflicts they believed were the driving force of history. Moreover, with the rise of multinational corporations and globalization, capitalism itself was changing and was becoming less tied to individual countries. Thus an analysis based on trade relationships between countries became somewhat outdated.

Can development be widespread, as modernization theory argues, or is the underdevelopment of some countries inherent in the capitalist world economy, as the dependency theorists believe? The issue is still in dispute. The search for new explanations and new solutions to the problems of development will continue as peoples throughout the world work to improve their lives.

---

**Questions** In what sense was 19th-century Latin America a dependent economy? Which explanation or prediction about dependency best fits world economic trends today?

their capital. British, French, German, and North American businesses and entrepreneurs invested in mining, railroads, public utilities, and banking. More than half the foreign investments in Latin America were British, which alone were 10 times more in 1913 than they had been in 1870. But British leadership was no longer uncontested; Germany and, increasingly, the United States provided competition. The United States was particularly active in the Caribbean region and Mexico, but not until after World War I did U.S. capital predominate in the region.

Foreign investments provided Latin America with needed capital and services but tended to place key industries, transportation facilities, and services in foreign hands. Foreign investments also constrained Latin American governments in their social, commercial, and diplomatic policies.

## Mexico and Argentina: Examples of Economic Transformation

We can use these two large Latin American nations as examples of different responses within the same general pattern. In Mexico, the liberal triumph of Juárez had set the stage for economic growth and constitutional government. In 1876, Porfirio Díaz, one of Juárez's generals, was elected president, and for the next 35 years he dominated politics. Díaz suppressed regional rebellions and imposed a strong centralized government. Financed by foreign capital, the railroad system grew rapidly, providing a new way to integrate Mexican regional economies, move goods to the ports for export, and allow the movement of government troops to keep order. Industrialization began to take place. Foreign investment was encouraged in mining, transportation, and other sectors of the economy, and financial policies were changed to promote investments. For example, United States investments expanded from about 30 million pesos in 1883 to more than $1 billion by 1911.

The forms of liberal democracy were maintained but were subverted to keep Díaz in power and to give his development plans an open track. Behind these policies were a number of advisors who were strongly influenced by positivist ideas and who wanted to impose a scientific approach on the national economy. These **cientificos** set the tone for Mexico while the government suppressed any political opposition to these policies. Díaz's Mexico projected an image of modernization led by a Europeanized elite who greatly profited from the economic growth and the imposition of order under Don Porfirio.

Growth often was bought at the expense of Mexico's large rural peasantry and its growing urban and working classes. This population was essentially native, because unlike Argentina and Brazil, Mexico had received few immigrants. They participated very little in the prosperity of export-led growth. Economic expansion at the expense of peasants and American Indian communal lands created a volatile situation.

Strikes and labor unrest increased, particularly among railroad workers, miners, and textile workers. In the countryside, a national police force, the Rurales, maintained order, and the army was mobilized when needed. At the regional level, political bosses linked to the Díaz regime in Mexico City delivered the votes in rigged elections.

For 35 years, Díaz reigned supreme and oversaw the transformation of the Mexican economy. His opponents were arrested or driven into exile, and the small middle class, the landowners, miners, and foreign investors celebrated the progress of Mexico. In 1910, however, a middle-class movement with limited political goals seeking electoral reform began to mushroom into a more general uprising in which the frustrations of the poor, the workers, the peasants, and nationalist intellectuals of various political persuasions erupted in a bloody 10-year civil war, the Mexican Revolution.

At the other end of the hemisphere, Argentina followed an alternative path of economic expansion. By 1880 the American Indians on the southern pampas had been conquered, and vast new tracts of land were opened to ranching. The strange relationship between Buenos Aires and the rest of the nation was resolved when Buenos Aires was made a federal district. With a rapidly expanding economy, it became "the Paris of South America," an expression that reflected the drive by wealthy Argentines to establish themselves as a modern nation. By 1914 Buenos Aires had more than 2 million inhabitants, or about one-fourth of the national population. Its political leaders, the "Generation of 1880," inherited the liberal program of Sarmiento and other liberals, and they were able to enact their programs because of the high levels of income the expanding economy generated.

Technological changes contributed to Argentine prosperity. Refrigerated ships allowed fresh beef to be sent directly to Europe, and this along with wool and wheat provided the basis of expansion. The flood of immigrants provided labor. Some were *golondrinas* (literally, "swallows"), who were able to work one harvest in Italy and then a second in Argentina because of the differences in seasons in the two hemispheres, but many immigrants elected to stay. Almost 3.5 million immigrants stayed in Argentina between 1857 and 1930, and unlike the Mexican population, by 1914 about one-third of the Argentine population was foreign born. Italians, Germans, Russians, and Jews came to "hacer America"—that is, "to make America"—and remained. In a way, they really did Europeanize Argentina, as did not happen in Mexico, introducing the folkways and ideologies of the European rural and working classes. The result was a fusion of cultures that produced not only a radical workers' movement but also the distinctive music of the tango, which combined Spanish, African, and other musical elements in the cafe and red-light districts of Buenos Aires. The tango became the music of the Argentine urban working class.

As the immigrant flood increased, workers began to seek political expression. A Socialist party was formed in the 1890s and tried to elect representatives to office. Anarchists hoped to smash the political system and called for strikes and walkouts. Inspired to

VISUALIZING THE PAST

## Images of the Spanish-American War

Although the United States had fought a war with Mexico in the 1840s and commercial ties were growing in the 1880s, the real push for expansion in Latin America came in 1898 with the Spanish-American War. The U.S. motives for the war were a mixture of altruism and the desire for strategic and commercial advantages. A great deal of popular support was mobilized in the United States by the popular press, not by celebrating imperial expansion but by emphasizing the oppression suffered by people still under Spain's colonial rule. Sympathy was especially strong for the Cubans who had fought a bloody rebellion for independence from 1868 to 1878. However, the U.S. press often portrayed Latin Americans as unruly children and emphasized their "racial" difference, creating an image quite typical for the period. During the war, Teddy Roosevelt's heroic feats and the American victories stimulated national pride, but the element of altruism was always part of the mix. As in Europe, the concept of a " white man's burden" could not be separated from the drive for empire.

Among the popular political magazines of the era were *Punch* and the *Judge*. The two cover images shown here from the period of the Spanish-American War reflect popular sentiments and attitudes at the time.

**Questions** In what way do images convey political messages more effectively than texts? When do calls for moral action justify intervention in the affairs of another country?

LIBERTY CALLS CUBA.

UNCLE SAM IS BOUND HAND AND FOOT—WHILE OUR CIVILIZATION DEMANDS THAT JUSTICE BE DONE THE PEOPLE OF CUBA.

FIGURE 30.7 The drive for opening of a sea route from the Atlantic to the Pacific moved the United States to back the creation of the Panama Canal. Between 1881 and 1914 the canal, a major engineering feat, was constructed. The nation of Panama was created in the process of securing rights to the canal when the United States backed an independence movement that separated Panama from Colombia. The Panama Canal changed the nature of international maritime commerce. This image is of the Gatlin cut, which was the major excavation on the canal.

some extent by European ideological battles, the struggle spilled into the streets. Violent strikes and government repression characterized the decade after 1910, culminating in a series of strikes in 1918 that led to extreme repression. Development had its social costs.

The Argentine oligarchy was capable of some internal reform, however. A new party representing the emerging middle class began to organize, aided by an electoral law in 1912 that called for secret ballots, universal male suffrage, and compulsory voting. With this change, the Radical party, promising political reform and more liberal policies for workers, came to power in 1916, but faced with labor unrest it acted as repressively as its predecessors. The oligarchy made room for middle-class politicians and interests, but the problems of Argentina's expanding labor force remained unresolved, and Argentina's economy remained closely tied to the international market for its exports.

With many variations, similar patterns of economic growth, political domination by oligarchies formed by traditional aristocracies and "progressive" middle classes, and a rising tide of labor unrest or rural rebellion can be noted elsewhere in Latin America. Modernization was not welcomed by all sectors of society. Messianic religious movements in Brazil, American Indian resistance to the loss of lands in Colombia, and banditry in Mexico were all to some extent reactions to the changes being forced on the societies by national governments tied to the ideology of progress and often insensitive to its effects.

## Uncle Sam Goes South

After its Civil War, the United States began to take a more direct and active interest in the politics and economies of Latin America. Commerce and investments began to expand rapidly in this period, especially in Mexico and Central America. American industry was seeking new markets and raw materials, while the growing population of the United States created a demand for Latin American products. Attempts were made to create inter-American cooperation. A major turning point came in 1898 with the outbreak of war between Spain and the United States, which began to join the nations of western Europe in the age of imperialism.

The war centered on Cuba and Puerto Rico, Spain's last colonies in the Americas. The Cuban economy had boomed in the 19th century on the basis of its exports of sugar and tobacco grown with slave labor. A 10-year civil war for independence, beginning in 1868, had failed in its main objective but had won the island some autonomy. A number of ardent Cuban nationalists, including journalist and poet José Martí, had gone into exile to continue the struggle. Fighting erupted again in 1895, and the United States joined in in 1898, declaring war on Spain and occupying Cuba, Puerto Rico, and the Philippines.

In fact, U.S. investments in Cuba had been increasing rapidly before the war, and the United States had become a major market for Cuban sugar. The **Spanish-American War** opened the door to direct U.S. involvement in the Caribbean. A U.S. government of occupation was imposed on Cuba and Puerto Rico, which had witnessed its own stirrings for independence in the 19th century. When the occupation of Cuba ended in 1902, a series of onerous conditions was imposed on independent Cuba that made it almost an American dependency—a status that was legally imposed in Puerto Rico.

For strategic, commercial, and economic reasons, Latin America, particularly the Caribbean and Mexico, began to attract American interest at the turn of the century. These considerations lay behind the drive to build a canal across Central America that would shorten the route between the Atlantic and Pacific. When Colombia proved reluctant to meet American proposals, the United States backed a Panamanian movement for independence and then signed a treaty with its representative that granted the United States extensive rights over the **Panama Canal** (Figure 30.7). President Theodore Roosevelt was a major force behind the canal, which was opened to traffic in 1914.

The Panama Canal was a remarkable engineering feat and a fitting symbol of the technological and industrial strength of the United States. North Americans were proud of these achievements and hoped to demonstrate the superiority of the "American way"—a feeling fed to some extent by racist ideas and a sense of cultural superiority. Latin Americans were wary of American power and intentions in the area. Many intellectuals cautioned against the expansionist designs of the United States and against what they saw as the materialism of American culture. Uruguayan José Enrique Rodó, in his essay *Ariel* (1900), contrasted the spirituality of Hispanic culture with the materialism of the United States. Elsewhere in Latin America, others offered similar critiques.

Latin American criticism had a variety of origins: nationalism, a Catholic defense of traditional values, and some socialist attacks on expansive capitalism. In a way, Latin America, which had achieved its political independence in the 19th century and had been part of European developments, was able to articulate the fears and the reactions of the areas that had become the colonies and semicolonies of western Europe and the United States in the age of empire.

GLOBAL CONNECTIONS

## New Latin American Nations and the World

During the 19th century, the nations of Latin America moved from the status of colonies to that of independent nation-states. The process was sometimes exhilarating and often painful, but during the course of the century, these nations were able to create governments and begin to address many social and economic problems. These problems were inherited from the colonial era and were intensified by internal political and ideological conflicts and foreign intervention. Moreover, the Latin American nations had to revive their economies after their struggles for independence and to confront their position within the world economic system as suppliers of agricultural products and consumers of manufactured goods.

To some extent Latin America ran against the currents of global history in the 19th century. During the great age of imperialism, Latin America cast off the previous colonial controls. Swept by the same winds of change that had transformed Europe's society and economy and led to the separation of England's North American colonies, Latin American countries struggled with the problems of nation-building while, like China and Russia, holding off colonial incursions. In this sense, and also in some efforts to define a Latin American cultural identity, Latin America became a bit more isolated in the world at large.

The heritage of the past weighed heavily on Latin America. Political and social changes were many, and pressures for these changes came from a variety of sources, such as progressive politicians, modernizing military men, a growing urban population, dissatisfied workers, and disadvantaged peasants. Still, in many ways Latin America remained remarkably unchanged. Revolts were frequent, but revolutions that changed the structure of society or the distribution of land and wealth were few, and the reforms intended to make such changes usually were unsuccessful. The elite controlled most of the economic resources, a growing but still small urban sector had emerged politically but either remained weak or had to accommodate the elite, and most of the population continued to labor on the land with little hope of improvement. Latin America had a distinctive civilization, culturally and politically sharing much of the Western tradition yet economically functioning more like areas of Asia and Africa. Latin America was the first non-Western area to face the problems of decolonization, and many aspects of its history that seemed so distinctive in the 19th century proved to be previews of what would follow: decolonization and nation-building elsewhere in the world in the 20th century

Latin America's global connections included ongoing political and cultural ties with the West. Efforts to imitate the West accelerated in some regions, for example, with the importation of sports like soccer. Growing influence and intervention from the United States was another outside force. New immigration, from southern Europe but also now from Asia, brought additional connections. But Latin America's most significant global link continued to involve its dependent economy, drawing goods, now including machinery, from the West while exporting a growing range of foods and raw materials.

## Further Readings

David Bushnell and Neil Macauley, *The Emergence of Latin America in the Nineteenth Century*, 2nd ed. (1994), provides an excellent overview that is critical of the dependency thesis. The classic study from the dependency perspective is Fernando Henrique Cardoso and Enzo Faletto, *Dependency and Development in Latin America* (1979), which provides a good economic analysis, as does S. Haber, *Why Latin America Fell Behind* (1997). The movements for independence are described in John Lynch, *The Spanish American Revolutions* (1973), which is a classic, as is Tulio Halperin Donghi, *The Aftermath of Revolution in Latin America* (1973), which analyzes the first half of the 19th century. Arlene Díaz, *Female Citizens, Patriarchs, and the Law in Venezuela, 1786–1904* (2004), shows how women were affected by the new states. Kenneth Andrien and Lyman Johnson, *The Political Economy of Spanish America in the Age of Revolution, 1750–1850* (1994), presents a series of recent studies. E. Bradford Burns, *Poverty or Progress: Latin America in the Nineteenth Century* (1973), provides a challenging attack on the liberal programs and a defense of a folk political tradition. Florencia Mallon, *Peasant and Nation* (1995), suggests a peasant origin for Latin American nationalism. Eric Van Young, *The Other Rebellion* (2001), examines Mexico's independence movement. Jean Franco, *The Modern Culture of Latin America: Society and the Artist* (1967), is a lively discussion of literature and the arts. Volumes 3 to 5 of *The Cambridge History of Latin America* (1985–1986) contain fine essays on major themes and individual countries. A good essay from the collection is Robert Freeman Smith's "Latin America, the United States, and the European Powers, 1830–1930," vol. 4, 83–120. On the complex relationship between the United States and Latin America, see the essays in G. Joseph, C. Legrand, and R. Salvatore, eds., *Close Encounters of Empire* (1998).

There are many single-volume country histories and monographs on particular topics. David Rock, *Argentina* (1985); Richard Slatta, *Gauchos and the Vanishing Frontier* (1985); José Moya, *Cousins and Strangers: Spanish Immigrants to Buenos Aires, 1850–1930* (1998); and Jeremy Adelman, *A Republic of Capital* (1999), provide a good start on Argentina. *Robert Levine, A History of Brazil* (1999); Michael Meyer and William Beezley, *The Oxford History of Mexico* (2000); and Herbert Klein, *Bolivia* (1982), are good examples of national histories. There are excellent rural histories, such as Stanley Stein, *Vassouras: A Brazilian Coffee County* (1989); B. J. Barickman, *A Bahian Counterpoint* (1998); and Charles Berquist, *Coffee and Conflict in Colombia, 1886–1910* (1978). Silvia Arrom, *The Women of Mexico City* (1985), is a fine example of the growing literature in women's history, as is Eileen J. Suárez Findlay, *Imposing Decency: The Politics of Sexuality and Race in Puerto Rico, 1870–1920* (1999). At the regional level of analysis Greg Grandin, *The Blood of Guatemala* (2000), discusses indigenous peoples' relation to the nation in that country. Charles Berquist, *Labor in Latin America* (1986), is a comparative interpretative essay that provides a good starting point.

## On the Web

Simon Bolívar's views on state formation and his ambivalent attitude toward the United States are examined at http://victorian.fortunecity.com/dadd/453 and http://www.emory.edu/COLLEGE/CULPEPER/BAKEWELL/texts/jamaica-letter.html. The life and career of his co-revolutionist in the south, José de San Martín, is beautifully illustrated at http://pachami.com/English/sanmartin1E.htm and described at http://geocities.com/TimesSquare/1848/martin.html.

Bolívar and San Martín lived to see their visions compromised or betrayed, but they avoided the tragic fate of the hero of the Mexican war for independence, Father Miguel de Hidalgo, who is discussed at http://www.mexconnect.com/mex_/travel/ganderson/gadeloresh.html. Postindependence leaders such as Mexico's Santa Anna (http://www.pbs.org/weta/thewest/people/s_z/santaanna.htm and http://www.mexconnect.com/mex_/history/jtuck/jtsantaanna.html) and Argentina's Domingo Sarmiento (http://www.mexconnect.com/mex_/history/jtuck/jtsantaanna.html) faced numerous difficulties when addressing the task of nation-building.

The Monroe Doctrine (http://www.yale.edu/lawweb/avalon/monroe.htm) and Thomas Jefferson's comments on its "imperial" implications (http://www.mtholyoke.edu/acad/intrel/thomas.htm) are worthy of close attention. Other sites, including http://usinfo.state.gov/usa/infousa/

facts/democrac/50.htm, stress that for all its later foreign policy implications, the Monroe Doctrine was merely a reflection of John Quincy Adams's domestic political concerns. However, discourse over the Monroe Doctrine illuminates the process by which the United States evolved from a revolutionary upstart to a world power. Jefferson rejected a seizure of Cuba on moral grounds but noted its value as a possible addition to his country. Other American leaders with fewer scruples would later seize land from their neighbors to the south, a topic addressed with some drama through primary sources and poetry at http://www.smplanet.com/imperialism/toc.html, http://www.english.uiuc.edu/maps/poets/a_f/espada/imperialism.htm, http://www.fordham.edu/halsall/mod/1913calderon.html, and http://www.fordham.edu/halsall/mod/modsbook32.html. The concept of Manifest Destiny as it relates to world history beyond the United States-Mexican conflict is discussed at http://odur.let.rug.nl/~usa/E/manifest/manifxx.htm and http://www.pbs.org/kera/usmexicanwar/dialogues/prelude/manifest/d2aeng.html.

For U.S. and Latin American relations generally, see http://www.uoregon.edu/~caguirre/uslatam.html.

CHAPTER 31

# Civilizations in Crisis: The Ottoman Empire, the Islamic Heartlands, and Qing China



Hong Xiuquan was a deeply troubled young man. One of five children from a struggling peasant family living in the Guangdong region on China's southeast coast, Hong had worked hard to excel in school so that he could take the exams that would provide entry into the lower rungs of the scholar-gentry-dominated bureaucracy. Counting on Hong's demonstrated aptitude for book learning to improve the family fortunes, his parents and kinsfolk scrimped to find the money needed to send him to school and hire tutors to prepare him for the rigorous examination process.

The pressure of such life-defining testing is invariably intense, but with the fate of his family in the balance and his community carefully monitoring his progress through the early 1830s, Hong found his failures deeply humiliating. Mortification was increasingly laced with anger as he tried and failed four times to pass the exams that would earn him the lowest official degree, which carried with it a modest stipend from the state and the right to wear the robes of the scholar-gentry.

Perhaps to escape the shame he felt in the company of family and friends who were well aware of his failures, Hong became an avid traveler. In 1836, in Whampoa, which was close to the great port city of Canton and not far from his home village, Hong first came into contact with Protestant missionaries from the United States. Through one of the Chinese converts who was helping the missionaries translate the Bible, Hong received a copy of a pamphlet entitled "Good Words for Exhorting the Age," which contained biblical passages. Apparently he paid the pamphlet little heed until after he failed the exams the third and fourth times. Those setbacks, which left him depressed and often delirious, not only prompted him to begin a serious study of the Bible but to connect its teachings to a strange dream he had experienced after his third failure in 1837. He concluded that the two men with whom he had conversed in his dream—the older of whom had given him a sword—were God the Father and Jesus Christ. Hong came to believe that he was the younger son of Jesus and that the sword had been given to him to rid the world of corrupt officials and other agents of the devil.

Hong was well educated (in a society where few went to school); he was also a charismatic speaker, given to trances and speaking in tongues, and he was convinced that he had a divine mission. He began to preach in public and was soon baptizing hundreds, then thousands of converts to his growing band

FIGURE 31.1 This panoramic scene painted by a Chinese witness to the Taiping rebellion shows the rebel forces besieging and burning an enemy town and a nearby estate house of a large landlord's family in central China.

of "God worshipers." Many of his early followers shared his minority background as members of the Hakka ethnic group, which the Han Chinese treated as distinctly inferior. Others were drawn from hard-pressed mountain tribal peoples as well as miners, charcoal burners, riverboat "coolies," and pawnbrokers—many of whom had been displaced by the heightened influx of Western commerce in the Canton region in the early 1800s. Often in very garbled renditions, Biblical teachings and Christian rituals were widely deployed by adherents to his sect, which became known as the Taipings (meaning "Great Peace"), after one of the Chinese titles Hong claimed for himself. Among these many recruits, Hong built an inner circle of advisors

| 1640 C.E. | 1800 C.E. | 1850 C.E. | 1875 C.E. | 1900 C.E. |
|---|---|---|---|---|
| **1644** Manchu nomads conquer China; Qing dynasty rules<br>**1664–1722** Reign of Kangxi emperor in China<br>**1727** First printing press set up in Ottoman Empire<br>**1736–1799** Reign of Qianlong emperor in China<br>**1768–1774** Disastrous Ottoman defeat in war with Russia<br>**1772** Safavid dynasty falls in Persia<br>**1789–1807** Reign of Ottoman Sultan Selim III<br>**1798** British embassy to Qianlong emperor in China; French invasion of Egypt; Napoleon defeats Egypt's Mamluk rulers | **1805–1849** Reign of Muhammad Ali in Egypt<br>**1807–1839** Reign of Ottoman Sultan Mahmud II<br>**1826** Ottoman Janissary corps destroyed<br>**1834** Postal system established in Ottoman Empire<br>**1838** Ottoman treaty with British removing trade restrictions in the empire<br>**1839–1841** Opium War in China<br>**1839–1876** *Tanzimat* reforms in the Ottoman Empire<br>**1839–1897** Life of Islamic thinker al-Afghani<br>**1849–1905** Life of Egyptian reformer Muhammad Abduh | **1850–1864** Taiping Rebellion in China<br>**1854–1856** Crimean War<br>**1856–1860** Anglo-French war against China<br>**1866** First railway begun in Ottoman Empire<br>**1869** Opening of the Suez Canal<br>**1870** Ottoman legal code reformed | **1876** Constitution promulgated for Ottoman Empire<br>**1876–1908** Reign of Ottoman Sultan Abdul Hamid<br>**1877** Treaty of San Stefano; Ottomans driven from most of the Balkans<br>**1882** British invasion and occupation of Egypt; failed Orabi revolt in Egypt<br>**1883** Mahdist victory over British-led Egyptian expeditionary force at Shakyan<br>**1889** Young Turks establish the Ottoman Society for Union and Progress in Paris<br>**1898** British-Egyptian army defeats the Mahdist army at Omdurman<br>**1898–1901** Boxer Rebellion and 100 Days of Reform in China | **1905** Fatherland Party established in Egypt<br>**1908** Young Turks seize power in Istanbul |

and military leaders who soon displayed great aptitude for their assigned tasks.

As his following grew into the tens of thousands, Hong's preaching became more strident and openly directed against the ruling Qing dynasty, which had been established in the mid-17th century by the nomadic Manchu people who lived to the north and east of the Great Wall. Hong charged that the Manchus were the source of all manner of earthly evils and responsible for China's recent defeats at the hands of the British and other European intruders. The Taiping revolutionary agenda was also aimed at the scholar-gentry and other fundamental aspects of the Confucian order. In rebel-controlled areas, ancestral tablets were smashed, land was seized from the local gentry to be distributed to Hong's followers on the basis of need, and the imperial examination system was abolished. The Taipings proclaimed that women were equal to men, adopted a Christian solar calendar, and sought to restore moral order by banning slavery, concubinage, arranged marriage, opium smoking, footbinding, judicial torture, and the worship of idols. After decisively defeating a Qing military force sent to put an end to the Taiping movement, Hong's followers launched one of the longest-lived and most deadly rebellions of the 19th century; in just thirteen years, tens of millions of Chinese died as a result of the rebellion.

Both Hong's personal crisis and the revolutionary movement his visions and teachings launched were catalyzed by the disintegration—beginning in the early 1800s—of Chinese civilization, which had been one of the world's most advanced for thousands of years. At the other end of Asia, the Ottomans, the last of the rival Muslim dynasties that had ruled the Middle East and south Asia in the early modern era, had gone into decline even earlier. In both cases, the sheer size, complexity, and persisting military power of each of these empires, combined with the ongoing rivalries among the European powers, prevented them from being formally colonized like much of the rest of Asia, Africa, and the Pacific. But, as we shall see, both dynasties and the civilizations they sought to uphold came under repeated assault during the 19th century.

The Taiping Rebellion was a violent, radical variant of a succession of movements in both China and the Middle East that sought either to reform or put an end to the existing social and political order. The Taiping

Rebellion and its counterpart in the Muslim Middle East, the Mahdist upheaval that raged in the Anglo-Egyptian Sudan for most of the last two decades of the century, were dedicated to bringing down an existing social order in order to replace it with a religiously inspired utopian society. At the other end of the political spectrum, Western-educated dissidents sought to build strong nation-states patterned after those of western Europe. The disruptions that resulted from the interventions of Western industrial powers in informally dominated areas, such as China and the Ottoman Empire, often contributed to the emergence of these empires. But growing internal divisions within the movements themselves played a far greater role in precipitating these great rebellions and determining their impact on China and the Middle East in the last half of the 19th century.

## From Empire to Nation: Ottoman Retreat and the Birth of Turkey

■ **Weakened by internal strife and unable to prevent European rivals from whittling away its territories on all sides, the Ottoman Empire appeared near disintegration. But in the late 18th century, able Ottoman rulers and committed reformers devised strategies that slowed the decline of the empire and the advance of the European powers.**

In part, the Ottoman crisis was brought on by a succession of weak rulers within a political and social order that was centered on the sultan at the top. Inactive or inept sultans opened the way for power struggles between rival ministers, religious experts, and the commanders of the Janissary corps. Competition between elite factions further eroded effective leadership within the empire, weakening its control over the population and resources it claimed to rule. Provincial officials colluded with the local land-owning classes, the ayan, to cheat the sultan of a good portion of the taxes due him, and they skimmed all the revenue they could from the already impoverished peasantry in the countryside.

At the same time, the position of the artisan workers in the towns deteriorated because of competition from imported manufactures from Europe. Particularly in the 18th and early 19th centuries, this led to urban riots in which members of artisan guilds and young men's associations often took a leading role. Merchants within the empire, especially those who belonged to minority religious communities such as the Jews and Christians, grew more and more dependent on commercial dealings with their European counterparts. This pattern accelerated the influx of Western manufactured goods that was steadily undermining handicraft industries within the empire. In this way, Ottoman economic dependence on some of its most threatening European political rivals increased alarmingly.

With the Ottoman leaders embroiled in internal squabbles and their armies deprived of the resources needed to match the great advances in weaponry and training made by European rivals, the far-flung Ottoman possessions proved an irresistible temptation for their neighbors (see Visualizing the Past feature, p. 712). In the early 18th century, the Austrian Habsburg dynasty was the main beneficiary of Ottoman decadence. The long-standing threat to Vienna was forever vanquished, and the Ottomans were pushed out of Hungary and the northern Balkans.

In the late 1700s, the Russian Empire, strengthened by Peter the Great's forced Westernization (see Chapter 23), became the main threat to the Ottomans' survival. As military setbacks mounted and the Russians advanced across the steppes toward warm-water ports on the Black Sea, the Ottomans' weakness was underscored by their attempts to forge alliances with other Christian powers. As the Russians gobbled up poorly defended Ottoman lands in the Caucasus and Crimea, the subject Christian peoples of the Balkans grew more and more restive under Ottoman rule. In 1804 a major uprising broke out in Serbia that was repressed only after years of difficult and costly military campaigns. But military force could not quell the Greek revolt that broke out in the early 1820s, and by 1830 the Greeks had regained their independence after centuries of Ottoman rule. In 1867 Serbia also gained its freedom, and by the late 1870s the Ottomans had been driven from nearly the whole of the Balkans and thus most of the European provinces of their empire. In the decades that followed, Istanbul was repeatedly threatened by Russian armies or those of the newly independent Balkan states.

### Reform and Survival

Despite almost two centuries of unrelieved defeats on the battlefield and steady losses of territory, the Ottoman Empire somehow managed to survive into the 20th century. Its survival resulted in part from divisions between the European powers, each of which feared that the others would gain more from the total dismemberment of the empire. In fact, the British concern to prevent the Russians from controlling Istanbul—thus gaining direct access to and threatening British naval dominance in the Mediterranean—led them to prop up the tottering Ottoman regime repeatedly in the last half of the 19th century. Ultimately, the Ottomans' survival depended on reforms from within, initiated by the sultans and their advisors at the top of the imperial system and carried out in stages over most of the 19th century. At each stage, reform initiatives increased

Southeast Europe and the Ottoman Empire

tensions within the ruling elite. Some factions advocated far-reaching change along European lines, others argued for reforms based on precedents from the early Ottoman period, and other elite groups had a vested interest in blocking change of any sort.

These deep divisions within the Ottoman elite made reform a dangerous enterprise. Although modest innovations, including the introduction of the first printing press in 1727, had been enacted in the 18th century, Sultan **Selim III** (r. 1789–1807) believed that bolder initiatives were needed if the dynasty and empire were to survive. But his reform efforts, aimed at improving administrative efficiency and building a new army and navy, angered powerful factions within the bureaucracy. They were also seen by the Janissary corps, which had long been the dominant force in the Ottoman military (see Chapter 26), as a direct threat. Selim's modest initiatives cost him his throne—he was toppled by a Janissary revolt in 1807—and his life.

Two decades later, a more skillful sultan, **Mahmud II,** succeeded where Selim III had failed. After secretly building a small professional army with the help of European advisors, in 1826 Mahmud II ordered his agents to incite a mutiny of the Janissaries. This began when the angry Janissaries overturned the huge soup kettles in their mess area. With little thought given to planning their next move, the Janissaries poured into the streets of Istanbul, more a mob than a military force. Once on the streets, they were shocked to be confronted by the sultan's well-trained new army. The confrontation ended in the slaughter of the Janissaries, their families, and the Janissaries' religious allies.

After cowing the ayan, or provincial notables, into at least formal submission to the throne, Mahmud II launched a program of much more far-reaching reforms than Selim III had attempted. Although the ulama, or religious experts, and some of Mahmud's advisors argued for self-strengthening through a return to the Ottoman and Islamic past, Mahmud II patterned his reform program on Western precedents. After all, the Western powers had made a shambles of his empire. He established a diplomatic corps on Western lines and exchanged ambassadors with the European powers (Figure 31.2). The westernization of the army was expanded from Mahmud's secret force to the whole military establishment. European military advisors, both army and navy, were imported to supervise the overhaul of Ottoman training, armament, and officers' education.

In the decades that followed, Western influences were pervasive at the upper levels of Ottoman society, particularly during the period of the **Tanzimat reforms** between 1839 and 1876. University education was reorganized on Western lines, and training in the European sciences and mathematics was introduced. State-run postal and telegraph systems were established in the 1830s, and railways were built in the 1860s. Newspapers were established in the major towns of the empire. Extensive legal reforms were enacted, and in 1876 a constitution, based heavily on European prototypes, was promulgated. These legal reforms greatly improved the position of minority religious groups, whose role in the Ottoman economy increased steadily.

Reform of the State as an Imperial Project: The Hatt-i Serif of Gülhane, November 3, 1839

Some groups were adversely affected by these changes, which opened the empire more and more to Western influences. This was especially true of the artisans, whose position was gravely weakened by an 1838 treaty with the British that removed import taxes and other barriers to foreign trade that had protected indigenous producers from competition from the

**FIGURE 31.2** In the courtyard of the Topkapi Palace in Istanbul, Sultan Selim III receives dignitaries from throughout the Ottoman Empire in the midst of a splendidly attired imperial entourage.

Women and Children Workers in an Ottoman Textile Mill, 1878

West. Other social groups gained little from the Tanzimat reforms. This was particularly true of women. Proposals for women's education and an end to seclusion, polygamy, and veiling were debated in Ottoman intellectual circles from the 1860s onward. But few improvements in the position of women, even among the elite classes, were won until after the last Ottoman sultan was driven from power in 1908.

## Repression and Revolt

The reforms initiated by the sultans and their advisors improved the Ottomans' ability to fend off, or at least deflect, the assaults of foreign aggressors. But they increasingly threatened the dynasty responsible for them. Western-educated bureaucrats, military officers, and professionals came increasingly to view the sultanate as a major barrier to even more radical reforms and the full transformation of society. The new elites also clashed with conservative but powerful groups, such as the ulama and the ayan, who had a vested interest in preserving as much as possible of the old order.

The Ottoman Sultan **Abdul Hamid** responded to the growing threat from westernized officers and civilians by attempting a return to despotic absolutism during his long reign from 1878 to 1908. He nullified the constitution and restricted civil liberties, particularly the freedom of the press. These measures deprived westernized elite groups of the power they had gained in forming imperial policies. Dissidents or even suspected troublemakers were imprisoned and sometimes tortured and killed. But the deep impact of decades of reform was demonstrated by the fact that even Abdul Hamid continued to push for westernization in certain areas. The military continued to adopt European arms and techniques, increasingly under the instruction of German advisors. In addition, railways, including the famous line that linked Berlin to Baghdad, and telegraph lines were built between the main population centers. Western-style educational institutions grew, and judicial reforms continued.

The Decline of the Ottoman Empire

The despotism of Abdul Hamid came to an abrupt end in the nearly bloodless coup of 1908. Resistance to his authoritarian rule had led exiled Turkish intellectuals and political agitators to found the **Ottoman Society for Union and Progress** in Paris in 1889. Professing their loyalty to the Ottoman regime, the Young Turks (Figure 31.3), as members of the society came to be known, were determined to restore the 1876 constitution and resume far-reaching reforms within the empire. Clandestine printing presses operated by the Young Turks turned out tracts denouncing the regime and outlining further steps to be taken to modernize and thus save the empire. Assassinations were attempted and coups plotted, but until 1908 all were undone by a combination of divisions within the ranks of the westernized dissidents and police countermeasures.

Political Oppression in the Ottoman Empire

Sympathy within the military for the 1908 coup had much to do with its success. Perhaps even more important was the fact that only a handful of the sultan's

**FIGURE 31.3** Taken after Turkey's defeat in World War I and the successful struggles of the Turks to prevent the partition of their heartlands in Asia Minor, this photo features a group of Young Turks who had survived these challenges and grown a good deal older. The man in the business suit in the center is Mustafa Kemal, or Ataturk, who emerged as a masterful military commander in the war and went on to become the founder of modern Turkey.

IN DEPTH

## Western Dominance and the Decline of Civilizations

As we have seen in our examination of the forces that led to the breakup of the great civilizations in human history, each civilization has a unique history. But some general patterns have been associated with the decline of civilizations. Internal weaknesses and external pressures have acted over time to erode the institutions and break down the defenses of even the largest and most sophisticated civilizations. In the preindustrial era, slow and vulnerable communication systems were a major barrier to the long-term cohesion of the political systems that held civilizations together. Ethnic, religious, and regional differences, which were overridden by the confidence and energy of the founders of civilizations, reemerged. Self-serving corruption and the pursuit of pleasure gradually eroded the sense of purpose of the elite groups that had played a pivotal role in civilized development. The resulting deterioration in governance and military strength increased social tensions and undermined fragile preindustrial economies.

*"A major factor in the fall of nearly every great civilization, from those of the Indus valley and Mesopotamia to Rome and the civilizations of Mesoamerica, was an influx of nomadic peoples, whom sedentary peoples almost invariably saw as barbarians."*

Growing social unrest from within was paralleled by increasing threats from without. A major factor in the fall of nearly every great civilization, from those of the Indus valley and Mesopotamia to Rome and the civilizations of Mesoamerica, was an influx of nomadic peoples, whom sedentary peoples almost invariably saw as barbarians. Nomadic assaults revealed the weaknesses of the ruling elites and destroyed their military base. Their raids also disrupted the agricultural routines and smashed the public works on which all civilizations rested. Normally, the nomadic invaders stayed to rule the sedentary peoples they had conquered, as has happened repeatedly in China, Mesoamerica, and the Islamic world. Elsewhere, as occurred after the disappearance of the Indus valley civilization in India and after the fall of Rome, the vanquished civilization was largely forgotten or lay dormant for centuries. But over time, the invading peoples living in its ruins managed to restore patterns of civilized life that were quite different from, though sometimes influenced by, the civilization their incursions had helped to destroy centuries earlier.

Neighboring civilizations sometimes clashed in wars on their frontiers, but it was rare for one civilization to play a major part in the demise of another. In areas such as Mesopotamia, where civilizations were crowded together in space and time in the latter millennia B.C.E., older, long-dominant civilizations were overthrown and absorbed by upstart rivals. In most cases, however, and often in Mesopotamia, external threats to civilizations came from nomadic peoples. This was true even of Islamic civilization, which proved the most expansive before

Young Turks Overthrow Abdul Hamid II, 1908

supporters were willing to die defending the regime. Although a group of officers came to power, they restored the constitution and press freedoms and promised reforms in education, administration, and even the status of women. The sultan was retained as a political figurehead and the highest religious authority in Islam.

Unfortunately, the officers soon became embroiled in factional fights that took up much of the limited time remaining before the outbreak of World War I. In addition, their hold on power was shaken when they lost a new round of wars in the Balkans and a conflict against Italy over Libya, the Ottomans' last remaining possession in north Africa. Just as the sultans had before them, however, the Young Turk officers managed to stave off the collapse of the empire by achieving last-gasp military victories and by playing the hostile European powers against each other.

The Young Turk Revolution, 1908

Although it is difficult to know how the Young Turks would have fared if it had not been for the outbreak of World War I, their failure to resolve several critical issues did not bode well for the future. They overthrew the sultan, but they could not bring themselves to give up the empire ruled by Turks for over 600 years. The peoples most affected by their decision to salvage what was left of the empire were the Arabs of the Fertile Crescent and coastal Arabia, who still remained under Ottoman control. Arab leaders in Beirut and Damascus had initially favored the 1908 coup because they believed it would bring about the end of their long domination by the Turks. To their dismay, the Arabs discovered that the Young Turks not only meant to continue their subjugation but were determined to enforce state control to a degree unthinkable to the later Ottoman sultans. The quarrels between the leaders of the Young Turk coalition and the growing resistance in the Arab portions of the emergence of Europe and whose rise and spread brought about the collapse of several long-established civilized centers. The initial Arab explosion from Arabia that felled Sasanian Persia and captured Egypt was nomadic. But the incursions of the Arab bedouins differed from earlier and later nomadic assaults on neighboring civilizations. The Arab armies carried a new religion with them from Arabia that provided the basis for a new civilization, which incorporated the older ones they conquered. Thus, like other nomadic conquerors, they borrowed heavily from the civilizations they overran.

The emergence of western Europe as an expansive global force radically changed long-standing patterns of interaction between civilizations as well as between civilizations and nomadic peoples. From the first years of overseas exploration, the aggressive Europeans proved a threat to other civilizations. Within decades of Columbus' arrival in 1492, European military assaults had destroyed two of the great centers of civilization in the Americas: the Aztec and Inca empires. The previous isolation of the Native American societies and their consequent susceptibility to European diseases, weapons, plants, and livestock made them more vulnerable than most of the peoples the Europeans encountered overseas. Therefore, in the first centuries of Western expansion, most of the existing civilizations in Africa and Asia proved capable of standing up to the Europeans, except on the sea. With the scientific discoveries and especially the technological innovations that transformed Europe in the 17th and 18th centuries, all of this gradually changed. The unparalleled extent of the western Europeans' mastery of the natural world gave them new sources of power for resource extraction, manufacture, and war. By the end of the 18th century, this power was being translated into the economic, military, and increasingly the political domination of other civilizations.

A century later, the Europeans had either conquered most of these civilizations or reduced them to spheres they controlled indirectly and threatened to annex. The adverse effects of economic influences from the West, and Western political domination, proved highly damaging to civilizations as diverse as those of west Africa, the Islamic heartlands, and China. For several decades before World War I, it appeared that the materially advanced and expansive West would level all other civilized centers. In that era, most leading European, and some African and Asian, thinkers and political leaders believed that the rest of humankind had no alternative (except perhaps a reversion to savagery or barbarism) other than to follow the path of development pioneered by the West. All non-Western peoples became preoccupied with coping with the powerful challenges posed by the industrial West to the survival of their civilized past and the course of their future development.

**Questions** Can you think of instances in which one preindustrial civilization was a major factor in the collapse of another? Why do you think such an occurrence was so rare? Discuss the advantages that the Native Americans' isolation from civilizations in Europe, Africa, and Asia gave the European intruders in the 16th century. What kinds of advantages did the scientific and industrial revolutions give the Europeans over all other civilized peoples from the 18th century onward? Is the West losing these advantages today?

what was left of the Ottoman Empire were suddenly cut short in August 1914.

## Western Intrusions and the Crisis in the Arab Islamic Heartlands

■ **The profound crisis of confidence brought on by successive reverses and the increasing strength of European rivals elicited a variety of responses in the Islamic world. Islamic thinkers debated the best way to reverse the decline and drive back the Europeans. Some argued for a return to the Islamic past; others favored a large-scale adoption of Western ways.**

By the early 1800s, the Arab peoples of the Fertile Crescent, Egypt, coastal Arabia, and north Africa had lived for centuries under Ottoman-Turkish rule. Although most Arabs resented Turkish domination, they could identify with the Ottomans as fellow Muslims, who were both ardent defenders of the faith and patrons of Islamic culture. Still, the steadily diminishing capacity of the Ottomans to defend the Arab Islamic heartlands left them at risk of conquest by the aggressive European powers. The European capture of outlying but highly developed Islamic states, from those in the Indonesian archipelago and India to Algeria in north Africa, engendered a sense of crisis among the Islamic faithful in the Middle Eastern heartlands. From the most powerful adversaries of Christendom, the Muslims had become the besieged. The Islamic world had been displaced by the West as the leading civilization in a wide range of endeavors, from scientific inquiry to monumental architecture.

## Muhammad Ali and the Failure of Westernization in Egypt

Although it did not establish a permanent European presence in the Islamic heartlands, Napoleon's invasion of Egypt in 1798 sent shock waves across what remained of the independent Muslim world. Significantly, Napoleon's motives for launching the expedition had little to do with designs for empire in the Middle East. Rather, he saw the Egyptian campaign as the prelude to destroying British power in India, where the French had come out on the short end of earlier wars for empire. Whatever his calculations, Napoleon managed to slip his fleet past the British blockade in the Mediterranean and put ashore his armies in July 1798 (see Visualizing the Past feature, p. 712). There followed one of the most lopsided military clashes in modern history. As they advanced inland, Napoleon's forces were met by tens of thousands of cavalry bent on defending the Mamluk regime that then ruled Egypt as a vassal of the Ottoman sultans. The term *Mamluk* literally meant slave, and it suggested the Turkic origins of the regime in Egypt. Beginning as slaves who served Muslim overlords, the Mamluks had centuries earlier risen in the ranks as military commanders and seized power in their own name. **Murad,** the head of the coalition of Mamluk households that shared power in Egypt at the time of Napoleon's arrival, dismissed the invader as a donkey boy whom he would soon drive from his lands.

Murad's contempt for the talented young French commander was symptomatic of the profound ignorance of events in Europe that was typical of the Islamic world at the time. This ignorance led to a series of crushing defeats, the most famous of which came in a battle fought beneath the pyramids of the ancient Egyptian pharaohs (see Figure 31.4). In that brief but bloody battle, the disciplined firepower of the French legions devastated the ranks of Mamluk cavalry, who were clad in

FIGURE 31.4 Napoleon's victory in the Battle of the Pyramids led to a short-lived, but transformative, French occupation of Egypt.

medieval armor and wielded spears against the artillery Napoleon used with such devastating effect.

Because the Mamluks had long been seen as fighters of great prowess in the Islamic world, their rout was traumatic. It revealed just how vulnerable even the Muslim core areas were to European aggression and how far the Muslims had fallen behind the Europeans in the capacity to wage war. Ironically, the successful invasion of Egypt brought little advantage to Napoleon or the French. The British caught up with the French fleet and sank most of it at the Battle of Aboukir in August 1798. With his supply line cut off, Napoleon was forced to abandon his army and sneak back to Paris, where his enemies were trying to use his reverses in Egypt to put an end to his rise to power. Thus, Egypt was spared European conquest for a time. But the reprieve brought little consolation to thoughtful Muslims because the British, not Egypt's Muslim defenders, had been responsible for the French retreat.

In the chaos that followed the French invasion and eventual withdrawal in 1801, a young officer of Albanian origins named **Muhammad Ali** emerged as the effective ruler of Egypt. Deeply impressed by the weapons and discipline of the French armies, the Albanian upstart devoted his energies and the resources of the land that he had brought under his rule to building an up-to-date European-style military force. He introduced Western-style conscription among the Egyptian peasantry, hired French officers to train his troops, imported Western arms, and adopted Western tactics and modes of organization and supply. Within years he had put together the most effective fighting force in the Middle East. With it, he flouted the authority of his nominal overlord, the Ottoman sultan, by successfully invading Syria and building a modern war fleet that threatened Istanbul on a number of occasions.

Although Muhammad Ali's efforts to introduce reforms patterned after Western precedents were not confined to the military, they fell far short of a fundamental transformation of Egyptian society. To shore up his economic base, he ordered the Egyptian peasantry to increase their production of cotton, hemp, indigo, and other crops that were in growing demand in industrial Europe. Efforts to improve Egyptian harbors and extend irrigation works met with some success and led to modest increases in the revenues that could be devoted to the continuing modernization of the military. Attempts to reform education were ambitious, but little was actually achieved. Numerous schemes to build up an Egyptian industrial sector were frustrated by the opposition of the European powers and the intense competition from imported, Western-manufactured goods.

The limited scope of Muhammad Ali's reforms ultimately checked his plans for territorial expansion and left Egypt open to inroads by the European powers. He died in 1848, embittered by the European opposition that had prevented him from mastering the Ottoman sultans and well aware that his empire beyond Egypt was crumbling. Lacking Muhammad Ali's ambition and ability, his successors were content to confine their claims to Egypt and the Sudanic lands that stretched from the banks of the upper Nile to the south. Intermarrying with Turkish families that had originally come to Egypt to govern in the name of the Ottoman sultans, Muhammad Ali's descendants provided a succession of rulers who were known as **khedives** after 1867. The khedives were the formal rulers of Egypt until they were overthrown by the military coup that brought Gamel Abdul Nasser to power in 1952.

## Bankruptcy, European Intervention, and Strategies of Resistance

Muhammad Ali's successors made a muddle of his efforts to reform and revitalize Egyptian society. While cotton production increased and the landlord class grew fat, the great majority of the peasants went hungry. The long-term consequences of these developments were equally troubling. The great expansion of cotton production at the expense of food grains and other crops rendered Egypt dependent on a single export. This meant that it was vulnerable to sharp fluctuations in demand (and thus price) on the European markets to which most of it was exported. Some further educational advances were made. But these were mainly at elite schools where French was the language of instruction.

Much of the revenue the khedives managed to collect, despite the resistance of the ayan, was wasted on the extravagant pastimes of the mostly idle elite connected to the palace. Most of what was left was squandered on fruitless military campaigns to assert Egyptian authority over the Sudanic peoples along the upper Nile. The increasing inability of the khedives to balance their books led in the mid-19th century to their growing indebtedness to European financiers. The latter lent money to the khedives and members of the Turkish elite because the financiers wanted continued access to Egypt's cheap cotton. By the 1850s, they had a second motive: a share in the potentially lucrative schemes to build a canal across the isthmus of Suez that would connect the Mediterranean and Red seas. The completion of the **Suez Canal** in 1869, depicted while still under construction in Figure 31.5, transformed Egypt into one of the most strategic places on earth. The canal soon became a vital commercial and military link between the European powers

Disraeli Purchasing Controlling Interest in the Suez Canal

**FIGURE 31.5** Building a canal across the desert isthmus of Suez was a remarkable engineering feat. A massive investment in up-to-date technology was needed. By creating a water route between the Mediterranean and Red seas, the canal greatly shortened the travel time between Europe and maritime Asia as well as the east coast of Africa. Combined with the growing predominance of steamships, it helped to expand global commerce as well as tourism, which became a major middle-class activity in the late 19th century.

and their colonial empires in Asia and east Africa. Controlling it became one of the key objectives of their peaceful rivalries and wartime operations through the first half of the 20th century.

The ineptitude of the khedival regime and the Ottoman sultans, who were their nominal overlords, prompted discussion among Muslim intellectuals and political activists as to how to ward off the growing European menace. In the mid-19th century, Egypt, and particularly Cairo's ancient Muslim University of al-Azhar, became key meeting places of these thinkers from throughout the Islamic world. Some prominent Islamic scholars called for a jihad to drive the infidels from Muslim lands. They also argued that the Muslim world could be saved only by a return to the patterns of religious observance and social interaction that they believed had existed in the golden age of Muhammad.

Other thinkers, such as **al-Afghani** (1839–1897) and his disciple **Muhammad Abduh** (1849–1905), stressed the need for Muslims to borrow scientific learning and technology from the West and to revive their earlier capacity to innovate. They argued that Islamic civilization had once taught the Europeans much in the sciences and mathematics, including such critical concepts as the Indian numerals. Thus, it was fitting that Muslims learn from the advances the Europeans had made with the help of Islamic borrowings. Those who advocated this approach also stressed the importance of the tradition of rational inquiry in Islamic history. They strongly disputed the views of religious scholars who contended that the Qur'an was the source of all truth and should be interpreted literally.

Although both religious revivalists and those who stressed the need for imports from the West agreed on the need for Muslim unity in the face of the growing European threat, they could not reconcile their very different approaches to Islamic renewal. Their differences, and the uncertainties they injected into Islamic efforts to cope with the challenges of the West, remain central problems in the Muslim world today.

Religious and Secular Opposition Within the Middle East

The mounting debts of the khedival regime and the strategic importance of the canal gave the European powers, particularly Britain and France, a growing stake in the stability and accessibility of Egypt. French and British bankers, who had bought up a good portion of the khedives' shares in the canal, urged their governments to intervene militarily when the khedives proved unable to meet their loan payments. In the early 1880s, a major challenge to the influence of foreign interests was mounted by the supporters of a charismatic young Egyptian officer named **Ahmad Orabi.** The son of a small farmer in lower Egypt, Orabi had attended Qur'anic school and studied under the reform-minded Muhammad Abduh at al-Azhar. Though a native Egyptian, Orabi had risen in the ranks of the khedival army and had become increasingly critical of the fact that the officer corps was dominated by Turks with strong ties to the khedival regime. An attempt by the khedive to save money by disbanding Egyptian regiments and dismissing Egyptian officers sparked a revolt led by Orabi in the summer of 1882. Riots in the city of Alexandria, associated with mutinies in the Egyptian armies, drove the frightened khedive to seek British assistance. After bombarding the coastal batteries set up by Orabi's troops, the British sent ashore an expeditionary force that crushed Orabi's rebellion and secured the position of the khedive.

Although Egypt was not formally colonized, the British intervention began decades of dominance both by British consuls, who ruled through the puppet khedives, and by British advisors to all high-ranking Egyptian administrators. British officials controlled Egypt's finances and foreign affairs; British troops ensured that their directives were heeded by Egyptian administrators. Direct European control over the Islamic heartlands had begun.

## Jihad: The Mahdist Revolt in the Sudan

As Egypt fell under British control, the invaders were drawn into the turmoil and conflict that gripped the Sudanic region to the south. Egyptian efforts to conquer and rule the Sudan, beginning in the 1820s, were resisted fiercely. The opposition forces were led by the camel- and cattle-herding nomads who occupied the vast, arid plains that stretched west and east from the upper Nile. The sedentary peoples who worked the narrow strip of fertile land along the river were more easily dominated. Thus, Egyptian authority, insofar as it existed, was concentrated in these areas and in river towns such as **Khartoum,** which was the center of Egyptian administration in the Sudan.

Even in the riverine areas, Egyptian rule was greatly resented. The Egyptian regime was notoriously corrupt, and its taxes placed a heavy burden on the peasants compelled to pay them. The Egyptians were clearly outsiders, and the favoritism they showed some of the Sudanic tribes alienated the others. In addition, nearly all groups in the Muslim areas in the north Sudan were angered by Egyptian attempts in the 1870s to eradicate the slave trade. The trade had long been a great source of profit for both the merchants of the Nile towns and the nomads, who attacked non-Muslim peoples, such as the Dinka in the south, to capture slaves.

By the late 1870s, Egyptian oppression and British intervention had aroused deep resentment and hostility. But a leader was needed to unite the diverse and often divided peoples of the region and to provide an ideology that would give focus and meaning to rebellion. **Muhammad Achmad** proved to be that leader. He was the son of a boat builder, and he had been educated by the head of a local Sufi brotherhood. The fact that his family claimed descent from Muhammad and that he had the physical signs—a cleft between his teeth and a mole on his right cheek—that the local people associated with the promised deliverer, or **Mahdi,** advanced his reputation. The visions he began to experience, after he had broken with his Sufi master and established his own sectarian following, also suggested that a remarkable future was in store. What was seen to be a miraculous escape from a bungled Egyptian effort to capture and imprison Muhammad Achmad soon led to his widespread acceptance as a divinely appointed leader of revolt against the foreign intruders.

The jihad that Muhammad Achmad, who came to be known to his followers as the Mahdi, proclaimed against both the Egyptian heretics and British infidels was one of a number of such movements that had swept through sub-Saharan Africa since the 18th century. It represented the most extreme and violent Islamic response to what was perceived as the dilution of Islam in the African environment and the growing threat of Europe. Muhammad Achmad promised to purge Islam of what he saw as superstitious beliefs and degrading practices that had built up over the centuries, thus returning the faith to what he claimed was its original purity. He led his followers in a violent assault on the Egyptians, whom he believed professed a corrupt version of Islam, and on the European infidels. At one point, his successors dreamed of toppling the Ottoman sultans and invading Europe.

The Mahdi's skillful use of guerrilla tactics and the confidence his followers placed in his blessings and magical charms earned his forces several stunning victories over the Egyptians. Within a few years the Mahdist forces were in control of an area corresponding roughly to the present-day nation of Sudan. At the peak of his power, the Mahdi fell ill with typhus and died. In contrast to many movements of this type,

VISUALIZING THE PAST

## Mapping the Decline of Civilizations

Throughout much of human history, the size of the empires associated with major civilizations was usually a pretty good gauge of the extent of the political power, economic prosperity, and cultural influence they enjoyed. Civilizations on the rise were expansive and compelled even neighboring peoples who were not directly ruled to acknowledge their dominance. By contrast, civilizations in decline lost control of their borderlands to rival empires or suffered invasions—often by nomadic peoples—into the heart of the vast domains that their ruling dynasties continued to claim long after they could effectively govern them.

In the 18th and 19th centuries, two of the largest and most enduring empires in human history, the Ottoman and Qing, spiraled into decline. The plight of each of these empires is illustrated by the maps included here, which trace the advance of rival powers and the rise of internal resistance.

**Questions** Which of the empires would have been harder to defend? Compare the timing and nature of the external threats posed for each of the empires by rival powers and other external enemies in the late 18th and 19th centuries. Why was China affected somewhat later? Why were the Qing so much slower to respond to the outside threat compared to the Ottomans? Why were the Chinese more reluctant than the Ottomans to adopt the weapons and methods of their enemies? Which of the empires was more threatened by internal rebellions? In what ways did these empires' territorial losses differ? Why did the Chinese nation that emerged from the collapse of the Qing empire hold onto more territory than did the modern nation of Turkey, which lost all of the Ottoman domains except Anatolia and a small corner of the Balkans west of Istanbul?

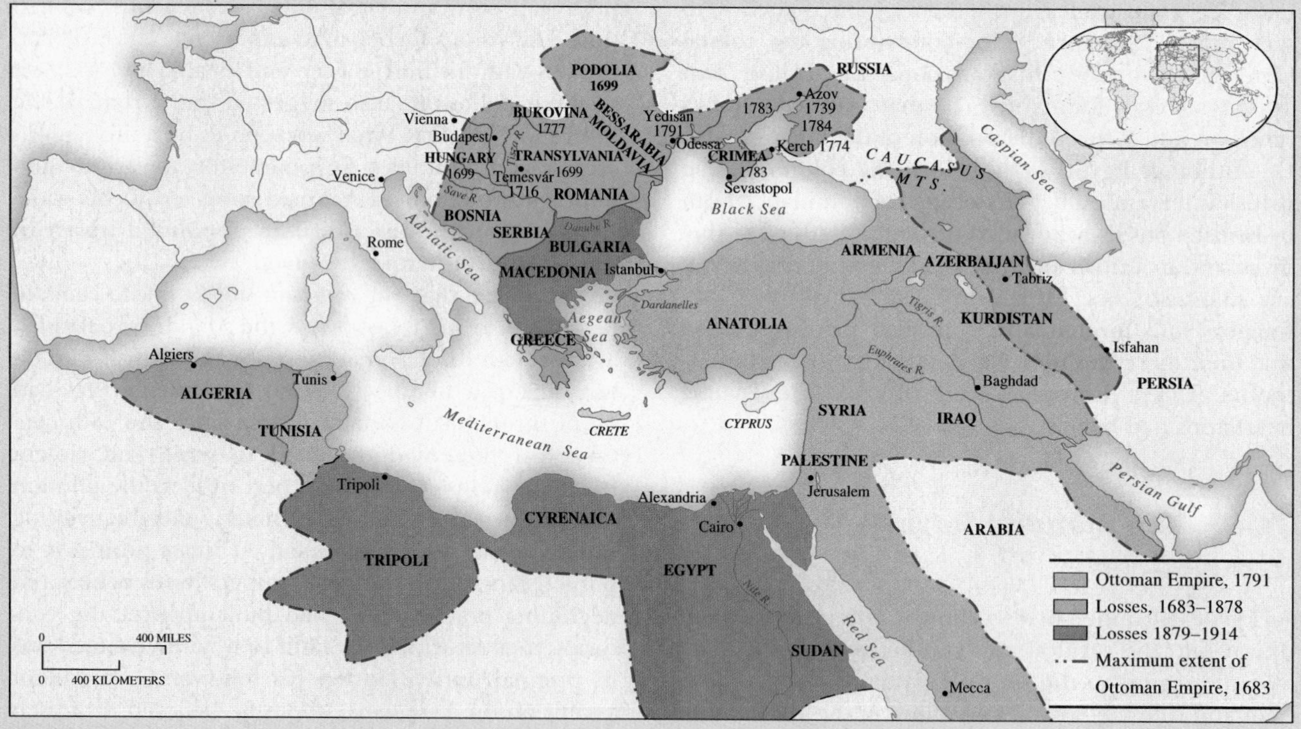


Ottoman Empire from Late 18th Century to World War I

which collapsed rapidly after the death of their prophetic leaders, the Mahdists found a capable successor for Muhammad Achmad. The **Khalifa Abdallahi** had been one of the Mahdi's most skillful military commanders. Under Abdallahi, the Mahdists built a strong, expansive state. They also sought to build a closely controlled society in which smoking, dancing, and alcoholic drink were forbidden, and theft, prostitution, and adultery were severely punished. Islamic religious and ritual practices were enforced rigorously. In addi-

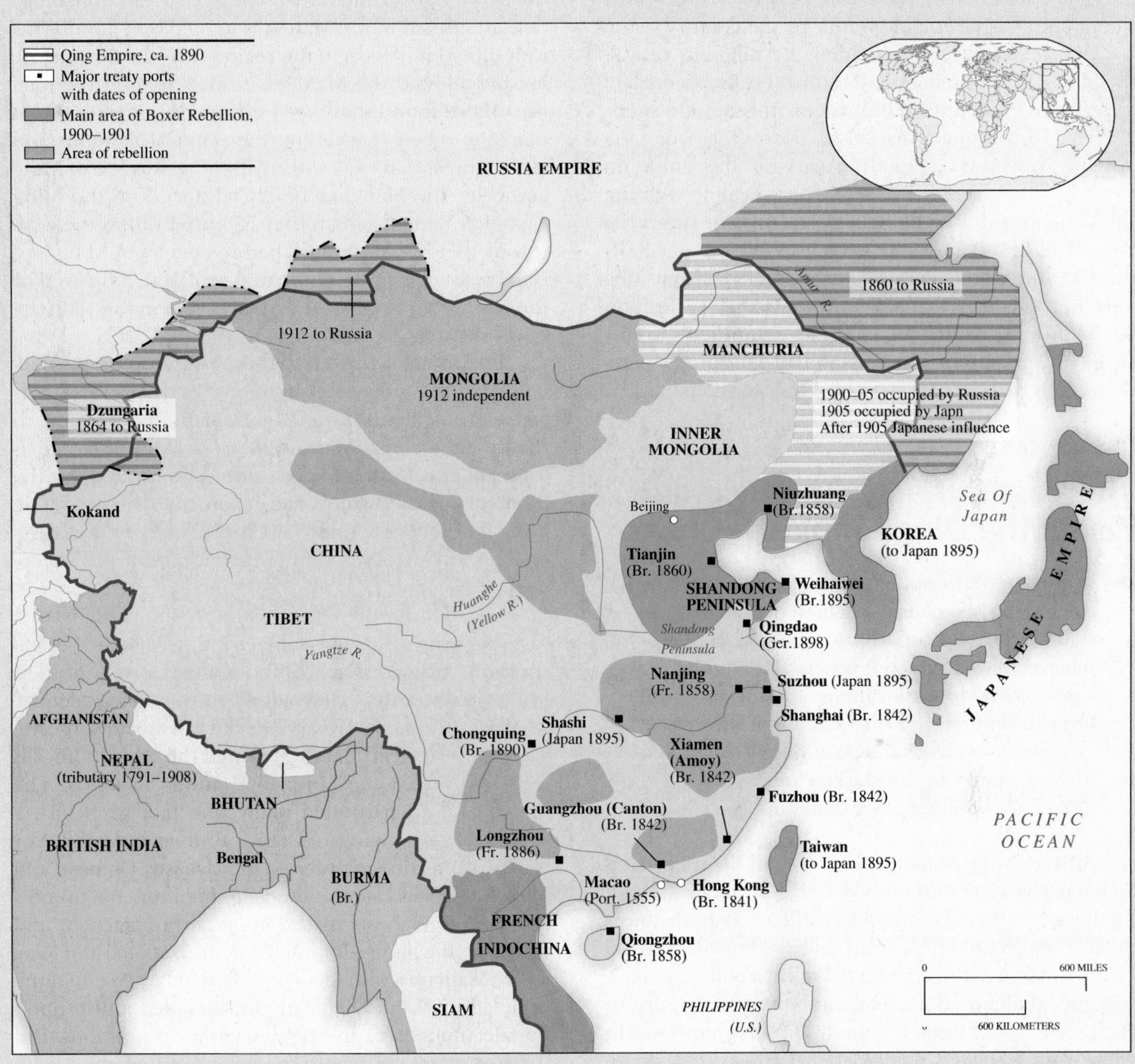


Qing Empire from Opium War of 1839–1841 to World War I

tion, most foreigners were imprisoned or expelled, and the ban on slavery was lifted.

For nearly a decade, Mahdist armies attacked or threatened neighboring states on all sides, including the Egyptians to the north. But in the fall of 1896, the famous British General Kitchener was sent with an expeditionary force to put an end to one of the most serious threats to European domination in Africa. The spears and magical garments of the Mahdist forces proved no match for the machine guns and artillery of

Kitchener's columns. At the battle of Omdurman in 1898, thousands of the Mahdist cavalry were slaughtered. Within a year the Mahdist state collapsed, and British power advanced yet again into the interior of Africa.

The 19th century was a time of severe reverses for the peoples of the Islamic world. By the century's end, it was clear that neither the religious revivalists, who called for a return to a purified Islam free of Western influences, nor the reformers, who argued that some borrowing from the West was essential for survival, had come up with a successful formula for dealing with the powerful challenges posed by the industrial West. Failing to find adequate responses and deeply divided, the Islamic community grew increasingly anxious over the dangers that lay ahead. Islamic civilization was by no means defeated. But its continued viability clearly was threatened by its powerful European neighbor, which had become master of the world.

The Middle East Enters the World Economy

## The Last Dynasty: The Rise and Fall of the Qing Empire in China

- **In the late 18th century, a long period of strong rule by the Manchus and a high degree of social stability, if not prosperity, for the Chinese people gave way to rampant official corruption, severe economic dislocations, and social unrest. Over the course of the 19th century, the Western powers took advantage of these weaknesses to force open China's markets and reduce its Qing rulers to little more than puppets.**

Although the Manchu nomads had been building an expansive state of their own north of the Great Wall for decades, their conquest of China was both unexpected and sudden. A local leader named **Nurhaci** (1559–1626) was the architect of unity among the quarrelsome Manchu tribes. He combined the cavalry of each tribe into extremely cohesive fighting units within eight **banner armies,** named after the flags that identified each. In the first decades of the 17th century, Nurhaci brought much of Manchuria, including a number of non-Manchu peoples, under his rule (see Visualizing the Past feature, p. 712). Although he remained the nominal vassal of the Chinese Ming emperor, Nurhaci's forces continually harassed the Chinese who lived north of the Great Wall. During this period, the Manchu elite's adoption of Chinese ways, which had begun much earlier, was greatly accelerated. The Manchu bureaucracy was organized along Chinese lines, Chinese court ceremonies were adopted, and Chinese scholar-officials found lucrative employment in the growing barbarian state north of the Great Wall.

The weakness of the declining Ming regime, rather than the Manchus' own strength, gave the Manchus an opportunity to seize control in China. Their entry into China resulted from a bit of luck. In 1644 an official of the Ming government in charge of the northern defenses called in the Manchus to help him put down a widespread rebellion in the region near the Great Wall. Having allowed the Manchus to pass beyond the wall, the official found that they were an even greater threat than the rebels. Exploiting the political divisions and social unrest that were destroying what was left of Ming authority, the Manchus boldly advanced on the Ming capital at Beijing, which they captured within the year. It took nearly two decades before centers of Ming and rebel resistance in the south and west were destroyed by the banner armies, but the Manchus soon found themselves the masters of China.

They quickly proved that they were up to the challenge of ruling the largest empire in the world. Their armies forced submission by nomadic peoples far to the west and compelled tribute from kingdoms such as Vietnam and Burma to the south. Within decades, the Manchu regime, which had taken the dynastic name **Qing** before its conquest of China, ruled an area larger than any previous Chinese dynasty with the exception of the Tang.

To reconcile the ethnic Chinese who made up the vast majority of their subjects, the Manchu rulers shrewdly retained much of the political system of their Ming predecessors. They added to the court calendar whatever Confucian rituals they did not already observe. They made it clear that they wanted the scholar-officials who had served the Ming to continue in office. The Manchus even pardoned many who had been instrumental in prolonging resistance to their conquest. For much of the first century of the dynasty, Chinese and Manchu officials were paired in appointments to most of the highest posts of the imperial bureaucracy, and Chinese officials predominated at the regional and local levels. Manchus, who made up less than 2 percent of the population of the Qing Empire, occupied a disproportionate number of the highest political positions. But there were few limits as to how high talented ethnic Chinese could rise in the imperial bureaucracy.

Unlike the Mongol conquerors who had abolished it, the Manchus retained the examination system and had their own sons educated in the Chinese classics. The Manchu emperors styled themselves the Sons of Heaven and rooted their claims to be the legitimate rulers of China in their practice of the traditional Confucian virtues. The early Manchu rulers were generous patrons of the Chinese arts, and at least one, **Kangxi** (1661–1722), was a significant Confucian scholar in his own right. Kangxi and other Manchu rulers employed thousands of scholars to compile great encyclopedias of Chinese learning.

## Economy and Society in the Early Centuries of Qing Rule

The Manchu determination to preserve much of the Chinese political system was paralleled by an equally conservative approach to Chinese society as a whole. In the early centuries of their reign, the writings of Zhu Xi, which had been so influential in the preceding dynastic eras, continued to dominate official thinking. Thus, long-nurtured values such as respect for rank and acceptance of hierarchy—that is, old over young, male over female, scholar-bureaucrat over commoner—were emphasized in education and imperial edicts. Among the elite classes, the extended family remained the core unit of the social order, and the state grew increasingly suspicious of any forms of social organization, such as guilds and especially secret societies, that rivaled it.

The lives of women at all social levels remained centered on or wholly confined to the household. There the dominance of elder men was upheld by familial pressures and the state. Male control was enhanced by the practice of choosing brides from families slightly lower in social status than those of the grooms. Because they were a loss to their parents' household at marriage and usually needed a sizeable dowry, daughters continued to be much less desirable than sons. Despite the poor quality of the statistics relating to the practice, there are indications that the incidence of female infanticide rose in this period. In the population as a whole, males considerably outnumbered females, the reverse of the balance between the two in contemporary industrial societies.

Beyond the family compound, the world pretty much belonged to men, although women from lower-class families continued to work in the fields and sell produce in the local markets. The best a married woman could hope for was strong backing from her father and brother after she had gone to her husband's home, as well as the good luck in the first place to be chosen as the wife rather than as a second or third partner in the form of a concubine. If they bore sons and lived long enough, wives took charge of running the household. In elite families they exercised control over other women and even younger men.

Some of the strongest measures the Manchus took after conquering China were aimed at alleviating the rural distress and unrest that had become so pronounced in the last years of Ming rule. Taxes and state labor demands were lowered. Incentives such as tax-free tenure were offered to those willing to resettle lands that had been abandoned in the turmoil of the preceding decades. A sizeable chunk of the imperial budget (up to 10 percent in the early years of the dynasty) was devoted to repairing existing dikes, canals, and roadways and extending irrigation works. Peasants were encouraged to plant new crops, including those for which there was market demand, and to grow two or even three crops per year on their holdings.

Given the growing population pressure on the cultivable acreage and the near disappearance in most areas of open lands that could be settled, the regime had very little success in its efforts to control the landlord classes. After several decades of holding steady, the landlord classes found that they could add to their estates by calling in loans to peasants or simply by buying them out. With a surplus of workers, tenants had less and less bargaining power in their dealings with landlords. If they objected to the share of the crop the landlords offered, they were turned off the land and replaced by those willing to accept even less. As a result, the gap between the rural gentry and ordinary peasants and laborers increased. One could not miss the old and new rich in the rural areas, as they rode or were carried in sedan chairs, decked out in silks and furs, to make social calls on their peers. To further display their superior social standing, many men of the gentry class let their nails grow long to demonstrate that they did not have to engage in physical labor.

The sector of Chinese society over which the Qing exercised the least control was also the most dynamic. The commercial and urban expansion that had begun in the Song era gained new strength in the long peace China enjoyed during the first century and a half of Manchu rule. Regional diversification in crops such as tea was matched by the development of new ways to finance agricultural and artisan production. Until the end of the 18th century, both the state and the mercantile classes profited enormously from the great influx of silver that poured into China in payment for its exports of tea, porcelain, and silk textiles. European and other foreign traders flocked to Canton, and Chinese merchants, freed from the restrictions against overseas travel of the late Ming, found lucrative market outlets overseas. Profits from overseas trade gave rise to a wealthy new group of merchants, the **compradors,** who specialized in the import-export trade on China's south coast. In the 19th century, these merchants proved to be one of the major links between China and the outside world.

## Rot from Within: Bureaucratic Breakdown and Social Disintegration

By the late 18th century, it was clear that like so many Chinese dynasties of the past, the Qing was in decline. The signs of decline were pervasive and familiar. The bureaucratic foundations of the Chinese Empire were rotting from within. The exam system, which had done well in selecting able and honest bureaucrats in the early decades of the dynasty, had become riddled with cheating and favoritism. Despite formal restrictions, sons of high officials often were ensured a place in the ever-growing bureaucracy. Even more disturbing was the fact that nearly anyone with enough money could buy a post for sons or brothers. Impoverished scholars could be paid to take the exams for poorly educated or not-so-bright relatives. Examiners could be bribed to approve weak credentials or look the other way when candidates consulted cheat sheets while taking their exams. In one of the most notorious cases of cheating, a merchant's son won high honors despite the fact that he had spent the days of testing in a brothel hundreds of miles from the examination site.

Cheating had become so blatant by the early 18th century that in 1711 students who had failed the exams at Yangzhou held a public demonstration to protest bribes given to the exam officials by wealthy salt merchants. The growing influx of merchants' and poorly educated landlords' sons into the bureaucracy was particularly troubling because few of them had received the classical Confucian education that stressed the responsibilities of the educated ruling classes and their obligation to serve the people. Increasingly, the wealthy saw positions in the bureaucracy as a means of influencing local officials and judges and enhancing family fortunes. Less and less concern was expressed for the effects of bureaucratic decisions on the peasantry and urban laborers.

Over several decades, the diversion of revenue from state projects to enrich individual families devastated Chinese society. For example, funds needed to maintain the armies and fleets that defended the huge empire fell off sharply. Not surprisingly, this resulted in a noticeable drop in the training and armament of the military. Even more critical for the masses were reductions in spending on public works projects. Of these, the most vital were the great dikes that confined the Huanghe (Yellow River) in northern China. Over the millennia, because of the silting of the river bottom and the constant repair of and additions to the dikes, the river and dikes were raised high above the densely populated farmlands through which they passed. Thus, when these great public works were neglected for lack of funds and proper official supervision of repairs, leaking dikes and the rampaging waters of the great river meant catastrophe for much of northeastern China.

Nowhere was this disaster more apparent than in the region of the Shandong peninsula (see Visualizing the Past feature, p. 713). Before the mid-19th century, the Huanghe emptied into the sea south of the peninsula. By the 1850s, however, the neglected dikes had broken down over much of the area, and the river had flooded hundreds of square miles of heavily cultivated farmland. By the 1860s, the main channel of the river flowed north of the peninsula. The lands in between had been flooded and the farms wiped out. Millions of peasants were left without livestock or land to cultivate. Tens—perhaps hundreds—of thousands of peasants died of famine and disease.

As the condition of the peasantry deteriorated in many parts of the empire, further signs of dynastic decline appeared. Food shortages and landlord demands prompted mass migrations. Vagabond bands clogged the roads, and beggars crowded the city streets. Banditry, long seen by the Chinese as one of the surest signs of dynastic decline, became a major problem in many districts. As the following verse from a popular ditty of the 1860s illustrates, the government's inability to deal with the bandits was seen as a further sign of Qing weakness:

> When the bandits arrive, where are the troops?
> When the troops come, the bandits have vanished.
> Alas, when will the bandits and troops meet?

The assumption then widely held by Chinese thinkers—that the dynastic cycle would again run its course and the Manchus would be replaced by a new and vigorous dynasty—was belied by the magnitude of the problems confronting the leaders of China. The belief that China's future could be predicted from the patterns of its past ignored the fact that there were no precedents for the critical changes that had occurred in China under Manchu rule. Some of these changes had their roots in the preceding Ming era (see Chapter 27), in which, for example, food crops from the Americas, such as corn and potatoes, had set in motion a population explosion. China desperately needed innovations in technology and organization that would increase its productivity to support its exploding population at a reasonable level. The corrupt and highly conservative late Manchu regime was increasingly an obstacle to, rather than a source of, these desperately needed changes.

## Barbarians at the Southern Gates: The Opium War and After

Another major difference between the forces sapping the strength of the Manchus and those that had brought down earlier dynasties was the nature of the "barbarians" who threatened the empire from outside. Out of ignorance, the Manchu rulers and their Chinese administrators treated the Europeans much like the nomads and other peoples they saw as barbarians. But the Europeans presented a very different sort of challenge. They came from a civilization that was China's equal in sophistication and complexity. In fact, although European nation-states such as Great Britain were much smaller in population (in the early 19th century, England had 7 million people to China's 400 million), the scientific and industrial revolutions allowed them to compensate for their smaller numbers with better organization and superior technology. These advantages proved critical in the wars between China and Britain and the other European powers that broke out in the mid-19th century.

The issue that was responsible for the initial hostilities between China and the British did little credit to the latter. For centuries, British merchants had eagerly exported silks, fine porcelains, tea, and other products from the Chinese empire. Finding that they had little in the way of manufactured goods or raw materials that the Chinese were willing to take in exchange for these products, the British were forced to trade growing amounts of silver bullion. Unhappy about the unfavorable terms of trade in China, British merchants hit on a possible solution in the form of opium, which was grown in the hills of eastern India. Although opium was also grown in China, the Indian variety was far more potent and was soon in great demand in the Middle Kingdom. By the early 19th century an annual average of 4500 chests of opium, each weighing 133 pounds, were sold, either legally or illegally, to merchants on the south China coast (Figure 31.6). By 1839, on the eve of the **Opium War,** nearly 40,000 chests were imported by the Chinese.

Although the British had found a way to reverse the trade balance in their favor, the Chinese soon realized that the opium traffic was a major threat to their economy and social order. Within years, China's favorable trade balance with the outside world was reversed, and silver began to flow in large quantities out of the country. As sources of capital for public works and trade expansion decreased, agricultural productivity stagnated or declined, and unemployment spread, especially in the hinterlands of the coastal trading areas. Wealthy Chinese, who could best afford it, squandered increasing amounts of China's wealth to support their opium habits. Opium dens spread in the

FIGURE 31.6 In the late 19th century, the Chinese were forced to concede port and warehouse areas, such as the one in this painting, to rival imperialist powers. These areas were, in effect, colonial enclaves. They were guarded by foreign troops, flew foreign flags, and were run by Western or Japanese merchant councils.

towns and villages of the empire at an alarming rate. It has been estimated that by 1838, 1 percent of China's more than 400 million people were addicted to the drug. Strung-out officials neglected their administrative responsibilities, the sons of prominent scholar-gentry families lost their ambition, and even laborers and peasants abandoned their work for the debilitating pleasures of the opium dens.

From the early 18th century, Qing emperors had issued edicts forbidding the opium traffic, but little had been done to enforce them. By the beginning of the 19th century, it was clear to the court and high officials that the opium trade had to be stopped. When serious efforts were finally undertaken in the early 1820s, they only drove the opium dealers from Canton to nearby islands and other hidden locations on the coast. Finally, in the late 1830s, the emperor sent one of the most distinguished officials in the empire, **Lin Zexu,** with orders to use every means available to stamp out the trade. Lin, who was famous for his incorruptibility, took his charge seriously. After being rebuffed in his attempts to win the cooperation of European merchants and naval officers in putting an end to the trade, Lin ordered the European trading areas in Canton blockaded, their warehouses searched, and all the opium confiscated and destroyed.

Lin Zexu: Letter to Queen Victoria (1839)

Not surprisingly, these actions enraged the European merchants, and they demanded military action to avenge their losses. Arguing that Lin's measures violated both the property rights of the merchants and principles of free trade, the British ordered the Chinese to stop their anti-opium campaign or risk military intervention. When Lin persisted, war broke out in late 1839. In the conflict that followed, the Chinese were routed first on the sea, where their antiquated war junks were no match for British gunboats. Then they were soundly defeated in their attempts to repel an expeditionary force the British sent ashore. With British warships and armies threatening the cities of the Yangtze River region, the Qing emperor was forced to sue for peace and send Lin into exile in a remote province of the empire.

Their victories in the Opium War and a second conflict, which erupted in the late 1850s, allowed the European powers to force China to open trade and diplomatic exchanges. After the first war, Hong Kong was established as an additional center of British commerce. European trade was also permitted at five other ports, where the Europeans were given land to build more warehouses and living quarters. By the 1890s, 90 ports of call were available to more than 300,000 European and American traders, missionaries, and diplomats. Britain, France, Germany, and Russia had won long-term leases of several ports and the surrounding territory.

Treaty Ports and the Boxer Rebellion in China

Although the treaty of 1842 made no reference to the opium trade, after China's defeat the drug poured unchecked into China. By the mid-19th century, China's foreign trade and customs were overseen by British officials. They were careful to ensure that European nationals had favored access to China's markets and that no protective tariffs, such as those the Americans were using at the time to protect their young industries, were established by the Chinese. Most humiliating of all for the Chinese was the fact that they were forced to accept European ambassadors at the Qing court. Not only were ambassadors traditionally (and usually quite rightly) seen as spies, but the exchange of diplomatic missions was a concession that European nations were equal in stature to China. Given the deeply entrenched Chinese conviction that their Middle Kingdom was the civilized center of the earth and that all other peoples were barbarians, this was a very difficult concession to make. European battleships and firepower gave them little choice.

The Treaty of Nanjing

## A Civilization at Risk: Rebellion and Failed Reforms

Although it was not immediately apparent, China's defeat in the Opium War greatly contributed to a building crisis that threatened not just the Qing dynasty, but Chinese civilization as a whole. Defeat and the dislocations in south China brought on by the growing commercial encroachments of the West spawned several rebellions that swept through much of south China in the 1850s and early 1860s and at one point threatened to overthrow the Qing dynasty. By far the greatest of these was the **Taiping Rebellion** led by the mentally unstable, semi-Christianized prophet **Hong Xiuquan.**

By the early 1850s, Hong's talented military commanders worked his growing numbers of followers into a formidable army that included regiments of Hakka women. Taiping fighters won a series of stunning victories against the demoralized and ill-disciplined Qing forces sent to destroy them. By the spring of 1853, they had captured a wide swath of territory in south-central China and established a capital at Nanjing, just west of Shanghai (see Visualizing the Past feature, p. 713).

Nineteenth-Century China

With the Qing dynasty tottering on the verge of collapse, the northward drive lost its momentum, and over the next half decade it imploded. With Nanjing and a number of other prosperous cities and their hinterlands under Taiping control, the rebel leaders, including Hong, began to plot and quarrel among themselves. As some were killed and others deserted the cause, the quality of the military commanders and the training of the God Worshipers' fighters declined precipitously. Taiping policies also alienated some of their own followers and increased the numbers of the enemies arrayed against them. None of their utopian measures to provide better lives for their followers were actually implemented, and their puritanical regulations were increasingly resented by their often hostile subjects. The ban on opium smoking and Hong's bizarre variations on Christian teachings alienated the Europeans, who threw their support behind the gravely imperiled Qing dynasty.

Of all of the rebellions that threatened to topple the Qing dynasty in the 19th century, the Taiping movement posed the most serious alternative—not only to the Qing dynasty but to Confucian civilization as a whole. The Taipings not only offered sweeping programs for social reform, land redistribution, and the liberation of women, but they also attacked the traditional Confucian elite and the learning on which its claims to authority rested. In addition to smashing ancestral tablets and shrines, the Taipings sought to develop a simplified script and mass literacy, which would have undermined some of the scholar-gentry's chief sources of power.

Their attack on the scholar-gentry was one of the main causes of the Taipings' ultimate defeat. Left no option but to rally to the Manchu regime, the provincial scholar-gentry became the focus of resistance to the Taipings. Honest and able Qing officials, such as Zeng Guofan, raised effective, provincially based military forces just in time to fend off the Taiping assault on northern China. Zeng and his allies in the government also carried out much needed reforms to root out corruption in the bureaucracy and revive the stagnating Chinese economy. In the late 19th century, these dynamic provincial leaders were the most responsible for China's **self-strengthening movement,** which was aimed at countering the challenge from the West. They encouraged Western investment in railways and factories in the areas they governed, and they modernized their armies. Combined with the breakdown of Taiping leadership and the declining appeal of a movement that could not deliver on its promises, the gentry's efforts brought about the very bloody suppression of the Taiping Rebellion. Hong died—due to illness or suicide—before his capital at Nanjing was retaken. Nearly 100,000 of his followers perished in battle or immolated themselves in mass fires.

Despite their clearly desperate situation by the late 19th century, including a shocking loss in a war with Japan in 1894 and 1895, the Manchu rulers stubbornly resisted the far-reaching reforms that were the only hope of saving the regime and, as it turned out, Chinese civilization. Manchu rulers occasionally supported officials who pushed for extensive political and social reforms, some of which were inspired by the example of the West. But their efforts were repeatedly frustrated by the backlash of members of the imperial household and their allies among the scholar-gentry, who were determined to preserve the old order with only minor changes and to make no concessions to the West.

The last decades of the dynasty were dominated by the ultraconservative dowager empress **Cixi,** who became the power behind the throne. In 1898 she and her faction crushed the most serious move toward reform. Her nephew, the emperor, was imprisoned in the Forbidden City, and leading advocates for reform were executed or driven from China. On one occasion, Cixi defied the Westernizers by rechanneling funds that had been raised to build modern warships into the building of a huge marble boat in one of the lakes in the imperial gardens. With genuine reform blocked by Cixi and her faction, the Manchus relied on divisions among the provincial officials and among the European powers to maintain their position. Members of the Qing household also secretly backed popular outbursts aimed at expelling the foreigners from China, such as the **Boxer Rebellion** (Figure 31.7). The Boxer uprising broke out in 1898 and was put down only through the intervention of the imperialist powers in 1901. Its failure led to even greater control over China's internal affairs by the Europeans and a further devolution of power to provincial officials.

American Cartoon on Western Powers Carving Up China

## The Fall of the Qing: The End of a Civilization?

By the beginning of the 20th century, the days of the Manchus were numbered. With the defeat of the Taipings, resistance to the Qing came to be centered in rival secret societies such as the Triads and the Society of Elders and Brothers. These underground organizations inspired numerous local uprisings against the dynasty in the late 19th century. All of these efforts failed because of lack of coordination and sufficient resources. But some of the secret society cells became a valuable training ground that prepared the way for a new sort of resistance to the Manchus.

By the end of the 19th century, the sons of some of the scholar-gentry and especially of the merchants in the port cities were becoming more and more involved in secret society operations and other activities aimed at overthrowing the regime. Because many of these

FIGURE 31.7 China's peril in the aftermath of the Boxer Rebellion and the military interventions by the imperialist powers that it prompted are brilliantly captured in this contemporary cartoon showing the aggressive and mutually hostile great powers circling the carcass of the Qing Empire.

young men had received European-style educations, their resistance was aimed at more than just getting rid of the Manchus. They envisioned power passing to Western-educated, reformist leaders who would build a new, strong nation-state in China patterned after those of the West, rather than simply establishing yet another imperial dynasty. For aspiring revolutionaries such as **Sun Yat-sen,** who emerged as one of their most articulate advocates, seizing power was also seen as a way to enact desperately needed social programs to relieve the misery of the peasants and urban workers.

Although they drew heavily on the West for ideas and organizational models, the revolutionaries from the rising middle classes were deeply hostile to the involvement of the imperialist powers in Chinese affairs. They also condemned the Manchus for failing to control the foreigners. Like the Taipings, the young rebels cut off their *queues* (braided ponytails) in defiance of the Manchu order that all ethnic Chinese wear their hair in this fashion. They joined in uprisings fomented by the secret societies or plotted assassinations and acts of sabotage on their own. Attempts to coordinate an all-China rising failed on several occasions because of personal animosities or incompetence. But in late 1911, opposition to the government's reliance on the Western powers for railway loans led to secret society uprisings, student demonstrations, and mutinies on the part of imperial troops. When key provincial officials refused to put down the spreading rebellion, the Manchus had no choice but to abdicate. In February 1912, the last emperor of China, a small boy named **Puyi,** was deposed, and one of the more powerful provincial lords was asked to establish a republican government in China.

The revolution of 1911 toppled the Qing dynasty, but in many ways a more important turning point for Chinese civilization was reached in 1905. In that year, the civil service exams were given for the last time. Reluctantly, even the ultraconservative advisors of the empress Cixi had concluded that solutions to China's predicament could no longer be found in the Confucian learning the exams tested. In fact, the abandonment of the exams signaled the end of a pattern of civilized life the Chinese had nurtured for nearly 2500 years. The mix of philosophies and values that had come to be known as the Confucian system, the massive civil bureaucracy, rule by an educated and cultivated scholar-gentry elite, and even the artistic accomplish-

DOCUMENT

## Building a New China

Faced with mounting intrusions by the Western powers into China, which the Manchu dynasty appeared powerless to resist, Chinese political leaders and intellectuals debated the ways by which China could renew itself and thus survive the challenges posed by the industrialized West. As the following passages from his journal *A People Made New* (published from 1902 to 1905) illustrate, Liang Qichao, one of the main advocates of major reforms in Chinese society, recognized the need for significant borrowing from Europe and the United States. At the same time, late 19th- and early 20th-century champions of renewal such as Liang wanted to preserve the basic features of Chinese society as they had developed over two millennia of history.

If we wish to make our nation strong, we must investigate extensively the methods followed by other nations in becoming independent. We should select their superior points and appropriate them to make up our own shortcomings. Now with regard to politics, academic learning, and techniques, our critics know how to take the superior points of others to make up for our own weakness; but they do not know that the people's virtue, the people's wisdom, and the people's vitality are the great basis of politics, academic learning, and techniques.

[Those who are for "renovation"] are worried about the situation and try hard to develop the nation and to promote well-being. But when asked about their methods, they would begin with diplomacy, training of troops, purchase of arms and manufacture of instruments; then they would proceed to commerce, mining, and railways; and finally they would come, as they did recently, to officers' training, police, and education. Are these not the most important and necessary things for modern civilized nations? Yes. But can we attain the level of modern civilization and place our nation in an invincible position by adopting a little of this and that, or taking a small step now and then? I know we cannot. . . .

Let me illustrate this by commerce. Economic competition is one of the big problems of the world today. It is the method whereby the powers attempt to conquer us. It is also the method whereby we should fight for our existence. The importance of improving our foreign trade has been recognized by all. But in order to promote foreign trade, it is necessary to protect the rights of our domestic trade and industry; and in order to protect these rights, it is necessary to issue a set of commercial laws. Commercial laws, however, cannot stand by themselves, and so it is necessary to complement them with other laws. A law which is not carried out is tantamount to no law; it is therefore necessary to define the powers of the judiciary. Bad legislation is worse than no legislation, and so it is necessary to decide where the legislative power should belong. If those who violate the law are not punished, laws will become void as soon as they are proclaimed; therefore, the duties of the judiciary must be defined. When all these are carried to the logical conclusion, it will be seen that foreign trade cannot be promoted without a constitution, a parliament, and a responsible government....

What, then, is the way to effect our salvation and to achieve progress? The answer is that we must shatter at a blow the despotic and confused governmental system of some thousands of years; we must sweep away the corrupt and sycophantic learning of these thousands of years.

**Questions** What does Liang see as the key sources of Western strength? What does he believe China needs most to borrow from Europe and the United States? Do his recommendations strike you as specific enough to rescue China from its many predicaments? If you were the emperor's advisor, what sorts of changes would you recommend, perhaps copying the approaches tried by the leaders of other civilizations in this era?

ments of the old order came under increasing criticism in the early 20th century. Many of these hallmarks of the most enduring civilization that has ever existed were violently destroyed.

GLOBAL CONNECTIONS

## Muslim and Chinese Decline and a Shifting Global Balance

Both Chinese and Islamic civilizations were severely weakened by internal disruptions during the 18th and 19th centuries, and each was thrown into prolonged crisis by the growing challenges posed by the West. Several key differences in the interaction between each civilization and the West do much to explain why Islam, though badly shaken, survived, whereas Chinese civilization collapsed under the burden of domestic upheavals and foreign aggression. For the Muslims, who had been warring and trading with Christian Europe since the Middle Ages, the Western threat had long existed. What was new was the much greater strength of the Europeans in the ongoing contest, which resulted from their global expansion and their scientific and industrial revolutions. For China, the challenges from the West came suddenly and brutally. Within decades, the Chinese had to revise their image of their empire as the center of the world and the source of civilization itself to take into account severe defeats at the hands of peoples they once dismissed as barbarians.

The Muslims could also take comfort from the fact that, in the Judeo-Christian and Greek traditions, they shared much with the ascendant Europeans. As a result, elements of their own civilization had played critical roles in the rise of the West. This made it easier to justify Muslim borrowing from the West, which in any case could be set in a long tradition of exchanges with other civilizations. Although some Chinese technology had passed to the West, Chinese and Western leaders were largely unaware of early exchanges and deeply impressed by the profound differences between their societies. For the Chinese, borrowing from the barbarians required a painful reassessment of their place in the world—a reassessment many were unwilling to make.

In countering the thrusts from the West, the Muslims gained from the fact that they had many centers to defend; the fall of a single dynasty or regime did not mean the end of Islamic independence. The Muslims also gained from the more gradual nature of the Western advance. They had time to learn from earlier mistakes and try out different responses to the Western challenges. For the Chinese, the defense of their civilization came to be equated with the survival of the Qing dynasty, a line of thinking that the Manchus did all they could to promote. When the dynasty collapsed in the early 20th century, the Chinese lost faith in the formula for civilization they had successfully followed for more than two millennia. Again, timing was critical. The crisis in China seemed to come without warning. Within decades, the Qing went from being the arrogant controller of the barbarians to being a defeated and humbled pawn of the European powers.

When the dynasty failed and it became clear that the "barbarians" had outdone the Chinese in so many fields of civilized endeavor, the Chinese had little to fall back on. Like the Europeans, they had excelled in social and political organization and in mastery of the material world. Unlike the Hindus or the Muslims, they had no great religious tradition with which to counter the European conceit that worldly dominance could be equated with inherent superiority. In the depths of their crisis, Muslim peoples clung to the conviction that theirs was the true faith, the last and fullest of God's revelations to humankind. That faith became the basis of their resistance and their strategies for renewal, the key to the survival of Islamic civilization and its continuing efforts to meet the challenges of the West in the 21st century.

Both China and the Islamic lands of the Middle East and north Africa faced common challenges through the unavoidable intrusion of Western-dominated globalism. While their responses differed, both civilizations were only partially colonized (in contrast to Africa). Their situation also differed from that of Latin America, where connections to the West ran deeper amid an older pattern of economic dependency. They differed, finally, from two other societies, near neighbors, who retained fuller independence amid the same global pressures: Russia and Japan.

## Further Readings

The best general introductions to the Ottoman decline and the origins of Turkey are Bernard Lewis, *The Emergence of Modern Turkey* (1968), and the chapter "The Later Ottoman Empire" by Halil Inalcik in *The Cambridge History of Islam*, vol. 1 (1973). Other recent studies on specific aspects of this process include C. V. Findley's studies of Ottoman bureaucratic reform and the development of a modern civil service in what is today Turkey; Ernest Ramsaur, *The Young Turks* (1957); Stanford Shaw, *Between Old and New* (1971); and David Kusher, *The Rise of Turkish Nationalism* (1977). On Egypt and the Islamic heartlands in this period, see P. M. Holt, *Egypt and the Fertile Crescent, 1516–1922* (1965), or P. J. Vatikiotis, *The History of Egypt* (1985). On the Mahdist movement in the Sudan, see P. M. Holt, *The Mahdist State in the Sudan* (1958), or the fine summary by L. Carl Brown in Robert Rotberg and Ali Mazrui, eds., *Protest and Power in Black Africa* (1970). The latter also includes many informative articles on African resistance to European conquest and rule. On women and changes in the family in the Ottoman realm, see Nermin Abadan-Unat, *Women in Turkish Society* (1981); in the Arab world, see Nawal el Saadawi, *The Hidden Face of Eve* (1980).

On the Manchu takeover in China, see Frederic Wakeman Jr., *The Great Enterprise* (1985), and Jonathan Spence and John E. Willis, eds., *Ming to Ch'ing* (1979). On Qing rule, among the most readable and useful works are Spence's *Emperor of China: Portrait of K'ang-hsi* (1974) and the relevant sections in his *The Search for Modern China* (1990); Susan Naquin and Evelyn Rawski, *Chinese Society in the 18th Century* (1987); and the essays in John Fairbank, ed., *The Cambridge History of China: Late Ch'ing 1800–1911* (1978). A good survey of the causes and course of the Opium War is provided in Hsin-pao Chang, *Commissioner Lin and the Opium War* (1964). The Taiping Rebellion is covered in Jen Yu-wen, *The Taiping Revolutionary Movement* (1973), and Jonathan D. Spence, *God's Chinese Son: Taiping Heavenly Kingdom of Hong Xiuquan* (1996). The rebellion heralding the last stage of Qing decline is examined in J. W. Esherick, *The Origins of the Boxer Rebellion* (1987).

The first stages of the Chinese nationalist movement are examined in the essays in Mary Wright, ed., *China in Revolution: The First Phase* (1968). The early sections of Elisabeth Croll, *Feminism and Socialism in China* (1980), provide an excellent overview of the status and condition of women in the Qing era.

## On the Web

The transitions from the Mongol to Ming to Qing dynasties are reviewed at http://www.bergen.org/AAST/Projects/ChinaHistory/MING.HTM. Links to resources for the study of the art of the Qing Empire can be found at http://www.art-and-archaeology.com/timelines/china/qing.html. The decline of the Qing (http://library.thinkquest.org/26469/history/1900.html) was accelerated by the failure of a reform effort which climaxed in the 103 days from June 11 to September 21, 1898 (http://www-chaos.umd.edu/history/modern3.html). This failure came on top of the Opium War (http://www.wsu.edu/~dee/CHING/OPIUM.HTM and http://www.cyber.law.harvard.edu/ChinaDragon/opiumwar.html). A site at http://web.jjay.cuny.edu/~jobrien/reference/ob29.html encourages discussion of Chinese Opium Commissioner Lin Zexu's letter to Queen Victoria.

The Taiping Rebellion (http://www.chaos.umd.edu/history/modern2.html) gravely weakened 2000 years of traditional Chinese government. The Boxer Rebellion (http://www.smplanet.com/imperialism/fists.html) provided the coup de grâce.

Major General Charles "Chinese" Gordon (http://www.bbc.co.uk/history/historic_figures/gordon_general_charles.shtml), who took part in the suppression of the antiforeign, anti-Qing Taiping Rebellion, also had to address another indigenous revolt in Egypt led by Muhammad Achmad, the Mahdi (http://en.wikipedia.org/wiki/Muhammad_ibn_Abdalla).

Unlike the Mahdi, who sought the path of militant revivalism, Mohammad Abduh and Jamal al-din Afghani (http://www.iranchamber.com/personalities/jasadabadi/jamal_odin_asadabadi.php) sought Western-style modernization within the context of Islam.

Earlier, Muhammad Ali, ruler of Egypt, had sought the same goal through economic transformation, but even the efforts of his successors to build the Suez Canal backfired due to European control over capital flow, which ultimately led to increased European control over Egypt (http://www.emayzine.com/lectures/egypt1798-1924.html). Much the same fate befell the Tanzimat reforms (http://www.scholars.nus.edu.sg/landow/victorian/history/dora/dora9.html), the Ottoman effort that paralleled the Qing reformist experiment.

CHAPTER 32

# Russia and Japan: Industrialization Outside the West



Yukichi Fukuzawa (1834–1904) was one of the most ardent educational reformers in late 19th-century Japan. Very soon after Japan began to have greater contact with the West, he concluded that Japan needed to change. He began to travel to the United States and Europe as early as 1860. He was not uncritical—he did not like the outspokenness of Western women or divisive debates in parliaments. But he firmly believed that, in key respects, Western education surpassed Japanese. As he put it in his autobiography, in 1899: "When I compare the two . . . as to wealth, armament, and the greatest happiness for the greatest number, I have to put the Orient below the Occident."

The problem in Japanese education, according to Fukuzawa, was Confucianism. The Confucian tradition, he believed, undervalued science and mathematics. It also suffered from a "lack of the idea of independence." Although independence was hard to define, Fukuzawa argued that it was essential if "mankind [was] to thrive" and if Japan was to "assert herself among the great nations of the world."

Japanese conservatives were deeply offended by this enthusiasm for Western education. Fukuzawa, a member of the elite and family friend of key conservatives, was sensitive to their criticism. In a letter to one observer, he seemed to back down. He talked of his commitment to "the teaching of filial piety and brotherly harmony." He said he worried that he was not being faithful to the memory of his own parents (who had been Confucianists). He admitted that he jumped into "Western studies" at a young age and did not know as much as he should about Confucianism. He even argued that (by the late 1870s) the traditions had reconciled: "Western and Confucian teachings have now grown into one, and no contradiction is seen."

Fukuzawa's dilemma was a common one for reformers: trying to prompt real change in a Western direction without unduly offending traditionalists and without wanting to become fully Western. Russian reformers, though different from the Japanese, faced similar problems, and handled them less successfully. Fukuzawa himself bent but did not break in his reformist zeal. In his autobiography he returned to defiance: "Again and again I had to rise up and denounce the all-important Chinese influence" even though "it was not altogether a safe road for my reckless spirit to follow."

**FIGURE 32.1** Japanese children at school. Showing children the latest in naval technology suggests the relationship between education and other aspects of Japanese development in the later 19th century.

| 1700 C.E. | 1800 C.E. | 1825 C.E. | 1850 C.E. | 1875 C.E. | 1900 C.E. |
|---|---|---|---|---|---|
| **1720** End ban on Western books in Japan<br>**1762–1796** Reign of Catherine the Great<br>**1773–1775** Pugachev Rebellion<br>**1772–1795** Partitioning of Poland | **1800–1850** Growth of "Dutch Studies" in Japan<br>**1812** Failure of Napoleon's invasion of Russia<br>**1815** Russia reacquires Poland through Treaty of Vienna; Alexander I and the Holy Alliance | **1825** Decembrist Revolt, Russia<br>**1825–1855** Heightening of repression by Tsar Nicholas I<br>**1829–1878** Serbia gains increasing autonomy in Ottoman Empire, then independence<br>**1830–1831** Polish nationalist revolt repressed<br>**1831** Greece wins independence after revolt against Ottomans<br>**1833, 1853** Russian–Ottoman wars<br>**1841–1843** Brief shogun reform effort | **1853** Perry expedition to Edo Bay<br>**1854** Follow-up American and British fleet visit<br>**1854–1856** Crimean War<br>**1856** Romania gains virtual independence<br>**1860–1868** Civil strife in Russia<br>**1860s–1870s** Alexander II reforms<br>**1861** Russian emancipation of serfs<br>**1865–1879** Russian conquests in central Asia<br>**1867** Mutsuhito, emperor of Japan<br>**1867** Russia sells Alaska to United States<br>**1868–1912** Meiji period in Japan<br>**1870** Ministry of Industry established in Japan<br>**1870–1940** Population growth in Russia<br>**1872** Universal military service established in Russia<br>**1872** Education Act, Japan | **1875–1877** Russian–Ottoman War; Russia wins new territory<br>**1877** Final samurai rising<br>**1878** Bulgaria gains independence<br>**1881** Anarchist assassination of Alexander II<br>**1881–1905** Growing repression and attacks on minorities in Russia<br>**1884–1887** New Russian gains in central Asia<br>**1884–1914** Beginnings of Russian industrialization; near-completion of trans-Siberian railway (full linkage 1916)<br>**1890** New constitution and legal code<br>**1892–1903** Sergei Witte, Minister of Finance<br>**1894–1895** Sino-Japanese War<br>**1898** Formation of Marxist Social Democratic Party, Russia | **1902** Loose alliance between Japan and Britain<br>**1904–1905** Russo-Japanese War; Japan defeats Russia<br>**1905–1906** Russian Revolution results in peasant reforms and duma (parliament)<br>**1910** Japan annexes Korea<br>**1912** Growing party strife in Russian duma<br>**1912–1918** Balkan Wars<br>**1914** World War I begins<br>**1916–1918** Japan seizes former German holdings in Pacific and China<br>**1917** Russian Revolution leads to Bolshevik victory |

This chapter deals with two important nations that defied the common pattern of growing Western domination during the 19th century. By 1914 Russia and Japan had managed to launch significant programs of industrialization and to make other changes designed to strengthen their political and social systems. Russia and Japan differed from the pattern of halting reforms characteristic of China and the Middle East in the 19th century. Theirs were the only societies outside the West to begin a wholesale process of industrialization before the 1960s. In the process, Japan pulled away from other Asian societies, while Russia ultimately enhanced its power in world affairs.

Russia and Japan did have some common characteristics, which help explain why both could maintain economic and political independence during the West's century of power. They both had prior experience of imitation: Japan from China, Russia from Byzantium and then the West. They knew that learning from outsiders could be profitable and need not destroy their native cultures. Both had improved their political effectiveness during the 17th and 18th centuries, through the Tokugawa shogunate and the tsarist empire, respectively. Both nations could use the state to sponsor changes that, in the West, had rested in part with private businesses. At the same time, change took distinctive directions in each society: Russia's process undercut social stability, while Japan's maintained greater social cohesion.

## Russia's Reforms and Industrial Advance

■ **Russia's reform period began in 1861 with the emancipation of the serfs. Russian leaders tried to combine change with continued tsarist autocracy.**

### Russia Before Reform

Russian rulers, beginning with Catherine the Great in her later years, sought ways to protect the country from the contagion of the French Revolution. The sense that Western policies might serve as models for Russia faded dramatically. Napoleon's 1812 invasion of Russia also led to a new concern with defense. Conservative intellectuals supported the move toward renewed isolation. In the eyes of these aristocratic writers, Russia knew the true meaning of community and stability. The system of serfdom provided ignorant peasants with the guidance and protection of paternalistic masters—an inaccurate social analysis but a comforting one. To resist Napoleon's pressure early in the 19th century, the government introduced some improvements in bureaucratic training. A new tsar, Alexander I, flirted with liberal rhetoric, but at the Congress of Vienna he sponsored the **Holy Alliance** idea. In this alliance, the conservative monarchies of Russia, Prussia, and Austria would combine in defense of religion and the established order. The idea of Russia as a bastion of sanity in a Europe gone mad was appealing, although in fact the alliance itself accomplished little.

Defending the status quo produced some important new tensions, however. Many intellectuals remained fascinated with Western progress. Some praised political freedom and educational and scientific advance. Others focused more purely on Western cultural styles. Early in the 19th century, Russia began to contribute creatively to Europe's cultural output. The poet Pushkin, for example, descended from an African slave, used romantic styles to celebrate the beauties of the Russian soul and the tragic dignity of the common people. Because of its compatibility with the use of folklore and a sense of nationalism, the romantic style took deep root in eastern Europe. Russian musical composers would soon make their contributions, again using folk themes and sonorous sentimentality within a Western stylistic context.

While Russia's ruling elite continued to welcome Western artistic styles and took great pride in Russia's growing cultural respectability, they increasingly censored intellectuals who tried to incorporate liberal or radical political values. A revolt of Western-oriented army officers in 1825—the **Decembrist uprising** (Figure 32.2)—inspired the new tsar, Nicholas I, to still more adamant conservatism. Repression of political opponents stiffened, and the secret police expanded. Newspapers and schools, already confined to a small minority, were tightly supervised. What political criticism there was flourished mainly in exile in places such as Paris and London; it had little impact on Russia.

Partly because of political repression, Russia avoided the wave of revolutions that spread through Europe in 1830 and 1848. Russia seemed to be operating in a different political orbit from that of the West, to the great delight of most Russian officials. In its role as Europe's conservative anchor, Russia even intervened in 1849 to help Austria put down the nationalist revolution in Hungary—a blow in favor of monarchy but

**FIGURE 32.2** The 1825 Decembrist revolt in St. Petersburg arose when there was a disagreement over the successor to Tsar Alexander I, who had no son. While the leaders of the revolt were well-educated aristocrats fighting for liberalization, many of their followers were illiterate and ill-informed subjects of the authoritarian regime. Soldiers who supported the accession of the dead tsar's liberal brother, Constantine, marched through the streets, chanting, "Constantine and Constitution." Many of these soldiers later admitted that they had assumed Constitution was the name of Constantine's wife. The revolt failed, and its leaders were executed or exiled to Siberia. Nicolas I, who became tsar, was even more repressive than his predecessor, but the courage of the Decembrists provided inspiration to future generations of reformers.

also a reminder of Russia's eagerness to flex its muscles in wider European affairs.

While turning more conservative than it had been in the 18th century, Russia maintained its tradition of territorial expansion. Russia had confirmed its hold over most of Poland at the Congress of Vienna in 1815 after Napoleon briefly sponsored a separate Polish duchy. Nationalist sentiment, inspired by the growth of romantic nationalism in Poland and backed by many Polish landowners with ties to western Europe, roused recurrent Polish opposition to Russian rule. An uprising occurred in 1830 and 1831, triggered by news of the revolutions in the West and led by liberal aristocrats and loyal Catholics who chafed under the rule of an Orthodox power. Tsar Nicholas I put down this revolt with great brutality, driving many leaders into exile.

At the same time, Russia continued its pressure on the Ottoman Empire, whose weakness attracted their eager attention. A war in the 1830s led to some territorial gains. France and Britain repeatedly tried to prop up Ottoman authority in the interest of countering Russian aggression. Russia also supported many nationalist movements in the Balkans, including the Greek independence war in the 1820s; here, a desire to cut back the Turks outweighed Russia's commitment to conservatism. Overall, although no massive acquisitions marked the early 19th century, Russia continued to be a dynamic diplomatic and military force (Map 32.1).

## Economic and Social Problems: The Peasant Question

Russia's economic position did not keep pace with its diplomatic aspirations. As the West industrialized and central European powers such as Prussia and Austria introduced at least the beginnings of industrialization, including some rail lines, Russia largely stood pat. This meant that it began to fall increasingly behind the West in technology and trade. Russian landlords eagerly took advantage of Western markets for grain, but they increased their exports not by improving their techniques but by tightening the labor obligations on their serfs. This was a common pattern in much of east-

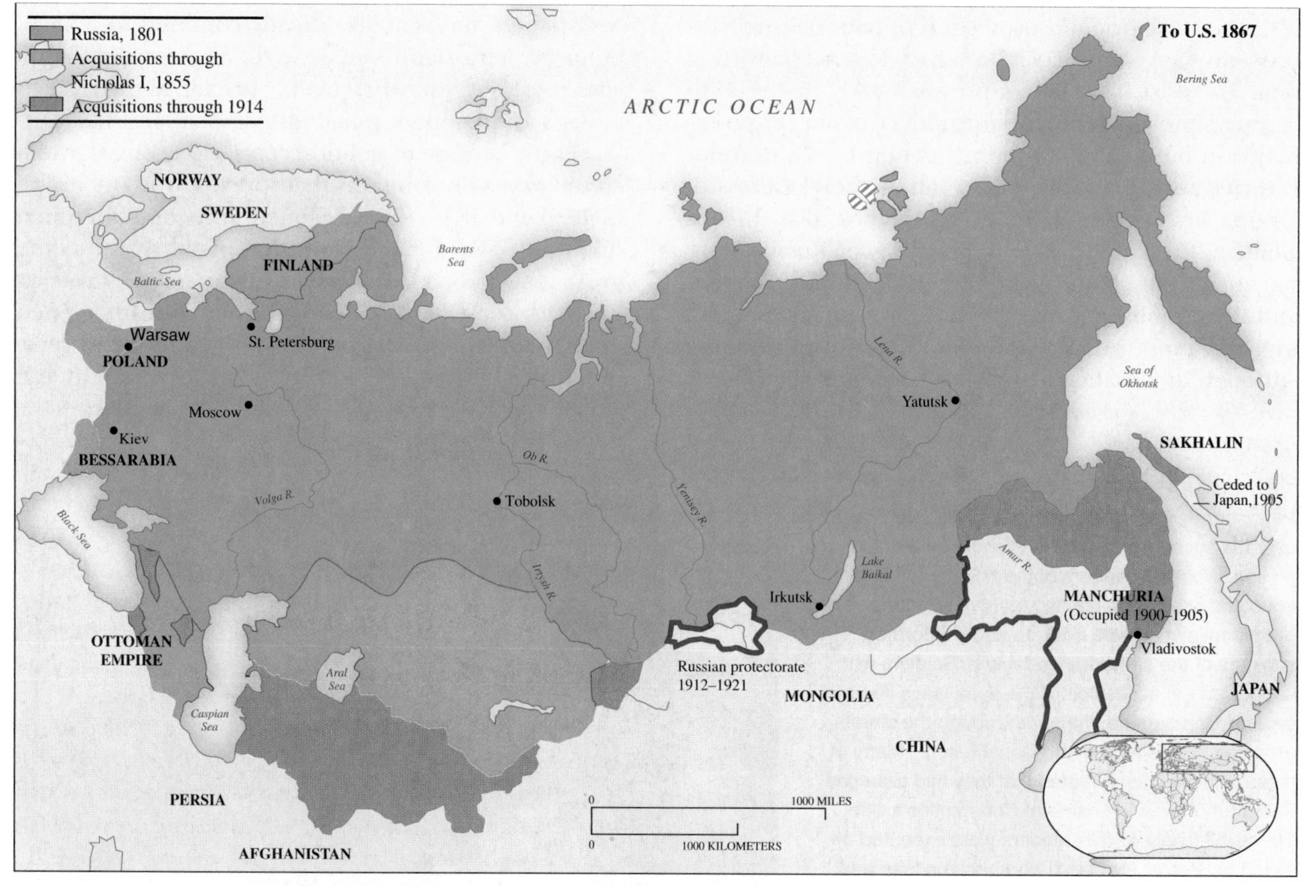


**MAP 32.1 Russian Expansion, 1815–1914.** Russia continued to push to the west, south, and east. At first, its main conflicts were with the Ottoman Empire. Later, however, conflicts in east Asia loomed larger.

ern Europe in the early 19th century, as Polish and Hungarian nobles also increased labor service to gain ground in the export market. In return for low-cost grain exports, Russia and other east European areas imported some Western machinery and other costly equipment as well as luxury goods for the great aristocrats to display as badges of cultured respectability. A few isolated factories that used foreign equipment were opened up in imitation of western European industrialization, but there was no significant change in overall manufacturing or transportation mechanisms. Russia remained a profoundly agricultural society based mainly on serf labor, but it was now a visibly stagnant society as well.

The widening gap between Russia and the West was driven home dramatically by a minor war in the Crimea between 1854 and 1856. Nicholas I provoked conflict with the Ottoman Empire in 1853, arguing among other things that Russia was responsible for protecting Christian interests in the Holy Land. This time, however, France and Britain were not content with diplomatic maneuverings to limit Russian gains but came directly to the sultan's aid. Britain was increasingly worried about any great power advance in the region that might threaten its hold on India, whereas France sought diplomatic glory and also represented itself as the Western champion of Christian rights. The resultant **Crimean War** was fought directly in Russia's backyard on the Black Sea, yet the Western forces won, driving the Russian armies from their entrenched positions. (Each side lost about 250,000 troops in a truly difficult struggle.) The loss was profoundly disturbing to Russian leadership, for the Western powers won this little war not because of great tactics or inspired principles but because of their industrial advantage. They had the ships to send masses of military supplies long distances, and their artillery and other weapons were vastly superior to Russia's home-produced models. This severe blow to a regime that prided itself on military vigor was a frightening portent for the future.

The Crimean War helped convince Russian leaders, including the new tsar, Alexander II, that it was time for a change. Reform was essential, not to copy the West but to allow sufficient economic adjustments for Russia to keep pace in the military arena. First and foremost, reform meant some resolution of Russia's leading social issue, the issue that most distinguished Russian society from that of the West: serfdom. Only if the status of serfs changed could Russia develop a more vigorous and mobile labor force and so be able to industrialize. Russian concern about this issue paralleled the attacks on slavery in the Americas in the same period, reflecting a desire to meet Western humanitarian standards and a need for cheap, flexible labor.

So for two decades Russia returned to a policy of reform, based on Western standards and examples; serfdom had been abolished in western Europe after 1789 and in east central regions such as Prussia and Hungary in the aftermath of the revolutions of 1848. As before, however, the intention was not to duplicate Western measures fully but to protect distinctive Russian institutions, including the landed aristocracy and tightly knit peasant communities. The result was an important series of changes that, with tragic irony, created more grievances than they resolved while opening the way to further economic change.

## The Reform Era and Early Industrialization

The final decision to emancipate the serfs in 1861 came at roughly the same time that the United States and Brazil decided to free slaves. Neither slavery nor rigorous serfdom suited the economic needs of a society seeking an independent position in Western-dominated world trade.

In some ways, the **emancipation of the serfs** was more generous than the liberation of slaves in the Americas. Although aristocrats retained part of the land, including the most fertile holdings, the serfs got most of it, in contrast to slaves, who received their freedom but nothing else. However, Russian emancipation was careful to preserve essential aristocratic power; the tsar was not interested in destroying the nobility, who remained his most reliable political allies and the source of most bureaucrats. Even more, emancipation was designed to retain the tight grip of the tsarist state. The serfs obtained no new political rights at a national level. They were still tied to their villages until they could pay for the land they were given. The redemption money went to the aristocrats to help preserve this class. Redemption payments added greatly to peasants' material hardship (Figure 32.3), and peasants thought that the land belonged to them with no need to pay for its return.

Emancipation did bring change; it helped create a larger urban labor force. But it did not spur a revolution in agricultural productivity because most peasants continued to use traditional methods on their small plots. And it did not bring contentment. Indeed, peasant uprisings became more common as hopes for a brighter future seemed dashed by the limits of change. Explosive rural unrest in Russia was furthered by substantial population growth as some of the factors that had earlier swelled the West's population now spread to Russia, including increased use of the potato. In sum, after 1861 Russia was a classic case of a society in the midst of rapid change where reform did not go far enough to satisfy key protest groups.

**FIGURE 32.3** This late 19th-century roadside scene depicts the poverty of a Russian peasant village. What forces produced such poor conditions, even after serfdom had been abolished?

To be sure, the reform movement did not end with emancipation. Alexander II introduced a host of further measures in the 1860s and early 1870s. New law codes cut back the traditional punishments now that serfs were legally free in the eyes of the law (though subject to important transitional restrictions). The tsar created local political councils, the **zemstvoes,** which had a voice in regulating roads, schools, and other regional policies. Some form of local government was essential now that the nobles no longer directly ruled the peasantry. The zemstvoes gave some Russians, particularly middle-class people such as doctors and lawyers, new political experience, and they undertook important inquiries into local problems. However, the councils had no influence on national policy; the tsar resolutely maintained his own authority and that of his extensive bureaucracy. Another important area of change was the army; the Crimean War had shown the need for reform. The officer corps was improved through promotion by merit and a new organization of essential services. Recruitment was extended, and many peasants learned new skills through their military service. Some strides also were made in providing state-sponsored basic education, although schools spread unevenly.

From the reform era onward, literacy increased rapidly in Russian society. A new market developed for popular reading matter that had some similarities to the mass reading culture developing in the West. Interestingly, Russian potboiler novels, displaying a pronounced taste for excitement and exotic adventure, also attested to distinctive values. For example, Russian "bad guys" never were glorified in the end but always were either returned to social loyalty or condemned—a clear sign of the limits to individualism. Women gained new positions in this climate of change. Some won access to higher education, and, as in the West, a minority of women mainly from the upper classes began to penetrate professions such as medicine. Even sexual habits began to change, as had occurred in the West a century earlier. Fathers' control over their children's behavior loosened a bit, particularly where nonagricultural jobs were available, and sexual activity before marriage increased.

The move toward industrialization was part of the wider process of change. State support was an industrial effort, for Russia lacked a preexisting middle class and capital. State enterprises had to make up part of the gap, in the tradition of economic activity that went back to Peter the Great.

Russia began to create an extensive railroad network in the 1870s. The establishment of the **trans-Siberian railroad,** which connected European Russia with the Pacific, was the crowning achievement of this drive when it was nearly completed by the end of the 1880s. The railroad boom directly stimulated expansion of Russia's iron and coal sectors. Railroad development also stimulated the export of grain to the West, which now became essential to earn foreign currency

DOCUMENT

## Conditions for Factory Workers in Russia's Industrialization

Russia passed several laws protecting workers, but enforcement was minimal. The Ministry of Finance established a factory inspectorate in the 1880s, which dutifully reported on conditions; these reports usually were ignored. The following passages deal with a number of Moscow factories in the 1880s.

In the majority of factories there are no special quarters for the workers. This applies to workers in paper, wool, and silk finishing. Skilled hand craftsmen like brocade weavers can earn good wages, and yet most of them sleep on or under their looms, for lack of anything else. Only in a few weaving factories are there special sleeping quarters, and these are provided not for the weavers, but for other workers—the winders and dyers, etc. Likewise, the velveteen cutters almost always sleep on the tables where they work. This habit is particularly unhealthy, since the work areas are always musty and the air is saturated with dye fumes—sometimes poisonous ones. Carpenters also generally sleep on their workbenches. In bastmatting factories, workers of both sexes and all ages sleep together on pieces and mats of bast which are often damp. Only the sick workers in these bast factories are allowed to sleep on the single stove. . . . Work at the mill never stops, day or night. There are two twelve-hour shifts a day, which begin at 6:00 A.M. and 6:00 P.M. The men have a half-hour for breakfast (8:30–9:00) and one hour for dinner (1:00–2:00).

The worst violations of hygienic regulations were those I saw in most of the flax-spinning mills where linen is produced. . . . Although in western Europe all the dust-producing carding and combing machines have long been covered and well ventilated, I saw only one Russian linen mill where such a machine was securely covered. Elsewhere, the spools of these machines were completely open to the air, and the scutching apparatus is inadequately ventilated. . . .

In many industrial establishments the grounds for fines and the sizes of fines are not fixed in advance. The factory rules may contain only one phrase like the following: "Those found violating company rules will be fined *at the discretion of the manager.*"

The degree of arbitrariness in the determination of fines, and thus also in the determination of the worker's wages, was unbelievably extreme in some factories. In Podolsk, for instance, in factories No. 131 and No. 135, there is a ten-ruble forfeit for leaving the factory before the expiration of one's contract. But as applied, this covers much more than voluntary breach of contract on the worker's part. This fine is exacted from every worker who for any reason has to leave the factory. Cases are known of persons who have had to pay this fine three times. Moreover, fines are levied for so many causes that falling under a severe fine is a constant possibility for each worker. For instance, workers who for any reason came into the office in a group, instead of singly, would be fined one ruble. After a second offense, the transgressors would be dismissed—leaving behind, of course, the ten-ruble fine for breach of contract.

In factory No. 135 the workers are still treated as serfs. Wages are paid out only twice a year, even then not in full but only enough to pay the workers' taxes (other necessities are supplied by the factory store). Furthermore this money is not given to the workers directly, but is sent by mail to their village elders and village clerks. Thus the workers are without money the year around. Besides they are also paying severe fines to the factory, and these sums will be subtracted from their wages at the final year-end accounting.

Extreme regulations and regimentation are very common in our factories—regulations entangle the workers at every step and burden them with more or less severe fines which are subtracted from their often already inadequate wages. Some factory administrators have become real virtuosos at thinking up new grounds for fines. A brief description of a few of the fines in factory No. 172 is an excellent example of this variety: on October 24, 1877, an announcement was posted of new fines to be set at the discretion of the office for fourteen different cases of failure to maintain silence and cleanliness. There were also dozens of minor fines prescribed for certain individual offenses: for example, on August 4, 1883, a huge fine of five rubles was set for singing in the factory courtyard after 9:30, or at any time in any unauthorized place. On June 3, 1881, a fine was to be levied from workers who took tea and sugar, bread, or any kind of foodstuffs into the weaving building, "in order to avoid breeding any insects or vermin." On May 14, 1880, a fine was set for anyone who wrote with pencil, chalk, or anything else on the walls in the dyeing or weaving buildings.

**Questions** What were the worst features of Russian factories? Were conditions worse than in western Europe during early industrialization, and if so in what ways and why? (Relatedly, what conditions probably were common in the first stages of factory industry everywhere?) How did working conditions and management attitudes help create a revolutionary mood among Russian workers? Think also about the nature of this source. Why would a conservative government sponsor such a critical report? What does the report suggest about tensions at the top of Russian society, between government and business? Would a conservative government be more likely to undertake this kind of inquiry than the more reform-minded regime that had existed a decade earlier? What do you think the results of such a report would be, in the Russian context, or indeed in any early industrial context?

needed in payment for advanced Western machinery. The railroads also opened Siberia up to new development, which in turn brought Russia into a more active and contested Asian role.

By the 1880s, when Russia's railroad network had almost quintupled since 1860, modern factories were beginning to spring up in Moscow, St. Petersburg, and several Polish cities, and an urban working class was growing rapidly. Printing factories and metalworking shops expanded the skilled artisanry in the cities, and metallurgy and textile plants recruited a still newer semiskilled industrial labor force from the troubled countryside.

Early Russian Factory

Under Count **Sergei Witte,** minister of finance from 1892 to 1903 and an ardent economic modernizer, the government enacted high tariffs to protect new Russian industry, improved its banking system, and encouraged Western investors to build great factories with advanced technology. As Witte put it, "The inflow of foreign capital is . . . the only way by which our industry will be able to supply our country quickly with abundant and cheap products." By 1900 approximately half of Russian industry was foreign owned and much of it was foreign operated, with British, German, and French industrialists taking the lead. Russia became a debtor nation as huge industrial development loans piled up. Russia had surged to fourth rank in the world in steel production and was second to the United States in the newer area of petroleum production and refining. Russian textile output was also impressive. Long-standing Russian economic lags were beginning to yield.

This industrial revolution was still in its early stages. Russia's world rank was a function more of its great size and population, along with its rich natural resources, than of thorough mechanization. Many Russian factories were vast—on average, the largest in the world—but they usually were not up to Western technical standards, nor was the labor force highly trained. Agriculture also remained backward, as peasants, often illiterate, had neither capital nor motives to change their ways.

Other reforms also produced ambiguous results. Russia remained a traditional peasant society in many ways. Beneath the official military reorganization, many peasant-soldiers continued to see their officers as landlord-patrons. Discipline and military efficiency were lax. It was not clear that the Russian masses had experienced the kinds of attitudinal changes that had occurred in the West at the time of initial industrialization or even before. Even more obvious was the absence of a large, self-confident middle class of the sort that had arisen earlier in the West. Businesspeople and professionals grew in numbers, but often they were dependent on state initiatives, such as zemstvo employment for doctors and economic guidance for businesspeople. They also lacked the numbers and tradition to become as assertive as their Western counterparts had been (for example, in challenging aristocratic power and values).

## Protest and Revolution in Russia

- **Change and also the limits of change destabilized Russian society. Marxist leaders helped focus unrest.**

### The Road to Revolution

Alexander II's reforms, as well as economic change and the greater population mobility it involved, encouraged minority nationalities to make demands of the great empire. Intellectuals explored the cultural traditions of Ukrainians and other groups. Nationalist beliefs initially were imported from western Europe, but here and elsewhere in eastern Europe, they encouraged divisive minority agitation that multinational states, such as Russia and Austria–Hungary, found very hard to handle. Nationalist pressures were not the main problem in Russia, but given Russia's mainstream nationalist insistence on the distinctive superiorities of a Russian tradition, they did cause concern.

Social protest was more vigorous still, and it was heightened not only by the limitations of reform but by industrialization itself. Recurrent famines provoked peasant uprisings. Peasants deeply resented redemption payments and taxes and often seized and burned the records that indicated what they owed.

Many educated Russians, including some aristocrats, also clamored for revolutionary change. Two strands developed. Many business and professional people, though not very aggressive, began to seek a fuller political voice and new rights such as greater freedom in the schools and press; they argued for liberal reforms. At the same time, a group of radical **intelligentsia**—a Russian term for articulate intellectuals as a class—became increasingly active. As Russian universities expanded, student groups grew as well, and many were impatient with Russia's slow development and with the visible restrictions on political activity.

Some intellectuals later toned down their goals as they entered the bureaucracy or business life. But many remained inspired by radical doctrines, and more than a few devoted their lives to a revolutionary cause. This kind of intellectual alienation rested on some of the principles that had roused intellectuals in the West, but it went deeper in Russia. It was the first example of a kind of intellectual radicalism, capable of motivating terrorism, which would characterize other societies caught in tense transitions during the 20th century. The Russian intelligentsia wanted political freedom and deep social reform while maintaining a Russian culture different from that of the West, which they saw as hopelessly materialistic. Their radicalism may have stemmed from the demanding task they set themselves: attacking key Russian institutions while building a new society that would not reproduce the injustices and crippling limitations of the Western world.

Many Russian radicals were **anarchists,** who sought to abolish all formal government. Although anarchism was not unknown in the West, it took on particular force in Russia in opposition to tsarist autocracy. Many early anarchists in the 1860s hoped that they could triumph by winning peasant support, and a host of upper-class radicals fanned out to teach the peasantry the beauties of political activism. Failure here led many anarchists to violent methods and thus to the formation of the first large terrorist movement in the modern world. Given the lack of popular support and other political outlets, assassinations and bombings seemed the only way to attack the existing order. As anarchist leader Bakunin put it,

> We have only one plan—general destruction. We want a national revolution of the peasants. We refuse to take any part in the working out of schemes to better the conditions of life; we regard as fruitless solely theoretical work. We consider destruction to be such an enormous and difficult task that we must devote all our powers to it, and we do not wish to deceive ourselves with the dream that we will have enough strength and knowledge for creation.

Not surprisingly, the recurrent waves of terrorism merely strengthened the tsarist regime's resolve to avoid further political change in what became a vicious circle in 19th-century Russian politics.

By the late 1870s, Alexander II was pulling back from his reform interest, fearing that change was getting out of hand. Censorship of newspapers and political meetings tightened; many dissidents were arrested and sent to Siberia. Alexander II was assassinated by a terrorist bomb in 1881 after a series of botched attempts. His successors, while increasing the effort to industrialize, continued to oppose further political reform. New measures of repression also were directed against minority nationalities, partly to dampen their unrest and partly to gain the support of upper-class conservatives. The Poles and other groups were supervised carefully. Russian language instruction was forced on peoples such as Ukrainians. Persecution of the large Jewish minority was stepped up, resulting in many mass attacks—called pogroms—and seizures of property. As a consequence, many Russian Jews emigrated.

By the 1890s, the currents of protest gained new force. Marxist doctrines spread from the Western socialist movement to a segment of the Russian intelligentsia, who became committed to a tightly organized proletarian revolution. One of the most active Marxist leaders was **Vladimir Ilyich Ulyanov,** known as Lenin. Lenin, a man from a bureaucratic family whose brother was hanged after a trial, following his arrest by the political police, introduced important innovations in Marxist theory to make it more appropriate for Russia. He argued that because of the spread of international capitalism, a proletariat was developing worldwide in advance of industrialization. Therefore, Russia could have a proletarian revolution without going through a distinct middle-class phase. Lenin also insisted on the importance of disciplined revolutionary cells that could maintain doctrinal purity and effective action even under severe police repression. Lenin's approach animated the group of Russian Marxists known as **Bolsheviks,** or majority party (though, ironically, they were actually a minority in the Russian Marxist movement as a whole). The approach proved ideal for Russian conditions.

Working-class unrest in the cities grew with the new currents among the intelligentsia. Russian workers became far more radical than their Western counterparts. They formed unions and conducted strikes—all illegal—but many of them also had firm political goals in mind. Their radicalism stemmed partly from the absence of legal political outlets. It arose also from rural unrest—for these new workers pulled in peasant grievances against the existing order—and from the severe conditions of early industrialization, with its large factories and frequent foreign ownership. Although many workers were not linked to any particular doctrine, some became interested in Bolshevism, and they were urged on by passionate organizers.

By 1900 the contradictory currents in Russian society may have made revolution inevitable. The forces demanding change were not united, but the importance of mass protest in both countryside and city, as well as the radical intelligentsia, made it difficult to find a compromise. Furthermore, the regime remained resolutely opposed to compromise. Conservative ministers urged a vigorous policy of resistance and repression.

## The Revolution of 1905

Military defeat in 1904 and 1905 finally lit this tinderbox. Russia had maintained its expansionist foreign policy through the late 19th century, in part because of tradition and in part because diplomatic success might draw the venom from internal unrest. It also wanted to match the imperialist strides of the Western great powers. A war with the Ottoman Empire in the 1870s brought substantial gains, which were then pushed back at the insistence of France and Britain. Russia also successfully aided the creation in the Balkans of new Slavic nations, such as Serbia and Bulgaria, the "little Slavic brothers" that filled nationalist hearts with pride. Some conservative writers even talked in terms of a pan-Slavic movement that would unite the Slavic people—

under Russian leadership, of course. Russia participated vigorously in other Middle Eastern and central Asian areas. Russia and Britain both increased their influence in Persia and Afghanistan, reaching some uneasy truces that divided spheres of activity early in the 20th century. Russia was also active in China. The development of the trans-Siberian railroad encouraged Russia to incorporate some northern portions of Manchuria, violating the 18th-century Amur River agreement. Russia also joined Western powers in obtaining long-term leases to Chinese territory during the 1890s.

These were important gains, but they did not satisfy growing Russian ambitions, and they also brought trouble. Russia risked an overextension because its diplomatic aspirations were not backed by real increases in military power. The problem first came to a head in 1904. Increasingly powerful Japan became worried about further Russian expansion in northern China and efforts to extend influence into Korea. The **Russo-Japanese War** broke out in 1904. Against all expectations save Japan's, the Japanese won. Russia could not move its fleet quickly to the Pacific, and its military organization proved too cumbersome to oppose the more effective Japanese maneuvers. Japan gained the opportunity to move into Korea as the balance of power in the Far East began to shift.

Unexpected defeat in war unleashed massive protests on the home front in the Russian Revolution of 1905 (Figure 32.4). Urban workers mounted well-organized general strikes that were designed above all for political gains. Peasants led a series of insurrections, and liberal groups also agitated. After trying brutal police repression, which only infuriated the urban crowds, the tsarist regime had to change course. It wooed liberals by creating a national parliament, the **duma.** The interior minister Piotyr Stolypin introduced an important series of reforms for the peasantry. Under the **Stolypin reforms,** peasants gained greater freedom from redemption payments and village controls. They could buy and sell land more freely. The goal was to create a stratified, market-oriented peasantry in which successful farmers would move away from the peasant masses, becoming rural capitalists. Indeed, peasant unrest did die down, and a minority of aggressive entrepreneurs, called **kulaks,** began to increase agricultural production and buy additional land. Yet the reform package quickly came unglued. Not only were a few new workers' rights withdrawn, triggering a new series of strikes and underground activities, but the duma was progressively stripped of power. Nicholas II, a weak man who was badly advised, could not surrender the tradition of autocratic rule, and the duma became a hollow institution, satisfying no one. Police repression also resumed, creating new opponents to the regime.

Pressed in the diplomatic arena by the Japanese advance yet eager to counter internal pressures with some foreign policy success, the Russian government turned once again to the Ottoman Empire and the Balkans. Various strategies to acquire new rights of access to the Mediterranean and to back Slavic allies in the Balkans yielded no concrete results, but they did stir the pot in this vulnerable area and helped lead to World War I. And this war, in which Russia participated to maintain its diplomatic standing and live up to the billing of Slavic protector, led to one of the great revolutions of modern times.

## Russia and Eastern Europe

A number of Russian patterns were paralleled in smaller eastern European states such as Hungary (joined to Austria but autonomous after 1866), Romania, Serbia, Bulgaria, and Greece. These were new

**FIGURE 32.4** Women marching in the Russian Revolution of 1905.

nations—unlike Russia. And emerging after long Ottoman dominance, they had no access to the diplomatic influence of their giant neighbor. Most of the new nations established parliaments, in imitation of Western forms, but carefully restricted voting rights and parliamentary powers. Kings—some of them new, as the Balkan nations had set up monarchies after gaining independence from the Ottoman Empire—ruled without many limits on their power. Most eastern European nations abolished serfdom either in 1848 or soon after Russia's move, but landlord power remained more extensive than in Russia, and peasant unrest followed. Most of the smaller eastern European nations industrialized much less extensively than Russia, and as agricultural exporters they remained far more dependent on Western markets.

Amid all the problems, eastern Europe enjoyed a period of glittering cultural productivity in the late 19th century, with Russia in the lead. Development of the romantic tradition and other Western styles continued. National dictionaries and histories, along with the collection of folktales and music, helped the smaller Slavic nations gain a sense of their heritage. The Russian novel enjoyed a period of unprecedented brilliance. Westernizers such as Turgenev wrote realistic novels that promoted what they saw as modern values, whereas writers such as Tolstoy and Dostoevsky tried to portray a special Russian spirit. Russian music moved from the romanticism of Tchaikovsky to more innovative, atonal styles of the early 20th century. Polish and Hungarian composers such as Chopin and Liszt also made an important mark. Russian painters began participating in modern art currents, producing important abstract work. Finally, scientific research advanced at levels of fundamental importance. A Czech scientist, Gregor Mendel, furthered the understanding of genetics, and a Russian physiologist, Ivan Pavlov, experimenting on conditioned reflexes, explained unconscious responses in human beings. Eastern Europe thus participated more fully than ever before in a cultural world it shared with the West.

## Japan: Transformation Without Revolution

■ **Western pressure forced Japan to consider reforms beginning in the 1850s. Japan was able to combine existing strengths and traditions with significant reform.**

### The Final Decades of the Shogunate

On the surface, Japan experienced little change during the first half of the 19th century, and certainly this was a quiet time compared with the earlier establishment of the Tokugawa shogunate (see Chapter 27) or the transformation introduced after the 1850s.

During the first half of the 19th century, the shogunate continued to combine a central bureaucracy with semifeudal alliances between the regional daimyos and the samurai. The government repeatedly ran into financial problems. Its taxes were based on agriculture, despite the growing commercialization of the Japanese economy; this was a severe constraint. At the same time, maintaining the feudal shell was costly. The government paid stipends to the samurai in return for their loyalty. A long budget reform spurt late in the 18th century built a successful momentum for a time, but a shorter effort between 1841 and 1843 was notably unsuccessful. This weakened the shogunate by the 1850s and hampered its response to the crisis induced by Western pressure.

Japanese intellectual life and culture also developed under the Tokugawa regime. Neo-Confucianism continued to gain among the ruling elite at the expense of Buddhism. Japan gradually became more secular, particularly among the upper classes. This was an important precondition for the nation's response to the Western challenge in that it precluded a strong religious-based resistance to change. Various Confucian schools actively debated into the mid-19th century, keeping Japanese intellectual life fairly creative. Schools and academies expanded, reaching well below the upper class through commoner schools, or **terakoya,** which taught reading, writing, and the rudiments of Confucianism to ordinary people. By 1859 more than 40 percent of all men and over 15 percent of all women were literate—a far higher percentage than anywhere else in the world outside the West, including Russia, and on a par with some of the fringe areas of the West (including the American South).

Although Confucianism remained the dominant ideology, there were important rivals. Tensions between traditionalists and reformist intellectuals were emerging, as in Russia in the same decades. A national studies group praised Japanese traditions, including the office of emperor and the Shinto religion. One national studies writer expressed a typical sentiment late in the 18th century: "The 'special dispensation of our Imperial Land' means that ours is the native land of the Heaven-Shining Goddess who casts her light over all countries in the four seas. Thus our country is the source and fountainhead of all other countries, and in all matters it excels all the others." The influence of the national studies school grew somewhat in the early 19th century, and it would help inspire ultranationalist sentiment at the end of the century and beyond.

A second minority group consisted of what the Japanese called **Dutch Studies.** Although major Western works had been banned when the policy of isolation was adopted, a group of Japanese translators kept alive the knowledge of Dutch to deal with the traders at Nagasaki. The ban on Western books was ended in 1720, and thereafter a group of Japanese scholars interested in "Dutch medicine" created a new interest in Western scientific advances, based on the realization that Western anatomy texts were superior to those of the Chinese. In 1850, there were schools of Dutch Studies in all major cities, and their students urged freer exchange with the West and a rejection of Chinese medicine and culture. "Our general opinion was that we should rid our country of the influences of the Chinese altogether. Whenever we met a young student of Chinese literature, we simply felt sorry for him."

Just as Japanese culture showed an important capacity for lively debate and fruitful internal tension, so the Japanese economy continued to develop into the 19th century. Commerce expanded as big merchant companies established monopoly privileges in many centers. Manufacturing gained ground in the countryside in such consumer goods industries as soy sauce and silks, and much of this was organized by city merchants. Some of these developments were comparable to slightly earlier changes in the West and have given rise to arguments that economically Japan had a running start on industrialization once the Western challenge revealed the necessity of further economic change.

By the 1850s, however, economic growth had slowed—a situation that has prompted some scholars to stress Japan's backwardness compared with the West. Technological limitations constrained agricultural expansion and population increase. At the same time, rural riots increased in many regions from the late 18th century onward. They were not overtly political but rather, like many rural protests, aimed at wealthy peasants, merchants, and landlord controls. Although the authorities put down this unrest with little difficulty, the protests contributed to a willingness to consider change when they were joined by challenge from the outside.

## The Challenge to Isolation

Some Japanese had become increasingly worried about potential outside threats. In 1791 a book was issued advocating a strong navy. Fears about the West's growing power and particularly Russia's Asian expansion fed these concerns in later decades. Fear became reality in 1853 when American Commodore **Matthew Perry** arrived with a squadron in Edo Bay near Tokyo and used threats of bombardment to insist that Americans be allowed to trade. The United States, increasingly an active part of the West's core economy, thus launched for Japan the same kind of pressure the Opium War had created for China: pressure from the heightened military superiority of the West and its insistence on opening markets for its burgeoning economy. In 1854 Perry returned and won the right to station an American consul in Japan; in 1856, through a formal treaty, two ports were opened to commerce. Britain, Russia, and Holland quickly won similar rights. As in China, this meant that Westerners living in Japan would be governed by their own representatives, not by Japanese law.

A Comic Dialogue, 1855

The bureaucrats of the shogunate saw no alternative but to open up Japan, given the superiority of Western navies. And of course, there were Japanese who had grown impatient with strict isolation; their numbers swelled as the Dutch schools began to expand. On the other hand, the daimyos, intensely conservative, were opposed to the new concessions, and their opposition forced the shogun to appeal to the emperor for support. Soon, samurai opponents of the bureaucracy were also appealing to the emperor, who began to emerge from his centuries-long confinement as a largely religious and ceremonial figure. Whereas most daimyos defended the status quo, the samurai were more divided. Some saw opportunity in change, including the possibility of unseating the shogunate. The fact was that the complex shogunate system had depended on the isolation policy; it could not survive the stresses of foreign influence and internal reactions. The result was not immediate collapse; indeed, into the late 1850s, Japanese life seemed to go on much as before.

Japanese Woodcut on Perry's Arrival

In the 1860s, political crisis came into the open. The crisis was spiced by samurai attacks on foreigners, including one murder of a British official, matched by Western naval bombardments of feudal forts. Civil war broke out in 1866 as the samurai eagerly armed themselves with American Civil War surplus weapons, causing Japan's aristocracy to come to terms with the advantages of Western armaments. When the samurai defeated a shogunate force, many Japanese were finally shocked out of their traditional reliance on their own superiority. One author argued that the nation, compared with the West with its technology, science, and humane laws, was only half civilized.

This multifaceted crisis came to an end in 1868 when the victorious reform group proclaimed a new emperor named Mutsuhito but commonly called "Meiji," or "Enlightened One." In his name, key samurai leaders managed to put down the troops of the shogunate. The crisis period had been shocking enough to allow further changes in Japan's basic political structure—changes that went much deeper at the political level than those introduced by Russia from 1861 onward.

IN DEPTH

# The Separate Paths of Japan and China

Japan's ability to change in response to new Western pressure contrasted strikingly with the sluggishness of Chinese reactions into the 20th century. The contrast draws particular attention because China and Japan had been part of the same civilization orbit for so long, which means that some of the assets Japan possessed in dealing with change were present in China as well. Indeed, Japan turned out to benefit, by the mid-19th century, from having become more like China in key respects during the Tokugawa period. The link between Chinese and Japanese traditions should not be exaggerated, of course, and earlier differences help explain the divergence that opened so clearly in the late 19th century. The east Asian world now split apart, with Japan seizing eagerly on Chinese weakness to mount a series of attacks from the 1890s to 1945, which only made China's troubles worse.

> *"Several aspects of Japanese tradition gave it a flexibility that China lacked."*

Japan and China had both chosen considerable isolation from larger world currents from about 1600 until the West forced new openings between 1830 and 1860. Japan's isolation was the more complete. Both countries lagged behind the West because of their self-containment, which was why Western industrialization caught them unprepared. China's power and wealth roused Western greed and interference first, which gave Japan some leeway.

However, China surpassed Japan in some areas that should have aided it in reacting to the Western challenge. Its leadership, devoted to Confucianism, was more thoroughly secular and bureaucratic in outlook. There was no need to brush aside otherworldly commitments or feudal distractions to deal with the West's material and organizational power. Government centralization, still an issue in Japan, had a long history in China. With a rich tradition of technological innovation and scientific discovery in its past as well, China might have appeared to be a natural to lead the Asian world in responding to the West.

However, that role fell to Japan. Several aspects of Japanese tradition gave it a flexibility that China lacked. It already knew the benefits of imitation, which China, save for its period of attraction to Buddhism, had never acknowledged. Japan's slower government growth had allowed a stronger, more autonomous merchant tradition even as both societies became more commercial in the 17th and early 18th centuries. Feudal traditions, though declining under the Tokugawa shogunate, also limited the heavy hand of government controls while stimulating a sense of military competitiveness, as in the West. In contrast, China's government probably tried to control too much by the 18th century and quashed initiative in the process.

China was also hampered by rapid population growth from the 17th century onward. This population pressure consumed great energy, leaving scant capital for other economic initiatives. Japan's population stability into the 19th century pressed resources less severely. Japan's island status made the nation more sensitive to Western naval pressures.

Finally, China and Japan were on somewhat different paths when the Western challenge intruded in the mid-19th century. China was suffering one of its recurrent dynastic declines. Government became less efficient, intellectual life stagnated, and popular unrest surged. A cycle of renewal might have followed, with a new dynasty seizing more vigorous reins. But Western interference disrupted this process, complicating reform and creating various new discontents that ultimately overturned the imperial office.

In contrast, Japan maintained political and economic vigor into the 19th century. Whereas by the late 19th century China needed Western guidance simply to handle such bureaucratic affairs as tariff collection and repression of peasant rebellion, Japan suffered no such breakdown of authority, using foreign advisors far more selectively.

Once a different pattern of response was established, every decade increased the gap. Western exploitation of Chinese assets and dilution of government power made conditions more chaotic, while Japanese strength grew steadily after a very brief period of uncertainty. By the 20th century, the two nations were enemies—with Japan, for the first time, the stronger—and seemed to be in different orbits. Japan enjoyed increasing industrial success and had a conservative state that would yield after World War II to a more fully parliamentary form. China, after decades of revolution, finally won its 20th-century political solution: communism.

Different Responses to Westernization

Yet today, at the onset of the 21st century, it is unclear whether east Asia was split as permanently as 19th- and early 20th-century developments had suggested. Japan's industrial lead remains, but China's economy is beginning to soar. Common cultural habits of group cooperation and decision making remind us that beneath different political systems, a fruitful shared heritage continues to operate. The heritage is quite different from that of the West but fully adaptable to the demands of economic change. And so Westerners begin to wonder whether a Pacific century is about to dawn.

**Questions** What civilization features had Japan and China shared before the 19th century? In what ways were Japanese political institutions more adaptable than Chinese institutions? Why was Russia also able to change earlier and more fundamentally than 19th-century China?

## Industrial and Political Change in the Meiji State

The new Meiji government promptly set about abolishing feudalism, replacing the daimyos in 1871 with a system of nationally appointed prefects (district administrators carefully chosen from different regions; the prefect system was copied from French practice). Political power was effectively centralized, and from this base the Meiji rulers—the emperor and his close advisors, drawn from loyal segments of the aristocracy—began to expand the power of the state to effect economic and social change.

Quickly, the Japanese government sent samurai officials abroad, to western Europe and the United States, to study economic and political institutions and technology. These samurai, deeply impressed by what they saw, pulled back from their earlier antiforeign position and gained increasing voice over other officials in the government. Their basic goal was Japan's domestic development, accompanied by a careful diplomatic policy that would avoid antagonizing the West.

Fundamental improvements in government finance soon followed. Between 1873 and 1876, the Meiji ministers introduced a real social revolution. They abolished the samurai class and the stipends this group had received. The tax on agriculture was converted to a wider tax, payable in money. The samurai were compensated by government-backed bonds, but these decreased in value, and most samurai became poor. This development sparked renewed conflict, and a final samurai uprising occurred in 1877. However, the government had introduced an army based on national conscription, and by 1878 the nation was militarily secure. Individual samurai found new opportunities in political and business areas as they adapted to change. One former samurai, Iwasaki Yataro (1834–1885), who started his career buying weapons for a feudal lord, set up the Mitsubishi company after 1868, winning government contracts for railroad and steamship lines designed to compete with British companies in the region (Figure 32.5). Despite his overbearing personality, Iwasaki built a loyal management group, including other former samurai, and by his death had a stake in shipbuilding, mining, and banking as well as transportation. The continued existence of the samurai, reflecting Japan's lack of outright revolution, would yield diverse results in later Japanese history.

The process of political reconstruction crested in the 1880s. Many former samurai organized political parties. Meiji leaders traveled abroad to discover modern political forms. In 1884 they created a new conservative nobility, stocked by former nobles and Meiji leaders, that would operate a British-style House of Peers. Next, the bureaucracy was reorganized, insulated from political pressures, and opened to talent on the basis of civil service examinations. The bureaucracy began to expand rapidly; it grew from 29,000 officials in 1890 to 72,000 in 1908. Finally, the constitution, issued in 1889, ensured major prerogatives for the emperor along with limited powers for the lower house of the **Diet,** as the new parliament was called. Here, Germany provided the model, for the emperor commanded the military directly (served by a German-style general staff) and also directly named his ministers. Both the institution and its members' clothing were Western, as the Visualizing the Past feature shows. The Diet could pass laws, upon agreement of both houses, and could approve budgets, but failure to pass a budget would simply reinstate the budget of the previous year. Parliament could thus advise government, but it could not control it. Finally, the conservative tone of this parliamentary experiment was confirmed by high property qualifications set for voting rights. Only about 5 percent of Japanese men had enough wealth to be allowed to vote for representatives to the lower house.

DOCUMENT

The Meiji Constitution, 1889

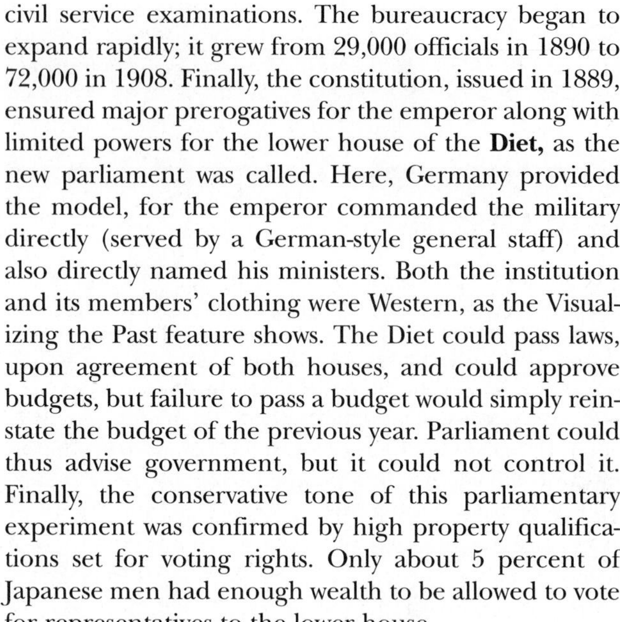

Japan's political structure thus came to involve centralized imperial rule, wielded by a handful of Meiji advisors, combined with limited representative institutions copied from the West. This combination gave great power to a group of wealthy businesspeople and former nobles who influenced the emperor and also pulled strings within the parliament. Political parties arose, but a coherent system overrode their divisions into the 20th century. Japan thus followed its new policy of imitating the West, but it retained its own identity. The Japanese political solution compared interestingly to Russian institutions after Alexander II's reforms. Both states were centralized and authoritarian, but Japan had incorporated business leaders into its governing structure, whereas Russia defended a more traditional social elite.

## Japan's Industrial Revolution

Political decisions were essential after the crisis of the 1860s, but they were soon matched by other initiatives. The new army, based on the universal conscription of young men, was further improved by formal officer training and by upgrading armaments according to Western standards. With the aid of Western advisors, a modern navy was established.

Attention also focused on creating the conditions necessary for industrialization. New government banks funded growing trade and provided capital for industry. State-built railroads spread across the country, and the islands were connected by rapid steamers. New methods raised agricultural output to feed the people of the growing cities.

The new economic structure depended on the destruction of many older restrictions. Guilds and internal road tariffs were abolished to create a national market. Land reform created clear individual own-

FIGURE 32.5 Born to an impoverished samurai family, the ambitious and forceful Iwasaki Yataro became one of the most powerful financiers and industrialists of late 19th-century Japan. He founded the company still known as Mitsubishi (which means Three Diamonds) in 1870 and made his fortune in shipping.

ership for many farmers, which helped motivate expansion of production and the introduction of new fertilizers and equipment.

Government initiative dominated manufacturing not only in the creation of transportation networks but also in state operation of mines, shipyards, and metallurgical plants. Scarce capital and the unfamiliarity of new technology seemed to compel state direction, as occurred in Russia at the same time. Government control also helped check the many foreign advisors needed by early Japanese industry; here, Japan maintained closer supervision than its Russian neighbor. Japan established the Ministry of Industry in 1870, and it quickly became one of the key government agencies, setting overall economic policy as well as operating specific sectors. By the 1880s, model shipyards, arsenals, and factories provided experience in new technology and disciplined work systems for many Japanese. Finally, by expanding technical training and education, setting up banks and post offices, and regularizing commercial laws, the government provided a structure within which Japan could develop on many fronts. Measures in this area largely copied established practices in the West, but with adaptation suitable for Japanese conditions; thus, well before any European university, Tokyo Imperial University had a faculty of agriculture.

Private enterprise quickly played a role in Japan's growing economy, particularly in the vital textile sector. Some businesspeople came from older merchant families, although some of the great houses had been ruined with the financial destruction of the samurai class. There were also newcomers, some rising from peasant ranks. Shuibuzawa Eiichi, for example, born a peasant, became a merchant and then an official of the Finance Ministry. He turned to banking in 1873, using other people's money to set up cotton-spinning mills and other textile operations. By the 1890s huge new industrial combines, later known as **zaibatsu,** were being formed as a result of accumulations of capital and far-flung merchant and industrial operations.

By 1900 the Japanese economy was fully launched in an industrial revolution. It rested on a political and social structure different from that of Russia—one that had in most respects changed more profoundly. Japan's success in organizing industrialization, including its careful management of foreign advice and models, proved to be one of the great developments of later 19th-century history.

It is important to keep these early phases of Japanese industrialization in perspective. Pre–World War I Japan was far from the West's equal. It depended on imports of Western equipment and raw materials such as coal; for industrial purposes, Japan was a resource-poor nation. Although economic growth and careful government policy allowed Japan to avoid Western domination, Japan was newly dependent on world economic conditions and was often at a disadvantage. It needed exports to pay for machine and resource imports, and these in turn took hordes of low-paid workers. Silk production grew rapidly, the bulk of it destined for Western markets. Much of this production was based on the labor of poorly paid women who worked at home or in sweatshops, not in mechanized factories. Some of these women were sold into service by farm families. Efforts at labor organization or other means of protest were met by vigorous repression.

## Social and Diplomatic Effects of Industrialization

The Industrial Revolution and the wider extensions of manufacturing and commercial agriculture, along with political change, had significant ramifications within Japanese culture and society. These changes also helped generate a more aggressive foreign policy. Japanese society was disrupted by massive population growth. Better nutrition and new medical provisions

VISUALIZING THE PAST

## Two Faces of Western Influence

Two Perspectives on Westerners in East Asia

These pictures show an 1850s cartoon portraying American Commodore Matthew Perry as a greedy warlord and the first meeting of the Japanese parliament in 1890.

**Questions** What was the cartoon meant to convey? What kinds of attitudes toward the West does it represent? What does the picture of parliament convey about attitudes toward the West? What was the model for the design of the meeting room? What do the two pictures suggest about uses of costume in a time of rapid change?

reduced death rates, and the upheaval of the rural masses cut into traditional restraints on births. The result was steady population growth that strained Japanese resources and stability, although it also ensured a constant supply of low-cost labor. This was one of the causes of Japan's class tensions.

The Japanese government introduced a universal education system, providing primary schools for all. This education stressed science and the importance of technical subjects along with political loyalty to the nation and emperor. Elite students at the university level also took courses that emphasized science, and many Japanese students went abroad to study technical subjects in other countries.

Education also revealed Japanese insistence on distinctive values. After a heady reform period in the 1870s, when hundreds of Western teachers were imported and a Rutgers University professor brought in for high-level advice about the whole system, the emperor and conservative advisors stepped back after 1879. This was when reformers like Yukichi Fukuzawa began to tone down their rhetoric. Innovation and individualism had gone too far. A traditional moral education was essential, along with new skills, which would stress "loyalty to the Imperial House, love of country, filial piety toward parents, respect for superiors, faith in friends, charity toward inferiors and respect for oneself." The use of foreign books on morality was prohibited, and intense government inspection of textbooks was intended to promote social order.

Many Japanese copied Western fashions as part of the effort to become modern. Western-style haircuts replaced the samurai shaved head with a topknot—another example of the westernization of hair in world history. Western standards of hygiene spread, and the Japanese became enthusiastic toothbrushers and consumers of patent medicines. Japan also adopted the Western calendar and the metric system. Few Japanese converted to Christianity, however, and despite Western popular cultural fads, the Japanese managed to preserve an emphasis on their own values. What the Japanese wanted and got from the West involved practical techniques; they planned to infuse them with a distinctively Japanese spirit. As an early Japanese visitor to the American White House wrote in a self-satisfied poem that captured the national mood,

> We suffered the barbarians to look upon
> The glory of our Eastern Empire of Japan.

Western-oriented enthusiasms were not meant to destroy a distinctive Japanese spirit.

Japanese family life retained many traditional emphases. The birth rate dropped as rapid population growth forced increasing numbers of people off the land. Meanwhile, the rise of factory industry, separating work from home, made children's labor less useful. This trend, developed earlier in the West, seems inseparable from successful industrialization. There were new signs of family instability as well; the divorce rate exploded until legal changes made procedures more difficult. On the more traditional side, the Japanese were eager to maintain the inferiority of women in the home. The position of Western women offended them. Japanese government visitors to the United States were appalled by what they saw as the bossy ways of women: "The way women are treated here is like the way parents are respected in our country." Standards of Japanese courtesy also contrasted with the more open and boisterous behavior of Westerners, particularly Americans. "Obscenity is inherent in the customs of this country," noted another samurai visitor to the United States. Certain Japanese religious values were also preserved. Buddhism lost some ground, although it remained important, but Shintoism, which appealed to the new nationalist concern with Japan's distinctive mission and the religious functions of the emperor, won new interest.

Economic change, and the tensions as well as the power it generated, also produced a shift in Japanese foreign policy. This shift was partly an imitation of Western models. New imperialism also relieved some strains within Japanese society, giving displaced samurai the chance to exercise their military talents elsewhere. Even more than Western countries, which used similar arguments for imperialism, the Japanese economy also needed access to markets and raw materials. Because Japan was poor in many basic materials, including coal and oil for energy, the pressure for expansion was particularly great.

Japan's quick victory over China in the **Sino-Japanese War** for influence in Korea (1894–1895) was a first step toward expansion (Map 32.2). Japan convincingly demonstrated its new superiority over all other Asian powers. Humiliated by Western insistence that it abandon the Liaodong peninsula it had just taken from China, the Japanese planned a war with Russia as a means of striking out against the nearest European state. A 1902 alliance with Britain was an important sign of Japan's arrival as an equal nation in the Western-dominated world diplomatic system. The Japanese were also eager to dent Russia's growing strength in east Asia after the development of the trans-Siberian railroad. Disputes over Russian influence in Manchuria and Japanese influence in Korea led to the Russo-Japanese War in 1904, which Japan won handily because of its superior navy. Japan annexed Korea in 1910, entering the ranks of imperialist powers.

Japanese Colonial Expansion to 1914

## The Strain of Modernization

Japanese achievement had its costs, including poor living standards in the crowded cities. Many Japanese conservatives resented the passion other Japanese displayed for Western fashions. Disputes between generations, with the old clinging to traditional standards and the young more interested in Western styles, were very troubling in a society that stressed the importance of parental authority.

Some tension entered political life. Political parties in Japan's parliament clashed with the emperor's

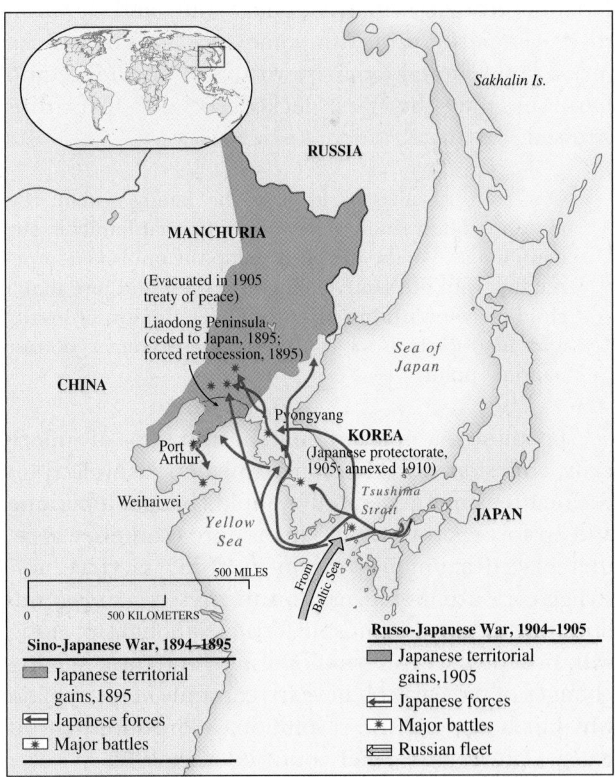


**MAP 32.2 Japanese Colonial Expansion to 1914.** What were the principal gains? Why was Japan frustrated by the ultimate results of its victories?

ministers over rights to determine policy. The government often had to dissolve the Diet and call for new elections, seeking a more workable parliamentary majority. Political assassinations and attempted assassinations reflected grievances, including direct action impulses in the samurai tradition.

Another kind of friction emerged in intellectual life. Many Japanese scholars copied Western philosophies and literary styles, and there was enough adaptation to prevent the emergence of a full Russian-style intelligentsia. Other intellectuals expressed a deep pessimism about the loss of identity in a changing world. The underlying theme was confusion about a Japan that was no longer traditional, but not Western either. What *was* it? Thus, some writers spoke of Japan's heading for a "nervous collapse from which we will not be able to recover." Others dealt with more personal conflicts such as those in the following poem:

> Do not be loved by others; do not accept their charity, do not promise anything. . . . Always wear a mask. Always be ready for a fight—be able to hit the next man on the head at any time. Don't forget that when you make friends with someone you are sooner or later certain to break with him.

As an antidote to social and cultural insecurity, Japanese leaders urged national loyalty and devotion to the emperor, and with some success. The official message promoted Japanese virtues of obedience and harmony that the West lacked. School texts thus stressed,

> Our country takes as its base the family system: the nation is but a single family, the imperial family is our main house. We the people worship the unbroken imperial line with the same feeling of respect and love that a child feels toward his parents. . . . The union of loyalty and filial piety is truly the special character of our national polity.

Japanese nationalism built on traditions of superiority, cohesion, and deference to rulers, as well as on the new tensions generated by rapid change. It became a deep force, probably in Japan more than elsewhere, that played a unique role in justifying sacrifice and struggle in a national mission to preserve independence and dignity in a hostile world. Nationalism, along with firm police repression of dissent and the sweeping changes of the early Meiji years, certainly helps explain why Japan avoided the revolutionary pressure that hit Russia, China, and other countries after 1900.

Yet Japan's very success reminds us of how unusual it was. No other society outside the Western world was yet able to match its achievements. Russia, responding to Western example in its own way, continued its growth as a world power, but amid such social disarray that further upheaval was inevitable. Most of the rest of the world faced the more immediate concern of adjusting to or resisting Western dominance; industrialization was a remote prospect. Even today, when many societies are striving for greater industrialization, the ability to emulate the Japanese pattern of rapid change seems very limited—with other parts of east Asia, interestingly enough, leading the pack.

## GLOBAL CONNECTIONS

# Russia and Japan in the World

Russia's world role, founded on its huge size and territorial expansion, had already been established in the early modern period. There were, however, new twists during the 19th century. Russian troops and diplomats periodically gained direct roles in western Europe. Russian forces entered France as part of the coalition that defeated Napoleon. A side result was the development of new restaurants in France, called bistros, based on the Russian word for quick. Russian armies helped put down the Hungarian revolution in 1849. Russian involvement in Middle Eastern diplomacy resulted from its steady pressure on the Ottoman Empire. By the later 19th century, Russia extended its influence in eastern Asia, seizing new territories in northern China and claiming a role elsewhere, in China and Korea alike. This set the collision course with Japan.

Japan's world role was much newer, and just emerging by 1914. Long isolated, Japan had experienced only one previous attempt at assertion beyond its borders, the late-16th century invasion of Korea. Now, however, ambitions increased, fueled by economic needs, growing industrial and military strength, and population pressure. Japan sought to be regarded as a great nation along Western imperialist lines. This would bring conflicts with China and Russia before 1914, and wider experiments thereafter. In the long run, it was Japan's striking economic success that would most clearly define its new place in the world. Initially, the unfolding of strength in the eastern Pacific region, along with the complex relationships to the West, marked Japan's dramatic entry as a force to be reckoned with.

The beginnings of serious industrialization in Russia and Japan, and the entry of Japan into world affairs, contributed important new ingredients to the global diplomatic picture by the early 20th century. These developments, along with the rise of the United States, added to the growing sense of competition between the established Western powers. Japan's surge promoted a fear in the West of a new **yellow peril** that should be opposed through greater imperialist efforts. Outright colonial acquisitions by the new powers added directly to the competitive atmosphere, particularly in the Far East.

## Further Readings

A. Gerschenkron, *Economic Backwardness in Historical Perspective: A Book of Essays* (1962), helps define the conditions of latecomer industrialization. The best survey of Russia in this transitional period is Hans Rogger, *Russia in the Age of Modernization and Revolution, 1881–1917* (1983). See also Geoffrey Hosking, *Russia: People and Empire, 1532–1917* (1997). Russian reforms and economic change are discussed in W. Blackwell, *The Industrialization of Russia* (1982), and Jerome Blum, *Lord and Peasant in Russia from the Ninth to the Nineteenth Century* (1961). Sidney Harcave, trans., *The Memoirs of Count Witte* (1990), includes a brief biographical sketch and his collected writings of this influential "modernizer." On social and cultural developments, see Victoria Bonnell, ed., *The Russian Worker: Life and Labor Under the Tsarist Regime* (1983); Barbara Engel, *Mothers and Daughters: Women of the Intelligentsia in Nineteenth Century Russia* (1983); and Jeffrey Brooks, *When Russia Learned to Read: Literacy and Popular Culture* (1987). On another vital area of eastern Europe, see A. Stavrianos, *The Balkans, 1815–1914* (1963).

Japan in the 19th century is viewed from a modernization perspective in R. Dore, ed., *Aspects of Social Change in Modern Japan* (1967). See also W. W. Lockwood, *The Economic Development of Japan: Growth and Structural Change 1868–1938* (1954); J. C. Abegglen, *The Japanese Factory: Aspects of Its Social Organization,* rev. ed. (1985); Andrew Gordon; *The Evolution of Labor Relations in Japan* (1985); and Hugh Patrick, ed., *Japanese Industrialization and Its Social Consequences* (1973). E. O. Reischauer's *Japan: The Story of a Nation* (1981) remains a good general history of the period. For more closely focused works on socioeconomic change, see S. Ericson, *The Sound of the Whistle: Railroads and the State in Meiji Japan* (1996); Peter N. Stearns, *Schools and Students in Industrial Society: Japan and the West* (1997); and E. P. Tsurumi, *Factory Girls: Women in the Thread Mills of Meiji Japan* (1990). *The Encyclopaedia Britannica* (including its online version) has a useful article on the life of Iwasaki Yataro, the founder of Mitsubishi, that puts a face on the modernization of Japan. Several works demonstrate that colonialism was an adjunct to industrialization in Japan as well as in Europe and in the Americas. These studies include R. H. Myers and M. R. Beattie, eds., *The Japanese Colonial Empire 1895–1945* (1984); W. G. Beasley, *Japanese Imperialism, 1894–1945* (1987); and P. Duus, *The Abacus and the Sword: The Japanese Penetration of Korea, 1895–1910* (1995).

## On the Web

The glories of tsarist Russia are revealed in a virtual tour of the Alexander Palace at http://www.alexanderpalace.org/palace/. However, the riches of the tsars could not conceal the dismal world of the Russian peasantry, whose lot was little improved by Russian economic modernization. This world and how it was illuminated by the works of the Russian writer Nikolai Gogol are addressed at http://www.kirjasto.sci.fi/gogol.htm, http://www.spartacus.schoolnet.co.uk/RUSserfs.htm, http://www.geocities.com/Athens/Forum/4123/krimlife.htm, and http://it.stlawu.edu/~rkreuzer/indv3/peasant.htm.

Russian liberalism reached its high-water mark with the abolition of serfdom, an institution whose rise and demise is described at http://bahai-library.org/resources/tablets-notes/lawh-malik-rus/bio.html and http://www.yale.edu/lawweb/avalon/econ/koval6.htm. A copy of the Emancipation Manifesto ending serfdom can be found at http://www.yurchenko.org/texts/hist_emancipation_manifesto.html. However, reaction soon set in.

The failure of the Revolution of 1905 (http://mars.acnet.wnec.edu/~grempel/courses/wc2/lectures/rev1905.html) to achieve any significant degree of political and social reform paved the way for those favoring more radical change, such as the Bolsheviks, led by Vladimir Ilyich Ulyanov, whose life and work is examined at http://www.marxists.org/archive/lenin/ and whose voice can be heard at http://www.aha.ru/~mausoleu/speaken2.htm. Count Sergei Witte's life and diplomatic and economic policies are glimpsed at http://www.fortunecity.com/victorian/hornton/890/RussiaNew3/Witte.html and http://members.tripod.com/~american_almanac/witte92b.htm. Marxist intellectual Leon Trotsky's brief evaluation of Witte, found at http://www.marxists.org/archive/trotsky/works/1905/ch10.htm, is dramatically written and full of interest.

The Meiji Restoration's industrial policy is discussed at http://www.japan-guide.com/e/e2130.html and http://kjs.nagaokaut.ac.jp/mikami/IDEAS/home.htm. Iwasaki Yataro's role in this process is illuminated at http://www.mitsubishi.or.jp/e/h/his.html. A key to the process of modernization in Japan is the Constitution of the Empire of Japan (1889), which is reproduced at http://history.hanover.edu/texts/1889con.html. For further insight into this process, this document can be compared with the Constitution of Japan (1947) at http://history.hanover.edu/texts/1947con.html. Life in Meiji Japan can be glimpsed through an exhibition of contemporary woodblock art at http://www.artgallery.sbc.edu/ukiyoe/historyofwoodblockprints.html and http://www.cjn.or.jp/ukiyo-e/.

Part V Retrospective

# THE DAWN OF THE INDUSTRIAL AGE, 1750–1914

## CONTACTS AND THEIR LIMITS

The long 19th century was an age of new contacts. Steamships, railroads, and the telegraph provided unprecedented speed and volume for the movement of people, goods, and news. The opening of the Suez and Panama canals added greatly to the ease of global travel. Within this essentially technological framework, the unrelenting pressure of European merchants, missionaries, and imperialists caused people in almost every society in the world to have to react to the West. As east Asia discovered, it was impossible to seek isolation. The question of what to do about Western culture and Western intrusion had become an inescapable global issue by the second half of the 19th century.

By this point, it is possible to speak of the beginnings of globalization as a new, more intense, and more demanding set of global contacts than had ever existed in world history. European and American corporations began setting up operations around the world, seeking raw materials and sales outlets. Many had factories in a variety of countries. By 1900, for example, Singer Sewing Machines, an American operation, was one of the largest companies in Russia.

Political globalization emerged as well, though it lagged behind international commerce. Two driving forces emerged. First, Western reformers began to take an interest in the human rights of distant peoples with whom they shared neither religion nor race but a common humanity. The origins of global human rights movements rest in the antislavery crusade of the late 18th and early 19th centuries, and the World Anti-Slavery Society, still active today from its base in London, was the first international organization that depended essentially on the moral pressure of world opinion. Other movements, such as the International Red Cross and conventions about the treatment of prisoners of war, followed from humanitarian concern applied internationally. Second, economic interests saw utility in new kinds of international agreements that would facilitate commercial activity. This resulted, for example, in new conventions against piracy and the establishment of international postal facilities. Building on both impulses, the 1880s saw a flurry of new international nongovernmental organizations around issues such as labor conditions and women's rights. At the end of the 19th century, an International Court, based in the Netherlands, began operations. It was designed to deal with international disputes and, ideally, to eliminate the need for war. Many of these movements had limited impact, but they showed a clear impulse to innovate in the global political arena. There was even a reformist effort to establish a blended international language, Esperanto.

Cultural globalization occurred as well. The popularity of Western sports was a case in point—for the first time popular culture spread directly from one region to the world at large. In the 1890s the Olympic Games were revived, this time as an international competition, in hopes that athletics could promote global harmony. By 1914 Hollywood was emerging as an international film capital.

While the level of international trade rose rapidly, there were limits to this first surge of globalization. It was clearly Western-dominated. The initial Olympics had athletes from North America and Australia joining European hosts—international, but hardly global. Global arrangements like the International Postal Union were truly important, but they were agreements among Western powers simply imposed on the rest of the world as part of enlightened imperialism.

Even aside from the limits of globalization, the range of contacts should not be exaggerated. Many societies participated in global trade, willingly or under pressure, without homogenizing. Japanese leaders ventured a brief period of unalloyed enthusiasm for things Western, but they pulled back quickly. In the 1880s, for example, the Japanese set clear limits to Western influence in education, instead emphasizing Japanese values. Japan managed a massive transformation without becoming "Western." On a still larger scale, Western missionaries, though hugely successful in Africa and Oceania, did not significantly impact most established centers of Islam, Hinduism, Buddhism, or Confucianism—Korea was a notable exception. Even in sub-Saharan Africa, Christian conversions were matched by new conversions to Islam.

Each region, including the West itself, continued to blend contacts with ongoing regional patterns in creative combinations. By 1914 the balance was clearly shifting toward globalization, but tremendous diversity persisted.

The spread of nationalism in fact permitted many regions to make new claims on real or imagined traditions as a reaction against too many concessions to global contacts. Nationalism was of course Western in origin. It rapidly spread to the United States, Latin America, and eastern Europe, and then to the Middle East (where it would be expressed in Arab, Turkish, and Zionist nationalisms), India, Japan, and China. Nationalism was a new political loyalty spreading, ironically, as a result of contact; it legitimized a degree of separation and a proud assertion of the validity of specific regional traditions. Nationalism could combat Western pressure, but it could also undermine non-Western regional entities such as the Ottoman Empire and, later, parts of Russia. In a world increasingly shaped by contacts, nationalism was an alternative, and largely disaggregating, force. ■

PART

# VI

# The Newest Stage of World History: 1914–Present



These maps help tell two of the biggest stories of the 20th century. First, the great Western empires and the Ottoman, Austro–Hungarian, and part of the Russian empires had imploded by the end of the century. More new nations arose during the 20th century than during any other span in history. These massive boundary changes were related to other upheavals. The typical political system in 1914 was either monarchy or empire; by the early 21st century, almost every country had a different kind of government from what it had had a century before, and some societies had had multiple kinds of government. The typical social system in 1914 was still dominated by a landed aristocracy or an aristocratic and big business blend. By the beginning of the 21st century, the landed aristocracy had faded dramatically, displaced by revolution or the rise of industry. New nations were thus paralleled by new political systems and new social structures.

But political maps are not the only story. While the current phase of world history involves the rise of the nation-state, the late 20th and early 21st centuries saw new challenges to the nation-state. A variety of new regional combinations formed, the strongest being the European Union. And multinational corporations often possessed powers far greater than any but the largest nations.

The age of empire has passed. But its replacement is less clear. Will it be a welter of new nations, each with a stake in its separate identity, or will it be new organizations associated with globalization? A period of world history has passed. The 19th century has ended far more than chronologically. But defining the new period is an ongoing challenge.

The problem is perspective: for past periods we know what the dominant trends and factors were, because we know the end of the story. For the current phase of world history, picking out the key themes amid the specific changes must be more tentative. Several clear conclusions must be mixed with several open questions.

## Triggers for Change

The world of European dominance began to come crashing down with World War I, and the destruction accelerated with the worldwide economic depres-

## Political Map of the World in 1914

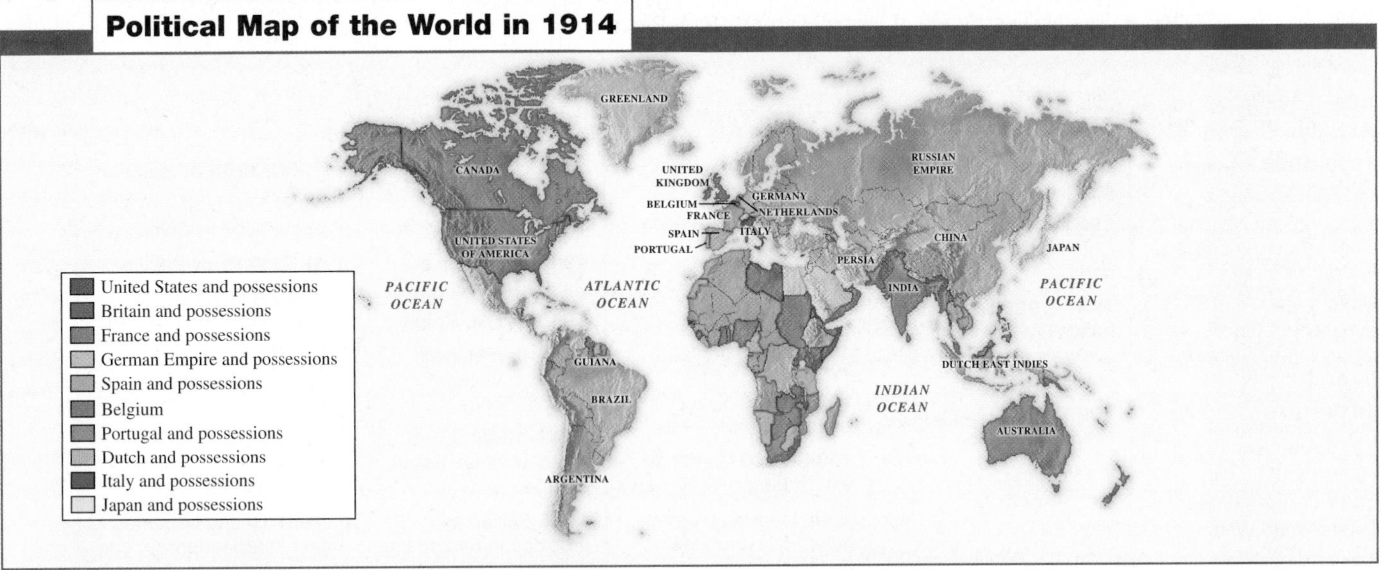


## Political Map of the Present-Day World

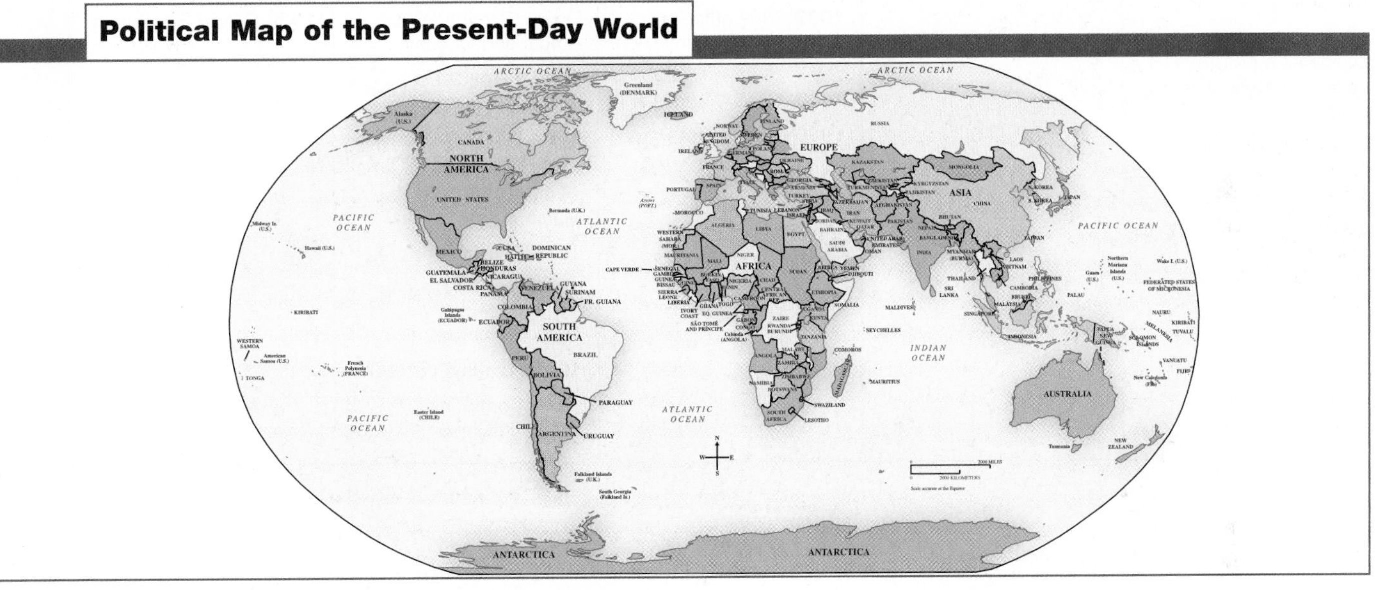


## Multinational Corporations in 2000

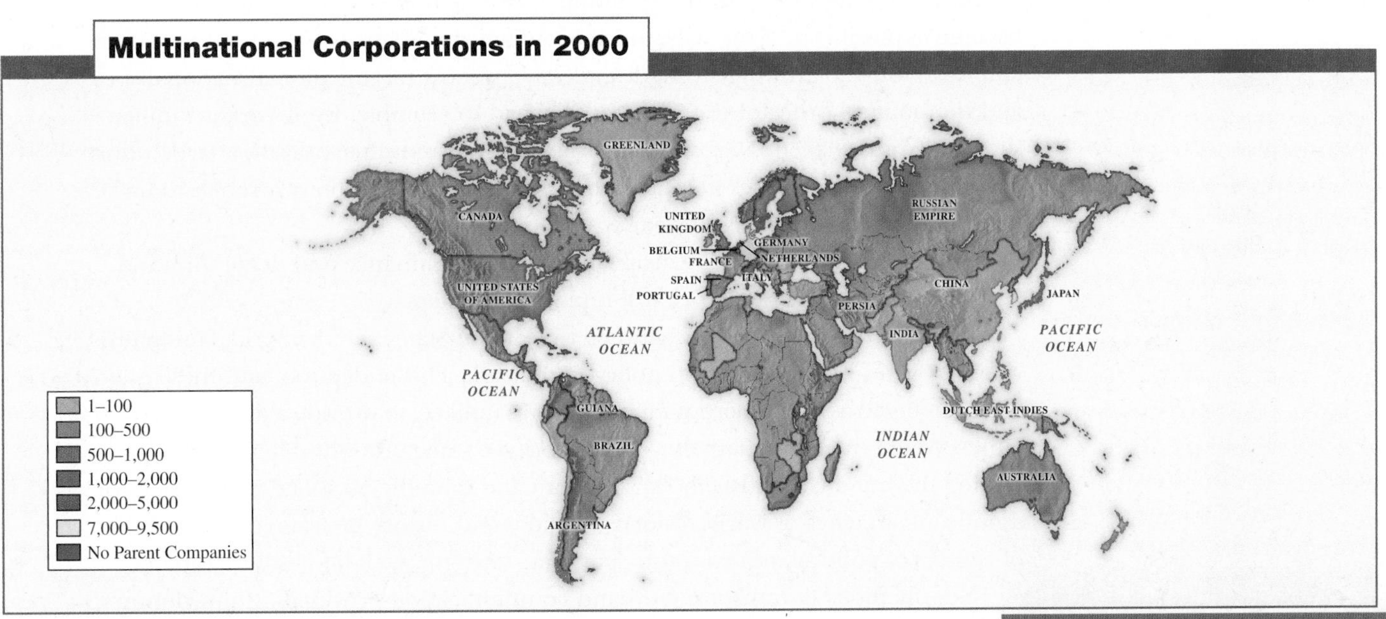

| 1910 C.E. | 1920 C.E. | 1930 C.E. | 1940 C.E. | 1950 C.E. |
|---|---|---|---|---|
| **1910–1920** Mexican Revolution<br>**1912** African National Congress party formed in South Africa<br>**1912** Fall of Qing dynasty in China; beginning of Chinese Revolution<br>**1914–1918** World War I<br>**1916** Arab revolts against Ottomans<br>**1917** United States enters World War I<br>**1917** Russian Revolution<br>**1917** Balfour Declaration promises Jews a homeland in Palestine<br>**1919** Versailles peace settlement, League of Nations<br>**1919** Revolt in Egypt, first Pan-African Nationalist Congress | **1920** Treaty of Sèvres reorganizes Middle East<br>**1921** Foundation of Chinese Communist party<br>**1927–1928** Stalin heads Soviet Union; five-year plans and collectivization<br>**1929–1933** Height of Great Depression | **1930–1945** Vargas regime in Brazil<br>**1931** Japan invades Manchuria<br>**1931–1947** Gandhi led resistance in India<br>**1933** Nazis rise to power in Germany<br>**1933–1939** New Deal in United States<br>**1934–1940** Cárdenas reform period in Mexico<br>**1935** German rearmament; Italy captures Ethiopia<br>**1937** Army officers in power in Japan; invasion of China<br>**1939–1945** World War II<br>**1939** Nazi–Soviet Pact | **1941** United States enters World War II<br>**1942–1945** Holocaust<br>**1945** Formation of United Nations<br>**1945** Atomic Bomb<br>**1945** Communists proclaim Vietnam independence<br>**1945–1948** Soviet takeover of eastern Europe<br>**1946** Philippines proclaim independence<br>**1946–1947** Decolonization in Asia, Africa, and Oceania<br>**1947** Peronism in Argentina<br>**1947** India and Pakistan gain independence<br>**1947–1975** Cold war; Marshall Plan<br>**1948** Division of Korea<br>**1948** Israel–Palestine partition; first Arab–Israeli war<br>**1949** Formation of NATO<br>**1949** Communist victory in China | **1950–1953** Korean War<br>**1951** End U.S. occupation in China<br>**1955** Warsaw Pact<br>**1955** Bandung conference; nonaligned movement<br>**1956** Partial end of Stalinism<br>**1957** European Economic Community (Common Market)<br>**1957** Ghana becomes first independent African nation<br>**1959** Cuban Revolution |

sion and then World War II. The two world wars were, in part, European civil wars, which caused massive loss of economic, demographic, and political vitality. It became impossible to cling to exclusive economic dominance, much less to overseas empires. Add the growing strength and effectiveness of anticolonial nationalisms, and the political order of the 19th century had to crumble. Even Western military supremacy was shaken. New challenges arose. Even more pervasively, a large number of the former colonies were able to develop sufficient military arsenals to make outside intervention dauntingly expensive.

*Trigger 1:* The collapse of European imperial dominance and decolonization.

*Question 1:* What framework will replace the system?

Initially the cold war rivalry between the United States and the Soviet Union provided a political, economic, and policy framework. This ended too, and the United States emerged as sole superpower, but this was unlikely to provide a durable pattern either. Would the next phase of world history see some other dominant civilization, playing the role that the Islamic Middle East and then the West had maintained for significant stretches of world history? Would world history be framed by a number of centers of political, military, and economic strength, with no absolute top dog?

New methods of transportation and communication provided a third defining feature and ushered in another stage in the capacity to move people, goods, and

| 1960 C.E. | 1970 C.E. | 1980 C.E. | 1990 C.E. | |
|---|---|---|---|---|
| **1960s** Civil rights movement in United States; revival of feminism<br>**1962** Algeria declares independence<br>**1965–1973** U.S. military intervention in Vietnam<br>**1965–1968** Cultural revolution in China<br>**1968–1973** Student protests in West | **1972, 1979** Oil crises; height of OPEC power<br>**1975** Communist victory in Vietnam<br>**1975–1998** Democratic regimes spread in Latin America<br>**1976** Death of Mao; new reform pattern in China<br>**1979** Iranian Revolution; spread of Islamic fundamentalism | **1980–1988** Iran–Iraq War<br>**1985 ff.** Gorbachev heads Soviet Union; reforms and unrest through eastern Europe<br>**1989** Reform movement in South Africa<br>**1989** New regimes throughout eastern Europe | **1990** Reunification of Germany<br>**1990–1991** Iraq invades Kuwait; Persian Gulf crisis; U.S.–Allied defeat of Iraq<br>**1991** Collapse of the Soviet Union<br>**1992** Full economic integration of Common Market<br>**1994** Palestinian autonomy in Israel; full democracy in South Africa, Nelson Mandela President<br>**1999** Rise of new conflicts, Palestinians, Israelis<br>**2003** U.S.–British war with Iraq | |

ideas worldwide. Radio, satellite transmissions, and the Internet shrunk the world as never before. New technology also redefined military life. From World War I onward, the destructive power of warfare steadily grew, boundaries between military personnel and civilians blurred, and even outside of outright war it became possible to kill more people more rapidly than ever before. From World War II onward, world history was marked by purges and genocides in which millions of people could die.

*Trigger 2:* Massive technological innovation.

*Question 2:* Which aspect—military capacity or global communications networks—should be emphasized?

Tremendous population growth provided the third defining feature of the new period in world history. New public health measures, introduced beginning in the 19th century, explain most of the growth. Improvements in food supply for the most part kept pace, though some regions experienced devastating famines. In many regions, population growth was accompanied by massive urbanization, often in advance of industrial growth, and new patterns of urban poverty played their own role, not just in regional but also in world history.

*Trigger 3:* The demographic explosion.

*Question 3:* Will historians look back on this as a framework for disaster, inevitably leading to exhaustion of resources, battles for space, and pollution; or will the new population levels prove manageable and self-correcting, as the rapid declines in birth rates by 2000 might suggest?

How should the story of the current period of world history be written? As military technology, population pressure, and environmental crises creating a catastrophe simply waiting to happen? Or as new global linkages, restraint in the use of military technology, and successful responses to population growth leading to change but also to new opportunities?

## THE BIG CHANGES

Revolutions in some countries and decolonization in many created the necessity for political innovation. The 20th century would toss up several possibilities: wider use of some sort of democracy; totalitarian governments—communist or fascist—seeking as full control over society as possible; or new forms of authoritarianism, including one-party rule. Political change was a dominant process. The need to accommodate new kinds of leaders, now that the aristocracy no longer served as primary source, contributed to this process.

With greater political independence and new political regimes, many parts of the world made systematic efforts to improve their position in the world economy. A few regions joined western Europe and the United States as advanced industrial societies at the top of the economic heap such as Japan and the Pacific Rim. A larger number of societies won some new voice at the global economic table. Some, like the oil-producing states, took advantage of new control over vital global resources. Some focused on replacing excessive reliance on the economic leaders with local manufacturing, in a process called import substitution. Others began to develop modern export sectors. Here, the biggest changes occurred from the 1970s onward. China became a global manufacturing engine. India enhanced its exports and developed as a center for the outsourcing of services. Brazil became the world's fourth largest computer exporter. Economic change and the advance of modern manufacturing were widespread. The result was a more complex world economy than that of the 19th century.

Cultural change occurred amid great dispute and resistance. Three cultural forces encouraged new secular loyalties. Nationalism won allegiance from many people. Marxism was a persuasive belief system for many people during much of the 20th century. From the West and Japan came leadership in consumer values and a faith in science. The cold war brought worldwide competition between Marxism and Western consumerism. Many people changed or modified their beliefs during the 20th and 21st centuries. But the major religions retained powerful support as well. Missionary activities were successful in Africa and elsewhere. From the 1970s onward, a strong commitment to what many argued were fundamental religious values gained ground, often making use of new technology to get the message across and characterized by a new level of intolerance. The result was a real contest for cultural preferences within societies such as the Middle East, India, and the United States.

The cultural debates, along with political and economic changes, frequently involved gender. The new period in world history saw important movements toward increases in education, new legal rights, and a stronger political voice for women. By the end of the 20th century, declining birth rates added another dimension to the changing lives of women. In some societies, women lost ground economically, as men took the more profitable jobs. Here was another mixed picture involving real change, new sets of questions, and unclear final outcomes.

A new round of globalization occurred in the second half of the 20th century. During the middle decades of the 20th century, globalization had receded. The Soviet Union pulled out of the international economic and political system, as did Nazi Germany and authoritarian Japan, as did China in the 1960s, as did the United States partially, during its two decades of isolationism. The technologies promoting further contacts continued to accelerate, however, and the major societies shifted position in the decades after World War II. Japan, Germany, and with slight hesitancy the United States became active global players. China reentered the global system in 1978, Russia after 1985. Not surprisingly, this second round of globalization proved even more intense than the first. Multinational corporations, for example, depended on much closer global integration than earlier international corporations. From the 1970s onward, a massive network of international nongovernmental organizations emerged, trying to deal with an array of issues from human rights to the environment to sweatshop labor. Global cultural change, around consumerism, became more extensive than ever before. Population growth encouraged new forms of migration that brought people from Africa, Asia, and Latin America to industrial centers in the United States, western Europe and to a degree Japan. Many migrants now went back and forth frequently, encouraging further cultural contact between their societies of origin and their new homes.

Globalization began also to involve new kinds of environmental change. Human impact on the environment had been largely regional. Now it took on an international dimension. Multinational corporations were involved with recurrent pollution crises, including oil spills and chemical disasters. Air pollution, causing acid rain, brought smoke from industrial regions to forests hundreds of miles away. Most scientists became convinced by the 21st century that air pollution and the destruction of tropical rain forests were creating global warming, which had implications for the entire planet. And while policymakers struggled to find global responses, there was again a lag between economic globalization and the political capacity to solve the problems it created.

## CONTINUITY

In the late 20th century, many people believed that change was accelerating more rapidly than at any previous point in world history. It was important, nevertheless, to recognize continuities. These fell into three related categories.

While a number of regions advanced industrialization, others continued to focus on low-cost production of raw materials and foods. During much of the 20th century industrial countries intensified their control over most African exports. Parts of Latin America and southeast Asia were also still dominated by older constraints in the world economy. Even within changing societies, such as India, rural regions often maintained older economic and social forms. Worldwide, by 2005, fewer than 30 percent of the world's people had access to the Internet—this was a huge minority, of course, and an impressive sign of change; but also a reminder of ongoing limitations. Overall, many economic inequalities had worsened by the early 21st century, both within regions and among them, and most of these gaps reflected older historical patterns.

There was great resistance to change in many parts of the world. Many societies hesitated over redefinitions of gender relations; this was one reason that, in places like Africa and the Middle East, girls continued to be less likely to receive primary education than boys. The increased influence of fundamentalist religions both reflected and encouraged resistance to many kinds of change, including the increasing inroads of consumer culture.

Even aside from outright resistance, many regions attempted to discipline change by combining it with older traditions. Early in the 21st century, in the southern Indian state of Kerala, for example, leaders attempted to organize beauty contests in which prizes would go to women with the best command of Keralan language and culture. This was an intriguing effort to use a new and popular aspect of global consumerism to revive regional tradition. The food chain McDonald's, even as it built a worldwide empire, accepted essential adjustments to local customs: serving wine and beer in its European outlets, more vegetarian fare in India, teriyaki burgers in Japan. Globalization did not entirely override continuity or opposition in the name of continuity.

Finally, even as they responded to change, many societies retained larger orientations derived from their traditions. Early in the 21st century it was clear that the United States continued to be extremely suspicious of participating in international agreements that might limit its sovereignty; several pacts, on the environment, on punishing war criminals, and on banning land mines, were rejected. China changed mightily during the 20th century at several points, but it continued to place an unusual emphasis on order and conformity. Government attacks on a Buddhist-derived religious movement, the Falun Gong, were uncannily similar to the repression of Buddhism itself under the Tang dynasty. Russia's return to greater authoritarianism in the early 21st century reminded many observers of the strong continuities between tsarist political systems, communism, and the new leadership—all intolerant of internal opposition and critique.

A key use of world history in interpreting contemporary conditions is in understanding how older regional or civilizational traditions continue to shape responses to current problems. The hand of the past does not prevent dramatic change, but it usually colors that change.

## Impact on Daily Life: Emotions and Behavior

Key developments in the 20th and 21st centuries impacted people's emotions and behavior. Emotions are to some extent hardwired and not subject to historical change. Many emotional and behavioral formulations reflect individual personality or particular cultures. And some emotional and behavioral standards continued to characterize specific civilizations in the 20th century. Thus Tahitians, according to anthropologists, were slower to anger than most people. Societies around the Mediterranean maintained traditions of angry or jealous responses to offenses.

Nevertheless, three kinds of change reflected and furthered the larger currents of world history. In many societies, efforts to destroy social inequality involved attempts to reverse emotional passivity. Mao Zedong, leader of the communist upheaval in China, urged peasants to cast off their traditional reluctance to show anger. Civil rights leaders in the United States wrote childrearing manuals to show African American parents how to instill new assertiveness in their children rather than more traditional deference.

Demographic changes had emotional and behavioral implications. When families drastically lowered their birth rates, emotional attachments to individual children increased. American families in the 20th century could rarely survive the death of a child without divorce. By the 1990s Chinese educators were noting growing debates with school officials over the proper treatment of particular children by teams of parents and grandparents, now focused intensely on the fate of a single child.

The spread of global consumerism affected some behaviors. When McDonald's set up its first restaurants in Soviet Russia, it had to teach workers to smile and pretend to be cheerful, a marked contrast to the surly style common among salespeople in the Soviet system. Flight attendants on international airlines received similar training in cheerfulness and service. Many consumer pitches played up emotions like romantic love and played down emotions like grief. Revealingly, when China opened up to the global economy after 1978, open expressions of romantic love increased, as did imports of foreign items that seemed to express loving care.

Emotions and behaviors hardly homogenized worldwide. Older distinctions persisted. New trends often contradicted each other: there were big differences, for example, between anger-fueled protest and the emotions suitable for consumerism. But there were some wider patterns nevertheless. A growing number of people, such as global businesspeople and immigrants who traveled back and forth between their old and new countries, learned a variety of behavioral rules depending on their setting, becoming fluent in global manners and also in the habits of particular societies.

## Societies and Trends

The section begins with Chapter 33 on World War I, in which some of the key trends of the 19th century were brutally reversed. Chapter 34 deals with major developments between the two world wars, including the rise of anticolonialism, dramatic new regimes in Russia, Germany, and Italy, and the global impact of economic depression. Chapter 35 describes World War II, which definitively ended the European order. Chapter 36 focuses on changes both in Western society and in eastern Europe during the cold war. Chapter 37 treats Latin America into the 21st century. Chapter 38 deals with decolonization and ensuing developments in Africa, the Middle East, and south Asia. Chapter 39 focuses on east Asia and the Pacific Rim, where complex developments and divisions had wide impact on the world at large. Chapters 40 and 41 describe key changes in the transition from the 20th to the 21st century.

Taken together, the chapters in this section illustrate the larger themes of this new period in world history. But they also recognize key stages within the past century: the world wars and interwar period as a time of transition; postwar developments dominated by the cold war and decolonization; and a third phase—our current phase—in which new alignments, within a framework of accelerating global contacts, hold pride of place.

CHAPTER 33

# Descent into the Abyss: World War I and the Crisis of the European Global Order



The British overlords were staggered and even some Egyptian nationalist leaders were taken aback by the thousands of women—young and old—who joined the mass demonstrations in the spring of 1919. Spreading from Cairo to towns and villages throughout the Protectorate, the protests shook the global British imperial edifice to its very foundations. Most accounts of the demonstrations, which in many instances turned into violent clashes, stress the role of students and working-class men. The participation of women is often mentioned. But most narratives deal only with elite women—some of whom are captured in the photograph here—who marched in the streets veiled to signal their defiance of the British colonizers. Predictably, we know a good deal about the backgrounds of these elite protesters and the causes they espoused. Little attention, however, has been given to working-class women who—though they have remained largely anonymous—marched in far larger numbers alongside the students and working-class men, and who took on much more aggressive roles during the political upheavals of the early 1920s.

It is not likely that young working-class women, such as Shafika Muhammad and Hamida Khalil, gave much thought to what contemporary reporters or later historians would write about their activities during the tumultuous months from 1919 to 1922 in Egypt. They were too deeply engaged in the tense demonstrations, which held the constant threat of serious injury or even death as Egyptians became more and more aggressive in their resistance to British attempts to crush the mounting popular protest. If they had known, however, that they would be lumped together with unveiled and scantily clad prostitutes in a report on the nationalist risings by a widely read British journalist, the young women would have been outraged. For even though they too marched in the streets unveiled, it was not a reflection of their lack of modesty. In contrast to the veiled well-to-do women from prominent families who had dominated the nationalist movement for decades, women who labored in the processing plants and farmlands of Egypt could not work effectively if restricted by veils and had never made much use of them. But unlike the prostitutes, working-class women made certain that their bodies were well covered, even if that meant wearing loose-fitting pants for some of the more dangerous revolutionary endeavors many were willing to undertake.

**FIGURE 33.1** In late May 1919, large numbers of veiled women joined the mass protests in Cairo and other Egyptian cities and towns that were sparked by the harsh wartime conditions that British demands had exacerbated and by the colonizers' refusal to give Egyptian leaders a hearing at the peace conference in Paris.

In important ways the grievances that sparked the popular risings all along the Nile Valley had much more to do with the lives of the working women than with the concerns of their elite counterparts. The former had always labored long hours at arduous tasks in the sweatshops or fields to earn meager wages or grow a little more food to share with their families. But the demands of the hard-pressed British rulers during World War I had proved devastating for the women and other ordinary Egyptians, who had begun to feel the effects of the global conflict within months of its outbreak in early August 1914.

The war triggered an export boom, especially in cotton, which was in great demand for uniforms, medical supplies, and many other wartime uses. For poor women like Shafika and Hamida, that meant jobs in the factories. And employment opportunities for women increased as the war dragged on, fed by the British decision to conscript Egyptian men in the tens of thousands. Most of the Egyptians worked as bearers, animal tenders, and purveyors of all sorts of services for the

| 1870 C.E. | 1890 C.E. | 1900 C.E. | 1910 C.E. | 1920 C.E. |
|---|---|---|---|---|
| **1870–1890** Cycle of economic depressions in Europe and the United States | **1890** End of the Three Emperors' Alliance (Russia, Austria–Hungary, Germany)<br>**1894** Franco-Russian alliance<br>**1899–1901** Anglo-Boer war in South Africa | **1904–1905** Japanese victory over Russia<br>**1906** Dinshawai incident in Egypt<br>**1909** Morley-Minto reforms in India | **1910** Union of South Africa formed<br>**1914–1918** World War I<br>**1916** Beginning of Arab revolt against Ottoman Empire<br>**1917** Russian Revolution<br>**1917** United States enters World War I<br>**1918** Treaty of Brest-Litovsk; Russia withdraws from war<br>**1919** Treaty of Versailles; League of Nations established<br>**1919** Gandhi leads first nonviolent protest movements in India; revolt in Egypt; Rowlatt Act in India | **1922** French and British mandates set up in Middle East<br>**1920s** Pan-African Congresses in Paris<br>**1923** Treaty of Lausanne recognizes independence of Turkey |

influx of British, Australian, and New Zealand armed forces that used Egypt as a staging area for attacks on Turkey and efforts to beat off German and Turkish threats to the Suez Canal. But the poorly paid and often dangerous jobs that became available to women like Shafika and Hamida could not begin to make up for the runaway inflation that plagued Egypt during the war years. Ordinary Egyptians were affected by sharply rising prices for all manner of household necessities, from bread to clothing to kerosene for lamps and cooking. The demands of garrisoning tens of thousands of soldiers from throughout the empire placed increasing demands on the already overstretched food supply of the Egyptian people, some of whom perished of malnutrition linked to the war. And widespread British confiscations of draft animals belonging to Egyptians enraged peasants and urban workers, both of whom depended on these animals for survival.

Although these and other abuses contributed to the buildup of social and political pressures during the war years, the British underestimated growing signs that a revolt was in the making, because they had long regarded the Egyptians as passive and pliable. Colonial officials were consequently ill-prepared to deal with the literal explosions of popular risings that occurred in the spring of 1919 in response to the British refusal to let Egyptian nationalist leaders travel to France to make the case for Egyptian independence. And none of the colonial leaders could figure out how to handle either the elite or the working-class women who displayed a great aptitude for political organization, dramatizing their causes and fearlessly confronting the police and armed forces. Working-class women even became involved in bombings and armed assaults directed against railways, telegraph stations, and government buildings during the waves of protest that swept across much of Egypt between 1919 and 1922. And, like Shafika Muhammad, who was killed by British soldiers who fired on crowds of unarmed demonstrators on March 14, 1919, some became martyrs of the national liberation movement. They were revered by ordinary Egyptians at the time (if neglected by subsequent historians) and for decades by the leaders of the nationalist movement.

Though far removed from the massive slaughter of young men in the trench warfare of Europe that we normally associate with World War I, the risings in Egypt and the emergence of women as a major force in resistance to continuing colonial domination underscore the importance of seeing the conflict as a truly global phenomenon with far-reaching repercussions for peoples and societies across much of Europe, the Middle East, Africa, Asia, North America, and the

Pacific—especially Australia and New Zealand. The fact that the three main adversaries in the war—Great Britain, France, and Germany—were colonial powers meant that when they plunged into war, they pulled their empires into the abyss with them.

Because the British controlled the sea approaches to Europe, they and their French allies were able to draw soldiers, laborers, raw materials, loans, and donations from their colonial possessions, and these proved critical to their ability to sustain the long war of attrition against Germany. In addition, there were major theaters of combat in the Middle East and Africa as well as clashes in China and the Pacific. The years of increasingly senseless slaughter on the Western Front made a mockery of European claims of superior rationality and a racially ingrained capacity to rule. Pressed by a shortage of trained officials, Europeans were willing to give Western-educated Africans and Indians roles in governance that would have been unimaginable without the war. When the British and French victors sought to renege on promises made to these elites and restore their prewar political prerogatives, the first wave of decolonization was set in motion in Egypt, India, Vietnam, and other colonial societies.

## The Coming of the Great War

**By 1914 diplomatic tensions among the major European powers had been escalating steadily for a generation. Colonial rivalries and arms races had led to the formation, beginning in the 1890s, of two increasingly hostile alliances.**

### The Long March to War

Fear of Germany's growing economic and military power had driven autocratic Russia to ally first with republican France and then with the even more democratic Britain (Map 33.1). Germany's growing power also menaced its neighbor to the west, France. From the early 1890s, the arrogance and aggressive posturing of Germany's new ruler, Kaiser Wilhelm II, only magnified the threat the emerging colossus seemed to pose for the rest of Europe. The French hoped that their alliance with Russia would lead to a two-front war that would brake Germany's rising supremacy and allow France to recover the provinces of Alsace and Lorraine, which France had lost to Germany through defeat in the Franco-Prussian War of 1870. Eclipsed by Germany economically, and increasingly threatened overseas by a growing German navy, Britain joined with Russia and France to form the Triple Entente in the early 1900s.

In the same years, the Triple Entente powers increasingly confronted a counteralliance consisting of Germany, Austria–Hungary, and (nominally at least) Italy that would become known as the Central Powers. With the accession of Kaiser Wilhelm II to power, Germany had moved away from a defensive triple alliance with Russia and Austria–Hungary to a growing dependence on the latter alone. Germany had also sought to draw Italy into its coalition with promises of support for its efforts at colonial expansion. But Italian hostility to Austria–Hungary, which still controlled lands the Italians claimed as their own, kept Italy's role as one of the Central Powers tentative and liable to shift with changing international circumstances. Italian ambivalence became all too clear after the outbreak of war when Italy not only refused to support Germany and Austria–Hungary but in 1915 entered the conflict on the side of the Triple Entente.

Europe, 1914

The alliance system, menacing in itself, was embittered by the atmosphere generated by imperial rivalries that were played out over most of the globe. In the decades leading up to the First World War, most of the European powers had been involved in empire-building overseas, and they came to equate the prestige of "great power" status with the possession of colonies. Their rivalries heightened nationalist sentiments in each country. But by 1900 most of the world's available territories had been colonized by one or another of the states in the two alliance systems. As a result, the scramble in the early 1900s for the few areas as yet unclaimed produced much greater tensions in the European diplomatic system. France maneuvered to annex Morocco to its north African colonies, which already included Algeria and Tunisia (Map 33.1). Germany twice threatened war if the French advance continued, only to back off when it was clear that none of the other European powers would support it. In the second of the international crises over Morocco in 1911, the Germans had to be bought off by a French concession of territory from their possessions in central Africa.

Imperialism in Asia, 1914

Africa on the Eve of World War I

Imperialist rivalries solidified the growing divisions between the two alliances and fed the jingoism (warlike nationalist sentiments that spread widely among the middle and working classes throughout Europe) that had much to do with the coming of the war. Most European leaders of both the great powers and smaller states like those in the Balkans were eager to vie for increased territories and obsessed with keeping their rivals from advancing at their country's expense (Figure 33.2).

Imperialism and the alliance system were both linked to ever more intense and costly arms races. Naval rivalry was the most apparent and fiercely contested. The Germans' decision to build a navy that could threaten Great Britain's long-standing control of the world's oceans was one of the key reasons for

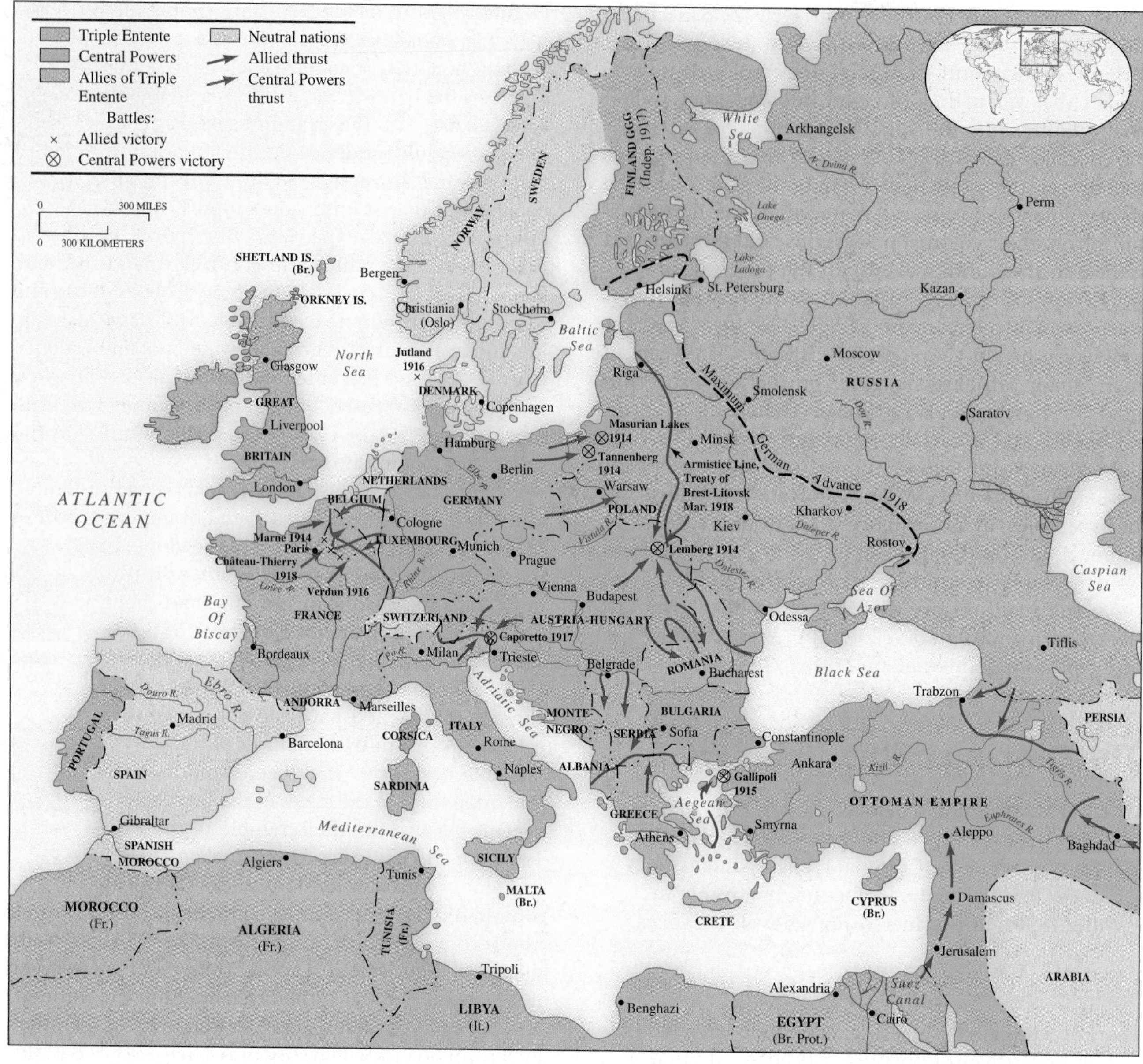


**MAP 33.1** World War I Fronts in Europe and the Middle East

Britain's move for military cooperation with France and (more grudgingly) Russia. It also touched off the greatest arms race in all of history to that time. Huge new warships, such as the *Dreadnought* battleship launched in 1906 and the German ships built in response, kept the naval rivalry at fever pitch. Serious hopes for arms limitations, much less reductions, faded. Armies grew steadily in size and firepower, and they practiced massive maneuvers that national leaders were prepared to implement in the event of the outbreak of a general war. Not surprisingly, the military buildup helped pave the way to war, as some in the German military in particular pushed for a preemptive strike before army reforms in Russia made it too powerful to overcome.

Diplomatic and military competition tied foreign policy to spiraling domestic tensions. All of the major industrial nations, and those in the process of industrializing like Russia, faced growing labor unrest after 1900. Strikes, the growth of trade unions, and votes for socialist parties mounted steadily in the decade and a half before 1914. The business classes and the political elites were alarmed by these challenges to their dominance. They sought diplomatic successes and confrontations with rival powers to distract their subjects from social problems at home. British ministers and the German kaiser, for example, appealed for labor peace in the name of national unity in the face of the threat of attack by powerful rivals. Those in power also supported military buildups because they provided

FIGURE 33.2 The obvious fear displayed by an assortment of European leaders in this 1912 *Punch* cartoon is eerily prescient of the bafflement and concern that later seized European and world leaders in the midst of the Balkan wars of the 1990s.

employment for the working classes and huge profits to industrialists who were pillars of support for each of the European regimes.

## The Outbreak of the War

In the years just before 1914, decades of rivalry and mounting tensions within the European state system were increasingly centered on the Balkans, where Russia sought to back Serbia in its determined resistance to the steady advance of the Austro-Hungarian empire. The complex ethnic divisions and interstate rivalries of the Balkan area mirrored the growing crisis of Europe as a whole. It was not surprising, then, that the event that precipitated the First World War occurred in the Balkans. In July 1914 a Serbian nationalist, Gavriel Princip, assassinated the heir apparent to the Austro-Hungarian throne, **Archduke Ferdinand,** and his wife in **Sarajevo,** the administrative center of the Bosnian province of the Austrian empire. Bolstered by the infamous "blank check" promised by German leaders for reprisals against Serbia, the Austro-Hungarians drew up a list of demands that it was impossible for the Serbs to accede to without surrendering their nation's sovereignty. The ruling circles of Austria–Hungary were determined to put an end to decades of Serbian challenges to their control over portions of the Balkans, and thus they were clearly intent on forcing a war.

Borijove Jevtic: The Murder of Archduke Franz Ferdinand at Sarajevo, 28 June 1914

When the Russians vowed to support their Slavic brethren in Serbia should war break out with the Austrians, the alliance systems that had been forged in the preceding decades quickly came into play. Within months the confrontation of the two blocs had transformed what might have been a regional war among the Balkan states and their Austrian or Russian backers into the threat of a general European war. Inept diplomacy and a widespread sense of resignation to the eventual outbreak of war, which some believed would sort out the quarrels and tensions that had been building for decades, led to the mobilization of the armies of the great powers in late July 1914.

Although the leaders of most of the powers had long regarded mobilization as a way of applying diplomatic pressure, for the Germans mobilization meant war. Because they had faced the possibility of massive combat on two fronts since the 1890s, the Germans had devised an intricate plan to first attack in the west and defeat France before turning to the more backward, and thus slower to mobilize, Russians in the east. Once Russia mobilized against Germany and the German armies moved to mobilize in retaliation according to a rigid railway timetable that plotted an invasion of neutral Belgium on the way to an all-out assault on France, the alliance systems were locked into a massive war. When the British entered the conflict, officially to defend tiny Belgium, which they had long before pledged to protect, a European conflict was transformed into a global one. Britain's naval ally Japan quickly jumped into the fray. British-ruled colonial territories, from the White Dominions of Canada, Australia, and New Zealand to Britain's extensive imperial possessions in India and across Africa and southeast Asia, were brought directly into the war. After nearly a century's lapse, Europe was again consumed by a general war that rapidly spread to other parts of the world.

The Schlieffen Plan, 1905

# A World at War

■ **Part of the reason that Europeans let their nations blunder into war in 1914 was that most of them expected the conflict to be brief and decisive. But after only a month, it was beginning to be clear that the world had been plunged into a conflict that was likely to go on for a good deal longer.**

## The War in Europe

Perhaps more than any other single factor, the failure of Germany's ambitious plan for a quick victory over France ensured that there would be a long war of stalemate and attrition. German political and military leaders counted on their country's superb railway system and huge armies to overwhelm the Belgians and defeat the French before they could even fully mobilize. The French obliged them by launching offensives against deeply entrenched German forces in Alsace-Lorraine that ended in the near destruction of some of France's best armies. But Belgium resisted bravely, slowing the German goliath, and the small but superbly trained British army suddenly appeared to contest the momentum of three German armies, each of which was larger than the total British forces. By the time they reached the frontiers of northern France, the German soldiers were tired and, having left the railways behind in southern Belgium, growing short of boots, food, and ammunition. Reeling from their defeats by the Germans in Alsace-Lorraine, the French forces fled toward Paris, where they regrouped, were reinforced (in part by a famous convoy of Parisian cab drivers), and prepared for the German onslaught. During a five-day battle along the Marne River in early September, the German advance was halted, then thrown back. Paris had been saved and the stage set for over three years of bloody stalemate on the **Western Front.**

Bravo, Belgium—British Cartoon, WWI

The Actual German Advance, 1914

To protect themselves from the withering firepower of the artillery and machine guns of the opposing armies, British and German soldiers began to dig into the ground during and after the clashes along the Marne. Soon northern and western France was crisscrossed by miles and miles of entrenchments that frustrated—with staggering levels of dead and wounded—all attempts to break the stalemate between the opposing forces until well into 1918. The almost unimaginable killing power of the industrial technology wielded by the opposing European armies favored the defensive. Devastating artillery, the withering fire of machine guns, barbed-wire barriers, and the use of poison gas turned the Western Front into a killing ground that offered no possibility of decisive victory to either side. The carnage reached unimaginable levels, with the Germans losing 850,000 troops, the French 700,000, and the British over 400,000 in the single year of 1916 on just the Western Front.

The Technology of War

A Typical British Trench System

By the millions, the youth of Europe was killed, maimed, and driven insane, or they waited for the next offensive catastrophe in rat- and lice-infested trenches. Like the so-called primitive peoples the Europeans had come to dominate overseas, soldiers were exposed to rain and cold and deprived of virtually all of the material comforts that large sections of western European societies had come to regard as their birthright. A German soldier, and later novelist, captured the constant fear, the almost unendurable anxiety the soldiers experienced:

1916 Debut of the British Tank

> The front is a cage in which we must await fearfully whatever may happen. We lie under the network of arching shells and live in a suspense of uncertainty. Over us chance hovers.

In so many ways, the war in Europe was centered on the ongoing and senseless slaughter in the trenches. Levels of dead and wounded that would have been unimaginable before the war rose ever higher between 1915 and 1918. They were all the more tragic because neither side could break the stalemate; hundreds of thousands were killed or maimed to gain small patches of ground that were soon lost in counterattacks. Years of carnage made all too evident the lack of imagination and utter incompetence of most of the generals on both sides of the conflict. Few understood that mass assaults on mechanized defenses had become suicidal at this point in the industrial age. The aged officers in the higher commands and overmatched politicians soon demoted or dismissed those who sought to find creative ways out of the trench morass. As the years passed, as a British war poet observed:

Life in the Trenches During WWI

Wilfred Owen

> Neither [side] had won or could win the war
> The war had won and would go on winning.

## The War in the East and in Italy

In the first weeks of the conflict, the Germans were alarmed by the rapidity with which the Russians were able to mount major offensives against both the Austro-Hungarians and eastern Germany. Having committed most of their forces to their own offensives against France, the German high command felt obliged to divert critical resources and manpower to check the advancing Russian armies. In late August the reorganized German forces virtually destroyed an entire Russian army (and sent a second into headlong retreat). In defeat, the Russian forces exhibited many of the weaknesses that resulted in, by far, the highest levels of casualties of any of the combatants and the ultimate and utter defeat of the tsarist armies. Aristocratic generals dispatched millions of mostly illiterate and poorly trained peasants to certain death in repeated assaults on better-armed and led German forces. Commands in critical battles were sent in uncoded format and readily picked up by their adversaries. Russian artillery, manned by upper-class personnel, usually provided little cover for massed peasant forces, which were reduced to little more than cannon and machine-gun fodder in assaults on the entrenched Germans.

Although the lines shifted over large areas in the east, they inexorably, with horrific human cost, moved east into the provinces of the Russian empire. The poor showing of the Russian commanders, including the hapless tsar **Nicholas II,** who insisted on taking control at the front, did much to spark the mutinies and peasant revolts that were critical forces in the revolutionary waves that destroyed the tsarist regime in 1917.

The Russians fared somewhat better on the Austro-Hungarian front (Map 33.1), where they faced even more inept generals and multiethnic armies whose soldiers' loyalty to the Austrian emperor was often lukewarm or nonexistent. But the Russians could not prevent the Austrians from crushing Serbia, which held out until the end of 1915. Thanks largely to timely interjections of German soldiers, the Austro-Hungarians managed, again at the cost of millions of casualties, to check repeated Russian offensives. The Austrian forces generally fought much better against the Italians, who entered the war in May 1915. Nine months earlier, Italian leaders had declined to march to war with their Central Power allies, who the Italians claimed had attacked first and thus nullified what was a defensive treaty. Having wrested British promises of substantial territorial gains, mostly at Austria–Hungary's expense, the Italians launched a series of offensives against the Austrians.

World War I

With the Austrians enjoying the high ground in the eastern Alps, the assaults all ended in disaster. Incompetent and corrupt generals, soldiers increasingly disgusted by costly campaigns that went nowhere, and venal politicians double-dealing behind the lines resulted in the near collapse of the Italian front in 1917. Although British and French reinforcements rushed from the Western Front eventually stalled the Austrian advance, Italian soldiers deserted in droves and the war plunged Italy into social and political turmoil. One of the Italian soldiers who was briefly at the front and slightly wounded, Benito Mussolini, would soon exploit this unrest to the fullest in his postwar drive to impose a fascist dictatorship on Italy.

The Eastern Front, 1915–1918

## The Home Fronts in Europe

As the war dragged on without any sign that decisive victories could be won by either side, soldiers at the fronts across Europe grew resentful of the civilians back home. Their anger was focused on political leaders who cheered them on from the safety of the sidelines far to the rear. But the soldiers were also disturbed more generally by the patriotic zeal and insensitivity of the civilian populace, which had little sense of the horrors that were endured at the front. In fact, the civilians behind the lines usually had a stronger commitment and more pronounced hatred for the enemy than did the soldiers in combat. Each of the powers remained able to mobilize ever larger numbers of soldiers and military resources, despite growing food shortages and privations on the home fronts. Governments responded by rationing resources and regulating production to head off potentially crippling labor disputes.

Whole industrial sectors, such as railways, were administered directly by the state. Executive branches of the combatants' governments gradually took over the power of elected parliaments—particularly in Germany, where by late 1916 the General Staff virtually ran the country. Dissent was suppressed, often by force, and newspapers and other media outlets (as well as the letters of the soldiers) were strictly censored. Governments developed propaganda departments that grew more sophisticated and strident as the war dragged on. The British proved the most adept at propaganda. Much of this was aimed at the United States in the hope that the Americans would be drawn into the war. The British and American public were bombarded with stories of German atrocities. As the war went into its second and third years, news of severe setbacks was increasingly denied to the German people. As a consequence, most Germans were stunned by what seemed their sudden defeat in 1918. The extent of the involvement of the civilian population (in some cases as targets of bombardments and aerial assaults) and the power of governments to mobilize men and women and control the information they received about the conflict made "the Great War" truly the first total war in human history.

The war sped up many developments already visible in industrial societies. The power of organization increased, particularly through the new interventions of governments. To maintain unified backing of the civilian population, socialists and trade union chiefs were given new recognition and allowed to serve on governing boards in charge of industrial production and negotiate improved working conditions. As their leaders became ever more drawn into the existing governmental system, some labor groups rejected their leadership and became ever more vocal critics of the war. As the war lumbered on, seemingly out of control, these trends became more pronounced, particularly in Russia and Germany. Labor protests in Moscow and St. Petersburg gave powerful momentum to the wave of discontent and mass protest that brought down the tsarist regime in February 1917 and propelled the Bolsheviks to power in October of the same year (see

**FIGURE 33.3** The drastic shortage of farm and factory workers caused by the insatiable military manpower needs of World War I generals provided abundant (but often dangerous, as the munitions work shown here suggests) job opportunities for young women.

Chapter 34). In Germany, labor agitation, very often sparked by growing shortages of food and fuel that were intensified by the British naval blockade, also loomed as a threat to the military commanders who ran the country in the last years of the conflict. As the German front in France and Belgium collapsed in the early summer of 1918, leftist leaders and angry laborers pushed the nation to the brink of revolution in late 1918 and 1919.

As a direct consequence of the war, women's participation in the labor force increased greatly, particularly in Germany, Britain, and the United States. Defying prevailing prewar notions about the "natural" gender roles, women proved very able to work even in heavy industry, where many were engaged in the very dangerous production of munitions (Figure 33.3). Better wages and the confidence they gained from their mastery of such demanding and critical roles as factory workers and nurses at the front sparked a broader liberation for women during the war years. From the rising hemlines of their dresses and their license to smoke in public to unchaperoned dating and greatly increased political activism, many women sought to recast gender roles and images.

At war's end, the loss of many of their jobs to men returning from the front as well as government programs consciously designed to force them back into the home reversed many of the gains that women had achieved during the conflict. But in Britain, Germany, and the United States, they gained the vote, which they had struggled for in the decades before 1914. The visibility and influence of the career-oriented and sophisticated "new women" of the 1920s, though a small minority even in Germany and the United States, gave promise of broader advances in the decades to come.

## The War Outside Europe

Except for Austria–Hungary, all of the major powers that went to war in 1914 had colonies outside Europe. When it became clear that the war was not to be the quick, decisive clash that most had anticipated, the manpower and resources of these imperial possessions were increasingly sucked into the spreading conflict. By 1915, fighting had spread to the Middle East, west and east Africa, across most of the seas and oceans of the world, and even to China and the islands of the Pacific. Troops from Canada, Australia, New Zealand, India, and throughout much of Africa had been recruited, mainly to fight for the Triple Entente allies. By 1917 the United States had entered the war, leaving only the nations of South America alone of all the continents not directly engaged in the struggle.

Britain's participation, more than that of any other power, contributed to the war's globalization. The British navy not only cut off Germany from its colonies in Africa, China, and the Pacific islands, but it hunted down German ships still on the high seas at the outbreak of war. Perhaps most critically, British naval supremacy meant that an effective blockade could be maintained that would deprive the Central Powers of supplies of food and raw materials from overseas throughout the war. Because the British also controlled trans-Atlantic cable links, they could easily outdo the Germans in propaganda efforts to convince the neutral United States to side with them in the war. The expensive and highly touted German navy fully engaged the British grand fleet only once during the war, in 1916 off Jutland in Denmark. Though the Germans sank more ships and killed more British sailors, the high seas fleet was driven back into port and proved of little use to the larger German effort for the rest of the war.

The British entry into the war also meant that its empire and allies were drawn into the fray. Japan, which had joined Britain in a naval pact in 1902, eagerly attacked German colonies in China and the Pacific. These acquisitions, especially the seizure of the Shandong peninsula, would provide great impetus to Japan's imperialist aspirations in China in the 1930s. The islands they captured from the Germans in World War I proved components of the defense perimeter they sought to build in the Pacific during World War II.

The British Dominions—Canada, Australia, and New Zealand—quickly marshalled considerable resources to support the war effort. These areas not only supplied food and critical raw materials, but in defiance of the German U-boat fleet in the Atlantic, they swelled the initially meager ranks of Britain's armed forces. Dominion troops were a mainstay of British operations in the Middle East, including the defense of the vital Suez Canal link and the ill-fated assault at **Gallipoli** in 1915. They fought valiantly on the Western Front throughout the war, at times bolstering British lines that were crumbling under massive German assaults. White settler colonials in south Africa also joined those from the Dominions in support of the British, despite bitter opposition from some segments of the Afrikaner population, which had suffered so greatly as a result of draconian British repression in the Anglo-Boer war just over a decade earlier.

The British and the French also received vital support from their nonsettler colonies in Africa, India, and southeast Asia. The massive army that the British had recruited in India for over a century and a half did much of the fighting in sub-Saharan Africa and the Middle East. The French deployed tens of thousands of non-European soldiers, recruited mainly in north and west Africa, on the Western Front, where many served with distinction but with scant reward. Unlike the British, who turned mainly to women to replace the millions of farmers and factory workers who went off to war, the French relied heavily on laborers recruited in their colonies from Africa to Vietnam.

Although the Germans quickly lost most of their colonies in Africa and the Far East, superbly led African soldiers recruited and trained in German East Africa (Tanzania today) held off hundreds of thousands of British-led Indian and south African troops until two weeks after the end of hostilities in Europe. But Germany's main support outside Europe came from the Ottoman Empire (Map 33.1), which entered the war in the fall of 1915. The Young Turk leaders, who had consolidated their power in Constantinople in the decade leading up to the war (see Chapter 31), had continued the Ottoman reliance on German military advisors and financiers. After fending off the British-led campaign to capture the Gallipoli peninsula, the Turks opened up fronts in southern Russia, where they suffered severe defeats, and the Middle East, where their fortunes were more mixed and they remained for years a threat to the British in Egypt and the Suez Canal zone.

The Young Turk leaders sought to transfer blame for the reverses on the Russian front to the Christian Armenian minority, which was concentrated in areas that spanned the two empires in eastern Anatolia and the Caucasus. In fact, remembering earlier pogroms launched by the Turks against them, some of the Armenians living in Turkish areas had backed the Russians. But most of the minority was loyal or neutral, and poor generalship and bad planning were the main causes of the Turkish military disasters. Struggling to cover their blunders, the Young Turk leaders launched an assault in 1915 against the Armenians. The ensuing **Armenian genocide** claimed as many as a million lives and sent hundreds of thousands of Armenians in flight to Russia and the Middle East.

A Turkish Officer Describes the Armenian Massacres

The last major combatant to enter the global conflagration was the United States, which declared war on Germany in the spring of 1917. The war made the United States into a major global power, culminating developments that had been underway for decades. By 1914 the United States had become an active force in international diplomacy and power politics. It had built a modest Pacific empire, centering on Hawaii and the Philippine islands, and had become increasingly forceful in its interventions in Central America and the Caribbean. The outbreak of the war was greeted with considerable ambivalence on the part of American leaders and the citizenry more generally. Distant from the battlefields, Americans disagreed over which side was in the right and whether or not they should intervene in quarrels that seemed to have little to do with them. But American businesses profited greatly from the war by selling food, raw materials, and eventually weapons, mainly (due to the British blockade) to the Entente allies. American mercantile interests, like their counterparts in Japan, also took advantage of the Europeans' need to concentrate their industrial production on the war effort by taking over new markets in Latin America and Asia. Rapidly rising exports, combined with huge loans to Britain, France, and Russia, which all needed credit to buy American goods, transformed the United States from an international debtor to the world's largest creditor and strongest economy.

Despite all of the gains that the United States had accrued through neutrality, American leadership and a majority of the American public was pro-British. British successes in the propaganda war and ever growing economic ties to the Entente allies did much to explain this sentiment. But clumsy German attempts to influence American opinion and, most critically, the German need to use submarines to counter the British blockade and control sea access to Europe did much to drive the United States into the war. Following the resumption of unrestricted submarine warfare in the Atlantic, which President Woodrow

Temporary Shelter for American Wounded

VISUALIZING THE PAST

## Trench Warfare

This World War I painting highlights soldiers in the trench fighting that dominated the conflict on the Western Front.

**Questions** What can be read from the picture? What were the trenches like? Can the expressions and poses of the soldiers be read to suggest what war meant to them? How did life in the trenches compare with their previous lives in industrial society and with expectations in an age that had vaunted manliness and nationalism? Does the painting raise issues of bias or staging on the part of the artist, or is it a neutral piece of evidence? Finally, can one move from this picture of war to some speculations about what peacetime life would be like for the veterans who returned home?

Wilson had earlier warned would force military retaliation by the United States, America entered the conflict in April 1917. American warships joined with the British to create a convoy system that eventually offset an intensified German submarine campaign designed to starve the British Isles into submission.

For much of 1917, the number of American troops sent to Europe was small and largely symbolic. But by early 1918, millions of young Americans were in training and hundreds of thousands arrived in Europe each week. The growing buildup of American reinforcements, and American-produced arms and supplies, convinced the German high command that they must launch a massive strike for a quick victory, before the full manpower and resources of the United States could be brought to bear against their weary soldiers.

## Endgame: The Return of Offensive Warfare

For several weeks in March and April 1918, the massive offensives launched by the Germans on the Western Front looked as if they might bring victory to the Central Powers. An entire British army had been shattered and another was in full retreat; the already demoralized French forces were also falling back toward Paris. Nearly a million German soldiers transferred from the **Eastern Front** after Russia was knocked out of the war, and new assault tactics and the deployment of storm troopers had restored the offensive and broken three long years of bloody stalemate. But just as Paris was again within the range of the great German guns, the advance slowed. Mounting casualties and sheer fatigue on the German side, counteroffensives, new weapons like tanks, and a rapidly increasing influx of fresh and enthusiastic American soldiers stalled the German drive and then began to push the German armies out of northern France. At the same time, the Austrian fronts broke down in both northeast Italy and the Balkans. The Austro-Hungarian empire fragmented along national lines, and the heir to the Habsburg throne abdicated as separate republics in Austria and Hungary sued the Entente allies for peace.

Fearing that their armies were on the verge of collapse and menaced by widespread rebellions at home, the German commanders agreed to an armistice on November 11, 1918. The generals sought to shift the blame for defeat to a civilian government that they had abruptly installed in Berlin. Made up of members of the Center and Socialist parties, Germany's new government was forced to both sue the Entente allies for peace and consent to an armistice agreement delivered by two British admirals and two French generals. Assuming that their armies were on the verge of victory just months before, the German people were stunned by the sudden reversal. Many accepted the myth that Germany had been betrayed by socialist and Jewish politicians, whose alleged "stab in the back" would become a rallying cry for **Adolf Hitler** and the Nazis' drive for power from the early 1920s.

After four years of slaughter, the casualty totals were staggering (see Table 33.1). At least 10 million soldiers were dead and 20 million more wounded. The losses were, by far, the heaviest among the great powers of Europe who had been the main adversaries in the conflict. From France to Russia, virtually every European family had a death to mourn. As the fighting ended, an additional calamity struck. Hundreds of thousands of soldiers and millions of civilians died in an influenza pandemic that began in Asia and spread like wildfire around the globe. Though the direct costs of the long and widespread war and the indirect economic losses it inflicted are almost impossible to calculate with certainty, both totals reached hundreds of billions of dollars. In Belgium and northern France, northern Italy, and across east central Europe, extensive swaths of fertile farmlands and bustling cites were reduced to smoldering ruins. This devastation and a postwar economic downturn that followed the armistice dislocated economies across the globe until well into the mid-1920s and fed into the Great Depression that was to follow a decade later.

**TABLE 33.1** World War I Losses

| | Dead | Wounded | Prisoner |
|---|---|---|---|
| Great Britain | 947,000 | 2,122,000 | 192,000 |
| France | 1,385,000 | 3,044,000 | 446,000 |
| Russia | 1,700,000 | 4,950,000 | 500,000 |
| Italy | 460,000 | 947,000 | 530,000 |
| United States | 115,000 | 206,000 | 4,500 |
| Germany | 1,808,000 | 4,247,000 | 618,000 |
| Austria–Hungary | 1,200,000 | 3,620,000 | 200,000 |
| Turkey | 325,000 | 400,000 | |

Note: The number of known dead (round numbers) was placed at about 10 million and the wounded at about 20 million, distributed among chief combatants.

## Failed Peace

**The widespread bitterness evoked by the war's unprecedented cost in lives and destruction was redoubled by the utter failure of the peace conference convened by the victorious allies in Paris.**

While the Italians and Japanese scrambled to obtain maximum advantage from their support of the Entente forces during the war, the French insisted that they had suffered the most and their losses had to be avenged. **Georges Clemenceau,** the French premier, pushed for the peace conference to brand the Germans the aggressors and thus force them to pay huge reparations to France and the other nations assaulted. He also worked to cut down the size of Germany and funnel its resources to France and the other powers.

Fearing that a reduced Germany would prove fertile ground for the spread of communist revolution, **David Lloyd George,** the British prime minister, attempted with little success to mediate between Clemenceau and Woodrow Wilson and to win enough reparations to satisfy a disgruntled electorate at home. All of the leaders of the victorious Entente powers, including Wilson, soon closed ranks against the demands welling up from peoples in colonized areas, from the Middle East to Vietnam (Figure 33.4). Dashing the expectations that

**FIGURE 33.4** At the Paris peace conference of 1919, the Arabs sought a new voice. The Arab representatives included Prince Feisal, later king of Iraq, and an Iraqi general. A British delegation member, T. E. Lawrence (third from the right), was a longtime friend of the Arabs. The Arabs did not win national self-determination for their homelands, as the British had promised during the war.

he had aroused by his ringing call for the right of peoples to **self-determination,** Wilson soon made it clear that the peoples he had in mind were white folk like the Poles, not Arabs or Vietnamese. With Wilson's blessing, the British and French set about shoring up, and in fact expanding, their battered empires, while the Japanese solidified their beachhead in China and island enclaves in the western Pacific. The triumvirate of Wilson, Lloyd George, and Clemenceau, which dominated the proceedings at Versailles, also made certain that a mild antiracist clause never made it into the final draft of the treaty.

IMAGE

The Mask Falls—German Cartoon Reacting to Treaty of Versailles

The Peace of Paris, which was the most important of a series of treaties that emerged from the gathering at Versailles, was nothing less than the *diktat* (dictated peace, without negotiations) that German politicians across the political spectrum sought to reverse in the postwar era. The German delegation was allowed no part in drafting the treaty, and they were given no opportunity to amend or refuse it. The German representatives were even humiliated by being brought in by the servants' entrance for the signing and being required to stand for hours while the entire draft of the treaty was read aloud before the assembled delegates. The Germans' main allies—the Austrians—were also major targets of the treaties that emerged from the conference. The Austro-Hungarian Empire was dismembered, as nationalist groups carved out the new nations of Czechoslovakia, Hungary, and Yugoslavia. Poland was also reborn, and like Czechoslovakia, it was given substantial chunks of what had been German territory before the war. This left a somewhat fragile Germanic Austria, cut off from its traditional markets, as one of many weak countries between a smaller Germany and a massive Soviet Union to the east.

Europe and the Middle East After World War I

The fatal flaws of the peace process extended far beyond calculated insults to the Germans. The new Bolshevik leaders of Russia, who would be treated as pariahs for decades, were not even invited to the conference. Wartime promises to the Arabs in return for their support for the Entente in the war were forgotten, as Britain and France divided the Arab heartlands of the Middle East between themselves. China's pleas for protection from Japanese occupation of the Shandong peninsula were dismissed, and a youthful Ho Chi Minh, the future leader of Vietnam, was rudely refused an audience with Woodrow Wilson. Denied their demand that Germany be permanently partitioned, French leaders turned inward on each other and waited despondently for the next German assault they were convinced was inevitable.

Even the United States, whose President Wilson had opened the peace conference with such exuberant expectations, repudiated what had been wrought at Versailles. Despite Wilson's literally near-fatal efforts to win popular support for the treaty, the American Congress voted down the critical clauses establishing the

**League of Nations** and later made a separate peace with Germany. Even as the delegates were still at work, it was clear to knowledgeable observers that Versailles was a disaster. One of the most perceptive chroniclers of the war years and their aftermath, Vera Brittain, wrote as the terms of the treaty began to be made public in the press:

> the Big Four were making a desert and calling it peace. When I thought about these negotiations . . . they did not seem to me to represent at all the kind of "victory" that the young men whom I had loved would have regarded as sufficient justification for their lost lives.

## The Nationalist Assault on the European Colonial Order

**Four long years of intra-European slaughter severely disrupted the systems of colonial domination that had been expanded and refined in the century leading up to World War I. The conflict also gave great impetus to the forces of resistance that had begun to well up in the decades before the war.**

Though the European colonizers had frequently quarreled over colonial possessions in the late 19th century, during World War I they actually fought each other in the colonies for the first time. African and Asian soldiers and laborers in the hundreds of thousands served on the Western Front and in the far-flung theaters of war in Egypt, Palestine, Mesopotamia, and east Africa. The colonies also supplied food for the home populations of the Triple Entente powers, as well as vital raw materials such as oil, jute, and cotton. Contrary to long-standing colonial policy, the hard-pressed British even encouraged a considerable expansion of industrial production in India to supplement the output of their overextended home factories. Thus, the war years contributed to the development in India of the largest industrial sector in the colonized world.

World War I presented the subjugated peoples of Africa and Asia with the spectacle of the self-styled civilizers of humankind sending their young men by the millions to be slaughtered in the horrific and barbaric trench stalemate on the Western Front. For the first time, African and Asian soldiers were ordered by their European officers to kill other Europeans. In the process, the vulnerability of the seemingly invincible Europeans and the deep divisions between them were starkly revealed. During the war years, European troops in the colonies were withdrawn to meet the need for manpower on the many war fronts. The garrisons that remained were dangerously understaffed. The need to recall administrative personnel from British and French colonies meant that colonial officials were compelled to fill their vacated posts with African and Asian administrators, many of whom enjoyed real responsibility for the first time.

To maintain the loyalty of their traditional allies among the colonized and to win the support of the Western-educated elites or new allies such as the Arabs, the British and French made many promises regarding the postwar settlement. Because these concessions often seriously compromised their prewar dominance or their plans for further colonial expansion, the leaders of the victorious allies repeatedly reneged on them in the years after the war. The betrayal of these pledges understandably contributed a great deal to postwar agitation against the continuance and spread of European colonial domination.

For intellectuals and political leaders throughout Africa and Asia, the appalling devastation of World War I cast doubt on the claims that the Europeans had made for over a century that they were, by virtue of their racial superiority, the fittest of all peoples to rule the globe. The social and economic disruptions caused by the war in key colonies, such as Egypt, India, and the Ivory Coast, made it possible for nationalist agitators to build a mass base for their anticolonial movements for the first time. But in these and other areas of the colonized world, the war gave added impetus to movements and processes already underway, rather than initiating new responses to European global domination. Therefore, it is essential to place wartime developments in the colonies and the postwar surge in anticolonial resistance in a longer-term context that takes into account African and Asian responses that extend in some cases back to the last decades of the 19th century. Since it is impossible to relate the history of the independence struggles in all of the European colonies, key movements, such as those that developed in India, Egypt, and British and French west Africa, will be considered in some depth. These specific movements will then be related to broader patterns of African and Asian nationalist agitation and the accelerating phenomenon of decolonization worldwide.

The West and the World: Changes in European Empires After World War I

### India: The Makings of the Nationalist Challenge to the British Raj

Because India and much of southeast Asia had been colonized long before Africa, movements for independence arose in Asian colonies somewhat earlier than in their African counterparts. By the last years of the 19th century, the Western-educated minority of the colonized in India and the Philippines had been

DOCUMENT

## Lessons for the Colonized from the Slaughter in the Trenches

The prolonged and senseless slaughter of the youth of Europe in the trench stalemate on the Western Front did much to erode the image of Europeans as superior, rational, and more civilized beings that they had worked hard to propagate among the colonized peoples in the decades before the Great War. The futility of the seemingly endless slaughter cast doubts on the Europeans' rationality and fitness to rule themselves, much less the rest of the world. The destructive uses to which their science and technology were put brought into question the Europeans' long-standing claims that these material advancements tangibly demonstrated their intellectual and organizational superiority over all other peoples. The excerpts below, taken from the writings of some of the leading thinkers and political leaders of the colonized peoples of Africa and Asia, reflect their disillusionment with the West as a result of the war and the continuing turmoil in Europe in the postwar era.

### Rabindranath Tagore

Bengali poet, playwright, and novelist Rabindranath Tagore was one of the earliest non-European recipients of the Nobel Prize for literature.

> Has not this truth already come home to you now when this cruel war has driven its claws into the vitals of Europe? When her hoard of wealth is bursting into smoke and her humanity is shattered on her battlefields? You ask in amazement what she has done to deserve this? The answer is, that the West has been systematically petrifying her moral nature in order to lay a solid foundation for her gigantic abstractions of efficiency. She has been all along starving the life of the personal man into that of the professional.

### Mohandas Gandhi

In the years after the First World War, Mohandas Gandhi emerged as India's leading nationalist figure.

> India's destiny lies not along the bloody way of the West, but along the bloodless way of peace that comes from a simple and godly life. India is in danger of losing her soul. . . . She must not, therefore, lazily and helplessly say, "I cannot escape the onrush from the West." She must be strong enough to resist it for her own sake and that of the world. I make bold to say that the Europeans themselves will have to remodel their outlooks if they are not to perish under the weight of the comforts to which they are becoming slaves.

### Léopold Sédar Senghor

Senegalese poet and political leader Léopold Sédar Senghor is widely regarded as one of the 20th century's finest writers in the French language.

> Lord, the snow of your Peace is your proposal to a divided world to a divided Europe
>
> To Spain torn apart.
>
> And I forget
>
> White hands that fired the shots which brought the empires crumbling
>
> Hands that flogged the slaves, that flogged You [Jesus Christ]
>
> Chalk-white hands that buffeted You, powdered painted hands that buffeted me
>
> Confident hands that delivered me to solitude to hatred
>
> White hands that felled the forest of palm trees once commanding Africa, in the heart of Africa.

From *Snow upon Paris*

### Aimé Césaire

West Indian poet Aimé Césaire was a founder of the négritude movement, which asserted black culture in the late 1920s.

> Heia [Praise] for those who have never invented anything
>
> those who never explored anything
>
> those who never tamed anything
>
> those who give themselves up to the essence of all things
>
> ignorant of surfaces but struck by the movement of all things.

From *Return to My Native Land*

---

**Questions** On the basis of this sample, what aspects of the West's claims to superiority would you say were called into question by the suicidal conflict of the leading powers within European civilization? What aspects of their own civilizations do these writers, both implicitly and explicitly, champion as alternatives to the ways of the West? Are these writers in danger of stereotyping both the West and their own civilizations?

organized politically for decades. Their counterparts in Burma and the Netherlands Indies were also beginning to form associations to give voice to their political concerns. Because of India's size and the pivotal role it played in the British Empire (by far the largest of the European imperialist empires), the Indian nationalist movement pioneered patterns of nationalist challenge and European retreat that were later followed in many other colonies. Though it had been under British control for only a matter of decades, Egypt also proved an influential center of nationalist organization and resistance in the pre–World War I era.

Local conditions elsewhere in Asia and in Africa made for important variations on the sequence of decolonization worked out in India and Egypt. But key themes—such as the lead taken by Western-educated elites, the importance of charismatic leaders in the spread of the anticolonial struggle to the peasant and urban masses, and a reliance on nonviolent forms of protest—were repeated again and again in other colonial settings.

The **National Congress party** led the Indians to independence and governed through most of the early decades of the postcolonial era. It grew out of regional associations of Western-educated Indians that were originally more like study clubs than political organizations in any meaningful sense of the term. These associations were centered in the cities of Bombay, Poona, Calcutta, and Madras (see Map 29.3). The Congress party that Indian leaders formed in 1885 had the blessing of a number of high-ranking British officials. These officials viewed it as a forum through which the opinions of educated Indians could be made known to the government, thereby heading off potential discontent and political protest.

For most of its first decades, the Congress party served these purposes quite well. The organization had no mass base and very few ongoing staff members or full-time politicians who could sustain lobbying efforts on issues raised at its annual meetings. Some members of the Congress party voiced concern for the growing poverty of the Indian masses and the drain of wealth from the subcontinent to Great Britain. But the Congress party's debates and petitions to the government were dominated by elite-centric issues, such as the removal of barriers to Indian employment in the colonial bureaucracy and increased Indian representation in all-Indian and local legislative bodies. Most of the members of the early Congress party were firmly loyal to the British rulers and confident that once their grievances were made known to the government, they would be remedied.

Many Western-educated Indians were increasingly troubled, however, by the growing virulence of British racism. This they were convinced had much to do with their poor salaries and limited opportunities for advancement in the colonial administration. In their annual meetings, members of the Congress, who were now able to converse and write in a common English language, discovered that no matter where they came from in India, they were treated in a similar fashion. The Indians' shared grievances, their similar educational and class backgrounds, and their growing contacts through the Congress party gave rise to a sense of common Indian identity that had never before existed in a south Asian environment that was more diverse linguistically, religiously, and ethnically than the continent of Europe.

## Social Foundations of a Mass Movement

By the last years of the 19th century, the Western-educated elites had begun to grope for causes that would draw a larger segment of the Indian population into their growing nationalist community. More than a century of British rule had generated in many areas of India the social and economic disruptions and the sort of discontent that produced substantial numbers of recruits for the nationalist campaigns. Indian businessmen, many of whom would become major financial backers of the Congress party, were angered by the favoritism the British rulers showed to British investors in establishing trade policies in India. Indian political leaders increasingly stressed these inequities and the more general loss to the Indian people resulting from what they termed the "drain" of Indian resources under colonial rule. Though the British rebuttal was that a price had to be paid for the peace and good government that had come with colonial rule, nationalist thinkers pointed out that the cost was too high.

A large portion of the government of India's budget went to cover the expenses of the huge army that mainly fought wars elsewhere in the British Empire. The Indian people also paid for the generous salaries and pensions of British administrators, who occupied positions that the Indians were qualified to assume. Whenever possible, as in the purchase of railway equipment or steel for public works projects, the government bought goods manufactured in Great Britain. This practice served to buttress a British economy that was fast losing ground to the United States and Germany. It also ensured that the classic colonial relationship between a manufacturing European colonizer and its raw-material-producing overseas dependencies was maintained.

Tragore, Letter on British Imperialism

In the villages of India, the shortcomings of British rule were equally apparent by the last decades of the 19th century. The needs of the British home economy had often dictated policies that pushed the Indian peasantry toward the production of cash crops such as cotton, jute, and indigo. The decline in food production that invariably resulted played a major role in the regional famines that struck repeatedly in the pre–World War I era. Radical Indian nationalists frequently charged that the British were callously indifferent to the suffering caused by food shortages and outbreaks of epidemic disease, and that they did far too little to alleviate the suffering that resulted. In many areas, landlessness and chronic poverty, already a problem before the establishment of British rule, increased markedly. In most places, British measures to control indebtedness and protect small landholders and tenants were too little and came too late.

## The Rise of Militant Nationalism

Some of the issues that Indian nationalist leaders stressed in their early attempts to build a mass base had great appeal for devout Hindus. This was particularly true of campaigns for the protection of cows, which have long had a special status for the Hindu population of south Asia. But these religious-oriented causes often strongly alienated the adherents of other faiths, especially the Muslims. Not only did Muslims eat beef, and thus slaughter cattle, but they made up nearly one-fourth of the population of the Indian Empire. Some leaders, such as **B. G. Tilak,** were little concerned by this split. They believed that since Hindus made up the overwhelming majority of the Indian population, nationalism should be built on appeals to Hindu religiosity. Tilak worked to promote the restoration and revival of what he believed to be the ancient traditions of Hinduism. On this basis, he opposed women's education and raising the very low marriage age for women. Tilak turned festivals for Hindu gods into occasions for mass political demonstrations. He broke with more moderate leaders of the Congress party by demanding the boycott of British-manufactured goods. Tilak also sought to persuade Indians to refuse to serve in the colonial administration and military. Tilak demanded full independence, with no deals or delays, and threatened violent rebellion if the British failed to comply.

Tilak's oratorical skills and religious appeal made him the first Indian nationalist leader with a genuine mass following. Nonetheless, his popularity was confined mainly to his home base in Bombay and in nearby areas in western India. At the same time, his promotion of a very reactionary sort of Hinduism offended and frightened moderate and progressive Hindus, Muslims, and followers of other religions, such as the Sikhs. When evidence was found connecting Tilak's writings to underground organizations that advocated violent revolt, the British, who had grown increasingly uneasy about his radical demands and mass appeal, arrested and imprisoned him. Six years of exile in Burma for Tilak had a dampening effect on the mass movement he had begun to build among the Hindu population.

The other major threat to the British in India before World War I came from Hindu communalists who advocated the violent overthrow of the colonial regime. But unlike Tilak and his followers, those who joined the terrorist movement favored clandestine operations over mass demonstrations. Though terrorists were active in several parts of India by the last decade of the 19th century, those in Bengal built perhaps the most extensive underground network. Considerable numbers of young Bengalis, impatient with the gradualist approach advocated by moderates in the Congress party, were attracted to underground secret societies. These were led by quasi-religious, guru-style leaders who exhorted them to build up their physiques with Western-style calisthenics and learn how to use firearms and make bombs. British officials and government buildings were the major targets of terrorist assassination plots and sabotage. On occasion the young revolutionaries also struck at European civilians and collaborators among the Indian population. But the terrorists' small numbers and limited support from the colonized populace as a whole rendered them highly vulnerable to British repressive measures. The very considerable resources the British devoted to crushing these violent threats to their rule had checked the terrorist threat by the outbreak of World War I.

Tilak's removal and the repression campaigns against the terrorists strengthened the hand of the more moderate politicians of the Congress party in the years before the war. Western-educated Indian lawyers became the dominant force in nationalist politics, and—as the careers of Gandhi, Jinnah, and Nehru demonstrate—they would provide many of the movement's key leaders throughout the struggle for independence. The approach of those who advocated a peaceful, constitutionalist route to decolonization was given added appeal by timely political concessions on the part of the British. The **Morley-Minto reforms** of 1909 provided educated Indians with considerably expanded opportunities both to vote for and serve on local and all-India legislative councils.

## The Emergence of Gandhi and the Spread of the Nationalist Struggle

In the months after the outbreak of World War I, the British could take great comfort from the way in which the peoples of the empire rallied to their defense. Of the many colonies among the tropical dependencies, none played as critical a role in the British war effort as India. The Indian princes offered substantial war loans; Indian soldiers bore the brunt of the war effort in east Africa and the Middle East; and nationalist leaders, including Gandhi and Tilak, toured India selling British war bonds. But as the war dragged on and Indians died on the battlefields or went hungry at home to sustain a conflict that had little to do with them, signs of unrest spread throughout the subcontinent.

Wartime inflation had adversely affected virtually all segments of the Indian population. Indian peasants were angered at the ceilings set on the price of their market produce, despite rising costs. They were also often upset by their inability to sell what they had produced because of shipping shortages linked to the war. Indian laborers saw their already meager wages drop steadily in the face of rising prices. At the same time, their bosses grew rich from profits earned in war production. Many localities suffered from famines, which were exacerbated by wartime transport shortages that impeded relief efforts.

After the end of the war in 1918, moderate Indian politicians were frustrated by the British refusal to honor wartime promises. Hard-pressed British leaders had promised the Indians that if they continued to support the war effort, India would move steadily to self-government within the empire once the conflict was over. Indian hopes for the fulfillment of these promises were raised by the **Montagu-Chelmsford reforms** of 1919. These measures increased the powers of Indian legislators at the all-India level and placed much of the provincial administration of India under their control. But the concessions granted in the reforms were offset by the passage later in the same year of the **Rowlatt Act,** which placed severe restrictions on key Indian civil rights, such as freedom of the press. These conditions fueled local protest during and immediately after the war. At the same time, **Mohandas Gandhi** emerged as a new leader who soon forged this localized protest into a sustained all-India campaign against the policies of the colonial overlords.

Gandhi's remarkable appeal to both the masses and the Western-educated nationalist politicians was due to a combination of factors. Perhaps the most important was the strategy for protest that he had worked out a decade earlier as the leader of a successful movement of resistance to the restrictive laws imposed on the Indian migrant community in south Africa. Gandhi's stress on nonviolent but quite aggressive protest tactics endeared him both to the moderates and to more radical elements within the nationalist movement. His advocacy of peaceful boycotts, strikes, noncooperation, and mass demonstrations—which he labeled collectively **satyagraha,** or truth force—proved an effective way of weakening British control while limiting opportunities for violent reprisals that would allow the British to make full use of their superior military strength.

Gandhi on Civil Disobedience

It is difficult to separate Gandhi's approach to mass protest from Gandhi as an individual and thinker. Though physically unimposing, he possessed an inner confidence and sense of moral purpose that sustained his followers and wore down his adversaries. He combined the career of a Western-educated lawyer with the attributes of a traditional Hindu ascetic and guru. The former had given him considerable exposure to the world beyond India and an astute understanding of the strengths and weaknesses of the British colonizers. These qualities and his soon legendary skill in negotiating with the British made it possible for Gandhi to build up a strong following among middle-class, Western-educated Indians, who had long been the dominant force behind the nationalist cause. But the success of Gandhi's protest tactics also hinged on the involvement of ever increasing numbers of the Indian people in anticolonial resistance. The image of a traditional mystic and guru that Gandhi projected was critical in gaining mass support from peasants and laborers alike. Many of these "ordinary" Indians would walk for miles when Gandhi was on tour. Many did so in order to honor a saint rather than listen to a political speech. Gandhi's widespread popular appeal, in turn, gave him even greater influence among nationalist politicians. The latter were very much aware of the leverage his mass following gave to them in their ongoing contests with the British overlords. Under Gandhi's leadership, nationalist protest surged in India during the 1920s and 1930s.

Gandhi

## Egypt and the Rise of Nationalism in the Middle East

Egypt is the one country in the Afro-Asian world in which the emergence of nationalism preceded European conquest and domination (Map 33.2). Risings touched off by the mutiny of Ahmad Orabi and other

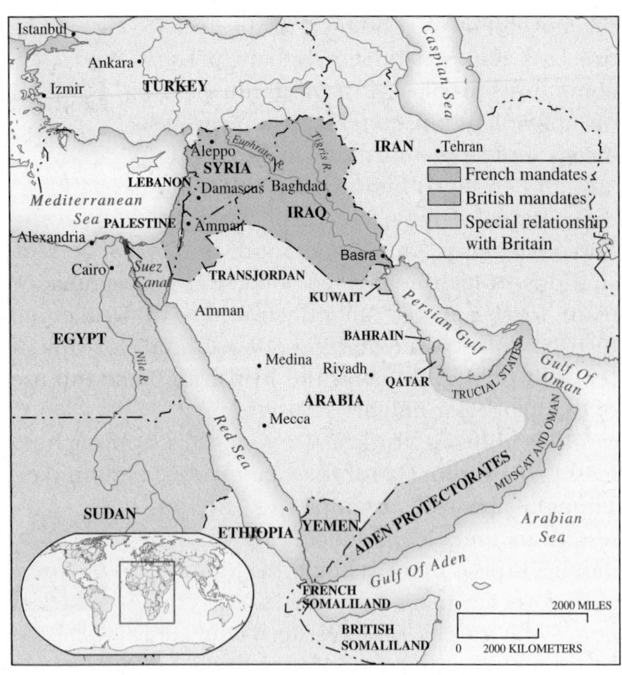


MAP 33.2 The Middle East After World War I

Egyptian officers (see Chapter 31), which led to the British occupation in 1882, were aimed at the liberation of the Egyptian people from their alien Turkish overlords as well as the meddling Europeans. British occupation meant, in effect, double colonization for the Egyptian people by the Turkish khedives (who were left in power) and their British advisors.

In the decades following the British conquest, government policy was dominated by the strong-willed and imperious **Lord Cromer.** As high commissioner of Egypt, he pushed for much-needed economic reforms that reduced but could not eliminate the debts of the puppet khedival regime. Cromer also oversaw sweeping reforms in the bureaucracy and the construction of irrigation systems and other public works projects. But the prosperity the British congratulated themselves for having brought to Egypt by the first decade of the 20th century was enjoyed largely by tiny middle and elite classes, often at the expense of the mass of the population. The leading beneficiaries included foreign merchants, the Turco-Egyptian political elite, a small Egyptian bourgeoisie in Cairo and other towns in the Nile delta, and the ayan, or the great landlords in the rural areas.

The latter were clearly among the biggest gainers. The British had been forced to rely heavily on local, estate-owning notables in extending their control into the rural areas. As a result, the ayan, not the impoverished mass of rural cultivators and laborers, received most of the benefits of the new irrigation works, the building of railways, and the increasing orientation of Egyptian agriculture to the production of raw cotton for the export market. Unfettered by legal restrictions, the ayan greedily amassed ever larger estates by turning smallholder owners into landless tenants and laborers. As their wealth grew, the contrast between the landlords' estate houses and the thatch and mud-walled villages of the great mass of the peasantry became more and more pronounced. Bored by life in the provinces, the well-heeled landed classes spent most of their time in the fashionable districts of Cairo or in resort towns such as Alexandria. Their estates were run by hired managers, who were little more than rent collectors as far as the peasants were concerned.

With the khedival regime and the great landlords closely allied to the British overlords, resistance to the occupation was left mainly to the middle class. Since the middle of the 19th century, this relatively new and small social class had been growing in numbers and influence, mainly in the towns in the Nile delta. With the memory of Orabi's revolt in 1882 still fresh, the cause of Egyptian independence was taken up mainly by the sons of the **effendi,** or the prosperous business and professional families that made up much of this new middle class. Even nationalist leaders who came from rural ayan families built their following among the urban middle classes. In contrast to India, where lawyers predominated in the nationalist leadership, in Egypt, journalists (a number of them educated in France) led the way.

In the 1890s and early 1900s, numerous newspapers in Arabic (and to a lesser extent French and English) vied to expose the mistakes of the British and the corruption of the khedival regime. Egyptian writers also attacked the British for their racist arrogance and their monopolization of well-paying positions in the Egyptian bureaucracy. Like their Indian counterparts, Egyptian critics argued that these could just as well have been filled by university-educated Egyptians. In the 1890s the first nationalist party was formed. But again in contrast to India, where the Congress party dominated the nationalist movement from the outset, a variety of rival parties proliferated in Egypt. There were three main alternatives by 1907, but none could be said to speak for the great majority of the Egyptians, who were illiterate, poorly paid, and largely ignored urban laborers and rural farmers.

In the years before the outbreak of World War I in 1914, heavy-handed British repression on several occasions put down student riots or retaliated for assassination attempts against high British and Turco-Egyptian officials. Despite the failure of the nationalist parties to unite or build a mass base in the decades before the war, the extent of the hostility felt by the Egyptian masses was demonstrated by the **Dinshawai incident** in

1906. This confrontation between the British and their Egyptian subjects exemplified the racial arrogance displayed by most of the European colonizers. Though the incident at Dinshawai was seemingly a small clash resulting in only limited numbers of fatalities, the excessive British response to it did much to undermine whatever support remained for their continued presence in Egypt.

Most Egyptian villages raised large numbers of pigeons, which served as an important supplement to the meager peasant diet. Over the years, some of the British had turned the hunting of the pigeons of selected villages into a holiday pastime. A party of British officers on leave was hunting the pigeons of the village of Dinshawai in the Nile delta when they accidentally shot the wife of the prayer leader of the local mosque. The angry villagers mobbed the greatly outnumbered shooting party, which in panic fired on the villagers. Both the villagers and the British soldiers suffered casualties in the clashes that followed. In reprisal for the death of one of the officers, the British summarily hung four of the villagers. Though the actual hanging was not photographed, the building of the scaffolding was captured in a photo (Figure 33.5). The British also ordered that other villagers connected to the incident be publicly flogged or sentenced to varying terms of hard labor.

The harsh British reprisals aroused a storm of protest in the Egyptian press and among the nationalist parties. Some Egyptian leaders later recounted how the incident convinced them that cooperation with the British was totally unacceptable and fixed their resolve to agitate for an end to Egypt's occupation. Popular protests in several areas, and the emergence of ayan support for the nationalist cause, also suggested the possibility of building a mass base for anti-British agitation. More than anything else, the incident at Dinshawai had galvanized support for popular protest across the communal and social boundaries that had so long divided the peoples of Egypt.

By 1913 the British had been sufficiently intimidated by the rising tide of Egyptian nationalism to grant a constitution and representation in a parliament elected indirectly by the men of wealth and influence. World War I and the British declaration of martial law put a temporary end to nationalist agitation. But, as in India, the war unleashed forces in Egypt that could not be stopped and that would soon lead to the revival of the drive for independence with even greater strength than before.

## War and Nationalist Movements in the Middle East

In the years after World War I, resistance to European colonial domination, which had been confined largely to Egypt in the prewar years, spread to much of the rest of the Middle East. Having sided with the Central Powers in the war, the Turks now shared in their defeat. The Ottoman Empire disappeared from history, as Britain and France carved up the Arab portions that had revolted against the Young Turk regime during the war. Italy and Greece attacked the Turkish rump of the empire around Constantinople and in Anatolia (Asia Minor) with the intent of sparking a partition of these areas in concert with the other Entente allies. But a skilled military commander, Mustafa Kemal, or **Ataturk,** had emerged for the Turkish officer

Ataturk (Mustafa Kemal)

**FIGURE 33.5** This photograph, probably taken without the knowledge of the British authorities, shows the construction of the gallows that were used to hang the four peasants who were executed in reprisal for the attacks on British soldiers at Dinshawai in 1906. The Dinshawai incident exemplified the colonizers' tendency to overreact to any sign of overt resistance on the part of the colonized.

corps during the war years. Ataturk rallied the Turkish forces and gradually drove back the Greek armies intent on colonizing the Turkish homeland.

By 1923 an independent Turkish republic had been established, but at the cost of the expulsion of tens of thousands of ethnic Greeks. As an integral part of the effort to establish a viable Turkish nation, Ataturk launched a sweeping program of reforms. Many of the often radical changes his government introduced in the 1920s and 1930s were modeled on Western precedents, including a new Latin alphabet, women's suffrage, and criticism of the veil. But in important ways his efforts to secularize and develop Turkey also represented the culmination of transformations made under the Ottomans over the preceding century (see Chapter 31).

The Six Arrows of Kemalism: The Principles of the Republican People's Party (RPP), 1935

With Turkish rule in the Arab heartlands ended by defeat in the war, Arab nationalists in Beirut, Damascus, and Baghdad turned to face the new threat presented by the victorious Entente powers, France and Britain. Betraying promises to preserve Arab independence that the British had made in 1915 and early 1916, French and British forces occupied much of the Middle East in the years after the war. **Hussein,** the sherif of Mecca, had used these promises to convince the Arabs to rise in support of Britain's war against the Turks, despite the fact that the latter were fellow Muslims. Consequently, the allies' postwar violation of these pledges humiliated and deeply angered Arabs throughout the Middle East. The occupying European powers faced stiff resistance from the Arabs in each of the **mandates** they carved out in Syria, Iraq, and Lebanon under the auspices of the League of Nations. Nationalist movements in these countries gained ground during the 1920s and 1930s. The Arabs' sense of humiliation and anger was greatly intensified by the disposition of Palestine, where British occupation was coupled with promises of a Jewish homeland.

The fact that the British had appeared to promise Palestine, for which they received a League of Nations mandate in 1922, to both the Jewish **Zionists** and the Arabs during the war greatly complicated an already confused situation. Despite repeated assurances to Hussein and other Arab leaders that they would be left in control of their own lands after the war, Lord Balfour, the British foreign secretary, promised prominent Zionist leaders in 1917 that his government would promote the establishment of a Jewish homeland in Palestine after the war. This pledge, the **Balfour Declaration,** fed existing Zionist aspirations for the Hebrew people to return to their ancient Middle Eastern lands of origin, which had been nurtured by the Jews of the diaspora for millennia. In the decades before the First World War, these dreams led to the formation of a number of organizations. Some of these were dedicated to promoting Jewish emigration to Palestine; others were committed to the eventual establishment of a Jewish state there.

These early moves were made in direct response to the persecution of the Jews of eastern Europe in the last decades of the 19th century. Particularly vicious *pogroms,* or violent assaults on the Jewish communities of Russia and Romania in the 1860s and 1870s, convinced Jewish intellectuals such as **Leon Pinsker** that assimilation of the Jews into, or even acceptance by, Christian European nations was impossible. Pinsker and other thinkers called for a return to the Holy Land. Like-minded individuals founded Zionist organizations, such as the Society for the Colonization of Israel, to promote Jewish migration to Palestine in the last decades of the 19th century. Until World War I, the numbers of Jews returning to Palestine were small—in the tens of thousands—though Zionist communities were established on lands purchased in the area.

Until the late 1890s, the Zionist effort was generally opposed by Jews in Germany, France, and other parts of western Europe who enjoyed citizenship and extensive civil rights. In addition, many in these communities had grown prosperous and powerful in their adopted lands. But a major defection to the Zionists occurred in 1894. **Theodor Herzl,** an established Austrian journalist, was stunned by French mobs shouting "Death to the Jews" as they taunted the hapless army officer **Alfred Dreyfus.** Dreyfus was a French Jew who had been falsely accused of passing military secrets to the Germans. His subsequent mistreatment, including exile to the infamous penal colony on Devil's Island, became the flashpoint for years of bitter debate between the left and right in France. Soon after this incident in 1897, Herzl and a number of other prominent western European Jews joined with Jewish leaders from eastern Europe to form the **World Zionist Organization.** As Herzl made clear in his writings, the central aim of this increasingly well-funded organization was to promote Jewish migration to and settlement in Palestine until a point was reached when a Zionist state could be established in the area. Herzl's nationalist ambitions, as well as his indifference to the Arabs already living in the area, were captured in the often-quoted view of one of his close associates that Palestine was "a land without people for a people [the Jews] without a land."

Lord Balfour's promises to the Zionists and the British takeover of Palestine struck the Arabs as a double betrayal of wartime assurances that Arab support for the Entente powers against the Turks would guarantee them independence after the war. This sense of betrayal was a critical source of the growing hostility the Arabs felt toward Jewish emigration to Palestine and their purchase of land in the area. Rising Arab opposition convinced many British officials, especially those who actually administered Palestine, to severely curtail the rather open-ended pledges that had been made to the Zionists during the war. This shift led in turn to Zionist mistrust of British policies and open resistance to them. It also fed the Zionists' determination to build up their own defenses against the increasingly violent Arab resistance to the Jewish presence in Palestine. But British attempts to limit Jewish emigration and settlement were not matched by efforts to encourage, through education and consultation, the emergence of strong leadership among the Arab population of Palestine. Consequently, in the critical struggles and diplomatic maneuvers of the 1930s and 1940s, the Arabs of Palestine were rarely able to speak for themselves. They were represented by Arab leaders from neighboring lands, who did not always understand Palestinian needs and desires. These non-Palestinian spokespersons also often acted more in the interests of Syrian or Lebanese Arabs than those of the Christian and Muslim Arab communities in Palestine.

## Revolt in Egypt, 1919

Because Egypt was already occupied by the British when the war broke out, and it had been formally declared a protectorate in 1914, it was not included in the promises made by the British to the sherif Hussein. As a result, the anticolonial struggle in Egypt was rooted in earlier agitation and the heavy toll the war had taken on the Egyptian people, particularly the peasantry. During the war, the defense of the Suez Canal was one of the top priorities for the British. To guard against possible Muslim uprisings in response to Turkish calls for a holy war, martial law was declared soon after hostilities began. Throughout the war, large contingents of Entente and empire forces were garrisoned in Egypt. These created a heavy drain on the increasingly scarce food supplies of the area. Forced labor and confiscations by the military of the precious draft animals of the peasantry also led to widespread discontent. As the war dragged on, this unrest was further inflamed by spiraling inflation as well as by food shortages and even starvation in some areas.

By the end of the war, Egypt was ripe for revolt. Mass discontent strengthened the resolve of the educated nationalist elite to demand a hearing at Versailles, where the victorious Allies were struggling to reach a postwar settlement. When a delegation (*wafd* in Arabic) of Egyptian leaders was denied permission to travel to France to put the case for Egyptian self-determination to the peacemakers at Versailles, most Egyptian leaders resigned from the government and called for mass demonstrations. What followed shocked even the most confident British officials. Student-led riots touched off outright insurrection over much of Egypt. At one point, Cairo was cut off from the outside world, and much of the countryside was hostile territory for the occupying power. Though the British army was able, at the cost of scores of deaths, to restore control, it was clear that some hearing had to be given to Egyptian demands. The emergence of the newly formed **Wafd party** under its hard-driving leader **Sa'd Zaghlul** provided the nationalists with a focus for unified action and a mass base that far excelled any they had attracted in the prewar decades.

When a special British commission of inquiry into the causes of the upheaval in Egypt met with widespread civil disobedience and continuing violent opposition, it recommended that the British begin negotiations for an eventual withdrawal from Egypt. Years of bargaining followed, which led to a highly qualified independence for the Egyptians. British withdrawal occurred in stages, beginning in 1922 and culminating in the British withdrawal to the Suez Canal zone in 1936. But though they pulled out of Egypt proper, the khedival regime was preserved and the British reserved the right to reoccupy Egypt should it be threatened by a foreign aggressor.

Though they had won a significant degree of political independence, the Egyptian leaders of the Wafd party, as well as its rivals in the Liberal Constitutionalist and Union parties, did little to relieve the increasing misery of the great majority of the Egyptian people. Most Egyptian politicians regarded the winning of office as an opportunity to increase their own and their families' fortunes. Many politicians from ayan households and from the professional and merchant classes used their influence and growing wealth to amass huge estates, which were worked by landless tenants and laborers. Locked in personal and interparty quarrels, as well as the ongoing contest with the khedival regime for control of the government, few political leaders had the time or inclination to push for the land reforms and public works projects that the peasantry so desperately needed.

The utter social bankruptcy of the 40 years of nationalist political dominance that preceded the military coup and social revolution led by Gamal Abdul Nasser in 1952 is suggested by some revealing statistics compiled by the United Nations in the early 1950s. By that time, nearly 70 percent of Egypt's cultivable land was owned by six percent of the population. Some 12,000 families alone controlled 37 percent of the

IN DEPTH

## Women in Asian and African Nationalist Movements

One important but often neglected dimension of the liberation struggles that Asian and African peoples waged against their colonial overlords was the emergence of a stratum of educated, articulate, and politically active women in most colonial societies. In this process, the educational opportunities provided by the European colonizers often played as vital a role as they had in the formation of male leadership in nationalist movements. Missionary girls' schools were confined in the early stages of European involvement in Africa and Asia to the daughters of low-class or marginal social groups. But by the end of the 19th century these schools had become quite respectable for women from the growing westernized business and professional classes. In fact, in many cases, some degree of Western education was essential if westernized men were to find wives with whom they could share their career concerns and intellectual pursuits.

> *"As nationalist leaders moved their anticolonial campaigns into the streets, women became involved in mass demonstrations."*

The seemingly insurmountable barriers that separated Westernized Asian and African men from their traditional—and thus usually without formal education—wives became a stock theme in the novels and short stories of the early nationalist era. This concern was perhaps best exemplified by the works of Rabindranath Tagore. The problem was felt so acutely by the first generation of Indian nationalist leaders that many took up the task of teaching their wives English and Western philosophy and literature at home. Thus, for many upper-class Asian and African women, colonization proved a liberating force. This trend was often offset by the male-centric nature of colonial education and the domestic focus of much of the curriculum in women's schools.

Although women played a small role in the early, elitist stages of Asian and African nationalist movements, they frequently became more and more prominent as the early study clubs and political associations reached out to build a mass base. In India, women who had been exposed to Western education and European ways, such as Tagore's famous heroine in the novel *The Home and the World,* came out of seclusion and took up supporting roles, though they were still usually behind the scenes. Gandhi's campaign to supplant imported, machine-made British cloth with homespun Indian cloth, for example, owed much of whatever success it had to female spinners and weavers. As nationalist leaders moved their anticolonial campaigns into the streets, women became involved in mass demonstrations. Throughout the 1920s and 1930s, Indian women braved the *lathi,* or billy club, assaults of the Indian police, suffered the indignities of imprisonment, and launched their own newspapers and lecture campaigns to mobilize female support for the nationalist struggle.

farmland. As for the mass of the people, 98 percent of the peasants were illiterate, malnutrition was chronic among both the urban and rural population, and an estimated 95 percent of rural Egyptians suffered from eye diseases. Such was the legacy of the very unrevolutionary process of decolonization in Egypt.

### The Beginnings of the Liberation Struggle in Africa

Most of Africa had come under European colonial rule only in the decades before the outbreak of World War I. Nonetheless, precolonial missionary efforts had produced small groups of Western-educated Africans in parts of west and south central Africa by the end of the 19th century. Like their counterparts in India, most Western-educated Africans were staunchly loyal to their British and French overlords during the First World War. With the backing of both Western-educated Africans and the traditional rulers, the British and especially the French were able to draw on their African possessions for manpower and raw materials throughout the war. But this reliance took its toll on their colonial domination in the long run. In addition to local rebellions in response to the forcible recruitment of African soldiers and laborers, the war effort seriously disrupted newly colonized African societies. African merchants and farmers suffered from shipping shortages and the sudden decline in demand for crops, such as cocoa. African villagers were not happy to go hungry so that their crops could feed the armies of the allies. As Lord Lugard, an influential colonial administrator, pointed out, the desperate plight of the British and French also forced them to teach tens of thousands of Africans:

In Egypt, the British made special note of the powerful effect that the participation of both veiled women and more westernized upper-class women had on mass demonstrations in 1919 and the early 1920s. These outpourings of popular support did much to give credibility to the Wafd party's demands for British withdrawal. In both India and Egypt, female nationalists addressed special appeals to British and American suffragettes to support their peoples' struggles for political and social liberation. In India in particular, their causes were advanced by feminists such as the English champion of Hinduism, Annie Besant, who became a major figure in the nationalist movement before and after World War I.

When African nationalism became a popularly supported movement in the post–World War II period, women, particularly the outspoken and fearless market women in west Africa, emerged as a major political force. In settler colonies, such as Algeria and Kenya, where violent revolt proved necessary to bring down deeply entrenched colonial regimes, women took on the dangerous tasks of messengers, bomb carriers, and guerrilla fighters. As Frantz Fanon argued decades ago, and as was later beautifully dramatized in the film *The Battle of Algiers,* this transformation was particularly painful for women who had been in seclusion right up to the time of the revolutionary upsurge. Cutting their hair and wearing lipstick and Western clothes often alienated them from their fathers and brothers, who equated such practices with prostitution.

In many cases, women's participation in struggles for the political liberation of their people was paralleled by campaigns for female rights in societies that, as we have seen, were dominated by males. Upper-class Egyptian women founded newspapers and educational associations that pushed for a higher age of marriage, educational opportunities for women, and an end to seclusion and veiling. Indian women took up many of these causes and also developed programs to improve hygiene and employment opportunities for lower-caste women. These early efforts, as well as the prominent place of women in nationalist struggles, had much to do with the granting of basic civil rights to women. These included suffrage and legal equality, which were key features of the constitutions of many newly independent Asian and African nations. The great majority of women in the new states of Africa and Asia have yet to enjoy most of these rights. Yet their inclusion in constitutions and postindependence laws provides crucial backing for the struggles for women's liberation in the nations of the postcolonial world.

**Questions** Why might missionary education for women in the colonies have stressed domestic skills? In what ways do you think measures to "modernize" colonial societies were oriented to males? Can you think of women who have been or are major political figures in contemporary Africa and Asia? Why have there not been more? What sorts of traditional constraints hamper the efforts of women to achieve economic and social equality and major political roles in newly independent nations?

> how to kill white men, around whom [they had] been taught to weave a web of sanctity of life. [They] also know how to handle bombs and Lewis guns and Maxims . . . and [they have] seen the white men budge when [they have] stood fast. Altogether [they have] acquired much knowledge that might be put to uncomfortable use someday.

The fact that the Europeans kept few of the promises of better jobs and public honors, which they had made during the war to induce young Africans to enlist in the armed forces or serve as colonial administrators, contributed a good deal to the unrest of the postwar years. This was particularly true of the French colonies, where opportunities for political organization, much less protest, were severely constricted before, during, and after the war. Major strikes and riots broke out repeatedly after the war. In the British colonies, where there was considerably more tolerance for political organization, there were also strikes and a number of outright rebellions. Throughout colonized Africa, protest intensified in the 1930s in response to the economic slump brought on by the Great Depression.

Though Western-educated politicians did not link up with urban workers or peasants in most African colonies until the 1940s, disenchanted members of the emerging African elite began to organize in the 1920s and 1930s. In the early stages of this process, charismatic African American political figures, such as **Marcus Garvey** and **W. E. B. Du Bois,** had a major impact on emerging African nationalist leaders. In the 1920s much effort was placed into attempts to arouse all-Africa loyalties and build **pan-African** organizations. However, the leadership of these organizations was mainly African American and West Indian, and the delegates from colonized areas in Africa faced very different challenges under different colonial overlords.

**FIGURE 33.6** After World War I, African and African American intellectuals such as Léopold Sédar Senghor (pictured here), W. E. B. Du Bois, and Aimé Césaire explored in their writings the ravages wrought on Africa by centuries of the slave trade and the forced diaspora that resulted. These intellectuals worked to affirm the genius of African culture and African patterns of social interaction.

Although these differences had much to do with the fact that pan-Africanism proved unworkable in Africa itself, its well-attended conferences, especially the early ones in Paris, did much to arouse anticolonial sentiments among Western-educated Africans.

By the mid-1920s, nationalists from French and British colonies were pretty much going separate ways. Because of restrictions in the colonies, and because small but well-educated groups of Africans were represented in the French parliament, French-speaking west Africans concentrated their organizational and ideological efforts in Paris in this period. The **négritude** literary movement nurtured by these exiles did much to combat the racial stereotyping that had so long held the Africans in psychological bondage to the Europeans. Writers such as the Senegalese poet **Léopold Sédar Senghor** (Figure 33.6), Léon Damas from French Guiana, and the West Indian Aimé Césaire celebrated the beauty of black skin and the African physique. They argued that in the precolonial era, African peoples had built societies where women were freer, old people were better cared for, and attitudes toward sex were far healthier than they had ever been in the so-called civilized West.

Except in settler colonies, such as Kenya and Rhodesia, Western-educated Africans in British territories were given greater opportunities to build political associations within Africa. In the early stages of this process, African leaders sought to nurture organizations that linked the emerging nationalists of different British colonies, such as the National Congress of British West Africa. By the late 1920s, these pan-colony associations gave way to political groupings concerned primarily with issues within individual colonies, such as Sierra Leone, the Gold Coast, or Nigeria. After the British granted some representation in colonial advisory councils to Western-educated Africans in this period, emphasis on colony-specific political mobilization became even more pronounced. Though most of these early political organizations were too loosely structured to be considered true political parties, there was a growing recognition by some leaders of the need to build a mass base. In the 1930s a new generation of leaders made much more vigorous attacks on the policies of the British. Through their newspapers and political associations, they also reached out to ordinary African villagers and the young, who had hitherto played little role in nationalist agitation. Their efforts to win a mass following would come to full fruition only after European divisions plunged humanity into a second global war.

## GLOBAL CONNECTIONS

## World War and Global Upheavals

The First World War—or the Great War as it was called by those who lived through it and did not know a second conflict of this magnitude lay in their future—was one of several key turning points of world history in the 20th century. The long conflict, particularly the horrific and draining stalemate in the trenches, did much to undermine Europe's prewar position of global dominance. The war severely disrupted Europe's economy and bolstered already emerging rivals, especially the United States and Japan, for preeminence in world trade and finance. Over much of Europe, the hardships endured by the civilian populations on the home front reignited long-standing class tensions. In Russia, but also elsewhere in east central Europe, growing social divisions sparked full-scale revolutions. In Britain, France, Germany, and other liberal democracies in western Europe, labor parties, some socialist or communist, emerged with much greater power after the conflict. Many shared power, both in coalitions with center parties or in their own right in the 1920s and 1930s. The war saw major changes in gender roles in spheres ranging from employment and marriage to sex and fashion. It also generated growing challenges to the rigid racial hierarchies that had dominated both scientific theorizing and popular attitudes in the decades leading up to the conflict.

The victorious Entente allies, especially the British and French but also the Belgians and Japanese, managed to hold on to, and in fact enlarge, their empires. But the hardships endured by colonized peoples and the empty promises made by their desperate colonial overloads during the war gave great impetus to resistance to their empires that spread from the Middle East and India to Vietnam and China. For African and Asian intellectuals at least, the psychological advantage that racial thinking and scientific and technological superiority had given the Europeans began to dissipate. The essential cooperation of nationalist leaders like Gandhi gave them and their ideologies of liberation access to ever larger numbers of colonized peoples. In the postwar decades, mass civil disobedience campaigns in India and Egypt, and peasant risings in Vietnam and China, established the protest techniques and demands that would ultimately bring down all of the European colonial empires. The revolutionary regime in Russia, which had come to power as a direct consequence of the war, actively abetted efforts to advance the cause of decolonization around the world. Two other industrial nations whose power had been greatly enhanced by the war, the United States and Japan, sought in different ways both to supplant the European colonizers and replace them as the economic and political power centers of the 20th century.

### Further Readings

There is a vast literature on the origins of the First World War. A somewhat dated, but still very readable, introduction is Laurence Lafore, *The Long Fuse* (1965). James Joll, *The Origins of the First World War* (1984), includes a much more detailed treatment of the many and highly contested interpretations of the causes of the conflict. Fritz Fisher, *Germany's Aims in the First World War* (1967), stirred great controversy by arguing that Germany's leaders purposely provoked the conflict, while Paul Kennedy, *The Rise of the Anglo-German Antagonism, 1860–1914* (1980), covers one of the key rivalries and especially the naval race with a good deal more balance. The impact of colonial disputes on the coming of the war is concisely and convincingly treated in L. F. C. Turner, *Origins of the First World War* (1970).

Of the many general histories of the war on land and sea, the more reliable and readable include *The World in the Crucible, 1914–1919* (1984) by Bernadotte Schmitt and Harold Vedeler, and most recently John Keegan's *The First World War* (1999). Marc Ferro's *The Great War* (1973) remains one of the most stimulating analyses of the conduct of the war. Three of the most successful attempts to understand the war from the participants' perspectives are Paul Fussell's *The Great War and Modern Memory* (1975) and John Cruickshank's *Variations on Catastrophe* (1982), which draw on literary works and memoirs, and Richard Cork's magisterial exploration of artistic images of the conflict in *A Bitter Truth: Avant-Garde Art and the Great War* (1994). Some of the better accounts by the participants include Erich Remarque, *All Quiet on the Western Front* (1929); Frederic Manning, *The Middle Parts of Fortune* (1929); Vera Brittain, *Testament of Youth* (1933); and Wilfred Owen, *Poems* (1920; reprinted as *The Collected Poems of Wilfred Owen*, 1964).

The disasters at Versailles and some of their consequences are also chronicled in numerous books and articles. Two of the most readable are Harold Nicholson's *Peace Making, 1919* (1965) and Charles L. Mee Jr.'s *The End of Order: Versailles, 1919* (1980). Samples of varying views on the many controversies surrounding the conference can be found in Ivo J. Lederer, ed., *The Versailles Settlement* (1960). The best book on the wider ramifications of the decisions made at or in connection with the conference is Arno Mayer, *Politics and Diplomacy of Peace-Making, 1918–1919* (1967).

A good general historical narrative of the impact of the war on the struggle for Indian independence can be found in Sumit Sarkar, *Modern India, 1885–1947* (1983). A closer analysis is offered in the essays in DeWitt C. Elinwood and S. D. Pradhan, eds., *India and World War I* (1978). The war also figures importantly in the early sections of Mohandas Gandhi's autobiographical *The Story of My Experiments with Truth* (1927). Louis Fischer's *Gandhi* (1950) still yields valuable insights into the personality of one of the great nationalist leaders and the workings of nationalist politics. Judith Brown's studies of Gandhi as a political leader, including *Gandhi's Rise to Power* (1972), and her recent biography of his life and career provide an approach more in tune with current research. The poems and novels of Rabindranath Tagore yield wonderful insights into the social and cultural life of India through much of this era.

P. J. Vatikiotis, *The History of Egypt* (especially the 1985 edition), has excellent sections on the war and early nationalist era in that country. Interesting but often less reliable is Jacques Berque, *Colonialism and Nationalism in Egypt* (1972). Leila Ahmed, *Women and Gender in Islam* (1992), has excellent chapters on the role of women at various stages of the nationalist struggle and in the postindependence era. A comprehensive treatment of working-class women protesters in Egypt is provided by Nawal El Saadawi, *The Hidden Face of Eve* (1980). George Antonius, *The Arab Awakening* (1946), is essential reading on British double dealing in the Middle East during the war, especially as this affected the Palestine question. Alternative perspectives are provided by Aaron Cohen, *The Arabs and Israel* (1970). David Fromkin, *A Peace to End All Peace* (1989), provides a more recent and superb account of wartime and postwar events in the Middle East as a whole.

The early stages of the nationalist struggle, including the war years, in west Africa are well covered by Michael Crowder, *West Africa under Colonial Rule* (1982). A narrative of the history of the First World War as a whole in sub-Saharan Africa can be found in Byron Farwell, *The Great War in Africa* (1986). The continued advance of European colonialism in the Middle East and Africa in the postwar years is analyzed in *France Overseas* (1981) by Christopher Andrew and A. S. Kanya-Forstner.

## On the Web

Recent interactive overviews of the Great War and its legacies are provided at http://www.bbc.co.uk/history/war/wwone/index.shtml, http://www.worldwar1.com/index.html, and at the Wilfred Owen multimedia archive at http://www.hcu.ox.ac.uk/jtap/. Wilfred Owen joined the British army to help relieve the suffering of soldiers in the field "directly by leading them as well as an officer can; indirectly, by watching their sufferings that I may speak of them as well as a pleader can." He accomplished both tasks. His life and war poetry are movingly presented at sites such as http://home.tiscali.be/ericlaermans/cultural/owen.html, http://www.pitt.edu/~pugachev/greatwar/owen.html, and http://www.bbc.co.uk/history/3d/trench.shtml, which includes a host of useful links to a wide variety of related subjects, including a virtual tour of a trench. The life and work of war poet and novelist Robert Graves, including excerpts from *Goodbye to All That,* are examined at http://www.spartacus.schoolnet.co.uk/Jgraves.htm, and http://www.oucs.ox.ac.uk/ltg/projects/jtap/rose/goodbye.html#the.

Life in the trenches, including related weapons such as chemical agents, is also explored at http://www.worldwar1.com/. But even this excellent site cannot compare in impact with the personal account of trench warfare found in the diary of Private Donald Fraser of the Canadian Expeditionary Force at http://www.fordham.edu/halsall/mod/1918fraser.html and at http://www.archives.ca/05/0518/05180105/0518010504_e.html, which also provides resources for the study of the battle of Vimy Ridge.

Two of the great battles in the trenches, the Somme and Verdun, are illuminated at http://www.stemnet.nf.ca/beaumont/somme2.htm and http://www.achtungpanzer.com/blitz.htm.

The home fronts of the combatant nations, from food rationing to the impact of the related influenza epidemic, are discussed at http://www.spartacus.schoolnet.co.uk/FWWhome.htm (scroll down to "War and the Home Front").

The text of the Zimmerman Telegram that provided the proximate cause of the U.S. entry into World War I can be found at http://www.firstworldwar.com/source/zimmerman.htm. The role of Canada and Latin America in the war and the war's impact on them are explored at http://www.archives.ca/05/0518_e.html and http://www.worldwar1.com/sfla.htm, respectively. The text of the Treaty of Versailles and many ancillary materials are offered at http://history.acusd.edu/gen/text/versaillestreaty/vercontents.html. A vast collection of other major documents related to the war is offered at http://www.ku.edu/~kansite/ww_one.

Colonial and postcolonial discourse that embraces issues such as négritude is the subject of analysis at http://www.wsu.edu/~amerstu/tm/poco.html and http://www.scholars.nus.edu.sg/landow/post/misc/postov.html, a site mirrored at http://www.postcolonialweb.org/ (go to Search Tool, enter "negritude" for links on this subject).

Insight into the casual brutality of imperialism that fuelled nationalist revolts can be derived from an account of the Dinshawai incident in Egypt (http://touregypt.net/denshwaymuseum.htm) and the Amritsar massacre in India (http://www.scholars.nus.edu.sg/landow/post/india/history/colonial/massacre.html, http://www.geocities.com/Broadway/Alley/5461/AMRITSAR.htm, and http://lachlan.bluehaze.com.au/churchill/am-man.htm). The African National Congress Party homepage at http://www.anc.org.za/ not only provides current information about the party but also materials on the freedom struggle in South Africa, such as the life histories, speeches, and writings of African National Congress freedom fighters.

Theodor Herzl's leadership of the early Jewish nationalist movement can be seen from both the Zionist (http://www.jewishvirtuallibrary.org/jsource/biography/Herzl.html) and Palestinian nationalist perspectives (http://www.arab2.com/biography/Arab-Israeli-Conflict.htm).

One of the early leaders of the Indian nationalist movement, Bal Gangadhar Tilak, is briefly examined at http://www.kamat.com/kalranga/itihas/tilak.htm. Mohandas Gandhi's leadership of that movement is explored at http://dwardmac.pitzer.edu/anarchist_archives/bright/gandhi/Gandhi.html. His famous Salt March (http://www.sscnet.ucla.edu/southasia/History/Gandhi/Dandi.html and http://www.algonet.se/~jviklund/gandhi/ENG.MKG.salt.html) is the subject of a film (http://harappa.com/wall/1930.html). His "Quit India" speech of 1942 is offered at http://www.ibiblio.org/pha/policy/1942/420427a.html. An appreciation of the character of Gandhi's close associate, Jawaharlal Nehru, and an audio file of his speeches is explored at http://www.indianchild.com/jawaharlal_nehru.htm and http://www.harappa.com/sounds/nehru.html. The poet laureate of the Indian independence movement, Rabindranath Tagore, is celebrated at http://nobelprize.org/literature/laureates/1913/tagore-bio.html. A review of the life of Muhammad Ali Jinnah, the Indian Muslim nationalist who led the campaign for the creation of the state of Pakistan and became its first president, is provided at http://www.rediff.com/news/1998/sep/10jinnah.htm, while a short movie made of him delivering one of his key speeches is available at http://www.harappa.com/jinnahmov.html.

CHAPTER

34

# The World Between the Wars: Revolutions, Depression, and Authoritarian Response



Russia's communist revolution in 1917 produced a regime that declared its commitment to workers. It was understandably less clear about its commitment to consumers. Department stores had spread in prerevolutionary Russia, almost exclusively for the rich. It was easy for the new communist rulers to decide to seize the stores. In their place, the government set up state department stores, headed by the chain called GUM (an acronym for State Universal Store, pronounced *goom*), with a flagship store right on Red Square in Moscow. It was also easy to proclaim that department stores were now available to all the people. GUM advertisements featured weathered peasants pondering new leather coats, and slogans trumpeted "Everything for Everybody" and "We Have Everything You Need at GUM."

There were, however, three problems. First, this was a poor society, and leaders were spending massive amounts of money on further industrialization and agricultural reform. There was not much left for abundant consumer goods. Second, communists were ambivalent about consumerism anyway. Sometimes they wanted consumerism for everybody, but sometimes they worried that consumerism was foreign, "bourgeois," and trivial. (Even in Western countries, Communist parties took some time to adjust to consumerism.) Third, the desire arose to protect workers in the stores from what the communists perceived as the demeaned status of those who "wait on" customers. The government stopped calling them clerks or salespeople, instead using the term "workers of the counter." Unfortunately, this led to clerks taking a surly attitude toward customers (now simply called "consumers").

The result of all this was that GUM stores became notorious for poor supplies and bad service. Customers were free to complain, and they often did, but government representatives rejected almost all the complaints with phrases like "does not correspond to reality." Communism and consumerism were both realities of the 20th century. Both movements could claim successes, but the two were not easy to combine.

FIGURE 34.1 The most famous link in the chain of Russian department stores known as GUM is the palatial pre-Communist era building on the right of this 1935 photograph of Red Square, Moscow.

The 1920s and 1930s—the interwar period—featured several crucial developments in addition to the immediate postwar adjustments and the rise of nationalist protest against European colonialism. The 1920s featured many innovations in industrial societies, but also a combination of structural weakness and misleading illusion. The key dynamics of the interwar period revolved around a wave of major revolutions, a global economic depression, and new authoritarian regimes spearheaded by German Nazism.

## The Roaring Twenties

- **In the West, consumerism and changes in women's roles gained ground. The United States and Japan registered economic gains and political tension. New authoritarian movements surfaced in eastern Europe and Italy.**

### Bouncing Back?

The postwar challenges to western European society were immense. Massive war deaths—over 10 million Europeans had died—combined with widespread injuries and tremendous blows to morale. Property damage and economic dislocation added to the problems: because wartime governments had printed new money rather than raise taxes, an unprecedented postwar inflation occurred, wiping out savings for many groups.

Superficially, however, a more buoyant attitude resumed by the middle of the decade. A new, democratic

| 1910 C.E. | 1920 C.E. | 1930 C.E. |
|---|---|---|
| **1917** Tsarist regime overthrown in February; Bolshevik revolution in October; Mexican constitution includes revolutionary changes<br>**1918** Armistice ends World War I in November<br>**1919** Versailles conference; Peace of Paris; leftist revolution defeated in Germany; May Fourth movement in China | **1920–1940** Muralist movement in Mexico<br>**1921** Albert Einstein wins the Nobel Prize; Chinese Communist party founded; Lenin's New Economic Policy begins in U.S.S.R.<br>**1922** Mussolini and the Fascists seize power in Italy; first commercial radio station in Pittsburgh<br>**1923–1924** Hyperinflation in Germany<br>**1923** Defeat of Japanese bill for universal suffrage; Tokyo earthquake<br>**1927** Charles Lindbergh's solo trans-Atlantic flight; Guomindang (Nationalists) capture north China, purge Communist party<br>**1927–1928** Stalin pushes the first five-year plan in the Soviet Union, collectivization begins; agricultural slump in United States<br>**1928–1929** Skyscraper craze in New York<br>**1929** Stock market crash | **1930** U.S. Congress passes the Smoot-Hawley tariff; economic downturn in western Europe and throughout European colonial empires; rapid rise of Nazi party in Germany<br>**1931** Statute of Westminster gives full autonomy to British Dominions of Canada, Australia, New Zealand, South Africa, and the Irish Free State; failed rebellion against Japanese rule in Korea; poor harvests and severe economic dislocations in Japan; Japanese invasion of Manchuria<br>**1932** Franklin Roosevelt begins four-term tenure as U.S. president and launches the New Deal<br>**1932–1934** Height of forced collectivization in U.S.S.R.; genocidal famine inflicted on the Ukraine and other areas<br>**1933** Adolf Hitler becomes chancellor of Germany<br>**1934–1940** Lázaro Cárdenas president of Mexico, extensive land reform<br>**1935** Nuremberg laws deprive Jews of German citizenship; Mussolini's armies invade Ethiopia; outbreak of civil war in Spain<br>**1936** Popular Front government formed in France; junior army officers revolt in Japan, key political leaders assassinated<br>**1936–1938** Height of Stalinist purges in U.S.S.R.<br>**1937** Full-scale Japanese invasion of China<br>**1938** *Kristallnacht* begins intensification of attacks on Jews in Germany; Munich agreement allows Hitler to begin destruction of Czechoslovakia<br>**1938** Japan's military leaders impose state control over economy and social system, Diet approves war budget<br>**1939** Hitler invades Poland, leading to outbreak of World War II |

The Art of Pablo Picasso

republic in Germany made some positive strides, despite the burdensome reparations payments the World War I victors had required. Artistic creativity included the **cubist movement,** led by Pablo Picasso, that rendered familiar objects in geometrical shapes, as in Figure 34.2. Writers and composers also challenged stylistic traditions. Modern design in architecture and furnishing gained ground (Figure 34.3). Important achievements in science included further work on Albert Einstein's groundbreaking theories of relativity in physics. Knowledge of atomic structure and also of genetics advanced.

New mass consumption items, like the radio, were important as well. Middle-class women gained new participation in popular culture, some of them going to nightclubs, smoking, and participating in dance crazes that often originated in the United States or Latin America (Figure 34.4). In several countries—Germany, Great Britain, the United States, and Turkey headed the list—women also gained the right to vote.

Aspects of the new culture, however, seemed frenzied, and certainly disturbed traditionalists. Key economic sectors—like agricultural and coal mining—did not really recover prosperity, and much of the British economy overall remained sluggish. Western Europe

FIGURE 34.2 Marcel Duchamp's *Nude Descending a Staircase, No. 2* (1912). Using a modified cubist style, Duchamp achieved a dramatic visual effect in an approach characteristic of Western art from the 1920s onward.

FIGURE 34.3 The skyscraper, developed first in the United States, became a major expression of artistic innovation and was the result of the use of new structural materials that allowed for unprecedented heights and dramatic effects. Buildings like this one—the Wrigley Building in Chicago—combined the new technology with elements of gothic architecture that recalled the great cathedrals of the Middle Ages, earning them the nickname "Cathedrals of Commerce."

did not regain export markets that had been taken over by the United States or Japan. Most western European countries also faced increasing political extremism. New communist parties on the left were matched by right-wing movements, often supported by many war veterans.

## Other Industrial Centers

Canada, Australia, and New Zealand gained rewards for their loyal participation in World War I. Australia, newly independent in 1901, gained particular pride in its military role. Several conferences in the 1920s confirmed the independence of the Dominions and their co-equal status with Britain (Map 34.1). The British Commonwealth of Nations was a free association of members, as British representation in the three Dominions became purely symbolic. The Dominions also registered solid export growth and population gains from immigration. Australia introduced extensive welfare measures, responding to a strong labor movement, and considerable economic planning.

U.S. economic and popular cultural initiatives advanced rapidly during the 1920s. The economy boomed throughout much of the decade. Corporations expanded and innovated, for example adding research and development operations to their portfolios. Organization of work systems changed. Henry Ford had introduced the assembly line for automobile production in 1913, using conveyor belts to move parts past semi-skilled workers doing small, repetitious tasks as each automobile was completed. During the 1920s industrial psychologists studied how to increase output further, for example by piping in music. These

FIGURE 34.4 The interwar decades saw the rise of a succession of dance crazes. Adults as well as young people were caught up in dancing to the new big bands.

production changes were widely imitated in Europe, Japan, and the Soviet Union. The United States also increased its popular cultural exports. Jazz spread from African American centers in the South to performances in Europe. Hollywood became the global film capital by 1920, and Hollywood stars, many of them foreign, became international staples.

The role of the United States worldwide had new complexities, however. The U.S. Senate rejected the Versailles treaty, refusing to enter the League of Nations. Diplomatically, the United States pursued an isolationist policy for two decades, refusing foreign alliances. Fear of communism also ran unusually high in the United States, with a "Red Scare" early in the decade heightening resistance to outside influences.

Japan entered a new phase of industrialization during the 1920s. Agricultural output improved with greater use of fertilizers and mechanical equipment. This freed labor for expanding factories. Japan rapidly augmented its heavy industrial sector, in metallurgy, shipbuilding, and electrical power, organized mainly by large industrial combines—the zaibatsu—linked to the state. Japan still depended heavily on cheap exports to the West, for it needed foreign earnings to cover the import of fuel and raw materials and to support rapid population growth. (A population of 45 million in 1900 had increased to 70 million by 1940.) Politically, tensions between Japan's military leaders

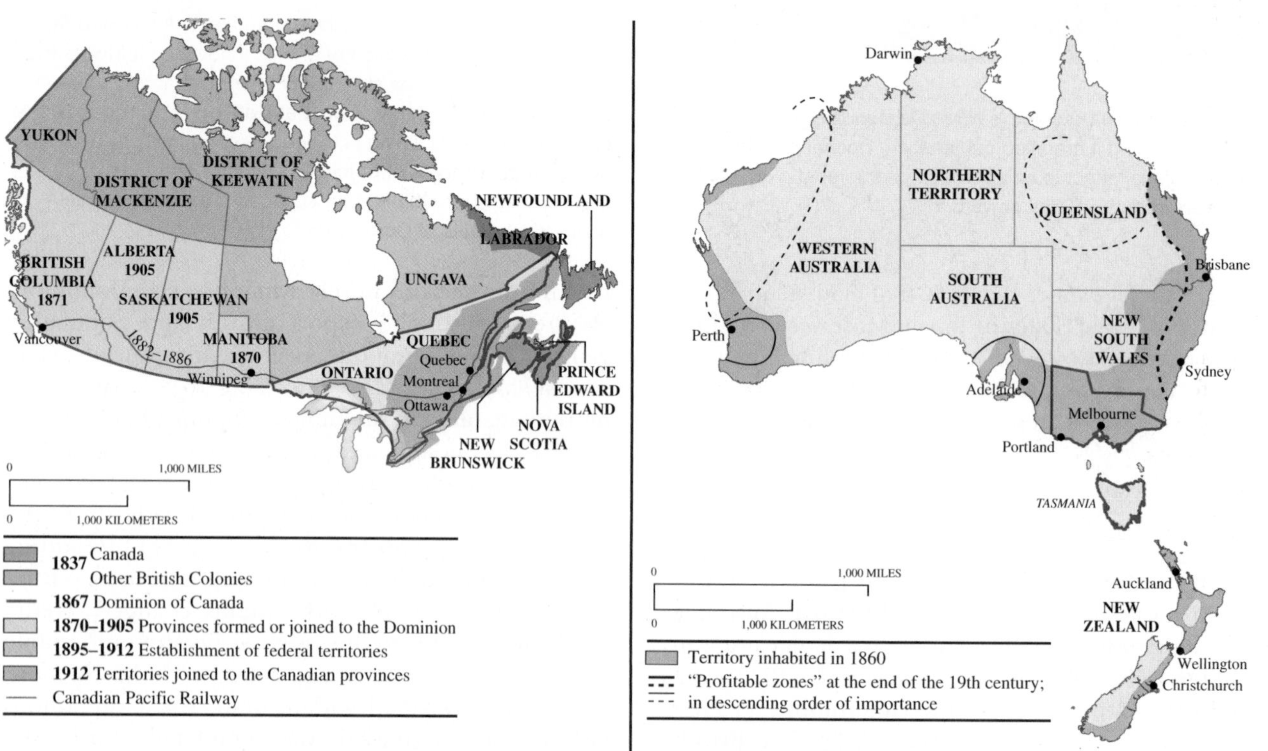


MAP 34.1 From Dominions to Nationhood: Formation of Canada, Australia, and New Zealand

FIGURE 34.5 One of the most ominous acts of Mussolini's fascist regime was the burning of books and other literature deemed "subversive."

and the civilian government increased during the decade. Military leaders, trained separately and reporting directly to the emperor, resented political controls that periodically reduced their budgets. Liberal politicians expanded voting rights to all adult males, but there was no full agreement on the appropriate political structure. The military, suspicious of growing consumerism in Japan, regarded itself as a guardian of tradition. It also exercised considerable independence in diplomacy, particularly concerning growing Japanese involvement in China.

## New Authoritarianism: The Rise of Fascism

Explicit hostility to liberal and democratic political systems emerged first on the fringes of western Europe. In 1919 a former socialist and (very briefly) former soldier, **Benito Mussolini,** formed the *fascio di combattimento,* or "union for struggle," in Italy. Italian fascists vaguely advocated a corporate state that would replace both capitalism and socialism with a new national unity. They pointed to the need for an aggressive, nationalistic foreign policy. Above all, fascists worked to seize power by any means and to build a strong state under a strong leader. They violently attacked rival political groups, seeking to promote an atmosphere of chaos.

**Fascism** had its roots in the late 19th century, with groups disenchanted with liberal, parliamentary systems and with social conflict. Various intellectuals, in many countries, began to urge the need for new, authoritarian leadership and devotion to nationalist values over capitalist profit-seeking and socialist class struggle.

Conditions in postwar Italy gave these impulses a huge boost. Nationalists resented the fact that Italy had gained so little new territory in World War I. Veterans often felt abandoned by civilian society, and some thirsted for new action. Labor unrest increased, which convinced some conservatives that new measures were essential against ineffective liberal leadership. The Italian parliament seemed incapable of decisive measures, as political factions jockeyed for personal advantage. In these conditions Mussolini, fascism's leading exponent, could make his mark even with a minority of direct supporters.

Amid growing political divisions and a rising threat from the working-class left, in 1922 the Italian king called on Mussolini to form a new government. Though the fascists had only limited popular support, they seemed the only hope to stem left-wing agitation and parliamentary ineptitude. Once in power, Mussolini eliminated most opposition (Figure 34.5), suspending elections outright in 1926, while seeking greater state direction of the economy and issuing strident propaganda about the glories of military conquest. This first fascist regime moved with some caution, fitting into the briefly hopeful negotiations among European states in the 1920s, but the principles it espoused suggested how far European politics had been unseated from the widespread prewar agreements on parliamentary rule.

## The New Nations of East Central Europe

Authoritarian regimes also took root in east central Europe during the 1920s, though they were not explicitly fascist. New nations in this region began with Western-style parliaments, but most could not maintain them amid economic difficulties.

Most of the new nations, from the Baltic states to Yugoslavia, were consumed by nationalist excitement at independence but also harbored intense grievances about territories they had not acquired. Hence there were bitter rivalries among the small eastern European states, which weakened them both diplomatically and economically (Map 34.2). Authoritarianism arrived either through a dictator (as in Poland) or by a monarch's seizure of new power (as in Yugoslavia, the new nation expanded from Serbia). This political pattern resulted from more underlying social tensions. Most eastern European countries remained primarily agricultural, heavily dependent on sales to western Europe. They were hard hit by the collapse of agricultural prices in the 1920s and then further damaged by the Depression. Furthermore, most countries refused to undertake serious land reform, despite widely professed intentions. Aristocratic estate owners thus sought desperately to repress peasant movements, which brought them to support authoritarian regimes, which often had vaguely fascist trappings. Peasant land hunger and continued problems of poverty and illiteracy were simply not addressed in most cases.

Europe in the 1920s and 1930s

## A Balance Sheet

Changes in Europe, other Western societies, and Japan during the 1920s were complex. Democratic and parliamentary political forms took further root in Germany and in places like Canada and Japan. Significant industrial and social change combined with signs of creativity in culture, in sciences and the arts. On the other hand, challenges to democracy arose in Italy and in much of east central Europe, while Japanese politics became less stable. The United States tried to isolate itself from world politics. Events would soon prove that the economic foundations of the major industrial powers were shaky as well. Even in the 1920s the economy of western Europe was newly challenged by the greater vigor of the United States and Japan.

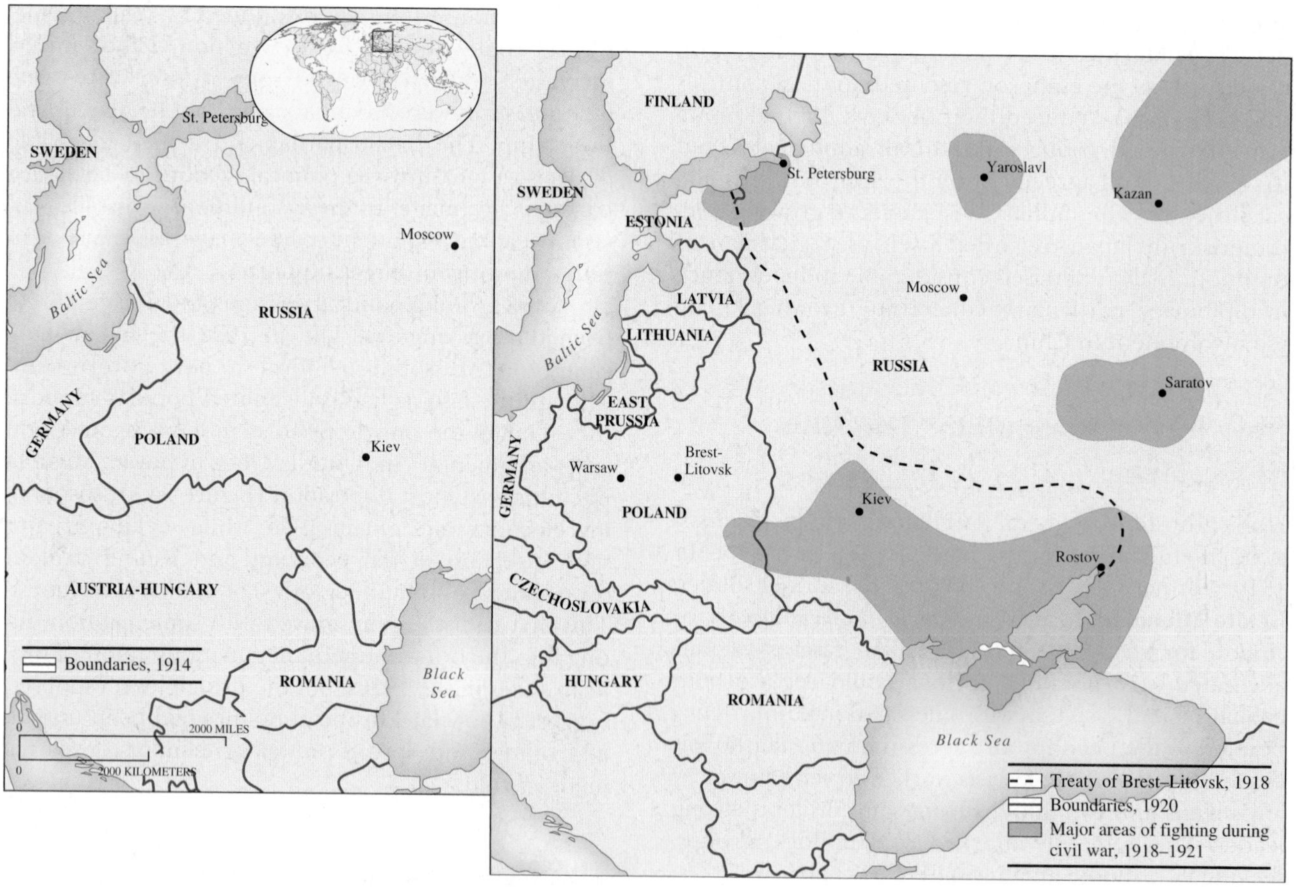

**MAP 34.2 Eastern Europe and the Soviet Union, 1919–1939.** The Soviet Union regained some territory ceded to Germany in the 1918 peace treaty, but it lost ground to a number of east European states.

## Revolution: The First Waves

■ **Major revolutions broke out in Mexico, Russia, and China before or during World War I. All three revolutions challenged Western dominance to some degree, and all reflected concerns about world economic relationships.**

A variety of social tensions affected Latin America early in the 20th century. Many countries continued to depend on a key export crop, like coffee. These crops provided profits to owners while Western demand was high, but they also depended on low wages for workers. During World War I, European manufactured goods were diverted. Several Latin American countries expanded their industrial output, in a process called import substitution. This mainly involved light industry (Figure 34.6), and the initiative receded after the war, leading to further poverty.

These developments did stimulate some political change. In Argentina a new 1912 election law gave voice to the middle classes. Labor agitation increased, some of it under the banners of **syndicalism,** which sought to use a general strike to seize power. Major strikes occurred from 1907 onward, usually brutally repressed by the state. An atmosphere of class conflict intensified. Only in Mexico, however, was there outright revolution.

FIGURE 34.6 The growing labor force that resulted from Latin American industrialization began to change the nature of urban life and politics. Here, women in Orizaba, Mexico, are making sacks for coffee.

### Mexico's Upheaval

Several cataclysmic events launched Latin America into the 20th century and set in motion trends that would determine much of the region's subsequent history. The first of these events was the 10-year civil war and political upheaval of the **Mexican Revolution,** caused primarily by internal forces. Eventually, the Mexican Revolution was also influenced by another major event: the outbreak of World War I. Although most Latin American nations avoided direct participation in the Great War, as World War I was called at the time, the disruption of traditional markets for Latin American exports and the elimination of European sources of goods caused a realignment of the economies of several nations in the region. They were forced to rely on themselves. A spurt of manufacturing continued the process begun after 1870, and some small steps were taken to overcome the traditional dependence on outside supply. Finally, at the end of World War I, the United States emerged as the dominant foreign power in the region, replacing Great Britain in both economic and political terms. That position created a reality that Latin Americans could not ignore and that greatly influenced the economic and political options in the region.

The regime of **Porfirio Díaz** had been in power since 1876 and seemed unshakable. During the Díaz dictatorship, tremendous economic changes had been made, and foreign concessions in mining, railroads, and other sectors of the economy had created a sense of prosperity among the Mexican elite. However, this progress had been bought at considerable expense. Foreigners controlled large sectors of the economy. The hacienda system of extensive landholdings by a small elite dominated certain regions of the country. The political system was corrupt, and any complaint was stifled. The government took repressive measures against workers, peasants, and American Indians who opposed the loss of their lands or the unbearable working conditions. Political opponents often were imprisoned or forced into exile. In short, Díaz ruled with an iron fist through an effective political machine.

Mexico nevertheless faced major issues. The economy, increasingly dependent on exports, lacked adequate investment funds. U.S. concerns owned 20 percent of the nation's territory. Growing nationalist resentment was similar to other reactions to widespread foreign control—a major spur to the revolutionary wave in general.

By 1910, moreover, Díaz was 80 years old and seemed willing to allow some political opposition. **Francisco Madero,** a wealthy son of an elite family, proposed to run against Díaz. Madero believed that some moderate democratic political reforms would relieve social tensions and allow the government to continue its economic development with a minimum of popular unrest. This was more than Díaz could stand. Madero was arrested, a rigged election put Díaz back in power, and things returned to normal. When Madero was released from prison, he called for a revolt.

A general rebellion developed. In the north, small farmers, railroaders, and cowboys coalesced under the colorful former bandit and able commander **Pancho Villa.** In the southern province of Morelos, an area of old conflicts between American Indian communities and large sugar estates, a peasant-based guerrilla movement began under **Emiliano Zapata,** whose goal of land reform was expressed in his motto "Tierra y Libertad" (Land and Liberty). Díaz was driven from power by this coalition of forces, but it soon became apparent that Madero's moderate programs would not resolve Mexico's continuing social problems. Zapata rose in revolt, demanding a sweeping land reform, and Madero steadily lost control of his subordinates. In 1913, with at least the tacit agreement of the U.S. ambassador in Mexico, who wanted to forestall revolutionary changes, a military coup removed Madero from government and he was then assassinated.

Plan de Ayala

General **Victoriano Huerta** sought to impose a Díaz-type dictatorship supported by the large landowners, the army, and the foreign companies, but the tide of revolution could not be stopped so easily. Villa and Zapata rose again against the government and were joined by other middle-class political opponents of Huerta's illegal rule. By 1914 Huerta was forced from power, but the victorious leaders now began to fight over the nature of the new regime and the mantle of leadership. An extended period of warfare followed, and the tides of battle shifted constantly. The railroad lines built under Díaz now moved large numbers of troops, including *soldaderas,* women who sometimes shouldered arms. Matters were also complicated by U.S. intervention, aimed at bringing order to the border regions, and by diplomatic maneuverings after the outbreak of World War I in Europe.

Villa and Zapata remained in control in their home territories, but they could not wrest the government from the control of the more moderate political leaders in Mexico City. **Alvaro Obregón,** an able general who had learned the new tactics of machine guns and trenches from the war raging in Europe and had beaten Villa's cavalry in a series of bloody battles in 1915, emerged as leader of the government.

By 1920 the civil war had ended and Mexico began to consolidate the changes that had taken place in the previous confused and bloody decade. Obregón was elected president in that year. He was followed by a series of presidents from the new "revolutionary elite" who tried to consolidate the new regime. There was much to be done. The revolution had devastated the country; 1.5 million people had died, major industries were destroyed, and ranching and farming were disrupted. But there was great hope because the revolution also promised (although it did not always deliver) real changes.

What were some of these changes? The new **Mexican Constitution of 1917** promised land reform, limited the foreign ownership of key resources, and guaranteed the rights of workers. It also placed restrictions on clerical education and church ownership of property, and promised educational reforms. The workers who had been mobilized were organized in a national confederation and were given representation in the government. The promised land reforms were slow in coming, though later, under President Lázaro Cárdenas (1934–1940), more than 40 million acres were distributed, most of it in the form of *ejidos,* or communal holdings. The government launched an extensive program of primary and especially rural education.

## Culture and Politics in Postrevolutionary Mexico

Nationalism and *indigenism,* or the concern for the indigenous peoples and their contribution to Mexican culture, lay beneath many reforms. Having failed to integrate the American Indians into national life for a century, Mexico now attempted to "Indianize" the nation through secular schools that emphasized nationalism and a vision of the Mexican past that glorified its American Indian heritage and denounced Western capitalism. Artists such as **Diego Rivera** and **José Clemente Orozco** recaptured that past and outlined a social program for the future in stunning murals on public buildings designed to inform, convince, and entertain at the same time. The Mexican muralist movement had a wide impact on artists throughout Latin America even though, as Orozco himself stated, it sometimes created simple solutions and strange utopias by mixing a romantic image of the American Indian past with Christian symbols and communist ideology.

Novelists, such as Mariano Azuela, found in the revolution a focus for the examination of Mexican reality. Popular culture celebrated the heroes and events of the revolution in scores of ballads (*corridos*) that were sung to celebrate and inform. In literature, music, and the arts, the revolution and its themes provided a stimulus to a tremendous burst of creativity, as in the following lines of poetry:

> Gabino Barrera rose in the mountains
> his cause was noble,
> protect the poor and give them the land.
> Remember the night he was murdered
> three leagues from Tlapehuala;
> 22 shots rang out
> leaving him time for nothing.
> Gabino Barrera and his loyal steed
> fell in the hail of rounds,
> the face of this man of the Revolution
> finally rested, his lips pressed to the ground.

The gains of the revolution were not made without opposition. Although the revolution preceded the Russian Revolution of 1917 and had no single ideological model, many of the ideas of Marxist socialism were held by leading Mexican intellectuals and a few politicians. The secularization of society and especially education met strong opposition from the Catholic church and the clergy, especially in states where socialist rhetoric and anticlericalism were extreme. In the 1920s, a conservative peasant movement backed by the church erupted in central Mexico. These **Cristeros,** backed by conservative politicians, fought to stop the slide toward secularization. The fighting lasted for years until a compromise was reached.

The United States intervened diplomatically and militarily during the revolution, motivated by a desire for order, fear of German influence on the new government, and economic interests. An incident provoked a short-lived U.S. seizure of Veracruz in 1914, and when Pancho Villa's forces raided across the border, the United States sent an expeditionary force into Mexico to catch him. The mission failed. For the most part, however, the war in Europe dominated U.S. foreign policy efforts until 1918. The United States was suspicious of the new government, and a serious conflict arose when U.S.-owned oil companies ran into problems with workers.

As in any revolution, the question of continuity arose when the fighting ended. The revolutionary leadership hoped to institutionalize the new regime by creating a one-party system. This organization, called the Party of the Institutionalized Revolution (PRI), developed slowly during the 1920s and 1930s into a dominant force in Mexican politics. It incorporated labor, peasant, military, and middle-class sectors and proved flexible enough to incorporate new interest groups as they developed. Although Mexico became a multiparty democracy in theory, in reality the PRI controlled politics and, by accommodation and sometimes repression, maintained its hold on national political life. Some presidents governed much like the strongmen in the 19th century had done, but the party structure and the need to incorporate various interests within the government coalition limited the worst aspects of caudillo, or personalist, rule. The presidents were strong, but the policy of limiting the presidency to one six-year term ensured some change in leadership. The question of whether a revolution could be institutionalized remained in debate. By the end of the 20th century, many Mexicans believed that little remained of the principles and programs of the revolutionaries of 1910.

## Revolution in Russia: Liberalism to Communism

In March 1917, strikes and food riots broke out in Russia's capital, St. Petersburg. The outbursts were spurred by wartime misery, including painful food shortages. They also and more basically protested the conditions of early industrialization set against incomplete rural reform and an unresponsive political system. And they quickly assumed revolutionary proportions. The rioters called not just for more food and work but for a new political regime as well. The tsar's forces struck back brutally but unsuccessfully. A council of workers, called a soviet, took over the city government and arrested the tsar's ministers. Unable to rely on his own soldiers, the tsar abdicated, thus ending the long period of imperial rule.

For eight months a liberal provisional government struggled to rule the country. Russia seemed thus to launch its revolution on a basis similar to France in 1789, where a liberal period set change in motion. Like Western liberals, Russian revolutionary leaders, such as **Alexander Kerensky,** were eager to see genuine parliamentary rule, religious and other freedoms, and a host of political and legal changes. But liberalism was not deeply rooted in Russia, if only because of the small middle class, so the analogies with the first phase of the French revolution cannot be pressed too far.

Furthermore, Russia's revolution took place in much more adverse circumstances, given the pressures of participation in the First World War. The initial liberal leaders were eager to maintain the war effort, which linked them with democratic France and Britain. Yet the nation was desperately war weary, and prolongation drastically worsened economic conditions while public morale plummeted. Liberal leaders also held back from the massive land reforms expected by the peasantry, for in good middle-class fashion they respected existing property arrangements and did not wish to rush into social change before a legitimate new political structure could be established. Hence serious popular unrest continued, and in November (October, by the Russian calendar) a second revolution took place, which expelled liberal leadership and soon brought to power the radical, Bolshevik wing of the Social Democratic party, soon renamed the Communist party, and Lenin, their dynamic chief (Figure 34.7).

The revolution was a godsend to Lenin. This devoted revolutionary had long been writing of Russia's readiness for a communist revolt because of the power of international capitalism and its creation of a massive proletariat, even in a society that had not directly passed through middle-class rule. Lenin quickly gained a strong position among the urban workers' councils in the major cities. This corresponded to his deeply rooted belief that revolution should come not from literal mass action but from tightly organized cells whose leaders espoused a coherent plan of action.

Once the liberals were toppled, Lenin and the Bolsheviks faced several immediate problems. One, the war, they handled by signing a humiliating peace treaty with Germany and giving up huge sections of western Russia in return for an end of hostilities. This treaty was soon nullified by Germany's defeat at the hands of the Western allies, but Russia was ignored at the Versailles peace conference—treated as a pariah by the fearful Western powers. Much former territory was converted into new nation-states. A revived Poland built heavily on land Russia had controlled for more than a century, and new, small Baltic states cut into even earlier acquisitions. Still, although Russia's deep grievances against the Versailles treaty would later help motivate renewed expansionism, the early end to the war was vital to Lenin's consolidation of power.

Although Lenin and the Bolsheviks had gained a majority role in the leading urban soviets, they were not the most popular revolutionary party, and this situation constituted the second problem faced at the end of 1917. The November seizure of power had led to the creation of the Council of People's Commissars, drawn from soviets across the nation and headed by Lenin, to govern the state. But a parliamentary election had already been called, and this produced a clear majority for the Social Revolutionary party, which emphasized peasant support and rural reform. Lenin, however, shut down the parliament, replacing it with a Bolshevik-dominated Congress of Soviets. He pressed the Social Revolutionaries to disband, arguing that "the people voted for a party which no longer existed." Russia was thus to have no Western-style, multiparty system but rather a Bolshevik monopoly in the name of the true people's will. Indeed, Communist party control of the government apparatus persisted from this point to 1989, a record for continuity much different from the fate of revolutionary groups earlier in the Western past.

Russia's revolution produced a backlash that revolutionaries in other eras would have recognized quite easily: foreign hostility and, even more important,

**FIGURE 34.7** Moscow workers guard the Bolshevik headquarters during the Russian Revolution of 1917.

domestic resistance. The world's leading nations—aside from Germany, now briefly irrelevant—were appalled at the communist success, which threatened principles of property and freedom they cherished deeply. As settled regimes, they also disliked the unexpected, and some were directly injured by Russia's renunciation of its heavy foreign debts. The result was an attempt at intervention, recalling the attacks on France in 1792. Britain, France, the United States, and Japan all sent troops. But this intervention, although it heightened Russian suspicion of outsiders, did relatively little damage. The Western powers, exhausted by World War I, pulled out quickly, and even Japan, though interested in lingering in Asiatic Russia, stepped back fairly soon.

The internal civil war, which foreign troops slightly abetted, was a more serious matter, as it raged from 1918 to 1921. Tsarist generals, religiously faithful peasants, and many minority nationalities made common cause against the communist regime. Their efforts were aided by continuing economic distress, the normal result of revolutionary disarray, but also heightened by earlier communist measures. Lenin had quickly decreed a redistribution of land to the peasantry and also launched a nationalization, or state takeover, of basic industry. Many already landed peasants resented the loss of property and incentive, and in reaction they lowered food production and the goods sent to markets. Industrial nationalization somewhat similarly disrupted manufacturing. Famine and unemployment created more economic hardship than the war had generated, which added fuel to the civil war fires. Even workers revolted in several cities, threatening the new regime's most obvious social base as well as its ideological mainstay.

Lenin Calls for Electrification of All Russia

## Stabilization of Russia's Communist Regime

Order was restored after the revolution on several key foundations. First, the construction of the powerful new army under the leadership of Leon Trotsky recruited able generals and masses of loyal conscripts. This **Red Army** was an early beneficiary of two ongoing sources of strength for communist Russia: a willingness to use people of humble background but great ability who could rise to great heights under the new order but who had been doomed to immobility under the old system, and an ability to inspire mass loyalty in the name of an end to previous injustice and a promise of a brighter future. Next, economic disarray was reduced in 1921 when Lenin issued his **New Economic Policy,** which promised considerable freedom of action for small business owners and peasant landowners. The state continued to set basic economic policies, but its efforts were now combined with individual initiative. Under this temporary policy, food production began to recover, and the regime gained time to prepare the more durable structures of the communist system.

By 1923 the Bolshevik revolution was an accomplished fact. There was a new capital: Moscow. And a new constitution set up a federal system of socialist republics. This system recognized the multinational character of the nation, which was called the **Union of Soviet Socialist Republics.** The dominance of ethnic Russians was preserved in the central state apparatus, however, and certain groups, notably Jews, were given no distinct representation. Since the separate republics were firmly controlled by the national Communist party and since basic decisions were as firmly centralized, the impact of the new nationalities policy was somewhat mixed; yet it was also true that direct nationalities' protests declined notably from the 1920s until the late 1980s.

The apparatus of the central state was another mixture of appearance and reality. The **Supreme Soviet** had many of the trappings of a parliament and was elected by universal suffrage. But competition in elections was normally prohibited, which meant that the Communist party easily controlled the body, which served mainly to ratify decisions taken by the party's central executive. Parallel systems of central bureaucracy and party bureaucracy further confirmed the Communists' monopoly on power and the ability to control major decisions from the center. The Soviet political system was elaborated over time. A new constitution in the 1930s spoke glowingly of human rights. In fact, the Communists had quickly reestablished an authoritarian system, making it more efficient than its tsarist predecessor had been, complete with updated versions of political police to ensure loyalty.

## Soviet Experimentation

The mid-1920s constituted a lively, experimental period in Soviet history, partly because of the jockeying for power at the top of the power pyramid. Despite the absence of Western-style political competition, a host of new groups found a voice. The Communist party, though not eager to recruit too many members lest it lose its tight organization and elite status, encouraged all sorts of subsidiary organizations. Youth movements, women's groups, and particularly organizations of workers all actively debated problems in their social environment and directions for future planning. Workers were able to influence management practices; women's leaders helped carve legal equality and new educational and work opportunities for their constituents.

One key to the creative mood of these years was the rapid spread of education promoted by the government, as well as educational and propaganda activities

IN DEPTH

## A Century of Revolutions

Not since the late 18th and early 19th centuries had there been a succession of revolutions like those in the early decades of the 20th century. In contrast to the revolutionary movements of the earlier period, however, the early 20th-century upheavals were just the first waves of a revolutionary tide that struck with renewed fury after 1945. A number of factors account for the successive surges of revolution in the 20th century. Rural discontent was crucial, for peasants provided vital contributions to 20th-century revolutions everywhere they occurred. Peasants were newly spurred by pressures of population growth, combined with resentment against big landowners. Modern state forms tended to increase taxes on the peasantry, while making traditional protests, like banditry, more difficult.

> *"Visions of the good life in peasant communes or workers' utopias were a powerful driving force for revolutionary currents throughout the century from Mexico to China."*

Equally fundamentally, the rise of revolutionary movements was fed by the underlying disruptions caused by the spread of the Industrial Revolution and the Western-centered, global market system. Handicraft producers thrown out of work by an influx of machine-manufactured goods, and peasants, such as those in central Mexico who lost their land to moneylenders, frequently rallied to calls to riot and, at times, ultimately became caught up in revolutionary currents. In the colonies, unemployed Western-educated African and Asian secondary school and college graduates became deeply committed to struggles for independence that promised them dignity and decent jobs. Urban laborers, enraged by the appalling working and living conditions that were characteristic of the early stages of industrialization in countries such as Russia and China, provided key support for revolutionary parties in many countries.

Although global economic slumps did much to fire the revolutionaries' longings, world wars proved even more fertile seedbeds of revolution. Returning soldiers and neglected veterans provided the shock troops for leftist revolutionaries and fascist pretenders alike. Defeated states witnessed the rapid erosion of their power to suppress internal enemies and floundered as their armies refused to defend them or joined movements dedicated to their overthrow. In this regard, the great increase in global interconnectedness in the 20th century was critical. The economic competition and military rivalries of the industrial powers drew them into unwanted wars that they could not sustain without raw materials and manpower drawn from their colonies and other neutral states.

Another key factor that contributed to the sharp rise in the incidence of revolutions in the 20th century was the underlying intellectual climate. Notions of progress and a belief in the perfectibility of human society, which were widely held in the 19th century, deeply influenced such communist theorists as Marx, Lenin, Mao Zedong, and Ho Chi Minh. These and other revolutionary ideologues sought, in part, to overthrow existing regimes that they viewed as exploitive and oppressive. But they were also deeply committed to building radically new societies that would bring justice and a decent livelihood to previously downtrodden social groups, especially the working classes, peasantry, and urban poor. Visions of the good life in peasant communes or workers' utopias were a powerful driving force for revolutionary currents throughout the century from Mexico to China. One measure of their influence is the extent to which highly competitive capitalist societies developed social welfare programs to curb social discontent that could spiral into active protest, and perhaps even revolutionary challenges to the existing social order.

A final common ingredient of 20th-century revolutions was the need to come to terms with Western influence and often to reassert greater national autonomy. Mexico, Russia, and China all sought to reduce Western economic control and cultural influence, seeking alternative models. Many revolutions involved active anti-Western sentiment and attacks on Western investments. In Russia, Stalinism went on the attack against "decadent" Western cultural influences.

---

**Questions** What internal and external forces weakened the governments of Mexico and China in the opening decades of the 20th century and unleashed the forces of revolution? What key social groups were behind the revolutions in Mexico, China, and Russia, and why were they so important in each case? What similarities and differences can you identify among these three early revolutions in the 20th century?

sponsored by various adult groups. Literacy gained ground quickly. The new educational system was also bent on reshaping popular culture away from older peasant traditions and, above all, religion, and toward beliefs in Communist political analysis and science. Access to new information, new modes of inquiry, and new values encouraged controversy.

The Soviet regime grappled with other key definitional issues in the 1920s. Rivalries among leaders at the top had to be sorted out. Lenin became ill and then died in 1924, creating an unexpected leadership gap. (St. Petersburg was renamed Leningrad in his honor, a name it retained until 1991.) A number of key lieutenants jostled for power, including the Red Army's flamboyant

Trotsky and a Communist party stalwart of worker origins who had taken the name **Stalin,** meaning steel. After a few years of jockeying, Joseph Stalin emerged as undisputed leader of the Soviet state, his victory a triumph also for party control over other branches of government.

Stalin's accession was more than a personal bureaucratic issue, however. Stalin represented a strongly nationalist version of communism, in contrast to the more ideological and international visions of many of his rivals. At the revolution's outset Lenin had believed that the Russian rising would be merely a prelude to a sweeping communist upheaval throughout the Western industrial world. Many revolutionary leaders actively encouraged communist parties in the West and set up a **Comintern,** or Communist International office, to guide this process. But revolution did not spill over, despite a few brief risings in Hungary and Germany right after World War I. Under Stalin, the revolutionary leadership, although still committed in theory to an international movement, pulled back to concentrate on Russian developments—building "socialism in one country," as Stalin put it. Stalin in many ways represented the anti-Western strain in Russian tradition, though in new guise. Rival leaders were killed or expelled, rival visions of the revolution downplayed. Stalin would also accelerate industrial development while attacking peasant land ownership with a new **collectivization** program (Figure 34.8).

Lenin, 1920, vs. Stalin, 1931

The Russian Revolution was one of the most successful risings in human history, at least for several decades. Building on widespread if diverse popular discontent and a firm belief in centralized leadership, the Bolsheviks beat back powerful odds to create a new, though not totally unprecedented, political regime. They used features of the tsarist system but managed to propel a wholly new leadership group to power not only at the top but also at all levels of the bureaucracy and army. The tsar and his hated ministers were gone, mostly executed, but so was the overweening aristocratic class that had loomed so large in Russian history for centuries.

## Toward Revolution in China

The abdication of Puyi, the Manchu boy-emperor in 1912, marked the end of a century-long losing struggle on the part of the Qing dynasty to protect Chinese civilization from foreign invaders and revolutionary threats from within, such as the massive Taiping movement (see Chapter 31). The fall of the Qing opened the way for an extended struggle over which leader or movement would be able to capture the mandate to rule the ancient society that had for millennia ordered the lives of at least one-fifth of humankind. Contenders included regional warlords; the loose alliance of students, middle-class politicians and secret societies, many of them attracted to a Western political model; and soon, Japanese intruders and a new communist movements as well. Internal divisions and foreign influences paved the way for the ultimate victory of the Chinese Communist party under Mao Zedong.

After the fall of the Qing dynasty, the best-positioned of the contenders for power were regionally based military commanders or warlords, who would dominate Chinese politics for the next three decades. Many of the warlords combined in cliques or alliances to protect their own territories and to

**FIGURE 34.8** Russian children help carry the propaganda for Stalin's campaign for collectivization of agriculture. The banner reads, "Everybody to the collective farms!" These happy faces belie the tragedy resulting from the collectivization program, in which millions fell victim to slaughter or starvation.

crush neighbors and annex their lands. The most powerful of these cliques, centered in north China, was headed by the unscrupulous **Yuan Shikai,** who hoped to seize the vacated Manchu throne and found a new dynasty. By virtue of their wealth, the merchants and bankers of coastal cities like Shanghai and Canton made up a second power center in post-Manchu China. Their involvement in politics resulted from their willingness to bankroll both favored warlords and Western-educated, middle-class politicians like Sun Yat-sen.

Sometimes supportive of the urban civilian politicians and sometimes wary of them, university students and their teachers, as well as independent intellectuals, provided yet another factor in the complex post-Qing political equation. Though the intellectuals and students played critical roles in shaping new ideologies to rebuild Chinese civilization, they were virtually defenseless in a situation in which force was essential to those who hoped to exert political influence. Deeply divided, but very strong in some regions, secret societies represented another contender for power. Like many in the military, members of these societies envisioned the restoration of monarchical rule, but under a Chinese, not a foreign, dynasty. As if the situation were not confused enough, it was further complicated by the continuing intervention of the Western powers, eager to profit from China's divisions and weakness. Their inroads, however, were increasingly overshadowed by the entry into the contest for the control of China by the newest imperialist power, Japan. From the mid-1890s, when the Japanese had humiliated their much larger neighbor by easily defeating it in war, until 1945, when Japan's surrender ended World War II, the Japanese were a major factor in the long and bloody contest for mastery of China.

## China's May Fourth Movement and the Rise of the Marxist Alternative

Sun Yat-sen headed the Revolutionary Alliance, a loose coalition of anti-Qing political groups that had spearheaded the 1911 revolt. After the Qing were toppled, Sun claimed that he and the parties of the alliance were the rightful claimants to the mandate to rule all of China. But he could do little to assert civilian control in the face of warlord opposition. The Revolutionary Alliance had little power and virtually no popular support outside the urban trading centers of the coastal areas in central and south China. Even in these areas, they were at the mercy of the local warlords. The alliance formally elected Sun president at the end of 1911, set up a parliament modeled after those in Europe, and chose cabinets with great fanfare. But their decisions had little effect on warlord-dominated China.

Sun Yat-sen conceded this reality when he resigned the acting presidency in favor of the northern warlord Yuan Shikai in 1912. As the most powerful of the northern clique of generals, Yuan appeared to have the best chance to unify China under a single government. He at first feigned sympathy for the democratic aims of the alliance leaders but soon revealed his true intentions. He took foreign loans to build up his military forces and buy out most of the bureaucrats in the capital at Beijing. When Sun and other leaders of the Revolutionary Alliance called for a second revolution to oust Yuan in the years after 1912, he made full use of his military power and more underhanded methods, such as assassinations, to put down their opposition. By 1915 it appeared that Yuan was well on his way to realizing his ambition of becoming China's next emperor. His schemes were foiled, however, by the continuing rivalry of other warlords, republican nationalists like Sun, and the growing influence of Japan in China. The latter increased dramatically as a result of World War I.

As England's ally according to terms of a 1902 treaty, Japan immediately entered the war on the side of the Entente, or Western allied powers. Moving much too quickly for the comfort of the British and the other Western powers, the Japanese seized German-held islands in the Pacific and occupied the Germans' concessionary areas in China. With all the great powers except the United States embroiled in war, the Japanese sought to establish a dominant hold over their giant neighbor. In early 1915, they presented Yuan's government with Twenty-One Demands, which, if accepted, would have reduced China to the status of a dependant protectorate. Though Sun and the Revolutionary Alliance lost much support by refusing to repudiate the Japanese demands, Yuan was no more decisive. He neither accepted nor rejected the demands but concentrated his energies on an effort to trump up popular enthusiasm for his accession to the throne. Disgusted by Yuan's weakness and ambition, one of his warlord rivals plotted his overthrow. Hostility to the Japanese won Yuan's rival widespread support, and in 1916, Yuan was forced to resign the presidency. His fall was the signal for a free-for-all power struggle between the remaining warlords for control of China.

As one of the victorious allies of World War I, Japan managed to solidify its hold on northern China by winning control of the former German concessions in the peace negotiations at Versailles in 1919. But the Chinese had also allied themselves to the Entente powers during the war. Enraged by what they viewed as a betrayal by the Entente powers, students and nationalist politicians organized mass demonstrations in numerous Chinese cities on May 4, 1919. The demonstrations began a prolonged period of protest against Japanese inroads. This protest soon expanded from marches and petitions to include strikes and mass boycotts of Japanese goods.

The fourth of May, 1919, the day when the resistance began, gave its name to a movement in which intellectuals and students played a leading role. Initially at least, the **May Fourth movement** was aimed at transforming China into a liberal democracy. Its program was enunciated in numerous speeches, pamphlets, novels, and newspaper articles. Confucianism was ridiculed and rejected in favor of a wholehearted acceptance of all that the Western democracies had to offer. Noted Western thinkers, such as Bertrand Russell and John Dewey, toured China, praising democracy and basking in the cheers of enthusiastic Chinese audiences. Chinese thinkers called for the liberation of women (including the abolition of footbinding), the simplification of the Chinese script in order to promote mass literacy, and the promotion of Western-style individualism. Many of these themes are captured in the literature of the period. In the novel *Family* by Ba Jin, for example, a younger brother audaciously informs his elder sibling that he will not accept the marriage partner the family has arranged for him. He clearly sees his refusal as part of a more general revolt of the youth of China against the ancient Confucian social code.

> Big Brother, I'm doing what no one in our family has ever dared do before—I'm running out on an arranged marriage. No one cares about my fate, so I've decided to walk my own road alone. I'm determined to struggle against the old forces to the end. Unless you cancel the match, I'll never come back. I'll die first.

However enthusiastically the program of the May Fourth movement was adopted by the urban youth of China, it was soon clear that mere emulation of the liberal democracies of the West could not provide effective solutions to China's prodigious problems. Civil liberties and democratic elections were meaningless in a China that was ruled by warlords. Gradualist solutions and parliamentary debates were folly in a nation where the great mass of the peasantry was destitute, much of them malnourished or dying of starvation. It soon became clear to many Chinese intellectuals and students, as well as to some of the nationalist politicians, that more radical solutions were needed. In the 1920s, this conviction gave rise to the communist left within the Chinese nationalist movement.

The Bolshevik victory and the programs launched to rebuild Russia prompted Chinese intellectuals to give serious attention to the works of Marx and other socialist thinkers and the potential they offered for the regeneration of China. But the careful study of the writings of Marx, Engels, Lenin, and Trotsky in the wake of the Russian Revolution also impressed a number of Chinese intellectuals with the necessity for major alterations in Marxist ideology if it was going to be of any relevance to China or other peasant societies. Marx, after all, had focused on advanced industrial societies and had regarded peasants as conservative or even reactionary. Taken literally, Marxism offering discouraging prospects for revolution in China.

The most influential of the thinkers who called for a reworking of Marxist ideology to fit China's situation was **Li Dazhao.** Li was from peasant origins, but he had excelled in school and eventually become a college teacher. He headed the Marxist study circle that developed after the 1919 upheavals at the University of Beijing. His interpretation of Marxist philosophy placed heavy emphasis on its capacity for promoting renewal and its ability to harness the energy and vitality of a nation's youth. In contrast to Lenin, Li saw the peasants, rather than the urban workers, as the vanguard of revolutionary change. He justified this shift from the orthodox Marxist emphasis on the working classes, which made up only a tiny fraction of China's population at the time, by characterizing the whole of Chinese society as proletarian. All of China, he argued, had been exploited by the bourgeois, industrialized West. Thus, the oppressed Chinese as a whole needed to unite and rise up against their exploiters.

Li's version of Marxism, with alterations or emphasis on elements that made it suitable for China, had great appeal for the students, including the young **Mao Zedong,** who joined Li's study circle. They, too, were angered by what they perceived as China's betrayal by the imperialist powers. They shared Li's hostility (very much a throwback to the attitudes of the Confucian era) to merchants and commerce, which appeared to dominate the West. They, too, longed for a return to a political system, like the Confucian, in which those who governed were deeply committed to social reform and social welfare. They also believed in an authoritarian state, which they felt ought to intervene constructively in all aspects of the peoples' lives. The Marxist study club societies that developed as a result of these discoveries soon spawned a number of more broadly based, politically activist organizations.

In the summer of 1921, in an attempt to unify the growing Marxist wing of the nationalist struggle, a handful of leaders from different parts of China met in secret in the city of Shanghai. At this meeting, closely watched by the agents of the local warlord and rival political organizations, the Communist party of China was born. The party was minuscule in terms of the numbers of their supporters, and at this time it was still dogmatically fixed on a revolutionary program oriented to the small and scattered working class. But the communists at least offered a clear alternative to fill the ideological and institutional void left by the collapse of the Confucian order.

## The Seizure of Power by China's Guomindang

In the years when the communist movement in China was being put together by urban students and intellectuals, the **Guomindang,** or Nationalist party, which was to prove the communists' great rival for the mandate to rule in China, was struggling to survive in the south. Sun Yat-sen, who was the acknowledged head of the nationalist struggle from the 1911 revolution until his death in early 1925, had gone into temporary exile in Japan in 1914, while warlords such as Yuan Shikai consolidated their regional power bases. After returning to China in 1919, Sun and his followers attempted to unify the diverse political organizations struggling for political influence in China by reorganizing the revolutionary movement and naming it the Nationalist party of China (the Guomindang).

The Nationalists began the slow process of forging alliances with key social groups and building an army of their own, which they now viewed as the only way to rid China of the warlord menace (Map 34.3). Sun strove to enunciate a nationalist ideology that gave something to everyone. It stressed the need to unify China under a strong central government, to bring the imperialist intruders under control, and to introduce social reforms that would alleviate the poverty of the peasants and the oppressive working conditions of laborers in China's cities. Unfortunately for the great majority of the Chinese people, for whom social reforms were the main concern, the Nationalist leaders concentrated on political and international issues, such as relations with the Western powers and Japan, and failed to implement most of the domestic programs they proposed, most especially land reform.

In this early stage Sun and the Nationalists built their power primarily on the support provided by urban businesspeople and merchants in coastal cities such as Canton. Sun forged an alliance with the communists that was officially proclaimed at the first Nationalist party conference in 1924. For the time being at least, the Nationalist leaders were content to let the communists serve as their major link to the peasants and the urban workers. Nationalist leaders also turned to Soviet Russia, and the Bolsheviks sent advisors and gave material assistance.

In 1924 the **Whampoa Military Academy** was founded with Soviet help and partially staffed by Russian instructors. The academy gave the Nationalists a critical military dimension to their political maneuvering. The first head of the academy was an ambitious young military officer named **Chiang Kai-shek.** The son of a poor salt merchant, Chiang had made his career in the military and by virtue of connections with powerful figures in the Shanghai underworld. He had received some military training in Japan and managed by the early 1920s to work his way into Sun Yat-sen's inner circle of advisors. Chiang was not happy with the communist alliance. But he was willing to bide his time until he had the military strength to deal with both the

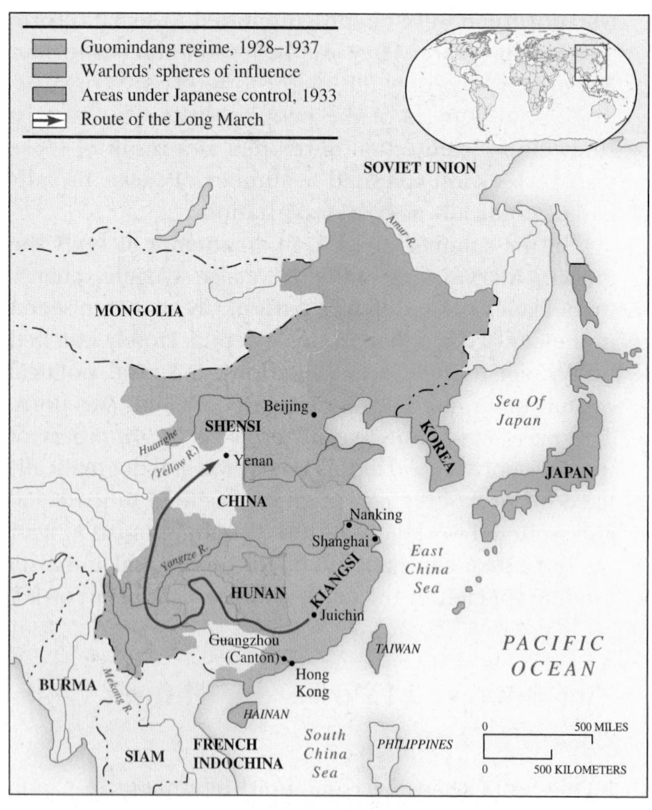


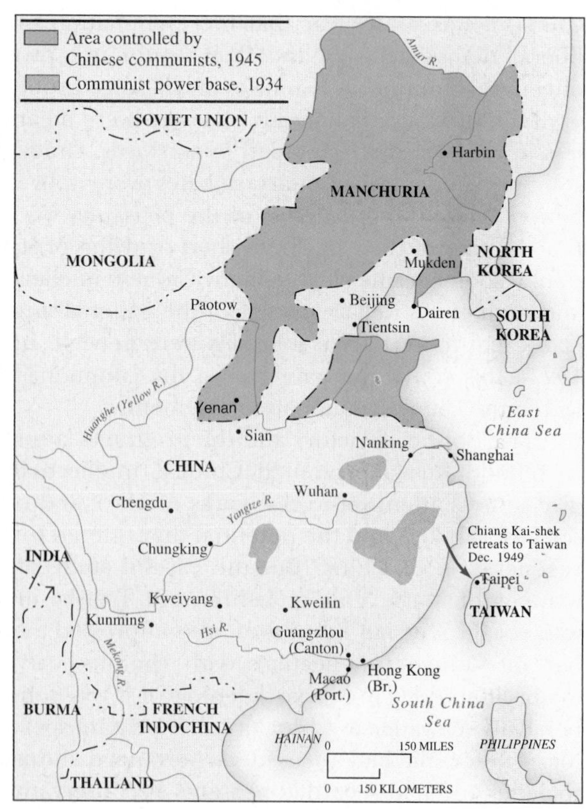


**MAP 34.3** China in the Era of Revolution and Civil War

communists and the warlords, who remained the major obstacles to the Nationalist seizure of power.

Political tensions distracted the Nationalist leaders from the growing deterioration of the economy. The peasantry, 90 percent of the population, suffered increasing misery following a long period of government ineffectiveness and depredations by the landlords. Famine and disease stalked the countryside, while irrigation systems deteriorated. Many peasants could not even bury their deceased parents, whose bodies were left for animals to devour.

Sun gave lip service to the Nationalist party's need to deal with the peasant problem. But his abysmal ignorance of rural conditions was revealed by statements in which he denied that China had exploitive landlords and his refusal to believe that there were "serious difficulties" between the great mass of the peasantry and the landowners.

## Mao and the Peasant Option

Though the son of a fairly prosperous peasant, Mao Zedong had rebelled early in his life against his father's exploitation of the tenants and laborers who worked the family fields. Receiving little assistance from his estranged father, Mao was forced to make his own way in the world. Through much of his youth and early adulthood, he struggled to educate himself in the history, philosophy, and economic theory that most other nationalist and revolutionary leaders mastered in private schools. Having moved to Beijing in the post–May Fourth era, Mao came under the influence of thinkers such as Li Dazhao, who placed considerable emphasis on solutions to the peasant problem as one of the keys to China's survival. As the following passage from Mao's early writings reveals, almost from the outset he was committed to revolutionary solutions that depended on peasant support:

> A revolution is an insurrection, an act of violence by which one class overthrows another. A rural revolution is a revolution by which the peasantry overthrows the power of the feudal landlord class. Without using the greatest force, the peasants cannot possibly overthrow the deep-rooted authority of the landlords which has lasted for thousands of years.

The Nationalists' successful drive for national power began only after Sun Yat-sen's death in 1925, which opened the way for Chiang Kai-shek and his warlord allies to seize control of the party. After winning over or eliminating the military chiefs in the Canton area, Chiang marched north with his newly created armies. His first campaign culminated in the Nationalists' seizure of the Yangtze River valley and Shanghai in early 1927. Later his forces also captured the capital at Beijing and the rest of the Huanghe river basin. The refusal of most of the warlords to end their feuding meant that Chiang could defeat them or buy them out, one by one. By the late 1920s, he was the master of China in name and international standing, if not in actual fact. He was, in effect, the head of a warlord hierarchy. But most political leaders within China and in the outside world recognized him as the new president of China.

**FIGURE 34.9** The Guomindang's brutal suppression of the workers' organizations in Shanghai in 1927 was a turning point in the history of modern China. The Guomindang–Communist party alliance was shattered, and Mao Zedong's call for a peasant-based revolution became imperative as the vulnerability of the small Chinese working class was exposed.

Chiang quickly turned against the communists, attacking them in various places. A brutal massacre occurred in Shanghai in 1927, with many workers gunned down or beheaded (Figure 34.9). Chiang carefully wooed support from western Europe and the United States, while lining up most police and landlord leaders at home. The offensive propelled Mao Zedong to leadership. An attack on the communist rural stronghold in south central China, supported by German advisors, caused Mao to spearhead a **Long March** of 90,000 followers in 1934, across thousands of miles to the more remote northwest. Here, in Shanxi, where some peasant communes had already been established, the new communist center took shape (Map 34.3).

While the Long March solidified Mao's leadership of Chinese communism and gave many followers a sense that they could not be defeated, it was the Japanese invasions of China in the 1930s that would begin to give communists a new advantage. Chiang had to ally with communists to fight the Japanese threat, while his own power base, along the coast, was eroded by the powerful Japanese advance. The Chinese revolution was far from over.

## The Global Great Depression

■ **The Great Depression was centered in the West but had global roots and impact. Western responses to the Depression varied, but none succeeded in ending the crisis.**

Coming barely a decade after the turmoil of World War I, the onset of global economic depression constituted a crucial next step in the mounting spiral of international crises. The crash of the New York stock market hit the headlines in 1929, but in fact the **Great Depression** had begun, sullenly, in many parts of the world economy even earlier. The Depression resulted from new problems in the industrial economy of Europe and the United States, combined with the long-term weakness in economies, like those of Latin America, that depended on sales of cheap exports in the international market. The result was a worldwide collapse that spared only a few economies and brought political as well as economic pressures on virtually every society.

### Causation

Structural problems affected many industrial societies during the 1920s, even after postwar recovery. Farmers throughout much of the Western world, including the United States, faced almost chronic overproduction of food and resulting low prices. Food production had soared in response to wartime needs; during the postwar inflation many farmers, both in western Europe and in North America, borrowed heavily to buy new equipment, overconfident that their good markets would be sustained. But rising European production combined with large imports from the Americas and New Zealand sent prices down, which lowered earnings and made debts harder to repay. One response was continued population flight from the countryside as urbanization continued. Remaining farmers were hard pressed and unable to sustain high demand for manufactured goods.

Thus although economies in France and Germany seemed to have recovered by 1925, problems continued: the fears massive postwar inflation had generated limited the capacity of governments to respond to other problems. Much of the mid-decade prosperity rested on exceedingly fragile grounds. Loans from U.S. banks to various European enterprises helped sustain demand for goods but on condition that additional loans pour in to help pay off the resultant debts.

Furthermore, most of the dependent areas in the world economy, colonies and noncolonies alike, were suffering badly. Pronounced tendencies toward overproduction developed in the smaller nations of eastern Europe, which sent agricultural goods to western Europe, as well as among tropical producers in Africa and Latin America. Here, continued efforts to win export revenue pressed local estate owners to drive up output in coffee, sugar, and rubber. As European governments and businesses organized their African colonies for more profitable exploitation, they set up large estates devoted to goods of this type. Again, production frequently exceeded demand, which drove prices and earnings down in both Africa and Latin America. This meant, in turn, that many colonies and dependant economies were unable to buy many industrial exports, which weakened demand for Western products precisely when output tended to rise amid growing U.S. and Japanese competition. Several food-exporting regions, including many of the new eastern European nations, fell into a depression, in terms of earnings and employment, by the mid-1920s, well before the full industrial catastrophe.

Governments of the leading industrial nations provided scant leadership during the emerging crisis of the 1920s. Knowledge of economics was often feeble within a Western leadership group not noteworthy for its quality even in more conventional areas. Nationalistic selfishness predominated. Western nations were more concerned about insisting on repayment of any debts owed to them or about constructing tariff barriers to protect their own industries than about facilitating balanced world economic growth. Protectionism, in particular, as practiced even by traditionally free-trade Great Britain and by the many nations in eastern Europe, simply reduced market opportunities and made a bad situation worse. By the later 1920s employment in key Western industrial sectors—coal (also beset by new competition from imported oil), iron, and textiles—began to decline, the foretaste of more general collapse.

### The Debacle

The formal advent of the Depression occurred in October 1929, when the New York stock market collapsed. Stock values tumbled as investors quickly lost confidence in prices that had been pushed ridiculously high. Banks, which had depended heavily on their stock investments, rapidly echoed the financial crisis, and many institutions failed, dragging their depositors along with them. Even before this crash, Americans had begun to call back earlier loans to Europe. Yet the European credit structure depended extensively on U.S. loans, which had fueled some industrial expansion but also less productive investments, such as German reparations payments and the construction of fancy town halls and other amenities. In Europe, as in the United States, many commercial enterprises existed on the basis not of real production power but of continued speculation. When one piece of the speculative spiral was withdrawn, the whole edifice quickly collapsed. Key bank failures in Austria and Germany followed the U.S. crisis. Throughout most of the industrial West, investment funds dried up as creditors went bankrupt or tried to pull in their horns.

With investment receding, industrial production quickly began to fall, beginning with the industries that produced capital goods and extending quickly to consumer products fields. Falling production—levels dropped by as much as one-third by 1932—meant falling employment and lower wages, which in turn withdrew still more demand from the economy and led to further hardship. Unemployed and underpaid workers could not buy goods whose production might give other workers jobs. The existing weakness of some markets, such as the farm sector or the nonindustrial world, was exacerbated as demand for foods and minerals plummeted. New and appalling problems developed among workers, now out of jobs or suffering from reduced hours and reduced pay (Figure 34.10), as well as among the middle classes. The Depression, in sum, fed on itself, growing steadily worse from 1929 to 1933. Even countries initially less hard hit, such as France and Italy, saw themselves drawn into the vortex by 1931.

DOCUMENT

The Great Depression: An Oral Account

In itself the Great Depression was not entirely unprecedented. Previous periods had seen slumps triggered by bank failures and overspeculation, yielding several years of falling production, unemployment, and hardship. But the intensity of the Great Depression had no precedent in the brief history of industrial societies. Its duration was also unprecedented; in many countries, full recovery came only after a decade and only with the forced production schedules provoked by World War II. Unlike earlier depressions, this one came on the heels of so much other distress—the economic hardships of war, for example, and the catastrophic inflation of the 1920s—and caught most governments totally unprepared.

The Depression was more, of course, than an economic event. It reached into countless lives, creating hardship and tension that would be recalled even as the crisis itself eased. Loss of earnings, loss of work, or simply fears that loss would come devastated people at all social levels. The suicides of ruined investors in New York were paralleled by the vagrants' camps and begging that spread among displaced workers. The statistics were grim: up to one-third of all blue-collar workers in the West lost their jobs for prolonged periods. White-collar unemployment, though not quite as severe, was also unparalleled. In Germany 600,000 of 4 million white-collar workers had lost their jobs by 1931. Graduating students could not find work or had to resort to jobs they regarded as insecure or demeaning. Six million overall unemployed in Germany and 22 percent of the labor force unemployed in Britain were statistics of stark misery and despair. Families were disrupted; men felt emasculated at their inability to provide, and women and children were disgusted with authority figures whose authority was now hollow. In some cases wives and mothers found it easier to gain jobs in a low-wage economy than their husbands did, and although this development had some promise in terms of new opportunities for women, it could also be confusing for standard family roles. For many, the agony and personal disruption of the Depression were desperately prolonged, with renewed recession around 1937 and with unemployment still averaging 10 percent or more in many countries as late as 1939.

The Depression, like World War I, was an event that blatantly contradicted the optimistic assumptions of the later 19th century. To many it showed the fragility of any idea of progress, while to others it seemed to condemn the system of parliamentary democracy. Because it was a second catastrophic event within a generation, the Depression led to even more extreme results than the war had done—more bizarre experiments, more paralysis in the face of deepening despair. To be sure, there were some escapist alternatives: Hollywood movies put up a cheerful front, and in 1938 a new American comic book figure, Superman, provided an alternative to the constraints of normal life. But these were modest alternatives at best.

**FIGURE 34.10** This famous photograph of a tenant farmer and her children in the American South was published in the book *Let Us Now Praise Famous Men.* It exemplifies the hardship and poverty endured by many during the Great Depression.

For most of the world outside the West, moreover, the Depression worsened an already bleak economic picture. Western markets could absorb fewer commodity imports as production fell and incomes dwindled. Hence the nations that produced foods and raw materials saw prices and earnings drop even more than before. Unemployment rose rapidly in the export sectors of the Latin American economy, creating a major political challenge not unlike that faced by the Western nations. Japan, a new industrial country, still heavily depended on export earnings for financing its imports of essential fuel and raw materials. The Japanese silk industry, an export staple, was already suffering from the advent of artificial silklike fibers produced by Western chemical giants. Now Western luxury purchases collapsed, leading to severe unemployment in Japan and a crucial political crisis. Between 1929 and 1931, the value of Japanese exports plummeted by 50 percent. Workers' real income dropped by almost one-third, and more than 3 million people were unemployed. Depression was compounded by poor harvests in several regions, leading to rural begging and near starvation. The Great Depression, though most familiar in its Western dimensions, was a truly international collapse.

## Responses to the Depression in Western Europe

Western governments, already weakened, responded to the onset of the economic catastrophe counterproductively. National tariffs were raised to keep out the goods of other countries, but this merely worsened the international economy and curbed sales for everyone. Most governments tried to cut spending, reflecting the decline in revenues that accompanied falling production. They were concerned about avoiding renewed inflation, but in fact their measures further reduced economic stimulus and pushed additional workers—government employees—out of jobs. Confidence in the normal political process deteriorated. In many countries the Depression heightened political polarization. People sought solutions from radical parties or movements, both on the left and on the right. Support for communist parties increased in many countries, and in important cases the authoritarian movement on the right gained increased attention. Even in relatively stable countries, such as Britain, battles between the Conservative party and the labor movement made decisive policy difficult. Class conflict rose to new levels, in and out of politics.

In key cases, the Great Depression led to one of two effects: either a parliamentary system that became increasingly incapacitated, unable to come to grips with the new economic dilemma and too divided to take vigorous action, even in foreign policy, or the outright overturning of the parliamentary system.

France was a prime example of the first pattern. The French government reacted sluggishly to the Depression. Voters responded by moving toward the political extremes. Socialist and then communist parties expanded. Rightist movements calling for a strong leader and fervent nationalism grew, their adherents often disrupting political meetings in order to discredit the parliamentary system by making orderly debate impossible. In response liberal, socialist, and communist parties formed the **Popular Front** in 1936 to win the election. The Popular Front government, however, was unable to take strong measures of social reform because of the ongoing strength of conservative republicans hostile to change and the authoritarian right that looked to forceful leadership to contain the lower classes. The same paralysis crept into foreign policy, as Popular Front leaders, initially eager to support the new liberal regime in Spain that was attacked by conservative army leaders in the Spanish Civil War, found themselves forced to pull back. The Popular Front fell in 1938, but even before this France was close to a standstill.

There were more constructive responses. Scandinavian states, most of them directed by moderate socialist parties, increased government spending, providing new levels of social insurance against illness and unemployment. This foreshadowed the welfare state. British policy was more tentative, but new industrial sectors emerged under the leadership of innovative businesspeople. The world's first television industry, for example, took shape in southern England in the late 1930s, though it was too small to break the hold of the Depression.

## The New Deal

After a few years of floundering, the United States generated another set of creative responses. Initial American policies, under President Herbert Hoover, resembled those of western Europe, in seeking higher tariffs and attempting to cut spending in reaction to falling revenues. The United States also sought to accelerate war debt repayments from Europe, which also made matters worse internationally. In 1933 a new administration took over, under Franklin Roosevelt, offering a "new deal" to the American people.

**New Deal** policies, as they unfolded during the 1930s, offered more direct aid to Americans at risk, through increased unemployment benefits and other measures. Many unemployed people were given jobs on public works projects. A crucial innovation was the Social Security system, based on contributions from workers and employers and designed to provide protection in unemployment and old age. The New Deal also undertook some economic planning and stimulus, for both industry and agriculture, while installing new regulations on banking.

The New Deal ushered in a period of rapid government growth, a watershed in American history particularly as it was followed by the massive expansion of military operations in World War II. The regime did not solve the Depression, which sputtered on until wartime spending ended it in the early 1940s. It also did not install a full welfare state, holding back, for example, from plans to offer a health insurance system. But the New Deal did restore the confidence of most Americans in their political system, preempting more extremist political movements and minimizing the kind of paralysis that afflicted Britain and France in the same years.

## The Authoritarian Response

- **European fascism expanded in response to the new crisis as Nazism took hold in Germany. New authoritarian regimes gained ground in Latin America. Military authoritarians won power in Japan. Stalin tightened the Soviet totalitarian system.**

### The Rise of Nazism

German patterns differed markedly from the wavering responses of Germany's neighbors, and from democratic welfare innovation as well. In Germany the impact of the Depression led directly to a new fascist regime. Germany had suffered the shock of loss in World War I, enhanced by treaty arrangements that cast primary blame for the war on the German nation, which had only recent and shaky parliamentary traditions. A number of factors, in sum, combined to make Germany a fertile breeding ground for fascism, though it took the Depression to bring this current to the fore.

Fascism in Germany, as in Italy, was a product of the war. The movement's advocates, many of them former veterans, attacked the weakness of parliamentary democracy and the corruption and class conflict of Western capitalism. They proposed a strong state ruled by a powerful leader who would revive the nation's forces through vigorous foreign and military policy. While fascists vaguely promised social reforms to alleviate class antagonisms, their attacks on trade unions as well as on socialist and communist parties pleased landlords and business groups. Although fascism won outright control only in Italy in the movement's early years, fascist parties complicated the political process in a number of other nations during the 1920s and beyond. But it was the advent of the National Socialist, or Nazi, regime in Germany under Adolf Hitler that made this new political movement a major force in world history. Here, a Western commitment to liberal, democratic political forms was challenged and reversed.

In his vote-gathering campaigns, in the later 1920s and early 1930s, Hitler repeated standard fascist arguments about the need for unity and the hopeless weakness of parliamentary politics. The state should provide guidance, for it was greater than the sum of individual interests, and the leader should guide the state. Hitler promised many groups a return to more traditional ways; thus many artisans voted for him in the belief that preindustrial economic institutions, such as the guilds, would be revived. Middle-class elements, including big-business leaders, were attracted to Hitler's commitment to a firm stance against socialism and communism. Hitler also focused grievances against various currents in modern life, from big department stores to feminism, by attacking what he claimed were Jewish influences in Germany. He promised a glorious foreign policy to undo the wrongs of the Versailles treaty. Finally, Hitler represented a hope for effective action against the Depression. Although the Nazis never won a majority vote in a free election, his party did win the largest single slice in 1932, and this enabled Hitler to make arrangements with other political leaders for his rise to power legally in 1933.

German Painting Idolizing Hitler

Once in power, Hitler quickly set about constructing a **totalitarian state**—a new kind of government that would exercise massive, direct control over virtually all the activities of its subjects. Hitler eliminated all opposition parties; he purged the bureaucracy and military, installing loyal Nazis in many posts. His secret police, the **Gestapo,** arrested hundreds of thousands of political opponents. Trade unions were replaced by government-sponsored bodies that tried to appease low-paid workers by offering full employment and various welfare benefits. Government economic planning helped restore production levels, with particular emphasis on armaments construction. Hitler cemented his regime by continual, well-staged propaganda bombardments (Figure 34.11), strident nationalism, and an incessant attack on Germany's large Jewish minority.

Hitler's hatred of Jews ran deep; he blamed them for various personal misfortunes and also for socialism and excessive capitalism—movements that in his view had weakened the German spirit. Obviously, anti-Semitism served as a catchall for a host of diverse dissatisfactions, and as such it appealed to many Germans. Anti-Semitism also played into Hitler's hands by providing a scapegoat that could rouse national passions and distract the population from other problems. Measures against Jews became more and more severe; they were forced to wear special emblems, their property was attacked and seized, and increasing numbers were sent to concentration camps. After 1940 Hitler's policy insanely turned to the literal elimination of European Jewry, as the Holocaust raged in the concentration camps of Germany and conquered territories (see Chapter 35).

FIGURE 34.11 The adulation that the German masses felt for Adolf Hitler in the mid-1930s is evident in this rally photo. Hitler's popularity rested primarily on his promises to rebuild Germany's deeply depressed economy and restore its world power status by reversing the 1919 treaty ending World War I.

Hitler's foreign and military policies were based on preparation for war. He wanted to not only recoup Germany's World War I losses but also create a land empire that would extend across much of Europe, particularly toward the east against what he saw as the inferior Slavic peoples. Progressively Hitler violated the limits on German armaments and annexed neighboring territories, provoking only weak response from the Western democracies.

The Expansion of Germany in the 1930s

## The Spread of Fascism and the Spanish Civil War

Nazi triumph in Germany inevitably spurred fascism in other parts of Europe. Many east central states, already authoritarian, took on fascist trappings. Explicit fascist movements emerged in Hungary and Romania. Fascism in Austria was vindicated when Hitler proclaimed the union of Austria and Germany in 1938, quickly spreading the apparatus of the Nazi party and state.

Hitler's advent galvanized the authoritarian regime of a nearby power, Italy, where a fascist state had been formed in the 1920s, led by Benito Mussolini. Like Hitler, Mussolini had promised an aggressive foreign policy and new nationalist glories, but his first decade had been rather moderate diplomatically. With Hitler in power, Mussolini began to experiment more boldly, if only to avoid being overshadowed completely.

In 1935 Mussolini attacked Ethiopia, planning to avenge Italy's failure to conquer this ancient land during the imperialist surge of the 1890s. The League of Nations condemned the action, but neither it nor the democratic powers in Europe and North America took action. Consequently, after some hard fighting, the Italians won their new colony. Here, then, was another destabilizing element in world politics.

Fascism also spread into Spain, leading to the **Spanish Civil War.** Here, forces supporting a parliamentary republic plus social reform had feuded since 1931 with advocates of a military-backed authoritarian state. In 1936 outright civil war broke out. Spanish military forces, led by General Francisco Franco, were backed by an explicitly fascist party, the Falange, as well as more conventionally conservative landowners and Catholic leaders.

Republican forces included various groups, with support from peasants and workers in various parts of the country. Communists and a large anarchist movement played a crucial role. They won some support also from volunteers from the United States and western Europe, and from the Soviet Union.

Bitter fighting consumed much of Spain for three years. German and Italian forces bombed several Spanish cities, a rehearsal for the bombing of civilians in World War II. France, Britain, and the United States made vague supporting gestures to the republican forces but offered no concrete aid, fearful of provoking a wider conflict and paralyzed by internal disagreements about foreign policy. Franco's forces won in 1939. The resultant regime was not fully fascist, but it maintained authoritarian controls and catered to landlords, church, and army for the next 25 years.

## Economic and Political Changes in Latin America

In the 1920s and 1930s, the limitations of liberalism became increasingly apparent in Latin America. A middle class had emerged and had begun to enter politics, but unlike its western European counterpart, it gained power only in conjunction with the traditional oligarchy or the military. In Latin America, the ideology of liberalism was not an expression of the strength

VISUALIZING THE PAST

## *Guernica* and the Images of War

This painting, probably the most famous work of art of the 20th century, was Spanish artist Pablo Picasso's protest against the bombing of the village of Guernica during the Spanish Civil War. On April 27, 1937, German and Italian planes bombarded the city for three hours. Guernica burned for three days, and more than 1500 people were killed.

**Questions** What was Picasso trying to say through the painting? Why did it have such a strong impact? Picasso, a Cubist artist, was working in a nonrepresentational style of art. Was his style effective for a contemporary statement about war, or would a more traditional artistic presentation have done the job better? Can you think of other works of art, including photographs, that have helped capture the notion of modern war? Does art make a difference where war is concerned?

Pablo Picasso's *Guernica.*

of the middle class but rather a series of ideas not particularly suited to the realities of Latin America, where large segments of the population were landless, uneducated, and destitute. Increasing industrialization did not dissolve the old class boundaries, nor did public education and other classic liberal programs produce as much social mobility as had been expected.

Disillusioned by liberalism and World War I, artists and intellectuals who had looked to Europe for inspiration turned to Latin America's own populations and history for values and solutions to Latin American problems. During the 1920s intellectuals complained that Latin America was on a race to nowhere. In literature and the arts, the ideas of rationality, progress, and order associated with liberalism and the outward appearances of democracy were under attack.

Ideas of reform and social change were in the air. University students in Córdoba, Argentina, began a reform of their university system that gave the university more autonomy and students more power within it. This movement soon spread to other countries. There were other responses as well. Socialist and communist parties were formed or grew in strength in several Latin American nations in this period, especially after the Russian Revolution of 1917. The strength of these parties of the left originated in local conditions but sometimes was aided by the international communist movement. Although criticism of existing governments and of liberalism as a political and economic philosophy came from these left-leaning parties, it also came from traditional elements in society such as the Roman Catholic church, which disliked the secularization represented by a capitalist society.

## The Great Crash and Latin American Responses

The economic dependency of Latin America and the internal weaknesses of the liberal regimes were made clear by the great world financial crisis. Export sales dropped rapidly. Amid growing poverty, reform movements gained momentum. More important, however, was the rise of a conservative response, hostile to class conflict and supported by church and military leaders. A corporatist movement, aimed at curbing capitalism while avoiding Marxism, won growing attention. **Corporatism** emphasized the organic nature of society, with the state as a mediator adjusting the interests of different social groups; the ideology appealed to conservative groups and the military, in European as well as Latin American societies. Some corporatist leaders sympathized with aspects of Italian and German fascism.

New regimes, as well as a new concern with social problems, characterized much of Latin America in the 1930s. One such reforming administration was that of President **Lázaro Cárdenas** (1934–1940) in Mexico, when land reform and many of the social aspects of the revolution were initiated on a large scale. Cárdenas distributed more than 40 million acres of land and created communal farms and a credit system to support them. He expropriated foreign oil companies that refused to obey Mexican law and created a state oil monopoly. He expanded rural education programs. These measures made him broadly popular in Mexico and seemed to give substance to the promise of the revolution.

Cárdenas in Mexico was perhaps the most successful example of the new political tide that could be seen elsewhere in Latin America. In Cuba, for example, the leaders of a nationalist revolution aimed at social reform and breaking the grip of the United States took power in 1933, and although their rule soon was taken over by moderate elements, important changes and reforms did take place. To some extent, such new departures underlined both the growing force of nationalism and the desire to integrate new forces into the political process. Nowhere was this more apparent than in the populist Vargas regime of Brazil.

## The Vargas Regime in Brazil

In Brazil, a contested political election in 1929, in which the state elites could not agree on the next president, resulted in a short civil war and the emergence of **Getúlio Vargas** (1872–1954) as the new president. The Brazilian economy, based on coffee exports, had collapsed in the 1929 crash. Vargas had promised liberal reforms and elimination of the worst abuses of the old system. Once in power, he launched a new kind of centralized political program, imposing federal administrators over the state governments. He held off attempted coups by the communists in 1935 and by the green-shirted fascist "Integralists" in 1937. With the support of the military, Vargas imposed a new constitution in 1937 that established the *Estado Novo* (New State), based on ideas from Mussolini's Italy. It imposed an authoritarian regime within the context of nationalism and economic reforms, limiting immigration and eliminating parties and groups that resisted national integration or opposed the government.

For a while, Vargas played off Germany and the Western powers in the hope of securing armaments and favorable trade arrangements. Despite Vargas's authoritarian sympathies, he eventually joined the Allies during World War II, supplied bases to the United States, and even sent troops to fight against the Axis powers in Italy. In return, Brazil obtained arms, financial support for industrial development, and trade advantages. Meanwhile, Vargas ran a corporatist government, allowing some room for labor negotiations under strict government supervision. Little open opposition to the government was allowed. The state organized many other aspects of the economy. Opposition to Vargas and his repressive policies was building in Brazil by 1945, but by then he was turning increasingly to the left, seeking support from organized labor and coming to terms with the Communist party leaders whom he had imprisoned.

Under criticism from both the right and the left, Vargas committed suicide in 1954. His suicide note emphasized his populist ties and blamed his death on Brazil's enemies:

> Once more the forces and interests which work against the people have organized themselves again and emerge against me. . . . I was a slave to the people, and today I am freeing myself for eternal life. But this people whose slave I was will no longer be slave to anyone. My sacrifice will remain forever in their souls and my blood will be the price of their ransom.

Much of Brazilian history since Vargas has been a struggle over his mantle of leadership. In death, Vargas became a martyr and a nationalist hero, even to those groups he had repressed and imprisoned in the 1930s.

## Argentina: Populism, Perón, and the Military

Argentina was something of an anomaly. There, the middle-class Radical party, which had held power during the 1920s, fell when the economy collapsed in 1929. A military coup backed by a strange coalition of nationalists, fascists, and socialists seized power, hoping to return Argentina to the golden days of the great export boom of the 1890s. The coup failed. Argentina became more dependent as foreign investments increased and markets for Argentine products declined. However, industry was growing, and with it grew the numbers and strength of industrial workers, many of whom had migrated from the countryside. By the 1940s the workers were organized in two major labor federations. Conservative governments backed by the traditional military held power through the 1930s, but in 1943 a military group once again took control of the government.

The new military rulers were nationalists who wanted to industrialize and modernize Argentina and make it the dominant power of South America. Some were admirers of the fascist powers and their programs. Although many of them were distrustful of the workers, the man who became the dominant political force in Argentina recognized the need to create a broader basis of support for the government. Colonel **Juan D. Perón** (1895–1974) emerged as a power in the government. Using his position in the Ministry of Labor, he appealed to workers, raising their salaries, improving their benefits, and generally supporting their demands. Attempts to displace him failed, and he increasingly gained popular support, aided by his wife, Eva Duarte, known as Evita. She became a public spokesperson for Perón among the lower classes. During World War II, Perón's admiration for the Axis powers was well known. In 1946, when the United States tried to discredit him because of his fascist sympathies, he turned the attempt into nationalist support for his presidential campaign.

As president, Perón forged an alliance among the workers, the industrialists, and the military. Like Vargas in Brazil, he learned the effectiveness of the radio, the press, and public speeches in mobilizing public support. He depended on his personal charisma and on repression of opponents to maintain his rule. The Peronist program was couched in nationalistic terms. The government nationalized the foreign-owned railroads and telephone companies, as well as the petroleum resources. The foreign debt was paid off, and for a while the Argentine economy boomed in the immediate postwar years. But by 1949 there were economic problems again. Meanwhile, Perón ruled by a combination of inducements and repression, while Evita Perón became a symbol to the *descamisados*, or the poor and downtrodden, who saw in Peronism a glimmer of hope. Her death in 1952 at age 33 caused an outpouring of national grief.

Perón's regime was a populist government with a broader base than had ever been attempted in Argentina. Nevertheless, holding the interests of the various components of the coalition together became increasingly difficult as the economy worsened. A democratic opposition developed and complained of Perón's control of the press and his violation of civil liberties. Industrialists disliked the strength of labor organizations. The military worried that Perón would arm the workers and cut back on the military's gains. The Peronist party became more radical and began a campaign against the Catholic church. In 1955, anti-Perón military officers drove him into exile.

Argentina spent the next 20 years in the shadow of Perón. The Peronist party was banned, and a succession of military-supported civilian governments tried to resolve the nation's economic problems and its continuing political instability. But Peronism could survive even without Perón, and the mass of urban workers and the strongly Peronist unions continued to agitate for his programs, especially as austerity measures began to affect the living conditions of the working class. Perón and his new wife, Isabel, returned to Argentina in 1973, and they won the presidential election in that year—she as vice president. When Perón died the next year, however, it was clear that Argentina's problems could not be solved by the old formulas. Argentina slid once more into military dictatorship.

## The Militarization of Japan

Authoritarian military rule took over in Japan even earlier than in the West. Not fascist outright, it had some clear affinities with the new regimes in Europe, including its aggressive military stance. As early as 1931, as the Depression hit Japan hard, military officials completed a conquest of the Chinese province of Manchuria, without the backing of the civilian government (Map 34.3).

As political divisions increased in response to the initial impact of the Depression, a variety of nationalist groups emerged, some advocating a return to Shintoist or Confucian principles against the more Western values of urban Japan. This was more than a political response to economic depression. As in Germany, a variety of groups used the occasion for a more sweeping protest against parliamentary forms; nationalism here seemed a counterpoise to alien Western values. Older military officers joined some bureaucrats in urging a more authoritarian state that could ignore party politics; some wanted further military expansion to protect Japan from the uncertainties of the world economy by providing secure markets and sources of raw materials.

In May 1932 a group of younger army officers attacked key government and banking officers and murdered the prime minister. They did not take over the state directly, but for the next four years moderate military leaders headed the executive branch, frustrating both the military firebrands and the political parties. Another attempted military coup in 1936 was put down by forces controlled by the established admirals and generals, but this group, including General Tojo Hideki, increasingly interfered with civilian cabinets, blocking the appointment of most liberal bureaucrats. The result, after 1936, was a series of increasingly militaristic prime ministers.

The military superseded civilian politics, particularly when renewed wars broke out between Japan and China in 1937. Japan, continuing to press the ruling Chinese government lest it gain sufficient strength to threaten Japanese gains, became involved in a skirmish with Chinese forces in the Beijing area in 1937. Fighting spread, initially quite unplanned. Most Japanese military leaders opposed more general war, arguing that the nation's only interest was to defend Manchuria and Korea. However, influential figures on the General Staff held that China's armies should be decisively defeated to prevent trouble in the future. This view prevailed, and Japanese forces quickly occupied the cities and railroads of eastern China. Several devastating bombing raids accompanied this invasion.

Although Japanese voters had continued to prefer more moderate policies, their wishes were swept away by military leaders in a tide of growing nationalism. By the end of 1938 Japan controlled a substantial regional empire, including Manchuria, Korea, and Taiwan (Formosa), within which the nation sold half its exports and from which it bought more than 40 percent of all imports, particularly food and raw materials. Both the military leadership, eager to justify further modernization of Japan's weaponry and to consolidate political control, and economic leaders, interested in rich resources of other parts of Asia—such as the rubber of British Malaya or the oil of the Dutch East Indies—soon pressed for wider conquests as Japan surged into World War II (Map 34.4).

Japan's Territorial Ambition

As war in Asia expanded, well before the formal outbreak of World War II, Japan also tightened its hold over its earlier empire, particularly in Korea. Efforts to suppress Korean culture were stepped up, and the Japanese military brutally put down any resistance. Japanese language and habits were forced on Korean teachers. Japanese industrialists dominated Korean resources, while peasants were required to produce rice for Japan at the expense of nutrition in Korea itself. Young men were pressed into labor groups, as the population was exhorted to join the Japanese people in "training to endure hardship."

## Industrialization and Recovery

Japan's policies in the 1930s quelled the effects of the Depression for Japan even more fully than Hitler's policies were able to do for Germany. While the Depression initially hit Japan hard—half of all factories were closed by 1931, children in some areas were reduced to begging for food from passengers on passing trains, and farmers were eating tree bark—active government policies quickly responded. As a result, Japan suffered far less than many Western nations did during the Depression decade as a whole. Under the 1930s minister of finance, Korekiyo Takahashi, the government increased its spending to provide jobs, which in turn generated new demands for food and manufactured items, yielding not only the export boom but also the virtual elimination of unemployment by 1936. The same policy helped support government military purchasing, but it is not clear that this constituted an essential response.

Indeed, Japan made a full turn toward industrialization after 1931, its economy growing much more rapidly than that of the West and rivaling the surge of the Soviet Union. Production of iron, steel, and chemicals soared. The spread of electric power was the most rapid in the world. The number of workers, mainly men, in the leading industries rose sevenfold during the 1930s. Quality of production increased as assembly-line methods were introduced, and Japanese manufacturing goods began to rival those of the West. As the level of Japanese industrial goods rose, the first Western outcry against Japanese exports was produced—even though in 1936 the Japanese controlled only 3.6 percent of world trade.

Japan also initiated a series of new industrial policies designed to stabilize the labor force and prevent social unrest. These paralleled the growing emphasis on mass patriotism and group loyalty developed by the government. Big companies began to offer lifetime contracts to a minority of skilled workers and to develop company entertainments and other activities designed to promote hard work and devotion. These distinctive Japanese policies, not part of its initial industrialization, proved to be a durable feature of Japanese society.

By 1937 Japan boasted the third largest and the newest merchant marine in the world. The nation became self-sufficient in machine tools and scientific equipment, the fruit of the growth in technical training. The basis had been set for the more significant economic expansion of the later 20th century, delayed by Japan's dash into World War II.

## Stalinism in the Soviet Union

The Soviet Union was buffered from the Depression by its separate economy. Soviet leaders made much of the nation's ongoing industrial growth, even as Western economies collapsed. But the 1930s saw a tightening of the communist system under Stalin in ways that echoed authoritarian responses in other societies.

Stalin devoted himself to a double task: to make the Soviet Union a fully industrial society and to do so under full control of the state rather than through private initiative and individual ownership of producing

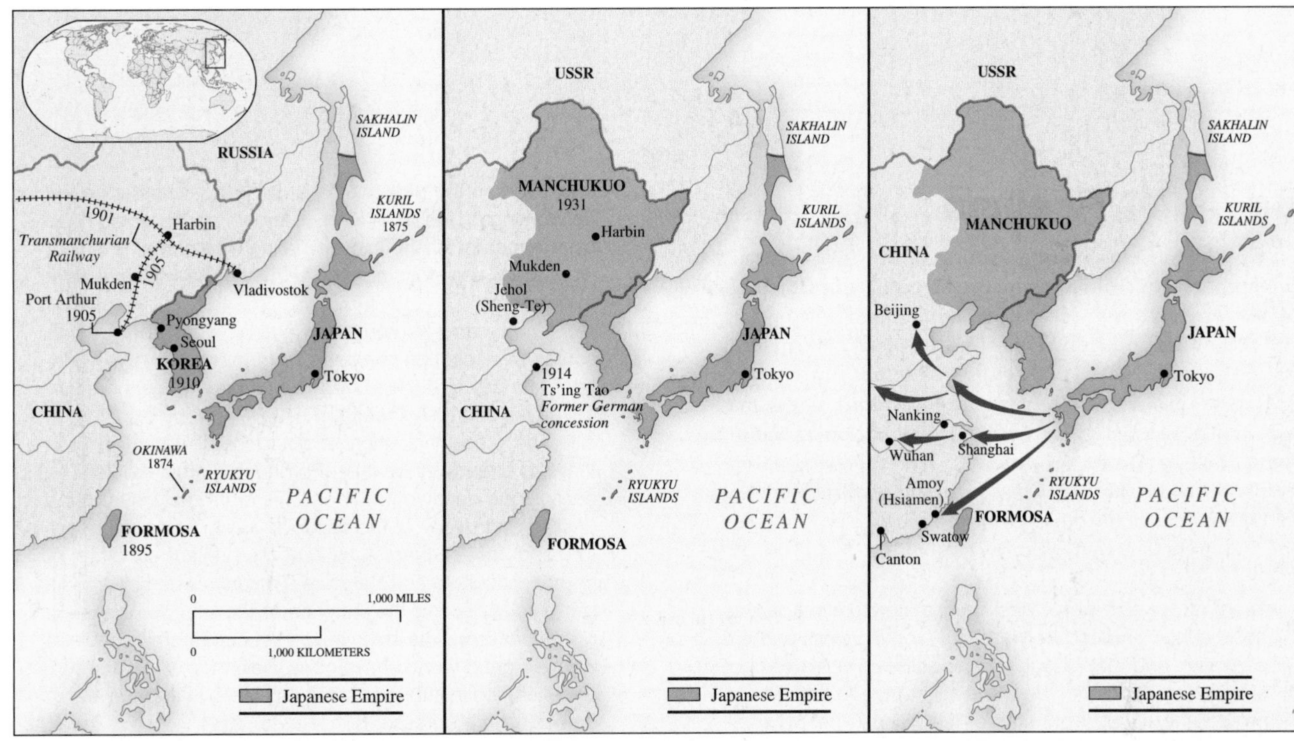


MAP 34.4 The Expansion of Japan to the Outbreak of World War II

Stalin Demands Rapid Industrialization of the U.S.S.R.

property. He reversed the more experimental mood of the 1920s, including tolerance for small private businesses and wealthy peasant farmers. In essence, Stalin wanted modernization but with a revolutionary, noncapitalist twist. Although he was willing to borrow Western techniques and advice, importing a small number of foreign engineers, for example, he insisted on Soviet control and largely Soviet endeavor.

## Economic Policies

A massive program to collectivize agriculture began in 1928. Collectivization meant the creation of large, state-run farms, rather than individual holdings as in the West. Communist party agitators pressed peasants to join in collectives. In addition to being distinctly socialistic, the collectives movement also further offered, at least in theory, the chance to mechanize agriculture most effectively, as collective farms could group scarce equipment, such as tractors and harvesters. Collectivization also allowed more efficient control over peasants, reflecting, though in radical new form, a traditional reluctance to leave peasants to their own devices. Government and party control was desirable not only for political reasons, but also because Stalin's hopes for a speedup of industrialization required that resources be taken from peasants, through taxation, in order to provide capital for industry.

The peasantry responded to collectivization with a decidedly mixed voice. Many laborers, resentful of kulak wealth, initially welcomed the opportunity to have more direct access to land. But most kulaks refused to cooperate voluntarily, often destroying livestock and other property rather than submit to collectivization. Devastating famine resulted from Stalin's insistence on pressing forward. In addition, millions of kulaks were killed or deported to Siberia during the early 1930s, in one of the most brutal oppressions of what turned out to be a brutal century in world history. Gradually, rural resistance collapsed and production began to increase once again; the decimation of the kulaks may indeed have weakened opportunities to oppose Stalin's increasingly authoritarian hold for a generation or two. But collectivization, though increasingly thorough, was not a smash success, for even those peasants who participated often seemed fairly unmotivated. Although the collective farms allowed peasants small plots of their own, as well as job security and considerable propagandizing by the omnipresent Communist party members, they created an atmosphere of factorylike discipline and rigid planning from above that antagonized many peasants. The centralized planning process allowed few incentives for special efforts and often complicated a smooth flow of supplies and equipment, a problem also exacerbated by the Stalinist regime's priority concentration on the industrial sector. Agricultural production remained a major

DOCUMENT

## Socialist Realism

One of the most fascinating features of the Soviet system was the attempt to create a distinctive art, different from the art of Western cultures (seen as decadent) and appropriate to the communist mission. This effort involved censorship and forced orthodoxy, but it also was an attempt to resolve earlier Russian problems of relating formal culture to the masses and trying to preserve a national distinctiveness amid the seductions of Western influence. The following effort to define Soviet artistic policy was written by Andrey Zhdanov in 1934, the year Stalin made him the party's spokesperson at the Congress of Soviet Writers.

There is not and never has been a literature making its basic subject-matter the life of the working class and the peasantry and their struggle for socialism. There does not exist in any country in the world a literature to defend and protect the equality of rights of the working people of all nations and the equality of rights of women. There is not, nor can there be in any bourgeois country, a literature to wage consistent war on all obscurantism, mysticism, hierarchic religious attitudes, and threats of hell-fire, as our literature does.

Only Soviet literature could become and has in fact become such an advanced, thought-imbued literature. It is one flesh and blood with our socialist construction. . . .

What can the bourgeois writer write or think of, where can he find passion, if the worker in the capitalist countries is not sure of his tomorrow, does not know whether he will have work, if the peasant does not know whether he will be working on his bit of land or thrown on the scrap heap by a capitalist crisis, if the working intellectual is out of work today and does not know whether he will have work tomorrow?

What can the bourgeois author write about, what source of inspiration can there be for him, when the world, from one day to the next, may be plunged once more into the abyss of a new imperialist war?

The present position of bourgeois literature is such that it is already incapable of producing great works. The decline and decay of bourgeois literature derives from the decline and decay of the capitalist system and are a feature and aspect characteristic of the present condition of bourgeois culture and literature. The days when bourgeois literature, reflecting the victories of the bourgeois system over feudalism, was in the heyday of capitalism capable of creating great works, have gone, never to return. Today a degeneration in subject matter, in talents, in authors and in heroes, is in progress. . . .

A riot of mysticism, religious mania, and pornography is characteristic of the decline and decay of bourgeois culture. The "celebrities" of that bourgeois literature which has sold its pen to capital are today thieves, detectives, prostitutes, pimps, and gangsters. . . .

The proletariat of the capitalist countries is already forging its army of writers and artists—revolutionary writers, the representatives of whom we are glad to be able to welcome here today at the first Soviet Writers' Congress. The number of revolutionary writers in the capitalist countries is still small but it is growing and will grow with every

weakness in the Soviet economy, demanding a higher percentage of the labor force than was common under industrialization.

The collective farms did, however, allow normally adequate if minimal food supplies once the messy transition period had ended, and they did free excess workers to be channeled into the ranks of urban labor. The late 1920s and early 1930s saw a massive flow of unskilled workers into the cities, as the Soviet Union's industrialization, already launched, shifted into high gear.

If Stalin's approach to agriculture had serious flaws, his handling of industry was in most ways a stunning success. A system of **five-year plans** under the state planning commission began to set clear priorities for industrial development, including expected output levels and new facilities. The government constructed massive factories in metallurgy, mining, and electric power to make the Soviet Union an industrial country independent of Western-dominated world banking and trading patterns. There was more than a hint of Peter the Great's policies here, in updating the economy without really westernizing it, save that industrialization constituted a more massive departure than anything Peter had contemplated. The focus, as earlier, was on heavy industry, which built on the nation's great natural resources and also served to prepare for possible war with Hitler's anticommunist Germany.

This distinctive industrialization, which slighted consumer goods production, was to remain characteristic of the Soviet version of industrial society. Further, Stalin sought to create an alternative not simply to private business ownership but also to the profit-oriented market mechanisms of the West. Thus he relied not on price competition but on formal, centralized resource allocation to distribute equipment and supplies. This led to many bottlenecks and considerable waste, as day's sharpening of the class struggle, with the growing strength of the world proletarian revolution.

We are firmly convinced that the few dozen foreign comrades we have welcomed here constitute the kernel, the embryo, of a mighty army of proletarian writers to be created by the world proletarian revolution in foreign countries. . . .

Comrade Stalin has called our writers "engineers of the human soul." What does this mean? What obligations does such an appellation put upon you?

It means, in the first place, that you must know life to be able to depict it truthfully in artistic creations, to depict it neither "scholastically" nor lifelessly, nor simply as "objective reality," but rather as reality in its revolutionary development. The truthfulness and historical exactitude of the artistic image must be linked with the task of ideological transformation, of the education of the working people in the spirit of socialism. This method in fiction and literary criticism is what we call the method of socialist realism.

Our Soviet literature is not afraid of being called tendentious, for in the epoch of class struggle there is not and cannot be "apolitical" literature.

And it seems to me that any and every Soviet writer may say to any dull-witted bourgeois, to any philistine or to any bourgeois writers who speak of the tendentiousness of our literature: "Yes, our Soviet literature is tendentious and we are proud of it, for our tendentiousness is to free the working people—and the whole of mankind—from the yoke of capitalist slavery."

To be an engineer of the human soul is to stand foursquare on real life. And this in turn means a break with old-style romanticism, with the romanticism which depicted a nonexistent life and nonexistent heroes, drawing the reader away from the contradictions and shackles of life into an unrealizable and utopian world. Romanticism is not alien to our literature, a literature standing firmly on a materialistic basis, but ours is a romanticism of a new type, revolutionary romanticism. We say that socialist realism is the fundamental method of Soviet fiction and literary criticism, and this implies that revolutionary romanticism will appear as an integral part of any literary creation, since the whole life of our Party, of the working class and its struggle, is a fusion of the hardest, most matter-of-fact practical work, with the greatest heroism and the vastest perspectives. The strength of our Party has always lain in the fact that it has united and unites efficiency and practicality with broad vision, with an incessant forward striving and the struggle to build a communist society.

Soviet literature must be able to portray our heroes and to see our tomorrow. This will not be utopian since our tomorrow is being prepared by planned and conscious work today.

**Questions** What were the reasons for culture according to Stalinist intellectuals? How did Soviet cultural leaders analyze Western intellectual life? What were the proper tasks of an artist in Soviet society? How were these tasks expressed in socialist realism? What would the Soviet response be to Western intellectuals who claimed objectivity for their work?

quotas for individual factories were set in Moscow, but there was no question that rapid industrial growth occurred. During the first two five-year plans, to 1937—that is, during the same period that the West was mired in the Depression—Soviet output of machinery and metal products grew 14-fold. The Soviet Union had become the world's third industrial power, behind only Germany and the United States. A long history of backwardness seemed to have ended.

## Toward an Industrial Society

For all its distinctive features, the industrialization process in the Soviet Union produced many results similar to those in the West. Increasing numbers of people were crowded into cities, often cramped in inadequate housing stock. Factory discipline was strict, as communist managers sought to instill new habits in a peasant-derived workforce. Incentive procedures were introduced to motivate workers to higher production. Particularly capable workers received bonuses and also elaborate public awards for their service to society. At the same time, communist policy quickly established a network of welfare services, surpassing the West in this area and reversing decades of tsarist neglect. Workers had meeting houses and recreational programs, often including vacations on the Black Sea, as well as protection in cases of illness and old age. Soviet industrial society provided only modest standards of living at this point, but a host of collective activities compensated to some degree.

Finally, although Soviet industry was directed from the top, with no legal outlet for worker grievances—strikes were outlawed, and the sole trade union movement was controlled by the party—worker concerns were studied, and identified problems were addressed.

The Soviet Union under Stalin used force and authority, but it also recognized the importance of maintaining worker support—so, informally, laborers were consulted as well.

## Totalitarian Rule

Stalinism instituted new controls over intellectual life. In the arts, Stalin insisted on uplifting styles that differed from the modern art themes of the West, which he condemned as capitalist decadence. (Hitler and Stalin, bitter enemies, both viewed contemporary Western culture as dangerous.) Artists and writers who did not toe the line risked exile to Siberian prison camps, and party loyalists in groups like the Writers Union helped ferret out dissidents. **Socialist realism** was the dominant school, emphasizing heroic idealizations of workers, soldiers, and peasants (Figure 34.12). Science was also controlled. Stalin clamped down hard on free scientific inquiry, insisting for example that evolutionary biology was wrong because it contradicted Marxism. A number of scientists were ruined by government persecution.

Stalin also combined his industrialization program with a new intensification of government police procedures; he used party and state apparatus to monopolize power, even more thoroughly than Hitler's totalitarian state attempted. Real and imagined opponents of his version of communism were executed. During the great purge of party leaders that culminated in 1937–1938, hundreds of people were intimidated into confessing imaginary crimes against the state, and most of them were then put to death. Many thousands more were sent to Siberian labor camps. News outlets were monopolized by the state and the party, and informal meetings also risked a visit from the ubiquitous secret police, renamed the MVD in 1934. Party congresses and meetings of the executive committee, or **Politburo,** became mere rubber stamps. An atmosphere of terror spread.

Stalin's purges, which included top army officials, ironically weakened the nation's ability to respond to growing foreign policy problems, notably the rising threat of Hitler. Soviet diplomatic initiatives after the 1917 revolution had been unwontedly modest, given the nation's traditions, largely because of the intense concentration on internal development. Diplomatic relations with major nations were gradually reestablished as the fact of communist leadership was accepted, and the Soviet Union was allowed into the League of Nations. A few secret military negotiations, as with Turkey in the early 1920s, showed a flicker of interest in more active diplomacy, and of course the nations continued to encourage and often guide internal Communist party activities in many other countries.

Hitler's rise was a clear signal that more active concern was necessary. A strong Germany was inevitably a threat to Russia from the west, and Hitler was vocal about his scorn for Slavic peoples and communism, and about his desire to create a "living room" for Germany to the east. Stalin initially hoped that he could

**FIGURE 34.12** In his 1949 painting *Creative Fellowship*, Soviet artist Shcherbakov shows the cooperation of scientists and workers in an idealized factory setting. The painting exemplifies the theories and purposes of socialist realism.

cooperate with the Western democracies in blocking the German threat. The Soviet Union thus tried to participate in a common response to German and Italian intervention during the Spanish Civil War, in 1936–1937. But France and Britain were incapable of forceful action and were in any event almost as suspicious of the Soviets as of the Nazis. So the Soviet Union, unready for war and greatly disappointed in the West, signed a historic agreement with Hitler in 1939. This pact bought some time for greater war preparation and also enabled Soviet troops to attack eastern Poland and Finland in an effort to regain territories lost in World War I. Here was the first sign of a revival of Russia's long interest in conquest, which would be intensified by the experience of World War II.

## GLOBAL CONNECTIONS

## Economic Depression, Authoritarian Response, and Democratic Retreat

The Great Depression of the 1930s promoted a growing wave of nationalist reactions and further weakened global ties. Western European countries and the United States increased their tariffs and refused to collaborate in measures the might have alleviated economic dislocation. Their narrow policies made economic collapse even worse. Japan, badly hurt by a new U.S. tariff that cut into silk exports, increased its own nationalism; here was the context for the growing power of younger army officers pushing for overseas expansion. Japan began to think of its own new empire in east Asia that could shield it from worldwide economic trends. Nazi Germany also pulled out of the international community, seeking to make Germany as economically self-sufficient as possible. The Soviet Union still mouthed communist commitment to internationalism, but in fact Stalin concentrated on standing alone, in a nationalist and isolationist version of the great Russian Revolution. The world was falling into pieces, and no society, certainly not the beleaguered West, seemed capable of putting it back together.

### Further Readings

Sally Marks, *The Ebbing of European Ascendancy: An International History of the World: 1914–1945* (2002), is the new standard introduction to the diplomacy of the period. The previous standard, her own *The Illusion of Peace* (1976), remains useful due to its brevity and clarity. Good overall studies of the political revolutions of the period include Eric Wolf, *Peasant Wars of the Twentieth Century* (1965); Theda Skocpol, *States and Social Revolutions* (1970); and John Dunn, *Modern Revolutions* (1972). Mark N. Katz, *Reflections on Revolutions* (1999), is an accessible survey of historical theories of revolution.

On the Russian Revolution, Sheila Fitzpatrick, *The Russian Revolution* (1994), is an overview with a rich bibliography. See also E. H. Carr, *The Bolshevik Revolution, 1917–1923* (1978). Rex Wade, *The Russian Revolution, 1917* (2000), is a comprehensive social and political history of the revolution's early years. Edmund Wilson, *To the Finland Station* (1972), offers a dramatic account of the revolution's early phase and the philosophical currents that informed Bolshevik thinking. On specific social groups, see John Keep, *The Russian Revolution: A Study in Mass Mobilization* (1976); and Victoria Bonnell, *Roots of Rebellion: Workers' Politics and Organizations in St. Petersburg and Moscow, 1900–1914* (1983). Leon Trotsky's *History of the Russian Revolution,* a gripping narrative by a participant, surveys social, economic, and political dimensions of the revolution.

On fascism in Italy, R. J. B. Bosworth, *The Italian Dictatorship: Problems and Perspectives in the Interpretation of Mussolini and Fascism* (1998), traces changing historical thinking. Philip Morgan, *Italian Fascism, 1919–1945* (1995), provides a general overview. Emilio Gentile, *The Sacralization of Politics in Fascist Italy,* trans. Keith Botsford (1996), examines popular political culture. C. F. Delzell, *Mediterranean Fascism, 1919–1945* (1970), provides documents and primary sources.

The economic history of Latin America is summarized in the classic by Brazilian economist Celso Furtado, *Economic Development of Latin America* (1976), and in John Sheahan, *Patterns of Development in Latin America* (1987). There are many good studies of Latin American politics, but Guillermo O'Donnell's *Modernization and Bureaucratic Authoritarianism* (1973) has influenced much recent scholarship. Also useful are Alan Knight's *The Mexican Revolution,* 2 vols. (1986), and John M. Hart's *Revolutionary Mexico* (1987), which provide excellent analyses of that event. Freidrich Katz, *The Life and Times of Pancho Villa* (1998), is an outstanding biography.

On the cultural aspects of the U.S. influence on Latin America there is Gilbert Joseph et al., eds., *Close Encounters Empire* (1998). The role of the United States is discussed in Abraham Lowenthal, *Partners in Conflict: The United States and Latin America* (1987). Lester D. Langley's *The United States and the Caribbean in the Twentieth Century* (1989) gives a clear account of the recent history of that region, and Walter La Feber's *Inevitable Revolutions* (1984) is a critical assessment of U.S. policy in Central America.

For the United States, William Leuchtenburg's *The Perils of Prosperity, 1914–32* (1958) and David Joseph Goldberg's *Discontented America: The United States in the 1920s* (1999) are both useful introductions. Robert Cruden, *Body and Soul: The Making of American Modernism* (2000), and Lynn Dumenil and Eric Foner, *The Modern Temper: American Culture and Society in the 1920s* (1995), offer intriguing analyses of the period. Robert Stern, Gregory Gilmartin, and Thomas Mellins, *New York: 1930* (1987), examines American architecture and urbanism between the two world wars. Steve Watson, *The Harlem Renaissance* (1995), is unsurpassed as a general study of African American culture and society in the "Roaring Twenties." Paula Fass, *The Damned and the Beautiful: American Youth in the 1920's* (1977), remains the best introduction to the "Lost Generation."

Some of the best general studies on China in the early 20th century include Lucian Bianco, *The Communist Revolution in China* (1967); C. P. Fitzgerald, *Birth of Communist China* (1964); Wolfgang Franke, *A Century of Chinese Revolution, 1851–1949* (1970); and Jonathan Spence, *The Search for Modern China* (1990). For firsthand accounts of conditions in the revolutionary era, see especially Graham Peck, *Two Kinds of Time* (1950); Edgar Snow, *Red Star over China* (1938); and Theodore White and Analee Jacoby, *Thunder out of China* (1946).

On the causes and onset of the Great Depression, C. Kindleberger's *The World in Depression, 1929–1939* (1973) is a solid introduction. See also J. Galbraith, *The Great Crash: 1929* (1980), and, for a useful collection of articles, W. Lacquer and G. L. Mosse, eds., *The Great Depression* (1970). Japan's experience is covered in I. Morris, ed., *Japan, 1931–1945: Militarism, Fascism, Japanism?* (1963).

Ronald Edsforth, *The New Deal: America's Response to the Great Depression* (2000), is a readable introduction to the political history of the New Deal. For a case study of social and political change in the United States during the period, see Lizabeth Cohen, *Making a New Deal: Industrial Workers in Chicago, 1919–1939* (1990). See also William Chafe, *Women and Equality: Changing Patterns in American Culture* (1984).

Alan Bullock's *Hitler: A Study in Tyranny* (1964) remains the best introduction to the Nazi leader. The methods and manner of the rise of German fascism are explored in William S. Allen, *Nazi Seizure of Power in a Single Town, 1930–1935* (1969); Russell G. Lemmons, *Goebbels and Der Angriff: Nazi Propaganda, 1927–1933* (1994); David Schoenbaum, *Hitler's Social Revolution: Class and Status in Nazi Germany* (1997); and Samuel W. Mitchum Jr., *Why Hitler? The Genesis of the Nazi Reich* (1996).

For a standard analysis of the Spanish Civil War, see Hugh Thomas, *The Spanish Civil War* (1977); Paul Preston, *The Spanish Civil War, 1936–1939* (1994); and Raymond Carr, *The Spanish Tragedy: The Civil War in Perspective* (1993). Peter Carroll's *The Odyssey of the Abraham Lincoln Brigade: Americans in the Spanish Civil War* (1994) deals with one of the civil war's many international aspects.

For the career of Juan Perón and Peronism, there is Frederick C. Turner, *Juan Peron and the Reshaping of Argentina* (1983). Robert M. Levine, *Getúlio Vargas: Father of the Poor* (1998), explores Brazil's corporatist state. Luis Aguilar, *Cuba 1933: Prologue to Revolution* (1972), demonstrates that, as in so many Asian and Latin American countries, the post–Second World War revolutionary movement in Cuba led by Fidel Castro was rooted in the events of the 1930s. Irwin Gellman's *Good Neighbor Diplomacy: United States Policy in Latin America, 1933–1945* (1980) and *Roosevelt and Batista: Good Neighbor Policy in Cuba, 1933–1945* (1973) address the U.S. role in shaping the regimes that were challenged by those later revolutionary movements.

On the Stalinist era, Robert Conquest's *The Great Terror: A Reassessment* (1990) and Roy Medvedev's *Let History Judge: The Origins and Consequences of Stalinism* (1989) are important studies of the period. Stephen Kotkin, *Magnetic Mountain: Stalinism as Civilization* (1995), assesses the cultural, social, and political impact of Stalin's industrialization program by looking at the experience of a planned industrial city. Sarah Davies, *Popular Opinion in Stalin's Russia: Terror, Propaganda, and Dissent, 1934–1941* (1997), offers a revealing portrayal of everyday cultural life under Stalin. Alan Bullock, *Hitler and Stalin: Parallel Lives* (1993), offers a comparative biography of the two totalitarian leaders.

Mark Selden's *The Yenan Way in Revolutionary China* (1971) provides the fullest account of the development of the communist movement after the Long March.

## On the Web

Web pages with links to superior sites exploring the Russian Revolution, including key documents of the revolution and addressing events such as the arrival of U.S. expeditionary forces in Siberia, are offered at http://www.uea.ac.uk/his/webcours/russia/links/, http://www.barnsdle.demon.co.uk/russ/rusrev.html, http://www.fordham.edu/halsall/mod/modsbook4.html#Russian%20Revolution, and http://www.historywiz.com/russia.htm. The initial program of the Russian Provisional Government (http://www.spartacus.schoolnet.co.uk/RUSprovisional.htm), its worst political blunders (http://www.historylearningsite.co.uk/provisional_government.htm), and the revealing shift of lyrical contents of the national anthem during the revolutionary period (http://www.stanford.edu/class/slavgen194a/hymn/anthem_history.htm and http://www.national-anthems.net/countries/index.php?id=rs#lyrics) are also accessible on the Web. The Lenin Archive (http://www.marxists.org/archive/lenin/) is a good place to find the works, a biography, and images of the Bolshevik leader. Other useful sites for further study of Lenin and other leaders of the early communist movement are http://www.marxists.org/ and http://www.anu.edu.au/polsci/marx/marx.html.

Benito Mussolini's vision of fascism can be glimpsed at http://www.fordham.edu/halsall/mod/mussolini-fascism.html. Italian fascism and life in fascist Italy is explained at http://www.library.wisc.edu/libraries/dpf/Fascism/Intro.html. An internal link at this site (http://www.library.wisc.edu/libraries/dpf/Fascism/Youth.html) offers a vivid look into the manner in which young fascists were indoctrinated via a magazine, whose front covers are alone worth a visit to the site.

Life in the United States in the 1920s is illuminated at http://cvip.fresno.com/~jsh33/roar.html and http://webtech.kennesaw.edu/jcheek3/roaring_twenties.htm. Other sites examine in detail the Scopes "Monkey Trial" (http://xroads.virginia.edu/~UG97/inherit/1925home.html), Prohibition (http://www.prohibition.history.ohio-state.edu/), and Harlem in the jazz age (http://www.nku.edu/~diesmanj/harlem_intro.html and http://www.si.umich.edu/CHICO/Harlem/index.html). The path that led to women's suffrage is traced at http://www.memory.loc.gov/ammem/naw/nawshome.html and http://www2.worldbook.com/features/whm/html/whm010.html, while the role of women peace activists during the Red Scare is examined at http://womhist.binghamton.edu/wilpf/intro.htm.

Links to sites illuminating key figures in the fall of the Qing empire can be found at a useful biography of Yuan Shikai at http://www.wikipedia.org/wiki/Yuan_Shikai. The emergence of Republican China, including Sun Yat-sen's early political platform, is treated at http://www-chaos.umd.edu/history/republican.html. The life of Chiang Kai-shek as seen against the background of nationalist politics is provided at http://www.wsu.edu:8001/~dee/MODCHINA/NATIONAL.HTM. An interesting reflection on the legacy of the student-led May Fourth Movement is offered at http://www.fas.harvard.edu/~asiactr/haq/199903/9903a003.htm. An excellent introduction to the life of Mao Zedong is provided at http://www.asiasource.org/society/mao.cfm.

The causes of the Great Depression are examined at http://www.sos.state.mi.us/history/museum/techstuf/depressn/teacup.html. Photographic records and personal remembrances of the Great Depression in the United States are recorded at http://memory.loc.gov/ammem/fsowhome.html and http://www.michigan.gov/hal/0,1607,7-160-17451_18670_18793-53511--,00.html. The American Dust Bowl is discussed at http://www.pbs.org/wgbh/amex/dustbowl/index.html.

The Franklin Delano Roosevelt Library (http://www.fdrlibrary.marist.edu/index.html) offers a gateway to the study of America's longest serving president. His response to the Great Depression, the New Deal, is examined at what is simply one of the finest of all Internet sites, http://www.newdeal.feri.org/.

The origins and future of Stalinism are explored at http://home.mira.net/~andy/bs/index.htm. Stalinism is seen through declassified documents at http://www.utoronto.ca/ceres/serap/. Stalin offers his view of Soviet industrialization at http://artsci.shu.edu/reesp/documents/Stalin—industrialization.htm. A transcript of one of Stalin's purge trials brings them alive at http://art-bin.com/art/omosc20e.html.

Leon Trotsky's role as an exiled critic of Stalin's regime (http://www.anu.edu.au/polsci/marx/contemp/pamsetc/socfrombel/sfb_7.htm) can be enlivened by a virtual visit to the house in Mexico where he was assassinated by a Stalinist agent (http://www.mexconnect.com/mex_/travel/jmitchell/jmtrotsky.html). Profiles of Nazi leaders and documents illustrating the rise of German fascism are offered at http://fcit.coedu.usf.edu/holocaust/people/perps.htm. The origins of Hitler's anti-Semitism are revealed at http://www2.h-net.msu.edu/~german/gtext/kaiserreich/hitler1.html. Trotsky's now classic critique of fascism has been made available at http://eserver.org/history/fighting-fascism/ and http://csf.colorado.edu/psn/marx/Other/Trotsky/Archive/1930-Ger.

A course lesson plan that offers a very good general introduction to German National Socialism and its totalitarian state and that includes useful definitions of key terms can be found at http://www.remember.org/guide/Facts.root.nazi.html.

The nature of the totalitarian state and the relationship between politics and art can be explored at http://www.calvin.edu/academic/cas/gpa/politart.htm and http://fcit.coedu.usf.edu/holocaust/arts/artReich.htm. The Spanish Civil War is analyzed at http://www.geocities.com/CapitolHill/9820/, while an excellent related photo file, including Robert Capra's famous "Moment of Death" photograph, can be found at http://history.sandiego.edu/cdr2/WW2Pics/13953.jpg.

The growth of militarism in Japan is traced at http://www.users.bigpond.com/battleforaustralia/historicalbackground/JapMilaggro.html. The course of that growth can be traced in the career of Hideki Tojo, minister for war and foreign affairs and prime minister of imperial Japan. Tojo's life, illuminated by selections from his diary, is explored at http://www.spartacus.schoolnet.co.uk/2WWtojo.htm. The cult of State Shinto used to drive the Japanese national and martial spirit is examined at http://www.britannica.com/eb/article-9069473.

The Web provides some vivid accounts of Latin America in the early decades of the 20th century at sites examining the lives of Pancho Villa (http://ojinaga.com/villa/ and http://www.mexconnect.com/mex_/history/panchovilla1.html), Fulgencio Batista (http://www.historyofcuba.com/history/batista.htm), Getúlio Vargas (search on http://historicaltextarchive.com/), and Juan Perón, whose followers maintain their own Web page (http://www.falange.us/peron.htm), which is devoid of critical analysis but has excellent contemporary photographs.

A guide to the poster art of the period, from revolution to counterrevolution and from women's rights to the Spanish Civil War, is provided at http://worldhistoryconnected.press.uiuc.edu/1.2/gilbert.html.

CHAPTER 35

# A Second Global Conflict and the End of the European World Order



Because the Japanese forces had come so swiftly to Padang early in World War II in the Pacific and had routed the Dutch defenders so thoroughly, Sukarno felt comfortable taking a walk through the town the morning after it had been captured. As the European global order in Asia came tumbling down in late 1941 and the first weeks of 1942, he explained to his young friend, Waworuntu, why the Japanese invaders ought to be seen as the liberators of the peoples of what was soon to be the nation of Indonesia, as well as much of the rest of southeast Asia. As he later recalled in an autobiographical account of his life related to an American reporter, Sukarno denounced the Dutch because they had long humiliated and exploited the colonized peoples of Indonesia. In addition, after posturing for centuries as a superior race, the Dutch had fled or stood by passively as the Japanese took their place as rulers of the archipelago.

In tandem with the successful Japanese sneak attack on Pearl Harbor in Hawaii, the Japanese navy and army had swept down into Malaya, Borneo, the Philippines, the Dutch East Indies (later Indonesia), and Burma (Map 35.1, p. 823). In a matter of weeks, the armed forces of the Western colonial powers—Britain, the Netherlands, and the United States, who had colonized these areas decades or in some cases centuries earlier, had been defeated. Like Sukarno and his fellow Indonesians, peoples across southeast Asia watched as bedraggled European and American soldiers, nurses, bureaucrats, and merchants were herded on long marches to prison camps; many died on the way to the camps and many more died in captivity. The Japanese intentionally staged marches, such as that depicted in Figure 35.1, to break the psychological hold "whites" had striven for centuries to establish over colonized peoples. And as they vanquished and discredited the former overlords, the Japanese sought to pass themselves off as liberators—fellow Asians whose rule would soon bring a new order and better lives to peoples so long subjected to alien rule.

Recalling this moment of profound transition decades later, Sukarno claimed that he saw through the Japanese propaganda, that he knew they were "fascists" and would be little better as rulers than the Western imperialists they had supplanted. Whether or not he had actually seen this outcome at

**FIGURE 35.1** The victorious Japanese armies subjected the tens of thousands European and American prisoners captured in their swift conquest of Southeast Asia in 1941–42 to forced marches to remote prison camps. Many of those who survived these "death marches" perished in the harsh conditions of internment. This photograph, stolen from Japanese files by Filipinos during Japan's three-year occupation, shows Japanese soldiers standing guard over American prisoners of war just before the "death march" began.

the time, his prediction was correct. The Indonesians and other peoples now colonized by the Japanese soon came to realize that they were going to be far more demanding and brutal masters than the Dutch, British, or Americans. Increasingly hard-pressed by the counterattacks of the Allied forces, the Japanese ruled their newly won empire with an iron fist. They tortured and killed those who were even suspected of being hostile and brutally repressed anyone who dared to disagree with, much less resist, their policies. The Japanese soon alienated the peasants and workers who made up the great majority of their subject peoples by introducing forced labor systems to extract the raw materials they so desperately needed to fight the Pacific war. Death rates in these *romusha* (forced labor) brigades often equaled or exceeded those for combatants in the war itself.

| 1930 C.E. | 1940 C.E. | 1950 C.E. | 1960 C.E. |
|---|---|---|---|
| **1930s** Great Depression<br>**1931** Japan invades Manchuria<br>**1933** Nazis come to power in Germany<br>**1935** Government of India Act<br>**1935** Italy invades Ethiopia<br>**1936–1939** Spanish Civil War<br>**1936–1939** Arab uprisings in Palestine<br>**1938** Germany's union (Anschluss) with Austria; Munich conference; German armies occupy the Sudetenland<br>**1939** Nazi-Soviet Pact<br>**1939** World War II begins | **1941** Japanese attack Pearl Harbor; United States enters World War II<br>**1941** German invasion of the Soviet Union<br>**1942** Fall of Singapore to the Japanese<br>**1942** Cripps mission to India; Quit India movement<br>**1945** Atomic bomb dropped on Japan; World War II ends; United Nations established<br>**1947** India and Pakistan gain independence, leading to wider decolonization<br>**1947** Cold war begins<br>**1948** Israel-Palestine partition, first Arab-Israeli war; beginning of apartheid legislation in South Africa | **1957** Ghana established as first independent African nation<br>**1958** Afrikaner Nationalist party declares independence of South Africa | **1960** Congo granted independence from Belgian rule<br>**1962** Algeria wins independence |

Before the coming of the Japanese, Sukarno had been involved for well over a decade in the nationalist struggle against the Dutch. His arrest, trial, imprisonment, and exile at the hands of the European colonizers had established him as a political personage to be reckoned with. As the Pacific war began to turn against the Japanese in mid-1942, the Japanese recruited nationalist leaders like Sukarno to mobilize colonized peoples to work and fight for their self-styled Japanese "liberators." Sukarno was later branded by some among the Allied leadership as a collaborator for becoming a front man for these campaigns. But a good deal of evidence bears out his impassioned insistence after the war that he was actually working to revitalize nationalist resistance to both the Japanese and Western colonizers.

A highly charismatic speaker, Sukarno cleverly foiled the intelligence officers who shadowed him at every step as he spoke at mass rallies and to paramilitary forces being trained by the Japanese. Drawing on incidents from the *wayang* shadow puppet plays based on the great Indian epics, the *Mahabharata* and the *Ramayana,* that had for centuries been central elements of Indonesian culture, Sukarno spoke in Javanese or Indonesian, so his Japanese handlers would not understand what he said. In a spirited oratorical style that suited the shadow dramas, he mocked the Japanese pretense that they were benevolent overlords by equating them with cruel rulers or treacherous characters from the epics.

Like many of the leaders of the decolonization movements that swept Asia and Africa after 1945, Sukarno used the power vacuum created by the weakening of the great powers on both sides during the Pacific war to arouse and organize nationalist resistance and, as the fighting wound down in 1945, to declare Indonesia's independence. Thus, as we shall see in this chapter, even more than the war between 1914 and 1918, World War II was a global conflict. The defeats suffered early in the war by the Western colonial powers doomed their empires. In part due to the success of their mobilizing efforts and agitation during the war years, Western-educated leaders like Sukarno in many cases inherited political power in the new nations that emerged from the fallen empires. Like Sukarno, many of these leaders lacked the skills and political base to deal effectively with the problems that faced their new states, which were often artificially patched together, ethnically and religiously divided, and economically disadvantaged. And many of these leaders shared Sukarno's fate, as his failures and the machinations of the superpowers locked in cold war rivalries led to his overthrow by military leaders who so often seized power in nations emerging from colonial rule.

## Old and New Causes of a Second World War

**The path to World War II was paved in large part by major social and political upheavals in several of the nations that had fought in World War I. Grievances related to World War I were compounded in each case by the economic havoc, and resulting social tensions, brought on by the Depression.**

The gradual militarization of Japan proceeded despite the solid majorities that moderate political parties continued to win until the end of the 1930s. And it developed in the context of a succession of regional diplomatic crises. During the later 1920s, nationalistic forces in China began to get the upper hand over the regional warlords who had dominated Chinese politics since the early 1900s. At the head of the Guomindang (or Nationalist) party, General Chiang Kai-shek in particular was able to win the support of intellectuals, students, the business classes, the rural gentry, and even members of the largely discredited Confucian elites and rival military leaders. His military successes against first the southern and later the northern warlords seemed destined to unify China under a strong central government for the first time in decades.

The success of the Guomindang worried Japan's army officers, who feared that a reunited China would move to resist the informal control the Japanese had exerted over Manchuria since their victory in the Russo-Japanese war in 1905. Fearful of curbs on their expansionist aims on the mainland and unimpeded by weak civilian governments at home, the Japanese military seized Manchuria in 1931 and proclaimed it the independent state of Manchukuo. The international crisis that resulted worked to the military's advantage because civilian politicians were reluctant to raise objections that might weaken Japan in negotiations with the United States and the other powers or undermine its armies of occupation in Manchuria and Korea, which the Japanese had declared a colony in 1910.

In contrast to the gradual shift of power to the military in Japan, the change of regimes in Germany was more abrupt and more radical. Parliamentary government in the Weimar era had been under siege from the time its civilian leaders had agreed to the armistice in 1918, and even more so after they signed the punitive treaty at Versailles. Weimar had survived these humiliations, civil war, and the hyperinflation of the mid-1920s, but just as economic recovery appeared to be gaining real momentum, the Great Depression struck. In the social discontent and political turmoil that followed, Adolf Hitler and the **National Socialist (Nazi)** party captured a steadily rising portion of the votes and parliamentary seats in a rapid succession of elections. The Nazis promised to put the German people back to work, restore political stability, and set in motion a remilitarization program that would allow Germany to throw off the shackles of what Hitler branded the diktat of Versailles. Hitler also promised to turn back the communist bid to capture power in Germany that had grown more and more serious as the Depression deepened. The threat of the communists within was linked to that of the Soviet Union to the east. From the early 1920s, Hitler and his lieutenants had stressed the need to invade and destroy the Soviet empire, and a key part of Hitler's racist vision for the future was to reduce the Russians and other Slavic peoples to virtual slaves in the service of the Aryan master race.

As we have seen in Chapter 34, a major part of the Nazis' political agenda once in power was a systematic dismantling of the political and diplomatic system created by the Versailles settlement. Rearmament from 1935, the militarization of the Rhineland in 1936, a forced union with Austria and the seizure of areas in Czechoslovakia where German-speakers were in the majority in 1938, and the occupation of the rest of the Czechoslovak republic the following year made a shambles of the agreements that had ended World War I. Hitler's successes emboldened Mussolini to embark on military adventures of his own, most infamously in Ethiopia, where Italian pilots bombed defenseless cities and highly mechanized armies made extensive use of poisonous gases against resistance forces armed with little more than rifles. The fascists stunned much of the rest of the world by routinely unleashing these weapons on a civilian population that had no means of defending itself.

Hitler and Mussolini also intervened militarily in the Spanish Civil War in the mid-1930s in the hope of establishing an allied regime. Once again, Mussolini's mechanized forces proved effective, this time against the overmatched, left-leaning armed forces of the Spanish republic. Both the Italian and German air forces used the Spanish conflict as a training ground for their air forces; in the absence of enemy planes or pilots, however, their main targets were ground forces and, ominously, civilians in Spain's cities and villages. The support of the Axis members was critical to Franco's destruction of the elected republican government and seizure of power, particularly since the Western democracies had refused to counter the Nazi and fascist interventions.

Excepting volunteer forces recruited in England, France, the United States, and other democracies, only the Soviet Union sought to provide military aid to Spain's republicans. Though valiant, these relief attempts proved futile in the face of relentless assaults by Franco's well-supplied legions and the Axis forces. Despite the critical assistance provided by his fellow fascists, Franco refused to join them in the global war that broke out soon after he had crushed the republic and begun a dictatorial rule in Spain that would last for decades.

## Unchecked Aggression and the Coming of War in Europe and the Pacific

**By the late 1930s, the leaders of the new totalitarian states acted on the lesson that international rivalries in the preceding decades seemed to offer–that blatant aggression would succeed and at little cost.**

World War II began officially on September 1, 1939, with the German invasion of Poland. But a succession of localized clashes, initiated by the Japanese seizure of Manchuria in 1931, can be seen as part of a global conflict that raged for well over a decade between 1930 and 1945. In contrast to the coming of World War I, which, as we have seen, the leaders of Europe more or less blundered into, World War II was provoked by the deliberate aggressions of Nazi Germany and a militarized and imperialist Japan. The failure of the Western democracies and the Soviet Union to respond resolutely to these challenges simply fed the militarist expansionism of what came to be called the Axis powers, in reference to the linkages, both real and imagined, between Berlin, Rome, and Tokyo.

Hitler and Mussolini discovered that Britain and France, and even more so the increasingly isolated United States, were quite willing to sacrifice small states, such as Spain and Czechoslovakia, in the false hope that fascist and especially Nazi territorial ambitions would be satisfied and thus war averted. Leaders like **Winston Churchill,** who warned that a major war was inevitable given Hitler's insatiable ambitions, were kept from power by voters who had no stomach for another world war. Rival politicians, such as Neville Chamberlain and the socialist leaders of France, also feared correctly that rearming as Churchill proposed would put an end to their ambitious schemes to build welfare states as an antidote to further economic depressions. But in the late 1930s, another round of provocative aggressions pushed the democracies into a war that none had the stomach for or was prepared at that point to fight.

Although Nazi aggressions traditionally have been stressed as the precipitants of World War II, the Japanese military actually moved first. In the second half of 1937, from their puppet state, Manchukuo, which had been carved out of Manchuria, they launched a massive invasion of China proper. Exploiting a trumped-up incident in early July that led to a fire fight between Japanese and Chinese troops, the army launched an ill-advised campaign to conquer the whole of China. Prominent naval leaders and civilian politicians had deep misgivings about this massive escalation of the war in China and were uneasy about American and British reactions to yet another major round of Japanese aggression. But they were largely cowed into silence by the threat of assassination by fanatical junior army officers and appeals to patriotic solidarity in a situation where Japanese soldiers were at risk.

At first, the advancing Japanese forces met with great success, occupying most of the coastal cities, including Shanghai and, by the end of 1938, Canton as well as the hinterlands behind cities in the north. The Japanese deployed extensive aerial bombing against Guomindang forces and especially the civilian population in the coastal cities. As Chinese resistance stiffened in some areas, Japanese soldiers resorted to draconian reprisals against both the Chinese fighters and civilians. In many instances, most infamously in the capture in December 1937 of the city of Nanjing, the evacuated Guomindang capital, Japanese forces took out their frustrations on retreating Chinese troops and the civilian population (Figure 35.2). The wanton destruction and

FIGURE 35.2 On December 13, 1937, Japanese troops took the city of Nanking and carried out orders to kill all of its inhabitants. Japanese officers used the occupation of the city as an opportunity to harden their troops for further battle, urging them to rape and torture Chinese POWs and civilians before killing them. Between 200,000 and 300,000 citizens of Nanking were murdered in the following weeks. The Japanese military sent news and photos of these killings back to Japan, where the mood of the country was so militaristic that the reports were hailed by many as good news.

IN DEPTH

## Total War

War had changed long before the 20th century. With state centralization, war lost its ritual characteristics. It became more commonly an all-out battle, using any tactics and weapons that would aid in victory. In other words, war became less restrained than it had been among less bureaucratized peoples who often used bluff and scare more than violence.

The 20th century most clearly saw the introduction of a fundamentally new kind of war, total war, in which vast resources and emotional commitments of the belligerent nations were marshaled to support military effort. The two world wars were thus novel not only in their geographic sweep, but in their mobilization of the major combatants. The features of total war also colored other forms of struggle, helping to explain brutal guerrilla and terrorist acts by groups not powerful enough to mount total wars but nonetheless affected by their methods and passions.

> *"[O]ne measure of total war was a blurring of the distinction between military and civilians, a distinction that had often limited war's impact earlier in world history."*

Total war resulted from the impact of industrialization on military effort, reflecting both the technological innovation and the organizational capacity that accompanied the industrial economy. Key steps in the development of total war emerged in the West at the end of the 18th century. The French Revolution, building new power for the state in contact with ordinary citizens, introduced mass conscription of men, forming larger armies than had ever before been possible. New citizen involvement was reflected in incitements to nationalism and stirring military songs, including aggressive national anthems—a new idea in itself. Industrial technology was first applied to war on a large scale in the U.S. Civil War. Railroads allowed wider movement of mass armies. Mass-produced guns and artillery made a mockery of earlier cavalry charges and redefined the kind of personal bravery needed to fight in war.

However, it was World War I that fully revealed the nature of total war. Steadily more destructive technology included battleships, submarines, tanks, airplanes, poison gas (which had been banned by international agreement before the war), machine guns, and long-range artillery. Organization for war included not only massive, compulsory recruitment—the draft—but also government control of economic activity via obligatory planning and rationing. Another factor was unprecedented control of media, not only through effective censorship and the containment of dissidents but through powerful propaganda designed to incite passionate, all-out commitment to the national cause and deep, unreasoned hatred of the enemy. Vivid posters, flaming speeches, and outright falsehood were combined in the emotional mobilization effort. All of these features returned with a vengeance in World War II, from the new technology of bombing, rocketry, and ultimately the atomic bomb to the enhanced economic mobilization organized by government planners.

The people most affected by the character of total war were the troops, who directly endured—bled from and died from—the new technology. But one measure of total war was a blurring of the distinction between military and civilians, a distinction that had often limited war's impact earlier in world history. Whole civilian populations, not just those unfortunate enough to be near the front lines, were forced into certain types of work and urged to certain types of beliefs. The bombing raids, including the German rockets directed against British cities late in World War II, subjected civilians to some of the most lethal weapons available as many belligerents deliberately focused their attacks on densely populated cities. Correspondingly, psychological suffering, though less common among civilians than among frontline soldiers, could spread throughout the populations involved in war.

Total war, like any major historical development, had mixed results. Greater government economic direction often included new measures to protect workers and give them a voice on management boards. Mobilization of the labor force often produced at least temporary breakthroughs for women. Intense efforts to organize technological research often produced side effects of more general economic benefit, such as the invention of synthetic rubber and other new materials.

Still, total war was notable especially for its devastation. The idea of throwing all possible resources into a military effort made war more economically disruptive than had been the case before. The emotions unleashed in total war produced embittered veterans who might vent their anger by attacking established political values. It certainly made postwar diplomacy more difficult. One result of total war was a tendency for the victor to be inflexible in negotiations at war's end. People who fought so hard found it difficult to treat enemies generously. The results of a quest for vengeance often produced new tensions that led directly, and quickly, to further conflict. War-induced passions and disruptions could also spark new violence at home; crime rates often soared not only right after the war ended (a traditional result) but for longer periods of time. Children's toys started to reflect the most modern weaponry. Thus, much of the nature of life in the 20th and 21st centuries has been determined by the consequences of total war.

---

**Questions** How did the experience of total war affect social and political patterns after World War II? Why do many historians believe that total war made rational peacetime settlements more difficult than did earlier types of warfare?

pillage, murder of innocent civilians, and rape of tens of thousands of undefended Chinese women that accompanied the Japanese occupation of the ancient city was but a prelude to the unparalleled human suffering of the world war that had now begun.

Deprived of the coastal cities and provinces that were the main centers of their power, Chiang and the Guomindang forces retreated up the Yangtze River, deep into the interior to the city of Chongqing, which became the nationalist capital for the rest of the war. Thus, long before the Japanese attacks on Pearl Harbor and Western colonies throughout southeast Asia in late 1941 that greatly expanded the war in Asia, Japan and China were engaged in a massive and deadly contest for control of all of east Asia.

The Japanese had plunged into war without coordination, or even serious consultation with their likely allies, Germany and Italy. In fact the Tripartite Pact, which joined the three expansive states in a loose alliance, was not signed until September 1940, when the war was well under way in both Europe and east Asia. In fact, Nazi military advisors had contributed greatly to the training of the Guomindang officers and troops that fought to contain the Japanese invasion of China.

With a pause to consolidate his stunning gains in central Europe from 1936 to 1938, Hitler now concentrated his forces on the drive to the Slavic east, which he had long staked out as the region that would provide living space for the Germanic master race. He bought time to prepare the way for the assault on the main target, the Soviet Union, by signing a nonaggression pact with Stalin in August 1939. Military emissaries of the two dictators negotiated a division of the smaller states that separated their empires, and Stalin swallowed short-term disappointments, such as the division of Poland, to prepare the Soviet Union for the invasion that most observers were now convinced was inevitable. Within days of signing the agreement, Hitler ordered the Wehrmacht, or Nazi armies, to overrun western Poland; the Soviets then occupied the eastern half of the country, which had been promised to them in the cynical pact just concluded with the Nazis.

The brutal Nazi invasion of Poland on September 1, 1939, put an end to any lingering doubts about Hitler's contempt for treaties and repeated assurances that Germany's territorial ambitions had been satisfied by the absorption of Czechoslovakia into the Nazi Reich (Figure 35.3). Although they were helpless to assist the overmatched Poles in their futile efforts to oppose the German advance, the British and French had no choice but to declare war on Germany. But the armies of both powers simply dug in along the defensive lines that had been established in eastern France in the late 1920s. There they waited for the Nazis to turn to the west for further conquests, and prepared for another defensive war like the one they had managed to survive, at such horrific cost, between 1914 and 1918. But a second major theater of what rapidly developed into a second world war had been opened, and this conflict would prove radically different in almost all major respects from the one to which the new configuration of powers in Europe and the Pacific believed they were committing themselves.

**FIGURE 35.3** Sober-faced and weeping Czechs watch the entry of the Nazi armies into Prague in the spring of 1939, as Hitler completes the takeover of the tiny democracy that was betrayed by the duplicity and cowardice of Allied leaders.

## The Conduct of a Second Global War

**The forces that gave rise to World War II meant that there would be more of a balance between a number of theaters spread across Europe, north Africa, and Asia. The largest and most costly front in lives lost and physical destruction resulted from the Nazi invasion of the vast expanses of the Soviet Union, but the Germans were also forced to defend a hastily built empire against an alliance that struck in north Africa, Italy, and by mid-1944 across northern Europe. After December 1941, the decade-long contest between Japan and China spread across southeast Asia and much of the Pacific; the United States and Great Britain emerged as Japan's most determined adversaries.**

The reluctance to rearm and react decisively displayed by both the Western democracies and the Soviet Union in the 1930s made possible crushing and almost unremitting victories and rapid territorial advances on the part of the main Axis powers, Germany and Japan, early in the war. But once the Nazis became bogged down in the expanses of the Russian steppes and the United States entered the war, the tide shifted steadily in favor of the Allies. Once the initial momentum of the Axis war machine was slowed, it became increasingly clear that the Anglo-American and Soviet alliance was decidedly more powerful in terms of population size, potential industrial production, technological innovation, and military capacity on land, in the seas, and in the air.

### Nazi Blitzkrieg, Stalemate, and the Long Retreat

As the Japanese bogged down in China and debated the necessity of tangling with the United States and the European colonial powers, the Nazi war machine captured France and the Low Countries with stunning speed, forced the British armies to beat a fast retreat to their island refuge, and then rolled over eastern Europe and drove deep into the Soviet Union (Map 35.1). Germany appeared unstoppable, and the fate of a large chunk of humanity seemed destined for a long period of tyrannical Nazi rule. From the outset, German strategy was centered on the concept of **blitzkrieg,** or "lightning war," which involved the rapid penetration of enemy territory by a combination of tanks and mechanized troop carriers, backup infantry, and supporting fighter aircraft and bombers. The effective deployment of these forces overwhelmed the Poles in 1939, and more critically routed the French and British within a matter of days in the spring of 1940, thereby accomplishing what the kaiser's armies failed to do through four long years of warfare between 1914 and 1918. German willingness to punish adversaries or civilian populations in areas that refused to yield greatly magnified the toll of death and destruction left in the wake of Hitler's armies. In early 1940, for example,

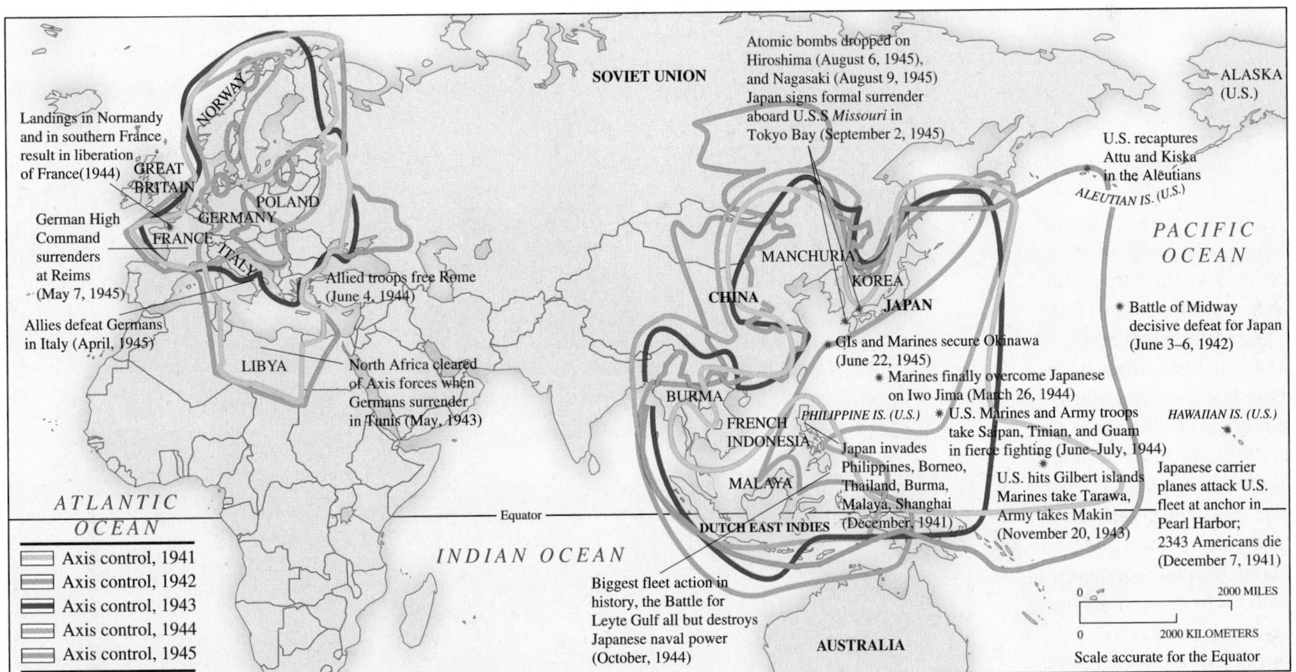


**MAP 35.1** The Main Theaters of World War II

the Dutch port of Rotterdam was virtually leveled by Nazi bombers, killing over 40,000 civilians.

The rapid collapse of France was, in part, a consequence of the divided and weak leadership the republic had displayed in the successive crises of the 1930s. Governments had come and gone as contemporaries quipped that they were moving in revolving doors. Left and right quarreled and stalemated over rearming, responding to the Nazis and allying with the British and the Soviets. When the war broke out, the citizenry of France was thoroughly demoralized, and the nation's defenses were outdated and extremely susceptible to the Wehrmacht's blitzkrieg offensives. By the summer of 1940, all of north and central France was in German hands; in the south, a Nazi puppet regime, centered on the city of **Vichy,** was in charge. With the Nazi occupations of Norway and Denmark in the preceding months, Britain alone of the western democracies in Europe survived. But what remained of the British armies had been driven from the continent, while the nation's people and cities were under heavy assault by a markedly superior German air force, which strove to open the way to cross-channel invasion by the much larger and more powerful land forces of the steadily growing Nazi empire.

Remarkably, under the courageous leadership of Winston Churchill, the British people weathered what their new prime minister had aptly pronounced the nation's "darkest hour." A smaller British air force proved able to withstand the Nazi air offensive, including saturation bombing of London and other British cities. Victory in what came to be known as the **Battle of Britain** was due to a mix of strong leadership by Churchill and a very able coalition cabinet, innovative air tactics made possible by the introduction of radar devices for tracking German assault aircraft, the bravery of Britain's royal family, and the high morale of the citizenry as a whole that the bombing raids seemed only to enhance. Unable to destroy Britain's air defenses or break the resolve of its people, Hitler and the Nazi high command had to abandon their plans for conquest of the British Isles. Without air superiority, the Germans could not prevent the Royal Navy from entering the channel and destroying the huge flotilla of landing craft that would be needed to carry the Nazi forces across the narrow but turbulent straits that had for nearly a millennium shielded Britain from outside invasion.

By mid-1941 the Germans controlled most of the continent of Europe and much of the Mediterranean. They had rescued the Italians' floundering campaign to conquer Albania and overrun Yugoslavia and Greece. They had conquered, or in the case of Sweden forced the neutralization of, the Scandinavian countries. They continued on to capture most of the islands of the Mediterranean and launched motorized offensives under the soon-to-be legendary commander Erwin Rommel (Figure 35.4) across north Africa and on to Egypt, with the goal of seizing the Suez Canal and cutting Britain off from its Asian empire. Once conquered, the hundreds of millions of peoples subjugated by Nazi aggression were compelled to provide resources, war materials, soldiers, and slave labor to a German war machine then being directed against even more ambitious targets.

The Nazi Empire in 1942

**FIGURE 35.4** Erwin Rommel was the Germans' most daring general, earning the nickname "the Desert Fox" when he fought in north Africa. In 1944, when it was clear that Germany was losing the war, he came under suspicion of having plotted to kill Hitler. Rommel was given the choice of taking poison and being buried as a hero or being tried for treason. He chose poison; his death was presented to the German public as the result of war injuries.

Frustrated by resolute British defiance, Hitler and the Nazi high command turned to the south and east to regain the momentum that had propelled them to so many victories in the first years of the war in Europe. As Nazi forces, numbering 3.5 million, drove the poorly prepared and understaffed Soviet forces out of Finland, Poland, the Baltic states, and much of Byelorussia and the Ukraine in the summer and early fall of 1941, Hitler's grandest victory of all—and unlimited access to cheap labor and such critical resources as oil—seemed within reach. But the Soviet armies, despite appalling losses, did not collapse; they retreated eastward rather than surrender. Stalin ordered Soviet industry relocated across the Ural Mountains to shield them from capture and German aerial attacks.

As with Napoleon's invasion nearly a century and a half earlier, Russian resistance stiffened as winter approached, and the German drive east stalled on the outskirts of Moscow and Leningrad. The harsh winter caught the German forces unprepared while their Russian adversaries used terrain and weather conditions they knew well to counterattack with ferocity on a wide front. The Nazis' mass killings and harsh treatment of the Slavic peoples, including the Ukrainians, many of whom initially were disposed to support the invaders, aroused guerrilla resistance by tens then hundreds of thousands of partisans, who fought behind German lines throughout the rest of the war.

Renewed German offensives in the spring of 1942 again drove deep into Russia but failed a second time to capture key cities like Moscow, Leningrad, and Stalingrad, and perhaps as critically the great Baku oil fields in the southern steppes. The two sides clashed in some of the greatest battles of the entire war—in fact of all human history—including Kursk, which featured thousands of tanks deployed (and destroyed) by each of the adversaries. As another winter approached, the Germans were further away from knocking the Soviets out of the war than the year before. In fact, the failed Nazi attempt to capture Stalingrad in the bitter winter of 1942 and 1943 ended in the destruction of an entire German army and proved a decisive turning point in the war in the east.

In 1943 the Red armies went on the offensive at numerous points along the overextended, undermanned, and vulnerable German front. With staggering losses in lives and equipment, the Nazi forces, despite Hitler's rantings that they die in place, began the long retreat from the Soviet Union. By late 1944, Red armies had cleared the Soviet Union of Nazi forces and captured Poland and much of east central Europe southward into the Balkans. As the Soviet forces advanced inexorably toward Germany, it was clear that the destruction of Hitler's "thousand-year reich" was only months away. It was also apparent that the almost unimaginable sacrifices and remarkable resilience of Russian soldiers, which included many women, had contributed mightily to the destruction of the vaunted Nazi armed forces.

## From Persecution to Genocide: Hitler's War Against the Jews

As the Nazi war machine bogged down in Russia, Hitler and his Nazi henchmen stepped up their vendetta against Gypsies, leftist politicians, homosexuals, and especially Jews. Jews, Polish intellectuals, and communists had been rounded up and killed in mass executions during the German offensives into eastern Europe and Russia in the early 1940s. But after a "final solution" for the "Jewish problem" was decided upon by prominent Nazi officials at the Wannsee Conference in February 1942, the regime directed its energies explicitly and systematically to genocide. The destruction, rather than the removal, of the Jewish people became the official policy of the Reich. The concentration camps that had been set up in the 1930s to incarcerate political enemies and groups branded as racially inferior—thus polluting to the Aryan people—were transformed into factories for the mass production of death.

Poland and the Death Camps

The more the war turned against Hitler and the Nazi high command, the more they pressed the genocidal campaign against the largely defenseless Jewish peoples of Europe. Vital resources were regularly diverted from the battle fronts for transportation, imprisonment, and mass murder in the camps, where the destruction of human life reached a frenetic pace in the last years of the regime. Jews and other "undesirables" were identified and arrested throughout the Nazi empire. Shipped to the camps in the east, those deemed physically fit were subjected to harsh forced labor that took a heavy toll in lives. The less fortunate, including the vast majority of the women and children, were systematically murdered, sometimes in experiments carried out by German physicians with the callous disregard for human suffering and humiliation that was a hallmark of the Nazi regime.

Emaciated Woman at Bergen-Belsen

As many as 12 million people were murdered in the genocidal orgy that has come to be known as the **Holocaust,** and which will perhaps prove to be what is remembered more than anything else about the Nazi regime. Of these, at least 6 million were Jews, and many millions of others were Slavic peoples mercilessly slaughtered on the Eastern Front. Without question, the Holocaust was by far the most costly genocide of the 20th century, which had begun with the Armenian massacres in 1915, and had the horrors of

The Holocaust: Memoirs from the Commandant of Auschwitz

Kampuchea, Rwanda, Bosnia, and Kosovo yet to come. With the possible exceptions of the massacres in the Soviet Ukraine in the 1930s and those carried out in the 1970s by the Khmer Rouge, more than any of the other major episodes of the 20th-century genocide, the Holocaust was notable for the degree to which it was premeditated, systematic, and carried out by the Nazi state apparatus and functionaries, who until the very end kept precise and detailed records of their noxious deeds. The Holocaust was at least passively abetted by denial on the part of the people of Germany and the occupied countries, though the Danes and Italians were notable for their resistance to Nazi demands that they turn over "their" Jews for incarceration.

The plight of the Jews of Europe was also greatly exacerbated by the refusal of the Western Allies to accept as immigrants any but the most affluent or skilled Jews fleeing Nazi atrocities, and by the failure of those same Allies to use their military assets to strike at the railway lines and killing chambers they clearly knew were in operation by the last months of the war. These responses to the Nazi horror only steeled the resolve of Zionist leaders in Palestine and elsewhere to facilitate, by negotiations with the hated Nazis if necessary, the flight of the European Jews. It also intensified their determination to establish a Jewish state in Palestine to ensure that there could never be another Holocaust.

Liberating the Concentration Camps

## Anglo-American Offensives, Encirclement, and the End of the 12-Year Reich

For nearly two years, the British were so absorbed in their own struggle for survival that they could provide little relief for their Soviet allies, hard-pressed by what some have seen as Hitler's foolhardy invasion of Russia. Even before the attack on Pearl Harbor in December 1941, the United States was providing substantial assistance, including military supplies, to beleaguered Britain. Franklin Roosevelt was quite openly sympathetic to the British cause and soon established a good working relationship with Churchill. American forces first entered the war in a major way in the campaigns to counter German U-boat attacks on shipping crossing the Atlantic. Then American tank divisions and infantry joined the British in reversing Rommel's gains in North Africa in 1942 and 1943. Having all but cleared Nazi forces from Africa and the Middle East, Anglo-American armies next struck across the Mediterranean at Sicily and then Italy proper. Their steady, but often costly, advance up the peninsula lasted into early 1945 but eventually toppled the fascist regime and prompted a Nazi takeover of northern Italy. Mussolini and the last of his many mistresses were captured and shot by partisans and enraged civilians and hung upside down on a lamp post near Lake Bellagio.

With significant German forces tied down on the Eastern Front and in Italy, the allied high command, with General Dwight Eisenhower at its head, prepared landings in northern France that would carry the war into the fortress the Nazis had been building in occupied Europe ever since their defeat in the Battle of Britain in 1940. In early June, against fierce resistance, the Allies established beachheads at Normandy, from which they launched liberation campaigns into the Low Countries and the rest of France. Despite Hitler's last-ditch effort to repel the invading Allied armies in what became known as the **Battle of the Bulge** in the winter of 1944–1945, by early in 1945, the Allies had invaded Germany from the west, while the Red armies were pouring in from the east.

Operation Overlord, Normandy, 1944

In late April, Russian and American troops linked up at the Elbe River, where they became caught up in spontaneous celebrations. The genuine camaraderie and mutual respect widely displayed by troops on both sides would soon be lost in high-stakes maneuvers by the political leaders in each camp to shape the postwar world order. On April 30, after haranguing his closest advisors for his betrayal by the German people, Adolf Hitler committed suicide in his Berlin bunker. Less than two weeks later, German military leaders surrendered their forces, putting an end to the war in the European and Mediterranean theaters. But the contest between the Anglo-American and Soviet allies for control of Germany had already commenced, and it would soon be extended to Europe as a whole and the rest of the world.

Allied Victory in Europe, 1942–1945

## The Rise and Fall of the Japanese Empire in the Pacific War

Long before their sneak attack on **Pearl Harbor** on December 7, 1941, the Japanese had been engaged in a major war on the Chinese mainland. Even after Pearl Harbor, roughly one-third of all Japanese military forces would remain bogged down in China, despite the sudden extension of the Japanese empire over much of southeast Asia and far out into the Pacific (Map 35.1). With the American Pacific fleet temporarily neutralized by the attack, Japan's combined air, sea, and army assaults quickly captured the colonial territories of the British in Hong Kong in south China as well as Malaya and Burma. They also overran the Dutch East Indies and the Philippines—despite more determined resistance—and completed the takeover of French Indochina. The Thais managed to stave off the invasion and occupation of Siam by retreating into neutrality and cooperating with the ascendant Japanese. Although Great Britain remained a major combatant, and Australia and New Zealand provided important support, the United States quickly emerged as the major counterforce to Japan's ever expanding Asian empire.

Though impressive in size and the speed with which it was formed, the Japanese empire soon proved highly vulnerable to the Allied forces committed to its destruction. The Japanese had risked alienating virtually all of the European colonial powers by their seizure of much of southeast Asia. They did so because they calculated that since the European metropoles had been overrun or were hard-pressed by the Nazis, the Europeans would not be able to reinforce their colonial enclaves. The Japanese leadership was also aware that the homeland's wartime economy was in desperate need of critical raw materials, including oil and staple foods, that could be imported from southeast Asia. But in their efforts to extract those resources, the Japanese imposed colonial regimes on the peoples of southeast Asia that were a good deal more brutally oppressive than those of any of the displaced Western colonizers. Over time, this produced growing resistance movements from Burma to the Philippines, which drew Japanese soldiers and substantial resources from the war in the Pacific against the advancing Allied forces.

Farthest Limits of Japanese Conquests

Resistance fighters also cooperated with British and American forces pushing into the area in the latter stages of the war. Southeast Asian guerrilla forces, which often had communist affiliations, played significant roles in sabotaging occupying forces and harassing retreating Japanese armies. The shipping lanes from distant colonial enclaves throughout southeast Asia also proved highly vulnerable to American submarines, which by late 1944 were able to sink a high percentage of the tons of foodstuffs and war materials shipped back to Japan.

The main front of the Pacific theater of the war centered on the widely scattered islands that Japan had begun to occupy before, and especially after, World War I, as well as those seized from the British and Americans after Pearl Harbor. No sooner had the Japanese garrisoned these enclaves than a hastily but well-prepared American advance into the central Pacific put them on the defensive. Having attacked Pearl Harbor when all of the major American aircraft carriers were at sea, the Japanese missed the chance to cripple the most potent weapons in the United States arsenal. Within six months, the United States naval and air forces fought the Japanese to a standoff at the **Battle of the Coral Sea.** In June, less than a month later, off **Midway Island,** they won a decisive victory over a powerful carrier force, commanded by Admiral Yamamoto, the architect of the Pearl Harbor attack. Once the Allied forces had gained the upper hand in the air and on the sea through these engagements, they could begin the assault on the double ring of Pacific island fortresses that protected the Japanese homeland (Figure 35.5).

War in the Pacific

**FIGURE 35.5** The United States advanced on Japan with the invasion and capture of Okinawa in March 1945. Note the enormous stores of munitions, food, and other supplies that have been brought ashore to supply the Allied armies that have only recently stormed the beaches of the island. This awesome material abundance touched off a new wave of "cargo cult" movements in the Pacific islands after the war.

DOCUMENT

## Japan and the Loss of World War II

Japan's defeat in World War II brought moral and material confusion. The government was so uncertain of the intentions of the victorious Americans that it evacuated its female employees to the countryside. The following excerpt from the 1945 diary of Yoshizawa Hisako (who became a writer on home economics) reveals more popular attitudes and the mixed ingredients that composed them. The passage also suggests how the American occupation force tried to present itself and the reception it received.

*August 15.* As I listened to the Emperor's voice announcing the surrender, every word acquired a special meaning and His Majesty's voice penetrated my mind. Tears streamed down my cheeks. I kept on telling myself that we must not fight ourselves and work hard for our common good. Yes, I pledged myself, I must work [for Japan's recovery].

The city was quiet.

I could not detect any special expression in people's faces. Were they too tired? However, somehow they seemed brighter, and I could catch an expression showing a sign of relief. It could have been a reflection of my own feelings. But I knew I could trust what I saw. . . .

The voluntary fighting unit was disbanded, and I was no longer a member of that unit. Each of us burned the insignia and other identifications.

I cannot foresee what kind of difficulty will befall me, but all I know is that I must learn to survive relying on my health and my will to live.

*August 16.* People do not wear expressions any different from other days. However, in place of a "good morning" or "good afternoon," people are now greeting each other with the phrase "What will become of us?"

During the morning, the city was still placed under air-raid alert.

My company announced that until everything becomes clearer, no female employees were to come to work and urged all of us to go to the countryside, adding that we should leave forwarding addresses. This measure was taken to conform to the step already taken by governmental bureaus. Are they thinking that the occupation army will do something to us girls? There are so many important questions we have to cope with, I cannot understand why governmental officials are so worried about these matters.

We did not have enough power and lost the war.

The Army continued to appeal to the people to resist the enemy to the end. This poses a lot of problems. People can show their true colors better when they are defeated than when they win. I just hope we, as a nation, can show our better side now.

Just because we have been defeated, I do not wish to see us destroying our national characteristics when we are dealing with foreign countries.

*August 17.* It was rumored that a number of lower echelon military officers were unhappy with the peace, and were making some secret moves. There were other rumors, and with the quiet evacuation of women and children from the cities, our fear seemed to have intensified. After all we have never experienced a defeat before. Our fear may simply be the manifestation of fear of the unknown.

Our airplanes dropped propaganda leaflets.

Keying their amphibious assaults on strategically vital islands, the joint air, sea, and land operations of the Allied forces had come within striking distance of Japan itself by early 1944, despite fierce and unrelenting Japanese resistance. In June of that year, the American air force began regular bomber assaults on the Japanese home islands. The high concentration of the Japanese population in urban areas and the wood and paper construction of most Japanese dwellings provided tempting targets for American bomber squadrons. In March 1945, General Curtis Le May, who was in charge of American air operations, ordered mass aerial bombardment of highly vulnerable Japanese cities. In Tokyo alone, these raids killed over 125,000 people, mostly civilians, and destroyed over 40 percent of the city within days. At the same time, Allied naval superiority and submarine attacks had largely cut the home islands off from what remained of the empire in China and southeast Asia.

Japan in 1945

By the early summer of 1945, Japanese leaders were sending out peace feelers, while the more fanatical elements in the army were promising to fight to the death. The end was sudden and terrifying. On August 6 and three days later on August 9, atomic bombs were dropped on Hiroshima and Nagasaki, respectively. In moments these cities, which to this point had been spared bombing, were reduced to ashes. Short-term casualties in both cities were well over 100,000, and deaths from radi-

An Eyewitness to Hiroshima

One of the leaflets was posted at the Kanda Station which said: "Both the Army and Navy are alive and well. We expect the nation to follow our lead." The leaflet was signed. I could understand how those military men felt. However, we already have the imperial rescript to surrender. If we are going to rebuild, we must open a new path. It is much easier to die than to live. In the long history of our nation, this defeat may become one of those insignificant happenings. However, the rebuilding after the defeat is likely to be treated as a far more important chapter in our history.

We did our best and lost, so there is nothing we have to say in our own defense. Only those people who did not do their best may now be feeling guilty, though.

Mr. C. said that everything he saw in the city was so repugnant that he wanted to retreat to the countryside. I was amazed by the narrowness of his thought process. I could say that he had a pure sense of devotion to the country, but that was only his own way of thinking. Beautiful perhaps, but it lacked firm foundation. I wish men like him would learn to broaden their perspectives.

*August 18.* Rationed bread distribution in the morning. I went to the distribution center with Mrs. A.

*August 21.* We heard that the Allied advance units will be airlifted and arrive in Japan on the 26th. And the following day, their fleet will also anchor in our harbors. The American Army will be airlifted and land in Atsugi airport.

According to someone who accompanied the Japanese delegation which went to accept surrender conditions, the Americans behaved like gentlemen. They explained to the Americans that certain conditions were unworkable in light of the present situation in Japan. The Americans immediately agreed to alter those conditions. They listened very carefully to what the Japanese delegation had to say.

An American paper, according to someone, reported that meeting as follows: "We cooked thick beefsteak expecting seven or eight Japanese would appear. But seventeen of them came, so we had to kill a turkey to prepare for them. We treated them well before they returned." . . . When I hear things like this, I immediately feel how exaggerated and inefficient our ways of doing things are. They say that Americans will tackle one item after another at a conference table, and do not waste even 30 seconds. . . .

In contrast, Japanese administration is conducted by many chairs and seals. For example when an auxiliary unit is asked to undertake a task for a governmental bureau, before anything can be done, twenty, or thirty seals of approval must be secured. So there is no concept of not wasting time. Even in war, they are too accustomed to doing things the way they have been doing and their many seals and chairs are nothing but a manifestation of their refusal to take individual responsibilities.

The fact of a defeat is a very serious matter and it is not easy to accept. However, it can bring some positive effects, if it can inculcate in our minds all the shortcomings we have had. I hope this will come true some day, and toward that end we must all endeavor. Even if we have to suffer hunger and other tribulations we must strive toward a positive goal.

**Questions** How did Japanese attitudes in defeat help prepare Japan for postwar redevelopment? Did defeat produce new divisions in attitudes among the Japanese? What other kinds of reactions might have been expected? How would you explain the rather calm and constructive outlook the passage suggests? Would American reactions to a Japanese victory have been similar?

Nagasaki Bomb Attack—August 1945

ation sickness increased this total greatly in the years, and even decades, that followed. Even more than in the European theater, the end of the long and most destructive war in human history came swiftly. As they had in dealing with Germany, the Allies demanded unconditional surrender by the Japanese. With the exception of retaining the emperor, which was finally allowed, the Japanese agreed to these terms and began to disarm. With the division of Germany that had begun some months earlier, the Allied occupation of the islands set the stage for the third main phase of the 20th century, which would be dominated by the cold war between the Soviet and American superpowers that would be waged amid the collapse of the European colonial order.

## War's End and the Emergence of the Superpower Standoff

■ **The final stages of World War II quickly led to a tense worldwide half-century of confrontation between the United States and the Soviet Union, each of which headed hostile alliances anchored in nations that had been major combatants during the war.**

World War II did not produce the sweeping peace settlements, misguided as most of them turned out to be, which had officially ended World War I. The leaders of the Allies opposed to the Axis powers met on several

Charter of the United Nations (excerpted)

occasions in an attempt to build the framework for a more lasting peace free of the vindictiveness that was so prominent at the Versailles gathering. A key result of Allied discussions was agreement on establishing the **United Nations (UN).** From the outset, this new international organization was more representative of the world's peoples, in both large and small nations, than the League of Nations. The United States pledged to join, played a major role in the United Nations' planning and finance, and provided a site on the East River in Manhattan for the organization's permanent headquarters. The Soviet Union was also a charter member, along with long-standing great powers, such as Britain and France. China, represented in the first decades after 1945 by the Guomindang, was grouped with these other global powers as a permanent member of the Security Council, the steering committee for United Nations operations. In the decades after the end of the war, the vanquished Axis powers were eventually granted membership, as were the former colonies, soon after each gained independence.

With the successful establishment of the United Nations, international diplomacy and assistance moved beyond the orbit of the Western powers, who had all but monopolized them for centuries, but through their vetoes in the Security Council they retained considerable control. The United Nations' primary mission was to provide a forum for negotiating international disputes. But it also took over the apparatus of more specialized international agencies, including the World Court of Justice, those concerned with human rights, and those that coordinated programs directed at specific groups and problems, ranging from labor organization and famine relief to agricultural development and women's concerns. Although UN interventions to preserve or restore peace to numerous regions have encountered much resistance by both the great powers and regional power brokers, they have repeatedly proved vital to reducing violent conflict and providing refugee relief throughout the globe. The United Nations has also sponsored initiatives, including critical international conferences, that have proved highly influential in shaping policies and programs affecting child labor, women's rights, and environmental protection.

United Nations: Universal Declaration of Human Rights

## From Hot War to Cold War

The cold war would last until the 1980s, with various points of crisis and confrontation. Direct conflict between the two superpowers did not occur, despite dire forebodings. Much of world history, however, was shaped by cold war maneuvering for over four decades.

The cold war began when the World War II allies turned, in the war's final conferences, to debate the nature of the postwar settlement. It quickly became apparent that the Soviet Union expected massive territorial gains and that Britain and the United States intended to limit these gains through their own areas of influence. Unresolved disputes—for World War II was never ended with a clear set of peace negotiations—then led to the full outbreak of the cold war between 1945 and 1949.

Tensions had clearly surfaced during the 1944 **Tehran Conference,** when the allies agreed on the invasion of Nazi-occupied France. The decision to focus on France rather than moving up from the Mediterranean gave the Soviet forces a free hand to move through the smaller nations of eastern Europe as they pushed the Nazi armies back. Britain negotiated separately with the Soviets to ensure Western preponderance in postwar Greece as well as equality in Hungary and Yugoslavia, with Soviet control of Romania and Bulgaria, but the United States resisted this kind of un-Wilsonian scorn for the rights of small nations.

The next settlement meeting was the **Yalta Conference** in the Soviet Crimea early in 1945. President Franklin Roosevelt of the United States was eager to press the Soviet Union for assistance against Japan and to this end promised the Soviets important territorial gains in Manchuria and the northern Japanese islands. The organization of the United Nations was confirmed. As to Europe, however, agreement was more difficult. The three powers easily arranged to divide Germany into four occupation zones (liberated France getting a chunk), which would be disarmed and purged of Nazi influence. Britain, however, resisted Soviet zeal to eliminate German industrial power, seeing a viable Germany as a potential ally in a subsequent Western–Soviet contest. Bitter dispute also raged over the smaller nations of eastern Europe. No one disagreed that they should be friendly to their Soviet neighbor, but the Western leaders also wanted them to be free and democratic. Stalin, the Soviet leader, had to make some concessions by including noncommunist leaders in what was already a Soviet-controlled government in liberated Poland—concessions that he soon violated.

The Big Three at Yalta

The final postwar conference occurred in the Berlin suburb of **Potsdam** in July 1945. Russian forces now occupied not only most of eastern Europe but eastern Germany as well. This de facto situation prompted agreement that the Soviet Union could take over much of what had been eastern Poland, with the Poles gaining part of eastern Germany in compensation. Germany was divided pending a final peace treaty (which was not to come for more than 40 years). Austria was also divided and occupied, gaining unity and independence only in 1956, on condition of neutrality between the United

States and the Soviet Union. Amid great difficulty, treaties were worked out for Germany's other allies, including Italy, but the United States and later the Soviet Union signed separate treaties with Japan.

All these maneuvers had several results. Japan was occupied by the United States and its wartime gains stripped away. Even Korea, taken earlier, was freed but was divided between U.S. and Soviet zones of occupation (the basis for the North Korea–South Korea division still in effect today). Former Asian colonies were returned to their old "masters," though often quite briefly, as new independence movements quickly challenged the control of the weakened imperialist powers. China regained most of its former territory, though here, too, stability was promptly challenged by renewed fighting between communist and nationalist forces within the nation, aided by the Soviet Union and the United States, respectively.

The effort to confirm old colonial regimes applied also to the Middle East, India, and Africa. Indian and African troops had fought for Britain during the war, as in World War I, though Britain imprisoned key nationalist leaders and put independence plans on hold. African leaders had participated actively in the French resistance to its authoritarian wartime government. The Middle East and north Africa had been shaken by German invasions and Allied counterattacks. Irritability increased, and so did expectations for change. With Europe's imperial powers further weakened by their war effort, adjustments seemed inevitable, as in those parts of Asia invaded by the Japanese.

In Europe the boundaries of the Soviet Union pushed westward, with virtually all the losses after World War I erased. Independent nations created in 1918 were for the most part restored (though the former Baltic states of Latvia, Lithuania, and Estonia became Soviet provinces because they had been Russian provinces before World War I). Except for Greece and Yugoslavia, the new nations quickly fell under Soviet domination, with communist governments forced on them and Soviet troops in occupation. The nations of western Europe were free to set up or confirm democratic regimes, but most of them lived under the shadow of growing U.S. influence, manifested in continued presence of U.S. troops, substantial economic aid and coordination, and no small amount of outright policy manipulation.

The stage was set, in other words, for two of the great movements that would shape the ensuing decades in world history. The first comprised challenges by subject peoples to the tired vestiges of control by the great European empires—the movement known as "decolonization" that in a few decades would create scores of new nations in Asia, Africa, and the West Indies. The second great theme was the confrontation between the two superpowers that emerged from the war—the United States and the Soviet Union, each with new international influence and new military might. Many believed that this cold war would soon become a war in a more literal and devastating sense. That these trends constituted a peace settlement was difficult to imagine in 1945 or 1947, yet they seemed the best that could be done.

## Nationalism and Decolonization

■ **A second global conflict between the industrial powers proved fatal to the already badly battered European colonial empires. From the Philippines to west Africa, independence was won in most of the nonsettler colonies with surprisingly little bloodshed and remarkable speed; the opposite was true in colonies with large settler communities, where liberation struggles were usually violent and prolonged.**

The Nazi rout of the French and the stunningly rapid Japanese capture of the French, Dutch, British, and U.S. colonies in southeast Asia put an end to whatever illusions the colonized peoples of Africa and Asia had left about the strength and innate superiority of their colonial overlords. Because the Japanese were non-Europeans, their early victories over the Europeans and Americans played a particularly critical role in destroying the myth of the white man's invincibility. The fall of the "impregnable" fortress at Singapore on the southern tip of Malaya and the Americans' reverses at Pearl Harbor and in the Philippines proved to be blows from which the colonizers never quite recovered, even though they went on to eventually defeat the Japanese. The sight of tens of thousands of British, Dutch, and American troops, struggling under the supervision of the victorious Japanese to survive the "death marches" to prison camps in their former colonies, left an indelible impression on the Asian villagers who saw them pass by. The harsh regimes and heavy demands the Japanese conquerors imposed on the peoples of southeast Asia during the war further strengthened the determination to fight for self-rule and to look to their own defenses after the conflict was over.

The devastation of World War II—a **total war** fought in the cities and countryside over much of Europe—drained the resources of the European powers. This devastating warfare also sapped the will of the European populace to hold increasingly resistant African and Asian peoples in bondage. The war also greatly enhanced the power and influence of the two giants on the European periphery: the United States and the Soviet Union. In Africa and the Middle East, as well as in the Pacific, the United States approached the war as a campaign of liberation. American propagandists made no secret of Franklin Roosevelt's hostility to colonialism in their efforts to win Asian and African support for the Allied war effort. In fact, American intentions in this regard were enshrined in the **Atlantic Charter of 1941.** This pact sealed an alliance between the United States and Great Britain that the latter desperately needed to survive in its war with Nazi Germany. In it Roosevelt persuaded a reluctant Churchill to include a clause that recognized the "right of all people to choose the form of government under which they live." The Soviets were equally vocal in their condemnation of colonialism and were even more forthcoming with material support for nationalist campaigns after the war. In the cold war world of the superpowers that emerged after 1945, there was little room for the domination that the much-reduced powers of western Europe had once exercised over much of the globe.

## The Winning of Independence in South and Southeast Asia

The outbreak of World War II soon put an end to the accommodation between the Indian National Congress and the British in the late 1930s. Congress leaders offered to support the Allies' war effort if the British would give them a significant share of power at the all-India level and commit themselves to Indian independence once the conflict was over. These conditions were staunchly rejected both by the viceroy in India and at home by Winston Churchill, who headed the coalition government that led Britain through the war. Labour members of the coalition government, however, indicated that they were quite willing to negotiate India's eventual independence. As tensions built between nationalist agitators and the British rulers, Sir Stafford Cripps was sent to India in early 1942 to see whether a deal could be struck with the Indian leaders. Indian divisions and British intransigence led to the collapse of Cripps's initiative and the renewal of mass civil disobedience campaigns under the guise of the **Quit India movement,** which began in the summer of 1942.

Indian Declaration of Independence

The British responded with repression and mass arrests, and for much of the remainder of the war, Gandhi, Nehru, and other major Congress politicians were imprisoned. Of the Indian nationalist parties, only the Communists—who were committed to the antifascist alliance—and, more ominously, the **Muslim League** rallied to the British cause. The League, now led by a former Congress party politician, the dour and uncompromising **Muhammad Ali Jinnah,** won much favor from the British for its wartime support. As their demands for a separate Muslim state in the subcontinent hardened, the links between the British and Jinnah and other League leaders became a key factor in the struggle for decolonization in south Asia.

Nehru

World War II brought disruptions to India similar to those caused by the earlier global conflict. Inflation stirred up urban unrest, while a widespread famine in 1943 and 1944, brought on in part by wartime transport shortages, engendered much bitterness in rural India. Winston Churchill's defeat in the first postwar British election in 1945 brought a Labour government

**FIGURE 35.6** As this photo of Mohandas Gandhi beside his spinning wheel suggests, he played many roles in the Indian nationalist struggle. The wheel represents India's traditional textile industry and the economic boycotts of British machine-made cloth that were central to Gandhi's civil disobedience campaigns. Gandhi's meditative position projects the image of a religious guru, which appealed to large segments of the Indian populace. The simplicity of his surroundings evokes the asceticism and detachment from the material world that had long been revered in Indian culture.

to power that was ready to deal with India's nationalist leaders. With independence in the near future tacitly conceded, the process of decolonization between 1945 and 1947 focused on what sort of state or states would be carved out of the subcontinent after the British withdrawal. Jinnah and the League had begun to build a mass following among the Muslims. In order to rally support, they played on widespread anxieties among the Muslim minority that a single Indian nation would be dominated by the Hindu majority, and that the Muslims would become the targets of increasing discrimination. It was therefore essential, they insisted, that a separate Muslim state called Pakistan be created from those areas in northwest and east India where Muslims were the most numerous.

As communal rioting spread throughout India, the British and key Congress party politicians reluctantly concluded that a bloodbath could be averted only by partition—the creation of two nations in the subcontinent: one secular, one Muslim. Thus, in the summer of 1947, the British handed power over to the leaders of the majority Congress party, who headed the new nation of India, and to Jinnah, who became the first president of Pakistan.

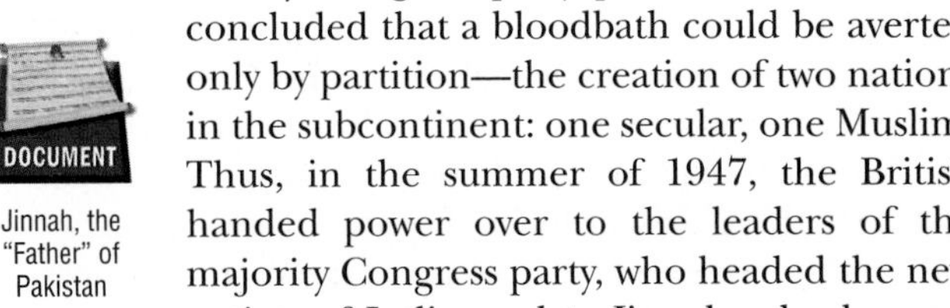
DOCUMENT

Jinnah, the "Father" of Pakistan

In part because of the haste with which the British withdrew their forces from the deeply divided subcontinent, a bloodbath occurred anyway. Vicious Hindu–Muslim and Muslim–Sikh communal rioting, in which neither women nor children were spared, took the lives of hundreds of thousands in the searing summer heat across the plains of northwest India. Whole villages were destroyed; trains were attacked and their passengers hacked to death by armed bands of rival religious adherents. These atrocities fed a massive exchange of refugee populations between Hindu, Sikh, and Muslim areas that may have totaled 10 million people. Those who fled were so terrified that they were willing to give up their land, their villages, and most of their worldly possessions. The losses of partition were compounded by the fact that there was soon no longer a Gandhi to preach tolerance and communal coexistence. On January 30, 1948, on the way to one of his regular prayer meetings, he was shot by a Hindu fanatic.

DOCUMENT

The Tandon Family at Partition

DOCUMENT

Gandhi Speaks Against the Partition of India

In granting independence to India, the British, in effect, removed the keystone from the arch of an empire that spanned three continents. Burma (known today as Myanmar) and Ceylon (now named Sri Lanka) won their independence peacefully in the following years. India's independence and Gandhi's civil disobedience campaigns, which had done so much to win a mass following for the nationalist cause, also inspired successful struggles for independence in Ghana, Nigeria, and other African colonies in the 1950s and 1960s.

The retreat of the most powerful of the imperial powers could not help but contribute to the weakening of lesser empires such as those of the Dutch, the French, and the Americans. In fact, the process of the transfer of power from U.S. officials to moderate, middle-class Filipino politicians was well under way before World War II broke out. The loyalty to the Americans that most Filipinos displayed during the war, as well as the stubborn guerrilla resistance they put up against the Japanese occupation, did much to bring about the rapid granting of independence to the Philippines once the war ended. The Dutch and French were less willing to follow the British example and relinquish their colonial possessions in the postwar era. From 1945 to 1949, the Dutch fought a losing war to destroy the nation of Indonesia, which nationalists in the Netherlands Indies had established when the Japanese hold over the islands broke down in mid-1945. The French struggled to retain Indochina. Communist revolutions in east Asia also emerged victorious in the postwar period. No sooner had the European colonizers suffered these losses than they were forced to deal with new threats to the last bastions of the imperial order in Africa.

## The Liberation of Nonsettler Africa

World War II proved even more disruptive to the colonial order imposed on Africa than the first global conflict of the European powers. Forced labor and confiscations of crops and minerals returned, and inflation and controlled markets again cut down on African earnings. African recruits in the hundreds of thousands were drawn once more into the conflict and had even greater opportunities to use the latest European weapons to destroy Europeans. African servicemen had witnessed British and French defeats in the Middle East and southeast Asia, and they fought bravely only to experience renewed racial discrimination once they returned home. Many were soon among the staunchest supporters of postwar nationalist campaigns in the African colonies of the British and French. The swift and humiliating rout of the French and Belgians by Nazi armies in the spring of 1940 shattered whatever was left of the colonizers' reputation for military prowess. It also led to a bitter and, in the circumstances, embarrassing struggle between the forces of the puppet Vichy regime and those of de Gaulle's Free French, who continued fighting the Nazis mainly in France's north and west African colonies.

The wartime needs of both the British and the Free French led to major departures from long-standing colonial policies that had restricted industrial development throughout Africa. Factories were established to process urgently needed vegetable oils, foods, and minerals in western and south central Africa. These in turn contributed to a growing migration on the part of African peasants to the towns and a sharp spurt in African urban growth. The inability of many of those who moved to the towns to find employment made for a reservoir of disgruntled, idle workers that would be skillfully tapped by nationalist politicians in the postwar decades.

There were essentially two main paths to decolonization in nonsettler Africa in the postwar era. The first was pioneered by Kwame Nkrumah and his followers in the British Gold Coast colony, which, as the independent nation of Ghana, launched the process of decolonization in Africa. Nkrumah epitomized the more radical sort of African leader that emerged throughout Africa after the war (see Visualizing the Past feature). Educated in African missionary schools and the United States, he had established wide contacts with nationalist leaders in both British and French West Africa and civil rights leaders in America prior to his return to the Gold Coast in the late 1940s. He returned to a land in ferment. The restrictions of government-controlled marketing boards and their favoritism for British merchants had led to widespread, but nonviolent, protest in the coastal cities. But after the police fired on a peaceful demonstration of ex-servicemen in 1948, rioting broke out in many towns.

Though both urban workers and cash crop farmers had supported the unrest, Western-educated African leaders were slow to organize these dissident groups into a sustained mass movement. Their reluctance arose in part from their fear of losing major political concessions, such as seats on colonial legislative councils, which the British had just made. Rejecting the caution urged by more established political leaders, Nkrumah resigned his position as chair of the dominant political party in the Gold Coast and established his own **Convention Peoples Party (CPP).** Even before the formal break, he had signaled the arrival of a new style of politics by organizing mass rallies, boycotts, and strikes.

In the mid-1950s, Nkrumah's mass following, and his growing stature as a leader who would not be deterred by imprisonment or British threats, won repeated concessions from the British. Educated Africans were given more and more representation in legislative bodies, and gradually they took over administration of the colony. The British recognition of Nkrumah as the prime minister of an independent Ghana in 1957 simply concluded a transfer of power from the European colonizers to the Western-educated African elite that had been under way for nearly a decade.

The peaceful devolution of power to African nationalists led to the independence of the British nonsettler colonies in black Africa by the mid-1960s. Independence in the comparable areas of the French and Belgian empires in Africa came in a somewhat different way. Hard-pressed by costly military struggles to hold on to their colonies in Indochina and Algeria, the French took a much more conciliatory line in dealing with the many peoples they ruled in west Africa. Ongoing negotiations with such highly westernized leaders as Senegal's Léopold Sédar Senghor and the Ivory Coast's Felix Houphouât-Boigny led to reforms and political concessions. The slow French retreat ensured that moderate African leaders, who were eager to retain French economic and cultural ties, would dominate the nationalist movements and the postindependence period in French west Africa. Between 1956 and 1960, the French colonies moved by stages toward nationhood—a process that sped up after de Gaulle's return to power in 1958. By 1960 all of France's west African colonies were free.

In the same year, the Belgians completed a much hastier retreat from their huge colonial possession in the Congo. Their virtual flight was epitomized by the fact that there was little in the way of an organized nationalist movement to pressure them into concessions of any kind. In fact, by design there were scarcely any well-educated Congolese to lead resistance to Belgian rule. At independence in 1960, there were only 16 African college graduates in a Congolese population that exceeded 13 million. Though the Portuguese still clung to their impoverished and scattered colonial territories, by the mid-1960s the European colonial era had come to an end in all but the settler societies of Africa.

## Repression and Guerrilla War: The Struggle for the Settler Colonies

The pattern of relatively peaceful withdrawal by stages that characterized the process of decolonization in most of Asia and Africa proved unworkable in most of the settler colonies. These included areas like Algeria, Kenya, and Southern Rhodesia, where substantial numbers of Europeans had gone intending to settle permanently in the 19th and early 20th centuries. South Africa, which had begun to be settled by Europeans centuries earlier, provided few openings for nationalist agitation except that mounted by the politically and economically dominant colonists of European descent. In each case, the presence of European settler communities, varying in size from millions in South Africa and Algeria to tens of thousands in Kenya and Southern Rhodesia, blocked both the rise of indigenous nationalist movements and concessions on the part of the colonial overlords.

Because the settlers regarded the colonies to which they had emigrated as their permanent homes,

VISUALIZING THE PAST

## On National Leadership

Throughout Africa and Asia, struggles for decolonization and national independence often led to the emergence of leaders with exceptional mass appeal and political skills. But the personal qualities, visions of the future, and leadership styles that made for widespread loyalty to these individuals varied widely depending on the cultures and social settings from which they emerged as well as the nature of the political contests that led to the colonizers' retreat and the establishment of new nations. The following are photos of four of the most charismatic and effective leaders of independence movements in Africa and Asia. Study these photos and the background information on each of these individuals that is provided in earlier sections of this chapter and the relevant sections of Chapter 34, and answer the questions about leadership styles and images that follow.

**Questions** What do the dress and poses of these leaders tell us about the image each projected? Why did the style and approach each adopted win widespread popular support in each of the very different societies in which they emerged as pivotal leaders in the struggles for independence? How well do you think that each of their approaches to leadership served them in dealings with the European colonizers and contests with the rival leaders and political parties they faced in each of the societies in which they arose? What did charisma mean in each of these settings?

Mohandas Gandhi, India.

Léopold Sédar Senghor, Senegal.

Gamal Abdul Nasser, Egypt.

Kwame Nkrumah, Ghana.

they fought all attempts to turn political control over to the African majority or even to grant them civil rights. They also doggedly refused all reforms by colonial administrators that required them to give up any of the lands they had occupied, often at the expense of indigenous African peoples. Unable to make headway through nonviolent protest tactics—which were forbidden—or negotiations with British or French officials, who were fearful of angering the highly vocal settler minority, many African leaders turned to violent, revolutionary struggles to win their independence.

The first of these erupted in Kenya in the early 1950s. Impatient with the failure of the nonviolent approach adopted by **Jomo Kenyatta** and the leading nationalist party, the **Kenya African Union (KAU)**, an underground organization coalesced around a group of more radical leaders. After forming the **Land Freedom Army** in the early 1950s, the radicals mounted a campaign of terror and guerrilla warfare against the British, the settlers, and Africans who were considered collaborators. At the height of the struggle in 1954, some 200,000 rebels were in action in the capital at Nairobi and in the forest reserves of the central Kenyan highlands. The British responded with an all-out military effort to crush the guerrilla movement, which was dismissed as an explosion of African savagery and labeled the "Mau Mau" by the colonizers, not the rebels. In the process, the British, at the settlers' insistence, imprisoned Kenyatta and the KAU organizers, thus eliminating the nonviolent alternative to the guerrillas.

The rebel movement had been militarily defeated by 1956 at the cost of thousands of lives. But the British were now in a mood to negotiate with the nationalists, despite strong objections from the European settlers. Kenyatta was released from prison, and he emerged as the spokesperson for the Africans of Kenya. By 1963 a multiracial Kenya had won its independence. Under what was, in effect, Kenyatta's one-party rule, it remained until the mid-1980s one of the most stable and more prosperous of the new African states.

The struggle of the Arab and Berber peoples of Algeria for independence was longer and even more vicious than that in Kenya. Algeria had for decades been regarded by the French as an integral part of France—a department just like Provence or Brittany. The presence of more than a million European settlers in the colony only served to bolster the resolve of French politicians to retain it at all costs. But in the decade after World War II, sporadic rioting grew into sustained guerrilla resistance. By the mid-1950s, the **National Liberation Front (FLN)** had mobilized large segments of the Arab and Berber population of the colony in a full-scale revolt against French rule and settler dominance. High-ranking French army officers came to see the defeat of this movement as a way to restore a reputation that had been badly tarnished by recent defeats in Vietnam (see Chapter 39). As in Kenya, the rebels were defeated in the field. But they gradually negotiated the independence of Algeria after de Gaulle came to power in 1958. The French people had wearied of the seemingly endless war, and de Gaulle became convinced that he could not restore France to great power status as long as its resources continued to be drained by the Algerian conflict.

In contrast to Kenya, the Algerian struggle was prolonged and brutalized by a violent settler backlash. Led after 1960 by the **Secret Army Organization (OAS),** it was directed against Arabs and Berbers as well as French who favored independence for the colony. With strong support from elements in the French military, earlier resistance by the settlers had managed to topple the government in Paris in 1958, thereby putting an end to the Fourth Republic. In the early 1960s, the OAS came close to assassinating de Gaulle and overthrowing the Fifth Republic, which his accession to power had brought into existence. In the end, however, the Algerians won their independence in 1962 (Figure 35.7). After the bitter civil war, the multiracial accommodation worked out in Kenya appeared out of the question as far as the settlers of Algeria were concerned. Over 900,000 left the new nation within months after its birth. In addition, tens of thousands of harkis, or Arabs and Berbers who had sided with the French in the long war for independence, fled to France. They, and later migrants, formed the core of the substantial Algerian population now present in France.

## The Persistence of White Supremacy in South Africa

In southern Africa, violent revolutions put an end to white settler dominance in the Portuguese colonies of Angola and Mozambique in 1975 and in Southern Rhodesia (now Zimbabwe) by 1980. Only in South Africa did the white minority manage to maintain its position of supremacy. Its ability to do so rested on several factors that distinguished it from other settler societies. To begin with, the white population of South Africa, roughly equally divided between the Dutch-descended Afrikaners and the more recently arrived English speakers, was a good deal larger than that of any of the other settler societies. Though they were only a small minority in a country of 23 million black Africans and 3.5 million East Indians and coloreds (mulattos, in American parlance), by the mid-1980s, South Africa's settler-descended population had reached 4.5 million.

Unlike the settlers in Kenya and Algeria, who had the option of retreating to Europe as full citizens of France or Great Britain, the Afrikaners in particular had no European homeland to fall back upon. They had lived in South Africa as long as other Europeans had in North America, and they considered themselves quite distinct from the Dutch. Over the centuries, the Afrikaners had also built up what was for them a persuasive ideology of white racist supremacy. Though crude by European or American standards, Afrikaner racism was far more explicit and elaborate than that developed by the settlers of any other colony. Afrikaner ideology was grounded in selected biblical quotations and the celebration of their his-

FIGURE 35.7 Algerians celebrated in Oran as French barricades were torn down by members of the local Arab militia and Arab civilians just after independence was announced in July 1962. The barricades had been erected throughout the colony to keep European residential areas off limits to the Arabs and Berbers, who made up the overwhelming majority of the population. Although cities such as Oran and Algiers had long been segregated into "native" and European quarters, the protracted and bloody war for independence had resulted in full-scale occupation by the French army and physical separation of settler and Arab-Berber areas.

toric struggle to "tame a beautiful but hard land" in the face of opposition from both the African "savages" and the British "imperialists."

Ironically, their defeat by the British in the Boer War from 1899 to 1902 also contributed much to the capacity of the white settler minority to maintain its place of dominance in South Africa. A sense of guilt, arising especially from their treatment of Boer women and children during the war—tens of thousands of whom died of disease in what the British called concentration camps—led the victors to make major concessions to the Afrikaners in the postwar decades. The most important of these was internal political control, which included turning over the fate of the black African majority to the openly racist supremacist Afrikaners. Not surprisingly, the continued subjugation of the black Africans became a central aim of the Afrikaner political organizations that emerged in the 1930s and 1940s, culminating in the **Afrikaner National Party.** From 1948, when it emerged as the majority party in the all-white South African legislature, the National party devoted itself to winning complete independence from Britain (which came without violence in 1961) and to establishing lasting white domination over the political, social, and economic life of the new nation.

A rigid system of racial segregation (which will be discussed more fully in Chapter 38), called **apartheid** by the Afrikaners, was established after 1948 through the passage of thousands of laws. Among other things, this legislation reserved the best jobs for whites and carefully defined the sorts of contacts permissible between different racial groups. The right to vote and political representation were denied to the black Africans, and ultimately to the coloreds and Indians. It was illegal for members of any of these groups to hold mass meetings or to organize political parties or labor unions. These restrictions, combined with very limited opportunities for higher education for black Africans, hampered the growth of black African political parties and their efforts to mobilize popular support for the struggle for decolonization. The Afrikaners' establishment of a vigilant and brutal police state to uphold apartheid, and their opportunistic cultivation of divisions between the diverse peoples in the black African population, also contributed to their ability to preserve a bastion of white supremacy in an otherwise liberated continent.

## Conflicting Nationalisms: Arabs, Israelis, and the Palestinian Question

Along with Egypt, several Middle Eastern states, including Iraq and Syria, had technically gained independence between the world wars, though European influence remained strong. With World War II, independence became more complete, though it was not until the 1970s that governments were strong enough to shake off Western dominance of the oil fields.

Egypt's 1952 revolt and independence movements in the rest of north Africa gained ground, though the struggle against France in Algeria was bitter and prolonged. Although virtually all Arab peoples who were not yet free by the end of World War II were liberated by the early 1960s, the fate of Palestine continued to present special problems. Hitler's campaign of genocide against the European Jews had provided powerful support for the Zionists' insistence that the Jews must have their own homeland, which more and more was conceived in terms of a modern national state. The brutal persecution of the Jews also won international sympathy for the Zionist cause. This was in part due to the fact that the leaders of many nations, including the United States and Great Britain, were reluctant to admit Jews fleeing the Nazi terror into their own countries. As Hitler's henchmen stepped up their race war against the Jews, the tide of Jewish immigration to Palestine rose sharply. But growing Arab resistance to Jewish settlement and land purchases in Palestine, which was often expressed in communal rioting and violent assaults on Zionist communities, led to increasing British restrictions on the entry of Jews into the colony.

A major Muslim revolt swept Palestine between 1936 and 1939. The British managed to put down this rising but only with great difficulty. It both decimated the leadership of the Palestinian Arab community and further strengthened the British resolve to stem the flow of Jewish immigrants to Palestine. Government measures to keep out Jewish refugees from Nazi oppression led in turn to violent Zionist resistance to the British presence in Palestine. The Zionist assault was spearheaded by a regular Zionist military force, the **Haganah,** and several underground terrorist organizations.

By the end of World War II, the major parties claiming Palestine were locked into a deadly stalemate. The Zionists were determined to carve out a Jewish state in the region. The Palestinian Arabs and their allies in neighboring Arab lands were equally determined to transform Palestine into a multireligious nation in which the position of the Arab majority would be ensured. Having badly bungled their mandatory responsibilities, and under attack from both sides, the British wanted more than anything else to scuttle and run. The 1937 report of a British commission of inquiry supplied a possible solution: partition. The newly created United Nations provided an international body that could give a semblance of legality to the proceedings. In 1948, with sympathy for the Jews running high because of the postwar revelations of the horrors of Hitler's Final Solution, the member states of the United Nations—with the United States and the Soviet Union in rare agreement—approved the partition of Palestine into Arab and Jewish countries (Map 35.2).

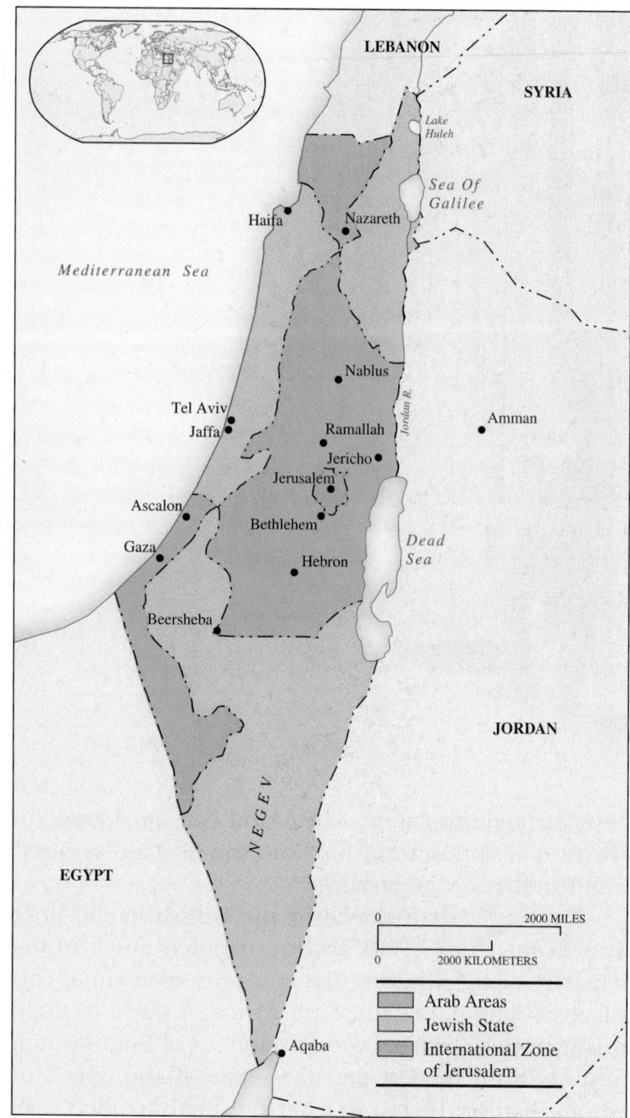


**MAP 35.2** The Partition of Palestine After World War II

The Arab states that bordered the newly created nation of Israel had vehemently opposed the UN action. Soon the two sides were engaged in all-out warfare. Though heavily outnumbered, the Zionists proved better armed and much better prepared to defend themselves than almost anyone could have expected. Not only did they hold onto the tiny, patchwork state they had been given by the United Nations, but they expanded it at the Arabs' expense. The brief but bloody war that ensued created hundreds of thousands of Palestinian Arab refugees. It also sealed the persist-

Israel and Its Neighbors

ing hostility between Arabs and Israelis that has been the all-consuming issue in the region and a major international problem to the present day. In Palestine, conflicting strains of nationalism had collided. As a result, the legacy of colonialism proved even more of a liability to social and economic development than in much of the rest of newly independent Africa and Asia.

## GLOBAL CONNECTIONS

## Persisting Trends in a World Transformed by War

Given the fragile foundations on which it rested, the rather rapid demise of the European colonial order is not really surprising. World War II completed the process that World War I and anticolonial nationalism had begun; the end of Western imperialism came quickly. In this sense, the global framework was transformed. However, the winning of political freedom in Asia and Africa also represented less of a break with the colonial past than the appearance of many new nations on the map of the world might lead one to assume.

The decidedly nonrevolutionary, elite-to-elite transfer of power that was central to the liberation process in most colonies, even those where there were violent guerrilla movements, limited the extent of the social and economic transformation that occurred. The Western-educated African and Asian classes moved into the offices and took the jobs—and often the former homes—of the European colonizers. But social gains for the rest of the population in most new nations were minimal or nonexistent. In Algeria, Kenya, and Zimbabwe (formerly Southern Rhodesia), abandoned European lands were distributed to Arab and African peasants and laborers. But in most former colonies, especially in Asia, the big landholders that remained were indigenous, and they have held on tenaciously to their holdings. Educational reforms were carried out to include more sciences in school curricula and the history of Asia or Africa rather than Europe. But Western cultural influences have remained strong in almost all of the former colonies. Indians and many west Africans with higher educations continue to communicate in English and French.

The liberation of the colonies also did little to disrupt Western dominance of the terms of international trade or the global economic order more generally. In fact, in the negotiations that led to decolonization, Asian and African leaders often explicitly promised to protect the interests of Western merchants and businesspeople in the postindependence era. These and other limits that sustained Western influence and often dominance, even after freedom was won, greatly reduced the options open to nationalist leaders struggling to build viable and prosperous nations. Though new forces have also played important roles, the postindependence history of colonized peoples cannot be understood without a consideration of the lingering effects of the colonial interlude in their history.

## Further Readings

Two of the most genuinely global histories of World War II, which also include extensive accounts of the origins of the war in both Europe and the Pacific, are Gerhard L. Weinberg, *A World at Arms: A Global History of World War II* (1994), and Peter Calvocoressi and Guy Wint, *Total War: Causes and Courses of the Second World War* (1972). For a good overview of the coming of the war in Europe from the British perspective, see Christopher Thorne, *The Approach of War 1938–1939* (1967), and from the German viewpoint, Gerhard L. Weinberg, *Germany, Hitler, and World War II* (1995). A fine analysis of the underlying patterns in the European theater can be found in Gordon Wright, *The Ordeal of Total War, 1939–1945* (1968).

From a prodigious literature on the Holocaust, some good works to begin with are Hannah Arendt's brilliant *Eichmann in Jerusalem* (1963) and Raul Hilberg's *Destruction of the European Jews* (1985). Christopher Browning's *Ordinary Men* (1992) provides a chilling account of some of those who actually carried out the killings, while Viktor Frankl's *Man's Search for Meaning* (1959) is one of the most poignant of the numerous autobiographical accounts of the concentration camps. Omer Bartov provides a thoughtful meditation on the wider meanings of the Holocaust for 20th-century history in *Murder in Our Midst* (1996).

On the causes of the Pacific war, see Michael Barnhart, *Japan Prepares for Total War* (1987), and William O'Neill, *A Democracy at War* (1993). Sukarno's reactions to the Japanese invasion of the Netherlands Indies are related in his *Autobiography* (1965) as related to Cindy Adams, which should be balanced by John Legge's *Sukarno: A Political Biography* (1972). On the course of the war in the Pacific from differing perspectives, see Ronald Spector, *Eagle Against the Sun* (1985); Saburò Ienaga, *The Pacific War, 1931–1945* (1978); and John Dower, *War Without Mercy: Race and Power in the Pacific War* (1986). On the end of the war and the forces that led to the cold war, see Martin Sherwin, *A World Destroyed: The Atomic Bomb and the Grand Alliance* (1975); William Craig, *The Fall of Japan* (1967); Herbert Feis, *From Trust to Terror: The Onset of the Cold War, 1945–1950* (1970); and Melvyn Leffler, *A Preponderance of Power: National Security, the Truman Administration, and the Cold War* (1992).

A thoughtful overview of the process of decolonization in the British empire as a whole can be found in the works of John Darwin. In addition to P. J. Vatikiotis's general *History of Egypt*, mentioned in Chapter 5, Jacques Berque's *Egypt: Imperialism and Revolution* (1972) and Peter Mansfield's *The British in Egypt* (1971) provide detailed accounts of the nationalist revolt and early years of quasi-independence. The struggles for decolonization in Africa are surveyed by Ali A. Mazrui and Michael Tidy in *Nationalism and New States in Africa* (1984); J. D. Hargreaves, *Decolonization in Africa* (1988); and W. R. Louis and P. Gifford, eds., *Decolonization in Africa* (1984).

From the very substantial literature on the rise of nationalism in settler societies, some of the best studies include C. Roseberg and J. Nottingham, *The Myth of "Mau Mau"* (1966), on Kenya; the writings of Terrence Ranger on Rhodesia; and Alastair Horne, *A Savage War of Peace* (1977), on Algeria. Of the many works on South Africa, the general histories of S. Throup, B. Bunting, T. D. Moodie, and Leonard Thompson provide a good introduction to the rise of Afrikaner power. The period of the partition and the first Arab-Israeli conflict have been the subject of much revisionist scholarship in recent years. Some of the best of this is included in important books by Benny Morris, Walid Khalidi, Ilan Pappé, and Tom Segev.

On the United States in the cold war decades, see Walter Lafeber, *America, Russia, and the Cold War, 1945–2004* (2004). Ronald Powaski, *The Cold War: The United States and the Soviet Union, 1917–1991* (1998), is a reliable and readable standard political history that synthesizes the historiography of the cold war. Ellen Schrecker, *Many Are the Crimes: McCarthyism in America* (1998), has a broad social history of the political and cultural legacy of the Red Scare. T. H. Etzold and J. L. Gaddis, eds., *Containment: Documents on American Policy and Strategy, 1945–1950* (1978), provides primary source material on the political history of the early cold war.

## On the Web

A superb starting point for the online study of World War II can be found at http://www.historywiz.com/worldwartwo.htm. The site features links to battle histories, oral histories, and exhibits, and offers an audio file of President's Truman's speech announcing the use of the atomic bomb against Japan. Other useful links can be found at http://history.acusd.edu/gen/ww2_links.html, which leads to sources organized by battles and by countries, including the battle for Stalingrad and the role of Russia in the war. Yale University provides a digital library for Second World War documents at http://www.yale.edu/lawweb/avalon/wwii/wwii.htm. Rutgers University offers records of personal experiences at http://fas-history.rutgers.edu/oralhistory/orlhom.htm, which can be supplemented by other collections at http://www.eyewitnesstohistory.com/, http://www.geocities.com/Athens/Oracle/2691/links.htm, and http://www.fsu.edu/~ww2/links.htm, which offer links to materials ranging from combat stories to prisoner of war experiences.

Dramatic recreations or virtual visits to key sites of this conflict abound on the Web. These sites include Hiroshima (http://titan.iwu.edu/~rwilson/hiroshima/), the 1941–1944 siege of Leningrad (http://www.cityvision2000.com/history/900days.htm), and Pearl Harbor (http://execpc.com/~dschaaf/mainmenu.html, and http://plasma.nationalgeographic.com/pearlharbor/). The concept of "lightning war" or blitzkrieg is explained at http://www.achtungpanzer.com/blitz.htm.

The role of the American home front and American women in World War II is explored through photographs and interviews at http://www.pomperaug.com/socstud/stumuseum/web/ARHhome.htm, http://www.u.arizona.edu/~kari/rosie.htm, http://www.wasp-wwii.org/, and http://www.stg.brown.edu/projects/WWII_Women/WomenInWWII.html.

The experience of internment and death camps for civilians and prisoners of war in German-, Russian-, and Japanese-held territories is examined at http://www.vikingphoenix.com/public/rongstad/military/pow/pow.htm and http://www.mansell.com/pow-index.html. The removal of the Japanese American population in America to internment camps during the war is discussed and links on the subject provided at http://www.geocities.com/Athens/8420/main.html. Many Japanese internment camps in America have their own dedicated Web site, such as that at http://www.nps.gov/manz/ and http://www.library.arizona.edu/wracamps/.

Overviews and interactive digital data bases for the Holocaust are provided at http://www.remember.org, http://www.holocaust-history.org, and http://www.ushmm.org. See also the excellent teacher's guide that offers study guides, documents, and essays at http://fcit.coedu.usf.edu/holocaust/resource/document/DocPropa.htm. A map of Nazi concentration camps is provided at http://history1900s.about.com/library/holocaust/blmap.htm. There are several Web pages devoted to those who struggled against the Holocaust, including Oskar Schindler (http://auschwitz.dk/Schindler2.htm) and Raul Wallenberg (http://www.us-israel.org/jsource/biography/wallenberg.html). The struggle against those who seek to deny the genocidal nature of the Nazi regime is addressed in articles offered at http://www.holocaust-history.org/. The search for meaning in the modern European Holocaust has been pioneered by one of its victims, Simon Wiesenthal (http://www.wiesenthal.com/). Virtual visits to the Anne Frank homepages (http://www.annefrank.nl/ and http://www.annefrank.com) and other links (see http://www.coollessons.org/holocaust.htm) lend a human face to both fascist oppression and the quest for a world without hatred.

That this Holocaust is but one of many human genocides is the subject of several sites that offer comparative analyses or links to other examples from Cambodia to Rwanda. These include http://www.yale.edu/cgp/, http://www.cybercambodia.com/dachs/, http://www.hawaii.edu/powerkills/SOD.CHAP4.HTM, http://news.bbc.co.uk/1/hi/world/africa/1288230.stm, http://www.hrw.org/reports/1999/rwanda/, and http://www.webster.edu/~woolflm/holocaust.html.

The winning of India's independence, Gandhi's last years, and his assassination did not end the struggle for *satyagraha* (http://www.colorado.edu/conflict/peace/example/wehr7496.htm). Many others have followed this path in India and abroad (see examples and resource lists at http://www.aforcemorepowerful.org/, http://www.transnational.org/forum/Nonviolence/

Nonviolence.html, and http://edition.cnn.com/WORLD/9708/India97/india/gandhi.legacy/). Gandhi can be seen in a short film of a visit to London and during the Salt March at http://www.historychannel.com/broadband/searchbrowse/index.jsp. Jawaharlal Nehru's life and role in the freedom movement is explored at http://www.pbs.org/wgbh/commandingheights/shared/minitextlo/prof_jawaharlalnehru.html. His "tryst with destiny speech" that inaugurated a new chapter in the history of the Indian subcontinent can be read at http://www.fordham.edu/halsall/mod/1947nehru1.html. It can be heard at http://www.harappa.com/sounds/nehru.html.

A newsreel covering the birth of Pakistan can be viewed at http://harappa.com/wall/pakistan.html, while the birth pangs of Bangladesh are traced at http://www.virtualbangladesh.com/.

The generation of leaders that helped secure Africa's freedom is well represented on the Internet. For Léopold Senghor, poet of négritude and president of Senegal, see http://web.uflib.ufl.edu/cm/africana/senghor.htm. Links to Tanzania's Julius Nyerere's life and speeches can be found at http://www.hartford-hwp.com/archives/30/index-fd.html. Jomo Kenyatta and his role in the Land Freedom Army and Mau Mau movements are listed at http://www.kenyaweb.com/history/struggle/ and http://www.ccs.neu.edu/home/feneric/maumau.html.

The African National Congress Party homepage at http://www.anc.org.za/ traces its anticolonial role from its earliest beginnings to Nelson Mandela. Apartheid in South Africa is discussed at http://www-cs-students.stanford.edu/~cale/cs201/apartheid.hist.html.

CHAPTER 36

# Western Society and Eastern Europe in the Decades of the Cold War



In 1954 the United States tested a nuclear weapon in the Marshall Islands that caused radioactive fallout to shower a Japanese fishing boat, ultimately killing one crew member and hospitalizing many others. International outrage ensued. Both the United States and the Soviet Union were conducting aboveground nuclear tests, and they would soon be joined by France and Britain. All sorts of people, in all sorts of places, rallied against these tests, in a striking manifestation of what media were beginning to label "world opinion."

Church groups, from Quakers to Roman Catholics, protested the tests. Buddhist voices were also strong. Japanese leadership was crucial; given the nation's experience at the end of World War II, it was hardly surprising that 86 percent of Japanese opposed nuclear testing. Australia and New Zealand vigorously objected to the use of the Pacific for tests, while Egypt and other Middle Eastern countries resisted French use of the Sahara. In Germany, with a new passion against war, hundreds of thousands of demonstrators marched before the U.S. embassy. African and Indian voices were also strong. In the United States many women joined protest groups—there was widespread concern that testing would lead to nuclear contamination of milk that would threaten the health of children.

The governments that were doing the testing initially resisted attempts to outlaw it. Many American leaders claimed the protests were a communist plot, and it was true that Soviet groups tried to use the rallies to their advantage. But finally the great powers reconsidered. In 1958 President Dwight Eisenhower, told by a scientist that further tests would create still more awesome bombs, replied: "The new thermonuclear weapons are tremendously powerful; however they are not as powerful as is world opinion today in obliging the United States to follow certain lines of policy." A testing moratorium was declared in 1958, and an initial test ban treaty was negotiated in 1963.

FIGURE 36.1 This 1958 Russian poster depicts a woman shielding her eyes from the light of a mushroom cloud and holding her hand up in a universal gesture of opposition. The lettering says "No!" The palm trees make clear that the reference is to testing in the Pacific. Why might the Soviets, who had themselves done aboveground nuclear testing, publish such a poster?

| 1940 C.E. | 1950 C.E. | 1960 C.E. | 1970 C.E. | 1980 C.E. | 1990 C.E. | 2000 C.E. |
|---|---|---|---|---|---|---|
| **1945** End of World War II<br>**1945–1948** Soviet takeover of eastern Europe; new constitutions in Italy, Germany, and France; Labour Party victory in Britain; growth of welfare states in western Europe<br>**1947** Marshall Plan<br>**1947–1960s** Cold war begins and reaches its peak<br>**1949** Separate East and West German regimes established<br>**1949** Soviet Union develops atomic bomb; North Atlantic Treaty Organization established | **1953** Stalin's death<br>**1955** Formation of Warsaw Pact<br>**1956** Khrushchev breaks with Stalinism<br>**1956** Hungarian revolt and its suppression<br>**1957** Establishment of European Economic Community or Common Market (basis of later European Union)<br>**1958** De Gaulle's Fifth Republic in France | **1960s** Civil rights and feminist movements in United States<br>**1961** Berlin Wall erected<br>**1962** Cuban missile crisis<br>**1968** Czechoslovakian revolt suppressed; Brezhnev Doctrine proclaims right to intervene in any socialist country<br>**1968–1973** Massive student protests in West | **1970s** Democratic regimes in Spain, Portugal, and Greece<br>**1973, 1977** Oil crises<br>**1979** Uprisings in Poland and their suppression; Thatcher and new conservatism in Britain; Soviet invasion of Afghanistan; significant economic recession | **1981–1988** Reagan president in United States<br>**1985–1991** Gorbachev heads Soviet Union<br>**1989** Berlin Wall division ends; new regimes throughout eastern Europe | **1992** End of economic restrictions within Common Market<br>**1993** Division of Czechoslovakia; Clinton inauguration ends three-term Republican tenure in White House | **2001** Euro currency introduced<br>**2001** Growing concern about terrorism |

Both western and eastern Europe had been devastated by World War II. Yet the Soviet Union emerged within a few years with a new European empire and status as a world superpower, rivaling the United States and its allies. Western Europe bounced back as well, though it did not recover its prewar world dominance. The United States, defying its earlier traditions, became very active in international affairs, maintaining a strong international presence and making massive military expenditures.

While the cold war set the framework for developments in the West and in eastern Europe, other changes may have been more important for the longer run. In the West, democratic political forms gained new vitality, along with rising consumer prosperity. In eastern Europe, dominated by the Soviet Union, the desire for economic development and cultural change vied with the wish to maintain superpower status.

## After World War II: A New International Setting for the West

■ **Western Europe had to adjust to its loss of world dominance after the war. Western European countries lost their colonies and became secondary players in the cold war between the superpowers.**

World War II left western Europe in shambles. The sheer physical destruction caused problems with housing and transportation. Downed bridges and rail lines complicated food shipments, leaving many people in France and Germany ill-fed and unable to work at full efficiency. Nazi Germany's use of forced foreign labor, as well as the many boundary changes resulting from the war, generated hundreds of thousands of refugees trying to return home or find new homes. For at least two years after 1945 it was unclear that recovery would be possible—mere survival proved difficult enough. Europe's postwar weakness after three decades of strife helped trigger a crescendo of nationalist sentiment in areas the West had colonized, as well as the fuller emergence of the United States and the Soviet Union, whose size and growing industrial strength now overshadowed Europe's proud nation-states.

## Europe and Its Colonies

The two larger changes provoked by the war—decolonization and the cold war—quickly intruded on the West. We have seen that colonies outside Europe, roused by the war, became increasingly restive. When the British returned to Malaya and the Dutch to Indonesia—areas from which they had been dislodged—they found a more hostile climate, with well-organized nationalist resistance. It was soon clear that many colonies could be maintained only at great cost, and in the main the European nations decided that the game was not worth the candle. A few cases proved messy. France tried to defend its holdings in Vietnam against communist guerrillas, yielding only in 1954 after some major defeats. The French clung even more fiercely to Algeria, the oldest African colony and one with a large European minority. The French military joined Algerian settlers in insisting on a war to the death against nationalist forces, and bitter fighting went on for years. The tension even threatened civil war in France, until a new president, Charles de Gaulle, realized the hopelessness of the struggle and negotiated Algeria's independence in 1962.

Overall, decolonization proceeded more smoothly than this between the late 1940s and the mid-1970s, without prolonged fighting that might drain the Western nations. Kenya, Vietnam, and the Algerian morass were bitter exceptions. Western governments typically retained important cultural relations with their former colonies and sometimes provided administrative and military help as well. Both France and Belgium, for example, frequently intervened in Africa after decolonization was officially complete. Finally, Western economic interests remained strong in most former colonies—particularly in Africa, which exploited mineral and agricultural resources in a pattern of trade not radically different from that of colonial days.

The impact of decolonization on the West should not, however, be minimized. Important minorities of former settlers and officials came home embittered, though, except briefly in France, they were not a significant political force. Europe's overt power in the world was dramatically reduced. Efforts by Britain and France to attack independent Egypt in 1956, to protest Egypt's nationalization of the Suez Canal, symbolized the new state of affairs. The United States and the Soviet Union forced a quick end to hostilities, and what was once a colonial lifeline came into non-Western hands. Yet although decolonization was a powerful change in world affairs, it did not, at least in the short run, overwhelm the West, as neither economic growth nor internal political stability suffered greatly.

## The Cold War

The final new ingredient of Europe's diplomatic framework, the **cold war** between the United States and the Soviet Union, had a more durable ongoing influence on politics and society within the West. The conflict took shape between 1945 and 1947. The last wartime meetings among the leaders of Britain, the United States, and the Soviet Union had rather vaguely staked out the boundaries of postwar Europe, which were certainly open to varied interpretations. By the war's end, Soviet troops firmly occupied most eastern European countries, and within three years the Soviets had installed communist regimes to their liking, while excluding opposition political movements. Thus an **eastern bloc** emerged that included Poland, Czechoslovakia, Bulgaria, Romania, and Hungary. And Soviet boundaries themselves had pushed west, reversing the decisions of the post–World War I Versailles conference. The Baltic states disappeared, and Poland lost territory to Russia, gaining some former German lands as compensation. Finally, Soviet occupation of the eastern zone of Germany gave Russia a base closer toward the heart of Europe than the tsars had ever dreamed possible (Map 36.1).

The Cold War Military Standoff

Offended by the Soviet Union's heavy-handed manipulation of eastern Europe, including its zone in eastern Germany, U.S. and British policymakers tried to counter. The new American president, **Harry Truman,** was less eager for smooth relations with the Soviets than Franklin Roosevelt had been; Truman was emboldened by the U.S. development of the atomic bomb in 1945. Britain's wartime leader, Winston Churchill, had long feared communist aggression; it was he who in 1946 coined the phrase **iron curtain** to describe the division between free and

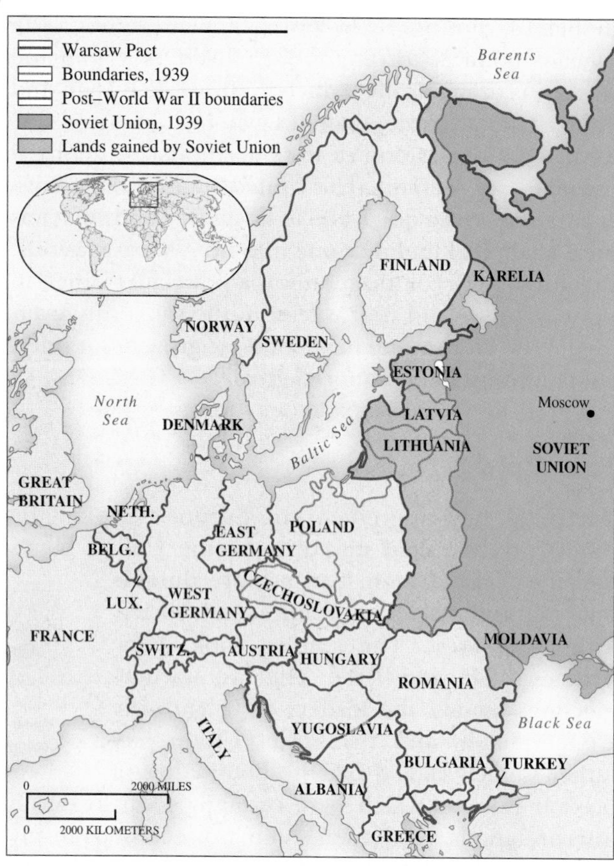


**MAP 36.1 Soviet and Eastern European Boundaries by 1948.** The new communist empire was joined in the Warsaw Pact, formed to respond to the West's North Atlantic Treaty Organization (itself formed in response to a perceived communist threat).

repressed societies that he saw taking shape in Europe. But Britain frankly lacked the power to resist Soviet pressure, and under the Labour government it explicitly left the initiative to the United States.

The United States responded to Soviet rivalry with vigor. It criticized Soviet policies and denied Soviet applications for reconstruction loans. It bolstered regimes in Iran, Turkey, and Greece that were under Soviet pressure. Then in 1947 the United States proclaimed its **Marshall Plan,** a program of substantial loans that was designed to aid Western nations rebuild from the war's devastation. In Soviet eyes the Marshall Plan was a vehicle for U.S. economic dominance, and indeed there is little question that in addition to humanitarian motives the United States intended to beat back domestic communist movements in countries such as France and Italy by promoting economic growth.

The focal point of the cold war in these early years was Germany, which after the war had been divided into four zones administered by the United States, Britain, France, and the Soviet Union (Map 36.2). Soviet policy in Germany initially concentrated on seizing goods and factories as reparation. The Western Allies soon prevented Soviet intervention in their own zones and turned to some rebuilding efforts in the interests of playing a modest "German card" against growing Soviet strength in the East. That is, although the West, led by the United States, did not intend to resurrect a powerful Germany, it soon began to think in terms of constructing a viable political and economic entity. Allied collaboration started building a unified West Germany in 1946, and local political structures followed by more national ones were established through elections. When in 1947 the West moved to promote German economic recovery by creating a stable currency, the Soviet Union responded by blockading the city of Berlin, the divided former capital that sat in the midst of the Soviet zone. The United States responded with a massive airlift to keep the city supplied, and the crisis finally ended in 1948, with two separate Germanies—East and West—beginning to take clear shape along a tense, heavily fortified frontier.

Cold war divisions spread from Germany to Europe more generally with the formation of two rival military alliances. The **North Atlantic Treaty Organization (NATO)** was formed in 1949, under U.S. leadership, to group most of the western European powers and Canada in a defensive alliance against possible Soviet aggression. The NATO pact soon legitimated some rearmament of West Germany in the context of resistance to communism, as well as the continued maintenance of a substantial U.S. military presence in Germany and in other member nations. In response, the Soviet Union organized the **Warsaw Pact** among its eastern European satellites. When in 1949 the Soviets developed their own nuclear capability, the world—particularly the European world—seemed indeed divided between two rival camps, each in turn dominated by its own superpower. Numerous U.S. and Soviet military units were permanently stationed in Europe on either side of the cold war divide.

Europe in the Cold War

The cold war had a number of implications for western Europe. It brought new influences from the United States on internal as well as foreign policy. Through the 1950s and beyond, the United States pressed for acceptance of German rearmament (though under some agreed-on limits); it lobbied for higher military expenditures in its old allies France and Britain; and it pressed for acceptance of U.S. forces and weapons systems. The Americans' wishes were not always met, but the United States had vital negotiating leverage in the economic aid it offered (and might withdraw), in the troops it stationed in Europe, and in the nuclear "umbrella" it developed (and might, in theory, also withdraw). Nuclear weapons seemed to offer the only realistic protection should the Soviet Union

U.S. Test Bomb over Uninhabited Pacific Island, 1952

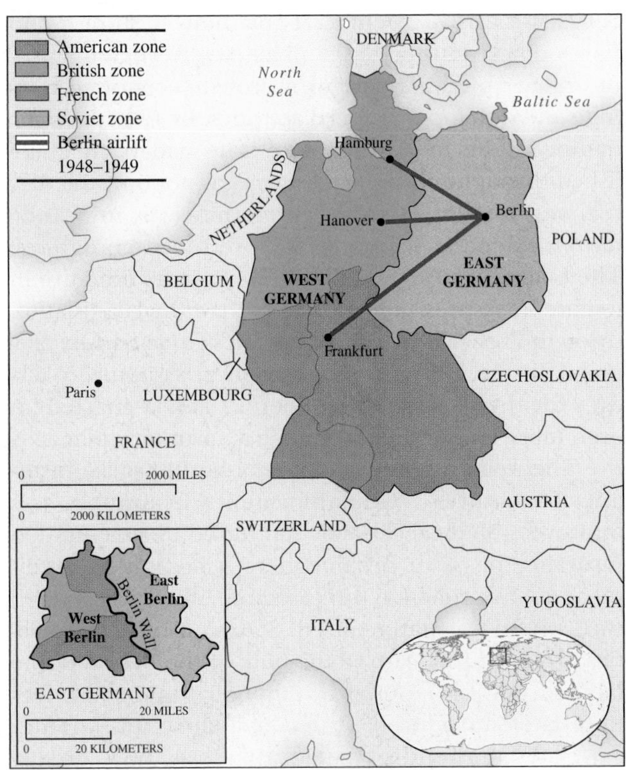


MAP 36.2 Germany After World War II

venture direct attack. The Soviets, for their part, influenced western Europe not only through perceived aggressive intent but also by funding and supporting substantial communist movements in France and Italy, which in turn affected but did not overwhelm the political process.

The cold war did not maintain within Europe the intensity it reached in the initial years. Centers of conflict shifted in part outside Europe as Korea, then Vietnam, and recurrently the Middle East became flashpoints. After 1958 France became more and more restive under what it viewed as Anglo-U.S. dominance of NATO, and it finally withdrew its forces from the joint NATO command, requiring also that U.S. troops leave French soil. In the 1970s Germany opened new negotiations with the Soviet Union and eastern bloc countries, wanting increased export opportunities and reduced diplomatic tension. Nevertheless, the cold war and the resultant alliance system continued to describe much of the framework of East–West relations in Europe and elsewhere in the world.

The shifting balance between the United States and Europe produced a crisscrossing of military relationships, whatever the larger implications of the shift. As western Europe abandoned military preeminence, the United States, never before a major peacetime military power, devoted growing resources to its military capacity and gave an increasing voice to its military leaders. Regardless of the political party in power, the percentage of the U.S. government budget going to the military remained stable from the 1950s to the 1980s—when it went up. In contrast, some European leaders boasted that their societies had made a transition toward preeminence of civilian values and goals. Although U.S. and European values and institutions became more similar in key respects after World War II, the difference in military roles signaled ongoing distinctions within Western society.

## The Resurgence of Western Europe

■ **Western Europeans introduced striking innovations in politics and the economy, though there were new sources of tension. Strides toward European unity cut through traditional enmities. Rapid economic growth sustained a strong European role in the world economy.**

A new set of leaders emerged in many European countries, some from wartime resistance movements, eager to avoid the mistakes that had led to economic depression and war. Their vision was not always realized, but from 1945 onward, western Europe did move forward on three important fronts: the extension of democratic political systems, a modification of nation-state rivalries within Europe, and a commitment to rapid economic growth that reduced previous social and gender tensions.

### The Spread of Liberal Democracy

In politics, defeat in war greatly discredited fascism and other rightist movements that had opposed parliamentary democracy. Several new political movements surfaced in western Europe, notably an important Christian Democratic current, which was wedded to democratic institutions and moderate social reform. Communist as well as socialist leaders largely accepted democratic procedures. Western Europe experienced a shift in the political spectrum toward fuller support for democratic constitutions and greater agreement on the need for government planning and welfare activities.

New regimes had to be constructed in Germany and Italy after the defeat of fascist and Nazi leadership. France established a new republic once occupation ended. In Germany, political reconstruction was delayed by the division of the nation by the victorious Allies. As the cold war took shape, however, France, Britain, and the United States progressively merged their zones into what became the Federal Republic of Germany (West Germany), encouraging a new constitution that would avoid the mistakes of Germany's earlier Weimar Republic by outlawing extremist political movements. Italy established a constitutional democracy. Women's voting rights spread throughout the region as well.

Western Europe's movement toward more consistent democracy continued in the 1970s, when Spain and Portugal moved from their authoritarian, semifascist constitutions (following the deaths of longtime strongmen) to democratic, parliamentary systems. Greece, increasingly linked to the West, followed the same pattern. By the 1980s western Europe had become more politically uniform than ever before in history.

## The Welfare State

The consolidation of democracy also entailed a general movement toward a **welfare state.** Resistance ideas and the shift leftward of the political spectrum helped explain the new activism of the state in economic policy and welfare issues. Wartime planning in the British government had pointed to the need for new programs to reduce the impact of economic inequality and to reward the lower classes for their loyalty (Figure 36.2). Not surprisingly, the governments that emerged at the war's end—Britain's Labour party and the Communist-Socialist–Christian Democrat coalitions in France and Italy—quickly moved to set up a new government apparatus that would play a vigorous role in economic planning and develop new social activities. By 1948 the basic nature of the modern welfare state had been established throughout western Europe, as not only the new regimes but also established reformists (as in Scandinavia) extended a variety of government programs. The United States, though somewhat more tentative in welfare measures, added to its New Deal legislation through President Lyndon Johnson's Great Society programs in the 1960s, creating medical assistance packages for the poor and the elderly. Canada enacted an even more comprehensive medical insurance plan.

The welfare state elaborated a host of social insurance measures. Unemployment insurance was improved. Medical care was supported by state-funded insurance or, as in Britain where it became a centerpiece to the new Labour program, the basic health care system was nationalized. State-run medical facilities provided free care to the bulk of the British population from 1947 onward, although some small fees were later introduced. Family assistance was another category, not entirely new, that was now greatly expanded. All western European governments provid-

FIGURE 36.2 This poster, published by the British Ministry of Health during the 1950s, was intended to increase public awareness of good health practices. Campaigns like these were part of a major shift in thinking about the role of government in Western societies: after World War II, most western European nations established "welfare states," intended to provide social services and economic assistance for citizens "from the cradle to the grave."

ed payments to families with several children, the amount increasing with family size. In the 1950s a French worker family with low earnings and five children could improve its income by as much as 40 percent through family aid. Governments also became more active in the housing field—a virtual necessity, given wartime destruction and postwar population growth. By the 1950s over one-fourth of the British population was housed in structures built and run by the government. The welfare state cushioned citizens against major expenses and unusual hardships, though it did not rearrange overall social structure.

The welfare state was undeniably expensive. It greatly enlarged government bureaucracies, in addition to channeling tax monies to new purposes. A new breed of bureaucrat, often called a **technocrat** because of intense training in engineering or economics and because of a devotion to the power of national planning, came to the fore in government offices. By the 1950s up to 25 percent of the gross national product of France and Holland was going to welfare purposes, and the figure tended to rise with time. As military expenses began to stabilize, welfare commitments became far and away the largest component of Western government budgets outside the United States. Here was a clear indication of the extent to which the western European state had altered its relationship to the wider society.

## New Challenges to Political Stability

The Western pattern of political compromise around the mechanisms of parliamentary democracy and the welfare state were severely jolted by a series of student protests that developed in the late 1960s. Even before this, in the United States a vigorous civil rights movement had developed to protest unequal treatment of African Americans (Figure 36.3). Massive demonstrations, particularly in cities in the American South, attacked segregation and limitations on African American voting rights.

Campus unrest was a Western-wide phenomenon in the 1960s. At major American universities, campus unrest focused on the nation's involvement in the war in Vietnam. Young people in Europe and the United States also targeted the materialism of their societies, including the stodginess of the welfare state, seeking more idealistic goals and greater justice. Student uprisings in France in 1968 created a near revolution. By the early 1970s new rights for students and other reforms, combined with police repression, ended the most intense student protests, whereas passage of civil rights legislation in the United States ultimately reduced urban

FIGURE 36.3 The great civil rights rally drew more than 250,000 people to Washington, D.C. in August 1963. The large numbers and high feelings expected at this rally caused much worry about civil unrest—liquor sales were suspended, thousands of troops were put on alert, police were brought in from other cities, and the public address system was set up so that government officials could shut it down if they thought it necessary—but the day was entirely peaceful.

rioting and demonstrations. The flexibility of postwar Western democracy seemed triumphant. Some additional political concerns, including a new wave of feminism focusing on economic rights and dignity for women, and environmentalist movements entered the arena during the 1970s, partly as an aftermath of the student explosion. The rise of the **Green movement** in several countries in the 1970s signaled a new political tone, hostile to uncontrolled economic growth. Green parliamentary deputies in Germany even refused to wear coats and ties in their efforts to defy established political habits.

As economic growth slowed in the 1970s and the Western world faced its greatest economic recession since the immediate postwar years, other signs of political change appeared. New leadership sprang up within the British Conservative party and the U.S. Republican party, seeking to reduce the costs and coverage of the welfare state. In 1979 British Conservative leader Margaret Thatcher began the longest-running prime-ministership in 20th-century British history, working to cut welfare and housing expenses and to promote free enterprise. Neither she nor her U.S. counterpart, Ronald Reagan, fully dismantled the welfare state, but they did reduce its impact. Despite important adjustments, however, the main line of postwar government in the West persisted into the 21st century.

## The Diplomatic Context

Along with the extension of democracy and the development of the welfare state, the West showed postwar vigor in addressing some traditional diplomatic problems, notably recurrent nationalistic rivalry, as well as specific manifestations, such as French–German enmity. U.S. guidance combined with innovative thinking in the new European governments.

During the war, many resistance leaders had tempered their hatred of Nazism with a plea for a reconstruction of the European spirit. The Christian Democratic movement, particularly, produced important new advocates of harmony among European nations. By 1947 U.S. leaders were also eager to spur western Europe's economic recovery, for which they judged coordination across national boundaries an essential precondition. Thus the Marshall Plan required discussion of tariffs and other development issues among recipient nations. With simultaneous U.S. insistence on the partial rearmament of Germany and German participation in NATO, the framework for diplomatic reform was complete.

Faced with these pressures and aware of the failure of nationalistic policies between the wars, France initiated coordination with Germany as a means of setting up a new Europe. The nations of the Low Countries and Italy were soon linked in these activities. The idea was to tie German economic activity to an international framework so that the nation's growing strength would not again threaten European peace. Institutions were established to link policies in heavy industry and later to develop atomic power. A measure to establish a united European military force proved too ambitious and collapsed under nationalist objections. But in 1958 the six western European nations (West Germany, France, Italy, Belgium, Luxembourg, and the Netherlands) set up the European Economic Community, or Common Market—later called the **European Union**—to begin to create a single economic entity across national political boundaries (Map 36.3). Tariffs were progressively reduced among the member nations, and a common tariff policy was set for the outside world. Free movement of labor and investment was encouraged. A Common Market bureaucracy was established, ultimately in Brussels, to oversee these operations. The Common Market set up a court system to adjudicate disputes and prevent violations of coordination rules; it also administered a development fund to spur economic growth in such laggard regions as southern Italy and western France.

European Union Flag

The Common Market did not move quickly toward a single government. Important national disputes limited the organization's further growth. France and Germany, for example, routinely quarreled over agricultural policy, with France seeking more payments to farmers as a matter of obvious self-interest. But although the European Union did not turn into full integration, on the whole it prospered. It even established an advisory international parliament, ultimately elected by direct vote. Further, in the 1980s firm arrangements were made to dismantle all trade and currency exchange barriers among member states in 1992, creating essentially complete economic unity. A single currency, the euro, was set up in many member countries by 2001. The European Union's success expanded its hold within western Europe. After long hesitations Britain, despite its tradition of proud island independence, decided to join, as did Ireland, Denmark, and later Greece, Spain, Portugal, Austria, Sweden, and Finland. By 2005 nine other nations, mostly in central Europe, were admitted to membership.

Contemporary Europe

Nationalist tensions within Europe receded to a lower point than ever before in modern European history. After the worst scares of the cold war, focused mainly on the division between communist East and semicapitalist West, Europe became a diplomatically placid continent, enjoying one of the longest periods of substantial internal peace in its history.

## Economic Expansion

After a surprisingly short, if agonizing, postwar rebuilding, striking economic growth accompanied political

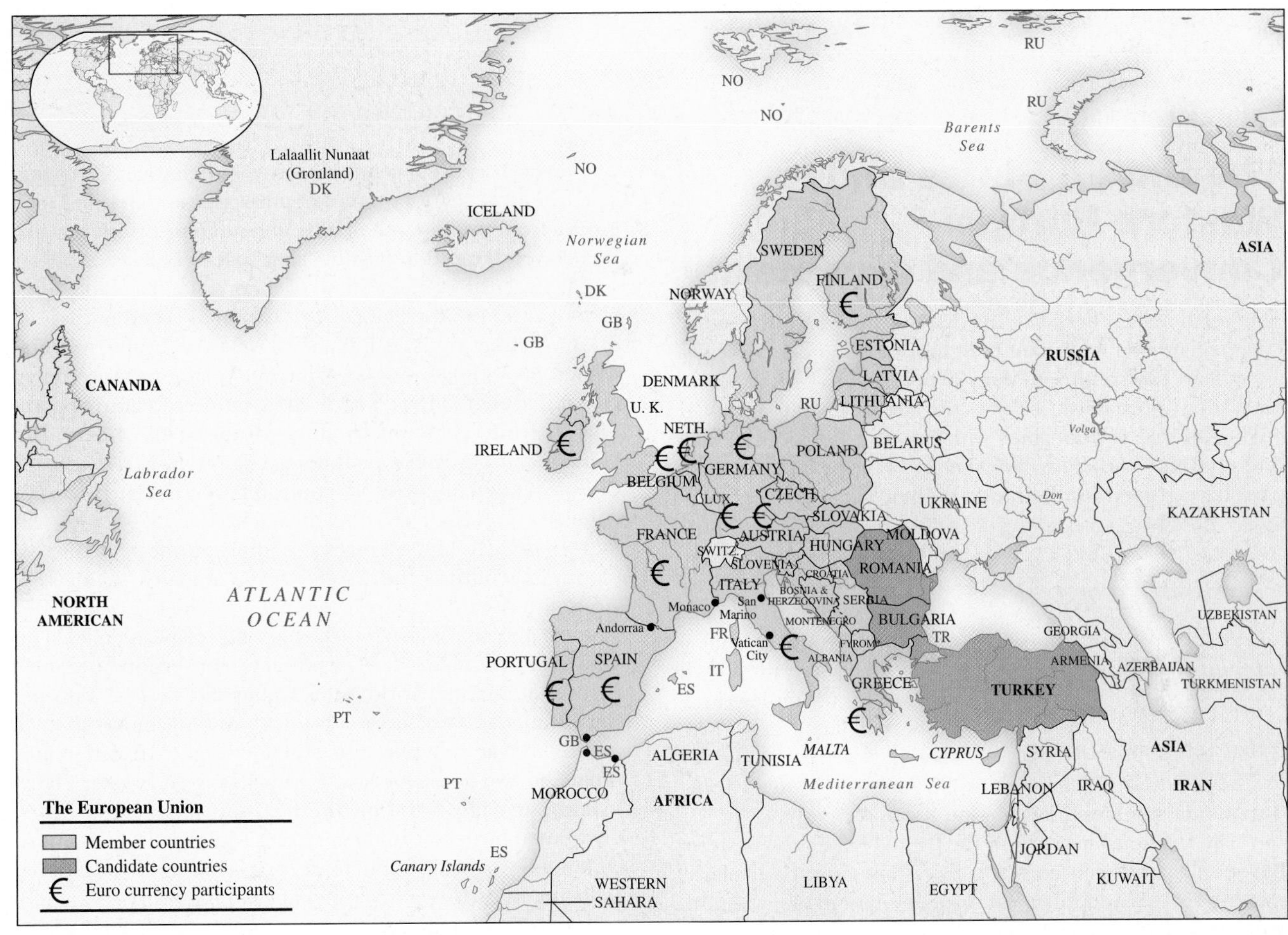


**MAP 36.3** Stages in the Development of the European Union

and diplomatic change. The welfare state and the European Union may have encouraged this growth by improving purchasing power for the masses and facilitating market expansion across national boundaries; certainly economic growth encouraged the success of new political and diplomatic systems.

There was no question that by the mid-1950s western Europe had entered a new economic phase. Agricultural production and productivity increased rapidly as peasant farmers, backed by technocrats, adopted new equipment and seeds. European agriculture was still less efficient than that of North America, which necessitated some much-resented tariff barriers by the Common Market. But food production easily met European needs, often with some to spare for export. Retooled industries poured out textiles and metallurgical products. Expensive consumer products, such as automobiles and appliances, supported rapidly growing factories. Western Europe also remained a leading center of weapons production, trailing only the United States and the Soviet Union in exports. Overall growth in gross national product surpassed the rates of any extended period since the Industrial Revolution began; it also surpassed the growth rates of the U.S. economy during the 1950s and 1960s.

By this point French, German, and Italian economies were growing between 6 percent and 11 percent annually. These growth rates depended on rapid technological change. Europe's rising food production was achieved with a steadily shrinking agricultural labor force. France's peasant population—16 percent of the labor force in the early 1950s—fell to 10 percent two decades later, but overall output was much higher than before. During the 1950s the industrial workforce grew as part of factory expansion, but by the 1960s the relative proportion of factory workers also began to drop, despite rising production. Workers in the service sector, filling functions as teachers, clerks, medical personnel, insurance and bank workers, and performers and other "leisure industry" personnel, rose rapidly in contrast. In France half of all paid workers were in the service sector by 1968, and the proportion rose steadily thereafter.

Another key change involved immigration. Many parts of the continent experienced a labor shortage and had to seek hundreds of thousands of workers

IN DEPTH

## The United States and Western Europe: Convergence and Complexity

The relationship between the United States and western Europe has been important both historically and analytically for at least two centuries. Many people in the United States have tried to establish a distinctive identity while acknowledging special relationships with Europe; isolationism was one response earlier in this century. Europeans, for their part, have groped for definition of their U.S. "cousins," particularly as U.S. military and cultural influence grew in the 20th century. Were U.S. innovations to be welcomed, as stemming from a kindred society with a special flair for technology and modern mass taste, or should they be resisted as emblems of a superficial, degenerate, and essentially un-European society?

> *"The United States constituted a more traditional society, in terms of values, in the later 20th century than did western Europe."*

The relationship between the United States and western Europe has not been constant. Over time, and particularly since 1945, U.S. and European societies have in many important respects converged. Because of heightened imitation and shared advanced industrial economies, some earlier differences have receded.

Western Europe, for example, no longer has a very distinct peasantry. Its farmers, though smaller scale than their U.S. agribusiness counterparts, are commercialized and simply so few in numbers that they no longer set their society apart. European workers, though less likely than those in the United States to call themselves middle class, are now relatively prosperous. They have moved away from some of the political radicalism that differentiated them from their U.S. counterparts earlier in the 20th century. Europe does not have as deep-seated a racial issue as the United States inherited from slavery, but the growing influx of people from the West Indies, north Africa, and Asia has duplicated in Europe some of the same racial tensions and inner-city problems that bedevil the United States. At the other end of the social scale, trained managers and professionals now form a similar upper class in both societies, the fruit of systems of higher education that differ in particulars but resemble each other in producing something of a meritocratic elite.

A shared popular culture has certainly emerged. Although it stemmed mainly from U.S. innovations before World War II, more recently it has involved mutual borrowing. The United States, for example, embraced miniskirts and rock groups from Britain in the 1960s, and not only British but also French youth raced to buy the latest style in blue jeans.

Differences remain, some of them going back to earlier historical traditions. The United States has relied more fully on free-market capitalism than did western Europe, with the United States possessing less complete planning, fewer environmental regulations, and a more modest welfare apparatus. The difference was heightened during the 1990s. The United States proved much more religious than did western Europe. Only a minority of people in most western European countries professed religious belief by the 1990s, with less than 10 percent in most cases attending church with any regularity. In contrast the United States remains highly religious, with up to 40 percent regular church attendance, and 70 to 80 percent of its people professing religious belief. The United States made a less complete conversion to a new leisure ethic after World War II than did western Europe; European vacation time advanced toward more than a month a year, whereas the average in the United States remained two weeks or less. Europeans were franker about teenage sexuality, following the 1960 sexual revolution. They distributed birth control materials to adolescents much more commonly than did their more prudish U.S. counterparts, reducing rates of teenage pregnancy in the process.

In certain important respects, then, the United States constituted a more traditional society, in terms of values, in the later 20th century than did western Europe. Some of the variation between the two societies related to long-established distinctions (as in the degree of suspicion of government power); others emerged for the first time, sometimes surprisingly, after World War II.

The biggest distinctions between the two societies in recent decades, however, followed from their increasingly divergent world roles. Western Europe, though still highly influential in culture and trade on a global scale, concentrated increasingly on its own regional arrangements, including the European Union trading bloc, and decreasingly on military development. The United States moved in the opposite direction. Thus a traditional distinction was reversed; the United States became the more military (and some would argue militaristic) society, and many Europeans became committed to more strictly civilian goals.

---

**Questions** Why did the United States and western Europe converge in new ways during the 20th century? Do the two societies remain part of a common civilization? What are the most important issues to resolve in making this judgment?

**FIGURE 36.4** In the United States, as well as in Japan and western Europe, advertisements increasingly tried to create the sense that a good life could be achieved by buying the right goods. Here, a new car was associated with a prosperous home, a loving family, and even happy pets.

from other areas—first from southern Europe, then, as this region industrialized, from Africa, the Middle East, and parts of Asia. The rise of immigrant minorities was a vital development in western Europe and also the United States, where the influx of Asian and Latin American immigrants stepped up markedly.

Unprecedented economic growth and low unemployment meant unprecedented improvements in incomes, even with the taxation necessary to sustain welfare programs. New spending money rapidly translated into huge increases in the purchase of durable consumer goods, as virtually the whole of Western civilization became an "affluent society."

Ownership of standard consumer goods like televisions and cars spread widely. Shopping malls and supermarkets migrated across the Atlantic. Advertising was not quite as ubiquitous in Europe as in the United States. But promptings to buy, to smell good, to look right, to express one's personality in the latest car style began quickly to describe European life (Figure 36.4). The frenzy to find good vacation spots was certainly intense. Millions of Germans poured annually into Italy and Spain, seeking the sun. Britons thronged to Spanish beaches. Europeans were bent on combining efficient work with indulgent leisure.

The West's economic advance was not without some dark spots. Many immigrant workers from Turkey, north Africa, Pakistan, and the West Indies suffered very low wages and unstable employment. These immigrants, euphemistically labeled "guest workers," were often residentially segregated and victims of discrimination by employers and police, as racism continued to be an important factor in Western society.

By the 1990s slower economic growth raised new unemployment problems in western Europe. Economic inequality increased throughout the West, though particularly in the United States. Nevertheless, the West's economic vitality, a marked contrast to the interwar decades, underpinned vital social transformations and played a major role in the global economic framework as well.

## Cold War Allies: The United States, Canada, Australia, and New Zealand

- **Many changes in the non-European West paralleled those in Europe, including the welfare state. The United States took a distinctive role, particularly because of its new position as a military superpower.**

Developments in the so-called overseas West in many ways paralleled those in western Europe, but without the sense of grappling with prior collapse. The sheer level of innovation in domestic policy was less great, in part because the crises of the first half of the 20th century had been less severe. Crucial adjustments occurred, however, in foreign policy. The United States led the way in making the changes in its own tradition that were necessary to develop a massive peacetime military force and a global set of alliances. With the decline of European, and particularly British, international power and the emergence of the cold war context, Australia, New Zealand, and Canada tightened their links with the United States and developed new contacts with other areas of the world.

## The Former Dominions

Canada forged ahead in welfare policies after World War II, establishing a greater stake in economic planning and state-run medical insurance than did the United States. At the same time, however, Canadian economic integration with the United States continued, with U.S. investments in Canadian resources and mutual exports and imports soaring steadily into the 1970s. By 1980 the Canadian government took some measures to limit further U.S. penetration, and a sense of Canadian nationalism sparked resentment of the giant to the south. In 1988, however, the two nations signed a free-trade agreement, creating a North American trading bloc at a time when European unity was increasing rapidly.

Continued emigration to Canada pointed in new directions also, with growing numbers of people arriving from various parts of Asia. Canada's most distinctive issue, however, involved growing agitation by French Canadians in Quebec for regional autonomy or even national independence. A new separatist party, founded in 1967, took control of the provincial government during the 1970s. Subsequent legislation limited the use of the English language in Quebec's public and commercial life, though referendums for full independence failed during the 1980s. A new Canadian constitution in 1982, however, granted greater voice to the provinces, both to counter French Canadian demand and also to recognize the growing economic strength of the resource-rich western provinces. Separatist tensions continue to simmer, however, into the 21st century.

From 1945 onward Australia and New Zealand moved steadily away from their traditional alignment with Great Britain and toward horizons around the Pacific. The two commonwealths joined a mutual defense pact with the United States in 1951, directed against potential communist aggression in the Pacific. Both nations cooperated with the United States in the Korean War, and Australia backed U.S. intervention in Vietnam. In 1966 the Australian prime minister declared, "Wherever the United States is resisting aggression . . . we will go a-waltzing Matilda with you." In the later 1970s and 1980s Australia and especially New Zealand began to distance themselves somewhat from U.S. foreign policy. New Zealand barred U.S. nuclear-armed vessels in 1985.

As Great Britain aligned with the European Union, Australian and New Zealand exports were increasingly directed toward other Pacific nations, notably Japan, whereas investment capital came mainly from the United States and Japan. Indeed, Australia became Japan's chief raw-materials supplier aside from oil. Asian emigration also increasingly altered the population mix, again particularly in Australia. Despite a long-held whites-only immigration policy, the Australian government was powerless to resist growing regional emigration, particularly from Indochina. By 1983 Asians accounted for 60 percent of the total immigrant population in Australia.

## The "U.S. Century"?

Amid a host of domestic issues, the big news in U.S. history after 1945 was its assumption—in many ways, its eager assumption—of the superpower mantle, opposing the Soviet Union and serving as the world's leading defender of democratic and capitalistic values. The United States hesitated briefly after 1945, demobilizing its World War II forces rather quickly with some hope that world peace would provide some respite from further international engagement. However, Great Britain's inability to continue to police the world for the West, together with rapid Soviet successes in installing communist governments in eastern Europe, prompted a decisive U.S. stance. In 1947 President Harry Truman promised support for "free peoples who are resisting subjugation by armed minorities or by outside pressures." The doctrine, specifically directed against communist pressures on Greece and Turkey, soon extended into the elaboration of Marshall Plan aid to rebuild the economies of western Europe against the possibility of communist subversion in these war-torn countries. The Republican party was initially tempted to resist these new international engagements, but the 1948 communist takeover of Czechoslovakia checked that impulse. For many decades basic U.S. foreign policy proceeded amid wide bipartisan agreement.

The plunge into the cold war took a toll on the home front, however. The United States entered a period of intense, even frenzied concern about internal communist conspiracies, ferreting out a host of suspected spies and subjecting people in many fields to dismissal from their jobs on grounds of suspected radical sympathies.

Cold war engagement prompted other policy changes in the federal government. The Defense

Department was set up in 1947 to coordinate military policy, and the Central Intelligence Agency was established to organize a worldwide information-gathering and espionage network. Military spending increased considerably, with the formation of the Strategic Air Command to stand in constant readiness in case of a Soviet bombing attack. A massive U.S. airlift thwarted Soviet pressure on the western sectors of occupied Berlin. The United States resisted the invasion of South Korea by the communist North, beginning in the 1950s; U.S. troops stationed in Japan were sent in to support the South Koreans. Under General Douglas MacArthur and backed by several allies under a hastily arranged United Nations mandate, the North Korean invasion was repulsed within a few months. The United States then authorized an invasion into North Korea, which brought a retaliatory intervention from communist China. The United States was pushed back, and more than two years of additional fighting ensued before peace was negotiated in 1953—with the new boundary line between the two Koreas relatively close to the previous line. In the meantime annual U.S. spending on the military had increased from $13.5 billion to $50 billion.

During the 1950s, under the presidency of Dwight Eisenhower, the United States settled into a policy of containment of the Soviet Union, which involved maintenance of large peacetime military forces. The United States also arranged alliances not only with western Europe, in NATO, but also with Australia and New Zealand, with several southeast Asian nations, and with several nations in the Middle East; this alliance system virtually surrounded the Soviet Union. Less novel was recurrent U.S. intervention in Central America against suspected communist movements; thus U.S. aid toppled a new Guatemalan government in 1954. The United States was unable to prevent a takeover in Cuba that eventually propelled Cuba into the communist camp, despite a U.S.-backed invasion attempt by anticommunist Cuban rebels. Nonetheless, the United States maintained its policy of vigilance (under President John Kennedy in 1962) by forcing the Soviet Union to withdraw its missile sites on the island.

The U.S. containment policy yielded a final test that took shape during the 1960s, when intervention against communist revolutionaries in South Vietnam gradually escalated. The U.S. Air Force began bombing communist North Vietnam in 1965. Later that year American troops were sent in, reaching a total of 550,000 by 1968. By this time the United States was spending $2 billion a week on a war that never produced convincing success and gradually bogged down in horrendous bloodshed on both sides. By 1970 more bombs had been dropped on Vietnam than had been dropped by anyone, anywhere previously in the 20th century. By 1968 domestic pressure against the war, centered particularly on U.S. college campuses, began to force changes in strategy. A new U.S. president, Richard Nixon, tried to expand the war to other parts of Indochina, to increase pressure on North Vietnam. Simultaneously, peace negotiations with North Vietnam were launched, resulting finally in an agreement on a cease-fire, in 1973. By 1975, as the United States speedily withdrew, all Vietnam lay in communist hands.

Furor over the Vietnam War led to agonizing policy reassessments in the United States. Some observers judged that new directions might be forged, as the United States had discovered that its massive military might could be stalemated by fervent guerrilla tactics. Both the U.S. military and the public grew more wary of regional wars. Although the national mood sobered, however, decisive policy changes did not ensue. A socialist government in Chile, for example, was ousted with the aid of covert U.S. pressure even as the Vietnam conflict wound down. The socialist government was replaced by a brutal military regime.

In 1980 the United States overwhelmingly elected a new president, Ronald Reagan, who combined conservative domestic policies with a commitment to bolster military spending and make sure that the United States would "ride tall" again in world affairs. The 1980s saw no major new international involvements, but several punitive raids were conducted against suspected terrorists in the Middle East, and the small West Indian island of Grenada was invaded to topple a leftist regime. President Reagan sponsored a number of expensive new weapons systems, which helped press an afflicted Soviet economy to virtual collapse as its leaders attempted to keep pace. The next president, George Bush, continued an interventionist policy by sending U.S. troops into Panama to evict and arrest an abrasive dictator and then by spearheading a Western and moderate Arab alliance against Iraq's invasion of Kuwait, during 1990–1991. Under President Bill Clinton, the United States led participation in military action against forces in the Balkans in the 1990s.

By this point, with the cold war over, the United States emerged as "the world's only superpower." It had taken over and expanded many of the international policing functions once held by Western nations like Britain. Other Western states sometimes resented American leadership, but they generated no clear alternative and usually supported U.S. initiatives.

## Culture and Society in the West

■ **The expansion of consumer culture marked recent Western history. Dramatic changes in gender relations also defined Western society.**

Political and economic changes in Western society progressively altered the contours of earlier industrial development. The West became the first example of an advanced industrial society, especially from the 1950s onward, and both the United States and western Europe shared in leading facets of change.

## Social Structure

Economic growth, bringing increasing prosperity to most groups, eased some earlier social conflicts throughout the West. Workers were still propertyless, but they had substantial holdings as consumers, and their sense of social inferiority often declined as a result. Social lines were also blurred by increasing social mobility, as educational opportunities opened further and the size of the white-collar sector expanded. Much unskilled labor was left to immigrants. Economic and political change also altered conditions for western Europe's peasantry, and not only by cutting its size. Peasants became increasingly commercial, eager for improvements in standards of living, and participants, through car trips and television, in urban culture. They also became more attuned to bureaucracies, as state regulations pushed them into cooperative organizations.

Social distinctions remained. Middle-class people had more abundant leisure opportunities and a more optimistic outlook than did most workers. Signs of tension continued. Crime rates went up throughout Western society after the 1940s, though the levels were particularly high in the United States. Race riots punctuated U.S. life in the 1950s and 1960s and exploded in immigrant sections of British cities in the 1980s and Germany in the early 1990s.

## The Women's Revolution

A key facet of postwar change involved women and the family, and again both western Europe and the United States participated fully in this upheaval. Although family ideals persisted in many ways—with workers, for example, urging that "a loving family is the finest thing, something to work for, to look to and to look after"—the realities of family life changed in many ways. Family leisure activities expanded. Extended-family contacts were facilitated by telephones and automobiles. More years of schooling increased the importance of peer groups for children, and the authority of parents undoubtedly declined.

The clearest innovation in family life came through the new working patterns of women. World War II brought increased factory and clerical jobs for women, as the earlier world war had done. After a few years of downward adjustment, the trends continued. From the early 1950s onward, the number of working women, particularly married women, rose steadily in western Europe, the United States, and Canada. (See Visualizing the Past feature.) Women's earlier educational gains had improved their work qualifications; the growing number of service jobs created a need for additional workers—and women, long associated with clerical jobs and paid less than men, were ideal candidates. Many women also sought entry into the labor force as a means of adding to personal or family income, to afford some of the consumer items now becoming feasible but not yet easy to buy, or as a means of personal fulfillment in a society that associated worth with work and earnings.

The growing employment of women, which by the 1970s brought the female segment of the labor force up to 44 percent of the total in most Western countries, represented particularly the employment of adult women, most of them married and many with children. Teenage employment dropped as more girls stayed in school, but long-term work commitments rose steadily. This was not, to be sure, a full stride to job equality. Women's pay lagged behind men's pay. Most women were concentrated in clerical jobs rather than spread through the occupational spectrum, despite a growing minority of middle-class women entering professional and management ranks. Clearly, however, the trends of the 19th-century Industrial Revolution, to keep women and family separate from work outside the home, had yielded to a dramatic new pattern.

Other new rights for women accompanied this shift. Where women had lacked the vote before, as in France, they now got it; of the western European nations, only Switzerland doggedly refused this concession at the national level until 1971. Gains in higher education were considerable, though again full equality remained elusive. Women constituted 23 percent of German university students in 1963, and under socialist governments in the 1970s the figure rose. Preferred subjects, however, remained different from those of men, as most women stayed out of engineering, science (except medicine), and management.

Family rights improved, at least in the judgment of most women's advocates. Access to divorce increased, which many observers viewed as particularly important to women. Abortion law eased, though more slowly in countries of Catholic background than in Britain or Scandinavia; it became increasingly easy for women to regulate their birth rate. Development of new birth control methods, such as the contraceptive pill introduced in 1960, as well as growing knowledge and acceptability of birth control, decreased unwanted pregnancies. Sex and procreation became increasingly separate considerations. Although women continued to differ from men in sexual outlook and behavior—more than twice as many French women as men, for example, hoped to link sex, marriage, and romantic love, according to 1960s polls—more women than before tended to define sex in terms of pleasure.

VISUALIZING THE PAST

## Women at Work in France and the United States

A statistical table of the sort presented here is essentially descriptive. What patterns are described? Is there a major change, and how can it be defined? What are the main differences between these two nations? Were they converging, becoming more similar, in 1962? In 1982? Do they end up in a similar situation with regard to women's work roles, or are they more different in 1982 than they were in 1946?

**Questions** From description, questions of causation arise. Statistical patterns provide a precise framework for a challenging analysis. Why were the United States and France so different in 1946? What might have caused the changes in patterns (for example, in the United States during the 1950s)? What was the role of new feminist demands in 1963? What might have caused the differences in the timing of trends in France and the United States?

**Women at Work: The Female Labor Force in France and the United States**

| | France | | United States | |
|---|---|---|---|---|
| | Women Workers (thousands) | Percentage of Total Force | Woman Workers (thousands) | Percentage of Total Force |
| 1946 | 7,880 | 37.90 | 16,840 | 27.83 |
| 1954 | 6,536 | 33.93 | 19,718 | 29.43 |
| 1962 | 6,478 | 33.23 | 24,047 | 32.74 |
| 1968 | 6,924 | 34.62 | 29,242 | 35.54 |
| 1975 | 7,675 | 36.48 | 37,553 | 39.34 |
| 1982 | 8,473 | 39.46 | 47,894 | 42.81 |

*Sources:* B. R. Mitchell, *International Historical Statistics: Europe, 1750-1988;* U.S. Bureau of the Census, *Historical Statistics of the United States, Colonial Times to 1970, Bicentennial Edition, Part 1;* U.S. Bureau of the Census, *Statistical Abstract of the United States: 1984.*

Predictably, of course, changes in the family, including the roles of women, brought new issues and redefined ideals of companionship. The first issue involved children. A brief increase in the Western birth rate ended in the early 1960s and a rapid decline ensued. Women working and the desire to use income for high consumer standards mitigated against children, or very many children, particularly in the middle class, where birth rates were lowest. Those children born were increasingly sent, often at an early age, to day-care centers, one of the amenities provided by the European welfare state and particularly essential where new fears about population growth began to surface. European families had few hesitations about replacing maternal care with collective care, and parents often claimed that the result was preferable for children. At the same time, however, some observers worried that Western society, and the Western family, were becoming indifferent to children in an eagerness for adult work and consumer achievements. American adults, for example, between the 1950s and 1980s, shifted their assessment of family satisfaction away from parenthood by concentrating on shared enjoyments between husbands and wives.

Family stability also opened new cracks. Pressures to readjust family roles, women working outside the family context, and growing legal freedoms for women caused men and women alike to turn more readily to divorce. In 1961, 9 percent of all British marriages ended in divorce; by 1965 the figure was 16 percent and rising. By the late 1970s, one-third of all British marriages ended in divorce, and the U.S. rate was higher still.

The development of a new surge of feminist protest, although it reflected much wider concerns than family life alone, showed the strains caused by women's new activities and continued limitations. Growing divorce produced many cases of impoverished women combining work and child care. New work roles revealed the persistent earnings gap between men and women. More generally, many women sought supporting values and organizations as they tried to define new identities less tied to the domestic roles and images of previous decades.

A **new feminism** began to take shape with the publication in 1949 of *The Second Sex* by the French intellectual Simone de Beauvoir. Echoed in the 1950s and 1960s by other works, such as *The Feminine Mystique*, by

**FIGURE 36.5** In Houston, in November 1977, the U.S. government sponsored a National Women's Conference. In order to symbolize the direct link between earlier American feminists and the women at the Conference, a torch was lit in Seneca Falls, New York—seat of the famous women's right convention of 1848—and carried 2600 miles by relay runners to Houston. In this photograph, feminist leaders accompany the torch and its three bearers on the last mile of the journey. Here, from left to right, are Susan B. Anthony II, Representative Bella Abzug, Sylvia Ortiz, Peggy Kokernot, and Michele Cearcy (the torch bearers), and Betty Friedan.

Betty Friedan of the United States (Figure 36.5), a new wave of women's rights agitation rose after three decades of relative calm. The new feminism tended to emphasize a more literal equality that would play down special domestic roles and qualities; therefore, it promoted not only specific reforms but also more basic redefinitions of what it meant to be male and female.

The new feminism did not win all women, even in the middle class, which was feminism's most avid audience. It also did not cause some of the most sweeping practical changes that were taking place, as in the new work roles. But it did support the revolution in roles. From the late 1960s onward it pressed Western governments for further change, raising issues that were difficult to fit into established political contexts. The movement both articulated and promoted the gap between new expectations and ongoing inequalities in gender. And the new feminism expressed and promoted some unanswered questions about family functions. In a real sense, later 20th-century feminism seemed to respond to the same desire for individuality and work identity in women that had earlier been urged on men as part of the new mentality suitable for a commercialized economy. Family remained important in the evolving outlook of women, although some feminist leaders attacked the institution outright as hopelessly repressive. Even for many less ideological women, however, family goals were less important than they had been before.

## Western Culture

Amid great innovations in politics, the economy, and social structure—including some pressing new problems—Western cultural life in many respects proceeded along established lines. A host of specific new movements arose, and a wealth of scientific data was assimilated, though basic frameworks had been set earlier, often in the more turbulent but intellectually creative decades of the early 20th century.

One key development was a shift of focus toward the United States. Greater political stability in the United States during the 1930s and 1940s, as well as Hitler's persecutions, had driven many prominent intellectuals to U.S. shores, where they often remained even as western Europe revived. As U.S. universities expanded, their greater wealth fueled more scientific research; what was called a "brain drain," based on dollar power, drew many leading European scientists to the United States even during the 1950s and 1960s. European science remained active, but the costliness of cutting-edge research produced a durable U.S. advantage. Money also mattered in art, as patronage became increasingly important, and thus New York replaced Paris as the center of international styles.

Europeans did participate in some of the leading scientific advances of the postwar years. Francis Crick, of Cambridge University in England, shared with the American James Watson key credit for the discovery of the basic structure of the genetic building block deoxyribonucleic acid (DNA), which in turn opened the way for rapid advances in genetic knowledge and industries based on artificial synthesis of genetic materials. By 2000 work on the human genome project was proceeding rapidly on both sides of the Atlantic. Europeans also participated in nuclear research, often through laboratories funded by the European Union or other inter-European agencies. European space research, slower to develop than Soviet or U.S. initiatives, nevertheless also produced noteworthy achievements by the 1970s, and again there were important commercial spin-offs in communications satellites and other activities.

Developments in the arts maintained earlier 20th-century themes quite clearly. Most artists continued to work in the "modern" modes set before World War I, which featured unconventional self-expression and a wide array of nonrepresentational techniques. The clearest change involved growing public acceptance of the modern styles. The shock that had greeted earlier innovations disappeared, and the public, even when preferring older styles displayed in museums or performed by symphony orchestras devoted to the classics, now seemed reconciled to the redefinition of artistic standards (Figure 36.6). New names were added to the roster of leading modern artists. In Paris Bernard Buffet scored important successes with gaunt, partially abstract figures. The British sculptor Henry Moore produced rounded figures and outright abstractions that conveyed some of the horrors of wartime life and postwar dislocations. A new group of "pop" artists in the 1960s tried to bridge the gap between art and commercial mass culture by incorporating cans and other products, comic strips, and advertisements into paintings, prints, and collages. As also held true in the realm of fully abstract painting, U.S. artists increasingly took the lead.

Europeans retained clearer advantages in artistic films. Italian directors produced a number of gripping, realistic films in the late 1940s, portraying both urban and peasant life without frills. Italy, France, and Sweden became centers of experimental filmmaking again in the 1960s. Jean-Luc Godard and Michelangelo Antonioni portrayed the emptiness of urban life, and

FIGURE 36.6 In the early 1960s the struggling pop artist Andy Warhol was casting about for subject matter. A friend advised him to paint whatever he liked best in the world. He painted soup cans and became an overnight sensation. His work, which also included repeated images of celebrities such as Marilyn Monroe and Marlon Brando, is understood by critics as a statement about the "fascinated yet indifferent" experience of consumers in a society saturated by marketing images.

Swedish director Ingmar Bergman produced a series of dark psychological dramas. Individual directors in Spain, Britain, and Germany also broke new ground, as Europeans remained more comfortable than their U.S. counterparts in producing films of high artistic merit, relatively free from commercial distractions.

Fragmentation occurred in the social sciences, with no commanding figure rising to the stature of Marx or Weber in previous generations, willing to posit fundamental social dynamics or sweeping theories. Many specific fields in the social sciences turned to massive data collections and pragmatic, detailed observations; in many of these, U.S. practitioners developed a decided advantage. Economics, in particular, became something of an American specialty in the post-Keynesian decades and focused on massive quantitative studies of economic cycles and money supplies. European influence was greater in several new theoretical formulations in the humanities. French intellectuals also contributed to a redefinition of historical study, building on innovations launched between the world wars. Social history, or the focus on changes in the lives of ordinary people, became increasingly the order of the day, giving a great spur to historical research throughout western Europe and the United States.

### A Lively Popular Culture

Western society displayed more vitality in its popular culture than in formal intellectual life, which reflected the results of economic and social change. As European economies struggled to recover from the war and as U.S. military forces spread certain enthusiasms more widely than before, some observers spoke of a U.S. "Coca-colanization" of Europe. U.S. soft drinks, blue-jean fashions, chewing gum, and other artifacts became increasingly common. U.S. films continued to wield substantial influence, although the lure of Hollywood declined somewhat. More important was the growing impact of U.S. television series. Blessed with a wide market and revenues generated from advertising, American television was quite simply "slicker" than its European counterparts, and the western drama *Bonanza,* the soap opera *Dallas,* and many other shows appeared regularly on European screens to define, for better or worse, an image of the United States.

In contrast to the interwar decades, however, European popular culture had its own power, and it even began to influence the United States. The most celebrated figures of popular culture in the 1960s were unquestionably the Beatles, from the British port city of Liverpool. Although they adopted popular music styles of the United States, including jazz and early rock, the Beatles added an authentic working-class touch in their impulsiveness and their mockery of authority. They also expressed a good-natured desire to enjoy the pleasures of life, which is a characteristic of modern Western popular culture regardless of national context. British popular music groups continued to set standards in the 1970s and had wide impact on western Europe more generally.

Other facets of popular culture displayed a new vigor. Again in Britain, youth fashions, separate from the standards of the upper class, showed an ability to innovate and sometimes to shock. Unconventional uses of color and cut, as in punk hairstyles of the later 1970s, bore some resemblance to the anti-conventional tone of modern painting and sculpture.

Sexual culture also changed in the West, building on earlier trends that linked sex to a larger pleasure-seeking mentality characteristic of growing consumerism and to a desire for personal expression. Films and television shows demonstrated increasingly relaxed standards about sexual display. In Britain, Holland, and Denmark, sex shops sold a wide array of erotic materials and products.

Like the United States, western Europe experienced important changes in sexual behavior starting around 1960, particularly among young people. Premarital sex became more common. The average age of first sexual intercourse began to go down. Expressive sexuality in western Europe was also evident in the growing number of nude bathing spots, again in interesting contrast to more hesitant initiatives in the United States. Although the association of modern popular culture with sexuality and body concern was not novel, the openness and diversity of expression unquestionably reached new levels and also demonstrated western Europe's new confidence in defining a vigorous, nontraditional mass culture of its own.

Critics of Western popular culture worried about its superficiality and its role in distracting ordinary people from ongoing problems such as social inequality. But there were no huge reactions, like those of Nazism against the cultural trends of the 1920s. Western popular culture played a major role in setting global cultural standards, enhancing the West's international influence even as its formal political dominance declined.

## Eastern Europe After World War II: A Soviet Empire

- **Soviet Russia expanded its effective empire. Amid new challenges, the Soviet system maintained distinctive political controls.**

### The Soviet Union as Superpower

By 1945 Soviet foreign policy had several ingredients. Desire to regain tsarist boundaries (though not carried through regarding Finland) joined with traditional interest in expansion and in playing an active role in

European diplomacy. Genuine revulsion at Germany's two invasions prompted a feverish desire to set up buffer zones, under Soviet control. As a result of Soviet industrialization and its World War II push westward, the nation also emerged as a world power, like the newcomer United States. Continued concentration on heavy industry and weapons development, combined with strategic alliances and links to communist movements in various parts of the world, helped maintain this status.

Soviet participation in the late phases of the war against Japan provided an opportunity to seize some islands in the northern Pacific. The Soviet Union established a protectorate over the communist regime of North Korea, to match the U.S. protectorate in South Korea. Soviet aid to the victorious Communist party in China brought new influence in that country for a time, and in the 1970s the Soviet Union gained a new ally in communist Vietnam, which provided naval bases for the Soviet fleet. Its growing military and economic strength gave the postwar Soviet Union new leverage in the Middle East, Africa, and even parts of Latin America; alliance with the new communist regime in Cuba was a key step here, during the 1960s. The Soviet Union's superpower status was confirmed by its development of the atomic and then hydrogen bombs, from 1949 onward, and by its deployment of missiles and naval forces to match the rapid expansion of U.S. arsenals. The Soviet Union had become a world power.

## The New Soviet Empire in Eastern Europe

As a superpower the Soviet Union developed increasing worldwide influence, with trade and cultural missions on all inhabited continents and military alliances with several Asian, African, and Latin American nations. But the clearest extension of the Soviet sphere developed right after World War II, in eastern Europe (Map 36.1). Here the Soviets made it plain that they intended to stay, pushing the Soviet effective sphere of influence farther to the west than ever before in history. Soviet insistence on this empire helped launch the cold war, as the Soviet Union displayed its willingness to confront the West rather than relax its grip.

The small nations of eastern Europe, mostly new or revived after World War I, had gone through a troubled period between the world wars. Other than democratic Czechoslovakia, they had failed to establish vigorous, independent economies or solid political systems. Then came the Nazi attack and ineffective Western response, as Czechoslovakia, Poland, and Yugoslavia were seized by German or Italian forces. Eastern Europe fell under Nazi control for four years. Although anti-Nazi governments formed abroad, only in Yugoslavia was a resistance movement strong enough to seriously affect postwar results.

By 1945 the dominant force in eastern Europe was the Soviet army, as it pushed the Germans back and remade the map. Through the combination of the Soviet military might and collaboration with local communist movements in the nations that remained technically independent, opposition parties were crushed and noncommunist regimes forced out by 1948. The only exceptions to this pattern were Greece, which moved toward the Western camp in diplomatic alignment and political and social systems; Albania, which formed a rigid Stalinist regime that ironically brought it into disagreement with Soviet post-Stalinist leaders; and Yugoslavia, where a communist regime formed under the resistance leader Tito quickly proclaimed its neutrality in the cold war, resisting Soviet direction and trying to form a more open-ended, responsive version of the communist economic and social system.

After what was in effect the Soviet takeover, a standard development dynamic emerged throughout most of eastern Europe by the early 1950s. The new Soviet-sponsored regimes attacked possible rivals for power, including, where relevant, the Roman Catholic church. Mass education and propaganda outlets were quickly developed. Collectivization of agriculture ended the large estate system, without creating a property-owning peasantry. Industrialization was pushed through successive five-year plans, though with some limitation due to Soviet insistence on access to key natural resources (such as Romanian oil) on favorable terms. Finally, a Soviet and eastern European trading zone became largely separate from the larger trends of international commerce.

After the formation of NATO in western Europe, the relevant eastern European nations were enfolded in a common defense alliance, the Warsaw Pact, and a common economic planning organization. Soviet troops continued to be stationed in most eastern European states, both to confront the Western alliance and to ensure the continuation of the new regimes and their loyalty to the common cause.

Although it responded to many social problems in the smaller nations of eastern Europe, as well as to the desire of the Soviet Union to expand its influence and guard against German or more general Western attack, the new Soviet system created obvious tensions. Particularly tight controls in East Germany brought a workers' rising there in 1953, vigorously repressed by Soviet troops. Faced with a widespread exodus to West Germany, the Soviets built the **Berlin Wall** in 1961 to stem the flow. All along the new borders of eastern Europe, barbed-wire fences and armed patrols kept the people in.

Escaping the Berlin Wall

In 1956 a relaxation of Stalinism within the Soviet Union created new hopes that controls might be loosened. More liberal communist leaders arose in Hungary and Poland, with massive popular backing, seeking to create states that, although communist, would permit greater diversity and certainly more freedom from Soviet domination. In Poland the Soviets accepted a new leader more popular with the Polish people. Among other results, Poland was allowed to halt agricultural collectivization, establishing widespread peasant ownership in its place, and the Catholic church, now the symbol of Polish independence, gained greater tolerance. But a new regime in Hungary was cruelly crushed by the Soviet army and a hard-line Stalinist leadership set up in its place (Figure 36.7).

Yet Soviet control over eastern Europe did loosen slightly overall, for the heavy-handed repression cost considerable prestige. Eastern European governments were given a freer hand in economic policy and were allowed limited room to experiment with greater cultural freedom. Several countries thus began to outstrip the prosperity of the Soviet Union itself. Contacts with the West expanded in several cases, with greater trade and tourism. Eastern Europe remained with the Soviet Union as a somewhat separate economic bloc in world trade, but there was room for limited diversity. Individual nations, such as Hungary, developed new intellectual vigor and experimented with slightly less centralized economic planning. The communist political system remained in full force, however, with its single-party dominance and strong police controls; diplomatic and military alignment with the Soviet Union remained essential.

The limits of experimentation in eastern Europe were brought home again in 1968, when a more liberal regime came to power in Czechoslovakia. Again the Soviet army responded, expelling the reformers and setting up a particularly rigid leader. A challenge came from Poland once more in the late 1970s, in the form of widespread Catholic unrest and an independent labor movement called **Solidarity,** all against the backdrop of a stagnant economy and low morale. Here response was slightly more muted, though key agitators were arrested; the Polish army took over the state, under careful Soviet supervision.

By the 1980s eastern Europe had been vastly transformed by several decades of communist rule. Important national diversity remained, visible both in industrial levels and in political styles. Catholic Poland thus differed from hard-line, neo-Stalinist Bulgaria or Romania. Important discontents remained as well. Yet a communist-imposed social revolution had brought considerable economic change and real social upheaval, through the abolition of the once dominant aristocracy and the remaking of the peasant masses through collectivization, new systems of mass education, and industrial, urban growth. Earlier cultural ties with the West, though still greater than in the Soviet Union itself, had been lessened; Russian, not French or English, was the first foreign language learned.

The expansion of Soviet influence answered important Soviet foreign policy goals, both traditional and new. The Soviets retained a military presence deep in Europe, which among other things reduced very real anxiety about yet another German threat. Eastern European allies aided Soviet ventures in other parts of the world, providing supplies and advisors for activities in Africa, Latin America, and elsewhere. Yet the recurrent unrest in eastern Europe served as something of a check on Soviet policy as well. The need for continued military presence may have diverted Soviet leaders from emphasizing expansionist ambitions in other directions, particularly where direct commitment of troops might be involved.

**FIGURE 36.7** As Soviet troops moved into Hungary to crush the revolt of 1956, freedom fighters in Budapest headed for the front with whatever weapons they could find. This truckload of supporters is being urged on by the crowd.

## Evolution of Domestic Policies

Within the Soviet Union the Stalinist system remained intact during the initial postwar years. The war encouraged growing use of nationalism as well as appeals for communist loyalty, as millions of Russians responded heroically to the new foreign threat. Elements of this mood were sustained as the cold war with the United States developed after 1947, with news media blasting the United States as an evil power and a distorted society. Many Soviets, fearful of a new war that U.S. aggressiveness seemed to them to threaten, agreed that strong government authority remained necessary. This attitude helped sustain the difficult rebuilding efforts after the war, which proceeded rapidly enough for the Soviet Union to regain its prewar industrial capacity and then proceed, during the 1950s, to impressive annual growth rates. The attitude also helped support Stalin's rigorous efforts to shield the Soviet populations from extensive contact with foreigners or foreign ideas. Strict limits on travel, outside media, or any uncensored glimpse of the outside world kept the Soviet Union unusually isolated in the mid-20th-century—its culture, like its economy, largely removed from world currents.

Red Square Military Parade

Stalin's political structure continued to emphasize central controls and the omnipresent party bureaucracy, leavened by the adulation accorded to Stalin and by the aging leader's endemic suspiciousness. Moscow-based direction of the national economy, along with the steady extension of education, welfare, and police operations, expanded the bureaucracy both of the government and of the parallel Communist party. Recruitment from the ranks of peasant and worker families continued into the 1940s, as educational opportunities, including growing secondary school and university facilities, allowed talented young people to rise from below. Party membership, the ticket to bureaucratic promotion, was deliberately kept low, at about 6 percent of the population, to ensure selection of the most dedicated elements. New candidates for the party, drawn mostly from the more broadly based communist youth organizations, had to be nominated by at least three party members. Party members vowed unswerving loyalty and group consciousness.

# Soviet Culture: Promoting New Beliefs and Institutions

- **Rapid industrialization caused significant social change in eastern Europe. Tensions increased over relationships with Western culture.**

The Soviet government was an impressive new product, not just a renewal of tsarist autocracy. It carried on a much wider array of functions than the tsars had ventured, not only in fostering industrialization but also in reaching out for the direct loyalties of individual citizens. The government and the party also maintained an active cultural agenda, and although this had been foreshadowed by the church and state links of tsarist days, it had no full precedent. The regime declared war on the Orthodox church and other religions soon after 1917, seeking to shape a secular population that would maintain a Marxist, scientific orthodoxy; vestigial church activities remained but under tight government regulation. Artistic and literary styles, as well as purely political writings, were carefully monitored to ensure adherence to the party line. The educational system was used not only to train and recruit technicians and bureaucrats but also to create a loyal, right-thinking citizenry. Mass ceremonies, such as May Day parades, stimulated devotion to the state and to communism.

Although the new regime did not attempt to abolish the Orthodox church outright, it greatly limited the church's outreach. Thus the church was barred from giving religious instruction to anyone under 18, and state schools vigorously preached the doctrine that religion was mere superstition. Although loyalties to the church persisted, they now seemed concentrated in a largely elderly minority. The Soviet regime also limited freedom of religion for the Jewish minority, often holding up Jews as enemies of the state in what was in fact a manipulation of traditional Russian anti-Semitism. The larger Muslim minority was given greater latitude, on condition of careful loyalty to the regime. On the whole, the traditional religious orientation of Soviet society declined in favor of a scientific outlook and Marxist explanations of history in terms of class conflict. Church attendance dwindled under government repression; by the 1950s only the elderly seemed particularly interested.

The Soviet state also continued to attack modern Western styles of art and literature, terming them decadent, but maintained some earlier Western styles, which were appropriated as Russian. Thus Russian orchestras performed a wide variety of classical music, and the Russian ballet, though rigid and conservative by 20th-century Western norms, commanded wide attention and enforced rigid standards of excellence. In the arts, socialist realist principles spread to eastern Europe after World War II, particularly in public displays and monuments. With some political loosening and cold war thaw after 1950, however, Soviet and eastern European artists began to adopt Western styles to some extent. At the popular level, jazz and rock music bands began to emerge by the 1980s, though official suspicion persisted.

Literature in the Soviet Union remained diverse and creative, despite official controls sponsored by the communist-dominated Writers' Union. Leading authors wrote movingly of the travails of World War II, maintaining the earlier tradition of sympathy with the people, great patriotism, and concern for the Russian soul. The most creative Soviet artists, particularly the writers, often skirted a fine line between conveying some of the sufferings of the Russian people in the 20th century and courting official disapproval. Their freedom also depended on leadership mood; censorship eased after Stalin and then tightened again somewhat in the late 1960s and 1970s, though not to previous levels. Yet even authors critical of aspects of the Soviet regime maintained distinctive Russian values. **Aleksandr Solzhenitsyn,** for example, exiled to the United States after the publication of his trilogy on Siberian prison camps, *The Gulag Archipelago,* found the West too materialistic and individualistic for his taste. Though barred from his homeland, he continued to seek an alternative both to communist policy and to westernization, with more than a hint of a continuing belief in the durable solidarity and faith of the Russian common people and a mysterious Russian national soul.

Along with interest in the arts and a genuine diversity of expressions despite official party lines, Soviet culture continued to place great emphasis on science and social science. Scientists enjoyed great prestige and wielded considerable power. Social scientific work, heavily colored by Marxist theory, nonetheless produced important analyses of current trends and of history. Scientific research was even more heavily funded, and Soviet scientists generated a number of fundamental discoveries in physics, chemistry, and mathematics. At times scientists felt the heavy hand of official disapproval. Biologists and psychiatrists, particularly, were urged to reject Western theories that called human rationality and social progress into question, though here as in other areas controls were most stringent in the Stalinist years. Thus Freudianism was banned, and under Stalin biologists who overemphasized the uncontrollability of genetic evolution were jailed. But Soviet scientists overall enjoyed considerable freedom and great prestige. As in the West, their work was often linked with advances in technology and weaponry. After the heyday of Stalinism, scientists gained greater freedom from ideological dictates, and exchanges with Western researchers became more common in what was, at base, a common scientific culture.

Shaped by substantial state control, 20th-century Soviet culture overall proved neither traditional nor Western. Considerable ambivalence about the West remained, as Soviets continued to utilize many art forms they developed in common with the West, such as the ballet, while instilling a comparable faith in science. Fear of cultural pollution—particularly through non-Marxist political tracts but also through modern art forms—remained lively, as Soviet leaders sought a culture that would enhance their goals of building a socialist society separate from the capitalist West (Figure 36.8).

## Economy and Society

The Soviet Union became a fully industrial society between the 1920s and the 1950s. Rapid growth of manufacturing and the rise of urban populations to more than 50 percent of the total were measures of this development. Most of the rest of eastern Europe was also fully industrialized by the 1950s. Eastern European modernization, however, had a number of distinctive features. State control of virtually all economic sectors was one key element; no other industrialized society gave so little leeway to private initiative. The unusual imbalance between heavy industrial goods and consumer items was another distinctive aspect. The Soviet Union lagged in the priorities it placed on consumer goods—not only such Western staples as automobiles but also housing construction and simple items, such as bathtub plugs. Consumer-goods industries were poorly funded and did not achieve the advanced technological level that characterized the heavy-manufacturing sector.

The Soviet need to amass capital for development in a traditionally poor society helped explain the inattention to consumer goods; so did the need to create, in a society that remained poorer overall, a massive armaments industry to rival that of the United States.

FIGURE 36.8 Work incentives were a problem in collectivized agriculture. This 1947 poster was designed to spur Soviet farm workers to greater productivity. It proclaims, "Work hard and abundant bread will be your reward."

Thus despite an occasional desire to beat the West at its own affluent-society game, eastern Europe did not develop the kind of consumer society that came to characterize the West. Living standards improved and extensive welfare services provided security for some groups not similarly supported in the West, but complaints about poor consumer products and long lines to obtain desired goods remained a feature of Soviet life.

Soviet industrialization also caused an unusual degree of environmental damage. The drive to produce at all costs created bleak zones around factories, where waste was dumped, and in agricultural and mining areas. Up to one-quarter of all Soviet territory (and that of the eastern bloc) was environmentally degraded, often leading to severe health damages for people in the affected areas.

The communist system throughout eastern Europe also failed to resolve problems with agriculture. Capital that might have gone into farming equipment was often diverted to armaments and heavy industry. The arduous climate of northern Europe and Asia was a factor as well, dooming a number of attempts to spread grain production to Siberia, for example. But it seemed clear that the eastern European peasantry continued to find the constraints and lack of individual incentive in collectivized agriculture deterrents to maximum effort. Thus eastern Europe had to retain a larger percentage of its labor force in agriculture than was true of the industrial West, but it still encountered problems with food supply and quality.

Despite the importance of distinctive political and economic characteristics, eastern European society echoed a number of the themes of contemporary Western social history—simply because of the shared fact of industrial life. Work rhythms, for example, became roughly similar. Industrialization brought massive efforts to speed the pace of work and to introduce regularized supervision. The incentive systems designed to encourage able workers resembled those used in Western factories. Along with similar work habits came similar leisure activities. For decades, sports have provided excitement for the peoples of eastern Europe, as have films and television. Family vacations to the beaches of the Black Sea became cherished respites. Here, too, there were some distinctive twists, as the communist states boosted sports efforts as part of their political program (in contrast to the Western view of sports as a combination of leisure and commercialism). East Germany, along with the Soviet Union, developed particularly extensive athletic programs under state sponsorship, winning international competitions in a host of fields.

Eastern European social structure also grew closer to that of the West, despite the continued importance of the rural population and despite the impact of Marxist theory. Particularly interesting was a tendency to divide urban society along class lines—between workers and a better-educated, managerial middle class. Wealth divisions remained much less great than in the West, to be sure, but the perquisites of managers and professional people—particularly for Communist party members—set them off from the standard of living of the masses.

Finally, the Soviet family reacted to some of the same pressures of industrialization as did the Western family. Massive movements to the cities and crowded housing enhanced the nuclear family unit, as ties to a wider network of relatives loosened. The birth rate dropped. Official Soviet policy on birth rates varied for a time, but the basic pressures became similar to those in the West. Falling infant death rates, with improved diets and medical care, together with increasing periods of schooling and some increase in consumer expectations, made large families less desirable than before. Wartime dislocations contributed to birth rate decline at points as well. By the 1970s the Soviet growth rate was about the same as that of the West. As in the West, some minority groups—particularly Muslims in the southern Soviet Union—maintained higher birth rates than the majority ethnic group—in this case, ethnic Russians—a differential that caused some concern about maintaining Russian cultural dominance.

Patterns of childrearing showed some similarities to those in the West, as parents, especially in the managerial middle class, devoted great attention to promoting their children's education and ensuring good jobs for the future. At the same time children were more strictly disciplined than in the West, both at home and in school, with an emphasis on authority that had political implications as well. Soviet families never afforded the domestic idealization of women that had prevailed in the West during industrialization. Most married women worked, an essential feature of an economy struggling to industrialize and offering relatively low wages to individual workers. As in the peasant past, women performed many heavy physical tasks. They also dominated some professions, such as medicine, though these professionals were much lower in status than were their male-dominated counterparts in the West. Soviet propagandists took pride in the constructive role of women and their official equality, but there were signs that many women were suffering burdens from demanding jobs with little help from their husbands at home.

## De-Stalinization

The rigid government apparatus created by Stalin and sustained after World War II by frequent arrests and exiles to forced labor camps was put to a major test after Stalin's death in 1953. The results gradually loosened, without totally reversing, Stalinist cultural isolation. Focus on one-man rule might have created immense succession problems, and indeed frequent jockeying for power did develop among aspiring candidates. Yet the system held together. Years of bureaucratic experience had given most Soviet leaders a taste for coordination and compromise, along with a reluctance to strike out in radical new directions that might cause controversy or arouse resistance from one of the key power blocs within the state. Stalin's death was followed by a ruling committee that balanced interest groups, notably the army, the police, and the party apparatus. This mechanism encouraged conservatism, as each bureaucratic sector defended its existing prerogatives, but it also ensured fundamental stability.

In 1956, however, **Nikita Khrushchev** emerged from the committee pack to gain primary power, though without seeking to match Stalin's eminence. Indeed, Khrushchev attacked Stalinism for its concentration of power and arbitrary dictatorship. In a stirring speech delivered to the Communist party congress, Khrushchev condemned Stalin for his treatment of political opponents, for his narrow interpretations of Marxist doctrine, even for his failure to adequately prepare for World War II. The implications of the de-Stalinization campaign within the Soviet Union suggested a more tolerant political climate and some decentralization of decision making. In fact, however, despite a change in tone, little concrete institutional reform occurred. Political trials became less common, and the most overt police repression eased. A few intellectuals were allowed to raise new issues, dealing, for example, with the purges and other Stalinist excesses. Outright critics of the regime were less likely to be executed and more likely to be sent to psychiatric institutions or, in the case of internationally visible figures, exiled to the West or confined to house arrest. Party control and centralized economic planning remained intact. Indeed, Khrushchev planned a major extension of state-directed initiative by opening new Siberian land to cultivation; his failure in this costly effort, combined with his antagonizing many Stalinist loyalists, led to his quiet downfall.

After the de-Stalinization furor and Khrushchev's fall from power, patterns in the Soviet Union remained stable into the 1980s, verging at times on stagnant. Economic growth continued but with no dramatic breakthroughs and with recurrent worries over sluggish productivity and especially over periodically inadequate harvests, which compelled expensive grain deals with Western nations, including the United States. A number of subsequent leadership changes occurred, but the transitions were handled smoothly.

Cold war policies eased somewhat after Stalin's death. Khrushchev vaunted the Soviet ability to outdo the West at its own industrial game, bragging on a visit to the United States that "we will bury you." The Khrushchev regime also produced one of the most intense moments of the cold war with the United States, as he probed for vulnerabilities. The Soviets installed missiles in Cuba, yielding only to a firm U.S. response in 1962 by removing their missiles but not their support of the communist regime on the island. Khrushchev had no desire for war, and overall he promoted a new policy of peaceful coexistence. He hoped to beat the West economically and actively expanded the Soviet space program; *Sputnik,* the first space satellite, was sent up in 1957, well in advance of its U.S. counterpart. Khrushchev maintained a competitive tone, but he shifted away from an exclusive military emphasis. Lowered cold war tensions with the West permitted a small influx of Western tourists by the 1960s as well as greater access to the Western media and a variety of cultural exchanges, which gave some Soviets a renewed sense of contact with a wider world and restored some of the earlier ambiguities about the nation's relationship to Western standards.

Nikita Khrushchev Challenges the West to Disarm and Advance World Prosperity

At the same time, the Soviet leadership continued a steady military buildup, adding increasingly sophisticated rocketry and bolstered by its unusually successful space program (Figure 36.9). The Soviets

**FIGURE 36.9** This Soviet postcard proclaims, "Glory! The world's first group flight in space, August, 1962," and depicts cosmonauts A. G. Nikolaev and P. R. Popovich. ("CCP" on the cosmonauts' helmets is Cyrillic lettering meaning "U.S.S.R.") Soviet advances in science and technology both surprised and threatened the United States and western Europe.

maintained a lead in manned space flights into the late 1980s. Both in space and in the arms race, the Soviet Union demonstrated great technical ability combined with a willingness to settle for somewhat simpler systems than those the United States attempted, which helped explain how it could maintain superpower parity even with a less prosperous overall economy. An active sports program, resulting in a growing array of victories in Olympic games competition, also showed the Soviet Union's new ability to compete on an international scale and its growing pride in international achievements.

The nation faced a number of new foreign policy problems, although maintaining superpower status. From the mid-1950s onward the Soviet Union experienced a growing rift with China, a communist nation with which it shared a long border. Successful courtship of many other nations—such as Egypt, a close diplomatic friend during the 1960s—often turned sour, though these developments were often balanced by new alignments elsewhere. The rise of Muslim awareness in the 1970s was deeply troubling to the Soviet Union, with its own large Muslim minority. This prompted a 1979 invasion of Afghanistan, to promote a friendly puppet regime, which bogged down amid guerrilla warfare into the late 1980s. On balance, the Soviet Union played a normally cautious diplomatic game, almost never engaging directly in warfare but maintaining a high level of preparedness (Figure 36.10).

Problems of work motivation and discipline loomed larger in the Soviet Union than in the West by the 1980s, after the heroic period of building an industrial society under Stalinist exhortation and threat. With highly bureaucratized and centralized work plans and the absence of abundant consumer goods, many workers found little reason for great diligence. High rates of alcoholism, so severe as to cause an increase in death rates, particularly among adult males, also burdened work performance and caused great concern to Soviet leaders. More familiar were problems of youth agitation. Although Soviet statistics tended to conceal outright crime rates, it is clear that many youth became impatient with the disciplined life and eager to have greater access to Western culture, including rock music and blue jeans.

Most observers thought the Soviet Union remained firmly established in the early 1980s, thanks

**FIGURE 36.10** May Day in the Soviet Union was an occasion for massive military parades including troops, missiles, jets, and tanks, showcasing the country's military power, and for glorification of the State and its leaders, past and present. Enormous banners with portraits of Marx, Engels, and Lenin were stretched high over Red Square, suggesting the current leadership's connection with these giants. In this photo of the 1947 May Day parade, top Soviet leaders watch from reviewing stands in front of Lenin's tomb. Behind them is the wall of the Kremlin.

DOCUMENT

## 1986: A New Wave of Soviet Reform

The following document reflects a wave of reform introduced in 1986 by a new Soviet leader, Mikhail Gorbachev. Gorbachev's policies ultimately ushered in a major new era of Russian history. At the time, however, they represented an attempt to save the key features of the Soviet state while recognizing ominous new problems. The document obviously invites analysis around several issues, including what features of the Soviet state Gorbachev sought to preserve, what new problems he identified, and how he intended to deal with them. You might also speculate about why the reforms eventually spun out of Soviet control.

> None of us can continue living in the old way. This is obvious. In this sense, we can say that a definite step toward acceleration has been made.
>
> However, there is a danger that the first step will be taken as success, that we will assume that the whole situation has been taken in hand. I said this in Vladivostok. I want to say it again in Khabarovsk. If we were to draw this conclusion, we would be making a big mistake, an error. What has been achieved cannot yet satisfy us in any way. In general, one should never flatter oneself with what has been accomplished. All of us must learn this well. Such are the lessons of the past decades—the last two, at least. And now this is especially dangerous.
>
> No profound qualitative changes that would reinforce the trend toward accelerated growth have taken place as yet. In general, comrades, important and intensive work lies ahead of us. To put it bluntly, the main thing is still to come. Our country's Party, the entire Party, should understand this well. . . .
>
> We should learn as we go along, accomplishing new tasks. And we must not be afraid of advancing boldly, of doing things on the march, in the course of the active accomplishment of economic and social tasks. . . .
>
> Restructuring is a capacious word. I would equate the word restructuring with the word revolution. Our transformations, the reforms mapped out in the decisions of the April plenary session of the Party Central Committee and the 27th CPSU [Communist Party of the Soviet Union] Congress, are a genuine revolution in the entire system of relations in society, in the minds and hearts of people, in the psychology and understanding of the present period and, above all, in the tasks engendered by rapid scientific and technical progress.
>
> There is a common understanding in the CPSU and in the country as a whole—we should look for answers to the questions raised by life not outside of socialism but within the framework of our system, disclosing the potential of a planned economy, socialist democracy and culture and the human factor, and relying on the people's vital creativity.
>
> Some people in the West do not like this. There everyone lies in wait for something that would mean a deviation from socialism, for us to go hat in hand to capitalism, for us to borrow its methods. We are receiving a great deal of "advice" from abroad as to how and where we should proceed. Various kinds of provocative broadcasts are made, and articles are published, aimed at casting aspersions on the changes taking place in our country and at driving a wedge between the Party leadership and the people. Such improper attempts are doomed to failure. The interests of the Party and the people are inseparable, and our choice and political course are firm and unshakable. On this main point, the people and the Party are united.
>
> But we also cannot allow ingrained dogmas to cloud our eyes, to impede our progress and keep us from creatively elaborating theory and applying it in practice, in the given, concrete historical stage through which our society is passing. We cannot allow this, either.
>
> I am saying this also because among us there are still, of course, people who have difficulty in accepting the word "restructuring" [perestroika] and who even sometimes can pronounce it only with difficulty. In this process of renewal, they often see not what it in fact contains but all but a shaking of foundations, all but a renunciation of our principles. Our political line is aimed at fully disclosing the potential and advantages of the socialist system, removing all barriers and all obstructions to our progress, and creating scope for factors of social progress.
>
> I want to say something else. The farther we advance into restructuring, the more the complexity of this task is revealed, and the more fully the enormous scale and volume of the forthcoming work is brought out. It is becoming clearer to what extent many notions about the economy and management, social questions, statehood and democracy, upbringing and education and moral demands still lag behind today's requirements and tasks, especially the tasks of further development.

to careful police control, vigorous propaganda, and real, popular pride in Soviet achievements. Even though the U.S. Central Intelligence Agency failed to see major problems, economic conditions were deteriorating rapidly, and the whole Soviet system would soon come unglued. Yet its collapse was all the more unsettling because of communism's huge success for many decades. At great cost to many people, the Soviet Union had attained world power. Many rejoiced in its fall, but many were also disoriented by it. What could and should replace a system that had dominated huge stretches of Europe and Asia for so long?

We will have to remove, layer by layer, the accumulated problems in all spheres of the life of society, freeing ourselves of what has outlived its time and boldly making creative decisions. . . .

Sometimes people ask: Well, just what is this odd business, restructuring? How do you understand it, "what do you eat it with," this restructuring? Yes, we're all for it, some say, but we don't know what to do. Many say this straight out. . . .

Restructuring proposes the creation of an atmosphere in society that will impel people to overcome accumulated inertia and indifference, to rid themselves, in work and in life, of everything that does not correspond to the principles of socialism, to our world views and way of life. Frankly, there is some work to be done here. But in this instance everyone must look first of all at himself, comrades—in the Politburo, in the primary Party organizations—and everyone must make a specific attempt to take himself in hand. In past years, we got used to some things in an atmosphere of insufficient criticism, openness and responsibility, things that do not all correspond to the principles of socialism. I apply this both to rank-and-file personnel and to officials. . . .

In general, comrades, we must change our style of work. It should be permeated with respect for the people and their opinions, with real, unfeigned closeness to them. We must actually go to people, listen to them, meet with them, inform them. And the more difficult things are, the more often we must meet with them and be with them when some task or other is being accomplished. In our country, people are responsive; they are a wonderful people, you can't find another people like them. Our people have the greatest endurance. Our people have the greatest political activeness. And now it is growing. This must be welcomed and encouraged in every way. Let us consider that we have come to an agreement on this in the Khabarovsk Party organization. [*Applause.*]

In this connection, some words about public openness [glasnost]. It is sometimes said: Well, why has the Central Committee launched criticism, self-criticism and openness on such a broad scale? I can tell you that so far we have lost nothing, we have only gained. The people have felt an influx of energy; they have become bolder and more active, both at work and in public life. Furthermore, you know that all those who had been trying to circumvent our laws immediately began to quiet down. Because there is nothing stronger than the force of public opinion, when it can be put into effect. And it can be put into effect only in conditions of criticism, self-criticism and broad public openness. . . .

Incidentally, it looks as if many local newspapers in cities and provinces are keeping quiet. The central newspapers are speaking out in full voice, supporting everything good and criticizing blunders and shortcomings. But the local papers are silent. When a group of editors assembled in the Central Committee's offices, they said bluntly: "Well, you tell this to our secretaries in the city and district Party committees." And indeed, why shouldn't people know what is going on in the district or the city? Why shouldn't they make a judgment on it and, if need be, express their opinion? This is what socialism is, comrades. Are there any editors present? [*A voice:* Yes, we're here.]

I hope that the secretaries of the city and district Party committees will take our talk into account. They are the managers. These are their newspapers. We must not be afraid of openness, comrades. We are strong, and the people are in favor of socialism, the Party's policy, changes and restructuring. In general, it is impermissible to approach openness with the yardsticks of traditional short-term campaigns. Public openness is not a one-shot measure but a norm of present-day Soviet life, a continuous, uninterrupted process during which some tasks are accomplished and new tasks—as a rule, still more complicated ones—arise. [*Applause.*]

I could say the same thing about criticism and self-criticism. If we do not criticize and analyze ourselves, what will happen? For us, this is a direct requirement, a vital necessity for purposes of the normal functioning of the Party and of society. . . .

*Source*: From a speech to the Communist party in Khabarovsk. From Alexander Dallin and Gail Lapidus, eds., *The Soviet System: From Crisis to Collapse* (1994), pp. 284–287.

**Questions** What did Gorbachev intend by the policies of glasnost and perestroika? What problems was he focusing on? What aspects of Soviet politics and society did Gorbachev hope to preserve? Why did the reform movement ultimately prove incompatible with the Soviet state?

## GLOBAL CONNECTIONS

# The Cold War and the World

The massive competition between the West and the Soviet alliance dominated many aspects of world history between 1945 and 1992. It played a key role in other major global themes, such as decolonization and nationalism. But the competition also gave other parts of the world some breathing room, as they could play one side against the other—a contrast to previous decades in which Western imperialism had dominated.

At the same time, Western and Soviet influences were not entirely contradictory. While Western consumerism and Soviet communism were quite different, both were largely secular. Both societies emphasized science. Both societies challenged key social traditions, including purely traditional roles for women. Both eagerly sold weapons on the world market. Both could stimulate hostility to new forms of outside influence and pressures to change. These factors, too, helped shape world history for a crucial half-century.

## Further Readings

Important overviews of recent European history are Walter Laqueur, *Europe Since Hitler* (1982); John Darwin, *Britain and Decolonization* (1988); Helen Wallace et al., *Policy-Making in the European Community* (1983); and Alfred Grosser, *The Western Alliance* (1982).

Some excellent national interpretations provide vital coverage of events since 1945 in key areas of Europe, including A. F. Havighurst's *Britain in Transition: The Twentieth Century* (1982) and John Ardagh's highly readable *The New French Revolution: A Social and Economic Survey of France* (1968) and *France in the 1980s* (1982). Volker Berghahn, *Modern Germany: Society, Economy, and Politics in the 20th Century* (1983), is also useful.

On post–World War II social and economic trends, see C. Kindleberger, *Europe's Postwar Growth* (1967); V. Bogdanor and R. Skidelsky, eds., *The Age of Affluence, 1951–1964* (1970); R. Dahrendorf, ed., *Europe's Economy in Crisis* (1982); and Peter Stearns and Herrick Chapman, *European Society in Upheaval* (1991). On the welfare state, see Stephen Cohen, *Modern Capitalist Planning: The French Model* (1977), and E. S. Einhorn and J. Logue, *Welfare States in Hard Times* (1982).

On Commonwealth nations, see Charles Doran, *Forgotten Partnership: U.S.-Canada Relations Today* (1983); Edward McWhinney, *Canada and the Constitution, 1979–1982* (1982); and Stephen Graubard, ed., *Australia: Terra Incognita?* (1985).

Postwar Soviet history is treated in Richard Barnet, *The Giants: Russia and America* (1977); A. Rubinstein, *Soviet Foreign Policy Since World War II* (1981); Alec Nove, *The Soviet Economic System* (1980); Stephen Cohen et al., eds., *The Soviet Union Since Stalin;* and Ben Eklof, *Gorbachev and the Reform Period* (1988).

On Soviet culture, Jeffrey Brooks, *Thank You, Comrade Stalin! Soviet Public Culture from Revolution to Cold War* (2000), is a cultural history of the communist press. James von Geldern and Richard Stites, eds., *Mass Culture in Soviet Russia: Tales, Poems, Songs, Movies, Plays, and Folklore, 1917–1953* (1995), is a valuable repository of primary cultural texts and documents.

Postwar eastern Europe is treated in H. Setson Watson, *Eastern Europe Between the Wars* (1962); F. Fetjo, *History of the People's Democracies: Eastern Europe Since Stalin* (1971); J. Tampke, *The People's Republics of Eastern Europe* (1983); Timothy Ash, *The Polish Revolution: Solidarity* (1984); H. G. Skilling, *Czechoslovakia: Interrupted Revolution* (1976) (on the 1968 uprising); and B. Kovrig, *Communism in Hungary from Kun to Kadar* (1979).

A major interpretation of the communist experience is T. Skocpol's *States and Social Revolutions* (1979). On women's experiences, see Barbara Engel and Christine Worobec, eds., *Russia's Women: Accommodation, Resistance, Transformation* (1990).

On the early signs of explosion in eastern Europe, see K. Dawisha, *Eastern Europe, Gorbachev, and Reform: The Great Challenge* (1988). Bohdan Nahaylo and Victor Swoboda's *Soviet Disunion: A History of the Nationalities Problem in the USSR* (1990) provides important background. See also Rose Brady, *Kapitalizm: Russia's Struggle to Free Its Economy* (1999). Joseph Rothschild, *Return to Diversity: A Political History of East Central Europe Since World War II* (2000), stands as the authoritative political history. Sabrina Ramet, ed., *Eastern Europe: Politics, Culture, and Society Since 1939* (1998), presents a cultural and social history survey through each country and includes a relevant bibliography.

James T. Patterson, *Grand Expectations: The United States, 1945–1974* (1996), offers a useful overview of the period. Trends in the postwar United States include the civil rights movement, movingly described in David J. Garrow, *Bearing the Cross: Martin Luther King Jr. and the Southern Leadership Conference, 1955–1968* (1986).

The transformation of America's cities is traced by Kenneth T. Jackson, *Crabgrass Frontier: The Suburbanization of the United States* (1985), and the growth of popular culture analyzed in R. Maltby, ed., *The Passing Parade: A History of Popular Culture in the Twentieth Century* (1989), and Lewis MacAdams, *The Birth of Cool: Beat, Bebop, and the American Avant-Garde* (2001). Arthur M. Schlesinger Jr., *A Thousand Days: John F. Kennedy in the White House* (1965); Doris Kearns, *Lyndon Johnson and the American Dream* (1976); and David Stockman, *The Triumph of Politics: Inside Story of the Reagan Revolution* (1987), offer accounts of American political aspirations during three key presidential administrations by authors closely identified with their subjects.

## On the Web

Stalin's death heralded much political infighting (http://www.1upinfo.com/country-guide-study/soviet-union/soviet-union65.html), which eventually saw the installation of Nikita Khrushchev (http://www.cnn.com/SPECIALS/cold.war/kbank/profiles/khrushchev/). Khrushchev's famous, but grossly misunderstood, "We will bury you" remarks at the United Nations in 1956 are analyzed at http://www.diplomacy.edu/Language/Translation/machine.htm. Soviet attacks on dissidents are noted at http://www.ibiblio.org/expo/soviet.exhibit/attack.html. The life and work of Russian cold war leader Leonid Brezhnev and the speech that announced what became known as the Brezhnev Doctrine can be found at http://www.cnn.com/SPECIALS/cold.war/episodes/14/documents/doctrine/ and http://www.cnn.com/SPECIALS/cold.war/kbank/profiles/brezhnev/. Links for the study of the Soviet space program are offered at http://www.cs.umd.edu/

~dekhtyar/space/. The role of that program in the cold war is examined at http://www.pbs.org/newshour/forum/october97/sputnik_10-13.html.

Excellent overviews of the cold war in text, images, and documents are available at http://www.coldwar.org/ and http://history.acusd.edu/gen/20th/coldwar0.html. American President John F. Kennedy's famous "Ich bin ein Berliner" speech is presented in written and audio format at http://www.coldwar.org/museum/berlin_wall_exhibit.html, a site that also traces the Berlin Wall's rise and demise. The cold war's impact on American domestic politics is illuminated at http://www.spartacus.schoolnet.co.uk/USAmccarthyism.htm. For other postwar developments in the United States, from the civil rights movement to urbanization, see http://vlib.iue.it/history/USA/ERAS/20TH/1960s.html, http://memory.loc.gov/ammem/aaohtml/exhibit/aopart9.html#09a (and succeeding articles), http://www.cnn.com/EVENTS/1997/mlk/links.html, http://college.hmco.com/history/readerscomp/rcah/html/ah_088600_urbanization.htm, http://www.ecb.org/tracks/mod9.htm, and http://cwis.usc.edu/dept/LAS/history/historylab/LAPUHK/index.html.

Czechoslovakia's effort to throw off the Stalinist yoke in 1968 is remembered at http://rferl.org/nca/special/invasion1968/. An overview of the later revolutions in eastern Europe that heralded the end of the Soviet empire can be found at http://mars.acnet.wnec.edu/~grempel/courses/wc2/lectures/rev89.html. The development of NATO is traced at http://www.nato.int/docu/facts/2000/origin.htm, http://www.zum.de/whkmla/region/europe/nato.html, and http://www.nato.int/docu/basics.htm.

Soviet–American competition in Latin America during the cold war and its legacies are examined at http://web.mit.edu/cascon/cases/case_els.html, http://www.hartford-hwp.com/archives/47/index-ca.html, http://www.coha.org/WRH_issues/wrh_21_15_nic.htm, and http://www.hartford-hwp.com/archives/47/index-fba.html.

The National Security Archives site offers audio tapes of related intelligence briefings, images of Soviet missile bases in Cuba, and minute by minute chronologies of the missile crisis at http://www.gwu.edu/~nsarchiv/nsa/cuba_mis_cri/.

Feminism and the place of Betty Friedan (http://womenshistory.about.com/library/qu/blqufrie.htm and http://search.eb.com/women/articles/Friedan_Betty_Naomi_Goldstein.html) in the American feminist movement left little doubt that this revolutionary effort ultimately sought the liberation of both men and women. An online archival site devoted to the women's liberation movement can be found at http://scriptorium.lib.duke.edu/wlm/.

CHAPTER 37

# Latin America: Revolution and Reaction into the 21st Century



In the late summer of 1973, everyone in Chile knew that a coup against the government was being hatched, but no one was quite sure whether it would come from the right-wing military or from the radical left. People turned on the radio each morning to learn whether the coup had taken place during the night. The country was almost at a standstill; the currency had no international value, public transportation did not function, and soldiers armed with machine guns guarded banks and gas stations. The atmosphere was tense; a political storm was coming. Since 1964 the military forces in various Latin American countries (Brazil, 1964; Argentina, 1966; Peru, 1968) had decided to take over their governments. Latin America, like much of the world, seemed divided between the backers of radical revolutionary change and those who wished to keep the status quo or to move very slowly toward any change.

The president of Chile at the time was Salvador Allende, a socialist politician who had been elected by a plurality in 1970 and who had begun to push through a series of reforms, including land redistribution and allowing workers to take control of their factories. He was pledged to peaceful change and respect for the Chilean constitution, but his political supporters in the "Popular Unity" movement were awash with enthusiasm. For them it seemed like a new era and their motto "A People united will never be defeated" became a rallying cry for the Left all over Latin America. Such a program would have generated enthusiasms and fears at any time, but this was the era of the cold war and the nations of Latin America were pulled into the struggle between the capitalist West aligned with the United States and the communist countries aligned with the Soviet Union. The United States did its best to destabilize and undercut the Allende regime. Allende's programs and the encouragement he received from Fidel Castro provoked conservative and middle-class elements in Chile. His insistence on remaining within the limits of the constitution bothered impatient radicals who wanted a government-led socialist revolution.

On the morning of September 11, 1973, it was the military, backed by conservative and anticommunist forces, that took action and seized the presidential palace. Allende died in the palace. His wife went into exile. The military crushed any resistance and imposed a regime of authoritarian control under General Augusto Pinochet. What followed next was almost two decades of

**FIGURE 37.1** On September 11, 1973, soldiers supporting the coup led by General Augusto Pinochet surrounded and bombed the Presidential Palace. Here, troops surrounding the palace take cover as bombs are dropped. Inside, the leftist-elected president, Salvador Allende, apparently committed suicide rather than be taken prisoner. Following the coup, Pinochet seized power for himself and a military junta rather than hold elections or return control to the civilian legislature.

repression. About 3000 people were killed or "disappeared," more than 80,000 people were arrested for political reasons, and more than 200,000 Chileans went into exile. This was an example of the kind of "dirty war" that could be seen elsewhere in Latin America in this era; it was the internalization of the ideological and political struggles of the cold war. During this period, however, neoliberal economics also restored economic stability to the country. The country returned to democracy in 1990, but the wounds on the nation's psyche were still fresh.

In 1998 General Augusto Pinochet, the elderly former commander in chief of the Chilean army and virtual dictator of his country from 1974 to 1990, was arrested in London on charges of crimes against humanity during his years in power. Pinochet and his supporters claimed he had no personal role in the abuses and that he had saved the country from anarchy and restored economic prosperity. His opponents looked on his regime as one of brutal oppression. The arrest became an international incident, and even though Pinochet was eventually released and for "reasons of health" was not forced to stand trial, some Chileans believed that at least a message had been sent to such dictators that crimes of oppression would not be tolerated or forgotten. But many Chileans—and Latin Americans in general—remained divided over what to do about the political struggles of the past. In Chile, Argentina, Brazil, Guatemala, and elsewhere, people asked whether it was better to seek reconciliation and move ahead, or to bring those who had committed abuses and crimes during the political struggles of the late 20th century to justice. The

| 1940 C.E. | 1960 C.E. | 1980 C.E. | 1990 C.E. | 2000 C.E. |
|---|---|---|---|---|
| **1942** Brazil joins Allies in World War II, sends troops to Europe<br>**1944–1954** Arevalo and Arbenz reforms in Guatemala<br>**1947** Juan Perón elected president of Argentina<br>**1952–1964** Bolivian revolution<br>**1954** Arbenz overthrown with help from United States<br>**1959** Castro leads revolution in Cuba | **1961** U.S.-backed invasion of Cuba is defeated<br>**1964** Military coup topples Brazilian government<br>**1970–1973** Salvador Allende's socialist government in Chile; Allende overthrown and assassinated by the military in 1973<br>**1979** Sandinista revolution in Nicaragua | **1982** Argentina and Great Britain clash over Falkland Islands (Islas Malvinas)<br>**1983** United States invades Grenada<br>**1989** Sandinistas lose election in Nicaragua<br>**1989** United States invades Panama, deposes General Noriega | **1994** Brazil stabilizes economy with new currency: the *real*<br>**1994** Zapatista uprising in Chiapas, Mexico<br>**1996** Return to civilian government in Guatemala<br>**1998** Colombian government initiates negotiations with FARC guerrillas but kidnappings and drug trade continue<br>**1998** Colonel Hugo Chávez elected president in Venezuela and new constitution approved in 1999 | **2000** PRI loses presidency of Mexico; Vicente Fox elected<br>**2001** Economic collapse of Argentina<br>**2002** "Lula" and Workers' party win Brazilian elections<br>**2003** Néstor Kirchner elected president of Argentina; one wing of the Peronist party returns to power<br>**2005** Lula's government faces major corruption scandal<br>**2005** Hugo Chávez, using nationalist rhetoric, opposes U.S.-sponsored free trade policies |

question divided these societies just as deeply as had the political struggles and alternative visions of society that originally generated the conflicts. For Latin America, much of the century had been an era of struggle between the forces of revolution and reaction.

The focus of the previous chapter—on the West and eastern Europe—involved societies with very different 20th-century institutions and experiences but with the common bond of being industrialized nations. The same holds true for the Pacific Rim, which will be discussed in Chapter 39. This chapter and the next deal with developing nations, societies grouped in what is sometimes called the **third world,** a term used in the cold war era to distinguish them from capitalist industrialized nations (the first world) and communist industrialized nations (the second world). The developing nations displayed great diversity in their cultural and political traditions—the presence or absence of revolutionary experience, for example. However, as part of their 20th-century history, they all faced issues of economic development as well as the challenge of what relationships to have with militarily and economically more powerful nations.

Latin America fit the third world definition closely, despite great regional variety, but it also showed how loose this definition was. From the second half of the 20th and into the 21st century, Latin America continued to take an intermediate position between the nations of the North Atlantic and the developing countries of Asia and Africa. Although Latin America shared many problems with these other developing areas, its earlier political independence and its often more Western social and political structures placed it in a distinct category. After 1945, and particularly from the 1970s onward, the Latin American elites led their nations into closer ties with the growing international capitalist economy over increasing objections from critics within their nations. Investments and initiative often came from Europe and the United States, and Latin American economies continued to concentrate on exports. As a result, Latin America became increasingly vulnerable to changes in the world financial system. For many Latin Americans, this dependency on the markets, the financial situation, and the economic decisions made outside the region was also reflected in a political and even cultural dependency in which foreign influence and foreign models shaped all aspects of national life.

Central America Today

South America Today

Throughout the 20th century, Latin Americans grappled with the problem of finding a basis for social justice, cultural autonomy, and economic security by adopting ideologies from abroad or by developing a specifically Latin American approach. Thus, in Latin America the struggle for decolonization has been primarily one of economic disengagement and a search for political and cultural forms appropriate to Latin American realities rather than a process of political separation and independence, as in Asia and Africa.

New groups began to appear on the political stage. Although Latin America continued its 19th-century emphasis on agricultural and mineral production, an industrial sector also grew in some places. As this movement gathered strength, workers' organizations began to emerge as a political force. Industrialization was accompanied by some emigration and by explosive urban growth in many places. A growing urban middle class linked to commerce, industry, and expanding state bureaucracies also began to play a role in the political process.

With variations from country to country, overall the economy and the political process were subject to a series of broad shifts. There was a pattern to these shifts, with economic expansion (accompanied by conservative regimes that, although sometimes willing to make gradual reforms, hoped to maintain a political status quo) alternating with periods of economic crisis during which attempts were made to provide social justice or to break old patterns. Thus, the political pendulum swung broadly across the region and often affected several countries at roughly the same time, indicating the relationship between international trends and the internal events in these nations.

Latin Americans have long debated the nature of their societies and the need for change. Although much of the rhetoric of Latin America stressed radical reform and revolutionary change in the 20th century, the region has remained remarkably unchanged. Revolutionaries have not been lacking since 1945, but the task of defeating the existing political and social order and creating a new one on which the majority of the population will agree is difficult, especially when this must be done within an international as well as a national context. Thus, the few revolutionary political changes that have had long-term effects stand in contrast to the general trends of the region's political history. At the same time, however, significant changes in education, social services, the position of women, and the role of industry have taken place over the past several decades and have begun to transform many areas of Latin American life.

## Latin America After World War II

- The end of World War II was not a turning point for Latin America, which was only modestly involved in the war, though the economies of many countries grew as a result of wartime demand. The cold war helped stimulate new revolutionary agitation in Latin America, partly under Marxist inspiration and with some Soviet backing. Although Latin America had been independent of foreign rule for more than a century, the third world decolonization movement encouraged restiveness about continued economic dependency.

In 1945 several key Latin American countries were still dominated by authoritarian reformers who had responded to the impact of the Great Depression. Getulio Vargas returned to power in Brazil in 1950 with a program of populist nationalism; the state took over the petroleum industry. Juan Perón (Figure 37.2) ruled in Argentina, again with a populist platform combined with severe political repression. A military group drove Perón from power in 1955, but the popularity of Peronism, particularly among workers, continued for two decades. This encouraged

Juan Perón and Postwar Populism

**FIGURE 37.2** The populist politics of Juan Perón and his wife Evita brought new forces, especially urban workers, into Argentine politics. Their personal charisma attracted support from groups formerly excluded from politics but eventually led to opposition from the Argentine military and Perón's overthrow in 1955.

FIGURE 37.3 On July 3, 2000, joyful supporters of the new Mexican president, Vicente Fox, celebrated their victory in electing an opposition candidate for the first time in more than a century.

severe political measures by the military dictators, including torture and execution of opponents in what was called the "dirty war." The military government involved Argentina in a war with Britain in 1982, over the Islas Malvinas, or Falkland Islands, which Britain controlled and Argentina claimed. The rulers hoped to gain nationalist support, but they lost the war and the regime was discredited.

## Mexico and the PRI

From the 1940s until a historic change in the 2000 election, Mexico was controlled by the Party of the Institutionalized Revolution, or **PRI** (Figure 37.3). By the last decades of the 20th century, the stability provided by the PRI's control of politics was undercut by corruption and a lack of social improvement. Many Mexicans believed that little remained of the revolutionary principles of the 1910 revolution. Charges of corruption and repression mounted for several decades. In 1994 an armed guerrilla movement burst forth in the heavily Indian southern state of Chiapas (Figure 37.4). Calling themselves **Zapatistas** in honor of Emiliano Zapata, the peasant leader in the 1910 revolution, the movement showed how key social issues remained unresolved. The Mexican government responded with a combination of repression and negotiation.

Also in the 1990s the government joined in negotiations for the North American Free Trade Agreement (NAFTA), hoping to spur Mexican industry. Results remained unclear by 2006, though trade with the United States increased and Mexico became the second largest U.S. trade partner, amid Mexican fears of loss of economic control and a growing gap between a sizeable middle class and the very poor, including most of Mexico's Indians. NAFTA also drew Mexico into closer political and economic ties with the United States.

In 2000 a national election ended the PRI political monopoly. Vicente Fox, leader of the conservative National Action party (PAN), became president on a platform of cleaning up corruption and improving conditions for Mexican workers in the United States. Again, long-term results remain unclear.

FIGURE 37.4 On January 1, 1994, the North American Free Trade Agreement (NAFTA) went into effect. On that day, Zapatista rebels in Chiapas, Mexico, seized control of several towns, announcing their opposition to NAFTA, seizing weapons, and freeing prisoners from jail. Although its natural resources are great, the people of Chiapas are among the poorest in Mexico. Their declaration read, in part: "We have nothing to lose, absolutely nothing, no decent roof over our heads, no land, no work, poor health, no food, no education, no right to freely and democratically choose our leaders, no independence from foreign interests, and no justice for ourselves or our children. . . . We are the descendants of those who truly built this nation, we are the millions of dispossessed, and we call upon all of our brethren to join our crusade, the only option to avoid dying of starvation!"

## Radical Options in the 1950s

■ After World War II, key Latin American nations continued earlier political patterns. But a surge of radical unrest in several smaller countries quickly brought cold war tensions into play. In Bolivia, Guatemala, and Cuba, revolutionaries tried to change the nature of government and society, but they had to accommodate the realities of the cold war and the interests of the United States.

The Argentine and Brazilian changes begun by Perón and Vargas were symptomatic of the continuing problems of Latin America, but their populist authoritarian solutions were only one possible response. By the 1940s, pressure for change had built up through much of Latin America. Across the political spectrum there was a desire to improve the social and economic conditions throughout the region and a general agreement that development and economic strength were the keys to a better future. How to achieve those goals remained in question. In Mexico, as we have seen, one-party rule continued, and the "revolution" became increasingly conservative and interested in economic growth rather than social justice. In a few countries, such as Venezuela and Costa Rica, reform-minded democratic parties were able to win elections in an open political system. In other places, such a solution was less likely or less attractive to those who wanted reform. Unlike the Mexican revolutionaries of

VISUALIZING THE PAST

## Murals and Posters: Art and Revolution

Public art for political purposes has been used since ancient Egypt, but with the development of lithography (a color printing process), the poster emerged as a major form of communication. First developed in the late 19th century as a cheap form of advertising using image and text to sell soap, wine, or chocolate or to advertise dance halls and theaters, by the 1880s posters were adapted to political purposes, and in World War I all the major combatants used them. But those opposed to governments could also use posters to convey a revolutionary message to a broad public. In Latin America, the Mexican Revolution made use of public art in great murals, but these were often expensive and took a long time to complete. The Cuban revolutionaries of the 1960s and the Nicaraguan revolutionaries of the 1980s turned to the poster as a way to convey their policies and goals to a broad public.

**Questions** What are the advantages of the poster over the mural, and vice versa? Is poster art really art? Why are images of the past often the subjects of revolutionary art? To whom is political art usually directed?

1910–1920, those seeking change in the post–World War II period could turn to the well-developed political philosophy of Marxian socialism as a guide. However, such models were fraught with dangers because of the context of the cold war and the ideological struggle between western Europe and the Soviet bloc.

Throughout Latin America, the failures of political democratization, economic development, and social reforms led to consideration of radical and revolutionary solutions to national problems. In some cases, the revolutions at first were successful but ultimately were unable to sustain the changes. In predominantly Indian Bolivia, where as late as 1950 90 percent of the land was owned by 6 percent of the population, a revolution erupted in 1952 in which miners, peasants, and urban middle-class groups participated. Although mines were nationalized and some land redistributed, fear of moving too far to the left brought the army back into power in 1964, and subsequent governments remained more interested in order than in reform.

### Guatemala: Reform and U.S. Intervention

The first place where more radical solutions were tried was Guatemala. This predominantly Indian nation had some of the worst of the region's problems. Its population was mostly illiterate and sufferd poor health conditions and high mortality rates. Land and wealth were distributed very unequally, and the whole economy depended on the highly volatile prices for its main exports of coffee and bananas. In 1944 a middle-class and labor coalition elected reformer **Juan José Arevalo** as president. Under a new constitution, he began a series of programs within the context of "spiritual socialism" that included land reform and an improvement in the rights and conditions of rural and industrial workers. These programs and Arevalo's sponsorship of an intense nationalism brought the government into direct conflict with foreign interests operating in Guatemala, especially the **United Fruit Company**, the largest and most important foreign concern there.

In 1951, after a free election, the presidency passed to Colonel Jacobo Arbenz, whose nationalist program was more radical. Arbenz announced several programs to improve or nationalize the transportation network, the hydroelectric system, and other areas of the economy. A move to expropriate unused lands on large estates in 1953 provoked opposition from the landed oligarchy and from United Fruit, which eventually was threatened with the loss of almost half a million acres of reserve land. The U.S. government, fearing "communist" penetration of the Arbenz government and under considerable pressure from the United Fruit Company, denounced the changes and began to impose economic and diplomatic restrictions on Guatemala. At the same time, the level of nationalist rhetoric intensified, and the government increasingly received the support of the political left in Latin America and in the socialist bloc.

In 1954, with the help of the U.S. Central Intelligence Agency, a dissident military force was organized and invaded Guatemala. The Arbenz government fell, and the pro-American regime that replaced it turned back the land reform and negotiated a settlement favorable to United Fruit. The reform experiment was thus brought to a halt. By the standards of the 1960s and later, the programs of Arevalo and Arbenz seem rather mild, although Arbenz's statements and supposedly his acceptance of arms from eastern Europe undoubtedly contributed to U.S. intervention.

The reforms promised by the U.S.-supported governments were minimal. Guatemala continued to have a low standard of living, especially for its Indian population. The series of military governments after the coup failed to address the nation's social and economic problems. That failure led to continual violence and political instability. Political life continued to be controlled by a coalition of coffee planters, foreign companies, and the military. A guerrilla movement grew and provoked brutal military repression, which fell particularly hard on the rural Indian population. Guatemala's attempt at radical change, an attempt that began with an eye toward improving the conditions of the people, failed because of external intervention. The failure was a warning that change would not come without internal and foreign opposition.

## The Cuban Revolution: Socialism in the Caribbean

The differences between Cuba and Guatemala underline the diversity of Latin America and the dangers of partial revolutions. The island nation had a population of about 6 million, most of whom were the descendants of Spaniards and the African slaves who had been imported to produce the sugar, tobacco, and hides that were the colony's mainstays. Cuba had a large middle class, and its literacy and health care levels were better than in most of the rest of the region. Rural areas lagged behind in these matters, however, and there the working and living conditions were poor, especially for the workers on the large sugar estates. Always in the shadow of the United States, Cuban politics and economy were rarely free of American interests. By the 1950s, about three-fourths of what Cuba imported came from the United States. American investments in the island were heavy during the 1940s and 1950s. Although the island experienced periods of prosperity, fluctuations in the world market for Cuba's main product, sugar, revealed the tenuous basis of the economy. Moreover, the disparity between the countryside and the growing middle class in Havana underlined the nation's continuing problems.

From 1934 to 1944, **Fulgencio Batista,** a strong-willed, authoritarian reformer who had risen through the lower ranks of the army, ruled Cuba. Among his reforms were a democratic constitution of 1940 that promised major changes, nationalization of natural resources, full employment, and land reform. However, Batista's programs of reform were marred by corruption, and when in 1952 he returned to the presidency, there was little left of the reformer but a great deal of the dictator. Opposition developed in various sectors of the society. Among the regime's opponents was **Fidel Castro,** a young lawyer experienced in leftist university politics and an ardent critic of the Batista government and the ills of Cuban society. On July 26, 1953, Castro and a few followers launched an unsuccessful attack on some military barracks. Captured, Castro faced a trial, an occasion he used to expound his revolutionary ideals, aimed mostly at a return to democracy, social justice, and the establishment of a less dependent economy.

Released from prison, Castro fled to exile in Mexico where, with the aid of **Ernesto "Che" Guevara,** a militant Argentine revolutionary, he gathered a small military force. They landed in Cuba in 1956 and slowly began to gather strength in the mountains. By 1958 the "26th of July Movement" had found support from students, some labor organizations, and rural

Soviet Deputy Premier in Cuba

workers and was able to conduct operations against Batista's army. The bearded rebels, or *barbudos,* won a series of victories. The dictator, under siege and isolated by the United States (which because of his excesses refused to support him any longer), was driven from power, and the rebels took Havana amid wild scenes of joy and relief (Figure 37.5).

What happened next is highly debatable, and Castro himself has offered alternative interpretations at different times. Whether Castro was already a Marxist-Leninist and had always intended to introduce a socialist regime (as he now claims) or whether the development of this program was the result of a series of pragmatic decisions is in question. Rather than simply returning to the constitution of 1940 and enacting moderate reforms, Castro launched a program of sweeping change. Foreign properties were expropriated, farms were collectivized, and a centralized socialist economy was put in place. Most of these changes were accompanied by a nationalist and anti-imperialist foreign policy. Relations with the United States were broken off in 1961, and Cuba increasingly depended on the financial support and arms of the Soviet Union to maintain its revolution. With that support in place, Castro was able to survive the increasingly hostile reaction of the United States. That reaction included a disastrous U.S.-sponsored invasion by Cuban exiles in 1961 and an embargo on trade with Cuba. Dependence on the Soviet Union led to a crisis in 1961, when Soviet nuclear missiles, perhaps placed in Cuba in case of another U.S. invasion, were discovered and a confrontation between the superpowers ensued. Despite these problems, to a large extent the Cuban revolution survived because of the global context. The politics of the cold war provided Cuba with a protector and a benefactor, the Soviet Union.

Fidel Castro Defends the Revolution

The Cold War and Cuba

The results of the revolution have been mixed. The social programs were extensive. Education, health, and housing have improved greatly and rank Cuba among the world's leaders—quite unlike most other nations of the region. This is especially true in the long-neglected rural areas. A wide variety of social and educational programs have mobilized all sectors of the population. The achievements have been accompanied by severe restrictions of basic freedoms.

Attempts to diversify and strengthen the economy have been less successful. An effort to industrialize in the 1960s failed, and Cuba turned again to its ability to produce sugar. The world's falling sugar and rising petroleum prices led to disaster. Only by subsidizing Cuban sugar and supplying petroleum below the world price could the Soviet Union maintain the Cuban economy. After the breakup of the Soviet Union in the 1990s, the Cuban situation deteriorated as Castro adhered to an inflexible socialist economic policy. Increasingly isolated—along with China and North

**FIGURE 37.5** Fidel Castro and his guerrilla army brought down the Batista government in January 1959, to the wild acclaim of many Cubans. Castro initiated sweeping reforms in Cuba that eventually led to the creation of a socialist regime and a sharp break with the United States.

Korea, Cuba was one of the last three communist governments in the world—Cuba no longer received much-needed Soviet aid and faced an uncertain future.

Despite these problems, the Cuban revolution offered an example that proved attractive to those seeking to transform Latin American societies. Early direct attempts to spread the model of the Cuban revolution, such as Che Guevara's guerrilla operation in Bolivia, where he lost his life in 1967, were failures, but the Cuban model and the island's ability to resist the pressure of a hostile United States proved attractive to other nations in the Caribbean and Central America, such as Grenada and Nicaragua, that also exercised the revolutionary option. U.S. reaction to such movements has been containment or intervention.

## The Search for Reform and the Military Option

- **Latin Americans continued to seek solutions to their problems using Catholic, Marxist, and capitalist doctrines. In the 1960s and 1970s nationalistic, pro-capitalist military governments created new "bureaucratic authoritarian" regimes which, for a while, served the cold war interests of the United States. By the 1980s, a new wave of democratic regimes was emerging.**

The revolutionary attempts of the 1950s, the durability of the Cuban revolution, and the general appeal of Marxist doctrines in developing nations underlined Latin America's tendency to undertake revolutionary change that left its economic and social structures unchanged. How could the traditional patterns of inequality and international dependency be overcome? What was the best path to the future?

For some, the answer was political stability, imposed if necessary, to promote capitalist economic growth. The one-party system of Mexico demonstrated its capacity for repression when student dissidents were brutally killed during disturbances in 1968. Mexico enjoyed some prosperity from its petroleum resources in the 1970s, but poor financial planning, corruption, and foreign debt again caused problems by the 1980s, and the PRI seemed to be losing its ability to maintain control of Mexican politics.

For others, the church, long a power in Latin America, provided a guide. Christian Democratic parties formed in Chile and Venezuela in the 1950s, hoping to bring reforms through popularly based mass parties that would preempt the radical left. The church often was divided politically, but the clergy took an increasingly engaged position and argued for social justice and human rights, often in support of government opponents. A few, such as Father Camilo Torres in Colombia, actually joined armed revolutionary groups in the 1960s.

More common was the emergence within the church hierarchy of an increased concern for social justice (Figure 37.6). By the 1970s, a **liberation theology** combined Catholic theology and socialist principles or used Marxist categories for understanding society in an effort to improve conditions for the poor. Liberation theologians stressed social equality as a

FIGURE 37.6 In September 1999, thousands of Brazilians attended a mass to celebrate the "Cry of the Excluded," a protest against the social and economic degradation of the nation's poor, who make up more than a third of the population.

DOCUMENT

## The People Speak

Scholarly analysis of general trends often fails to convey the way in which historical events and patterns affect the lives of people or the fact that history is made up of the collective experience of individuals. It is often very difficult to know about the lives of common people in the past or to learn about their perceptions of their lives. In recent years in Latin America, however, a growing literature of autobiographies, interpreted autobiographies (in which another writer puts the story down and edits it), and collections of interviews have provided a vision of the lives of common people. These statements, like any historical document, must be used carefully because their authors or editors sometimes have political purposes, because they reflect individual opinions, or because the events they report may be atypical. Nevertheless, these personal statements put flesh and blood on the bones of history and provide an important perspective from those whose voice in history often is lost.

### A Bolivian Woman Describes Her Life

Domitilia Barrios de Chungara was a miner's wife who became active in the mine workers' political movement. Her presence at the United Nations–sponsored International Woman's Year Tribunal in 1975 moved a Brazilian journalist to organize her statements into a book about her life. This excerpt provides a picture of her everyday struggle for life.

> My day begins at four in the morning, especially when my compañero is on the first shift. I prepare his breakfast. Then I have to prepare salteñas [small meat pastries] because I make about one hundred salteñas every day and I sell them on the street. I do this in order to make up for what my husband's wage doesn't cover in terms of our necessities. The night before, we prepare the dough and at four in the morning I make the salteñas while I feed the kids. The kids help me.
>
> Then the ones that go to school in the morning have to get ready, while I wash the clothes left soaking over night.
>
> At eight I go out to sell. The kids that go to school in the afternoon help me. We have to go to the company store and bring home the staples. And in the store there are immensely long lines and you have to wait there until eleven in order to stock up. You have to line up for meat, for vegetables, for oil. So it's just one line after another. Since everything is in a different place, that's how it has to be.
>
> From what we earn between my husband and me, we can eat and dress. Food is very expensive: 28 pesos for a kilo of meat, 4 pesos for carrots, 6 pesos for onions. . . . Considering that my compañero earns 28 pesos a day, that's hardly enough is it?
>
> We don't ever buy ready made clothes. We buy wool and knit. At the beginning of each year, I also spend about 2000 pesos on cloth and a pair of shoes for each of us. And the company discounts some of that each month from my husband's wage. On the pay slips that's referred to as the "bundle." And what happens is that before we finish paying the "bundle" our shoes are worn out. That's how it is.
>
> Well, from eight to eleven in the morning I sell the salteñas. I do the shopping in the grocery store, and I also work at the Housewives Committee talking with the sisters who go there for advice.
>
> At noon, lunch has to be ready because the rest of the kids have to go to school.

form of personal salvation. When criticized for promoting communism in his native Brazil, Dom Helder da Camara, archbishop of Pernambuco, remarked, "The trouble with Brazil is not an excess of communist doctrine but a lack of Christian justice." The position of the Catholic church in Latin American societies was changing, but there was no single program for this new stance or even agreement among the clergy about its validity. Still, this activist position provoked attacks against clergy such as the courageous Archbishop Oscar Romero of El Salvador, who was assassinated in 1980 for speaking out for social reform, and even against nuns involved in social programs. The church, however, played an important role in the fall of the Paraguayan dictatorship in 1988.

Liberation Theology Challenged

## Out of the Barracks: Soldiers Take Power

The success of the Cuban revolution impressed and worried those who feared revolutionary change within a communist political system. The military forces in Latin America had been involved in politics since the days of the caudillos in the 19th century, and in several nations military interventions had been common. As the Latin American military became more professionalized, however, a new philosophy underlay the military's involvement in politics. The soldiers began to see themselves as above the selfish interests of political parties and as the true representatives of the nation. With technical training and organizational skills, military officers by the 1920s and 1930s believed that they were best equipped to

In the afternoon I have to wash clothes. There are no laundries. We use troughs and have to get the water from a pump.

I've got to correct the kids' homework and prepare everything I'll need to make the next day's salteñas.

## From Peasant to Revolutionary

Rigoberta Menchú, a Quiché Indian from the Guatemalan highlands, came from a peasant family that had been drawn into politics during the repression of Indian communities and human rights in the 1970s. In these excerpts, she reveals her disillusionment with the government and her realization of the ethnic division between Indians and ladinos, or mestizos, that complicates political action in Guatemala.

The CUC [Peasant Union] started growing; it spread like wildfire among the peasants in Guatemala. We began to understand that the root of all our problems was exploitation. That there were rich and poor and that the rich exploited the poor—our sweat, our labor. That's how the rich got richer and richer. The fact that we were always waiting in offices, always bowing to the authorities was part of the discrimination that we Indians suffered.

The situation got worse when the murderous generals came to power although I did not actually know who was the president at the time. I began to know them from 1974 when General Kjell Langerud came to power. He came to our region and said: "We're going to solve the land problem. The land belongs to you. You cultivate the land and I will share it out among you." We trusted him. I was at the meeting when [he] spoke. And what did he give us? My father tortured and imprisoned.

Later I had the opportunity of meeting other Indians. Achi Indians, the group that lives closest to us. And I got to know some Mam Indians too. They all told me: "The rich are bad. But not all ladinos are bad." And I started wondering: Could it be that not all ladinos are Achi Indians, the group that lives closest to us? And I know some Mam Indians too. They all told me: "The rich are bad." . . . There were poor ladinos as well as rich ladinos, and they were exploited as well. That's when I began recognizing exploitation. I kept on going to the finca [large farm] but now I really wanted to find out, to prove if that was true and learn the details. There were poor ladinos on the finca. They worked the same, and their children's bellies were swollen like my little brother's . . . .I was just beginning to speak a little Spanish in those days and I began to talk to them. I said to one poor ladino: "You are a poor ladino, aren't you?" And he nearly hit me. He said: "What do you know about it, Indian!" I wondered: "Why is that when I say poor ladinos are like us, I'm spurned?" I didn't know then that the same system which tries to isolate us Indians also puts barriers between Indians and ladinos. . . . Soon afterwards, I was with the nuns and we went to a village in Uspantán where mostly ladinos live. The nun asked a little boy if they were poor and he said: "Yes, we're poor but we're not Indians." That stayed with me. The nun didn't notice, she went on talking. She was foreign, she wasn't Guatemalan. She asked someone else the same question and he said: "Yes, we're poor but we're not Indians." It was very painful for me to accept that an Indian was inferior to a ladino. I kept on worrying about it. It's a big barrier they've sown between us, between Indian and ladino. I didn't understand it.

**Questions** What was distinctive about lower-class life and outlook in late 20th-century Latin America? How had lower-class life changed since the 19th century?

solve their nations' problems, even if that meant sacrificing the democratic process and imposing martial law.

In the 1960s, the Latin American military establishments, made nervous by the Cuban success and the swing to leftist or populist regimes, began to intervene directly in the political process, not simply to clean out a disliked president or party, as they had done in the past, but to take over government itself. In 1964 the Brazilian military (with the support of the United States and the Brazilian middle class) overthrew the elected president after he threatened to make sweeping social reforms. In Argentina, growing polarization between the Peronists and the middle class led to a military intervention in 1966. In 1973 the Chilean military, which until then had remained for the most part out of politics, overthrew the socialist government of President **Salvador Allende,** as described in the chapter opening.

The soldiers in power imposed a new type of bureaucratic authoritarian regime. Their governments were supposed to stand above the competing demands of various sectors and establish economic stability. Now, as arbiters of politics, the soldiers would place the national interest above selfish interests by imposing dictatorships. Government was essentially a presidency, controlled by the military, in which policies were formulated and applied by a bureaucracy organized like a military chain of command. Political repression and torture were used to silence critics, and stringent measures were imposed to control inflation and strengthen the countries' economies. In Argentina, violent opposition to military rule led to a counteroffensive and the "dirty war" in which thousands of people "disappeared."

Government economic policies fell heaviest on the working class. The goal of the military in Brazil and Argentina was development. To some extent, in Brazil at least, economic improvements were achieved, although income distribution became even more unequal than it had been. Inflation was reduced, industrialization increased, and gains were made in literacy and health, but basic structural problems such as land ownership and social conditions for the poorest people remained unchanged.

There were variations within these military regimes, but all were nationalistic. The Peruvian military tried to create a popular base for its programs and to mobilize support among the peasantry. It had a real social program, including extensive land reform, and was not simply a surrogate for the conservatives in Peruvian society. In Chile and Uruguay, the military was fiercely anticommunist. In Argentina, nationalism and a desire to gain popular support in the face of a worsening economy led to a confrontation with Great Britain over the Falkland Islands (Islas Malvinas), which both nations claimed. The war stimulated pride in Argentina and its soldiers and sailors, but defeat caused a loss of the military's credibility.

## The New Democratic Trends

In Argentina and elsewhere in South America, by the mid-1980s the military had begun to return government to civilian politicians. Continuing economic problems and the pressures of containing opponents wore heavily on the military leaders, who began to realize that their solutions were no more destined to success than those of civilian governments. Moreover, the populist parties, such as the Peronists and Apristas, seemed less of a threat, and the fear of Cuban-style communism had diminished. Also, the end of the cold war meant that the United States was less interested in sponsoring regimes that, though "safe," were also repressive. In Argentina, elections were held in 1983. Brazil began to restore democratic government after 1985 and in 1989 chose its first popularly elected president since the military takeover. The South American military bureaucrats and modernizers were returning to their barracks.

Brazil's Constitution of 1988

The process of redemocratization was not easy, nor was it universal. In Peru, Sendero Luminoso (Shining Path), a long-sustained leftist guerrilla movement, controlled areas of the countryside and tried to disrupt national elections in 1990. In Central America, the military cast a long shadow over the government in El Salvador, but return to civilian government took place in 1992. In Nicaragua, the elections of 1990, held under threat of a U.S. embargo, removed the **Sandinista party** from control in Nicaragua. In subsequent elections the party of the Sandinistas could still muster much support, but it could not win back the presidency. The trend toward a return to electoral democracy could be seen in Guatemala as well. By 1996 civilian government had returned to Guatemala as the country struggled to overcome the history of repression and rebellion and the animosities they had created. The United States demonstrated its continuing power in the region in its invasion of Panama and the arrest of its strongman leader, Manuel Noriega.

Latin American governments in the last decades of the 20th century faced tremendous problems. Large foreign loans taken in the 1970s for the purpose of development, sometimes for unnecessary projects, had created a tremendous level of debt that threatened the economic stability of countries such as Brazil, Peru, and Mexico. In 2002 the Argentine government defaulted on its debt and faced economic crisis. High rates of inflation provoked social instability as real wages fell. Pressure from the international banking community to curb inflation by cutting government spending and reducing wages often ignored the social and political consequences of such actions. An international commerce in drugs, which produced tremendous profits, stimulated criminal activity and created powerful international cartels that could even threaten national sovereignty. In Colombia a leftist guerrilla movement controlled large areas of the country and funded itself from the drug trade. It destabilized the country and the government's legitimacy. In countries as diverse as Cuba, Panama, and Bolivia, the narcotics trade penetrated the highest government circles.

But despite the problems, the 1990s seemed to demonstrate that the democratic trends were well established. In Central America there was a return to civilian government. In Venezuela and Brazil, corruption in government led to the fall of presidents and as we have mentioned led to a major political change in Mexico in 2000. But dissatisfaction with NAFTA and continuing economic problems continued. In Brazil a leftist working-class presidential candidate, Lula (Luiz Inacio Lula da Silva), was elected in 2002, but by 2005 little change in social inequalities had taken place and major figures his government faced charges of corruption. More radical options were also still possible. In Colombia the insurgency supported by ties to the drug trade continued to threaten the nation's stability. In Venezuela a populist military leader, Hugo Chávez, survived a coup in 2002 and threatened to move the country toward a more independent foreign policy. By 2005 he had mobilized support among other nations in Latin America. In other countries the military was sometimes troublesome, but a commitment to a more open political system in most of the region seemed firm.

## The United States and Latin America: Continuing Presence

As a backdrop to the political and economic story we have traced thus far stands the continuing presence of the United States. After World War I, the United States emerged as the predominant power in the hemisphere, a position it had already begun to assume at the end of the 19th century with the Cuban–Spanish–American war and the building of the Panama Canal. European nations were displaced as the leading investors in Latin America by the United States. In South America, private investments by American companies and entrepreneurs, as well as loans from the American government, were the chief means of U.S. influence. U.S. investments rose to more than $5 billion by 1929, or more than one-third of all U.S. investments abroad.

Cuba and Puerto Rico experienced direct U.S. involvement and almost a protectorate status. But in the Caribbean and Central America, the face of U.S. power, economic interest, and disregard for the sovereignty of weaker neighbors was most apparent. Military interventions to protect U.S.-owned properties and investments became so common that there were more than 30 before 1933 (Map 37.1). Haiti, Nicaragua, the Dominican Republic, Mexico, and Cuba all experienced direct interventions by U.S. troops. Central America was a peculiar case because the level of private

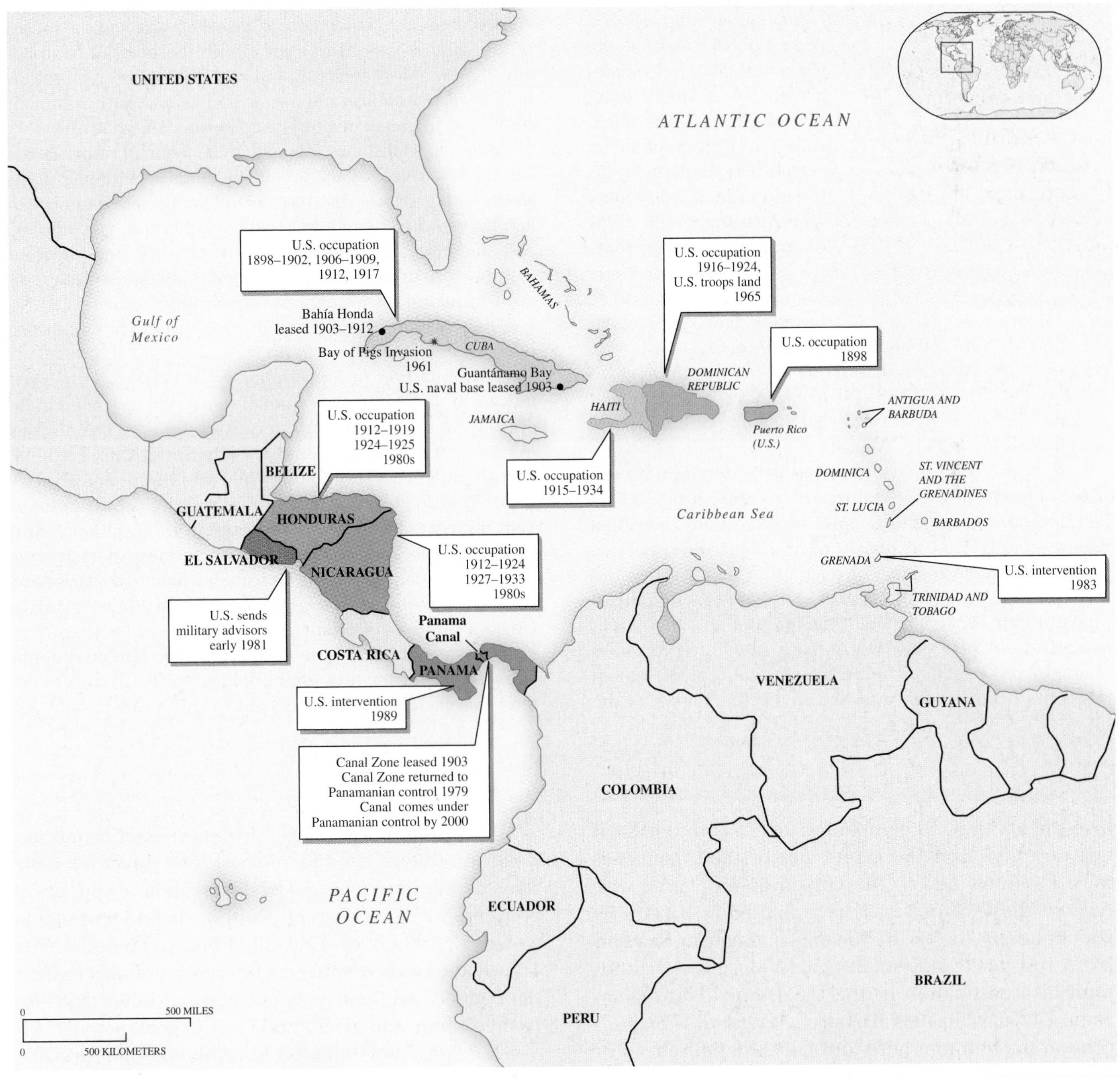


**MAP 37.1** U.S. Military Interventions, 1898–2000

IN DEPTH

## Human Rights in the 20th Century

In Latin America, the question of human rights became a burning issue in the 1960s and continued thereafter. The use of torture by repressive governments, the mobilization of death squads and other vigilante groups with government acquiescence, and the use of terrorism against political opponents by the state and by groups opposed to the state became all too common in the region. Latin America's record on the violation of human rights was no worse than that of some other areas of the world. However, the demonstrations by the Argentine "Mothers of the Plaza del Mayo" to focus attention on their disappeared children; the publication of prison memoirs recounting human rights violations in Brazil, Cuba, and Argentina; and films dramatizing events such as the assassination of Archbishop Oscar Romero in El Salvador have all focused attention on the problem in Latin America. Moreover, because Latin America shares in the cultural heritage of Western societies, it is difficult to make an argument that human rights there have a different meaning or importance than in Europe or North America.

> *"Whereas developing nations view the right to development as a human right, it is viewed as a political and economic demand in wealthier nations of the West."*

The concept of human rights—that is, certain universal rights enjoyed by all people because they are justified by a moral standard that stands above the laws of any individual nation—may go back to ancient Greece. The concept of natural law and the protection of religious or ethnic minorities also moved nations in the 19th century toward a defense of human rights. To some extent, the international movement to abolish the slave trade was an early human rights movement. In modern times, however, the concept of human rights has been strongly attached to the foundation of the United Nations. In 1948 that body, with the experience of World War II in mind, issued a Universal Declaration of Human Rights and created a commission to oversee the human rights situation. The Universal Declaration, which guaranteed basic liberties and freedoms regardless of color, sex, or religion, proclaimed that it should be the "common standard for all peoples and nations." However, one critic has stated that of the 160 nations in the United Nations, only about 30 have a consistently good record on human rights.

A major problem for the international community has been enforcing the Universal Declaration. The United Nations commission did not have any specific powers of enforcement, and much debate has taken place on the power of the United Nations to intervene in the internal affairs of any nation. More recently, various regional organizations have tried to establish the norms that should govern human rights and to create institutions to enforce these norms.

One specialist has claimed that "human rights is the world's first universal ideology." The defense of human rights seems to be a cause that most people and governments can accept without hesitation, but the question is complex. Although the rights to life, liberty, security, and freedom from torture or degrading punishment are generally accepted in principle by all nations, other rights remain open to question. What is a right, and to what extent are definitions of rights determined by culture?

The question of universality versus relativism emerged quickly in the debate over human rights. What seemed to be obvious human rights in Western societies were less obvious in other parts of the world, where other priorities were held. For example, laws prohibiting child labor were enforced by most Western societies, but throughout the world perhaps 150 million children worked, often in unhealthy and exploitive conditions. They worked because of economic necessity in many cases, but in some societies such labor was considered moral and proper. Such cultural differences have led to a position of relativism, which recognizes that there are profound cultural variations in what is considered moral and just. Critics of the original Universal Declaration contend that its advocacy of the right to own property and the

---

investments by U.S. companies such as United Fruit was very high and the economies of these countries were so closely tied to the United States. Those who resisted the U.S. presence were treated as bandits by expeditionary forces. In Nicaragua, **Augusto Sandino** led a resistance movement against occupying troops until his assassination by the U.S.-trained Nicaraguan National Guard in 1934. His struggle against U.S. intervention made him a hero and later the figurehead of the Sandinista party, which carried out a socialist revolution in Nicaragua in the 1980s.

The grounds for these interventions were economic, political, strategic, and ideological. The direct interventions usually were followed by the creation or support of conservative governments, often dictatorships that would be friendly to the United States. These became known as **banana republics,** a reference not only to their dependence on the export of tropical products but also to their often subservient and corrupt governments.

Foreign interventions contributed to a growing nationalist reaction. Central America with its continuing political problems became a symbol of Latin America's right to vote imposed Western political and economic values as universals. Cultural relativism had the advantage of recognizing the variety of cultures and standards in the world, but it has also been used as a shield to deflect criticism and to excuse the continued violation of human rights.

The definition of human rights is also political. The West emphasizes the civil and political rights of the individual. The socialist nations placed social and economic justice above individual rights, although by the 1990s movements in eastern Europe and China indicated that there was pressure to modify this approach. In the developing nations, an argument for peoples' rights has emerged in which the "right to development," which calls for a major structural redistribution of the world's resources and economic opportunities, is a central concept. As Léopold Senghor of Senegal put it, "Human rights begin with breakfast"; or as a report on Ghana stated, " 'One man, one vote' is meaningless unless accompanied by the principle of 'one man, one bread.' " Whereas developing nations view the right to development as a human right, it is viewed as a political and economic demand in wealthier nations of the West.

Another dimension of human rights is the extent to which it influences national foreign policies. Governments may make statements pledging respect for human rights in their foreign policies, but considerations of national defense, security, sovereignty, war against terrorism, or other goals often move human rights concerns into a secondary position. Disputes over the role of human rights in foreign policy sometimes are posed as a conflict between "moralistic utopians" who see the world as it should be and "pragmatists" who see the world as it is. Neither approach necessarily denies the importance of human rights, but there are differences in priority and strategy. Pragmatists might argue that it is better to maintain relations with a nation violating human rights in order to be able to exercise some influence over it in the future, or that other policy considerations must be weighed along with those of human rights in establishing foreign policy. Moralists would prefer to bring pressure by isolating and condemning a nation that violates international standards.

These different approaches have been reflected in the U.S. policy shifts toward Latin America. In the 1950s, human rights considerations were secondary to opposing the spread of communism in the hemisphere, and the United States was willing to support governments that violated human rights as long as they were anticommunist allies. During the 1960s, this policy continued, but increasing and systematic abuses by military regimes in Brazil, Uruguay, Chile, Nicaragua, and elsewhere in Latin America began to elicit some changes. In 1977 President Carter initiated a new policy in which human rights considerations would be given high priority in U.S. foreign policy. The U.S. refusal to support or aid governments that violated human rights contributed to the weakening of some regimes and stimulated resistance to human rights violations in Latin America, but by the 1980s a more pragmatic approach had returned to U.S. policy. Criticism of human rights violations sometimes was made selectively, and abuses in "friendly" governments were dismissed. The extent to which human rights concerns must be balanced against issues such as security, the maintenance of peace, and nonintervention continues to preoccupy policymakers. The issue became particularly thorny in the United States in the aftermath of the terrorist attack of September 11, 2001. In 2004 the United States suspended normal legal protections and restraints against torture in the treatment of military prisoners from the wars in Iraq and Afghanistan and in dealing with potential terrorists at home.

Attention to human rights will continue to play an important role in international affairs. Problems of definition still remain, and there is no universal agreement on the exact nature of human rights. Controversy on the weight of political and civil rights and social, cultural, and economic rights continues to divide richer and poorer nations. Still, the United Nations Declaration of Human Rights, to which 160 nations are signatories, provides a basic guide and an outline for the future.

**Questions** Why might various regimes oppose human rights, and on what basis? Is the human rights movement a Western replacement for imperialism as a way to exert international political influence? Have international human rights movements produced political change?

weakness in the face of foreign influence and interference, especially by the United States. The Nobel Prize–winning Chilean communist poet Pablo Neruda, in his poem "The United Fruit Co." (1950), spoke of the dictators of Central America as "circus flies, wise flies, learned in tyranny" who buzzed over the graves of the people. He wrote the following eight lines with passion:

> When the trumpet sounded, all was prepared in the land,
> and Jehovah divided the world between Coca Cola Inc.,
> Anaconda, Ford Motors, and other companies:
> United Fruit Co. reserved for itself the juiciest part,
> the central coast of my land,
> the sweet waist of America
> and baptized again its lands
> as Banana Republics.

The actions of the United States changed for a time after 1937. In that year, President Franklin D. Roosevelt introduced the **Good Neighbor Policy,** which promised to deal more fairly with Latin America and to stop direct interventions. After World War II, however, the U.S. preoccupation with containment of the Soviet Union and communism as an ideology led to new strategies in Latin America. They included participation in regional organizations, the support of governments that at least expressed democratic or anticommunist principles, the covert undermining of governments considered unfriendly to U.S. interests, and when necessary, direct intervention. Underlying much of this policy was also a firm belief that economic development would eliminate the conditions that contributed to radical political solutions. Thus, U.S. programs such as the **Alliance for Progress,** begun in 1961, aimed to develop the region as an alternative to those solutions. The alliance had limited success despite good intentions and more than $10 billion in aid, but many Latin Americans perceived that it benefited the elites rather than the poor. Because of its record, Latin Americans and North Americans both began to question the assumption that development was basically a problem of capital and resources and that appropriate strategies would lead to social and economic improvement, which in turn would forestall revolution.

During the 1970s and 1980s, U.S. policy often was pragmatic, accepting Latin America as it was, which meant dealing on friendly terms with the military dictatorships. President Jimmy Carter (1976–1980) made a new initiative to deal with Latin America and to influence governments there to observe civil liberties. Most significantly, a treaty was signed with Panama that ceded to that nation eventual control of the Panama Canal. Increasing violence in Central America in the 1980s and the more conservative presidencies of Ronald Reagan and George H. Bush led the United States back to policies based on strategic, economic, and defense considerations in which direct intervention or support of counterrevolutionary forces such as the Contras in Nicaragua played a part. Thus, in 1989 and 1990, the United States toppled a government in Panama that was authoritarian, defied U.S. policies, and promoted drug smuggling, replacing it with a cooperative regime backed by American troops.

After 2000 U.S. concerns with Latin America continued to focus on the issues of commerce, immigration, the drug trade, and political stability. Militarization of the campaign against drugs and increasing concern with terrorism meant that by 2003 almost 60 percent of U.S. aid to Latin America was pledged to military purposes. Globalization for Latin America did increase national economic growth, but free trade arrangements did not protect workers and well over 30 percent of the region's population still fell below the poverty line. That fact contributed to the growing tide of Latin American migration—legal and illegal—to the United States. By 2004 there were 40 million Hispanics in the United States, about 40 percent of them immigrants.

## Societies in Search of Change

■ **Social relations changed slowly in Latin America. Population growth, urbanization, and the migration of workers continued to challenge the region.**

Despite frustrated Latin American attempts at profound reform, there were great changes during the 20th century. Social and gender relations changed during the century. We have already seen how countries such as Mexico, Peru, and Bolivia sought to enfranchise their Indian populations during this century in different ways and with differing degrees of success. National ideologies and actual practice often are not the same, and discrimination on the basis of ethnicity continues. To be called Indian is still an insult in many places in Latin America. Although ethnic and cultural mixture characterizes many Latin American populations and makes Indian and African elements important features of national identity, relations with Indian populations often continue to be marked by exploitation and discrimination in nations as diverse as Brazil, Nicaragua, and Guatemala.

### Slow Change in Women's Roles

The role of women has changed slowly. After World War I, women in Latin America continued to live under inequalities in the workplace and in politics. Women were denied the right to vote anywhere in Latin America until Ecuador enfranchised women in 1929 and Brazil and Cuba did the same in 1932. Throughout most of the region, those examples were not followed until the 1940s and 1950s. In some nations, the traditional associations of women with religion and the Catholic church in Hispanic life made reformers and revolutionaries fear that women would become a conservative force in national politics. This attitude, combined with traditional male attitudes that women should be concerned only with home and family, led to a continued exclusion of women from political life. In response, women formed various associations and clubs and began to push for the vote and other issues of interest to them.

Feminist organizations, suffrage movements, and international pressures eventually combined to bring about change. In Argentina, 15 bills for female suffrage were introduced in the senate before the vote was won in 1945. Sometimes the victory was a matter of political expediency for those in power: In the Dominican Republic and some other countries, the enfranchisement of women was a strategy used by conservative groups to add more conservative voters to the electorate in an effort to hold off political change. In Argentina, recently enfranchised women became a major pillar of the Peronist regime, although that regime also suppressed female political opponents such as Victoria Ocampo, editor of the important literary magazine *Sur.*

Women eventually discovered that the ability to vote did not in itself guarantee political rights or the ability to have their specific issues heard. After achieving the vote, women tended to join the national political parties, where traditional prejudices against women in public life limited their ability to influence political programs. In Argentina, Brazil, Colombia, and Chile, for example, the integration of women into national political programs has been slow, and women have not participated in proportion to their numbers. In a few cases, however, women played a crucial role in elections.

Some of the earliest examples of mobilization of women and their integration into the national labor force of various Latin American nations came in the period just before World War I and continued thereafter. The classic roles of women as homemakers, mothers, and agricultural workers were expanded as women entered the industrial labor force in growing numbers. By 1911 in Argentina, for example, women made up almost 80 percent of the textile and clothing industry's workers. But women found that their salaries often were below those of comparable male workers and that their jobs, regardless of the skill levels demanded, were considered unskilled and thus less well paid. Under these conditions, women, like other workers, joined the anarchist, socialist, and other labor unions and organizations.

Labor organizations are only a small part of the story of women in the labor force. In countries such as Peru, Bolivia, and Ecuador, women working in the markets control much small-scale commerce and have become increasingly active politically. In the growing service sectors, women have also become an important part of the labor force. Shifts in attitudes about women's roles have come more slowly than political and economic changes. Even in revolutionary Cuba, where a Law of the Family guaranteed equal rights and responsibilities within the home, enforcement has been difficult.

By the mid-1990s, the position of women in Latin America was closer to that in western Europe and North America than to the other areas of the world. Women made up 9 percent of the legislators in Latin America, a percentage higher than in any other region of the world. In terms of demographic patterns, health, education, and place in the workforce, the comparative position of women reinforced Latin America's intermediate position between industrialized and developing nations.

## The Movement of People

In 1950 the populations of North America (United States and Canada) and Latin America were both about 165 million, but by 1985 North America's population was 265 million, while Latin America's had grown to more than 400 million. Declining mortality and continuing high fertility were responsible for this situation.

At the beginning of the 20th century, the major trend of population movement was immigration to Latin America, but the region has long experienced internal migration and the movement of people within the hemisphere. By the 1980s, this movement had reached significant levels, fed by the flow of workers seeking jobs, the demands of capital for cheap labor, and the flight of political refugees seeking basic freedoms. During World War II, government programs to supply laborers were set up between the United States and Mexico, but these were always accompanied by extralegal migration, which fluctuated with the economy. Conditions for migrant laborers often were deplorable, although the extension of social welfare to them in the 1960s began to address some of the problems. By the 1970s, more than 750,000 illegal Mexican migrants a year were crossing the border—some more than once—as the United States continued to attract migrants.

This internationalization of the labor market was comparable in many ways with the movement of workers from poorer countries such as Turkey, Morocco, Portugal, and Spain to the stronger economies of West Germany and France. In Latin America it also reflected the fact that industrialization in the 20th century depended on highly mechanized industry that did not create enough new jobs to meet the needs of the growing population. Much of the migration has been to the United States, but there has also been movement across Latin American frontiers: Haitians migrate to work in the Dominican Republic, and Colombians illegally migrate to Venezuela. By the 1970s, about 5 million people per year were migrating in Latin America and the Caribbean.

Politics has also been a major impulse for migration. Haitians fleeing political repression and abysmal conditions have risked great dangers in small open boats to reach the United States. The Cuban revolution caused one of the great political migrations of the century. Beginning in 1959, when the Cuban middle class fled socialism, and continuing into the 1980s with the flight of Cuban workers, almost 1 million Cubans left the island. The revolutionary upheaval in Nicaragua, political violence in Central America, and poverty in Haiti have contributed to the flight of refugees. Often, it is difficult to separate political and economic factors in the movement of people from their homelands.

International migration is only part of the story. During the 20th century, there was a marked movement in Latin America from rural to urban areas (Table 37.1). Whereas in the 19th century Latin America was an agrarian region, by the 1980s about one-half of the population lived in cities of more than 20,000, and more than 25 of these cities had populations of more than 1 million. Some of these cities had reached enormous size. In 1999 Mexico City had more than 18 million inhabitants, São Paulo had almost 18 million, and Buenos Aires had over 12 million. Latin America was by far the most urbanized area of the developing world and only slightly less urbanized than western Europe.

The problem is not simply size but rate of growth. The urban populations grew at a rate about three times that of the population as a whole, which itself has grown rapidly. Urban economies have not been able to create enough jobs for the rapidly increasing population. Often recent migrants lived in marginal neighborhoods or in shantytowns, which have become characteristic of the rapidly growing cities of Latin America. These *favelas,* to use the Brazilian term, have created awful living conditions, but over time some have become poorer neighborhoods within the cities, and community cooperation and action within them have secured basic urban services. More recently, the rate of urban growth has slowed, but the social problems in the cities remain a major challenge.

Although Latin American urbanization increased rapidly after 1940, the percentage of its people living in cities is still less than in western Europe but more than in Asia and Africa. Unlike the 19th-century European experience, the lack of employment in Latin American cities has kept rural migrants from becoming part of a laboring class with a strong identification with fellow workers. Those who do succeed in securing industrial jobs often join paternalistic labor organizations that are linked to the government. Thus, there is a separation between the chronically underemployed urban lower class and the industrial labor force. Whereas industrialization and urbanization promoted a strong class solidarity in 19th-century Europe, which led to the gains of organized labor, in contemporary Latin America nationalist and populist politics have weakened the ability of the working class to operate effectively in politics.

## Cultural Reflections of Despair and Hope

Latin America remains an amalgamation of cultures and peoples trying to adjust to changing world realities. Protestant denominations have made some inroads, but the vast majority of Latin Americans are still Catholic. Hispanic traditions of family, gender relations, business, and social interaction influence everyday life and help to determine responses to the modern world.

Latin American popular culture remains vibrant. It draws on African and Indian traditional crafts, images, and techniques but arranges them in new ways. Music is also part of popular culture. The Argentine tango of the turn of the century began in the music halls of lower-class working districts of Buenos Aires and became an international craze. The African-influenced Brazilian samba and the Caribbean salsa have spread widely. They are a Latin American contribution to world civilization.

**TABLE 37.1 Population of Capital Cities as a Percentage of Total Population in 10 Latin American Nations**

| Nation | Capital | 1880 | 1930 | 1960 | 1983 | 2003 |
|---|---|---|---|---|---|---|
| Argentina | Buenos Aires | 12 | 20 | 32 | 34 | 33 |
| Brazil | Rio de Janeiro | 3 | 4 | 7 | 4* | 3* |
| Chile | Santiago | 6 | 13 | 22 | 37 | 29 |
| Colombia | Bogotá | 1 | 2 | 8 | 11 | 15 |
| Cuba | Havana | 13 | 15 | 18 | 20 | 20 |
| Mexico | Mexico City | 3 | 5 | 15 | 20 | 9 |
| Panama | Panama City | 7 | 16 | 25 | 20 | 15 |
| Peru | Lima | 3 | 5 | 19 | 27 | 30 |
| Uruguay | Montevideo | 12 | 28 | 31 | 40 | 39 |
| Venezuela | Caracas | 3 | 7 | 20 | 18 | 7 |

*No longer the capital city.

*Sources:* From J. P. Cole, *Latin America: An Economic and Social Geography* (1965), 417; and http://www.world-gazetteer.com.

The struggle for social justice, economic security, and political formulas in keeping with the cultural and social realities of their nations has provided a dynamic tension that has produced tremendous artistic achievements. Latin American poets and novelists have gained worldwide recognition. We have already noted the artistic accomplishments of the Mexican Revolution. In 1922 Brazilian artists, composers, and authors staged a Modern Art Week in São Paulo, which emphasized a search for a national artistic expression that reflected Brazilian realities.

That theme also preoccupied authors elsewhere in Latin America. The social criticism of the 1930s produced powerful realist novels, which revealed the exploitation of the poor, the peasantry, and the Indians. Whether in the heights of the Andes or in the dark streets of the growing urban slums, the plight of the common folk provided a generation of authors with themes worthy of their effort. Social and political criticism has remained a central feature of Latin American literature and art and has played an important role in the development of newer art forms such as film.

The inability to bring about social justice or to influence politics has also sometimes led Latin American artists and intellectuals to follow other paths. In the 1960s a wave of literature took place in which novels that mixed the political, the historical, the erotic, and the fantastic were produced by a generation of authors who used "magical realism" because they found the reality of Latin America too absurd to be described by the traditional forms or logic. Writers such as the Argentine Jorge Luis Borges (1899–1980) and the Colombian Gabriel García Marquez (b. 1928) won acclaim throughout the world. García Marquez's *One Hundred Years of Solitude* (1967) used the history of a family in a mythical town called Macondo as an allegory of Latin America and traced the evils that befell the family and the community as they moved from naive isolation to a maturity that included oppression, exploitation, war, revolution, and natural disaster but never subdued the spirit of its people. In that way, his book outlined the trajectory of Latin America in the 20th century.

## GLOBAL CONNECTIONS

## Struggling Toward the Future in a Global Economy

As Latin America entered the 21st century, it continued to search for economic growth, social justice, and political stability. No easy solutions were available. In many ways, Latin American societies remained "unrevolutionary"—unable to bring about needed changes because of deeply entrenched class interests, international conditions, or power politics. However, the struggle for change had produced some important results. The Mexican and Cuban revolutions brought profound changes in those countries and had a broad impact on the rest of the hemisphere, either as models to copy or as dangers to be avoided. Other nations, such as Bolivia, Peru, and Nicaragua, attempted their own versions of radical change with greater or lesser success. New forms of politics, sometimes populist and sometimes militarist, were tried. New political and social ideas, such as those of liberation theology, grew out of the struggle to find a just and effective formula for change. Latin American authors and artists served as a conscience for their societies and received worldwide recognition for their depiction of the sometimes bizarre reality they observed. Although tremendous problems continued to face the region, Latin America remained the most advanced part of the developing world. Levels of literacy, for example, easily surpassed those in most of Asia and in Africa.

In the age of globalization, Latin America faces new challenges. The new world economy has created opportunities for expansion, and in the 1990s Latin American economies grew considerably, but this growth has made the problems of the distribution of wealth in Latin America even more acute. Over a third of the population still lives in poverty. Brazil has one of the strongest economies in the region, but the gap between rich and poor is among the world's worst. Other problems also result from economic changes. The northern part of Mexico near the border with the United States has benefited from new trade opportunities while southern Mexico has gotten poorer. Then too, integration into the world economy often threatens traditional cultures. Since the 1980s, various Indian political movements have sought to protect traditional cultures while seeking political and economic opportunities. Frustrated by continuing social problems and its disadvantages in the global economy of free trade and privatization, Latin America seemed to be moving toward the left. By 2006, Leftist presidents had been elected in Chile and Bolivia, joining those already in power in Cuba, Venezuela, Brazil, Argentina, and Uruguay, and there was concern that Peru, Mexico, and Nicaragua would also soon move in that direction. This trend revealed collective discontent and sometimes a rhetoric of opposition to U.S. policies, but it also demonstrated that democratic politics were functioning through much of the region.

Cultural issues remain unresolved as well. Partly reflecting divisions in wealth and urbanism, Latin Americans have participated variously in global consumer currents. Middle-class Mexicans, for example, began to copy United States patterns in celebrating Halloween (previously an important traditional holiday focused on the forces of death) and Christmas. To some Mexican intellectuals, this represented a crucial abandonment of identity, and to others the new interests seemed either alien or unobtainable. The spread of new religious movements, including fundamentalist Protestantism, signaled an attempt to provide alternatives to global culture, particularly among urban slum-dwellers. About 10 percent of Latin Americans are now members of Protestant denominations. At the same time, Latin American filmmakers, artists, and popular musicians have contributed directly to global culture, often incorporating traditional elements in the process. Latin America's global position has become increasingly complex.

## Further Readings

A considerable literature in many disciplines deals with Latin America as a whole, and there are many country-specific studies. Two good introductory texts, both of which present variations of the "dependency" interpretation, are E. Bradford Burns, *Latin America: A Concise Interpretative History* (1986), and Thomas E. Skidmore and Peter H. Smith, *Modern Latin America* (1989). John Charles Chasteen, *Born in Fire and Blood* (2001), gives a good overview.

The economic history of Latin America is summarized ably in Victor Bulmer-Thomas, *The Economic History of Latin America Since Independence* (1994), and in John Sheahan, *Patterns of Development in Latin America* (1987). An overview is provided by Richard Salvucci, ed., in *Latin America and the World Economy* (1996).

Three excellent studies of labor are the general study in Charles Berquist, *Labor in Latin America* (1986); the analysis of the case of Brazil in John French, *Drowning in Laws: Labor Law and Brazilian Political Culture* (2004); and June Nash, *We Eat the Mines and the Mines Eat Us* (1979), which provides the worldview of Bolivian miners.

There are many good studies of Latin American politics, but Guillermo O'Donnell, *Modernization and Bureaucratic Authoritarianism* (1973), influenced a generation of scholars. The role of the United States is discussed in Peter Smith, *Talons of the Eagle: Dynamics of U.S.–Latin American Relations* (1996). Anthony Maingot, *The United States and the Caribbean* (1994), gives a clear account of the recent history in that region, and John Coatsworth, *Central America and the United States* (1994), is a critical assessment of U.S. policy in that region. Recent scholarship has emphasized the cultural dimensions of this relationship. Frederick Pike, *The United States and Latin America: Myths and Stereotypes of Civilization and Nature* (1992), set the outlines of cultural relations. Gilbert Joseph et al., eds., *Close Encounters of Empire* (1998), presents suggestive essays. Lars Schoultz, *Human Rights and United States Policy Toward Latin America*(1981), details the influence of human rights on foreign policy and the challenges of setting consistent policies. Steve Stern, *Remembering Pinochet's Chile* (2004), discusses the difficulty of national reconciliation when those rights are violated.

A few good monographs on important topics represent the high level of scholarship on Latin America. Alan Knight, *The Mexican Revolution,* 2 vols. (1986), and John M. Hart, *Revolutionary Mexico* (1987), provide excellent analyses of that event. Freidrich Katz, *The Life and Times of Pancho Villa* (1998), is an outstanding biography. Florencia Mallon, *The Defense of Community in Peru's Central Highlands* (1983), looks at national change from a community perspective. The Cuban revolution and its implications are treated in Louis Perez, *On Becoming Cuban: Identity, Nationality, and Culture* (1999). David Kunzle et al. examine the role of Che Guevara in the Cuban revolution and its legacy for the wider world in *Che Guevara: Icon, Myth, and Message* (2002).

Frank McCann, *Soldiers of the Patria* (2004), on the military in Brazil, is one of the most in-depth studies of a Latin American military establishment, and Richard Gott, *Guerrilla Movements in Latin America* (1972), was a valuable book that presented analysis and documents on the movements seeking revolutionary change at that time. On some of the major themes of the 21st century, there is Juan Gonzalez, *Harvest of Empire: A History of Latinos in America* (2000); Michael Coniff, ed., *Populism in Latin America* (1999); Steve Ellner and Daniel Hellinger, *Venezuela Politics in the Chávez Era* (2003); and Carol Wise, ed., *The Post-NAFTA Political Economy: Mexico and the Western Hemisphere* (1998).

## On the Web

A great deal on Latin American politics and social conditions can be gathered from the Internet. From a well-researched critical stance, see the North American Congress on Latin America (NACLA) reports at http://www.nacla.org. Case studies and other approaches to the revolution in Chile (http://www.hartford-hwp.com/archives/42a/130.html or http://www.soc.ucsb.edu/projects/casemethod/foran.html), Cuba (http://www.worldsocialist-cwi.org/publications/Cuba/index2.html?/publications/Cuba/cuapp1.html), Guatemala (http://www2.truman.edu/~marc/webpages/revsfall98/guatemala/guatemala.html, http://www.hartford-hwp.com/archives/47/index-ce.html, and http://www.gwu.edu/~nsarchiv/NSAEBB/NSAEBB4/), and Nicaragua (http://ww.jcrnian.com/san.html and http://www.socialistworker.org/2004_2/506/506_8_08_Nicaragua.shtml) demonstrate how they inspired both joy and deadly reaction.

The lives of the leaders of these movements receive close treatment on the Web, including sites devoted to Cuba's Castro (http://www.cnn.com/SPECIALS/cold.war/kbank/profiles/castro/ and http://www.marxists.org/history/cuba/archive/castro/index.htm), Mexico's Emiliano Zapata (http://www.cs.utk.edu/~miturria/project/

zapata.html and http://www.mexconnect.com/mex_/history/ezapata1.html), and the women of the Mexican Revolution (http://www.u.arizona.edu/ic/mcbride/ws200/mex-jand.htm) often seem larger than life, none more so than Ernesto "Che" Guevara (http://www.pbs.org/newshour/forum/november97/che.html, http://www.marxists.org/archive/guevara/ and http://www.che_lives.com/home/), whose image remains as current as an icon of revolution today as it did almost a half-century ago.

The hopes of many Latin Americans for a more egalitarian society were celebrated in the works of artists such as Diego Rivera (http://www.diegorivera.com/index.php) and Jose Orozco (http://hoodmuseum.dartmouth.edu/collections/crozco_murals.html). These hopes were ultimately broken on the anvil of the cold war (http://www.coldwar.org and http://www.turnerlearning.com/cnn/coldwar/backyard/byrd_ttl.html). They now largely rest with those who see the free market as the solution to poverty and inequality. There are doubts, however, that the free market is the panacea for the region's long-standing economic and social ills. This doubt is particularly strong among the Mayan farmers of Chiapas (http://nativenet.uthscsa.edu/archive/nl/9407/0164.html, http://lanic.utexas.edu/project/Zapatistas/, http://www.american.edu/ted/chiapas.htm, and http://www.zapatistas.org).

CHAPTER

38

# Africa, the Middle East, and Asia in the Era of Independence



As she had so often in the past, Indira Gandhi refused to heed those who urged her to be cautious. She had audaciously ordered the army to drive the extreme separatist Sikhs from the sacred grounds of the Golden Temple in Amritsar in northwest India. Indian troops had carried out her orders all too well. They had evicted the Sikh radicals, who demanded an independent state, which they called Khalistan. But in the process the troops had killed thousands of Sikhs inside the temple grounds and destroyed or badly damaged many revered shrines, including the library housing the Sikhs' holy scriptures. Now her advisors pleaded with her to replace her Sikh bodyguards with elite army units that had no religious or kinship ties to the aggrieved Sikh community. But Prime Minister Gandhi insisted that the Sikh units that had traditionally guarded her—and her father and British colonial rulers before him—were loyal and placed their honor as soldiers and duty to the nation above whatever sympathy they might feel for radical elements among the Sikh faithful.

So Sikh soldiers were on guard several months later as Indira Gandhi walked from her home through her beloved garden to her nearby office. As she approached the garden gate, she was challenged by two of her most trusted protectors, both Sikhs, who opened fire at close range and riddled her body with bullets. The assassination sparked anti-Sikh riots across India's capital that left thousands dead and sections of the city smoldering ruins. Her son Rajiv, who had only recently taken up a political career, was soon sworn in as her successor. But across the world's largest democracy, Indira was mourned as the lost "mother of the nation" and a relentless champion of the poor and powerless.

As was the case with so many of the women who emerged as leaders in developing nations in the postcolonial era, few Indian politicians expected Indira Gandhi to be a forceful, dynamic prime minister with a vision of her own. As the daughter of Jawaharlal Nehru, who was second only to Gandhi among those who fashioned the nationalist revolt and one of the most influential leaders of the early cold war decades, Indira Gandhi inherited close links to the powerful. But though she became her father's confidant and close companion, she was regarded by India's numerous time-tested and ambitious

FIGURE 38.1 As this photograph of Indian Prime Minister Indira Gandhi on the campaign trail in 1979 strikingly reveals, she reveled in direct contact with the ordinary people of India. Seeing herself as the champion of the poor and defenseless, she refused to be isolated by the phalanxes of bodyguards commonly associated with national leaders across the globe.

politicians as a shy young woman who was content to be her father's helpmate. Seeing her as someone they could control, several of the power brokers of the Congress party backed her as the successor to Lal Bahadur Shastri, who had become prime minister on the death of her father two years before, only to die suddenly himself of a heart attack in early 1966. Gandhi soon made it clear that she was as strong-willed as her father, and as determined to pursue her own agenda for the uplift of India's peoples and extending the nation's influence in international affairs.

With the exception of a three-year hiatus after she had been defeated in national elections in 1977, Indira Gandhi dominated Indian politics from 1966 until her assassination in 1984. Like other activist postcolonial leaders, she faced prodigious challenges. These issues and the often very different strategies for tackling them adopted by different African and Asian leaders are the focus of the chapter that follows. On a resource base depleted by millennia of use, Prime Minister Gandhi sought to find ways first to feed the people and then to improve the living standards of one of the poorest and most populous nations on earth. Like other leaders of developing nations, she had to find a way to balance the demands of the U.S. and Soviet superpowers while maintaining India's nonaligned status in a world threatened by nuclear conflagration. And as demonstrated by the confrontation with the Sikh separatists—only one of a number of highly inflammatory ethnoreligious divisions she had to deal with—like other leaders in the emerging nations, Indira Gandhi spent a great deal of her energy and political capital just holding the country together.

Like the majority of postcolonial heads of state in the developing world, Gandhi sought to centralize power in her own hands, and she resorted at times to preemptive strikes against her political opponents or used force to put down what she perceived as enemies of the new nation. And like so many of her counterparts in the often artificial and unstable political entities carved out of the Euro-American colonial empires, she was violently removed from power. Indira Gandhi's regime ended with her assassination by loyalists turned into implacable enemies by her violent

| 1910 C.E. | 1920 C.E. | 1930 C.E. | 1940 C.E. | 1950 C.E. | 1960 C.E. | 1970 C.E. | 1980 C.E. | 1990 C.E. |
|---|---|---|---|---|---|---|---|---|
| **1912** African National Congress party formed<br>**1919** First Pan-African Nationalist Congress | **1928** Founding of the Muslim Brotherhood in Egypt | **1930s** Free Officers movement develops in Egypt | **1947** India and Pakistan achieve independence<br>**1948** First Arab-Israeli War; Afrikaner Nationalist party comes to power in South Africa, bringing the beginning of apartheid<br>**1949** Hassan al-Banna assassinated in Egypt | **1951** India's first five-year plan for economic development launched<br>**1952** Farouk and khedival regime overthrown in Egypt; Nasser and Free Officers come to power<br>**1955** Bandung Conference; beginning of nonaligned movement<br>**1956** Aborted British-French-Israeli intervention in Suez<br>**1958** South Africa completely independent of Great Britain | **1960** Sharpeville shootings in South Africa<br>**1966** Nkrumah overthrown by military coup in Ghana<br>**1966–1970** Biafran secessionist war in Nigeria<br>**1967** Six-Day War between Israel and Arab nations | **1970s** Peak period for OPEC cartel<br>**1971** Bangladesh revolt against West Pakistan; Indo-Pakistani War<br>**1972** Bangladesh becomes independent nation<br>**1973** Third Arab-Israeli War<br>**1979** Shah of Iran overthrown; Islamic republic declared | **1980–1988** Iran-Iraq War<br>**1989** De Klerk charts path of peaceful reform in South Africa | **1990** Nelson Mandela released from South African prison; Iraqi invasion of Kuwait<br>**1991** Persian Gulf War<br>**1994** First democratic elections in South Africa |

attempt to suppress separatist forces similar to those that have threatened to pull apart virtually all of the new nations of the developing world.

## The Challenges of Independence

■ **In the early decades of independence, the very existence of the nation-states that were carved out of the Western colonial empires was often challenged by internal rivalries, and in some cases civil wars, between different social and ethnic groups. Economic growth was hampered by unprecedented rates of population increase, the structure of the international market, and the underdeveloped state of most colonial economies at the time of independence.**

The nationalist movements that won independence for most of the peoples of Africa, the Middle East, and Asia usually involved some degree of mass mobilization. Peasants and working-class townspeople, who hitherto had little voice in politics beyond their village boundaries or local labor associations, were drawn into political contests that toppled empires and established new nations. To win the support of these groups, nationalist leaders promised them jobs, civil rights, and equality once independence was won. The leaders of many nationalist movements nurtured visions of postindependence utopias in the minds of their followers. The people were told that once the Europeans, who monopolized the best jobs, were driven away and their exploitive hold on the economy was brought to an end, there would be enough to give everyone a good life.

After Empire: Africa and the Middle East

Unfortunately, postindependence realities in almost all of the new nations made it impossible for nationalist leaders to fulfill the expectations they had aroused among their followers and, in varying degrees, among the colonized populace at large. Even with the Europeans gone and the terms of economic exchange

New Nations in Africa

with more developed countries somewhat improved, there was simply not enough to go around. Thus, the socialist-inspired ideologies that nationalist leaders had often embraced and promoted were misleading. The problem was not just that goods and services were unequally distributed, leaving some people rich and the great majority poor. The problem was that there were not enough resources to take care of everybody, even if it was possible to distribute them equitably.

When utopia failed to materialize, personal rivalries and long-standing divisions between different classes and ethnic groups (communalism), which had been muted by the common struggle against the alien colonizers, resurfaced or intensified. The European colonizers had established arbitrary boundaries (Maps 38.1 and

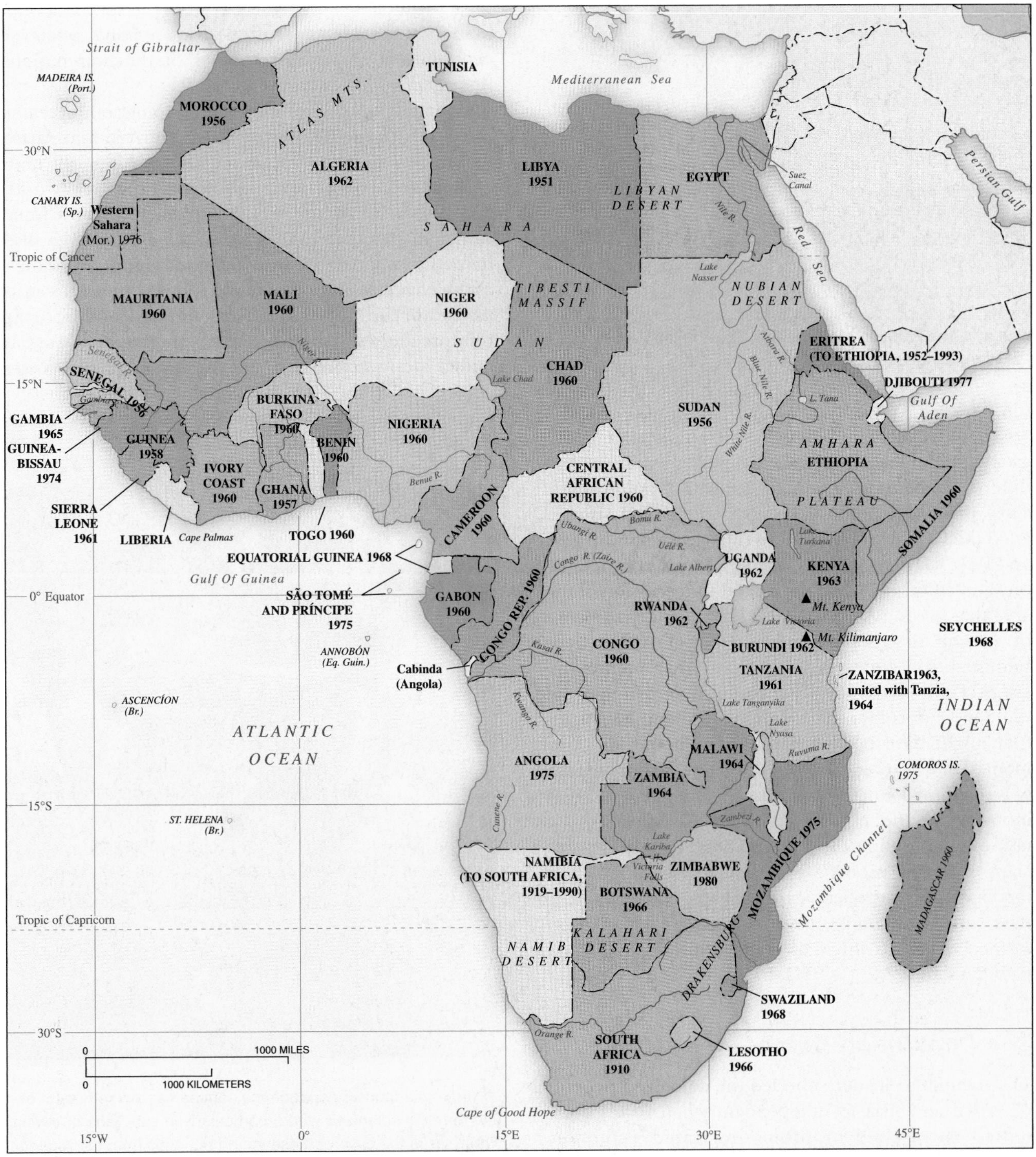

**MAP 38.1** The Colonial Division of Africa and the Emergence of New Nations

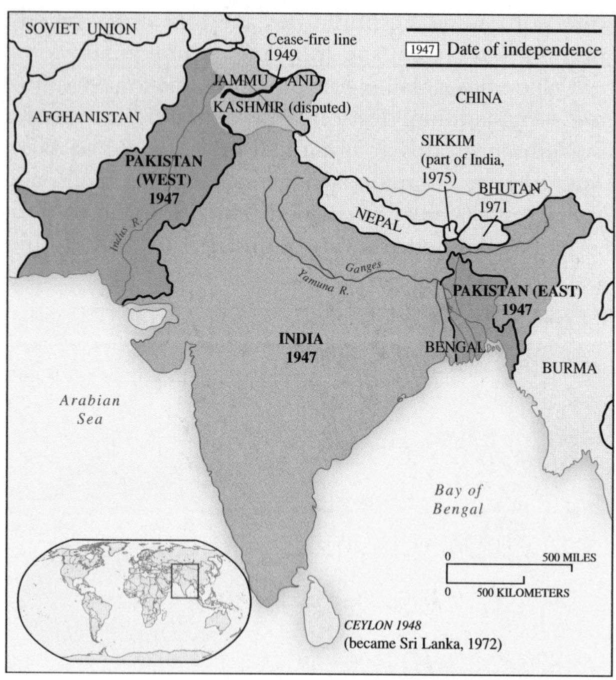


**MAP 38.2 The Partition of South Asia: The Formation of India, Pakistan, Bangladesh, and Sri Lanka**

38.2), sometimes combining hostile ethnic or religious groups. In almost all the new states, these rivalries and differences became dominant features of political life. They produced political instability and often threatened the viability of the nations themselves, as with East and West Pakistan, where extreme contrasts of topography and culture led to violence and the secession of the area that became **Bangladesh.** The recurring problems of famine and starvation in parts of Africa have stemmed from human conflicts more than natural disasters (Figure 38.2). Rivalries and civil wars in many of the newly decolonized nations consumed resources that might have been devoted to economic development. They also blocked—in the name of the defense of subnational interests—measures designed to build more viable and prosperous states. Absorbed by the task of just holding their new nations together, politicians neglected problems—such as soaring population increases, uncontrolled urban growth, rural landlessness, and environmental deterioration—that soon formed as large a threat as political instability to their young nations.

## The Population Bomb

The nationalist leaders who led the colonized peoples of Africa and Asia to independence had firmly committed themselves to promoting rapid economic development once colonial restraints were removed. In keeping with their Western-educated backgrounds, most of these leaders saw their nations following the path of industrialization that had brought national prosperity and international power to much of western Europe and the United States. This course of development was also fostered by representatives of the Soviet bloc, who had emphasized heavy industry in their state-directed drives to modernize their economies and societies. Of the many barriers to the rapid economic breakthroughs postcolonial leaders hoped for, the most formidable and persistent were the spiraling population increases that often overwhelmed whatever economic advances the peoples of the new nations managed to make (Figure 38.3).

Factors making for sustained population increases in already densely populated areas of Asia and Africa had begun to take effect even before the era of high colonialism. Food crops, mostly from the New World, contributed to dramatic population growth in China, India, and Java as early as the 17th century. They also helped sustain high levels of population in areas such as the Niger delta in west Africa, despite heavy losses as a result of the slave trade. The coming of colonial rule reinforced these upward trends in a number of ways. It ended local warfare that had caused population losses

**FIGURE 38.2 Since independence, famine has stalked much of the formerly colonized world, particularly in sub-Saharan Africa. Often, as in the case of these young refugees from the Nigerian civil war photographed in the late 1960s, starvation has been caused by human conflicts rather than natural disasters.**

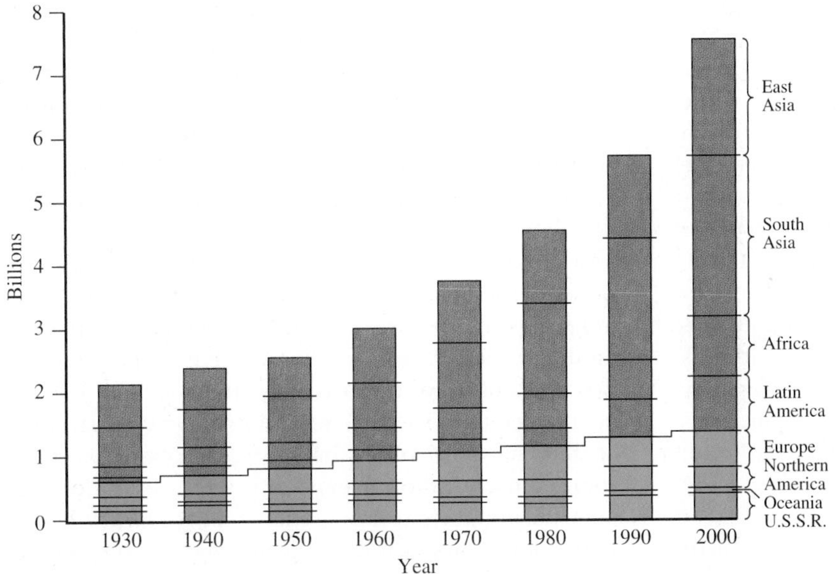


**FIGURE 38.3** This graph shows the growth of the world population by major global geographic areas between 1930 and 2000. It illustrates the near-stabilization of the upswing in populations of the West and the states of the former Soviet Union that began with industrialization in the 18th century. It charts the explosion that occurred in recent decades in the areas of the globe that were colonized, both formally and informally, by the industrial powers in the 19th and early 20th centuries. These increases surpass those of any other epoch in human history.

and, perhaps more significantly, had indirectly promoted the spread of epidemic diseases and famine. The new railroad and steamship links established by the colonizers to foster the spread of the market economy also cut down on the regional famines that had been a major check against sustained population increase since ancient times. Large amounts of food could be shipped from areas where harvests were good to those where drought or floods threatened the local inhabitants with starvation.

With war and famine—two of the main barriers to population increase—much reduced, growth began to speed up. This was particularly true in areas such as India and Java that had been under European control for decades. Death rates declined, but birth rates remained much the same, leading to increasingly larger net increases. Improved hygiene and medical treatment played little part in this rise until the early 20th century. From that time, efforts to eradicate tropical diseases, as well as global scourges such as smallpox, and to improve sewage systems and purify drinking water have led to further population increases.

Nearly all leaders of the emerging nations headed societies in which population was increasing at unprecedented levels. This increase continued in the early years of independence. In much of Asia, it has begun to level off in recent decades. But in most of Africa, population growth continues at very high rates. In some cases, most notably south Asia, moderate growth rates have produced huge total populations because they were adding to an already large base. Population experts predicted in the 1970s that south Asia's population of more than 600 million would more than double by the year 2000. With more than 1 billion people in India alone at present, the prophecy has more than been fulfilled.

In Africa, by contrast, which began with low population levels relative to its large land area, very high birth rates and diminished mortality rates have resulted in very steep population increases in recent decades. Some population experts predict that if present growth rates continue, by the mid-21st century Nigeria will have a population equal to that of present-day China. In view of the AIDS epidemic that has spread through much of central and eastern Africa since the 1980s, some of the estimates for population increases in Africa as a whole may have to be revised downward. But recent measures of African productivity and per capita incomes suggest that even more moderate increases in population may be difficult to support at reasonable living standards. This prospect is underscored by estimates that the 400 million peoples of Africa are supported by a continental economy with a productive capacity equal to just 6 percent of that of the United States, or roughly equal to that of the state of Illinois.

On the face of it, the conquest of war, disease, and famine was one of the great achievements of European colonial regimes. It was certainly an accomplishment that colonial officials never tired of citing in defense of continued European dominance. But the European policy of limiting industrialization in their colonial dependencies meant that one of the key ways by which Europe had met its own population boom in the 19th and early 20th centuries was not available to the new nations. They lacked the factories to employ the exploding population that moved to the cities from the rural areas, as well as the technology to produce the necessities of life for more and more people. Unlike the Europeans and the Americans, the emerging nations found it difficult to draw food and mineral

The Wretched of the Earth

resources from the rest of the world to feed this growing population. In fact, these were the very things the colonized peoples had been set up to sell to the industrialized nations. Even in countries such as India, where impressive advances in industrialization were made in the postcolonial era, gains in productivity were swallowed up rapidly by the population explosion.

In most African and Asian countries, there has been resistance to birth control efforts aimed at controlling population growth. Some of this resistance is linked to deeply entrenched social patterns and religious beliefs. In many of these societies, procreation is seen as a sign of male virility. In addition, the capacity to bear children, preferably male children, continues to be critical to the social standing of women. In some cases, resistance to birth control is linked to specific cultural norms. For example, Hindus believe that a deceased man's soul cannot begin the cycle of rebirth until his eldest son has performed special ceremonies over his funeral pyre. This belief increases the already great pressure on Indian women to have children, and it encourages families to have several sons to ensure that at least one survives the father.

In Africa, children are seen as indispensable additions to the *lineage:* the extended network of relatives (and deceased ancestors) that, much more than the nuclear family, makes up the core social group over much of the subcontinent. As in India, sons are essential for continuing the patrilineal family line and performing burial and ancestral rites. The key roles played by women in agricultural production and marketing make girls highly valued in African societies. This is not true in many Asian societies, where high dowries and occupational restrictions limit their contribution to family welfare.

Before the 20th century, the high rates of stillbirths and infant mortality meant that mothers could expect to lose many of the children they conceived. Ten or 12 deaths of 15 or 16 children conceived was not unheard of. Beyond the obvious psychological scars left by these high death rates, they also fostered the conviction that it was necessary to have many children to ensure that some would outlive the parents. In societies where welfare systems and old-age pensions were meager or unknown, surviving children took on special urgency because they were the only ones who would care for parents who could no longer work for themselves. The persistence of these attitudes in recent decades, when medical advances have greatly reduced infant mortality, has been a major factor contributing to soaring population growth.

In the early decades after independence, many African and Asian leaders were deeply opposed to state measures to promote family planning and birth control. Some saw these as Western attempts to meddle in their internal affairs; others proudly declared that the socialist societies they were building would be able to take care of the additional population. As it has become increasingly clear that excessive population increase makes significant economic advances impossible, many of these leaders have begun to reassess their attitudes toward birth control. A particular cause for alarm is the fact that in many developing countries a high percentage of the population is under age 15 (as high as 40 percent in some areas) and thus dependent on others for support. But even for those who now want to promote family planning, the obstacles are staggering. In addition to the cultural and social factors just discussed, leaders often find they lack sufficient resources and the educated personnel needed to make these programs effective. High rates of illiteracy, particularly among women, must be overcome, but education is expensive. Perhaps no form of financial and technical assistance from the industrialized to the developing world will be as critical in the coming decades as that devoted to family planning.

## Parasitic Cities and Endangered Ecosystems

As population increase in the rural areas of emerging nations outstripped the land and employment opportunities available to the peasantry, mass migrations to urban areas ensued. The massive movement of population from overcrowded villages to the cities was one of the most dramatic developments in the postcolonial history of most new nations. Ambitious youths and the rural poor crowded into port centers and capital cities in search of jobs and a chance to find the "good life" that the big hotels and restaurants and the neon lights of the city center appeared to offer to all comers. But because most of these cities lacked the rapidly expanding industrial sectors that had made possible the absorption of a similar migrant influx earlier in the West, they were often dead ends for migrants from the rural areas. There were few jobs, and heavy competition for them ensured that wages would remain low for most workers. The growing numbers of underemployed or unemployed migrants turned to street vending, scavenging, huckstering, begging, or petty crime to survive.

The urban poor have become a volatile factor in the political struggles of the elite. They form the crowds willing for a price to cheer on one contender or jeer down another, and ready to riot and loot in times of government crisis. In deeply divided societies, the poor, working-class, or idle youths of the urban areas often form the shock troops in communal clashes between rival ethnic and religious groups. Fear of outbursts by urban "mobs" has forced Asian, Middle Eastern, and African regimes to spend scarce resources to subsidize and thus keep low the price of bread, kerosene, and other necessities.

The sudden population influx from the rural areas to cities without sufficient jobs or the infrastructure to support them has greatly skewed urban growth in the emerging nations. Within decades, Asian cities have become some of the largest in the world, and Middle Eastern and African urban areas have sprawled far beyond their modest limits in colonial times. As Figure 38.4 dramatically illustrates, the wealth of the upper- and middle-class areas, dominated by glitzy hotels and high-rises, contrasts disturbingly with the poverty of the vast slums that stretch in all directions from the city centers. Little or no planning was possible for the slum quarters that expanded as squatters erected makeshift shelters wherever open land or derelict buildings could be found. Originally, most of the slum areas lacked electricity, running water, or even the most basic sewage facilities. As shanties were gradually converted into ramshackle dwellings, many governments scrapped plans to level slum settlements and instead tried to provide them with electrical and sanitary systems. As an increasing number of development specialists have reluctantly concluded, slums often provide the only housing urban dwellers are likely to find for some time to come.

Overpopulation in Cairo

These conditions have burdened many postcolonial societies with parasitic rather than productive cities. This means that they are heavily dependent for survival on food and resources drawn from their own countryside or from abroad. In contrast to the cities of western Europe and North America, even during the decades of rapid urban expansion in the 19th century, few cities of the emerging nations have had the manufacturing base needed to generate growth in their surrounding regions or the nation as a whole. They take from the already impoverished countryside, but they are able to give little in return. Urban dependence on the countryside further stretches the already overextended resources of the rural areas.

Rural overpopulation in the decades after independence has led to soil depletion in many areas that have been worked for centuries or millennia. It has also resulted in an alarming rate of deforestation throughout Africa and Asia. Peasant villagers cut trees for fuel or clear land for farming and livestock grazing. Deforestation and overgrazing not only pose major threats to wild animal life but also upset the balance in fragile tropical ecosystems, producing further soil depletion and erosion and encouraging desertification. This environmental degradation is intensified by industrial pollution from both the developed countries and the emerging nations themselves. Although the industrial sectors in the latter are small, pollution tends to be proportionally greater than in the developed world because developing nations rarely can afford the antipollution technology introduced over the last few decades in western Europe, Japan, and North America.

FIGURE 38.4 In the urban areas of undeveloped nations, the contrast between the wealth of the few and the poverty of the majority is revealed by the juxtaposition of the high-rise apartments of the affluent middle classes and the shantytowns of the urban poor. The city centers in emerging nations are much like those of the industrial West or Japan. But the cities as a whole often are more like collections of large villages than integrated urban units. Many of these villages are vast shantytowns with varying levels of basic services such as running water, sewer systems, and transportation networks to the city center.

## Women's Subordination and the Nature of Feminist Struggles in the Postcolonial Era

The example of both the Western democracies and the communist republics of eastern Europe, where women had won the right to vote in the early and mid-20th century, encouraged the founders of many emerging nations to write female suffrage into their constitutions. The very active part women played in many nationalist struggles was perhaps even more critical to their earning the right to vote and run for political office. Women's activism also produced some semblance of equality in legal rights, education, and occupational opportunities under the laws of many new nations.

However, the equality that was proclaimed on paper often bore little resemblance to the actual rights that most women could exercise. It also had little bearing on the conditions under which they lived their daily lives. Even the rise to power of individual women such as **Indira Gandhi,** whose career and downfall were profiled in the opening section, or **Corazon Aquino,** president of the Philippines in the post-Marcos era of the late 1980s, is deceptive. In most instances, female heads of state in the emerging nations entered politics and initially won political support because they were connected to powerful men. As we have seen, Indira Gandhi was the daughter of **Jawaharlal Nehru,** India's first prime minister. Corazon Aquino's husband was the martyred leader of the Filipino opposition to Ferdinand Marcos. **Benazir Bhutto,** a prime minister of Pakistan, was the daughter of a domineering Pakistani prime minister who had been toppled by a military coup and executed in the late 1970s. Lacking these sorts of connections, most African, Middle Eastern, and Asian women have been at best relegated to peripheral political positions and at worst allowed no participation in the political process.

The limited gains made by women in the political sphere are paralleled by the second-class position to which most are consigned in many societies. In some respects, their handicaps are comparable to those that constrict women in the industrialized democracies and communist nations. But the obstacles to female self-fulfillment, and in many cases mere survival, in emerging nations are usually much more blatant and fundamental than the restrictions women have to contend with in developed societies. To begin with, early marriage ages for women and large families are still the norm in most African, Middle Eastern, and Asian societies. This means that women spend their youthful and middle-age years having children. There is little time to think of higher education or a career.

The Search for Justice: Nâzim Hikmet and Nazik al-Mala'ika (20th Century)

Because of the low level of sanitation in many postcolonial societies and the scarcity of food, all but elite and upper-middle-class women experience chronic anxiety about such basic issues as adequate nutrition for their children and their susceptibility to disease. The persistence of male-centric customs directly affects the health and life expectancy of women. For example, the Indian tradition that dictates that women first serve their husbands and sons and then eat what is left has obvious disadvantages. The quantity and nutritional content of the leftovers is likely to be lower than that of the original meals, and in tropical environments flies and other disease-bearing insects are more likely to have fouled the food.

The demographic consequences of these social patterns can be dramatic. In the 1970s, for example, it was estimated that as much as 20 percent of the female population of India was malnourished and that another 30 percent had a diet that was well below acceptable United Nations levels. In sharp contrast to the industrial societies of Japan, the United States, and Europe, where women outnumber (because on the average they outlive) men, in India there are only 930 females for every 1000 males.

Although the highly secular property and divorce laws many new states passed after independence have given women much greater legal protection, many of these measures are ignored in practice. Very often, women have neither the education nor the resources to exercise their legal rights. The spread of **religious revivalism** in many cases has further eroded these rights, even though advocates of a return to tradition often argue that practices such as veiling and stoning for women (but not men) caught in adultery actually enhance their dignity and status. Most Asian, Middle Eastern, and African women continue to be dominated by male family members, are much more limited than men in their career opportunities, and are likely to be less well fed, educated, and healthy than men at comparable social levels.

## Neocolonialism, Cold War Rivalries, and Stunted Development

The schemes of nationalist leaders aimed at building an industrial base that would support the rapidly increasing populations of their new nations soon yielded to the economic realities of the postcolonial world. Not only did most of the nations that emerged from colonialism have little in the way of an industrial base, but their means of obtaining one were meager. To buy the machines and hire or train the technical experts that were essential to get industrialization going, the new nations needed to earn capital they could invest for these ends. Some funds could be accumulated by saving a portion of the state revenues collected from the peasantry. In most cases, however, there was little left once the bureaucrats had been paid, essential public works and education had been funded, and other state expenses had been met. Thus, most emerging nations have relied on the sale of cash crops and minerals to earn the money they need to finance industrialization. As their leaders soon discovered, the structure of the world market worked against them.

DOCUMENT

## Cultural Creativity in the Emerging Nations: Some Literary Samples

Despite, or perhaps because of, political instability and chronic economic difficulties, postcolonial societies have generated a high level of artistic creativity over the past four or five decades. Nowhere has this creativity been more prominent and brilliant than in literary works for which African, Middle Eastern, and Asian writers have earned Nobel prizes and won a wide readership far beyond their own nations. The selections that follow are only a small sample of the vast and varied works of these talented writers, from poetry and drama to novels and short stories.

Many of these writers focus on the predicament of the Western-educated elites who dominate the new nations that emerged from the European colonial empires. In the following stanza from the poem "I Run Around with Them," Indonesian poet Chairil Anwar reflects on the lack of purpose and malaise he believed to be widespread among the children of these elite groups.

> I run around with them, what else can I do, now—
>
> Changing my face at the edge of the street, I use their eyes
>
> And tag along to visit the fun house:
>
> These are the facts as I know them
>
> (A new American flic at the Capitol,
>
> The new songs they dance to).
>
> We go home: there's nothing doing
>
> Though this kind of Death is our neighbor, our friend, now.
>
> Hanging around at the corner, we wait for the city bus
>
> That glows night to day like a gold tooth;
>
> Lame, deformed, negative, we
>
> Lean our bony asses against lamp poles
>
> And jaw away the years.

In the next quotation, from the novel *No Longer at Ease,* widely read Nigerian author Chinua Achebe identifies another dilemma: the pull between Western culture and the ancient civilization of one's own land.

> Nothing gave him greater pleasure than to find another Ibo-speaking student in a London bus. But when he had to speak in English with a Nigerian student from another tribe he lowered his voice. It was humiliating to have to speak to one's countryman in a foreign language, especially in the presence of the proud owners of that language. They would naturally assume that one had no language of one's own. He wished they were here today to see. Let them come to Umuofia [the protagonist's home village] now and listen to the talk of men who made a great art of conversation. Let them come and see men and women and children who knew how to live, whose joy of life had not yet been killed by those who claimed to teach other nations how to live.

Like many of the more famous novelists of the emerging nations, V. S. Naipaul is an expatriate, born in the Caribbean and now living in rural England. In his moving and controversial account of his return to his Indian ancestral home, titled *An Area of Darkness,* Naipaul confronts the problem of massive poverty and the responses of foreigners and the Indian elite to it.

> To see [India's] poverty is to make an observation of no value; a thousand newcomers to the country before you have seen and said as you. And not only newcomers. Our own sons and daughters, when they return from Europe and America, have spoken in your very words. Do not think that your anger and contempt are marks of your sensitivity. You might have seen more: the smiles on the faces of the begging children, that domestic group among the pavement sleepers waking in the cool Bombay morning, father, mother and baby in a trinity of love, so self-contained that they are as private as if walls had separated them from you; it is your gaze that violates them, your sense of outrage that outrages them. . . . It is your surprise, your anger that denies [them] humanity.

**Questions** Can you think of parallels in U.S. history or contemporary society to the situations and responses conveyed in these passages from recent postcolonial writings? Do they suggest that it is possible to communicate even intimate feelings across cultures, or do you find them alien, different? What other issues would you expect African, Middle Eastern, and Asian postcolonial artists to deal with in their work?

The pattern of exchange promoted in the colonial era left most newly independent countries dependent on the export production of two or three food crops or industrial raw materials. The former included cocoa, palm oil, coffee, jute, and hemp. Key among the latter were minerals, such as copper, bauxite, and oil, for which there was a high demand in the industrialized economies of Europe, North America, and increasingly Japan. Since World War II, the prices of these exports—which economists call **primary products—**

IN DEPTH

## Artificial Nations and the Rising Tide of Communal Strife

Again and again in the postcolonial era, new states have been torn by internal strife. Often much of what we in the industrialized West know of these areas in Africa, the Middle East, and Asia is connected to the breakdown of their political systems and the human suffering that has resulted. In just the last few years, for example, international news reports have featured descriptions of famines generated by civil wars in Somalia, the Sudan, and Mozambique; by harrowing images of refugees fleeing for their lives from Rwanda, Angola, and Cambodia; by religious riots in India, and mass slaughter in Timor. Western observers are often tempted to take this instability and suffering as proof that the people of these decolonized areas are unfit to rule themselves, that they are incapable of building viable political systems.

*"Any analysis of the recurring political crises of Africa, the Middle East, and Asia should begin with the realization that nearly all the nations that emerged from decolonization were artificial creations."*

Although these responses are understandable given the crisis-focused coverage of the emerging nations by international news agencies, they fail to take into account the daunting obstacles that have confronted African, Middle Eastern, and Asian nation-builders. They ignore the important ways in which Western colonialism contributed to the internal divisions and political weaknesses of newly independent states. They also overlook the deep, often highly disruptive social divisions within Western societies (the long history of racial conflict in the United States, for example, or the vicious civil war in the former European nation of Yugoslavia). Any analysis of the recurring political crises of Africa, the Middle East, and Asia should begin with the realization that nearly all the nations that emerged from decolonization were artificial creations. The division of Africa and Asia by the Western imperialist powers was arbitrary (see, for example, Maps 38.1 and 38.2). Some colonial boundaries cut peoples apart: the Shans of southeast Asia, the Kurds of the Middle East, the Somalis of the horn of east Africa. Some imposed boundaries tossed together tens, sometimes hundreds, of very different and often hostile ethnic or religious groups. The roads and railways built by the colonizers, the marketing systems they established, and the educational policies they pursued all hardened the unnatural boundaries and divisions established in the late 19th century. It was these artificial units, these motley combinations of peoples that defied the logic of history and cultural affinity, that African, Middle Eastern, and Asian nationalist leaders had to try to meld into nations after World War II.

The point is not that there was perfect harmony or unity among the peoples of these areas before the coming of colonial rule. As we have seen, there was a great diversity of ethnicity, languages, and religions among the peoples who built civilizations in these areas in the precolonial era. Intense competition, communal conflict, and countless wars occurred between different ethnic and religious groups. European colonization worsened these divisions while suppressing violent confrontations between different communities. In fact, European colonial regimes were built and maintained by divide-and-rule tactics. Very often the colonizers selectively recruited minority ethnic or religious groups into their armies, bureaucracies, and police forces. For example, the Tutsi minority in strife-torn Rwanda and Burundi was much favored by first the Belgians and later the French. In the colonial period, the Tutsis had greater access than the Hutu majority to missionary education, military training, and government positions. These advantages gained a disproportionate share of political power and social standing for the Tutsis after independence. But they also made them the obvious target for persecution by disgruntled Hutus. Rivalry and violent conflict between the two groups has often made a shambles of nation-building initiatives in Rwanda and Burundi over the past several decades and reached catastrophic levels in the mid-1990s. It has continued to simmer in the years since, at times spilling over into political struggles in neighboring states such as Congo.

The inequities of the colonial order were compounded by the increasingly frequent use of divide-and-rule policies by European officials in the last years of their rule. In addition, the colonizers' desire to scuttle and run from their colonial responsibilities when it was clear that the days of colonial rule were numbered opened the way for ethnic and religious strife. Communal violence in turn prompted the exodus of refugees that accompanied the winning of independence in many colonies, most notably in south Asia, Nigeria, the Belgian

have not only fluctuated widely but have declined steadily compared to the prices of most of the manufactured goods emerging nations usually buy from the industrialized world. Price fluctuations have created nightmares for planners in developing nations. Revenue estimates from the sale of coffee or copper in years when the price is high are used to plan government projects for building roads, factories, and dams. Market slumps can wipe out these critical funds, thereby retarding economic growth and throwing countries deeply into debt.

Congo, and Palestine. The Western-educated leaders who came to power in these and other newly independent states soon realized that only a small portion of the population was committed to an overarching nationalist identity. Even among the Westernized elite classes, which had led the decolonization struggle, national loyalties were often shallow and overridden by older, subnational ethnic and religious identities. As a result, many of the new nations of Africa and southeast Asia have been threatened by secessionist movements.

The most spectacular collapse of a new state came in Pakistan, the unwieldy patchwork of a nation the British threw together at the last minute in 1947 to satisfy Jinnah's demands for majority rule in Muslim areas of the Indian subcontinent (Map 38.2). A glance at the map reveals the vulnerability of Pakistan, split into two parts: West and East Pakistan, separated by India's more than 1000 miles of hostile territory. East and West Pakistan also differed greatly in their natural environments and in the ethnic makeup of their peoples and the languages they used. They even differed in their approaches to the Islamic faith that had justified including them in the same country in the first place.

Fragile national ties were eroded rapidly by the East Pakistanis' perception that they had been in effect recolonized by West Pakistan. West Pakistanis held highly disproportionate shares of government jobs and military positions, and West Pakistan received the lion's share of state revenues although East Pakistan generated most of the new nation's foreign earnings. By the early 1970s, East and West Pakistan were locked in a bloody civil war, which ended with the creation of the nation of Bangladesh from East Pakistan in 1972.

India, which relished the chance to contribute to the breakup of Pakistan, has itself been repeatedly threatened by civil strife between different linguistic, religious, and ethnic groups. In the early 1980s, Sikh guerrillas carried on a violent campaign for separation in the north, and the Indian government was forced to intervene militarily in the violent struggle between different ethnic and religious groups in Sri Lanka (Ceylon), its neighbor to the south. In 1997 an avowedly Hindu communalist party came to power in New Delhi, in defiance of the staunch adherence to the principle of a secular state upheld by leading Indian nationalist figures in the colonial era and all of the earlier postindependence governments. The victory of the Bharatya Janata party (BJP) has intensified the anxieties of the large Muslim minority and other non-Hindu religious groups about the possibility of discrimination and even open persecution.

In Africa, where there was even less of a common historical and cultural basis on which to build nationalism than in south or southeast Asia, separatist movements have been a prominent feature of the political life of new states. Secessionist movements have raged from Morocco in the northwest to Ethiopia in the east and Angola in the south (Map 38.1). Civil wars, such as the struggle of the non-Muslim peoples of the southern Sudan against the Muslim rulers from the northern parts of that country, have also abounded. Thus far, none of the secessionist movements have succeeded, although that of the Ibo peoples of eastern Nigeria, who proclaimed an independent state of Biafra in 1967, led to three years of bloody warfare in Africa's most populous nation.

In all cases, the artificial nature of the new nations of Africa, the Middle East, and Asia has proved costly. In addition to internal divisions, boundary disputes between newly independent nations have often led to border clashes and open warfare. India and Pakistan have fought three such wars since 1947. Iraq's Saddam Hussein justified his 1990 annexation of Kuwait with the argument that the tiny but oil-rich Arab "sheikhdom" was an artificial creation of the British colonizers, who had carved Kuwait out of land that historically had been part of Iraq.

Democracy has often been one of the main victims of the tensions between rival ethnic groups within many emerging nations and threats from neighbors without. Politicians in nearly all the new states have been quick to play on communal fears as well as on ethnic and religious loyalties to win votes. As a result, freely elected legislatures have often been dominated by parties representing these special interests. Suspicions that those in power were favoring their own or allied groups has led to endless bickering and stalemates in national legislatures, which have become tempting targets for coup attempts by military strongmen. One of the more predictable reasons these usurpers have given for dictatorial rule has been the need to contain the communal tensions aroused by democratic election campaigns.

**Questions** How might colonial policies have been changed to reduce the tensions between different ethnic and religious communities? Why were these measures not taken? What can be done now to alleviate these divisions? Should the United Nations or industrialized nations such as the United States or Japan intervene directly to contain communal clashes or civil wars in Africa and Asia? What is to be done with the rapidly growing refugee populations created by these conflicts?

African, Middle Eastern, and Asian leaders have been quick to blame the legacy of colonialism and what they have called the **neocolonial economy**—the global economy dominated by the industrialized nations—for the limited returns yielded thus far by their development schemes. Although there is much truth to these accusations, they do not tell the whole story. These leaders must also share the responsibility for the slow pace of economic growth in much of the developing world. The members of the educated classes that came to dominate the political and business life of newly independent nations often used their positions to enrich themselves and their relatives at the expense of their societies as a whole. Corruption has been notoriously widespread in most of the new nations. Government controls on the import of goods such as automobiles, television sets, and stereos, which are luxury items beyond the reach of most of the people, have often been lax. As a result, tax revenues and export earnings that could have fueled development have often gone to provide the good life for small minorities within emerging nations. The inability or refusal of many regimes to carry out key social reforms, such as land redistribution, which would spread the limited resources available more equitably over the population, has contributed vitally to the persistence of these patterns.

Badly strapped for investment funds and essential technology, emerging African, Middle Eastern, and Asian nations have often turned to international organizations, such as the World Bank and the International Monetary Fund, or to rival industrial nations for assistance. Although resources for development have been gained in this way, the price for international assistance has often been high. The industrialized nations have demanded major concessions in return for their aid. These have ranged from commitments to buy the products of, and favor investors from, the lending countries to entering into alliances and permitting military bases on the territory of the client state.

Loans from international lending agencies almost invariably have been granted only after the needy nation agreed to structural adjustments. These are regulations that determine how the money is to be invested and repaid, and they usually involve promises to make major changes in the economy of the borrowing nation. In recent years, these promises have often included a commitment to remove or reduce state subsidies on food and other essential consumer items. State subsidies were designed to keep prices for staple goods at a level that the urban and rural poor—the great majority of the people in almost all emerging nations—could afford. When carried out, subsidy reductions often have led to widespread social unrest, riots, and the collapse or near collapse of postcolonial regimes.

# Paths to Economic Growth and Social Justice

■ **The leaders of the new nations of Africa, the Middle East, and Asia soon felt the need to deliver on the promises of social reform and economic well-being that had rallied support to the nationalist cause. Strategies ranged from populism to dictatorship to rejection of the West.**

Depending on their own skills, the talents of their advisors and lieutenants, and the resources at their disposal, leaders in the emerging nations have tackled the daunting task of development with varying degrees of success. Ways have been found to raise the living standards of a significant percentage of the population of some of the emerging nations. But these strategies have rarely benefited the majority. It may be too early to judge the outcomes of many development schemes. But so far, none has proved to be the path to the social justice and general economic development that nationalist leaders saw as the ultimate outcome of struggles for decolonization. Although some countries have done much better than others, successful overall strategies to deal with the challenges facing emerging nations have yet to be devised.

## Charismatic Populists and One-Party Rule

One of the least successful responses on the part of leaders who found their dreams for national renewal frustrated has been a retreat into authoritarian rule. This approach has often been disguised by calculated, charismatic appeals for support from the disenfranchised masses. Perhaps the career of Kwame Nkrumah, the leader of Ghana's independence movement, illustrates this pattern best. There is little question that Nkrumah was genuinely committed to social reform and economic uplift for the Ghanaian people during the years of his rise to become the first prime minister of the newly independent west African nation of Ghana in 1957 (Map 38.3). After assuming power, he moved vigorously to initiate programs that would translate his high aspirations for his people into reality. But his ambitious schemes for everything from universal education to industrial development soon ran into trouble.

Kwame Nkrumah

Rival political parties, some representing regional interests and ethnic groups long hostile to Nkrumah, repeatedly challenged his initiatives and tried to block the efforts to carry out his plans. His leftist leanings won support from the Soviet bloc but frightened away Western investors, who had a good deal more capital to plow into Ghana's economy. They also led to growing hostility on the part of the United States, Great Britain, and other influential noncommunist countries. Most devastatingly, soon after independence, the price of cocoa—by far Ghana's largest export crop—began to fall sharply. Tens of thousands of Ghanaian cocoa farmers were hard hit and the resources for Nkrumah's development plans suddenly dried up.

Nkrumah's response to these growing problems was increasingly dictatorial. He refused to give up or cut back on his development plans. As a result, most

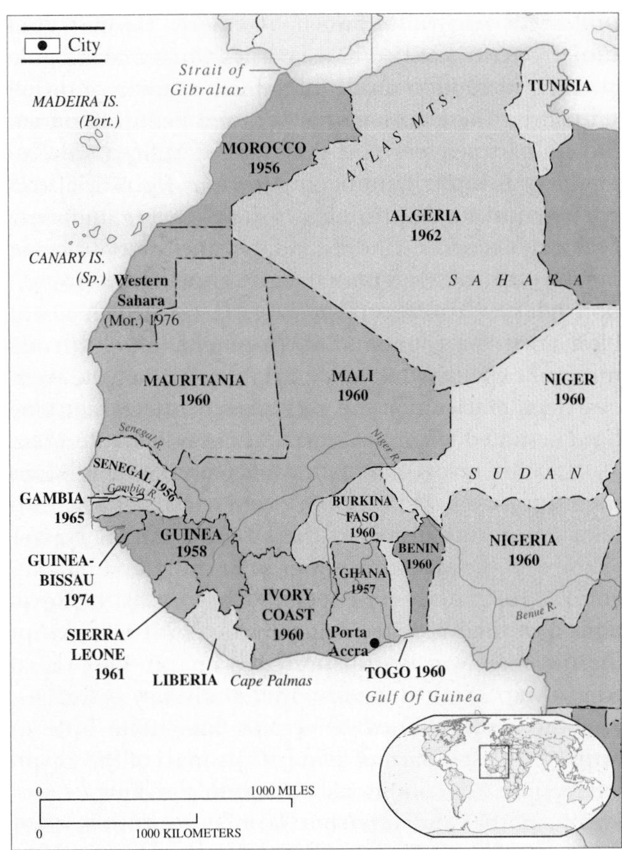


MAP 38.3 The New West African Nations

Kwame Nkrumah on African Unity

failed miserably because of the lack of key supplies and official mismanagement. In the early 1960s, he forcibly crushed all political opposition by banning rival parties and jailing other political leaders. He assumed dictatorial powers and ruled through functionaries in his own Convention People's party.

Nkrumah also sought to hold on to the loyalty of the masses and mobilize their energies by highly staged "events" and the manipulation of largely invented symbols and traditions that were said to be derived from Ghana's past. Thus, he tried to justify his policies and leadership style with references to a uniquely African brand of socialism and the need to revive African traditions and African civilization. Even before independence, he had taken to wearing the traditional garb of the Ghanaian elite. The very name *Ghana,* which Nkrumah himself proposed for the new nation that emerged from the former Gold Coast colony, had been taken from an ancient African kingdom. The original Ghanaian kingdom actually was centered much farther to the north and had little to do with the peoples of the Gold Coast.

Nkrumah went about the country giving fiery speeches, dedicating monuments to the "revolution," which often consisted of giant statues of himself (Figure 38.5). He also assumed a prominent role in the nonaligned movement that was then sweeping the newly independent nations. His followers' adulation knew no bounds. Members of his captive parliament compared him to Confucius, Muhammad, Shakespeare, and Napoleon and predicted that his birthplace would serve as a "Mecca" for all of Africa's leaders. But his suppression of all opposition and his growing ties to the Communist party, coupled with the rapid deterioration of the Ghanaian economy, increased the ranks of his enemies, who waited for a chance to strike. That chance came early in 1966, when Nkrumah went off on one of his many trips, this time a peace mission to Vietnam. In his absence, he was deposed by a military coup. Nkrumah died in exile in 1972, and Ghana moved in a very different direction under its new military rulers.

FIGURE 38.5 Many monumental statues of Kwame Nkrumah, such as this one, rose in the towns and villages of Ghana as he tried to cover the failure of his socialist-inspired development programs with dictatorial rule and self-glorification. Although Nkrumah's efforts to cover his regime's failures through self-glorifying displays and pageantry were extreme, they were not unique. The many images of the "great leader" of the moment that one finds in many developing nations are a variation on Nkrumah's tactics. These state campaigns to glorify the dictatorial figures are reminiscent of those mounted by the leaders of the communist revolutions in Russia, China, and Cuba.

## Military Responses: Dictatorships and Revolutions

Given the difficulties that leaders such as Nkrumah faced after independence and the advantages the military have in crisis situations, the proliferation of coups in the emerging nations is not surprising. Armed forces have at times been divided by the religious and ethnic rivalries that have been so disruptive in new nations. But the regimentation and emphasis on discipline and in-group solidarity in military training often render soldiers more resistant than other social groups to these forces. In conditions of political breakdown and social conflict, the military possesses the monopoly—or near monopoly—of force that is often essential for restoring order. Their occupational conditioning makes soldiers not only more ready than civilian leaders to use the force at their disposal but less concerned with its destructive consequences. Military personnel also tend to have some degree of technical training, which was usually lacking in the humanities-oriented education of civilian nationalist leaders. Because most military leaders have been staunchly anticommunist, they have often attracted covert technical and financial assistance from Western governments.

Once in control, military leaders have banned civilian political parties and imposed military regimes of varying degrees of repression and authoritarian control. Yet the ends to which these regimes have put their dictatorial powers have differed greatly. At their worst, military regimes—such as those in Uganda (especially under Idi Amin), Myanmar (formerly Burma), and Congo—have quashed civil liberties while making little attempt to reduce social inequities or improve living standards. These regimes have existed mainly to enrich the military leaders and their allies. Military governments of this sort have been notorious for official corruption and for imprisoning, torturing, or eliminating political dissidents. Understandably uneasy about being overthrown, these regimes have diverted a high proportion of their nations' meager resources, which might have gone for economic development, into expenditures on expensive military hardware. Neither the Western democracies nor the countries of the Soviet bloc have hesitated to supply arms to these military despots.

In a few cases, military leaders have been radical in their approaches to economic and social reform. Perhaps none was more so than **Gamal Abdul Nasser** (Figure 38.6), who took power in Egypt after a military coup in 1952. As we have seen in Chapter 33, the Egyptians won their independence in the mid-1930s except for the lingering British presence in the Suez Canal zone (Map 38.4). But self-centered civilian politicians and the corrupt khedival regime had done little to improve the standard of living of the mass of the Egyptian people. As conditions worsened and Egypt's governing parties did little but rake in wealth for their elitist memberships, revolutionary forces emerged in Egyptian society.

The radical movement that succeeded in gaining power, the **Free Officers movement,** evolved from a secret organization established in the Egyptian army in

FIGURE 38.6 After the Free Officers seized power in the 1952 coup, a young general named Nasser emerged as the most charismatic and able of a number of rivals for power. Here cheering crowds climb toward a balcony where the new leader of Egypt has been addressing them, and Nasser is embraced by one enthusiastic supporter.

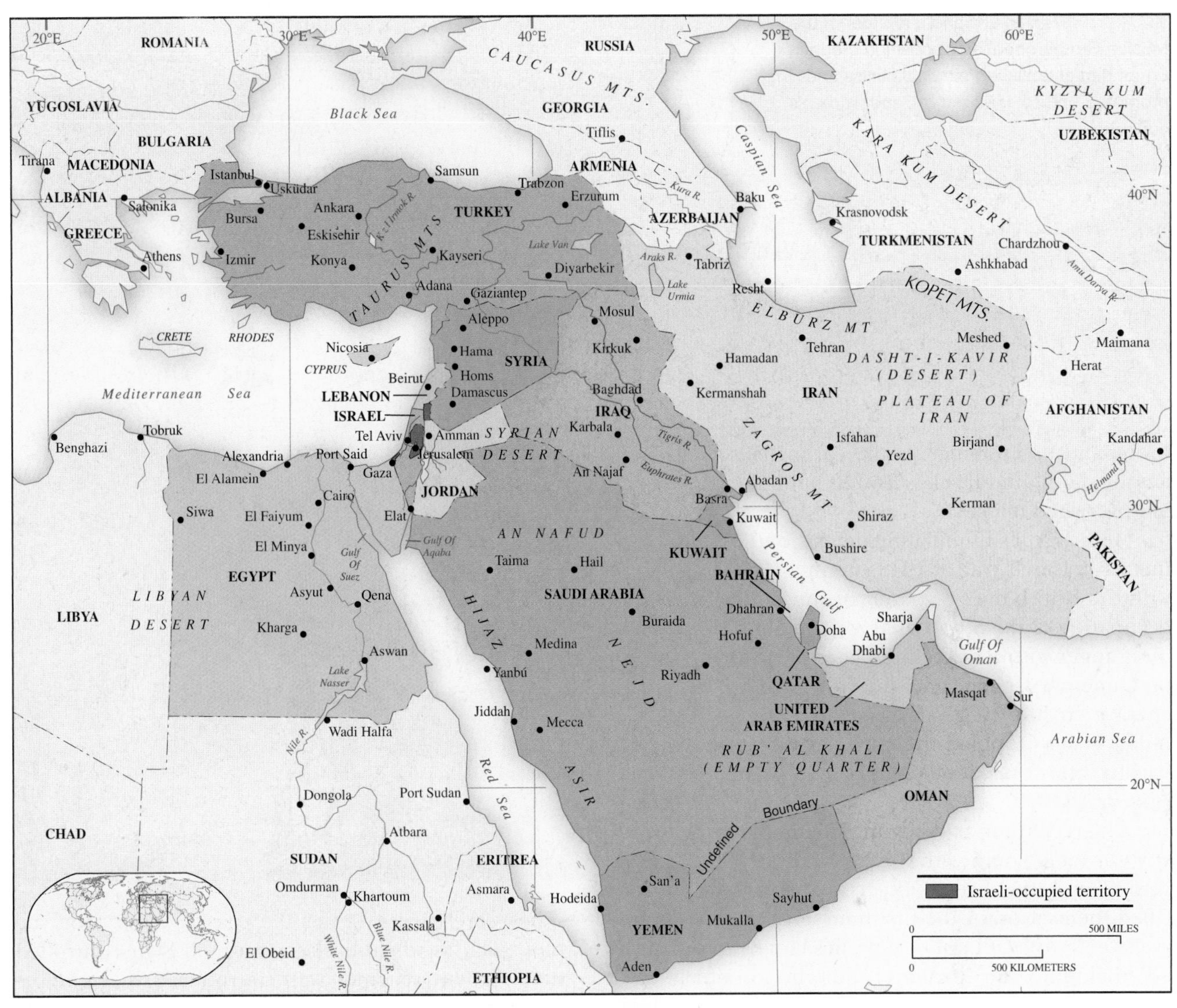


**MAP 38.4** The Middle East in the Cold War Era

the 1930s. Founded by idealistic young officers of Egyptian rather than Turco-Egyptian descent, the secret Revolutionary Command Council studied conditions in the country and prepared to seize power in the name of a genuine revolution. For many decades, it was loosely allied to the **Muslim Brotherhood,** another revolutionary alternative to the khedival regime.

The brotherhood was founded by Hasan al-Banna (Figure 38.7) in 1928. Al-Banna was a schoolteacher who had studied in his youth with the famous Muslim reformer Muhammad Abduh. While at Al-Azhar University in Cairo in the years after World War I, al-Banna had combined a deep interest in scientific subjects with active involvement in student demonstrations in support of Wafd demands for Egyptian independence. In this period, like many other Egyptian students, al-Banna developed contempt for the wealthy minority of Egyptians and Europeans who flourished in the midst of the appalling poverty of most of his people.

To remedy these injustices and rid Egypt of its foreign oppressors, al-Banna founded the Muslim Brotherhood in 1928. Although members of the organization were committed to a revivalist approach to Islam, the brotherhood's main focus, particularly in the early years, was on a program of social uplift and sweeping reforms. The organization became involved in a wide range of activities, from promoting trade unions and building medical clinics to educating women and pushing for land reform. By the late 1930s, the brotherhood's social service had become highly politicized. Al-Banna's followers fomented strikes and urban riots and established militant youth organizations and paramilitary assassination squads. Despite the murder of al-Banna by the khedive Farouk's assassins in 1949, the members of the brotherhood continued

FIGURE 38.7 Hasan al-Banna, founder of the Muslim Brotherhood, an opposition group in Egypt that established medical clinics and promoted unions, land reform, and women's education.

to expand its influence in the early 1950s among both middle-class youths and the impoverished masses.

After Egypt's humiliating defeats in the first Arab-Israeli War of 1948 and in a clash with the British over the latter's continuing occupation of the Suez Canal zone in 1952, mass anger with a discredited khedival and parliamentary regime gave the officers their chance. In July 1952, an almost bloodless military coup toppled the corrupt khedive Farouk from his jewel-encrusted throne (Figure 38.8).

The revolution had begun. The monarchy was ended, and with the installation of Nasser and the Free Officers, Egyptians ruled themselves for the first time since the 6th century B.C.E. By 1954 all political parties had been disbanded, including the Muslim Brotherhood, which had clashed with its former allies in the military and had been suppressed after an attempt on Nasser's life. Nasser was only one of several officers at the head of the Free Officers movement, and by no means was he initially the most charismatic. But after months of internal power struggles in the officer corps, he emerged as the head of a military government that was deeply committed to revolution.

Nasser and his fellow officers used the dictatorial powers they had won in the coup to force through programs that they believed would uplift the long-oppressed Egyptian masses. They were convinced that only the state had the power to carry out essential social and economic reforms, and thus they began to intervene in all aspects of Egyptian life. Land reform measures were enacted: limits were placed on how much land an individual could own, and excess lands were seized and redistributed to landless peasants. State-financed education through the college level was made available to Egyptians. The government became Egypt's main employer; by 1980, more than 30 percent of Egypt's workforce was on the state payroll. State subsidies were used to lower the price of basic food staples, such as wheat and cooking oil. State-controlled development schemes were introduced that emphasized industrial growth, modeled after the five-year plans of the Soviet Union.

To establish Egypt's economic independence, stiff restrictions were placed on foreign investment. In some cases foreign properties were seized and redistributed to Egyptian investors. Nasser also embarked on an interventionist foreign policy that stressed the struggle to destroy the newly established Israeli state, forge Arab unity, and foment socialist revolutions in neighboring lands. His greatest foreign policy coup came in 1956, when he rallied international opinion to finally oust the British and their French allies from the Suez Canal zone. Despite the setbacks suffered by Egyptian military forces, Nasser made good use of the rare combined backing of the United States and the Soviet Union to achieve his aims in the crisis.

However well intentioned, many of Nasser's initiatives misfired. Land reform efforts were frustrated by bureaucratic corruption and the clever strategies devised by the landlord class to hold on to their estates. State development schemes often lacked proper funding and failed because of mismanagement and miscal-

**FIGURE 38.8** Growing Egyptian resistance to the British occupation of the Suez Canal zone was expressed in this effigy of a British soldier that was strung up on a Cairo street corner in January 1952. The Arabic banner that accompanies the mock hanging reminds Egyptians of the Dinshawai incident, discussed in Chapter 33, and the need to sustain resistance to British domination. Within months of this protest, mass demonstrations and a military coup freed the Egyptian people from both the British occupation and the repressive khedival regime.

culations. Even the Aswan Dam project, the cornerstone of Nasser's development drive, was a fiasco. Egypt's continuing population boom quickly canceled out the additional cultivable lands the dam produced. The dam's interference with the flow of the Nile resulted in increasing numbers of parasites that cause blindness. It also led to a decline in the fertility of farmlands in the lower Nile delta, which were deprived of the rich silt that normally was washed down by the river. Foreign investment funds from the West, which Egypt desperately needed, soon dried up. Aid from the much poorer Soviet bloc could not begin to match what was lost, and much of this assistance was military. In the absence of sufficient foreign investment and with Egypt's uncontrolled population rising at an alarming rate, the state simply could not afford all the ambitious schemes to which Nasser and the revolutionary officers had committed it. The gap between aspirations and means was increased in the later years of Nasser's reign (in the 1960s) by the heavy costs of his mostly failed foreign adventures, including the disastrous Six-Day War with Israel in 1967.

Although he had to move slowly at first, Nasser's successor, **Anwar Sadat,** had little choice but to dismantle the massive state apparatus that had been created. He favored private rather than state initiatives. During Sadat's tenure in office the middle class, which had been greatly restricted by Nasser, emerged again as a powerful force. After fighting the Israelis to a stalemate in 1973, Sadat also moved to end the costly confrontation with Israel as well as Egypt's support for revolutionary movements in the Arab world. He expelled the Russians and opened Egypt to aid and investment from the United States and western Europe.

Sadat's shift in direction has been continued by his successor, **Hosni Mubarak.** But neither the attempt at genuine revolution led by Nasser nor the move to capitalism and more pro-West positions under his successors has done much to check Egypt's alarming population increases and the corruption of its bloated bureaucracy. Neither path to development has had much effect on the glaring gap between the living conditions of Egypt's rich minority and its impoverished masses. No better gauge of the discontent that is bred by these inequities can be found than the proliferation of Muslim fundamentalist movements. One of these succeeded in assassinating Sadat; others have sustained terrorist campaigns aimed at overthrowing the Mubarak regime.

## The Indian Alternative: Development for Some of the People

Although the approach to nation-building and economic development followed by the leaders of independent

India has shared the Nasserite emphasis on socialism and state intervention, India's experience has differed from Egypt's in several significant ways. To begin with, the Indians have managed to preserve civilian rule throughout the nearly five decades since they won their independence from Great Britain. In fact, in India the military has consistently defended secular democracy against religious extremism and other would-be authoritarian trends. In addition, although India, like Egypt, has been saddled with a crushing burden of overpopulation, it came to independence with a larger industrial and scientific sector, a better communication system and bureaucratic grid, and a larger and more skilled middle class in proportion to its total population than most other emerging nations.

During the first decades of its freedom, India had the good fortune to be governed by leaders such as Jawaharlal Nehru and his allies in the Congress party, who were deeply committed to social reform and economic development as well as the preservation of civil rights and democracy. India's success at the latter has been remarkable. Despite continuous threats of secession by religious and linguistic minorities, as well as poverty, unemployment, and recurring natural disasters, India remains the world's largest functioning democracy. Except for brief periods of rule by coalitions of opposition parties, the Congress party has ruled at the center for most of the independence era. But opposition parties have controlled many state and local governments, and they remain vocal and active in the national parliament. Civil liberties, exemplified by a very outspoken press and free elections, have been upheld to an extent that sets India off from much of the rest of the emerging nations.

Nehru's approach to government and development also differed from Nasser's in his more moderate mix of state and private initiatives. Nehru and his successors pushed state intervention in some sectors but also encouraged foreign investment from countries in both of the rival blocs in the cold war. As a consequence, India has been able to build on its initial advantages in industrial infrastructure and its skilled managerial and labor endowment. Its significant capitalist sector has encouraged ambitious farmers, such as those in the Punjab in the northwest, to invest heavily in the **Green Revolution**—the introduction of improved seed strains, fertilizers, and irrigation as a means of producing higher crop yields. Industrial and agrarian growth has generated the revenue necessary for the Indian government to promote literacy and village development schemes, as well as family planning, village electrification, and other improvement projects in recent decades. Indians have also developed one of the largest and most sophisticated high-tech sectors in the postcolonial world, including its own "silicon valleys" in cities like Bangalore in southern India. From the late 1980s India also provided tens of thousands of computer and Internet experts for advanced industrial societies such as those found in the United States and Europe.

Despite its successes, India has suffered from the same gap between needs and resources that all developing nations have had to face. Whatever the government's intentions—and India has been hit by corruption and self-serving politicians, like most nations—there have simply not been the resources to raise the living standards of even a majority of its huge population. The middle class has grown, perhaps as rapidly as that of any postcolonial nation. Its presence is striking in the affluent neighborhoods of cities such as Mombai and Delhi and is proclaimed by the Indian film industry, the world's largest, and in many sitcoms and dramas about the lives of Indian-style yuppies. But as many as 50 percent of India's people have gained little from the development plans and economic growth that have occurred since independence.

In part, this is because population growth has offset economic gains. But social reform has been slow in most areas, both rural and urban. Groups such as the wealthy landlords, who supported the nationalist drive for independence, have continued to dominate the great mass of tenants and landless laborers, just as they did in the precolonial and colonial eras. Some development measures, most notably those associated with the Green Revolution, have greatly favored cultivators with the resources to invest in new seeds and fertilizer. They have increased the gap between rich and poor people over much of rural India. Thus, the poor have paid and will continue to pay the price for Indian gradualism.

## Iran: Religious Revivalism and the Rejection of the West

No path of development adopted by a postcolonial society has provided more fundamental challenges to the existing world order than revolutionary Iran under the direction of the **Ayatollah Ruhollah Khomeini.** In many respects, the Khomeini revolution of 1979 was a throwback to the religious fervor of such anticolonial resistance movements as that led by the Mahdi of the Sudan in the 1880s. Core motivations for the followers of both movements were provided by the emphasis on religious purification and the rejoining of religion and politics, which leaders such as the Mahdi and Khomeini have seen as central to the Islamic tradition. The call for a return to the kind of society believed to have existed in the past "golden age" of the prophet Muhammad was central to the policies pursued by both the Mahdist and Iranian

Ayatollah Khomeini

regimes once they had gained power. Both movements were aimed at toppling Western-backed governments: the Mahdists' the Anglo-Egyptian presence in the Sudan, Khomeini's the autocratic Iranian shah and the Pahlavi dynasty.

Although they came from the Sunni and Shi'a religious traditions, respectively, both the Mahdi and Khomeini claimed to be divinely inspired deliverers. Each promised to rescue the Islamic faithful from imperialist Westerners and from corrupt and heretical leaders within the Muslim world. Both leaders promised their followers magical protection and instant paradise should they fall while waging the holy war against the heretics and infidels. Each leader sought to build a lasting state and social order on the basis of what were believed to be Islamic precedents. Thus, each revivalist movement aimed at defending and restoring what its leaders believed to be the true beliefs, traditions, and institutions of Islamic civilization. The leaders of both movements sought to spread their revolutions to surrounding areas, both Muslim and infidel, and each believed he was setting in motion forces that would eventually sweep the entire globe.

Though proclaimed as an alternative path for development that could be followed by the rest of the emerging nations, Khomeini's revolution owed its initial success in seizing power to a combination of circumstances that was unique to Iran (Map 38.4). Like China, Iran had not been formally colonized by the European powers but rather had been reduced to a sphere of informal influence, divided between Great Britain and Russia. As a result, neither the bureaucratic nor the communication infrastructures that accompanied colonial takeovers were highly developed there. Nor did a substantial Western-educated middle class emerge. Thus, the impetus for "modernization" came suddenly and was imposed from above by the Pahlavi shahs. The initiatives taken by the second shah in particular, which were supported by Iran's considerable oil wealth, wrenched Iran out of the isolation and backwardness in which most of the nation lived until the mid-20th century. The shah had fled Iran in the early 1950s after a staunch nationalist leader named Mohammed Mosaddeq rose to power, but the shah was restored by a CIA-engineered coup in 1953. Once back in power, he tried to impose economic development and social change through government directives. Although advances occurred, the regime managed to alienate the great mass of the Iranian people in the process.

The shah's dictatorial and repressive regime deeply offended the emerging middle classes, whom he considered his strongest potential supporters. His flaunting of Islamic conventions and his neglect of Islamic worship and religious institutions enraged the *ayatollahs,* or religious experts. They also alienated the *mullahs,* or local prayer leaders and mosque attendants, who guided the religious and personal lives of the great majority of the Iranian population. The favoritism the shahs showed foreign investors and a handful of big Iranian entrepreneurs with personal connections to highly placed officials angered the smaller bazaar merchants, who had long maintained close links with the mullahs and other religious leaders. The shah's half-hearted land reform schemes alienated the land-owning classes without doing much to improve the condition of the rural poor. Even the urban workers, who benefited most from the boom in construction and light industrialization the shah's development efforts had stimulated, were dissatisfied. In the years before the 1979 revolution, a fall in oil prices resulted in an economic slump and widespread unemployment in urban areas such as the capital, Tehran.

Although he had treated his officers well, the shah had badly neglected the military rank-and-file, especially in the army. So when the crisis came in 1978, the shah found that few soldiers were prepared to defend his regime. His armies refused to fire on the growing crowds that demonstrated for his removal and the return of Khomeini, then in exile in Paris. Dying of cancer and disheartened by what he saw as betrayal by his people and by allies such as the United States, the shah fled without much of a fight. Khomeini's revolution triumphed over a regime that looked powerful but proved exceptionally vulnerable.

After coming to power, Khomeini, defying the predictions of most Western "experts" on Iranian affairs, followed through on his promises of radical change. Constitutional and leftist parties allied to the revolutionary movement were brutally repressed. Moderate leaders were replaced quickly by radical religious figures who were eager to obey Khomeini's every command. The "satanic" influences of the United States and western Europe were purged. At the same time, Iran also distanced itself from the atheistic communist world. Secular influences in law and government were supplanted by strict Islamic legal codes, which included such punishments as the amputation of limbs for theft and stoning for women caught in adultery. Veiling became obligatory for all women, and the career prospects for women of the educated middle classes, who had been among the most favored by the shah's reforms, suddenly were limited drastically (Figure 38.9).

Islam and the State in the Middle East: Ayatollah Khomeini's Vision of Islamic Government

Khomeini's planners also drew up grand schemes for land reform, religious education, and economic development that accorded with the dictates of Islam. Most of these measures came to little because soon

FIGURE 38.9 Women played a vital role in the mass demonstrations that toppled the shah of Iran and brought Ayatollah Khomeini to power in 1979. In many ways women's support for political movements in the postcolonial period was a continuation of their active participation in earlier struggles against European colonial domination. But increasingly in the postcolonial era, women have organized not only to promote political change, but to force social and economic reforms intended to improve the quality of their own lives as women.

after the revolution, Saddam Hussein, the military leader of neighboring Iraq, sought to take advantage of the turmoil in Iran by annexing its western, oil-rich provinces. The Iran-Iraq War that resulted swallowed up Iranian energies and resources for almost the entire decade after Khomeini came to power. The struggle became a highly personal vendetta for Khomeini, who was determined to destroy Saddam Hussein and punish the Iraqis. His refusal to negotiate peace caused heavy losses and untold suffering to the Iranian people. This suffering continued long after it was clear that the Iranians' aging military equipment and handful of allies were no match for Hussein's more advanced military hardware and an Iraqi war machine bankrolled by its oil-rich Arab neighbors, who were fearful that Khomeini's revolution might spread to their own countries.

As the support of the Western powers, including the United States (despite protestations of neutrality), for the Iraqis increased, the position of the isolated Iranians became increasingly intolerable. Hundreds of thousands of poorly armed and half-trained Iranian conscripts, including tens of thousands of untrained and nearly weaponless boys, died before Khomeini finally agreed to a humiliating armistice in 1988. Peace found revolutionary Iran in shambles. Few of its development initiatives had been pursued, and shortages in food, fuel, and the other necessities of life were widespread.

Iran's decade-long absorption in the war and its continuing isolation makes it impossible to assess the potential of the religious revivalist, anti-Western option for other postcolonial nations. What had seemed at first a viable path to independent development had become mired in brutal internal repression and misguided and failed development schemes. By the 1990s, however, although control by Islamic leaders continued, more open elections began to occur in Iran, presenting new alternatives for the future.

## South Africa: The Apartheid State and Its Demise

South Africa was by no means the only area still under some form of colonial dominance decades after India gained its independence in 1947. Portugal, the oldest and long considered the weakest of the European colonizers, held onto Angola, Mozambique, and its other African possessions until the mid-1970s. Until 1980, Zimbabwe (formerly Southern Rhodesia) was run by white settlers, who had unilaterally declared their independence from Great Britain. Southwest Africa became fully free of South African control only in 1989, and some of the smaller islands in the West Indies and the Pacific remain under European or American rule to the present day.

By the 1970s, however, South Africa was by far the largest, most populous, richest, and most strategic area where most of the population had yet to be liberated from colonial domination. Since the 1940s, the white settlers, particularly the Dutch-descended Afrikaners, had solidified their internal control of the country under the leadership of the Nationalist party. In stages and through a series of elections in which the blacks, who made up the majority of South Africans, were not allowed to vote, the Nationalists won complete independence from Great Britain in 1960. From 1948, when the Nationalist party first came to power, the Afrikaners moved to institutionalize white supremacy and white minority rule by passing thousands of laws that, taken together, made up the system of apartheid (see Chapter 35) that dominated all aspects of South African life until the 1990s.

Apartheid was designed not only to ensure a monopoly of political power and economic dominance for the white minority, both British- and Dutch-descended, but also to impose a system of extreme segregation on all races of South Africa in all aspects of their lives. Separate and patently unequal facilities were established for different racial groups for recreation, education, housing, work, and medical care. Dating and sexual intercourse across racial lines were strictly prohibited, skilled and high-paying jobs were reserved for white workers, and nonwhites were required to carry passes that listed the parts of South Africa where they were allowed to work and live. If caught by the police without their passes or in areas where they were not permitted to travel, nonwhite South Africans were routinely given stiff jail sentences.

Spatial separation was also organized on a grander scale by the creation of numerous **homelands** within South Africa, each designated for the main ethnolinguistic or "tribal" groups within the black African population. Though touted by the Afrikaners as the ultimate solution to the racial "problem," the homelands scheme would have left the black African majority with a small portion of some of the poorest land in South Africa. Because the homelands were overpopulated and poverty-stricken, the white minority was guaranteed a ready supply of cheap black labor to work in their factories and mines and on their farms. Denied citizenship in South Africa proper, these laborers would have been forced eventually to return to the homelands, where they had left their wives and children while emigrating in search of work.

To maintain the blatantly racist and inequitable system of apartheid, the white minority had to build a police state and expend a large portion of the federal budget on a sophisticated and well-trained military establishment. Because of the land's great mineral wealth, the Afrikaner nationalists were able to find the resources to fund their garrison state for decades. Until the late 1980s, the government prohibited all forms of black protest and brutally repressed even nonviolent resistance. Black organizations such as the **African National Congress** were declared illegal, and African leaders such as **Walter Sisulu** and **Nelson Mandela** were shipped off to maximum-security prisons. Other leaders, such as **Steve Biko,** one of the young organizers of the Black Consciousness movement, were murdered while in police custody.

A Liberal White Journalist on Apartheid

Through spies and police informers, the regime tried to capitalize on personal and ethnic divisions within the black majority community. Favoritism was shown to some leaders and groups to keep them from uniting with others in all-out opposition to apartheid. With all avenues of constitutional negotiation and peaceful protest closed, many advocates of black majority rule in a multiracial society turned to guerrilla resistance from the 1960s onward. The South African government responded in the 1980s by declaring a state of emergency, which simply intensified the restrictions already in place in the garrison state. The government repeatedly justified its repression by labeling virtually all black protest as communist-inspired and playing on the racial fears of the white minority.

Through most of the 1970s and early 1980s, it appeared that the hardening hostility between the unyielding white minority and the frustrated black majority was building to a very violent upheaval. But from the late 1980s, countervailing forces were taking hold in South African society. An international boycott greatly weakened the South African economy. In addition, the South African army's costly and futile involvement in wars in neighboring Namibia and Angola seemed to presage never-ending struggles against black liberation movements within the country. Led by the courageous **F. W. de Klerk,** moderate Afrikaner leaders pushed for reforms that began to dismantle the system of apartheid. The release of key black political prisoners, such as the dramatic freeing of Nelson Mandela in 1990, signaled that at long last the leaders of the white majority were ready to negotiate the future of South African politics and society. Permission for peaceful mass demonstrations and ultimately the enfranchisement of all adult South Africans for the 1994 elections provided a way out of the dead end in which the nation was trapped under apartheid.

Voters Waiting to Vote in South Africa's First Open Election, 1994

The well-run and remarkably participatory 1994 elections brought to power the African National Congress party, led by Nelson Mandela, who became the first black president of South Africa. Mandela proved to be one of the most skillful and respected political leaders on the world scene as well as a moderating force in the potentially volatile South African arena. The peaceful surrender of power by F. W. de Klerk's losing party, which was supported by most of the white minority, suggested that a pluralist democracy might well succeed in South Africa (Figure 38.10). But major obstacles remain. Bitter interethnic rivalries within the black majority community, which periodically flared into bloody battles between Zulus and Xhosas in 1990s, have yet to be fully resolved. Hard-line white supremacist organizations among the Afrikaners continue to defy the new regime. And the tasks of reforming the institutions and redistributing the wealth of South Africa in ways that will make for a just and equitable social order are formidable. Well into the 21st century, South Africa is likely to remain one of the most interesting and promising social experiments of an age in which communalism and ethnic hostility threatened to engulf much of the globe.

## Comparisons of Emerging Nations

This chapter has focused on many of the common problems faced by newly independent nations in Asia, the Middle East, and Africa in the final decades of the 20th century. Some of these problems, obviously, resemble issues in Latin America discussed in Chapter 37, where new nations' problems were less salient than for the regions discussed here but where population pressure, environmental change, and considerable economic dependence also loomed large.

Despite common issues, it is also important to distinguish particular patterns in the late 20th century, some of which reflected older traditions in key civilizations. India's success in maintaining democracy, for example, contrasts with the experience of most of the Middle East and, until recently, much of Africa. India was less completely a new nation than its counterparts

**FIGURE 38.10** This photograph of a long line of newly enfranchised citizens waiting to vote in South Africa provides a striking contrast with the decreasing participation in elections in the United States and other older democracies in the West. For the first time, the Bantu-speaking peoples, coloreds, and Indians who make up the vast majority of South Africa's population were allowed to vote in free elections. Their determination to exercise their hard-won right to vote was demonstrated by the peoples' willingness to wait, often in stifling heat, for many hours in the long lines that stretched from polling stations throughout the country.

VISUALIZING THE PAST

## Globalization and Postcolonial Societies

Although many of the areas colonized by the industrialized nations of the West had participated in long-distance trade from early times, colonial rule greatly intensified their integration into the capitalist-dominated world system. Colonization also brought more remote areas that had been only marginally affected by cross-cultural trade into the world system for the first time. As we have seen in Chapter 29 and the present chapter, new market linkages not only affected the elites and trading classes of African, Middle Eastern, and Asian societies, but they also increasingly involved the peasants, who made up the great majority of the population of colonial societies, as well as smaller numbers of workers in the towns and cities.

In the postcolonial era, this process of global market integration has accelerated steadily. One key feature of advancing globalization has been the specialized production of mineral and agricultural exports for foreign consumption. Another has been the growing proportion of uprooted farmers and urban laborers in postcolonial societies employed in factories manufacturing clothing, household furnishings, audiovisual equipment, and other consumer goods for sale overseas, particularly in wealthy societies such as those in North America, western Europe, and Japan. These shifts have greatly increased trading links and economic independence between postcolonial societies and those that had formerly colonized them.

The pervasiveness of these connections in the daily lives of peoples around the globe can be readily seen in the shoes, clothing, and watches worn by the teacher and students in your class, and by the equipment and furnishings of your classrooms. Poll the class to determine where these items and other school supplies were produced. Discuss household and other personal items that were likely to have been manufactured, or at least assembled, in similar locales. Then consider the conditions under which the laborers who made these products were likely to have worked, and the international corporations that oversee and market these products.

**Questions** Who benefits the most from the profits made in the international marketing of goods from postcolonial societies? How does the fact they are imported in massive quantities affect the wages and working conditions of American factory laborers? What measures can be taken to improve the situation of both workers in emerging nations and those in the United States, or are the interests of the two irreconcilable?

elsewhere. It reflected enlightened leadership and its complex relationship with Great Britain. Earlier Indian traditions of considerable decentralization showed in the federal system of the huge democracy. The abolition of the caste system, a massive change, did not remove considerable social inequality based in part on the caste heritage. While it too changed in some ways, the persistence of Hinduism as the majority religion marked India as well.

Developments in the Middle East reflected massive changes, ranging from the tensions over Israel to the region's growing control over its oil revenues. Despite distinguished traditions, most nations in this region were new, and political patterns also reflected the absence of a dominant regional state since the fall of the Ottoman Empire. Important tensions continued between secular and religious leaders. The significance of Islam, as in the Iranian revolution, also linked this region to earlier traditions, raising issues about the relationship between religion and politics and the role of women that had distinctive regional elements as well.

Africa had particular features of its own. The new nations of sub-Saharan Africa came late to independence, and they had been subjected to increasing Western economic dominance well into the postcolonial decades. This was one reason that Africa was poorer than most of Asia by the century's end. Massive cultural changes included growing conversions to Islam or Christianity: by 2000, about 40 percent of all sub-Saharan Africans were Muslim, about 40 percent Christian, while the number of traditional polytheists had shrunk to 20 percent (from 80 percent) during the course of the century. Nationalism, consumer culture, and some Marxism constituted other new cultural components. Yet here too, some observers found important elements of tradition. Many Africans combined older beliefs and artistic styles with their new religions. In some nations, emphasis on powerful authoritarian rulers reflected not only the tensions of new nationhood, but an earlier tradition of "Big Man" rule.

GLOBAL CONNECTIONS

## Postcolonial Nations in the Cold War World Order

The years of independence for the nations that emerged from the colonial empires in Asia, the Middle East, and Africa have been filled with political and economic crises and social turmoil, and tensions between tradition and change. At the same time, it is important to put the recent history of these areas in a larger perspective. Most of the new nations that emerged from colonialism have been in existence for only a few decades. They came to independence with severe handicaps, many of which were a direct legacy of their colonial experiences. It is also important to remember that developed countries, such as the United States, took decades filled with numerous boundary disputes and outright wars to reach their current size and structure. Nearly a century after the original 13 colonies broke from Great Britain and formed the United States, a civil war, the most costly war in the nation's history, was needed to preserve the union. If one takes into account the artificial nature of the emerging nations, most have held together rather well.

What is true in politics is true of all other aspects of the postcolonial experience of the African, Middle Eastern, and Asian peoples. With much lower populations and far fewer industrial competitors, as well as the capacity to draw on the resources of much of the rest of the world, European and North American nations had to struggle to industrialize and thereby achieve a reasonable standard of living for most of their people. Even with these advantages, the human cost in terms of horrific working conditions and urban squalor was enormous, and we are still paying the high ecological price. African, Middle Eastern, and Asian countries (and, as we saw in Chapter 32, this includes Japan) have had few or none of the West's advantages. Most of the emerging nations have begun the "great ascent" to development burdened by excessive and rapidly increasing populations that overwhelm the limited resources that developing nations often must export to earn the capital to buy food and machines. The emerging nations struggle to establish a place in the world market system that is structured in favor of the established industrial powers.

Despite the cultural dominance of the West, which was one of the great legacies or burdens of the colonial era, Asian, Middle Eastern, and African thinkers and artists have achieved a great deal. If much of this achievement has depended on Western models, one should not be surprised, given the educational backgrounds and personal experiences of the emerging nations' first generations of leaders. The challenge for the coming generations will be to find genuinely African, Middle Eastern, and Asian solutions to the problems that have stunted political and economic development in the postcolonial nations. The solutions arrived at are likely to vary a great deal, given the diversity of the nations and societies involved. They are also likely to be forged from a combination of Western influences and the ancient and distinguished traditions of civilized life that have been nurtured by African, Middle Eastern, and Asian peoples for millennia.

## Further Readings

Much of the prolific literature on political and economic development in the emerging nations is focused on individual countries, and it is more helpful to know several cases in some depth than to try to master them all. Robert Heilbroner's writings, starting with *The Great Ascent* (1961), still provide the most sensible introduction to challenges to the new states in the early decades of independence. Peter Worsley's *The Third World* (1964) provides a provocative, if somewhat disjointed, supplement to Heilbroner's many works. Though focused mainly on south and southeast Asia, Gunnar Myrdal's *Asian Drama,* 3 vols. (1968), is the best exploration in a single cultural area of the complexities of the challenges to development. A good overview of the history of postindependence south Asia can be found in W. N. Brown, *The United States and India, Pakistan, and Bangladesh* (1984), despite its misleadingly Western-centric title. Perhaps the best account of Indian politics is contained in Paul Brass, *The Politics of India Since Independence* (1990), in the *New Cambridge History of India* series. On development policy in India, see Francine R. Frankel, *India's Political Economy, 1947–1977* (1978).

Ali Mazrui and Michael Tidy, *Nationalism and New States in Africa* (1984), provides a good survey of developments throughout Africa. Also useful are S. A. Akintoye, *Emergent African States* (1976), and H. Bretton, *Power and Politics in Africa* (1973). For the Middle East, John Waterbury, *The Egypt of Nasser and Sadat* (1983), provides a detailed account of the politics of development, and Peter Mansfield, *The Arabs* (1978), supplies a decent (if now a bit dated) overview.

On military coups, see Ruth First, *The Barrel of a Gun* (1971), and S. Decalo, *Coups and Army Rule in Africa* (1976). Shaul Bakhash, *The Reign of the Ayatollahs* (1984), is perhaps the most insightful of several books that have appeared about Iran since the revolution. Brian Bunting, *The Rise of the South African Reich* (1964), traces the rise of the apartheid regime in great (and polemical) detail, while Gail Gerhart, *Black Power in South Africa* (1978), is one of the better studies devoted to efforts to tear that system down. Among the many fine African, Middle Eastern, and Asian authors whose works are available in English, some of the best include (for Africa) Chinua Achebe, Wole Soyinka, and Ousmene Sembene; (for India) R. K. Narayan and V. S. Naipaul; (for Egypt) Nawal el Saadawi and Naguib Mahfouz; and (for Indonesia) Mochtar Lubis and P. A. Toer. For white perspectives on the South African situation, the fictional works of Nadine Gordimer and J. M. Coetzee are superb.

## On the Web

A timeline for decolonization is provided at http://smccd.net/accounts/helton/decoloni.htm and http://campus.northpark.edu/history/WebChron/World/

Decolonization.html. An overview of famed African novelist Chinua Achebe's writing on imperialism and decolonization can be found at http://www.postcolonialweb.org/achebe/achebeov.html and http://www.webster.edu/~barrettb/achebe.htm.

Kwame Nkrumah's classic indictment of neocolonialism can be found at http://www.fhsu.edu/history/virtual/nkrumah.htm, while a classically neoconservative view condemning neocolonialism, but not modernization, is offered at http://www.afbis.com/analysis/neo-colonialism.html. The postcolonial burdens of African leaders are addressed at sites devoted to Léopold Senghor (http://web.uflib.ufl.edu/cm/africana/senghor.htm) and the life and speeches of Tanzania's Julius Nyerere (http://www.hartford-hwp.com/archives/30/index-fd.html).

Gamal Abdul Nasser's cold war era experiments with Arab socialism as the best means of negotiating modernization are discussed at http://www.arab.net/egypt/et_nasser.htm and http://www.1upinfo.com/country-guide-study/egypt/egypt44.html.

The debate over the role of religion as a solution to the moral malaise as well as the disparity of wealth that has come to characterize the postmodern era is illuminated by the works of Hasan al-Banna of the Muslim Brotherhood (http://www.glue.umd.edu/~kareem/rasayil/, http://www.nmhschool.org/tthornton/hasan_al.htm, and http://www.ummah.org.uk/ikhwan/) and the life of Iran's Ayatollah Ruhollah Khomeini (http://www.iranchamber.com/history/rkhomeini/ayatollah_khomeini.php and http://www.asiasource.org/society/khomeini.cfm). For further information regarding Khomeini's role as the supreme leader of the Islamic revolution in Iran, see http://www.bbc.co.uk/persian/revolution/rev_01.shtml and http://www.fordham.edu/halsall/mod/1979khom1.html. Possible moderating trends in this seedbed of the Islamic movement are analyzed at http://www.brown.edu/Departments/Anthropology/publications/IranisChanging.htm and http://www.brown.edu/Departments/Anthropology/Beeman.html.

A useful review of India's first 50 years of independence may be found at http://www.itihaas.com/independent/contrib7.html. Jawaharlal Nehru's views on Marxism, capitalism, and nonalignment are available at http://www.fordham.edu/halsall/mod/1941nehru.html. His commitment to world disarmament (http://www.indianembassy.org/policy/Disarmament/India_Disarmament.htm) failed to move the world, and as a result, India later went down the path to nuclear confrontation with Pakistan. The growing place of religion in Indian political life, which Nehru would have also opposed, is embodied in the platform of the Bharatiya Janata Party (http://www.bjp.com). Indira Gandhi's role in postcolonial India is explored at http://www.sscnet.ucla.edu/southasia/History/Independent/Indira.html. Two views of the modernization policies pursued by her son are offered at http://www.sscnet.ucla.edu/southasia/History/Independent/Rajiv.html and http://en.wikipedia.org/wiki/Rajiv_Gandhi.

CHAPTER 39

# Rebirth and Revolution: Nation-building in East Asia and the Pacific Rim



Well into young adulthood, Yun Ruo seemed to be a person blessed by good fortune. Though he grew up in post-1945 China, a nation wracked by revolutionary turmoil and state repression, Yun lived a life of relative privilege and security—until the late 1960s. His father, Liu Shaoqui, had long been one of the most prominent leaders of the Communist party, and his family was firmly ensconced in the elite strata of the People's Republic. Yun was a brilliant and hard-working student who in his late teens had gained admission into the highly competitive and prestigious Beijing Aeronautics Institute. In the late 1950s, he was rewarded for his academic accomplishments by being offered the opportunity to further his technical training in the Soviet Union, which at the time was a major supporter of the struggling People's Republic of China.

In Russia, as in China, Yun went from one career achievement to the next, unaffected by the state's forcible mobilization of teachers, students, and other professionals into labor brigades ordered to join the Maoists' misguided Great Leap Forward campaign, which was launched in 1958. But when the assault on the elite social strata broadened to doctors, government officials, scientists, and technicians during the Cultural Revolution of 1967–1970, Yun found himself caught up in the persecution by the Red Guards and other political factions proclaiming their fanatical loyalty to Chairman Mao. In this more radical surge of anti-elitism in the People's Republic, intellectuals and party functionaries were not only sent into the countryside to labor among the peasants, but many were publicly purged, imprisoned, and killed.

Reflecting the deep paranoia and widespread persecution of the times, Yun was branded an enemy of the revolution, ostensibly because he had fallen in love with a Russian woman while a student in the Soviet Union. Once Communist China's main backer, the Soviet Union had increasingly distanced itself from China beginning in the early 1960s, and by the end of the decade it was denounced as antirevolutionary and a threat to the People's Republic. But Yun's romantic ties were largely a pretext to use him in a campaign of vilification against his father, Liu Shaoqui.

**FIGURE 39.1** Mass demonstrations, such as the one in the photo that was staged in front of the Gate of Heavenly Peace in Beijing at the height of the Cultural Revolution in the mid-1960s, demonstrated both the participants' adulation of Mao Zedong and their capacity to intimidate his political rivals.

In response to political pressures surrounding the shifting Maoist stance toward the Soviets, Yun's family forbade him to marry his Russian lover. His family confiscated the couple's love letters, which had allowed them to sustain a long-distance relationship after Yun returned to China, and the letters were passed on to government functionaries. No less a personage than Jiang Qing (Mao's wife) branded Yun a spy, and he was later convicted of treason by a "people's court." Sentenced to eight years in prison, Yun was released in 1974, when the fervor of the Cultural Revolution had begun to fade. But his experiences in prison left him mentally unbalanced, and he died several years later of a lung disease that was probably contracted during his imprisonment.

| 1940 C.E. | 1955 C.E. | 1970 C.E. |
|---|---|---|
| **1942** Japanese occupation of French Indochina | **Mid–1950s** Buildup of U.S. advisors in South Vietnam | **1975** Communist victory in Vietnam; collapse of Republic of South Vietnam |
| **1945** Ho Chi Minh proclaims the Republic of Vietnam | **1957** "Let a Hundred Flowers Bloom" campaign in China | **1976** Deaths of Zhou Enlai and Mao Zedong; purge of Gang of Four |
| **1948** U.S.-sponsored Republic of (South) Korea established | **1958–1960** "Great Leap Forward" in China | **1994** Death of North Korean leader Kim Il-Sung |
| **1949** Communist victory in China; People's Republic of China established | **1960** South Korean nationalist leader Syngman Rhee forced from office by student demonstrations | |
| **1950–1951** Purge of the landlord class in China | **1963** Beginning of state family planning in China | |
| **1950–1953** Korean War | **1965–1968** Cultural Revolution in China | |
| **1952** U.S. occupation of Japan ends | **1965–1973** Direct U.S. military intervention in Vietnam | |
| **1953** Beginning of China's first five-year plan | **1968** Tet offensive in Vietnam | |
| **1954** French defeated at Dien Bien Phu; Geneva accords, French withdrawal from Vietnam; beginning of the Sino-Soviet split | | |

The turmoil and uncertainty—and finally brutality—that enveloped Yun Ruo's life were dominant motifs throughout much of east and southeast Asia during the post–World War II era. Societies across both regions had been deeply disrupted, even devastated, by the Pacific war. Most of Japan's cities were smoldering ruins; its islands were occupied and ruled by the U.S. military, and its people were threatened by starvation, disease, homelessness, and utter despair. China, Vietnam, and Korea, which had been caught up in the war to varying degrees, were embroiled in civil wars that in Korea and Vietnam would prolong wartime privations and destruction for many years. The long civil war in China was decided by the victory of the Communists in 1949 and the flight of the Guomindang to Taiwan. But persecution of the fledgling regime's perceived enemies would continue through much of the following decade and, as we have seen through the experience of Yun Ruo, spread to loyal supporters of the revolution and across society at large by the late 1950s and 1960s.

By the 1980s a number of other nations on the **Pacific Rim,** including Japan, Korea, Singapore, Taiwan, Thailand, and Malaysia, had joined the ranks of developed nations. Their economic successes and political stability, as well as some of the challenges they have posed in recent decades for older developing societies, such as the United States, will be considered in the following chapter. By the 1980s both Vietnam and China had also begun to recover from foreign occupations, civil strife, and revolutionary turmoil. Since then, China in particular has emerged as a global economic power, and Vietnam has increasingly opened its tightly controlled society to the outside world. Altogether the nations of east Asia and the Pacific Rim have become major economic, and potentially political, players in the international arena of the early 21st century.

## East Asia in the Postwar Settlements

- **At the end of World War II, a zone of reasonably stable noncommunist states developed along the Pacific Rim. Linked to the West, these states maintained a neo-Confucian emphasis on the importance of conservative politics and a strong state.**

### New Divisions and the End of Empires

The victors in World War II had some reasonably clear ideas about how east Asia was to be restructured. Korea was divided between a Russian zone of occupation in the north and an American zone in the south. The island of **Taiwan** was restored to China, which in principle was ruled by a Guomindang government headed by Chiang Kai-shek. The United States regained the Philippines and pledged to grant independence quickly, retaining some key military bases. European powers restored control over their holdings in Vietnam, Malaya, and Indonesia. Japan was occupied by American forces bent on introducing major changes that would prevent a recurrence of military aggression.

After Empire: Independent Asia

Not surprisingly, the Pacific regions of Asia did not quickly settle into agreed-upon patterns. A decade after the war's end, not only the Philippines but also Indonesia and Malaya were independent, as part of the postwar tide of decolonization (Map 39.1). Taiwan was still ruled by Chiang Kai-shek, but the Chinese mainland was in the hands of a new and powerful communist regime. Chiang's nationalist regime claimed a mission to recover China, but in fact Taiwan was a separate republic. Korea remained divided but had undergone a brutal north–south conflict in which only U.S. intervention preserved South Korea's independence. Japan was one of the few Pacific regions where matters had proceeded somewhat according to plan, as the nation began to recover while accepting a very different political structure.

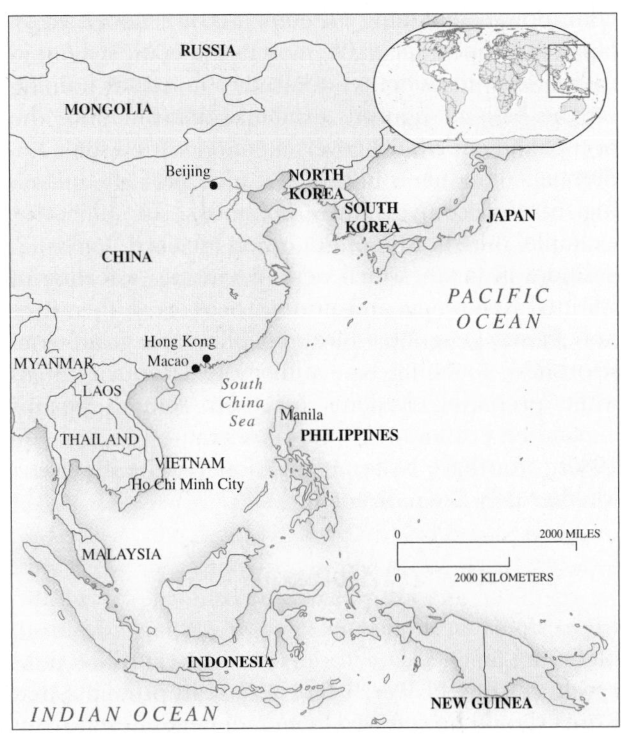


**MAP 39.1 The Pacific Rim Area by 1960.** Geographic locations and political systems created new contacts and alignments.

## Japanese Recovery

Japan in 1945 was in shambles. Its cities were burned, its factories destroyed or idle, its people impoverished and shocked by the fact of surrender and the trauma of bombing, including the atomic devastation of Hiroshima and Nagasaki. However, like the industrial nations of the West, Japan was capable of reestablishing a vigorous economy with surprising speed. Its occupation by U.S. forces, eager to reform Japan but also eager to avoid punitive measures, provided an opportunity for a new period of selective westernization.

The American occupation government, headed by General Douglas MacArthur, worked quickly to tear down Japan's wartime political structure. (Occupation lasted until 1952, a year after Japan signed a peace treaty with most of its wartime opponents.) Japan's military forces were disbanded, the police decentralized, many officials removed, and political prisoners released. For the long run, American authorities pressed for a democratization of Japanese society by giving women the vote, encouraging labor unions, and abolishing Shintoism as a state religion. Several economic reforms were also introduced, breaking up landed estates for the benefit of small farmers—who quickly became politically conservative—and dissolving the holdings of the zaibatsu combines, a measure that had little lasting effect as Japanese big business regrouped quickly.

A new constitution tried to cut through older limitations by making the parliament the supreme government body. Several civil liberties were guaranteed, along with gender equality in marriage and collective bargaining rights. Military forces with "war potential" were abolished forever, making Japan a unique major nation in its limited military strength. The emperor became merely a symbolic figurehead, without political power and with no claims to Shinto divinity. Even as Japan accepted many political and legal concepts, it inserted its own values into the new constitution. Thus, a 1963 law called for special social obligations to the elderly, in obvious contrast to Western approaches: "The elders shall be loved and respected as those who have for many years contributed toward the development of society, and a wholesome and peaceful life shall be guaranteed to them."

The Constitution of Japan, Two Versions

These new constitutional measures were embraced by the Japanese people, many of whom became avid opponents of any hint of military revival. Military power and responsibility in the region were retained by the United States, which long after the occupation period kept important bases in Japan. Many of the political features of the new constitution worked smoothly—in large part because the Japanese had experienced parliamentary and political party activity for extended periods in previous decades. Two moderate parties merged in 1955 into the new **Liberal Democratic party,** which monopolized Japan's government into the 1990s.

Japan became a genuine multiparty democracy but with unusual emphasis on one-party control in the interests of order and elite control. It granted women the vote, but women's conditions differed markedly from men's. In education, American occupation forces insisted on reducing the nationalism in textbooks and opening secondary schools to more social groups. These changes merged with existing Japanese enthusiasm for education, heightening the emphasis on school success. Japan developed one of the most meritocratic systems in the world, with students advanced to university training on the basis of rigorous examinations. But once the occupation ended, the government reasserted some traditional components in this education package, including careful controls over textbooks. In 1966, for example, the Ministry of Education attacked "egotistic" attitudes in Japan, which were producing "a feeling of spiritual hollowness and unrest." Schools in this situation should generate ethical discipline and group consciousness, touching base with more customary goals while preparing students for their role in Japan's expanding economy. As one conservative put it in the 1980s, "You have to teach tradition [to the children] whether they like it or not."

## Korea: Intervention and War

Korea's postwar adjustment period was far more troubled than Japan's. The leaders of the great Allied powers during World War II had agreed in principle that Korea should be restored as an independent state. But the United States' eagerness to obtain Soviet help against Japan resulted in Soviet occupation of the northern part of the peninsula. As the cold war intensified, American and Soviet authorities could not agree on unification of the zones, and in 1948 the United States sponsored a **Republic of Korea** in the south, matched by a Soviet-dominated **People's Democratic Republic of Korea** in the north. North Korea's regime drew on an earlier Korean Communist party founded in exile in the 1900s. North Korea quickly became a communist state with a Stalinist-type emphasis on the power of the leader, Kim Il-Sung, until his death in 1994. The South Korean regime, bolstered by an ongoing American military presence, was headed by nationalist Syngman Rhee. Rhee's South Korea developed institutions that were parliamentary in form but maintained a strongly authoritarian tone.

In June 1950, North Korean forces attacked South Korea, hoping to impose unification on their own terms (Figure 39.2). The United States reacted quickly (after some confusing signals about whether South Korea was inside the U.S. "defense perimeter"). President Truman insisted on drawing another line against communist aggression, and he orchestrated United Nations sponsorship of a largely American "police action" in support of South Korean troops. In the ensuing **Korean War,** under General MacArthur's lead-

FIGURE 39.2 The internationalization of the civil conflict between the regimes of North and South Korea in the late 1940s led to the flight of hundreds of thousands of refugees from one region to another. As this photo so starkly portrays, these migrations often occurred in the harsh winter season when many of those in flight died of the cold and hunger.

ership, Allied forces pushed North Korea back, driving on toward the Chinese border; this action roused concern on the part of China's communist regime, which sent "volunteers" to force American troops back toward the south. The front stabilized in 1952 near the original north–south border. The stalemate dragged on until 1953, when a new American administration was able to agree to an armistice.

Korea then continued its dual pattern of development. North Korea produced an unusually isolated version of one-man rule as Kim concentrated his powers over the only legal political party, the military, and the government. Even Soviet liberalization in the late 1980s brought little change. South Korea and the United States concluded a mutual defense treaty in 1954; American troop levels were reduced, but the South Korean army gained more sophisticated military equipment and the United States poured economic aid into the country, initially to prevent starvation in a war-ravaged land. The political tenor of South Korea continued to be authoritarian. In 1961 army officers took over effective rule of the country, although sometimes a civilian government served as a front.

However, economic change began to gain ground in South Korea, ushering in a new phase of activity and international impact. Tensions between the two Koreas continued to run high, with many border clashes and sabotage, but outright warfare was avoided.

### Emerging Stability in Taiwan, Hong Kong, and Singapore

Postwar adjustments in Taiwan involved yet another set of issues. As the communist revolutionary armies gained the upper hand in mainland China, between 1946 and 1948 the Guomindang (Nationalist) regime prepared to fall back on its newly reacquired island, which the communists could not threaten because they had no navy. The result was imposition over the Taiwanese majority of a new leadership plus a massive military force drawn from the mainland.

The authoritarian political patterns the nationalists had developed in China, centered on Chiang Kai-shek's personal control of the government, were amplified by the need to keep disaffected Taiwanese in check. Hostility with the communist regime across the Taiwan Strait ran high. In 1955 and 1958, the communists bombarded two small islands controlled by the nationalists, Quemoy and Matsu, and wider conflict threatened as the United States backed up its ally. Tensions were defused when communist China agreed to fire on the islands only on alternate days, while U.S. ships supplied them on the off-days, thus salvaging national honor. Finally, the United States induced Chiang to renounce any intentions of attacking the mainland, and conflict eased into mutual bombardments of propaganda leaflets. During this period, as in South Korea, the United States gave economic aid to Taiwan, ending assistance only in the 1960s when growing prosperity seemed assured.

Two other participants in the economic advances of the Pacific Rim were distinguished by special ties to Britain. **Hong Kong** remained a British colony after World War II; only in the 1980s was an agreement reached between Britain and China for its 1997 return to the Chinese fold. Hong Kong gained increasing autonomy from direct British rule. Its Chinese population swelled at various points after 1946 as a result of flights from communist rule.

IMAGE
Modern Hong Kong

Singapore retained a large British naval base until 1971, when Britain abandoned all pretense of power in east Asia. Singapore grew into a vigorous free port, and it became an independent nation in 1965.

Overall, by the end of the 1950s a certain stability had emerged in the political situation of many smaller east Asian nations. From the 1960s onward these same areas, combining Western contacts with important traditions of group loyalty, moved from impressive economic recovery to new international influence on the basis of manufacturing and trade.

## Japan, Incorporated

- **The keynotes of Japanese history from the 1950s onward were an intense concentration on economic growth and distinctive political and cultural forms as the nation proved that industrial success did not depend on a strict Western pattern.**

### Japan's Distinctive Political and Cultural Style

The chief emphasis of Japanese politics lay in conservative stability. The Liberal Democratic party held the reins of government from 1955 onward. This meant that Japan, uniquely among the democratic nations of the postwar world, had no experience with shifts in party administration until 1993. Changes in leadership, which at times were frequent, were handled through negotiations among the Liberal Democratic elite, not directly as a result of shifts in voter preference.

Clearly, this system revived many of the oligarchic features of Meiji Japan and the Japan of the 1920s. During the prosperous 1970s and 1980s, economic progress and the Liberal Democrats' willingness to consult opposition leaders about major legislation reinforced Japan's effective political unity. Only at the end of the 1980s, when several Liberal Democratic leaders were branded by corruption of various sorts, were new questions raised.

Japan's distinctive political atmosphere showed clearly in strong cooperation with business. The state set production and investment goals while actively lending public resources to encourage investment and limit imports. The government–business coordination to promote economic growth and export expansion prompted the half-admiring, half-derisory Western label "Japan, Incorporated."

The government actively campaigned to promote birth control and abortion, and population growth slowed. This was another product of the strong national tradition of state-sponsored discipline.

As in politics and education, Japanese culture preserved important traditional elements, which provided aesthetic and spiritual satisfactions amid rapid economic change (Figure 39.3). Customary styles in poetry, painting, tea ceremonies, and flower arrangements continued. Each New Year's Day, for example, the emperor presided at a poetry contest, and masters of traditional arts were honored by being designated as Living National Treasures. Kabuki and No theater also flourished. Japanese films and novels often recalled the country's earlier history. Japanese painters and architects participated actively in the "international style" pioneered in the West, but they often infused it with earlier Japanese motifs such as stylized nature painting. City orchestras played the works of Western composers and native compositions that incorporated passages played on the Japanese flute and zither. At the same time, aside from interior decoration and film, Japanese contributions to world culture were negligible; this was not where national creativity showed an international face.

Cultural combinations were not always smooth. Both before and after World War II, key intellectuals used art and literature to protest change, not merely to blend Western and traditional styles. The flamboyant postwar writer Hiraoka Kimitoke (pen name Yukio Mishima, 1925–1970) was a case in point. His novels and dramas, which began to appear in 1949, dealt with controversial themes such as homosexuality while also updating versions of the No plays. A passionate nationalist, he was too sickly for military service in World War II, though he later built up his body. At first he enjoyed many Western contacts and interests, but he came to hate Western ways. In 1968 he formed a private army centered on restoring Japanese ideals. After finishing a final major novel, Mishima performed his own ritual suicide in 1970. He wrote to an American friend shortly before his death, "I came to wish to sacrifice myself for this old beautiful tradition of Japan, which is disappearing very quickly day by day."

**FIGURE 39.3** The blending of ancient Japanese culture (*kimonos*) and modern consumer goods (umbrellas, backpacks, and thermoses) is evident in this photo of three young women dressed for an evening out on the town.

## The Economic Surge

Particularly after the mid-1950s, rapid economic growth made Japan's clearest mark internationally and commanded the most intense energies at home. By 1983 the total national product was equal to the combined totals of China, both Koreas, Taiwan, India, Pakistan, Australia, and Brazil. Per capita income, though still slightly behind that of the leading Western nations such as West Germany, had passed that of many countries, including Britain. Annual economic growth reached at least 10 percent regularly from the mid-1950s onward, surpassing the regular levels of every other nation during the 1960s and 1970s, as Japan became one of the top two or three economic powers in the world (Figure 39.4). Leading Japanese corporations, such as the great automobile manufacturers and electronic equipment producers, became known not

Japanese Technician Testing Equipment

FIGURE 39.4 Tokyo at night at the beginning of the 21st century epitomizes the resurgence of Asian economies following World War II.

simply for the volume of their international exports but for the high quality of their goods.

A host of factors fed this astounding economic performance. Active government encouragement was a major ingredient. Educational expansion played a major role as Japan began to turn out far more engineers than did more populous competitors such as the United States. Foreign policy also played a role. Japan was able to devote almost its whole capital to investment in productive technology, for its military expenses were negligible given its reliance on United States protection.

Japan's distinctive labor policies functioned well. Workers were organized mainly in company unions that were careful not to impair their companies' productivity. Leading corporations solidified this cooperation, which spurred zealous work from most employees. Social activities, including group exercise sessions before the start of the working day, promoted and expressed group loyalty, and managers took active interest in suggestions by employees. The Japanese system also ensured lifetime employment to an important part of the labor force, a policy aided by economic growth, low average unemployment rates, and an early retirement age. This network of policies and attitudes made Japanese labor seem both less class-conscious and less individualistic than labor forces in the advanced industrial nations of the West; it reflected older traditions of group solidarity in Japan, going back to feudal patterns.

Japanese management displayed a distinctive spirit, again as a result of adapting older traditions of leadership. There was more group consciousness, including a willingness to abide by collective decisions and less concern for quick personal profits than was characteristic of the West, particularly the United States. Few corporate bureaucrats changed firms, which meant that their efforts were concentrated on their company's success. Leisure life remained meager by Western standards, and many Japanese were reluctant to take regular vacations.

Japan's distinctiveness extended to family life, despite some features similar to the West's industrial experience. Japanese women, though increasingly well educated and experiencing an important decline in birth rates, did not follow Western patterns precisely. A feminist movement was confined to a small number of intellectuals. Within the family, women shared fewer leisure activities with their husbands, concentrating more heavily on domestic duties and intensive child-rearing than was true in the West by the 1970s. In child-rearing, conformity to group standards was emphasized far more than in the West or in communist China. A comparative study of nursery schools showed that Japanese teachers were bent on effacing their own authority in the interests of developing strong bonds between the children. Shame was directed toward non-conformist behaviors, a disciplinary approach the West had largely abandoned in the early 19th century. Japanese television game shows, superficially copied from those of the West, imposed elaborate, dishonoring punishment on losing contestants.

The nation had few lawyers, for it was assumed that people could make and abide by firm arrangements through mutual agreement. Psychiatrists reported far fewer problems of loneliness and individual alienation than in the West. Conversely, situations that promoted competition between individuals, such as university entrance tests, produced far higher stress levels than did analogous Western experiences. The Japanese had particular ways to relieve tension. Bouts of heavy drinking were more readily tolerated than in the West, seen as a time when normal codes of conduct could be suspended under the helpful eyes of friends. Businessmen and some politicians had recourse to traditional geisha houses for female-supplied cosseting, a normal and publicly accepted activity.

Japanese popular culture was not static, both because of ongoing attraction to Western standards and because of rapid urbanization and economic growth (Figure 39.5). The U.S. presence after World War II brought a growing fascination with baseball, and professional teams flourished. Japanese athletes began also to excel in such sports as tennis and golf. In the mid-1980s, the government, appalled to discover that a majority of Japanese children did not use chopsticks but preferred knives and forks in order to eat more rapidly, invested money to promote chopsticks training in the

**FIGURE 39.5** As this photo of an ultra-modern skyscraper in Hong Kong amply illustrates, some of the most innovative architecture of the age of globalization can be found in the great commercial centers along the Pacific Rim. The region also boasts the world's tallest building, a twin-tower office complex in the Malaysian capital of Kuala Lumpur.

schools. This was a minor development, but it indicates the ongoing tension between change, with its Western connotations, and a commitment to Japanese identity. The veneration of old age was challenged by some youthful assertiveness and by the sheer cost of supporting the rapidly growing percentage of older people, for Japan relied heavily on family support for elders.

Other issues were associated with change. By the 1960s, pollution became a serious problem as cities and industry expanded rapidly; traffic police, for example, sometimes wore masks to protect their lungs. The government (eager to preempt a potential opposition issue) paid increasing attention to environmental issues after 1970.

The 1990s brought some new questions to Japan. Mired in political corruption, the Liberal Democrats were replaced by shaky coalition governments. A severe economic recession caused widespread unemployment. Even as Japanese methods were being touted in the West as a basis for economic and social revitalization, some of the critical patterns of postwar development were at least temporarily disrupted.

## The Pacific Rim: New Japans?

- **Economic and political developments in several nations and city-states on Asia's Pacific coast echoed important elements of Japan's 20th-century history. Political authoritarianism was characteristic of most Pacific Rim states, though there were periodic bows to parliamentary forms and protests from dissidents who wanted greater freedom.**

### The Korean Miracle

South Korea was the most obvious example of the spread of new economic dynamism to other parts of the Pacific Rim. The Korean government rested normally in the hands of a political strongman, usually from army ranks. Syngman Rhee was forced out of office by student demonstrations in 1960; a year later, a military general, Park Chung-hee, seized power. He retained his authority until his assassination in 1979 by his director of intelligence. Then another general seized power. Intense student protest, backed by wider popular support, pressed the military from power at the end of the 1980s, but a conservative politician won the ensuing general election, and it was not clear how much the political situation had changed. Opposition activity was possible in South Korea, though usually heavily circumscribed, and many leaders were jailed. There was some freedom of the press although it did not extend to publications from communist countries.

As in postwar Japan, the South Korean government from the mid-1950s onward placed its primary emphasis on economic growth, which in this case started from a much lower base after the Korean War and previous Japanese exploitation. Huge industrial firms were created by a combination of government aid and active entrepreneurship. By the 1970s, when growth rates in Korea began to match those of Japan, Korea was competing successfully in the area of cheap consumer goods, as well as in steel and automobiles, in a variety of international markets. In steel, Korea's surge—based on the most up-to-date technology, a skilled engineering sector, and low wages—pushed past Japan's. The same held true in textiles, where Korean growth (along with that of Taiwan) erased almost one-third of the jobs held in the industry in Japan.

Huge industrial groups such as Daewoo and **Hyundai** resembled the great Japanese holding companies before and after World War II and wielded great political influence. For example, Hyundai was the creation of entrepreneur Chung Ju Yung, a modern folk hero who walked 150 miles to Seoul, South Korea's capital, from his native village to take his first job as a day laborer at age 16. By the 1980s, when Chung was in his 60s, his firm had 135,000 employees and 42 overseas offices throughout the world. Hyundai virtually governed Korea's southeastern coast. It built ships, including petroleum supertankers; it built thousands of housing units sold to low-paid workers at below-market rates; it built schools, a technical college, and an arena for the practice of the traditional Korean martial art Tae Kwon Do. With their lives carefully provided for, Hyundai workers responded in kind, putting in six-day weeks with three vacation days per year and participating in almost worshipful ceremonies when a fleet of cars was shipped abroad or a new tanker launched (Figure 39.6).

South Korea Enters the U. S. Auto Market

South Korea's rapid entry into the ranks of newly industrialized countries produced a host of more general changes. The population soared. By the 1980s more than 40 million people lived in a nation about the size of the state of Indiana, producing one of the highest population densities on earth: about 1000 people per square mile. This was one reason, even amid growing prosperity, why many Koreans emigrated. The government gradually began to encourage couples to limit their birth rates. Seoul expanded to embrace 9 million people; it developed intense air pollution and a hothouse atmosphere of deals and business maneuvers. Per capita income grew despite the population increase, rising almost 10 times from the early 1950s to the early 1980s, but to a level still only one-ninth that of Japan. Huge fortunes coexisted with widespread poverty in this setting, although the poor were better off than those of less developed nations.

FIGURE 39.6 Hyundai loading dock for export to the United States.

## Advances in Taiwan and the City-States

The Republic of China, as the government of Taiwan came to call itself, experienced a high rate of economic development. Productivity in both agriculture and industry increased rapidly, the former spurred by land reform that benefited small commercial farmers. The government concentrated increasingly on economic gains as its involvement in plans for military action against the mainland communist regime declined. As in Japan and Korea, formal economic planning reached high levels, though allowing latitude for private business. Money was poured into education, and literacy rates and levels of technical training rose rapidly. The result was important cultural and economic change for the Taiwanese people. Traditional medical practices and ritualistic popular religion remained lively but were expanded to allow simultaneous use of modern, Western-derived medicine and some of the urban entertainment forms popular elsewhere.

The assimilation of rapid change gave the Taiwanese government great stability despite a host of new concerns. The U.S. recognition of the People's Republic of China brought with it a steadily decreasing official commitment to Taiwan. In 1978 the United States severed diplomatic ties with the Taiwanese regime, although unofficial contacts—through the American Institute in Taiwan and the Coordination Council for North American Affairs, established by the republic in Washington—remained strong. The Taiwanese also built important regional contacts with other governments in eastern and southeastern Asia that facilitated trade. For example, Japan served as the nation's most important single trading partner, purchasing foodstuffs, manufactured textiles, chemicals, and other industrial goods.

Taiwan also developed some informal links with the communist regime in Beijing, although the latter continued to claim the island as part of its territory. The republic survived the death of Chiang Kai-shek and the accession of his son, **Chiang Ching-kuo,** in 1978. The young Chiang emphasized personal authority less than his father had, and he reduced somewhat the gap between mainland-born military personnel and native Taiwanese in government ranks. However, a strong authoritarian strain continued, and political diversity was not encouraged.

Conditions in the city-state of Singapore, though less tied to great power politics, resembled those in Taiwan in many ways. Prime Minister **Lee Kuan Yew** took office in 1965, when the area first gained independence, and held power for the next three decades. The government established tight controls over its citizens, going beyond anything attempted elsewhere in the Pacific Rim. Sexual behavior and potential economic corruption, as well as more standard aspects of municipal regulation and economic planning, were scrutinized carefully. The government proclaimed the necessity of unusual discipline and restraint because such a large population crowded into a limited space. One result was unusually low reported crime rates, and another was the near impossibility of serious political protest. The dominant People's Action party suppressed opposition movements. The authoritarian political style was rendered somewhat more palatable by extraordinarily successful economic development, based on a combination of government controls and initiatives and free enterprise. Already the

Clean-Room Disc Manufacturing in Singapore

VISUALIZING THE PAST

## Pacific Rim Growth

**Questions** How can the figures in the table be used to illustrate the industrial emergence of the Pacific Rim (Japan, South Korea, Singapore, Hong Kong)? Which countries most clearly have been undergoing an industrial revolution since the 1960s, and how can this be measured? How do the key Pacific Rim areas compare in growth to the neighboring "little tigers" Indonesia, Malaysia, and Thailand? Do the Philippines constitute another "little tiger"? How do Japanese patterns compare with the newer areas of the Pacific Rim, and how can this relationship be explained?

**Indices of Growth and Change in the Pacific Rim: Gross National Product (GNP) 1965–1996**

| | Per Capita GNP East and Southeast Asia, annual growth rates (%) | |
|---|---|---|
| | **1965** | **1996** |
| China | 8.5 | 6.7 |
| Hong Kong | 7.5 | 5.6 |
| Indonesia | 6.7 | 4.6 |
| Japan | 4.5 | 3.6 |
| Korea (South) | 8.9 | 7.3 |
| Malaysia | 6.8 | 4.1 |
| Philippines | 3.5 | 0.9 |
| Singapore | 8.3 | 6.3 |
| Thailand | 7.3 | 5.0 |
| **For comparison** | | |
| All preexisting industrial countries | 3.0 | 2.2 |
| United States | 2.4 | 1.4 |
| India | 4.5 | 2.3 |

**Social and Economic Data**

| | % labor force in agriculture | | % population urban | |
|---|---|---|---|---|
| | **1965** | **1996** | **1965** | **1996** |
| China | 78 | 72 | 17 | 31 |
| Indonesia | 66 | 55 | 41 | 82 |
| Japan | 20 | 7 | 71 | 78 |
| Korea (South) | 49 | 18 | 41 | 82 |
| Malaysia | 54 | 27 | 34 | 54 |
| Thailand | 80 | 64 | 13 | 20 |

*Note:* Growth at 2.3 percent per year doubles the category in 30 years; 7 percent per year doubles in 10 years.
*Source:* Adapted from World Bank, *World Development Indicators* (Washington, D.C., 1998).

world's fourth largest port, Singapore saw manufacturing and banking surpass shipping as sources of revenue. Electronics, textiles, and oil refining joined shipbuilding as major sectors. By the 1980s Singapore's population enjoyed the second highest per capita income in Asia. Educational levels and health conditions improved accordingly.

Finally, Hong Kong retained its status as a major world port and branched out as a center of international banking, serving as a bridge between the communist regime in China and the wider world. Export production combined high-speed technology with low wages and long hours for the labor force, yielding highly competitive results. Textiles and clothing formed 39 percent of total exports by the 1980s, but other sectors, including heavy industry, developed impressively as well. As in other Pacific Rim nations, a prosperous middle class emerged, with links to many other parts of the world, Western and Asian alike. In 1997, after careful negotiation with the British, Hong Kong was

IN DEPTH

## The Pacific Rim as a U.S. Policy Issue

Any change in the power balance between nations or larger civilizations results in a host of policy issues for all who are involved. The rise of the Pacific Rim economies posed some important questions for the West, particularly for the United States because of its military role in the Pacific as well as its world economic position. The United States had actively promoted economic growth in Japan, Korea, and Taiwan as part of its desire to discourage the spread of communism. Although American aid was not solely responsible for Pacific Rim advances, and although it tapered off by the 1960s, the United States took some satisfaction in demonstrating the vitality of noncommunist economies. The United States also was not eager to relinquish its military superiority in the region, which gave it a stake in Asian opinion.

> *"Asian leaders recognized the need for some change, but they did not welcome advice that seemed to ignore successful components from the past and threatened some of the privileges of established political and business elites."*

Yet the threats posed by increasing Pacific Rim economic competition were real and growing. Japan seemed to wield a permanent balance-of-payments superiority; its exports to the United States regularly exceeded imports by the 1970s and 1980s, which contributed greatly to the United States' unfavorable overall trade balance. Japanese investment in American companies and real estate increased the United States' growing indebtedness to foreign nations. The symbolic problems were real as well. Japanese observers pointed out with some justice that Americans seemed more worried about Japanese investments than about larger British holdings in the United States, an imbalance that smacked of racism. Certainly, Americans found it harder to accept Asian competition than they did European, if only because it was less familiar. Japanese ability to gain near monopolies in key industries such as electronic recording systems as well as the growing Korean challenge in steel and automobiles meant or seemed to mean loss of jobs and perhaps a threat of more fundamental economic decline in years to come.

In the 1980s, several observers urged American imitation of the bases of Pacific Rim success: The United States should open more partnerships between government and private industry and do more economic planning, it should teach managers to commit themselves to group harmony rather than individual profit seeking, and it should build a new concord between management and labor, based on greater job security and cooperative social programs. Some firms in the United States did introduce certain Japanese management methods, including more consultation with workers, with some success.

Other observers, also concerned about long-term erosion of American power on the Pacific Rim, urged a more antagonistic stance. A few wanted the United States to pull out of costly Japanese and Korean military bases so that the Pacific Rim would be forced to shoulder more of its own defense costs. Others wanted to impose tariffs on Asian goods, at least until the Pacific Rim nations made it easier for American firms to compete in Asian markets. Aggrieved American workers sometimes smashed imported cars and threatened Asian immigrants, although many American consumers continued to prefer Pacific Rim products. The options were complex, and no clear change in American policy emerged.

Pacific Rim nations also faced choices about their orientation toward the West, particularly the United States. Questions that arose earlier about what Western patterns to copy and what to avoid continued to be important, as the Japanese concern about forks and chopsticks suggests. Added were issues about how to express pride and confidence in modern achievements against what were seen as Western tendencies to belittle and patronize. In 1988 the summer Olympic games were held in South Korea, a sign of Korea's international advance and a source of great national pride. During the games, Korean nationalism flared against the U.S. athletes and television commentators, based on their real or imagined tendencies to seek out faults in Korean society. South Korea, like Japan, continued to rely on Western markets and U.S. military assistance, but there was a clear desire to put the relationship on a more fully equal footing. This desire reflected widespread public opinion, and it could have policy implications.

The Pacific Rim crisis in 1998 raised a new set of questions. American leaders urged assistance to beleaguered economies such as those of South Korea and Indonesia, but they also, with some self-satisfaction, tried to insist on introducing a more Western-style market economy. Asian leaders recognized the need for some change, but they did not welcome advice that seemed to ignore successful components from the past and threatened some of the privileges of established political and business elites.

---

**Questions** How great were the challenges posed by the Pacific Rim to the U.S. world position and well-being? What are the most likely changes in American and Pacific Rim relations over the next two decades?

returned to China. The communist government promised to respect the territory's free market economic system and maintain democratic political rights, although the changeover raised questions for the future.

## Common Themes and New Problems

The Pacific Rim states had more in common than their rapid growth rates and expanding exports. They all stressed group loyalties against excessive individualism or protest and in support of hard work. Confucian morality often was used, implicitly or explicitly, as part of this effort. The Pacific Rim states also shared reliance on government planning and direction amid limitations on dissent and instability. Of course, they benefited greatly from the expansion of the Japanese market for factory goods, such as textiles, as well as raw materials.

The dynamism of the Pacific Rim spilled over to neighboring parts of southeast Asia by the 1980s. "Little tigers" such as Indonesia, Malaysia, and Thailand began to experience rapid economic growth, along with the pollution problems that accompanied new manufacturing and larger cities.

River Market in Thailand

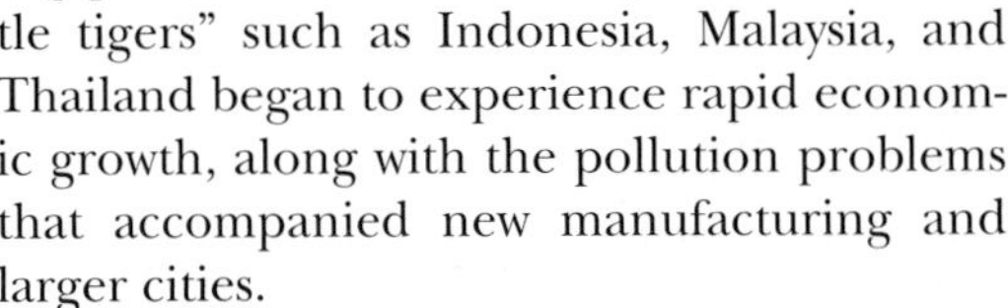

However, the final years of the 20th century revealed unexpected weaknesses in this dynamic region. Growth faltered, unemployment rose, and currencies from South Korea to Indonesia took a drastic hit. Many Western observers argued that this crisis could be resolved only by reducing the links between governments and major firms and introducing more free market competition. In essence, they contended that only a Western industrial model could be successful, and agencies such as the World Bank tried to insist on reforms in this direction as a condition for economic assistance. In the meantime, political pressures increased amid economic distress, and in 1998 the longtime authoritarian ruler of Indonesia was overturned in favor of pledges for future democracy. By 1999, however, economic growth rates in the region began to pick up. It was not clear that basic patterns had to be rethought.

# Mao's China and Beyond

- **After their victory in the long civil war against the Guomindang in 1949, Chinese communists faced the formidable task of governing a vast nation in ruins. In their pursuit of economic development and social reform, the communists sought to build on the base they had established in the "liberated" zones during their struggle for power.**

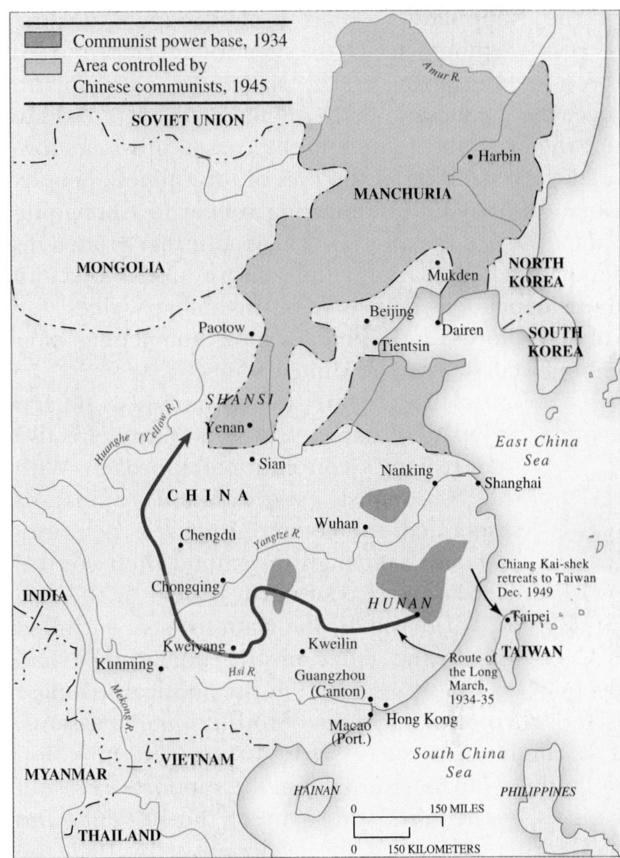


**MAP 39.2** China in the Years of Japanese Occupation and Civil War, 1931–1949

Just as he was convinced that he was on the verge of victory, Chiang Kai-shek's anticommunist crusade had been rudely interrupted by the Japanese invasion of the Chinese mainland (see Chapter 35). Obsessed with the communists, Chiang had done little to block the steady advance of Japanese forces in the early 1930s into Manchuria and the islands along China's coast. Even after the Japanese launched their assaults, aimed at conquering China, Chiang wanted to continue the struggle against the communists (Map 39.2).

Forced by his military commanders to concentrate on the Japanese threat, Chiang grudgingly formed a military alliance with the communists. Although he did all he could to undermine the alliance and continue the anticommunist struggle by underhanded means, for the next seven years the war against Japan took priority over the civil war in the contest for control of China.

Although it brought more suffering to the Chinese people, the Japanese invasion was enormously advantageous for the Communist party. The Japanese invaders captured much of the Chinese coast, where the cities were the centers of the business and mercantile backers of the Nationalists. Chiang's conventional military forces were pummeled by the superior air, land, and sea forces of the Japanese. The Nationalists' attempts to meet the Japanese in conventional battles led to disaster; their inability to defend the coastal provinces lowered their standing in the eyes of the Chinese people. Chiang's hasty and humiliating retreat to Chongqing (Map 39.2), in the interior of China, further eroded his reputation as the savior of the nation and rendered him more dependent than ever on his military allies, the rural landlords, and—perhaps most humiliating—foreign powers such as the United States.

The guerrilla warfare the communists waged against the Japanese armies proved far more effective than Chiang's conventional approach. With the Nationalist extermination campaigns suspended, the communists used their anti-Japanese campaigns to extend their control over large areas of north China. By the end of World War II, the Nationalists controlled mainly the cities in the north; they had become (as Mao prescribed in his political writings) islands surrounded by a sea of revolutionary peasants. The communists' successes and their determination to fight the Japanese won them the support of most of China's intellectuals and many of the students who had earlier supported the Nationalists. By 1945 the balance of power within China was clearly shifting in the communists' favor. In the four-year civil war that followed, communist soldiers, who were well treated and fought for a cause, consistently routed the much-abused soldiers of the Nationalists, many of whom switched to the communist side. By 1949 it was over. Chiang and what was left of his armies fled to the island of Formosa, renamed Taiwan, and Mao proclaimed the establishment of the **People's Republic of China** in Beijing.

China in Civil War and Revolution

The Japanese invasion proved critical in the communist drive to victory. But equally important were the communists' social and economic reform programs, which eventually won the great majority of the peasantry, the students and intellectuals, and even many of the bureaucrats to their side. Whereas Chiang, whatever his intentions, was able to do little to improve the condition of the great mass of the people, Mao made uplifting the peasants the central element in his drive for power (Figure 39.7). Land reforms, access to education, and improved health care gave the peasantry a real stake in Mao's revolutionary movement and good reason to defend their soviets against both the Nationalists and the Japanese. In contrast to Chiang's armies, whose arrival meant theft, rape, and murder to China's villagers, Mao's soldiers were indoctrinated with the need to protect the peasantry and win their support. Lest they forget, harsh penalties were levied, such as execution for stealing an egg.

As guerrilla fighters, Mao's soldiers had a much better chance to survive and advance in the ranks than did the forcibly conscripted, brutally treated foot soldiers of the Nationalists. Mao and the commanders around him, such as **Lin Biao,** who had been trained at Chiang's Whampoa Academy in the 1920s, proved far more gifted—even in conventional warfare—than the often corrupt and inept Nationalist generals. Thus, although the importance of the Japanese invasion cannot be discounted, the communists won the mandate to govern China because they offered solutions to China's fundamental social and economic problems. Even more critically, they actually put their programs into action in the areas that came under their control. In a situation in which revolutionary changes appeared to be essential, the communists alone convinced the Chinese people that they had the leaders and the program that could improve their lives.

**FIGURE 39.7** This propaganda poster features Mao Zedong as the friend and father of the people. Soldiers, peasants, women, children, and peoples from the many regions of China are pictured here joyously rallying to Mao's vision of a strong, just, and prosperous China.

## The Communists Come to Power

The communists' long struggle for control had left the party with a strong political and military organization that was rooted in the **party cadres** and the **People's Liberation Army.** The continuing importance of the army was indicated by the fact that most of China was administered by military officials for five years after the communists came to power. But the army remained clearly subordinate to the party. Cadre advisors were attached to military contingents at all levels, and the central committees of the party were dominated by nonmilitary personnel.

With this strong political framework in place, the communists moved quickly to assert China's traditional preeminence in east and much of southeast Asia. Potential secessionist movements were forcibly repressed in Inner Mongolia and Tibet, although resistance in the latter has erupted periodically and continues to the present day. In the early 1950s, the Chinese intervened militarily in the conflict between North and South Korea, an intervention that was critical in forcing the United States to settle for a stalemate and a lasting division of the peninsula. Refusing to accept a similar but far more lopsided two-nation outcome of the struggle in China itself, the communist leadership has periodically threatened to invade the Nationalists' refuge on Taiwan, often touching off international incidents. China also played an increasingly important role in the liberation struggle of the Vietnamese to the south, although that did not peak until the height of American involvement in the conflict in the 1960s.

By the late 1950s, the close collaboration between the Soviet Union and China that marked the early years of Mao's rule had broken down. Border disputes, focusing on territories the Russians had seized during the period of Qing decline, and the Chinese refusal to play second fiddle to Russia, especially after Stalin was succeeded by the less imposing Khrushchev, were key causes of the split. These causes of the breakdown in collaboration worsened the differences resulting from the meager economic assistance provided by the Soviet "comrades." They also fed Mao's sense that with the passing of Stalin, he was the chief theoretician and leader of the communist world. In the early 1960s, the Chinese flexed their military and technological muscle by defeating India in a brief war that resulted from a border dispute. More startling, however, was the Chinese success in exploding the first nuclear device developed by a nonindustrial nation.

## Planning for Economic Growth and Social Justice

On the domestic front, the new leaders of China moved with equal vigor, though with a good deal less success. Their first priority was to complete the social revolution in the rural areas that had been carried through to some extent in communist-controlled areas during the wars against the Japanese and Guomindang. Between 1950 and 1952, the landlord class and the large landholders, most of whom had been spared in the earlier stages of the revolution, were dispossessed and purged. Village tribunals, overseen by party cadre members, gave tenants and laborers a chance to get even for decades of oppression. Perhaps as many as 3 million people who were denounced as members of the exploitive landlord class were executed. At the same time, the land taken from the land-owning classes was distributed to peasants who had none or little. For a brief time at least, one of the central pledges of the communist revolutionaries was fulfilled: China became a land of peasant smallholders.

However, communist planners saw rapid industrialization, not peasant farmers, as the key to successful development. With the introduction of the first Stalinist-style five-year plan in 1953, the communist leaders turned away from the peasantry, which had brought them to power, to the urban workers as the hope for a new China. With little foreign assistance from either the West or the Soviet bloc, the state resorted to stringent measures to draw resources from the countryside to finance industrial growth. Some advances were made in industrialization, particularly in heavy industries such as steel. But the shift in direction had consequences that were increasingly unacceptable to Mao and his more radical supporters in the party. State planning and centralization were stressed, party bureaucrats greatly increased their power and influence, and an urban-based privileged class of technocrats began to develop. These changes, and the external threat to China posed by the U.S. intervention in Korea and continuing U.S.-China friction, led Mao and his followers to force a change of strategies in the mid-1950s.

Mao had long nurtured a deep hostility toward elitism, which he associated with the discredited Confucian system. He had little use for Lenin's vision of revolution from above, led by a disciplined cadre of professional political activists. He distrusted intellectuals, disliked specialization, and clung to his faith in the peasants rather than the workers as the repository of basic virtue and the driving force of the revolution. Acting to stem the trend toward an elitist, urban-industrial focus, Mao and his supporters pushed the **Mass Line** approach, beginning with the formation of agricultural cooperatives in 1955. In the following year, cooperatives became farming collectives that soon accounted for more than 90 percent of China's peasant population. The peasants had enjoyed their own holdings for less than three years. As had occurred earlier in the Soviet Union, the leaders of the revolution, who had originally given the land over to the mass of the peasants, later took it away from them through collectivization.

In 1957 Mao struck at the intellectuals through what may have been a miscalculation or perhaps a clever ruse. Announcing that he wanted to "let a hundred flowers bloom," Mao encouraged professors, artists, and other intellectuals to speak out on the course of development under communist rule. His request stirred up a storm of angry protest and criticism of communist schemes. Having flushed the critics into the open (if the campaign was indeed a ruse) or having been shocked by the vehemence of the response, the party struck with demotions, prison sentences, and banishment to hard labor on the collectives. The flowers rapidly wilted in the face of this betrayal.

## The Great Leap Backward

With political opposition within the party and army apparently in check (or in prison), Mao and his supporters launched the **Great Leap Forward** in 1958. The programs of the Great Leap were a further effort to revitalize the flagging revolution by restoring its mass, rural base. Rather than huge plants located in the cities, industrialization would be pushed through small-scale projects integrated into the peasant communes. Instead of the communes' surplus being siphoned off to build steel mills, industrial development would be aimed at producing tractors, cement for irrigation projects, and other manufactures needed by the peasantry. Enormous publicity was given to efforts to produce steel in "backyard" furnaces (Figure 39.8) that relied on labor rather than machine-intensive techniques. Mao preached the benefits of backwardness and the joys of mass involvement, and he looked forward to the withering away of the meddling bureaucracy. Emphasis was placed on self-reliance within the peasant communes. All aspects of the lives of their members were regulated and regimented by the commune leaders and the heads of the local labor brigades.

Within months after it was launched, all indicators suggested that the Great Leap Forward and rapid collectivization were leading to economic disaster. Peasant resistance to collectivization, the abuses of commune leaders, and the dismal output of the backyard factories combined with drought to turn the Great Leap into a giant step backward. The worst famine of the communist era spread across China. For the first time since 1949, China had to import large amounts of grain to feed its people, and the numbers of Chinese to feed continued to grow at an alarming rate. Defiantly rejecting Western and United Nations proposals for family planning, Mao and like-thinking radicals charged that socialist China could care for its people, no matter how many they were. Birth control was seen as a symptom of capitalist selfishness and inability to provide a decent living for all of the people.

Like those of India, China's birth rates were actually a good deal lower than those of many emerging nations. Also like India, however, the Chinese were adding people to a massive population base. At the time of the communist rise to power, China had approximately 550 million people. By 1965 this had risen to approximately 750 million. By the year 2000, China's population was approximately 1.3 billion.

In the face of the environmental degradation and overcrowding that this leap in population produced, even the party ideologues came around to the view that something must be done to curb the birth rate. Beginning in the mid-1960s, the government launched a nationwide family planning campaign designed to limit urban couples to two children and those in rural areas to one. By the early 1970s, these targets had been revised to two children for either urban or rural cou-

FIGURE 39.8 The famous backyard steel furnaces became a symbol of China's failed drive for self-sufficiency during the disastrous "Great Leap Forward" of the late 1950s.

DOCUMENT

China's One-Child Family Policy

ples. By the 1980s, however, just one child per family was allowed. Although there is evidence of official excesses—undue pressure for women to have abortions, for example—these programs have greatly reduced the birth rate and have begun to slow China's overall population increase. But again, the base to which new births are added is already so large that China's population will not stabilize until well into the 21st century. By that time there will be far more people than now to educate, feed, house, and provide with productive work.

Advances made in the first decade of the new regime were lost through amateurish blunders, excesses of overzealous cadre leaders, and students' meddling. China's national productivity fell by as much as 25 percent. Population increase soon overwhelmed the stagnating productivity of the agricultural and industrial sectors. By 1960 it was clear that the Great Leap must be ended and a new course of development adopted. Mao lost his position as state chairman (although he remained the head of the party's Central Committee). The **pragmatists,** including Mao's old ally **Zhou Enlai,** along with **Liu Shaoqui** and **Deng Xiaoping,** came to power determined to restore state direction and market incentives at the local level.

## "Women Hold Up Half of the Heavens"

In Mao's struggles to renew the revolutionary fervor of the Chinese people, his wife, **Jiang Qing,** played an increasingly prominent role. Mao's reliance on her was consistent with the commitment to the liberation of Chinese women he had acted upon throughout his political career. As a young man he had been deeply moved by a newspaper story about a young girl who had committed suicide rather than be forced by her family to submit to the marriage they had arranged for her with a rich but very old man. From that point onward, women's issues and women's support for the communist movement became important parts of Mao's revolutionary strategy. Here he was drawing on a well-established revolutionary tradition, for women had been very active in the Taiping Rebellion of the mid-19th century, the Boxer revolt in 1900, and the 1911 revolution that had toppled the Manchu regime. One of the key causes taken up by the May Fourth intellectuals, who had a great impact on the youthful Mao Zedong, was women's rights. Their efforts put an end to footbinding. They also did much to advance campaigns to end female seclusion, win legal rights for women, and open educational and career opportunities to them.

The attempts by the Nationalists in the late 1920s and 1930s to reverse many of the gains made by women in the early revolution brought many women into the communist camp. Led by Chiang's wife, Madam Chiang Kai-shek, the Nationalist counteroffensive (like comparable movements in the fascist countries of Europe at the time) tried to return Chinese women to the home and hearth. Madam Chiang proclaimed a special Good Mother's Day and declared that for women, "virtue was more important than learning." She taught that it was immoral for a wife to criticize her husband (an ethical precept she herself ignored regularly).

The Nationalist campaign to restore Chinese women to their traditional domestic roles and dependence on men contrasted sharply with the communists' extensive employment of women to advance the revolutionary cause. Women served as teachers, nurses, spies, truck drivers, and laborers on projects ranging from growing food to building machine-gun bunkers. Although the party preferred to use them in these support roles, in moments of crisis women became soldiers on the front lines. Many won distinction for their bravery under fire. Some rose to become cadre leaders, and many were prominent in the antilandlord campaigns and agrarian reform. Their contribution to the victory of the revolutionary cause bore out Mao's early dictum that the energies and talents of women had to be harnessed to the national cause because "women hold up half of the heavens."

As was the case in many other Asian and African countries, the victory of the revolution brought women legal equality with men—in itself a revolutionary development in a society such as China's. For example, women were given the right to choose their marriage partners without familial interference. But arranged marriages persist today, especially in rural areas, and the need to have party approval for all marriages is a new form of control. Since 1949 women have also been expected to work outside the home. Their opportunities for education and professional careers have improved greatly. As in other socialist states, however, openings for employment outside the home have proved to be a burden for Chinese women. Until the late 1970s, traditional attitudes toward childrearing and home care prevailed. As a result, women were required not only to hold down a regular job but also to raise a family, cook meals, clean, and shop, all without the benefit of the modern appliances available in Western societies.

Although many women held cadre posts at the middle and lower levels of the party and bureaucracy, the upper echelons of both were overwhelmingly controlled by men. The short-lived but impressive power amassed by Jiang Qing in the early 1970s ran counter to these overall trends, but Jiang Qing got to the top because she was married to Mao. She exercised power mainly in his name and was toppled soon after his death when she tried to rule in her own right.

DOCUMENT

## Women in the Revolutionary Struggle

Even more than in the nationalist movements in colonized areas such as India and Egypt, women were drawn in large numbers into revolutionary struggles in areas such as China and Vietnam. The breakdown of the political and social systems weakened the legal and family restrictions that had subordinated women and limited their career choices. The collapse of the Confucian order also ushered in decades of severe crisis and brutal conflict in which women's survival depended on their assumption of radically new roles and their active involvement in revolutionary activities. The following quotations are taken from Vietnamese and Chinese revolutionary writings and interviews with women involved in revolutionary movements in each country. They express the women's goals, their struggle to be taken seriously in the uncharacteristic political roles they had assumed, and some of the many ways women found self-respect and redress for their grievances as a result of the changes wrought by the spread of the new social order.

> Women must first of all be masters of themselves. They must strive to become skilled workers . . . and, at the same time, they must strictly observe family planning. Another major question is the responsibility of husbands to help their wives look after children and other housework.

> We intellectuals had had little contact with the peasants and when we first walked through the village in our Chinese gowns or skirts the people would just stare at us and talk behind our backs. When the village head beat gongs to call out the women to the meeting we were holding for them, only men and old women came, but no young ones. Later we found out that the landlords and rich peasants had spread slanders among the masses saying "They are a pack of wild women. Their words are not for young brides to hear."

> Brave wives and daughters-in-law, untrammelled by the presence of their menfolk, could voice their own bitterness . . . encourage their poor sisters to do likewise, and thus eventually bring to the village-wide gatherings the strength of "half of China" as the more enlightened women, very much in earnest, like to call themselves. By "speaking pains to recall pains," the women found that they had as many if not more grievances than the men, and that given a chance to speak in public, they were as good at it as their fathers and husbands.

> In Chingtsun the work team found a woman whose husband thought her ugly and wanted to divorce her. She was very depressed until she learned that under the Draft Law [of the Communist party] she could have her own share of land. Then she cheered up immediately. "If he divorces me, never mind," she said. "I'll get my share and the children will get theirs. We can live a good life without him."

**Questions** On the basis of these quotations, identify the traditional roles and attitudes toward women (explored in earlier chapters on China and Vietnam) that women engaged in revolutionary movements in China and Vietnam have rejected. What do they believe is essential if women are to gain equality with men? How do the demands of the women supporting these revolutionary movements compare with those of women's rights advocates in the United States?

### Mao's Last Campaign and the Fall of the Gang of Four

Having lost his position as head of state but still the most powerful and popular leader in the Communist party, Mao worked throughout the early 1960s to establish grassroots support for yet another renewal of the revolutionary struggle. He fiercely opposed the efforts of Deng Xiaoping and his pragmatist allies to scale back the communes, promote peasant production on what were in effect private plots, and push economic growth over political orthodoxy. By late 1965, Mao was convinced that his support among the students, peasants, and military was strong enough to launch what would turn out to be his last campaign, the **Cultural Revolution.** With mass student demonstrations paving the way, he launched an all-out assault on the "capitalist-roaders" in the party.

Waving "little red books" of Mao's pronouncements on all manner of issues, the infamous **Red Guard** student brigades (Figure 39.9) publicly ridiculed and abused Mao's political rivals. Liu Shaoqui was killed, Deng Xiaoping was imprisoned, and Zhou Enlai was driven into seclusion. The aroused students and the rank and file of the People's Liberation Army were used to pull down the bureaucrats from their positions of power and privilege. College professors, plant managers, and the children of the bureaucratic elite were berated and forced to confess publicly their many crimes against "the people." Those who were not imprisoned or, more rarely, killed were forced to do manual labor on rural communes to enable them to understand the hardships endured by China's peasantry. In cities such as Shanghai, workers seized control of the factories and local bureaucracy. As Mao had hoped, the centralized state and technocratic elites that

FIGURE 39.9 Mao Zedong and his allies launched the Cultural Revolution during the mid-1960s in an effort to restore the revolutionary fervor that they felt had been eroded by the growing bureaucratization of China. In this photo a crowd of Mao's zealous young supporters rally in Beijing. The vicious assaults on anyone branded as elitist or pro-Western led to torture, imprisonment, and killings on a scale that is not yet fully understood. As the movement degenerated into mindless radicalism for its own sake, many of the gains a more moderate approach had made in the preceding decade were lost.

had grown steadily since the first revolution won power in 1949 were being torn apart by the rage of the people.

However satisfying for advocates of continuing revolution such as Mao, it was soon clear that the Cultural Revolution threatened to return China to the chaos and vulnerability of the prerevolutionary era. The rank-and-file threat to the leaders of the People's Liberation Army eventually proved decisive in prompting countermeasures that forced Mao to call off the campaign by late 1968. The heads of the armed forces moved to bring the rank and file back into line; the student and worker movements were disbanded and in some cases forcibly repressed. By the early 1970s, Mao's old rivals had begun to surface again. For the next half decade, a hard-fought struggle was waged at the upper levels of the party and the army for control of the government. The reconciliation between China and the United States that was negotiated in the early 1970s suggested that, at least in foreign policy, the pragmatists were gaining the upper hand over the ideologues. Deng's growing role in policy formation from 1973 onward also represented a major setback for Jiang Qing, who led the notorious **Gang of Four** that increasingly contested power on behalf of the aging Mao.

The death in early 1976 of Zhou Enlai, who was second only to Mao in stature as a revolutionary hero and who had consistently backed the pragmatists, appeared to be a major blow to those whom the Gang of Four had marked out as "capitalist-roaders" and betrayers of the revolution. But Mao's death later in the same year cleared the way for an open clash between the rival factions. While the Gang of Four plotted to seize control of the government, the pragmatists acted in alliance with some of the more influential military leaders. The Gang of Four were arrested, and their supporters' attempts to foment popular insurrections were foiled easily. Later tried for their crimes against the people, Jiang Qing and the members of her clique were purged from the party and imprisoned for life after their death sentences were commuted.

Since the death of Mao, the pragmatists have been ascendant, and leaders such as Deng Xiaoping have opened China to Western influences and capitalist development, if not yet democratic reform. Under Deng and his allies, the farming communes were discontinued and private peasant production for the market was encouraged. Private enterprise has also been promoted in the industrial sector, and experiments have been made with such capitalist institutions as a stock exchange and foreign hotel chains.

Although it has become fashionable to dismiss the development schemes of the communist states as misguided failures, the achievements of the communist regime in China in the late 20th and early 21st centuries have been impressive. Despite severe economic setbacks, political turmoil, and a low level of foreign assistance, the communists have managed a truly revolutionary redistribution of the wealth of the country. China's very large population remains poor, but in education, health care, housing, working conditions, and the availability of food, most of it is far better off than it was in the prerevolutionary era. The Chinese have managed to provide a decent standard of living for a higher proportion of their people than perhaps any other large developing country. They have also achieved higher rates of industrial and agricultural growth than neighboring India, with its mixed state–capitalist economy and democratic polity. The Chinese have done all of this with much less foreign assistance than most developing nations have had. If the pragmatists remain in power and the champions of the market economy are right, China's growth in the 21st century should be even more impressive. But the central challenge for China's leaders will be to nurture that growth and the improved living standards without a recurrence of the economic inequities and social injustice that brought about the revolution in the first place.

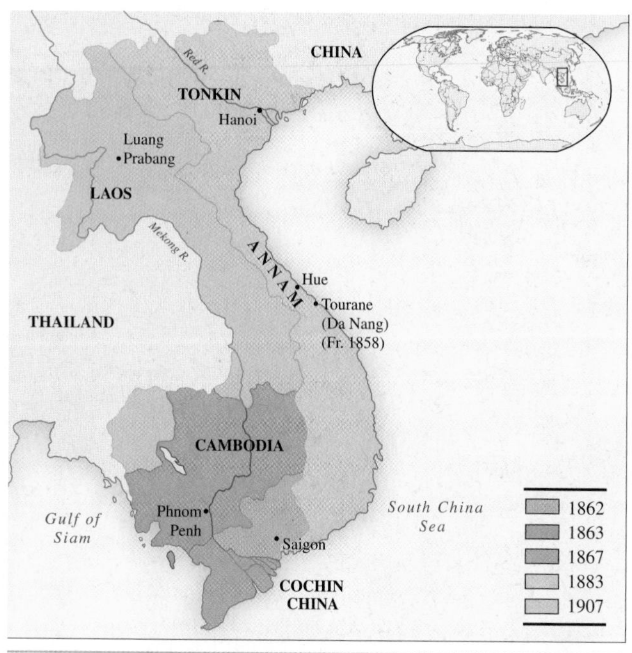

MAP 39.3 Vietnam: Divisions in the Nguyen and French Periods

## Colonialism and Revolution in Vietnam

**The Vietnamese, as well as their neighbors in Laos and Cambodia, were brought under European colonial rule in the second half of the 19th century. As in China, the collapse of the Confucian system around which the Vietnamese had organized civilized life for nearly two millennia led to violent revolution and a search for a viable social and political order that brought a communist regime to power.**

French interest in Vietnam reached back as far as the 17th century. Driven from Japan by the founders of the Tokugawa shogunate, French missionaries fell back on coastal Vietnam. Vietnam attracted them both because its Confucian elite seemed similar to that of the Japanese and because the continuing wars between rival dynastic houses in the Red River valley and central Vietnam gave the missionaries ample openings for their conversion efforts (Map 39.3). From this time onward, French rulers, who considered themselves the protectors of the Catholic missions overseas, took an interest in Vietnamese affairs. As the numbers of converts grew into the tens of thousands and French merchants began to trade at Vietnamese ports, the French stake in the region increased.

By the late 18th century, French involvement had become distinctly political as a result of the power struggles that convulsed the whole region. In the south, a genuine peasant rebellion, the **Tayson Rebellion,** toppled the Nguyen dynasty in the late 1770s. In the years that followed, the Trinh dynasty, the northern rival of the Nguyen, was also dethroned. The Tayson controlled most of the country, eliminated the Trinh, and all but wiped out the Nguyen. Seeing a chance to win influence in the ruling house, the French head of the Vietnam mission, the bishop of Adran, threw his support behind the one surviving prince of the southern house, **Nguyen Anh.**

Anh had fled into the Mekong wilderness with a handful of supporters, thus escaping death at the hands of the Tayson. With the arms and advice of the French, he rallied local support for the dynasty and soon fielded a large army. After driving the Tayson from the south, Nguyen Anh launched an invasion of Tayson strongholds in the north. His task of conquest was made easier by bitter quarrels between the Tayson leaders. By 1802 the Nguyen armies had prevailed, and Nguyen Anh had proclaimed himself the Gia Long emperor of Vietnam.

Gia Long made the old Nguyen capital at Hue in central Vietnam the imperial capital of a unified Vietnam. His French missionary allies were rewarded with a special place at court, and French traders were given greater access to the port of Saigon, which was rapidly emerging as the leading city of the Mekong River valley region in the south. The Nguyen dynasty was the first in centuries to rule all of Vietnam and the first to rule a Vietnamese kingdom that included both the Red River and Mekong deltas. In fact, the Mekong region had only begun to be settled extensively by Vietnamese in the century or so before Gia Long rose to power.

Gia Long and his successors proved to be archtraditionalists deeply committed to strengthening Confucianism in Vietnam. Their capital at Hue was intended to be a perfect miniature of the imperial palace at Beijing. The dynasty patronized Confucian schools and built its administration around scholar-bureaucrats who were well versed in Confucian learning. The second emperor, **Minh Mang** (1820–1841), prided himself on his knowledge of the Confucian classics and his mastery of the Chinese script. He even had the audacity to criticize the brushwork of the reigning Chinese emperor, who was not any more Chinese than Minh Mang but was descended from Manchu nomads. All of this proved deeply disappointing to the French missionaries, who hoped to baptize Gia Long and then carry out through the Vietnamese the sort of top-down conversion that the Jesuits had hoped for ever since their arrival in Asia.

Things actually got much worse. Gia Long's ultra-Confucian successor, Minh Mang, came to see the Catholics as a danger to the dynasty. His persecution of the Vietnamese Catholic community not only enraged the missionaries but also contributed to the growing political and military intervention of the French government in the region. Pushed both by political pressures at home and military defeats in Europe, French adventurers and soldiers exploited quarrels with the Nguyen rulers to justify the piecemeal conquest of Vietnam and neighboring Cambodia and Laos beginning in the late 1840s (Map 39.3). By the 1890s, the whole of the country was under French control, and the Nguyen dynasty had been reduced to the status of puppet princes. In the decades that followed, the French concentrated on drawing revenue and resources from Vietnam while providing very little in return.

The French determination to make Vietnam a colony that was profitable for the homeland worsened social and economic problems that were already severe under the Nguyen rulers. Most of the densely packed peasant population of the north lacked enough land for a subsistence livelihood. French taxes and the burden of obligatory purchases by each village of set amounts of government-sold opium and alcohol drove many peasants into labor in the mines. Even larger numbers left their ancestral villages and migrated to the Mekong region to work on the plantations established there by French and Chinese entrepreneurs. Other migrants chose to become tenants on the great estates that had been carved out of sparsely settled frontier regions by Vietnamese and Chinese landlords.

Migration brought little relief. Plantation workers were paid little and were treated much like slave laborers. The unchecked demands of the Mekong landlords left their tenants with scarcely enough of the crops they grew to feed, clothe, and house their families. The exploitive nature of French colonialism in Vietnam was graphically revealed by the statistics the French themselves collected. These showed a sharp drop in the food consumed by the peasantry in all parts of the colony between the early 1900s and the 1930s, a drop that occurred despite the fact that Vietnam became one of the world's major rice-exporting areas.

## Vietnamese Nationalism: Bourgeois Dead Ends and Communist Survival

The failure of the Nguyen rulers after Minh Mang to rally the forces of resistance against the French did much to discredit the dynasty. But from the 1880s into the first decades of the 20th century, guerrilla warfare was waged in various parts of the country in support of the "Save the King" movement. Because this resistance was localized and small, the French were able to crush it on a piecemeal basis. In any case, French control over the puppet emperors who remained on the throne at Hue left the rebels with little cause worth fighting for. The failure of the Nguyen and the Confucian bureaucratic classes to defend Vietnam against the French did much to discredit the old order in the eyes of the new generations that came of age in the early decades of French rule. Perhaps because it was imported rather than homegrown, the Vietnamese were quicker than the Chinese to reject Confucianism once its failings were clear, and they did so with a good deal less trauma. But its demise left an ideological and institutional vacuum that the Vietnamese, again like the Chinese, would struggle for decades to fill.

In the early 20th century, a new Western-educated middle class, similar to that found in other colonial settings (see Chapters 29 and 33), was formed. It was made up mainly of the children of the traditional Confucian elite and the emerging landlord class in the Mekong region. Some, taking advantage of their parents' wealth, went to French schools and emerged speaking fluent French and with a taste for French fashions and frequent holiday jaunts to Paris and the French Riviera. Many of them went to work for the French as colonial administrators, bank managers, and even labor recruiters. Others pursued independent careers as lawyers, doctors, and journalists. Many who opted for French educations and French lifestyles were soon drawn into nationalist organizations. Like their counterparts elsewhere in the colonies, the members of these organizations initially concentrated on protesting French racism and discrimination, improving their wages, and gaining access to positions in the colonial government held by French people.

As in other colonies, nationalist newspapers and magazines proliferated. These became the focal point of an extended debate over the approach that should be taken toward winning freedom from French rule and, increasingly, what needed to be done to rebuild Vietnam as a whole. Because the French forcibly repressed all attempts to mount peaceful mass demonstrations or organize constitutional agitation, those who argued for violent resistance eventually gained the upper hand. In the early 1920s, the nationalist struggle was centered in the clandestine **Vietnamese Nationalist party** (Vietnamese Quoc Dan Dong, or VNQDD), which was committed to violent revolution against the French colonizers. Although the VNQDD made some attempt to organize urban laborers and peasant villagers, the party members were drawn overwhelmingly from the children of the landlord elite and urban professional classes. Their secret codes and elaborate rituals proved little protection against the dreaded Sûreté, or French secret police. A series of failed uprisings, culminating in a 1929 attempt to spark a general revolution with the assassination of a much-hated French official in charge of labor recruitment, decimated the party. It was particularly hard hit by the ensuing French campaign of repression, execution, and imprisonment. From that point onward, the bourgeois nationalists were never again the dominant force in the struggle for independence.

The demise of the VNQDD left its major rival, the **Communist party of Vietnam,** as the main focus of nationalist resistance in Vietnam. As in China and Korea, the communist wing of the nationalist movement had developed in Vietnam during the 1920s, often at the initiative of leaders in exile. By the late 1920s, the party was dominated by the charismatic young Nguyen Ai Quoc, who would later be known as **Ho Chi Minh.** Ho had discovered Marxism while studying in France and Russia during and after World War I. Disillusioned by his failure to gain a hearing for his plea for the Vietnamese right to self-determination at the post–World War I Paris Peace Conference, Ho dedicated himself to a revolutionary struggle to drive the French from Indochina.

Frantz Fanon and Ho Chi Minh Speak Out Against Imperialism

In the early 1930s, the Communist party still held to the rigid but unrealistic orthodox vision of a revolution based on the urban working classes. Because the workers in Vietnam made up as small a percentage of the population as they had in China, the orthodox strategy made little headway. A sudden shift in the early 1930s to a peasant emphasis, in part to take advantage of widespread but not communist-inspired peasant uprisings in central Vietnam, led to a disaster almost as great as that which had overtaken the VNQDD a year before. French repression smashed the party hierarchy and drove most of the major communist leaders into exile. But the superior underground organization of the communists and the support they received from the Comintern helped them survive the French onslaught. When the French were weakened by the Japanese invasion of Indochina in 1941, the Vietnamese communists were ready to use the colonizers' setbacks to advance the struggle for national liberation.

## The War of Liberation Against the French

During World War II, operating out of bases in south China, the communist-dominated nationalist movement, known as the **Viet Minh,** established liberated areas throughout the northern Red River delta (Map 39.3). The abrupt end of Japanese rule left a vacuum in Vietnam, which only the Viet Minh was prepared to fill. Its programs for land reform and mass education had wide appeal among the hard-pressed peasants of the north, where they had been propagated during the 1930s and especially during the war. The fact that the Viet Minh actually put their reform and community-building programs into effect in the areas they controlled won them very solid support among the rural population. The Viet Minh's efforts to provide assistance to the peasants during the terrible famine of 1944 and 1945 also convinced the much-abused Vietnamese people that here at last was a political organization genuinely committed to improving their lot.

Under the leadership of general **Vo Nguyen Giap,** the Viet Minh skillfully used guerrilla tactics similar to those devised by Mao in China. These offset the advantages that first the French and then the Japanese enjoyed in conventional firepower. With a strong base of support in much of the rural north and the hill regions, where they had won the support of key non-Vietnamese "tribal" peoples, the Viet Minh forces advanced triumphantly into the Red River delta as the Japanese withdrew. By August 1945, the Viet Minh were in control of Hanoi, where Ho Chi Minh proclaimed the establishment of the independent nation of Vietnam.

Vietnamese Declaration of Independence

Although the Viet Minh had liberated much of the north, they had very little control in the south. In that part of Vietnam a variety of communist and bourgeois nationalist parties jostled for power. The French, eager to reclaim their colonial empire and put behind them their humiliations at the hands of the Nazis, were quick to exploit this turmoil. With British assistance, the French reoccupied Saigon and much of south and central Vietnam. In March 1946, they denounced the August declaration of Vietnamese independence and moved to reassert their colonial control over the whole of Vietnam and the rest of Indochina. An unsteady truce between the French and the Viet Minh quickly broke down. Soon Vietnam was consumed by a renewal of the Viet Minh's guerrilla war for liberation, as well as bloody infighting between the different factions of the Vietnamese.

After nearly a decade of indecisive struggle, the Viet Minh had gained control of much of the Vietnamese countryside, and the French, with increasing American financial and military aid, clung to the fortified towns. In 1954 the Viet Minh decisively defeated the French by capturing the giant fortress they had built at **Dien Bien Phu** in the mountain highlands hear the Laotian border. The victory gained international recognition at a 1954 conference in Geneva for an independent state, the Democratic Republic of Vietnam, in the north. At Geneva, elections throughout

Vietnam were also promised in the treaty within two years to decide who should govern a reunited north and the still politically fragmented south.

## The War of Liberation Against the United States

In Geneva, some hoped that free elections would eventually be held to determine who should govern a united Vietnam. However, this electoral contest never materialized. Like the rest of east Asia, Vietnam had become entangled in the cold war maneuvers of the United States and the Soviet Union. Despite very amicable cooperation between the Viet Minh and U.S. armed forces during the war against Japan, U.S. support for the French in the First Indochina War and the growing fame of Ho Chi Minh as a communist leader drove the two further and further into opposition. The anticommunist hysteria in the United States in the early 1950s fed the perception of influential American leaders that South Vietnam, like South Korea, must be protected from communist takeover.

The search for a leader to build a government in the south that the United States could prop up with economic and military assistance led to **Ngo Dinh Diem.** Diem appeared to have impeccable nationalist credentials. In fact, he had gone into exile rather than give up the struggle against the French. His sojourn in the United States in the 1940s and the fact that he was Catholic also recommended him to American politicians and clergy. Unfortunately, these same attributes would alienate him from the great majority of the Vietnamese people.

With U.S. backing, Diem was installed as the president of Vietnam. He tried to legitimatize his status in the late 1950s by holding rigged elections in the south, in which the communists were not permitted to run. Diem also mounted a series of campaigns to eliminate by force all possible political rivals. Because the communists posed the biggest threat (and were of the greatest concern to Diem's American backers), the suppression campaign increasingly focused on the communist cadres that remained in the south after Vietnam had been divided at Geneva. By the mid-1950s, the **Viet Cong** (as the Diem regime dubbed the communist resistance) were threatened with extermination. In response to this threat, the communist regime in the north began to send weapons, advisors, and other resources to the southern cadres, which were reorganized as the National Liberation Front in 1960.

As guerrilla warfare spread and Diem's military responses expanded, both the United States and the North Vietnamese escalated their support for the warring parties. When Diem proved unable to stem the communist tide in the countryside, the United States authorized his generals to overthrow him and take direct charge of the war. When the Vietnamese military could make little headway, the United States stepped up its military intervention.

From thousands of special advisors in the early 1950s, the U.S. commitment rose to nearly 500,000 men and women, who made up a massive force of occupation by 1968. But despite the loss of nearly 60,000 American lives and millions of Vietnamese casualties, the Americans could not defeat the communist movement. In part, their failure resulted from their very presence, which made it possible for the communists to convince the great majority of the Vietnamese people that they were fighting for their independence from yet another imperialist aggressor.

Although more explosives were dropped on tiny Vietnam, North and South, than in all of the theaters of World War II, and the United States resorted to chemical warfare against the very environment of the South Vietnamese they claimed to be trying to save, the communists would not yield. The Vietnamese emerged as the victors of the Second Indochina War. In the early 1970s, U.S. diplomats negotiated an end to direct American involvement in the conflict. Without that support, the unpopular military regime in the south fell apart by 1975 (Figure 39.10). The communists united Vietnam under a single government for

**FIGURE 39.10** April 30, 1975. As the victorious Viet Cong entered Saigon, a photographer captured the image of a lone woman hurrying along a road strewn with uniforms abandoned by former South Vietnamese soldiers fearful of being identified as having fought on the losing side.

the first time since the late 1850s. But the nation they governed was shattered and impoverished by decades of civil war, revolution, and armed conflict with two major colonial powers and the most powerful nation of the second half of the 20th century.

## After Victory: The Struggle to Rebuild Vietnam

In the years since 1975 and the end of what was, for the Vietnamese, decades of wars for liberation, communist efforts to complete the revolution by rebuilding Vietnamese society have failed. In part, this failure can be linked to Vietnam's isolation from much of the rest of the international community. This isolation resulted in part from pressures applied by a vengeful United States against relief from international agencies. It was increased by border clashes with China that were linked to ancient rivalries between the two countries. Deprived of assistance from abroad and faced with a shattered economy and a devastated environment at home, Vietnam's aging revolutionary leaders pushed hard-line Marxist-Leninist (and even Stalinist) political and economic agendas. Like their Chinese counterparts, they devoted their energies to persecuting old enemies (thus setting off mass migrations from what had been South Vietnam) and imposed a dictatorial regime that left little room for popular responses to government initiatives. In contrast to the Chinese in the past decade, however, the Vietnamese leadership also tried to maintain a highly centralized command economy. The rigid system that resulted stifled growth and, if anything, left the Vietnamese people almost as impoverished as they had been after a century of colonialism and decades of civil war.

By the late 1980s, the obvious failure of these approaches and the collapse of communist regimes throughout eastern Europe prompted measures aimed at liberalizing and expanding the market sector within the Vietnamese economy. The encouraging responses of Japanese and European corporations, eager to open up Vietnamese markets, have done much to stimulate growth in the Vietnamese economy. Growing investments by their industrial rivals have placed increasing pressure on American firms to move into the Vietnamese market (Figure 39.11). These trends have been strengthened by the genuine willingness shown by Vietnamese leaders in the past decade to work with U.S. officials to resolve questions about prisoners of war and soldiers missing in action from the Vietnam War. But, like many other postcolonial nations, Vietnam has paid a high price for its efforts at integration into the globalizing economy. Many of its workers have had to endure the sweatshop conditions widely found in foreign factories, social inequality has increased markedly, and the free education system and other public services once provided by the communist state have declined or have entirely disappeared.

**FIGURE 39.11** By the mid-1990s, the failed efforts of the United States to isolate Vietnam gave way to increasing economic and diplomatic contacts. One example of American corporate penetration is depicted in this street scene from Hanoi in 1993. The opening of Vietnam to foreign investment, assistance, and tourism accelerated through the 1990s. In this atmosphere it has been possible to begin to heal the deep wounds and animosities generated by decades of warfare waged by the Vietnamese people against advanced industrial nations such as Japan, France, and the United States.

GLOBAL CONNECTIONS

## East Asia and the Pacific Rim in the Contemporary World

In many respects, the recent histories of China and the peoples of Japan, Korea, and Vietnam, whose cultures were so profoundly affected by Chinese civilization, have been fundamentally different from those of much of the rest of Asia and Africa. Particularly in the past century, the experience of the Japanese has diverged the most from those of other Asian and African peoples. The ethnically homogeneous, politically unified, and militarily adept Japanese not only were able to beat off Western imperialist advances against their island home but they have been one of the few non-Western peoples to achieve a high level of industrialization. Within decades of the forced "opening" of Japan by the United States in the 1850s, it also became the only African or Asian nation to join the ranks of the great powers. In imitation of its Western rivals, Japan embarked on its own campaign of imperialist expansion overseas. Although Korea was colonized early in the 20th century by its powerful Japanese neighbor, in the decades since World War II it has emerged as one of the leading industrial centers of the Pacific Rim. Since World War II, Taiwan and several other east Asian centers experienced rapid industrial advances, propelling the Pacific Rim to new importance in world affairs.

In contrast to industrialized Japan and to Korea in the past four decades or so, with their high standards of living and global economic power, China and Vietnam have had a good deal in common with the rest of the emerging nations. China and Vietnam suffered heavily from the assaults and exploitive terms of exchange imposed by imperialist powers, both Western and Japanese. Each has had to contend with underdevelopment, overpopulation, poverty, and environmental degradation. But unlike most of the rest of the formerly colonized peoples, the Chinese and the Vietnamese have had to deal with these awesome challenges in the midst of the collapse of the patterns of civilized life each had followed for thousands of years.

As disruptive as imperialist conquest and its effects were in the rest of the Asian and African worlds, most colonized peoples managed to preserve much of their precolonial cultures and modes of social organization. The defense and revival of traditional customs, religious beliefs, and social arrangements played a key role in their struggles for decolonization. This was not the case in China and Vietnam, where a combination of external aggression and internal upheavals discredited and destroyed the Confucian system that had long been synonymous with civilized life. With their traditional order in shambles, the peoples of China and Vietnam had no choice but to embark on full-scale revolutions that would clear away the rubble of the failed Confucian system. They needed to remove the obstacles posed by imperialist dominance and build new, viable states and societies. In contrast to much of the rest of the colonized world, the countries of China and Vietnam derived few benefits from European domination, either informal or formal. Imperialist pressures eroded and smashed their political institutions rather than building up a bureaucratic grid and imparting political ideologies that could form the basis for nation-building. Both China and Vietnam already had the strong sense of identity, common language, and unifying polity that were among the major legacies of colonialism in other areas.

Because of economic development (in the Pacific Rim, and more recently in China and Vietnam) and the forces of revolution, east Asia has been fundamentally recast in the decades since World War II and has gained new importance in world affairs. Patterns vary, between the combination of industrialization and reform of the Pacific Rim, in close connection to the West, and the fluctuations of major revolutionary movements, followed by a post-Maoist adoption of what one observer aptly dubbed "Market-Leninism" in China and Vietnam in recent decades. The legacy of earlier patterns in east Asia, including Confucianism, has similarly been redefined and utilized in different ways. But the themes of growing independence and self-assertion have been combined across east Asia in recent years with ongoing or new experiments in Western-style capitalism, replacing Confucianism as the state ideology and providing the philosophical basis for the new social order.

Revolution and economic change have combined to make east Asia a growing force in world affairs by the early 21st century—and of course, largely independent of Western control in contrast to the previous period of imperialism. China's size and post-revolutionary economic surge, which has come to exceed even that of the rest of the Pacific Rim nations, has prompted some observers to wonder if the twenty-first century will be the "century of east Asia." China, Japan, and South Korea have become centers of multinational corporations, along with the West. East Asian exports, including toys like Pokemon and animated films are now staples of global consumer culture. Japanese, Korean, and more recently Chinese scientific capacity in areas like supercomputing have made them major global innovators, while China and Japan have come to play growing roles in space technology. China, Japan, and Korea have also become prominent participants in global athletic competitions. In various ways, including standard diplomatic and economic channels, the nations of east Asia have come to exert more influence in world affairs than ever before. Their growing predominance in all of these areas ensures that the peoples of east Asia will shape human history in the 21st century in major, perhaps transformative, ways.

## Further Readings

The best account of contemporary Japanese society and politics is E. O. Reischauer, *The Japanese* (1988). For a recent history, see M. Hane, *Modern Japan: A Historical Survey* (1992); William G. Beasley, *The Rise of Modern Japan* (1995); and Edward R. Beauchamp, ed., *Women and Women's Issues in Post World War II Japan* (1998).

Several novels and literary collections are accessible and useful. J. Tanizaki, *The Makioka Sisters* (1957), deals with a merchant family in the 1930s; see also H. Hibbett, ed., *Contemporary Japanese Literature: An Anthology of Fiction, Film, and Other Writing Since 1945* (1992). An important study of change, focusing on postwar rural society, is G. Bernstein, *Haruko's World: A Japanese Farm Woman and Her Community* (1983). Another complex 20th-century topic is assessed in R. Storry, *The Double Patriots: A Story of Japanese Nationalism* (1973).

On the Pacific Rim concept and its implications in terms of the world economy, see David Aikman, *Pacific Rim: Area of Change, Area of Opportunity* (1986); Philip West et al., eds., *The Pacific Rim and the Western World: Strategic, Economic, and Cultural Perspectives* (1987); Stephen Haggard and Chung-In Moon, *Pacific Dynamics: The International Politics of Industrial Change* (1988); and Roland A. Morse et al., *Pacific Basin: Concept and Challenge* (1986). Vera Simone, *The Asian Pacific: Political and Economic Development in a Global Context* (1995), is a comparative survey of postcolonial state building and international cultural connections. Also see S. Ichimura, *The Political Economy of Japanese and Asian Development* (1998).

Excellent introductions to recent Korean history are Bruce Cumings, *The Two Koreas* (1984) and *Korea's Place in the Sun: A Modern History* (1997), and David Rees, *A Short History of Modern Korea* (1988). A variety of special topics are addressed in Marshal R. Pihl, ed., *Listening to Korea: Economic Transformation and Social Change* (1989). See also Paul Kuznet, *Economic Growth and Structure in the Republic of Korea* (1977), and Dennis McNamara, *The Colonial Origins of Korean Enterprise, 1910–1945* (1990).

For a fascinating exploration of cultural change and continuity in Taiwan regarding issues in health and medicine, see Arthur Kleinman, *Patients and Healers in the Context of Culture* (1979). On Singapore, Janet W. Salaff, *State and Family in Singapore* (1988), is an excellent study; see also R. N. Kearney, ed., *Politics and Modernization in South and Southeast Asia* (1975).

A good summary of the final stages of the civil war in China is provided in Lucien Bianco, *Origins of the Chinese Revolution, 1915–1949* (1971). Perhaps the best overview of modern Chinese history from the Qing dynasty era through the Tiananmen Square massacres can be found in Jonathan D. Spence, *The Search for Modern China* (1990). Other useful accounts of the post-1949 era include Maurice Meisner, *Mao's China and After 1984* (1984); Michael Gasster, *China's Struggle to Modernize* (1987); and Immanuel C. Y. Hsu, *China Without Mao* (1983). On the pivotal period of the Cultural Revolution, see Roderick MacFarquhar, *The Origins of the Cultural Revolution*, 2 vols. (1974, 1983), and Lowell Dittmer, *Liu Shao-ch'i and the Chinese Cultural Revolution* (1974). For a highly critical assessment of the Maoist era, it is difficult to surpass Simon Leys, *Chinese Shadows* (1977). On cultural life in the postrevolutionary era, see the essays in R. MacFarquhar, ed., *The Hundred Flowers Campaign and the Chinese Intellectuals*, and Lois Wheeler Snow, *China on Stage* (1972). Elisabeth Croll, *Feminism and Socialism in China* (1978), remains by far the best single work on the position of women in revolutionary and Maoist China.

The first war of liberation in Vietnam is covered in Ellen J. Hammer, *The Struggle for Indochina, 1940–1955* (1966). The best of many surveys of the second war, often called the American War in Vietnam, is Marilyn Young, *The Vietnam Wars, 1945–1990* (1989). Of a number of fine studies on the origins of American intervention in the area, two of the best are Archimedes Patti, *Why Vietnam?* (1980), and Lloyd Gardner, *Approaching Vietnam* (1988). On the conduct of the war, Jeffrey Races, *The War Comes to Long An* (1972); Eric Bergerud, *The Dynamics of Defeat: The Vietnam War in Hau Nghia Province* (1991); and Marc Jason Gilbert, ed., *Why the North Won the Vietnam War* (2002), are useful for the stress they place on the role of the Vietnamese in determining this conflict's course and ultimate outcome. Powerful firsthand accounts of the guerrilla war and U.S. combat include Mark Baker, *Nam* (1981); Philip Caputo, *A Rumor of War* (1977); and Troung Nhu Tang, *A Viet Cong Memoir* (1985).

## On the Web

The career arc of leading personalities in the rise of modern Korea, such as Syngman Rhee (http://www.hartford-hwp.com/archives/55a/186.html and http://us.cnn.com/SPECIALS/cold.war/kbank/profiles/rhee/) and much of the history of postwar Japan was shaped by the Korean War (http://mcel.pacificu.edu/as/students/stanley/home.html). The nature of the Korean economy and the dominant role of large corporate entities, *chaebol*, in postwar Korea are explored at http://www.country-data.com/cgi-bin/query/r-12303.html and http://news.bbc.co.uk/1/hi/in_depth/business/2000/review/1037276.stm, where they are compared with Japanese *keiretsu*.

The life of General Douglas MacArthur and the art and society of the occupation or "Confusion" era in Japan are the subject of a brilliant Smithsonian exhibition available online at http://www.smithsonianeducation.org/migrations/sackler/saltfore.html. Japan's difficulty in accepting responsibility for its wartime atrocities, particularly the abuse of Korean and other Asian women by Japanese occupation troops, is discussed at http://online.sfsu.edu/~soh/comfortwomen.html, http://online.sfsu.edu/~soh/cw-links.htm (a links page), and http://taiwan.yam.org.tw/womenweb/conf_women/index_e.html.

Korekiyo Takahashi's role in the building of the modern Japanese economy and his conflict with the war party led by Tojo Hideki is examined at http://

www.ndl.go.jp/portrait/e/datas/122.html?c=0 and http://www.ier.hitu.ac.jp/common/publication/DP/DP395.pdf. The place of Takahashi's policies in today's Japan is examined at http://www.atimes.com/Japan-econ/AB12Dh01.html.

Much of the postwar recovery of east Asian economies was due to close cooperation between business and government, which recently has been criticized even in Japan, where politicians have been caught with trunks full of cash provided by leading Japanese companies. This pattern was followed by the eastern Pacific Rim's economic tigers as part of an authoritarian development strategy, most clearly expressed by Singapore's Lee Kwan Yew, who has made comparisons between himself and Machiavelli (http://www.sfdonline.org/Link%20Pages/Link%20Folders/Political%20Freedom/Machiavelli.html). However, a recent economic recession in the region, discussed in an audio file by Lee Kwan Yew himself at http://www.rice.edu/rtv/speeches/19981023lee.html, has forced some to question whether the east Asian model of economic growth is worthy of emulation elsewhere. A close look at the causes and lessons of the Asian economic crisis of the 1990s (and just now abating) is explored at http://www.parliament.uk/commons/lib/research/rp99/rp99-014.pdf.

CHAPTER

40

# The End of the Cold War and the Shape of a New Era: World History 1990–2006



A human rights activist in Guatemala put the situation this way in the mid-1980s:

> If it were not for the international assistance, primarily from Americas Watch, Amnesty International, the World Council of Churches, solidarity organizations from democratic countries, Canadian organizations, organizations of Guatemalans working in the United States, Canada or Europe, without the moral and political help of those organizations, I believe we would have been dead many years ago, the army would not have permitted our organization to develop. . . . If you don't have the contacts, if the people who are doing the killing know that nobody is going to do anything if you disappear, then you disappear. . . . It was vital to have contacts so that information could go outside.

Many Central American regimes were repressive at the beginning of the 1990s. Their hostility to communism and social revolution earned them support from a conservative president in the United States. Free elections were impossible and many resistance figures were jailed or worse. But the situation changed. Local agitation for democracy would not cease. Instead, it spread in many parts of Latin America. Movement of people between countries played a key role, bringing opportunities for new contacts and for free expression. International human rights organizations took up the cause, organizing massive petition campaigns on behalf of victims. Church groups were active. Labor organizations, from the United States and elsewhere, chimed in, as did European Common Market (European Union) and United Nations human rights groups. Despite the power of the local military and the strength of U.S. policy, there was a new international counterweight, able to publicize abuse and prevent its concealment. Activities of local "death squads" received wide media attention, as did attacks on foreign Christian missionaries. Ultimately, these pressures forced the United States to change its policies, and fledgling democratic regimes began to take shape throughout the region.

Enthusiasm for international definitions of political rights had never run higher. There was a new force in world politics. At the same time, the force had clear limits. In some areas, particularly in conflict-torn regions of Africa, ruling groups resisted international criticism and made no effective effort to stop human rights abuses. How much was the world changing?

FIGURE 40.1 During more than three decades of brutal civil conflict, 200,000 Guatemalans were killed or "disappeared" and more than a million were forced out of their homes. After a peace agreement was signed in 1996, a church commission headed by Bishop Juan José Gerardi investigated the atrocities committed during the civil war and issued a scathing report in which he found that 90 percent of the abuses had been committed by the government. Two days later, the 75-year-old bishop was bludgeoned to death. Here, throngs of mourners witness his funeral procession.

In the last two decades of the 20th century, global history took an abrupt turn. With the remarkably sudden collapse of the Soviet Union and the communist regimes of eastern Europe, the long and tense cold war came to an end. A larger current of expanding democracy provided a context for these developments as well. At the same time, a new set of regional conflicts complicated post–cold war politics, while the emergence of the United States as sole superpower had its own pluses and minuses.

## The End of the Cold War

■ **Strains within the Soviet empire forced reforms that led to its downfall.**

The cold war had lasted for 30 years when its context began to shift. The Russian empire had been expanding, off and on, for 500 years, interrupted only briefly by World War I and the initial phases of the Russian Revolution before it resumed its growth, to unprecedented levels. What could cause these two firmly established patterns, the cold war and the Russian empire, to change course dramatically?

Leadership was surely one component. After Stalin and then Khrushchev, Soviet leadership had turned conservative. Party bureaucrats, eager to protect the status quo, often advanced only mediocre people to top posts, men whose major leadership characteristic was their unwillingness to rock the boat. Many of these leaders then continued to hold power when their own aptitude declined with illness and age.

Of more general significance was the reassertion of initiative from some parts of the world surrounding the Soviet Union, despite continued pressures from the superpowers. The rise of Islamic fervor, evident in the Iranian Revolution of 1979, inevitably created anxiety in the Soviet Union with its large Muslim minority. To reduce this new threat, late in 1979 the Soviets invaded neighboring Afghanistan, hoping to set up a

| 1980 C.E. | 1990 C.E. | 2000 C.E. |
|---|---|---|
| **1988** Soviet withdrawal from Afghanistan<br>**1988–1991** Independence movements in eastern Europe and in minority states in Soviet Union<br>**1989–1990** Collapse of Soviet Union and Warsaw Pact regimes | **1990** Iraqi invasion of Kuwait<br>**1991** Breakup of Soviet Union; Yeltsin to power in Russia; civil wars begin in Yugoslavia; Slovenia and Croatia secede; Persian Gulf War, Iraq defeated<br>**1992** North American Free Trade Agreement (NAFTA) inaugurated; Bosnia withdraws from Yugoslavia; first World Environmental Conference in Brazil<br>**1992–1993** UN-U.S. interventions in Somalia<br>**1994** Mass genocide in Rwanda<br>**1994** U.S. intervention in Haiti<br>**1995** U.S.-NATO interventions in Bosnia<br>**1997** Second World Environmental Conference, Kyoto, Japan<br>**1998** Serbian assault on Albanians in Kosovo<br>**1999** U.S.-NATO war against Yugoslavia; Putin becomes president of Russia | **2000** International Human Rights Conference, South Africa; Milosevic forced out as Serbian president; end of Yugoslav civil wars<br>**2000–2002** Second Intifada in Palestine and Israel<br>**2001** Mass demonstrations against World Trade Organization in Genoa; terrorist attacks on World Trade Center and Pentagon; U.S.–Northern Alliance coalition topples Taliban regime in Afghanistan<br>**2002** India and Pakistan mobilize armies over Kashmir dispute; euro becomes common currency in much of European Union<br>**2003** U.S. and allies bring down Saddam Hussein's government in Iraq<br>**2004–2005** Democratic regimes begin in Georgia, Ukraine; new protests begin in central Asia |

puppet regime that would protect Russian interests; the move drew widespread international disapproval. The war proved difficult, as Afghan guerrillas, with some backing from the United States, held their ground fiercely. Costs and casualties mounted, and the war—the first formal action the Soviets had indulged in since World War II—quickly proved unpopular at home.

At the same time, the success of western Europe's economy pushed communism into a defensive and retreating posture throughout eastern Europe. The attraction of Western institutions and consumer standards gained ground. Within the Soviet empire itself, a free trade union movement resumed in Poland, linked to the Catholic church, and while it was repressed through Soviet-mandated martial law in 1981, the stress of keeping the lid on was likely to increase.

Changes in Chinese policy entered in. China of course had separated itself from Soviet direction in the 1960s. But in 1978 the regime made a choice to participate in the world economy and to admit more market forces and competitive free enterprise in the internal economy as well. There was no relaxation of political controls, and a democratic movement was vigorously quashed in 1989. But the Chinese economy now differed dramatically from that of the Soviet Union, and change was quickly rewarded, both with international investment and with rapid growth. The Soviets now had to contend not only with China's massive population but with its superior economic performance.

Finally, U.S. diplomatic policy tightened. While President Jimmy Carter hoped to reduce tensions in the late 1970s, he was a vigorous human rights advocate, particularly eager to point out Soviet deficiencies. American conservatives heightened their own opposition to the Soviet Union. A new strategic arms limitation agreement (SALT II) was negotiated in 1979 but quickly encountered resistance in the U.S. Senate. Then came the Soviet move into Afghanistan. President Carter reacted vigorously, claiming that the move was a "stepping stone to their possible control over much of the world's oil supplies" and, even more dramatically, the "gravest threat to world peace since World War II." American participation in the 1980 Moscow Olympics was cancelled.

Then, in 1980, the new, conservative president, Ronald Reagan, who had denounced the Soviet Union as an "evil empire," announced a massive increase in U.S. defense spending. The size of domestic programs declined relative to the federal budget as a whole, and some programs were cut outright (promoting, among other things, a surge in homelessness), but conservatives accepted a growing budget deficit in favor of the new military outlays. The president also announced a "Reagan doctrine" of assisting anticommunism anywhere, and followed it up with an invasion of a small, Marxist-controlled Caribbean island, Grenada, and support for anti-Marxist military action in Central America.

These moves put new pressure on the Soviets, already stretched to the limit to maintain military and global competition with the United States, and beset with an unpopular war and new regional pressures as well. The stage was set for the events that, initially promoted for quite different reasons, undid the cold war.

## The Explosion of the 1980s and 1990s

From 1985 onward the Soviet Union entered a period of intensive reform, soon matched by new political movements in eastern Europe that effectively dismantled the Soviet empire. The initial trigger for this extraordinary and unanticipated upheaval lay in the deteriorating Soviet economic performance, intensified by the costs of military rivalry with the United States. There were reasons for pride in the Soviet system, and many observers believed that public attitudes by the 1980s were shaped much less by terror than by satisfaction with the Soviet Union's world prestige and the improvements the communist regime had fostered in education and welfare. But to a degree unperceived outside the Soviet Union, the economy was grinding to a standstill. Forced industrialization had produced extensive environmental deterioration throughout eastern Europe. According to Soviet estimates, half of all agricultural land was endangered by the late 1980s; more than 20 percent of Soviet citizens lived in regions of ecological disaster. Rates and severity of respiratory and other diseases rose, impairing both morale and economic performance. Infant mortality rates also rose in several regions, sometimes nearing the highest levels in the world.

More directly, industrial production began to stagnate and even drop as a result of rigid central planning, health problems, and poor worker morale. Growing inadequacy of housing and consumer goods resulted, further lowering motivation. As economic growth stopped, the percentage of resources allocated to military production escalated, toward a third of all national income. This reduced funds available for other investments or for consumer needs. At first only privately, younger leaders began to recognize that the system was near collapse.

## The Age of Reform

Yet the Soviet system was not changeless, despite its heavy bureaucratization. Problems and dissatisfactions, though controlled, could provoke response beyond renewed repression. After a succession of leaders whose age or health precluded major initiatives, the Soviet Union in 1985 brought a new, younger official to the fore. **Mikhail Gorbachev** quickly renewed some of the earlier attacks on Stalinist rigidity and replaced some of the old-line party bureaucrats (Figure 40.2). He conveyed a new, more Western style, dressing in

FIGURE 40.2 Early in his first administration, President Ronald Reagan referred to the Soviet Union as the "Evil Empire" and showed little interest in cooperating in any way with Moscow. After the accession of Mikhail Gorbachev, Reagan changed his attitude, and the two men worked closely to ease tensions between the two great powers.

fashionable clothes (and accompanied by his stylish wife), holding relatively open press conferences, and even allowing the Soviet media to engage in active debate and report on problems as well as successes. Gorbachev also further altered the Soviet Union's modified cold war stance. He urged a reduction in nuclear armament, and in 1987 he negotiated a new agreement with the United States that limited medium-range missiles in Europe. He ended the war in Afghanistan, bringing Soviet troops home.

Internally, Gorbachev proclaimed a policy of **glasnost,** or openness, which implied new freedom to comment and criticize. He pressed particularly for a reduction in bureaucratic inefficiency and unproductive labor in the Soviet economy, encouraging more decentralized decision making and the use of some market incentives to stimulate greater output. The sweep of Gorbachev's reforms, as opposed to an undeniable new tone in Soviet public relations, remained difficult to assess. Strong limits on political freedom persisted, and it was unclear whether Gorbachev could cut through the centralized planning apparatus that controlled the main lines of the Soviet economy. There was also uncertainty about how well the new leader could balance reform and stability.

Indeed, questions about Gorbachev's prospects recalled many basic issues in Soviet history. In many ways Gorbachev's policies constituted a return to a characteristic ambivalence about the West. He reduced Soviet isolation while continuing to criticize aspects of Western political and social structure. Gorbachev clearly hoped to use some Western management techniques and was open to certain Western cultural styles without, however, intending to abandon basic control of the communist state. Western analysts wondered if the Soviet economy could improve worker motivation without embracing a Western-style consumerism or whether computers could be more widely introduced without allowing freedom for information exchange.

Gorbachev also sought to open the Soviet Union to fuller participation in the world economy, recognizing that isolation in a separate empire had restricted access to new technology and limited motivation to change. Although the new leadership did not rush to make foreign trade or investment too easy—considerable suspicion persisted—the economic initiatives brought symbolic changes, such as the opening of a McDonald's restaurant in Moscow and a whole array of new contacts between Soviet citizens and foreigners (Figure 40.3).

Gorbachev's initial policies did not quickly stir the Soviet economy, but they had immediate political effects, some of which the reform leader had almost certainly not anticipated. The keynote of the reform program was **perestroika,** or economic restructuring, which Gorbachev translated into more leeway for private ownership and decentralized control in industry and agriculture. Farmers, for example, could now lease land for 50 years, with rights of inheritance, and industrial concerns were authorized to buy from either private or state operations. Foreign investment was encouraged. Gorbachev pressed for reductions in Soviet military commitments, particularly through agreements with the United States on troop reductions and limitations on nuclear weaponry, in order to free resources for consumer goods industries. He urged more self-help among the Soviets, including a reduction in drinking, arguing that he wanted to "rid public opinion of . . . faith in a 'good Tsar,' the all powerful center, the notion that someone can bring about order and organize perestroika from on high."

Mikhail Gorbachev on the Need for Economic Reform

Politically, Gorbachev encouraged a new constitution in 1988, giving considerable power to a new parliament, the Congress of People's Deputies, and

FIGURE 40.3 After 14 years of negotiations between McDonald's executives and Soviet government officials, the first McDonald's restaurant opened in Moscow in 1990. Lines formed around the block to get a first taste of the famous fast food.

abolishing the Communist monopoly on elections. Important opposition groups developed both inside and outside the party, pressing Gorbachev between radicals who wanted a faster pace of reform and conservative hard-liners. Gorbachev himself was elected to a new, powerful presidency of the Soviet Union in 1990.

Reform amid continued economic stagnation provoked agitation among minority nationalities in the Soviet Union, from 1988 onward. Muslims and Armenian Christians rioted in the south, both against each other and against the central state. Baltic nationalist and other European minorities also stirred, some insisting on full independence, some only pressing for greater autonomy. Again, results of this diverse unrest were difficult to forecast, but some observers predicted the end of Soviet control of central Asia and the European borderlands.

Even social issues were given uncertain new twists. Gorbachev noted that Soviet efforts to establish equality between the sexes had burdened women with a combination of work and household duties. His solution—to allow women to "return to their purely womanly missions" of housework, childrearing, and "the creation of a good family atmosphere"—had a somewhat old-fashioned ring to it.

## Dismantling the Soviet Empire

Gorbachev's new approach, including his desire for better relations with Western powers, prompted more definitive results outside the Soviet Union than within, as the smaller states of eastern Europe uniformly pushed for greater independence and internal reforms. Bulgaria moved for economic liberalization in 1987 but was held back by the Soviets; pressure resumed in 1989 as the party leader was ousted and free elections were arranged. Hungary changed leadership in 1988 and installed a noncommunist president. A new constitution and free elections were planned; the Communist party renamed itself Socialist. Hungary also reviewed its great 1956 rising, formally declaring it "a popular uprising . . . against an oligarchic system . . . which had humiliated the nation." Hungary moved rapidly toward a free-market economy. Poland installed a noncommunist government in 1988 and again moved quickly to dismantle the state-run economy; prices rose rapidly as government subsidies were withdrawn. The Solidarity movement, born a decade before through a merger of noncommunist labor leaders and Catholic intellectuals, became the dominant political force. East Germany displaced its communist government in 1989, expelling key leaders and moving rapidly toward unification with West Germany. The Berlin Wall was dismantled, and in 1990 noncommunists won a free election (Figure 40.4). German unification occurred in 1991, a dramatic sign of the collapse of postwar Soviet foreign policy. Czechoslovakia installed a new government in 1989, headed by a playwright, and sought to introduce free elections and a more market-driven economy.

Although mass demonstrations played a key role in several of these political upheavals, only in Romania was there outright violence, as an exceptionally authoritarian communist leader was swept out by force. As in Bulgaria, the Communist party retained considerable power, though under new leadership, and reforms moved less rapidly than in Hungary and Czechoslovakia. The same held true for Albania, where

FIGURE 40.4 Breaching the Berlin Wall in 1989: West and East Germany meet.

the unreconstructed Stalinist regime was dislodged and a more flexible communist leadership installed.

New divergences in the nature and extent of reform in eastern Europe were exacerbated by clashes among nationalities, as in the Soviet Union. Change and uncertainty brought older attachments to the fore. Romanians and ethnic Hungarians clashed; Bulgarians attacked a Turkish minority left over from the Ottoman period. In 1991 the Yugoslavian communist regime, though not Soviet dominated, also came under attack, and a civil war boiled up from disputes among nationalities. Minority nationality areas, notably Slovenia, Croatia, and Bosnia-Herzegovina, proclaimed independence, but the national, Serbian-dominated army applied massive force to preserve the Yugoslav nation.

Amid this rapid and unexpected change, prospects for the future became unpredictable. Few of the new governments fully defined their constitutional structure, and amid innovation the range of new political parties almost compelled later consolidations. Like the Soviet Union itself, all the eastern European states suffered from sluggish production, massive pollution, and economic problems that might well lead to new political discontent.

With state controls and protection abruptly withdrawn by 1991, tensions over the first results of the introduction of the market economy in Poland brought rising unemployment and further price increases. These in turn produced growing disaffection from the Solidarity leadership. Diplomatic linkages among small states—a critical problem area between the two world wars—also had yet to be resolved.

The massive change in Soviet policy was clear. Gorbachev reversed postwar imperialism completely, stating that "any nation has the right to decide its fate by itself." In several cases, notably Hungary, Soviet troops were rapidly withdrawn, and generally it seemed unlikely that a repressive attempt to reestablish an empire would be possible (Map 40.1). New contacts with Western nations, particularly in the European Economic Community (European Union), seemed to promise further realignment in the future.

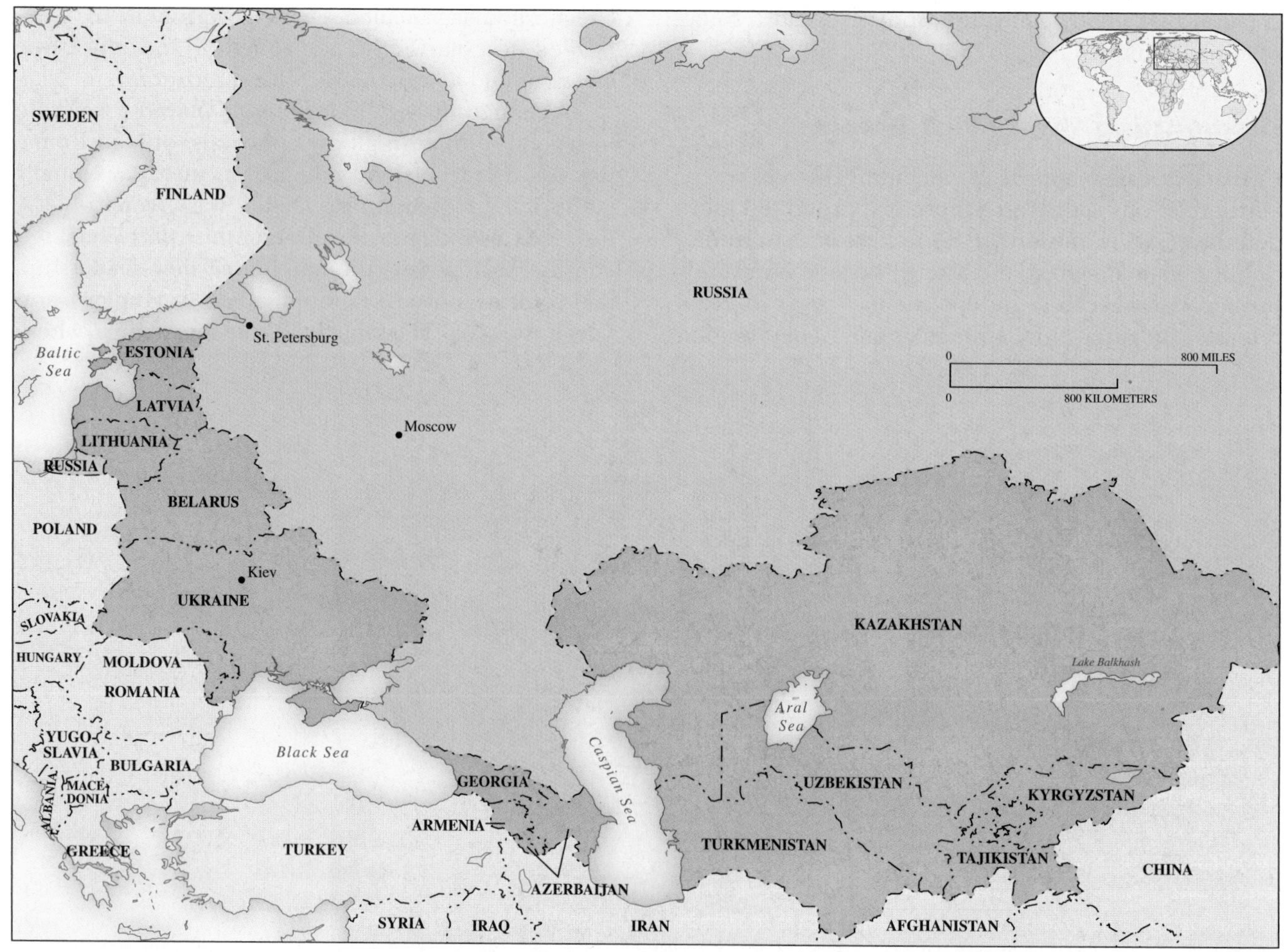


**MAP 40.1 Post–Soviet Union Russia, Eastern Europe, and Central Asia.** With the collapse of the Soviet Union, the boundaries of eastern Europe and central Asia were substantially redrawn.

VISUALIZING THE PAST

## Symbolism in the Breakdown of the Soviet Bloc

Although the majority of Latvians strongly opposed the Soviet takeover of their government in 1939, for fifty years most had been afraid to express their views. After World War II, a strong nationalist resistance movement had arisen, but was harshly suppressed. Tens of thousands of Latvians were killed and many more were imprisoned or deported to Siberia. When, in the late 1980s, Perestroika opened possibilities for change in the Soviet Union, Latvians were quick to act. They elected a new parliament that, in 1990, proclaimed its intention of beginning a transition to independence. Although Soviet hard-liners tried to crack down on Latvian independence advocates, the failed August 1991 coup in Moscow opened the door to Latvian independence. One of the first acts of the Latvians was to topple statues of Soviet leaders like this one of Lenin.

**Questions** Imagine the toppled Lenin statue as it stood on the day it was erected. What do you think the Soviets intended to express to the Latvian people when they placed this statue? What effect might they have hoped it would have? How do you think the Latvians who opposed Soviet rule might have viewed the meaning of the statue? What was the symbolism of toppling the statue? Why might it be one of the first acts of a people liberated from foreign occupation? If you had been in charge of commissioning a statue that would ease tensions between Latvians and their Soviet occupiers, what might you have suggested as a theme? Do you think art can serve the purpose of uniting people in a situation like this one?

As part of the independence of the Baltic nation of Latvia, crowds toppled Soviet symbols—in this case, a giant statue of Lenin—in 1991.

### Renewed Turmoil in the 1990s

The uncertainties of the situation within the Soviet Union were confirmed in the summer of 1991, when an attempted coup was mounted by military and police elements. Gorbachev's presidency and democratic decentralization were both threatened. Massive popular demonstrations, however, asserted the strong democratic current that had developed in the Soviet Union since 1986. The contrast with earlier Soviet history and the suppression of democracy in China two years before was striking.

In the aftermath of the attempted coup, Gorbachev's authority weakened. Leadership of the key republics, including the massive Russian Republic, became relatively stronger. The three Baltic states used the occasion to gain full independence though economic links with the Soviet Union remained. Other minority republics proclaimed independence as well, but Gorbachev struggled to win agreement on continued economic union and some other coordination. By the end of 1991 leaders of the major republics, including Russia's **Boris Yeltsin,** proclaimed the end of the Soviet Union, projecting a commonwealth of the leading republics, including the economically crucial Ukraine, in its stead. Amid the disputes Gorbachev fell from power, doomed by his attempts to salvage a presidency that depended on some survival of a greater Soviet Union. His leadership role was taken over by Boris Yeltsin, who as president of Russia and an early renouncer of communism now emerged as the leading, though quickly beleaguered, political figure. Yeltsin soon used force to bring Russia's parliament under some control (Figure 40.5).

Statue of Lenin Toppled During Soviet Collapse

The former Soviet Union gave way to the loose Commonwealth of Independent States, which won tentative agreement from most of the now independent republics. But tensions immediately surfaced about economic coordination amid rapid dismantling of state controls; about control of the military, where Russia—still by far the largest unit—sought predominance, including nuclear control amid challenges from the Ukraine and from Kazakhstan (two of the other republics with nuclear weaponry on their soil); and about relationships between the European-dominated republics, including Russia, and the cluster of central Asian states. How much unity might survive in the former Soviet Union was unclear. The fate of economic reform was also uncertain. Russian leaders hesitated to convert to a full market system lest transitional disruption further antagonize the population.

Break-up of the Soviet Union

Scientists Examine Russia's Economy and Environment, 1991–1993

**FIGURE 40.5** In the fall of 1993, the Soviet Union teetered on the brink of civil war as Boris Yeltsin's opponents, meeting in the Russian parliament building, sought to remove him from office. Mass street demonstrations led to fighting in which hundreds of people were killed and wounded. Faced with a complete breakdown of public order, the military threw its support to Yeltsin and crushed his opponents in early October. Two months later, a new constitution gave Yeltsin broad powers to carry out his reforms.

By the late 1990s, the leadership of Boris Yeltsin deteriorated as the economy performed badly, individual profiteers pulled in huge fortunes, and Yeltsin's health worsened. A bitter civil war broke out with the Muslim region of Chechnya: terrorist acts by the rebels and brutal military repression seemed to feed each other. A new president, Vladimir Putin, was named in 1999, vowing to clean up corruption and install more effective government controls over separate provinces. Putin declared his commitment to democracy and a free press but also sponsored new attacks on dissident television stations and newspapers. Many Russians seemed to agree that stronger measures were needed—why should a leader tolerate public criticism? Others longed for a return to the Soviet days of greater economic security and national glory. Reformists were able to voice their concerns, but Putin tightened his hold on the state and media, even attacking independent-minded business leaders. He also resisted appeals to compromise on the Chechnya revolt.

## The Spread of Democracy

■ **A dramatic surge of democracy began in the 1970s, spreading worldwide. Fed by the fall of international communism, democracy spread further between 1989 and 2005. Important holdouts and regressions complicated the trend.**

The end of the cold war was associated with another large trend in the world at the end of the 20th century: the spread of multiparty democracy with (reasonably) free elections (Figure 40.6). We have seen that, through much of the century, several different forms of government competed for success amid a general climate of change: communism, fascism, and other forms of authoritarianism, and democracy. But from the late 1970s onward, the tide seemed to turn toward democracy in many regions that had long been inhospitable.

Economic and political success in western Europe, including the drawing power of the Common Market, helped propel Spain, Portugal, and Greece to democratic systems in the mid-1970s, after long periods of authoritarian control. Then the democratic wave hit Latin America, backed by U.S. and western European support. Beginning with new regimes in Argentina and Brazil, authoritarian controls were replaced by free elections (see Chapter 37). The process continued through the 1990s, when literally all Latin American countries except Cuba were in the democratic camp. Revolutionaries in Central America accepted the system in the late 1980s; Paraguay was the final authoritarian regime to yield a decade later. In 2000 Mexico elected its first president from a party other than the PRI, the party that had monopolized control since the revolution.

Democratic systems gained ground in South Korea and Taiwan in the 1980s. In the Philippines, an authoritarian ruler was cast aside, amid considerable popular pressure, in favor of an elected government. By this point, of course, the democratic current captured the Soviet bloc, with democratic systems winning out in most of east central Europe and in Russia itself.

While most of Africa remained authoritarian, democratic change spread to this region by the 1990s, headed with the triumph of democracy over

FIGURE 40.6 This was one of the key elections in which Russians had the chance to choose among many competing parties.

DOCUMENT

## Democratic Protest and Repression in China

On June 4, 1989, Chinese troops marched on political protesters, many of them students, camped in Beijing's central Tiananmen Square. The protesters had been agitating for weeks for a more open, democratic system, as against communist one-party control. The military move caused hundreds of deaths and additional political imprisonments and exiles. It crushed the protest movement, differentiating China from the many other societies that were establishing new democracies at that time. (The imminent visit of Russia's democratizing president, Mikhail Gorbachev, was one spur to the protesters.) China continued, instead, its interesting experiment with authoritarian politics amid rapid economic change.

The following document, from a leading communist party official, Li Peng, establishes the kind of reasoning that, to the government, justified its later repression; it comes from a speech on Chinese television in mid-May. The document mixes some standard government claims about the nature of protest with some specific Chinese as well as communist traditions concerning politics and order.

> Comrades, in accordance with a decision made by the Standing Committee of the CPC Central Committee, the party Central Committee and the State Council have convened a meeting here of cadres from party, government, and army organs at the central and Beijing municipal levels, calling on everyone to mobilize in this emergency and to adopt resolute and effective measures to curb turmoil in a clear-cut manner, to restore normal order in society, and to maintain stability and unity in order to ensure the triumphant implementation of our reform and open policy and the program of socialist modernization [*applause*].
>
> The current situation in the capital is quite grim. The anarchic state is going from bad to worse. Law and discipline have been undermined. Prior to the beginning of May, the situation had begun to cool down as a result of great efforts. However, the situation has become more turbulent since the beginning of May. More and more students and other people have been involved in demonstrations. Many institutions of higher learning have come to a standstill. Traffic jams have taken place everywhere. The party and government leading organs have been affected, and public security has been rapidly deteriorating. All this has seriously disturbed and undermined the normal order of production, work, study, and everyday life of the people in the whole municipality. Some activities on the agenda for state affairs of the Sino-Soviet summit that attracted worldwide attention had to be canceled, greatly damaging China's international image and prestige.
>
> The activities of some of the students on hunger strike at Tiananmen Square have not yet been stopped completely. Their health is seriously deteriorating and some of their lives are still in imminent danger. In fact, a handful of persons are using the hunger strikes as hostages to coerce and force the party and the government to yield to their political demands. In this regard, they have not one iota of humanity [*applause*].
>
> The party and the government have, on one hand, taken every possible measure, to treat and rescue the fasting students. On the other hand, they have held several dialogues with representatives of the fasting students and have earnestly promised to continue to listen to their opinions in the future, in the hope that the students would stop their hunger strike immediately. But, the dialogues did not yield results as expected. The square is packed with extremely excited crowds who keep shouting demagogic slogans. Right now, representatives of the hunger striking students say that they can no longer control the situation. If we fail to promptly put an end to such a state of affairs and let it go unchecked, it will likely lead to serious consequences which none of us want to see.
>
> The situation in Beijing is still developing, and has already affected many other cities in the country. In many places, the number of demonstrators and protestors is

apartheid in South Africa. After new assertions of military control, Nigeria, the continent's most populous country, turned to democracy in 1999. At this point also, a near-revolution toppled the authoritarian system in Indonesia and replaced it with competitive elections.

Another surge occurred in 2004–2005. Largely peaceful risings in Georgia and Ukraine replaced authoritarian leaders with democratic elections (against Russian opposition). Stirrings also occurred in former Soviet republics in central Asia, although in Uzbekistan they were brutally repressed.

Spurred in part by the American invasion of Iraq, which toppled a classic authoritarian regime and led to new elections, several Arab countries experimented with greater democracy. Openly contested local elections occurred in some cases, including Saudi Arabia. Kuwait granted the vote to women. A Syrian withdrawal from Lebanon opened the possibility of a more open political system. Palestinians conducted an open increasing. In some places, there have been many incidents of people breaking into local party and government organs, along with beating, smashing, looting, burning, and other undermining activities that seriously violated the law. Some trains running on major railway lines have even been intercepted, causing communications to stop. Something has happened to our trunk line, the Beijing-Guangzhou line. Today, a train from Fuzhou was intercepted. The train was unable to move out for several hours.

All these incidents demonstrate that we will have nationwide major turmoil if no quick action is taken to turn and stabilize the situation. Our nation's reforms and opening to the outside world, the cause of the modernization [program], and even the fate and future of the People's Republic of China, built by many revolutionary martyrs with their blood, are facing a serious threat [*applause*].

Our party and government have pointed out time and time again that the vast numbers of young students are kindhearted, that subjectively they do not want turmoil, and that they have fervent patriotic spirit, wishing to push forward reform, develop democracy, and overcome corruption. This is also in line with the goals which the party and government have striven to accomplish. It should be said that many of the questions and views they raise have already exerted and will continue to exert positive influence on improving the work of the party and government. However, willfully using various forms of demonstrations, boycotts of class, and even hunger strikes to make petitions have damaged social stability and will not be beneficial to solving the problems. . . .

One important reason for us to take a clear-cut stand in opposing the turmoil and exposing the political conspiracy of a handful of people is to distinguish the masses of young students from the handful of people who incited the turmoil. For almost a month, we adopted an extremely tolerant and restrained attitude in handling the student unrest. No government in the world would be so tolerant. The reason that we were so tolerant was out of our loving care for the masses of youths and students. We regard them as our own children and the future of China. We do not want to hurt good people, particularly not the young students. However, the handful of behind-the-scenes people, who were plotting and inciting the turmoil, miscalculated and took the tolerance as weakness on the part of the party and government. They continued to cook up stories to confuse and poison the masses, in an attempt to worsen the situation. This has caused the situation in the capital and many localities across the country to become increasingly acute. Under such circumstances, the CPC, as a ruling party and a government responsible to the people, is forced to take resolute and decisive measures to put an end to the turmoil [*applause*].

Comrades, our party is a party in power and our government is a people's government. To be responsible to our sacred motherland and to all people, we must adopt firm and resolute measures to end the turmoil swiftly, to maintain the leadership of the party as well as the socialist system. We believe that our actions will surely have the support of all members of the Communist Party and the Communist Youth League, as well as workers, peasants, intellectuals, democratic parties, people in various circles, and the broad masses [*applause*]. We believe that we will certainly have the backing of the People's Liberation Army [PLA], which is entrusted by the Constitution with guarding the country and the peaceful work of the people [*applause*]. At the same time, we also hope that the broad masses will fully support the PLA, the public security cadres, and the police in their efforts to maintain order in the capital [*applause*].

**Questions** Why does Li Peng object to the protest movement? How does he try to persuade ordinary Chinese that the protest should cease? What arguments resemble those many governments use against protest? What arguments reflect more distinctively Chinese traditions or communist values? Why did the Chinese decide to repress political democracy?

election in their autonomous territory in Israel. These developments remained tentative, and key regimes, such as Egypt, continued to repress political opposition. At the least, some new questions were on the region's agenda.

## Democracy and Its Limits

Never before had democracy spread so widely, among so many otherwise different societies. Only China, North Korea, and parts of the Middle East and central Asia seemed to hold apart completely. In China the major democratic demonstration in Beijing in 1989 echoed the global democratic current but was brutally put down. Elsewhere, the political stability, cultural prestige, and economic success of Western democracy, supplemented by the strength of democratic systems in Japan and India, seemed to win the day. The fall of European communism both

North and South Korea Accord, June 2000

reflected and encouraged the trend. One of democracy's main competitors was now discredited. The end of the cold war worked to the same effect, reducing the need for great powers to support authoritarian systems in return for military alliance. The United States, in particular, became more consistent in its encouragement to democratic reforms, under Jimmy Carter and again in the 1990s. International agencies and human rights groups also supported the trend.

Huge questions remained about democracy's future. The link to economic expectations—the sense that democracy was a precondition for freer markets and economic growth that supported many Latin American conversions and also Gorbachev's reforms in Russia—was an obvious vulnerability. What if the economy did not improve?

New uncertainties emerged after 2000. The United States voiced great support for the spread of democracy, but it also allied with authoritarian regimes—in Egypt, Pakistan, and Uzbekistan, for example—that promised support against terrorism. Russia's retreat from full democracy, under President Putin, was an important development. Democratic systems struggled against poverty and social unrest in several Latin American countries, particularly in the Andes region. A new Venezuelan strongman, Hugo Chávez, recalled earlier populist authoritarians in Latin America.

Important questions also involved the definition of democracy. Iran, for example, was partly ruled by conservative Muslim clerics who were not elected and who put great pressure on other officials. But elections did occur, and they were contested to a degree. Despite uncertainties, a global trend was undeniable, at least for several decades. And despite significant holdouts and backslidings, there had never, in modern world history, been such wide international agreement on political standards.

## The Great Powers and New Disputes

**The collapse of the Soviet system created new, often bitter, regional disputes. Conflicts in other regions often led to massive bloodshed.**

The end of the cold war framework highlighted certain regional rivalries. Many of them were not new, but they became more acute as the controlling influence of U.S.-Soviet rivalry disappeared. The surge of conflicts significantly constrained the spread of democracy. The United States and the United Nations sought to keep the peace in most instances, but their efforts were not always successful.

### The Former Soviet Empire

The Soviet Union, with its totalitarian government, opposition to religion, and emphasis on class rather than ethnic conflict, had kept a lid on hosts of potential internal disputes. When it collapsed, the lid came off. Ethnic and religious clashes occurred in several of the new nations. The Chechnya rising was a case in point within Russia itself. Armenia and Azerbaijan, now nations, conducted low-level warfare over disputed regions claimed by different ethnic groups. Disagreements between Czechs and Slovaks resulted in a split of Czechoslovakia, though in this instance the adjustment was peaceful.

The most important post-Soviet clash occurred in Yugoslavia (Map 40.2). Long-standing tensions divided different Slavic groups (Orthodox Serbs and Catholic Croats; Serbs and Muslim Bosnians) and also minority nationalities like Albanians. The communist regime had held the pieces together, particularly under Marshall Tito, who died in 1980. Amid Soviet collapse, two regions, more prosperous than the country as a whole, declared independence in 1991: Slovenia and Croatia. Serbians, eager to hold Yugoslavia together under their leadership, warred with Croatia but failed. Conflict spread to Bosnia, where Serbs attacked not only Croats but also Muslims. Brutal assaults on civilians caused massive deaths and were ultimately judged acts of genocide. After long hesitation, NATO intervened and protected a new nation in Bosnia-Herzegovina.

The Former Yugoslavia

MAP 40.2 The Implosion of Yugoslavia, 1991–1999

A second conflict developed at the end of the 1990s, over the province of Kosovo. Albanian pressure for independence was met by Serbian resistance, again with acts of genocide under the label "ethnic cleansing." Again, NATO intervention, including air attacks, ended the violence and led to a new, more democratic regime in Serbia. Only ongoing military occupation, however, protected the peace. In the process, the federated nation of Serbia and Montenegro replaced the now defunct Yugoslavia.

## Endemic Conflicts

The end of the cold war did not cause several of the most troubling regional conflicts. However, the reduction of cold war tension and controls contributed to new regional latitude (Figure 40.7). The Middle East remained a trouble spot during the 1990s. Even before the end of the cold war, Iraq and Iran had conducted a long, casualty-filled war, with the ambitions of Iraq's dictatorial leader, Saddam Hussein, pitted against the Islamic revolutionary regime in Iran. Iraq prevailed, and then later, in 1990, invaded the small oil-rich state of Kuwait. This galvanized an international coalition of Western and moderate Arab states, which defeated Iraq in the 1991 **Persian Gulf War** while leaving Saddam Hussein in power. The United States maintained a large military presence in the Persian Gulf region, which drew criticism from many Arabs and Muslims.

Israeli–Palestinian tensions served as another Middle Eastern flashpoint. Israeli relations with the huge Palestinian minority deteriorated after the cold war ended, despite some promising peace moves in the mid-1990s. Though an autonomous Palestinian government was set up over two territories within Israel, tensions continued. Bitter violence between Israelis and Palestinians revived between 2001 and 2003. A wave of suicide bombings by Palestinians targeted Israeli civilians, while the Israeli government attacked Palestinian cities and refugee camps in turn. Clearly, key issues in this complex region remain to be resolved.

Israel-PLO Declaration of Principles on Interim Self-Government Arrangements, September 13, 1993

The Modern Middle East

Tensions between India and Pakistan also escalated, with various border clashes particularly around the disputed territory of Kashmir. By 2000 both countries had conducted tests of nuclear weapons. This was the most open case of nuclear dissemination, as the limited nuclear group of

FIGURE 40.7 Image of the road to Baghdad after bombing in the Gulf War.

the cold war began to expand. Increased Hindu nationalism within India was matched by fiercer Muslim rhetoric in Pakistan.

## Ethnic and Other Conflicts: A New Surge

The upsurge of ethnic conflict in several areas constituted a striking new feature of the post–cold war scene. Ethnic rivalries were not new, of course, but several components helped explain the new and troubling outbreak. New levels of global interaction, for example, increased the potential for group identities to generate hostilities. Some groups clearly increased their investment in ethnic identity as a means of countering outside influences and global pressures.

Within Europe, a number of ethnic groups developed new opportunities for expression as the hold of the classic nation-state declined. The British government gave limited autonomy to Scottish and Welsh governments. France and Spain became more tolerant toward linguistic minorities such as the Bretons and the Catalans. During the 1990s, a number of European countries saw the rise of new political movements bent on reducing immigration in favor of protecting jobs and cultural identity for the majority national group. A National Front group in France won up to 10 percent of all votes during the mid-1990s, though it then fell back a bit. Austria generated a controversial right-wing national government rhetorically hostile to immigrants, and in 2001 a new government leader in Italy emphasized an antiforeign plank. Violence against immigrant groups, such as Turks in Germany, flared recurrently as well.

In the 1990s a set of far bloodier conflicts broke out in central Africa, pitting tribal groups, the Hutus and the Tutsis, against each other particularly in the nation of Rwanda (Figure 40.8). Here, too, old rivalries blended with disputes over current power; the Tutsis had long ruled, but they were outnumbered by resentful Hutus. Intervention from neighboring states like Uganda contributed to the confusion. Tremendous slaughter resulted, with hundreds of thousands killed and many more—over 2 million—driven from their homes. While outside powers, the Organization of African States, and the United Nations urged peace, there was no decisive outside intervention. Bloodshed finally ran its course, but ethnic disputes continued in central Africa, contributing to civil war in countries like Congo. Ethnic and religious disputes were also involved in a number of other African trouble spots, including battles between government forces and various groups in Sudan, and warfare among military gangs in countries like Sierra Leone and Liberia. Violence frequently involved heavily armed children, or "boy soldiers." Sudanese conflicts resulted in over 2 million killed, and endemic warfare in the Congo (in which activities by neighboring states as well as internal ethnic struggle intensified the problems) killed almost the same number. Massive dislocations of refugees accompanied all these conflicts.

Clearly, ethnic tensions were leading not just to warfare, but to renewed acts of genocide that targeted whole populations of civilians, including women and children. Reactions from the world at large varied. In some instances, violence seemed sufficiently menacing

**FIGURE 40.8** In the last decades of the 20th century, the specter of genocide returned to a century that had seen more examples of this extreme form of violence against whole peoples than any other period in world history. Genocide infected the Balkans and, as this picture shows, the nation of Rwanda in east central Africa.

to major powers that some intervention occurred, though never without great hesitation. No policies emerged that offered great promise of pushing back the potential for ethnic conflict.

## The United States as Sole Superpower

**U.S. military power had no global rival by the 1990s, but a variety of reactions constrained American power. A new round of terrorism targeted the United States.**

The decline of Russian power left the United States without a clear military competitor. Faced with economic problems, Russian leaders scaled back military expenses, which by 2001 totaled only 4 percent of American levels. Russia enjoyed some influence over neighboring states and retained a nuclear arsenal, but its global military presence essentially vanished. In contrast, U.S. military commitments remained high. By 2005 the nation was spending more on defense than the next 25 countries combined.

This level of American power obviously worried many (Figure 40.9). China increased its military arsenal, along with its growing power in the global economy. Periodic collaborations among powers like China, Russia, and Iran countered American interests, but they did not lead to permanent alignments. European countries, though allied with the United States, had their own concerns. Several nations discussed a joint military force independent of NATO, though on the whole European military outlays continued to decline.

The growth and success of the European Union (EU) sketched a potential counterweight to the United States. The new currency shared by most EU member states, the euro, surpassed the strength of the dollar. Expansion to 25 members was another key move. But an ambitious EU constitution that might provide more coordination in foreign affairs met widespread criticism

**FIGURE 40.9** In this cartoon from the *Ottawa Citizen,* Uncle Sam is portrayed as a vaudeville entertainer entirely absorbed in his act who is about to lose his place in the spotlight. In the wings, China waits to go on. The "fifteen minutes" is a reference to American artist Andy Warhol's much-quoted statement, "In the future everyone will be world-famous for fifteen minutes." What feelings toward the United States does this cartoon express?

IN DEPTH

# Terrorism, Then and Now

In the last years of the 20th century, terrorism became a major issue for the international media, the world's political and military leaders, and increasingly for civilians across the globe who became both targets and mass victims of increasingly indiscriminate violent assaults. For Americans terrorism on home soil arrived gradually as the initial, and largely failed, attempt to bomb the World Trade Center in New York City in 1993 faded from memory. By contrast, for much of the rest of the world, fear of and precautions against terrorist violence had become ongoing and a major concern as early as the late 1960s. From Basque separatists in Spain and Protestant and Catholic paramilitary units in Northern Ireland to Tamil suicide bombers in Sri Lanka and cult plotters in Japan, terrorism has become an ever-present menace in the lives of leaders and ordinary citizens alike over much of the globe. This is particularly true in the growing conurbations where much of humanity has come to be concentrated. The well-coordinated and appallingly destructive attacks of September 11, 2001, on the World Trade Center in New York and the Pentagon in Washington, D.C., brought these concerns and their vulnerability to terrorism home to Americans with mind-numbing force.

*"Although current commentators often treat the late-20th-century global epidemic of terrorism as a phenomenon without historical precedent, in fact in the decades before the First World War terrorist attacks were also a major concern and were carried out by dissident groups in many areas of the globe."*

Although current commentators often treat the late 20th-century global epidemic of terrorism as a phenomenon without historical precedent, in fact in the decades before the First World War terrorist attacks were also a major concern and were carried out by dissident groups in many areas of the globe. From the capitals and metropolitan centers of Europe (especially those of tsarist Russia) and the United States to the port cities and imperial centers of the far-flung colonial empires of the great industrial powers, assassinations and bombs killed and maimed, disoriented societies, and challenged political regimes. But in critical ways—including the nature and causes espoused by terrorist groups, the targets they favored, and the amount of damage or numbers of casualties their attacks caused—terrorism in the 1880s or the early 1900s differed significantly from its counterpart in the 1970s or 1990s. An exploration of some of these key differences can tell us a great deal not only about the transformation of terrorists' motivations and operations, but also about key contrasts in terms of the global and local contexts in which each wave of terrorism occurred.

In both time periods, the main sources of terrorist assaults were small, secret, and highly politically motivated organizations. In both the early 20th century and in the decades at its end, the main objective of the members of these organizations was to discredit, weaken, and ultimately overthrow political regimes that they believed were oppressive and supportive of exploitation at the national and international levels. Their operations were also designed to advertise the causes these extremist groups espoused and draw attention to injustices they believed could not be effectively addressed through less violent or less confrontational modes of protest. But in the pre–World War I era, most terrorists were driven either by (1) anarchist aspirations to destroy increasingly centralized states, (2) radical Marxist programs for workers to overthrow the capitalist world order, or (3) struggles for the liberation of colonized peoples, from Ireland to India. The most spectacular terrorist assault of the era was of the latter type: Bosnian Serb Gavril Princip's assassination of the Archduke Ferdinand and his wife, Sophie, which precipitated the crisis that led to the First World War.

At the turn of the 21st century, by contrast, terrorist assaults have come mainly from sectarian extremists claiming affiliation with one of the world's great religious traditions—including Christianity, Hinduism, Judaism, and Islam—or from subnationalist groups, such as the Basques in Spain or Protestant and Catholic militias in Northern Ireland. Interethnic civil wars, such as those that have raged in Lebanon, Cyprus, Bosnia, and Sri Lanka in recent decades, have also proved to be major sources of terrorist activities. Periodically, radical environmentalists and groups opposing international institutions, such as the International Monetary Fund and World Trade Organization, that promote economic globalization have also resorted to terrorist tactics.

The targets terrorists select often tell us a good deal about the differing causes they espouse. Many of the regimes that anarchists struck at in the pre–World War I period—for example, the tsarist empire or the British Raj in India—were in fact autocratic, often indifferent to the oppressive living conditions of the great majority of their subjects, and prone to respond to even peaceful protest with violent repression, including torture. Scholarly investigations of these and current causes of terrorist activities have made us aware of the frequent resort to terrorist tactics by bureaucrats, the military, and state officials who so vehemently condemn dissident violence. In fact, terrorist activities have often proved far less lethal and destructive than the violence employed by regimes in power. Though these discoveries do not justify violence, particularly that directed against innocent civilians, they help us to understand in part why terrorist groups resort to violence rather than trusting the state to carry through with reforms or to negotiate with them peacefully and in good faith.

In both time periods, terrorist acts were carried out mainly by young men. But in the decades at the turn of the 20th century, many of the operatives were middle-aged, and separatist activists in both eras have included young women. Targets differed significantly in each phase of the 20th century. In the decades before World War I, individuals—monarchs (and their spouses), government officials (including President McKinley of the United States), business tycoons, and colonial officials—were most often chosen, in part because of the propaganda value of striking at the powerful and wealthy. At times, bombs placed in public areas were used to instill mass panic and disrupt normal social life. In the case of anarchist and Marxist extremists, indiscriminate mass killings and widespread destruction in fashionable quarters of urban areas were seen as symbolic assaults on the bourgeois, capitalist global order.

At the turn of the 21st century, indiscriminate assaults on defenseless civilians have become the preferred tactic of terrorists in Ireland, Spain, Israel and the Palestinian territories, Sri Lanka, Japan, and other areas. Technological advances that allowed terrorist operatives to miniaturize bombs and automatic firearms contributed to this preference. But perhaps more critical were great advances in surveillance devices and the elaborate security measures taken to defend national and world leaders. Quite simply, it became more and more dangerous to target soldiers, police, and political leaders, and increasingly even economic magnates or religious figures.

Technological change affected the nature of terrorist operations in other important ways. The spread of communications technologies such as the telephone and television, complex networks for delivering electric power and fuels like natural gas, and nuclear reactors and centers of scientific experimentation created a whole new range of what have often proved to be very vulnerable targets. Trains, buses, and airplanes have also become tempting objects for capture or destruction at the hands of hijackers and bombers. Finally, invention and scientific experimentation have made a whole new generation of terrorist weapons feasible, including gases like Sarin, which wreaked havoc on Tokyo's subways, toxic bacterial agents like anthrax, and miniaturized nuclear devices that, theoretically at least, can be packed in the proverbial suitcase and carried into the heart of major urban centers.

Between the 1970s and the 1990s, these shifts in science and technology greatly reduced the odds of success in operations aimed at well-defended leaders, government institutions, or military organizations. This situation turned unarmed civilians going about their daily lives into ever more tempting targets for terrorists with guns or bombs. The emergence of suicide bombers, particularly in the 1990s, made this pattern even more disturbing. Terrorist organizations were confident that these attacks would serve several purposes. To begin with, they dramatically publicized the grievances that inspired armed resistance. Highly lethal attacks on civilians were also seen to destabilize target societies and deprive citizens of the sense of security required to live productive and fulfilled lives. Both outcomes, in turn, were believed to discredit targeted political regimes. The dissident groups who launched the assaults hoped they would weaken governments in power to the point where they would either make major concessions or prove vulnerable to even more ambitious attempts to overthrow them.

These expected outcomes have very rarely come to pass. In fact, indiscriminate terrorist acts have usually outraged public and world opinion, and obscured or distorted the causes that dissident groups were attempting to publicize. They have also greatly enhanced the latitude of retaliatory responses open to national governments and international agencies as well as public support for these measures. This has been true even in situations where large numbers of new civilian casualties occurred as a result. Equally critical, the terrorists' willingness to launch mass assaults on innocent civilians has tended to be equated with religious fanaticism or political radicalism that is so extreme as to preclude negotiation and even rational explanation. As a consequence, violent repression has very often been deemed the only viable response to the death and suffering visited upon innocent civilians by terrorist true believers.

These shifts in the nature and targets of terrorist assaults between the pre–World War I era and the last decades of the 20th century have in most instances greatly increased the cost in human lives and property. The magnitude of these losses has also been linked to the growing globalization of terrorist networks. This has meant a proliferation of complex linkages between dissident groups in different nations and regions, who are very often espousing radically different causes. Perhaps most sobering in this regard was the way in which the attacks on September 11, 2001, demonstrated the possibilities for well-funded and organized terrorist groups to turn highly advanced civilian technologies, embodied in modern passenger planes, into appallingly lethal weapons that could be aimed at innocent and unsuspecting civilian victims. The collapse of the World Trade Towers after each had been struck by hijacked airliners also revealed the vulnerability of even the most imposing modern buildings to this sort of assault. The nearly simultaneous crash of another airliner into the Pentagon demonstrated that even the headquarters of the world's most powerful military organization was not immune to terrorist attack. These events may mark a fundamental shift in the nature of violent protest and warfare that will be played out in the century to come.

---

**Questions** What are some of the specific technologies that have shaped changes in terrorist operations over the 20th century? What sorts of systems and devices have been used by states and military organizations to counter these shifts? In what instances have terrorist organizations been successful politically? What does success mean in these situations? Is terrorism likely to become the dominant mode of warfare in the 21st century?

**A Challenge** What kinds of measures might be taken to bring terrorism under control in the coming decades? Pick one 20th-century case where a cause that generated terrorism was ultimately resolved. What lessons does it provide for current terrorist campaigns?

in 2005 by nations concerned about their own independence of action. France and Holland voted nay, and the whole project was in doubt. The EU might be a real force, but it was no match for American military and diplomatic power.

What was the United States to do with its world power? Americans debated how much they should try to police regional conflicts, often questioning the idea of serving as some kind of global enforcer. In 1993, for example, an American military intervention to halt civil strife in Somalia led to widespread resistance and loss of life, and the United States pulled out. At the same time, U.S. leaders clearly felt emboldened to tell other parts of the world how to organize their societies. Both business and political experts argued that the U.S. model of a free market economy should be widely adopted. U.S. leaders also worried about several medium-sized powers that had or might develop nuclear weapons or that might sponsor terrorism. Efforts to mobilize the world community against countries like Iran, Iraq, and North Korea had varying degrees of success, suggesting some limits to American power as well.

The United States became increasingly suspicious of international agreements that might limit its sovereignty, particularly after George W. Bush became president in 2001. Treaties designed to protect the environment or prevent the use of land mines were rejected, despite wide international support. These gestures of independence provoked criticism in various parts of the world.

## Anti-American Terrorism and Response

American interests had periodically been the targets of terrorist attacks since the 1960s. Hijacking of airplanes and other moves frequently expressed hostility to U.S. policies. But the massive attacks on the World Trade Center and the Pentagon by Islamic militants on September 11, 2001, created a new level of threat (Figure 40.10). The attacks reflected concern about specific U.S. policies in the Middle East, including support for authoritarian governments, the alliance with Israel, and the stationing of troops on "sacred ground" in Saudi Arabia. The terrorists were also hostile to wider U.S. power, or as they termed it, arrogance. Their response, hijacking airliners to crash into buildings that symbolized American financial and military might, killed about 3000 people. The terrorists regarded this as justifiable action against a nation they could not hope to fight by conventional means.

**FIGURE 40.10** At 10:05 on the morning of September 11, 2001, the south tower of the World Trade Center collapsed after having been hit by a hijacked commercial plane. The north tower, shown here in flames, collapsed less than half an hour later. This terrorist attack and the ensuing "War on Terror" changed the course of history, not just in the United States, but around the world, as terrorism became the focus of American foreign policy.

The attacks clearly altered U.S. policy and focused the administration on a war against terrorism. "War on Terror" was the new catchphrase, and a number of measures were taken, including heightened screening of international visitors. The problem dominated American foreign policy. A first response involved a military attack that successfully topped the Islamic fundamentalist regime in Afghanistan that had harbored the Al Qaeda group behind the September 11 attacks. World opinion largely supported this move. The United States established new military bases near several possible centers of terrorist activity.

In 2003 U.S. attention turned to Iraq, which was accused of amassing dangerous weaponry and aiding terrorists. Evidence for these charges proved largely erroneous, and world opinion turned heavily against the American move, with millions of demonstrators protesting the impending war in February 2003. But the United States, joined by several allies, including Britain, invaded and quickly conquered the country. The ensuing occupation, however, was extremely troubled, as the United States could not clearly restore order against a variety of insurgents. The results of this war, in terms of Iraq's future, broader global reactions to the United States, and the flexibility of American policy itself, are not yet clear.

GLOBAL CONNECTIONS

## New Global Standards, New Divisions

The end of the cold war reduced divisions in the world and dramatically lowered the danger of all-out nuclear war. The larger spread of democracy also suggested new kinds of global linkages and agreements. A few optimistic observers argued that there would be an "end of history"—that democracy and peace would predominate, ending the contentious historical processes that had defined the human experience since the dawn of civilization.

But the escalation of regional conflicts, with their tragic violence and dislocation, argued against this kind of optimism. Democracy was spreading, but not winning everywhere, and peaceful solutions to many tensions seemed impossible to achieve. The emergence of the United States as the sole superpower also caused much ambivalence. On the one hand, the disproportion of American power gave the nation true global influence. On the other hand, reactions to this power, and American uses of it, raised new disputes. The United States did not in fact have the power to reshape the world. Its policies raised new tensions with segments of Islam. The military confrontation between the United States and terrorism was far different from that of the cold war, but the deep ideological roots of the hostilities seemed distressingly familiar to some observers.

## Further Readings

On the struggle to build the European Economic Community that became the European Union, see G. W. White, *Nationalism and Territory: Constructing Group Identity in Southeastern Europe* (2000); T. L. Friedman, *The Lexus and the Olive Tree: Understanding Globalization* (2000); and Andrew Valls, ed., *Ethics in International Affairs: Themes and Cases* (2000).

For the explosion of the 1980s and 1990s, David Kotz and Fred Weir, *Revolution from Above: The Demise of the Soviet System* (1997), explores the internal dissolution of the Soviet leadership. Mikhail Gorbachev's *Memoirs* (1995) is the central participant's reflections on the end of the Soviet Union. Raymond L. Garthoff, *The Great Transition: American-Soviet Relations at the End of the Cold War* (1994), provides the foreign policy context. Karen Dawisha and Bruce Parrott, eds., *The Consolidation of Democracy in East-Central Europe* (1997), discusses recent experiences in the direction of democratization and includes a country-by-country survey. Nanette Funk and Magda Mueller, *Gender Politics and Post-Communism: Reflections from Eastern Europe and the Former Soviet Union* (1993), deals with women's role in the transition. Tina Rosenberg, *The Haunted Land: Facing Europe's Ghosts After Communism* (1995), is an engaging narrative that explores the legacies of repression in Germany, Poland, and the Czech Republic. Also see Paul Hockenos, *Free to Hate: The Rise of the Right in Post-Communist Eastern Europe* (1994).

For a detailed, long-term historical perspective on the successive conflicts in the Balkans, see Misha Glenny, *The Balkans: Nationalism, War, and the Great Powers, 1804–1999* (2000). On the religious dimensions of the Yugoslavian wars, see the essays in Paul Mojzes, ed., *Religion and War in Yugoslavia* (1998). On the successive conflicts of the mid-1990s more specifically, see Misha Glenny, *The Fall of Yugoslavia* (1992); Laura Silber and Allan Little, *Yugoslavia: Death of a Nation* (1995); Tim Judah, *Kosovo: War and Revenge* (2000); and *Noel Malcolm, Kosovo* (1998). From the very substantial literature that has developed on the Rwanda crisis, Gérard Prunier, *The Rwanda Crisis: History of a Genocide* (1999), is one of the most detailed accounts, and Mahmood Mamdani, *When Victims Become Killers* (2001), is an interesting analysis of the conflict's larger political and philosophical implications. Levon Chorbajian and George Shirinian, *Studies in Comparative Genocide* (1999), is a good place to begin an exploration of the darker side of 20th-century history.

Of the numerous and highly contentious writings on Islamic revivalism, Dilip Hiro, *Holy Wars: The Rise of Islamic Fundamentalism* (1989), is insightful and more balanced than most. A counterpart on Judaism is Arthur Hertzberg, *Jewish Fundamentalism* (1991). For Hinduism, see Gurdas Ahuja, *BJP and Indian Politics* (1994). For a comparative view covering Christian movements, see Richard Antoun, *Understanding Fundamentalism* (2001).

September 11, 2001, and persisting communal struggles, such as those in Northern Ireland and over Israel and Palestine, have produced a great proliferation of journalistic books and articles on terrorism in recent decades. A manageable place to begin an investigation of this highly contested and fluid category of social movement is Alexander Yonan et al., eds., *Terrorism: Theory and Practice* (1979). A historical overview with a global range for the modern period can be found in Albert Parry, *Terrorism* (2002). George Woodcock, *Anarchism* (1970), remains the classic account of movements that were often connected to terrorism in the late 19th century.

A very substantial literature has developed on the 1991 Persian Gulf War. The essays in Ibrahim Ibrahim, ed., *The Gulf Crisis* (1992) provide a good historical introduction to the conflict. Two of the better general accounts of the war itself are Lawrence Freedman and Efraim Karsh, *The Gulf Conflict, 1990–1991* (1993); and Michael Gordon and Bernard Trainor, *The General's War* (1995). An Arab viewpoint on the conflict is provided in Mohamed Heikal, *Illusions of Triumph* (1992), and a strong critique of the media coverage and technowar aspects of the conflict is the focus of *The Persian Gulf TV War* (1992) by Douglas Kellner.

For a provocative and detailed account of U.S. interventionism since the end of the cold war, a good place to begin is David Halberstam, *War in a Time of Peace* (2001). Less compellingly written, but useful for differing perspectives, is Lester Brune, *The United States and Post-Cold War Interventions* (1998). On specific flashpoints that provoked extensive international involvement and policy debate in the United States and elsewhere, some of the best work is on Somalia, including Mark Bowden's superb recounting of the mission in crisis in *Black Hawk Down* (1990) and Jonathan Stevenson's more policy-oriented *Losing Mogadishu* (1995).

Recent work includes *Congressional Quarterly, World at Risk: A Global Issues Sourcebook* (2002); Ronnie Lipshutz, *After Authority: War, Peace, and Global Politics in the 21st Century* (2000); Stanley Brunn, *11 September and Its Aftermath: The Geopolitics of Terror* (2004); Lee Harris, *Civilization and Its Enemies: The Next Stage of History* (2004); Ronald Glossop, *Confronting War: An Examination of Humanity's Most Pressing Problem* (2001); Barbara Walter and Jack Snyder, eds., *Civil Wars, Insecurity, and Intervention* (1999); and Immanuel Wallerstein, *The Decline of American Power: The U.S. in a Chaotic World* (2003).

## On the Web

As NATO and the Warsaw Pact seem to be merging, it is appropriate to examine their parallel histories and the impact of their past antagonisms on world history, an effort attempted at http://www.isn.ethz.ch/php/. An examination of the nature and future of NATO, and analyses of recent events and significant speeches in Europe, as well as analyses of NATO actions, can be found at http://www.nato.int/. The European quest for union is explored at http://www.eurunion.org and http://europa.eu.int/index_en.htm. Resources for the study of the collapse of communism and changes within the former Soviet Union since 1991 (including the attempted breakaway of Chechnya from the Russian Federation) are explored at http://www.learner.org/exhibits/russia. The emergence of a post–cold war "New World Order" is traced at http://www.historyteacher.net/APEuroCourse/WebLinks/WebLinks-NewWorldOrder.htm.

A survey of the lives of Alexander Dubcek (http://rferl.org/nca/special/invasion1968), Vaclav Havel and his Velvet Revolution (http://www.radio.cz/history/history15.html), and Lech Walesa (http://www.achievement.org/autodoc/page/wal1int-1) illuminate the process that led to the fall of the Berlin Wall. Both the rise and demise of that wall is traced in text, video, and photographs at http://www.coldwar.org/museum/berlin_wall_exhibit.html and http://members.aol.com/johball/berlinw2.htm. The history of Lenin's mausoleum, perhaps the greatest relic of the communist era in Russia, is examined at http:/www.aha.ru/~mausoleu/m-hist_e.htm.

For the breakup of Yugoslavia and the genocidal war in the Balkans, see http://www.truthinmedia.org and http://www.historyguy.com/balkan_war_third.htm. For links to documents on conflicts in that region, go to http://www.mtholyoke.edu/acad/intrel/bosnia.htm. Some examples of ethnic violence elsewhere in Europe and around the globe are addressed at http://www.stanford.edu/~jfearon/papers/ethreview.pdf, http://www.globalsecurity.org/military/library/news/1999/07/990729-nigeria.htm, http://hrw.org/english/docs/2000/11/01/slanka617.htm, http://www.financialsense.com/stormwatch/geo/pastanalysis/2005/1111.html, http://www.american.edu/projects/mandala/TED/ice/kaliman.htm, http://www.payvand.com/news/05/may/1078.html, and http://en.wikipedia.org/wiki/Darfur_conflict.

Efforts to prevent genocide and ethnic violence by expanding access to basic human rights around the world are traced at http://www.hrw.org/. A copy of the Universal Declaration of Human Rights can be found at http://www.un.org/Overview/rights.html. Other related documents, biographies of human rights leaders, and information about regional movements are provided at http://www1.umn.edu/humanrts/ and http://www.un.org/rights/. The current expansion of democracy is examined at http://www.democracywatch.org/ and at links provided at http://www.dmoz.org/Society/Politics/Democracy/. The meaning of democracy in China is explored at http://www.tsquare.tv/themes/essay.html.

Many forces are running counter to the expansion of secular democracy, including religious fundamentalism. Several sites offer good definitions and histories of religious fundamentalism within many religious traditions, though it is difficult to find scholarly studies that offer balanced views. The best, but by no means perfect, of these sites include http://www.purifymind.com/Fundamentalism.htm and http://jbe.gold.ac.uk/6/fenn991.html. For information about Christianity, see http://religiousmovements.lib.virginia.edu/nrms/fund.html and http://www.nhc.rtp.nc.us:8080/tserve/twenty/tkeyinfo/fundam.htm. On Islam, see http://bglatzer.de/aga/funda.htm, http://www.csmonitor.com/2001/1004/p25s1-wosc.html, http://www.islamfortoday.com/fundamnetalism.htm, and http://www.awesomelibrary.org/Muslims-Rage.html. On Judaism, see http://www.sas.upenn.edu/penncip/lustick/. For information about

Hinduism, go to http://www.class.uidaho.edu/ngier/hindfund.htm, http://www.cbc.ca/india/hindufundamentalism.html, http://waf.gn.apc.org/j5p42.htm, and for two opposing views http://www.boloji.com/analysis/016.htm and http://www.angelfire.com/ca/Hinduism/frawley.html.

The terrorist threat to the new world order can be traced through documents at http://www.yale.edu/lawweb/avalon/terrorism/terror.htm. The terrorist attacks on September 11, 2001, on New York City and Washington, D.C., are recounted and documented from many perspectives at http://www.freepint.com/gary/91101.html and http://www.lib.umich.edu/govdocs/usterror.html. For a moving account of that event, see http://www.September11news.com and http://911digitalarchive.org/. For critical analysis of U.S. policy in the wake of the attacks, see http://www.gwu.edu/~nsarchiv/NSAEBB/NSAEBB55/index1.html.

For general coverage of the 1991 Persian Gulf War, also called Operation Desert Storm or Desert Shield, see http://www.pbs.org/wgbh/pages/frontline/gulf/index.html. For the debate over the inconclusive end of the war and continuing conflict in the region, see http://www.pbs.org/wgbh/pages/frontline/shows/syndrome/.

The 1991 actions called Operation Desert Storm and Operation Desert Shield are explored at http://www.desert-storm.com/ and http://www.gwu.edu/~nsarchiv/NSAEBB/NSAEBB39/. The war witnessed a larger role for women in modern warfare, a transformation explored at http://userpages.aug.com/captbarb/femvetsds.html.

The Second Gulf War or Iraqi War and the parallel American intervention in Afghanistan have proved more controversial than its predecessor, both for the apparent inaccuracy of the intelligence on which the war was based and also the mid-war course change by the United States to a nation-building strategy in both countries. These developments as well as military operations are explored at http://www.globalsecurity.org/military/ops/enduring-freedom.htm, http://www.ips-dc.org/iraq/primer.htm, http://www.comw.org/pda/0201strangevic.html, http://hrw.org/reports/2004/afghanistan0304/, http://www.nationalgeographic.com/landincrisis/, and http://www.parliament.uk/commons/lib/research/rp2001/rp01-081.pdf. The earlier UN-U.S. intervention in Somalia and its troubling outcomes are considered from different vantage points at http://www.netnomad.com/ and http://www.unsomalia.org/.

Threats to the global ecology are explored at http://www.unep.org/ and http://portal.unesco.org/. Take a virtual tour of the expanding hole in the ozone layer at http://www.atm.ch.cam.ac.uk/tour/. See also the links provided at http://www.sosig.ac.uk/roads/subject-listing/World-cat/envthreat.html.

CHAPTER 41

# Globalization and Resistance



A recent movie about a family in Kerala (a state in southern India) makes the point inescapably. A baby girl is turned over to her "good" brother for care: he lives in the village and provides for her a simple, idyllic life. But when she enters college, she goes to the city to live with a childless aunt and uncle. They shower her with new clothes, including blue jeans, Western-style skirts, and cosmetics. She enters and wins a college beauty pageant. She gets in with a heavy-drinking, rowdy group of men and is disgraced—finally returning to the village where, in shame, she assumes the traditional costume.

By the early 21st century, Kerala had become a quiet battleground. Many residents worked abroad, mainly in the Persian Gulf. Television Channel V, the Indian version of MTV, piped in Japanese, Filipino, and Arab as well as Indian music, with disk jockeys—all women of Indian origin from Britain or North America—speaking English. Beauty pageants had spread widely after an Indian woman won the Miss Universe contest in the 1990s. A word derived from lower-caste slang, *chetu,* came to mean "cool"—denoting jeans, cars, a new motorbike. But there was also bitter opposition to a local Coca-Cola bottling plant, which was accused of contaminating the local water. Hindu nationalists condemned beauty contests: "In India, the woman is not meant to be sold." Compromise efforts to hold a pageant in which women were tested in their knowledge of Keralan culture failed because the women who entered such competitions did not have the relevant information. It was a confusing situation, with change and continuity warring for dominance and dividing the people of Kerala.

Along with the end of the cold war and its aftermath, a larger process, called globalization, was unfolding around the world. While the new global contacts were powerful, they did not monopolize the world scene. Important alternatives were nationalism and religion. And there was explicit resistance to globalization as well. These tensions, like the uncertainties surrounding the post–cold war diplomatic and military framework, raise intriguing questions about the relationship between world history and world future.

**FIGURE 41.1** Indian university students in New Delhi protest India's hosting of the Indian Miss World contest by burning contestants in effigy. Like these students, some Indian conservatives see beauty pageants as decadent imports from the West that are destructive of their culture's traditional values.

## Globalization: Causes and Processes

■ **Globalization is a result of political, demographic, and cultural as well as technological changes. Economic globalization involves unprecedented interconnection among the world's peoples. New political arrangements have responded to globalization.**

**Globalization** is the increasing interconnectedness of all parts of the world, particularly in communication and commerce but in culture and politics as well. It means openness to exchanges around the world.

The surge of globalization at the end of the 20th century was launched in part by political decisions to rejoin international economic exchange. Crucial here was China's decision, in 1978, to develop more export activity and to open to international exchange. Similar decisions in the Soviet Union, from 1985 onward, and then the collapse of the Soviet empire brought huge stretches of eastern Europe and central Asia into the same process. Beginning in the 1970s, an even larger number of societies in south Asia and Latin America began to adopt free-market policies with less government control. Sometimes this reflected pressure from international economic organizations, but the result contributed further to the creation of global economic links.

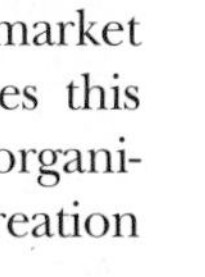

Asia, 2000

By the 1990s only a few nations, such as Myanmar and North Korea, remained isolated. While many states maintained concerns about some aspects of globalization, few raised systematic barriers to exchanges of goods, ideas, and people. Tentatively, growing numbers of people around the world became accustomed to global connections (Figure 41.2). At least in some areas, intensive nationalism declined in favor of a more cosmopolitan interest in wider influences and contacts. The spread of English as a world language, though incomplete and often resented, was part of this connection. English served airline travel, many sports, and the early Internet as a common language. This encouraged and reflected other facets of global change.

## The New Technology

A globalization guru tells the following story. In 1988 a U.S. government official traveling to Chicago was assigned a limousine with a cellular phone. He was so delighted to have this novelty that he called his wife just to brag. Nine years later, in 1997, the same official was visiting a remote village in Côte d'Ivoire, in west Africa, that was accessible only by dugout canoe. As he prepared to leave, a Côte d'Ivoire official told him he had a call from Washington and handed him a cellular phone. Cellular phones had become increasingly common. They were among the key new communication devices that, by the 1990s, had made almost constant contact with other parts of the world feasible, and for some people unavoidable. Western Europe and east Asia led in the cellular phone revolution, but people in all parts of the world participated.

During the 1980s steady improvements in miniaturization made computers increasingly efficient. By the 1990s the amount of information that could be stored on microchips increased by more than 60 percent each year. Linkages among computers improved

FIGURE 41.2 Midnight, December 31, 1999: celebration of the new millennium in Sydney, Australia. New Year's Eve 1999 was not without worry. Some experts predicted that the turn of the century would wreak havoc on the internal calendars of computers worldwide, possibly leading to massive power failures, loss of data bases by businesses and governments, and disruptions in the supply of the most basic necessities of life. In some places, panicky shoppers stripped store shelves of bottled water, canned goods, flashlights, batteries, and other emergency supplies. But "Y2K," as this potential disaster came to be called, never materialized. Thanks to fully functional telecommunications, festivities in most time zones were broadcast worldwide, making for a great global party.

as well, starting with halting efforts in the 1960s mainly for defense purposes. E-mail was introduced in 1972. In 1990 a British software engineer working in Switzerland, Tim Berners, developed the World Wide Web, and the true age of the Internet was born. Almost instantaneous contact by computer became possible around the world, and with it came the capacity to send vast amounts of information, from text, to videos and other imagery, to music. While the Internet was not available to everyone—by 2005 only 30 percent of the world's population had access—it did provide global contacts for some regions otherwise fairly remote. In eastern Russia, for example, international mail service was agonizingly slow, telephone access often interrupted—but a student could sit at an Internet cafe in Vladivostok and communicate easily with friends in the United States or Brazil.

Satellite linkages for television formed a final communications revolution, making simultaneous broadcasts possible around the world. A full quarter of the world's population now could, and sometimes did, watch the same sporting event—usually World Cup soccer or the Olympics—a phenomenon never before possible or even approachable in world history. Global technology gained new meaning.

## Economic Globalization: Business Organization and Investment

Thanks in part to new technology, in part to more open political boundaries, international investment accelerated rapidly at the end of the 20th century. Stock exchanges featured holdings in Chinese utilities or Brazilian steel companies as well as the great corporations of the West and Japan. U.S. investments abroad multiplied rapidly, almost doubling in the first half of the 1970s. By the 1980s foreign operations were generating between 25 and 40 percent of all corporate profits in the United States. Japan's foreign investment rose 15-fold during the 1970s. During the 1980s Japanese car manufacturers set up factories in the United States, Europe, and other areas. German cars, French tires, German chemicals and pharmaceuticals, and Dutch petroleum all had substantial U.S. operations. At the end of the 1990s the German Volkswagen firm introduced an updated version of the automobile affectionately known as the "bug," whose initial design went back to Hitler's Germany. Its production facilities were entirely based in Mexico, but it was marketed in the United States and around the world.

Globalization in business involved rapid increases in exports and imports, the extension of business organization across political boundaries—resulting in **multinational corporations**—and division of labor on a worldwide basis. Cars that were made in the United States were assembled from parts made in Japan, Korea, Mexico, and elsewhere. Japanese cars often had more American-made parts in them than Detroit products had. Firms set up operations not simply to produce closer to markets to save transportation costs; they also sought to reduce costs by looking for cheap labor and minimal environmental regulations. Computer boards were made by West Indian and African women. India developed a huge software industry, subcontracting for firms in the United States and western Europe. The linkages were dazzling.

International firms continued to seek cheap raw materials. For example, companies in Japan and the West competed for access to oil and minerals in the newly independent nations of central Asia after the collapse of the Soviet Union. International investments also followed interest rates. During the 1990s relatively attractive U.S. interest rates drew extensive investment from Europe, Japan, and the oil-rich regions in the Middle East.

While multinational corporations sometimes faced government regulation, many of them had more power, and far more resources, than the governments of most of the countries within which they operated. Thus, they could determine most aspects of labor and environmental policy. They could and did pull up stakes in one region if more attractive opportunities opened elsewhere, regardless of the impact on the workers and facilities they left behind. Early in the 21st century, for example, many multinationals pulled jobs from Mexico in favor of expansion to China or Vietnam, where wages were lower. Even clerical jobs were outsourced: telephone services for many American companies, for example, were set up in India, where wages were lower and English was widely spoken. The spread of multinationals promoted industrial skills in many previously agricultural regions and depended on improvements in communications and transportation that could bring wider changes for the people of the lands in which they hired workers (Figure 41.3).

American factories located in northern Mexico, designed to produce goods for sale back in the United States, showed the complexity of the new international economy. The owners of these factories unquestionably sought cheap labor and lax regulations. Their factories often leaked chemical waste. Wages were barely 10 percent of what U.S. workers would earn. Nonetheless these factories often paid better than their Mexican counterparts. Many workers, including large numbers of women, found the labor policies more enlightened and the foremen better behaved in the foreign firms. A key question, not yet answerable, is whether the poverty-level wages for workers in such factories will improve and whether the industrial skills they learn will make possible a widening range of opportunities.

Efforts to tally the overall economic effects of globalization are complex and contested. Some parts of Africa lost traditional manufacturing jobs to new global

FIGURE 41.3 Change and continuity in rural India. New irrigation and electrification combine with traditional methods of tilling the soil as agricultural production rises.

competition, and in these regions, unemployment rates of 30 percent or more were common. Prostitution and even the sale of body organs showed the increasingly desperate poverty in some societies. Not only global competition but reductions in government services, in the name of free-market principles, contributed to new problems. In south and southeast Asia, rates of child labor rose, though the larger global patterns were different. On the other hand, new global opportunities permitted an increase in per capita income in places like China and India.

It was clear that there were winners and losers in economic globalization, both among different parts of the world and within individual societies—even within industrial societies like the United States. Gaps widened between the poor and those with higher incomes. A growing middle class developed in Latin America, India, and China, but urban slums and exploited labor expanded as well.

## Migration

Broad international patterns of migration had developed by the 1950s and 1960s, with the use of "guest workers" from Turkey and north Africa in Europe for example. Here, patterns in the 1990s built clearly on previous trends. But easier travel, along with the continued gap between slowly growing populations in the industrial countries and rapidly growing populations in Latin America, Africa, and parts of Asia, maintained high levels of exchange. A few areas, including Italy, Greece, and Japan, had almost ceased internal population growth by the 1990s, which meant that new labor needs, particularly at the lower skill levels, had to be supplied by immigration.

Japan hoped to avoid too much influx by relying on high-technology solutions, but even here worker groups were brought in from the Philippines and southeast Asia. Migration into Europe and the United States was far more extensive, producing truly multinational populations in key urban and commercial centers. By 2000 at least 25 percent of all Americans, mostly people of color, came from households where English was not the first language. Ten percent of the French population in 2003 was Muslim (Figure 41.4). Here was an important source of tension, with local populations often fearing foreigners and worried about job competition. Here also was a new opportunity, not just for new laborers but for new cultural inspiration.

Migration was hardly new in world history. But new levels of migration from distant regions had novel qualities. So did the resulting mixture of migrants and locals in the cities of North America, western Europe, or the Persian Gulf states of the Middle East. So, finally, did the new facility of traveling back and forth: many migrants, returning home to Turkey or India on vacation or permanently, brought back new styles and ideas, maintaining their own commitment to at least two different cultures.

## Cultural Globalization

Thanks in part to global technologies and business organization, plus reduced political barriers, the pace of cultural exchange and contact around the world accelerated at the end of the 1990s. Much of this involved mass consumer goods, spread from the United States, western Europe, and Japan. But art shows, symphony exchanges, scientific conferences, and Internet contact increased as well. Music conductors and artists held posts literally around the world, sometimes juggling commitments among cities like Tokyo, Berlin, and Chicago within a single season. Science laboratories filled with researchers from around the world, collaborating (usually in English) with little regard for national origin.

The spread of fast-food restaurants from the United States, headed by McDonald's, formed one of the most striking international cultural influences from the 1970s onward. The company began in Illinois in

**FIGURE 41.4** The mixtures of peoples and cultures that had become a prominent feature of world history by the end of the 20th century are wonderfully illustrated by this group of Muslim schoolchildren in a French school. By 2007, more than 10 percent of the French population will be Islamic. In 2006, riots broke out in Islamic areas of French cities revealing tensions over the gap between opportunities available to immigrants and those available to the majority population.

1955 and started its international career in 1967 with outlets in Canada and Puerto Rico. From then on, the company entered an average of two new nations per year and accelerated the pace in the 1990s. By 1998 it was operating in 109 countries overall. The company won quick success in Japan, where it gained its largest foreign audience; "makadonaldo" first opened in Tokyo's world famous Ginza, already known for cosmopolitan department stores, in 1971. McDonald's entry into the Soviet Union in 1990 was a major sign of the ending of cold war rivalries and the growing Russian passion for international consumer goods. The restaurants won massive patronage despite (by Russian standards) very high prices. Even in gourmet-conscious France, McDonald's and other fast-food outlets were winning 26 percent of all restaurant dining by the 1990s. Not everyone who patronized McDonald's really liked the food. Many patrons in Hong Kong, for example, said they went mainly to see and be seen, and to feel part of the global world.

Cultural globalization obviously involved increasing exposure to American movies and television shows. Series like *Baywatch* won massive foreign audiences. Movie and amusement park icons like Mickey Mouse, and products and dolls derived from them, had international currency. Western beauty standards, based on the models and film stars, won wide exposure, expressed among other things in widely sought international beauty pageants. MTV spread Western images and sounds to youth audiences almost everywhere.

Holidays took on an international air. American-style Christmas trappings, including gift giving, lights, and Santa Claus, spread not only to countries of Christian background, like France, but also places like Muslim Istanbul. Northern Mexico picked up American Halloween trick-or-treating, as it displaced the more traditional Catholic observance of All Saints' Day. Muslim observance of Ramadan, the month of self-denial, began to include greeting cards and presents for children, a clear echo of new consumerism. The American jingle "happy birthday," with its implications about individualism and entertainment for children, was translated into virtually every language.

Consumer internationalization was not just American. Japanese rock groups gained wide audience. The Pokémon toy series, derived from Japanese cultural traditions, won a frenzied audience among American children in the 1990s, who for several years could not get enough. A Japanese soap opera heroine became the most admired woman in Muslim Iran. South Korea, historically hostile to Japan, proved open to popular Japanese music groups and cartoon animation. European popular culture, including fashion and music groups, gained large followings around the world as well.

Dress was internationalized to an unprecedented extent. American-style blue jeans showed up almost everywhere. A major export item for Chinese manufacturing involved Western clothing pirated from famous brand names. A "Chinese market" in the cities of eastern Russia contained entirely Western-style items, mainly clothing and shoes.

Tradition vs. Modernity

The international expansion of middle-class consumerism also generated a global epidemic of obesity, particularly for children. Available foods increased along with more sedentary lives and entertainments, producing echoes in Shanghai and Bangalore of problems more obvious in Houston or Birmingham.

DOCUMENT

## Protests Against Globalization

In December 1999, a series of protests rocked Seattle on the occasion of a World Trade Organization (WTO) meeting designed to discuss further international tariff cuts in the interests of promoting global trade. The following passage was written by Jeffrey St. Clair, a radical journalist who is co-editor of the political newsletter *CounterPunch*. St. Clair describes the atmosphere of the Seattle protests and some of the groups involved. The Seattle protests foreshadowed a regular sequence of popular demonstrations at the meetings of such groups as the World Bank, which continue into the 21st century, involving many of the same groups and issues.

Monday

And the revolution will be started by: sea turtles. At noon about 2000 people massed at the United Methodist Church, the HQ of the grassroots [organizations], for a march to the convention center. It was Environment Day and the Earth Island Institute had prepared more than 500 sea turtle costumes for marchers to wear. The sea turtle became the prime symbol of the WTO's threats to environmental laws when a WTO tribunal ruled that the U.S. Endangered Species Act, which requires shrimp to be caught with turtle excluder devices, was an unfair trade barrier.

But the environmentalists weren't the only ones on the street Monday morning. In the first showing of a new solidarity, labor union members from the Steelworkers and the Longshoremen showed up to join the march. In fact, Steelworker Don Kegley led the march, alongside environmentalist Ben White. (White was later clubbed in the back of the head by a young man who was apparently angry that he couldn't do his Christmas shopping. The police pulled the youth away from White, but the man wasn't arrested. White played down the incident.) The throng of sea turtles and blue-jacketed union folk took off to the rhythm of a familiar chant that would echo down the streets of Seattle for days: "The people will never be divided!"

I walked next to Brad Spann, a Longshoreman from Tacoma, who hoisted up one of my favorite signs of the entire week: "Teamsters and Turtles Together at Last!" Brad winked at me and said, "What the hell do you think old Hoffa [former Teamster leader] thinks of that?"

The march, which was too fast and courteous for my taste, was escorted by motorcycle police and ended essentially in a cage, a protest pen next to a construction site near the convention center. A large stage had been erected there hours earlier and Carl Pope, the director of the Sierra Club, was called forth to give the opening speech. The Club is the nation's most venerable environmental group. . . .

Standing near the stage I saw Brent Blackwelder, the head of Friends of the Earth. Behind his glasses and somewhat shambling manner, Blackwelder looks ever so professional. And he is by far the smartest of the environmental CEOs. But he is also the most radical politically, the most willing to challenge the tired complacency of his fellow green executives. . . .

Blackwelder's speech was a good one, strong and defiant. He excoriated the WTO as a kind of global security force for transnational corporations whose mission is "to stuff unwanted products, like genetically engineered foods, down our throats." . . .

After the speechifying most of the marchers headed back to the church. But a contingent of about 200 ended up in front of McDonald's where a group of French farmers had mustered to denounce U.S. policy on biotech foods. Their leader was José Bove, a sheep farmer from Millau in southwest France and a leader of Confederation Paysanne, a French environmental group. In August, Bove had been jailed in France for leading a raid on a McDonald's restaurant under construction in Larzac. At the time, he was already awaiting charges that he destroyed a cache of Novartis' genetically engineered corn. Bove said his raid on the Larzac McDonald's was promoted by the U.S. decision to impose a heavy tariff on Roquefort cheese in retaliation for the European Union's refusal to import American hormone-treated beef. Bove's act of defiance earned him the praise of Jacques Chirac and Friends of the Earth. Bove said he was prepared to start a militant worldwide campaign against "Frankenstein" foods. "These actions will only stop when this mad logic comes to a halt," Bove said. "I don't demand clemency but justice."

Bove showed up at the Seattle McDonald's with rounds of Roquefort cheese, which he handed out to the crowd. After listening to a rousing speech against the evils of Monsanto, and its bovine growth hormone and Roundup Ready soybeans, the crowd stormed the McDonald's breaking its windows and urging customers and workers to join the marchers on the streets. This was the first shot in the battle for Seattle.

Who were these direct action warriors on the front lines? Earth First, the Alliance for Sustainable Jobs and the

The penetration of cultural globalization varied—in part by wealth and urbanization, in part according to degrees of cultural tolerance (Figure 41.5). There were obvious resource limits: by 2005, only 30 percent of the world's people had access to the Internet, a huge figure but nevertheless a reminder that global signals had clear limits. Blending of global and local signals was another key development. Foreign models were often adapted to local customs. Thus foods in McDonald's in India (where the chain was not very

Environment (the new enviro-steelworker alliance), the Ruckus Society (a direct action training center), Jobs with Justice, Rainforest Action Network, Food Not Bombs, Global Exchange, and a small contingent of Anarchists, the dreaded Black Bloc.

There was also a robust international contingent on the streets Tuesday morning: French farmers, Korean greens [environmentalists], Canadian wheat growers, Mexican environmentalists, Chinese dissidents, Ecuadorian anti-dam organizers, U'wa tribespeople from the Columbian rainforest, and British campaigners against genetically modified foods. Indeed earlier, a group of Brits had cornered two Monsanto lobbyists behind an abandoned truck carrying an ad for the *Financial Times*. They detained the corporate flacks long enough to deliver a stern warning about the threat of frankencrops to wildlife, such as the Monarch butterfly. Then a wave of tear gas wafted over them and the Monsanto men fled, covering their eyes with their neckties. . . .

As the march turned up toward the Sheraton and was beaten back by cops on horses, I teamed up with Etienne Vernet and Ronnie Cumming. Cumming is the head of one of the feistiest groups in the U.S., the PureFood Campaign, Monsanto's chief pain in the ass. Cumming hails from the oil town of Port Arthur, Texas. He went to Cambridge with another great foe of industrial agriculture, Prince Charles. Cumming was a civil rights organizer in Houston during the mid-sixties. "The energy here is incredible," Cumming said. "Black and white, labor and green, Americans, Europeans, Africans, and Asians arm in arm. It's the most hopeful I've felt since the height of the civil rights movement."

Vernet lives in Paris, where he is the leader of the radical green group EcoRopa. At that very moment the European delegates inside the convention were capitulating on a key issue: The EU, which had banned import of genetically engineered crops and hormone-treated beef, had agreed to a U.S. proposal to establish a scientific committee to evaluate the health and environmental risks of biotech foods, a sure first step toward undermining the moratorium. Still Vernet was in a jolly mood, lively and invigorated, if a little bemused by the decorous nature of the crowd. "Americans seem to have been out of practice in these things," he told me. "Everyone's so polite. The only things on fire are dumpsters filled with refuse." He pointed to a shiny black Lexus parked on Pine Street, which throngs of protesters had scrupulously avoided. In the windshield was a placard identifying it as belonging to a WTO delegate. "In Paris that car would be burning."

[David] Brower [environmental leader] was joined by David Foster, Director for District 11 of the United Steelworkers of America, one of the most articulate and unflinching labor leaders in America. Earlier this year, Brower and Foster formed an unlikely union, a coalition of radical environmentalists and Steelworkers called the Alliance for Sustainable Jobs and the Environment, which had just run an amusing ad in the *New York Times* asking, "Have You Heard the One about the Environmentalist and the Steelworker?" The groups had found they had a common enemy: Charles Hurwitz, the corporate raider. Hurwitz owned the Pacific Lumber company, the northern California timber firm that is slaughtering some of the last stands of ancient redwoods on the planet. At the same time, Hurwitz, who also controlled Kaiser Aluminum, had locked out 3000 Steelworkers at Kaiser's factories in Washington, Ohio, and Louisiana. "The companies that attack the environment most mercilessly are often also the ones that are the most anti-union," Foster told me. "More unites us than divides us."

I came away thinking that for all its promise this tenuous marriage might end badly. Brower, the master of ceremonies, isn't going to be around forever to heal the wounds and cover up the divisions. There are deep, inescapable issues that will, inevitably, pit Steelworkers, fighting for their jobs in an ever-tightening economy, against greens, defending dwindling species like sockeye salmon that are being killed off by hydrodams that power the aluminum plants that offer employment to steel workers. When asked about this potential both Brower and Foster danced around it skillfully. But it was a dance of denial. The tensions won't go away simply because the parties agree not to mention them in public. Indeed, they might even build, like a pressure cooker left unwatched. I shook the thought from my head. For this moment, the new, powerful solidarity was too seductive to let such broodings intrude for long.

From Alexander Cockburn, Jeffrey St. Clair, and Allan Sekula, *5 Days That Shook the World* (London: Verso, 2000), 16–21, 28, 29, 36–37.

**Questions** What were the principal groups involved in the globalization protests? Why did they feel such passion? Was this a global protest, or did different parts of the world have different issues? Is the movement likely to hold together? Can you think of other reasons to oppose globalization? What were the key arguments of defenders of globalization who disapproved of this kind of protest and of its goals?

popular in any event) included vegetarian items not found elsewhere. Comic books in Mexico, originally derived from U.S. models, took on Mexican cultural images, including frequent triumphs over "gringo" supermen. Regions in India tried to adapt a consumer staple—the beauty pageant—to local conditions by requiring knowledge of traditional language and culture from contestants. A host of combinations emerged. Cultural internationalization was a real development, but it was complex and incomplete.

FIGURE 41.5 Pokémon, a children's game invented in Japan that quickly spread to become an international phenomenon and multibillion dollar industry, is often cited as an example of the globalization of culture in the early 21st century.

### Institutions of Globalization

On the whole, political institutions globalized less rapidly than technology or business, or even consumer culture. Many people worried about the gap between political supervision and control and the larger globalization process. UN activity accelerated a bit in the 1990s. With the end of the cold war, more diplomatic hotspots invited intervention by multinational military forces. UN forces tried to calm or prevent disputes in a number of parts of Africa, the Balkans, and the Middle East. Growing refugee populations called for UN humanitarian intervention, often aided by other international groups. UN conferences broadened their scope, dealing for example with gender and population control issues. While the results of the conferences were not always clear, a number of countries did incorporate international standards into domestic law. Women in many African countries, for example, were able to appeal to UN proclamations on gender equality as a basis for seeking new property rights in the courts. By 2001 the United Nations became increasingly active as well in encouraging assistance to stem the AIDS epidemic.

The World Health Organization also expanded its range directly. A threatened global outbreak of Sudden Acute Respiratory Syndrome (SARS), after occurrences in east Asia and Canada in 2003, met with prompt controls under international guidance.

Another area of innovation involved international nongovernmental organizations (INGOs). Amnesty International, a London-based human rights agency, began in 1961. The 1970s saw a more rapid proliferation of INGOs for human rights, labor, environmental, and other issues, often with networks of local affiliates. By the 1990s Internet-based petitions against torture, labor abuses, or the death penalty became standard fare, sometimes winning significant policy responses. The range of criteria for INGOs expanded steadily as well: rape, for example, was internationally recognized as a war crime by the 1990s, a major innovation.

As more nations participated actively in international trade, the importance of organizations in this arena grew. The International Monetary Fund (IMF) and the World Bank had been founded after World War II to promote trade. Guided by the major industrial powers, these organizations offered loans and guidance to developing areas and also to regions that encountered temporary economic setbacks. Loans to Mexico and to southeast Asia during the 1990s were intended to promote recovery from recessions that threatened to affect other areas. Loans were usually accompanied by requirements for economic reform, usually through reduced government spending and the promotion of more open competition. These guidelines were not always welcomed by the regions involved. The IMF and the World Bank were widely viewed as primary promoters of the capitalist global economy.

World Bank-Supported Day Care Programs in Uganda

Annual meetings of the heads of the seven leading industrial powers (four from Europe, two from North America, plus Japan) also promoted global trade and policies toward developing regions. Finally, the regional economic arrangements that had blossomed from the 1950s onward gained growing importance as globalization accelerated. The European Union headed the list, but the **North American Free Trade Agreement (NAFTA)** and other regional consortiums in Latin America and east Asia also pushed for lower tariffs and greater economic coordination.

## Resistance and Alternatives

- **Globalization generated direct protest at the end of the 20th century. Nationalism and religion, overlapping globalization, provided alternative sets of loyalties.**

### Protest and Economic Uncertainties

Accelerating globalization attracted a vigorous new protest movement. Meetings of the World Bank or the industrial leaders were increasingly marked by huge demonstrations and some violence. The current movement began with massive protests in Seattle in 1999, and the protests continued at key gatherings thereafter. Protesters came from various parts of the world and raised a number of issues. Many people believed that rapid global economic development was threatening the environment. Others blasted the use of cheap labor by international corporations, which was seen as damaging labor conditions even in industrial nations. Rampant consumerism was another target.

Many critics claimed that globalization was working to the benefit of rich nations and the wealthy generally, rather than the bulk of the world's population. They pointed to figures that suggested growing inequalities of wealth, with the top quarter of the world's population growing richer during the 1990s while the rest of the people increasingly suffered (Figure 41.6). This division operated between regions, widening the gap between affluent nations and the more populous developing areas. It also operated within regions, including the United States and parts of western Europe, where income gaps were on the rise. Bitter disagreements increasingly divided the supporters and opponents of globalization.

**FIGURE 41.6** The increasing gap between rich and poor is a controversial problem in the age of globalization. Here, a man in Western dress talking on a cell phone passes a ragged beggar on a Hong Kong sidewalk.

## Nationalism and New Religious Currents

Several trends ran counter to globalization as the 21st century began. Nationalism was one. While many nations were partially bypassed by globalization—many countries were much less powerful than the multinational corporations—nationalist resistance to globalization surfaced in many ways. Many countries opposed the erosion of traditions by global cultural patterns. Thus the Japanese government subsidized training in the use of chopsticks, because so many Japanese children seemed to be relying on forks and fast foods instead of traditional customs. The French government periodically resisted the incorporation of English words into the French language. Many European countries tried to regulate the number of immigrants from Africa, Asia, and the West Indies, in the interest of preserving dominance for families and workers of European background. The United States rejected a wide variety of international treaties, including a provision for regulation against war crimes, because they might interfere with national sovereignty. China and other states periodically bristled against international criticism of internal policies concerning political prisoners.

It was religion, however, that posed the most interesting challenge to globalization in the final decades of the 20th century. Most religious movements were not necessarily opposed to globalization, but they tended to insist on their distinctiveness, against any uniform global culture, and they also bred suspicions of the consumerism and sexuality highlighted in many manifestations of globalization, including films and tourism.

As communism collapsed in eastern Europe, many people returned to previous religious beliefs, including Orthodox Christianity. Protestant fundamentalists, often from the United States, were also busy in the region. Protestant fundamentalism also spread rapidly in parts of Latin America, such as Guatemala and Brazil. In India, Hindu fundamentalism surged by the 1990s, with Hindu nationalist politicians capturing the nation's presidency. In China, an intriguing spinoff from Buddhism, the Falun Gong, won wide support, despite bitter repression by the government.

Fundamentalism also gained ground in Islam, particularly in the Middle East and nearby parts of Africa and south central Asia. The Taliban, who followed a

IN DEPTH

## How Much Historical Change?

As the cold war drew to a close, a number of analysts, primarily in the United States, looked forward to dramatic shifts in human affairs. There were two related lines of argument. The "end of history" concept emphasized the new dominance of the democratic form of government. According to this view, the contest among political and economic systems, particularly between democracy and communism, was over; democracy would now sweep over the world. With this, the need for basic questioning about political institutions would also end: democracy worked best, and it was here to stay. Further, the change in political structure also had implications for power rivalries. Some analysts contend that democracies never war on each other. Once the people control affairs of state through their votes, the selfishness and power trips that lead to war will end. Ordinary people understand the horror of war. They appreciate the common humanity they share with other democratic peoples. Just as democracy resolves internal conflicts through votes, democracies would come to resolve external conflicts through bargaining and compromise. They argue that, in the main, people do not vote for wars of aggression, at most sanctioning defense against attack.

> *"The 'end of history' concept emphasized the new dominance of the democratic form of government."*

Another argument, which might be combined with the democracy approach, focused on the spread of consumer capitalism around the world. As put forward by a U.S. journalist in a popular book called *The Lexus and the Olive Tree,* the consumer capitalism approach emphasized the benefits of a global economy. In this, everyone would gain access to greater material abundance and the wonders of consumerism, and no one would wish to jeopardize prosperity by waging war. Shared interests, rather than traditional disputes over limited resources, it is alleged, would carry the day. However, history suggests that capitalism is not necessarily compatible with democracy: the drive for material wealth has often led to corruption within democratic societies, sapping the effectiveness of their institutions. The proponents of the idea that history will end in the triumph of capitalism have voiced concern that growing disparities of wealth even within the most prosperous capitalist nations might spark violent unrest that could derail the drive toward a free-market utopia.

This is a challenging kind of forecasting because it cannot easily be disproved—until the future does not correspond to the dramatic projections. The consumerism argument, particularly, has no precedent. At the same time, the predictions also could not be proved, for example, merely by pointing to some prior historical analogy. How, then, should they be assessed?

---

**Questions** Following the end of the cold war, did the world change as rapidly and fundamentally as these predictions implied? Did new systems spread as uniformly and consistently as the democracy and global consumerism arguments implied? Were past rivalries and cultural and institutional commitments to war and dispute so easily wiped away? These predictions were issued in the wake of the excitement surrounding the cold war's end. Developments later in the 1990s and in 2001 did not necessarily live up to the idea of fundamental transformation. How wrong were the predictions, and why did very intelligent people find them plausible in the first place? Or was the world in the early stages of the kinds of transition the forecasters suggested? How significant, in other words, was the cold war's end in reshaping global relationships?

---

particular version of Islamic fundamentalism, gained control of the state in Afghanistan, initially in opposition to Soviet occupation. Islamic fundamentalists argued for a return to religious law, opposing more secular governments in the region as well as the lures of global consumerism. Whether Christian, Hindu, or Islamic, fundamentalists tended to urge a return to the primacy of religion and religious laws and often opposed greater freedoms for women. Frequently, fundamentalists urged government support for religious values.

Religious fundamentalism ran counter to globalization in several ways, even though many religious leaders became adept at using new global technologies such as the Internet. It tended to appeal particularly to impoverished urban groups who seemed to be left behind in the global economy. Fundamentalism also tended to increase intolerance, even in religious traditions that had historically been reasonably open. Hindu fundamentalism, for example, was more fiercely exclusive than had been true in the past, while also more eager to seek support from the state. While some advocates of globalization assumed that religious traditionalism would decline, the balance was in fact unclear as the 21st century opened.

Religious differences contributed to many regional conflicts. Catholic, Serbian Orthodox, and Muslim clashes complicated the ethnic rivalries in the former Yugoslavia. Battles between Muslims and Christians occurred in Indonesia and the Sudan, and clashes between Hindus and Muslims intensified in India during the 1990s. Judaism and Islam, and Christianity as well, generated tensions not only in Israel but also in Lebanon. Tensions between Christian fundamentalists and other groups intensified political divisions within the United States.

Religious-based terrorism was explicitly against globalization. Choice of the World Trade Center in New York as a target for the September 2001 attacks involved its symbolic role in international, and not just American, capitalism. A bloody bombing attack on a hotel in Bali, Indonesia, lashed out at Australian tourists and the consumerist lifestyle of an international resort. Reactions to terrorism, for example in generating new limitations on international travel, compounded the impact.

Most of the religious movements were not, of course, mainly terroristic, nor were they defined simply by opposition to globalization. Different strands of fundamentalism emerged: for example, many Iranian religious leaders, though eager to support religious law, regarded the Taliban in Afghanistan as crude and excessive. Many religious leaders were far more focused on local issues—like the secular regimes in the Middle East—than on global ones. Fundamentalists did, however, provide alternative identities and standards, compared to globalization. They generated debate within a large number of societies about what kind of future people should strive for.

## The Global Environment

■ **Globalization generated unfamiliar environmental problems. These problems fed resistance to globalization and also efforts at corrective reform.**

Human impact on the environment was not new, but its global level was unprecedented. Industrial competition, in the context of globalization, increased the number of societies eager for economic growth regardless of environmental consequences. New technologies expanded global impact directly. Huge tankers periodically leaked massive amounts of oil into the oceans, affecting many regions. Tall smokestacks, designed to reduce local pollution in the American Midwest or the German Ruhr, spread acidity to the forests of Canada or Scandinavia. Multinationals, seeking loose environmental controls, often spilled chemicals. Above all, the pressure to expand production, in agriculture as well as industry, steadily cut into tropical rain forests, in places like Brazil, causing regional economic damage and contributing to global warming.

A key issue was the expansion of intensive industrial development goals. The Soviet Union and its satellites, pressing production during the cold war, had already caused extensive environmental damage, particularly in regions like central Asia. By the 1990s, China's headlong industrial drive raised new concerns. China's population of over a billion people was building on a resource base that was already severely depleted and degraded—including widespread water shortages. Perpetual smoke covered large regions of the country, thanks to rapid industrial growth. The Chinese called it the "yellow dragon." Beijing planned to shut down manufacturing operations during the 2008 Olympics to provide a brief, internationally pleasant respite. The nation became the second greatest air polluter, after the United States, by 2001.

Equally alarming were reports on the ecological fallout of rapid development in southeast Asia, where multinationals based in Japan and in the newly industrialized countries of east Asia are extracting resources with abandon and where the rain forest is disappearing even more rapidly than in Brazil. Similar trends have been documented in sub-Saharan Africa, where imminent economic collapse and environmental demise are now routinely predicted.

By the end of the 20th century, the wealthy one-fifth of humanity living in the industrialized nations consumed four-fifths of all marketed goods and resources. They also produced over 70 percent of the earth's pollution. In 1998 tiny Belgium, with 9 million people, had a gross domestic product (GDP) equal to that of the 40 countries of sub-Saharan Africa, whose combined population was 450 million. It has been estimated that, at present rates of economic growth, it would take most developing nations 150 years to reach the average levels of productivity achieved in 1980 by wealthy nations like the United States, Japan, and those of western Europe. Many of these societies may not have even a fraction of this time to find sustainable solutions to dilemmas of mass poverty, overpopulation, and environmental degradation. The general issues became abundantly clear in Mexico City, where oxygen is now widely sold by peddlers in the streets. A journalist, Marc Cooper, put it this way:

> the city's poised on the abyss of a world-class bio/technic disaster . . . its infrastructure is crumbling, . . . the drinking water mixes with sewer effluent, . . . many of the scars of the 1985 killer quake won't be healed before the next tremblor strikes. [And even then] Mexico City still beats the eternally depressed, sun-baked countryside.

### Environmental Issues as Global Concerns

At the turn of the 21st century, environmental issues have emerged as focal points of public debate and government policy in most human societies (Figure 41.7). After a century of unprecedented levels of mechanized

**FIGURE 41.7** In April 1986, nuclear chain reactions in the Chernobyl nuclear power plant in Ukraine (then part of the Soviet Union) leapt out of control, creating a fireball that blew the steel and concrete lid off of the reactor. Radioactive material was spewed into the open air and drifted across Europe. The area surrounding the plant, which is now closed, remains a contaminated wasteland. The Chernobyl catastrophe was unique, but it added to the larger environmental damage in many parts of the former Soviet Union.

warfare, scientific experimentation, and the spread of industrialization, a wide variety of complex and often interrelated environmental disruptions threaten not only humanity but all other life forms on the planet Earth (Figure 41.8).

Most scientists now agree that the greenhouse effect caused by the buildup in the atmosphere of excessive amounts of carbon dioxide and other heat-trapping gases has led to a substantial warming of the planet in recent decades. Some of the chief sources of the pollutants responsible for the atmospheric buildup are industrial wastes—including those resulting from energy production through the burning of fossil fuels like coal—and exhaust from millions of cars, trucks, and other machines run by internal combustion engines that burn petroleum. But other major sources of the greenhouse effect are both surprising and at present essential to the survival of large portions of humanity. Methane, another greenhouse gas, is introduced into the atmosphere in massive quantities as a by-product of the stew of fertilized soil and water in irrigated rice paddies, which feed a majority of the peoples of Asia, the world's most populous continent. Methane is also released by flatulent cattle, which produce milk and meat for human populations over much of the globe. Other gases have had equally alarming effects. Chlorofluorocarbons (CFCs), for example, which were once widely used in refrigeration, air conditioning, and spray cans, deplete the ozone layer, thereby removing atmospheric protection from the ultraviolet rays emanating from the sun.

If scientific predictions are correct, global warming will increasingly cause major shifts in temperatures and rainfall throughout much of the globe. Fertile and well-watered areas now highly productive in foods for humans and animals may well be overwhelmed by droughts and famine. If widely accepted computer simulations are correct, coastal areas at sea level—which from Bangladesh to the Netherlands to New Jersey are among the most densely populated in the world—are likely to be inundated. These coastal areas are threatened not just by rising water levels in the world's oceans but by hurricanes and tropical storms that may in the coming decades generate winds up to 200 miles an hour. As climates are drastically altered, vegetation and wildlife in many areas will be radically altered. Temperate forests, for example, may die off in many regions

**FIGURE 41.8** The powerful December 2004 earthquake beneath the Indian Ocean generated *tsunami* (tidal waves) that devastated large areas of Indonesia, Sri Lanka, India, and Thailand. These waves, up to 100 feet high, killed close to 200,000 people in the Indian Ocean basin and caused deaths even as far away as South Africa. Some scientists argue that global warming and overdevelopment of the world's coastlines made the damage caused by the tsunami more severe than it otherwise would have been. Here, survivors walk amid debris from the tsunami in Banda Aceh, Sumatra, almost three weeks after the wave hit.

and be replaced by scrub, tropical vegetation, or desert flora. Some animal species may migrate or adapt and survive, but many, unable to adjust to such rapid climatic changes, will become extinct.

Not all of the sources of global warming are the product of the Industrial Revolution and its rapid spread and intensification, which has been a major theme in 20th-century world history. Most human societies have raised cattle and sheep for millennia, and methane has been flowing from rice paddies into the atmosphere since the Neolithic revolution, which began in some areas as early as the middle of the 9th millennium B.C.E. But the intensification of industrial processes and resource demands has accelerated the greenhouse effect and global warming. The cutting and burning of the world's forests is one of the more notable examples. Not only does the smoke produced contribute massively to carbon dioxide buildup in the atmosphere, but the destruction of the rain forests, in particular, deprives the earth of the natural "sinks" of plant life that suck up carbon dioxide and turn it into oxygen.

The destruction of the rain forests is especially troublesome since, unlike the temperate woodlands, they cannot regenerate themselves. And in terms of evolution, the rain forests have been the source of most of the species of plant and animal life that now inhabit the earth. In this and other ways, human interventions now affect global climate and weather in the short term and will determine the fate of the planetary environment in the centuries, perhaps millennia, to come.

The Rain Forest

International discussions of environmental regulation increased from 1997 onward. A major conference in Kyoto, Japan, set limits on greenhouse gas emissions, in order to curtail global warming. It was not clear, however, whether these limits would have any effect. Many individual nations, including the United States by 2001, opposed the limits proposed because of potential damage to national economies. Here was another area where global politics did not seem to be keeping pace with globalization.

VISUALIZING THE PAST

## Two Faces of Globalization

Early in the 21st century the city of Dubai, in the United Arab Emirates, became a world commercial center, with banking, telecommunications, and other services. Many international corporations located regional offices there. The city was a beehive of construction, including work on the world's newest tallest skyscraper. Most of the buildings were in characteristic modern style, often designed by Western firms and often strikingly beautiful. This Arab center was becoming increasingly cosmopolitan, with little overt protest. But there was another face. Workers in Dubai, most of them immigrants from places like Pakistan, Palestine, and the Philippines, often had relatively low pay. Few were citizens, which limited their access to benefits such as higher education. While they wanted the work for conditions in their host country were better than at home they were not reaping the benefits of globalization in a way comparable to the citizens of Dubai, and their work was extremely physically challenging in a demanding climate.

**Questions** What does this picture say about globalization? There is an obvious side: the march of gleaming city centers in many parts of the world. A less obvious side is the people whose work built the global economy. The picture provides evidence about both sides.

## Disease

Changes in global contacts have usually involved disease, and globalization is no exception. Rapid international travel helped spread the AIDS epidemic from 1980 onward. Southern and eastern Africa were hit most severely, but AIDS also spread to the United States and western Europe. The epidemic took on even larger proportions in places like Brazil. By the early 21st century, rates of increase in parts of Asia and in Russia began to accelerate. These were regions that had initially felt relatively safe but where global contact ultimately brought new levels of contagion. In 2003 a small but persistent outbreak of a new illness, Severe Acute Respiratory Syndrome (SARS), raised fears of another global contagion.

The result, to be sure, was less severe than some of the earlier epidemics associated with global contacts, though some experts warned of even greater disease problems in the future. Environmental issues, newer on the global scale, may have replaced disease as the clearest downside of international connections.

## Toward the Future

- **Forecasts about the future use history, but in different ways. Key issues for the future emerge from recent trends and tensions.**

Human beings have always wanted to know what the future will hold. Various societies looked to the configurations of the stars for predictions, and astrology still has partisans in the contemporary world. Some societies generated beliefs in cycles, predicting that the future would repeat patterns already seen in the past; many Chinese scholars developed a cyclical approach. Still other societies assume that the future will differ from the past; from the Enlightenment onward, Western culture developed an additional belief in progress.

History suggests the futility of many efforts at forecasting. It has been estimated that well over half of the "expert" forecasts generated in the United States since World War II have been wrong. This includes predictions that by 2000 most Americans would be riding to and from work in some kind of airship, or that families would be replaced by promiscuous communes. Yet if history debunks forecasts, it also provides the basis for thinking about the future.

### Projecting from Trends

The most obvious connection between history and the future involves the assessment of trends that are likely to continue at least for several decades. Thus we "know" that global population growth will slow up, because it is already slowing up. Many forecasts see stabilization by 2050, based on rapidly falling birth rates around the world. We also "know" that populations will become older; that is, the percentage of older citizens will increase. This is already happening in western Europe, the United States, and Japan and will occur elsewhere as birth rates drop. What we don't "know" of course is how societies will react to the demands of the increasing numbers of older people, or how much the environment will have deteriorated by the time global population stabilizes. Even trend-based forecasts can be thrown off by unexpected events, like wars. In the 1930s experts "knew" that the American birth rate would fall, because it was already falling, but then war and prosperity created a totally unexpected baby boom, and the experts were wrong for at least two decades.

Trend-based forecasting is even chancier when the trends are already fragile. The late 20th century saw a genuine global spread of democracy, though admittedly not to every region. It was possible to venture predictions about the triumph of this form of government. But by 2002 it was hard to be confident that democracies were entirely secure in parts of Latin America or even in Russia. The hold of earlier, less democratic political traditions or the sheer pressure of economic stagnation might unseat the trend.

Forecasting is at least as complex when two different trends are in play. The 20th century saw a fairly steady rise in consumerism, which spread to all parts of the world. The appeal of mass media, commercialized sports, and global fashions reaches across traditional boundaries. But the last 30 years have also seen a pronounced increase in religious interest, in many if not all parts of the world. Some people participate in both trends, but overall, the priorities are different. Is one of the two trends likely to predominate? Or should we think of the future in terms of division and tension among cultural interests?

### Big Changes

Some analysts have looked at the world's future in terms of stark departures from its past. They argue that trend analysis is inadequate because we are on the verge of a major shift in framework. In the 1960s a "population bomb" analysis won considerable attention. The argument was that rapid population growth was about to overwhelm all other developments, leading to resource depletion, new wars over resources, and a world far different from what we had previously known. In fact, this particular scenario has fallen from favor, despite continued rapid population growth. The slowing rate of growth, combined with the fact that food production has on the whole kept pace, has displaced this disturbing scenario. But other forecasts, of dramatic climate change and of resource exhaustion, provide some environmentalists with another dire picture of the world's future, in which other issues, like the fate of particular political systems, fade in importance.

Another scenario that has enjoyed recurrent popularity is the vision of a postindustrial world. Some pundits argue that computer technology, genetic engineering, and other technological advances are undermining the conditions of industrial society. Information, not production, becomes the key to economic growth and to social structures. The functions of cities shift from production to entertainment. Work will become more individualized and less time consuming, creating a new premium for expressive leisure. Again, the emphasis is on a dramatically different future. Here too, however, critics express doubts. Many parts of the world are not yet industrial, much less postindustrial. Work does not seem to be heading toward less routine; for example, computers promote repetitious activities as much as new creativity. As is always true with intriguing predictions of massive change, the jury is still out.

## The Problem of the Contemporary Period

One of the reasons prediction is particularly difficult—though also compelling—is that world history has undergone so many fundamental changes during the past century. We know, for example, that the dominance of western Europe, for centuries a staple of world history, is a thing of the past, despite the continued vitality of the region. But what will replace it? Continued United States ascendancy, with military outposts in many parts of the world? Or the rise of China or east Asia? Or perhaps no single dominant region at all? We know there's a question about the world balance that will replace Western control, but the answer is unclear.

The same applies to conditions for women. Improvements in women's education plus the decline of the birth rate add up to significant changes for women around the world. The pace of change varies with the region, to be sure. Many regions also have given new legal and political rights to women. But is there a new model for women's roles that might be applicable around the world? Continued disputes about women's work roles, significant male backlash against change, and even disputes by women themselves about the relevance of a Western model for women's lives make forecasting difficult. We can assume continued change, but it's hard to pinpoint the results.

GLOBAL CONNECTIONS

## Civilizations and Global Forces

A key question for the future involves the fate of individual civilizations. World history has been shaped by the characteristics of key civilizations for over 5000 years, granting that not everyone has been part of a major civilization and that in some cases civilizations are not easy to define. Some observes argue that, by the 21st century, the separate characteristics of civilizations are beginning to yield to homogenizing forces. Many scientists, athletes, and businesspeople feel more commitment to their professional interests than to their region of origin—which means that global professional identities can override civilizational loyalties. The downtowns of most cities around the world look very much alike. The same products, stores, and restaurants can be found in most urban areas. Globalization may be outpacing regional labels.

Yet we have also seen that globalization can falter, as it did in the middle decades of the 20th century. Even when it accelerates, as in the 1990s, it brings efforts to reassert separate identities. Even as it participates in the global economy, China remains different, reflecting for example some of the political characteristics that were launched 3000 years ago. The Japanese easily move in global economics and culture, but with an emphasis on group identity measurably different from the personal goals emphasized in the United States. Major religions like Hinduism and Islam continue to mark their regions, and in some ways their influence seems to be on the rise.

World history has long been defined by a tension between regional features and larger connections. The specifics change, for example with shifts in technology and organizational capacity. But it may be premature to assume that some kind of global homogeneity is going to change the equation altogether.

## Further Readings

Walter Laqueur, *Fascism: Past, Present, Future* (1997), is the authoritative analysis of present-day fascism, with an excellent bibliographical essay and several solid regional studies of far-right political movements. Paul Hockenos, *Free to Hate: The Rise of the Right in Post-Communist Eastern Europe* (1994), provides accessible reportage that explores neofascist movements on a country-by-country basis. J. Luccassen and L. Luccassen, eds., *Migration, Migration, History, History: Old Paradigms and New Perspectives* (1997), is a recent comparative social history—in addition to an extensive bibliography it includes chapters on conceptual issues (periodization, definitions, etc.) and several regional historical case studies. Alistair Ager, *Refugees: Perspectives on the Experience of Forced Migration* (1998), is a useful survey.

For very different takes on the resurgence of globalization since 1989, see Thomas Friedman's cautious celebration in *The Lexus and the Olive Tree: Understanding Globalization* (2000), John Gray's more sober appraisal in *False Dawn* (2000), and Thomas Frank's lively critique in *One Market Under God* (2000). Differing perspectives on the cultural ramifications of the new global economic order are provided by Peter Stearns, *Consumerism in World History* (2001); Walter LaFeber, *Michael Jordan and the New Global Capitalism* (2000); and the contributions to James Watson, ed., *Golden Arches East: McDonald's in East Asia* (1998). See also Lewis Solomon, *Multinational Corporations and the Emerging World Order* (1978); Stephen Rees, *American Films Abroad* (1997); Theodore von Laue, *The World Revolution of Westernization* (1997); Peter N. Stearns, *The Industrial Revolution in World History* (1998); and Bruce Mazlish and Ralph Buultjens, eds., *Conceptualizing Global History* (1993).

For genuinely global perspectives on environmental issues, see Bill McKibben, *The End of Nature* (1999 ed.); Mark Hertsgaard, *Earth Odyssey* (1998); and Ramachandra Guha, *Environmentalism: A Global History* (2000). The best accounts of environmental degradation in key regions of the world include Susanna Hecht and Alexander Cockburn, *The Fate of the Forest* (1990), about Brazil; Judith Shapiro, *Mao's War against Nature* (2001); Vaclav Smil, *The Bad Earth* (1984) and *China's Environmental Crisis* (1993); Murray Feshback and Alfred Friendly Jr., *Ecocide in the USSR* (1992); Marc Reisner, *Cadillac Desert* (1993), about the United States; and Madhav Gadgil and Ramachandra Guha, *Ecology and Equity* (1995), about India.

Several serious books (as well as many more simplistic, popularized efforts) attempt to sketch the future of the world or the West. On the concept of the postindustrial society, see Daniel Bell, *The Coming of Post-Industrial Society* (1974). For other projections, consult R. L. Heilbroner, *An Inquiry into the Human Prospect* (1974); and L. Stavrianos, *The Promise of the Coming Dark Age* (1976).

On environment and resource issues, see D. H. Meadows and D. L. Meadows, *The Limits to Growth* (1974); Al Gore, *Earth in the Balance* (1992); and L. Herbert, *Our Synthetic Environment* (1962). M. ul Haq's *The Poverty Curtain: Choices for the Third World* (1976) and L. Solomon's *Multinational Corporations and the Emerging World Order* (1978) cover economic issues, in part from a non-Western perspective. On a leading social issue, see P. Huston, *Third World Women Speak Out* (1979).

## On the Web

Analyses and links to both sides of the globalization debate are offered at http://globalization.about.com/library/weekly/aa080701a.htm and http://www.emory.edu/SOC/globalization/. Of the many other sites on globalization, some of the more interesting and historically grounded include http://www.stephweb.com/capstone/index.htm and http://www.epinet.org/subjectpages/trade.html, which reports on international trade. One site highly critical of economic globalization (http://www.ifg.org/analysis.htm) offers a dark analysis of the role of the World Trade Organization, the World Bank, and the United Nations in this process. The World Bank (http://www1.worldbank.org/economicpolicy/globalization/) and the International Monetary Fund offer their own more roseate view of globalization at http://www.imf.org/external/np/exr/ib/2000/041200.htm. Another site (http://www.pbs.org/globalization/) examines the impact of globalization on human rights.

A militant view of the alleged ills of the affluent society and the growing dominance of multinational and nonstate organizations in the postmodern era is presented at http://www.socialconscience.com/. A less radical view that nonetheless suggests that the twin pillars of Western civilization (the market economy and democracy) are more likely to undermine than support each other can be found at http://www.mtholyoke.edu/acad/intrel/attali.html.

An indispensable discussion of recent trends in Islamic nationalism/fundamentalism is provided at http://wrc.lingnet.org/islamf.htm.

Links to virtually every aspect of recent conflicts within Islamist states and with non-Islamist nations, including the origins of the Taliban and counter-Taliban attacks on Afghanistan by much of the world community, can be found at http://www.library.vanderbilt.edu/romans/terrorism/afghanistan.html. The roots and results of the Taliban movement can currently be studied via an online version of David B. Edwards, *Before Taliban: Genealogies of the Afghan Jihad* (2002), at http://ark.cdlib.org/ark:/13030/ft3p30056w/. For the place of Hamas in Islamist efforts, see http://www.prisonplanet.com/news_lert_hamas2.html and http://www.meta-religion.com/Hate_Groups/extremism_islamic.htm.

The text of, and debate over the accuracy of, Samuel Huntington's argument that the world is heading toward a "clash of civilizations" can be found at http://www.alamut.com/subj/economics/misc/clash.html, http://www.lander.edu/atannenbaum/Tannenbaum%20courses%20folder/POLS%20103%20World%20Politics/103_huntington_clash_of_civilizations_full_text.htm, http://www.shunya.net/Text/Articles/EdwardSaid.htm, http://csf.colorado.edu/wsystems/jwsr/archive/vol4/v4n2r2.htm, and http://www.ndsu.nodak.edu/ndsu/ambrosio/civ.html.

A site that seeks to debunk concerns over global warming (http://www.globalwarming.org/about.htm) may be usefully compared with other public interest sites expressing those concerns (http://www.sierraclub.org/globalwarming/dangerousexperiment/ and http://www.climatehotmap.org/). Pace University's site, http://www.law.pace.edu/env/energy/globalwarming.html, offers useful links to all sides of this controversy. The text of the Kyoto protocol on global warming that the United States has refused to sign is offered at http://www.cnn.com/SPECIALS/1997/global.warming/stories/treaty/. Another interesting site (http://www.americans-world.org/digest/global_issues/global_warming/gw2.cfm) is devoted to analyzing shifts in public opinion on the Kyoto protocols.

# Document Analysis

## Part IV • The Early Modern Period, 1450–1750: The World Shrinks

**I. What can these documents tell us about the motives of the Europeans and the consequences of their encounters with the indigenous peoples of the Americas? What additional types of documents might be helpful in answering these questions? Background: European travel and exploration in the Americas expanded steadily after 1492; records of native reactions are rarer but some records were preserved.**

**1. Letter of Amerigo Vespucci: his first voyage to the New World c. 1497**

Amongst those people we did not learn that they had any law, nor can they be called Moors nor Jews, and (they are) worse than pagans: because we did not observe that they offered any sacrifice: nor even had they a house of prayer: their manner of living I judge to be Epicurean: their dwellings are in common: and their houses (are) made in the style of huts, but strongly made, and constructed with very large trees, and covered over with palm-leaves, secure against storms and winds: and in some places (they are) of so great breadth and length, that in one single house we found there were 600 souls . . . every eight or ten years they change their habitations: and when asked why they did so: (they said it was) because of the soil which, from its filthiness, was already unhealthy and corrupted, and that it bred aches in their bodies, which seemed to us a good reason: their riches consist of bird's plumes of many colours, or of rosaries which they make from fishbones, or of white or green stones which they put in their cheeks and in their lips and ears, and of many other things which we in no wise value: they use no trade, they neither buy nor sell. In fine, they live and are contended with that which nature gives them. The wealth that we enjoy in this our Europe and elsewhere, such as gold, jewels, pearls, and other riches, they hold as nothing; and although they have them in their own lands, they do not labour to obtain them, nor do they value them. They are liberal in giving, for it is rarely they deny you anything: and on the other hand, liberal in asking, when they shew themselves your friends. . . .

**2. Dr. Diego Alverez Chanca, participant in Columbus's second voyage, on the Caribe Indians, in a published account c. 1500**

The way of life of these *caribe* people is bestial. . . .

These people raid the other islands and carry off the women whom they can take, especially the young and beautiful ones, whom they keep to serve them and have as concubines, and they carry off so many that in fifty houses nobody was found, and of the captives more than twenty were young girls. These women also say that they are treated with a cruelty which seems incredible, for sons whom they have from them are eaten and they only rear those whom they have from their native women. The men whom they are able to take, those who are alive they bring to their houses to butcher for meat, and those who are dead are eaten there and then. They say that men's flesh is so good that there is nothing like it in the world, and it certainly seems so for the bones which we found in these houses had been gnawed of everything they could gnaw, so that nothing was left on them except what was much too tough to be eaten.

**3. Spanish explorer Hernando Cortés in Mexico, writing to the Spanish government c. 1520**

Captain Hernando Cortés . . . decided . . . to depart; and so hoisting sail they left that Island of Cozumel . . . very peaceably inclined, so much so that if it were proposed to found a colony there the natives would be ready without coercion to serve their Spanish masters. The chiefs in particular were left contented and at ease with what the Captain had told them on behalf of your Majesties and with the numerous articles of finery which he had given them for their own persons. I think there can be no doubt that all Spaniards who may happen to come to this Island in the future will be as well received as if they were arriving in a land which had been long time colonized.

Your Majesties must know that when the Captain told the chiefs in his first interview with them that they must live no longer in the pagan faith which they held they begged him to acquaint them with the law under which they were henceforth to live. The Captain accordingly informed them to the best of his ability in the Catholic Faith . . . and gave them to understand very fully what they must do to be good Christians, all of which they manifestly received with very good will, and so we left them very happy and contented. . . .

**4. French explorer Samuel de Champlain in North America, reporting to his government c. 1632**

All these savages from the Island Cape wear neither robes nor furs, except very rarely. . . . They have only the sexual parts concealed with a small piece of leather; so likewise the women, with whom it comes down a little lower behind than with the men, all the rest of the body being naked. . . . Their bodies are well-proportioned. I cannot tell what government they have, but I think that in this respect they resemble their neighbors, who have none at all. They know not how to worship or pray; yet, like the other savages, they have some superstitions, which I shall describe in the place. . . . Even a slight intercourse with them gives you at once a knowledge of them. They are great thieves and, if they cannot lay hold of any thing with their hands, they try to do so with their feet, as we have oftentimes learned by experience. I am of opinion that, if they had any thing to exchange with us, they would not give themselves to thieving. They bartered away to us their bows, arrows, and quivers, for pins and buttons; and if they had had any thing else better they would have done the same with it. It is necessary to be on one's guard against this people, and live in a state of distrust with them, yet without letting them perceive it.

**5. Aztec reactions to the European encounter 16th Century**

The messengers [of the Aztec leader Motecuhzoma, returning from the Spanish explorer Hernando Cortés] also said: "Their trappings and arms are all made of iron. They dress in iron and wear iron casques on their heads. Their swords are iron; their bows are iron; their shields are iron, their spears are iron. Their deer carry them on their backs wherever they wish to go. These deer, our lord, are as tall as the roof of a house.

"The strangers' bodies are completely covered, so that only their faces can be seen. Their skin is white, as if it were made of lime. They have yellow hair, though some of them have black. Their beards are long and yellow, and their moustaches are also yellow. Their hair is curly, with very fine strands."

When Motecuhzoma heard this report, he was filled with terror. It was as if his heart had fainted, as if it had shriveled. It was as if he were conquered by despair.

While the Spaniards were in Tlaxcala, a great plague broke out in Tenochtitlan. It began to spread . . . striking everywhere in the city and killing a vast number of our people. Sores erupted on our faces, our breasts, our bellies; we were covered with agonizing sores from head to foot.

**II. Evaluate the cultural, economic, and political calculations that were made by Russians, Asians, and Africans as a result of the sudden increase in the West European role in world trade. What additional types of documents might assist in addressing this question? Background: Europe's world trade expanded steadily from about 1500 onward, drawing various reactions and policies in Asia, Russia, and Africa.**

**1. Russia: Decree of Tsar Peter the Great Regarding the Study of Navigation Abroad c. 1714**

3. Discover as much as possible how to put ships to sea during a naval battle. Those who cannot succeed in this effort must diligently ascertain what action should be taken by the vessels that do and those that do not put to sea during such a situation [naval battle]. Obtain from [foreign] naval officers written statements, bearing their signatures and seals, of how adequately you [Russian students] are prepared for [naval] duties.
4. If, upon his return, anyone wishes to receive [from the Tsar] greater favors for himself, he should learn, in addition to the above enumerated instructions, how to construct those vessels aboard which he would like to demonstrate his skills.
5. Upon his return to Moscow, every [foreign-trained Russian] should bring with him at his own expense, for which he will later be reimbursed, at least two experienced masters of naval science.

**2. China: Memorial of bureaucrat Hsu Kuang-Chi (to the Emperor) c. 1617**

Knowing full well that the arts and sciences of the foreigners are in a high degree correct, your majesty's humble servant earnestly begs of his sacred Intelligence, the illustrious honor of issuing a manifesto on their behalf. . . .

As your servant for years past has been thus accustomed to engage in discussions and investigations with these [European] courtiers, he has become well acquainted with them, and knows that they are not only in deportment and in heart wholly free from anything which can excite suspicion, but that they are indeed worthies and sages; that their doctrines are most correct; their regimen most strict, their learning most extensive; their knowledge most refined; their hearts most true; their views most steady. . . . Now the reason of their coming thousands of miles eastward, is because hearing that the teachers, the sages and worthies of China, served Heaven by the cultivation of personal virtue . . . they desired, notwithstanding the difficulties and dangers by land and by sea, to give their seal to the truth. . . .

**3. Muslim Indian reactions: Abu Taleb Khan's book about his travels to England 18th Century**

The first and greatest defect I observed in the English is their want of faith in religion, and their great inclination to philosophy [atheism]: The effect of these principles, or rather want of principle, is very conspicuous in the lower orders of people, who are totally devoid of honesty. They are, indeed, cautious how they transgress against the laws, from fear of punishment; but whenever an opportunity offers of stealing anything without the risk of detection, they never pass it by. . . .

Their third defect is a passion for acquiring money and their attachment to worldly affairs. Although these bad qualities are not so reprehensible in them as in countries more subject to the vicissitudes of fortune, (because, in England, property is so well protected by the laws that every person reaps the fruits of his industry, and, in his old age, enjoys the earnings or economy of his youth,) yet sordid habits are generally found to accompany avarice; on the contrary, generosity, if it does not launch into prodigality, but is guided by the hand of prudence, will render a man respected and esteemed. . . .

**4. Reactions to the first Portuguese arrivals in East Africa, from a Swahili chronicle c. 1520**

During al-Fudail's reign there came news from the land of Mozambique that men had come from Europe. They had three ships, and the name of their captain was al-Mirati [Dom Vasco da Gama]. After a few days there came word that the ships had passed Kilwa and had gone on to Mafia. The lord of Mafia rejoiced, for they thought they [the Europeans] were good and honest men. But those who knew the truth confirmed that they were corrupt and dishonest persons who had only come to spy out the land in order to seize it. And they determined to cut the anchors of their ships so that they should drift ashore and be wrecked by the Muslims. The Europeans learnt of this and went on to Malindi. When the people of Malindi saw them, they knew they were bringers of war and corruption, and were troubled with very great fear. They gave them all they asked, water, food, firewood, and everything else. And the Europeans asked for a pilot to guide them to India, and after that back to their own land—God curse it!

**5. Japanese exclusion of the Portuguese c. 1639**

1. The matter relating to the banning of Christianity is known [to the Portuguese]. However, heretofore they have secretly transported those who are going to propagate that religion.
2. If those who believe in that religion band together in an attempt to do evil things, they must be subjected to punishment.
3. While those who believe in the preaching of the priests are in hiding, there are incidents in which that country [Portugal] has sent gifts to them for their sustenance.

In view of the above, hereafter entry by the Portuguese ships is forbidden. If they insist on coming [to Japan], the ships must be destroyed and anyone aboard those ships must be beheaded. We have received the above order and are thus transmitting it to you accordingly.

The above concerns our disposition with regard to the *galeota*.

**III. Based on the following documents, evaluate attitudes about the role Native American labor served in the Spanish colonies in the Americas in the 16th and 17th centuries. Explain what kind of additional document(s) would help you evaluate these attitudes.**

*Historical background: The Spanish Empire in the Americas, which began in 1492, was organized into 4 viceroyalties, each with a royally- appointed Viceroy and royally-appointed judges in courts known as Audencias. The viceroyalties of Peru and New*

*Spain (Mexico) contained the major silver mines, while other viceroyalties had economies based on agriculture and trade. The Spanish adapted the Inca traditional labor organization of the mita (a labor tax, which required that one's family—allyu—must do some unpaid labor for local aristocrats, religious communities, or the royal court) to their own uses in Peru. The Catholic Church sought to convert the Amerindians to Catholicism through missionaries and then a well-established and organized hierarchy similar to European models, including schools, universities, monasteries, and convents.*

1.

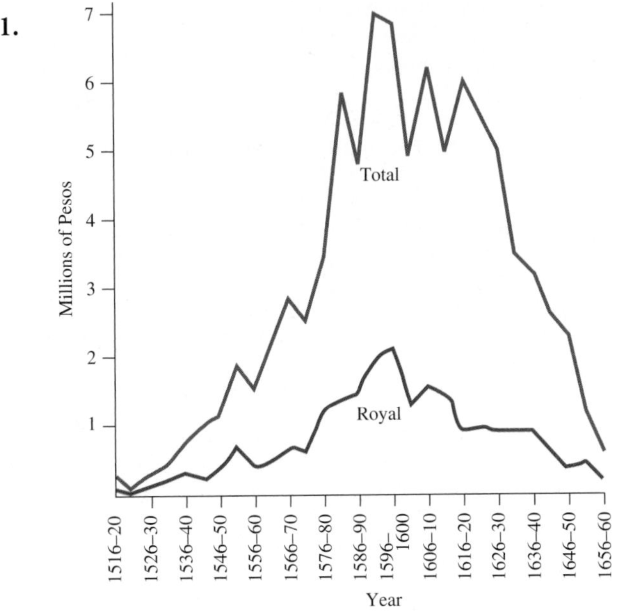


*Source:* Silver Production in Spanish America, 1516–1660.

2.

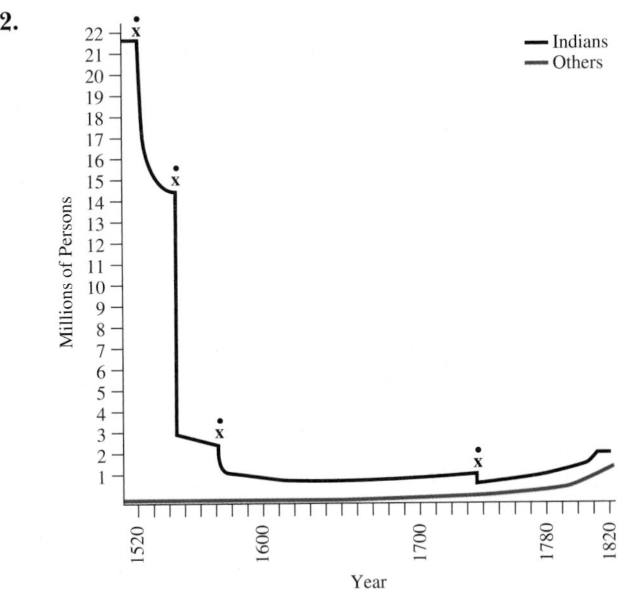


*Source:* Population Decline in New Spain, 1520–1820.

3. ***The Laws and Ordinances Newly made by His Majesty [Charles I] for the Government of the Indies and Good Treatment and Preservation of the Indians*, Spain, 1542**

***Source: From* The New Laws of the Indies, *ed. Henry Stevens (London: The Chiswick Press, 1893), pp. iii–xvii, passim. Accessed at http://www.fordham.edu/halsall/mod/1542newlawsindies.html 1/23/06. Document has been edited slightly for length and clarity of vocabulary.***

Whereas one of the most important things in which the Audiencias [royally-appointed courts in each of the viceroyalties] are to serve us is in taking very especial care of the good treatment of the Indians and preservation of them, We command that the said Audiencias enquire continually into the excesses or ill treatment which are or shall be done to them by governors or private persons. [...]

As We have ordered provision to be made that from henceforward the Indians in no way be made slaves, including those who until now have been enslaved against all reason and right and contrary to the provisions and instructions thereupon, We ordain and command that the Audiencias having first summoned the parties to their presence, without any further judicial form, but in a summary way, so that the truth may be ascertained, speedily set the said Indians at liberty unless the persons who hold them for slaves show title why they should hold and possess them legitimately.

Also, We command that with regard to the loading of the said Indians with cargo, the Audiencias take especial care that they be not loaded with cargo, or in case that in some parts this cannot be avoided that it be in such a manner that no risk of life, health and preservation of the said Indians may ensue from an immoderate burden; and that against their own will and without their being paid, in no case be it permitted that they be loaded with cargo, punishing very severely him who shall act contrary to this. In this there is to be no remission out of respect to any person.

4. **Excerpt from *New Chronicle and Good Government*, Guaman Poma de Ayala [Andean noble and Christian convert who served Spanish priests as interpreter of Quechua, the Indian language of Central and Southern Andes], Peru, c. 1615**

The aforementioned priests, fathers, and pastors who stand for God and his saints in the parishes of this kingdom of Peru do not act like the blessed priests who preceded them. Rather, they give themselves over to greed for silver, clothing, and things of the world, and sins of the flesh, appetites, and unspeakable misdeeds.

These fathers and parish priests in this kingdom all keep *mita* [corvée labor] Indians busy: two Indians in the kitchen, another looking after the horses, another in the garden, another as janitor, others to bring firewood and fodder, others as shepherds, harvesters, messengers, field workers, and tenders of chicken, goats, sheep, cows, mares, and pigs. And in other things they insolently put the aforementioned hapless Indian men and women of this kingdom to work without pay. And for this reason they leave their homes.

These Parish priests pasture ten mules and others belonging to their friends, which they fatten up at the expense of the Indians and single women who must take care of them. Some have many cows; also a thousand head of goats or sheep and pigs . . . one or two hundred chickens and rabbits; and planted fields. And people are put in charge of all these things with the corrals and buildings, keeping the poor Indians busy. . . and they [the workers] are neither paid nor fed.

These parish priests have thread spun and woven, oppressing the widows and unmarried women, making them work without pay on the pretext that they were living in illicit unions.

5. **"The Potosí Mine and Indian Forced Labor in Peru," Antonio Vásquez de Espinosa [a Carmelite monk traveling through Spanish America between 1612–1620], Spain.**

These Indians are sent out every year under a captain whom they choose in each village or tribe . . . every year they have a new election, for as some go out, others come in. This works out very badly, with great losses and gaps in the quotas of Indians, the villages being depopulated. . . .

These 13,330 are divided up every 4 months into 3 *mitas*, each consisting of 4,433 Indians, to work in the mines on the range and in the 120 smelters. . . . These mita Indians each earn each day 4 *reales*. Besides these there are others not under obligation, who are mingados or hire themselves out voluntarily: these get 12 to 16 *reales*. . . . They and the *mita* Indians go up every Monday morning to . . . the foot of the range; the Corregidor arrives . . . and he there checks off and reports to each mine and smelter owner the number of Indians assigned him. . . .

After each has eaten his ration, they climb up the hill, each to his mine, and go in, staying there from that hour until Saturday evening without coming out of the mine; their wives bring them food, but they stay constantly underground, excavating and carrying out ore from which they get the silver. They all have tallow candles, lighted day and night; that is the light they work with . . . .

**6.**

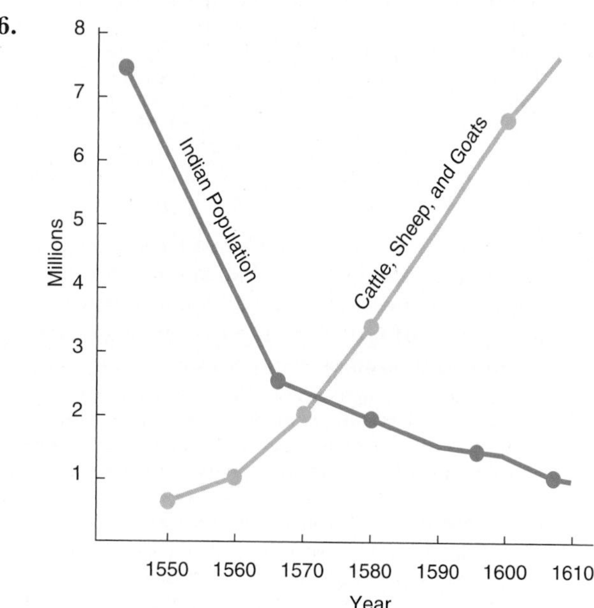


A comparison of human and livestock populations in central Mexico.

**7.**

**TABLE 25.2 Estimated Slave Imports into the Americas by Importing Region, 1519–1866**

| Region and Country | Slaves |
|---|---|
| Brazil | 3,902,000 |
| British Caribbean | 2,238,200 |
| Spanish America | 1,267,800 |
| French Caribbean | 1,092,600 |
| Guianas[a] | 403,700 |
| British North America | 361,100 |
| Dutch Caribbean | 129,700 |
| Danish Caribbean | 73,100 |
| | 9,468,200 |

[a]Includes Dutch, French and British colonies, namely Berbice, Cayenne, Demerara, Essequebo, and Surinam.

# Document Analysis

## Part V • The Dawn of the Industrial Age, 1750–1914

**I. What was the relationship between nationalism on the one hand, and liberalism and conservatism on the other in the 18th and 19th centuries? What additional types of documents would help in understanding this relationship? Background: Nationalist ideals first developed on an intellectual level in later 18th-century Europe; liberal ideals date in part from the 18th century Enlightenment; formal conservatism emerged during the 1790s. All were enhanced and further shaped by the French and other revolutions from 1789 into the early 19th century; developments like the Mexican republic of the later 1860s and conservative reactions to Russian reforms in the 1860s also brought new political statements.**

**1. Decree of the revolutionary National Convention in France 1792**

Henceforth the French nation proclaims the sovereignty of the people, the suppression of all civil and military authorities which have governed you up to the present, and of all taxes which you sustain, in whatever form they exist; the abolition of the tithe, of feudalism, of seigneurial [feudal] rights . . . of real and personal servitude, of aristocratic hunting and fishing privileges, [labor service and all manorial taxes], and generally of every species of contributions with which you have been burdened by your usurpers; it proclaims also the abolition among you of all prerogatives and privileges that are contrary to equality. You are henceforth, brothers and friends, all citizens, all equal in rights, and all equally summoned to govern, to serve, and to defend your *Patrie* [fatherland].

**2. Prussian government proclamation rousing the people against Napoleon 1813**

Brandenburgers, Prussians, Silesians, Pomeranians, Lithuanians! You know what you have borne for the past seven years; you know the sad fate that awaits you if we do not bring this war to an honorable end. Think of the times gone by,—of the Great Elector, the great Frederick! Remember the blessings for which your forefathers fought under their leadership and which they paid for with their blood,—freedom of conscience, national honor, independence, commerce, industry, learning.

Great sacrifices will be demanded from every class of the people, for our undertaking is a great one, and the number and resources of our enemies far from insignificant. But would you not rather make these sacrifices for the fatherland and for your own rightful king than for a foreign ruler, who, as he has shown by many examples, will use you and your sons and your uttermost farthing for ends which are nothing to you?

**3. Speech of Simón Bolívar to the Legislature of Venezuela after Independence 1819**

All our moral powers will not suffice to save our infant republic from this chaos unless we fuse the mass of the people, the government, the legislation, and the national spirit into a unified single body. Unity, unity, unity must be our motto in all things. The blood of our citizens is varied: let it be mixed for the sake of unity. Our constitution has divided our powers of government: let them be bound together to secure unity. Our laws are but a sad relic of ancient and modern despotism. Let this monstrous edifice crumble and fall; and, having removed even its ruins, let us erect a temple to Justice; and, guided, by its sacred inspiration, let us write a code of Venezuelan laws.

**4. Speech of the Mexican intellectual Gabino Barreda c. 1867**

Fellow citizens: in the future let our motto be Liberty, Order, and Progress; Liberty as means; Order as a base, and Progress as an end; it is a triple motto represented by the tricolor on our beautiful flag, that same flag which became in 1821 a blessed emblem of our independence . . . the emblem which . . . assured the future of America and the world by rescuing republican institutions.

In the future, may a complete freedom of conscience and an absolute freedom of expression permitting all ideas and inspirations, concede an enlightenment everywhere and make all disturbance not spiritual and all revolution which is not merely intellectual, unnecessary and impossible. May the physical order, conserved and maintained by all governors and respected by the governed, be a sure guarantor and the best way forever along the florid path of progress and civilization.

**5. Slavic nationalist Nikolai Danilevsky c. 1869**

In the socio-economic sphere, Russia is the only large state which has solid ground under its feet, in which there are no landless masses, and in which, consequently, the social edifice does not rest on the misery of the majority of the citizens and on the insecurity of their situation. In Russia only there cannot and does not exist any contradiction between political and economic ideals. This contradiction threatens disaster to European life, a life which has embarked on its historical voyage in the dangerous seas between . . . military despotism and . . . social revolution. The factors that give such superiority to the Russian social structure over the European, and give it an unshakable stability, are the peasant's land and its common ownership. On this health of Russia's socio-economic structure we found our hope for the great socio-economic significance of the Slav cultural-historical type. This type has been able for the first time to create a just and normal system of human activity, which embraces not only human relations in the moral and political sphere, but also man's mastery of nature, which is a means of satisfying human needs and requirements. Thus it establishes not only formal equality in the relations between citizens, but a real and concrete equality. Under the wise authority of our Emperor, Russians benefit from political order, not the corrupt agitation of Western politicians.

**II. How did leaders in Europe, the United States, and Japan justify the expansion of educational opportunity in the 19th century? What additional types of documents would assist in this evaluation? Background: Discussions of educational reform blossomed in France and the United States in the 1830s and 1840s, when new public school systems were launched; Japanese discussion followed from the establishment of mass education in 1872.**

1. **France: Writings of Albertine-Adrienne Necker de Saussure 1838**

But this part of our celestial nature which education should constantly seek to bring out, man has scarcely taken into account. He has had this life only in view, and has shut his eyes upon whatever limited his rights here. He has seen only the wife in the woman—in the young girl only the future wife. All the faculties, the qualities which have no immediate relation to his interests, have seemed to him worthless. Yet there are many of the gifts bestowed upon woman that have no relation to the state of a wife. This state, although natural, is not necessary—perhaps half the women who now exist, have not been, or are no longer, married. In the indigent classes, the girl who is able to maintain herself, quits her parents, and supports herself by industry for a long time, perhaps for life, without requiring aid from man. No social arrangements oblige her to become dependent. It is therefore important, that education should unfold in the young girl the qualities which give the surest promise of wisdom, happiness, usefulness, and dignity, whatever may be her lot. . . .

2. **Reform leader Horace Mann's *The Goals of Education* c. 1840**

One of the highest and most valuable objects, to which the influences of a school can be made conducive, consists in training our children to self-government. . . . So tremendous, too, are the evils of anarchy and lawlessness, that a government by mere force, however arbitrary and cruel, has been preferable to no-government. But self-government, self-control, a voluntary compliance with the laws of reason and duty, have been justly considered as the highest point of excellence attainable by a human being. No one, however, can consciously obey the laws of reason and duty, until he understands them. Hence the preliminary necessity of their being clearly explained, of their being made to stand out, broad, lofty, and as conspicuous as a mountain against a clear sky. There may be blind obedience without a knowledge of the law, but only of the will of the lawgiver; but the first step towards rational obedience is a knowledge of the rule to be obeyed, and of the reasons on which it is founded.

3. **United States: Eliza Duffy on Education 1874**

If there is really a radical mental difference in men and women founded upon sex, you *cannot* educate them alike, however much you try. If women *cannot* study unremittingly, why then they *will* not, and you *cannot make them.* But because they do, because they choose so to do, because they will do so in spite of you, should be accepted as evidence that they can, and, all other things being equal, can with impunity. Instead of our race dying out through these women, they are the hope of the country—the women with broad chests, large limbs and full veins, perfect muscular and digestive systems and harmonious sexual organs, who will keep pace with men either in a foot or an intellectual race, who know perfectly their own powers and are not afraid to tax them to their utmost, knowing as they do that action generates force. These are the mothers of the coming race. . . . The result will be truly "the survival of the fittest."

4. **Japan: Imperial Rescript on Education 1890**

Our Imperial Ancestors have founded Our Empire on a basis broad and everlasting, and have deeply and firmly implanted virtue; Our subjects ever united in loyalty and filial piety have from generation to generation illustrated the beauty thereof. This is the glory of the fundamental character of Our Empire, and herein also lies the source of Our education. Ye, Our subjects, . . . pursue learning and cultivate arts; and thereby develop intellectual faculties and perfect moral powers; furthermore advance public good and promote common interests; always respect the Constitution and observe the laws; should emergency arise, offer yourselves courageously to the State; and thus guard and maintain the prosperity of Our Imperial Throne coeval with heaven and earth. So shall ye not only be Our good and faithful subjects, but render illustrious the best traditions of our forefathers.

5. **Japan: Educational reformer Yukichi Fukuzawa's *Autobiography* 1899**

In the education of the East, so often saturated with Confucian teaching, I find two things lacking; that is to say, a lack of studies in the number and reason in material culture, and a lack of the idea of independence in spiritual culture. But in the West I think I see why their states then are successful in managing their national affairs, and the businessmen in theirs, and the people generally ardent in their patriotism and happy in their family circles.

I regret that in our country I have to acknowledge that people are not formed on these two principles, though I believe no one can escape the laws of number and reason, nor can anyone depend on anything but the doctrine of independence as long as nations are to exist and mankind is to thrive. Japan could not assert herself among the great nations of the world without full recognition of these two principles. And I reasoned that Chinese philosophy as the root of education was responsible for our obvious shortcomings.

## III. Analyze the similarities and differences in the motives claimed by leaders who supported independence movements in the Atlantic World in the late 18th and early 19th centuries. Explain what additional document(s) would help you analyze their motives.

1. **Thomas Jefferson, *The Declaration of Independence*, Philadelphia, Pennsylvania, June 1776**

[*The following selection was deleted from the final draft of the* Declaration of Independence *by the Second Continental Congress in the American English colonies. Emphasis is in the original.*]

He [King George III of England] has waged cruel war against human nature itself, violating its most sacred rights of life and liberty in the persons of a distant people who never offended him, captivating and carrying them into slavery in another hemisphere, or to incur miserable death in their transportation hither. [ . . . ] [A]nd . . . he is now exciting those very people to rise in arms among us, and to purchase that liberty of which *he* had deprived them, by murdering the people upon whom *he* also obtruded them: thus paying off former crimes committed against the *liberties* of one people, with crimes which he urges them to commit against the *lives* of another.

[*The following sections were* not *deleted, and are found in the* Declaration of Independence *as it was signed on July 4, 1776.*]

For cutting off our trade with all parts of the world;

For imposing taxes on us without our consent;

For taking away our charters, abolishing our most valuable laws, and altering fundamentally the forms of our governments;

He [King George III] has abdicated government here, by declaring us out of his protection and waging war against us.

A prince, whose character is thus marked by every act which may define a tyrant, is unfit to be the ruler of a free people.

[ . . . ]

We, therefore, the representatives of the United States of America, in General Congress assembled, appealing to the Supreme Judge of the world for the rectitude of our intentions, do, in the name and by the authority of the good people of these colonies solemnly publish and declare, That these United Colonies are, and of right ought to be, ***FREE AND INDEPENDENT STATES;*** that they are absolved from all allegiance to the British crown and that all political connection between them and the state of Great Britain is, and ought to be, totally dissolved; and that, as free and independent states, they have full power to levy war, conclude peace, contract alliances, establish commerce, and do all other acts and things which independent states may of right do.

**2. National Assembly, *Declaration of the Rights of Man and Citizen*, Paris, France, 1789**

[ . . . ]Therefore the National Assembly recognizes and proclaims, in the presence and under the auspices of the Supreme Being, the following rights of man and of the citizen:

[ . . . ]

6. Law is the expression of the general will. Every citizen has a right to participate personally, or through his representative, in its formation. It must be the same for all, whether it protects or punishes. All citizen, being equal in the eyes of the law, are equally eligible to all dignities and to all public positions and occupations, according to their abilities, and without distinction except that of their virtues and talents.
7. No person shall be accused, arrested, or imprisoned except in the cases and according to the forms prescribed by law.

[ . . . ]

13. A common contribution is essential for the maintenance of the public forces and for the cost of administration. This should be equitably distributed among all the citizens in proportion to their means.

**3. Cartoon, "Patience, Monsignor, Your Turn Will Come!" Paris, France, 1789 (Note: Monsignor is an honorific term for a priest.)**

At George Mason University's Center for History and New Media, http://chnm.gmu.edu/revolution/searchfr.php?function=find&keyword=&topReligion=1&sourceImage=1&Find=Find#

**4. Olympe de Gouges, *Declaration of the Rights of Woman and Citizeness**, Paris, France, 1791**

Mothers, daughters, sisters, female representatives of the nation ask to be constituted as a national assembly. [ . . . ] In consequence, the sex that is superior in beauty as in courage, needed in maternal sufferings, recognizes and declares, in the presence and under the auspices of the Supreme Being, the following rights of woman and citizeness:

[ . . . ]

1. Woman is born free and remains equal to man in rights. Social distinctions may be based only on common utility.
6. The law should be the expression of the general will. All citizenesses and citizens should take part, in person or by their representatives, in its formation. It must be the same for everyone. All citizenesses and citizens, being equal in its eyes, should be equally admissible to all public dignities, offices, and employments, according to their ability, and with no other distinction than that of their virtues and talents. . . .
13. For the maintenance of pubic authority and for expenses of administration, taxation of women and men is equal; she take part in all forces labor service, in all painful tasks; she must therefore have the same proportion in the distribution of places, employment, offices, dignities, and in industry. . . .

*In French, a male citizen is *le citoyen* and the spelling for a female citizen is *la citoyenne.* "Citizeness" is an awkward English translation used to indicate the feminine form of the word and "citizen" is used for the male form of the word.

**5. Jean Jacques Dessallines, *Announcement of Independence of St. Domingo* (Haiti), Haiti, Nov. 1803**

In the name of the Black People, and the Men of Color of St. Domingo:

The Independence of St. Domingo is proclaimed. Restored to our primitive dignity, we have asserted our rights; we swear never to yield them to any power on earth; the frightful veil of prejudice is torn to pieces, be it so forever. Woe be to them who would dare to put together its bloody tatters.

[ . . . ]

We have sworn not to listen with clemency towards all those who would date to speak of slavery; we will be inexorable, perhaps even cruel, towards all troops who, themselves forgetting the object for which they have not ceased fighting since 1780, should come from Europe to bring among us death and servitude. Nothing is too dear, and all means are lawful to men from whom it is wished to tear the first of all blessings.

**6. Simón Bolivar, *Advice to the Congress of Angostura* (Argentina), 1819**

We are not Europeans; we are not Indians; we are but a mixed species of aborigines and Spaniards. Americans by birth and Europeans by law, we find ourselves engaged in a dual conflict: we are disputing with the natives for titles of ownership, and at the same time we are struggling to maintain ourselves in the country that gave us birth against the opposition of the invaders.

[ . . . ]

Venezuela had, has, and should have a republican government. Its principles should be the sovereignty of the people, divisions of powers, civil liberty, proscription of slavery, and the abolition of monarchy and privileges. We need equality to recast, so to speak into a unified nation, the classes of men, political opinions, and public customs.

[ . . . ]

If the Senate were hereditary rather than elective, it would, in my opinion, be the basis, the tie, the very soul of our republic. In political storms this body would arrest the thunderbolts of the government and would repel any violent popular reaction.

# DOCUMENT ANALYSIS

## PART VI • THE NEWEST STAGE OF WORLD HISTORY, 1914–PRESENT

**I. To what extent did the Cold War affect the goals of leaders of decolonization movements and new nations in the 1950s and 1960s? What additional types of documents would help in answering this question? Background: The Cold War conflict between the United States and the Soviet Union, and their respective allies, emerged in the late 1940s; it was reflected in movements like Ho Chi Minh's communist revolt against French colonialism in Vietnam and Castro's 1959 revolution in Cuba.**

### 1. Vietnam: Manifesto of the Laodong Party 1951

[Note: By this time China and the Soviet Union had recognized the Party's regime in Vietnam, but it was still struggling for control.]

The main task of the Viet Nam Laodong Party now is:

To unite and lead the working class, the working masses and the entire people of Viet Nam in their struggle to wipe out the French colonialists and defeat the American interventionists; to bring the liberation war of the Viet Nam people to complete victory, thereby making Viet Nam a genuinely independent and united country. . . .

In the field of external affairs, the Viet Nam Laodong Party recommends: The Viet Nam people must actively support the national liberation movements of oppressed peoples; unite closely with the Soviet Union, China and other people's democracies; form close alliances with the peoples of France and the French colonies so as to contribute to the anti-imperialist struggle to defend world peace and democracy!

### 2. Indonesia: President Sukarno at the opening of the Bandung Conference 1955

No task is more urgent than that of preserving peace. Without peace our independence means little. The rehabilitation and upbuilding of our countries will have little meaning. Our revolutions will not be allowed to run their course. . . .

What can we do? We can do much! We can inject the voice of reason into world affairs. We can mobilise all the spiritual, all the moral, all the political strength of Asia and Africa on the side of peace. Yes, we! We, the peoples of Asia and Africa, 1,400,000,000 strong, far more than half the human population of the world, we can mobilise what I have called the Moral Violence of Nations in favour of peace. We can demonstrate to the minority of the world which lives on the other continents that we, the majority, are for peace, not for war.

### 3. Speech of Jawaharlal Nehru, first Prime Minister of India 1956

The preservation of peace forms the central aim of India's policy. It is in the pursuit of this policy that we have chosen the path of nonalignment in any military or like pact of alliance [including Cold War alliances]. Nonalignment does not mean passivity of mind or action, lack of faith or conviction. It does not mean submission to what we consider evil. It is a positive and dynamic approach to such problems that confront us. We believe that each country has not only the right to freedom but also to decide its own policy and way of life. Only thus can true freedom flourish and a people grow according to their own genius.

We believe, therefore, in nonaggression and non-interference by one country in the affairs of another and the growth of tolerance between them and the capacity for peaceful coexistence. We think that by the free exchange of ideas and trade and other contacts between nations each will learn from the other and truth will prevail. We therefore endeavor to maintain friendly relations with all countries, even though we may disagree with them in their policies or structure of government. We think that by this approach we can serve not only our country but also the larger causes of peace and good fellowship in the world.

### 4. Egypt: Anwar al-Sadat at the First Afro-Asian People's Solidarity Conference 1957

We cannot live peacefully in a world threatened by the shadow of war. We can no longer enjoy the products of our hands and the fruits of our labour in a world where plunder prevails and flourishes. We can no longer build and reconstruct in a world which manufactures weapons for destruction and devastation. We can no longer raise the standard of living of our peoples and stamp out diseases and epidemics in a world where nations vie with each other for the production of lethal weapons of massacre and annihilation. Gone for ever is the era where the future of war and peace was decided upon in a few European capitals, because today we happen to be strong enough to make the decision ourselves in that respect.

Our weight in the international balance has now become preponderant. Only think of the colossal number of our people, our natural resources, the vastness of the area covered by our respective countries, and our strategic positions. You will surely come to the conclusion that the outbreak of war is impossible so long as we insist on peace, especially if we do not content ourselves with a mere negative attitude, but assume one of positiveness in favour of Peace. This transition from the negative to the positive is a fundamental basis worthy of our adoption.

### 5. Cuban leader Fidel Castro: Second Declaration of Havana 1962

Since the end of the Second World War, the Latin American nations are becoming pauperized constantly. The value of their per capita income falls. The dreadful percentages of child death rate do not decrease, the number of illiterates grows higher, the peoples lack employment, land, adequate housing, schools, hospitals, communication systems and the means of subsistence. On the other hand, North America investments exceed 10 billion dollars. Latin America, moreover, supplies cheap raw materials and pays high prices for manufactured articles. Like the first Spanish conquerors, who exchanged mirrors and trinkets with the Indians for silver and gold, so the United States trades with Latin America. . . .

The duty of every revolutionary is to make revolution. We know that in America and throughout the world the revolution will be victorious. But revolutionaries cannot sit in the doorways of their homes to watch the corpse of imperialism pass by. The role of Job does not behoove a revolutionary. Each year by which America's liberation may be hastened will mean millions of children rescued from death, millions of minds freed for learning, infinitudes of sorrow spared the peoples.

## II. In a context of rapidly growing world population, what was the nature of debate over family planning at the 1994 United Nations Population and Development Conference, and how did the United Nations handle the debate? What additional types of documents would be useful in analyzing this debate? Background: From the 1970s onward, the United Nations sponsored recurrent conferences, widely attended by member states, on issues such as women's conditions, rights of children, and population policy.

### 1. Statement of the Norwegian Prime Minister at the United Nations Population and Development Conference 1994

I am pleased by the emerging consensus that everyone should have access to the whole range of family-planning services at an affordable price. Sometimes religion is a major obstacle. This happens when family planning is made a moral issue. But morality cannot only be a question of controlling sexuality and protecting unborn life. Morality is also a question of giving individuals the opportunity of choice, of suppressing coercion of all kinds and abolishing the criminalization of individual tragedy. Morality becomes hypocrisy if it means accepting mothers' suffering or dying in connection with unwanted pregnancies and illegal abortions, and unwanted children living in misery.

Women's education is the single most important path to higher productivity, lower infant mortality and lower fertility. The economic returns on investment in women's education are generally comparable to those for men, but the social returns in terms of health and fertility by far exceed what we gain from men's education. So let us pledge to watch over the numbers of school-enrollment for girls.

Population growth is one of the most serious obstacles to world prosperity and sustainable development. We may soon be facing new famine, mass migration, and war as peoples compete for ever more scarce land and water resources.

### 2. Interview with the Iranian Minister Hossain Malekafzali attending the United Nations Population and Development Conference 1994

First of all, is the abortion. We do not accept abortion as it is in the text, as a family planning tool, but also we think that we should have . . . a good quality of services for family planning. Do not take the abortion, so abortion is not permitted, except in a very few cases, when the life of the mother, for example, is in danger . . . and also, the second point is the child education, or adults and education, regarding the sex education. This also is not permitted in Islamic countries like Iran, but when the men and women are in the age of marriage, then it is OK. We can have the sex education for those people who are ready to get married. This is the second point, and the third point is the importance of the family because the thing [is] that the family is the basic unit of the society, and the family role is very clear.

### 3. Statement of the representative of the United Arab Emirates

The delegation of the United Arab Emirates believes in protecting man and promoting his welfare and enhancing his role in the family and in the State and at the international level. We consider also that man is the central object and the means for attaining sustainable development. We do not consider abortion as a means of family planning, and we adhere to the principles of Islamic law also in matters of inheritance.

We wish to express reservations on everything that contravenes the principles and precepts of our religion Islam, a tolerant religion, and our laws.

### 4. Statement of the representative of the Holy See [Vatican]

But there are other aspects of the final document which the Holy See cannot support. Together with so many people around the world, the Holy See affirms that human life begins at the moment of conception. That life must be defended and protected. The Holy See can therefore never condone abortion or policies which favor abortion. The final document, recognizes abortion as a dimension of population policy even though it does stress that abortion should not be promoted as a means of family planning and urges nations to find alternatives to abortion.

The chapters also contain references which could be seen as accepting extramarital sexual activity, especially among adolescents. They would seem to assert that abortion services belong within primary health care as a method of choice. . . .

### 5. Statement by the representative of the Syrian Arab Republic

I should like to put on record that the Syrian Arab Republic will deal with an address the concepts contained in the Programme of Action . . . in full accordance with the ethical, cultural and religious concepts and convictions of our society in order to serve the unit of the family, which is the nucleus of society, and in order to enhance prosperity in our societies.

### 6. U.N. Report from the United Nations Population and Development Conference 1994

The aim of family-planning programmes must be to enable couples and individuals to decide freely and responsibly the number and spacing of their children and to have the information and means to do so and to ensure informed choices and make available a full range of safe and effective methods. The success of population education and family planning programmes in a variety of settings demonstrates that informed individuals can and will act responsibly in the light of their own needs and those of their families and communities. The principle of informed free choice is essential to the long-term success of family-planning programmes. Any form of coercion has no part to play.

Family-planning programmes have contributed considerably to the decline in average fertility rates for developing countries. However, the full range of modern family-planning methods still remains unavailable to at least 350 million couples world wide. Survey data suggest that approximately 120 million additional women world wide could be currently using a modern family-planning method if more accurate information and affordable services were easily available, and if partners, extended families and the community were more supportive.

As part of the effort to meet unmet needs, all countries should seek to identify and remove all the major remaining barriers to the utilization of family-planning services. Some of those barriers are related to the inadequacy, poor quality and cost of existing family-planning services. It should be the goal of public, private and non-governmental family planning organizations to remove all programme-related barriers to family-planning use by the year 2005. . . .

## III. Based on the following documents, assess the relative importance of common ingredients or individual dynamics in explaining the causes of late 20th- and early 21st-century outbreaks of ethnic conflicts. Explain what kind(s) of additional documents would help you assess these reasons.

*Historical background*

*After the initial collapses of Eastern bloc communist governments in 1989–1990, Serbian Communist Slobodan Milosevic was elected President of Serbia, a state within Yugoslavia. Civil war ensured in Yugoslavia between 1991–1999.*

*Wales has been part of the British kingdom since the 14th century. In the 1990s, a Welsh nationalist party called Plaid Cymru began calling for Welsh independence.*

*When Rwanda achieved independence from the Belgians in 1962, hundreds of thousands of the Tutsi, an ethnic group favored by the Belgians but a minority of the population, fled to neighboring Uganda, fearing the majority Hutu. Supporters of Hutu President Habyarimana routinely killed opposition Tutsi and Hutu politicians within Rwanda. On April 6, 1994, a plane carrying Habyarimana was shot down by unknown assailants. The shooting down of a plane was used by a small group of Habyarimana's associates to justify systematically killing opponents, and particularly Tutsi.*

### 1. Slobodan Milosevic, quoted by the British Broadcasting Service (BBC), Former Yugoslavia, 2000

(Accessed 12/31/05 at http://news.bbc.co.uk.hi/english/static/in_depth/europe/2000/milosevic_yugoslavia/croatia.stm )

After Croatia declared independence [in 1991], the Serb minority in Croatia—who had proclaimed regional autonomy in Krajina—looked to Milosevic for support. He responded with typical bravado: "We believe that Serbs have the legitimate right to live in one country. If we must fight then by God, we will fight," he said.

When Bosnia declared independence in April 1992, following a referendum, violence broke out throughout the republic. Milosevic vowed to defend Serbs from what he called "Croatian genocide" and "Islamic fundamentalism." More than three years of war followed—the bloodiest in Europe since World War II.

### 2. The International Criminal Tribunal for the Former Yugoslavia, Indictment of Slobodan Milosevic, United Nations, New York, 2002

(Accessed 12/31/05 at http://www.un.org/icty/cases-e/index-sre.htm)

[F]rom 1987 until late 2000, Slobodan Milosevic was the dominant political figure in Serbia and the Federal Republic of Yugoslavia. It is alleged that Slobodan Milosevic, acted alone and in the joint criminal enterprise in the following ways:

(a) He exerted effective control over the elements of the Yugoslav People's Army ("JNA") and the Yugoslav Army ("VJ") which participated in the planning, preparation, facilitation and execution of the forcible removal of the majority of non-Serbs, principally Bosnian Muslims and Bosnian Croats, from large areas of Bosnia and Herzegovina. [ . . . ]

(d) He participated in the planning and preparation of the take-over of municipalities in Bosnia and Herzegovina and the subsequent forcible removal of the majority of non-Serbs. He provided the financial, material and logistical support for such a take-over. [ . . . ]

(g) He controlled, manipulated or otherwise utilized Serbian state-run media to spread false messages of ethnically-based attacks by Bosnian Muslims and Croats against Serbs intended to create an atmosphere of fear and hatred among Serbs living in Serbia, Croatia and Bosnia and Herzegovina which contributed to the forcible removal of the majority of non-Serbs.

### 3. Plaid Cymru [a Welsh political party], "A Manifesto for the European Parliament Elections," Wales, United Kingdom, 2004

(Accessed at www.plaidcymru.org/europeanmanifesto.pdf on 2/5/2006)

Plaid Cymru wishes Wales to be a positive role model as a nation of proactive and influential Europeans. With our two Plaid Cymru MEPs [Members of the European Parliament] Jill Evans and Eurig Wyn, Wales has achieved a prominent place in Brussels. As a result significant steps have been taken towards improving the conditions and rights of people in Wales, across Europe and further afield. [...]

Plaid Cymru is the only political party in Wales that has consistently represented the values and interests of Wales on national and international issues.

Plaid Cymru represents the distinctive interests of Welsh farmers, not large ranchers in South East England. Welsh farmers' interests are what drive our policy interventions in agriculture. We do not follow the British government's line on the war in Iraq or other foreign affairs issues. Instead, we tell the world what Wales thinks on such highly important matters.

We do not bow to the interests of the London stock exchange at the expense of Welsh manufacturing jobs. Plaid Cymru is free to truly represent Wales in Europe. [...]

We supported the move to include a reference to respecting the rich cultural and linguistic diversity of the Union in the text of the draft European Constitution [which reads:]

We will:

1. Continue to fight for the rights of minority language speakers in the European Union;
2. Continue working to ensure a legal basis to support minority languages in Europe in order to facilitate European funding;
3. Continue fighting to mainstream minority language matters in European programs;
4. Continue raising the profile of the Welsh language in Europe;
5. Continue building alliances with other European stateless nations and minority communities to advance the cause of minority language rights.

### 4. National Assembly for Wales, "Your Guide to the Assembly," Wales, United Kingdom, 2006

(Accessed at www.wales.gov.uk/pubinfaboutassembly/pdfs/english.pdf on 2/5/06)

In July 1997, the Government published a White Paper, A Voice for Wales, which outlined proposals for devolution in Wales [transfer of power to govern from the English Parliament to a Welsh National Assembly]. These proposals were endorsed in the referendum of 18 September 1997. Parliament passed the Government of Wales Act 1998, which established the National Assembly for Wales, and the National Assembly for Wales (Transfer of Functions) Order 1999, which enabled the transfer of the devolved powers and responsibilities from the Secretary of

State for Wales to the Assembly to take place on 1 July 1999. Subsequently many acts of Parliament have given new powers to the Assembly.

Wales remains part of the UK and the Secretary of State for Wales and Members of Parliament (MPs) from Welsh constituencies continue to have seats in Westminster. Laws passed by Parliament in Westminster still apply to Wales.

The Assembly has considerable power to develop and implement policy within a range of areas: agriculture, ancient monuments and historic buildings, culture, economic development, education and training, the environment, health and health services, highways, housing, industry, local government, social services, sport and leisure, tourism, town and country planning, transport and roads, [and] the Welsh language.

### 5. Bureau of Intelligence and Research [Intelligence arm of the U.S. Department of State], Declassified Confidential Memo, "Rwanda: Genocide and Partition," April 26, 1994

(Accessed at http://www.gwu.edu/%7Ensarchiv/NSAEBB/NSAEBB117/index.htm)

Heavy fighting yesterday continued in Kigali after the government failed to show up for weekend peace talks in Tanzania and the Rwandan Patriotic Front (RPF—Tutsi) did not appear in Zaire for separate talks to which it apparently was not invited, according to press reports. Both sides announced unilateral, conditional cease-fire declarations that were to take effect yesterday.

The ICRC [International Committee of the Red Cross] delegate for Africa is certain at least 100,000 Rwandans have been killed since April 6, believes the actual number is closer to 300,000, and notes ICRC personnel in country think the total could be 500,000 according to Mission Geneva. The ICRC is concerned that the situation could worsen, citing some Hutu extremists who speak of a "final solution" to eliminate all Tutsis. The ICRC and other NGOs have withdrawn all their workers for the country, except for a small number in Kigali.

Comment: the butchery shows no sign on ending. The inability of either side to conquer the other—and the intensity of ethnic slaughter—make it increasingly probably Rwanda will divide into zones controlled by the RPF in the north and east and by Hutu forces linked to the interim government in the northwest, the south and most of Kigali. Though a cease-fire may be possible in the days ahead, Hutu hardliners ascendant behind government lines totally distrust the RPF and will reject any interim political settlement based on sharing power with the rebels.

### 6. Human Rights Watch, "Report on the Rwandan Genocide," New York, 1999

http://www.hrw.org/reports/1999/rwanda/Geno1-3-02.htm#P22_7285 accessed through http://www.pbs.org/wgbh/pages/frontline/shows/evil/

[Note: Human Rights Watch is a privately funded, non-governmental, non-partisan, so-called watchdog group, with international offices in North America and Europe.]

President Juvenal Habyarimana, nearing the end of two decades in power, was losing popularity among Rwandans when the RPF [Tutsi *Rwandese Patriotic Front*] attacked from Uganda on October 1, 1990. At first Habyarimana did not see the rebels as a serious threat, although they stated their intention to remove him as well as to make possible the return of the hundreds of thousands of Rwandan [Tutsi] refugees who had lived in exile for a generation. The president and his close colleagues decided, however, to exaggerate the RPF threat as a way to pull dissident Hutu back to his side and they began portraying Tutsi inside Rwanda as RPF collaborators. For three and a half years, this elite worked to redefine the population of Rwanda into "Rwandans," meaning those who backed the president, and the "ibyitso" or "accomplices of the enemy," meaning the Tutsi minority and Hutu opposed to him.

[. . .]

This leaves 507,000 Tutsi killed, and represents the annihilation of about 77 percent of the population registered as Tutsi. Using other data from Butare prefecture, our researchers computed an estimated loss of 75 percent of the Tutsi population in that prefecture. Based on these preliminary data, we would conclude that at least half a million persons were killed in the genocide, a loss that represented about three-quarters of the Tutsi population of Rwanda.

# Glossary

Pronunciation guidance is supplied in square brackets, [ ], after difficult words. The symbols used for pronunciation are found in the table below. Syllables for primary stress are *italicized.*

| | | | | | |
|---|---|---|---|---|---|
| a | act, bat, marry | I | bite, ice | u | sum, up |
| AY | age, rate | j | just, tragic | U | sue, blew, through |
| âr | ar, dare | k | keep, cop | ûr | turn, urge, cur |
| ä | ah, part, calm | ng | sing | zh | vision, pleasure |
| ch | chief, beach | o | ox, hot | uh | *a*lone, syst*e*m, eas*i*ly, gall*o*p, circ*us* |
| e | edge, set | O | hope, over | A | as in French *a*mi |
| EE | equal, seat, bee | ô | order, ball | KH | as in German a*ch*, i*ch* |
| EER | here, ear | oi | oil, joint | N | as in French bo*n* |
| g | give, trigger | oo | book, tour | OE | as in French d*eux* |
| h | here | ou | plow, out | R | as in French *r*ouge |
| hw | which, when | sh | she, fashion | Y | as in German f*ü*hlen |
| i | if, big | th | thin, ether | | |

**Abbas the Great** Safavid ruler from 1587 to 1629; extended Safavid domain to greatest extent; created slave regiments based on captured Russians, who monopolized firearms within Safavid armies; incorporated Western military technology. (p. 579)

**Abdallahi, Khalifa** [uh dool *ä hEE*] Successor of Muhammad Achmad as leader of Mahdists in Sudan; established state in Sudan; defeated by British General Kitchener in 1598. (p. 712)

**Abduh, Muhammad** Disciple of al-Afghani; Muslim thinker at end of 19th century; stressed need for adoption of Western scientific learning and technology, recognized importance of tradition of rational inquiry. (p. 710)

**Abdul Hamid** Ottoman sultan who attempted to return to despotic absolutism during reign from 1878 to 1908; nullified constitution and restricted civil liberties; deposed in coup in 1908. (p. 705)

**absolute monarchy** Concept of government developed during rise of nation-states in western Europe during the 17th century; featured monarchs who passed laws without parliaments, appointed professionalized armies and bureaucracies, established state churches, imposed state economic policies. (p. 489)

**Achmad, Muhammad** Head of a Sudanic Sufi brotherhood; claimed descent from prophet Muhammad; proclaimed both Egyptians and British as infidels; launched revolt to purge Islam of impurities; took Khartoum in 1883; also known as the Mahdi. (p. 711)

**African National Congress** Black political organization within South Africa; pressed for end to policies of apartheid; sought open democracy leading to black majority rule; until the 1990s declared illegal in South Africa. (p. 915)

**Afrikaner National Party** Emerged as the majority party in the all-white South African legislature after 1948; advocated complete independence from Britain; favored a rigid system of racial segregation called apartheid. (p. 837)

**age of revolution** Period of political upheaval beginning roughly with the American Revolution in 1775 and continuing through the French Revolution of 1789 and other movements for change up to 1848. (p. 624)

**Akbar** (1542–1605) Son and successor of Humayan; oversaw building of military and administrative systems that became typical of Mughal rule in India; pursued policy of cooperation with Hindu princes; attempted to create new religion to bind Muslim and Hindu populations of India. (p. 583)

**al-Afghani** Muslim thinker at the end of the 19th century; stressed need for adoption of Western scientific learning and technology; recognized importance of tradition of rational inquiry. (p. 710)

**Ali, Muhammad** Won power struggle in Egypt following fall of Mamluks; established mastery of all Egypt by 1811; introduced effective army based on Western tactics and supply and a variety of other reforms; by 1830s was able to challenge Ottoman government in Constantinople; died in 1848. (p. 709)

**Allende, Salvador** [ä *yAHn* dAY, ä *yen* dEE] President of Chile; nationalized industries and banks; sponsored peasant and worker expropriations of lands and foreign-owned factories; overthrown in 1973 by revolt of Chilean military with the support of the United States. (p. 883)

**Alliance for Progress** Begun in 1961 by the United States to develop Latin America as an alternative to radical political solutions; enjoyed only limited success; failure of development programs led to renewal of direct intervention. (p. 888)

**Amaru, Tupac, II** (1738–1781) Mestizo leader of Indian revolt in Peru; supported by many among lower social classes; revolt eventually failed because of Creole fears of real social revolution. (p. 539)

**American Civil War** Fought from 1861 to 1865; first application of Industrial Revolution to warfare; resulted in abolition of slavery in the United States and reunification of North and South. (p. 635)

**American Revolution** Rebellion of English American colonies along Atlantic seaboard between 1775 and 1783; resulted in independence for former British colonies and eventual formation of United States of America. (p. 625)

**amigos del país** [uh *mEE* gOs, ä *mEE*-, del päEEs] Clubs and associations dedicated to improvements and reform in Spanish colonies; flourished during the 18th century; called for material improvements rather than political reform. (p. 536)

**anarchists** Political groups seeking abolition of all formal government; formed in many parts of Europe and Americas in late 19th and early 20th centuries; particularly prevalent in

Russia, opposing tsarist autocracy and becoming a terrorist movement responsible for assassination of Alexander II in 1881. (p. 733)

**Anglican church** Form of Protestantism set up in England after 1534; established by Henry VIII with himself as head, at least in part to obtain a divorce from his first wife; became increasingly Protestant following Henry's death. (p. 482)

**Anschluss** Hitler's union of Germany with the German-speaking population of Austria; took place in 1938, despite complaints of other European nations. (p. 816)

**apartheid** Policy of strict racial segregation imposed in South Africa to permit the continued dominance of whites politically and economically. (p. 837)

**Aquino, Corazon** (b. 1933) First president of the Philippines in the post-Marcos era of late 1980s; she served from 1986 to 1992; Aquino, whose husband was assassinated by thugs in the pay of the Marcos regime, was one of the key leaders in the popular movement that toppled the dictator. (p. 902)

**Arevalo, Juan José** Elected president of Guatemala in 1944; began series of socialist reforms including land reform; nationalist program directed against foreign-owned companies such as United Fruit Company. (p. 878)

**Argentine Republic** Replaced state of Buenos Aires in 1862; result of compromise between centralists and federalists. (p. 686)

**Armenian genocide** Assault carried out by mainly Turkish military forces against Armenian population in Anatolia in 1915; over a million Armenians perished and thousands fled to Russia and the Middle East. (p. 763)

**Asante Empire** [uh *san* tEE, uh *sän*] Established in Gold Coast among Akan people settled around Kumasi; dominated by Oyoko clan; many clans linked under Osei Tutu after 1650. (p. 552)

**asantehene** [un san tAY hAY nAY] Title taken by ruler of Asante Empire; supreme civil and religious leader; authority symbolized by golden stool. (p. 552)

**Asian sea trading network** Prior to intervention of Europeans, consisted of three zones: Arab zone based on glass, carpets, and tapestries; India based on cotton textiles; China based on paper, porcelain, and silks. (p. 595)

**Ataturk** Also known as Mustafa Kemal; leader of Turkish republic formed in 1923; reformed Turkish nation using Western models. (p. 773)

**Atlantic Charter of 1941** World War II alliance agreement between the United States and Britain; included a clause that recognized the right of all people to choose the form of government under which they live; indicated sympathy for decolonization. (p. 832)

**audiencia** Royal court of appeals established in Spanish colonies of New World; there were 10 in each viceroyalty; part of colonial administrative system; staffed by professional magistrates. (p. 529)

**Aurangzeb** [*ôr* uhng zeb] Son and successor of Shah Jahan in Mughal India; determined to extend Mughal control over whole of subcontinent; wished to purify Islam of Hindu influences; incessant warfare exhausted empire despite military successes; died in 1707. (p. 587)

**Babur** Founder of Mughal dynasty in India; descended from Turkic warriors; first led invasion of India in 1526; died in 1530. (p. 583)

**Balboa, Vasco de** (c. 1475–1519) First Spanish captain to begin settlement on the mainland of Mesoamerica in 1509; initial settlement eventually led to conquest of Aztec and Inca empires by other captains. (p. 469)

**Balfour Declaration** British minister Lord Balfour's promise of support for the establishment of Jewish settlement in Palestine issued in 1917. (p. 774)

**Balkan nationalism** Movements to create independent nations within the Balkan possessions of the Ottoman Empire; provoked a series of crises within the European alliance system; eventually led to World War I. (p. 644)

**banana republics** Term given to governments supported or created by the United States in Central America; believed to be either corrupt or subservient to U.S. interests. (p. 886)

**Bangladesh** Founded as an independent nation in 1972; formerly East Pakistan. (p. 898)

**banner armies** Eight armies of the Manchu tribes identified by separate flags; created by Nurhaci in early 17th century; utilized to defeat Ming emperor and establish Qing dynasty. (p. 714)

**Batavia** Dutch fortress located after 1620 on the island of Java. (p. 599)

**Batista, Fulgencio** Dictator of Cuba from 1934 to 1944; returned to presidency in 1952; ousted from government by revolution led by Fidel Castro. (p. 879)

**Battle of Britain** The 1940 Nazi air offensive including saturation bombing of London and other British cities, countered by British innovative air tactics and radar tracking of German assault aircraft. (p. 824)

**Battle of the Bulge** Hitler's last-ditch effort to repel the invading Allied armies in the winter of 1944–1945. (p. 826)

**Battle of the Coral Sea** World War II Pacific battle; United States and Japanese forces fought to a standoff. (p. 827)

**Berlin Wall** Built in 1961 to halt the flow of immigration from East Berlin to West Berlin; immigration was in response to lack of consumer goods and close Soviet control of economy and politics; torn down at end of cold war in 1991. (p. 861)

**Bhutto, Benazir** Twice prime minister of Pakistan in the 1980s and 1990s; first ran for office to avenge her father's execution by the military clique then in power. (p. 902)

**Biko, Steve** (1946–1977) An organizer of Black Consciousness movement in South Africa, in opposition to apartheid; murdered while in police custody. (p. 915)

**Bismarck, Otto von** Conservative prime minister of Prussia; architect of German unification under Prussian king in 1870; utilized liberal reforms to attract support for conservative causes. (p. 634)

**blitzkrieg** German term for lightning warfare; involved rapid movement of airplanes, tanks, and mechanized troop carriers; resulted in early German victories over Belgium, Holland, and France in World War II. (p. 823)

**Boers** Dutch settlers in Cape Colony, in southern Africa. (p. 474)

**Boer Republics** Transvaal and Orange Free State in southern Africa; established to assert independence of Boers from British colonial government in Cape Colony in 1850s; discovery of diamonds and precious metals caused British migration into the Boer areas in 1860s. (p. 668)

**Boer War** Fought between 1899 and 1902 over the continued independence of Boer republics; resulted in British victory, but began the process of decolonization for whites in South Africa. (p. 668)

**Bolívar, Simon** Creole military officer in northern South America; won series of victories in Venezuela, Colombia, and Ecuador between 1817 and 1822; military success led to creation of independent state of Gran Colombia. (p. 676)

**Bolsheviks** Literally, the majority party; the most radical branch of the Russian Marxist movement; led by V. I. Lenin and dedicated to his concept of social revolution; actually a minority in the Russian Marxist political scheme until its triumph in the 1917 revolution. (p. 733)

**Bonaparte, Napoleon** Rose within the French army during the wars of the French Revolution; eventually became general; led a coup that ended the French Revolution; established French Empire under his rule; defeated and deposed in 1815. (p. 627)

**Boxer Rebellion** Popular outburst in 1898 aimed at expelling foreigners from China; failed because of intervention of armies of Western powers in China; defeat of Chinese enhanced control by Europeans and the power of provincial officials. (p. 719)

**British East India Company** Joint stock company that obtained government monopoly over trade in India; acted as virtually independent government in regions it claimed. (p. 465)

**British Raj** British political establishment in India; developed as a result of the rivalry between France and Britain in India. (p. 653)

**Cabral, Pedro Alvares** Portuguese leader of an expedition to India; blown off course in 1500 and landed in Brazil. (p. 531)

**Calcutta** Headquarters of British East India Company in Bengal in Indian subcontinent; located on Ganges; captured in 1756 during early part of Seven Years War; later became administrative center for all of Bengal. (p. 474)

**Calvin, Jean** French Protestant (16th century) who stressed doctrine of predestination; established center of his group at Swiss canton of Geneva; encouraged ideas of wider access to government, wider public education; Calvinism spread from Switzerland to northern Europe and North America. (p. 482)

**candomble** [kan dom *blä*] African religious ideas and practices in Brazil, particularly among the Yoruba people. (p. 562)

**Canton** One of two port cities in which Europeans were permitted to trade in China during the Ming dynasty. (p. 605)

**Cape Colony** Dutch colony established at Cape of Good Hope in 1652 initially to provide a coastal station for the Dutch seaborne empire; by 1770 settlements had expanded sufficiently to come into conflict with Bantus. (p. 474)

**Cape of Good Hope** Southern tip of Africa; first circumnavigated in 1488 by Portuguese in search of direct route to India. (p. 461)

**capitaincies** Strips of land along Brazilian coast granted to minor Portuguese nobles for development; enjoyed limited success in developing the colony. (p. 531)

**caravels** Slender, long-hulled vessels utilized by Portuguese; highly maneuverable and able to sail against the wind; key to development of Portuguese trade empire in Asia. (p. 594)

**Cárdenas, Lázaro** President of Mexico from 1934 to 1940; responsible for redistribution of land, primarily to create ejidos, or communal farms; also began program of primary and rural education. (p. 806)

**Caribbean** First area of Spanish exploration and settlement; served as experimental region for nature of Spanish colonial experience; encomienda system of colonial management initiated here. (p. 518)

**Castro, Fidel** Cuban revolutionary; overthrew dictator Fulgencio Batista in 1958; initiated series of socialist reforms; came to depend almost exclusively on Soviet Union. (p. 879)

**Catherine the Great** German-born Russian tsarina in the 18th century; ruled after assassination of her husband; gave appearance of enlightened rule; accepted Western cultural influence; maintained nobility as service aristocracy by granting them new power over peasantry. (p. 505)

**Catholic Reformation** Restatement of traditional Catholic beliefs in response to Protestant Reformation (16th century); established councils that revived Catholic doctrine and refuted Protestant beliefs. (p. 482)

**caudillos** [kou *thEE* lyos, *-thEE* yos] Independent leaders who dominated local areas by force in defiance of national policies; sometimes seized national governments to impose their concept of rule; typical throughout newly independent countries of Latin America. (p. 679)

**Cavour, Count Camillo di** [kä *voor*] Architect of Italian unification in 1858; formed an alliance with France to attack Austrian control of northern Italy; resulted in creation of constitutional monarchy under Piedmontese king. (p. 634)

**centralists** Latin American politicians who wished to create strong, centralized national governments with broad powers; often supported by politicians who described themselves as conservatives. (p. 679)

**Chaldiran** [chäl duh *rán*] Site of battle between Safavids and Ottomans in 1514; Safavids severely defeated by Ottomans; checked western advance of Safavid Empire. (p. 577)

**Charles III** Spanish enlightened monarch; ruled from 1759 to 1788; instituted fiscal, administrative, and military reforms in Spain and its empire. (p. 537)

**Chartist movement** Attempt by artisans and workers in Britain to gain the vote during the 1840s; demands for reform beyond the Reform Bill of 1832 were incorporated into a series of petitions; movement failed. (p. 629)

**Chiang Ching-kuo** [jEE *äng ching gwO*] Son and successor of Chiang Kai-shek as ruler of Taiwanese government in 1978; continued authoritarian government; attempted to lessen gap between followers of his father and indigenous islanders. (p. 930)

**Chiang Kai-shek** [chang kiy shek] A military officer who succeeded Sun Yat-sen as the leader of the Guomindang or Nationalist party in China in the mid-1920s; became the most powerful leader in China in the early 1930s, but his Nationalist forces were defeated and driven from China by the Communists after World War II. (p. 798)

**Chongzhen** [*choong juhn*] Last of the Ming emperors; committed suicide in 1644 in the face of a Jurchen capture of the Forbidden City at Beijing. (p. 609)

**Churchill, Winston** (1874–1965) British prime minister during World War II; responsible for British resistance to German air assaults. (p. 820)

**cientificos** Advisors of government of Porfirio Díaz who were strongly influenced by positivist ideas; permitted Mexican government to project image of modernization. (p. 694)

**Cixi** [*tsU shEE*] Ultraconservative dowager empress who dominated the last decades of the Qing dynasty; supported Boxer Rebellion in 1898 as a means of driving out Westerners. (p. 719)

**Clemenceau, Georges** French prime minister in last years of World War I and during Versailles Conference of 1919; pushed for heavy reparations from Germans. (p. 765)

**Clive, Robert** (1725–1774) Architect of British victory at Plassey in 1757; established foundations of British Raj in northern India (18th century). (p. 654)

**cold war** The state of relations between the United States and its allies and the Soviet Union and its allies between the end of World War II and 1990; based on creation of political spheres of influence and a nuclear arms race rather than actual warfare. (p. 845)

**collectivization** Creation of large, state-run farms rather than individual holdings; allowed more efficient control over peasants, though often lowered food production; part of Stalin's economic and political planning; often adopted in other communist regimes. (p. 795)

**Columbian exchange** Biological and ecological exchange that took place following Spanish establishment of colonies in New World; peoples of Europe and Africa came to New World; animals, plants, and diseases of two hemispheres were transferred. (p. 526)

**Columbus, Christopher** Genoese captain in service of king and queen of Castile and Aragon; successfully sailed to New World and returned in 1492; initiated European discoveries in Americas. (p. 461)

**Comintern** International office of communism under U.S.S.R. dominance established to encourage the formation of Communist parties in Europe and elsewhere. (p. 795)

**Communist party of Vietnam** Originally a wing of nationalist movement; became primary nationalist party after decline of VNQDD in 1929; led in late 1920s by Nguyen Ai Quoc, alias Ho Chi Minh. (p. 942)

**compradors** Wealthy new group of Chinese merchants under the Qing dynasty; specialized in the import-export trade on China's south coast; one of the major links between China and the outside world. (p. 715)

**Comte, Auguste** [koNt] French philosopher (19th century); founder of positivism, a philosophy that stressed observation and scientific approaches to the problems of society. (p. 683)

**Comunero Revolt** One of popular revolts against Spanish colonial rule in New Granada (Colombia) in 1781; suppressed as a result of divisions among rebels. (p. 539)

**Congress of Vienna** Meeting in the aftermath of Napoleonic Wars (1815) to restore political stability in Europe and settle diplomatic disputes. (p. 628)

**conservative** Political viewpoint with origins in western Europe during the 19th century; opposed revolutionary goals; advocated restoration of monarchy and defense of church. (p. 629)

**consulado** Merchant guild of Seville; enjoyed virtual monopoly rights over goods shipped to America and handled much of the silver received in return. (p. 529)

**Convention Peoples party (CPP)** Political party established by Kwame Nkrumah in opposition to British control of colonial legislature in Gold Coast. (p. 834)

**Cook, Captain James** Made voyages to Hawaii from 1777 to 1779 resulting in opening of islands to the West; convinced Kamehameha to establish unified kingdom in the islands. (p. 669)

**Copernicus** Polish monk and astronomer (16th century); disproved Hellenistic belief that the earth was at the center of the universe. (p. 486)

**core nations** Nations, usually European, that enjoyed profit from world economy; controlled international banking and commercial services such as shipping; exported manufactured goods for raw materials. (p. 466)

**Cornwallis, Lord Charles** Reformer of the East India Company administration of India in the 1790s; reduced power of local British administrators; checked widespread corruption. (p. 658)

**Coronado, Francisco Vázquez de** (c. 1510–1554) Leader of Spanish expedition into northern frontier region of New Spain; entered what is now United States in search of mythical cities of gold. (p. 522)

**corporatism** Political ideology that emphasized the organic nature of society and made the state a mediator, adjusting the interests of different social groups; appealed to conservative groups in European and Latin American societies and to the military. (p. 806)

**Cortés, Hernán** Led expedition of 600 to coast of Mexico in 1519; conquistador responsible for defeat of Aztec Empire; captured Tenochtitlan. (p. 522)

**cossacks** Peasants recruited to migrate to newly seized lands in Russia, particularly in south; combined agriculture with military conquests; spurred additional frontier conquests and settlements. (p. 501)

**Council of the Indies** Body within the Castilian government that issued all laws and advised king on all matters dealing with the Spanish colonies of the New World. (p. 529)

**Creoles** Whites born in the New World; dominated local Latin American economies and ranked just beneath peninsulares. (p. 535)

**Creole slaves** American-born descendants of saltwater slaves; result of sexual exploitation of slave women or process of miscegenation. (p. 560)

**Crimean War** Fought between 1854 and 1856; began as Russian attempt to attack Ottoman Empire; Russia opposed by France and Britain as well; resulted in Russian defeat in the face of Western industrial technology; led to Russian reforms under Tsar Alexander II. (p. 729)

**Cristeros** Conservative peasant movement in Mexico during the 1920s; most active in central Mexico; attempted to halt slide toward secularism; movement resulted in armed violence. (p. 791)

**Cromer, Lord** (1841–1917) British proconsul in khedival Egypt from 1883 to 1907; pushed for economic reforms that reduced but failed to eliminate the debts of the khedival regime. (p. 772)

**cubist movement** 20th-century art style; best represented by Spanish artist Pablo Picasso; rendered familiar objects as geometrical shapes. (p. 784)

**Cultural Revolution** Movement initiated in 1965 by Mao Zedong to restore his dominance over pragmatists; used mobs to ridicule Mao's political rivals; campaign was called off in 1968. (p. 938)

**Dahomey** Kingdom developed among Fon or Aja peoples in 17th century; center at Abomey 70 miles from coast; under King Agaja expanded to control coastline and port of Whydah by 1727; accepted Western firearms and goods in return for African slaves. (p. 553)

**Darwin, Charles** Biologist who developed theory of evolution of species (1859); argued that all living species evolved into their present form through the ability to adapt in a struggle for survival. (p. 638)

**Decembrist uprising** Political revolt in Russia in 1825; led by middle-level army officers who advocated reforms; put down by Tsar Nicholas I. (p. 727)

**Declaration of the Rights of Man and the Citizen** Adopted during the liberal phase of the French Revolution (1789); stated the fundamental equality of all French citizens; later became a political source for other liberal movements. (p. 626)

**Deism** Concept of God current during the Scientific Revolution; role of divinity was to set natural laws in motion, not to regulate once process was begun. (p. 487)

**de Klerk, F. W.** White South African prime minister in the late 1980s and early 1990s. Working with Nelson Mandela and the African National Congress, de Klerk helped to dismantle the apartheid system and opened the way for a democratically elected government that represented all South Africans for the first time. (p. 915)

**de la Cruz, Sor Juana Inés** (1651–1695) Author, poet, and musician of New Spain; eventually gave up secular concerns to concentrate on spiritual matters. (p. 530)

**Deng Xiaoping** [dung shee ow ping] One of the more pragmatic, least ideological of the major Communist leaders of China; joined the party as a young man in the 1920s, survived the legendary Long March and persecution during the Cultural Revolution of the 1960s, and emerged as China's most influential leader in the early 1980s. (p. 937)

**Descartes, René** [dAY *kärt*] Established importance of skeptical review of all received wisdom (17th century); argued that human reason could then develop laws that would explain the fundamental workings of nature. (p. 487)

**Deshima** Island in Nagasaki Bay; only port open to non-Japanese after closure of the islands in the 1640s; only Chinese and Dutch ships were permitted to enter. (p. 612)

**Díaz, Porfirio** One of Juárez's generals; elected president of Mexico in 1876; dominated Mexican politics for 35 years; imposed strong central government. (p. 789)

**Diem, Ngo Dinh** Political leader of South Vietnam; established as president with United States support in the 1950s; opposed Communist government of North Vietnam; overthrown by military coup approved by United States. (p. 943)

**Dien Bien Phu** Most significant victory of the Viet Minh over French colonial forces in 1954; gave the Viet Minh control of northern Vietnam. (p. 942)

**Diet** Japanese parliament established as part of the new constitution of 1889; part of Meiji reforms; could pass laws and approve budgets; able to advise government, but not to control it. (p. 738)

**Din-i-Ilahi** [din i i lä hee, dEEn] Religion initiated by Akbar in Mughal India; blended elements of the many faiths of the subcontinent; key to efforts to reconcile Hindus and Muslims in India, but failed. (p. 584)

**Dinshawai incident** [din shä wAY] Clash between British soldiers and Egyptian villagers in 1906; arose over hunting accident along Nile River where wife of prayer leader of mosque was accidentally shot by army officers hunting pigeons; led to Egyptian protest movement. (p. 772)

**Disraeli, Benjamin** Leading conservative political figure in Britain in the second half of the 19th century; took initiative of granting vote to working-class males in 1867; typical of conservative politician making use of popular politics. (p. 634)

**Dreyfus, Alfred** (1859–1935) French Jew falsely accused of passing military secrets to the Germans; his mistreatment and exile to Devil's Island provided flash-point for years of bitter debate between the left and right in France. (p. 774)

**Du Bois, W. E. B.** African American political leader; had a major impact on emerging African nationalist leaders in the 1920s and 1930s. (p. 777)

**duma** National parliament created in Russia in the aftermath of the Revolution of 1905; progressively stripped of power during the reign of Tsar Nicholas II; failed to forestall further revolution. (p. 734)

**Dutch East India Company** Joint stock company that obtained government monopoly over trade in Asia; acted as virtually independent government in regions it claimed. (p. 465)

**Dutch Studies** Group of Japanese scholars interested in implications of Western science and technology beginning in the 17th century; urged freer exchange with West; based studies on few Dutch texts available in Japan. (p. 735)

**Dutch trading empire** The Dutch system extending into Asia with fortified towns and factories, warships on patrol, and monopoly control of a limited number of products. (p. 599)

**eastern bloc** Nations favorable to the Soviet Union in eastern Europe during the cold war—particularly Poland, Czechoslovakia, Bulgaria, Romania, Hungary, and East Germany. (p. 845)

**Eastern Front** Most mobile of the fronts established during World War I; after early successes, military defeats led to downfall of the tsarist government in Russia. (p. 765)

**edict of Nantes** Grant of tolerance to Protestants in France in 1598; granted only after lengthy civil war between Catholic and Protestant factions. (p. 483)

**Edo** Tokugawa capital city; modern-day Tokyo; center of the Tokugawa Shogunate. (p. 610)

**effendi** Class of prosperous business and professional urban families in khedival Egypt; as a class generally favored Egyptian independence. (p. 772)

**Einstein, Albert** Developed mathematical theories to explain the behavior of planetary motion and the movement of electrical particles; after 1900 issued theory of relativity. (p. 638)

**El Mina** Most important of early Portuguese trading factories in forest zone of Africa. (p. 545)

**emancipation of the serfs** Tsar Alexander II ended rigorous serfdom in Russia in 1861; serfs obtained no political rights; required to stay in villages until they could repay aristocracy for land. (p. 729)

**encomendero** [AYn kO mAYn *dAU* rO] The holder of a grant of Indians who were required to pay a tribute or provide labor. The encomendero was responsible for their integration into the church. (p. 518)

**encomienda** Grants of Indian laborers made to Spanish conquerors and settlers in Mesoamerica and South America; basis for earliest forms of coerced labor in Spanish colonies. (p. 517)

**English Civil War** Conflict from 1640 to 1660; featured religious disputes mixed with constitutional issues concerning the powers of the monarchy; ended with restoration of the monarchy in 1660 following execution of previous king. (p. 483)

**Enlightenment** Intellectual movement centered in France during the 18th century; featured scientific advance, application of scientific methods to study of human society; belief that rational laws could describe social behavior. (p. 492)

**European-style family** Originated in 15th century among peasants and artisans of western Europe, featuring late marriage age, emphasis on the nuclear family, and a large minority who never married. (p. 482)

**European Union** Began as European Economic Community (or Common Market), an alliance of Germany, France, Italy, Belgium, Luxembourg, and the Netherlands, to create a single economic entity across national boundaries in 1958; later joined by Britain, Ireland, Denmark, Greece, Spain, Portugal, Sweden, Austria, Finland, and other nations for further European economic integration. (p. 850)

**factories** European trading fortresses and compounds with resident merchants; utilized throughout Portuguese trading empire to assure secure landing places and commerce. (p. 545)

**fascism** Political philosophy that became predominant in Italy and then Germany during the 1920s and 1930s; attacked weakness of democracy, corruption of capitalism; promised vigorous foreign and military programs; undertook state control of economy to reduce social friction. (p. 787)

**fazendas** Coffee estates that spread within interior of Brazil between 1840 and 1860; created major export commodity for Brazilian trade; led to intensification of slavery in Brazil. (p. 688)

**federalists** Latin American politicians who wanted policies, especially fiscal and commercial regulation, to be set by regional governments rather than centralized national administrations; often supported by politicians who described themselves as liberals. (p. 679)

**feminist movements** Sought various legal and economic gains for women, including equal access to professions and higher education; came to concentrate on right to vote; won support particularly from middle-class women; active in western Europe at the end of the 19th century; revived in light of other issues in the 1960s. (p. 636)

**Ferdinand, Archduke Franz** (1863–1914) Heir apparent to the Austro-Hungarian throne whose assassination in Sarajevo set in motion the events that started World War I. (p. 759)

**Ferdinand of Aragon** (r. 1479–1516) Along with Isabella of Castile, monarch of largest Christian kingdoms in Iberia; marriage to Isabella created united Spain; responsible for reconquest of Granada, initiation of exploration of New World. (p. 517)

**five-year plans** Stalin's plans to hasten industrialization of U.S.S.R.; constructed massive factories in metallurgy, mining, and electric power; led to massive state-planned industrialization at cost of availability of consumer products. (p. 810)

**Francis I** King of France in the 16th century; regarded as Renaissance monarch; patron of arts; imposed new controls on Catholic church; ally of Ottoman sultan against Holy Roman emperor. (p. 481)

**Frederick the Great** Prussian king of the 18th century; attempted to introduce Enlightenment reforms into Germany; built on military and bureaucratic foundations of his predecessors; introduced freedom of religion; increased state control of economy. (p. 492)

**Free Officers movement** Military nationalist movement in Egypt founded in the 1930s; often allied with the Muslim Brotherhood; led coup to seize Egyptian government from khedive in July 1952. (p. 908)

**French Revolution** Revolution in France between 1789 and 1800; resulted in overthrow of Bourbon monarchy and old regimes; ended with establishment of French Empire under Napoleon Bonaparte; source of many liberal movements and constitutions in Europe. (p. 626)

**Freud, Sigmund** (1856–1939) Viennese physician who developed theories of the workings of the human subconscious; argued that behavior is determined by impulses. (p. 639)

**Fulani** [*fU* lā nEE, foo *lā*-] Pastoral people of western Sudan; adopted purifying Sufi variant of Islam; under Usuman Dan Fodio in 1804, launched revolt against Hausa kingdoms; established state centered on Sokoto. (p. 556)

**Galileo** Published Copernicus's findings (17th century); added own discoveries concerning laws of gravity and planetary motion; condemned by the Catholic church for his work. (p. 487)

**galleons** Large, heavily armed ships used to carry silver from New World colonies to Spain; basis for convoy system utilized by Spain for transportation of bullion. (p. 529)

**Gallipoli** Peninsula south of Istanbul; site of decisive 1915 Turkish victory over Australian and New Zealand forces under British command during World War I. (p. 763)

**Gálvez, José de** (1720–1787) Spanish minister of the West Indies and chief architect of colonial reform; moved to eliminate Creoles from upper bureaucracy of the colonies; created intendants for local government. (p. 537)

**Gandhi, Indira** Daughter of Jawaharlal Nehru (no relation to Mahatma Gandhi); installed as a figurehead prime minister by the Congress party bosses in 1966; a strong-willed and astute politician, she soon became the central figure in India politics, a position she maintained through the 1970s and passed on to her sons. (p. 902)

**Gandhi, Mohandas** (1869–1948) Led sustained all-India campaign for independence from British Empire after World War I; stressed nonviolent but aggressive mass protest. (p. 771)

**Gang of Four** Jiang Qing and four political allies who attempted to seize control of Communist government in China from the pragmatists; arrested and sentenced to life imprisonment in 1976 following Mao Zedong's death. (p. 939)

**Garvey, Marcus** African American political leader; had a major impact on emerging African nationalist leaders in the 1920s and 1930s. (p. 777)

**Gestapo** Secret police in Nazi Germany, known for brutal tactics. (p. 803)

**Giap, Vo Nguyen** Chief military commander of the Viet Minh; architect of the Vietnamese victory over the French at Dien Bien Phu in 1954. (p. 942)

**glasnost** Policy of openness or political liberation in Soviet Union put forward by Mikhail Gorbachev in the late 1980s. (p. 952)

**globalization** The increasing interconnectedness of all parts of the world, particularly in communication and commerce but also in culture and politics. (p. 971)

**Glorious Revolution** English overthrow of James II in 1688; resulted in affirmation of parliament as having basic sovereignty over the king. (p. 489)

**Goa** Portuguese factory or fortified trade town located on western India coast; site for forcible entry into Asian sea trade network. (p. 597)

**Good Neighbor Policy** Established by Franklin D. Roosevelt for dealing with Latin America in 1933; intended to halt direct intervention in Latin American politics. (p. 887)

**Gorbachev, Mikhail** U.S.S.R. premier after 1985; renewed attacks on Stalinism; urged reduction in nuclear armament; proclaimed policies of glasnost and perestroika. (p. 951)

**Gran Colombia** Independent state created in South America as a result of military successes of Simon Bolívar; existed only until 1830, at which time Colombia, Venezuela, and Ecuador became separate nations. (p. 676)

**Great Depression** International economic crisis following the First World War; began with collapse of American stock market in 1929; actual causes included collapse of agricultural prices in 1920s; included collapse of banking houses in the United States and western Europe, massive unemployment; contradicted optimistic assumptions of 19th century. (p. 800)

**Great Leap Forward** Economic policy of Mao Zedong introduced in 1958; proposed industrialization of small-scale projects integrated into peasant communes; led to economic disaster; ended in 1960. (p.936)

**Great Trek** Movement of Boer settlers in Cape Colony of southern Africa to escape influence of British colonial government in 1834; led to settlement of regions north of Orange River and Natal. (p. 557)

**Greek Revolution** Rebellion in Greece against the Ottoman Empire in 1820; key step in gradually dismantling the Ottoman Empire in the Balkans. (p. 629)

**Green movement** Political parties, especially in Europe, focusing on environmental issues and control over economic growth. (p. 850)

**Green Revolution** Introduction of improved seed strains, fertilizers, and irrigation as a means of producing higher yields in crops such as rice, wheat, and corn; particularly important in the densely populated countries of Asia. (p. 912)

**guano** Bird droppings utilized as fertilizer; exported from Peru as a major item of trade between 1850 and 1880; income from trade permitted end to American Indian tribute and abolition of slavery. (p. 682)

**Guevara, Ernesto "Che"** Argentine revolutionary; aided Fidel Castro in overthrow of Fulgencio Batista regime in Cuba; died while directing guerrilla movement in Bolivia in 1967. (p. 879)

**guillotine** [*gil* uh tEEn, *gEE* uh-, gil uh *tEEn*, gEE uh-] Introduced as a method of humane execution; utilized to execute thousands during the most radical phase of the French Revolution known as the Reign of Terror. (p. 626)

**Guomindang** [*gwo min däng*] Chinese Nationalist party founded by Sun Yat-sen in 1919; drew support from local warlords and Chinese criminal underworld; initially forged alliance with Communists in 1924; dominated by Chiang Kai-shek after 1925. (p. 797)

**Gutenberg, Johannes** Introduced movable type to western Europe in 15th century; credited with greatly expanded availability of printed books and pamphlets. (p. 481)

**Habsburg, Maximilian von** Proclaimed Emperor Maximilian of Mexico following intervention of France in 1862; ruled until overthrow and execution by liberal revolutionaries under Benito Juárez in 1867. (p. 685)

**haciendas** Rural estates in Spanish colonies in New World; produced agricultural products for consumers in America; basis of wealth and power for local aristocracy. (p. 528)

**Haganah** Zionist military force engaged in violent resistance to British presence in Palestine in the 1940s. (p. 838)

**Harvey, William** English physician (17th century) who demonstrated circular movement of blood in animals, function of heart as pump. (p. 487)

**Herzl, Theodor** [*hûrt* suhl, *hârt*-] Austrian journalist and Zionist; formed World Zionist Organization in 1897; promoted Jewish migration to Palestine and formation of a Jewish state. (p. 774)

**Hidalgo, Father Miguel de** Mexican priest who established independence movement among American Indians and mestizos in 1810; despite early victories, was captured and executed. (p. 675)

**Hideyoshi, Toyotomi** [tO yO tO mAY] General under Nobunaga; succeeded as leading military power in central Japan; continued efforts to break power of daimyos; constructed a series of alliances that made him military master of Japan in 1590; died in 1598. (p. 609)

**Hispaniola** First island in Caribbean settled by Spaniards; settlement founded by Columbus on second voyage to New World; Spanish base of operations for further discoveries in New World. (p. 518)

**Hitler, Adolf** Nazi leader of fascist Germany from 1933 to his suicide in 1945; created a strongly centralized state in Germany; eliminated all rivals; launched Germany on aggressive foreign policy leading to World War II; responsible for attempted genocide of European Jews. (p. 765)

**Ho Chi Minh** Also known as Nguyen Ai Quoc; led Vietnamese Communist party in struggle for liberation from French and U.S. dominance and to unify north and south Vietnam. (p. 942)

**Holocaust** Term for Hitler's attempted genocide of European Jews during World War II; resulted in deaths of 6 million Jews. (p. 825)

**Holy Alliance** Alliance among Russia, Prussia, and Austria in defense of religion and the established order; formed at Congress of Vienna by most conservative monarchies of Europe. (p. 727)

**homelands** Under apartheid, areas in South Africa designated for ethno-linguistic groups within the black African population; such areas tend to be overpopulated and poverty-stricken. (p. 915)

**Hong Kong** British colony on Chinese mainland; major commercial center; agreement reached between Britain and People's Republic of China returned colony to China in 1997. (p. 925)

**Hongwu** First Ming emperor in 1368; originally of peasant lineage; original name Zhu Yuanzhang; drove out Mongol influence; restored position of scholar-gentry. (p. 601)

**Hong Xiuquan** [*hoong* shEE *U* chY *än*] (1812–1864) Leader of the Taiping rebellion; converted to specifically Chinese form of Christianity; attacked traditional Confucian teachings of Chinese elite. (p. 718)

**Huancavelica** [wäng kuh vuh *lEE* kuh] Location of greatest deposit of mercury in South America; aided in American silver production; linked with Potosí. (p. 528)

**Huerta, Victoriano** Attempted to reestablish centralized dictatorship in Mexico following the removal of Madero in 1913; forced from power in 1914 by Villa and Zapata. (p. 790)

**humanism** Focus on humankind as center of intellectual and artistic endeavor; method of study that emphasized the superiority of classical forms over medieval styles, in particular the study of ancient languages. (p. 481)

**Humayan** Son and successor of Babur; expelled from India in 1540, but restored Mughal rule by 1556; died shortly thereafter. (p. 583)

**Hussein** Sherif of Mecca from 1908 to 1917; used British promise of independence to convince Arabs to support Britain against the Turks in World War I; angered by Britain's failure to keep promise; died 1931. (p. 774)

**Hyundai** Example of huge industrial groups that wield great power in modern South Korea; virtually governed Korea's southeastern coast; vertical economic organization with ships, supertankers, factories, schools, and housing units. (p. 929)

**Ieyasu, Tokugawa** [tO koog ä wä] Vassal of Toyotomi Hideyoshi; succeeded him as most powerful military figure in Japan; granted title of shogun in 1603 and established Tokugawa Shogunate; established political unity in Japan. (p. 610)

**imams** According to Shi'ism, rulers who could trace descent from the successors of Ali. (p. 580)

**import substitution** Typical of Latin American economies; domestic production of goods during the 20th century that had previously been imported; led to light industrialization. (p. 787)

**Indies piece** Term used within the complex exchange system established by the Spanish for African trade; referred to the value of an adult male slave. (p. 550)

**Industrial Revolution** Series of changes in economy of Western nations between 1740 and 20th century; stimulated by rapid population growth, increase in agricultural productivity, commercial revolution of 17th century, and development of new means of transportation; in essence involved technological change and the application of machines to the process of production. (p. 623)

**intelligentsia** [in teli *jent* sEE uh, *gent-*] Russian term denoting articulate intellectuals as a class; 19th-century group bent on radical change in Russian political and social system; often wished to maintain a Russian culture distinct from that of the West. (p. 732)

**iron curtain** Phrase coined by Winston Churchill to describe the division between free and communist societies taking shape in Europe after 1946. (p. 845)

**Isabella of Castile** (1451–1504) Along with Ferdinand of Aragon, monarch of largest Christian kingdoms in Iberia; marriage to Ferdinand created united Spain; responsible for reconquest of Granada, initiation of exploration of New World. (p. 517)

**Isandhlwana** [EE sän dl *wä* nuh] Location of battle fought in 1879 between the British and Zulu armies in south Africa; resulted in defeat of British; one of few victories of African forces over western Europeans. (p. 662)

**Isfahan** [is fuh *hän*] (1592–1629) Safavid capital under Abbas the Great; planned city laid out according to shah's plan; example of Safavid architecture. (p. 581)

**Ismâ'il** (1487–1524) Sufi commander who conquered city of Tabriz in 1501; first Safavid to be proclaimed shah or emperor. (p. 576)

**Iturbide, Augustín de** (1783–1824) Conservative Creole officer in Mexican army who signed agreement with insurgent forces of independence; combined forces entered Mexico City in 1821; later proclaimed emperor of Mexico until its collapse in 1824. (p. 675)

**Ivan III** (1440–1505) Also known as Ivan the Great; prince of Duchy of Moscow; claimed descent from Rurik; responsible for freeing Russia from Mongols after 1462; took title of tsar or Caesar—equivalent of emperor. (p. 500)

**Ivan IV** (1530–1584) Also known as Ivan the Terrible; confirmed power of tsarist autocracy by attacking authority of boyars (aristocrats); continued policy of Russian expansion; established contacts with western European commerce and culture. (p. 500)

**Janissaries** Ottoman infantry divisions that dominated Ottoman armies; forcibly conscripted as boys in conquered areas of Balkans, legally slaves; translated military service into political influence, particularly after 15th century. (p. 571)

**Jesuits** A new religious order founded during the Catholic Reformation; active in politics, education, and missionary work; sponsored missions to South America, North American, and Asia. (p. 482)

**Jiang Qing** [*jyäng ching*] (1914–1991) Wife of Mao Zedong; one of Gang of Four; opposed pragmatists and supported Cultural Revolution of 1965; arrested and imprisoned for life in 1976. (p. 937)

**Jinnah, Muhammad Ali** (1876–1948) Muslim nationalist leader in India; originally a member of the National Congress party; became leader of Muslim League; traded Muslim support for British during World War II for promises of a separate Muslim state after the war; first president of Pakistan. (p. 832)

**João VI** Portuguese monarch who established seat of government in Brazil from 1808 to 1820 as a result of Napoleonic invasion of Iberian peninsula; made Brazil seat of empire with capital at Rio de Janeiro. (p. 677)

**Juárez, Benito** (1806–1872) Indian governor of state of Oaxaca in Mexico; leader of liberal rebellion against Santa Anna; liberal government defeated by French intervention under Emperor Napoleon III of France and establishment of Mexican Empire under Maximilian; restored to power in 1867 until his death in 1872. (p. 684)

**Kangxi** [*käng shEE*] Confucian scholar and Manchu emperor of Qing dynasty from 1661 to 1722; established high degree of Sinification among the Manchus. (p. 714)

**Kenya African Union (KAU)** Leading nationalist party in Kenya; adopted nonviolent approach to ending British control in the 1950s. (p. 836)

**Kenyatta, Jomo** (1946–1978) Leader of the nonviolent nationalist party in Kenya; organized the Kenya Africa Union (KAU); failed to win concessions because of resistance of white settlers; came to power only after suppression of the Land Freedom Army, or Mau Mau. (p. 835)

**Kerensky, Alexander** (1881–1970) Liberal revolutionary leader during the early stages of the Russian Revolution of 1917; sought development of parliamentary rule, religious freedom. (p. 791)

**Khartoum** River town that was administrative center of Egyptian authority in Sudan. (p. 711)

**khedives** [kuh *dEEv*] Descendants of Muhammad Ali in Egypt after 1867; formal rulers of Egypt despite French and English intervention until overthrown by military coup in 1952. (p. 709)

**Khomeini, Ayatollah Ruhollah** [KHO *mAY* nEE, kO-, äyuh *tO* luh] (1900–1989) Religious ruler of Iran following revolution of 1979 to expel the Pahlavi shah of Iran; emphasized religious purification; tried to eliminate Western influences and establish purely Islamic government. (p. 912)

**Khrushchev, Nikita** [*kroosh* chef, chof, *krUsh*-] Stalin's successor as head of U.S.S.R. from 1953 to 1964; attacked Stalinism in 1956 for concentration of power and arbitrary dictatorship; failure of Siberian development program and antagonism of Stalinists led to downfall. (p. 866)

**Korean War** Fought from 1950 to 1953; North supported by U.S.S.R. and later People's Republic of China; South supported by United States and small international United Nations force; ended in stalemate and continued division of Korea. (p. 924)

**kulaks** Agricultural entrepreneurs who utilized the Stolypin and later NEP reforms to increase agricultural production and buy additional land. (p. 734)

**Land Freedom Army** Radical organization for independence in Kenya; frustrated by failure of nonviolent means, initiated campaign of terror in 1952; referred to by British as the Mau Mau. (p. 836)

**Las Casas, Bartolomé de** (1484–1566) Dominican friar who supported peaceful conversion of the Native American population of the Spanish colonies; opposed forced labor and advocated Indian rights. (p. 520)

**League of Nations** International diplomatic and peace organization created in the Treaty of Versailles that ended World War I; one of the chief goals of President Woodrow Wilson of the United States in the peace negotiations; the United States was never a member. (p. 767)

**Lee Kuan Yew** Ruler of Singapore from independence in 1959 through three decades; established tightly controlled authoritarian government; ruled through People's Action party to suppress political diversity. (p. 930)

**Lepanto** Naval battle between the Spanish and the Ottoman Empire resulting in a Spanish victory in 1571. (p. 466)

**Lesotho** Southern African state that survived mfecane; not based on Zulu model; less emphasis on military organization, less authoritarian government. (p. 557)

**letrados** University-trained lawyers from Spain in the New World; juridical core of Spanish colonial bureaucracy; exercised both legislative and administrative functions. (p. 529)

**liberal** Political viewpoint with origins in western Europe during the 19th century; stressed limited state interference in individual life, representation of propertied people in government; urged importance of constitutional rule and parliaments. (p. 629)

**Liberal Democratic party** Monopolized Japanese government from its formation in 1955 into the 1990s; largely responsible for the economic reconstruction of Japan. (p. 923)

**liberation theology** Combined Catholic theology and socialist principles in effort to bring about improved conditions for the poor in Latin America in 20th century. (p. 881)

**Li Dazhao** [*lEE dä jaU*] (1888–1927) Chinese intellectual who gave serious attention to Marxist philosophy; headed study circle at the University of Beijing; saw peasants as vanguard of revolutionary communism in China. (p. 797)

**Lin Biao** (1907–1971) Chinese commander under Mao; trained at Chiang Kaishek's Whampoa Academy in the 1920s. (p. 934)

**Lin Zexu** (1785–1850) Distinguished Chinese official charged with stamping out opium trade in southern China; ordered blockade of European trading areas in Canton and confiscation of opium; sent into exile following the Opium War. (p. 718)

**Liu Shaoqui** Chinese Communist pragmatist; with Deng Xiaoping, came to power in 1959 after Mao was replaced; determined to restore state direction and market incentives at local level; purged in 1966 as Mao returned to power. (p. 937)

**Lloyd George, David** Prime minister of Great Britain who headed a coalition government through much of World War I and the turbulent years that followed. (p. 765)

**Locke, John** (1632–1704) English philosopher who argued that people could learn everything through senses and reason and that power of government came from the people, not divine right of kings; offered possibility of revolution to overthrow tyrants. (p. 487)

**Long March** Communist escape from Hunan province during civil war with Guomindang in 1934; center of Communist power moved to Shaanxi province; firmly established Mao Zedong as head of the Communist party in China. (p. 799)

**Louis XIV** (1638–1715) French monarch of the late 17th century who personified absolute monarchy. (p. 487)

**Louis XVI** (1754–1793) Bourbon monarch of France who was executed during the radical phase of the French Revolution. (p. 626)

**L'Overture, Toussaint** [lU veR *tYR*] (1743–1803) Leader of slave rebellion on the French sugar island of St. Domingue in 1791 that led to creation of independent republic of Haiti in 1804. (p. 675)

**Luanda** Portuguese factory established in 1520s south of Kongo; became basis for Portuguese colony of Angola. (p. 546)

**Luo** Nilotic people who migrated from upper Nile valley; established dynasty among existing Bantu population in lake region of central eastern Africa; center at Bunyoro. (p. 555)

**Luther, Martin** (1483–1546) German monk; initiated Protestant Reformation in 1517 by nailing 95 theses to door of Wittenberg church; emphasized primacy of faith over works stressed in Catholic church; accepted state control of church. (p. 482)

**Luzon** Northern island of Philippines; conquered by Spain during the 1560s; site of major Catholic missionary effort. (p. 599)

**Macao** One of two ports in which Europeans were permitted to trade in China during the Ming dynasty. (p. 605)

**Machiavelli, Niccolo** [mak EE uh *vel* EE] (1469–1527) Author of *The Prince* (16th century); emphasized realistic discussions of how to seize and maintain power; one of most influential authors of Italian Renaissance. (p. 481)

**Madero, Francisco** (1873–1913) Moderate democratic reformer in Mexico; proposed moderate reforms in 1910; arrested by Porfirio Díaz; initiated revolution against Díaz when released from prison; temporarily gained power, but removed and assassinated in 1913. (p. 790)

**Magellan, Ferdinand** (1480–1521) Spanish captain who in 1519 initiated first circumnavigation of the globe; died during the voyage; allowed Spain to claim Philippines. (p. 462)

**Mahdi** In Sufi belief system, a promised deliverer; also name given to Muhammad Achmad, leader of late 19th-century revolt against Egyptians and British in the Sudan. (p. 711)

**Mahmud II** (1785–1839) Ottoman sultan; built a private, professional army; fomented revolution of Janissaries and crushed them with private army; destroyed power of Janissaries and their religious allies; initiated reform of Ottoman Empire on Western precedents. (p. 704)

**mandates** Governments entrusted to European nations in the Middle East in the aftermath of World War I; Britain occupied mandates in Syria, Iraq, Lebanon, and Palestine after 1922. (p. 774)

**Mandela, Nelson** (b. 1918) Long-imprisoned leader of the African National

Congress party; worked with the ANC leadership and F. W. de Klerk's supporters to dismantle the apartheid system from the mid-1980s onward; in 1994, became the first black prime minister of South Africa after the ANC won the first genuinely democratic elections in the country's history. (p. 915)

**manifest destiny** Belief of the government of the United States that it was destined to rule the continent from coast to coast; led to annexation of Texas and Mexican-American War. (p. 684)

**Mao Zedong** (1893–1976) Communist leader in revolutionary China; advocated rural reform and role of peasantry in Nationalist revolution; influenced by Li Dazhao; led Communist reaction against Guomindang purges in 1920s, culminating in Long March of 1934; seized control of all of mainland China by 1949; initiated Great Leap Forward in 1958. (p. 797)

**Marattas** Western India peoples who rebelled against Mughal control early in 18th century. (p. 589)

**Marquis of Pombal** Prime minister of Portugal from 1755 to 1776; acted to strengthen royal authority in Brazil; expelled Jesuits; enacted fiscal reforms and established monopoly companies to stimulate the colonial economy. (p. 538)

**Marshall Plan** Program of substantial loans initiated by the United States in 1947; designed to aid Western nations in rebuilding from the war's devastation; vehicle for American economic dominance. (p. 846)

**Marx, Karl** (1818–1883) German socialist who blasted earlier socialist movements as utopian; saw history as defined by class struggle between groups out of power and those controlling the means of production; preached necessity of social revolution to create proletarian dictatorship. (p. 636)

**mass leisure culture** An aspect of the later Industrial Revolution; based on newspapers, music halls, popular theater, vacation trips, and team sports. (p. 638)

**Mass Line** Economic policy of Mao Zedong; led to formation of agricultural cooperatives in 1955; cooperatives became farming collectives in 1956. (p. 935)

**Mataram** Kingdom that controlled interior regions of Java in 17th century; Dutch East India Company paid tribute to the kingdom for rights of trade at Batavia; weakness of kingdom after 1670s allowed Dutch to exert control over all of Java. (p. 652)

**May Fourth movement** Resistance to Japanese encroachments in China began on this date in 1919; spawned movement of intellectuals aimed at transforming China into a liberal democracy; rejected Confucianism. (p. 797)

**Mehmed II** [me *met*] (1432–1481) Ottoman sultan called the "Conqueror"; responsible for conquest of Constantinople in 1453; destroyed what remained of Byzantine Empire. (p. 570)

**mercantilism** Economic theory that stressed governments' promotion of limitation of imports from other nations and internal economies in order to improve tax revenues; popular during 17th and 18th centuries in Europe. (p. 466)

**mestizos** People of mixed European and Indian ancestry in Mesoamerica and South America; particularly prevalent in areas colonized by Spain; often part of forced labor system. (p. 467)

**Mexican-American War** Fought between Mexico and the United States from 1846 to 1848; led to devastating defeat of Mexican forces, loss of about one-half of Mexico's national territory to the United States. (p. 684)

**Mexican Constitution of 1917** Promised land reform, limited foreign ownership of key resources, guaranteed the rights of workers, and placed restrictions on clerical education; marked formal end of Mexican Revolution. (p. 790)

**Mexican Revolution** Fought over a period of almost ten years from 1910; resulted in ouster of Porfirio Díaz from power; opposition forces led by Pancho Villa and Emiliano Zapata. (p. 789)

**Mexico City** Capital of New Spain; built on ruins of Aztec capital of Tenochtitlan. (p. 522)

**mfecane** [um fuh *ka* nAY] Wars of 19th century in southern Africa; created by Zulu expansion under Shaka; revolutionized political organization of southern Africa. (p. 557)

**Middle Passage** Slave voyage from Africa to the Americas (16th–18th centuries); generally a traumatic experience for black slaves, although it failed to strip Africans of their culture. (p. 559)

**Midway Island** World War II Pacific battle; decisive U.S. victory over powerful Japanese carrier force. (p. 827)

**Minas Gerais** [*mEE* nuhs zhi *RIs*] Region of Brazil located in mountainous interior where gold strikes were discovered in 1695; became location for gold rush. (p. 532)

**Mindanao** Southern island of Philippines; a Muslim kingdom that was able to successfully resist Spanish conquest. (p. 599)

**Minh Mang** [*min mäng*] Second emperor of a united Vietnam; successor of Nguyen Anh; ruled from 1820 to 1841; sponsored emphasis of Confucianism; persecuted Catholics. (p. 941)

**Moctezuma II** [mok te *sU* mä] (1480–1520) Last independent Aztec emperor; killed during Hernán Cortés's conquest of Tenochtitlan. (p. 522)

**Monroe Doctrine** American declaration stated in 1823; established that any attempt of a European country to colonize in the Americas would be considered an unfriendly act by the United States; supported by Great Britain as a means of opening Latin American trade. (p. 682)

**Montagu-Chelmsford reforms** Increased the powers of Indian legislators at the all-India level and placed much of the provincial administration of India under local ministries controlled by legislative bodies with substantial numbers of elected Indians; passed in 1919. (p. 771)

**Morley-Minto reforms** Provided educated Indians with considerably expanded opportunities to elect and serve on local and all-India legislative councils. (p. 770)

**Mubarak, Hosni** President of Egypt since 1981, succeeding Anwar Sadat and continuing his policies of cooperation with the West. (p. 911)

**Mughal Empire** Established by Babur in India in 1526; the name is taken from the supposed Mongol descent of Babur, but there is little indication of any Mongol influence in the dynasty; became weak after rule of Aurangzeb in first decades of 18th century. (p. 568)

**mullahs** Local mosque officials and prayer leaders within the Safavid Empire; agents of Safavid religious campaign to convert all of population to Shi'ism. (p. 580)

**multinational corporations** Powerful companies, mainly from the West or Pacific Rim, with production as well as distribution operations in many different countries. Multinationals surged in the decades after World War II. (p. 973)

**Mumtaz Mahal** (1593–1631) Wife of Shah Jahan; took an active political role in Mughal court; entombed in Taj Mahal. (p. 588)

**Murad** (1790–1820) Head of the coalition of Mamluk rulers in Egypt; opposed Napoleonic invasion of Egypt and suffered devastating defeat; failure destroyed Mamluk government in Egypt and revealed vulnerability of Muslim core. (p. 708)

**Muslim Brotherhood** Egyptian nationalist movement founded by Hasan al-Banna in 1928; committed to fundamentalist movement in Islam; fostered strikes and urban riots against the khedival government. (p. 909)

**Muslim League** Founded in 1906 to better support demands of Muslims for separate electorates and legislative seats in Hindu-dominated India; represented division within Indian nationalist movement. (p. 832)

**Mussolini, Benito** Italian fascist leader after World War I; created first fascist government (1922–1943) based on aggressive foreign policy and new nationalist glories. (p. 787)

**Mvemba, Nzinga** King of Kongo south of Zaire River from 1507 to 1543; converted to

Christianity and took title Alfonso I; under Portuguese influence attempted to Christianize all of kingdom. (p. 545)

**nabobs** Name given to British representatives of the East India Company who went briefly to India to make fortunes through graft and exploitation. (p. 658)

**Nadir Khan Afshar** (1688–1747) Soldier-adventurer following fall of Safavid dynasty in 1722; proclaimed himself shah in 1736; established short-lived dynasty in reduced kingdom. (p. 583)

**Nasser, Gamal Abdul** (1918-1970) Took power in Egypt following a military coup in 1952; enacted land reforms and used state resources to reduce unemployment; ousted Britain from the Suez Canal zone in 1956. (p. 908)

**Natal** British colony in south Africa; developed after Boer trek north from Cape Colony; major commercial outpost at Durban. (p. 668)

**National Congress party** Grew out of regional associations of Western-educated Indians; originally centered in cities of Bombay, Poona, Calcutta, and Madras; became political party in 1885; focus of nationalist movement in India; governed through most of postcolonial period. (p. 769)

**National Liberation Front (FLN)** Radical nationalist movement in Algeria; launched sustained guerilla war against France in the 1950s; success of attacks led to independence of Algeria in 1958. (p. 836)

**National Socialist (Nazi) party** Also known as the Nazi party; led by Adolf Hitler in Germany; picked up political support during the economic chaos of the Great Depression; advocated authoritarian state under a single leader, aggressive foreign policy to reverse humiliation of the Versailles treaty; took power in Germany in 1933. (p. 819)

**nationalism** Political viewpoint with origins in western Europe; often allied with other "isms"; urged importance of national unity; valued a collective identity based on culture, race, or ethnic origin. (p. 627)

**négritude** Literary movement in Africa; attempted to combat racial stereotypes of African culture; celebrated the beauty of black skin and African physique; associated with origins of African nationalist movements. (p. 778)

**Nehru, Jawaharlal** [*nAY* rU, *nâr* U] (1889–1964) One of Gandhi's disciples; governed India after independence (1947); committed to program of social reform and economic development; preserved civil rights and democracy. (p. 902)

**neocolonial economy** Industrialized nations' continued dominance of the world economy; ability of the industrialized nations to maintain economic colonialism without political colonialism. (p. 905)

**New Deal** President Franklin Roosevelt's precursor of the modern welfare state (1933–1939); programs to combat economic depression enacted a number of social insurance measures and used government spending to stimulate the economy; increased power of the state and the state's intervention in U.S. social and economic life. (p. 802)

**New Economic Policy** Initiated by Lenin in 1921; state continued to set basic economic policies, but efforts were now combined with individual initiative; policy allowed food production to recover. (p. 793)

**new feminism** New wave of women's rights agitation dating from 1949; emphasized more literal equality that would play down domestic roles and qualities for women; promoted specific reforms and redefinition of what it meant to be female. (p. 858)

**New France** French colonies in North America; extended from St. Lawrence River along Great Lakes and down Mississippi River valley system. (p. 471)

**New Spain** Spanish colonial possessions in Mesoamerica; included most of central Mexico; based on imperial system of Aztecs. (p. 522)

**Newton, Isaac** (1643–1727) English scientist; author of *Principia*; drew together astronomical and physical observations and wider theories into a neat framework of natural laws; established principles of motion; defined forces of gravity. (p. 487)

**Nguyen Anh** [ngI *en, ngu yen än*] (1762–1820) Last surviving member of Nguyen dynasty following Tayson Rebellion in Vietnam; with French support retook southern Vietnam; drove Tayson from northern Vietnam by 1802; proclaimed himself emperor with capital at Hue; also known as Gia Long. (p. 940)

**Nicholas II** Tsar of Russia 1894–1917; forcefully suppressed political opposition and resisted constitutional government; deposed by revolution in 1917. (p. 761)

**Nobili, Robert di** (1577–1656) Italian Jesuit missionary; worked in India during the early 1600s; introduced strategy to convert elites first; strategy later widely adopted by Jesuits in various parts of Asia; mission eventually failed. (p. 600)

**Nobunaga** (1534–1582) Japanese daimyo; first to make extensive use of firearms; in 1573 deposed last of Ashikaga shoguns; unified much of central Honshu under his command. (p. 609)

**North American Free Trade Agreement (NAFTA)** Agreement that created an essentially free trade zone among Mexico, Canada, and the United States, in hopes of encouraging economic growth in all three nations; after difficult negotiations, went into effect January 1, 1994. (p. 978)

**North Atlantic Treaty Organization (NATO)** Created in 1949 under United States leadership to group most of the western European powers plus Canada in a defensive alliance against possible Soviet aggression. (p. 846)

**Northern Renaissance** Cultural and intellectual movement of northern Europe; began later than Italian Renaissance c. 1450; centered in France, Low Countries, England, and Germany; featured greater emphasis on religion than Italian Renaissance. (p. 481)

**Nurhaci** (1559-1626) Architect of Manchu unity; created distinctive Manchu banner armies; controlled most of Manchuria; adopted Chinese bureaucracy and court ceremonies in Manchuria; entered China and successfully captured Ming capital at Beijing. (p. 714)

**Nur Jahan** (1577–1645) Wife of Jahangir; amassed power in court and created faction of male relatives who dominated Mughal empire during later years of Jahangir's reign. (p. 587)

**obeah** African religious ideas and practices in the English and French Caribbean islands. (p. 562)

**Obregón, Alvaro** (1880–1928) Emerged as leader of the Mexican government in 1915; elected president in 1920. (p. 790)

**Old Believers** Russians who refused to accept the ecclesiastical reforms of Alexis Romanov (17th century); many exiled to Siberia or southern Russia, where they became part of Russian colonization. (p. 502)

**Opium War** Fought between the British and Qing China beginning in 1839; fought to protect British trade in opium; resulted in resounding British victory, opening of Hong Kong as British port of trade. (p. 717)

**Orabi, Ahmad** (1841–1911) Student of Muhammad Abduh; led revolt in 1882 against Turkish influence in Egyptian army; forced khedive to call on British army for support. (p. 711)

**Ormuz** Portuguese factory or fortified trade town located at southern end of Persian Gulf; site for forcible entry into Asian sea trade network. (p. 597)

**Orozco, José Clemente** (1883–1949) Mexican muralist of the period after the Mexican Revolution; like Rivera's, his work featured romantic images of the Indian past with Christian symbols and Marxist ideology. (p. 790)

**Ottoman Empire** Turkic empire established in Asia Minor and eventually extending throughout Middle East; responsible for conquest of Constantinople and end of Byzantine Empire in 1453; succeeded Seljuk Turks following retreat of Mongols. (p. 568)

**Ottomans** Turkic people who advanced from strongholds in Asia Minor during 1350s; conquered large part of Balkans; unified under Mehmed I; captured

Constantinople in 1453; established empire from Balkans that included most of Arab world. (p. 570)

**Ottoman Society for Union and Progress** Organization of political agitators in opposition to rule of Abdul Harmid; also called "Young Turks"; desired to restore 1876 constitution. (p. 705)

**Pacific Rim** Region including Japan, South Korea, Singapore, Hong Kong, Taiwan; typified by rapid growth rates, expanding exports, and industrialization; either Chinese or strongly influenced by Confucian values; considerable reliance on government planning and direction, limitations on dissent and instability. (p. 922)

**Palmares** Kingdom of runaway slaves with a population of 8000 to 10,000 people; located in Brazil during the 17th century; leadership was Angolan. (p. 562)

**pan-African** Organization that brought together intellectuals and political leaders from areas of Africa and African diaspora before and after World War I. (p. 777)

**Panama Canal** An aspect of American intervention in Latin America; resulted from United States support for a Panamanian independence movement in return for a grant to exclusive rights to a canal across the Panama isthmus; provided short route between Atlantic and Pacific oceans; completed 1914. (p. 697)

**parliamentary monarchy** Originated in England and Holland, 17th century, with kings partially checked by significant legislative powers in parliaments. (p. 490)

**partition of Poland** Division of Polish territory among Russia, Prussia, and Austria in 1772, 1793, and 1795; eliminated Poland as independent state; part of expansion of Russian influence in eastern Europe. (p. 506)

**party cadres** Basis of China's communist government organization; cadre advisors were attached to military contingents at all levels. (p. 935)

**Pasteur, Louis** French scientist who discovered relationship between germs and disease in 19th century, leading to better sanitation. (p. 633)

**Paulistas** Backwoodsmen from São Paulo in Brazil; penetrated Brazilian interior in search of precious metals during 17th century. (p. 532)

**Pearl Harbor** American naval base in Hawaii; attack by Japanese on this facility in December 1941 crippled American fleet in the Pacific and caused entry of United States into World War II. (p. 826)

**Pedro I** (1798–1834) Son and successor of João VI in Brazil; aided in the declaration of Brazilian independence from Portugal in 1822; became constitutional emperor of Brazil. (p. 677)

**peninsulares** People living in the New World Spanish colonies but born in Spain. (p. 535)

**People's Democratic Republic of Korea** Northern half of Korea dominated by U.S.S.R.; long headed by Kim Il-Sung; attacked south in 1950 and initiated Korean War; retained independence as a communist state after the war. (p. 924)

**People's Liberation Army** Chinese Communist army; administered much of country under People's Republic of China. (p. 935)

**People's Republic of China** Communist government of mainland China; proclaimed in 1949 following military success of Mao Zedong over forces of Chiang Kai-shek and the Guomindang. (p. 934)

**perestroika** [per uh *stroi* kuh] Policy of Mikhail Gorbachev calling for economic restructuring in the U.S.S.R. in the late 1980s; more leeway for private ownership and decentralized control in industry and agriculture. (p. 952)

**Pericles** Athenian political leader during 5th century B.C.E.; guided development of Athenian Empire; died during early stages of Peloponnesian War. (p. 99)

**Perón, Juan D.** Military leader in Argentina who became dominant political figure after military coup in 1943; used position as Minister of Labor to appeal to working groups and the poor; became president in 1946; forced into exile in 1955; returned and won presidency in 1973. (p. 807)

**Perry, Matthew** American commodore who visited Edo Bay with American fleet in 1853; insisted on opening ports to American trade on threat of naval bombardment; won rights for American trade with Japan in 1854. (p. 736)

**Persian Gulf War** 1991 war led by United States and various European and Middle Eastern allies, against Iraqi occupation of Kuwait. The war led to Iraqi withdrawal and a long confrontation with Iraq about armaments and political regime. (p. 961)

**Peter I** Also known as Peter the Great; son of Alexis Romanov; ruled from 1689 to 1725; continued growth of absolutism and conquest; included more definite interest in changing selected aspects of economy and culture through imitation of western European models. (p. 502)

**Pinsker, Leon** (1821–1891) European Zionist who believed that Jewish assimilation into Christian European nations was impossible; argued for return to Middle Eastern Holy Land. (p. 774)

**Pizarro, Francisco** Led conquest of Inca Empire of Peru beginning in 1535; by 1540, most of Inca possessions fell to the Spanish. (p. 469)

**Plassey** Battle in 1757 between troops of the British East India Company and an Indian army under Sirāj ud-daula, ruler of Bengal; British victory resulted in control of northern India. (p. 654)

**Politburo** Executive committee of the Soviet Communist party; 20 members. (p. 812)

**polyandry** [*pol* EE an drEE, pol EE *an*-] Marriage practice in which one woman had several husbands; recounted in Aryan epics. (p. 54)

**Popular Front** Combination of socialist and communist political parties in France; won election in 1936; unable to take strong measures of social reform because of continuing strength of conservatives; fell from power in 1938. (p. 802)

**population revolution** Huge growth in population in western Europe beginning about 1730; prelude to Industrial Revolution; population of France increased 50 percent, England and Prussia 100 percent. (p. 625)

**positivism** French philosophy based on observation and scientific approach to problems of society; adopted by many Latin American liberals in the aftermath of independence. (p. 683)

**Potosí** Mine located in upper Peru (modern Bolivia); largest of New World silver mines; produced 80 percent of all Peruvian silver. (p. 527)

**Potsdam Conference** Meeting among leaders of the United States, Britain, and the Soviet Union just before the end of World War II in 1945; Allies agreed upon Soviet domination in eastern Europe; Germany and Austria to be divided among victorious Allies. (p. 830)

**pragmatists** Chinese Communist politicians such as Zhou Enlai, Deng Xiaoping, and Liu Shaoqui; determined to restore state direction and market incentives at the local level; opposed Great Leap Forward. (p. 937)

**presidencies** Three districts that made up the bulk of the directly ruled British territories in India; capitals at Madras, Calcutta, and Bombay. (p. 655)

**PRI** Party of the Institutionalized Revolution; dominant political party in Mexico; developed during the 1920s and 1930s; incorporated labor, peasant, military, and middle-class sectors; controlled other political organizations in Mexico. (p. 876)

**primary products** Food or industrial crops for which there is a high demand in industrialized economies; prices of such products tend to fluctuate widely; typically the primary exports of Third World economies. (p. 903)

**princely states** Domains of Indian princes allied with the British Raj; agents of East India Company were stationed at the rulers' courts to ensure compliance; made up over one-third of the British Indian Empire. (p. 655)

**proletariat** Class of working people without access to producing property; typically manufacturing workers, paid laborers in agricultural economy, or urban poor; in Europe, product of economic changes of 16th and 17th centuries. (p. 485)

**Protestantism** General wave of religious dissent against Catholic church; generally held to have begun with Martin Luther's attack on Catholic beliefs in 1517; included many varieties of religious belief. (p. 482)

**proto-industrialization** Preliminary shift away from agricultural economy in Europe; workers become full- or part-time producers of textile and metal products, working at home but in a capitalist system in which materials, work orders, and ultimate sales depended on urban merchants; prelude to Industrial Revolution. (p. 625)

**Pugachev rebellion** During 1770s in reign of Catherine the Great; led by cossack Emelian Pugachev, who claimed to be legitimate tsar; eventually crushed; typical of peasant unrest during the 18th century and thereafter. (p. 506)

**Puyi** Last emperor of China; deposed as emperor while still a small boy in 1912. (p. 720)

**Qing** Manchu dynasty that seized control of China in mid-17th century after decline of Ming; forced submission of nomadic peoples far to the west and compelled tribute from Vietnam and Burma to the south. (p. 714)

**Quit India movement** Mass civil disobedience campaign that began in the summer of 1942 to end British control of India. (p. 832)

**radical** Political viewpoint with origins in western Europe during the 19th century; advocated broader voting rights than liberals; in some cases advocated outright democracy; urged reforms in favor of the lower classes. (p. 629)

**Recopilación** [rAY kO pEEl ä sEE *On*] Body of laws collected in 1681 for Spanish possessions in New World; basis of law in the Indies. (p. 529)

**Red Army** Military organization constructed under leadership of Leon Trotsky, Bolshevik follower of Lenin; made use of people of humble background. (p. 793)

**Red Guard** Student brigades utilized by Mao Zedong and his political allies during the Cultural Revolution to discredit Mao's political enemies. (p. 938)

**Red Heads** Name given to Safavid followers because of their distinctive red headgear. (p. 576)

**Reform Bill of 1832** Legislation passed in Great Britain that extended the vote to most members of the middle class; failed to produce democracy in Britain. (p. 629)

**Reforma, La** The liberal rebellion of Benito Juárez against the forces of Santa Anna. (p. 684)

**religious revivalism** An approach to religious belief and practice that stresses the literal interpretation of texts sacred to the religion in question and the application of their precepts to all aspects of social life; increasingly associated with revivalist movements in a number of world religions, including Christianity, Islam, Judaism, and Hinduism. (p. 902)

**Republic of Korea** Southern half of Korea sponsored by United States following World War II; headed by nationalist Syngman Rhee; developed parliamentary institutions but maintained authoritarian government; defended by UN forces during Korean War; underwent industrialization and economic emergence after 1950s. (p. 924)

**revisionism** Socialist movements that at least tacitly disavowed Marxist revolutionary doctrine; believed social success could be achieved gradually through political institutions. (p. 636)

**Rhodes, Cecil** British entrepreneur in south Africa around 1900; manipulated political situation in south Africa to gain entry to resources of Boer republics; encouraged Boer War as means of destroying Boer independence. (p. 668)

**Ricci, Matteo** [*rEEt* chEE] (1552–1610) Along with Adam Schall, Jesuit scholar in court of Ming emperors; skilled scientist; won few converts to Christianity. (p. 607)

**Rio de Janeiro** Brazilian port; close to mines of Minas Gerais; importance grew with gold strikes; became colonial capital in 1763. (p. 533)

**Rivera, Diego** [ri *vär* uh] (1886–1957) Mexican artist of the period after the Mexican Revolution; famous for murals painted on walls of public buildings; mixed romantic images of the Indian past with Christian symbols and Marxist ideology. (p. 790)

**Romanov, Alexis** Second Romanov tsar (r. 1645–1676) ; abolished assemblies of nobles; gained new powers over Russian Orthodox church. (p. 502)

**Romanov dynasty** Dynasty elected in 1613 at end of Time of Troubles; ruled Russia until 1917. (p. 502)

**romanticism** Artistic and literary movement of the 19th century in Europe; held that emotion and impression, not reason, were the keys to the mysteries of human experience and nature; sought to portray passions, not calm reflection. (p. 639)

**Rosas, Juan Manuel de** Strongman leader in Buenos Aires; took power in 1831; commanded loyalty of gauchos; restored local autonomy. (p. 679)

**Rowlatt Act** Placed severe restrictions on key Indian civil rights such as freedom of the press; acted to offset the concessions granted under Montagu-Chelmsford reforms of 1919. (p. 771)

**Roy, Ram Mohun** Western-educated Indian leader, early 19th century; cooperated with British to outlaw sati. (p. 658)

**Royal African Company** Chartered in 1660s to establish a monopoly over the slave trade among British merchants; supplied African slaves to colonies in Barbados, Jamaica, and Virginia. (p. 550)

**Russo-Japanese War** War between Japan and Russia (1904-1905) over territory in Manchuria; Japan defeated the Russians, largely because of its naval power; Japan annexed Korea in 1910 as a result of military dominance. (p. 734)

**Sadat, Anwar** Successor to Gamal Abdul Nasser as ruler of Egypt; acted to dismantle costly state programs; accepted peace treaty with Israel in 1973; opened Egypt to investment by Western nations. (p. 911)

**Safavid dynasty** Originally a Turkic nomadic group; family originated in Sufi mystic group; espoused Shi'ism; conquered territory and established kingdom in region equivalent to modern Iran; lasted until 1722. (p. 568)

**Sail al-Din** [sä EEl al din, dEEn] Early 14th-century Sufi mystic; began campaign to purify Islam; first member of Safavid dynasty. (p. 576)

**saltwater slaves** Slaves transported from Africa; almost invariably black. (p. 560)

**Sandinista party** Nicaraguan socialist movement named after Augusto Sandino; successfully carried out a socialist revolution in Nicaragua during the 1980s. (p. 884)

**Sandino, Augusto** Led a guerrilla resistance movement against U.S. occupation forces in Nicaragua; assassinated by Nicaraguan National Guard in 1934; became national hero and symbol of resistance to U.S. influence in Central America. (p. 886)

**San Martín, José de** Leader of independence movement in Rio de la Plata; led to independence of the United Provinces of the Rio de la Plata by 1816; later led independence movement in Chile and Peru as well. (p. 676)

**Santa Anna, General Antonio López de** Seized power in Mexico after collapse of empire of Mexico in 1824; after brief reign of liberals, seized power in 1835 as caudillo; defeated by Texans in war for independence in 1836; defeated by United States in Mexican-American War in 1848; unseated by liberal rebellion in 1854. (p. 679)

**Santa Cruz, Andrés** Mestizo general who established union of independent Peru and Bolivia between 1829 and 1839. (p. 678)

**Sarajevo** Administrative center of the Bosnian province of Austrian Empire; assassination there of Archduke Ferdinand in 1914 started World War I. (p. 759)

**Sarmiento, Domingo F.** (1811–1888) Liberal politician and president of Argentine Republic from 1868 to 1874; author of *Facundo,* a critique of caudillo politics; increased international trade, launched internal reforms in education and transportation. (p. 686)

**satyagraha** [*sut* yuh gruhuh, suht *yä* gruh-] Literally, "truth-force"; strategy of nonviolent protest developed by Mohandas Gandhi and his followers in India; later deployed throughout the colonized world and in the United States. (p. 771)

**Schall, Adam** (1591-1666) Along with Matteo Ricci, Jesuit scholar in court of Ming emperors; skilled scientist; won few converts to Christianity. (p. 607)

**school of National Learning** New ideology that laid emphasis on Japan's unique historical experience and the revival of indigenous culture at the expense of Chinese imports such as Confucianism; typical of Japan in 18th century. (p. 612)

**Scientific Revolution** Culminated in 17th century; period of empirical advances associated with the development of wider theoretical generalizations; resulted in change in traditional beliefs of Middle Ages. (p. 486)

**Secret Army Organization (OAS)** Organization of French settlers in Algeria; led guerrilla war following independence during the 1960s; assaults directed against Arabs, Berbers, and French who advocated independence. (p. 836)

**self-determination** Right of people in a region to determine whether to be independent or not. (p. 766)

**self-strengthening movement** Late 19th-century movement in China to counter the challenge from the West; led by provincial leaders. (p. 719)

**Selim III** Sultan who ruled Ottoman Empire from 1789 to 1807; aimed at improving administrative efficiency and building a new army and navy; toppled by Janissaries in 1807. (p. 704)

**Senghor, Léopold Sédar** (1906–2001) One of the post–World War I writers of the négritude literary movement that urged pride in African values; president of Senegal from 1960 to 1980. (p. 778)

**sepoys** Troops that served the British East India Company; recruited from various warlike peoples of India. (p. 653)

**settlement colonies** Areas, such as North America and Australia, that were both conquered by European invaders and settled by large numbers of European migrants who made the colonized areas their permanent home and dispersed and decimated the indigenous inhabitants. (p. 662)

**Seven Years War** Fought both in continental Europe and also in overseas colonies between 1756 and 1763; resulted in Prussian seizures of land from Austria, English seizures of colonies in India and North America. (p. 472)

**Sikhs** Sect in northwest India; early leaders tried to bridge differences between Hindu and Muslim, but Mughal persecution led to anti-Muslim feeling. (p. 589)

**Sino-Japanese War** War fought between Japan and Qing China between 1894 and 1895; resulted in Japanese victory; frustrated Japanese imperial aims because of Western insistence that Japan withdraw from Liaodong peninsula. (p. 741)

**Sisulu, Walter** (1912–2003) Black African leader who, along with Nelson Mandela, opposed apartheid system in South Africa. (p. 915)

**Smith, Adam** Established liberal economics (*Wealth of Nations,* 1776); argued that government should avoid regulation of economy in favor of the operation of market forces. (p. 492)

**social question** Issues relating to repressed classes in western Europe during the Industrial Revolution, particularly workers and women; became more critical than constitutional issues after 1870. (p. 635)

**socialism** Political movement with origins in western Europe during the 19th century; urged an attack on private property in the name of equality; wanted state control of means of production, end to capitalist exploitation of the working man. (p. 636)

**socialist realism** Attempt within the U.S.S.R. to relate formal culture to the masses in order to avoid the adoption of western European cultural forms; begun under Joseph Stalin; fundamental method of Soviet fiction, art, and literary criticism. (p. 812)

**sociedad de castas** American social system based on racial origins; Europeans or whites at top, black slaves or Native Americans at bottom, mixed races in middle. (p. 533)

**Solidarity** Polish labor movement formed in 1970s under Lech Walesa; challenged U.S.S.R.-dominated government of Poland. (p. 862)

**Solzhenitsyn, Aleksandr** [sOl zhuh *nEEt* sin, sol-] (b. 1918) Russian author critical of the Soviet regime but also of Western materialism; published trilogy on the Siberian prison camps, *The Gulag Archipelago* (1978). (p. 864)

**Spanish-American War** War fought between Spain and the United States beginning in 1898; centered on Cuba and Puerto Rico; permitted American intervention in Caribbean, annexation of Puerto Rico and the Philippines. (p. 697)

**Spanish Civil War** War pitting authoritarian and military leaders in Spain against republicans and leftists between 1936 and 1939; Germany and Italy supported the royalists; the Soviet Union supported the republicans; led to victory of the royalist forces. (p. 804)

**Stalin, Joseph** Successor to Lenin as head of the U.S.S.R.; strongly nationalist view of communism; represented anti-Western strain of Russian tradition; crushed opposition to his rule; established series of five-year plans to replace New Economic Policy; fostered agricultural collectivization; led U.S.S.R. through World War II; furthered cold war with western Europe and the United States; died in 1953. (p. 795)

**Stolypin reforms** Reforms introduced by the Russian interior minister Piotyr Stolypin intended to placate the peasantry in the aftermath of the Revolution of 1905; included reduction in redemption payments, attempt to create market-oriented peasantry. (p. 734)

**Suez Canal** Built across Isthmus of Suez to connect Mediterranean Sea with Red Sea in 1869; financed by European investors; with increasing indebtedness of khedives, permitted intervention of British into Egyptian politics to protect their investment. (p. 709)

**Sun Yat-sen** Head of Revolutionary Alliance, organization that led 1911 revolt against Qing dynasty in China; briefly elected president in 1911, but yielded in favor of Yuan Shikai in 1912; created Nationalist party of China (Guomindang) in 1919; died in 1925. (p. 720)

**Supreme Soviet** Parliament of Union of Soviet Socialist Republics; elected by universal suffrage; actually controlled by Communist party; served to ratify party decisions. (p. 793)

**Suriname** Formerly a Dutch plantation colony on the coast of South America; location of runaway slave kingdom in 18th century; able to retain independence despite attempts to crush guerrilla resistance. (p. 562)

**Swazi** New African state formed on model of Zulu chiefdom; survived mfecane. (p. 557)

**syndicalism** Economic and political system based on the organization of labor; imported in Latin America from European political movements; militant force in Latin American politics. (p. 789)

**Taiping Rebellion** Broke out in south China in the 1850s and early 1860s; led by Hong Xiuquan, a semi-Christianized prophet; sought to overthrow Qing dynasty and Confucian basis of scholar-gentry. (p. 718)

**Taiwan** Island off Chinese mainland; became refuge for Nationalist Chinese regime under Chiang Kai-shek as Republic of China in 1948; successfully retained independence with aid of United States; rapidly industrialized after 1950s. (p. 922)

**Taj Mahal** Most famous architectural achievement of Mughal India; originally built as a mausoleum for the wife of Shah Jahan, Mumtaz Mahal. (p. 587)

**Tanzimat reforms** Series of reforms in Ottoman Empire between 1839 and 1876; established Western-style university, state postal system, railways, extensive legal reforms; resulted in creation of new constitution in 1876. (p. 704)

**Tayson Rebellion** Peasant revolution in southern Vietnam during the late 1770s; succeeded in toppling the Nguyen dynasty; subsequently unseated the Trinh dynasty of northern Vietnam. (p. 940)

**technocrat** New type of bureaucrat; intensely trained in engineering or economics and devoted to the power of national planning; came to fore in offices of governments following World War II. (p. 849)

**Tehran Conference** Meeting among leaders of the United States, Britain, and the Soviet Union in 1943; agreed to the opening of a new front in France. (p. 830)

**terakoya** Commoner schools founded during the Tokugawa Shogunate in Japan to teach reading, writing, and the rudiments of Confucianism; resulted in high literacy rate, approaching 40 percent, of Japanese males. (p. 735)

**third Rome** Russian claim to be successor state to Roman and Byzantine empires; based in part on continuity of Orthodox church in Russia following fall of Constantinople in 1453. (p. 500)

**third world** Also known as developing nations; nations outside the capitalist industrial nations of the first world and the industrialized communist nations of the second world; generally less economically powerful, but with varied economies. (p. 874)

**Thirty Years War** War within the Holy Roman Empire between German Protestants and their allies (Sweden, Denmark, France) and the emperor and his ally, Spain; ended in 1648 after great destruction with Treaty of Westphalia. (p. 483)

**Tilak, B. G.** (1856–1920) Believed that nationalism in India should be based on appeals to Hindu religiosity; worked to promote the restoration and revival of ancient Hindu traditions; offended Muslims and other religious groups; first populist leader in Indian nationalist movement. (p. 770)

**Time of Troubles** Followed death of Russian tsar Ivan IV without heir early in 17th century; boyars attempted to use vacuum of power to reestablish their authority; ended with selection of Michael Romanov as tsar in 1613. (p. 502)

**Tokugawa Shogunate** Founded 1603 when Tokugawa Ieyasu was made shogun by Japanese emperor; ended the civil wars and brought political unity to Japan. (p. 610)

**totalitarian state** A new kind of government in the 20th century that exercised massive, direct control over virtually all the activities of its subjects; existed in Germany, Italy, and the Soviet Union. (p. 803)

**total war** Warfare of the 20th century; vast resources and emotional commitments of belligerent nations were marshaled to support military effort; resulted from impact of industrialization on the military effort reflecting technological innovation and organizational capacity. (p. 831)

**trans-Siberian railroad** Constructed in 1870s to connect European Russia with the Pacific; completed by the end of the 1880s; brought Russia into a more active Asian role. (p. 730)

**trasformismo** Political system in late 19th-century Italy that promoted alliance of conservatives and liberals; parliamentary deputies of all parties supported the status quo. (p. 635)

**Treaty of Guadalupe-Hidalgo** Agreement that ended the Mexican-American War; provided for loss of Texas and California to the United States; left legacy of distrust of the United States in Latin America. (p. 684)

**Treaty of Paris** Arranged in 1763 following Seven Years War; granted New France to England in exchange for return of French sugar island in Caribbean. (p. 472)

**Treaty of Tordesillas** [tor duh *sEEl* yäs, *-sEE-*] Signed in 1494 between Castile and Portugal; clarified spheres of influence and rights of possession in New World; reserved Brazil and all newly discovered lands east of Brazil to Portugal; granted all lands west of Brazil to Spain. (p. 529)

**Treaty of Westphalia** Ended Thirty Years War in 1648; granted right to individual rulers within the Holy Roman Empire to choose their own religion—either Protestant or Catholic. (p. 483)

**triangular trade** Commerce linking Africa, the New World colonies, and Europe; slaves carried to America for sugar and tobacco transported to Europe. (p. 550)

**Triple Alliance** Alliance among Germany, Austria-Hungary, and Italy at the end of the 19th century; part of European alliance system and balance of power prior to World War I. (p. 644)

**Triple Entente** Alliance among Britain, Russia, and France at the outset of the 20th century; part of European alliance system and balance of power prior to World War I. (p. 644)

**Truman, Harry** American president from 1945 to 1952; less eager for smooth relations with the Soviet Union than Franklin Roosevelt; authorized use of atomic bomb during World War II; architect of American diplomacy that initiated the cold war. (p. 845)

**Tutu, Osei** [*tU* tU] (r. 1675–1717) Member of Oyoko clan of Akan peoples in Gold Coast region of Africa; responsible for creating unified Asante Empire in 1701; utilized Western firearms. (p. 552)

**Ulyanov, Vladimir Ilyich** [Ul *yä* nuhf] Better known as Lenin; most active Russian Marxist leader; insisted on importance of disciplined revolutionary cells; leader of Bolshevik Revolution of 1917. (p. 733)

**Union of Soviet Socialist Republics** Federal system of socialist republics established in 1923 in various ethnic regions of Russia; firmly controlled by Communist party; diminished nationalities protest under Bolsheviks; dissolved 1991. (p. 793)

**United Fruit Company** Most important foreign economic concern in Guatemala during the 20th century; attempted land reform aimed at United Fruit caused U.S. intervention in Guatemalan politics leading to ouster of reform government in 1954. (p. 879)

**United Nations** International organization formed in the aftermath of World War II; included all of the victorious Allies; its primary mission was to provide a forum for negotiating disputes. (p. 830)

**Valdivia, Pedro de** Spanish conquistador; conquered Araucanian Indians of Chile and established city of Santiago in 1541. (p. 522)

**Vargas, Getúlio** [*vär* guhs] Elected president of Brazil in 1929; launched centralized political program by imposing federal administrators over state governments; held off coups by communists in 1935 and fascists in 1937; imposed a new constitution based on Mussolini's Italy; leaned to communists after 1949; committed suicide in 1954. (p. 806)

**viceroyalties** Two major divisions of Spanish colonies in New World; one based in Lima; the other in Mexico City; direct representatives of the king. (p. 529)

**Vichy** French collaborationist government established in 1940 in southern France following defeat of French armies by the Germans. (p. 822)

**Viet Cong** Name given by Diem regime to communist guerrilla movement in southern Vietnam; reorganized with northern Vietnamese assistance as the National Liberation Front in 1958. (p. 943)

**Viet Minh** Communist-dominated Vietnamese nationalist movement; operated out of base in southern China during World War II; employed guerrilla tactics similar to the Maoists in China. (p. 942)

**Vietnamese Nationalist party** Also known as the Vietnamese Quoc Dan Dong or VNQDD; active in 1920s as revolutionary force committed to violent overthrow of French colonialism. (p. 941)

**Villa, Pancho** [*vEE* uh] (1878–1923) Mexican revolutionary and military commander in northern Mexico during the Mexican Revolution; succeeded along with Emiliano Zapata in removing Díaz from power in 1911; also participated in campaigns that removed Madero and Huerta. (p. 790)

**vizier** [vi *zEEr, viz* yuhr] Ottoman equivalent of the Abbasid wazir; head of the Ottoman bureaucracy; after 5th century often more powerful than sultan. (p. 572)

**vodun** African religious ideas and practices among descendants of African slaves in Haiti. (p. 562)

**Wafd party** [wäft] Egyptian nationalist party that emerged after an Egyptian delegation was refused a hearing at the Versailles treaty negotiations following World War I; led by Sa'd Zaghlul; negotiations eventually led to limited Egyptian independence beginning in 1922. (p. 775)

**War of the Spanish Succession** Resulted from Bourbon family's succession to Spanish throne in 1701; ended by Treaty of Utrecht in 1713; resulted in recognition of Bourbons, loss of some lands, grants of commercial rights to English and French. (p. 536)

**Warsaw Pact** Alliance organized by Soviet Union with its eastern European satellites to balance formation of NATO by Western powers in 1949. (p. 846)

**welfare state** New activism of the western European state in economic policy and welfare issues after World War II; introduced programs to reduce the impact of economic inequality; typically included medical programs and economic planning. (p. 848)

**Western Front** Front established in World War I; generally along line from Belgium to Switzerland; featured trench warfare and horrendous casualties for all sides in the conflict. (p. 760)

**Whampoa Military Academy** Founded in 1924; military wing of the Guomindang; first head of the academy was Chiang Kai-shek. (p. 798)

**White Dominions** Colonies in which European settlers made up the overwhelming majority of the population; small numbers of native inhabitants were typically reduced by disease and wars of conquest; typical of British holdings in North America and Australia with growing independence in the 19th century. (p. 662)

**white racial supremacy** Belief in the inherent mental, moral, and cultural superiority of whites; peaked in acceptance in decades before World War I; supported by social science doctrines of social Darwinists such as Herbert Spencer. (p. 664)

**Wilberforce, William** British statesman and reformer; leader of abolitionist movement in English parliament that led to end of English slave trade in 1807. (p. 563)

**witchcraft persecution** Reflected resentment against the poor, uncertainties about religious truth; resulted in death of over 100,000 Europeans between 1590 and 1650; particularly common in Protestant areas. (p. 486)

**Witte, Sergei** [*vit* uh] Russian minister of finance from 1892 to 1903; economic modernizer responsible for high tariffs, improved banking system; encouraged Western investors to build factories in Russia. (p. 732)

**Wollstonecraft, Mary** (1759–1797) Enlightenment feminist thinker in England; argued that new political rights should extend to women. (p. 494)

**world economy** Established by Europeans by the 16th century; based on control of seas, including the Atlantic and Pacific; created international exchange of foods, diseases, and manufactured products. (p. 458)

**World Zionist Organization** Founded by Theodor Herzl to promote Jewish migration to and settlement in Palestine to form a Zionist state. (p. 774)

**Xavier, Francis** [*zAY* vEE uhr, *zav* EE-, *zAY* vyuhr] Spanish Jesuit missionary; worked in India in 1540s among the outcaste and lower caste groups; made little headway among elites. (p. 600)

**Yalta Conference** Meeting among leaders of the United States, Britain, and the Soviet Union in 1945; agreed to Soviet entry into the Pacific war in return for possessions in Manchuria, organization of the United Nations; disputed the division of political organization in the eastern European states to be reestablished after the war. (p. 830)

**yellow peril** Western term for perceived threat of Japanese imperialism around 1900; met by increased Western imperialism in region. (p. 742)

**Yeltsin, Boris** Russian leader who stood up to coup attempt in 1991 that would have displaced Gorbachev; president of the Russian republic following dissolution of Soviet Union. (p. 956)

**Yuan Shikai** [yU *än shEE kI, yYän*] Warlord in northern China after fall of Qing dynasty; hoped to seize imperial throne; president of China after 1912; resigned in the face of Japanese invasion in 1916. (p. 796)

**Zaghlul, Sa'd** Leader of Egypt's nationalist Wafd party; their negotiations with British led to limited Egyptian independence in 1922. (p. 775)

**zaibatsu** [zI *bät* sU] Huge industrial combines created in Japan in the 1890s as part of the process of industrialization. (p. 739)

**Zapata, Emiliano** Mexican revolutionary and military commander of peasant guerrilla movement after 1910 centered in Morelos; succeeded along with Pancho Villa in removing Díaz from power; also participated in campaigns that removed Madero and Huerta; demanded sweeping land reform. (p. 790)

**Zapatistas** Guerrilla movement named in honor of Emiliano Zapata; originated in 1994 in Mexico's southern state of Chiapas; government responded with a combination of repression and negotiation. (p. 876)

**zemstvoes** [*zemst* vO, pl. -stvos] Local political councils created as part of reforms of Tsar Alexander II (1860s); gave some Russians, particularly middle-class professionals, some experience in government; councils had no impact on national policy. (p. 730)

**Zhou Enlai** [*jO* en *lI*] After Mao Zedong, the most important leader of the Communist party in China from the 1930s until his death in 1976; premier of China from 1954; notable as perhaps the most cosmopolitan and moderate of the inner circle of Communist leaders. (p. 937)

**Zionism** Movement originating in eastern Europe during the 1860s and 1870s that argued that the Jews must return to a Middle Eastern holy land; eventually identified with the settlement of Palestine. (p. 774)

# Credits

## Literary Credits

### PART IV

#### Chapter 23

From *Imperial Russia: A Source Book, 1700–1917* edited by Basil Dmytryshyn. Copyright Academic International Press, Gulf Breeze, Fla. Used by permission.

#### Chapter 25

Reprinted by permission of Waveland Press, Inc. from Philip D. Curtin, *Africa Remembered: Narratives by West Africans from the Era of the Slave Trade.* (Long Grove, IL; Waveland Press, Inc. 1967 [reissued 1997]). All rights reserved.

#### Chapter 27

Maps, Japan in the Imperial and Warlord Periods, Japan During the Rise of the Tokugawa Shogunate, Japanese Colonial Expansion, used by permission of Brown Reference Group.

### PART V

#### Chapter 29

Map adapted from *A Short History of Indonesia* by Alis Zainu'ddin, copyright © 1970. Reproduced with permission of Greenwood Publishing Group, Inc., Westport, CT.

#### Chapter 31

Abridgement of "A People Made New (1902–1905)" by Liang Qichso from *Sources of Chinese Tradition* by William T. deBary, 1960. Used by permission of Columbia University Press.

#### Chapter 32

From *Readings in Russian Civilization,* edited by T. Riha, 1969. Reprinted by permission of The University of Chicago Press.

#### Chapter 32

Maps, Japan in the Imperial and Warlord Periods, Japan During the Rise of the Tokugawa Shogunate, Japanese Colonial Expansion, used by permission of Brown Reference Group.

### PART VI

#### Chapter 33

"Snow Upon Paris" from *Selected Poems* by L. S. Senghor, translated by J. Reed and Clive Wake, 1964. Reprinted with permission of the University of Virginia Press and Oxford University Press.

#### Chapter 33

"Snow Upon Paris" from *Selected Poems* by L. S. Senghor, translated by J. Reed and Clive Wake, 1964. Reprinted with permission of the University of Virginia Press and Oxford University Press.

#### Chapter 34

Map "The Civil War" from *The World Atlas of Revolutions* by Andrew Wheatcroft (Hamish Hamilton 1983), pp. 84–87. Text copyright © 1983 Andrew Wheatcroft. Cartography copyright © 1983 Hamish Hamilton Ltd. Reproduced by permission of Penguin Books Ltd.

#### Chapter 34

Adaptation of two maps, "China in the Era of Revolution and Civil War" from *The Atlas of World History* edited by G. Barraclough, copyright © 1984, Times Books, p. 262. Reprinted by permission of HarperCollins Publishers Ltd., http://harpercollins.co.uk.

#### Chapter 35

From *Readings in Russian Civilization,* edited by T. Riha, 1969. Reprinted by permission of The University of Chicago Press.

## Photo Credits

### PART IV

#### Chapter 21

**Figure 21.1** The Granger Collection, NY; **21.2** The Granger Collection, NY; **21.4** The Granger Collection, NY; **21.5** The Granger Collection, NY; **21.6** The Granger Collection, NY; **21.7** The Granger Collection, NY; **21.8** Victoria and Albert Museum, London, UK

#### Chapter 22

**Figure 22.1** Private Collection/Bridgeman Art Library; **22.3** The Granger Collection, NY; **22.4** Science Museum, London, Great Britain/Art Resource, NY; **Visualizing the Past** Musee du Chateau de Versailles/Dagli Orti/The Art Archive; **22.5** Louvre, Paris, France/Erich Lessing/Art Resource, NY

#### Chapter 23

**Figure 23.1** The Bridgeman Art Library; **23.2** Sovfoto; **23.3** Hermitage/Art Resource, NY; **Visualizing the Past** Sovfoto; **23.4** Sovfoto

#### Chapter 24

**Figure 24.1** Museo Pedro de Osma Lima/Mireille Vautier/The Art Archive; **24.2** The Bridgeman Art Library; **24.3** The Granger Collection, NY; **24.4** The Granger Collection, NY; **24.6** Museo Nacional del Virreinato, Tepotzotlan, Mexico/Schalkwijk/Art Resource, NY; **24.8** Museo de American, Madrid, Spain/Erich Lessing/Art Resource, NY; **24.9** De Bry, America, 1565; **24.10** Laurie Platt Winfrey/Carousel, Inc.

#### Chapter 25

**Figure 25.1** The Bridgeman Art Library; **25.2** Courtesy of the Trustees of the British Museum, London (MM0318787); **25.3** The British Library; **25.4** The Granger Collection; **25.5** Museo Preshistorico e Ethnografico, Rome/Ministero per i Beni e le Attivita Culturali; **Visualizing the Past** Photograph © Doran H. Ross; **25.6** Local History Museum Collection Durban, S. A.; **25.7** UCLA Fowler Museum

#### Chapter 26

**Figure 26.1** Victoria and Albert Museum, London/Art Resource, NY; **26.2** Bettmann/Corbis; **26.3** Luigi Mayer/Bridgeman Art Library; **26.4** National Maritime Museum, Greenwich, England; **26.5** British Museum; **26.7** Tretyakov Gallery, Moscow, Russia/Scala/Art Resource, NY; **26.8** Arthur Thevenart/Corbis

#### Chapter 27

**Figure 27.1** Bridgeman Art Library; **27.2** Bridgeman Art Library; **27.3** Bildarchiv Preussischer Kulturbesitz/Art Resource, NY; **27.5** The British Museum; **27.6** Private Collection/Giraudon/The Bridgeman Art Library; **27.7** The Granger Collection, NY; **27.8** The Granger Collection, NY

### PART V

#### Chapter 28

**Figure 28.1** The Granger Collection; **Visualizing the Past** Bridgeman Art Library; **28.2** The Granger Collection; **28.3** Mary Evans Picture Library; **28.4** The Granger Collection; **28.5** National Gallery, London, Great Britain/Erich Lessing/Art Resource, NY; **28.6** Philadelphia Museum of Art/Art Resource, NY

#### Chapter 29

**Figure 29.1** National Army Museum, London; **29.2** The British Library; **29.3** Royal Tropical Institute/APA Photo Agency; **29.4** National Maritime Museum; **29.5** The Granger Collection; **29.6** Collection Musee de l'Homme (C35.1495.467); **29.7** The Art Archive

#### Chapter 30

**Figure 30.1** Staedtische Kunsthalle, Mannheim, Germany/Erich Lessing/Art Resource, NY; **30.2** Reproduced with permission of the General Secretariat of the Organization of American States; **30.4** Robert Frerck/Odyssey Productions, Chicago; **30.5** Bettmann/Corbis **30.6** Paulo Zanettini; **Visualizing the Past Image 1** Culver Pictures; **Image 2** Private Collection; **30.7** The Granger Collection

#### Chapter 31

**Figure 31.1** The Granger Collection; **31.1** Topkapi Palace Museum, Istanbul, Turkey/Giraudon/Art Resource, NY; **31.2** Bettmann/Corbis; **31.3** Musee des Beaux-Arts, Lille, France/Erich Lessing/Art Resource, NY; **31.4** Bildarchiv Preussischer Kulturbesitz/Art Resource, NY; **31.5** Metropolitan Museum of Art, Gift of Lincoln Kirstein. 1959 (JP 3346) Photograph © Metropolitan Museum of Art; **31.6** The Granger Collection

#### Chapter 32

**Figure 32.1** Mary Evans Picture Library; **32.2** State Historical Museum, Moscow; **32.3** California Museum of Photography, Riverside; **32.4** Sovfoto; **Visualizing the Past Image 1** Bettmann/Corbis; **Image 2** The Granger Collection

### PART VI

#### Chapter 33

**Figure 33.1** Bettmann/Corbis; **33.2** *Punch,* 1912; **33.3** Imperial War Museum, London; **Visualizing the Past** Imperial War Museum, London; **33.4** Bettmann/Corbis; **33.5** The Granger Collection, New York; **33.6** Camera Press/Globe Photos

#### Chapter 34

**Figure 34.1** Sovfoto; **34.2** Philadelphia Museum of Art, The Louise and Walter Arensberg Collection/© 2006 Artists Rights Society (ARS); **34.3** Neil Beer/Corbis; **34.4** Hulton Archive/Getty Images; **34.5** Bettmann/Corbis; **34.6** Library of Congress; **34.7** Bildarchiv Preussischer Kulturbesitz; **34.8** Sovfoto; **34.9** Bettmann/Corbis; **34.10** Library of Congress; **Visualizing the Past** Museo Nacional Centro de Arte Reina Sofia, Madrid, Spain/Erich Lessing/© 2003 Estate of Pablo Picasso/Arts Rights Society (ARS), New York. Photograph John Bigelow Taylor/Art Resource, NY; **34.13** Sovfoto

#### Chapter 35

**Figure 35.1** AP/Wide World Photos; **35.2** Ullstein-bild/The Granger Collection; **35.3** AP/ Wide World Photos; **35.4** Topham/The Image Works; **35.5** AP/Wide World Photos; **35.6** Margaret Bourke-White/Time Life Pictures/Getty Images; **Visualizing the Past Image 1** Camera Press/Globe Photos; **Image 2** Corbis; **Image 3** Margaret Bourke-White/Time Life Pictures/Getty Images; **Image 4** Corbis; **35.7** AP/Wide World Photos

#### Chapter 36

**Figure 36.1** The Granger Collection; **36.2** British Ministry of Health/National Archives, Kew, UK; **36.3** AP/Wide World Photos; **36.4** The Granger Collection; **36.5** Time & Life Pictures/Getty Images; **36.7** Bettmann/Corbis; **36.8** The Granger Collection; **36.9** The Art Archive; **36.10** Topham/The Image Works

#### Chapter 37

**Figure 37.1** AP/Wide World Photos; **37.2** Bettmann/Corbis; **37.3** AP/Wide World Photos; **37.4** Alyx Kellington/ Liaison/Getty Images; **Visualizing the Past Image 1** Tim Page/Corbis; **Image 2** National Palace, Mexico City, DF/Schalwijk/Art Resource, NY; **37.5** AP/Wide World Photos; **37.6** AP/Wide World Photos

#### Chapter 38

**Figure 38.1** Kapoor Baldev/Sygma/Corbis; **38.2** Sovfoto; **38.4** Stock, Boston; **38.5** Bettmann/Corbis; **38.6** Bettmann/Corbis; **38.7** University of California Press, Berkeley; **38.8** Bettmann/Corbis; **38.9** Corbis; **38.10** Peter Turnley/Corbis

#### Chapter 39

**Figure 39.1** Bettmann/Corbis; **39.2** Bettmann/Corbis; **39.3** B.S.P.I./Corbis; **39.4** Kevin R. Morris/Corbis; **39.5** Getty Images; **39.6** Koichi Kamoshida/Getty Images; **39.7** The Granger Collection; **39.8** Sovfoto; **39.9** AP/Wide World Photos; **39.10** Jacques Pavlovsky/Sygma/Corbis; **39.11** Bettmann/Corbis

#### Chapter 40

**Figure 40.1** AP/Wide World Photos; **40.2** Bettmann/Corbis; **40.3** Mark Stephenson/Corbis; **40.4** Tom Stoddart/Woodfin Camp & Associates; **40.5** Anthony Suau/Liaison Agency/Getty Images; **40.6** Tom Sobolik/Black Star/Stockphoto.com; **40.7** Peter Turnley/Corbis; **40.8** Peter Turnley/Corbis; **40.9** Cagle Cartoons, Inc.; **40.10** AP/Wide World

#### Chapter 41

**Figure 41.1** AP/Wide World Photos; **41.2** Reuters New Media/Corbis; **41.3** Bettmann/Corbis; **41.4** Jacques Pavlovsky/Corbis Sygma; **41.5** Time & Life Pictures/ Getty Images; **41.6** Time & Life Pictures/Getty Images; **41.7** Igor Kostin/Corbis; **41.8** Kimimasa Mayama/ Reuters/Landov **Visualizing the Past** AFP/Getty Images

# INDEX

*Note:* Page numbers followed by *f*, *m*, and *t* indicate figures, maps, and tables, respectively.

## A

## D



## E

# Contemporary Political Map of the World

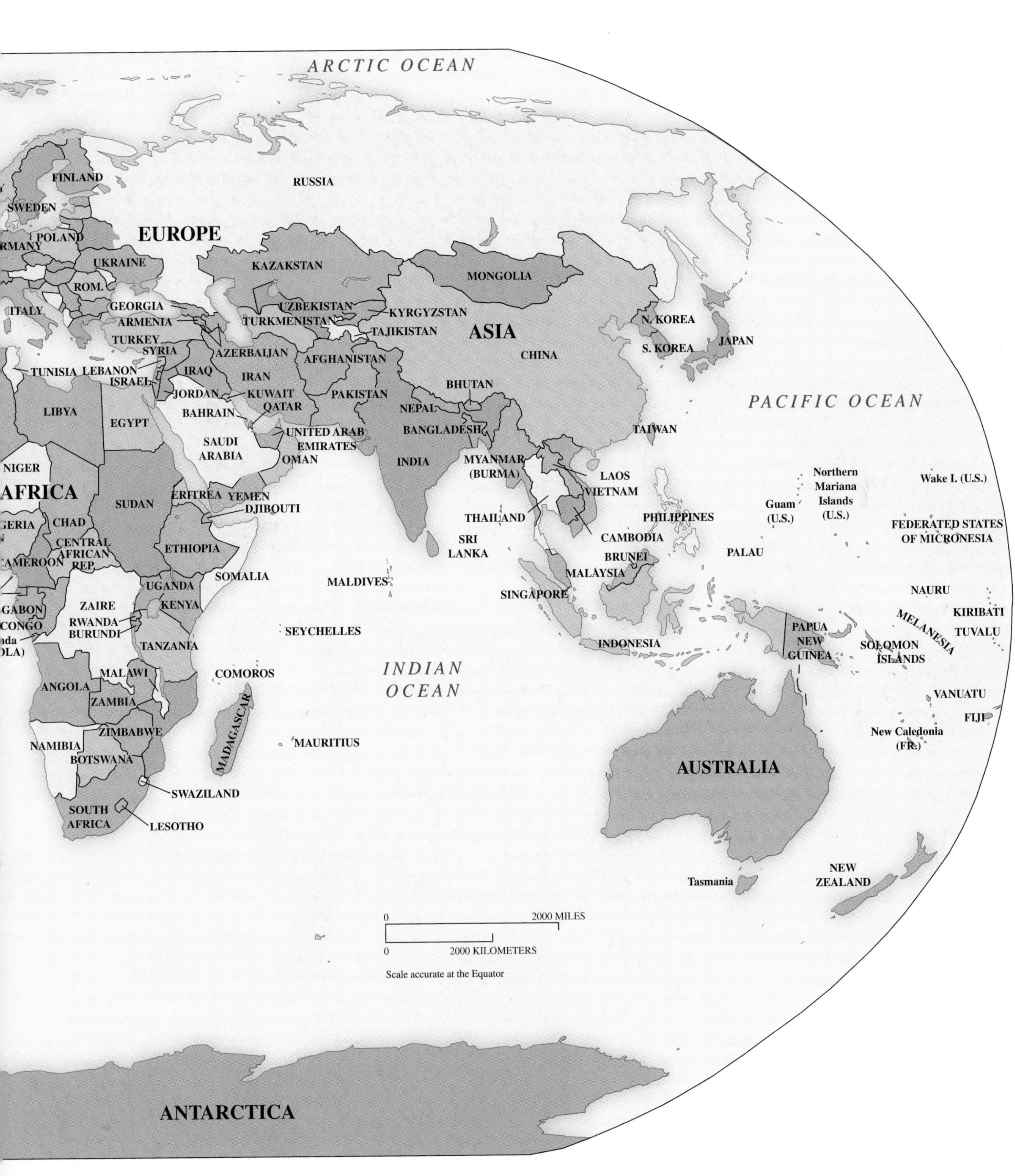
ARCTIC OCEAN
RUSSIA
FINLAND
SWEDEN
EUROPE
POLAND
RMANY
UKRAINE
KAZAKSTAN
MONGOLIA
ROM.
ITALY
GEORGIA
ARMENIA
UZBEKISTAN
TURKMENISTAN
KYRGYZSTAN
TAJIKISTAN
ASIA
N. KOREA
S. KOREA
JAPAN
CHINA
TURKEY
SYRIA
AZERBAIJAN
AFGHANISTAN
TUNISIA
LEBANON
ISRAEL
IRAQ
IRAN
JORDAN
KUWAIT
QATAR
BAHRAIN
PAKISTAN
BHUTAN
NEPAL
LIBYA
EGYPT
PACIFIC OCEAN
UNITED ARAB EMIRATES
BANGLADESH
TAIWAN
SAUDI ARABIA
OMAN
INDIA
MYANMAR (BURMA)
NIGER
AFRICA
SUDAN
ERITREA
YEMEN
DJIBOUTI
LAOS
VIETNAM
Northern Mariana Islands (U.S.)
Guam (U.S.)
Wake I. (U.S.)
THAILAND
PHILIPPINES
FEDERATED STATES OF MICRONESIA
CHAD
CENTRAL AFRICAN REP.
ETHIOPIA
SRI LANKA
CAMBODIA
BRUNEI
PALAU
CAMEROON
SOMALIA
MALDIVES
MALAYSIA
UGANDA
SINGAPORE
NAURU
KENYA
ZAIRE
GABON
CONGO
RWANDA
BURUNDI
MELANESIA
KIRIBATI
SEYCHELLES
TUVALU
TANZANIA
INDONESIA
PAPUA NEW GUINEA
SOLOMON ISLANDS
MALAWI
COMOROS
INDIAN OCEAN
ANGOLA
ZAMBIA
VANUATU
MADAGASCAR
FIJI
ZIMBABWE
New Caledonia (FR.)
NAMIBIA
MAURITIUS
BOTSWANA
AUSTRALIA
SWAZILAND
SOUTH AFRICA
LESOTHO
NEW ZEALAND
Tasmania
0
2000 MILES
0
2000 KILOMETERS
Scale accurate at the Equator
ANTARCTICA